American Government

8-850
855-945
950-1040
1045-1135

American Government

Continuity and Change

Alternate 2002 Edition
Election Update

KAREN O'CONNOR

Professor of Government
American University

LARRY J. SABATO

Robert Kent Gooch Professor
of Government and Foreign Affairs
University of Virginia

Longman

New York San Francisco Boston
London Toronto Sydney Tokyo Singapore Madrid
Mexico City Munich Paris Cape Town Hong Kong Montreal

Vice President/Publisher: Priscilla McGeehon
Senior Acquisitions Editor: Eric Stano
Development Director: Lisa Pinto
Senior Development Editor: Dawn Groundwater
Senior Marketing Manager: Megan Galvin-Fak
Media Supplements Editor: Patrick McCarthy
Senior Production Manager: Eric Jorgensen
Project Coordination, Text Design, Art Studio,
    and Electronic Page Makeup: Electronic Publishing Services Inc., NYC
Project Management for Election Update: Sunflower Publishing Services
Cover Designer/Manager: Nancy Danahy
Photo Research: Photosearch, Inc.
Manufacturing Buyer: Lucy Hebard
Printer and Binder: RR Donnelly & Sons, Co.
Cover Printer: Phoenix Color Corp.

For permission to use copyrighted material, grateful acknowledgment is made to the copyright
holders on the pages where the material appears.

Library of Congress Cataloging-in-Publication Data

O'Connor, Karen,
    American government : continuity and change / Karen O'Connor, Larry J. Sabato.--
2002 alternate ed.
        p. cm.
    Includes bibliographical references and index.
    ISBN 0-321-12181-3 (pbk.)
        1. United States—Politics and government. I. Sabato, Larry. II. Title.

JK274 .O263b 2002
320.473--dc21

                                                            2001029102

Please visit our website at http://www.ablongman.com

ISBN 0–321–12181-3 (Alternate edition, paperback)

12345678910—DOW—04 03 02 01

To Meghan,
who grew up with this book

Karen O'Connor

To my Government 101 students
over the years, who all know that
"politics is a good thing"

Larry Sabato

BRIEF CONTENTS

DETAILED CONTENTS

PREFACE

The terrorist attacks of September 11, 2001. Corporate scandals accompanying a downturn in the economy and the burst of the technology "bubble." A sweep in the 2002 midterm elections, where the Republicans bucked historical trends, solidified their hold on the House, and retook control of the Senate.

When we first started writing this text over a decade ago, we could never have envisioned that each passing edition would chronicle such dramatic changes in American government and politics. In just over a decade, we experienced 1992's "Year of the Woman" that produced record numbers of women elected to national office, and 1994's "Year of the Angry Male Voter" that produced a Republican revolution in Congress. The editions that followed those years appeared during various phases of the Clinton scandals, including the second impeachment trial of a U.S. President. Then came the 2000 election, when the outcome did not occur until December and then appeared to many to be decided by a single Justice when the Court ruled in George W. Bush's favor.

It can never be said that American politics is boring. For every edition of this text something unexpected or extraordinarily unusual has occured giving question to the old adage, "Politics as usual." At least on the national level, there appears to be little that is usual. Politics and policy is a vital, fascinating process that affects all our daily lives and we hope that this text reflects that phenomenon and provides you with the tools to understand politics as an evolutionary process where history matters.

In less than a decade, our perceptions of politics, the role of the media, and the utility of voting appear to have undergone tremendous change. Over the last six editions, this text has tried diligently to reflect those changes and to present information about politics in a manner to engage students actively—many of whom have little interest in politics when they come into the classroom. In this edition, we try to build on a solid tried-and-true base and at the same time to present information about how politics now seems to be changing at an ever more rapid pace. Thus, we present new information that we hope will whet students' appetites to learn more about politics while providing them with all of the information they need to make informed decisions about their government, politics, and politicians. We very much want our students to make such decisions. We very much want them to *participate*. Our goal with this text is to transmit just this sort of practical, useful information while creating and fostering student interest in American politics despite growing national skepticism about government and government officials at all levels. In fact, we hope that this new edition of our text will explain the national mood about politics and put it in a better context for students to understand their important role in a changing America.

APPROACH

We believe that one cannot fully understand the actions, issues, and policy decisions facing the U.S. government, its constituent states, or "the people" unless these issues are examined from the perspective of how they have evolved over time. Consequently, the title of this book is *American Government: Continuity and Change*. In its pages we try to examine how the United States is governed today by looking not just at present behavior but also at the Framers' intentions and how they have been implemented and adapted over the years. For example, we believe that it is critical to an understanding of the role of political parties in the United States to understand the Framers' fears of factionalism, how parties evolved, and when and why realignments in party identification occurred.

In addition to questions raised by the Framers, we explore issues that the Framers could never have envisioned, and how the basic institutions of government have changed in responding to these new demands. For instance, no one more than two centuries ago could have foreseen election campaigns in an age when nearly all American homes contain television sets, and the Internet and fax machines allow instant access to information. Moreover, increasing citizen demands and expectations have routinely forced government reforms, making an understanding of the dynamics of change essential for introductory students.

Our overriding concern is that students understand their government as it exists today, so that they may become better citizens and make better choices. In spite of current voter apathy, we believe that by providing students with information about government, explaining why it is important, and why their participation counts, students will come to see that politics can be a good thing.

To understand their government at all levels, students must understand how it was designed in the Constitution. Each chapter, therefore, approaches its topics from a combination of perspectives which we believe will facilitate this approach. In writing this book, we chose to put the institutions of government (Part Two) before political behavior (Part Three). Both sections, however, were written independently, making them easy to switch for those who prefer to teach about the actors in government and elections before discussing its institutions. To test the book, each of us has taught from it in both orders, with no pedagogical problems.

WHAT'S CHANGED IN THIS EDITION?

In this Election Update of the 2002 Edition of *American Government: Continuity and Change*, we have retained our basic approach to the study of politics as a constantly changing and often unpredictable enterprise. But we also discuss the dizzying array of important events that have taken place since the book last published. We include in-depth coverage of the terrorist attacks of September 11, 2001, their impact on numerous aspects of American government and life in the United States, and the subsequent "war on terror." We examine closely the evolving presidency of George W. Bush and the work of the 107th Congress, leading up to the 2002 midterm elections. Finally, we provide detailed analyses of the 2002 midterm elections in which a popular George W. Bush reinvested his political capital, vigorously campaigned for his party, and helped the Republican shake historical trends by gaining seats in the House and retaking the Senate.

Chapter Changes

These and many other changes join those made for the 2002 Edition. **Chapter 1** includes new data on the 2000 Census. **Chapter 2** includes revised coverage on the Great Compromise and an expanded discussion on Articles IV through VII. **Chapter 3** includes a revised section on federalism and the Supreme Court. **Chapter 4** is reorganized so that the section on Indian nations comes after a basic overview of state and local governments and includes a new map on 2000 party control of state governorships. **Chapter 5** has new coverage on the Supreme Court's 2000 rulings on student-initiated prayer, *Miranda*, partial-birth abortion, and the Boy Scouts' exclusion of gay men. **Chapter 7** includes updated coverage on the 108th Congress and its new members and provides a new case study—the China Trade Act of 2000—to illustrate how a bill really becomes a law. **Chapter 8** provides new coverage on postmodern presidents and presidential expectations, new material on vice-presidential power sharing, the Bush Cabinet, and a new section on ruling through regulation. **Chapter 10** has new coverage of the Supreme Court's role in the outcome of the 2000 presidential election. **Chapter 11** has new coverage on the Voter News Service's role in the 2000 and 2002 elections, the shortcomings of exit polling, gender differences in political knowledge during the 2000 election, and online election forecasting. **Chapter 12** includes analysis of Ralph Nader's impact on the 2000 election and the rise and the fall of the Reform Party. **Chapter 13** provides new analysis on electoral college reforms in the wake of the 2000 elections, results of the 2002 congressional elections, new coverage of ballot systems, an updated discussion of redistricting that reflects the 2000 census, and an analysis of the 2000 voter turnout. **Chapter 14** offers comprehensive coverage of the 2000 presidential campaign, from the nomination battle to the Supreme Court's historic ruling. **Chapter 15** includes updated coverage of how the press covers the presidency, how media influences the public, and media conflict of interest. **Chapter 16** includes new coverage of the role of the NRA and the Christian Coalition in state and national elections as well as the policy process and new coverage on the mobilization of unions during the 2000 election.

We have also made a major effort to make certain that this edition contains the most up-to-date scholarship by political scientists, not only on how government works, but what they have said on contemporary debates.

In addition to chapter-by-chapter changes, we have developed new features designed to enhance student understanding of the political processes, institutions, and policies of American government.

Point/Counterpoint   To involve students in more decision-making issues, we developed a Point/Counterpoint feature that examines a provocative issue from two opposing points of view. Topics like chapter 2's "Is There a Constitutional Right to Privacy?" or chapter 8's "Does the President Need a Mandate to Govern?" are designed to prompt students to take sides in the debate. At the end of each Point/Counterpoint, students are encouraged to take part in an online student bulletin board to post their own views.

Analyzing the Data   A feature designed to encourage visual literacy, *Analyzing the Data* helps students make sense of quantitative information and enables them to get the most out of graphic representations. Topics range from chapter 1's "Changing Age Composition of the United States" to chapter 8's "Presidential Approval Ratings Since 1938." Using annotated leaders and pointers to explain data in bar graphs, line graphs, maps, and charts, these visual learning features appear once in every chapter.

FEATURES

The Election Update of the 2002 Edition has retained the best features and pedagogy from previous editions and added exciting new ones.

Historical Perspective

Every chapter uses history to serve three purposes: first, to show how institutions and processes have evolved to their present states; second, to provide some of the color that makes information memorable; and third, to provide students with a more thorough appreciation that our government was born amid burning issues of representation and power, issues that continue to smolder today. A richer historical texture helps to explain the present.

Comparative Perspective

Changes in the Japanese economy, Russia, Eastern Europe, North America, and Asia all remind us of the preeminence of democracy, in theory if not always in fact. As new democratic experiments spring up around the globe, it becomes increasingly important for students to understand the rudiments of presidential versus parliamentary government and of multiparty versus two-party systems. To put American government in perspective, we continue to draw comparisons with Great Britain within the text discussion. Global Politics boxes compare U. S. politics and institutions with industrialized democracies and non-western countries such as Russia, China, and Indonesia.

Enhanced Pedagogy

We have revised and enhanced many pedagogical features to help students become stronger political thinkers and to echo the book's theme of evolving change.

Preview and Review   To pique students' interest and draw them into each chapter, we begin each chapter with a contemporary vignette. These vignettes, including how eighteen-year-olds acquired the vote, how special interests are lobbying Congress for laws to allow them to go after student debtors, and congressional efforts to deal with violence in public schools in the aftermath of the Columbine shooting, frequently deal with issues of high interest to students, which we hope will whet their appetites to read the rest of the chapter. Each vignette is followed by a bridge paragraph linking the vignette with the chapter's topics and a roadmap previewing the chapter's major headings. Chapter Summaries restate the major points made under each of these same major headings.

Key Terms   Glossary definitions are included in the margins of the text for all bold-faced key terms. Key terms are listed once more at the end of each chapter, with page references for review and study.

Special Features   Each chapter contains several boxed features in keeping with its theme of continuity and change:

- *Roots of Government*   These boxes highlight the role that a particular institution, process, or person has played in the course of American politics as it has evolved to the present. Chapter 11, for example, profiles George Gallup, the founder of modern polling, while chapter 9 looks at Mary Anderson, the first head of the federal Women's Bureau.

- *Global Politics*   To put American government in perspective, these boxes compare U.S. politics with that of other nations. Many of these boxes now include comparisons to non-Western nations such as China, Russia, and Indonesia; some now focus on specific issues such such as chapter 16's Labor Unions in Comparative Perspective and chapter 14's Americanization of Parliamentary Campaigns.

- *Politics Now*   These boxes act as a counterpoint to the text's traditional focus on "roots." Based on current clippings, editorials, and moments in time, these boxes are designed to encourage students to think about current issues in the context of the continuing evolution of the American political system. Chapter 5, for example examines DNA and changing views about the death penalty.

- *Highlight*   These boxes focus on high student-interest material outside the stream of the text discussion. Chapter 5, for example, looks at political speech and mandatory student fees. Chapter 2 describes how one college student's term paper led to the ratification of a constitutional amendment.

■ ***Continuity & Change***   These sections conclude each chapter. They encourage students to think critically and tie in with the book's theme of change in America. Many of these sections in the 2002 Edition heve been revised in order to focus on the evolution of a specific issue. Chapter 3, for example, examines the evolution of marriage in the federal system. We have retained the popular "Cast Your Vote" student polling questions found at the end of each Continuity and Change section.

Web Explorations

Each chapter contains several links to the World Wide Web through our book-specific Web site. Identified in the margins with an 🌐 icon, Web Explorations encourage students to learn more about a specific issue or concept (e.g., "For more about local gun initiatives, go to **www.ablongman.com/oconnor**).

LongmanParticipate.com, Version 2.0

Each chapter also contains several links to interactive activities found on Longman's distinctive Web site for American Government, *LongmanParticipate.com* (go to www.coursecompass.com to register). Identified in the margins with an icon, exercises on LongmanParticipate.com help students understand important concepts—and make learning them fun—by getting students involved in several types of activities (e.g., simulations in which the student takes to role of the President, a member of Congress, a police officer, and more).

THE ANCILLARY PACKAGE

The ancillary package for the Election Update of *American Government: Continuity and Change, 2002 Edition*, reflects the pedagogical goals of the text: to provide information in a useful context and with colorful examples. We have tried especially hard to provide materials that are useful for instructors and helpful to students.

Instructor Supplements

Instructor's Manual   Includes chapter overviews, chapter outlines, learning objectives, key terms, and valuable teaching suggestions. Written by Sue Davis of the American Political Science Association.

Test Bank   Contains hundreds of challenging and thoroughly revised multiple choice, true-false, and essay questions along with an answer key. Written by Sue Davis of the American Political Science Association.

TestGen EQ CD-ROM   The printed Test Bank is also available through our computerized testing system, TestGen EQ. This fully-networkable, user-friendly program enables instructors to view and edit questions, add their own questions, and print tests in a variety of formats.

Faculty Guide to accompany **LongmanParticipate.com 2.0** ***Web site***   Contains chapter-by-chapter detailed summaries for each of the site's interactive activities, as well as a list of concepts covered, recommendations about how to integrate the site into coursework, and discussion questions and paper topics for every excercise. Instructors may use the table of contents in the front of the guide to locate information on a given activity icon that appears in the margin of this textbook. This guide also provides instructors with detailed instructions and screen shots showing how to register on the site and how to set up and use the administration center. The introductory chapter describes the numerous additional resources included on the Web site. Written by Scott Furlong at the University of Wisconsin.

American Government Presentation Library CD-ROM   This complete multimedia presentation tool provides: a built-in presentation-maker, 200 photographs, 200 figures and graphs from Longman texts, 20 minutes of audio clips, 20 video clips, and links to over 200 Web sites. Media items can be imported into PowerPoint® and Persuasion® presentation programs.

PowerPoint® CD-ROM   A lecture outline PowerPoint® presentation of the new edition along with graphics from the book. Written by Robert Sterken of the University of Texas at Tyler.

Transparencies   Full-color acetates of the figures from all 26 chapters of the book.

Interactive American Government Video   Contains 27 video segments on topics ranging from the term limit debate to Internet pornography to women in the Citadel. Critical thinking questions accompany each clip, encouraging students to 'interact' with the videos by analyzing their content and the concepts they address.

Politics in Action Video   Eleven "lecture-launchers" covering subjects from conducting a campaign to the passage of a bill. Includes narrated videos, interviews, edited documentaries, original footage, and political ads.

American Government Video Program   Qualified adopters can peruse our list of videos for the American government classroom.

Active Learning Guide for American Government   This unique guide offers an abundance of innovative suggestions for classroom projects and teaching strategies—including scenarios, role plays and debates—that will get students actively involved in course material. Written by Richard H. Foster, Mark K. McBeth, Joseph Morris, Sean K. Anderson, and Mark Mussman.

Online Course Management   Longman offers comprehensive online course management systems such as CourseCompass, WebCT, and Blackboard in conjunction with this text. These systems provide complete content, class roster, online quizzing and testing, grade administration, and more, over the Internet. **CourseCompass** combines the strength of Longman content with state-of-the-art eLearning tools! **CourseCompass** is a nationally-hosted, dynamic, interactive online course management system powered by BlackBoard, leaders in the development of Internet-based learning tools. This easy-to-use and customizable program enables professors to tailor content and functionality to meet individual course needs! Every **CourseCompass** course includes a range of pre-loaded content such as testing and assessment question pools. Instructors can redeem pin codes and set up access at *www.coursecompass.com.* Please contact your local Allyn & Bacon/Longman representative for more information.

Student Supplements

LongmanParticipate.com 2.0 (go to www.coursecompass.com to register)   FREE 6-month student subscription in every new copy of the text. More interactive, more comprehensive and more in depth than any American government Web site currently available, *LongmanParticipate.com* offers instructors and students an exciting new resource for teaching and learning about our political system that's easy to integrate into any course.

- *Simulations* put students in the role of a political actor.
- *Visual Literacy* exercises get students interpreting, manipulating, and applying data.
- *Interactive Timelines* through which students experience the evolution of an aspect of government.
- *Participation* activities personalize politics by either getting students involved or exploring their own thoughts and opinions about our system.
- *Comparative* exercises in which students compare aspects of our system to those of other countries.

Students receive feedback at every step and instructors can track student work through the gradebook feature offered by Coursecompass. The various activities and features were written by instructors from around the country:

Paul Benson, *Tarrant County Community College*
Quentin Kidd, *Christopher Newport University*
Stephen Sandweiss, *Tacoma Community College*

Activities and content for Version 1.0 were also written by:

James Brent, *San Jose State University*
Laura Roselle, *Elon College*
Denise Scheberle, *University of Wisconsin*
B. Thomas Schuman, *University of New Hampshire*
Sharon Spray, *Elon College*
Cara Strebe, *San Francisco State University*
Ruth Ann Strickland, *Appalachian State University*
Kaare Strøm, *University of California, San Diego*
David Tabb, *San Francisco State University*

Interactive Edition CD-ROM Offering students a complete multimedia learning experience, this CD-ROM contains the full text of the comprehensive book on CD with hyperlinks to various media—video clips, Web links, practices tests, photos and graphics, primary sources, and much more! FREE when ordered packaged with the text.

Companion Web Site **(www.ablongman.com/oconnor)**

- *Web Explorations*—critical thinking web exercises (referenced in the text through icons in the margins).
- *Practice Tests*—multiple choice, true/false, fill-in-the-blank, and essay questions.
- *Summaries*
- *Online Research and Citation Guide*
- *Chatroom and Message Board*

Study Guide The printed study guide features chapter outlines, key terms, a variety of practice tests, and critical thinking questions to help students learn. This supplement also covers the seven additional chapters on Texas in this edition.

StudyWizard CD-ROM This interactive study guide helps students master concepts in the text through practice tests, chapter and topic summaries, and a comprehensive interactive glossary. Students receive immediate feedback on practice tests in the form of answer explanations and page references in the text to go to for extra help. FREE when ordered packaged with the text. Written by David Dupree at Victor Valley College.

Getting Involved: A Student Guide to Citizenship   A unique and practical handbook that guides students through political participation with concrete advice and extensive sample material—letters, telephone scripts, student interviews, and real-life anecdotes-for getting involved and making a difference in their lives and communities. FREE when ordered packaged with the text. Written by Mark Kann, Todd Belt, Gabriella Cowperthwaite, and Steven Horn.

Ten Things Every American Government Student Should Read *by Karen O'Connor*   We asked American Government instructors across the country to vote for the ten things beyond the text that they believed every student should read. The top vote-getter in each category was put into this unique reader. FREE when ordered packaged with the text.

Discount Subscription to Newsweek *magazine*   Students receive 12 issues of *Newsweek* at more than 80% off the regular price. An excellent way to keep students up on current events.

CHOICES: An American Government Reader   This customizable reader allows instructors to choose from a database of over 300 readings to create a reader that exactly matches their course needs. Database includes some of the most important documents from the 2000 Election.

Penguin-Putnam Paperback Titles at a Deep Discount   Longman offers 25 Penguin-Putnam titles at more than a 60% discount when packaged with O'Connor & Sabato's text. Titles include De Tocqueville's *Democracy in America* and Lewis' *The Jungle*. Go to www.ablongman.com/penguin for a complete list.

Guide to the Internet for American Government   This easy-to-use guide presents a series of American government exercises using the Internet. It also includes a thorough discussion on evaluating sites for academic usefulness. FREE when ordered packaged. Written by Carol Hays.

Writing in Political Science 2/e *by Diane Schmidt*   Taking students step-by-step through all aspects of writing in political science, this guide features samples from actual students and expanded information about using the Internet. Available at a significant discount when ordered packaged.

Texas Politics Supplement 2/e *by Debra St. John*   90-page primer on state and local government and issues in Texas. FREE when packaged with the book.

California Politics Supplement 2/e *by Barbara Stone*   70-page primer on state and local government and issues in California. FREE when packaged with the book.

ACKNOWLEDGMENTS

Karen O'Connor thanks the thousand-plus students in her American Government courses at Emory and American University who, over the years, have pushed her to learn more about American government and to have fun in the process. She especially thanks her American University colleagues who offered books and suggestions for this most recent revision—especially Gregg Ivers and David Lublin. Her former professor and long-time friend and coauthor, Nancy E. McGlen, has offered support for more than two decades. Her former students, too, have contributed in various ways to this project, especially John R. Hermann, Paul Fabrizio, Bernadette Nye, Sue Davis, Laura van Assendelft, and Sarah Brewer.

For this edition of the book, Ali Yanus, a brilliant undergraduate, offered invaluable assistance. Her fresh perspectives on politics and ideas about things of interest to students, as well as her keen eye for typos, has greatly benefited the book. Her unbelievable hard work has made this a much better book.

Larry J. Sabato would like to acknowledge the students, past and present in his University of Virginia Government 101 class, who have offered many valuable suggestions and much thoughtful feedback. He would also like to thank the past and present staff and interns at the UVA Center for Governmental Studies—especially Joshua Scott and Matthew Wikswo, who were truly instrumental in the process of reviewing this edition. Other staff member, interns, and colleagues who helped with this and previous editions of the textbook include, but are not limited to: Allison Barrett, Zene Colt, Whitney Duff, Howard Ernst, Brett Ferrell, Ed Fields, Emily Harding, Louisa Jilcott, Bruce Larson, Ade Patton, Dan Payne, and Moshin Syed. Finally, he extends his thanks to the faculty and staff of the Department of Government and Foreign Affairs at the University of Virginia, especially Nancy Rae, Lawrence Schack, and Shirley Mayes.

Particular thanks from both of us go to Dennis L. Dresang at the University of Wisconsin–Madison, who coauthored chapter 4 (State and Local Government), David Potter of the University of Northern Kentucky, who prepared the Global Politics features, and Sue Davis at APSA for her help with many of the Point/Counterpoint features.

In the now many years we have been writing and rewriting this book, we have been blessed to have been helped by many people at Macmillan, Allyn & Bacon, and now Longman. Eric Stano has been a fantastic editor as well as fun to work with. Our development editor, Dawn Groundwater, and our marketing manager, Megan Galvin-Fak, have also done terrific jobs and made this a better book. We would also like to acknowledge the tireless efforts of the Allyn & Bacon/Longman sales force. In the end, we hope that all of these talented people see how much their work and support have helped us to write a better book.

Many of our peers reviewed past editions of the book and earned our gratitude in the process:

Danny Adkison *Oklahoma State University*

Weston H. Agor *University of Texas at El Paso*

Victor Aikhionbare *Salt Lake Community College*

James Anderson *Texas A & M University*

Judith Baer *Texas A & M University*

Ruth Bamberger *Drury College*

Christine Barbour *Indiana University*

Jon Bond *Texas A&M University*

Stephen A. Borrelli *University of Alabama*

Ann Bowman *University of South Carolina*

Robert C. Bradley *Illinois State University*

Gary Brown *Montgomery College*

John Francis Burke *University of Houston–Downtown*

Greg Caldeira *Ohio State University*

David E. Camacho *Northern Arizona University*

Alan R. Carter *Schenectady County Community College*

Carl D. Cavalli *North Georgia College and State University*

Steve Chan *University of Colorado*

Richard Christofferson Sr. *University of Wisconsin–Stevens Point*

David Cingranelli *SUNY, Binghamton*

Clarke E. Cochran *Texas Tech University*

Anne N. Costain *University of Colorado*

Cary Covington *University of Iowa*

Stephen C. Craig *University of Florida*

Lane Crothers *Illinois State University*

Abraham L. Davis *Morehouse College*

Robert DiClerico *West Virginia University*

John Domino *Sam Houston State University*

Keith L. Doughtery *St. Mary's College of Maryland*

David E. Dupree *Victor Valley College*

Craig F. Emmert *Texas Tech University*

Walle Engedayehu *Prairie View A & M University*

Alan S. Engel *Miami University*

Frank B. Feigert *University of North Texas*

Evelyn Fink *University of Nebraska*

Scott R. Furlong *University of Wisconsin–Green Bay*

James D. Gleason *Victoria College*

Sheldon Goldman *University of Massachusetts, Amherst*

Doris Graber *University of Illinois at Chicago*

Jeffrey D. Green *University of Montana*

Roger W. Green *University of North Dakota*

Charles Hadley *University of New Orleans*

William K. Hall *Bradley University*

Robert L. Hardgrave Jr. *The University of Texas at Austin*

Chip Hauss *George Mason University/University of Reading*

Stacia L. Haynie *Louisiana State University*

John R. Hermann *Trinity University*

Marjorie Hershey *Indiana University*

Steven Alan Holmes *Bakersfield College*

Cornell Hooton *Emory University*

Jon Hurwitz *University of Pittsburgh*

Joseph Ignagni *University of Texas–Arlington*

Willoughby Jarrell *Kennesaw State College*

Susan M. Johnson *University of Wisconsin–Whitewater*

Dennis Judd *University of Missouri–St. Louis*

Carol J. Kamper *Rochester Community College*

Kenneth Kennedy *College of San Mateo*

Donald F. Kettl *University of Wisconsin*

John Kincaid *University of North Texas*

Karen M. King *Bowling Green State University*

Jonathan E. Kranz *John Jay College of Criminal Justice*

Mark Landis *Hofstra University*

Sue Lee *North Lake College*

Ted Lewis *Collin County Community College*

Brad Lockerbie *University of Georgia*

Larry Martinez *California State University–Long Beach*

Lynn Mather *Dartmouth College*

Laurel A. Mayer *Sinclair Community College*

Steve Mazurana *University of Northern Colorado*

Clifton McCleskey *University of Virginia*

James L. McDowell *Indiana State University*

Carl E. Meacham *SUNY–Oneonta*

Mark C. Miller *Clark University*

Kenneth F. Mott *Gettysburg College*

Joseph Nogee *University of Houston*

Mary Alice Nye *University of North Texas*

John O'Callaghan *Suffolk University*

Bruce Oppenheimer *Vanderbilt University*

Richard Pacelle *University of Missouri–St. Louis*

Marian Lief Palley *University of Delaware*

David R. Penna *Gallaudet University*

Richard M. Pious *Columbia University*

David H. Provost *California State University–Fresno*

Lawrence J. Redlinger *University of Texas at Dallas*

Leroy N. Rieselbach *Indiana University*

David Robertson *Public Policy Research Centers, University of Missouri–St. Louis*

David Robinson *University of Houston–Downtown*

David W. Rohde *Michigan State University*

Frank Rourke *Johns Hopkins University*

Ronald Rubin *City University of New York Borough of Manhattan Community College*

Bruce L. Sanders *MacComb Community College*

Gaye Lynn Scott *Austin Community College*

Daniel M. Shea *University of Akron*

Denise Scheberle *The University of Wisconsin–Green Bay*

Martin P. Sellers *Campbell University*

John N. Short *University of Arkansas–Monticello*

Mark Silverstein *Boston University*

James R. Simmons *University of Wisconsin–Oshkosh*

Andrea Simpson *University of Washington*

Philip M. Simpson *Cameron University*

Elliott E. Slotnick *Ohio State University*

Michael W. Sonnleitner *Portland Community College*

Frank J. Sorauf *University of Minnesota*

Gerald Stanglin *Cedar Valley College*

C. S. Tai *University of Arkansas–Pine Bluff*

Richard J. Timpone *SUNY–Stony Brook*

Brian Walsh *University of Maryland*

Shirley Anne Warshaw *Gettysburg College*

Matt Wetstein *San Joaquin Delta College*

Richard Whaley *Marian College*

Rich Whisonant *York Technical College*

Martin Wiseman *Mississippi State University*

Finally, we'd also like to thank our peers who reviewed and aided in the development of the current edition:

John Dinan *Wake Forest University*
Mel Hailey *Abilence Christian*
Thomas Hyde *Pfeiffer University*
Quentin Kidd *Christopher Newport University*
Alec Kirby *Univerity of Wisconsin–Stout*
John C. Kuzenski *The Citadel*
Cecilia Manrique *University of Wisconsin–La Crosse*

Stephen S. Meinhold *University of North Carolina–Wilmington*
David R. Penna *GalludetUniversiy*
James A. Rhodes *Luther College*
Donald Roy *Ferris State University*
Michael Eric Siegel *American University*
Kevan Yenerall *Bridgewater College*

American Government

1 The Political Landscape

*We the People of the United States, in Order to form a more
perfect Union, establish Justice, insure domestic Tranquility,
provide for the common defense, promote the general Welfare,
and secure the Blessings of Liberty to ourselves and our
Posterity, do ordain and establish the Constitution for the
United States of America.*

So begins the Preamble to the United States Constitution. Written in 1787, this document has guided our nation, its government, its politics, its institutions, and its inhabitants for over 200 years.

Back when the Constitution was written, the phrases "We the People" and "ourselves" meant something very different than they do today. Although the Framers—the men who wrote the Constitution—probably intended to include nearly all white men and women, they still envisioned an electorate that was made up of less than half of those who lived in the thirteen original states. After all, voting was largely limited to property-owning white males. Indians, slaves, and women could not vote. Today, through the expansion of the right to vote, the phrase "the People" encompasses men and women of all races, ethnic origins, and social and economic status—a variety of peoples and interests the Framers could not have imagined, although most of those who are eligible to vote today do not.

In the goals it outlines, the Preamble to the Constitution describes what the people of the United States can expect from their government. But many Americans today are questioning how well the country and its government can deliver on these goals. Few Americans today would classify the Union as "perfect"; many feel excluded from "Justice" and the "Blessings of Liberty"; many more do not feel our domestic situation is particularly tranquil. Furthermore, judging from recent poll results and economic statistics, many Americans feel that their general welfare is not very well promoted by their government. Others simply do not care about government much at all.

Change. If there has been one constant in the life of the United States, it is change. The Framers would be astonished to see the forms and functions that the institutions they so carefully outlined in the Constitution have taken on, and the number of additional political institutions that have arisen to support and fuel the functioning of the national government. The Framers also would be amazed at the array of services and programs the government— especially the national government—provides. They would be further surprised to see how the physical boundaries and the composition of the population have changed in more than 200 years. And they might well wonder, "How did we get here?"

It is part of the American creed that each generation should hand down to the next not only a better America, but an improved economic, educational, and social status. In general, Americans long have been optimistic about our nation, its institutions, and its future. Thomas Jefferson saw the United States as the world's "best hope"; Abraham Lincoln echoed these sentiments when he called it the "last, best hope of earth."[1] But during the 1990s, for the first time in decades, some of that optimism faded. Many Americans were dismayed by the Clinton/Lewinsky affair, campaign finance abuses, and often even government in general.

This disenchantment, some believe, led to the continued low voter turnout in the 2000 election. Still, most Americans report that their lives are better than their parents' and most are very optimistic about the future although in the aftermath of the drawn out process of the 2000 presidential election and the 2001 stock market collapse, many are uncertain about what the future holds.

WEB EXPLORATION
To connect with others who are interested in politics, see
www.ablongman.com/oconnor

In this text we present you with the tools that you need to understand how our political system has evolved, and to prepare you to understand the changes that are yet to come. If you approach the study of American government and politics with an open mind, it should help you become a better citizen. We hope that you learn to ask questions, to understand how various issues have come to be important, and to see why a particular law was enacted and how it was implemented. With such understanding, we further hope that you will learn not to accept at face value everything you see on the television news, hear on the radio, or read in the newspaper. Work to understand your government, and use your vote and other forms of participation to help ensure that your government works for you.

We recognize that the discourse of politics has changed dramatically in just the last few years, and more and more Americans—especially the young—are turned off to politics, especially at the national level. The 2000 presidential election, and its failure to produce a clear presidential winner, as well as the record amount of money spent and the negativity of many 2002 campaigns, have left many people wondering about the nature of the political process itself.

We believe that a thorough understanding of the workings of government will allow you to question and think about the system—the good parts and the bad—and decide for yourself the advantages and disadvantages of possible changes and reforms. Equipped with such an understanding, we hope you will become better informed and more active participants in the political process.

Every long journey begins with a single step. In this chapter we'll examine the following topics:

- First, we will look at the *roots of American government.* To understand how the U.S. government and our political system work today, it is critical to understand the philosophies that guided the American colonists as they created a system of governance different from those then in existence.

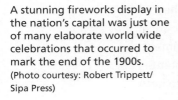

A stunning fireworks display in the nation's capital was just one of many elaborate world wide celebrations that occurred to mark the end of the 1900s. (Photo courtesy: Robert Trippett/ Sipa Press)

- Second, we will explore the *characteristics of American democracy*. Several enduring characteristics have defined American democracy since its beginning and continue to influence our nation's government and politics today.
- Third, we will explore the *changing political culture and characteristics of the American people*. Because government derives its power from the people it governs, an understanding of who the American people are and how they are changing is critical to an understanding of American politics.
- Fourth, we will discuss *political culture and Americans' views about government* and the role that government plays in their lives.

THE ROOTS OF AMERICAN GOVERNMENT: WHERE DID THE IDEAS COME FROM?

The current American political system did not spring into being overnight. It is the result of philosophy, trial and error, and yes, even luck. To begin our examination of why we have the type of government we have today, we look at the theories of government that influenced the Framers: those men who gathered in Philadelphia and drafted a new Constitution, thereby creating the United States of America.

From Aristotle to the Enlightenment

Aristotle (384–322 B.C.) and the Greeks were the first to articulate the notion of **natural law,** the doctrine that human affairs should be governed by certain ethical principles. Being nothing more nor less than the nature of things, these principles can be understood by reason. In the thirteenth century, the Italian priest and philosopher Thomas Aquinas (1225–1274) gave the idea of natural law a new, Christian framework. He argued that natural law and Christianity were compatible because God created the natural law that established individual rights to life and liberty. In contradiction to this view, kings throughout Europe continued to rule as absolute monarchs, claiming this divine right came directly from God. Thus citizens were bound by the government under which they found themselves, regardless of whether they had a say in its workings: If government reflected God's will, who could argue with it?

   In the early sixteenth century, a religious movement to reform the doctrine and institutions of Roman Catholicism began to sweep through Europe. In many cases these efforts at reform resulted in the founding of Protestant churches separate from their Catholic source. During this period, known as the Reformation, the resultant growth in the Protestant faith promoted the belief that people could talk directly to God without the intervention of a priest and altered the nature of government as people began to believe they could also have a say in their own governance.

   During the Enlightenment period, the ideas of philosophers and scientists such as Isaac Newton (1642–1727) worked further to affect peoples' views of government. Newton and others argued that the world could be improved through the use of human reason, science, and religious toleration. He and other theorists directly challenged earlier notions that fate alone controlled an individual's destiny and that kings ruled by divine right. Together the intellectual and religious developments of the Reformation and Enlightenment periods encouraged people to seek alternatives to absolute monarchy and to ponder new methods of governing.

A Growing Idea: Popular Consent

In the late sixteenth century in England, "separatists" split from the Anglican Church. They believed that their ability to speak one-on-one to God gave them the power to participate directly in the governing of their own local assemblies. They established

The media often shapes how Americans perceive politics, as when several newspapers prematurely proclaimed Bush the victor the day after Election Day in 2000. The final outcome in the presidential contest was not known for weeks afterward. (Photo courtesy: NYT Pictures)

natural law
A doctrine that society should be governed by certain ethical principles that are part of nature and, as such, can be understood by reason.

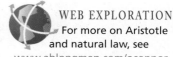

WEB EXPLORATION
For more on Aristotle and natural law, see
www.ablongman.com/oconnor

self-governing congregations, and were responsible for the first widespread appearance of self-government in the form of social compacts. When some separatists settled in America during the 1600s, they brought along their beliefs about self-governance. The Mayflower Compact, deemed sufficiently important to be written while that ship was still at sea, reflects this tradition. Although it addressed itself to secular government, the Pilgrims called it a "covenant" and its form was akin to other common religious covenants adopted by Congregationalists, Presbyterians, and Baptists.[2]

Two English theorists of the seventeenth century, Thomas Hobbes (1588–1679) and John Locke (1632–1704), built on conventional notions about the role of government and the relationship of the government to the people in proposing a **social contract theory** of government (see Roots of Government: The Philosophies of Thomas Hobbes and John Locke). They argued that, even before the creation of God-ordained governments theorized by Aquinas, all individuals were free and equal by natural right. This freedom, in turn, required that all men give their consent to be governed.

social contract theory
The belief that people are free and equal by God-given right and that this in turn requires that all people give their consent to be governed; espoused by John Locke and influential in the writing of the Declaration of Independence.

Hobbes and Locke. In his now-classic political treatise *Leviathan* (1651), in which he argued for King Charles's restoration to the throne (which finally occurred in 1661), Hobbes argued pessimistically that man's natural state was war. Government, Hobbes theorized, particularly a monarchy, was necessary to restrain man's bestial tendencies because life without government was a "state of nature." Without written, enforceable rules, people would live like animals—foraging for food, stealing, and killing when necessary. To escape the horrors of the natural state and to protect their lives, Hobbes argued, men must give up to government certain rights. Without government, Hobbes warned, life would basically be "solitary, poor, nasty, brutish, and short"—a constant struggle to survive against the evil of others. For this reason, governments had to intrude on people's rights and liberties to better control society and provide the necessary safeguards for property.[3]

Hobbes argued strongly for a single ruler, no matter how evil, to guarantee the rights of the weak against the strong. Leviathan, a biblical sea monster, was his characterization of an all-powerful government. Strict adherence to Leviathan's laws, however encompassing or intrusive on liberty, was but a small price to pay for living in a civilized society, or even for life itself.

In contrast, John Locke—like many other political philosophers of the era—took the basic survival of humanity for granted. He argued that government's major responsibility was the preservation of private property, an idea that ultimately found its way into the Constitution of the United States. In two of his works (*Essay Concerning Human Understanding* [1690] and *Second Treatise on Civil Government* [1689]), Locke responded to King James II's abuses of power, which were largely directed at the Anglican Church and Parliament. Locke not only denied the divine right of kings to govern, but argued that men were born equal and with natural rights that no king had the power to void. Under what Locke termed social contract theory, the consent of the people is the only true basis of any sov-

The title page from Thomas Hobbes's *Leviathan*, 1651. (Photo courtesy: Bettmann/Corbis)

ROOTS OF GOVERNMENT

THE PHILOSOPHIES OF THOMAS HOBBES AND JOHN LOCKE

In almost any newspaper or TV news report, on any given day, you can find stories that show Americans grappling with questions about the proper role of government in their lives. These questions are not new. Centuries ago, Thomas Hobbes and John Locke both wrote extensively on these issues. Their ideas, however, differed remarkably. For Hobbes, who viewed humans as basically evil, a government that regulated all kinds of conduct was necessary. Locke, who was more optimistic, saw the need only for more limited government.

Hobbes — *viewed everyone as evil*

Thomas Hobbes was born in 1588 in Gloucestershire (Glouster), England, and began his formal education at the age of four. By the age of six he was learning Latin and Greek, and by the age of nineteen he had obtained his bachelor's degree from Oxford University. In 1608 Hobbes accepted a position as a family tutor with the earl of Devonshire, a post he retained for the rest of his life.

Hobbes was greatly influenced by the chaos of the English Civil War during the mid-seventeenth century. Its impact is evident in his most famous work, *Leviathan* (1651), a treatise on governmental theory that states his views on Man and Citizen. *Leviathan* is commonly described as a book about politics, but it also deals with religion and moral philosophy.

Hobbes characterized humans as selfishly individualistic and constantly at war with one another. Thus he believed that people must surrender themselves to rulers in exchange for protection from their neighbors.

Locke — *OPTIMISTIC*

John Locke, born in England in 1632, was admitted to an outstanding public school at the age of fifteen. It was there that he began to question his upbringing in the Puritan faith. At twenty he went on to study at Oxford, where he later became a lecturer in Aristotelian philosophy. Soon, however, he found a new interest in medicine and experimental science.

In 1666 Locke met Anthony Ashley Cooper, the first earl of Shaftesbury, and a politician who believed in individual rights and parliamentary reform. It was through Cooper that Locke discovered his own talent for philosophy. In 1689 Locke published his most famous work, *Second Treatise on Civil Government*, in which he set forth a theory of natural rights. He used natural rights to support his "social contract [theory]— the view that the consent of the people is the only true basis of any sovereign's right to rule." A government exists, he argued, because individuals agree, through a contract, to form a government to protect their rights under natural law. By agreeing to be governed, individuals agree to abide by decisions made by majority vote in the resolution of disputes.

Both men, as you can see, relied on wealthy royal patrons to allow them the time to work on their philosophies of government. While Hobbes and Locke agreed that government was a social contract between the people and their rulers, they differed significantly about the proper scope of government. Which man's views about government (and people) reflect your views?

---

ereign's right to rule. According to Locke, men form governments largely to preserve life, liberty, and property, and to assure justice. If governments act improperly, they break their contract with the people and therefore no longer enjoy the consent of the governed. Because he believed that true justice comes from laws, Locke argued that the branch of government that makes laws—as opposed to the one that enforces or interprets laws—should be the most powerful.

Locke believed that having a chief executive to administer laws was important, but that he should necessarily be limited by law or by the social contract with the governed. Locke's writings influenced many American colonists, especially Thomas Jefferson, whose original draft of the Declaration of Independence noted the rights to "life, liberty, and property" as key reasons to split from England.[4] This document was "pure Locke" because it based the justification for the split with England on the English government's violation of the social contract implicit in its dealings with the American colonies.

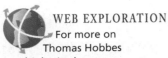

WEB EXPLORATION
For more on
Thomas Hobbes
and John Locke, see
www.ablongman.com/oconnor

monarchy
A form of government in which power is vested in hereditary kings and queens.

oligarchy
A form of government in which the right to participate is always conditioned on the possession of wealth, social status, military position, or achievement.

aristocracy
A system of government in which control is based on rule of the highest.

democracy
A system of government that gives power to the people, whether directly or through their elected representatives.

direct democracy
A system of government in which members of the polity meet to discuss all policy decisions and then agree to abide by majority rule.

indirect (representative) democracy
A system of government that gives citizens the opportunity to vote for representatives who will work on their behalf.

republic
A government rooted in the consent of the governed; a representative or indirect democracy.

Devising a National Government

Although social contract theorists agreed on the need for government, they did not necessarily agree on the form that a government should take. Thomas Hobbes argued for a single leader; John Locke and Jean-Jacques Rousseau, a French philosopher (1712–1778), saw the need for less centralized power.

The colonists rejected a system with a strong ruler like the British **monarchy,** as soon as they declared their independence. Most European monarchical systems gave hereditary rulers absolute power over all forms of activity. Many of the colonists had fled Great Britain to avoid religious persecution and other harsh manifestations of power wielded by George II, whom they viewed as a malevolent despot. They naturally were reluctant to put themselves in the same position in their new nation.

While some colonies, such as Massachusetts, originally established theocracies in which religious leaders eventually ruled claiming divine guidance, they later looked to more secular forms of governance. Colonists also did not want to create an **oligarchy,** or "rule by the few or an elite," in which the right to participate is conditioned on the possession of wealth, property, social status, military position, or achievement. Aristotle defined this form of government as a perversion of an **aristocracy,** or "rule of the highest." Again, the colonists were fearful of replicating the landed and titled system of the British aristocracy, and viewed the formation of a representative form of government as far more in keeping with the ideas of social contract theorists. But the **democracy** in which we live, as settled on by the Framers, is difficult to define. Nowhere is the word mentioned in the Declaration of Independence or the U.S. Constitution. The term comes from two Greek words: *demos* (the people) and *kratia* (power or authority). Thus democracy can be interpreted as a form of government that gives power to the people. The question, then, is how and to which people is this power given?

The Theory of Democratic Government

As evidenced by the creation in 1619 of the Virginia House of Burgesses as the first representative assembly in North America, and its objections to "taxation without representation," the colonists were quick to create participatory forms of government in which most men were allowed to take part. The New England town meeting, where all citizens gather to discuss and decide issues facing the town, today stands as a surviving example of a **direct democracy,** such as was used in ancient Greece when all free, male citizens came together periodically to pass laws and "elect" leaders by lot (see Politics Now: The Internet and Our Changing Society).

Direct democracies, in which the people rather than their elected representatives make political decisions, soon proved unworkable in the colonies. But as more and more settlers came to the New World, many town meetings were replaced by a system called an **indirect democracy** (this is also called *representative democracy*). This system of government, in which representatives of the people are chosen by ballot, was considered undemocratic by ancient Greeks, who believed that all citizens must have a direct say in their governance.[5] Later, in the 1760s, the French political philosopher Jean-Jacques Rousseau would also argue that true democracy is impossible unless all citizens participate in governmental decision making. Nevertheless, indirect democracy was the form of government opted for throughout most of the colonies.

Representative or indirect democracies, which call for the election of representatives to a governmental decision-making body, were formed first in the colonies and then in the new Union. Many citizens were uncomfortable with the term "democracy" and used the term "republic" to avoid any confusion between the system adopted and direct democracy. Historically, the term **republic** implied a system of government in which the interests of the people were represented by more educated or wealthier citizens who were responsible to those who elected them. Today, representative democracies are more commonly called "republics," and the words "democracy" and "republic" often are used interchangeably.

POINT/COUNTERPOINT

IS GOVERNMENT A POSITIVE FORCE OR A NEGATIVE NECESSITY?

Political polls continue to show that most Americans believe government does not do very much for them. Some people feel government ought to be more active in providing services and promoting quality of life. Others believe that government shouldn't be involved in so many facets of daily life. Should there be more or less government? Let's examine these two points of view.

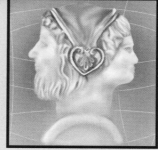

Many people, such as Democrats and Populists, believe that government regulation is good, especially when dealing with protections for the poor, groups that are difficult to mobilize (such as consumers), and public safety. From the cradle to the grave, the government works to provide safety and security, from child safety standards on cribs, car seats, and pajamas to minimum standards of care for nursing homes to protect the elderly and infirm. Other examples of the positive role government plays in our lives include: Social Security, a program created in the 1930s to assist those too old to work; the Family Leave and Medical Emergency Act that was passed in 1993 to assure maternity leave and leave to care for elderly ill relatives; helmet and seat-belt laws, which have been passed in most states; and many more. These services help provide the life, liberty, and happiness promised in the founding documents of our country.

The government also provides for national defense, regulates the skies and public airwaves, and funds educational programs such as *Sesame Street* and National Public Radio. It also works to guarantee the safety of food and drugs and even requires standardized food labeling so we can compare the nutritional value of our foods. Local and state governments provide sewer systems, garbage collection, recycling programs, roads, and free public education at the elementary and secondary levels, plus low-cost junior colleges and state universities.

Both federal and local governments regulate businesses and even the conduct of private individuals through an extensive code of criminal and civil laws. Without government and its research and development funding, we might not have cellular phones, satellite communications, the Internet, silicon chips (and thus the computer), cable and dish TV, fax machines, Velcro, freeze-dried foods, or four-wheel-drive vehicles.

However, many people, such as Republicans and Libertarians, believe that government regulation is bad. It inhibits freedom and liberty, warps the market forces of the economy, and interferes in areas the government should have nothing to do with. These people believe that government is not a positive force for good but an evil necessity to perform only those functions that individuals cannot do alone. For example, government ought to provide for the national defense, border and immigration controls, and the collection of some minimum level of taxation to pay for the above duties but not for things like the war on drugs and gun control.

Advocates for less government believe that government should not interfere in the lives of individuals and that, by and large, the market and individuals ought to take care of social and economic problems. For example, if the elderly need help, their family or church ought to step in. The government shouldn't provide for services such as day care because the market will provide for day care if there is a need for it. People ought to be responsible for their own safety. If they choose not to wear a helmet or a seat belt, then that is their choice and their responsibility. In addition, they believe that businesses ought to be able to pursue their line of work without undue government interference. In specific policy terms, this viewpoint argues that the problems with Social Security can be fixed by privatizing the program, and that schools can be improved by the introduction of competition through vouchers.

Less government allows for more individual freedom and liberty. No government should be able to tell you that you can't own a gun, smoke a cigarette in a public building, or eat popcorn at the movies. You should be free to read the books you choose to read, watch the movies you choose to watch, and get together with people whom you enjoy, all without government interference.

Smaller, more limited governments would be less likely to be corrupt and could be held accountable more easily than large government. The activities of government would be more transparent because there would be fewer of them, so people would always know what the government was doing.

Government is considered less efficient than the private sector. Proponents of less government argue that if a government agency takes on a task, it will spend more money, hire more people, and produce less than if a private firm or individual were to do the same task. In order to be efficient, supply and demand as well as cost must be an integral part of decision making, and government tends to ignore those principles. The private sector innovates and responds more quickly to changing needs as well.

What do you think? Is government a positive force or a negative necessity? Should we prefer less government or more government?
Go to www.ablongman.com/oconnor

POLITICS NOW

THE INTERNET AND OUR CHANGING SOCIETY

It is hard to believe that the Internet as we know it was not around when the first edition of this text was published in 1993. What began in 1969 as ARPANET, a communications network developed by the U.S. Department of Defense for its employees to maintain contact with defense contractors and universities in the case of a nuclear attack, has revolutionized how students write papers, people seek information, and even how some individuals date. The Internet is now a vast resource for those interested in politics and may have enormous consequences in the near future as it becomes as critical a part of our daily lives as televisions and telephones.

For the first decade of its existence, the Internet was largely used for e-mail and access to distant data bases, and to facilitate communication among governmental agencies, corporations, and universities.[a] During the early 1980s, all of the interrelated research networks converted to a new protocol that allowed for easy back-and-forth transfer of information; ARPANET became the backbone of the new system, facilitating by 1983 the birth of the Internet we know today.

Only a decade ago, HTML, a hypertext Internet protocol that allowed graphic information to be transmitted over the Internet, was devised. This allowed for the creation of graphic pages—called Web sites—which then became "part of a huge, virtual hypertext network called the World Wide Web."[b] This new, improved Internet was then christened the Web.

By 2000, over 64 percent of all adult Americans reported that they had used the Internet themselves. The vast major-

ity of those aged 8 to 25, however, had used the Web. Almost all schools have Internet access. By 2001, over 50 million households were online. In 2000, female Internet usage surpassed male usage for the first time. Usage by teenage girls soared 126 percent in just four years.[c] Thus, given estimates that computer ownership and Web access are increasing at remarkable rates, the Web's impact on democracy must be considered.

Near-universal usage of home telephones, for example, changed the way that public opinion was measured, and television eventually changed the way that candidates and their supporters reached potential voters. What kinds of political changes can we foresee given the rise of the Web?

- Increased reliance on candidate and party Web sites to raise money and supporters
- A more informed electorate given easier access to information about candidates and issues
- A more effective grassroots mechanism for citizens to contact officials, policy makers, large corporations, and so on
- The eventual use of the Internet to conduct polling research
- The use of the Internet to enhance voter turnout
- Online voting.

[a]"Internet History," http://ww.tdi.uregina.ca/~ursc/internet/history.html
[b]"Internet History."
[c]Leslie Walker, "Teen Girls Help Create Female Majority Online," *The Washington Post* (August 20, 2000): E3.

Longman
Participate.com
2.0
Participation
Democracy and the Internet

free market economy
The economic system in which the "invisible hand" of the market regulates prices, wages, product mix, and so on.

capitalism
The economic system that favors private control of business and minimal governmental regulation of private industry.

Why a Capitalist System?

In addition to fashioning a democratic form of government, the colonists also were confronted with the dilemma of what kind of role the government should play in the economy. Concerns with liberty, both personal and economic, were always at the forefront of their actions and decisions in creating a new government. They were well aware of the need for a well-functioning economy and saw that government had a key role in maintaining one. What a malfunction in the economy is, however, and what steps the government should take to remedy it, were questions that dogged the Framers and continue to puzzle politicians and theorists today.

The American economy is characterized by (1) the private ownership of property and (2) a **free market economy**—two key tenets of **capitalism,** a form of economic system that favors private control of business and minimal governmental regulation of private industry. In capitalist systems the laws of supply and demand, interacting freely in the marketplace, set prices of goods and drive production. Under capitalism, sales occur for the profit of the individual. Capitalists believe that both national and individual production is greatest when individuals are free to do with their property or goods as they wish. The government, however, plays an indispensable role in creating and enforcing the rules of the game.

In 1776, in the same year as the signing of the Declaration of Independence, Adam Smith (1723–1790) argued that free trade would result in full production and economic health. These ideas were greeted with great enthusiasm in the colonies as independence was proclaimed. Colonists no longer wanted to participate in the mercantile system of Great Britain and other Western European nations. **Mercantile systems** bound trade and its administration to national governments. Smith and his supporters saw free trade as "the invisible hand" that produced the wealth of nations. This wealth, in turn, became the inspiration and justification for capitalism.

First Lady Laura Bush visits a D.C. public school to encourage students to read. (Photo courtesy: Robin Weiner/WirePix/The Image Works)

From the mid- to late eighteenth century, and through the mid-1930s in the United States and in much of the Western world, the idea of *laissez-faire* economics (from the French, "to leave alone") enjoyed considerable popularity. While most states regulated and intervened heavily in their economies well into the nineteenth century, the U.S. national government routinely followed a "hands-off" economic policy. By the late 1800s, however, the national government felt increasing pressure to regulate some aspects of the economy (often in part because of the difficulties states faced in regulating large, multistate industries such as the railroads, and from industry's desire to override the patchwork regulatory scheme produced by the states). Thereafter, the Great Depression of the 1930s forced the national government to take a much larger role in the economy. Afterward, any pretense that the United States was a purely capitalist system was abandoned. The worldwide extent of this trend, however, varied by country and over time. In post–World War II Britain, for example, the extent of government economic regulation of industry and social welfare was much greater than that attempted by American policy makers in the same period.

For most of U.S. history, capitalism and the American dream have been alive and well: Hard work has been rewarded with steady jobs and increased earning power and wages, and Americans have expected to hand down improved economic, social, and educational status to their children. In many ways World War II ushered in the era of the American dream: Men returned from the war and went to college, their tuition paid for by the G.I. Bill. Prior to the war, a college education was mainly the preserve of the rich; the G.I. Bill made it available to men from all walks of life. Many men got the education they needed to succeed and do much better than their parents before them. In addition, low-interest-rate mortgages were made available through the Veterans' Administration, and the American dream of owning a home became a reality for millions. Capitalism worked and made their efforts to preserve it worthwhile.

mercantile system
A system that binds trade and its administration to the national government.

Longman
Participate.com
2.0
Timeline
Major
Technological
Innovations
that Have
Changed the
Political
Landscape

Other Economic Systems

Capitalism is just one type of economic system. Others include socialism, communism, and totalitarianism.

Socialism.   Socialism is a philosophy that advocates collective ownership and control of the means of economic production. Socialists call for governmental—rather than

socialism
An economic system that advocates for collective ownership and control of the means of production.

private—ownership of all land, property, and industry and, in turn, an equitable distribution of the income from those holdings. In addition, socialism seeks to replace the profit motive and competition with cooperation and social responsibility.

Some Socialists actually tolerate capitalism as long as the government maintains some kind of control over the economy. Others reject capitalism outright and insist on the abolition of all private enterprise.

Some Socialists, especially in Western Europe, have argued that socialism can evolve through democratic processes. Thus, in nations like Great Britain, certain critical industries or services such as health care or the coal industry have been nationalized, or taken over by the state, to provide for more efficient supervision and to avoid the major concentrations of wealth that occur when individuals privately own key industries.

communism
An economic system in which workers own the means of production and control the distribution of resources.

Communism.   The German philosopher Karl Marx argued that government was simply a manifestation of underlying economic forces and could be understood according to types of economic production. In *Das Kapital* (1867), Marx argued that capitalism would always be replaced by socialist states in which the working class would own the means of production and distribution and be able to redistribute the wealth to meet its needs.

Marx believed that it was inevitable for each society to pass through the stages of history: feudalism, capitalism, socialism, and then **communism**. When society reached communism, Marx theorized, all class differences would be abolished and government would become unnecessary. A system of common ownership of the means of sustenance and production would lead to greater social justice. In practice, most notably under Vladimir Ilyich Ulyanov, under the pseudonym Lenin, and the Soviet dictator Joseph Stalin (also a pseudonym; his real name was Josif Vissarionivich Dzhugashvili), many of the tenets of Marxism were changed or modified.

Marx saw the change coming first in highly industrialized countries such as Britain and Germany, where a fully mature capitalism would pave the way for a socialist revolution. But Lenin and the Bolshevik Party wanted to have such a revolution in underdeveloped Russia. So, instead of relying on the historical inevitability of the communist future (as Marx envisioned), they advocated forcing that change. Lenin argued that by establishing an elite vanguard party of permanent revolutionaries and a dictatorship of the proletariat (working class), they could achieve socialism and communism without waiting for the historical forces to work. In the 1940s China followed the Leninist path led by Mao Ze Dong (formerly transliterated as Mao Tse Tung).

In practice, the communist states rejected free markets as a capitalist and exploitative way of organizing production and turned instead to planning and state regulation. In capitalist economies, the market sets prices, wages, product mix, and so on. Under a planned economy, government makes conscious choices to determine prices, wages, product mix, and so on.

totalitarianism
An economic system in which the government has total control over the economy.

Totalitarianism.   A totalitarian system is basically a modern form of extreme authoritarian rule. In contrast to governments based on democratic beliefs, totalitarian governments have total authority over their people and their economic system. The tools of **totalitarianism** are secret police, terror, propaganda, and an almost total prohibition on civil rights and liberties. These systems also tend to be ruled in the name of an ideology or a personality cult organized around a supreme leader. The reign of Saddam Hussein in Iraq comes close to the total control of forms of production, the airwaves, education, the arts, and even sports implied by totalitarianism. Some communist systems also approached totalitarianism.

CHARACTERISTICS OF AMERICAN DEMOCRACY

The United States, as created by the Framers, is an indirect democracy with several underlying concepts and distinguishing characteristics. Many of these characteristics are often in conflict, a factor that has led to some of the political discontent present in the population and simply turned off others. The political system, for example, is based on an underlying notion of the importance of balance among the legislative, executive, and judicial branches, between the state and federal governments, between the wants of the majority and the minority, between the rights of the individual and the best interests of the nation as a whole. The Framers built the system on the idea that there would be statesmen who would act for the good of the system. Without such statespersons, the system necessitates constant vigilance to keep a balance as the pendulum swings back and forth between various desires, demands, and responsibilities. To some, government may be a necessary evil; but a good government is less evil if it can keep things in balance as it operates in various spheres. The ideas of balance permeate many of the concepts and characteristics of American democracy presented below.

Popular Consent

Popular consent, the idea that governments must draw their powers from the consent of the governed, is one distinguishing characteristic of American democracy. Derived from Locke's social contract theory, the notion of popular consent was central to the Declaration of Independence. A citizen's willingness to vote represents his or her consent to be governed and is thus an essential premise of democracy. Growing numbers of nonvoters can threaten the operation and legitimacy of a truly democratic system. So, too, can voting systems where certain kinds of ballots, such as many of those used in Florida in 2000, appeared not to count many of the votes cast.

popular consent
The idea that governments must draw their powers from the consent of the governed.

Popular Sovereignty

The notion of **popular sovereignty,** the right of the majority to govern themselves, has its basis in natural law: Ultimately, political authority rests with the people, who can create, abolish, or alter their governments. The idea that all governments derive their power from the people is found in the Declaration of Independence and the U.S. Constitution, but the term itself did not come into wide use until pre–Civil War debates over slavery. At that time, supporters of popular sovereignty argued that the citizens of new states seeking admission to the Union should be able to decide whether or not their states would allow slavery within their borders. (See Highlight: Who Makes Decisions in America? for some theories about who makes decisions about governing.) Today, public opinion polls are often used as instantaneous measures of the popular will.

popular sovereignty
The right of the majority to govern themselves.

Majority Rule

Majority rule, another basic democratic principle, means that the majority (normally) of citizens in any political unit should elect officials and determine policies (50 percent of the total votes cast plus 1). This principle holds for both voters and their elected representatives. Yet the American system also stresses the need to preserve minority rights, as evidenced by the myriad protections of individual rights and liberties found in the Bill of Rights.

The concept of the preservation of minority rights has changed dramatically in the United States. It wasn't until after the Civil War that slaves were freed and African Americans began to enjoy minimal citizenship rights. By the 1960s, however, rage at America's failure to guarantee minority rights in all sections of the nation fueled the civil rights movement, which ultimately led to congressional passage of the Civil Rights Act of 1964 and the Voting Rights Act of 1965, both designed to further minority rights. Today, attacks on affirmative action are often fueled by cries that majority rights are being trampled.

Concepts of majority rule today are threatened by a tradition of political apathy that has emerged slowly over time within the American electorate. Since 1960, the number of eligible voters who have cast ballots generally has continued to decline. In the 2000 presidential election, just more than 50 percent of those eligible voted. In the 2002 midterm elections, 39.3 percent of the eligibles voted, up slightly from 1998. This increase

majority rule
The central premise of direct democracy in which only policies that collectively garner the support of a majority of voters will be made into law.

HIGHLIGHT

How conflicts are resolved is often determined by how the government is operated and by whom. All of these theories provide interesting ways to think about how policy decisions are made, whether we are looking at local, state, or national policies.

Elite Theory

Elite theory posits that all important decisions in society are made by the few, called the elite, so that government is increasingly alienated from the people and rarely responsive to their wishes. In *The Power Elite* (1956), American sociologist C. Wright Mills argued that important policies were set by a loose coalition of three groups with some overlap among each.[a] According to his elite theory, these three major influencers of policy—corporate leaders, military leaders, and a small group of key governmental leaders—are the true "power elite" in America. Other elite theorists have argued that the news media should be included as a fourth source of political power in the United States.

Another proponent of elite theory, political scientist Thomas R. Dye, contends that all societies are divided into elites and masses. The elite are the few who have power, and the masses are the many who don't.[b] This distribution of functions and powers in society is inevitable. Elites, however, are not immune from public opinion, nor do they by definition oppress the masses. Dye argues that in a complex society, such as ours, only a "tiny minority" actually make policy.

Bureaucratic Theory

Max Weber (1864–1920), the founder of modern sociology, argued that all institutions, governmental and nongovernmental, have fallen under the control of a large and ever-growing bureaucracy that carry out policy on a day-to-day basis using standardized procedures. Because all institutions have grown more complex, Weber concluded that the expertise and competence of bureaucrats allows them to wrest power from others, especially elected officials.

Interest Group Theory

David Truman argues that interest groups—not elites, sets of elites, or bureaucrats—control the governmental process.[c] He believes there are so many potential pressure points in the three branches of the federal government—as well as at the state level—that groups can step in on any number of competing sides. The government then becomes the equilibrium point in the system as it mediates between competing interests.

Pluralist Theory

According to some political scientists, the structure of our democratic government allows only for a pluralistic model of democracy.[d] Borrowing from Truman's work, Robert Dahl argues that resources are scattered so widely in our diverse democracy that no single elite group can ever have a monopoly over any substantial area of policy.

Adding to this debate, Theodore J. Lowi has described how political decision making takes place today in an era of what he terms "interest group liberalism." According to Lowi, participants in every political controversy get something; thus, each has some impact on how political decisions are made. Lowi also states that governments rarely say no to any well-organized interests. Thus, all interests ultimately receive some benefits or rewards. Lowi bemoans the fact that the public interest—that is, what is good for the public at large—often tends to lose in this system.[e]

---

[a]C. Wright Mills, *The Power Elite* (New York: Oxford University Press, 1956).
[b]Thomas R. Dye, *Who's Running America?* (New York: Prentice Hall, 1976).
[c]David B. Truman, *The Governmental Process* (New York: Knopf, 1951).
[d]Robert A. Dahl, *Preface to Democratic Theory* (Chicago: University of Chicago Press, 1956).
[e]Theodore J. Lowi, *The End of Liberalism* (New York: Norton, 1979).

---

was attributed to unprecedented Republican get-out-the-vote efforts. Although one in five of those who admitted that they did not vote said they didn't do so because they couldn't take time off from work or were "too busy,"[6] others lay blame on the political process then noting that low voter turnout is a message to politicians.[7] In the 2000 presidential election, however, the proportion of voters edged up slightly to just above 50 percent. Whatever reasons are offered for nonvoting, it is an important phenomenon to keep in mind when we talk about majority rule. Most discussions of elections as the voice of the majority are really better cast as discussions of the wishes of the majority who voted.

Individualism

Tremendous value is placed on the individual in American democracy and culture. All individuals are deemed rational and fair, and endowed, as Thomas Jefferson proclaimed in the Declaration of Independence, "with certain unalienable rights." Even today, many view individualism, which holds that the primary function of government is to enable the individual to achieve his or her highest level of development, as a mixed blessing. It is also a concept whose meaning has changed over time. The rugged individualism of the western frontier, for example, was altered as more citizens moved westward, cities developed, and demands for government services increased.

Equality

Another key characteristic of our democracy is the American emphasis on political equality, the definition of which has varied considerably over time (as discussed in chapter 6). The importance of political equality is another reflection of American stress on the importance of the individual. Although some individuals clearly wield more political clout than others, the adage "One man, one vote" implies a sense of political equality for all.

Personal Liberty

Personal liberty is perhaps the single most important characteristic of American democracy. The Constitution itself was written to assure "life" and "liberty." Over the years, however, our concepts of liberty have changed and evolved from "freedom *from*" to "freedom *to.*" The Framers intended Americans to be free from governmental infringements on freedom of religion and speech, from unreasonable search and seizure, and so on (see chapter 5). The addition of the Fourteenth Amendment to the Constitution and its emphasis on equal protection of the laws and subsequent passage of laws guaranteeing civil rights, however, expanded Americans' concept of liberty to include demands for "freedom to" be free from discrimination. Debates over how much the government should do to guarantee these rights or liberties illustrate the conflicts that continue to occur in our democratic system.

personal liberty
A key characteristic of U.S. democracy. Initially meaning freedom from governmental interference, today it includes demands for freedom to engage in a variety of practices free from governmental discrimination.

THE CHANGING POLITICAL CULTURE AND CHARACTERISTICS OF THE AMERICAN PEOPLE

The concept **political culture** has been defined as the "attitudes toward the political system and its various parts, and attitudes toward the role of the self in the system." It is a set of orientations toward a special set of social objects and processes.[8] Where you live, how you were raised, and even your age or age cohort can affect how you view the government or a governmental program.

Americans are very divided on some issues; politicians, media commentators, and even the citizenry itself also tend to focus on how different Americans are. But before we explore some of those differences, which have profound implications on policy and individual preferences, we must note the similarities of Americans. Most Americans share a common language—English—and have similar aspirations for themselves and their families. Most agree that they would rather live in the United States than anywhere else; and that democracy, with all of its warts, is still the best system for most. Most Americans highly value education and want to send their children to the best schools possible, viewing an education as the key to success.

Still, at the heart of the American political system is change, be it in population, demographics, or interest in politics. But while it is true that America and its population are undergoing rapid change, this is not necessarily a new phenomenon. It is simply new to

political culture
Attitudes toward the political system and its various parts, and attitudes toward the role of the self in the system.

Longman
participate.com
2.0
Simulation
**How to Satisfy
Aunt Martha**

most of us. In the pages that follow, we take a look at some of the characteristics of the American population and its political culture. Because the people of the United States are the basis of political power and authority, these characteristics and attitudes have important implications for how America is governed and how and what policies are made.

Changing Size and Population

WEB EXPLORATION
To get a minute-by-minute update on U.S. population, see
www.ablongman.com/oconnor

One year after the Constitution was ratified, less than 4 million Americans lived in the thirteen states. They were united by a single language and opposition to the king. Most shared a similar Protestant-Christian heritage, and those who voted were white male property owners. The Constitution mandated that each of the sixty-five members of the original House of Representatives should represent 30,000 citizens. However, due to rapid growth, that number often was much higher. Anti-Federalists, who opposed a strong national government during the founding period, at least took solace in the fact that members of the House of Representatives, who generally represented far fewer people than senators, would be more in touch with "the people."

As revealed in Figure 1.1, as the nation grew westward, the absolute population of the country also grew. Although the physical size of the United States has remained

FIGURE 1.1   U.S. Population, 1790–2050
Since around 1890, when more and more immigrants came to America, the population of the United States, although largely fueled by new births and increased longevity, has continued to rise.

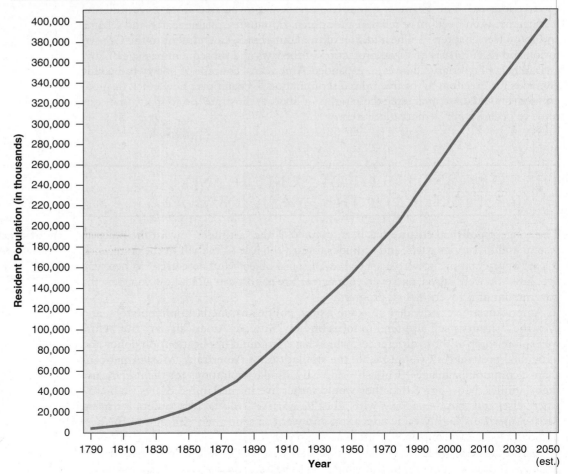

Source: U.S. Census Bureau, *U.S. Census of Population: 1920–1990, vol. 1;* Population Projections of the Total Resident Population, 1999–2101, www.census.gov/prod/1

stable since the addition of Alaska and Hawaii in 1959, there are now more than 281.4 million Americans. In 2002, a single member of the House of Representatives from Montana represented as many as 900,000 people.

As a result of this growth, most citizens today feel far removed from the national government and their elected representatives. Members of Congress, too, feel this change. Often they represent diverse constituencies with a variety of needs, concerns, and expectations, and they can meet only a relative few of these people in face-to-face electioneering.

Changing Demographics of the U.S. Population

As the physical size and population of the United States have changed, so have many of the assumptions on which it was founded. Some of the dynamism of the American system actually stems from the racial and ethnic changes that have taken place throughout our history, a notion that often gets lost in debates about immigration policy. Moreover, for the first time, the U.S. population is getting much older. This "graying" of America also will assuredly lead to changes in our expectations of government and in our public policy demands. The current debate over what to do with the budget surplus is illustrative of that phenomenon. Below, we look at some demographic facts (that is, information on characteristics of America's population), and then discuss some implications of these changes for how our nation is governed and what policy issues might arise.

Changes in Racial and Ethnic Distributions. From the start, the population of America has been constantly changed by the arrival of various kinds of immigrants to its shores—Western Europeans fleeing religious persecution in the 1600s to early 1700s, Irish Catholics escaping the potato famine in the 1850s, Chinese laborers arriving to work on the railroads, Northern and Eastern Europeans from the 1880s to 1910s, and most recently, Southeast Asians, Cubans, Mexicans, and others.

Immigration to the United States peaked in the first decade of the 1900s, when nearly 9 million people, many of them from Eastern Europe, entered the country. The United States did not see another major wave of immigration until the late 1980s, when nearly 2 million immigrants were admitted in one year, as illustrated in Figure 1.2. Unlike the arrivals in other periods of high immigration, however, these "new" Americans were often "nonwhite"; many were Southeast Asians or Latin Americans. In fact, in 1997, a poll commissioned by PBS revealed that 45 percent of Americans polled thought "too many" immigrants were entering the United States from Latin American countries.[9]

While immigration has been a continual source of changing demographics in America, race has also played a major role in the development and course of politics in the United States. As revealed in Analyzing the Data: Changing Age Composition of the United States, the racial balance in America is changing dramatically. In 2000, for example, whites made up 75.1 percent of the U.S. population, African Americans 12.3 percent, and Hispanics 12.5 percent, surpassing the number of African Americans in the United States for the first time. Originally, demographers did not anticipate Hispanics surpassing African Americans to occur until 2050. In some states, Hispanic population is rivaling white, non-Hispanic populations.

Changes in Age Cohort Composition. Just as the racial and ethnic composition of the American population is changing, so too is the average age of the population. "For decades, the U.S. was described as a nation of the young because the

Elian Gonzalez holds American and Cuban flags as a crowd of supporters grows outside his uncle's home. The large Cuban community is a powerful force in Miami politics and objected strenuously to Elian's return to Cuba. (Photo courtesy: AFP/Corbis)

(Photo courtesy: Culver Pictures)

That immigration problem again!

FIGURE 1.2   Race and Ethnicity in America: 2000 and Beyond

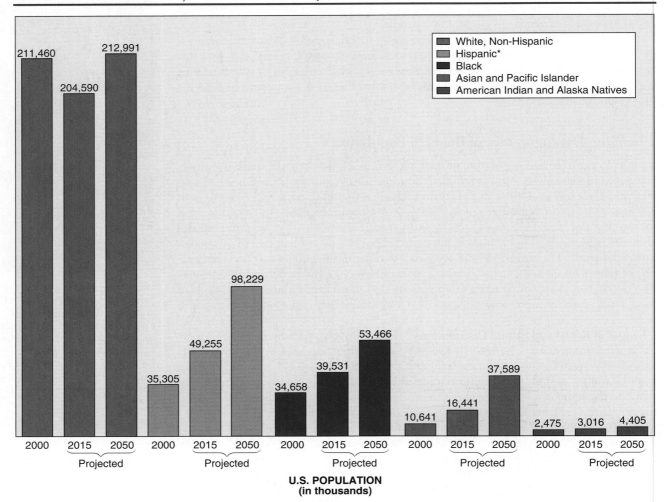

	White, Non-Hispanic
	Hispanic*
	Black
	Asian and Pacific Islander
	American Indian and Alaska Natives

U.S. POPULATION
(in thousands)

*Persons of Hispanic origin can be of any race.

Source: U.S. Census Bureau, www.census.gov/population/projections

Longman
Participate.com 2.0
Participation
**The Debate
Over
Immigration**

Longman
Participate.com 2.0
Visual Literacy
**Understanding
Who We Are**

number of persons under the age of twenty greatly outnumber(ed) those sixty-five and older,"[10] but this is no longer the case. Due to changes in patterns of fertility, life expectancy, and immigration, the nation's age profile has changed drastically.[11] When the United States was founded, the average life expectancy was thirty-five years; by 2000, it was nearly eighty years for women and seventy-four years for men. As people live longer, the types of services and policies they demand from government differ dramatically. In Florida, for example, which leads the nation in the percentage of its population over age sixty-five,[12] citizens are far less concerned with the quality of public schools (especially if they are being taxed for those schools) than the citizens in states with far lower proportions of the elderly.

As the age profile of the U.S. population has changed, political scientists and others have found it useful to assign labels to various generations. Such labels can be useful in understanding the various pressures put on our nation and its government, because when people were born and the kinds of events they experienced can have important consequences on how they view other political, economic, and social events. For example, those 76.8 million people born after World War II (1946–1964) are often referred to as "Baby Boomers." These individuals grew up in a very different America than did their parents and now are reaching retirement age, which will put a major strain on the

A N A L Y Z I N G   T H E   D A T A

CHANGING AGE COMPOSITION OF THE UNITED STATES

The elderly are the fastest-growing group in the United States due to increased life expectancy, immigration, and advanced medical technology. The percentage of elderly individuals is projected to exceed the percentage of young people under seventeen years old by 2030. This is a dramatic increase from 1900, when the elderly comprised only 4 percent of the population. How does this impact government? In one respect, as elderly people steadily retire from the labor force, the proportion of nonworking adults will generate ever-greater demands for social programs like Social Security and health care.

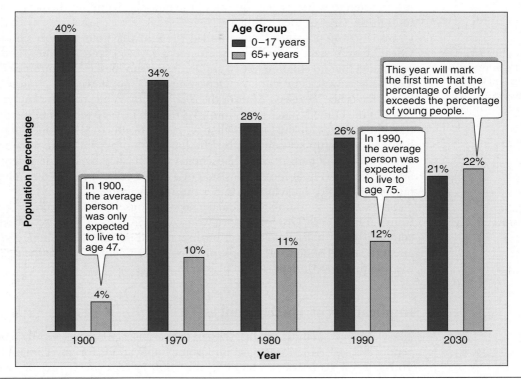

Source: From *Young vs. Old: Generational Combat in the 21st Century* by Susan A. McManus, Copyright © 1995 by Westview Press, Inc. Reprinted by permission of Westview Press, a member of Perseus Books, L.L.C.

already overburdened Social Security system.[13] In contrast, their children are often called Generation X-ers, the name of an early 1980s punk band and, later, a novel.[14] Soon, however, *Time* and *Newsweek* used the term to christen the 50 million who were born in the late 1960s and early 1970s to the Baby Boomers.

This group experienced the economic downturn of the 1980s. Jobs were scarce when they graduated from college, and many initially had a hard time paying off their college loans. They overwhelmingly believe that political leaders ignore them, and they distrust the political process. X-ers work longer, are better educated, and are more grassroots oriented politically than their parents.[15] Moreover, it is a very libertarian generation. According to one commentator, a difference between Generation X-ers and the liberal Baby Boomers is that X-ers "see capitalism as something that's not necessarily evil." X-ers believe they "can use capitalism for social change. It's one way to make government and big business stand up and take notice."[16]

In contrast, the fastest-growing group under age sixty-five is called "Generation Y," those aged ten to twenty-four. This group, unlike their Generation X predecessors,

WEB EXPLORATION
For more detail on population projections, see
www.ablongman.com/oconnor

WEB EXPLORATION
To learn more about Generation Y, see
www.ablongman.com/oconnor

"has grown up in good times and [they] have nothing but optimism about their future."[17] This group is very Internet savvy and much more globally focused than any generation before it.

Changes in Family and Family Size.   Family size and household arrangements can be affected by several factors, including age at first marriage, divorce rates, economic conditions, longevity rates, and improvements in health care. In the past, large families were the norm (in part because so many children died early) and gender roles were clearly defined. Women did housework and men worked in the fields. Large families were imperative; children were the source of cheap farm labor.

Industrialization and knowledge of birth control methods, no matter how primitive, began to put a dent in the size of American families by the early 1900s. No longer needing children to work for the survival of the household unit on the farm, couples began to limit the sizes of their families.

By 1949, 49 percent of those polled thought that four or more children was the "ideal" family size; in 1997, only 8 percent favored large families, and 54 percent responded that no children to two children were the "best."[18] As chronicled in the popular press as well as by the U.S. Department of Commerce, the American family no longer looks like *The Cosby Show* or the *Brady Bunch*. While the actual number of households in the United States grew from 93.3 million in 1970 to 103 million in 2000, what those households looked like has changed dramatically. In 1940, nine out of ten households were family households; by 2000, only 55.6 percent were two-parent family households, 14.9 percent of all households were headed by a single parent, and nearly 30 percent of all households consisted of a single person. Fewer than one-half of the family households had children under the age of eighteen.

Since 1970, the number of female-headed households has increased dramatically from 5.5 million to 12.8 million—a whopping 133 percent increase. These changes in composition of households, lower birthrates, and prevalence of single-parent families affect the kinds of demands people place on government as well as their perceptions of the role that government should play in their lives.

Implications of These Changes

The varied races, ethnic origins, sizes of the various age cohorts, family types, and even gender roles of Americans have important implications for government and politics. Today, a few Americans, including the 2000 Reform Party presidential candidate Patrick Buchanan, believe that immigrants (legal and illegal) are flooding onto our shores with disastrous consequences. Such anti-immigration sentiments are hardly new—in fact, American history is replete with examples of "Americans" set against any new immigration. In the 1840s, for example, the Know Nothing Party arose in part to oppose immigration from Roman Catholic nations, charging that the pope was going to organize the slaughter of all Protestants in the United States. In the 1920s the Ku Klux Klan, which had over 5 million members, called for barring immigration to stem the tide of Roman Catholics and Jews into the nation.

Today, even though almost all Americans have ancestors who immigrated to the United States, most Americans oppose unrestricted access to the United States and react negatively to reports that the foreign-born population is increasing. Hostility to immigrants manifests itself in a variety of ways. Some bemoan the fact that the nation is becoming "less white," or criticize those who refuse to adopt "American" ways as they cling to the customs, language, and traditions of their old country. Immigrants, too, often face blame from the citizenry or elected officials for lost jobs or depressed wages (because they are often willing to take low-wage jobs).

In the presidential campaign of 1996, immigration (legal and illegal) was a big issue. Many Americans believed (erroneously, for the most part) that floods of immigrants were putting Americans out of work and putting a strain on our already overburdened

WEB EXPLORATION
For more information on families and household composition, see
www.ablongman.com/oconnor

state and federal resources, especially school systems and welfare programs. In 1998, for example, California voters passed Proposition 227 abolishing bilingual education programs in public elementary and secondary schools, a measure many viewed as anti-immigrant. But by 2000, when the U.S. unemployment rate was at near record lows, this issue faded.

Changing racial, ethnic, and even age and family demographics also seem to intensify—at least for some—an "us" versus "them" attitude. For example, government affirmative action programs, which were created in the 1960s to redress decades of overt racial discrimination, are now under attack because some people believe that they give minorities and women unfair advantages in the job market, as well as easier access to higher education opportunities. As more and more women graduated from college and entered the workforce, for example, some men criticized efforts to widen opportunities for women, while many women complained that a "glass ceiling" barred their advancement to the highest levels in most occupations. Dramatic changes in educational and employment opportunities, revealed in Table 1.1, also underscore these tensions.

With the slowing of the U.S. economy after several years of economic growth, anti-immigration sentiment is surfacing once again. (Photo courtesy: Essdras Suarez/ Liaison Agency)

Sociologist James Davison Hunter defines the culture conflict that is the result of changing demographics as "political and social hostility rooted in very different systems of moral understanding."[19] These different worldviews—worker versus CEO; educated versus uneducated, young versus old, white versus black, male versus female, native-born versus immigrant—can create deep cleavages in society, as exemplified by the "polarizing impulses or tendencies" in American society.[20] Just as the two parties at times seem to be pushed to take extreme positions on many issues, so are many of those who speak out on those issues.

Demographics also affect politics and government because an individual's perspective often influences how he or she *hears* the debate on various issues. Thus, many African Americans viewed O. J. Simpson's acquittal as vindication for decades of unjust treatment experienced by blacks in the criminal justice system and the wealthy view proposals for a flat tax with much more enthusiasm than do many of the poor.

TABLE 1.1　Men and Women in a Changing Society

	1970		2000	
	Men	*Women*	*Men*	*Women*
Estimated life expectancy	67.1	74.1	74.24	79.9
% high school graduates	53	52	87	88
% of BAs awarded	57	43	45	55
% of MAs awarded	60	40	45	55
% of PhDs awarded	87	13	61	39
% in legal profession	95	5	70	30
Median earnings	$26,760	$14,232	$35,345	$25,862
Single parents	1.2 million	5.6 million	n/a	n/a

Sources: for 1970: *1996 Statistical Abstract*, U.S Dept. of Commerce, Economics and Statistics Administration, Bureau of the census. 2000 data: National Center for Education Statistics http://nces.ed.gov/fastfacts.

These cleavages and the emphasis many politicians put on our demographic differences play out in many ways in American politics. Baby Boomers and the elderly object to any changes in Social Security or Medicare, while those in Generation X vote for politicians who support change, if they vote at all. Many policies are targeted at one group or the other, further exacerbating differences—real or imagined—and lawmakers often find themselves the target of many different factions. All of this makes it difficult to devise coherent policies to "promote the general welfare," as promised in the Constitution.

The Ideology of the American Public

political ideology
An individual's coherent set of values and beliefs about the purpose and scope of government.

Political ideology is a term used by political scientists to refer to the more or less consistent set of values that historically have been reflected in the political system, economic order, social goals, and moral values of any given society. "It is the means by which the basic values held by a party, class, group or individual are articulated."[21] Most Americans espouse liberalism or conservatism, although a growing number call themselves libertarians, who do not place themselves on traditional liberal/conservative continuums used by political scientists (see Figure 1.3).

You probably already have a good idea of what the terms liberal and conservative mean, but you may not be aware that the meaning of these terms has changed dramatically over time. During the nineteenth century, for example, conservatives supported governmental power and favored a role for religion in public life; in contrast, liberals supported freedom from undue governmental control. (See Table 1.2 for additional information about these terms.) In general, your ideology often is a good predictor of where you stand on a variety of issues (see Table 1.2) as well as how you view the proper role of government.

conservative
One thought to believe that a government is best that governs least and that big government can only infringe on individual, personal, and economic rights.

Conservativism.   According to William Safire's *New Political Dictionary,* a **conservative** "is a defender of the status quo who, when change becomes necessary in tested institutions or practices, prefers that it come slowly, and in moderation."[22] Conservatives are thought to believe that a government is best that governs least, and that big government can only infringe on individual, personal, and economic rights. They want less government, especially in terms of regulation of the economy. Conservatives favor local and state action over federal action, and emphasize fiscal responsibility, most notably in the

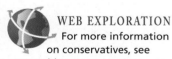

WEB EXPLORATION
For more information on conservatives, see
www.ablongman.com/oconnor

FIGURE 1.3   Self-Identification as Liberal, Moderate, or Conservative, 1974–2000
After several years of stagnation, fewer Americans are beginning to characterize themselves as liberal as the number of conservatives increased again.

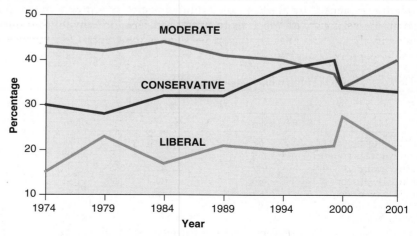

Note: "Liberal" equals the combined percentages of those identifying themselves as extremely liberal, liberal, or slightly liberal; "conservative" equals the combined percentages of those identifying themselves as extremely conservative, conservative, or slightly

Source: Roper Center at the University of Connecticut, *Public Opinion Online.*

TABLE 1.2   Liberal? Conservative? Libertarian? Chart Your Views on These Issues

| | | | | ISSUES | | | Government Support of: | |
	Abortion Rights	Environmental Regulation	Organized School Prayer	Gun Control Laws	Anti-Discrimination Laws	Poor	School Vouchers
Conservative	Oppose	Oppose	Favor	Oppose	Oppose	Oppose	Favor
Liberal	Favor ✓	Favor ✓	Oppose ✓	Favor	Favor ✓	Favor ✓	Oppose
Libertarian	Favor	Oppose	Oppose	Oppose	Oppose	Oppose	Oppose

form of balanced budgets. Conservatives are likely to support smaller, less activist governments and believe that domestic problems like homelessness, poverty, and discrimination are better dealt with by the private sector than by the government. Less rigid conservatives see the need for governmental action in some fields and for steady change in many areas. They seek to achieve such change within the framework of existing institutions, occasionally changing the institutions when they show a need for it.

Liberalism.   Liberalism is a political view held by those who "seek to change the political, economic, or social status quo to foster the development and well-being of the individual."[23] Safire defines a **liberal** as "currently one who believes in more government action to meet individual needs, originally one who resisted government encroachments on individual liberties."[24] Liberals now are considered to favor a big government that plays an active role in the economy. They also stress the need for the government to provide for the poor and homeless, to provide a wide array of other social services, and to take an activist role in protecting the rights of women, the elderly, minorities, and the environment. It is a political philosophy that has roots in the American Revolution and eighteenth-century liberalism. Today, many of its supporters refer to it as the "modern revival of classical liberalism."[25]

liberal
One considered to favor extensive governmental involvement in the economy and the provision of social services and to take an activist role in protecting the rights of women, the elderly, minorities, and the environment.

Libertarianism.   Libertarianism is a political philosophy based largely on individual freedom and the curtailment of state power. **Libertarians** have long believed in the evils of big government and stress that government should not involve itself in the plight of the people or attempt to remedy any social ills. Basically, libertarians, although a very diverse lot, favor a free market economy and an end to governmental intrusion in the area of personal liberties. Generation X-ers are more libertarian in political philosophy than any other age cohort and credited with the election of Governor Jesse Ventura of Minnesota, who ran as the Reform Party candidate, became an Independent after election, and claims to be a libertarian. Liberals criticize libertarian calls for elimination of all government sponsored welfare and public works programs; conservatives bemoan libertarian calls for reductions in the defense budget and elimination of federal agencies such as the Central Intelligence Agency and the Federal Bureau of Investigation.

libertarian
One who favors a free market economy and no governmental interference in personal liberties.

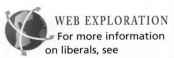
WEB EXPLORATION
For more information on liberals, see
www.ablongman.com/oconnor

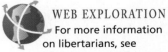
WEB EXPLORATION
For more information on libertarians, see
www.ablongman.com/oconnor

WEB EXPLORATION
To find out your ideological stance, go to
www.ablongman.com/oconnor

Problems with Political Labels

When considering what it means when someone identifies himself or herself as a conservative, liberal, libertarian, or some other political philosophy, it is important to remember that the labels such as "conservative" and "liberal" can be quite misleading and do not necessarily allow us to predict political opinions. In a perfect world, liberals would be liberal and conservatives would be conservative. Studies reveal, however, that many people who call themselves conservative actually take fairly liberal positions on many policy issues. In fact, anywhere from 20 percent to 60 percent will take a traditionally "conservative" position on one issue and a traditionally "liberal" position on another.[26] People who take conservative stances against "big government," for example, often support increases in spending for the elderly, education, or health care. It is also not unusual to encounter a person who could be considered liberal on social issues such

Dick Armey (R–TX), House majority leader in the 107th session and chairman of the House Select Committee on Homeland Security, talks to House Democratic Whip Nancy Pelosi (D-CA) as the committee begins debate on legislation creating a department of homeland security. In the House, they stand at opposite ends of the liberal (Pelosi) and conservative (Armey) spectrum. (Photo courtesy: Dennis Cook/AP/Wide World Photos.)

as abortion and civil rights but conservative on economic or "pocketbook" issues. Moreover, libertarians, for example, often are against any governmental restrictions on abortion (a liberal view) but against any kind of welfare spending (a conservative view). Today, like libertarians, most Americans' positions on specific issues cut across liberal/conservative ideological boundaries to such a degree that new, more varied ideological categories may soon be needed to capture division within American political thought. (See Table 1.2 to see where your political views place you.)

POLITICAL CULTURE AND VIEWS OF GOVERNMENT

Americans' views about and expectations of government affect the political system at all levels. It has now become part of our political culture to expect negative campaigns, dishonest politicians, and political pundits who make their living bashing politicians and the political process. How Americans view politics, the economy, and their ability to achieve the American dream is also influenced by their political ideology as well as by their social, economic, educational, and personal circumstances.

Since the early 1990s, the major sources of most individuals' on-the-air news—the three major networks (ABC, CBS, and NBC) along with CNN and C-SPAN—have been supplemented dramatically as the number of news and quasi-news outlets have multiplied like rabbits. First there were weekly programs including *Dateline* and *Primetime Live* on the regular networks. Then came the rapid expansion of cable programming beginning with CNN and C-SPAN, then the new FOX network, MSNBC, and CNBC—all competing for similar audiences. By Election Night 2000, most people turned to a cable news program to learn about who won, never suspecting that the results weren't to be final for five more weeks. These networks' news programming also has been supplemented by the phenomenal development of the Internet as an instantaneous source of news as well as rumor about politics. One online newsletter, the *Drudge Report*, was actually the first to break the story about President Clinton and Monica Lewinsky.

As more and more news programs developed, the pressure on each network or news program to be "the first" with the news—often whether it actually is verifiable or not—multiplied exponentially as was illustrated on Election Night 2000, as all rushed to "call" states for a particular candidate and to be the first to predict the overall winner. So has their focus on political scandals. This phenomenon is well illustrated by the debate over whether *Newsweek* erred in delaying breaking the initial story of Bill Clinton's affair with Monica Lewinsky. For seven months the nation got a daily diet of speculation and conjecture about "Bill and Monica" until the president finally admitted to an "improper relationship."

The competition for news stories, as well as the instantaneous nature of these communications, often highlights the negative, the sensational, the sound bite, and usually the extremes. It's hard to remain upbeat about America or politics amidst the media's focus on personality and scandal. It's hard to remain positive about the fate of Americans and their families if you listen to talk radio or watch talk shows like *Jerry Springer* or *Ricki Lake*. It was far easier for the press to focus on the Clinton/Lewinsky matter than to devote time and space to a story of a teenage mother who, aided by government programs, went to college, got a job, and became an

During the 2000 campaign, George W. Bush appeared on informal talk shows like *Oprah Winfrey* and *Live with Regis* in an effort to appeal to women voters. (Photo courtesy: Tannen Maury/The Image Works)

involved parent and citizen. Those kinds of success stories are generally showcased only in State of the Union addresses or at presidential nominating conventions.

This frustration and discontent with government and its institutions are a relatively new phenomenon in the United States. In the nineteenth and early twentieth centuries, immigrants who came to America lived in small, ethnic urban enclaves, but they made learning English and adopting American ways their first priority. At school, their children were taught pride in the United States and its symbols. Compulsory civics classes taught them about the Framers and how to be good citizens. The public schools, in essence, were engaged in state building, and there was general agreement about America and what it stood for and what government should do.[27]

High Expectations

In roughly the first 150 years of our nation's history, the federal government had few responsibilities, and its citizens had few expectations of it beyond national defense, printing money, collecting tariffs and taxes, and so on. The state governments were generally far more powerful than the federal government in matters affecting the everyday lives of Americans (see chapter 3).

As the nation and its economy grew in size and complexity, the federal government took on more responsibilities such as regulating some businesses, providing poverty relief, and inspecting food. Then, in the 1930s, in response to the Great Depression, President Franklin D. Roosevelt's New Deal government programs proliferated in almost every area of American life (job creation, income security, aid to the poor, and so on). Since then, until recently, Americans have looked to the government for solutions to all kinds of problems.

Politicians, too, have often contributed to rising public expectations by promising far more than they or government could deliver. Although President Clinton's vow to end "welfare as we know it" was realized by the end of his first term, his ambitious promises to overhaul the health care system went nowhere. Similarly, several key provisions of the Republicans' highly ambitious Contract with America failed to see the legislative light of day. Term limits, for example, a battle cry of Republicans running

Doris "Granny D" Haddock looks out from the U.S. Capitol steps as she completes a 14-month, 3,200-mile trek across America to agitate for campaign finance reform. (Photo courtesy: Reuters/Jamal Wilson/Archive Photos)

for the 104th Congress in 1994, were not really so attractive to them once they took over control of Congress. These rising expectations about government's ability to reform itself, as well as to cure all social and economic ills, have led to cynicism about government and apathy, as evidenced in low voter turnout. It may be that Americans have come to expect too much from the national government and must simply readjust their expectations. Nevertheless, as revealed in Table 1.3, confidence in most institutions was up, at least before the 2000 presidential election, the Supreme Court's 5–4 decision essentially deciding that election, and the convening of a highly partisan, closely divided 107th Congress.

A Missing Appreciation of the Good

During the Revolutionary period, average citizens were passionate about politics because the stakes—the very survival of the new nation—were so high. Today the stakes aren't readily apparent to many, and the government is no longer perceived as central to the achievement of "the good life." If you don't have faith in America, its institutions, or symbols (and Table 1.3 shows that many of us don't), it becomes even easier to blame the government for all kinds of woes—personal as well as societal—or to fail to credit governments for the things governments do well. Many Americans, for example, enjoy a remarkably high standard of living and much of it is due to governmental programs, practices, and protections (see Table 1.4 for quality of life measures).

Even in the short time between when you get up in the morning and when you leave for classes or work, the government—or its rulings or regulations—pervades your life. The national or state governments, for example, set the standards for whether you wake up on Eastern, Central, Mountain, or Pacific Standard Time. The national government regulates the airwaves and licenses the radio or television broadcasts you might listen to or glance at as you eat and get dressed. States, too, regulate and tax telecommunications. Whether or not the water you use as you brush your teeth contains fluoride is a state or local governmental issue. The federal Food and Drug Administration inspects your breakfast meat and sets standards for the advertising on your cereal box, orange juice carton, and other food packaging. States set standards for food labeling. Are they really "lite," "high in fiber," or "fresh squeezed"? Usually, one or more levels of government is authorized to decide these matters.

Although all governments have problems, it is important to stress the good they can do. In the aftermath of the Great Depression in the United States, for example, the government created the Social Security program, which dramatically decreased poverty among the elderly. Our contract laws and judicial system provide an efficient framework for business, assuring people that they have a recourse in the courts should someone fail to deliver as promised. Government-guaranteed student loan programs make

TABLE 1.3   Faith in Institutions

	PERCENTAGE OF AMERICANS DECLARING THEY HAD A "GREAT DEAL" OF CONFIDENCE IN THE INSTITUTION				
	1966	1975	1986	1996	2000
Congress	42%	13%	16%	8%	7%
Executive branch	41	13	21	10	15
The press	29	26	18	11	12
Business & industry	55	19	24	23	9
Colleges/universities	61	36	28	23	37
Medicine	73	51	46	45	39

Sources: Newsweek (January 8, 1996): 32; and The Public Perspective 8 (February/March 1994): 4. Data for 2000: Gallup Poll, Confidence in Institutions, June 22–25, 2000.

A truck sprays pesticide in the Canarsie section of Brooklyn, New York. A dead crow that tested positive for the West Nile virus was found in the neighborhood in August 2000, precipitating spraying, much to the concern of many local residents and environmentalists. (Photo courtesy: Chris Hondros/Newsmakers/ Online USA)

it possible for many students to attend college. And even something as seemingly mundane as our uniform bankruptcy laws help protect both a business enterprise and its creditors when the enterprise collapses.

Mistrust of Politicians

It's not difficult to see why Americans might be distrustful of politicians. In August 1998 after President Clinton announced to the American public that he had misled them concerning his relationship with Monica Lewinsky, 45 percent said they were disgusted, 33 percent they were angry, but only 18 percent were surprised, according to a poll conducted by the *Washington Post.* Only 19 percent responded that the president had "high personal, moral and ethical standards," down from 45 percent two years earlier.[28]

WEB EXPLORATION
For more information on the American electorate, see
www.ablongman.com/oconnor

TABLE 1.4   How Americans Are Really Doing

	1945	1970	2000
Population	132 million	203 million	281.4 million
Life expectancy	65.9	70.8	77
Per capita income (1987 constant dollars)	$6,367	$9,875	19,241[d]
Adults who are high school grads	25%[a]	55%	83%[e]
Adults who are college grads	5%[a]	11%	27%[e]
Households with phones	46%	87%	94%[b]
Households with televisions	0%	95%	98%[e]
Households with cable TV	0%	4%	65.3%[c]
Households with computers	n/a	n/a	50%
Women in labor force	29%	38%	67%[e]
Own their own home	46%	63%	65%[e]
Annual airline passengers	7 million	170 million	551 million[‡e]
Poverty rate	39.7%[†]	12.6%	13.3%[c]
Divorce rate (per 1,000 people)	3.5	3.5	9.9[a]
Children born out of wedlock	3.9%	16.7%	32%[d]

[a]1940 figure.   [†]1949 figure.   [b]1996 figure.   [‡]Estimate.   [c]1996 figure.   [d]1997 figure.   [e]1998 figure.

Sources: U.S. Census Bureau, Dept. of Economic Analysis, National Center for Health Statistics, Dept. of Education, *Statistical Abstract*, Bureau of Labor Statistics, the Air Transport Association.

"AT LAST, A CAMPAIGN ABOUT THE _REAL_ ISSUES!"

(Photo courtesy: Henry Payne. Reprinted by permission of United Feature Syndicate, Inc.)

President Clinton wasn't the only politician to incur the public's distrust. One 1998 poll conducted by the Pew Charitable Trusts found that 40 percent of those polled thought that most politicians were "crooks."[29] The low levels of public confidence in Congress, the executive branch, and the media revealed in Table 1.4 underscore this view. Character counts and the electorate has concluded—rightly or wrongly—that on this measure many elected officials can be found wanting. Even high proportions of the public questioned the motives of many justices of the U.S. Supreme Court in the wake of their decisions concerning the outcome of the 2000 presidential contest.

Voter Apathy

"Campaigns are the conversation of democracy," an observer once said.[30] But a Gallup poll conducted after the 1988 presidential contest between George Bush and Michael Dukakis found that 30 percent of those who voted would have preferred to check off a "no confidence in either" box had they been given the choice.

Americans, unlike voters in most other societies, get an opportunity to vote on a host of candidates and issues, but some say those choices may just be too numbing. Responsible voters may simply opt not to go to the polls, fearing that they lack sufficient information of the vast array of candidates and issues facing them.

A Census Bureau report examining the reasons that over 5 million eligible voters stayed home from the polls on Election Day in 1996 showed that "[t]ime constraints [were] the single biggest reason Americans" gave for not voting.[31] The head of the Committee for the Study of the American Electorate thinks that time is an excuse.[32] Instead, he faults the lack of real choices facing voters. Why vote, if your vote won't make much difference? In fact, unsuccessful Green Party presidential candidate Ralph Nader tried to run as an alternative to the two major parties, arguing that there was little difference between Republicans and Democrats.

Some commentators have noted that nonvoting may not even be a sign of contentment. If things are good, or you perceive that there is no need for change, why vote?

Whatever the reason, declining voter participation is cause for concern. If information is truly a problem, it may be that the Internet, access to information, and new ways to

GLOBAL POLITICS

THE UNITED STATES IN COMPARATIVE CONTEXT

Two scholars of American politics recently published books examining their field of study in comparative context. The title of one, *America the Unusual*, speaks volumes about how Americans perceive their national politics. The other, *Only in America?*, wonders whether the political differences make that much difference.* Do political institutions and practices in the United States truly differ from politics elsewhere?

To give you a sense of how different, and in many cases how similar, politics in this country is to politics in other countries, each chapter of this book will include a Global Politics box that compares some aspect of American politics with that in other countries. One line of comparison will be with Canada, France, Germany, Italy, Japan, the United Kingdom, and the United States (known as the G-7) which represent a variety of experiences within a common framework. They are all industrial democracies, holding among the highest GNPs in the world and enjoying a comparatively high standard of living. Since the mid-1990's the group has become known as the G-8 by the addition of the Russian president to the annual summit. In this book we continue the G-7 shorthand to stand for a set of advanced capitalist industrial democracies. Even though Russia is now officially a member of this "leadership club," its situation as a country making the transition to capitalism and parliamentary democracy from a socialist economy and political system make its recent political experience qualitatively different from the original G-7 members.

There is, however, variation among the G-7 on specific indicators. Note, for example, the variations in country size. The United States is far larger than any of its counterparts except Canada. It has more than twice the population of Japan, the next most populous country in the group. More women are in the U.S. workforce, even as a proportion of total adult female population. The United States also has a low unemployment rate, especially compared to the European countries. Thus, the industrial democracies provide a pool of good cases for comparison of politics.

Industrial democracies, however, do not represent the majority of political systems in the world. Of the other 190 or so nation-states in existence today, we will consider China, Indonesia, Mexico, and Russia as representative examples. The first three are typically classified as developing countries; the indicators above show lower levels of economic development. Mexico is often characterized as a semidemocracy; Indonesia and Russia have only begun the transition to democracy recently. All in one way or another demonstrate the problems many countries face in achieving democracy. China is a socialist country, and as such differs from the G-7 even as to basic definitions of democracy. Russia is classified as a transitional democracy, attempting to move from the socialist political and economic pattern of the former Soviet Union to parliamentary democracy and a capitalist economy.

*John W. Kingdon, *America the Unusual* (New York: Worth Publishers, 1999). Graham K. Wilson, *Only in America?* (Chatham, NJ: Chatham House, 1998).

Vital Statistics of Selected Countries

Country	Population (million, 2000)	Area (1,000 km²)	GDP/ Capita ($,1995)	Life Expectancy	Televisions 1,000 people (1996)	Women in the Labor Force (% of Total Women)
Canada	31.1	9,971	19,439	78.9	714	58
China	1,284.9	9,597	777(a)	68.6	319	73
France	59.0	552	24,739	77.9	591	48
Germany	82.0	357	26,183	76.5	564	48
Indonesia	212.1	1,905	478	62.7	67	50
Italy	57.2	301	20,659	78.1	524	35
Japan	126.7	378	29,956	80.5	684	50
Mexico	98.8	1,958	4,324	71.5	270	39
Russia	146.9	17,075	1,936	64.9	405	50
UK	58.8	243	23,934	76.8	516	54
USA	278.3	9,364	31,059	76.1	805	60

Sources: Japan, 2000: An International Comparison (Tokyo: Japan Institute for Social and Economic Affairs, 1999). Sekai no Tokei 2000 (Tokyo: Somucho Tokeikyoku, 2000). United Nations Statistics Division, online. http://www.Un.org/Depts/unsd/social/.

vote may change the course of elections in the future. In the aftermath of the 2000 election, when for the first time it became clear to many Americans that absentee ballots are not always counted, or that some kinds of ballots produce large numbers of unreadable ballots, may only serve to exacerbate that problem at worst, or, for the best, lead to reforms.

There can be no doubt, however, that today, many citizens are disengaged from the political process. One 1999 poll found that 59 percent of those queried thought that "public officials don't care much what people like me think," and that only 28 percent believed that "having elections makes the government pay attention to what the people think."[33]

Redefining Our Expectations

politics
The process by which policy decisions are made.

Just as it is important to recognize that governments serve many important purposes, it is also important to recognize that government and **politics**—the process by which policy decisions are made—are not static. Politics, moreover, involves conflicts over different and sometimes opposing ideologies, and these ideologies are very much influenced by one's racial, economic, or historical experiences. These divisions are real and affect the political process at all levels. It is clear to most Americans today that politics and government no longer can be counted on to cure all of America's ills. Government, however, will always play a major role. True political leaders will need to help Americans come to terms with America as it is today—not as it was in the past—real or imaginary. Perhaps a discussion on how "community" is necessary for everybody to get along (and necessary for democracy) is in order. Some democratic theorists suggest that the citizen-activist must be ultimately responsible for the resolution of these divisions.

The current frustration and dissatisfaction about politics and government may be just another phase, as the changing American body politic seeks to redefine its ideas about government. This process is one that is likely to define politics well into the future, but the individualistic nature of the American system will have long-lasting consequences on how it can be accomplished. Americans want less government; but as they get older, they don't want less Social Security. They want lower taxes and better roads, but they don't want to pay for toll roads. They want better education for their children but lower expenditures on schools. Some clearly want less for others but not themselves, which puts politicians in the position of nearly always disappointing voters. This inability to please voters and find a middle ground undoubtedly led to the unprecedented retirements of members of Congress in 1994 and 1996.

Politicians, as well as their constituents, are looking for ways to redefine the role of government, much in the same way that the Framers did when they met in Philadelphia to forge a solution between Americans' quest for liberty and freedom tempered by order and governmental authority. While citizens charge that it is still government as usual, a change is taking place in Washington, D.C. The federal government, like most American organizations, is downsizing. Sacrosanct programs such as Social Security and welfare continually are being reexamined, and power and responsibility are slowly being returned to the states. Thus, the times may be different, but the questions about government and its role in our lives remain the same.

Although the Civil War and other national crises, such as the Great Depression and even the Watergate scandal (see chapter 8), created major turmoil, they demonstrated that our system can survive and even change in the face of enormous political, societal, and even institutional pressures. Often, these crises have produced considerable reforms. The Civil War led to the dismantling of the slavery system and to the passage of the Thirteenth, Fourteenth, and Fifteenth Amendments (see chapter 6), which led to the seeds of recognition of African Americans as American citizens. The Great Depression led to the New Deal and the creation of a government more actively involved in economic and social regulation. In the 1970s, the Watergate scandal and resignation of President Richard M. Nixon resulted in stricter ethics laws that have led to the resignation or removal of many unethical elected officials.

Continuity & Change

The Face of America

When the original settlers came to what is now the United States, they did so for a variety of reasons. Still, they recognized the critical role that government could play for them in the New World. So even though the colonists considered themselves British subjects, they knew the importance of fashioning some form of governance, as illustrated by their signatures of agreement on the Mayflower Compact. Those who signed that historic document were largely British, male, and Caucasian. They expected the government to be best that governed least, but they also recognized the importance of order and protection of property and were willing to give up some rights in return for government preservation of those ideals.

Over time, young men in a variety of large and not so large wars fought for what they believed was the American ideal. At the same time, women often left their homes to work in hospitals or factories to help the war effort, generally forgoing their personal goals. Immigrants and native-born citizens alike all shared the American dream.

Today, the American dream is more difficult to see. A new wave of immigrants in the 1980s has changed the composition of many U.S. cities and states, often straining scarce resources such as access to quality public education, which has always been at the forefront of the American political socialization process. Several states, especially California, have attempted to restrict the rights and privileges of aliens in recently unprecedented ways. It is a system of majority rule, where the rights of those newest to our borders often lose out.

As illustrated by Figure 1.2, however, the ethnic "look" of America is changing, and in some places such as California and Florida it is changing especially quickly. These changes prompt several questions.

1. What challenges do you believe national and state governments will face as the racial and ethnic composition of their citizenry changes dramatically?
2. In the wake of the 2000 Census that found Hispanics now to be the largest U.S. minority group, do you foresee any changes in how minorities, especially Hispanics, will be treated?

Cast Your Vote. What other challenges do you think national and state governments will face in the twenty-first century? To cast your vote, go to **www.ablongman.com/oconnor**

Elections themselves, which often seem chaotic, help generation after generation remake the political landscape as new representatives seek to shake up the established order. Thus, while elections can seem like chaos, from this chaos comes order and often the explosive productivity of a democratic society.

SUMMARY

In this chapter we have made the following points:

1. **The Roots of American Government. Where Did the Ideas Come From?**
   The American political system was based on several notions that have their roots in classical Greek ideas, including natural law, the doctrine that human affairs should be governed by certain ethical principles that can be understood by reason. The ideas of social contract theorists John Locke and Thomas Hobbes, who held the belief that people are free and equal by God-given right, have continuing implications for our ideas of the proper role of government in our indirect democracy.

2. **Characteristics of American Democracy**
   Key characteristics of this democracy established by the Framers are popular consent, popular sovereignty, majority rule and the preservation of minority rights, equality, individualism, and personal liberty, as is the Framers' option for a capitalistic system.

3. **The Changing Political Culture and Characteristics of the American People**
   Several characteristics of the American electorate can help us understand how the system continues to evolve and change. Chief among these are changes in size and population, demographics, racial and ethnic makeup, family and family size, age patterns, and ideological beliefs.

4. **Political Culture and Views of Government**
   Americans have high and often unrealistic expectations of government. At the same time, they often fail to appreciate how much their government actually does for them. Some of this failure may be due to Americans' general mistrust of politicians, which may explain some of the apathy evidenced in the electorate.

KEY TERMS

aristocracy, p. 8
capitalism, p. 10
communism, p. 12
conservative, p. 22
democracy, p. 8
direct democracy, p. 8
free market economy, p. 10
indirect (representative)
   democracy, p. 8

liberal, p. 23
libertarian, p. 23
majority rule, p. 13
mercantile system, p. 11
monarchy, p. 8
natural law, p. 5
oligarchy, p. 8
personal liberty, p. 15
political culture, p. 15

political ideology, p. 22
politics, p. 30
popular consent, p. 13
popular sovereignty, p. 13
republic, p. 8
social contract theory, p. 6
socialism, p. 11
totalitarianism, p. 12

SELECTED READINGS

Almond, Gabriel A., and Sidney Verba. *Civic Culture: Political Attitudes and Democracy in Five Nations.* Princeton, N.J.: Princeton University Press, 1963.

Craig, Stephen C., and Stephen Earl Bennett, eds. *After the Boom: The Politics of Generation X.* Lanham, Md.: Rowman & Littlefield, 1997.

Dahl, Robert A. *Polyarchy: Participation and Opposition.* New Haven, Conn.: Yale University Press, 1971.

Elshtain, Jean Bethke. *Democracy on Trial.* New York: Basic Books, 1995.

Glendon, Mary Ann. *Rights Talk: The Impoverishment of Political Discourse.* New York: Free Press, 1991.

Grossman, Lawrence K. *The Electronic Republic: Reshaping Democracy in the Information Age.* New York: Viking, 1995.

Hobbes, Thomas. *Leviathan.* ed. Richard Tuck. New York: Cambridge University Press, 1996.

Hochschild, Jennifer, L. *Facing Up to the American Dream: Race, Class, and the Soul of the Nation.* Princeton, N.J.: Princeton University Press, 1995.

Hunter, James Davison, *Culture Wars: The Struggle to Define America.* New York: Basic Books, 1991.

Jamieson, Kathleen Hall. *Dirty Politics: Deception, Distraction, and Democracy.* New York: Oxford University Press, 1992.

Locke, John. *Two Treatises of Government,* ed. Peter Lasleti. New York: Cambridge University Press, 1988.

Lowi, Theodore J. *The End of Liberalism.* New York: Norton, 1979.

Putnam, Robert D. *Bowling Alone: The Collapse and Revival of the American Community.* New York: Simon & Schuster, 2000.

Skocpol, Theda and Morris Fiorina, eds. *Civic Engagement in American Democracy.* Washington, D.C.: Brookings Institution Press, 1999.

Truman, David B. *The Governmental Process.* New York: Knopf, 1951.

Verba, Sidney, Kay Schlozman, and Henry Brady. *Voice and Equality: Civic Volunteerism in American Politics.* Cambridge, Mass.: Harvard University Press, 1995.

NOTES

1. Thomas Byrne Edsall, "The Era of Bad Feelings," *Civilization* (March/April 1996): 37.

2. The English and Scots often signed covenants with their churches in a pledge to defend and further their religion. In the Bible, covenants were solemn promises made to humanity by God. In the colonial context, then, covenants were formal agreements sworn to a new government to abide by its terms.

3. The term "men" is used here because only males were considered fit to vote.

4. Jack C. Plano and Milton Greenberg, *The American Political Dictionary,* 6th ed. (New York: Holt, Rinehart and Winston, 1982).

5. Frank Michelman, "The Republican Civic Tradition," *Yale Law Journal 97* (1988): 1503.

6. Lynne Casper and Loretta Bass, "Hectic Lifestyles Make for Record-Low Election Turnout, Census Bureau Reports," U.S. Census Bureau News (August 17, 1998).

7. "Apathetic Voters? No, Disgusted," *The Ledger* (July 12, 1998): A14.

8. Gabriel A. Almond and Sidney Verba, *The Civic Culture: Political Attitudes and Democracy in Five Nations* (Princeton, N.J.: Princeton University Press, 1963), 4.

9. "The USA's New Immigrants," *USA Today* (October 13, 1997): 11A.

10. Susan A. MacManus, *Young v. Old: Generational Combat in the 21st Century* (Boulder, Colo.: Westview Press, 1995), 3.

11. MacManus, *Young v. Old,* 4.

12. "Sixty-Five Plus in the United States," http://www.census.gov/socdemo/www/agebrief.html.

13. See William Strauss and Neil Howe, *Generations: The History, of America's Future, 1984–2069* (New York: William Morrow, 1991), and Fernando Torres-Gil, *The New Aging: Politics and Generational Change in America* (New York: Auburn House, 1992).

14. William R. Buck and Tracey Rembert, "Not Just Doing It: Generation X Proves That Actions Speak Louder than Words: Age Group Born in Late 1960s and Early 1970s," *Earth Action Network* (September 19, 1997): 28.

15. Buck and Rembert, "Not Just Doing It."

16. Buck and Rembert, "Not Just Doing It."

17. Teresa Gubbins, "Teens Push Aside the Boomers, Emerge as New Kings of Cool," *The Times-Picayune* (April 11, 1999): B3.

18. Kavita Varma, "Family Values," *USA Today* (March 11, 1997): 6D.

19. James Davison Hunter. Culture Wars: *The Struggle to Define America* (New York: Basic Books, 1991), 42.

20. Hunter, *Culture Wars,* 42.

21. Plano and Greenberg, *The American Political Dictionary,* 10.

22. William Safire, *Safire's New Political Dictionary* (New York: Random House. 1993), 144–45.

23. Jack C. Plano and Milton Greenberg. *The American Political Dictionary, 9th ed.* (Fort Worth, Tex.: Harcourt Brace. 1993), 16.

24. Safire, Safire's New Political Dictionary.

25. Plano and Greenberg, *The American Political Dictionary,* 16.

26. Philip E. Converse, "The Nature of Belief Systems in Mass Publics," in David E. Apter, ed., *Ideology and Discontent* (New York: Free Press, 1964), 206–21.

27. Ben J. Wattenberg, *Values Matter Most* (New York: Free Press, 1995); and Hunter, *Culture Wars*, chapter 8.

28. David Broder and Richard Morin, "Americans See 2 Distinct Bill Clintons," *The Washington Post* (August 23, 1998): A10.

29. Howard Wilkinson and Patrick Crowly, "Campaign '98: Races Offer Definite Choices." *The Cincinnati Enquirer*, September 7, 1998, Bl.

30. "Apathetic Voters? No, Disgusted," *The Ledger* (July 12, 1998): A14.

31. Scott Shepard, "Non-voters Too Busy or Apathetic?" *The Palm Beach Post* (August, 1998): 6A.

32. Shepard, "Non-voters."

33. 1999 Poll Questions on the Federal Government, National Journal's *Cloak Room Poll Track*. Questions from the Center of Policy Attitudes, conducted January 26–31, 1999.

2 The Constitution

At age eighteen, all American citizens today are eligible to vote in state and national elections. This has not always been the case. It took an amendment to the U.S. Constitution—one of only seventeen that have been added since the Bill of Rights in 1791—to guarantee the franchise to those under twenty-one years of age.

In 1942, during World War II, Rep. Jennings Randolph (D–W.Va.) proposed that the voting age be lowered to eighteen believing that since young men were old enough to be drafted to fight and die for their country, they also should be allowed to vote. He continued to reintroduce his proposal during every session of Congress, and in 1954 President Eisenhower endorsed the idea in his State of the Union message. Presidents Johnson and Nixon—both men who called upon the nation's young men to fight on foreign shores—also echoed his appeal.[1]

By the 1960s, the campaign to lower the voting age took on a new sense of urgency as hundreds of thousands of young men were drafted to fight in Vietnam and thousands were killed in action. "Old Enough to Fight, Old Enough to Vote," was one popular slogan of the day. By 1970, four states—who under the U.S. Constitution are allowed to set the eligibility requirements for their voters—had lowered their voting ages to eighteen, and under considerable pressure from Baby Boomers, Congress passed legislation lowering the voting age in national, state, and local elections to eighteen.

The state of Oregon, however, challenged the constitutionality of the law in court, arguing that Congress had not been given the authority to establish a uniform voting age in state and local government under the Constitution. The U.S. Supreme Court agreed.[2] The decision from the sharply divided Court meant that those under age twenty-one could vote in national elections but that the states were free to prohibit them from voting in state and local elections. The decision presented the states with a logistical nightmare in keeping two sets of registration books—one for those twenty-one and over, and one for those who were not.

Jennings Randolph, now a senator from West Virginia, reintroduced his proposed amendment.[3] Within three months of the Supreme Court's decision, Congress sent the proposed Twenty-Sixth Amendment to the states for their ratification. The required three-fourths of the states ratified the amendment within three months—making its adoption, on June 30, 1971, the quickest in the history of the constitutional amending process.

In spite of winning the right to vote through a change in the U.S. Constitution, young people never have voted in large numbers. In spite of issues of concern to those under the age of twenty-five, including Internet privacy, the fate of Napster, reproductive rights, and the continuance of student loan programs, this group has very low voter turnout rates. The most recent national elections showed little change in this phenomenon.

The Constitution was intentionally written to forestall the need for amendment, and the process by which it could be changed or amended was made intentionally time-consuming and difficult. Over the years, thousands of amendments—including those to prohibit child labor, provide equal rights for women, grant statehood to the District of Columbia, and balance the budget—have been debated or sent to the states for their approval, only to die slow deaths. Only twenty-seven amendments have successfully made their way into the Constitution. What the Framers came up with in Philadelphia has continued to work, in spite of continually increasing demands on and dissatisfaction with our national government. Perhaps Americans are happier with the system of government created by the Framers than they realize.

The ideas that went into the making of the Constitution and how the Constitution has evolved to address the problems of a growing and ever-changing nation are at the core of our discussion in this chapter.

- First, we will examine the *origins of the new nation* and the circumstances surrounding the break with Great Britain.
- Second, we will discuss the *Declaration of Independence* and the ideas that lay at its core.
- Third, we will discuss the *first attempts at American government* created by the *Articles of Confederation*.
- Fourth, we will examine the circumstances surrounding the drafting of a *new Constitution* in Philadelphia.
- Fifth, we will review the results of the Framers' efforts—the *U.S. Constitution*.
- Sixth, we will present the *drive for ratification* of the new government.
- Seventh, we will address the *formal methods of amending the Constitution*.
- Eighth, we will explore the informal methods of amending the Constitution.

THE ORIGINS OF A NEW NATION

Starting in the early seventeenth century, colonists came to the New World for a variety of reasons. Often it was to escape religious persecution. Others came seeking a new start on a continent where land was plentiful. The independence and diversity of the settlers in the New World made the question of how best to rule the new colonies a tricky one. More than merely an ocean separated England from the colonies; the colonists were independent people, and it soon became clear that the Crown could not govern the colonies with the same close rein used at home. King James I thus allowed some local participation in decision making through arrangements such as the first elected colonial assembly, the Virginia House of Burgesses, and the elected General Court that governed the Massachusetts Bay colony after 1629. Almost all the colonists agreed that the king ruled by divine right; but English monarchs allowed the colonists significant liberties in terms of self-government, religious practices, and economic organization. For 140 years, this system worked fairly well.[4]

By the early 1760s, however, a century and a half of physical separation, colonial development, and the relative self-governance of the colonies had led to weakening ties with—and loyalties to—the Crown. By this time, each of the thirteen colonies had drafted its own written constitution, which provided the fundamental rules or laws for each colony. Moreover, many of the most oppressive British traditions—feudalism, a rigid class system, and the absolute authority of church and king—were absent in the New World. Land was abundant. The restrictive guild and craft systems that severely limited entry into many skilled professions in England did not exist in the colonies. Although the role of religion was central to the lives of most colonists, there was no single state church, and the British practice of compulsory tithing (giving a fixed percentage of one's earnings to the state-sanctioned and -supported church) was nonexistent.

Trade and Taxation

Mercantilism, an economic theory based on the belief that a nation's wealth is measured by the amount of gold and silver in its treasury, justified Britain's maintenance of strict import/export controls on the colonies. After 1650, for example, Parliament passed a series of navigation acts to prevent its chief rival, Holland, from trading with the English colonies. From 1650 until well into the 1700s, England tried to regulate colonial imports and exports, believing that it was critical to export more goods than it imported as a way of increasing the gold and silver in its treasury. These policies, however, were difficult to enforce and were widely ignored by the colonists, who saw little self-benefit in them. Thus, for years, an unwritten agreement existed. The colonists relinquished to the Crown and the British Parliament the authority to regulate trade and conduct international affairs, but they retained the right to levy their own taxes.

This fragile agreement was soon put to the test. The French and Indian War, fought from 1756 to 1763 on the "western frontier" of the colonies and in Canada, was part of a global war initiated by the British. The American phase of the Seven Years' War was fought between England and France with its Indian allies. In North America, its immediate cause was the rival claims of those two European nations for the lands between the Allegheny Mountains and the Mississippi River. The Treaty of Paris (signed in 1763) signaled the end of the war. The colonists expected that with the "Indian problem" on the western frontier now "under control," westward migration and settlement could begin in earnest. They were shocked when the Crown decreed in 1763 that there was to be no further westward movement by British subjects. Parliament believed that expansion into Indian territory would lead to new expenditures for the defense of the settlers, draining the British treasury, which had yet to recover from the high cost of waging the war.

To raise money to pay for the war as well as the expenses of administering the colonies, Parliament enacted the Sugar Act in 1764, which placed taxes on sugar, wine, coffee, and other products commonly exported to the colonies. A postwar colonial depression heightened resentment of the tax. Around the colonies the political cry "No taxation without representation" was heard. Major protest, however, failed to materialize until imposition of the Stamp Act by the British Parliament in 1765. This law required the colonists to purchase stamps for all documents, including newspapers, magazines, and commercial papers. To add insult to injury, in 1765 Parliament passed the Mutiny or Quartering Act, which required the colonists to furnish barracks or provide living quarters within their own homes for British troops.

Most colonists, especially those in New England, where these acts hit hardest, were outraged. Men throughout the colonies organized the Sons of Liberty, under the leadership of Samuel Adams (see Roots of Government: Samuel Adams) and Patrick Henry. Whereas the Sugar Act was a tax on trade—still viewed as being within the legitimate authority of the Crown—the Stamp Act was a direct tax on many items not traditionally under the control of the king, and protests against it were violent and loud. Riots, often led by the Sons of Liberty, broke out. They were especially violent in Boston, where the colonial governor's home was burned by an angry mob, and British stamp agents charged with collecting the tax were threatened. A boycott of goods needing the stamps as well as British imports was also organized.

First Steps Toward Independence

In 1765 the colonists called for the **Stamp Act Congress,** the first official meeting of the colonies and the first step toward a unified nation. Nine of the thirteen colonies sent representatives to a meeting in New York City, where a detailed list of Crown violations of their fundamental rights was drawn up. Attendees defined what they thought to be the proper relationship between the various colonial governments and the British Parliament; they ardently believed that Parliament had no authority to tax them without colonial representation in the British Parliament. In contrast, the British

Stamp Act Congress
Meeting of representatives of nine of the thirteen colonies held in New York City in 1765, during which representatives drafted a document to send to the king listing how their rights had been violated.

ROOTS OF GOVERNMENT

SAMUEL ADAMS

Although Samuel Adams (1722–1803) today perhaps is known best for the beer that bears his name, his original claim to fame was as a leader against British and loyalist oppressors (although he did bankrupt his family's brewery business). A second cousin of President John Adams, Samuel Adams was a signer of the Declaration of Independence and a member of Massachusetts's constitutional convention that ratified the U.S. Constitution. He served as governor of Massachusetts from 1794 to 1797.

Adams was heavily influenced by John Locke's belief in man's natural right to be self-governing and free from taxation without representation. As a member of the Massachusetts legislature, he advocated defiance of the

Stamp Act. With the passage of the Townshend Acts in 1767, he organized a letter-writing campaign urging other colonies to join in resistance. Later, in 1772, he founded the Committees of Correspondence to unite the colonies.

Painting by John Singleton Copley. (Photo courtesy: Painting by John Singleton Copely. Courtesy, Museum of Fine Arts, Boston. Reproduced with permission. ©2001 Museum of Fine Arts, Boston. All Rights Reserved.)

believed that direct representation of the colonists was impractical and that members of Parliament represented the best interests of all the English, including the colonists.

The Stamp Act Congress and its petitions to the Crown did little to stop the onslaught of taxing measures. Parliament did, however, repeal the Stamp Act and revise the Sugar Act in 1766, largely because of the uproar made by British merchants who were losing large sums of money as a result of the boycotts. Rather than appeasing the colonists, however, these actions emboldened them to increase their resistance. In 1767 Parliament enacted the Townshend Acts, which imposed duties on all kinds of colonial imports, including tea. Response from the Sons of Liberty was immediate. Another boycott was announced, and almost all colonists gave up their favorite drink in a united show of resistance to the tax and British authority.[5] Tensions continued to run high, especially after the British sent 4,000 troops to Boston. On March 5, 1770, English troops opened fire on a mob that included disgruntled dock workers, whose jobs had been taken by British soldiers, and members of the Sons of Liberty who were taunting the soldiers in front of the Boston Customs House. Five colonists were killed in what became known as the Boston Massacre. Following this confrontation, all duties except those on tea were lifted. The tea tax, however, continued to be a symbolic irritant. In 1772, at the suggestion of Samuel Adams, Boston and other towns around Massachusetts set up **Committees of Correspondence** to articulate ideas and keep communications open around the colony. By 1774 twelve colonies had formed committees to maintain a flow of information among like-minded colonists.

Meanwhile, despite dissent in England over the treatment of the colonies, Parliament passed another tea tax designed to shore up the sagging sales of the East India Company. The colonists' boycott had left that British trading house with more than 18 million pounds of tea in its warehouses. To rescue British merchants from disaster, in 1773 Parliament passed the Tea Act, granting a monopoly to the financially strapped East India Company to sell the tea imported from Britain. The company was allowed to funnel business to American merchants loyal to the Crown, thereby undercutting

Committees of Correspondence
Organizations in each of the American colonies created to keep colonists abreast of developments with the British; served as powerful molders of public opinion against the British.

20,000 brains are improperly taken

Associated Press

LONDON – The brains of at least 20,000 people, many of them depressed or mentally ill when they died, were removed without their families' consent during 30-year period, a senior government doctor reported Monday.

Some brains were removed to help diagnose cause of death, while others were collected for neuropsychiatric research, Dr. Jeremy Metters, the royal inspector of anatomy, said in a report that followed an 18-month investigation.

In one case, a hospital mortician was paid $16 for each brain he provided for research. In another, more than 200 brains were kept for a Manchester University research project that studied the brains of people who had suffered from mental illness and those of healthy "controls" for comparison.

Removing organs without families' permission was explicitly outlawed in 1999. A law passed in 1961 said organs may be taken from corpses only if relatives did not object, but Metters said permission was seldom sought.

Metters said many of those involved in retaining organs didn't know they were breaking the law.

"There was a widespread belief that organ and tissue retention was in the 'public interest' and that retention was lawful because the post mortem was carried out for the coroner," he wrote.

The 20,000 figure may be far lower than the actual number of brains taken. It includes only brains still held by hospitals and universities in England, and Metters said many more could have been examined and destroyed.

The government ordered the investigation after a woman learned her husband's brain had been removed without her permission when he committed suicide in 1987. The couple's Jewish faith decrees a person must be buried intact.

Elaine Isaacs said the secrecy surrounding the case of her husband, Cyril, was "nothing short of collusion," and she expected authorities to take action against those responsible.

"I'm very, very angry about being here today," said Isaacs, who attended the launch of the report.

Hopefuls

▶ From Page 1A

debate.

Toss in former Vermont Gov. Howard Dean, who has stirred the most grass-roots enthusiasm, and the result is a race that has "tiered a little bit," separating those five candidates from the rest of the field, said Bill Carrick, a Gephardt strategist. "But I don't think you can say anybody is the front-runner."

Given that, the next phase of the campaign seems obvious, as the Democrats begin to focus less on their criticisms of President Bush and more on the differences among themselves. After all, "Just beating the hell out of Bush doesn't offer much distinction," as David Doak, an unaffiliated Democratic strategist, put it.

So while the candidates continue their long-running argument over the Iraq war, with Dean leading the opposition, they have broadened their debate to include a discussion of taxes, health care, energy policy and the proper size and scope of the federal government. Those issues may resurface Saturday when the Democratic hopefuls share a stage again in Des Moines, at a forum hosted by the American Federation of State, County and Municipal Employees.

Some fret over the increased pushing and shoving, fearing it only helps the opposition. Others welcome the fight.

"We don't need a nominee right now," said Donna Brazile, who managed Al Gore's 2000 presidential campaign. "This is an opportunity for the party to recapture the imagination not just of Democrats but to figure out how we as a party can win again.

"We need a good comprehensive message," Brazile said. "Not just, 'Me too, I'm against terrorism,' but saying what Democrats believe."

The emerging differences among the presidential contenders came into sharpest relief at their May 3 debate,

revealing
as perso
were po
Columb
some of
the next

It
Kerry
almos
Each
Han
shov
to h
thei

C
mean
midd
et D
Edw
prop
ever
call
"ta
poc

mor
help

L
cons

River

▶ From Page 1A

to relieve the county of that responsibility.

The Joint Drainage Board of Noble and LaGrange Counties, made up of two LaGrange County commissioners, two Noble County representen and the Steuben County suren examis this issue

That would allow the county to assess taxes from people who live in the watershed area to pay for maintenance work along the river. The river and its branches drain about two-thirds of Noble County and portions of LaGrange County.

State law allows counties to deepen, widen or change the channel of regulated drains, as well as divert the course of the water and remove obstructions. Opponents fear the

ing
natu
vatio

Z
drai
cutti
the c

F
peri
me
and
do

Paul Revere's engraving of the Boston Massacre was a potent piece of political propaganda. Five men were killed, not seven, as the legend states, and the rioters in front of the State House (left) were scarcely as docile as Revere portrayed them. (Photo courtesy: Collection of the New York Historical Society, negative # 29405)

colonial merchants, who could sell only tea imported from other nations. The effect was to drive down the price of tea and to hurt colonial merchants, who were forced to buy tea at the higher prices from other sources.

When the next shipment of tea arrived in Boston from Great Britain, the colonists responded by throwing the Boston Tea Party. Similar "tea parties" were held in other colonies. When the news of these actions reached King George, he flew into a rage against the actions of his disloyal subjects. "The die is now cast," the king told his prime minister. "The colonies must either submit or triumph."

His first act was to persuade Parliament to pass the Coercive Acts in 1774. Known in the colonies as the Intolerable Acts, they contained a key provision calling for a total blockade of Boston Harbor until restitution was made for the tea. Another provision reinforced the Quartering Act, giving royal governors the authority to quarter in the homes of private citizens the additional 4,000 British soldiers sent to patrol Boston.

The First Continental Congress

The British could never have guessed how the cumulative impact of these actions would unite the colonists. Samuel Adams's Committees of Correspondence spread the word, and food and money were sent to the people of Boston from all over the thirteen colonies. The tax itself was no longer the key issue; now the extent of British authority over the colonies was the far more important question. At the request of the colonial assemblies of Massachusetts and Virginia, all but one colonial assembly agreed to select a group of delegates to attend a continental congress authorized to communicate with the king on behalf of the now-united colonies.

The **First Continental Congress** met in Philadelphia from September 5 to October 26, 1774. It was made up of fifty-six delegates from every colony except Georgia. The colonists had yet to think of breaking with Great Britain; at this point, they simply wanted to iron out their differences with the king. By October they had agreed on a series of resolutions to oppose the Coercive Acts and to establish a formal organization to boycott British goods. The Congress also drafted a Declaration of Rights and Resolves, which called for colonial rights of petition and assembly, trial by peers, freedom from a standing army, and the selection of representative councils to levy taxes. The Congress further agreed that if the king did not capitulate to their demands, they would meet again in Philadelphia in May 1775.

The Second Continental Congress

King George refused to yield, tensions continued to rise, and a **Second Continental Congress** was called. Before it could meet, fighting broke out early in the morning of April 19, 1775, at Lexington and Concord, Massachusetts, with what Ralph Waldo Emerson called "the shot heard round the world." Eight colonial soldiers, called Minutemen, were killed, and 16,000 British troops besieged Boston.

When the Second Continental Congress convened in Philadelphia on May 10, 1775, delegates were united by their increased hostility to Great Britain. The bloodshed at Lexington left no other course but war. To solidify colonial support, a Southerner, George Washington of Virginia, was selected as the commander of the new Continental Army, since up to that date, British oppression had been felt most keenly in the Northeast. That task complete, the Congress then sent envoys to France to ask its assistance against France's perennial enemy. In a final attempt to avert conflict, the Second Continental Congress adopted the Olive Branch Petition on July 5, 1775, asking the king to end hostilities. King George rejected the petition and sent an additional 20,000 troops to quell the rebellion. The stage was set for war.

In January 1776, Thomas Paine, with the support and encouragement of Benjamin Franklin, issued (at first anonymously) *Common Sense,* a pamphlet forcefully arguing for independence from Great Britain. In frank, easy-to-understand language, Paine denounced the corrupt British monarchy and offered reasons for breaking with Great Britain. "The blood of the slain, the weeping voice of nature cries 'Tis Time to Part,'" wrote Paine. *Common Sense,* widely read throughout the colonies, was instrumental in changing minds in a very short time. In its first three months of publication, the forty-seven-page *Common Sense* sold 120,000 copies, the equivalent of approximately 18.75 million books today (given the U.S. population today). One copy of *Common Sense* was in distribution for every thirteen people in the colonies—a truly astonishing number, given the low literacy rate.

THE DECLARATION OF INDEPENDENCE

Common Sense galvanized the American public against reconciliation with England. As the mood in the colonies changed, so did that of the Second Continental Congress. On May 15, 1776, Virginia became the first colony to call for independence, instructing one of its delegates to the Second Continental Congress to introduce a resolution to that effect. On June 7, 1776, Richard Henry Lee of Virginia rose to move "that these United Colonies are, and of right ought to be, free and independent States, and that all

---

First Continental Congress
Meeting held in Philadelphia from September 5 to October 26, 1774, in which fifty-six delegates (from every colony except Georgia) adopted a resolution that opposed the Coercive Acts.

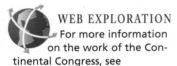

WEB EXPLORATION
For more information on the work of the Continental Congress, see
www.ablongman.com/oconnor

Second Continental Congress
Meeting that convened in Philadelphia on May 10, 1775, at which it was decided that an army should be raised and George Washington of Virginia was named commander-in-chief.

After the success of *Common Sense,* Thomas Paine wrote a series of essays collectively entitled *The Crisis* to arouse colonists' support for the Revolutionary War. The first *Crisis* papers contain the famous words "These are the times that try men's souls." (Photo courtesy: Stock Montage, Inc.)

connection between them and the State of Great Britain is, and ought to be, dissolved." His three-part resolution—which called for independence, the formation of foreign alliances, and preparation of a plan of **confederation**—triggered hot debate among the delegates. A proclamation of independence from Great Britain was treason, a crime punishable by death. Although six of the thirteen colonies had already instructed their delegates to vote for independence, the Second Continental Congress was suspended to allow its delegates to return home to their respective colonial legislatures for final instructions. Independence was not a move to be taken lightly.

At the same time, committees were set up to consider each point of Lee's proposal. A committee of five was selected to begin work on a **Declaration of Independence.** The Congress selected Benjamin Franklin, John Adams, Robert Livingston, and Roger Sherman as members. Adams lobbied hard for a Southerner to add balance. Thus, owing to his Southern origin as well as his "peculiar felicity of expression," Thomas Jefferson was selected as chair.

On July 2, 1776, twelve of the thirteen colonies (with New York abstaining) voted for independence. Two days later the Second Continental Congress voted to adopt the Declaration of Independence penned by Thomas Jefferson. On July 9, 1776, the Declaration, now with the approval of New York, was read aloud in Philadelphia.[6]

A Theoretical Basis for a New Government

In simple but eloquent language, Jefferson set out the reasons for the colonies' separation from Great Britain. Most of his stirring rhetoric drew heavily on the works of seventeenth- and eighteenth-century political philosophers, particularly the English philosopher John Locke (see Roots of Government: Hobbes and Locke in chapter 1), who had written South Carolina's first constitution, a colonial charter drawn up in 1663 when South Carolina was formed by King Charles II and mercantile houses in England. In fact, many of the words in the opening of the Declaration of Independence closely resemble passages from Locke's *Two Treatises of Government.*

confederation
Type of government in which the national government derives its powers from the states; a league of independent states.

Declaration of Independence
Document drafted by Thomas Jefferson in 1776 that proclaimed the right of the American colonies to separate from Great Britain.

American Renaissance man Thomas Jefferson (1743–1826)—author of the Declaration of Independence and the third president of the United States—voiced the aspirations of a new America as no other individual of his era. In the wake of scientific evidence appearing to prove he fathered at least one child by his slave Sally Hemmings, historians are now reassessing his writings and political thought. Some of her descendants, below, gather at Monticello. (Photo courtesy: Raab Shanna/Corbis Sygma)

Locke was a proponent of *social contract theory,* a philosophy of government that held that governments exist based on the consent of the governed. According to Locke, people leave the state of nature and agree to set up a government largely for the protection of property. In colonial times "property" did not mean just land. Locke's notion of property rights included life, liberty, and material possessions. Furthermore, argued Locke, individuals who give their consent to be governed have the right to resist or remove rulers who deviate from those purposes. Such a government exists for the good of its subjects and not for the benefit of those who govern. Thus, rebellion was the ultimate sanction against a government that violated the rights of its citizens.

It is easy to see the colonists' debt to John Locke. In ringing language the Declaration of Independence proclaims:

> We hold these truths to be self-evident, that all men are created equal, that they are endowed by their Creator with certain unalienable Rights, that among these are Life, Liberty and the pursuit of Happiness.

Jefferson and others in attendance at the Second Continental Congress wanted to have a document that would stand for all time, justifying their break with the Crown and clarifying their notions of the proper form of government. So, Jefferson continued:

> That to secure these rights, Governments are instituted among Men, deriving their just powers from the consent of the governed. That whenever any Form of Government becomes destructive of these ends, it is the Right of the People to alter or abolish it, and to institute new Government, laying its foundation on such Principles and organizing its Powers in such form, as to them shall seem most likely to effect their Safety and Happiness.

After this stirring preamble, the Declaration went on to enumerate the wrongs that the colonists had suffered under British rule. All pertained to the denial of personal rights and liberties, many of which would later be guaranteed by the U.S. Constitution through the Bill of Rights.

After the Declaration was signed and transmitted to the king, the Revolutionary War was fought with a greater vengeance. At a September 1776 peace conference on Staten Island (New York), British General William Howe demanded revocation of the Declaration of Independence. The Americans refused, and the war raged on while the Congress attempted to fashion a new united government.

THE FIRST ATTEMPT AT GOVERNMENT: THE ARTICLES OF CONFEDERATION

As noted earlier, the British had no written constitution. The colonists in the Second Continental Congress were attempting to codify arrangements that had never before been put into legal terminology. To make things more complicated, the delegates had to arrive at these decisions in a wartime atmosphere. Nevertheless, in late 1777 the **Articles of Confederation,** creating a loose "league of friendship" between the sovereign or independent states, were passed by the Congress and presented to the states for their ratification.

The Articles created a type of government called a confederation or confederacy. Unlike the unitary system of government in England, wherein all of the powers of the government reside in the national government, the national government in a confederation derives all of its powers directly from the states. Thus the national government in a confederacy is weaker than the sum of its parts, and the states often consider themselves independent states linked together only for limited purposes such as national defense. Key provisions in the Articles that created the confederacy included:

- A national government with a Congress empowered to make peace, coin money, appoint officers for an army, control the post office, and negotiate with Indian tribes.

Articles of Confederation
The compact among the thirteen original states that was the basis of their government. Written in 1776, the Articles were not ratified by all the states until 1781.

WEB EXPLORATION
For a full text
of the Articles of
Confederation, see
www.ablongman.com/oconnor

- Each state's retention of its independence and sovereignty, or ultimate authority to govern within its territories.
- One vote in the Continental Congress for each state, regardless of size.
- The vote of nine states to pass any measure (a unanimous vote for any amendment).
- The selection and payment of delegates to the Congress by their respective state legislatures.

Thus the Articles—finally ratified by all thirteen states in March 1781—fashioned a government well reflective of the political philosophy of the times.[7] Although it had its flaws, the government under the Articles of Confederation saw the nation through the Revolutionary War. However, once the British surrendered in 1781 and the new nation found itself no longer united by the war effort, the government quickly fell into chaos.

Problems Under the Articles of Confederation

In today's America we ship goods, travel by car and airplane across state lines, make interstate phone calls, and more. Over 250 years ago, Americans had great loyalties to their states and often did not even think of themselves as Americans. This lack of national sentiment or loyalty in the absence of a war to unite the citizenry fostered a reluctance to give any power to the national government. Thus, by 1784, just one year after the Revolutionary Army was disbanded, governing the new nation under the Articles of Confederation proved unworkable.[8] Congress could rarely assemble the required quorum of nine states to conduct business. Even when it could, there was little agreement among the states. To raise revenue to pay off war debts and run the government, various land, poll, and liquor taxes were proposed. But since Congress had no specific power to tax, all these proposals were rejected. At one point Congress was even driven out of Philadelphia (then the capital) by its own unpaid army.

Although the national government could coin money, it had no resources to back up the value of its currency. Continental dollars were worth little, and trade between states became chaotic as some states began to coin their own money. Another weakness of the Articles was their failure to allow Congress to regulate commerce among the states and with foreign nations. As a result individual states attempted to enter into agreements with other countries, and foreign nations were suspicious of trade agreements made with the United States. In 1785, for example, Massachusetts banned the export of goods in British ships, and Pennsylvania levied heavy duties on ships of nations that did not have a treaty with the U.S. government.

Fearful of a chief executive who would rule tyrannically, moreover, the draftees of the Articles had made no provision for an executive branch of government that would be responsible for executing, or implementing, laws passed by the legislative branch. Instead, the "president" was merely the presiding officer at meetings. John Hanson, a former member of the Maryland House of Delegates and of the First Continental Congress, was the first person to preside over the Congress of the Confederation, as the new government under the Articles was called. Therefore he is often referred to as the first president of the United States.

With Daniel Shays in the lead, a group of farmers and Revolutionary War veterans marched on the courthouse in Springfield, Massachusetts to stop the bank from foreclosing on farmers' mortgages. (Photo courtesy: Bettmann/Corbis)

In addition, the Articles of Confederation had no provision for a judicial system to handle the growing number of economic conflicts and boundary disputes among the individual states. Several states claimed the same lands to the west; Pennsylvania and Virginia went to war with each other; Vermont threatened to annex itself to Canada.

The Articles' greatest weakness, however, was their lack of creation of a strong central government. While states had operated independently before the war, during the war they acceded to the national government's authority to wage armed conflict. Once the war was over, however, each state resumed its sovereign status, and was unwilling to give up rights, such as the power to tax, to an untested national government. Consequently, the government was unable to force the states to abide by the provisions of the Treaty of Paris, signed in 1783, which had officially ended the war. For example, states passed laws to stay the bills of debtors who owed money to Great Britain. They also failed to restore property to many who had remained loyal to Britain during the war. Both actions were in violation of the treaty.

The crumbling economy and a series of bad harvests that failed to produce cash crops, making it difficult for farmers to get out of debt quickly, took their toll on the new nation. George Washington and Alexander Hamilton, both interested in the questions of trade and frontier expansion, soon saw the need for a stronger national government with the authority to act to solve some of these problems. They were not alone. In 1785 and 1786, some state governments began to discuss ways to strengthen the national government. Finally, several states joined together to call for a convention in Philadelphia in 1787.

Before that meeting could take place, however, new unrest broke out in America. In 1780 Massachusetts adopted a state constitution that appeared to favor the interests of the wealthy. Property-owning requirements barred the lower and middle classes from voting and office holding. And, as the economy of Massachusetts worsened, banks foreclosed on farms to pay off debts to Massachusetts Continental Army veterans who were waiting for promised bonuses. The last straw came in 1786, when the Massachusetts legislature enacted a new law requiring the payment of all debts in cash. Frustration and outrage at the new law caused Daniel Shays, a former Revolutionary War army captain, and 1,500 armed, disgruntled, and angry farmers to march to Springfield. This group forcibly restrained the state court from foreclosing on mortgages on their farms.

The Congress immediately authorized the secretary of war to call for a new national militia. A $530,000 appropriation was made for this purpose, but every state except Virginia refused the Congress's request for money. The governor of Massachusetts then tried to raise a state militia, but because of the poor economy, funds were unavailable in the state treasury. Frantic attempts at private support were made, and a militia was finally assembled. By February 4, 1787, this privately paid force put a stop to what was called **Shays's Rebellion.** The failure of the Congress to muster an army to put down the rebellion was yet another example of the weaknesses inherent in the Articles of Confederation.

Shays's Rebellion
A 1786 rebellion in which an army of 1,500 disgruntled and angry farmers led by Daniel Shays marched to Springfield, Massachusetts, and forcibly restrained the state court from foreclosing mortgages on their farms.

THE MIRACLE AT PHILADELPHIA: WRITING A CONSTITUTION

On February 21, 1787—in the throes of economic turmoil and with domestic tranquility gone haywire—the Congress passed an official resolution. It called for a Constitutional Convention in Philadelphia for "the sole and express purpose of revising the Articles of Confederation." All states but Rhode Island sent delegates.

Twenty-nine individuals met in sweltering Philadelphia on May 14. Many at that initial meeting were intellectuals, others were shrewd farmers or businessmen, and still others were astute politicians. All recognized that what they were doing could be considered treasonous. Revising the Articles of Confederation was one thing; to call for an entirely new government, as suggested by the Virginia delegation, was another. So they took their work quite seriously, even to the point of adopting a pledge of secrecy. George Washington, who was unanimously elected the convention's presiding officer, warned:

> Nothing spoken or written can be revealed to anyone—not even your family—until we have adjourned permanently. Gossip or misunderstanding can easily ruin all the hard work we shall have to do this summer.[9]

So concerned about leaks were those in attendance that the delegates agreed to accompany Benjamin Franklin to all of his meals. They feared that the normally gregarious gentleman might get carried away with the mood or by liquor and inadvertently let news of the proceedings slip from his tongue.

The Framers

Fifty-five out of the seventy-four delegates ultimately chosen by their state legislatures to attend the Constitutional Convention labored long and hard that hot summer behind closed doors in Philadelphia. All of them were men; hence they are often referred to as the "Founding Fathers." Most of them, however, were quite young; many were in their twenties and thirties, and only one—Benjamin Franklin, at eighty-one—was very old. (See Analyzing the Data: Who Were the Framers?) Here we generally refer to those delegates as Framers because their work provided the framework for our new government. The Framers brought with them a vast amount of political, educational, legal, and business experience. Although some scholarly debate continues concerning the motives of the Framers for shaping the new national government, it is clear that they were an exceptional lot who ultimately produced a brilliant document reflecting the best efforts of all present.

WEB EXPLORATION
For demographic background on the Framers, see
www.ablongman.com/oconnor

Motives of the Framers.   Debate about the Framers' motives filled the air during the ratification struggle and has provided grist for the mill of historians and political scientists over the years. Anti-Federalists, who opposed the new Constitution, charged that Federalist supporters of the Constitution were a self-serving, landed, and propertied elite with a vested interest in the capitalistic system that had evolved in the colonies. Federalists countered that they were simply trying to preserve the nation.

In his *Economic Interpretation of the Constitution of the United States* (1913), the highly respected political scientist and historian Charles A. Beard argued that the 1780s were a "critical period" (as the time under governance by the Articles of Confederation had come to be known) not for the nation as a whole, but rather for businessmen.[10] These men feared that a weak, decentralized government could harm their economic interests. Beard argued that the merchants wanted a strong national government to promote industry and trade, protect private property, and most importantly, ensure payment of the public debt—much of which was owed to them. Therefore, according to Beard, the Constitution represents "an economic document drawn with superb skill by men whose property interests were immediately at stake."[11]

By the 1950s this view had fallen into disfavor when other historians were unable to find direct links between wealth and the Framers' motives for establishing the Constitution.[12] Robert Brown, for example, faulted Beard's economic approach and his failure to consider the impact of religion and individual views about government.[13] In the 1960s, however, another group of historians began to argue that social and economic factors were, in fact, important motives for supporting the Constitution. In *The Anti-Federalists* (1961), Jackson Turner Main posited that while the Constitution's supporters might not have been the united group of creditors suggested by Beard, they were wealthier, came from high social strata, and had greater concern for maintaining the prevailing social order than the general public.[14]

A N A L Y Z I N G   T H E   D A T A

WHO WERE THE FRAMERS?

Who were the Framers? Of the fifty-five delegates who attended some portion of the Philadelphia meeting, seventeen were slaveholders who owned approximately 1,400 slaves (Washington, Mason, and Rutledge were the three largest slaveholders at the time of the Philadelphia Convention). In terms of education, thirty-one went to college, twenty-four did not. Those who did not were mostly business, legal, or printing apprentices.

Seven delegates signed both the U.S. Constitution and the Declaration of Independence.

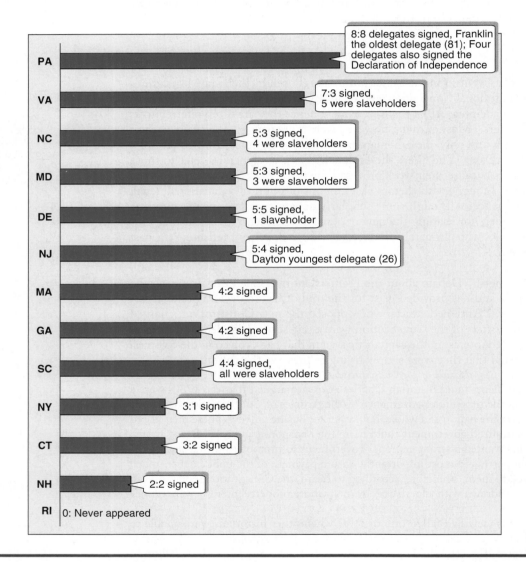

PA — 8:8 delegates signed, Franklin the oldest delegate (81); Four delegates also signed the Declaration of Independence

VA — 7:3 signed, 5 were slaveholders

NC — 5:3 signed, 4 were slaveholders

MD — 5:3 signed, 3 were slaveholders

DE — 5:5 signed, 1 slaveholder

NJ — 5:4 signed, Dayton youngest delegate (26)

MA — 4:2 signed

GA — 4:2 signed

SC — 4:4 signed, all were slaveholders

NY — 3:1 signed

CT — 3:2 signed

NH — 2:2 signed

RI — 0: Never appeared

In 1969, Gordon S. Wood's *The Creation of the American Republic* resurrected this debate. Wood deemphasized economics to argue that major social divisions explained different groups' support for (or opposition to) the new Constitution. He concluded that the Framers were representatives of a class that favored order and stability over some of the more radical ideas that had inspired the Revolution.[15]

The Virginia and New Jersey Plans

The less populous states were concerned with being lost in any new system of government where states were not treated as equals regardless of population. It is not surprising that a large state and then a small one, Virginia and New Jersey, respectively weighed in with ideas about how the new government should operate.

The **Virginia Plan** called for a national system based heavily on the European nation-state model, wherein the national government derives its powers from the people and not from the member states.

Its key features included:

- Creation of a powerful central government with three branches—the legislative, executive, and judicial.
- A two-house legislature with one house elected directly by the people; the other chosen from among persons nominated by the state legislatures.

In general, smaller states felt comfortable with the arrangements under the Articles of Confederation. These states offered another model of government, the **New Jersey Plan.** Its key features included:

- Strengthening the Articles, *not* replacing them.
- Creating a one-house legislature with one vote for each state with representatives chosen by state legislatures.
- Giving the Congress the power to raise revenue from duties and a post office.

Constitutional Compromises

The most serious disagreement between the Virginia and New Jersey plans concerned representation in Congress. When a deadlock on this point loomed, Connecticut offered its own compromise. Each state would have an equal vote in the Senate. Again, there was a stalemate. As Benjamin Franklin put it:

> The diversity of opinions turns on two points. If a proportional representation takes place, the small states contend that their liberties will be in danger. If an equality of votes is to be put in its place, large states say that their money will be in danger.... When a broad table is to be made and the edges of a plank do not fit, the artist takes a little from both sides and makes a good joint. In like manner, both sides must part with some of their demands, in order that they both join in some accommodating position.[16]

A committee to work out an agreement soon reported back what became known as the **Great Compromise.** Taking ideas from both the Virginia and New Jersey plans, it recommended:

1. In one house of the legislature (later called the House of Representatives), there should be sixty-five representatives—one representative for every 30,000 inhabitants.
2. That house should have the power to originate all bills for raising and spending money.
3. In the second house of the legislature (later called the Senate), each state should have an equal vote, and representatives would be selected by the state legislatures.[17]

The Great Compromise ultimately met with the approval of all states in attendance. The smaller states were pleased because they got equal representation in the Senate; the larger states were satisfied with the proportional representation in the House of Representatives. The small states then would dominate the Senate while the large states, such as Virginia and New York, would control the House. But because both houses had to pass any legislation, neither body could dominate the other.

The Great Compromise dealt with one major concern of the Framers—how best to treat the differences in large and small states—but other problems stemming largely from regional differences remained. Slavery was one of the thorniest. Southerners feared

Virginia Plan
The first general plan for the Constitution, proposed by James Madison. Its key points were a bicameral legislature, an executive chosen by the legislature, and a judiciary also named by the legislature.

New Jersey Plan
A framework for the Constitution proposed by a group of small states; its key points were a one-house legislature with one vote for each state, a multiperson "executive," the establishment of the acts of Congress as the "supreme law" of the land, and a supreme judiciary with limited power.

Great Compromise
A decision made during the Philadelphia Convention to give each state the same number of representatives in the Senate regardless of size; representation in the House was determined by population.

that the new national government would interfere with its lucrative cotton trade as well as slavery. Thus, when the national government was given the authority to regulate foreign commerce, the national government was banned from taxing exports or regulating the slave trade until 1808, and the Senate was required to cast a two-thirds vote to pass treaties. Thus, the Southern states, which made up more than one-third of the new union at that time, would be able to check the Senate's power, the cotton trade was protected, and it was believed that there would be an adequate supply of slaves by 1808.

Another sticking point concerning slavery remained: how to determine state population for purposes of representation in the House of Representatives. Slaves could not vote, but the Southern states wanted them included for purposes of determining population. After considerable dissension, it was decided that population for purposes of representation and the apportionment of direct taxes would be calculated by adding the "whole Number of Free Persons" to "three-fifths of all other Persons." "All other Persons" was the delegates' "tactful" way of referring to slaves. Known as the **Three-Fifths Compromise,** this highly political deal assured that the South would hold 47 percent of the House—enough to prevent attacks on slavery but not so much as to foster the spread of slavery northward.

Unfinished Business

The Framers next turned to fashioning an executive branch. While they agreed on the idea of a one-person executive, they could not settle on the length of the term of office, nor on how the chief executive should be selected. With Shays's Rebellion still fresh in their minds, the delegates feared putting too much power, including selection of a president, into the hands of the lower classes. At the same time, representatives from the smaller states feared that the selection of the chief executive by the legislature would put additional power into the hands of the large states.

Amid these fears the Committee on Unfinished Portions, whose sole responsibility was to iron out problems and disagreements concerning the office of chief executive, conducted its work. The committee recommended that the presidential term of office be fixed at four years instead of seven, as had earlier been proposed. By choosing not to mention a period of time within which the chief executive would be eligible for reelection, they made it possible for a president to serve more than one term.

The Framers also created the electoral college and drafted rules concerning removal of a sitting president. The electoral college system gave individual states a key role, because each state would select electors equal to the number of representatives it had in the House and Senate. It was a vague compromise that removed election of the president and vice president from both the Congress and the people and put it in the hands of electors whose method of selection would be left to the states. As Alexander Hamilton noted in *Federalist No. 68*, the electoral college was fashioned to avoid "turmolt and disorder" that the Framers feared could result if the "masses" were allowed to vote directly for president. Instead, the selection of the president was left to a small number of men (the electoral college) who "possess[ed] the information and discernment requisite" to decide, in Hamilton's words, the "complicated" business of selecting the president. (See Politics Now: The 2000 Election and Calls to Amend the Constitution for more on the electoral college.)

In drafting the new Constitution, the Framers also were careful to include a provision for removal of the chief executive. The House of Representatives was given the sole responsibility of investigating and charging a president or vice president with "Treason, Bribery, or other high Crimes and Misdemeanors." A majority vote would then result in issuing articles of impeachment against the president. In turn, the Senate was given sole responsibility to try the chief executive on the charges issued by the House. A two-thirds vote of the Senate was required to convict and remove the president from office. The chief justice of the United States was to preside over the Senate proceedings in place of the vice president (that body's usual leader) in order to prevent any appearance of impropriety on the vice president's part.

Three-Fifths Compromise Agreement reached at the Constitutional Convention stipulating that each slave was to be counted as three-fifths of a person for purposes of determining population for representation in the U.S. House of Representatives.

POLITICS NOW

THE 2000 ELECTION AND CALLS TO AMEND THE CONSTITUTION

After controversial Supreme Court decisions, it is not unusual to hear calls to amend the Constitution. The Court's decision ruling that laws forbidding flag burning are unconstitutional, for example, have elicited proposals to amend the Constitution to forbid the practice in every session of Congress since the Court's decision in 1985. The closeness of the 2000 presidential election, however, began to generate calls to abolish or modify the electoral college created by the Framers in Article II, almost immediately after the November 8 election and before the U.S. Supreme Court got involved in the fray. Other suggestions to amend the Constitution soon also were forthcoming. These include:

1. Abolish the electoral college and allow the candidate with the highest number of popular votes to win thereby creating the direct popular election of the president. A CNN/Gallup/*USA Today* poll found that 61 percent of the public agreed with this just one week after the 2000 election—one month before the process ended.[a]

2. Alter the electoral college to encourage the states to distribute their electors in proportion to the state vote for each candidate. Maine and Nebraska already do this.

3. Establish a nationwide standard for types of voting mechanisms including voting machines and absentee ballots.

4. Changing the Constitution's grant of life terms to Supreme Court justices to 18 year terms.

What are the merits or drawbacks of each of these proposals? Do you believe that any have a chance of becoming amendments?

[a]William Wichterman, "No Small Matter," *Sunday Gazette Mail*, December 10, 2000, 1C.

THE U.S. CONSTITUTION

After the compromise on the presidency, work proceeded quickly on the remaining resolutions of the Constitution. The Preamble to the Constitution, the last section to be drafted, contains exceptionally powerful language that forms the bedrock of American political tradition. Its opening line, "We the People of the United States," boldly proclaimed that a loose confederation of independent states no longer existed. Instead, there was but one American people and nation. The original version of the Preamble opened with:

> We the people of the States of New Hampshire, Massachusetts, Rhode Island and the Providence Plantations, Connecticut, New Jersey, New York, Pennsylvania, Delaware, Maryland, Virginia, North Carolina, South Carolina and Georgia, do ordain, declare and establish the following Constitution for the government of ourselves and our Posterity.

The simple phrase "We the people" ended, at least for the time being, the question of whence the government derived its power: It came directly from the people, not from the states. The next phrase of the Constitution explained the need for the new outline of government. "[I]n Order to form a more perfect Union" indirectly acknowledged the weaknesses of the Articles of Confederation in governing a growing nation. Next, the optimistic goals of the Framers for the new nation were set out: to "establish Justice, insure domestic Tranquility, provide for the common defense, promote the general Welfare, and secure the Blessings of Liberty to ourselves and our Posterity"; followed by the formal creation of a new government: "do ordain and establish this Constitution for the United States of America."

On September 17, 1787, the Constitution was approved by the delegates from all twelve states in attendance. While the completed document did not satisfy all the delegates, of the forty-one in attendance, thirty-nine ultimately signed it. The sentiments uttered by Benjamin Franklin probably well reflected those of many others: "Thus, I consent, Sir, to this Constitution because I expect no better, and because I am not sure that it is not the best."[18]

The Basic Principles of the Constitution

The ideas of political philosophers, especially two political philosophers, the French Montesquieu (1689–1755) and the English John Locke (see Roots of Government: Hobbes and Locke in chapter 1), heavily influenced the shape and nature of the government proposed by the Framers. Montesquieu, who actually drew many of his ideas about government from the works of Greek political philosopher Aristotle, was heavily quoted during the Constitutional Convention.

The proposed structure of the new national government owed much to the writings of Montesquieu, who advocated distinct functions for each branch of government, called **separation of powers,** with a system of **checks and balances** between each branch. The Constitution's concern with the distribution of power between states and the national government also reveals the heavy influence of political philosophers, as well as the colonists' experience under the Articles of Confederation.[19]

separation of powers
A way of dividing power among three branches of government in which members of the House of Representatives, members of the Senate, the president, and the federal courts are selected by and responsible to different constituencies.

checks and balances
A governmental structure that gives each of the three branches of government some degree of oversight and control over the actions of the others.

federal system
Plan of government created in the U.S. Constitution in which power is divided between the national government and the state governments and in which independent states are bound together under one national government.

Federalism.   Today, in spite of current calls for the national government to return power to the states, the question before and during the Convention was how much power states would give up to the national government. Given the nation's experiences under the Articles of Confederation, the Framers believed that a strong national government was necessary for the new nation's survival. However, they were reluctant to create a powerful government after the model of Britain, the country from which they had just won their independence. Its unitary system was not even considered by the colonists. Instead, they fashioned a system now known as the **federal system,** which divides the power of government between a strong national government and the individual states. This system, as the Court reaffirmed in 1995 in considering term limits, was based on the principle that the federal, or national, government derived its power from the citizens, not the states, as the national government had done under the Articles of Confederation.

Opponents of this system feared that a strong national government would infringe on their liberty. But James Madison argued that a strong national government with distinct state governments could, if properly directed by constitutional arrangements, actually be a source of expanded liberties and national unity. The Framers viewed the division of governmental authority between the national government and the states as a means of checking power with power, and providing the people with "double security" against governmental tyranny. Later, the passage of the Tenth Amendment, which stated that powers not given to the national government were reserved by the states or the people, further clarified the federal structure (see chapter 3).

Separation of Powers.   Madison and many of the Framers clearly feared putting too much power into the hands of any one individual or branch of government. His famous words, "Ambition must be made to counteract ambition," were widely believed at the Philadelphia convention.

Separation of powers is simply a way of parceling out power among the three branches of government. It has three key features:

1. Three distinct branches of government: the legislative, the executive, and the judicial.
2. Three separately staffed branches of government to exercise these functions.
3. Constitutional equality and independence of each branch.

As illustrated in Figure 2.1, the Framers were careful to create a system in which law-making, law-enforcing, and law-interpreting functions were assigned to inde-

FIGURE 2.1 Separation of Powers and Checks and Balances Illustrated

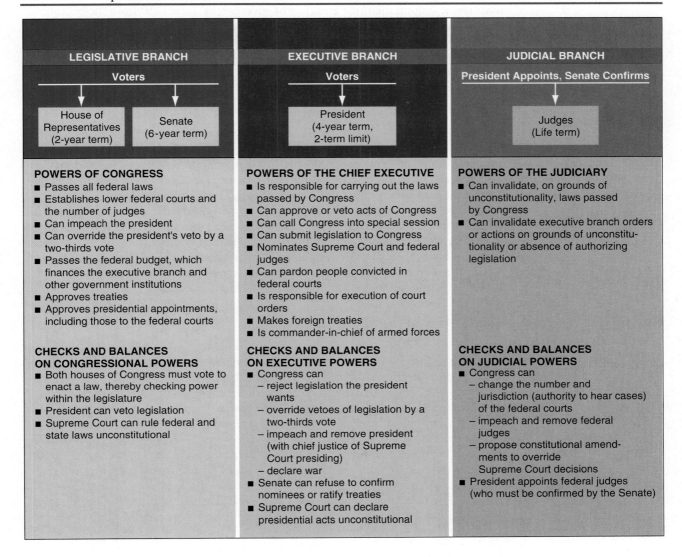

LEGISLATIVE BRANCH

Voters

House of Representatives (2-year term) Senate (6-year term)

POWERS OF CONGRESS
- Passes all federal laws
- Establishes lower federal courts and the number of judges
- Can impeach the president
- Can override the president's veto by a two-thirds vote
- Passes the federal budget, which finances the executive branch and other government institutions
- Approves treaties
- Approves presidential appointments, including those to the federal courts

CHECKS AND BALANCES ON CONGRESSIONAL POWERS
- Both houses of Congress must vote to enact a law, thereby checking power within the legislature
- President can veto legislation
- Supreme Court can rule federal and state laws unconstitutional

EXECUTIVE BRANCH

Voters

President (4-year term, 2-term limit)

POWERS OF THE CHIEF EXECUTIVE
- Is responsible for carrying out the laws passed by Congress
- Can approve or veto acts of Congress
- Can call Congress into special session
- Can submit legislation to Congress
- Nominates Supreme Court and federal judges
- Can pardon people convicted in federal courts
- Is responsible for execution of court orders
- Makes foreign treaties
- Is commander-in-chief of armed forces

CHECKS AND BALANCES ON EXECUTIVE POWERS
- Congress can
  - reject legislation the president wants
  - override vetoes of legislation by a two-thirds vote
  - impeach and remove president (with chief justice of Supreme Court presiding)
  - declare war
- Senate can refuse to confirm nominees or ratify treaties
- Supreme Court can declare presidential acts unconstitutional

JUDICIAL BRANCH

President Appoints, Senate Confirms

Judges (Life term)

POWERS OF THE JUDICIARY
- Can invalidate, on grounds of unconstitutionality, laws passed by Congress
- Can invalidate executive branch orders or actions on grounds of unconstitutionality or absence of authorizing legislation

CHECKS AND BALANCES ON JUDICIAL POWERS
- Congress can
  - change the number and jurisdiction (authority to hear cases) of the federal courts
  - impeach and remove federal judges
  - propose constitutional amendments to override Supreme Court decisions
- President appoints federal judges (who must be confirmed by the Senate)

pendent branches of government. On the national level (and in most states), only the legislature has the authority to make laws; the chief executive enforces laws, and the judiciary interprets them. Moreover, members of the House of Representatives, members of the Senate, the president, and members of the federal courts are selected by and are therefore responsible to different constituencies. Madison believed that the scheme devised by the Framers would divide the offices of the new government and their methods of selection among many individuals, providing each office holder with the "necessary means and personal motives to resist encroachment" on his or her power.

The Framers could not have foreseen the intermingling of governmental functions that has since evolved. Locke, in fact, cautioned against giving a legislature the ability to delegate its powers. In Article I of the Constitution, the legislative power is vested in the Congress. But the president is also given legislative powers via his ability to veto legislation, although his veto can be overridden by a two-thirds vote in Congress. Judicial interpretation then helps to clarify the implementation of legislation enacted through this process.

So instead of a pure system of separation of powers, a symbiotic, or interdependent, relationship among the three branches of government has existed from the beginning. Or, as one scholar has explained, there are "separated institutions sharing powers."[20] While Congress is still entrusted with making the laws, most proposals for legislation originate with the president. And although the Supreme Court's major function is to interpret the law, its involvement in areas such as criminal procedure, abortion, and other fields has led many to charge that it has surpassed its constitutional authority and become a law-making body.

Checks and Balances.   The separation of powers among the three branches of the national government is not complete. According to Montesquieu and the Framers, the powers of each branch (as well as the two houses of the national legislature and between the states and the national government) could be used to check the powers of the other two branches of government. The power of each branch of government is checked, or limited, and balanced because the legislative, executive, and judicial branches share some authority and no branch has exclusive domain over any activity. The creation of this system allowed the Framers to minimize the threat of tyranny from any one branch. Thus, for almost every power granted to one branch, an equal control was established in the other two branches. The Congress could "check" the power of the president, the Supreme Court, and so on, carefully creating "balance" among the three branches.

The Articles of the Constitution

The document finally signed by the Framers condensed numerous resolutions into a Preamble and seven separate articles. The first three articles established the three branches of government, defined their internal operations, and clarified their relationships with one another. All branches of government were technically considered equal, yet some initially appeared more "equal" than others. It is likely that the order in which the articles appear, and especially the relative amount of detail in the first three articles, reflects the Framers' concern that the branches of the government might abuse their powers. The four remaining articles define the relationships among the states, declare national law to be supreme, and set out methods of amending the Constitution.

Article I: The Legislative Branch.   Article I vests all legislative powers in the Congress and establishes a bicameral legislature, consisting of the Senate and the House of Representatives. It also sets out the qualifications for holding office in each house, the terms of office, methods of selection of representatives and senators, and the system of apportionment among the states to determine membership in the House of Representatives. Article I, section 2, specifies that an "enumeration" of the citizenry must take place every ten years in a manner to be directed by the U.S. Congress. Continuity and Change: Counting Americans reveals how complex and partisan that task has become. Operating procedures and the officers for each house are also outlined and described in Article I.

One of the most important sections of Article I is section 8. It carefully lists the powers the Framers wished the new Congress to possess. These specified or **enumerated powers** contain many key provisions that had been denied to the Continental Congress under the Articles of Confederation. For example, one of the major weaknesses of the Articles was Congress's lack of authority to deal with trade wars. The Constitution remedied this problem by authorizing Congress to "regulate Commerce with foreign Nations, and among the several States." Congress was also given the authority to coin money.

Today, Congress often enacts legislation that no specific clause of Article 1, section 8, appears to authorize. Laws dealing with the environment, welfare, education, and communications, among others, are often justified by reference to a particular power plus the necessary and proper clause. After careful enumeration of seventeen powers of Congress in Article 1, section 8, a final, general clause authorizing Congress to "make all Laws which shall be necessary and proper for carrying into Execution the foregoing Powers" was added to Article I. Often referred to as the elastic

Longman
Participate.com
2.0
Visual Literacy
The American System of Checks and Balances

enumerated powers
Seventeen specific powers granted to Congress under Article I, section 8, of the U.S. Constitution; these powers include taxation, coinage of money, regulation of commerce, and the authority to provide for a national defense.

clause, the **necessary and proper clause** has been a source of tremendous congressional activity never anticipated by the Framers, as definitions of "necessary" and "proper" have been stretched to accommodate changing needs and times. The clause is the basis for Congress's **implied powers** that it uses to execute its other powers. The Supreme Court, for example, has coupled Congress's authority to regulate commerce with the necessary and proper clause to allow Congress to ban prostitution (where travel across state lines is involved), regulate trains and planes, establish uniform federal minimum-wage and maximum-hour laws, and mandate drug testing for certain workers.

Article II: The Executive Branch.   Article II vests the executive power, that is, the authority to execute the laws of the nation, in a president of the United States. Section 1 sets the president's term of office at four years and explains the electoral college. It also states qualifications for office and describes a mechanism to replace the president in case of death, disability, or removal.

The powers and duties of the president are set out in section 3. Among the most important of these are the president's role as commander-in-chief of the armed forces, the authority to make treaties with the consent of the Senate, and the authority to "appoint Ambassadors, other public Ministers and Consuls, the Judges of the supreme Court, and all other Officers of the United States." Other sections of Article II instruct the president to report directly to Congress "from time to time," in what has come to be known as the State of the Union Address, and to "take Care that the Laws be faithfully executed." Section 4 provides the mechanism for removal of the president, vice president, and other officers of the United States for "Treason, Bribery, or other high Crimes and Misdemeanors" (see chapter 8).

Article III: The Judicial Branch.   Article III establishes a Supreme Court and defines its jurisdiction. During the Philadelphia meeting, the small and large states differed significantly as to the desirability of an independent judiciary and on the role of state courts in the national court system. The smaller states feared that a strong unelected judiciary would trample on their liberties. In compromise, Congress was permitted, but not required, to establish lower national courts. Thus, state courts and the national court system would exist side by side with distinct areas of authority. Federal courts were given authority to decide cases arising under federal law. The Supreme Court was also given the power to settle disputes between states, or between a state and the national government. Ultimately, it was up to the Supreme Court to determine what any provisions of the Constitution actually meant.

Although some delegates to the convention had urged that the president be allowed to remove federal judges, ultimately judges were given appointments for life, presuming "good behavior." And, like the president's, their salaries cannot be lowered while they hold office. This provision was adopted to ensure that the legislature did not attempt to punish the Supreme Court or any other judges for unpopular decisions.

Articles IV Through VII.   The remainder of the Articles attempted to anticipate problems that might occur in the operation of the new national government as well as its relations to the states. Article IV begins with what is called the full faith and credit clause, which mandates that states honor the laws and judicial proceedings of the other states. In 1996, when it appeared that Hawaii might legalize same-sex marriages, the U.S. Congress passed the Defense of Marriage Act to allow states to disregard gay marriages even if they are legal in other states. Vermont recognized the legality of same-sex partnerships in 2000, but no state has yet to legalize same-sex marriages (although the Vermont legislation bestows most rights of married couples to those who formalize their same-sex unions) and thus the constitutionality of this act has not been challenged in the federal courts. But since the full faith and credit clause mandates that states recognize the laws of other states, some question about the legality of the federal law remains. Article IV also includes the mechanisms for admitting new states to the Union.

necessary and proper clause
Found in the final paragraph of Article I, section 8, of the U.S. Constitution, it gives Congress the authority to pass all laws "necessary and proper" to carry out the enumerated powers specified in the Constitution.

implied powers
Powers given to the national government through the interference from enumerated powers.

Article V (discussed in greater detail on p. 58) specifies how amendments can be added to the Constitution. The Bill of Rights, which added ten amendments to the Constitution in 1791, was one of the one of the first items of business in the First Congress in 1789. Since then, only seventeen additional amendments have been ratified.

supremacy clause
The law of the national government stands above any state law or state constitution.

Article VI contains the supremacy clause, which asserts the basic primacy of the Constitution and national law over state laws and constitutions. The **supremacy clause** provides that the "Constitution, and the laws of the United States" as well as all treaties are to be the supreme law of the land. All national and state officers and judges are bound by national law and take oaths to support the federal Constitution above any state law or constitution. Because of the supremacy clause, any legitimate exercise of national power supercedes any state laws or action, in a process that is called preemption. Without the supremacy clause and the federal court's ability to invoke it, the national government would have little actual enforceable power; thus many commentators call the supremacy clause the linchpin of the entire federal system.

Mindful of the potential problems that could occur if church and state were too enmeshed, Article VI also specifies that no religious test shall be required for holding any office. This mandate strengthens the separation of church and state guarantee that was quickly added to the Constitution when the First Amendment was ratified.

The seventh and final article of the Constitution concerns the procedures for ratification of the new Constitution: Nine of the thirteen states would have to agree to, or ratify, its new provisions before it would become the supreme law of the land.

THE DRIVE FOR RATIFICATION

While delegates to the Constitutional Convention labored in Philadelphia, the Second Continental Congress continued to govern the former colonies under the Articles of Confederation. The day after the Constitution was signed, William Jackson, the secretary of the Constitutional Convention, left for New York City, then the nation's capital, to deliver the official copy of the document to the Congress. He also took with him a resolution of the delegates calling upon each of the states to vote on the new Constitution. Anticipating resistance from the representatives in the state legislatures, however, the Framers required the states to call special ratifying conventions to consider the proposed Constitution.

Jackson carried a letter from General George Washington with the proposed Constitution. In a few eloquent words, Washington summed up the sentiments of the Framers and the spirit of compromise that had permeated the long weeks in Philadelphia:

> That it will meet the full and entire approbation of every state is not perhaps to be expected, but each [state] will doubtless consider, that had her interest alone been consulted, the consequences might have been particularly disagreeable or injurious to others; that it is liable to as few exceptions as could reasonably have been expected, we hope and believe; that it may promote lasting welfare of that country so dear to us all, and secure her freedom and happiness is our ardent wish.[21]

The Second Continental Congress immediately accepted the work of the convention and forwarded the proposed Constitution to the states for their vote. It was by no means certain, however, that the new Constitution would be adopted. From the fall of 1787 to the summer of 1788, the proposed Constitution was debated hotly around the nation. State politicians understandably feared a strong central government. Farmers and other working-class people were fearful of a distant national government. And those who had accrued substantial debts during the economic chaos following the Revolutionary War feared that a new government with a new financial policy would plunge them into even greater debt. The public in general was very leery of taxes—these were the same people who had revolted against the king's taxes. At the heart of many of their concerns was an underlying fear of the massive changes that would be brought about by a new system. Favoring the Constitution were wealthy merchants, lawyers, bankers, and those who believed that the new nation could not continue to exist under the Articles of Confederation. For them, it all boiled down to one simple question offered by Madison: "Whether or not the Union shall or shall not be continued."

Federalists Versus Anti-Federalists

Almost as soon as the ink was dry on the last signature to the Constitution, those who favored the new strong national government chose to call themselves **Federalists.** They were well aware that many still generally opposed the notion of a strong national government. Thus they did not want to risk being labeled "nationalists," so they tried to get the upper hand in the debate by nicknaming their opponents **Anti-Federalists.** Those put in the latter category insisted that they were instead "Federal Republicans" who believed in a federal system. As noted in Table 2.1, Anti-Federalists argued that they simply wanted to protect state governments from the tyranny of a too-powerful national government.[22]

Federalists and Anti-Federalists participated in the mass meetings that were held in state legislatures to discuss the pros and cons of the new plan. Tempers ran high at public meetings, where differences between the opposing groups were highlighted. Fervent debates were published in newspapers. Indeed, newspapers played a powerful role in the adoption process. The entire Constitution, in fact, was printed in the *Pennsylvania Packet* just two days after the convention's end. Other major papers quickly followed suit. Soon articles on both sides of the adoption issue began to appear around the nation, often written under pseudonyms such as "Caesar" or "Constant Reader," as was the custom of the day.

One name stood out from all the rest: "Publius" (Latin for "the people"). Between October 1787 and May 1788, eighty-five articles written under that pen name routinely appeared in newspapers in New York, a state where ratification was in doubt. Most were written by Alexander Hamilton and James Madison. Hamilton, a young, fiery New Yorker born in the British West Indies, wrote fifty-one, Madison wrote twenty-six, and jointly they penned another three. John Jay, also of New York, and later the first chief justice of the United States, wrote five of the pieces. These eighty-five essays became known as ***The Federalist Papers.***

Today *The Federalist Papers* are considered masterful explanations of the Framers' intentions as they drafted the new Constitution. At the time, although they were reprinted widely, they were far too theoretical to have much impact on those who would ultimately vote on the proposed Constitution. Dry and scholarly, they lacked the fervor

Federalists
Those who favored a stronger national government and supported the proposed U.S. Constitution; later became the first U.S. political party.

Anti-Federalists
Those who favored strong state governments and a weak national government; opposed the ratification of the U.S. Constitution.

The Federalist Papers
A series of eighty-five political papers written by John Jay, Alexander Hamilton, and James Madison in support of ratification of the U.S. Constitution.

TABLE 2.1   Federalists and Anti-Federalists Compared

	Federalists	*Anti-Federalists*
Who were they?	Property owners, landed rich, merchants of Northeast and Middle Atlantic states	Small farmers, shopkeepers, laborers
Political philosophy	Elitist: saw themselves and those of their class as most fit to govern (others were to be governed)	Believed in the decency of the common man and in participatory democracy; viewed elites as corrupt; sought greater protection of individual rights
Type of government favored	Powerful central government; two-house legislature; upper house (six-year term) further removed from the people, whom they distrusted	Wanted stronger state governments (closer to the people) at the expense of the powers of the national government. Sought smaller electoral districts, frequent elections, referendum and recall, and a large unicameral legislature to provide for greater class and occupational representation
Alliances	Pro-British Anti-French	Anti-British Pro-French

of much of the political rhetoric that was then in use. *The Federalist Papers* did, however, highlight the reasons for the structure of the new government and its benefits. According to *Federalist No. 10,* for example, the new Constitution was called "a republican remedy for the disease incident to republican government." Moreover, these musings of Madison, Hamilton, and Jay continue to be the best single source of the political theories and philosophies at the heart of our Constitution.

WEB EXPLORATION
To compare the *The Federalist Papers* with the *Anti-Federalist Papers,* see
www.ablongman.com/oconnor

Forced on the defensive, the Anti-Federalists responded with their own series of "letters" written by Anti-Federalists adopting the pen names of "Brutus" and "Cato," two ancient Romans famous for their intolerance of tyranny. These "letters" (actually essays) undertook a line-by-line critique of the Constitution and were designed to counteract *The Federalist Papers.*

Anti-Federalists argued that a strong central government would render the states powerless.[23] They stressed the strengths the government had been granted under the Articles of Confederation, and argued that these Articles, not the proposed Constitution, created a true federal system. Moreover, they argued that the strong national government would tax heavily, that the Supreme Court would overwhelm the states by invalidating state laws, and that the president eventually would have too much power, as commander-in-chief of a large and powerful army.[24]

In particular, the Anti-Federalists feared the power of the national government to run roughshod over the liberties of the people. They proposed that the taxing power of Congress be limited, that the executive be curbed by a council, that the military consist of state militias rather than a national force, and that the jurisdiction of the Supreme Court be limited to prevent it from reviewing and potentially overturning the decisions of state courts. But their most effective argument concerned the absence of a bill of rights in the Constitution. James Madison answered these criticisms in *Federalists Nos.*

Alexander Hamilton (left), James Madison (center), and John Jay (right) were important early Federalist leaders. Jay wrote five of *The Federalist Papers* and Madison and Hamilton wrote the rest. Madison served in the House of Representatives (1789–1797) and as secretary of state in the Jefferson administration (1801–1808). In 1808 he was elected fourth president of the United States and served two terms (1809–1817). Hamilton became the first secretary of the treasury (1789–1795). He was killed in 1804 in a duel with Vice President Aaron Burr, who was angered by Hamilton's negative comments about his character. Jay became the first chief justice of the United States (1789–1795) and negotiated the Jay Treaty with Great Britain in 1794. He then served as governor of New York from 1795 to 1801. (Photos courtesy: left, The Metropolitan Museum of Art, Gift of Henry G. Marquand; 1881 (81.11) copyright ©1987 by The Metropolitan Museum of Art; center, Colonial Williamsburg Foundation; right, Bettman/Corbis)

10 and *51*. (The texts of these two essays are printed in the Appendix.) In *Federalist No. 10*, he pointed out that the voters would not always succeed in electing "enlightened statesmen" as their representatives. The greatest threat to individual liberties would therefore come from factions within the government, who might place narrow interests above broader national interests and the rights of citizens. While recognizing that no form of government could protect the country from unscrupulous politicians, Madison argued that the organization of the new government would minimize the effects of political factions. The great advantage of a federal system, Madison maintained, was that it created the "happy combination" of a national government too large to be controlled by any single faction, and several state governments that would be smaller and more responsive to local needs. Moreover, he argued in *Federalist No. 51* that the proposed federal government's separation of powers would prohibit any one branch from either dominating the national government or violating the rights of citizens.

Debate continued in the thirteen states as votes were taken from December 1787 to June 1788, in accordance with the ratifying process laid out in Article VII of the proposed Constitution. Three states acted quickly to ratify the new Constitution. Two small states, Delaware and New Jersey, voted to ratify before the large states could rethink the notion of equal representation of the states in the Senate. Pennsylvania, where Federalists were well organized, was one of the first three states to ratify. Massachusetts assented to the new government but tempered its support by calling for an immediate addition of amendments including one protecting personal rights. New Hampshire became the crucial ninth state to ratify on June 21, 1788. This action completed the ratification process outlined in Article VII of the Constitution and marked the beginning of a new nation. But because New York and Virginia (which between them accounted for more than 40 percent of the new nation's population) had not yet ratified the Constitution, the practical future of the new nation remained in doubt.

Hamilton in New York and Madison in Virginia worked feverishly to convince delegates to their state conventions to vote for the new government. In New York, sentiment against it was high. In Albany, fighting broke out over the proposed Constitution, resulting in injuries and death. When news of Virginia's acceptance of the Constitution reached the New York convention, Hamilton was finally able to convince a majority of those present to follow suit by a narrow margin of three votes. Both states also recommended the addition of a series of structural amendments, and a bill of rights.

Two of the original states—North Carolina and Rhode Island—continued to hold out against ratification. Both had recently printed new currencies and feared that values would plummet in a federal system where the Congress was authorized to coin money. On August 2, 1788, North Carolina became the first state to reject the

Longman
Participate.com
2.0
Simulation
You Are James Madison

Eagles on the backs of quarters are being replaced with designs from each of the fifty states. Five states will be featured each year from 1999 to 2008 based on the order in which they ratified the Constitution or were admitted to statehood. (Photo courtesy: U.S. Treasury, U.S. Mint)

Bill of Rights
The first ten amendments to the
U.S. Constitution.

Constitution on the grounds that no Anti-Federalist amendments were included. Soon after, owing much to the Anti-Federalist pressure for additional protections from the national government, Congress submitted a **Bill of Rights** in September 1789. North Carolina then ratified the Constitution by a vote of 194 to 77. Rhode Island, the only state that had not sent representatives to Philadelphia, remained out of the Union until 1790. Finally, under threats from its largest cities to secede from the state, the legislature called a convention that ratified the Constitution by only two votes (34 to 32)—one year after George Washington became the first president of the United States.

FORMAL METHODS OF AMENDING THE CONSTITUTION

Longman
Participate.com
2.0
Timeline
**The History of
Constitutional
Amendments**

Once the Constitution was ratified, elections were held. When Congress convened, it immediately sent a set of amendments to the states for their ratification. An amendment authorizing the enlargement of the House of Representatives and another to prevent members of the House from raising their own salaries failed to garner favorable votes in the necessary three-fourths of the states. (See Highlight: A Student's Revenge: The Twenty-Seventh [Madison] Amendment.) The remaining ten amendments, known as the Bill of Rights, were ratified by 1791 in accordance with the procedures set out in the Constitution. Sought by Anti-Federalists as a protection for individual liberties, they offered numerous specific limitations on the national government's ability to interfere with a wide variety of personal liberties, some of which were already guaranteed by many state constitutions (see chapters 5 and 6).

The Bill of Rights includes numerous specific protections of personal rights. Freedom of expression, speech, press, religion, and assembly are guaranteed by the First Amendment. The Bill of Rights also contains numerous safeguards for those accused of crimes.

In addition to guaranteeing these important rights, two of the amendments of the Bill of Rights were reactions to British rule—the right to bear arms (Second Amendment) and the right not to have soldiers quartered in private homes (Third Amendment). More general rights are also included in the Bill of Rights. The Ninth Amendment notes that these enumerated rights are not inclusive, meaning they are not the only rights to be enjoyed by the people, and the Tenth Amendment states that powers not given to the national government are reserved by the states or the people.

The Amendment Process

Article V of the Constitution creates a two-stage amendment process: proposal and ratification.[25] The Constitution specifies two ways to accomplish each stage. As illustrated in Figure 2.2, amendments to the Constitution can be proposed by:

1. A vote of two-thirds of the members in both houses of Congress; or

FIGURE 2.2   **Methods of Amending the Constitution**

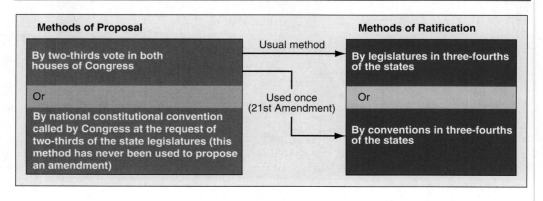

Methods of Proposal

By two-thirds vote in both houses of Congress

Or

By national constitutional convention called by Congress at the request of two-thirds of the state legislatures (this method has never been used to propose an amendment)

Usual method

Used once
(21st Amendment)

Methods of Ratification

By legislatures in three-fourths of the states

Or

By conventions in three-fourths of the states

H I G H L I G H T

A STUDENT'S REVENGE: THE TWENTY-SEVENTH (MADISON) AMENDMENT

On June 8, 1789, in a speech before the House of Representatives, James Madison stated.

[T]here is seeming impropriety in leaving any set of men without controul [sic] to put their hand into the public coffers, to take out money to put into their pockets. . . . I have gone therefore so far as to fix it, that no law, varying the compensation, shall operate until there is a change in the legislation.

When Madison spoke these words about his proposal, now known as the Twenty-Seventh Amendment, he had no way of knowing that more than two centuries would pass before it would become an official part of the Constitution. In fact, Madison deemed it worthy of addition only because the conventions of three states (Virginia, New York, and North Carolina) had demanded that it be included.

By 1791, when the Bill of Rights was added to the Constitution, only six states had ratified Madison's amendment, and it seemed destined to fade into obscurity. In 1982, however, Gregory Watson, a sophomore majoring in economics at the University of Texas-Austin, discovered the unratified compensation amendment while looking for a paper topic for an American government class. Intrigued, Watson wrote a paper arguing that the proposed amendment was still viable because it had no internal time limit and, therefore, should still be ratified. Watson received a "C" on the paper.

Despite his grade, Watson began a ten-year, $6,000 self-financed crusade to renew interest in the compensation amendment. Watson and his allies reasoned that the amendment should be revived because of the public's growing anger with the fact that members of Congress had sought to raise their salaries without going on the record as having done so. Watson's perseverance paid off, and on May 7, 1992, the amendment was ratified by the requisite thirty-eight states. On May 18, the United

States Archivist certified that the amendment was part of the Constitution, a decision that was overwhelmingly confirmed by the House of Representatives on May 19 and by the Senate on May 20.

At the same time that the Senate approved the Twenty-Seventh Amendment, it also took action to ensure that a similar situation would never occur by declaring "dead" four other amendments.

Source: Fordham Law Review (December 1992): 497–539, and Anne Marie Kilday, "Amendment Expert Agrees with Congressional Pay Ruling," *Dallas Morning News* (February 14, 1993): 13A.

Gregory Watson with a document that contains the first ten amendments to the Constitution, as well as the compensation amendment ("Article the second: No law varying the compensation for the services of the Senators and Representatives shall take effect until an election of Representatives shall have intervened"), which was finally ratified as the Twenty-Seventh Amendment in 1992. (Photo courtesy: Ziggy Kaluzny/People Weekly © 1993)

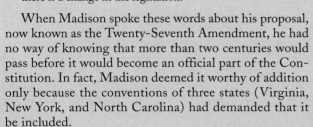

2. A vote of two-thirds of the state legislatures specifically requesting Congress to call a national convention to propose amendments.

The second method has never been used. Historically, it has served as a fairly effective threat, forcing Congress to consider amendments that might otherwise never have been debated. In the 1980s, for example, several states called on Congress to enact a balanced-budget amendment. To forestall the need for a special constitutional convention, in 1985 Congress enacted the Gramm-Rudman-Hollings Act, which called for a balanced budget by the 1991 fiscal year. But Congress could not meet that

GLOBAL POLITICS

COMPARING CONSTITUTIONS

Americans are used to the idea of a durable written constitution. The U.S. Constitution stands out not only for being the first written constitution in the modern world (Poland followed soon after, in 1790), but because it remains the Constitution of the United States today. In fact, the American case is rather anomalous, both in the number of constitutions it has had (two, if we count the Articles of Confederation) and in the continuity of the basic political rules it outlined. Among the cases surveyed here, only Canada and the United Kingdom have had similar experience with a single constitution. Yet Canada's constitutional history is nearly a century shorter than that of the United States. Britain's single constitution is unwritten and has evolved over centuries (parts of it date to the Middle Ages), rendering it difficult to compare with a written constitution. More typically, the European countries and Japan have had multiple constitutions. France is the extreme example, with fifteen constitutional regimes since 1789 (five in the first decade after the French Revolution). External events such as World War II, independence in Asia and Africa, and the collapse of the Soviet Union have had significant impacts on constitution building around the world.

Interestingly, these constitutions have established a wide range of political systems. Since 1789, France has had monarchies, republics, a commune, and a dictatorship in collaboration with a foreign occupier. The first constitutions in Germany, Italy, and Japan were within anti-democratic monarchies. Italy and Germany had fascist constitutional systems in the 1930s and early 1940s. Germany, moreover, had two competing constitutional systems during the Cold War, with a parliamentary democracy in West Germany and a Soviet-style socialist political system in East Germany. In Germany and Japan, postwar occupations by outside powers led to new constitutions. Constitutional amendment practices vary as well. Unlike the Framers' desire to make constitutional change difficult, the European parliamentary systems have rather simple amendment procedures: passage by both houses of the legislature is typically sufficient to effect amendment. The Russian and French presidents have the option to submit an amendment to referendum by the public (both countries' current constitutions were ratified in this manner); French President Chirac exercised the option in 2000. Informal extraconstitutional methods have tended to prevail in nondemocratic settings. Indonesia's 1945 constitution was restored in 1959 amidst civil disorder, and the reality of political power over the next forty years was increasingly remote from constitutional intent. China's three constitutions since 1949 have been largely modifications of their predecessors.

In sum, the United States' constitutional history is rather remarkable for its continuity under a single written document.

Constitutions in 11 Countries

Country	Number of Constitutions	Year Current Constitution Was Established
Canada	1	1867
China	4	1982
France	15	1958
Germany	5	1949
Indonesia	2	1945
Italy	3	1945
Japan	2	1947
Mexico	5	1917
Russia	5	1993
United Kingdom	n/a	n/a
United States	2	1789

WEB EXPLORATION
For the text of these failed amendments, see
www.ablongman.com/oconnor

target. The act was amended repeatedly until 1993, when Congress postponed the call for a balanced budget, the need for which has faded in light of current surpluses. The act also was ruled unconstitutional by a three-judge district court that declared the law violated separation of powers principles.

Of the more than 10,000 amendments that have been introduced on one or both floors of the Congress, only thirty-three mustered the two-thirds vote required for them to be sent to the states for debate and ratification through 2003. Only six proposed amendments sent to the states failed to be ratified.

For all its moral foundation in groups such as the Women's Christian Temperance Union (WCTU), whose members invaded bars to protest the sale of alcoholic beverages (left), the Eighteenth (Prohibition) Amendment was a disaster. Among its side effects were the rise of powerful crime organizations responsible for (among other things) the cache of over 3,000 bags of bottled beverages uncovered by federal agents (right). Once proposed, it took only ten months to ratify the Twenty-First Amendment, which repealed the Prohibition amendment. (Photos courtesy: left, Hulton Getty/Liaison Agency; right, AP/Wide World Photos)

The ratification process is fairly straightforward. When Congress votes to propose an amendment, the Constitution specifies that the ratification process must occur in one of two ways:

1. A favorable vote in three-fourths of the state legislatures; or
2. A favorable vote in specially called ratifying conventions in three-fourths of the states.

The Constitution itself, however, was to be ratified by specially called ratifying conventions. The Framers feared that the power of special interests in state legislatures would prevent a positive vote on the new Constitution. Since ratification of the Constitution, however, only one ratifying convention has been called. The Eighteenth Amendment, which caused the Prohibition era by outlawing the sale of alcoholic beverages, was ratified by the first method—a vote in state legislatures. Millions broke the law, others died from drinking homemade liquor, and still others made their fortunes selling bootleg or illegal liquor. After a decade of these problems, Congress decided to act. An additional amendment—the Twenty-First—was proposed to repeal the Eighteenth Amendment. It was sent to the states for ratification, but with a call for ratifying conventions, not a vote in the state legislatures.[26] Members of Congress correctly predicted that the move to repeal the Eighteenth Amendment would encounter opposition in the statehouses, which were largely controlled by conservative rural interests. Thus, Congress's decision to use the convention method led to quick approval of the Twenty-First Amendment.

The intensity of efforts to amend the Constitution has varied considerably, depending on the nature of the change proposed. Whereas the Twenty-First Amendment took only

Longman
Participate.com
2.0
Comparative
**Comparing
Constitutions**

ten months to ratify, an equal rights amendment (ERA) was introduced in every session of Congress from 1923 until 1972, when Congress finally voted favorably on it. Even then, years of lobbying by women's groups were insufficient to garner necessary state support. By 1982, the congressionally mandated date for ratification, only thirty-five states—three short of the number required—had voted favorably on the amendment.[27]

More recently, in 1998, to reverse what its supporters called three decades of court rulings that have stifled religious expression, the House of Representatives voted 224–203 for what was called the religious freedom constitutional amendment. As drafted, it would have allowed prayer in public schools, religious icons on government land and property, and state support of parochial schools. The amendment, however, fell 65 votes short of the two-thirds needed to send it to the states for their ratification.

In April 1999, the Senate Judiciary Subcommittee on the Constitution, Federalism, and Property Rights approved SJR 114 on a party line vote to override *Texas* v. *Johnson* (1989), in which the Supreme Court ruled that flag burning was a form of political speech protected by the First Amendment (see chapter 5).[28] This was the third attempt by the Republican-led Congress to overrule the 5–4 Supreme Court decision.[29] In May 1999, however, supporters again fell short of the two-thirds vote needed to send the amendment to the states.

Interestingly, the proposed amendment has public support. In 1999, 63 percent of those polled said that it was "worth it" to amend the Constitution to make flag burning illegal.[30] Nearly three-fourths of the men (74 percent) and 83.5 percent of the women polled believed that it should be illegal to burn the American flag.[31]

INFORMAL METHODS OF AMENDING THE CONSTITUTION

The Framers did not want to fashion a government that could respond to the whims of the people. The separation of powers and the checks and balances systems are just two indications of the Framers' recognition of the importance of deliberation and thought as a check against both government tyranny and the rash judgments of intemperate majorities. James Madison, in particular, wanted to draft a system of government that would pit faction against faction, and ambition against ambition, to design a system of representation and policy making that would strengthen minority factions against possible encroachments by majority factions. Although it took a long time, the Constitution was eventually amended to protect the rights of African Americans through the addition of the Thirteenth, Fourteenth, and Fifteenth amendments.

The Framers also made the formal amendment process a slow one to ensure that amendments were not added lightly to the Constitution. But the formal amendment process is not the only way that the Constitution has been changed over time. Judicial interpretation and cultural and social change also have had a major impact on the way the Constitution has evolved.

Judicial Interpretation

As early as 1803, under the leadership of Chief Justice John Marshall, the Supreme Court declared that the federal courts had the power to nullify acts of the nation's government when they were found to be in conflict with the Constitution. Over the years, this check on the other branches of government and on the states has increased the authority of the Court and has significantly altered the meaning of various provisions of the Constitution, a fact that prompted Woodrow Wilson to call the Supreme Court "a constitutional convention in continuous session." (More detail on the Supreme

DOONESBURY   Garry Trudeau

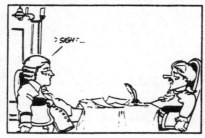

Court's role in interpreting the Constitution is found in chapters 5, 6, and 10 especially, as well as in other chapters in the book.)

Today some argue that the original intent of the Framers, as evidenced in *The Federalist Papers* as well as in private notes taken by James Madison at the Constitutional Convention, should govern judicial interpretation of the Constitution.[32] Others argue that the Framers knew that a changing society needed an elastic, flexible document that could conform to the ages.[33] In all likelihood, the vagueness of the document was purposeful. Those in attendance in Philadelphia recognized that they could not agree on everything and that it was wiser to leave interpretation to those who would follow them.

Recently, law professor Mark V. Tushnet has offered a particularly stinging criticism of any kind of judicial review and exclusive reliance on the courts to say what the Constitution means.[34] He believes that we must create a "populist" constitutional law that allows people to believe that they have the right to enforce the Constitution and not leave it up to the courts. To give this power to the courts, says Tushnet, necessarily means that "We, the People," envisioned by the Framers, lose sight of the true meaning of the Constitution.

Social, Cultural, and Legal Change

Even the most far-sighted of those in attendance at the Constitutional Convention could not have anticipated the vast changes that have occurred in the United States. For example, although many were uncomfortable with the Three-Fifths Compromise and others hoped for the abolition of slavery, none could have imagined the status of African Americans today, or that Colin Powell could serve as the U.S. secretary of state and have been frequently mentioned as a viable candidate for president or vice president. Likewise, few of the Framers could have anticipated the diverse roles that women would come to play in American society. The Constitution has often been bent to accommodate such social and cultural changes. Thus, although there is no specific amendment guaranteeing women equal protection of the law, the federal courts have

POINT/COUNTERPOINT

IS THERE A CONSTITUTIONAL RIGHT TO PRIVACY?

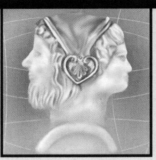

Since the mid 1960s, there has been substantial debate about whether there is a constitutional right to privacy in the United States. Privacy is defined simply as areas in which government should not and cannot legislate or otherwise make rules that infringe upon private dealings. In 1965, the Supreme Court, in the case *Griswold* v. *Connecticut*, ruled that the Constitution implied a right to privacy. The Court argued that although the word "privacy" was not specifically mentioned in the Constitution, the concept was so fundamental to our way of thinking and our political system that it is constitutionally protected. Since that time, there have been numerous arguments about whether the Supreme Court went too far in declaring an implied right to privacy that is constitutionally protected or whether the Constitution does protect that right. Is there a constitutional right to privacy? Let's examine these two viewpoints.

Griswold v. *Connecticut* concerned a Connecticut law that prohibited the sale and distribution of birth control and information about contraception to married persons in the state. In its ruling, the Court said that the right of a married couple to plan a family is a fundamental constitutional right protected by the right to privacy implied from several amendments: The First Amendment's right to freedom of speech implies a freedom of association and therefore privacy; the Fourth Amendment's protection against unreasonable search and seizure implies a right to privacy in one's home and person; the Fifth Amendment's right to avoid self-incrimination implies a zone of privacy in one's person; the Ninth Amendment guarantees that a person's rights are not limited solely to those written into the Constitution and so allows the Court to use implied rights and not simply enumerate or list rights.

The case in favor of a right to privacy starts with the ruling in *Griswold* that there is a fundamental right for married couples to be free from unwarranted governmental intrusion about matters of contraception. The privacy doctrine articulated by the Court in this case also was used in *Roe* v. *Wade* (1973). There, a majority of the Court ruled that a woman has a constitutional right to privacy in determining whether or not to end a pregnancy.

Those in favor of a constitutional right to privacy, such as so-called judicial activists, the Libertarian Party, and the National Abortion and Reproductive Rights Action League (NARAL), argue that the Framers understood that society would change over time and therefore gave the justices broad authority to interpret the Constitution to reflect the changing times and mores of society. The Framers never intended the Constitution's protections to be limited to the enumerated rights found in the document. Instead, they gave the country a flexible, living document that could cover myriad contingencies in a changing world.

The idea of a right to privacy has been most contentious because it is often thought of in terms of the abortion debate and contraceptive issues. However, proponents of a right to privacy contend that the right to privacy debate includes many other issues, such as Internet privacy (can you be traced online and how can this information be used), online credit card purchases, Social Security and health care information available online or for sale, your credit history, the sale of personal profiles, and even the encoding of information on the back of your driver's license. The right to privacy inherently limits the amount of governmental intrusion into your life and protects you and your right to own information about yourself and your personal habits and movements.

Critics of the idea, sometimes called Originalists, oppose implied rights in the Constitution, refer to the right to privacy as judicially created or judicial policy making and argue that the Court does not have the power to infer or imply rights. The Constitution does not mention privacy and therefore there is no constitutionally protected right to privacy. Thus, while some actions may be private and beyond the scope of governmental reach or regulation, opponents of a constitutional right to privacy argue that these rights need to be protected by laws, not by the Constitution.

The U.S. Constitution, in this view, does not provide the Court with the authority to invalidate the thoughtful laws of the states regulating public health and welfare because these powers are specifically reserved to the states by the Tenth Amendment. The correct bodies for making laws are the Congress and state legislatures; the courts can only rule on what is specifically written in the Constitution or in laws and statutes. Judicial bodies cannot make laws.

Originalists also care deeply about issues of privacy but do not claim there is a constitutional right that justifies it. Concerns for privacy and issues such as the Internet and whether you can be tracked by your subway ticket or by your cell-phone emissions are important but should be dealt with through laws by state legislatures or Congress, not by the courts.

 What do you think? Should there be a constitutional right to privacy or not?
Go to www.ablongman.com/oconnor

interpreted the Constitution to prohibit many forms of gender discrimination, thereby recognizing cultural and societal change.

Social change has also caused changes in the way institutions of government act. Thus, as problems such as the Great Depression appeared national in scope, Congress took on more and more power at the expense of the states to solve the economic and social crisis. In fact, Yale law professor Bruce Ackerman argues that on certain occasions, extraordinary times call for extraordinary measures such as the New Deal that, in effect, amend the Constitution. Thus, Congress's passage (and the Supreme Court's eventual acceptance) of sweeping New Deal legislation that altered the balance of power between the national government and the states, while possibly bordering on illegality, truly changed the Constitution without benefit of amendment.[35] Today, however, Congress is moving to return power to the states, although post 9/11 has meant some increase in federal powers. The actions of recent Congresses to return powers and responsibilities to the states may be viewed as an *informal* attempt not necessarily to amend the Constitution, but to realign the balance of power between the national and state government. Again, within the parameters of its constitutional powers, the Congress acted as the Framers intended without changing the document itself.

Advances in technology have also brought about constitutional change. Wiretapping and other forms of electronic surveillance, for example, are now regulated by the First and Fourth Amendments. Similarly, HIV testing must be balanced against constitutional protections and all kinds of new constitutional questions are posed in the wake of congressional efforts to regulate what kinds of information can be disseminated on the Internet. Still, in spite of these massive changes, the Constitution still survives, changed and ever changing after more than 200 years.

Continuity & Change

Counting Americans

The U.S. Constitution specifically requires that "representatives and direct Taxes shall be apportioned among the several States ... according to their respective numbers.... The actual Enumeration shall be made within three Years after the first Meeting of the Congress of the United States, and within every subsequent Term of ten Years in such a Manner as they shall by Law direct." In response to this, the first national census was taken in 1790.[36] But the process itself was very crude. U.S. marshals and their assistants, providing their own paper, took eighteen months to collect all of the data. And, unlike today, when all personal census survey data is confidential, law required that all local reports be posted in at least two public places.

For years, census data were tabulated by hand. In 1890 a punch card tabulating system was created, revolutionizing the process and allowing for quicker tabulation of data. Over time, the compiling of the U.S. Census has become more and more complex in response to changing governmental needs and well as changing technology. And, as the national government has grown, so have the kinds of data collected by the Census Bureau.

By 1990 the nation had grown so large that even the Census Bureau admitted that, for the first time, its report was more inaccurate than the one before it.[37] Millions of people, especially the poor, homeless, and minorities, were undercounted. Since the allocation of federal dollars, as well as congressional representation, is based on the results of the diennial censuses, urban centers and the Democratic Party cried foul since they believed that they were the most hurt by the undercounting of as many as 5.3 million people. Lawsuits were filed even before the 1990 Census challenging its methods, and in 1991 Congress passed legislation to compel the Census Bureau to contract with the nonpartisan National Academy of Sciences to study more accurate means for the 2000 Census. One of the means suggested was to sample the population. Actually, the Census Bureau began to use sampling in 1940, asking only every fourth household some more detailed questions.

But this is not the kind of sampling that was suggested by the Clinton administration and subsequently rejected by the Supreme Court in 1999.[38] It wanted to be able to adjust the count to include people that the

(continued)

current system was likely to miss. The Court, however, ruled that sampling could not be used to count citizens for the purposes of reallocating congressional seats among the states, although it didn't prohibit the use of sampling-adjusted numbers when states draw their own congressional and legislative district lines.

The 2000 Census was one of the most unique on record. To get Americans enthused about filling out their forms, a lavish campaign and outreach to minorities and immigrants were augmented with a variety of clever television advertisement throughout the nation, publicizing the importance of an accurate count to the distribution of federal dollars to states and local governments. This enormously expensive campaign worked: Early reports reveal that more Americans filled out their forms than in 1980 or 1990. Sixty-seven percent of all households filled out and returned their questionnaires. Response in the Hispanic community was, to some, surprisingly strong as Hispanics became the largest minority in the U.S.

In spite of these higher returns, the Clinton administration, to the outrage of Republicans in the Congress, also used sampling to revise the census count to add millions more people, particularly minorities. The Court's 1999 decision made it clear that sampling could not be used to apportion congressional seats but it did leave the door open to the use of sampling to redraw legislative boundaries within a state as well as to distribute federal dollars.[39]

The Census has far more political overtones than the Framers envisioned. Sampling is a well-recognized statistical technique, yet its use to "remedy" undercounting is highly contentious. In the future, the Census Bureau will continue to be challenged to come up with more accurate measures to count the population. With increasing use of multiple data bases, one might envision some sort of super-data base that could be combined and refigured to enhance the chances that everyone gets counted.

1. What kind of process might be developed to make sure that undercounting, particularly of certain populations with discrete interests, does not occur in the future?
2. How critical do you believe a totally accurate census is to the national government's ability to maintain a representative democracy?

Cast Your Vote. Which method of census-taking do you prefer? To cast your vote, go to **www.ablongman.com/oconnor**

This ad for U.S. Census 2000, which targets the Native American community, was among the many aimed at groups the Census traditionally had difficulty tracking. (Photo courtesy: United States Census 2000, G & G Advertising)

SUMMARY

The U.S. Constitution has proven to be a remarkably enduring document. In explaining how and why the Constitution came into being, this chapter has covered the following points:

1. **The Origins of a New Nation**
   While settlers came to the New World for a variety of reasons, most remained loyal to Great Britain and considered themselves subjects of the king. Over the years, as new generations of Americans were born on colonial soil, those ties weakened. A series of taxes levied by the Crown ultimately led the colonists to convene a Continental Congress and to declare their independence.

2. **The Declaration of Independence**
   The Declaration of Independence (1776), which drew heavily on the writings of John Locke, carefully enumerated the wrongs of the Crown and galvanized pub-

lic resentment and willingness to take up arms against Great Britain in the Revolutionary War (1775–1782).

3. **The First Attempt at Government: The Articles of Confederation**
   The Articles of Confederation (1781) created a loose league of friendship between the new national government and the states. Numerous weaknesses in the new government became apparent by 1784. Among the major flaws were Congress's inability to tax or regulate commerce, the absence of an executive to administer the government, and a weak central government.

4. **The Miracle at Philadelphia: Writing a Constitution**
   When the weaknesses under the Articles of Confederation became apparent, the states called for a meeting to reform them. The Constitutional Convention (1787) quickly threw out the Articles of Confederation and fashioned a new, more workable form of government. The Constitution was the result of a series of compromises, including those over representation, questions involving large and small states, and over how to determine population. Compromises were also made about how members of each branch of government were to be selected. The electoral college was created to give states a key role in the selection of the president.

5. **The U.S. Constitution**
   The proposed U.S. Constitution created a federal system that drew heavily on Montesquieu's ideas about separation of powers. These ideas concerned a way of parceling out power among the three branches of government, and checks and balances to prevent any one branch from having too much power.

6. **The Drive for Ratification**
   The drive for ratification became a fierce fight between Federalists and Anti-Federalists. Federalists lobbied for the strong national government created by the Constitution; Anti-Federalists favored greater state power.

7. **Formal Methods of Amending the Constitution**
   The Framers created a formal two-stage amendment process to include the Congress and the states. Amendments could be proposed by a two-thirds vote in Congress or of state legislatures requesting that Congress call a national convention to propose amendments. Amendments could be ratified by a positive vote of three-fourths of the state legislatures or specially called state ratifying conventions.

8. **Informal Methods of Amending the Constitution**
   The formal amendment process is not the only way that the Constitution can be changed. Judicial interpretation and social, cultural, and legal changes have also produced constitutional change.

KEY TERMS

Anti-Federalists, p. 55
Articles of Confederation, p. 42
Bill of Rights, p. 58
checks and balances, p. 50
Committees of Correspondence, p. 38
confederation, p. 41
Declaration of Independence, p. 41
enumerated powers, p. 52

federal system, p. 50
The Federalist Papers, p. 55
Federalists, p. 55
First Continental Congress, p. 40
Great Compromise, p. 47
implied powers, p. 53
necessary and proper clause, p. 53
New Jersey Plan, p. 47

Second Continental Congress, p. 40
separation of powers, p. 50
Shays's Rebellion, p. 44
Stamp Act Congress, p. 37
supremacy clause, p. 54
Three-Fifths Compromise, p. 48
Virginia Plan, p. 47

SELECTED READINGS

Ackerman, Bruce. *We the People.* Cambridge, Mass.: Belknap Press, 1991.

Bailyn, Bernard. *The Ideological Origins of the American Revolution.* Cambridge, Mass.: Belknap Press, 1967.

Beard, Charles. *An Economic Interpretation of the Constitution of the United States.* (reissue edition) New York: Free Press, 1996.

Bernstein, Richard B., with Jerome Agel. *Amending America.* Lawrence: University of Kansas Press, 1995.

Bowen, Catherine Drinker. *Miracle at Philadelphia.* Boston: Little, Brown, 1986.

Brinkley, Alan, Nelson W. Polsby and Kathleen M. Sullivan, *New Federalist Papers: Essays in Defense of the Constitution.* New York: Norton, 1997.

Hamilton, Alexander, James Madison, and John Jay. *The Federalist Papers.* New York: Bantam Books, 1989 (first published in 1788).

Ketchman, Ralph, ed. *The Anti-Federalist Papers and the Constitutional Convention Debated.* New York: Mentor Books, 1996.

Kyvig, David E. *Explicit and Authentic Acts: Amending the U.S. Constitution, 1776–1995.* Lawrence: University of Kansas Press, 1996.

Levy, Leonard W., ed. *Essays on the Making of the Constitution*, 2nd ed. New York: Oxford University Press, 1987.

Main, Jackson Turner. *The Social Structure of Revolutionary America*. Princeton, N.J.: Princeton University Press, 1965.

Rossiter, Clinton. *1787: Grand Convention*. (reissue edition) New York: Norton, 1987.

Stoner, James R., Jr. *Common Law and Liberal Theory*. Lawrence: University Press of Kansas, 1992.

Storing, Herbert J. *What the Anti-Federalists Were For*. Chicago: University of Chicago Press, 1981.

Vile, John R. *Encyclopedia of Constitutional Amendments, and Amending Issues, 1789–1995*. Santa Barbara, Calif.: ABC-CLIO, 1996.

Wood, Gordon S. *The Creation of the American Republic, 1776–1787*. (reissue edition) New York: Norton, 1993.

NOTES

1. See Richard B. Bernstein with Jerome Agel, *Amending America* (New York: New York Times Books, 1993), 138–140.
2. *Oregon* v. *Mitchell*, 400 U.S. *112* (1970).
3. Bernstein with Agel, *Amending America*, 139.
4. For an account of the early development of the colonies, see D. W. Meining, *The Shaping of America*, vol. 1: *Atlantic America, 1492–1800* (New Haven, Conn.: Yale University Press, 1986).
5. For an excellent chronology of the events leading up to the writing of the Declaration of Independence and the colonists' break with Great Britain, see Calvin D. Lonton, ed., *The Bicentennial Almanac* (Nashville, Tenn.: Thomas Nelson, 1975).
6. See Gary Wills, *Inventing America: Jefferson's Declaration of Independence* (New York: Random House, 1978). Wills argues that the Declaration was signed solely to secure foreign aid for the ongoing war effort.
7. See Gordon S. Wood, *The Creation of the American Republic, 1776–1787* (Chapel Hill: University of North Carolina Press, 1969).
8. For more about the Articles of Confederation, see Merrill Jensen, *The Articles of Confederation* (Madison: University of Wisconsin Press, 1940).
9. Quoted in Selma R. Williams, *Fifty-Five Fathers: The Story of the Constitutional Convention* (New York: Dodd, Mead, 1970), 10.
10. Charles A. Beard, *An Economic Interpretation of the Constitution of the United States* (reissue edition) New York: Free Press, 1996.
11. Quoted in Richard N. Current, et al., *American History: A Survey*, 6th ed. (New York: Knopf, 1983), 170.
12. John Patrick Diggins, "Power and Authority in American History: The Case of Charles A. Beard and His Critics," *The American Historical Review* 86 (October 1981): 701–30.
13. Robert Brown, *Charles Beard and the Constitution: A Critical Analysis of "An Economic Interpretation of the Constitution"* (Princeton, N.J.: Princeton University Press 1956).
14. Jackson Turner Main, *The Anti-Federalists* (Chapel Hill: University of North Carolina, 1961).
15. Gordon S. Wood, *The Creation of the American Republic, 1776–1787* (reissue edition) (New York: Norton, 1969).
16. Quoted in Doris Faber and Harold Faber, *We the People* (New York: Charles Scribner's Sons, 1987), 31.
17. For more on the political nature of compromise at the convention, see Calvin C. Jillson, *Constitution Making: Conflict and Consensus in the Federal Constitution of 1787* (New York: Agathon, 1988).
18. Quoted in Richard N. Current, et al., *American History: A Survey*, 6th ed. (New York: Random House, 1983), 168.
19. Bernard Bailyn, *The Ideological Origins of the American Revolution* (Cambridge, Mass.: Belknap Press, 1967).
20. Richard E. Neustadt, *Presidential Power: The Politics of Leadership from FDR to Carter* (New York: Macmillan, 1980), 26.
21. Quoted in Faber and Faber, *We the People*, 51–52.
22. Federal Republicans favored a republican or representative form of government (do not confuse this term with the modern Republican Party, which came into being in 1854; see chapter 12). Ultimately, the word *federal* came to mean the form of government embodied in the new Constitution, just as *confederation* meant the "league of states" under the Articles, and later came to mean the "Confederacy" of 1861–65.
23. See Ralph Ketcham, ed., *The Anti-Federalist Papers and the Constitutional Debates* (New York: New American Library, 1986).
24. See Herbert J. Storing *What the Anti-Federalists Were For* (Chicago: University of Chicago Press, 1981), for a fuller discussion of Anti-Federalist views.
25. See Alan P. Grimes, *Democracy and the Amendments to the Constitution* (Lexington, Mass.: Lexington Books, 1978).
26. David E. Kyvig, *Repealing National Prohibition* (Chicago: University of Chicago Press, 1978).
27. See Jane J. Mansbridge, *Why We Lost the ERA* (Chicago: University of Chicago Press, 1986).
28. Molly Peterson, "Senate Panel Approves Constitutional Ban on Flag Desecration," LEGI-SLATE, http://www.legislate.com/xp/p-daily/i-19990422101/a-924733492/article.view
29. The Washington Post Opinion Research Archive.
30. The Washington Post Opinion Research Archive.
31. Ben White, "Bipartisan Panel Urges Restraint on Constitutional Amendments," *The Washington Post* (May 14, 1999): A9.
32. Speech by Attorney General Edwin Meese III before the American Bar Association, July 9, 1985, Washington, D.C. See also Antonin Scalia and Amy Gutman, eds. *A Matter of Interpretation: Federal Courts and the Law* (Princeton, N.J.: Princeton University Press, 1998).
33. Speech by William J. Brennan, Jr., at Georgetown University, Text and Teaching Symposium, October 10, 1985, Washington, D.C.
34. Mark V. Tushnet, *Taking the Constitution Away from the Courts* (Princeton, N.J.: Princeton University Press, 1999).
35. Bruce Ackerman, *We the People: Foundations* (Cambridge, Mass.: Belknap Press, 1991).
36. This box draws heavily on information provided by the U.S. Department of Commerce. See U.S. Census Bureau "History and Organization," May 1988. Mimeo.

37. *Wisconsin* v. *City of New York*, 517 U.S. 1 (1996), and Sheldon T. Bradshaw, Note, "Death, Taxes, and Census Litigation: Do the Equal Protection and Apportionment Clauses Guarantee a Constitutional Right to Census Accuracy?" *George Washington University Law Review* 64 (January 1996): 379-413.

38. *DOC* v. *United States House of Representatives*, 119 S.Ct. 765 (1999).

39. D'Vera Cohn, "Clinton to Keep Political Appointees Out of Decision on Census," *The Washington Post* (June 14, 2000): A21.

3 Federalism

(Photo courtesy: Ed Bailey/AP/Wide World Photos)

A 1998 ruling by the U.S. Supreme Court brought an end to a long controversy between New York and New Jersey over title to Ellis Island, part of the Statue of Liberty national monument where a museum dedicated to chronicling the history of U.S. immigration is housed.[1] An 1834 compact between the two states set the boundary lines between them as the middle of the Hudson River and gave New York authority over the island even though Ellis Island was on the New Jersey side of the Hudson. New Jersey, however, retained rights to submerged lands on its side. In 1993, New Jersey finally filed suit to gain a final resolution of the land dispute.

Between 1892 and 1954, approximately 12 million steerage and third-class passengers who entered the United States through the Port of New York were processed through Ellis Island, where they were examined by physicians and their legal status reviewed. During that time, the U.S. government also began to fill in around the island's natural shoreline. Eventually 24.5 acres were added to the original island, increasing its size considerably.

While the outcome of the lawsuit filed by New Jersey would have little practical impact, prestige was on the line. Both states wanted bragging rights to this major tourist attraction.[2]

Because two states were involved, the U.S. Supreme Court had what is called original jurisdiction over the case, a term discussed in greater detail in chapter 9. A Special Master was appointed by the Court to investigate the dispute and to report back his findings to the justices. In 1998 the Court ultimately ruled that although New York claimed the land, New Jersey actually had all the rights to the "new lands" added by the federal government to the island. New York retained title to the visitors center and museum.

The states didn't go to war over this boundary dispute; they went to court. When the Framers created the federal system, they were mindful that disputes might arise between the states. Thus, they empowered the Supreme Court to serve as a trial court in these circumstances to provide each state with as fair of a hearing as possible.

WEB EXPLORATION
For a directory of
federalism links, see
www.ablongman.com/oconnor

WEB EXPLORATION
For more on your state
and local governments, see
www.ablongman.com/oconnor

The Framers were mindful of the need for government as well as one unifying body of law, and that was the U.S. Constitution. Thus over 87,000 different state and local governments, including New Jersey and New York, are ultimately bound by its provisions (see Figure 3.1). This is not to say, however, that many citizens and their elected representatives have been working through legal channels to divest the national government of some of the enormous powers it has amassed over the years since the states initially ratified the Constitution. Many Americans simply believe that the national government takes far too great a role in issues such as welfare, education, land use, and health care.

According to a poll conducted in 1995 for *Time*/CNN, 75 percent of Americans support having the "states take over more responsibilities now performed by the federal government."[3] Many, however, have probably not considered all of the ramifications of such a devolution. What happens if one state allows companies to pollute waterways that flow into adjoining states? Are state governments and state bureaucracies better equipped to handle welfare, medical care, job training, or other problems associated with poverty? And with more responsibilities comes the need for more funds. Will states begin to raise taxes? It's unlikely. With states taking on more responsibilities but having less money to execute them, everyone may have to make do with fewer governmental programs, no matter how beneficial or laudatory their goals.

From its very beginning, the challenge for the United States of America was to preserve the traditional independence and rights of the states while establishing an effective national government. In *Federalist No. 51,* James Madison highlighted the unique structure of governmental powers created by the Framers:

> The power surrendered by the people is first divided between two distinct governments, and then ... subdivided among distinct and separate departments. Hence, a double security arises to the rights of the people.

The Framers, fearing tyranny, divided powers between the state and the national governments. At each level, moreover, powers were divided among executive, legislative, and judicial branches.

Although most of the delegates to the Constitutional Convention favored a strong federal government, they knew that some compromise about the distribution of powers would be necessary. Some of the Framers wanted to continue with the confederate form of government defined in the Articles of Confederation; others wanted a more centralized system, like that of Great Britain. Their solution was to create the world's first federal system, in which the thirteen sovereign or independent states were bound together

FIGURE 3.1   Number of Governments in the United States

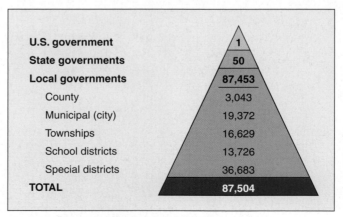

U.S. government	1
State governments	50
Local governments	87,453
County	3,043
Municipal (city)	19,372
Townships	16,629
School districts	13,726
Special districts	36,683
TOTAL	87,504

Source: U.S. Bureau of the Census, http://www.census.gov/govs/www/gid.html

under one national government. The result was a system of government that was "neither wholly national nor wholly federal," as Madison explained in *The Federalist Papers.*

The nature of the federal relationship between the national government and the states, including their respective duties, obligations, and powers, is outlined in the U.S. Constitution, although the word "federal" does not appear in that document. Throughout history, however, this system and the rules that guide it have been continually stretched, reshaped, and reinterpreted by crises, historical evolution, public expectations, and judicial interpretation. All these forces have had tremendous influence on who makes policy decisions and how these decisions get made.

Issues involving the distribution of power between the national government and the states affect you on a daily basis. You do not, for example, need a passport to go from Texas to Oklahoma. There is one national currency and a national minimum wage. But many differences exist among the laws of the various states: The age at which you may marry is a state issue, as are laws governing divorce, child custody, and the purchase of guns.

Although some policies or programs are under the authority of the state or local government, others, such as air traffic regulation, are solely within the province of the national government.[4] In many areas, however, the national and state governments work together cooperatively in a system of shared powers. The national government, for example, provides significant assistance to states to improve local schools in a variety of ways from subsidized breakfasts and lunches for students to support for special education teachers. But states and local government retain control over curricula.

At times, the national government cooperates with or supports programs only if the states meet certain conditions. To receive federal funds for the construction and maintenance of highways, for example, states must follow federal rules about the kinds of roads they build.

To understand the current relationship between the states and the federal government and to better grasp some of the issues that arise from this constantly changing relationship, in this chapter, we'll examine the following topics:

- First, we will look at the *roots of the federal system* created by the Framers, and at their attempt to divide the power and the functions of government between one national and several state governments.
- Second, we will analyze the allocation of the *powers of government* between the national and state governments in the *federal system.*
- Third, we will examine the *evolution and development of federalism.*
- Fourth, we will explore the relationship between *federalism* and the Supreme Court.

THE ROOTS OF THE FEDERAL SYSTEM

The Framers worked to create a particular form of government: One that would be familiar to Americans yet unlike the unitary system found in Great Britain, and one that would remedy many of the problems experienced by the confederated government established by the Articles of Confederation (see chapter 2). (Figure 3.2 illustrates these different forms of government.) The relationship between the national and state governments, and their intertwined powers, are the heart of **federalism** (from the Latin *foedus,* or "covenant"), the philosophy that defines the allocation of power between the national government and the states. Ironically, as discussed in chapter 2, those who supported the government under the Articles of Confederation argued for what they called a federal system. But the fear of being labeled "nationalists" prompted supporters of the new Constitution to call themselves "Federalists," thus co-opting this popular term of the day. Federalist supporters of the new Constitution articulated three major arguments for federalism: (1) the prevention of tyranny; (2) the provision for increased participation in politics; and (3) the use of the states as testing grounds or "laboratories" for new policies and programs.

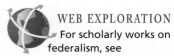

WEB EXPLORATION
For scholarly works on federalism, see
www.ablongman.com/oconnor

federalism
The philosophy that describes the governmental system created by the Framers; see also federal system.

FIGURE 3.2   The Federal, Confederation, and Unitary Systems of Government
The source of governmental authority and power differs dramatically in various systems of government.

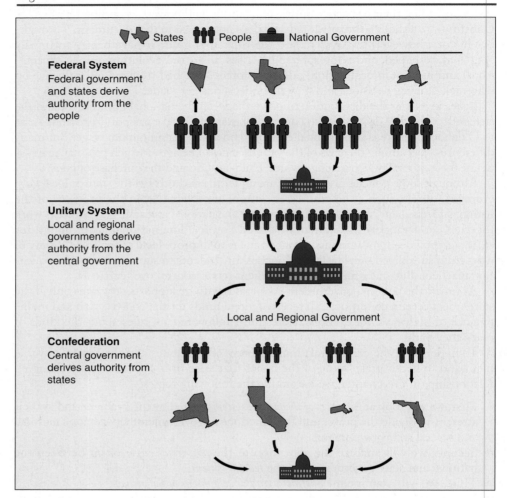

The national government created by the Framers draws its powers directly from the people, so that both national and state governments are ultimately directly accountable to the public. While each government has certain powers in common with the other (such as the ability to tax) and has its own set of public officials, the Framers also envisioned each government to be supreme in some spheres, as depicted in Figure 3.3. In *Federalist No. 51*, James Madison explained what he perceived to be the beauty of this system: The shifting support of the electorate between the two governments would serve to keep each in balance. In fashioning the new federal system of government, the Framers recognized that they could not define precisely how all the relations between the national government and the individual states would work. But the Constitution makes it clear that separate spheres of government were to be at the very core of the federal system, with some allowances made for concurrent powers. The addition of Article VI to the federal Constitution underscored the notion that the national government was always to be supreme in situations of conflict between state and national law. It declares that the U.S. Constitution, the laws of the United States, and its treaties are to be "the supreme Law of the Land; and the Judges in every State shall be bound thereby."

In spite of this explicit language, the meaning of what is called the **supremacy clause** has been subject to continuous judicial interpretation and reinterpretation. In

supremacy clause
Portion of Article VI of the U.S. Constitution that mandates that national law is supreme to (that is, supersedes) all other laws passed by the states or by any other subdivision of government.

FIGURE 3.3   The Distribution of Governmental Power in the Federal System

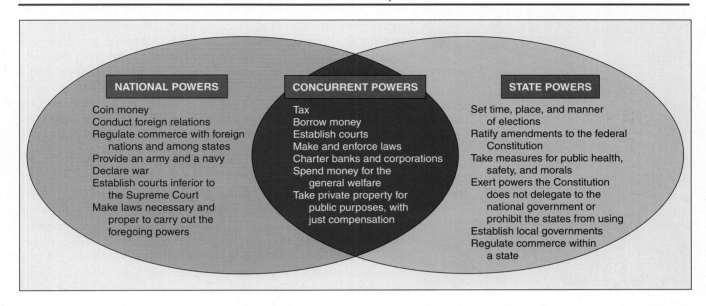

1920, for example, Missouri sought to prevent a U.S. game warden from enforcing the Migratory Bird Treaty Act of 1918, which prohibited the killing or capturing of many species of birds as they made their annual migration across the international border from Canada to parts of the United States.[5] Missouri argued that the Tenth Amendment, which reserved a state's powers to legislate for the general welfare of its citizens, allowed Missouri to regulate hunting. But the Court ruled that since the treaty was legal, it must be considered the supreme law of the land. Thus, when national law and state law come into conflict, national law (including treaties) is supreme. (See also *McCulloch* v. *Maryland* [1819].)

The federal government's right to tax was also clearly set out in the new Constitution. The Framers wanted to avoid the financial problems that the national government had experienced under the Articles of Confederation. To survive as a strong national government, the power of the national government to raise revenue had to be unquestionable.

The new Constitution left the qualifications of suffrage to the individual states. Thus, over time, the right to vote even in national elections has varied.

THE POWERS OF GOVERNMENT IN THE FEDERAL SYSTEM

The distribution of powers in the federal system is often described as two overlapping systems, as illustrated in Figure 3.3. On the left are powers that were specifically granted to Congress in Article I. Chief among the exclusive powers delegated to the national government are the authorities to coin money, conduct foreign relations, provide for an army and navy, declare war, and establish a national court system. All of these powers set out in Article I, section 8, of the Constitution are called enumerated powers. Article I, section 8, also contains the **necessary and proper clause,** which gives Congress the authority to enact any laws "necessary and proper" for carrying out any of its **enumerated powers**. Thus, for example, Congress's power to charter a national bank was held to be an **implied power** derived from its enumerated power to tax and spend.[6]

The Constitution does not specifically delegate or enumerate many specific powers to the states. Because states had all the power at the time the Constitution was written,

necessary and proper clause
The final paragraph of Article I, section 8, of the U.S. Constitution, which gives Congress the authority to pass all laws "necessary and proper" to carry out the enumerated powers specified in the Constitution; also called the "elastic" clause.

enumerated powers
Seventeen specific powers granted to Congress under Article I, section 8, of the U.S. Constitution; these powers include taxation, coinage of money, regulation of commerce, and the authority to provide for a national defense.

implied power
A power derived from an enumerated power and the necessary and proper clause. These powers are not stated specifically but are considered to be reasonably implied through the exercise of delegated powers.

Here, in an example of concurrent state and national power: birds are protected by both governments. (Photo courtesy: Judy Gelles/Stock Boston, Inc.)

reserve (or police) powers
Powers reserved to the states by the Tenth Amendment that lie at the foundation of a state's right to legislate for the public health and welfare of its citizens.

concurrent powers
Powers shared by the national and state governments.

bill of attainder
A law declaring an act illegal without a judicial trial.

ex post facto **law**
Law passed after the fact, thereby making previously legal activity illegal and subject to current penalty; prohibited by the U.S. Constitution.

the Framers felt no need, as they did for the new national government, to list and restate the powers of the states. Article I, however, allows states to set the "Times, Places and Manner, for holding elections for senators and representatives," and Article II requires that each state appoint electors to vote for president. States were also given the power to ratify amendments to the U.S. Constitution. Nevertheless, the enumeration of so many specific powers to the national government and so few to the states is a clear indication of the Federalist leanings of the Framers. It was not until the addition of the Bill of Rights and the Tenth Amendment that the states' powers were better described: "The powers not delegated to the United States by the Constitution, nor prohibited by it to the States, are reserved to the States respectively, or to the people." These powers, often called the states' **reserve** or **police powers,** include the ability to legislate for the public health, safety, and morals of their citizens. The states' rights to legislate under their police powers today are used as the rationale for many states' restrictions on abortion, including twenty-four-hour waiting requirements and provisions requiring minors to obtain parental consent. Police powers are also the basis for state criminal laws. That is why some states have the death penalty and others do not. So long as the U.S. Supreme Court continues to find that the death penalty does not violate the U.S. Constitution, the states may impose it, be it by lethal injection, gas chamber, or the electric chair.

As revealed in Figure 3.3, national and state powers also overlap. The area where the systems overlap represents **concurrent powers**— powers shared by the national and state governments. States already had the power to tax; the Constitution extended this power to the national government as well. Other important concurrent powers include the right to borrow money, establish courts, and make and enforce laws necessary to carry out these powers.

Denied Powers

Article I denies certain powers to the national and state governments. In keeping with the Framers' desire to forge a national economy, states are prohibited from entering treaties, coining money, or impairing obligation of contracts. States are also prohibited from entering into "compacts" with other states without express congressional approval. In a similar vein, Congress is barred from favoring one state over another in regulating commerce, and it cannot lay duties on items exported from any state.

Both the national and state governments are denied the authority to take arbitrary actions affecting constitutional rights and liberties. Neither national nor state governments may pass a **bill of attainder,** a law declaring an act illegal without a judicial trial. The Constitution also bars either from passing *ex post facto* **laws**, laws that make an act punishable as a crime even if the action was legal at the time it was committed.

Guarantees to the States

In return for giving up some of their powers, the states received several guarantees in the Constitution. Among them:

- Article I guarantees each state two members in the U.S. Senate and guarantees that Congress would not limit the slave trade before 1808.
- Article IV guarantees the citizens of each state the privileges and immunities of citizens of all other states; it also guarantees each state a "Republican Form of Government," meaning one that represents the citizens of the state; and it guarantees that the national government will protect the states against foreign attacks and domestic rebellion.

On May 18, 1999, the U.S. Supreme Court dusted off the privileges and immunities clause of the Fourteenth Amendment, which had not been used by the Court to anchor a decision in 126 years. The Court's dramatic 7–2 decision came in a case involving a challenge to a California law that allowed it to pay lower welfare benefits to new state residents.[7] Women who fled from abusive relationships in other states were ineligible for higher California state benefits although they still faced higher California cost of living expenses. Under the challenged provision, California paid new residents only the amounts that they were eligible for in the states that they left. So if a person traveled from Oklahoma, they would get but $341 their first year in California. Former Alabamans were eligible for only $120, while long-time Californians could receive $631. "The states' legitimate interest in saving money provides no justification for its decision to discriminate among equally eligible citizens," said Justice John Paul Stevens writing for the Court.[8]

The Court said that this two-level benefits system violated citizens' constitutional right to travel and was the justices' first decision dealing with any of the new welfare reform efforts, which critics charge violate the constitutional rights of many of America's poor. The ruling is also important because of the Court's "revival of a constitutional doctrine making citizens of all states equal."[9] Scores of constitutional scholars immediately weighed in, speculating that the Court's use of the privileges and immunities clause could mean far greater protection for what the Court views as fundamental rights.

WEB EXPLORATION
For perspectives on the federal system, see
www.ablongman.com/oconnor

Relations Among the States

The Constitution was designed to improve relations among the squabbling states. To that end it provides that disputes between states are to be settled directly by the U.S. Supreme Court under its original jurisdiction to avoid any sense of favoritism (see chapter 10). Moreover, Article IV requires that each state give "Full Faith and Credit . . . to the public Acts, Records and judicial Proceedings of every other State." This clause ensures that judicial decrees and contracts made in one state will be binding and enforceable in another, thereby facilitating trade and other commercial relationships. Interestingly, the Violence Against Women Act specifically requires states to give full faith and credit to protective orders issued by sister states.[10] (See Politics Now: Legislating Against Violence Against Women")

Article IV also requires states to extradite, or return, criminals to states where they have been convicted or are to stand trial. For example, Timothy Reed, an Indian-rights activist, spent five years in New Mexico fighting extradition to Ohio.[11] In 1998, the New Mexico Supreme Court ordered him released from custody in spite of an order from the New Mexico governor ordering his extradition to Ohio. Reed feared that his parole in Ohio would be revoked without due process, he would be returned to prison, and subject to bodily harm. The U.S. Supreme Court found that the Supreme Court of New Mexico went beyond its authority.[12]

States don't always get along however. As our opening vignette about Ellis Island illustrates, the U.S. Constitution gives the Supreme Court the final authority to decide controversies between the states. These kinds of land disputes always are decided by the Supreme Court under its original jurisdiction as mandated by Article III of the Constitution.

THE EVOLUTION AND DEVELOPMENT OF FEDERALISM

The victory of the Federalists—those who supported a strong national government—had long-lasting consequences on the future of the nation. Over the course of our nation's history, the nature of federalism and its allocation of power between the

Interstate speed limits are federalism issues. (Photo courtesy: Mark Leffingwell/AP/Wide World Photos)

national government and the states have changed dramatically. The debate continues today, too, as many Americans, frustrated with the national government's performance on a number of issues, look for a return of more power to the states. Because the distribution of power between the national and state governments is not clearly delineated in the Constitution, over the years the U.S. Supreme Court has played a major role in defining the nature of the federal system.

Early Pronouncements on Federalism

The first few years that the Supreme Court sat, it handled few major cases. As described in chapter 9, the Supreme Court was viewed as weak and many declined the "honor" of serving as a Supreme Court justice. The appointment of Chief Justice John Marshall, however, changed all of this. In a series of decisions, he and his associates carved out an important role for the Court, especially in defining the nature of the federal/state relationship as well as the power of the Court itself.

McCulloch v. _Maryland_ (1819)
The Supreme Court upheld the power of the national government and denied the right of a state to tax the bank. The Court's broad interpretation of the necessary and proper clause paved the way for later rulings upholding expansive federal powers.

McCulloch v. _Maryland_ (1819). **_McCulloch_ v. _Maryland_** was the first major decision of the Marshall Court to define the relationship between the national and state governments. In 1816 Congress chartered the Second Bank of the United States. (The charter of the First Bank had been allowed to expire.) In 1818 the Democratic-Republican-controlled Maryland state legislature levied a tax requiring all banks not chartered by Maryland (that is, the Second Bank of the United States) to (1) buy stamped paper from the state on which the Second Bank's notes were to be issued; (2) pay the state $15,000 a year; or (3) go out of business. James McCulloch, the head cashier of the Baltimore branch of the Bank of the United States, refused to pay the tax, and Maryland brought suit against him.

After losing in a Maryland court, McCulloch appealed his conviction to the U.S. Supreme Court by order of the U.S. secretary of the treasury. In a unanimous opinion, the Court answered the two central questions that had been put to it: First, did Congress have the authority to charter a bank? And, second, if it did, could a state tax it?

Chief Justice Marshall's answer to the first question—whether Congress had the right to establish a bank or another type of corporation, given that the Constitution does not explicitly mention such a power—continues to stand as the classic exposition of the doctrine of implied powers, and as a reaffirmation of the propriety of a strong national government. Although the word "bank" cannot be found in the Constitution, the Constitution enumerates powers that give Congress the authority to levy and collect taxes, issue a currency, and borrow funds. From these enumerated powers, Marshall found, it was reasonable to imply that Congress had the power to charter a bank, which could be considered "necessary and proper" to the exercise of its enumerated powers.

Marshall next addressed the question of whether a federal bank could be taxed by any state government. To Marshall, this was not a difficult question. The national government was dependent on the people, not the states, for its powers. In addition, Marshall noted, the Constitution specifically calls for the national law to be supreme. "The power to tax involves the power to destroy," wrote Marshall.[13] Thus, the state tax violated the supremacy clause, because individual states cannot interfere with the operations of the national government, whose laws are supreme.

Gibbons v. *Ogden* (1824).   Shortly after *McCulloch,* the Marshall Court had another opportunity to rule in favor of a broad interpretation of the scope of national power. *Gibbons* v. *Ogden* involved a dispute that arose after the New York State legislature granted to Robert Fulton the exclusive right to operate steamboats on the Hudson River. Simultaneously, Congress licensed a ship to sail on the same waters. By the time the case reached the Supreme Court, it was complicated both factually and procedurally. Suffice it to say that both New York and New Jersey wanted to control shipping on the lower Hudson River. But *Gibbons* actually addressed one simple, very important question: What was the scope of Congress's authority under the commerce clause? The states argued that "commerce," as mentioned in Article I, should be interpreted narrowly to include only direct dealings in products. In *Gibbons,* however, the Supreme Court ruled that Congress's power to regulate interstate commerce included the power to regulate commercial activity as well, and that the commerce power had no limits except those specifically found in the Constitution. Thus, New York had

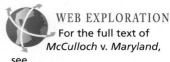

WEB EXPLORATION
For the full text of
McCulloch v. *Maryland,*
see
www.ablongman.com/oconnor

Gibbons v. *Ogden* (1824)
The Court upheld broad congressional power over interstate commerce.

WEB EXPLORATION
For the full text of
Gibbons v. *Ogden,* see
www.ablongman.com/oconnor

The *Gibbons* v. *Ogden* decision opened the waters to free competition; this is the New York waterfront in 1839. (Photo courtesy: I. N. Phelps Stokes Collection, Miriam and Ira D. Wallach Division of Art, Prints, and Photographs, The New York Public Library Astor, Lenox and Tilden Foundations)

no constitutional authority to grant a monopoly to a single steamboat operator, thereby interfering with interstate commerce.[14]

Dual Federalism

dual federalism
The belief that having separate and equally powerful levels of government is the best arrangement.

In spite of these nationalist Marshall Court decisions, strong debate continued in the United States over national versus state power. It was under the leadership of Chief Justice Marshall's successor, Roger B. Taney (1835–1863), that the Supreme Court articulated the notions of concurrent power, the belief that separate and equally powerful levels of government is the best arrangement; and **dual federalism,** which holds that the national government should not exceed its enumerated powers expressly set out in the Constitution.

Federalism and Slavery.   During the Taney era, the comfortable role of the Court as the arbiter of competing national and state interests became troublesome when the Court found itself called upon to deal with the highly political issue of slavery. In cases such as *Dred Scott* v. *Sandford* (1857) and others, the Court tried to manage the slavery issue by resolving questions of ownership, the status of fugitive slaves, and slavery in the new territories. These cases generally were settled in favor of slavery and states' rights within the framework of dual federalism. In its treatment of slavery (see Roots of Government: Dred Scott) the Taney Court erred grievously and thereby contributed to the coming of the Civil War, since its decision seemed to rule out any political (legislative) solution to slavery by the national government.

The Civil War and Beyond

The Civil War (1861–1865) forever changed the nature of federalism, but the Supreme Court continued to adhere to its belief in the concept of dual federalism. The importance and powers of the states were not diminished in spite of the addition of the Thirteenth, Fourteenth, and Fifteenth Amendments to the Constitution, or by Abraham Lincoln's appointment of the first Republican chief justice, Salmon Chase (1864–1873).

Between 1865 (the end of the Civil War) and 1933 (when the next major change in the federal system occurred), the Court generally continued to support dual federalism along several lines. State courts, for example, were considered to have the final say on the construction of laws affecting local affairs.[15] Generally, the Court upheld any laws passed under the states' police powers, which allow states to pass laws to protect the general welfare of their citizens. These laws included those affecting commerce, labor relations, and manufacturing. After the Court's decision in *Plessy* v. *Ferguson* (1896), in which the Court ruled that state maintenance of "separate but equal" facilities for blacks and whites was constitutional, most civil rights and voting cases also became state matters, in spite of the Civil War amendments.[16]

The Court also developed legal doctrine in a series of cases that reinforced the national government's ability to regulate commerce. By the 1930s these two somewhat contradictory approaches led to confusion: States, for example, could not tax gasoline used by federal vehicles,[17] and the national government could not tax the sale of motorcycles to the city police department.[18] In this period the Court did recognize the need for national control over new technological developments, such as the telegraph.[19] And beginning in the 1880s, the Court allowed Congress to regulate many aspects of economic relationships such as outlawing monopolies, a type of regulation or power formerly thought to be in the exclusive realm of the states. Passage of laws such as the Interstate Commerce Act in 1887 and the Sherman Anti-Trust Act in 1890 allowed Congress to establish itself as an important player in the growing national economy.

Despite finding that most of these federal laws were constitutional, the Supreme Court did not consistently enlarge the scope of national power. In 1895, for example, the United States filed suit against four sugar refiners, alleging that their sale would give their buyer control of 98 percent of the U.S. sugar-refining business. The Supreme Court

ROOTS OF GOVERNMENT

DRED SCOTT

Dred Scott, born into slavery around 1795, became the named plaintiff in a case that was to have major ramifications on the nature of the federal system. In 1833 Scott was sold by his original owners, the Blow family, to Dr. Emerson, an army surgeon in St. Louis, Missouri. The next year he was taken to Illinois and later to the Wisconsin Territory, returning to St. Louis in 1838.*

When Dr. Emerson died in 1843, Scott tried to buy his freedom. Before he could, however, he was transferred to Emerson's widow, who moved to New York leaving Scott in the custody of his first owners, the Blows. Some of the Blows (Henry Blow later founded the antislavery Free Soil Party) and other abolitionists gave money to support a test case seeking Scott's freedom: They believed that his residence in Illinois and later in the Wisconsin Territory, both of which prohibited slavery, made him a free man.

After many delays, the U.S. Supreme Court ruled seven to two that Scott was not a citizen of the United States. "Slaves," said the Court, "were never thought of or spoken of except as property."

At the urging of President James Buchanan, Chief Justice Roger B. Taney tried to fashion a broad ruling to settle the slavery question. In *Dred Scott* v. *Sandford* (1857), he concluded that the Congress of the United States lacked the constitutional authority to bar slavery in the territories. The decision narrowed the scope of national power while it enhanced that of the states. Moreover, for the first time since *Marbury* v. *Madison* (1803), the Court found an act of Congress—the Missouri Compromise—unconstitutional. And, by limiting what the national government could do concerning slavery, it in all likelihood quickened the march toward the Civil War.

*Don E. Ferenbacher, "The Dred Scott Case," in *Quarrels That Have Shaped the Constitution*, John A. Garraty, ed. (New York: Harper & Row, 1964), ch. 6.

(Photo courtesy: Missouri Historical Society)

---

ruled that congressional efforts to control monopolies (through passage of the Sherman Anti-Trust Act) did not give Congress the authority to prevent the sale of these sugar-refining businesses, because manufacturing was not commerce. Therefore the companies and their actions were beyond the scope of Congress's authority to regulate.[20]

Cooperative Federalism

The era of dual federalism came to an abrupt end in the 1930s. Its demise began in a series of economic events that ended in the cataclysm of the Great Depression:

- In 1921 the nation experienced a severe slump in agricultural prices.
- In 1926 the construction industry went into decline.
- In the summer of 1929, inventories of consumer goods and automobiles were at an all-time high.
- Throughout the 1920s, bank failures had become common.
- On October 29, 1929, stock prices, which had risen steadily since 1926, crashed, taking with them the entire national economy.

WEB EXPLORATION
For more information
on the Depression, see
www.ablongman.com/oconnor

The New Deal. Rampant unemployment (historians estimate it was as high as 40 percent to 50 percent) was the hallmark of the Great Depression. To combat this unemployment and a host of other problems facing the nation, newly elected President Franklin D. Roosevelt (FDR) proposed in 1933 a variety of innovative programs under the rubric "the New Deal" and ushered in a new era in American politics. FDR used the full power of the office of president as well as his highly effective communication skills to sell the American public and Congress on a whole new ideology of government. Not only were the scope and role of national government remarkably altered, but so was the relationship between each state and the national government. It is, in fact, the growth in the federal government that began with the New Deal that many who urge less federal power bemoan today.

The New Deal period (1933–1939) was characterized by intense government activity on the national level. It was clear to most politicians that to find national solutions to the Depression, which was affecting the citizens of every state in the Union, the national government would have to exercise tremendous authority.

In the first few weeks of the legislative session after FDR's inauguration, Congress and the president acted quickly to bolster confidence in the national government. Soon after, Congress passed a series of acts creating programs proposed by the president. These new agencies, often known by their initials, created what many termed an "alphabetocracy." Among the more significant programs were the Federal Housing Administration (FHA), which provided federal financing for new home construction; the Civilian Conservation Corps (CCC), a work relief program for farmers and homeowners; and the Agricultural Adjustment Administration (AAA) and the National Recovery Administration (NRA), both of which imposed restrictions on production in agriculture and many industries.

These programs tremendously enlarged the scope of the national government. Those who feared this unprecedented use of national power quickly challenged the constitutionality of New Deal programs in court. And, at least initially, the Supreme Court often agreed with them.

One of the hallmarks of the New Deal and FDR's presidency was the national government's new involvement of cities in the federal system. Here, New York City Mayor Fiorello La Guardia (for whom one New York airport is named) is commissioned as director of civil defense by FDR. (Photo courtesy: AP/Wide World Photos)

Through the mid-1930s, the Supreme Court continued to rule that certain aspects of the New Deal went beyond the authority of Congress to regulate commerce. In fact, many believe that the Court considered the Depression to be no more than the sum of the economic woes of the individual states and that it was a problem most appropriately handled by the states. The Court's *laissez-faire,* or "hands-off," attitude toward the economy was reflected in a series of decisions ruling various aspects of New Deal programs unconstitutional.

FDR and the Congress were outraged. FDR's frustration with the *laissez-faire* attitude of the Court prompted him to suggest what was ultimately nicknamed his "Court-packing plan." Knowing that he could do little to change the minds of those already on the Court, FDR suggested enlarging its size from nine to thirteen justices. This would have given him the opportunity to "pack" the Court with a majority of justices predisposed to the constitutional validity of the New Deal.

Even though Roosevelt was popular, the Court-packing plan was not. Congress and the public were outraged that he even suggested tampering with an institution of government. Nevertheless, the Court appeared to respond to this threat. In 1937 it reversed its series of anti–New Deal decisions, concluding that Congress (and therefore the national government) had the authority to legislate in areas that only *affected* commerce. Congress then used this newly recognized power to legislate in a wide array of areas, including maximum hour and minimum wage laws, and regulation of child labor. Moreover, the Court also upheld the constitutionality of the bulk of the massive New Deal relief programs, such as the National Labor Relations Act of 1935, which authorized collective bargaining between unions and employees in *NLRB* v. *Jones and Laughlin Steel Co.* (1937);[21] the Fair Labor Standards Act of 1938, which prohibited the interstate shipment of goods made by employees earning less than the federally mandated minimum wage;[22] and the Agriculture Adjustment Act of 1938, which provided crop subsidies to farmers.[23]

The New Deal programs forced all levels of government to work cooperatively with one another. Indeed, local governments—mainly in big cities—became a third partner in the federal system, as FDR relied on big-city Democratic political machines to turn out voters to support his programs. For the first time in U.S. history, in essence, cities were embraced as equal partners in an intergovernmental system and became players in the national political arena because many in the national legislature wanted to bypass state legislatures, where urban interests were usually significantly underrepresented.

The Changing Nature of Federalism: From Layer Cake to Marble Cake.   Before the Depression and the New Deal, most political scientists likened the federal system to a layer cake: Each level or layer of government—national, state, and local—had clearly defined powers and responsibilities. After the New Deal, however, the nature of the federal system changed. Government now looked something like a marble cake:

> Wherever you slice through it you reveal an inseparable mixture of differently colored ingredients.... Vertical and diagonal lines almost obliterate the horizontal ones, and in some places there are unexpected whirls and an imperceptible merging of colors, so that it is difficult to tell where one ends and the other begins.[24]

This kind of "marble cake" federalism is often called **cooperative federalism,** a term that describes the relationship between the national, state, and local governments that began with the New Deal as a stronger, more influential national government was created in response to economic and social crises. States began to take a secondary, albeit important, "cooperative" role in the scheme of governance, as did many cities. Nowhere is this shift in power from the states *to* the national government more clear than in the growth of federal grant programs that began in earnest during the New Deal. The tremendous growth in these programs and in federal government spending in general, as illustrated in Table 3.1, changed the nature and discussion of federalism from that time to 1995: from "How much power should the national government have?" to "How much say in the policies of

cooperative federalism
A term used to characterize the relationship between the national and state governments that began with the New Deal.

TABLE 3.1   Federal Grants-in-Aid Outlays, 1940–2004

Year	Total Grants–in-Aid (billions)	Federal Grants as a Percentage of Federal Outlays[a]			
		Total	Domestic Programs[b]	State and Local Expenditures[c]	Gross Domestic Product
1940	$0.9	9.2	—	—	0.9
1945	0.9	0.9	—	—	0.4
1950	2.3	5.3	—	—	0.8
1955	3.2	4.7	—	—	0.8
1960	7.0	7.6	18.0	19.0	1.4
1965	10.9	9.2	18.0	20.0	1.6
1970	24.1	12.3	23.0	24.0	2.4
1975	49.8	15.0	22.0	27.0	3.2
1980	91.4	15.5	22.0	31.0	3.4
1985	105.9	11.2	18.0	25.0	2.6
1986	112.3	11.3	—	—	2.6
1987	108.4	10.8	—	—	2.4
1988	115.3	10.8	—	—	2.3
1989	121.9	10.7	—	—	2.3
1990	135.3	10.8	17.0	21.0	2.4
1991	154.5	11.7	—	—	2.6
1992	178.1	12.9	—	—	2.9
1993	193.6	13.7	—	—	3.0
1994	210.6	14.4	—	—	3.1
1995	225.0	14.8	22.0	25.0	3.1
1996	227.8	14.6	21.0	24.0	3.0
1997	234.2	14.6	21.0	—	2.9
1998	246.1	14.9	21.0	—	2.9
1999	262.2	15.2	21.0	—	3.0
2000	283.5	16.1	22.0	—	3.1
2001[(est)]	300.7	16.7	22.0	—	3.2
2002[(est)]	310.3	17.0	23.0	—	3.1
2003[(est)]	323.6	17.1	23.0	—	3.1
2004[(est)]	338.8	17.3	23.0	—	3.1

Note: "—" indicates not available. Amounts in current dollars. Fiscal years.

[a]Includes off-budget outlays; all grants are on-budget.

[b]Excludes outlays for national defense, international affairs, and net interest.

[c]As defined in the national income and product accounts.

Source: Harold W. Stanley and Richard G. Niemi, *Vital Statistics on American Politics*, 7th ed. (Washington, D.C.: CQ Press, 2000), 319. Reprinted by permission of Congressional Quarterly Inc.

the states can the national government buy?" The national government initially imposed a national fifty-five-miles-per-hour speed limit on the states, for example, and forced states to adopt minimum-age drink restrictions in order to obtain federal transportation funds. (See Highlight: Do You Have ID? Setting a National Alcohol Policy.)

Federal Grants.   As early as 1790, Congress appropriated funds for the states to pay debts incurred during the Revolutionary War. But it wasn't until the Civil War that Congress enacted its first true federal grant program, which allocated federal funds to the states for a specific purpose.

Most view the start of this redistribution of funds with the Morrill Land Grant Act of 1862, which gave each state 30,000 acres of public land for each representative in

HIGHLIGHT

DO YOU HAVE ID? SETTING A NATIONAL ALCOHOL POLICY

The number of fatal crashes involving drivers aged eighteen to twenty-one fell by 14.3 percent from 1983 to 1994. Why? In 1984, after years of often highly emotional lobbying by Mothers Against Drunk Drivers (MADD) and other concerned citizens groups, Congress passed an amendment to the Surface Transportation Act of 1982 designed to withhold 5 percent of federal highway funds from states that did not prohibit those under the age of twenty-one from drinking alcoholic beverages. Prior to that time, MADD had lobbied most state legislators to raise their state drinking ages with mixed success. Then, its leaders turned their eyes on Congress.[a] In 1984, only sixteen U.S. senators voted against the amendment.

Because the national government did not have the power to regulate the drinking age, it resorted to the carrot-and-stick nature of federalism, whereby the national government dangles money in front of the states but places conditions on its use. To force states to raise their drinking age to twenty-one by 1988, Congress initially decided to withhold 5 percent of all federal highway grants to the recalcitrant states. (This was later raised to 10 percent.) In other words, no raised drinking age, no federal dollars. Even most conservative Republican senators—those most attached to the notion of states' rights—supported the provision, in spite of the fact that it imposed a national ideal on the states. After congressional action, the bill was signed into law by Ronald Reagan, another conservative long concerned with how the national government had trampled on state power.

States still retain the power to decide who is legally drunk, however. In 1998, Mothers Against Drunk Driving pressured members of Congress to adopt a national blood alcohol level of 0.08 to indicate drunkenness, but that effort failed.[b] Thus, the blood alcohol content required for determining legal intoxication varied dramatically, from a low of 0.05 in Colorado to a high of 0.1 in several states.

In 1999, however, President Clinton signed legislation that contained incentives for states to lower their blood alcohol levels defining drunk driving to 0.08. By late 2000, eighteen states and the District of Columbia adopted that standard. On the twentieth anniversary of its founding, MADD members rallied to convince Congress to set the 0.08 limit as a mandatory national standard, an action supported by a majority of Americans according to a recent Gallup poll.[c] In October 2000, President Clinton signed the Federal Transportation Appropriations bill, which gave states until October 1, 2003 to enact 0.08 limits or lose 2 percent of their annual federal highway funds per year.

[a]Ruth Gastel, "Drunk Driving and Liquor Liability," *Insurance Issues Updates*, April 1999.
[b]Steve Piacente, "Blood Alcohol Limits Under Fierce Debate," *The Post and Courier*, May 27, 1998: B1.
[c]Arthur Santana, "On 20th Anniversary, MADD Urges National 0.08% Standard," *The Washington Post* (September 7, 2000): A6.

Congress. Income from the sale of these lands was to be earmarked for the establishment and support of agricultural and mechanical arts colleges. Sixty-nine land-grant colleges—including Texas A&M University, the University of Georgia, and Michigan State University—were founded, making this grant program the single most important piece of education legislation passed in the United States up to that time.

Franklin D. Roosevelt's New Deal program increased the flow of federal dollars to the states with the infusion of massive federal dollars for a variety of public works programs, including building and road construction. These grants made the imposition of national goals on the states easier. No state wanted to decline funds, so states often secured funds for any programs for which money was available—whether they needed it for that specific purpose or not.

In the boom times of World War II, even more new federal programs were introduced; and by the 1950s and 1960s, federal grant-in-aid programs were well entrenched. They often defined federal/state relationships and made the national government a major player in domestic policy. Until the 1960s, however, most

categorical grant
Grant for which Congress appropriates funds for a specific purpose.

federal grant programs were constructed in cooperation with the states and were designed to assist the states in furthering their traditional responsibilities to protect the health, welfare, and safety of their citizens. Most of these programs were **categorical grants,** ones for which Congress appropriates funds for specific purposes. Funds are allocated by a precise formula and are subject to detailed conditions imposed by the national government, often on a matching basis; that is, states must contribute money to match federal funds, although the national government may pay as much as 90 percent of the total.

Creative Federalism

By the early 1960s, as concern about the poor and minorities rose, and as states (especially in the South) were blamed for perpetuating discrimination, those in power in the national government saw grants as a way to force states to behave in ways desired by the national government.[25] If the states would not cooperate with the national government to further its goals, it would withhold funds.

In 1964, the Democratic administration of President Lyndon B. Johnson (LBJ) (1963–1969) launched its renowned "Great Society" program, which included what LBJ called a "War on Poverty." The Great Society program was a broad attempt to combat poverty and discrimination. In a frenzy of activity in Washington not seen since the New Deal, federal funds were channeled to states, to local governments, and even directly to citizen action groups in an effort to alleviate social ills that the states had been unable or unwilling to remedy. There was money for urban renewal, education, and poverty programs, including Head Start and job training. The move to fund local groups directly was made by the most liberal members of Congress in order to bypass not only conservative state legislatures, but also conservative mayors and councils in cities like Chicago, who were not frequently moved to help their poor, often African-American, constituencies. Thus these programs often pitted governors and mayors against community activists, who became key players in the distribution of federal dollars.

These new grants altered the fragile federal/state balance of power that had been at the core of most older federal grant programs. During the Johnson administration, the national government began to use federal grants as a way to further what federal (and not state) officials perceived to be national needs. Grants based on what states wanted or believed they needed began to decline, while grants based on what the national government wanted states to do in order to foster national goals increased dramatically. Soon states routinely asked Washington for help: "Pollution, transportation, recreation, economic development, law enforcement and even rat control evoked the same response from politicians: create a federal grant." [26] By 1970, federal aid accounted for 20 percent of all state and local government spending; this amount of money made the states ever more dependent on the national government.

New Federalism and the Reagan Revolution

In 1976, Jimmy Carter, a former governor of Georgia, successfully ran for president as an "outsider" opposed to big government and federal grants that mandated state spending for a variety of programs, including education and pollution-reduction programs. The unfunded mandates discussed later in the chapter were programs passed by Congress requiring state compliance but that came with no funds for the states to meet federal standards. Although Carter was the first president to reduce

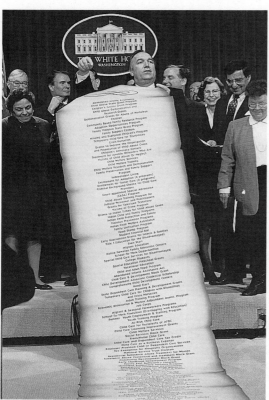

Michigan Governor John Engler unfurls a scroll of nearly 3,000 federal antipoverty programs that several Republican governors wanted dismantled in favor of lump-sum block grants to allow the states to decide where federal dollars in the states are best spent. (Photo courtesy: Jym Wilson/Gannett News Service)

Cincinatti Red and Head Start alum Deion Sanders helps children at a California Head Start center. Sanders was there to launch an educational outreach program designed to provide computers, software, and staff training to selected Head Start centers on the West Coast. (Photo courtesy: Jill Connelly HO/AP/Wide World Photos)

intergovernmental grant expenditures, the reforms in federal grant programs Carter introduced were insufficient to override the rest of his political woes, and in 1980, former California Governor Ronald Reagan was elected president. Reagan pledged to advance what he called a "New Federalism" and a return of power back to the states.

Reagan's New Federalism had many facets. The Republican "Reagan Revolution" as begun by President Reagan and continued by President George Bush had at its heart strong views about the role of states in the federal system. While many argued that grants-in-aid were an effective way to raise the level of services provided to the poor, others, including Reagan, attacked them as imposing national priorities on the states. Policy decisions were made at the national level, and the states, always in search of funds, were forced to follow the priorities of the national government. States found it very hard to resist the lure of grants, even though many were contingent on some sort of state investment of matching or proportional funds.

Shortly after taking office, Reagan proposed massive cuts in federal domestic programs (which had not become federal functions until the New Deal) and drastic income tax cuts. The Reagan administration's budget and its policies dramatically altered the relationships among federal, state, and local governments. For the first time in thirty years, federal aid to state and local governments declined.[27] Reagan persuaded Congress to consolidate many categorical grants (for specific programs that often require matching funds) into far fewer, less restrictive **block grants**—broad grants to states for specified activities such as secondary education or health services, with few strings attached.

By the end of the Bush administration in 1992, most block grants fell into one of four categories—health, income security, education, or transportation; yet many politicians, including most state governors, urged the consolidation of even more programs into block grants. Calls to reform the welfare system—particularly to allow more latitude to the states in an effort to get back to the Hamiltonian notion of states as laboratories of experiment—seem especially popular with citizens and governments alike, as the New Federalism took hold.

block grant
Broad grant with few strings attached are given to states by the federal government for specified activities, such as secondary education or health services.

Reagan's New "Republican" Federalism initially changed the nature of state politics. Many state governments—as well as cities within a single state—found themselves competing for funds. States were faced with revenue shortfalls caused by the recession of the early 1990s, legal requirements mandating balanced budgets, and growing demands for new social services and the replacement of some formerly provided by the federal government. Many governors around the nation found themselves in political trouble as they had to slash services and ask for tax increases. "A governor with over a 50 percent approval is more the exception than the rule now, and that just wasn't true three or four years ago," noted one pollster in 1991.[28] That same year legislators in forty-six states narrowly missed deadlines for their new budget authorizations because of rising costs.

Not only do individual governments lobby the national government, but myriad types of governments with shared or similar interests also have banded together to advance their collective interests. Some have individual offices in Washington. Others hire full-time or part-time lobbyists to work solely on their behalf to keep abreast of funding opportunities or to lobby for programs that could be useful back home. Others lobby as well as litigate to make sure that their interests are represented before the courts.[29]

What scholars term the "Big Seven," which include the National Governors' Association (NGA) and the National League of Cities, among others, are widely recognized as the premier **intergovernmental lobbies** (see Table 3.2). These groups, primarily founded from the turn of the century to the New Deal era, are well organized and well established.

Several of the Big Seven focus on state issues. The NGA is composed of incumbent governors from each state. The governors meet twice a year but have a staff and standing committees that meet more regularly. Adoption of policy positions requires a quorum and vote of three-quarters of the governors. Small states tend to be more active within the group than larger states. The Council of State Governments, located in Washington, D.C., is an umbrella organization designed to gather information and provide assistance to the states. The National Conference of State Legislatures, headquartered in Denver, publishes a monthly magazine, *State Legislatures,*

intergovernmental lobby
The pressure group or groups that are created when state and local governments hire lobbyists to lobby the national government.

TABLE 3.2   The "Big Seven" Intergovernmental Associations

Association (Current Title)	Date Founded	Membership
National Governors' Association (NGA)	1908	Incumbent governors
Council of State Governments (CSG)	1933	Direct membership by states and territories; serves all branches of government; has dozens of affiliate organizations of specialists
National Conference of State Legislatures (NCSL)	1948	State legislators and staff
National League of Cities (NLC)	1924	Direct, by cities and state leagues of cities
National Association of Counties (NAC)	1935	Direct by counties; loosely linked state associations; affiliate membership for county professional specialists
United States Conference of Mayors (USCM)	1933	Direct membership by cities with population over 30,000
International City/County Management Association (ICMA)	1914	Direct membership by appointed city and county managers, and other professionals

Source: Allan J. Cigler and Burdett A. Loomis, *Interest Group Politics,* 4th ed. (Washington D.C.: CQ Press, 1995), p. 135. Reprinted by permission of Congressional Quarterly Inc.

and uses its Washington office to monitor and publish information about the federal government that is useful to the states. It provides a variety of legislative services to all fifty state legislatures plus Puerto Rico.

Three other groups often are called the "urban lobby." The National League of Cities represents medium and small cities, the U.S. Conference of Mayors represents large cities, and the National Association of Counties represents rural, suburban, and urban counties. The remaining member of the Big Seven is the International City/County Management Association, which represents the country's appointed local chief executives.

In 1999, President Clinton and the Big Seven finally agreed on a proposed executive order to substantially strengthen and develop the federal/state relationship. A year earlier, Clinton caused a political firestorm when he released Executive Order 13083 on federalism. Within months, pressure from Republicans in Congress and the Big Seven, including the National Governors' Association, forced him to withdraw that attempt to update two previous executive orders on federalism.[30] Their major objection was that he proposed order "contained vague wording that may have given the federal government broad powers over states' affairs.[31] The Clinton administration insisted that it wasn't trying to usurp power from the states; instead, officials claimed that they were only trying to clarify the federal government's relationship to the states in light of recent Supreme Court cases and the

In spite of winning Florida with his brother Jeb's help, George W. Bush rebuffed personal appeals from the Florida governor not to allow drilling for natural gas and oil off the Florida Coast. (Photo courtesy: Reuters/Jeff Mitchell/Archive Photos)

Unfunded Mandates Reform Act (discussed later in this chapter). This was the Clinton administration's third effort to draft a new executive order.[32] Both earlier versions were also opposed by the Big Seven, who claimed not to have been consulted before they were proposed. The new order directs agencies to access any federal actions that limit state and local discretion and construe federal laws that preempt state law only where direct conflicts with federal power exist.[33]

WEB EXPLORATION
For more on National Governors' Association (NGA), see
www.ablongman.com/oconnor

The Devolution Revolution

In 1994 Republicans swept Congress, and every Republican governor who sought reelection was victorious, while some popular Democratic governors, such as Ann Richards of Texas, lost. In *Federalist No. 17*, Alexander Hamilton noted that "it will always be far more easy for the State government to encroach upon the national authorities than for the national government to encroach upon the State authorities." He was wrong. Today, some argue, the federal/state relationship has moved from "cooperation to coercion,"[34] a fact that in 1994 led many state governors and the Republican Party (remember, both increases in federal power—the New Deal and Great Society program—were launched during Democratic administrations) to rebel openly against this growth of national power.

Preemption.   One method the federal government has used to cut into the authority of the states to set their own policy preferences derives from the Constitution's supremacy clause. This practice, known as **preemption,** allows the national government to override, or preempt, state or local actions in certain areas.[35] The Tenth Amendment expressly reserves to the states and the people all powers not delegated to the national government. The phenomenal growth of preemption statutes, laws that Congress has passed to allow

preemption
A concept derived from the Constitution's supremacy clause that allows the national government to override or preempt state or local actions in certain areas.

the federal government to assume partial and/or full responsibility for traditional state and local governmental functions, began in 1965 during the Johnson administration. Since then, Congress routinely used its authority under the commerce clause to pre-empt state laws. These statutes not only took authority away from states, they often imposed significant costs on them in the form of unfunded mandates. In fact, the cost to the states—along with the perceived federal interference with local matters—is one reason that the electorate so willingly embraced the campaign message of the Republican Party in 1994.

The **Contract with America,** proposed by then House Minority Whip Newt Gingrich, was a campaign document signed by nearly all Republican candidates (and incumbents) for the House of Representatives in 1994. In it, Republican candidates pledged themselves to force a national debate on the role of the national government in regard to the states. A top priority was scaling back the federal government. Said then–House Budget Committee Chair John R. Kasich (R–Ohio). Congress wanted to "return money, power, and responsibility to the states," which some called the "devolution evolution."[36] Poll after poll, moreover, revealed that Americans believed the national government had too much power (48 percent) and that they favored their states assuming many of the powers and functions now exercised by the federal government (59 percent).[37]

Republicans lambasted the growth of federal power over the states and were particularly critical of several features of the federal-state relationship that they believed robbed the states of their power to set policy for the health and welfare of their citizens. A key component of the Contract was a commitment to end unfunded mandates.

Unfunded Mandates.   From the beginning, most categorical grants were matching grants that came with a variety of strings attached. As categorical grants declined, the national government continued to exercise a significant role in state policy priorities through **mandates**—laws that direct states or local governments to comply with federal rules or regulations (such as clean air or water standards) under threat of civil or criminal penalties or as a condition of receipt of any federal grants (a city might not get federal transportation funds, for example, unless the disabled have access to particular means of transportation).

Prior to 1995, the federal government required the states to shoulder the cost of federal programs it did not fund. Unfunded mandates often made up as much as 30 percent of a local government's annual operating budget. Between 1983 and 1990, it is estimated that the cumulative cost of unfunded mandates to state and local governments was between 8.9 and 12.7 billion dollars.[38]

The enactment of federal regulations requiring state and local spending increased tremendously through 1990. During the 1980s, for example, Congress added twenty-seven new programs requiring state spending, and many expensive unfunded provisions were attached to existing grant-in-aid programs. Columbus, Ohio, for example, with 633,000 residents, faced a $1 billion bill to comply with the federal Clean Water Act and the Safe Drinking Water Act at an estimated cost of $685 a year per household.

Unlike the national government, most states are required to have balanced budgets, and these federally mandated outlays were playing havoc with state budgets. In 1993, some state legislatures even passed laws summoning home their senators and representatives to explain why they were imposing costly national regulations on states without providing funds to implement these programs. It is not surprising, then, that the Republican majority was able to secure passage of the Unfunded Mandates Reform Act of 1995 barring Congress from passing costly programs without debate on how to fund them.

By 1999, the cumulative impact of the federal government's moving some powers back to the states, an improved economy, and decreasing federal mandates produced record federal and state budget surpluses. The late 1990s found the fifty states

---

Contract with America
Campaign pledge signed by most Republican candidates in 1994 to guide their legislative agenda.

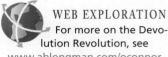

WEB EXPLORATION
For more on the Devolution Revolution, see
www.ablongman.com/oconnor

mandates
National laws that direct states or local governments to comply with federal rules or regulations (such as clean air or water standards) under threat of civil or criminal penalties or as a condition of receipt of any federal grants.

Longman
Participate.com 2.0
Visual Literacy
Federalism
and
Regulations

FIGURE 3.4   Change in Rainy-Day Funds for All States, 1991–2000
As state revenues decline after nearly a decade of growth, governors and state legislatures will face hard choices.

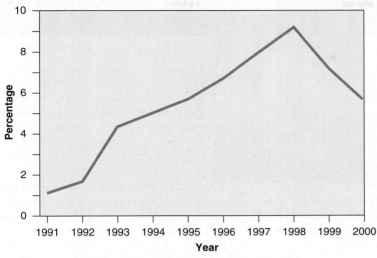

Source: USA Today, July 10, 2000, p. A1. Copyright 2000, USA TODAY. Reprinted with permission.

in the best fiscal shape that they had been in since the 1970s, before federal mandates hurt their ability to prioritize spending. According to the National Conference of State Legislatures, total state budget surpluses in 1998 exceeded $30 billion.

These tax surpluses allowed many states to increase spending, while other states offered their residents steep tax cuts. Mississippi, for example, increased its per capita spending by 42.4 percent, while Alaska opted to reduce taxes by 44.2 percent.[39]

The unprecedented growth in the national economy in the 1990s produced huge budget surpluses for most states. But, by 2000, state revenues were beginning to fall, costs of health care and education continued to rise, and sales tax revenue fell. Figure 3.4 reveals how state budget surpluses fell over 4 percent from 1999 to 2000. A report by the liberal Center on Budget and Policy Priorities found that forty-five of the forty-eight states it examined had inadequate reserve funds to weather any kind of a recession without cutting spending or raising taxes.[40] In the wake of the fall of the stock market, declining surpluses and a push for tax cuts, hard choices soon will have to be made by state and local legislators.

FEDERALISM AND THE SUPREME COURT

Historically, the role of the Supreme Court in determining the parameters of federalism cannot be underestimated. As we have seen in chapter 2, although Congress passed sweeping New Deal legislation that some have argued amended the Constitution, it was not until the Supreme Court finally reversed itself and found those programs to be constitutional that any real change occurred in the federal-state relationship. From the New Deal until the 1980s, the Supreme Court's impact on the nature of the federal system could be found in several areas, but especially in education, the electoral process, and the commerce clause and the functioning of the states.

Through grants-in-aid programs like the Morrill Land Grant Act of 1862, and into the 1950s, Congress long has tried to encourage the states to develop their university and educational systems. Still, education was usually considered a function of the states

WEB EXPLORATION
To analyze where your state stands relative to other states, see
www.ablongman.com/oconnor

GLOBAL POLITICS

FEDERALISM IN COMPARATIVE PERSPECTIVE

All governments face the issue of how to divide political authority geographically. Of the variations presented in the table, federal and unitary systems are the most prevalent throughout the world. The Commonwealth of Independent States (made up of most of the former republics of the Soviet Union) is the rare example a confederation. The countries presented here are split almost evenly between federal and unitary systems, with the latter slightly more common. While these federal systems divide political authority between national and local government, the near balance suggests that there is nothing inherently better, or even more democratic, in a federal system.

Whether a country adopts one or the other tends to be the result of its political history. The United States and Germany were created out of existing confederacies, so the new governments accommodated theoretically strong state governments as the price of union. Canada was formed in 1867 out of three British provinces that voluntarily sought union. In France, Italy, and Japan, the creation of modern nation-states was driven by central authorities that imposed geographic political arrangements on their provinces. In all three cases, subnational territories were created by national governments intent on obliterating then-existing regional identities. China and Russia have always had traditions of strong central government, which makes recent Russian federalism a puzzle.

The ability of the national government to alter local government at will remains a key feature of unitary systems. No better current example can be found than in the British Parliament's decision in 1998 to provide home parliaments for Scotland, Wales, and Northern Ireland. But what Parliament created can be abolished by that body at any time: In 2000, dissatisfied with the lack of progress in peace negotiations in Northern Ireland, the Blair government suspended that region's home parliament and reintroduced direct rule by the Parliament in London.

Power is divided differently even among the federal systems. Canada has had a strong federal government

with correspondingly weak provinces, although the latter have asserted their power in recent decades. Quebec is the clearest case, with its threat to separate from the rest of the country forcing the federal government to make concessions on issues like the national language and education. Unlike American states, German state governments cannot raise their own taxes, but they retain sole control over state police forces, the highest level of regular law enforcement. The Mexican and post-communist Russian federal systems have also been highly centralized. In the original spirit of the U.S. Constitution, Canadian, German, and Russian regional governments are represented in the upper houses of their respective federal parliaments. This gives state governments a direct say in national lawmaking.

Geographic Distribution of Authority

Country	System	Major Subnational Divisions
Canada	federal	10 provinces, 3 territories
China	unitary	23 provinces, 9 other units
France	unitary	96 departments
Germany	federal	16 states
Indonesia	unitary	23 provinces, 3 other units
Italy	unitary	20 regions
Japan	unitary	47 prefectures
Mexico	federal	31 states, 1 federal district
Russia	federal	49 oblasts, 21 republics, 13 other units
United Kingdom	unitary	53 counties
United States	**federal**	**50 states, 1 federal district**

Source: CIA World Factbook 2000 online. URL http://www.odci.gov/cia.publications/factbook/geos/. Searched September 20, 2000.

Longman
Participate.com 2.0
Comparative
Comparing Federal and Unitary Systems

under their police powers, which allow the states to provide for public health and welfare. That tradition was shattered when the Supreme Court ruled in *Brown* v. *Board of Education* (1954) that state-mandated segregation has no place in the public schools (see chapter 6). *Brown* forced states to dismantle their segregated school systems and ultimately led the federal courts to play an important role in monitoring the efforts of state and local governments to tear down the vestiges of segregation.

A decade after *Brown* v. *Board of Education*, the Supreme Court again involved itself in one of the most sacred areas of state regulation in the federal system—the conduct of elections. As a trade-off for giving the national government more powers, the Constitutional Convention allowed the states control over voter qualifications in national elections as well as over how elections were to be conducted. But in 1964, the Court began to limit the states' ability to control the process of congressional redistricting. In 1966, for example, the Supreme Court invalidated the poll tax, a state-imposed tax ranging from one to five dollars levied on those who wished to vote. The poll tax was widely used in the Southern states to curtail voting by the poor, who often were black.[41] Most Southern legislators assailed the Court's decision, viewing it as illegal interference with their powers to regulate elections under the Constitution, and as a violation of state sovereignty.

Since the New Deal, until recently, the commerce clause has been the rationale for virtually any federal intervention in state and local governmental affairs. In *Garcia* v. *San Antonio Metropolitan Transit Authority* (1985), for example, which involved the constitutionality of applying federally imposed minimum wage and maximum hour provisions to state governments, the Court ruled that Congress has broad power to impose its will on state and local governments, even in areas that traditionally have been left to their discretion. The Court ruled that the "political process ensures that laws that unduly burden the states will not be promulgated" and that it should not be up to an "unelected" judiciary to preserve state powers.[42] Furthermore, the majority of the Court concluded that the Tenth Amendment, which ensures that any powers not given to the national government be reserved for the states, was—at least for the time being—essentially meaningless!

"I GUESS I JUST HADN'T NOTICED IT BEFORE"

Unlike what the majority did in *Bush* v. *Gore*, generally the conservative Court usually defers to state courts as well as judgements of the state legislatures. (Photo courtesy: Copyright 2000 by Herblock in The Washington Post)

The Devolution Revolution and the Court

Growth in federal grants-in-aid programs and unfunded mandates to the states, as well as the Court's apparent bestowal of free rein on the authority of Congress to regulate under the commerce clause, left many states to rethink their position in the federal system. Most were unhappy with it. Some argued that one of the original reasons for federal grants—perceived overrepresentation of rural interests in state legislatures—has been removed, as the Supreme Court has ordered redistricting to ensure better representation of urban and suburban interests. Moreover, state legislatures have become more professional, state and local bureaucracies more responsive, and the delivery of services betters. In fact, the greatest growth in government hiring continues to be in the state and local sectors.

Beginning in the late 1980s, however, in what many term a devolution revolution, the Court began to changes its willingness to allow Congress to regulate in a variety of area. Once Ronald Reagan was elected president, he attempted to fashion a Supreme Court in his own image—one of new justices committed to notions of state rights and rolling back federal intervention in matters that he and many Republicans believed properly resided within the province of the states and not Congress or the federal courts.

Mario M. Cuomo, the former liberal Democratic New York governor, has referred to the decisions of what he called the Reagan-Bush Court as creating "a kind of new judicial federalism." According to Cuomo, this new federalism can be characterized by

Longman
Participate.com
2.0
Timeline
Federalism
and the
Supreme
Court

POINT/COUNTERPOINT

WHO SHOULD CONTROL EDUCATION?

Traditionally, control over public schools has rested with local school districts. But beginning with federal enforcement of civil rights laws and the Great Society programs in the 1950s and 1960s, the national government has been more and more involved in education issues. In 1979, President Jimmy Carter created the U.S. Department of Education, separating it from the Department of Health, Education and Welfare and in 1994 President Bill Clinton signed into law Goals 2000 or the Educate America Act, which set out eight national education goals and provided money to help states meet them. Among those goals are that children in grades 4, 8, and 12 need to demonstrate competency in English, mathematics, science, foreign languages, civics and government, economics, arts, history, and geography. This particular clause has led to a discussion of nationally mandated standards and to large numbers of standardized tests. The tests are lauded as "outcomes-based assessment" by their supporters and are criticized as interference with the prerogatives of parents and teachers by opponents. But standardized tests is only one aspect of the larger issue of federal involvement in public schools. Vouchers, or school choice, are another proposal designed to address failing schools. Introducing market-based forces into the public schools by allowing parents and students to leave failing schools and take money with them to a better functioning school is designed to increase competition and the quality of education. Opponents argue that vouchers merely undercut the public school system. Let's examine these points of view.

Advocates of strong federal involvement with public education, including many Democrats, argue that schools need national education standards to guarantee that all American children get a quality education, regardless of whether they are lucky enough to live in rich school districts or certain states. Advocates for federal involvement also argue that national education standards provide a benchmark with which to measure school reforms and quality. Further, only the federal government seems to be able to guarantee equal treatment for minorities and women.

In addition, the testing and assessment of students in critical grades (4, 8, and 12) is deemed essential to measuring quality and determining whether school reform is working and how well schools are teaching their students. Testing allows teachers and students to have an objective measure of how well they perform compared with local, state, and national averages.

Advocates of federal involvement are often adamantly opposed to vouchers. If parents opt to send their children to private or parochial schools and are allowed to bring state and federal monies with them, the national education system will be threatened. The worst case scenario is that only the poor and the disadvantaged will be left in public schools. The voucher arguments may also be based on a false assumption: that our public schools are failing. While the problem exists, in many respects public education seems to be improving and is generally high quality. The United States has more of its children going on to college than any country in the world.

Critics of federal involvement, including many Republicans and teachers' unions, argue that state and local authorities, coupled with parents, know and understand what is best for their children and for public education. They fiercely oppose national standards as an effort to impose a national curriculum. They also argue that the education bureaucracy is already expensive and bloated, *so* why add another layer by increasing the size of the federal education bureaucracy.

The critics also argue that testing is actually having a negative effect on learning. Multiple-choice tests, as most of them are, test only passive recognition, not cognitive ability. Many minority students, women, and students from poor families tend to perform less well on standardized tests. Instead of exploring ways of getting students excited about learning, teachers who teach to the test reduce the quality of education instead of enhancing it.

Many critics of federal involvement also favor vouchers. They see serious flaws in the educational system that, they feel, can be addressed by introducing competition and market forces into the system. If parents start removing their children, and government funding goes with them, poor schools will be forced to change and in the end all children will benefit from higher educational standards.

 What do you think? Who Should control education?
Go to www.ablongman.com/oconnor

the Court's withdrawal of "rights and emphases previously thought to be national."[43] Perhaps most illustrative of this trend are the Supreme Court's decisions in *Webster* v. *Reproductive Health Services* (1989)[44] and *Casey* v. *Planned Parenthood of Southeastern Pennsylvania* (1992).[45] In *Webster* the Court first gave new latitude—and even encouragement—to the states to fashion more restrictive abortion laws, as underscored in Table 3.3. Since *Webster*, one or more new restrictions on abortion, such as spousal or parental consent, informed consent or waiting periods, and bans on late-term abortions. (See Analyzing the Data: State-by-State Report Card on Access to Abortion.) The Court has consistently upheld the authority of the individual states to limit a minor's access to abortion through imposition of parental consent or notification laws. And it has consistently declined to review other restrictions, including twenty-four-hour waiting period requirements. In 2000, however, badly divided 5–4, the Court struck down a Nebraska ban on so-called "partial birth" abortions (as discussed in chapter 5).

Personal rights and liberties were not the only issues affected by a Court that became more and more conservative through the Reagan-Bush years. The addition of two justices by President Clinton did little to stem the course of the Court bent on rebalancing the nature of the federal system. Since 1989 the Supreme Court has decided several major cases dealing with the nature of the federal system. Most of these have been 5–4 decisions and most have been decided against increased congressional power or in a manner to provide the states with greater authority over a variety of issues and policies. In *U.S.* v. *Lopez* (1995), for example, which involved the conviction of a student charged with carrying a concealed handgun onto school property, a five-person majority of the Court ruled that Congress lacked constitutional authority under the commerce clause to regulate guns within 1,000 feet of a school.[46] The majority concluded that local gun control in the schools was a state, not a federal, matter. In the same year, the Court reined in state power the electoral process. In *U.S. Term Limits* v. *Thornton*, by a 5–4 margin, the Court struck down as unconstitutional

WEB EXPLORATION
For more information on state abortion restrictions, see
www.ablongman.com/oconnor

WEB EXPLORATION
For more about local gun control initiatives, see
www.ablongman.com/oconnor

TABLE 3.3 Major Cases in the Supreme Court Devolution of Power Back to the States

Case	Year	Issue	Decision	Vote
Webster v. *Reproductive Health Services*	1989	The constitutionality of several state abortion restrictions	In upholding most of the restrictions, the Court invites the states to begin to enact new state restrictions	5–4
N.Y. v. *Smith*	1992	Does the Low-Level Waste Act, which requires states to dispose of radioactive waste within their borders, violate the tenth Amendment?	Section of the act that requires the states to take legal ownership of waste was found unconstitutional because it would force states into the service of the federal government	6–3
U.S. Term Limits v. *Thornton*	1995	Can the states set qualifications for members of Congress?	States do not have the authority to enact term limits for federal elected officials	5–4
U.S. v. *Lopez*	1995	Does Congress have the authority to regulate guns within 1,000 feet of a public school?	Only states have this authority; no connection to commerce found here	5–4
Seminole Tribe v. *Florida*	1996	Can Congress impose a duty on the states to negotiate with Indian tribes?	Federal courts held to have no jurisdiction over Indian tribe's suit to force the state to comply with the Indian Gaming Regulations Act, thus upholding the state's sovereign immunity	5–4
Boerne v. *Flores*	1997	The constitutionality of the Religious Freedom Restoration Act and its application of local zoning ordinances to a church (see chapter 5)	Sections of the act are beyond the power of Congress to force on the states	5–4
Printz v. *U.S.*	1997	Constitutionality of requiring local law enforcement officials to conduct background checks on handgun purchasers temporarily	Congress lacks the authority to compel state officers to execute federal laws	5–4
Florida Prepaid v. *College Savings Bank*	1999	Can Congress change patent laws to affect state sovereign immunity (immunity from a lawsuit)?	Congress does not have authority under the commerce clause or the patent clause to abrogate state sovereign immunity from lawsuits	5–4
Alden v. *Maine*	1999	Can Congress void state immunity from lawsuit in state courts?	Congress lacks the authority to abrogate a state's immunity in its own courts	5–4

ANALYZING THE DATA

STATE-BY-STATE REPORT CARD ON ACCESS TO ABORTION

The National Abortion and Reproductive Rights Action League (NARAL) rated each state and the District of Columbia in fourteen categories, including bans on abortion procedures and counseling, clinic violence, the length of waiting periods, access for minors, and pubic funding. Several states have banned so-called "partial-birth abortions," but in many of these states courts or attorneys general have blocked enforcement.

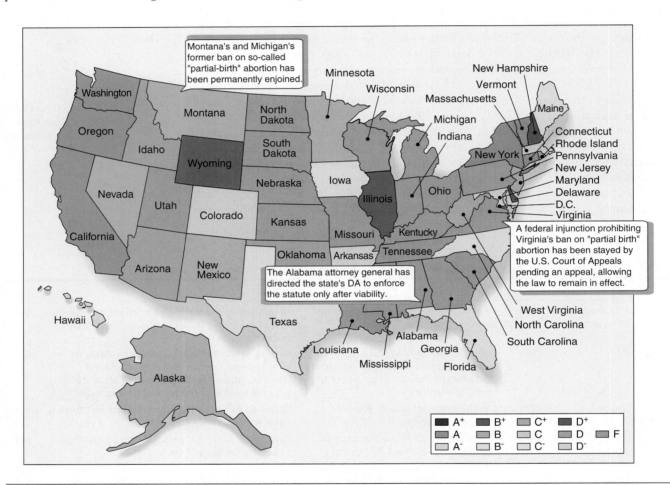

Montana's and Michigan's former ban on so-called "partial-birth" abortion has been permanently enjoined.

A federal injunction prohibiting Virginia's ban on "partial birth" abortion has been stayed by the U.S. Court of Appeals pending an appeal, allowing the law to remain in effect.

The Alabama attorney general has directed the state's DA to enforce the statute only after viability.

Legend: A+ B+ C+ D+ | A B C D F | A- B- C- D-

Source: From NARAL Resources, "State-by-State Report Card on Access to Abortion." Reprinted by permission from The NARAL Foundation.

sovereign immunity
The right of a state to be free from lawsuit unless it gives permission to the suit. Under the Eleventh Amendment, all states are considered sovereign.

state-imposed term limits on members of Congress.[47] States themselves, of course, are free to set limits on the terms of state lawmakers.

One year later, again a badly divided Court ruled that Congress lacked the authority to require the states to negotiate with Indian tribes about gaming.[48] The U.S. Constitution specifically gives Congress the right to deal with Indian tribes, but the Court found that Florida's **sovereign immunity** protected it from this kind of congressional directive about how to conduct its business. In 1997, the Court decided two more major cases dealing with the scope of Congress's authority to regulate in areas historically left

POLITICS NOW

LEGISLATING AGAINST VIOLENCE AGAINST WOMEN: A CASUALTY OF THE DEVOLUTION REVOLUTION?

As originally enacted, the Violence Against Women Act (VAWA) allowed women to file civil lawsuits in federal court if they could prove that they were the victim of rape, domestic violence, or other crimes "motivated by gender." VAWA was first enacted in 1994 and widely and widely praised as an effective mechanism to combat domestic violence. In its first five years, $1.6 million was allocated for states and local governments to pay for a variety of programs including a national toll-free hotline for victims of violence that averages 13,000 calls per month, funding for special police sex crime units, and civil and legal assistance for women in need of restraining orders.[a]

had overstepped its authority because the alleged crimes were "within the exclusive purview of the states."[c] The Clinton administration and the National Organization for Women Legal Defense and Education Fund unsuccessfully appealed this decision to the Supreme Court.

---

[a]Juliet Eilperin, "Reauthorization of Domestic Violence Act is at Risk," *Washington Post*, September 13, 2000, A6.
[b]*U.S. v. Morrison*, 120 S. Ct. 1740 (2000).
[c]Tony Mauro, "Court will review laws of protection," *USA Today*, September 29, 1999, 4A.

Most of the publicity surrounding the act has stemmed from a challenge to but one of its provisions; the decision from the Court easily can be viewed as part of the Rehnquist Court's reluctance to allow Congress to interfere in areas of traditional state interest. In 2000, five justices of the Supreme Court, including Justice Sandra Day O'Connor, ruled that Congress had no authority under the commerce clause to enact a provision of the Violence Against Women Act providing a federal remedy to victims of gender motivated violence.[b]

The suit brought by Christy Brzonkala was the first brought under the act's civil damages to provision. While she was a student at Virginia Polytechnic Institute, Brzonkala alleged that two football players there raped her. After the university took no action against the students, she sued the school and the students. No criminal charges were ever filed in her case. The conservative federal appeals court in Richmond, Virginia—in spite of rulings to the contrary in seventeen other courts—ruled that Congress

Christy Brzonkala, the petitioner in *U.S.* v. *Morrison*. (Photo courtesy: Cindy Pinkston, January, 1996)

---

to the province of the states: zoning and local law enforcement. In *Boerne* v. *Flores* (1997) a majority of the Court ruled that sections of the Religious Freedom Restoration Act were unconstitutional because Congress lacked the authority to meddle in local zoning regulations, even if a church was involved.[49] In *Printz* v. *U.S.* (1997), again a 5–4 majority of the Court ruled that Congress lacked the authority to require local law enforcement officials to conduct background checks on handgun purchasers until the federal government was able to implement a national system.[50] In 1999, in another case involving sovereign immunity, a slim majority of the Supreme Court ruled that Congress lacked the authority to change patent laws in a manner that would negatively affect a state's right to assert its immunity from suit.[51]

Longman
Participate.com 2.0
Simulation
You Are a Federal Judge

Longman
Participate.com
2.0
Participation
**Is Federalism
Dead and
Should It Be?**

The combined impact of all of these cases makes it clear that the Court will no longer countenance federal excursions into powers reserved to the states. (See also, Politics Now: Legislating Against Violence Against Women.) As the power of Congress to legislate in a wide array of areas has been limited, the hands of the states have been strengthened.

In 2000, the Supreme Court's decision to stay a ruling of the Florida State Supreme Court ordering a manual recount of ballots in several counties as originally requested by the Gore team, surprised many observers given the majority of the Court's reluctance over the last decade to interfere in areas historically left to the states. Thus, the Court's 5–4 majority decision in *Bush* v. *Gore* (2000), which followed fairly observable liberal/conservative lines, was surprising only in that justices normally opposed to federal intervention in state matters found that the Florida Supreme Court, which purportedly based its decisions solely on its interpretation of Florida law, violated federal law and the U.S. Constitution. Thus, the conservative, historically pro-states rights majority, used federal law to justify their decision, which had the effect of settling the election outcome in favor of George W. Bush, who would be likely to appoint more justices to tip the balance of the Court toward states rights at the expense of national power even further.

Continuity & Change

Marriage in the Federal System

When the Framers drafted the Constitution, most of them had clear ideas about what marriage was and the authority of the state (as well as the church) to sanction it. Marriage and the laws surrounding it (as well as its dissolution) were solely within the purview of state authority. Under English common law, when a woman married, she ceased to exist in the eyes of the law; in other words, she was civilly dead and could not make contracts or enter into any other kinds of legal arrangements. Beginning in the 1830s, however, most states began to change their laws to give women more rights in marriage. States regularly determine age at marriage (until the 1970s, it was frequently different for males and females), degree of relationship allowed (can cousins marry?), how married individuals can dispose of property (inheritance laws), pay their taxes, or even whether they can testify against each other in court.[52] Marriage is not only a legal contract recognized by the state,

Lois Farnham and Holly Puterbaugh challenged Vermont's refusal to allow them to marry, which eventually led to passage of Vermont's civil union law. (Photo courtsesy: Jym Wilson/ © 2000 USA Today. Reprinted with permission.)

but it carries certain rights and responsibilities with it. Only when some type of law or practice was viewed as discriminatory under the U.S. Constitution has the force of the federal government come into play. Thus, the Supreme Court has struck down as unconstitutional state laws that prohibit interracial marriages,[53] set differential ages for the age of legal capacity for men and women,[54] or allow only women to receive alimony upon dissolution of a marriage.[55] As public perceptions of what was appropriate changed, these changes were marked by changes in state law, and when that didn't happen, sometimes by the federal courts.

Until the 1980s, most people in America thought of marriage as a legal relationship between a male and a female. In the 1980s, however, some cities began recognizing what are termed domestic partnerships. Depending on the locale, these domestic partnership ordinances allowed same-sex couples to register with government

(continued)

officials to ensure that their union could be recognized in some way. In some cases, this provided the force of the state in matters of death and inheritances as well as other issues, including a person's ability to make decisions for an incapacitated partner over the wishes of other familial members. Many employers followed suit and began to offer health and insurance benefits to same-sex couples in committed relationships.

In 1993, a decision of the Hawaiian Supreme Court called that state's ban on homosexual marriages into constitutional question. While Hawaii was grappling with this issue, several state legislatures and the U.S. Congress were whipped into a frenzy about the specter of gay and lesbian marriages. In 1996 and 1997 alone, half of the states passed provisions to bar legal recognition of same-sex marriages. The U.S. Congress also got into the act and passed the Defense of Marriage Act, which allows states to disregard gay marriages even if they are legal in other states. (The questionable constitutionality of this provision under the full faith and credit clause is discussed on p. 53.)

In spite of these moves by so many of the states and the federal government, in 2000, Vermont became the first state in the union to sanction civil unions between same-sex couples. These are not marriages; instead, the Vermont law calls them "civil unions." Couples need only pay $20 to receive a license from a town clerk (there are no residency or blood test requirements) and have a ceremony performed by a judge or clergy member. Once so united, the couple is entitled to all of the benefits, protections, and responsibilities that are granted to married couples under Vermont law.

The idea of gay marriage is still upsetting to some, much as interracial marriage was in many sections of the South. Still, there can be no doubt that our notions of what a family is, as well as what (or who) makes up a married couple, are changing, and changing quite rapidly.

1. Are civil union states a good political compromise to diffuse this issue?

2. Should states be pressed to recognize Vermont civil unions under the full faith and credit clause of the U.S. Constitution?

Cast Your Vote. Should other states adopt a civil union law similar to that in Vermont? To cast your vote, go to **www.ablongman.com/oconnor**

SUMMARY

The inadequacies of the confederate form of government created by the Articles of Confederation led the Framers to create an entirely new, federal system of government. From the summer of 1776 until today, the tension between the national and state governments has been at the core of our federal system. In describing the origins of that tension and the renewed debate about the role of the national government in the federal system, we have made the following points:

1. **The Roots of the Federal System**
   The Framers created a federal system to replace the confederate form of government that had existed under the Articles of Confederation.

2. **The Powers of Government in the Federal System**
   The national government has both enumerated and implied powers, and also exercises concurrent powers with the states. Certain powers are denied to both the state and national governments. Certain guarantees concerning representation in Congress and protection against foreign attacks and domestic rebellion were made to the states in return for giving up some of their powers in the new federal system. Despite limitations, the national government is ultimately supreme.

3. **The Evolution and Development of Federalism**
   Over the years, the powers of the national government have increased tremendously at the expense of the states. The Supreme Court, in particular, has played a

key role in defining the relationship and powers of the national government through its broad interpretations of the supremacy and commerce clauses. For many years, however, it adhered to the notion of dual federalism, which tended to limit the national government's authority in areas such as slavery and, after the Civil War, civil rights. This notion of a limited role for the national government in some spheres ultimately fell by the wayside after the Great Depression.

The rapid creation of New Deal programs to alleviate many problems caused by the Depression led to a tremendous expansion of the federal government through the growth of federal services and grant-in-aid programs. This growth escalated during the Johnson administration and in the mid- to late 1970s. After his election in 1980, Ronald Reagan, upset by the growth of federal services, tried to reverse the tide through what he termed New Federalism. He built on earlier efforts by Richard M. Nixon to consolidate categorical grants into fewer block grant programs, and to give state and local governments greater control over programs. Since 1993 the national government and the states have been in a constant dialogue to reframe the structure of the federal-state relationship.

4. **Federalism and the Supreme Court**
   Over the years, the Supreme Court has been a major player in changing trends in the federal-state relationship.

Historically, its decisions in the areas of education, the electoral process, and the performance of state functions gave the federal government a wide role in the day-to-day functioning of the states, and limited the scope of the states' police powers. Since the Rea-gan-Bush era, however, the Supreme Court has been willing to draw the line on congressional power and return important powers to the states while limiting Congress's authority to legislate in areas it believes are the responsibility of the states.

KEY TERMS

bill of attainder, p. 76
block grant, p. 87
categorical grant, p. 86
concurrent powers, p. 76
Contract with America, p. 90
cooperative federalism, p. 83
dual federalism, p. 80

enumerated powers, p. 75
ex post facto law, p. 76
federalism, p. 73
Gibbons v. *Ogden* (1824), p. 79
implied power, p. 75
intergovernmental lobby, p. 88
mandates, p. 90

McCulloch v. *Maryland* (1819), p. 78
necessary and proper clause, p. 75
preemption, p. 89
reserve (or police) powers, p. 76
sovereign immunity, p. 96
supremacy clause, p. 74

SELECTED READINGS

Bowman, Ann O'M., and Richard C. Kearney. *State and Local Government*, 4th ed. Boston: Houghton Mifflin, 1999.

Conlan, Timothy J. *From New Federalism to Devolution: Twenty-Five Years of Intergovernmental Reform*. Washington, D.C.: Brookings, 1998.

Derthick, Martha. *The Influence of Federal Grants*. Cambridge, Mass.: Harvard University Press, 1970.

Elazar, Daniel J., and John Kincaid, eds. *The Covenant Connection: From Federal Theology to Modern Federalism*. Lexington, Mass.: Lexington Books, 2000.

Feingold, Kenneth, and Theda Skocpol. *State and Party in America's New Deal*. Madison: University of Wisconsin Press, 1995.

Gillespie, Ed, and Bob Schellhas, eds. *Contract with America*. New York: Times Books, 1994.

Grodzins, Morton. *The American System*. Chicago: Rand McNally, 1966.

Kenyon, Daphne A., and John Kincaid, eds. *Competition Among States and Local Governments*. Washington, D.C.: Urban Institute Press, 1991.

Ostrom, Vincent. *The Meaning of Federalism*. New York: Institute for Contemporary Studies, 1999.

Riker, William H. *Federalism: Origin, Operation, Significance*. Boston: Little, Brown, 1964.

Rivlin, Alice M. *Reviving the American Dream: The Economy, the States, and the Federal Government*. Washington, D.C.: Brookings Institution, 1993.

Walker, David B. *The Rebirth of Federalism*. Chatham, N.J.: Chatham House, 1994.

Zimmerman, Joseph F. *Interstate Relations: The Neglected Dimension of Federalism*. New York: Praeger, 1996.

NOTES

1. *New Jersey* v. *New York*, 523 U.S. 767 (1998).
2. Linda Greenhouse, "Skeptical High Court Hears Case over Pride and Acreage on Ellis I," *The New York Times* (January 13, 1998): B1. See also Lisa Anderson, "Land of the Free, Home of the Silly Dispute," *The Chicago Tribune* (June 5, 1998): 8.
3. "How Much Government—Devolution," *Public Perspective* (April/May 1995): 26.
4. In *City of Burbank* v. *Lockheed*, 411 U.S. 624 (1973), the U.S. Supreme Court ruled that the city could not impose curfews on plane takeoff or landing times. The Court said that one uniform *national* standard was critical for safety and the national interest.
5. *Missouri* v. *Holland*, 252 U.S. 416 (1920).
6. *McCulloch* v. *Maryland*, 4 Wheat. 316 (1819).
7. *Saenz* v. *Roe*, 1999 LEXIS 3174.
8. *Saenz* v. *Roe*, 1999 LEXIS 3174.
9. Joan Biskupic, "New-Resident Limits on Welfare Rejected," *The Washington Post* (May 18, 1999): A1.

10. Catherine F. Klein, "Full Faith and Credit: Interstate Enforcement of Protection Orders Under the Violence Against Women Act of 1994," *Family Law Quarterly* 29 (1995): 253.
11. Nancy Plevin, "Ohio Frees Indian-Rights Activist 'Little Rock' Reed," *Santa Fe New Mexican* (March 12, 1999): B1.
12. *New Mexico ex rel. Ortiz* v. *Reed*, 524 U.S. 151 (1998).
13. *McCulloch* v. *Maryland*, 4 Wheat. 316 (1819).
14. *Gibbons* v. *Ogden*, 22 U.S. 1 (1824).
15. *Lane County* v. *Oregon*, 74 U.S. 71 (1869).
16. 163 U.S. 537 (1896).
17. *Panhandle Oil Co.* v. *Knox*, 277 U.S. 71 (1928).
18. *Indian Motorcycle Co.* v. *United States*, 238 U.S. 570 (1931).
19. *Pensacola Telegraph* v. *Western Union*, 96 U.S. 1 (1877).
20. *United States* v. *E. C. Knight*, 156 U.S. 1 (1895).
21. 301 U.S. 1 (1937).
22. *United States* v. *Darby*, 312 U.S. 1 (1937).
23. *Wickard* v. *Filburn*, 317 U.S. 111 (1942).

24. Morton Grodzins, "Centralization and Decentralization in the American Federal System," in Robert A. Goldwin, ed. *A Nation of States* (Chicago: Rand McNally, 1963), 3–4.

25. Alice M. Rivlin, *Reviving the American Dream* (Washington, D.C.: Brookings Institution, 1992), 92.

26. Rivlin, *Reviving the American Dream,* 98.

27. Richard P. Nathan, *et al., Reagan and the States* (Princeton, N.J.: Princeton University Press, 1987), 4.

28. Quoted in David E. Anderson, "Conservative Think Tanks Go Local," *UPI* (June 10, 1991).

29. Stephen G. Bragaw, "Federalism's Defense Fund: The Intergovernmental Lobby and the Supreme Court, 1982–1997," paper delivered at the 1999 annual meeting of the Midwest Political Science Association.

30. Executive Order 13095, suspending Executive Order 13083.

31. Daniel Meisler, "State and Local Finance: White House Ready to Respond to Groups' Plea for Delay of Federalism Edict," *Bond Buyer* (September 11, 1998): 5.

32. Meisler, "State and Local Finance."

33. Executive Order 12612.

34. John Kincaid, "From Cooperation to Coercion in American Federalism: Housing, Fragmentation, and Preemption, 1789–1992," *Journal of Law and Politics* 9 (Winter 1993): 333–430.

35. This discussion of preemption relies heavily on Joseph F. Zimmerman, *Contemporary American Federalism: The Growth of National Power* (New York: Praeger, 1992), 55–81.

36. The Close Up Foundation, "Federalism," http://www.closeup.org/federal.html

37. "Devolutionary Thinking Is Now Part of a Larger Critique of Modern Governmental Experience," *Public Perspective* (April/May 1995): 28.

38. Timothy J. Conlan and David R. Beam, "Federal Mandates: The Record of Reform and Future Prospects," *Intergovernmental Perspectives* (Fall 1992): 9.

39. Richard Wolf, "States Bracing for Leaner Times," *USA Today* (July 10, 2000): A1.

40. Wolf, "States Bracing," A2.

41. *Harper* v. *Virginia Board of Elections,* 383 U.S. 663 (1966).

42. 469 U.S. 528 (1985).

43. Marianne Arneberg, "Cuomo Assails Judicial Hodgepodge," *Newsday* (August 15, 1990): 15.

44. 492 U.S. 490 (1989).

45. 112 S.Ct. 931 (1992).

46. 115 U.S. 1624 (1995).

47. 115 S.Ct. 1842 (1995).

48. *Stenberg* v. *Carhart,* 120 S.Ct. 2597 (2000).

48. *Seminole Tribe* v. *Florida,* 517 U.S. 44 (1996).

49. 521 U.S. 507 (1997).

50. 521 U.S. 898 (1997).

51. *Florida Prepaid* v. *College Savings Bank,* 527 U.S. 627 (1999).

52. *Bush* v. *Gore,* 121 S.Ct. 525 (2000).

53. *Loving* v. *Virginia,* 388 U.S. 1 (1967).

54. *Stanton* v. *Stanton,* 421 U.S. 7 (1975).

55. *Orr* v. *Orr,* 400 U.S. 268 (1979).

4 State and Local Government

As the twenty-first century begins, Hartford, Connecticut's capital, seems at a crossroad. The city has been through some rough and embarrassing times. Between 1990 and 2000, twenty police officers were arrested and there have been two grand jury investigations into police corruption. The city went for months without having its parks mowed. When finally some extra workers were hired to cut the grass, the city did not have the equipment for them to get the job done. The state has taken over the Hartford schools and oversees the effort to develop the downtown area. A study of the fire department concluded that it was vastly overstaffed and too expensive to run.[1]

On the other hand, Mike Peters, Hartford's popular mayor, and Saundra Kee Borges, the city's able and respected administrator, have made some notable achievements. Progress has been made in curtailing gang activity. A dysfunctional public housing complex has been torn down and replaced with single-family homes and an industrial park. Ambitious projects like an expansion of the civic auditorium, a massive new retail, entertainment, and housing development, and a new football stadium promise revitalization of the city.

Despite encouraging developments, there is a strong sense that Hartford is not governed well. The city council severely limits what the mayor and city administrator can do. Divided largely along ethnic lines, Hartford's council abolished the city planning department, thereby hampering future developments. Accomplishments are haphazard, not the result of an overall vision for the community. Members of the city's business elite and officials in Connecticut state government are pushing for reforms that would reduce the power of the city council and strengthen the executive.

Local governments, like Hartford, do not have the checks and balances built into the relationships of the institutions of the federal government. Most elected local officials have full-time jobs outside of government, making their public service part-time, despite the challenges faced by communities. State governments are responsible for local governments—how they are structured, what they can do, and what taxes they can levy. The problems faced by cities like Hartford are concerns on the agendas of governors and state legislators.

Governance in the United States is by multiple authorities, sometimes in conflict with one another and sometimes in harmony. It is easy for a school district, for example, to sidestep gang and youth violence issues and to define them as a problem for city police or for county social workers. The police might act only if a crime has actually been committed and refuse to get involved in prevention or intervention efforts, unless perhaps more money is put into their budget. Or various agencies and governments might get together informally to address a problem, more out of a common concern than because of a requirement.

The relationships among the various governments in our country are dynamic. The legal authority, the financial resources, and the political will of the federal government, state and municipal governments, tribal governments, school districts, water districts, and all the other public bodies are constantly changing. On the one hand, this provides groups and individuals with many points of access to government. On the other hand, the multiple, changing jurisdictions that govern our society can be a challenging puzzle, so complex that in effect citizens will have very little access and influence.

This chapter will present the basic patterns and principles of state and local governance so that you might readily understand how public policies in your community are made and applied.

■ First, we will review the *history of state and local governments.*
■ Second, we will identify the nature of *power and politics in communities.*
■ Third, we will describe the *development of state constitutions* and the major institutions of *state governments,* including trends in state elections.
■ Fourth, we will examine the different types of *local governments* and explain the bases for their authority as well as the special traits of their institutions.
■ Fifth, we will discuss relationships between federal and state governments and the Indian nations.
■ Sixth, we will explain the budgeting process for state and local *finances.*

THE EVOLUTION OF STATE AND LOCAL GOVERNMENTS

As pointed out in chapter 3, the basic, original unit of government in this country was the state. The thirteen colonial governments became thirteen state governments and their constitutions preceded the U.S. Constitution. The states initially were loosely tied together in the Articles of Confederation, but then formed a closer union and more powerful national government.

State governments, likewise, determined the existence of local governments. As we will later discuss in more detail, in some cases—like counties and, for most states, school districts—state laws *create* local governments. In others, like towns and cities, states *recognize* and *authorize* local governments in response to petitions from citizens.

In other words, the history of governance in the United States is not one built from the bottom. Local communities do not form states, which then form the United States. Instead, states are the basic units, which on the one hand establish local governments and on the other hand are the building blocks of the federal government.

In the past, state and local governments were primarily part-time governments. This has changed somewhat, but it will never change entirely. Initially, almost all state and local elected officials were part-time. Except for governors and a handful of big-city mayors, people in office were farmers, teachers, lawyers, and shop owners who did public service during their spare time. This was true as well for many judges and local government bureaucrats.

ROOTS OF GOVERNMENT

BAKER V. CARR (1962)

State governments have increased with capacity to govern in a dramatic and steady manner since the mid-1960s. A major reason for this is the implementation of the U.S. Supreme Court decision in *Baker* v. *Carr* in 1962. As in most states, Tennessee's legislature had not revised the boundaries of the districts from which lawmakers were elected as urban areas grew. The result was that one legislator from a rural district might represent 700 people while a legislator from an urban area would have 27,000 constituents. The Supreme Court ruled that state legislative boundaries had to be drawn to apply the principle of one-person, one-vote. In other words, the Court realized that rural votes in

Tennessee had more impact than urban votes. It mandated that each legislative district within a state have about the same number of people.

The end of rural overrepresentation in state legislatures meant that state governments treated the concerns and issues of everyone throughout the state seriously. States became relevant policy makers. Individuals who seriously wanted to perform public service found state governments attractive. State legislatures and administrative agencies became more professional.

Baker v. *Carr* demonstrated that the democratic principle of one-person, one-vote is important not only for representation, but for professionalism and competence.

As the responsibilities and challenges of government grew, more state and local officials became full-time. Increases in the need for urban services led to more full-time local governments. Likewise, states with high levels of urbanization, industrialization, and economic development needed larger, more professional, and full-time legislatures, courts, and administrative agencies. These states did not, however, always get their needs met. The boundaries of districts from which state legislators got elected did not change in response to population shifts in the post–Civil War period. As a result, state legislatures did not represent the character of their respective states. One legislator from a rural area might represent 50,000 people, whereas a legislator from an urban setting may represent as many as 500,000 constituents. Such a pattern led to low priority for urban needs.

This kind of misrepresentation remained in place until the 1960s. The 1962 ruling by the U.S. Supreme Court in *Baker* v. *Carr* became watershed in the evolution of state and local governments. The Court applied the Fourteenth Amendment to the U.S. Constitution and decreed that equal protection and the **one-person, one-vote** principles required that there be the same number of people in each of the legislative districts within a single state. As a result, state legislatures became more representative and the agendas of state governments became much more relevant than they had been. This in turn attracted more professional and serious individuals to seek administrative and elective positions in state governments.

The 1960s and 1970s were a period in which the federal government added both to the responsibilities and to the competence of state and local governments. Federal programs to combat poverty, revitalize urban areas, and protect the environment were designed to be administered by state and local officials rather than federal agencies. With this came assistance and sometimes mandates to improve the capacities of subnational governments.

In the past two decades, some trends in federalism have enhanced the importance of state and local governments. Conscious efforts since the Nixon administration were made to reverse the aggregation of power and authority in Washington, D.C. In part, this was philosophical, but it was also necessary. The federal government found itself

one-person, one-vote
The principle that each legislative district within a state should have the same number of eligible voters so that representation is equitably based on population.

unable to expand or even to maintain its presence in domestic policy areas. During the Reagan administration, the debt of the federal government more than tripled and there was no choice but to cut severely the flow of federal money and mandates that fueled much of the growth of state and local governments.

In 1995 the U.S. Supreme Court placed limitations on the federal government and reasserted the importance of state and local governments. This is best reflected in *U.S. v. Lopez,* where the Court ruled that Congress and the president did not have authority to require the establishment of gun-free zones around local schools and that it was a matter for state and local governments. The Court left open, however, the commonly used option of the federal government attaching conditions states had to meet to receive federal funds. This power had previously been affirmed in *South Dakota* v. *Dole* (1987), in which the Court said it was permissible for the federal government to require states that wanted transportation funds to pass laws setting twenty-one as the legal age for drinking. Congress and the president nonetheless seemed inclined to eliminate strings and to give state and local governments more discretion. For example, they removed the requirement that states have certain speed limits in order to receive federal transportation funds and gave local governments more leeway in determining how they would meet clean water standards.

The twentieth century closed with many changes and uncertainties, but with a clear message that state and local governments will have roles and responsibilities of increasing importance. For the most part, these jurisdictions relish these developments. Some states and cities, for example, are taking bold initiatives and even establishing direct ties with other countries in order to spur economic growth.[2] Others, especially in smaller and medium-sized communities, are overwhelmed with all there is to do.

GRASSROOTS POWER AND POLITICS

The most powerful and influential people in a state or community are not necessarily those who hold offices in government. While there is always a distinction between formal and informal power, the face-to-face character of governance at the grassroots level almost invites informal ties and influence. The part-time officials in particular have a more ambiguous identity than do full-time government officials.

In small to medium-sized communities it is common for a single family or a traditional elite to be the major decision maker, whether or not they have one of their members in a formal governmental position.[3] If you want to advocate for some improvements in a local park, a curriculum change in the schools, or a different set of priorities for the police department, it may be more important to get the support of a few key community leaders than the sympathy of the village president or the head of the school board. A newcomer interested in starting a business in a town likewise would be well advised to identify and court the informal elite and not just focus on those who hold a formal office.

Political participation in state and, especially, local politics is both more personal and more issue-oriented than at the national level. Much of what happens is outside the framework of political parties. Elections for some state and local government offices, in fact, are **nonpartisan elections,** which means parties do not nominate candidates and ballots do not include any party identification of those running for office. Access and approaches are usually direct. School board members receive phone calls at their homes. Members of the city council and county board bump into constituents while shopping for groceries or cheering their children in youth sports. The concerns that are communicated tend to be specific and neither partisan nor ideological. A particular grade school teacher is unfair and ineffective. Playground equipment is unsafe. It seems

nonpartisan election
A contest in which candidates run without formal identification or association with a political party.

to be taking forever for the city to issue a building permit so that you can get started on a remodeling project.

In this setting, local news media invariably play a key role. The major newspaper in the state and what might be the only newspaper in a community can shape the agendas of government bodies and the images of government officials. The mere fact that a problem is covered makes it an issue. If gang or cult activity is just a group of kids acting weird and dressing the same way, public officials might ignore it. News coverage of this or certainly of a violent incident, on the other hand, assures attention. Then the question is how the media define the issue—as an isolated and unusual event or as a signal that certain needs are not being met?

Ad hoc, issue-specific organizations are prevalent in state and local governments.[4] Individuals opposed to the plans of a state department of transportation to expand a stretch of highway from two to four lanes will organize, raise funds, and lobby hard to stop the project. Once the project is stopped or completed, that organization will go out of existence. Likewise, neighbors will organize to support or oppose specific development projects or to press for revitalization assistance, and then they will disband once the decision is made. The sporadic but intense activity focused on specific local or regional concerns is an important supplement to the ongoing work of parties and interest groups in state and local governments. A full understanding of what happens at the grass roots requires an appreciation of ad hoc, issue-specific politics as well as the institutions and processes through which state and local governments make and implement public policies.

STATE GOVERNMENTS

State governments have primary responsibility for education, public health, transportation, economic development, and criminal justice. States also are the unit of government that licenses and regulates various professions, such as doctors, lawyers, barbers, and architects. State governments have been active in welfare and the environment, in part as agents administering federal programs and in part on their own. National Guard and health agencies in states are key to homeland security.

State officials, in other words, have been and continue to be in charge of fundamental components of our society. They have also been challenged with problems that seem to defy solutions. Crime, for example, seems to be beyond our ability to do more than try to minimize it. Poverty is another such challenge. Likewise, we have not been fully satisfied with our efforts to provide appropriate high-quality education for every child. Despite these awesome responsibilities, there has been a historic reluctance to make state governments fully capable institutions.

State Constitutions

Whereas a major goal of the writers of the U.S. Constitution in 1787 was to *empower* the national government, the authors of the original **state constitutions** wanted to *limit* government. The Constitutional Convention in Philadelphia was convened, as you recall from chapter 2, because of the perception that the national government under the Articles of Confederation was not strong enough. The debates were primarily over how strong the national, or federal, government should be.

In contrast, the assumption of the authors of the first thirteen state constitutions, based on their backgrounds in the philosophy and experiences of monarchical rule, was that government was all-powerful, and so the question was how to limit it. The state constitutions were written and adopted before the Philadelphia Convention and included provisions that government may not interfere with basic individual liberties.

WEB EXPLORATION
To find statistics on any branch of government in the fifty states, see
www.ablongman.com/oconnor

state constitution
The document that describes the basic policies, procedures, and institutions of the government of a specific state, much like the U.S. Constitution does for the federal government.

These provisions, which were *integral* parts of each of the state constitutions, were *added* to the federal constitution as the first ten amendments, often called the Bill of Rights.

The first state constitutions provided for the institutions of government, such as governors, legislatures, and courts, with an emphasis on limiting the authority of each institution.[5] These constitutions did not fully embrace the principle of checks and balances that is found in the U.S. Constitution. The office of governor was particularly weak. Not surprisingly, the most powerful institution was the legislature. In fact, initially only South Carolina, New York, and Massachusetts gave their governors the authority to veto legislation. After over 200 years, the state of North Carolina still does not let its governor use a veto.

The first state constitutions set the pattern for what was to come. In one of its last actions, the national Congress under the Articles of Confederation passed the Northwest Ordinance of 1787, which addressed how new states might join the Union. Lawmakers were responding primarily to settlers in what is now Ohio but extended coverage to the territory that includes Minnesota, Wisconsin, Iowa, Illinois, Michigan, and Indiana—which the people in the original states considered the "northwest." The basic blueprint included in the ordinance was that a territory might successfully petition for statehood if it had at least 60,000 free inhabitants (slaves and American Indians did not count) and a constitution that was both similar to the documents of existing states and compatible with the national constitution. The first white settlers in the territory covered by the Northwest Ordinance were originally from New York and Massachusetts, with some individuals and families direct from Europe. Not surprisingly, the initial constitutions of these states were almost identical to those of New York and Massachusetts.[6]

The traumas of slavery and the Civil War had a profound impact on the constitutions of southern states. Events that led to the secession of Southern states included the Missouri Compromise of 1820–1821, which simultaneously admitted Missouri and Maine, the former with a constitution that legalized slavery and the latter as a "free state." The Missouri Compromise also included an agreement that no more states would be admitted that had constitutions allowing slavery. When, in 1854, that provision was violated by the admission of Kansas as a slave state and Nebraska as a free state, the confrontation between the two sides escalated.[7]

Slavery was a unique and very emotional issue. It raised the general question of the extent to which the national Congress could insist on specific clauses in state constitutions. The Civil War, of course, answered that question. That war also precipitated an era in which the states in the Confederacy wrote and discarded constitutions at a rapid pace and ended the process with documents that established state governments that were even weaker than those of the first thirteen states.

Southern states adopted new constitutions when they seceded and formed the Confederacy. After the Civil War, they had to adopt new constitutions acceptable to the Congress in Washington, D.C. These constitutions typically provided former slaves with considerable power and disenfranchised those who had been active in the Confederacy. These were not realistic constitutions. They divorced political power from economic wealth and social status, formal authority from informal influence. White communities simply ignored government and ruled themselves informally as much as possible. After less than ten years of this, whites reasserted political control and rewrote state constitutions.

The new documents reflected white distrust and provided for a narrow scope of authority for state governments and for weak, fragmented institutions. Governors could serve for only two-year terms. Legislatures could only meet for short periods of time and in some cases only once every other year. Law enforcement authority, both police and justices of the peace, rested squarely in local community power structures.

Western states entered the Union with constitutions that also envisioned weak governments. Here the central concerns were not slavery or national government interference, but rather political machines. In large cities in the Northeast and Midwest, machines based on bloc voting by new, non-English-speaking immigrants wrested political control

HIGHLIGHT

THE HAWAIIAN CONSTITUTION: A SPECIAL CASE

Hawaii was a kingdom ruled by an absolute monarch through the reign of Kamehameha the Great (1782–1819). Out of deference to the traditions of this monarchy, when the federal government ruled Hawaii as a territory (1900–1959), it established an executive that was more powerful than is common in states. Also, the government did not foster local governments but instead relied on the sugar and pineapple plantations to provide their own police and fire protection and other basic services.

As a legacy of this history, Hawaii's constitution provides for a more centralized governance than any of the other states. Public education, police and fire protection, library services, and health and welfare programs commonly run by local governments are operated directly by state government in Hawaii.

Another unique feature of Hawaii's constitution is the special attention to the welfare of native Hawaiians. Anyone who is at least 50 percent descended from the islands' indigenous inhabitants has land rights that are specially protected. Also the native Hawaiians benefit from income from certain land, originally designated by the federal government and now by state government. By contrast, other states may be affected by treaties agreed to by the federal government and American Indian tribes. Hawaiians relate directly to the state for governance, whereas American Indians continue to have their primary relationship with the federal government.

---

and, sometimes in corrupt ways, began amassing economic wealth. New states in the West sought to keep machine politics from ever getting started in the first place.

The most effective national anti-machine effort was the **Progressive Movement,** led by such figures as Woodrow Wilson, Theodore Roosevelt, Robert M. La Follette, and Hiram Johnson, who advocated changes that involved direct voter participation and bypassed traditional institutions.[8] These reforms included the use of primaries for nominating candidates instead of closed party processes, the initiative for allowing voters to enact laws directly rather than go through legislatures and governors, and the recall for constituents to remove officials from office in the middle of their term. Progressives succeeded in getting their proposals adopted as statutes in existing states and in the constitutions of new states emerging from western territories.

Though weak state government institutions may have been a reasonable response to earlier concerns, they are inappropriate for current issues. The trend since the 1960s, throughout the United States, has been to amend state constitutions in order to enhance the capacity of governors, legislatures, and courts to address problems. In the 1970s alone, over 300 amendments to state constitutions were adopted. Most were to lengthen the terms of governors and provide chief executives with more authority over spending and administration, to streamline courts, and to make legislatures professional and full-time.[9]

Constitutional changes have also reflected some ambivalence. While there has been widespread recognition that state governments must be more capable, there is also concern about what that might mean in taxes and in the entrenchment of power. Thus, reforms have included severe restrictions on the ability of state and local governments to raise taxes and limits on how long legislators in some states might serve. Historic distrust of government continues.

As compared with the U.S. Constitution, state constitutions are relatively easy to amend. Every state allows for the convening of a constitutional convention, and over 200 have been held. Also, every state has a process whereby the legislature can pass an amendment to the constitution, usually by a two-thirds or three-fourths vote, and then submit the change to the voters for their approval in a referendum. Seventeen states,

Progressive Movement
Advocate of measures to destroy political machines and instead have direct participation by voters in the nomination of candidates and the establishment of public policy.

Longman
Participate.com
2.0
Participation
Explore Your State Constitution

mostly in the West, allow for amendments simply by getting the proposal on a statewide ballot, without involvement of the legislature or governor.

An implication of the relatively simple amendment processes is frequent changes. All but nineteen states have adopted wholly new constitutions since they were first admitted, and almost six thousand specific amendments have been adopted. Another effect of the process is that state constitutions tend to be longer than the U.S. Constitution and include provisions that more appropriately should be statutes or administrative rules. The California constitution, for example, not only establishes state government institutions and protects individual rights, but also defines how long a wrestling match may be. Arkansas includes in its constitution what colors should be used for copies of registration documents. Clearly, these are details that do not belong in a constitution.

Governors

Governors have always been the most visible elected officials in state governments. Initially, that visibility supported the ceremonial role of governors as their primary function. Now that visibility serves governors as they set the agenda and provide leadership for others in state governments.

The most important role that current governors play is in identifying the most pressing problems facing their respective states and proposing solutions to those problems. Governors first establish agendas when they campaign for office. After inauguration, the most effective way for the chief executive to initiate policy changes is when submitting the budget for legislative approval.

Budgets are critical to the business of state governments. The ways in which money is raised and spent say a lot about the priorities of decision makers. Until the 1920s, state legislatures commonly compiled and passed budgets and then submitted them for gubernatorial approval or veto. As part of the efforts to strengthen the capacities of state governments, governors were, like presidents, given the major responsibility for starting the budget process. Now all but four states have their governors propose budgets.

The role of governor as budget initiator is especially important when coupled with the governor's veto authority and executive responsibilities. Like presidents, governors also have **package** or **general veto** authority, which rejects a bill in its entirety. In addition, governors in all but seven states may exercise a **line-item veto** on bills that involve spending or taxing. A line-item veto strikes only part of a bill that has been passed by the legislature. It allows a chief executive to delete a particular program or expenditure from a budget bill and let the remaining provisions become law. The intent of this authority is to enable governors to revise the work of legislators in order to produce a balanced budget.

Governor Tommy Thompson of Wisconsin has been among the most extensive and creative users of the line-item veto. He reversed the intent of legislation by vetoing the word "not" in a sentence and created entirely new laws by eliminating specific letters and numerals to make new words and numbers. Voters in Wisconsin were so upset with this free use of the veto pen that in 1993 they passed the "Vanna White amendment" to the state constitution, prohibiting the governor from striking letters within words and numerals within numbers. Not to be outmaneuvered, Governor Thompson then used his veto authority to actually *insert* new words and numbers in bills that had passed the legislature. The state supreme court, in 1995, upheld this interpretation of veto, as long as the net effect of the vetoes was not to increase spending.

While the Wisconsin case is extreme, it illustrates the significant power that veto authority can provide. Legislators can override vetoes, usually with a two-thirds vote in each of the chambers. But this rarely happens. Only 6 percent of gubernatorial vetoes are overturned,[10] and Governor Thompson had enough support from his party to sustain all of his.

The executive responsibilities of governors provide an opportunity to affect public policies after laws have been passed. Agencies are responsible for implementing the

governor
Chief elected executive in state government.

WEB EXPLORATION
To learn about issues that governors nationwide deem most important, see www.ablongman.com/oconnor

package or general veto
The authority of a chief executive to void an entire bill that has been passed by the legislature. This veto applies to all bills, whether or not they have taxing or spending components, and the legislature may override this veto, usually with a two-thirds majority of each chamber.

line-item veto
The authority of a chief executive to delete part of a bill passed by the legislature that involves taxing and/or spending. The legislature may override a veto, usually with a two-thirds majority of each chamber.

Governors generally need to demonstrate to their constituents that they are tough on crime. Here, New York Governor George Pataki, surrounded by state legislators, police officials, and crime victims' advocates, signs a stringent anti-crime bill. (Photo courtesy: Marty Lederhandler/AP/Wide World Photos)

laws. That may mean improving a road, enforcing a regulation, or providing a service. The speed and care with which implementation occurs are often under the influence of the governor.[11] Likewise, governors can affect the many details and interpretations that must be decided. State statutes require drivers of vehicles to have a license, but they typically let an agency decide exactly what one must do to get a license, where one can take the tests, and what happens if someone fails a test. Governors can influence these decisions primarily through appointing the heads of state administrative agencies.

One of the methods of limiting gubernatorial power is to curtail appointment authority.[12] Unlike the federal government, for example, states have some major agencies headed by individuals who are elected rather than appointed by the chief executive. Forty-three states, for example, elect their attorney general, a position that is part of the president's Cabinet. The positions of secretary of state, treasurer, and auditor are also usually filled by elected rather than appointed officials. Some states elect their head of education, agriculture, or labor. The movement throughout states to strengthen the institutions of their governments has included increasing the number of senior positions that are filled by gubernatorial appointments so that governors, like heads of major corporations, can assemble their own policy and management teams.

Another position that is filled by presidential appointment in the federal government but, in most cases, elected in state governments is judge. The structure of state courts and how judges are selected will be discussed later in the chapter. This is one more example of approaches that have been taken to restrict the authority of governors.

Nonetheless, governors are major actors in the judicial system. With the legislature, they define what is a crime within a state and attach penalties that should be meted out to those convicted of committing crimes. Once someone has been convicted, they will be institutionalized and/or supervised by an agency that is, in every state, headed by a

Specific issues arise from the grassroots to make their way onto the state and national political agendas. Sentiment among residents of the Mojave Desert town of Needles, California, obviously runs strongly against development of a nuclear waste dump in the Ward Valley, some twenty miles west of town. (Photo courtesy: Reed Saxon/AP/Wide World Photos)

pardon

The authority of a governor to cancel someone's conviction of a crime by a court and to eliminate all sanctions and punishments resulting from the conviction.

commute

The authority of a governor to cancel all or part of the sentence of someone convicted of a crime, while keeping the conviction on the record.

parole

The authority of a governor to release a prisoner before his or her full sentence has been completed and to specify conditions that must be met as part of the release.

extradite

The authority of a governor to send someone against his or her will to another state to face criminal charges.

gubernatorial appointment. Moreover, governors have authority to **pardon** someone who has been convicted, thereby eliminating all penalties and wiping the court action from an individual's record. Governors may also **commute** all or part of a sentence, which leaves the conviction on record even though the penalty is reduced.

In addition, governors grant **parole** to prisoners who have served part of their terms. Typically, governors are advised by a parole board on whether or not to grant a parole. Paroles usually have conditions that must be met, like staying in a certain area, avoiding contact with certain people or organizations, and participating in therapy or a work program. Violation of these conditions could mean a return to prison. Beginning in the mid-1990s, a number of states began eliminating parole and requiring convicts to serve their full sentences. This movement was known as "truth in sentencing."

Finally, under the U.S. Constitution, governors have the discretion to **extradite** individuals. This means that a governor may decide to send someone, against his or her will, to another state to face criminal charges. When Mario Cuomo, who opposed the death penalty, was governor of New York, he refused to extradite someone to a state that used capital punishment. That refusal became an issue in Governor Cuomo's bid for reelection in 1994. Shortly after he was inaugurated, the newly elected governor, George Pataki, ordered the extradition. In fact, with the support of Governor Pataki, New York itself adopted the death penalty.

Gubernatorial participation in the judicial process has led to some of the most colorful controversies in state politics. James E. Ferguson, as governor of Texas, granted 2,253 pardons between 1915 and 1917. His successor, William P. Hobby, granted 1,518 during the next two years, and then Governor Miriam "Ma" Ferguson outdid her husband by issuing almost 3,800 during her term. Texans were used to shady wheeling and dealing in politics, but this volume of pardons seemed a bit excessive. The Texas constitution was amended to remove authority to grant pardons and paroles from the governor; this power was placed in the hands of a board. Governors of the Lone Star State now have the lowest amount of authority among the fifty state chief executives to check actions of the judiciary.[13]

The general trend since the 1960s, as has been noted, has been to increase rather than decrease the power and authority of governors.[14] Given the historic desire to have weak chief executives, some of the enhancement of gubernatorial powers has come at the cost of the prerogatives of other institutions. This is particularly the case with veto

FIGURE 4.1   **Party of State Governors, 2002**
Democrats made gains in the 2002 elections and there is now an even distribution of governors between the two major parties.

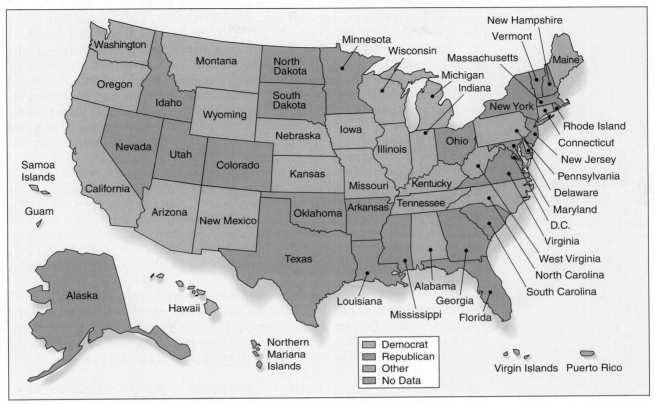

Note: At press time, a recount had been ordered in Alabama.
Source: By author.

authority and the role in the budgetary process. Capacity, however, has both absolute and relative dimensions. Legislatures and courts have also developed into more capable institutions since the 1960s.

State Legislatures

The principles of representative democracy are embodied primarily in the legislature. Legislatures, as mentioned above, were initially established to be the most powerful of the institutions of state government. In over half of the original states, legislatures began without the check of a gubernatorial veto. Until the twentieth century, most state legislatures were responsible for executive chores such as formulating a budget and making administrative appointments.

These tasks were, even more than was envisioned for the U.S. Congress, to be done by "citizen legislators" as a part-time responsibility. The image was that individuals would convene in the state capitol for short periods of time to conduct the state's business. State constitutions and statutes specified the part-time operation of the legislature and provided only limited compensation for those who served.

As mentioned earlier, the one-person, one-vote ruling of the U.S. Supreme Court in *Baker* v. *Carr* (1962) marked a turning point in the history of state legislatures, and state governments generally. Once legislatures more accurately represented their states, agendas became more relevant and policies were more appropriate.[15] State legislatures not only became more representative, they became more professional. Legislators worked more days—some of them full-time. In 1960, only eighteen state legislatures met annually. In 1995, forty-three met every year and only seven every other year. Moreover, the floor sessions were longer, and between sessions legislators and their staff increasingly did committee work and conducted special studies.[16]

Ideally, bills are drafted and votes are cast based on informed evaluations. Along with passing laws, legislatures must monitor and assess the activities of administrative agencies. Legislatures need to consider the many initiatives for policy change that come from agencies. To develop the capacity to provide oversight, conduct analyses, and serve constituents, state legislatures increased their staff by almost 130 percent between 1968 and 1974.[17] Growth since then has been at a rather steady 4 percent rate. Staff resources have been supplemented by the services of the National Conference of State Legislatures, established in 1973, and increasingly by computer technology and information sharing on the Internet. Like Congress, state legislatures have established library reference services and audit agencies to help serve their needs.

All states except Nebraska have two legislative houses. One, the senate, typically has fewer members than the other, usually called the "house" or the "assembly." The most common ratio between the two chambers is 1:3. In fourteen states the ratio is 1:2, and in New Hampshire it is 1:16. Another difference between the two bodies in thirty-four of the states is that senators serve four-year terms, whereas representatives in the larger house serve two-year terms. In eleven states everyone in both houses serves two-year terms, and in the remaining, including Nebraska, everyone serves for four years.

Although it has been common to have limits on how many terms someone may serve as governor, **term limits** for legislators is a development of the 1980s and 1990s. By 2002, sixteen states had measures limiting the number of years one might be a state legislator. In eight states, the limit is eight consecutive years per house. In five states the limit is twelve years, and in the others the number varies with each house and ranges from six to twelve. (See Table 4.1.)

Proponents of term limits included minority party leaders who calculated—sometimes in error—that they stood a better chance of gaining seats if incumbents had to leave after a certain period of time. Others saw term limits as a way of making the ideal

WEB EXPLORATION
To learn about the policy issues being addressed in your state legislature, see
www.ablongman.com/oconnor

term limits
Restrictions that exist in some states about how long an individual may serve in state and/or local elected offices.

TABLE 4.1   States With Term Limits

When each state's term limits affect the House and the Senate:

| | House | | Senate | |
	Takes Effect	Limit (years)	Takes Effect	Limit (years)
Maine	1996	8	1996	8
California	1996	6	1998	8
Colorado	1998	8	1998	8
Arkansas	1998	6	2000	8
Michigan	1998	6	2002	8
Florida	2000	8	2000	8
Missouri1	2002	8	2002	8
Ohio	2000	8	2000	8
South Dakota	2000	8	2000	8
Montana	2000	8	2000	8
Arizona	2000	8	2000	8
Oklahoma	2004	12	2004	12
Nevada	2008	12	2008	12
Utah	2006	12	2006	12
Wyoming	2006	12	2006	12
Louisiana	2007	12	2007	12

[1]Because of special elections, term limits are effective in 1998 for one senator and in 2001 for five House members.
Source: www.ncsl.org/programs/legman/about/states.htm. Reprinted with permission.

of citizen–legislator more probable. They saw intuitive appeal in the concept of having people being a legislator in addition to whatever else they did in life, as opposed to pursuing a career as an elected official.[18]

The movement to limit legislative service is a contrast to the pattern that evolved since the *Baker* v. *Carr* ruling. With an end to rural overrepresentation, state legislatures became relevant and more capable. Urban and economic development issues got serious attention. State budgets included a wider array of programs. The wider scope of state issues, enhanced when the federal government shed some of its responsibilities to the states, attracted individuals seriously interested in public service and required increased staff to help with analysis and evaluation.

State legislatures, although much more capable and serious institutions than they were prior to the early 1960s, are still primarily part-time, citizen bodies.[19] Every election puts new members in about one-fourth of the seats. Only a handful of legislators in each state envision careers as state lawmakers. Those with long-term political aspirations tend to view service in a state chamber as a step on a journey to some other office, in the state capitol or in Washington, D.C. For some, their goal is to don a black robe and preside in a courtroom.

State Courts

Almost everyone is in a courtroom at some point. It may be as a judge, a juror, an attorney, a court officer, or a litigant. It may also be for some administrative function like an adoption, a name change, or the implementation of a will. Few of us will ever be in a federal court; almost all of us will be in a state court.

Longman
Participate.com 2.0
Visual Literacy
**Explaining
Differences in
State Laws**

The primary function of courts is to settle disputes, and most disputes are matters of state, not federal, laws. For the most part, criminal behavior is defined by state legislatures. Family law, dealing with marriage, divorce, adoption, child custody, and the like, is found in state statutes. Contracts, liability, land use, and much that is fundamental to everyday business activity and economic development also are part of state governance.

A common misunderstanding is that the courts in the United States are all part of a single system, with the U.S. Supreme Court at the head. In fact, state and federal courts are separate, with their own rules, procedures, and routes for appeal. The only time state and federal courts converge is when a case involves both federal and state laws or constitutions.

A famous example of overlap between state and federal courts was in 1994, when Los Angeles police officers arrested Rodney King for a traffic violation. An amateur photographer videotaped the arrest and captured shots of the police officers severely beating King. The officers were first tried in California state court for using excessive force. They convinced the jury that King was resisting and thus force was justified. Federal prosecutors nonetheless proceeded to try the officers for violating King's civil rights, a federal crime. In federal court, the jury came to a different conclusion and convicted the officers.

Although the state and federal courts had essentially the same facts, the laws that applied here were somewhat different. The central question posed by state law was whether the police officers used more force than professionally acceptable. The issue focused on professional standards. The federal law centered on racial discrimination and Rodney King's civil rights. Here the racial slurs and jokes made by police officers weighed more heavily and were more relevant than for the state issue of whether excessive force was used.

Sometimes federal and state laws are directly related. If there is a contradiction between the two, then federal law prevails. A state statute that allowed or encouraged racial hiring, for example, would directly conflict with the 1964 federal Civil Rights Act. Through a rule known as **inclusion,** state courts would be obliged to enforce the federal law.

inclusion
The principle that state courts will apply federal laws when those laws directly conflict with the laws of a state.

The issue may be "more or less" rather than "either–or." Since the 1970s, the U.S. Supreme Court has generally taken the position that, especially with regard to individual rights protected in the Constitution, state courts should be encouraged to regard the federal government as setting minimums.[20] If state constitutions and laws provide additional protections or benefits, then state courts should enforce those standards.

State judges must incorporate **common law** as well as federal law into their analyses. Common law begins with the decisions made by judges in England in the thirteenth century; it has evolved with the interpretation and application of those rulings over the years. While some states and communities have made parts of common law into written laws, most of the rulings and rationale remain unwritten. Courts nonetheless are expected to apply traditional common law as they rule on family disputes, disorderly conduct, charges of indecency, and social conflicts in a community. Louisiana used to follow the Napoleonic Code of French tradition, but like other states now subscribes to fundamental edicts of Anglo-American common law and culture.

Another important distinction is between criminal law and civil law. **Criminal law** consists of instances where someone has been killed or injured or has suffered a loss or damage to property. These actions generally involve a victim, but they are considered to be crimes against society. A district attorney or state's attorney, representing society as a whole, prosecutes the alleged criminal. Penalties for those convicted include fines or incarceration or, in some states, death. **Civil law,** on the other hand, involves a dispute between two individuals and/or organizations. At issue may be a verbal or written contract. At stake is usually money. One party typically sues the other for compensation because of damages due to the violation of a contract or agreement. District attorneys or state's attorneys are not involved in civil law cases unless a state agency is suing or being sued.

Like other state government institutions, courts have modernized in the past few decades. Virtually extinct now is the justice of the peace, a judicial position that became part of American lore, humor, and dismay. These were part-time judges. (Some of the ridicule aimed at justices of the peace identified their "other" job as the sheriff!) One might count on a justice of the peace for a quick wedding (or divorce), but rarely for consistent, impartial, well-reasoned rulings.

Many states reorganized their court systems in the 1970s to follow a model that relied on full-time, qualified judges, simplified appeal routes, and enabled state supreme courts to have a manageable workload. Figure 4.2 illustrates the court structure that is now common among the states.

common law
Legal traditions of society that are for the most part unwritten but based on the aggregation of rulings and interpretations of judges beginning in thirteenth-century England.

criminal law
Codes of behavior related to the protection of property and individual safety.

civil law
Codes of behavior related to business and contractual relationships between groups and individuals.

FIGURE 4.2   The Federal, Confederation, and Unitary Systems of Government
Most state courts have the basic organization shown in the figure below.

	Jury or Bench Trials	Jurisdiction	Judges
STATE SUPREME COURT	Bench only	Appeal (limited)	Panel of judges, elected/appointed for fixed term
APPEALS COURTS	Bench only	Appeal (readily granted)	Panel of judges, elected/appointed for fixed term
CIRCUIT OR COUNTY COURTS	Jury and Bench	Original and appeal	One judge per court, elected/appointed for fixed term
MUNICIPAL AND SPECIAL COURTS	Bench only	Original	One judge per court, elected/appointed for fixed term

Most court cases in urban areas begin in a court that specializes in issues like family disputes, traffic, small claims (less than $500 or $1,000), or probate (wills) or in a general jurisdiction municipal court. Small towns and rural areas usually do not have specialized courts. Cases here start in county-level courts that deal with the full array of disputes.

The specialized courts do not use juries. A single judge hears the case and decides. Other courts at this level do have juries if requested by the litigants. A major responsibility of the judges and juries that deliberate on cases when they are originated is to evaluate the credibility of the witnesses and evidence. Although mistakes can be made, judges and jurors have the opportunity to see and consider the demeanor and apparent confidence of witnesses. When cases are heard on appeal, the only individuals making oral presentations are attorneys.

Appellate courts have panels of judges. There are no juries in these courtrooms. An important feature of the court reorganizations of the 1970s is that a court of appeals exists between the circuit or county courts and the state supreme court. This court is to cover part of the state and is supposed to accept all appeals. In part, this appellate level is to allow supreme courts to decide whether or not it will hear a case. The basic principle is that all litigants should have at least one opportunity to appeal a decision. If the state supreme court is the only place where an appeal can be lodged, that court is almost inevitably going to have too heavy a caseload and unreasonable backlogs will develop.

Most state judges are elected to the bench for a specific term. The first states had their legislatures elect judges, and that is still the case in Connecticut, Rhode Island, South Carolina, Vermont, and Virginia. As Table 4.2 shows, in sixteen states, voters

TABLE 4.2   Judicial Selection Patterns

Partisan Election	Nonpartisan Election	
Alabama	Arizona	
Arkansas	California	
Georgia	Florida	
Indiana	Idaho	
Illinois	Kentucky	
Kansas	Michigan	
Louisiana	Minnesota	
Mississippi	Montana	
Missouri	Nevada	
New Mexico	North Dakota	
New York	Ohio	
North Carolina	Oregon	
Pennsylvania	Oklahoma	
Tennessee	South Dakota	
Texas	Washington	
West Virginia	Wisconsin	

Election by Legislature	Appointment by Governor	
Connecticut	Delaware	
Rhode Island	Hawaii	
South Carolina	Maryland	
Vermont	Massachusetts	
Virginia	New Hampshire	
	New Jersey	

Missouri Plan		
Alaska	Iowa	Oklahoma
California	Kansas	Tennessee
Colorado	Missouri	Utah
Indiana	Nebraska	Wyoming

Source: The Book of the States, 2000–2001, pp 137-139. Copyright 2000, The Council of State Governments. Reprinted with permission.

Missouri Plan
A method of selecting judges in which a governor must appoint someone from a list provided by an independent panel. Judges are then kept in office if they get a majority of "yes" votes in general elections.

elect judges and use party identification. Another sixteen use nonpartisan elections. Only six states use gubernatorial appointments. The remaining states follow what is referred to as the **Missouri Plan,** in which the governor, who must select someone from a list prepared by an independent panel, initially appoints judges for a specific term of years. If a judge wishes to serve for an additional term, he or she must receive approval from the voters, who express themselves on a "yes–no" ballot. If a majority of voters cast a "no" ballot, the process starts all over. Five states (California, Kansas, Missouri, Oklahoma, and Tennessee) use the Missouri Plan for some judicial positions and elections for the others.

Elections

Elections are the vehicle for determining who will fill major state government positions and who will direct the institutions of state government. Almost all contests for state government posts are partisan. The major exceptions are judicial elections in many states, as noted above, and the senate in Nebraska's unicameral legislature. Although party labels are not used and political parties are not formally participants in nonpartisan races, the party identity of some candidates may be known and may have some influence.

Political parties have different histories and roles in the various states. The chart in Analyzing the Data: Patterns of Party Competition in State Legislatures shows the trends in how many state legislative seats have been won by Republicans and Democrats. Most states have experienced significant competition between Republicans and Democrats since the Civil War. These states usually have party control split between the two houses of the legislature and the governor's office or have frequent changes in party control of state government. This pattern has applied to Southern sates only once since the 1990s.

The Democratic Party has been dominant in Arkansas, Louisiana, Mississippi, Alabama, and Georgia since 1865. This means Democrats have elected the governor and majorities in both houses of the legislature over 60 percent of the time. The Republican Party has occasionally won the governor's race in some of these states, and there have been small blocs of Republicans in state legislatures. No state has experienced long-term dominance by Republicans similar to the Democratic control of these five states.

States are classified as having "majority party rule" if a single party wins the governorship at least 40 percent of the time and both houses of the legislature over 50 percent of the time. Both parties in these states typically win at least 40 percent of the votes cast. There has been Republican majority rule in only two states, New Hampshire and South Dakota. The states of Hawaii, New Mexico, Texas, Oklahoma, Florida, South Carolina, North Carolina, Kentucky, Rhode Island, and Maryland have had Democratic Party majority rule.

Elections from 1994 through 1997 provided evidence that the Republican Party is acquiring significant, long-term strength that will enhance party competition generally and perhaps lead to stable Republican dominance in some states. Republicans notched impressive victories throughout the country for federal and state offices. They gained control of the U.S. Senate and House of Representatives, won gubernatorial contests in populous states like New York, Texas, California, Florida, Illinois, and Pennsylvania, and secured the majority of seats in more state legislative chambers than ever before captured by the Republican Party. Democrats made somewhat of a comeback in 1998 and won the governor's race in California, but they lost Florida and generally had to concede that Republican gains in the 1990s were based on long-term changes in the political leanings of the population.

One of the reasons for Republican success is that voters in the South who had been voting for conservative Democrats began voting for conservative Republicans. Southerners have supported Republican presidential candidates since the Democratic Party began

WEB EXPLORATION
To understand how campaigns are financed in state governments, see
www.ablongman.com/oconnor

A N A L Y Z I N G   T H E   D A T A

PATTERNS OF PARTY COMPETITION IN STATE LEGISLATURES

This figure presents the trends of the Republican and Democratic Party success in winning seats in state legislatures. From 1938 to 1962, the Democrats won over 90% of state legislative seats in Southern states. In 1998 and 2000, in contrast, the Democratic share dropped below 60%. This regional pattern has affected the national picture. The Democratic dominance nationally from the mid-1950s through the mid-1990s has been transformed into a rather even balance in recent years. While some individual states have large Republican or Democratic majorities, the overall picture nationally is very even and competitive between the two parties.

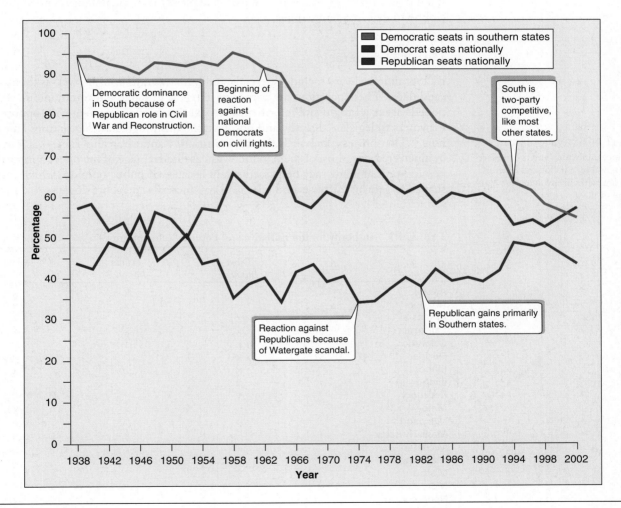

Source: Updated by author.

asserting leadership for civil rights following World War II. Alignment with Republicans in contests for state and congressional positions, however, has been much slower and more the exception than the rule. The 1994 elections may represent a threshold. After the votes were counted, six of the eleven Southern states had Republican governors. Republicans controlled the Florida state legislature and the house in North Carolina and came close in many chambers throughout the South. This pattern, with slight variations, continued through the rest of the decade. In short, Southerners no longer represent a significant minority within the national Democratic Party, but instead are part of the majority within the Republican Party—nationally and regionally.

It is easy to exaggerate the importance of partisanship in state politics. Whether at the state or the national level, the differences between Republicans and Democrats are important but not drastic. While party labels and organizations matter, campaigns are primarily centered on individual candidates. Voters usually have an opportunity to meet face-to-face with those contending for state government offices. A common strategy of candidates is to downplay their party identification, both to emphasize their strengths as an individual and to appeal to independent voters. After the election, party labels are important in determining who is in the majority in the legislature and therefore who will control committees and who will preside. That affects the agenda and the dynamics of policy making, but even here parties typically lack the homogeneity and the discipline to determine outcomes.

Direct Democracy

direct initiative
A process in which voters can place a proposal on a ballot and enact it into law without involving the legislature or the governor.

Ballots almost always include referenda and initiative questions, as well as the names of candidates. These questions are part of governance in states and communities. As mentioned earlier, a Progressive reform meant to weaken parties was to provide opportunities for voters to legislate directly, and not have to go through state legislatures and governors.[21] That process, known as the **direct initiative** and, shown in Table 4.3, is available in nineteen states, most of them in the West. A disadvantage of the direct initiative is the possibility that a law may be passed solely because of public opinion, which might be shaped largely by thirty-second television commercials and short slogans.

TABLE 4.3   Authority for the Initiative and Popular Referendum

State	Direct Initiative	Indirect Initiative	Popular Referendum
Alaska		X	X
Arizona		X	X
Arkansas	X		X
California	X		X
Colorado	X		
Florida	X		
Idaho	X		X
Illinois	X		
Kentucky			X
Maine		X	X
Maryland			X
Massachusetts		X	X
Michigan	X	X	X
Mississippi		X	
Missouri	X		X
Montana	X		X
Nebraska	X		X
Nevada	X	X	X
New Mexico			X
North Dakota	X		X
Ohio	X	X	X
Oklahoma	X		X
Oregon	X		X
South Dakota	X		X
Utah	X	X	X
Washington	X	X	X
Wyoming		X	X

Source: The Book of the States, 2000–2001, p. 211. Copyright 2000, The Council of State Governments. Reprinted with permission from The Book of the States.

POINT / COUNTERPOINT

SHOULD VOTERS BE ABLE TO ENACT LAWS?

Nineteen states—most of them in the West—allow voters to place a proposed law on the ballots for fall and spring elections, a process called direct initiative. If the majority of voters approve, the proposal becomes law without having to go through the legislature or the governor, a process known as direct initiative.

Advocates of direct initiative, such as U.S. Term Limits, Inc., the Public Affairs Research Institute of New Jersey, Philadelphia II, and numerous ad hoc anti-tax groups believe it is the essence of democracy. Historically, this process was established in reaction to political machines, in which bosses controlled the legislature and determined what would become law. Direct initiative is a way to counter the influence of special interest groups and allow the people to act when, for whatever reason, their government doesn't.

Proponents of direct initiative argue that voters are capable of understanding a policy issue, just as they are capable of making decisions about whom they elect. Democracy respects voters and is designed to reflect their will. Most decisions will continue to be made through the legislative process. But direct initiative provides an opportunity for voters to act on issues of major concern and a check on an unresponsive legislature.

Special interests are naturally going to participate in campaigns on initiatives that affect them. Their arguments and information can be valuable to voters as they consider how to cast their ballot. What is different from their involvement in the legislative process and their involvement in initiatives is that the latter is much more visible and direct.

Opponents of direct initiative, such as Common Cause and People for the American Way, believe that, as a representative democracy, we elect individuals to deliberate over the details of public policies and then to make sound, well-informed decisions on our behalf. The issues facing our society are too complex for voters to grasp all the implications. Individuals can vote only "yes" or "no" on a ballot even when the proposal needs to be revised in order to meet the needed objectives, whereas in a legislative body there is an opportunity for debate and amendment.

Special interest groups can influence a popular vote just as effectively as they do a legislature's decision. The National Rifle Association, environmental groups, tobacco companies, pharmaceutical companies, teachers' unions, and the like have spent millions of dollars running political advertisements on television, trying to sway voters about to vote in a direct initiative.

Opponents of direct initiative point out that special interest groups have sponsored direct initiatives when they have been rebuffed in the legislature. They form front organizations that solicit signatures on petitions to get something on the ballot, and they pay professionals a set fee for every signature they get. Then they flood the airwaves with their thirty-second ads, which provide more spin than information.

The Framers valued representative democracy and checks and balances between the major branches of government. The U.S. Constitution does not allow direct initiative at the national level. Opponents of direct initiative argue that some proposals get onto a ballot even if they violate the federal or state constitution, and then the initiative has to be set aside. This illustrates the need for taking good ideas or taking the concerns reflected in initiatives and having them developed and debated in a legislature to ensure that they become good law.

What do you think? Should laws be made through the legislative process or directly by voters?

Go to www.ablongman.com/oconnor

An issue is placed on the ballot by securing enough signatures on a petition. There is no guarantee that those who sign the petition or those who cast votes have considered the issue thoroughly or secured all the relevant evidence. Direct initiatives do not allow for the debate and amendment process available in a legislature. Voters are presented with a simple yes or no question.

Sometimes initiatives are passed and then set aside by courts because they violate the state and/or federal constitution or because the federal government preempts the state. When California, for example, passed Proposition 187 in 1994 denying most public services to unregistered immigrants, federal courts kept the state from

Longman
Participate.com
2.0
Timeline
The Initiative and the Referendum

implementing the law because it trespassed on federal immigration policy and violated the U.S. Constitution.

Debate, deliberation, and amendment are included in the **indirect initiative.** In this process, legislatures first consider the issue and then pass a bill that will become law if approved by the voters. The governor plays no role. Of the eight states that have the indirect initiative, five also have the direct initiative.

Voters in twenty-four states have the opportunity to veto some bills. In these states, voters may circulate a petition objecting to a particular law passed in a recent session of the legislature. If enough signatures are collected, then an item appears on the next statewide ballot, giving the electorate the chance to object and therefore veto the legislation. This is known as a **direct** or **popular referendum.**

All state and local legislative bodies may place an **advisory referendum** on a ballot. As the name implies, this is a device to take the pulse of the voters on a particular issue and has no binding effect. In addition, voter approval is required in a referendum to amend constitutions and, in some cases, to allow a governmental unit to borrow money through issuing bonds.

LOCAL GOVERNMENTS

The institutions and politics of local governance are even more personalized than state governments. In part this is because officials are friends, neighbors, and acquaintances living in the communities they serve. Except in large cities, most elected officials fulfill their responsibilities on a part-time basis. In part, the personal nature of local governance is due to the immediacy of the issues. The responsibilities of local governments include public health and safety in their communities, education of children in the area, jobs and economic vitality, zoning land for particular uses, and assistance to those in need. Local government policies and activities are the stuff of everyday living.

Charters

Romantic notions of democracy in America regard local governments as the building blocks of governance by the people. Alexis de Tocqueville, the critic credited with capturing the essence of early America, described government in the new country as a series of social contracts starting at the grass roots. He said, "the township was organized

---

indirect initiative
A process in which the legislature places a proposal on a ballot and allows voters to enact it into law, without involving the governor or further action by the legislature.

direct (popular) referendum
A process in which voters can veto a bill recently passed in the legislature by placing the issue on a ballot and expressing disapproval.

advisory referendum
A process in which voters cast nonbinding ballots on an issue or proposal.

WEB EXPLORATION
To learn more about the issues currently of concern to local government, see
www.ablongman.com/oconnor

Responsibilities of local governments are wide-ranging—from collecting the garbage in Minneapolis and filling potholes in Buffalo to patrolling the beach at Corpus Christi on spring break. (Photo courtesy: Bob Daemmrich/ Stock Boston, Inc.)

before the county, the county before the state, the state before the union."[22] It sounds good, but it's wrong.

A more accurate description comes from Judge John F. Dillon. In an 1868 ruling, known as **Dillon's Rule,** Dillon proclaimed:

> The true view is this: Municipal corporations owe their origins to and derive their power and rights wholly from the (state) legislature. It breathes into them the breath without which they cannot exist. As it creates, so it may destroy. If it may destroy, it may abridge and control.[23]

Dillon's Rule applies to all types of local governments.

There are many categories of local governments. Some of these are created in a somewhat arbitrary way by state governments. Counties and school districts are good examples. State statutes establish the authority for these jurisdictions, set the boundaries, and determine what these governments may and may not do and how they can generate funds.

Some local governments emerge as people and industries locate together and form a community. These governments must have a **charter** that is acceptable to the state legislature, much as states must have a constitution acceptable to Congress. Charters describe the institutions of government, the processes used to make legally binding decisions, and the scope of issues and services that fall within the jurisdiction of the governmental bodies. There are five basic types of charters:

1. **Special Charters.** Historically, as urban areas emerged, each one developed and sought approval for its own charter. To avoid inconsistencies, most state constitutions now prohibit the granting of special charters.
2. **General Charters.** Some states use a standard charter for all jurisdictions, regardless of size or circumstance.
3. **Classified Charters.** This approach classifies cities according to population and then has a standard charter for each classification.
4. **Optional Charters.** A more recent development is for the state to provide several acceptable charters and then let voters in a community choose from these.
5. **Home Rule Charters.** Increasingly, states are specifying the major requirements that a charter must meet and then allowing communities to draft and amend their own charters. State government must still approve the final product. Every state allows this process except Alabama, Indiana, Illinois, Kentucky, North Carolina, and Virginia.

An important feature of home rule is that the local government is authorized to legislate on any issue that does not conflict with existing state or federal laws. Other approaches list the subjects that a town or city may address.

In the early 1990s, Minnesota, California, and Colorado extended the concept of charters to public schools. They allowed teachers, parents, and/or community leaders to operate a school according to a charter instead of the standard rules and regulations of the state and the school district. To establish a **charter school,** a document would have to be approved that described the administration of the school, its curricula, admission policies, facilities, and general philosophy. States throughout the country have been authorizing charter schools as part of efforts to improve public education. Most states now allow for charter schools.

Types of Local Governments

There are about 87,000 local governments in the United States. Table 4.4 presents the major categories.

1. **Counties.** Every state except Connecticut and Rhode Island has **counties,** although in Louisiana they are called parishes and in Alaska, boroughs. With few exceptions, counties have very broad responsibilities and are used by state

Dillon's Rule
A court ruling that local governments do not have any inherent sovereignty, but instead must be authorized by state government.

charter
A document that, like a constitution, specifies the basic policies, procedures, and institutions of a municipality.

charter school
Public schools sanctioned by a specific agreement that allows the program to operate outside the usual rules and regulations.

county
A geographic district created within a state with a government that has general responsibilities for land, welfare, environment, and, where appropriate, rural service policies.

POLITICS NOW

SCHOOL REFORMS

In 1999 Florida, Ohio, and Wisconsin had new programs that tested the boundaries between church and state. Parents in these states can get public funds to pay tuition at private schools, including religious schools. The intent of these programs is to satisfy a longtime, fundamental responsibility of state governments: to provide a quality educational opportunity to every child. The traditional approach has been to establish public schools where parents, regardless of their income or location, can send their children to school through the twelfth grade for little or no cost, other than the general taxes that they and everyone else pay. Parents who want to send their children to a private school, of course, may do so but must pay whatever extra costs are involved.

Advocates for reform contend that parents should be able to choose the school that best meets the needs of their children and that competition among schools will inevitably lead to higher quality. States like Minnesota, California, and Oregon have provided alternatives within the public schools. These states also allow parents to educate their children at home. Only Florida, Ohio, and Wisconsin have extended the choice to religious schools, contending that the taxpayer money is going to parents, not directly to the schools, so that technically the separation between church and state is maintained. In 2002 the U.S. Supreme Court ruled that this approach is constitutional.

Those opposed to school choice argue that competitive market analogies don't apply when some parents cannot afford the time or money to transport children away from their neighborhood schools, and that attention and resources should be focused on providing good education for everyone. They regard public funds going indirectly to religious schools as a violation of the spirit of the federal and state constitutions, even if it can be argued as technically allowed.

The controversy over what, if any, choices parents should have is fueled by more than differences in philosophies. There is perennial conflict over whether schools should include subjects like sex education or creationism. Parents sometimes get very concerned about the quality of teachers their children have and the approaches taken to learning language and mathematical skills. They recognize how important schools are to the development of their children.

Education politics is typically intense and emotional. The issues of values and taxes are of fundamental importance, and the consequences are often immediate and personal.

---

governments as basic administrative units for welfare and environmental programs, courts, and the registration of land, births, and deaths. County and city boundaries may and do overlap, although state actions have merged city and county in New York, San Francisco, Denver, St. Louis, Nashville, and Honolulu.

2. **Towns.** In the first states and in the Midwest, "town" refers to a form of government in which everyone in a community is invited to an annual meeting to elect officers, adopt ordinances, and pass a budget. Another use of this term is simply to refer to a medium-sized city.

3. **Municipalities.** Villages, towns, and cities are established as **municipalities** and authorized by state governments as individuals congregate and form communities. Some of the most intense struggles among governments within the United States are over the boundaries, scope of authority, and sources of revenue for municipal governments.

4. **Special Districts. Special districts** are the most numerous form of government. A special district is restricted to a particular policy or service area. School districts are the most common form of special district. Others exist for library service, sewerage, water, and parks. Special districts are governed through a variety of structures. Some have elected heads and others, appointed. Some of these jurisdictions levy a fee to generate their revenues, whereas others depend on appropriations from a state, city, or county. A reason for the recent proliferation of special districts is to avoid restrictions on funds faced by municipalities, schools, or other jurisdictions. The creation of a special park district, for example, may enable the park to have its own budget and sources of funding and relieve a city or county treasury.

municipality
A government with general responsibilities, such as a city, town, or village government, that is created in response to the emergence of relatively densely populated areas.

special district
A local government that is responsible for a particular function, such as K–12 education, water, sewerage, or parks.

The reasons that an individual local government was established and given the authority it has are generally sound, but the multiple governments serving the same community and controlling the same area create incredible complexity and confusion. The challenge is to bridge the separation between cities, school districts, counties, and state agencies to effectively address an issue. A specific response to youth violence, for example, may be to provide a youth center and/or skateboard rink for young people in a community to hang out in a safe and healthy setting. Such a project poses questions about which jurisdictions will provide funding and ensure staffing. Land may have to be rezoned and building permits acquired. Will a park district be involved? Will schools count on this facility for after-school programming? What will be the role and approach of the police department? Who will be in charge?

There are examples of formal and informal arrangements among local governments to cooperate and coordinate their work in a single community. Miami and Dade County in Florida have been an early and visible example. The two jurisdictions have merged their public health services, jointly administer parks, operate a unified mass transit system, and together plan for development and land use. Saint Paul and Minneapolis in Minnesota have also pioneered cooperative arrangements. The establishment of the 911 emergency service can be a catalyst for cooperation by various police, fire, and paramedical agencies in a metropolitan area. The norm, however, continues to be conflict and often a failure to even communicate. Local officials and citizens alike find the legacies of past actions creating local governments a serious challenge.

Executives and Legislatures

Except for the traditional New England **town meeting,** where anyone who attends has the authority to vote on policy and management issues, local governments have some or all of the following decision-making offices:

1. Elected executive, like a mayor, village president, or county executive
2. Elected council or commission, like a city council, school board, or county board
3. Appointed manager, like a city manager or school superintendent

Local government institutions are not necessarily bound to the principles of separation of powers or checks and balances that the U.S. Constitution requires of the federal government and most state constitutions require of their governments. School boards, for example, commonly have both legislative and executive authority. They make policies regarding instruction and facilities, and they do the hiring and contracting to

town meeting
Form of local government in which all eligible voters are invited to attend a meeting at which budgets and ordinances are proposed and voted on.

TABLE 4.4   Major Forms of Municipal Government

Population Group	All Cities	Form of Government (Number and Percentage)			
		Mayor–Council	Council–Manager	Commission	Town Meeting[a]
Over 1,000,000	8	6 (75%)	2 (25%)	0 (0%)	0 (0%)
500,000 to 1,000,000	16	13 (81%)	3 (19%)	0 (0%)	0 (0%)
250,000 to 499,999	39	16 (41%)	22 (56%)	1 (3%)	0 (0%)
25,000 to 249,999	1137	407 (36%)	681 (60%)	22 (2%)	27 (2%)
10,000 to 24,999	1602	676 (42%)	751 (47%)	52 (3%)	123 (8%)
2,500 to 9,999	3792	2192 (58%)	1240 (33%)	73 (2%)	287 (8%)
Total (all cities over 2,500)	6594	3310 (50%)	2699 (41%)	148 (2%)	437 (7%)

[a]Includes representative town meeting

Note: The mayor–council form of government is most popular in very large and very small cities. The council–manager form is most popular in medium-sized cities. The commission form continues to lose popularity.

Source: The Municipal Year Book 1993 (Washington, D.C.: International City/County Management Association, 1993), Table 2, p. xi. Reprinted with permission.

One type of informal local government body is the neighborhood association. Whether or not such associations succeed in communicating clearly and resolving their problems is an open question. (Photo courtesy: Kevin Jacobus/The Image Works)

mayor
Chief elected executive of a city.

city council
The legislature in a city government.

political machine
An organization designed to solicit votes from certain neighborhoods or communities for a particular political party in return for services and jobs if that party wins.

manager
A professional executive hired by a city council or county board to manage daily operations and to recommend policy changes.

district-based elections
Elections in which candidates run for an office that represents only the voters of a specific district within the jurisdiction.

at-large elections
Elections in which candidates for office must compete throughout the jurisdiction as a whole.

implement those policies. School board members are, with few exceptions, part-time officials, so they hire superintendents and rely heavily on them for day-to-day management and for new policy ideas. The legislative and executive authority and responsibility, nonetheless, remains with the school board.

The patterns of executive and legislative institutions in local government have their roots in some of the most profound events in our history. The influx of non-English-speaking immigrants into urban areas in the North after the Civil War prompted the growth of political machines.[24] New immigrants needed help getting settled. They naturally got much of that help from ethnic neighborhoods, where, for example, a family from Poland would find people who spoke Polish, restaurants with Polish food, and stores and churches with links to the old country. Politicians dealt with these ethnic neighborhoods. If the neighborhood voted to help provide victory for particular candidates for **mayor** and **city council**, then city jobs and services would be provided. **Political machines** were built on these quid pro quo arrangements. The bosses of those machines were either the elected officials or people who controlled the elected officials.

As part of their efforts to destroy the political machines, Progressives sought reforms that minimized the politics in local government institutions.[25] Progressives favored local governments headed by professional **managers** instead of elected executives. Managers would be appointed by councils, the members of which were elected on a nonpartisan ballot, thus removing the role of parties.

As another way of sapping the strength of ethnic bloc voting, Progressive reformers advocated that council members be elected from the city at large rather than from neighborhood districts. The choice between **district-based** and **at-large elections** now, however, raises concerns about discrimination against Hispanics and African Americans. At-large elections may keep those communities a minority, rather than to divide the city into districts that might have an ethnic group constitute a majority within a district. The at-large elections, in short, have the same minimizing effect on these ethnic groups that was intended by Progressives on white ethnic groups.

As two-term mayor of New York City, Rudy Guiliani lowered the crime rate, improved living standards, and sparred with the city's powerful teachers' union. When terrorists attacked New York City on September 11, 2001, Mayor Guiliani lead the city and the country in mourning the victims and resolving to rebuild. (Photo courtesy: AFP/Corbis)

Progressives argued that the **commission** form of government was an acceptable alternative to mayors and boss politics. The commission evolved as a response to a tidal wave in 1900 that killed over 5,000 people in southern Texas. After the disaster, a group of prominent business leaders in Galveston formed a task force, with each member of the force assuming responsibility for a specific area, such as housing, public safety, and finance. Task force members essentially assumed the roles of both legislators making policy and managers implementing policy. The citizens of Galveston were so impressed with how well this worked that they amended their charter to replace the mayor and city council with a commission, elected at-large and on a nonpartisan basis. The model spread quickly, and by 1917 almost 500 cities had adopted the commission form of government.

As Table 4.4 indicates, half of all U.S. cities have an elected mayor and a council. Mayors differ in how much authority they have. Some are strong and have the power to veto city council action, appoint agency heads, and initiate as well as execute budgets. The charters of other cities do not provide mayors with these formal powers. Except for the largest cities, mayors serve on a part-time basis.

Slightly more than 40 percent of the municipalities have the Progressive model of government, with an appointed, professional manager and an elected city council. This is the most common pattern among medium-sized cities, whereas the very large and the very small have mayors and councils. Some jurisdictions have both mayors and managers.

Only 2 percent of U.S. cities still use the commission form of government. Tulsa, Oklahoma, and Portland, Oregon, are the largest cities run by commissions. Galveston itself is one of the cities that has abandoned this structure.

Over 1,800 of the almost 3,000 county governments are run by boards or councils that are elected from geographic districts and without any executive. Committees of the county board manage personnel, finance, roads, parks, social services, and the like. Almost 400 counties elect an executive as well as a board, and thus follow the mayor–council model. Almost 800 hire a professional manager.

commission
Form of local government in which several officials are elected to top positions that have both legislative and executive responsibilities.

public corpoations (authorities)
Government organizations established to provide a particular service or to run a particular facility that are independent of other city or state agencies and supposed to be operated like a business. Examples include a port authority or a mass transit system.

domestic dependent nation
A type of sovereignty that makes an Indian tribe in the United States outside the authority of state governments but reliant on the federal government for the definition of tribal authority.

WEB EXPLORATION
To learn more about American Indian nations and specific tribes, see
www.ablongman.com/oconnor

compact
A formal, legal agreement between a state and a tribe.

reservation land
Land designated in a treaty that is under the authority of an Indian nation and is exempt from most state laws and taxes.

trust land
Land owned by an Indian nation and designated by the federal Bureau of Indian Affairs as exempt from most state laws and taxes.

School districts, with very few exceptions, follow the council–manager model. Other special districts have boards, sometimes called **public corporations** or **authorities,** that are elected or appointed by elected officials. If the district is responsible for services like water, sewerage, or mass transit, the board is likely to hire and then supervise a manager.

RELATIONS WITH INDIAN NATIONS

Treaties between the federal government and American Indian nations directly affect thirty-four states. Most of these states are west of the Mississippi River, but New York, Michigan, Florida, Connecticut, and Wisconsin are also included. Although the treaties were between two nations, the United States and an American Indian tribal nation, invariably the tribal leaders signed because of actual or threatened military defeat. The legal status of the various tribes in the United States is that of a **domestic dependent nation,** where they retain their individual identity and sovereignty, but must rely on the U.S. federal government for the interpretation and application of treaty provisions. State and local governments are clearly affected by federal–tribal relations but have little influence and virtually no legal authority over these relations.

The policy approach of the federal government toward Indians has varied widely. (See Table 4.5) From 1830 to 1871, a major goal was to move all Indians to land west of the Mississippi. The policy between 1871 to 1934 was to assimilate Indians into the white culture of the United States. From 1934 until 1953 and then again from 1973 to today, the formal policy was to respect tribal customs, strengthen tribal governments, and promote economic self-determination. Between 1953 and 1973, the federal government terminated the legal status of various tribes, ended services to them, and refused to recognize their treaty rights. This generated protests and led to a resumption of the general policy begun in 1934.[26] While some would argue that the federal government has not been serious or effective enough in supporting treaty rights and self-determination, the current policy received new emphasis with the inclusion of tribes in steps to devolve responsibilities from Washington to states and local communities.

States are not parties to the treaties between the United States and American Indian nations and have no direct legal authority over tribes. The federal government has in several specific areas granted some powers to states. The Indian Gaming Regulatory Act of 1988, for example, gives state governments limited authority to negotiate agreements, called **compacts,** with tribes who wish to have casino gambling. Also, in 1953, Congress passed Public Law 280, which allows some states to pursue Indians suspected of criminal behavior even if they are on reservation land.

For the most part, however, federal–tribal relations provide given constraints and opportunities as states and communities engage in planning and problem solving. The two most important features of federal–tribal relations for state and local governments are land rights and treaty provisions for hunting, fishing, and gathering. Tribes have **reservation land** and **trust land,** neither of which is subject to taxation or regulation by state or local governments. The former was designated in the treaty.

TABLE 4.5   Federal Policies Toward Indian Nations

Up to 1830	Mix conquest and coexistence. Make treaties.
1830–1871	Force all tribes west of Mississippi. Make treaties.
1871–1934	Assimilate Indians into white culture.
1934–1953	Respect tribal customs and government. Encourage economic self-determination.
1953–1973	Terminate legal status of tribes. Ignore treaty provisions.
1973–present	Recognize tribes and treaty rights. Encourage constitutions and self-determination.

Tribes can acquire trust land by purchasing or otherwise securing ownership of a parcel and then seeking to have it placed in trust status by the secretary of the Department of the Interior. Since a tribe can get trust land at any time and any place, there is the potential for disruption of a community's development plans or tax base and an obvious challenge to cordial, working relationships between tribes, the federal government, and state or local government.

Hunting, fishing, and gathering activities have important cultural and religious significance for many American Indian nations. Treaty provisions giving rights to tribes to hunt, fish, and gather wild rice or berries on their own land and on public lands and waterways in land they once owned are key to tribal identity and dignity. These treaty rights supersede regulations enacted for environmental and recreational purposes. Non-Indian anglers and hunters sometimes protest that Indians have special privileges. Environmental planners worry about the potential implications of unregulated Indian activity. In 1999, for example, the Makah tribe in the Northwest celebrated the successful capture and killing of a whale. While the tribe applauded the preservation of an important cultural tradition, wildlife advocates bemoaned the treaty rights that allowed this destruction of a valued animal. For some, the discord is more racial in nature than based in real environmental or recreational issues. For the states affected, the challenge is to promote harmony between groups and individuals and to deal effectively with any substantive issues that do materialize.

Since Congress passed the Indian Self-Determination and Education Assistance Act in 1975, the federal government has been trying to strengthen tribal governments by encouraging the adoption of constitutions. The Bureau of Indian Affairs offers assistance in writing the constitutions and other federal agencies, such as the Environmental Protection Agency, are willing to devolve some of their authority to tribes that have constitutions.

While a tribe may include some traditional patterns of governance in their constitutions, the basic concept of a constitution is alien to Indian tribes. The documents read very much like state constitutions, with preambles that espouse principles of democracy and provisions that provide for a familiar separation of powers among executive, legislative, and judicial branches. Not surprisingly, some nations struggle with the mandates of their constitutions and the informal but real power of their traditions.

An advertisement from the Department of the Interior (c.1911) luring individuals to purchase land designated as surplus after tribal allotments were made to Indians. (Photo courtesy: Library of Congress)

FINANCES

State, tribal, and local governments must, of course, have money. Getting that money is one of the most challenging and thankless tasks of public officials. Unique to state and local governments is the requirement to balance budgets. Unlike the federal government, state and local units may not continually spend more money than they have. Unlike private businesses, state and local governments may not spend less money

FIGURE 4.3   State and Local Government Revenues (percentage of total revenues)

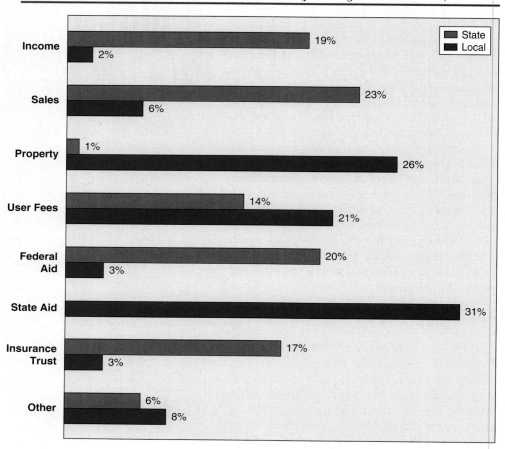

	State	Local
Income	19%	2%
Sales	23%	6%
Property	1%	26%
User Fees	14%	21%
Federal Aid	20%	3%
State Aid		31%
Insurance Trust	17%	3%
Other	6%	8%

In the aftermath of the devastating 1900 hurricane in Galveston, Texas, the commission form of city government came into being. Although Galveston has abandoned the commission form, the model spread quickly, and by 1917 almost 500 cities had adopted the commission form of government. (Photo courtesy: Bettmann/Corbis)

than they have. Whereas the goal of a private business is to have significantly more income than expenses, a governor, mayor, or other local public executive would be criticized for taxing too heavily if something akin to profits appeared on the books.

The budgeting process involves making projections of expenses and revenues. State and local officials face some special uncertainties when they make these guesses. One important factor is the health of the economy. If one is taxing sales or income, those will vary with levels of employment and economic growth. Moreover, the public sector faces double jeopardy when the economy declines. Revenues will go down as sales and incomes decline, and at the same time expenses go up as more families and individuals need assistance during harsh times.

Another important factor affecting state and local government budgets is the level of funding that governments give to one another. States have been getting about one-fourth of their funds from Washington, D.C. That level has varied over time and, especially with the pattern of deficit spending practiced by the federal government, is likely to decline. The amount of the decline will depend as much on political dynamics as it will on the health of the national economy. Local governments do not receive as much, but water and sewerage districts have been getting about 15 percent of their funds from the federal government.

Local governments depend heavily on aid from state governments. The pattern varies from one state to another, but on average, school districts get slightly over half of their funds from state governments, counties get almost one-third, and cities about 20 percent.[27]

Different governments depend on different types of taxes and fees. Figure 4.3 presents the pattern of funding for state and local governments. Unlike the federal government, which relies primarily on the income tax, state governments rely almost equally on income taxes and sales taxes. States differ among themselves, of course.

GLOBAL POLITICS

LOCAL AND PROVINCIAL POLITICS IN COMPARATIVE PERSPECTIVE

The United States has a long tradition of vigorous political activity at the state and local levels. This is not necessarily the case elsewhere. While the relationship between national and local government in the other countries shows a range of variation (in Britain's unitary system, there is no constitutional distinction made between national and local government; in Canada's federal system, local government is directly responsible only to provincial government, not to the federal government in Ottawa), national government and politics often take center stage. Japanese textbooks on politics in that country, for example, include chapters on local autonomy (from national authority) rather than local politics per se. In the centralized political systems of Britain and France, devolution—the decentralization of government authority—has been an important trend in the last two decades, but the national government in each case has retained control over the scope and pace of the changes.

That is not to say that localities play no roles in these countries. Local and provincial governments have often been controlled by the parties out of power at the national level, and elections at the lower levels often act as barometers for upcoming national elections. In France, the far right National Front built up political support at the local level, from which it expanded to national significance in the 1990s. Municipal governments controlled by the National Front have introduced anti-immigrant policies (see Global Politics, chapter 6) that are at odds with

national policy. In the 1999 elections for the newly created Scottish home parliament, the Scottish Nationalist Party, a minor party in the House of Commons, emerged with the second largest number of seats and denied the local Labour Party a majority. Even China is experimenting with elections at the township and county levels, although few experts see this as necessarily leading to competitive elections at the national level. The government's experiment with local competitive elections has been a top-down process in which the central government has tried to stave off further calls for democracy as provincial and local governments take on more responsibilities for economic development.

The provinces and municipalities have also served as centers of citizen political participation. Public opinion polls taken in postwar Japan suggest that citizens tend to identify with local political symbols more than with national ones, including the Parliament. Environmental movements in Europe began as local organizations, and they remain largely that way in Japan. Those movements have often used the local referendum and recall, borrowed from American practice, to try to remove municipal officials or change their policies.

Vigorous local politics is equated with democracy in the United States. In other countries it is often associated with the loss of central government control. Canada, Indonesia, Mexico, and Russia all face territorial independence movements, with armed insurgencies (e.g., in Chiapas and Chechnya) in the latter three.

Alaska, Delaware, Montana, New Hampshire, and Oregon have no sales tax at all, whereas some of the Southern states have a double-digit sales tax. Likewise, Alaska, Florida, Nevada, South Dakota, Texas, Washington, and Wyoming do not tax personal incomes. Tax rates differ among those states that do have an income tax, but the levels are generally less than 10 percent.

Local governments rely primarily on property taxes, have little from levies on sales, and receive virtually nothing from income. Schools, in particular, depend on property taxes for funding. Both local and state governments levy user fees, such as admission to parks, licenses for hunting and fishing, tuition for public universities, and charges based on water use. States, more than local governments, administer retirement systems and insurance programs for public employees. Income from the investment of retirement funds is listed but is not generally available for any use other than paying retirement benefits. Similarly, user fees are typically placed in **segregated funds,** which means they can only be used to provide the service for which the fee was charged. Tuition must, in other words, be used by the university and cannot pay for prison costs or maintaining highways.

Most people accept user fees as the fairest type of taxation. The problem is that the income is both limited and segregated. In general, taxes can be evaluated according to

Longman
Comparative
Comparing State and Local Governments

Longman
Simulation
You Are a Restaurant Owner

segregated funds
Money that comes in from a certain tax or fee and then is restricted to a specific use, such as a gasoline tax that is used for road maintenance.

how much money they can raise, whether the revenue is certain, and who bears the burden. Income taxes generate large sums of money, although there will be variations with how well the economy is doing, how many people are employed, and the like. Of all the taxes, those based on income are the most **progressive taxes,** which means that they are based on the ability to pay.

progressive tax
The level of tax increases with the wealth or ability of an individual or business to pay.

Sales taxes also generate lots of money and they vary with how well the economy is doing. These are not based on earnings, but on purchases. Since those with a low income must spend virtually all that they earn in order to live, sales taxes are **regressive taxes.** To counter the regressive nature of sales taxes, some states exempt food, medicine, and other necessities.

regressive tax
The level of tax increases as the wealth or ability of an individual or business to pay decreases.

The property tax varies with the value of one's property, not one's current income or spending. Thus farmers and those with a fixed income, like retired persons, might bear more of a burden than their current wealth suggests they should carry. The property tax can be a good revenue earner and is stable, since a jurisdiction can set a tax rate that virtually guarantees a certain level of revenue, regardless of economic trends. The local officials who set these rates invariably hear complaints about the regressive, arbitrary nature of property taxes.

Continuity &Change

Increased Role of State, Local, and Tribal Governments

By design, state governments initially were weak. In response to the colonial experience, the founders established governments that were very limited in their powers, responsibilities, and abilities. Governors and the executive branch were especially limited. Likewise, governance at the local level was minimal. Officials were part-time, concerns were few, and funds were low. The federal government controlled Indian nations and gave them very little authority to make their own decisions. Tribes found themselves at the receiving end of federal policies that changed drastically, ranging from neglect to assimilation to some forms of self-determination.

The limitations of state, local, and tribal governments became a major problem as technological and economic developments made American society increasingly complex. Crises emerged in the middle of the twentieth century as urban areas emerged and basic government services were lacking. State legislatures commonly had more representatives from rural areas than from urban areas, and city issues got low priority on agendas. Finally, in a 1962 case, the U.S. Supreme Court declared that states had to adhere to the principle of one-person, one-vote and allocate legislative seats according to population. That decision, *Baker* v. *Carr,* marked a threshold. People had a more effective voice and demanded that their state and local governments develop the capacity to address major concerns and issues. On a parallel track, the federal government adopted a policy of promoting more self-governance for the Indian nations.

Subnational units of government today are considerably more competent and more responsive than their predecessors. The governments that provide the services that affect us most directly and regularly have more capable people and more efficient processes than they have ever had before. Although most state, local, and tribal elected officials are still part-time, increasingly professional, full-time staff serves them. Governments run by our neighbors, friends, and co-workers tend to be more accessible and more responsive to our needs.

The challenges of the future rest with reconciling the traditions of desiring a limited government and avoiding high taxes with the demands of a society that is increasingly complex. The federal government has shed much of its responsibilities and many of its programs for local and tribal communities, in part in recognition of the advantages of allowing problem solving by those most directly affected by issues. States, similarly, delegate considerable authority to their local governments. But federal and state funds do not always follow delegation. The health and vitality of local communities will depend greatly on the creativity of their leaders in meeting the challenges of increased responsibilities and limitations on funds.

1. What regulations and services that have affected you during the past week were the responsibilities of state and local government respectively?
2. In what ways can you influence elective and appointed officials in your state and local governments?

Cast Your Vote. What kind of policies, if any, should the federal government impose on state, local, and tribal governments? To cast your vote, go to **www.ablongman.com/oconnor**

SUMMARY

The expectations are that state and local governments are readily accessible to citizens and that they are likely to be responsive to the needs and wishes of a particular community. In this chapter we have examined the changing character of governance at the state and local levels in order to appreciate both the variation and the common patterns in subnational governments. In this chapter we have made the following points:

1. **Evolution of Sate and Local Governments**
   The initial intent was to limit the capacity and scope of state and local governments. That changed with the increased complexity of our society and economy and with the ruling of the U.S. Supreme Court that legislative districts within a state must each have the same number of people. The trend since the 1960s has been for more representative and more professional state and local governments. These jurisdictions and the federal government are forming partnerships with each other and with the private sector to address issues and provide services.

2. **Grassroots Power and Politics**
   Those who wield the most influence over the making and implementation of public policy in a community are not always the ones elected to formal offices. Sometimes power is in the hands of a family, a small number of individuals, or the local media. Whether or not those who are most powerful are the ones in government offices, governance at the grass roots is face-to-face, between neighbors, friends, and former high school classmates.

3. **State Governments**
   State governments have traditionally had primary responsibility for criminal justice, education, public health, and economic development. Recently, state officials have assumed a larger role in welfare and environmental policy. State constitutions, which reflect major historical developments in American society, provide the basic framework of institutions and values in which state governments fulfill their roles. Since the 1960s, these governments have dramatically become more competent, professional, and accessible to the general public.

4. **Local Governments**
   Local governance in the United States is conducted by a myriad collection of almost 87,000 units, most of which are run by part-time officials. These governments range from general jurisdictions covering densely urbanized areas to special districts functioning for a specific, narrow purpose. The forms of local governments also differ. There are town meetings in which all eligible voters in a community gather to conduct business, elected and appointed boards that have both executive and legislative powers, and governments with distinct legislative councils, elected executives, and professional managers. Local politics is frequently nonpartisan, thanks in part to conscious efforts to prevent control by political party machines.

5. **Relations with Indian Nations**
   American Indian nations obviously affect and are affected by state and local governments. But, due to treaty rights and the domestic dependent sovereignty of the tribes, the Indian nations have a special relationship with the federal government. Tribes have important protections from the potential vagaries of state and local governments. Conversely, the special status of the tribes poses challenges to coherent and consistent policies in a community. Currently, the federal government is encouraging tribal governments to move to self-determination economically and politically and to enter into agreements with state and local governments on financial and policy matters.

6. **Finances**
   Funding government is complex. Revenues are hard to project because governments tax personal and business incomes, sales, and property value—none of which governments can control. State, local, and tribal governments also rely heavily on money given to them by other jurisdictions, including the federal government. The challenge is, given these uncertainties and the general hostility toward taxes, to budget for required services and popular programs.

KEY TERMS

advisory referendum, p. 122
at-large elections, p. 126
charter, p. 123
charter school, p. 123
city council, p. 126
civil law, p. 116
commission, p. 127

common law, p. 116
commute, p. 112
compact, p. 128
county, p. 123
criminal law, p. 116
Dillon's Rule, p. 123
direct initiative, p. 120

direct (popular) referendum, p. 122
district-based elections, p. 126
domestic dependent nation, p. 128
extradite, p. 112
governor, p. 110
inclusion, p. 115
indirect initiative, p. 122

line-item veto, p. 110
manager, p. 126
mayor, p. 126
Missouri Plan, p. 118
municipality, p. 124
nonpartisan election, p. 106
one-person, one-vote, p. 105
package or general veto, p. 110

pardon, p. 112
parole, p. 112
political machine, p. 126
Progressive Movement, p. 109
progressive tax, p. 132
public corporations (authorities) p. 128
regressive tax, p. 132

reservation land, p. 128
segregated funds, p. 131
special district, p. 124
state constitutions, p. 107
term limits, p. 114
town meeting p. 125
trust land, p. 128

SELECTED READINGS

Banfield, Edward C. *The Unheavenly City.* Boston: Little, Brown, 1970.

Benjamin, Gerald, and Michael J. Malbin, eds. *Limiting Legislative Terms.* Washington, D.C.: Congressional Quarterly Press, 1992.

Burns, Nancy E. *The Formation of American Local Governments: Private Values in Public Institutions.* New York: Oxford University Press, 1994.

Crenson, Matthew A. *Neighborhood Politics.* Cambridge, Mass.: Harvard University Press, 1983.

Dahl, Robert A. *Who Governs? Democracy and Power in an American City.* New Haven, Conn.: Yale University Press.

Erie, Steven P. *Rainbow's End: Irish Americans and the Dilemmas of Urban Machine Politics, 1840–1985.* Berkeley: University of California Press, 1988.

Erikson, Robert S., Gerald C. Wright, and John P. McIver, *Statehouse Democracy: Public Opinion and Policy in the American States.* Cambridge, England: Cambridge University Press, 1993.

Jewell, Malcolm E., and Marcia Lynn Whicker. *Legislative Leadership in the American States.* Ann Arbor: University of Michigan Press, 1994.

Stone, Clarence N. *Regime Politics: Governing Atlanta, 1946–1988.* Lawrence: University of Kansas Press, 1989.

Woliver, Laura R. *From Outrage to Action: The Politics of Grass-Roots Dissent.* Urbana: University of Illinois Press, 1993.

NOTES

1. Rob Gurwitt, "Rudderless in Hartford," *Governing* (September 2000): 75-78.

2. Peter K. Eisinger, *The Rise of the Entrepreneurial State* (Madison: University of Wisconsin Press, 1988).

3. Raymond Wolfinger, "Reputation and Reality in the Study of Community Power," *American Sociological Review* 25 (October 1960), 636–44; Nelson Polsby, *Community Power and Political Theory* (New Haven, Conn.: Yale University Press, 1963); and Robert E. Agger, Daniel Goldrich, and Bert Swanson, *The Rulers and the Ruled: Political Power and Impotence in American Communities* (New York: Wiley, 1964).

4. Laura R. Woliver, *From Outrage to Action: The Politics of Grass-Roots Dissent* (Urbana: University of Illinois Press, 1993); and Matthew A. Crenson, *Neighborhood Politics* (Cambridge, Mass.: Harvard University Press, 1983).

5. Albert L. Sturm, "The Development of American State Constitutions," *Publius* 12 (Winter 1982): 62–68.

6. Albert L. Kohlmeier. *The Old Northwest as the Keystone of the Arch of the American Federal Union* (Bloomington, Ind.: Principia Press, 1938); and *Pathways to the Old Northwest* (Indianapolis: Indiana Historical Society, 1988).

7. Theodore Clarke Smith, *Parties and Slavery* (New York: Harper and Brothers, 1906); and Arthur Charles Cole, *The Irrepressible Conflict, 1850–1865* (New York: Macmillan, 1934).

8. George E. Mowry, *The Progressive Era, 1900–1920* (Washington, D.C.: American Historical Association, 1972).

9. Janice C. May, "Constitutional Amendment and Revision Revisited," *Publius* 12 (Winter 1982): 153–79.

10. Charles Wiggins, "Executive Vetoes and Legislative Overrides in the American States," *Journal of Politics* 54 (November 1980): 42. Also see Glenn Abney and Thomas Lauth, "The Line-Item Veto in the States," *Public Administration Review* 45 (January/February 1985): 66–79.

11. F. Ted Hebert, Jeffrey L. Brudney, and Deil S. Wright, "Gubernatorial Influence and State Bureaucracy," *American Politics Quarterly* 11 (April 1983): 37–52; and Abney and Lauth, "The Governor as Chief Administrator," *Public Administration Quarterly* 3 (January/February 1983): 40–49.

12. Thad L. Beyle and Robert Dalton, "Appointment Power: Does It Belong to the Governor?" *State Government* 54, (1) (Winter 1981): 6.

13. Leon W. Blevins, *Texas Government in National Perspective* (Englewood Cliffs, N.J.: Prentice-Hall, 1987), 169.

14. James L. Garnett, *Reorganizing State Government: The Executive Branch* (Boulder, Colo.: Westview, 1980, 8 and 9; and Diane Kincaid Blair, "The Gubernatorial Appointment Power: Too Much of a Good Thing?" *State Government* 55 (Summer 1982): 88–91.

15. Timothy O'Rourke, *The Impact of Reapportionment* (New Brunswick, N.J.: Transaction Books, 1980).

16. Alan Rosenthal, *Governors and Legislatures* (Washington, D.C.: Congressional Quarterly Press, 1990); and Malcolm E. Jewell and Marcia Lynn Whicker, *Legislative Leadership in the American States* (Ann Arbor: University of Michigan Press, 1994).

17. Gary T. Clarke and Charles R. Grezlak, "Legislative Staffs Show Improvement," *National Civic Review* 65 (June 1976): 292.

18. Gerald Benjamin and Michael J. Malin, eds. *Limiting Legislative Terms* (Washington, D.C.: Congressional Quarterly Press, 1992).

19. Diana Gordon, "Citizen Legislators—Alive and Well," *State Legislatures* 20 (January 1994): 24–27.

20. Earl M. Maltz, "Federalism and State Court Activism," *Intergovernmental Perspective* (Spring 1987): 23–26.

21. Thomas E. Cronin, *Direct Democracy* (Cambridge, Mass.: Harvard University Press, 1989); and David B. Magleby, *Direct Legislation* (Baltimore, Md.: Johns Hopkins University Press, 1984).

22. Alex de Tocqueville, *Democracy in America,* ed. by Phillips Bradley (New York: Knopf, 1945), 40.

23. *City of Clinton* v. *Cedar Rapids and Missouri River Railroad Co.* (Iowa, 1868).

24. Steven P. Erie, *Rainbow's End: Irish-Americans and the Dilemmas of Urban Machine Politics, 1840–1985* (Berkeley: University of California Press, 1988); Alfred Steinberg, *The Bosses* (New York: New American Library, 1972); Seymour Mandelbaum, *Boss Tweed's New York* (New York: Wiley, 1955); and Milton Rakove, *Don't Make No Waves—Don't Back No Losers: An Insider's Analysis of the Daley Machine* (Bloomington: Indiana University Press, 1975).

25. Samuel P. Hays, "The Politics of Reform in Municipal Government in the Progressive Era," *Pacific Northwest Quarterly* 55 (October 1964): 157–66.

26. Sharon O'Brien, *American Indian Tribal Governments* (Norman: University of Oklahoma Press, 1989), 261–97.

27. U.S. Census Bureau, *Government Finances in 1993–1994* (Washington, D.C.: Government Printing Office, 1994), 12–19.

5 Civil Liberties

In spring 2000, the principal of predominantly African American Highland Springs High School in Virginia entered Liz Armstrong's tenth-grade biology class to announce a "random search."[1] In spite of the cry that went up from the class, the principal and other administrators forced students to empty their pockets, pocketbooks, and backpacks. No weapons or drugs were found.

Armstrong, a nine-year veteran of the classroom, was outraged and promised her students that she would find out more about the school district's search policy as well as contact the American Civil Liberties Union (ACLU) on her students' behalf. The next day she received a letter from the president of the Virginia ACLU informing her that the search was "clearly illegal" because it violated not only the students' Fourth Amendment right to be free from unlawful and unwarranted searches and seizures, but also the guidelines of the Virginia Board of Education regarding student searches. Upon receipt of the letter, Armstrong sent a letter to her principal informing him of the unlawfulness of the search and suggesting how a legal policy could be implemented.

Armstrong was suspended a few days later. She wasn't charged with speaking up for her students; instead, she was charged with violating "effective use of instructional time." How did Armstrong do that? By talking to her students about the search. In May, she was dismissed from her position.

In the wake of the 1999 shootings at Columbine High School in Colorado, many school boards and districts instituted zero-tolerance weapons policies for students and teachers. In spite of federal rulings to the contrary, students often fall prey to overzealous administrators as they attempt to keep order in their schools. This balancing of rights—in this case the right of students to be free from unreasonable searches and seizures, as well as to some expectation of privacy on their persons and their belongings, versus a community's and other students' right to be free from violence and harm in the classroom—points out how relevant the writings of John Locke and Thomas Hobbes are today. While these students were victims of an unlawful search, unless they wish to sue, they have little other recourse.

When the Bill of Rights, which contains many of the most important protections of individual rights, was written, its drafters were not thinking about issues such as abortion, gay rights, physician-assisted suicide, or many of the personal liberties discussed in this chapter. Civil liberties issues often present complex problems. The balancing of civil liberties, especially when competing interests are at stake, is made even more difficult by the nonabsolute nature of most civil liberties. Frequently, courts or policy makers are called on to balance competing interests and rights. As a society, for example, how much infringement on our personal liberties do we want to give the police? Do we want to have different rules for our homes, classrooms, lockers, dorm rooms, or cars? Similarly, as we discuss later in this chapter, policy makers continue to grapple with the scope of free speech rights on the Internet. Should citizens have unfettered discretion to write and print what they want, or should government impose limits? Even Congress's placing of the Starr Report and its graphic discussion of sex in the Oval Office drew critics about what information should be available over the Internet.

In many of the cases discussed in the chapter, there is a conflict between an individual or group of individuals seeking to exercise what they believe to be a right, and the government—local, state, or national—seeking to control the exercise of that right in an attempt to keep order and preserve the rights of others. In others, two liberties are in conflict, such as a physician's and her patients' rights to easy acces to a clinic versus a pro-lifer's liberty to picket that clinic. It generally falls to the judiciary to balance those interests. And, depending on the composition of the Supreme Court and the times, the balance may lean toward civil liberties or toward the power of the government to limit those rights.

In this chapter we explore the various dimensions of civil liberties guarantees contained in the U.S. Constitution and the Bill of Rights. **Civil liberties** are the personal rights and freedoms that the federal government cannot abridge, either by law, constitution, or judicial interpretation. Civil liberties guarantees place limitations on the power of the government to restrain or dictate how individuals act. Thus, when we discuss civil liberties such as those found in the Bill of Rights, we are concerned with limits on what governments can and cannot do. Civil rights, in contrast, refer to the positive actions of the government taken to protect individuals against arbitrary or discriminatory treatment. Civil rights are discussed in chapter 6.

In this chapter we explore the various dimensions of civil liberties guarantees contained in the U.S. Constitution and the Bill of Rights:

- First, we will discuss the *Bill of Rights,* the reasons for its addition to the Constitution, and its eventual application to the states via the incorporation doctrine.
- Second, we will survey the meaning of the *First Amendment's guarantees of freedom of religion.*
- Third, we will discuss the meanings of the *free speech and press guarantees found in the First Amendment.*
- Fourth, we will discuss the *right to keep and bear arms found in the Second Amendment.*
- Fifth, we will analyze the reasons for many of the *criminal defendants' rights* found in the Bill of Rights and how those rights have been expanded and contracted by the U.S. Supreme Court.
- Sixth, we will discuss the meaning of the *right to privacy* and how that concept has been interpreted by the Court.

civil liberties

The personal rights and freedoms that the federal government cannot abridge by law, constitution, or judicial interpretation.

THE FIRST CONSTITUTIONAL AMENDMENTS: THE BILL OF RIGHTS

In 1787, most state constitutions explicitly protected a variety of personal liberties: speech, religion, freedom from unreasonable searches and seizures, trial by jury, and

WEB EXPLORATION
To view an original copy of the Bill of Rights, see
www.ablongman.com/oconnor

more. It was clear that the new Constitution would redistribute power in the new federal system between the national government and the states. Without an explicit guarantee of specific civil liberties, could the national government be trusted to uphold the freedoms already granted to citizens by their states?

Recognition of the increased power that would be held by the new national government led Anti-Federalists to stress the need for a bill of rights. Anti-Federalists and many others were confident that they could control the actions of their own state legislators, but didn't trust the national government to be so protective of their civil liberties.

The notion of adding a bill of rights to the Constitution was not a popular one at the Constitutional Convention. When George Mason of Virginia proposed that such a bill be added to the preface of the proposed Constitution, for example, his resolution was defeated unanimously.[2] In the subsequent ratification debates, Federalists argued that a bill of rights was unnecessary. Not only did most state constitutions already contain those protections, Federalists believed it was foolhardy to list things that the national government had no power to do since the proposed Constitution didn't give the national government the power to regulate speech, religion, and the like.

Some Federalists, however, supported the idea. After the Philadelphia convention, for example, James Madison conducted a lively correspondence about the need for a national bill of rights with Thomas Jefferson. Jefferson was far quicker to support such guarantees than was Madison, who continued to doubt their utility because he believed that a list of "protected" rights might suggest that those not enumerated were not protected. Politics soon intervened, however, when Madison found himself in a close race against James Monroe for a seat in the House of Representatives in the First Congress. The district was largely Anti-Federalist. So to garner support, Madison, in an act of political expediency, issued a new series of public letters similar to the earlier *Federalist Papers,* in which he vowed to support a bill of rights.

Once elected to the House, Madison made good on his promise. He became the prime mover and author of the Bill of Rights, although he considered the Congress to have far more important matters to handle and viewed his labors on the Bill of Rights "a nauseous project."[3]

The insistence of Anti-Federalists on a bill of rights, the fact that some states conditioned their ratification of the Constitution on the addition of these guarantees, and the disagreement among Federalists about writing specific liberty guarantees into the Constitution led to prompt congressional action to put an end to further controversy. This was a time when national stability and support for the new government were particularly needed. Thus, in 1789, the proposed Bill of Rights was sent to the states by Congress for ratification, which was finally achieved in 1791.

The **Bill of Rights,** the first ten amendments to the Constitution, contains numerous specific guarantees, including those of free speech, press, and religion (see Appendix II for the full text). The Ninth and Tenth amendments in particular highlight Anti-Federalist fears of a too-powerful national government. The Ninth Amendment, strongly favored by Madison, makes it clear that this special listing of rights does not mean that others don't exist; and the Tenth Amendment simply reiterates that powers not delegated to the national government are reserved to the states or the people.

Bill of Rights
The first ten amendments to the U.S. Constitution, which guarantee specific rights and liberties.

The Incorporation Doctrine: The Bill of Rights Made Applicable to the States

The Bill of Rights was intended to limit the powers of the national government to infringe on the rights and liberties of the citizenry. In *Barron* v. *Baltimore* (1833), the

due process clause
Clause contained in the Fifth and Fourteenth Amendments. Over the years, it has been construed to guarantee to individuals a variety of rights ranging from economic liberty to criminal procedural rights to protection from arbitrary governmental action.

substantive due process
Principle in which the Supreme Court has held that most, but not all, of the specific guarantees in the Bill of Rights limit state and local governments by making those guarantees applicable to the states through the due process clause of the Fourteenth Amendment.

incorporation doctrine
An interpretation of the Constitution that holds that the due process clause of the Fourteenth Amendment requires that state and local governments also guarantee those rights.

Until *Gitlow* v. *New York* (1925), involving Benjamin Gitlow, the executive secretary of the Socialist Party, it was generally thought that the Fourteenth Amendment did not apply the protections of the Bill of Rights to the states. Here Gitlow is shown testifying before the Dies Committee, which was investigating un-American activities. (Photo courtesy: AP/Wide World Photos)

Supreme Court ruled that the federal Bill of Rights limited only the U.S. government and not the states.[4] In 1868, however, the Fourteenth Amendment was added to the U.S. Constitution. Its language suggested the possibility that some or even all of the protections guaranteed in the Bill of Rights might be interpreted to prevent state infringement of those rights. Section 1 of the Fourteenth Amendment reads: "No State shall … deprive any person of life, liberty, or property, without due process of law."

Until nearly the turn of the century, the Supreme Court steadfastly rejected numerous arguments urging it to interpret the **due process clause** found in the Fourteenth Amendment as making various provisions contained in the Bill of Rights applicable to the states. In 1897, however, the Court began to increase its jurisdiction over the states.[5] It began to hold states to a **substantive due process** standard whereby state laws had to be shown to be a valid exercise of the state's power to regulate the health, welfare, or public morals of its citizens. Interferences with state power, however, were rare. As a consequence, states continued to pass sedition laws (laws that made it illegal to speak or write any political criticism that threatened to diminish respect for the government, its laws, or public officials), expecting that the Supreme Court would uphold their constitutional validity. Then, in 1925, all of this changed dramatically. Benjamin Gitlow, a member of the Left Wing Section of the Socialist Party, was convicted of violating a New York law that in language very similar to that of the federal Espionage Act—prohibited the advocacy of the violent overthrow of the government. Gitlow had printed 16,000 copies of a manifesto in which he urged workers to rise up to overthrow the U.S. government. Although Gitlow's conviction was upheld, in *Gitlow* v. *New York* (1925) the Supreme Court noted that the states were not completely free to limit forms of political expression:

> For present purposes we may and do assume that freedom of speech and of the press—which are protected by the First Amendment from abridgement by Congress—are among the *fundamental personal rights and "liberties"* protected by the due process clause of the Fourteenth Amendment from impairment by the states [emphasis added].[6]

Gitlow, with its finding that states could not abridge free speech protections, was the first step in the slow development of the **incorporation doctrine**. After *Gitlow*, it took the Court six more years to "incorporate" another First Amendment freedom—that of the press. *Near* v. *Minnesota* (1931) was the first case in which the Supreme Court found that a state law violated freedom of the press as protected by the First Amendment. Jay Near, the publisher of a weekly Minneapolis newspaper, regularly attacked a variety of groups—African Americans, Catholics, Jews, and labor union leaders. Few escaped his hatred. Near's paper was closed under the authority of a state criminal libel law banning "malicious, scandalous, or defamatory" publications. Near appealed the closing of his paper, and the Supreme Court ruled that "The fact that the liberty of the press may be abused by miscreant purveyors of scandal does not make any the less necessary the immunity of the press from previous restraint."[7]

As revealed in Table 5.1, not all the specific guarantees in the Bill of Rights have been made applicable to the states through the due process clause of the Fourteenth Amendment. Instead, the Court has selectively chosen to limit the rights of states by protecting the rights it considers most fundamental, and thus subject to the Court's most rigorous strict scrutiny review. This process is referred to as *selective incorporation* discussed below.

Selective incorporation requires the states to respect freedoms of press, speech, and assembly among other rights. Other guarantees contained in the Second, Third, and Seventh amendments, such as the right to bear arms, have not been incorporated because the Court has yet to consider them sufficiently fundamental to national notions of liberty and justice.

TABLE 5.1   The Selective Incorporation of the Bill of Rights

Date	Amendment	Right	Case
1925	I.	Speech	*Gitlow* v. *New York*
1931		Press	*Near* v. *Minnesota*
1937		Assembly	*DeJonge* v. *Oregon*
1940		Religion	*Cantwell* v. *Connecticut*
	II.	Right to bear arms	*not incorporated* (Generally, the Supreme Court has upheld reasonable regulations of the right of private citizens to bear arms. Should a tough gun-control law be adopted by a state or local government and a challenge to it be made, a test of incorporation might be presented to the Court in the future.)
	III.	No quartering of soldiers	*not incorporated* (The quartering problem has not recurred since colonial times.)
1949	IV.	Unreasonable searches and seizures	*Wolf* v. *Colorado*
1961		The exclusionary rule	*Mapp* v. *Ohio*
1897	V.	Just compensation	*Chicago, B&O R.R. Co.* v. *Chicago*
1964		Self-incrimination	*Malloy* v. *Hogan*
1969		Double jeopardy	*Benton* v. *Maryland*
		Grand jury indictment	*not incorporated* (The trend in state criminal cases is away from grand juries and toward reliance on the sworn written accusation of the prosecuting attorney.)
1948	VI.	Public trial	*In re Oliver*
1963		Right to counsel	*Gideon* v. *Wainwright*
1965		Confrontation of witnesses	*Pointer* v. *Texas*
1966		Impartial trial	*Parker* v. *Gladden*
1967		Speedy trial	*Klopfer* v. *North Carolina*
1967		Compulsory trial	*Washington* v. *Texas*
1968		Jury trial	*Duncan* v. *Louisiana*
	VII.	Right to jury trial in civil cases	*not incorporated* (While Warren Burger was chief justice, he conducted a campaign to abolish jury trials in civil cases to save time and money, among other reasons.)
1962	VIII.	Freedom from cruel and unusual punishment	*Robinson* v. *California*
		Freedom from excessive fines or bail	*not incorporated*

Selective Incorporation and Fundamental Freedoms

The rationale for **selective incorporation**, the judicial application to the states of only some of the rights enumerated by the Bill of Rights, was set out by the Court in 1937 in its decision in *Palko* v. *Connecticut*.[8] Frank Palko was charged with first-degree murder for killing two Connecticut police officers, found guilty of a lesser charge of second-degree murder, and sentenced to life imprisonment. Connecticut appealed. Palko was retried, found guilty of first-degree murder, and resentenced to death. Palko then appealed his second conviction on the grounds that it violated the Fifth Amendment's prohibition against double jeopardy because the Fifth Amendment had been made applicable to the states by the due process clause of the Fourteenth Amendment.

The Supreme Court upheld Palko's second conviction and the death sentence, thereby choosing not to bind states to the Fifth Amendment's double jeopardy clause. This decision set forth principles that were to guide the Court's interpretation of the incorporation doctrine for the next several decades. Some protections found in the Bill

selective incorporation
A judicial doctrine whereby most but not all of the protections found in the Bill of Rights are made applicable to the states via the Fourteenth Amendment.

of Rights were absorbed into the concept of due process only because they are so fundamental to our notions of liberty and justice that they cannot be denied by the states unless the state can show what is called a compelling reason for the liberties' curtailment. This is a very high burden of proof for the state. Thus abridgment of a fundamental right is not often sustained by the Court. Because the Court concluded that the protection against double jeopardy was *not* a fundamental right, Palko's appeal was rejected and he died in Connecticut's gas chamber one year later. Those rights deemed fundamental are not only those selectively drawn from the Bill of Rights and incorporated into the due process clause of the Fourteenth Amendment to apply to the states. Fundamental rights include not only less than the whole of the Bill of Rights, but more—that is, other unenumerated rights, such as the right to privacy. The term *selective incorporation plus* suggests the reality of those rights recognized as fundamental and thus within the meaning of liberty protected by the due process clause of the Fourteenth Amendment.

WEB EXPLORATION
For groups with opposing views on how the First Amendment should be interpreted, see www.ablongman.com/oconnor

FIRST AMENDMENT GUARANTEES: FREEDOM OF RELIGION

Today, many lawmakers bemoan the absence of religion in the public schools and voice their concerns that America is becoming a godless nation in spite of the fact that nearly 70 percent of all Americans belong to a church or synagogue. Many of the Framers were religious men, but they knew what evils could arise if the new nation was not founded with religious freedom as one of its core ideals. Despite the fact that many colonists had fled Europe primarily to escape religious persecution, most colonies actively persecuted those who did not belong to their predominant religious groups. Pennsylvania, for example, was a Quaker colony. The Congregationalist Church of Massachusetts, a Puritan colony, taxed and harassed those who held other religious beliefs. Nevertheless, the colonists were uniformly outraged in 1774 when the British Parliament passed a law establishing Anglicanism and Roman Catholicism as official religions in the colonies. The First Continental Congress immediately sent a letter of protest announcing its "astonishment that a British Parliament should ever consent to establish . . . a religion [Catholicism] that has deluged [England] in blood and dispersed bigotry, persecution, murder and rebellion through every part of the world."[9]

This distaste for a national church or religion was reflected in the Constitution. Article VI, for example, provides that "no religious Test shall ever be required as a Qualification to any Office or Public Trust under the United States." This simple statement, however, did not reassure those who feared the new Constitution would curtail individual liberty. Thus, the First Amendment to the Constitution was ultimately ratified to lay those fears to rest.

The First Amendment to the Constitution begins, "Congress shall make no law respecting an establishment of religion, or prohibiting the free exercise thereof." This statement sets the boundaries of governmental action. The **establishment clause** ("Congress shall make no law respecting an establishment of religion") directs the national government not to involve itself in religion. It creates, in Thomas Jefferson's words, a "wall of separation" between church and state. The **free exercise clause** ("or prohibiting the free exercise thereof") guarantees citizens that the national government will not interfere with their practice of religion. These guarantees, however, are not absolute. In the mid-1800s, Mormons traditionally practiced and preached polygamy, the taking of multiple wives. In 1879, when it was first called on to interpret the free exercise clause, the Supreme Court upheld the conviction of a Mormon under a federal law barring polygamy. The Court reasoned that to do otherwise would provide constitutional protections to a full range of religious beliefs, including those as extreme as human sacrifice. "Laws are made for the government of actions," noted the Court, "and

establishment clause
The first clause in the First Amendment. It prohibits the national government from establishing a national religion.

free exercise clause
The second clause of the First Amendment. It prohibits the U.S. government from interfering with a citizen's right to practice his or her religion.

while they cannot interfere with mere religious belief and opinions, they may with practices."[10] Later, in 1940, the Supreme Court observed that the First Amendment "embraces two concepts—freedom to believe and freedom to act. The first is absolute, but in the nature of things, the second cannot be. Conduct remains subject to regulation of society."[11]

The Establishment Clause

Over the years, the Court has been divided over how to interpret the establishment clause. Does this clause erect a total wall between church and state, or is some governmental accommodation of religion allowed? While the Supreme Court has upheld the constitutionality of many kinds of church/state entanglements such as public funding to provide sign language interpreters for deaf students in religious schools,[12] the Court has held fast to the rule of strict separation between church and state when issues of prayer in school are involved. In *Engel* v. *Vitale* (1962), the Court first ruled that the recitation in public school classrooms of a twenty-two-word nondenominational prayer drafted by the New Hyde Park, New York, school board was unconstitutional.[13] In 1992, the Court continued its unwillingness to allow prayer in public schools by finding unconstitutional the saying of prayer at a middle school graduation.[14] In 2000, the Court ruled that student-led, student-initiated prayer at high-school football games violated the establishment clause.[15]

The Court has gone back and forth in its effort to come up with a workable way to deal with church/state questions. Since 1980, however, the Supreme Court has appeared more willing to lower the wall between church and state as long as school prayer is not involved. In 1981, for example, the Court ruled unconstitutional a Missouri law prohibiting the use of state university buildings and grounds for "purposes of religious worship," which had been used to ban religious groups from using school facilities.[16]

This decision was taken by many members of Congress as a sign that this principle could be extended to secondary and even primary schools. In 1984, Congress passed the Equal Access Act, which bars public schools from discriminating against groups of students on the basis of "religious, political, philosophical or other content

Before members of various faith-based organizations, President George W. Bush signs a presidential executive order creating the controversial Office of Faith Based Initiatives, which some fear is a lowering of the wall between church and state. (Photo Courtesy: AFP/Corbis.)

Santa Fe (Texas) High School Senior Marian Ward delivers a prayer before a football game. In 2000, the Supreme Court ruled that student-led prayer at high school football games violated the establishment clause. (Photo courtesy Brian K. Diggs/Austin American-Statesman)

of the speech at such meetings." The constitutionality of this law was upheld in 1990 when the Court ruled that a school board's refusal to allow a Christian Bible club to meet in a public high school classroom during a twice-weekly "activity period" violated the act. According to the decision, the primary effect of the act was neither to advance religion nor to excessively entangle government and religion—even though religious meetings would be held on school grounds with a faculty sponsor. The important factor seemed to be that the students had complete choice in their selection of activities with numerous nonreligious options.[17] In 1993, the Court also ruled that religious groups must be allowed to use public schools after hours if that access is also given to other community groups.[18]

Many believed that the 1993 replacement of Justice Byron White by Ruth Bader Ginsburg, a former attorney for the ACLU (see Roots of Government: The American Civil Liberties Union), would halt the trend toward lowering the wall between church and state. But in 1995, the Court signalled that it was willing to lower the wall even further. Ironically, it did so in a case involving Thomas Jefferson's own University of Virginia. In a 5–4 decision, the majority held that the university violated the First Amendment's establishment of religion clause by failing to fund a religious student magazine written by a fundamentalist Christian student group even though it funded similar magazines published by 118 other student groups, some of which were religiously based.[19] In dissent, the importance of this decision was highlighted by Justice David Souter, who noted: "The Court today, for the first time, approves direct funding of core religious activities by an arm of the state."[20]

WEB EXPLORATION

For more information on the *Agostini* v. *Felton* case, see www.ablongman.com/oconnor

In 1997, in *Agostini* v. *Felton,* the Supreme Court okayed a New York program that sent public school teachers into parochial schools during school hours to provide remedial education to disadvantaged students. The Court concluded that this was not an excessive entanglement of church and state and therefore was not a violation of the Establishment clause.[21] Neither is the lending of computers and library materials to parochial schools.[22]

The Free Exercise Clause

The free exercise clause of the First Amendment proclaims that "Congress shall make no law . . . prohibiting the free exercise [of religion]." Although the free exercise clause of the First Amendment guarantees individuals the right to be free from governmental interference in the exercise of their religion, this guarantee, like other First Amendment freedoms, is not absolute. When secular law comes into conflict with

Snake handling, once more common as part of certain fundamentalist Christian religious services, is banned by law in many parts of the South. (Photo courtesy: Bettmann/Corbis)

ROOTS OF GOVERNMENT

THE AMERICAN CIVIL LIBERTIES UNION

The American Civil Liberties Union (ACLU) was created in 1920 by a group that had tried to defend the civil liberties of those who were conscientious objectors to World War I. As the nation's oldest, largest, and premier nonpartisan civil liberties organization, the ACLU works in three major areas of the law: freedom of speech and religion, due process, and equality before the law. It lobbies for legislation affecting these areas and litigates to maintain these rights and liberties.

In its own words, the ACLU "has been a zealous advocate of the First Amendment and has steadfastly opposed government efforts to regulate either free speech or free thought, no matter how well-intentioned those efforts might be."* It regularly brings cases to court or files *amicus curiae*, or friend of the court briefs, in cases in which it is not lead counsel. *Amicus* briefs are a vehicle by which interested parties, usually interest groups or professional associations, can inform the Court of the policy and legal implications of its decision—from, of course, the filing group's perspective.

Over time, the national ACLU or one of its state affiliates (as was the case in our opening vignette) has been involved in one way or another in almost every major civil liberties case discussed in this chapter. It was at the fore of the sedition cases brought in the wake of World War I and was involved in the famous *Scopes* case in 1925, which challenged a Tennessee law that made it a crime to teach evolution. It has represented flag burners, Nazis, and skinheads in its zealous and often unpopular defense of the Bill of Rights. Among some of the major cases it has participated in historically are:

First Amendment rights:

- *Tinker* v. *Des Moines Independent School Board* (1969): Upheld the right of students to wear black armbands in protest of the Vietnam War.

- *Lynch* v. *Donnelly* (1984): In a defeat for the ACLU, the Court held that a city's inclusion of a crèche in its annual Christmas display in a private park did not violate the establishment clause.

Criminal defendant's rights:

- *Mapp* v. *Ohio* (1961): Established that illegally obtained evidence can't be used at trial.
- *Gideon* v. *Wainwright* (1963): Granted indigents the right to counsel.
- *Miranda* v. *Arizona* (1966): Guaranteed all suspects a right to counsel.

Privacy rights:

- *Roe* v. *Wade* and *Doe* v. *Bolton* (1973): Established a woman's right to an abortion.
- *Bowers* v. *Hardwick* (1986): An unsuccessful challenge to Georgia's sodomy law.
- *Planned Parenthood* v. *Casey* (1992): An unsuccessful challenge to Pennsylvania's restrictive abortion regulations.

More recently, it has participated in *Boy Scouts of America* v. *Dale, Stenberg* v. *Carhart* (partial-birth abortion), and *Santa Fe Independent School District* v. *Doe* (student-led prayer at football games), cases discussed in greater detail in this chapter.

---

*Brief Amicus Curiae, *Wisconsin* v. *Mitchell*, October Term, 1992, LEXIS.

---

religious law, the right to exercise one's religious beliefs is often denied—especially if the religious beliefs in question are held by a minority or by an unpopular or "suspicious" religious group. State statutes barring the use of certain illegal drugs, snake handling, and polygamy—all practices of particular religious sects—have been upheld as constitutional when states have shown compelling reasons to regulate these practices. Nonetheless, the Court has made it clear that the free exercise clause requires that a state or the national government remain neutral toward religion.

Many critics of rigid enforcement of such neutrality argue that the government should do what it can to accommodate the religious diversity in our nation. Nevertheless, the Court has interpreted the Constitution to mean that governmental interests can outweigh free exercise rights. In 1990, for example, the Supreme Court ruled that

GLOBAL POLITICS

RELIGIOUS FREEDOM

As we saw in earlier chapters, the First Amendment to the U.S. Constitution was based in an understanding of comparative politics. The Framers had seen what religious intolerance meant in Europe, and furthermore understood the establishment of official religions as a basic violation of civil liberties.

In terms of constitutional guarantees of religious freedom, the United States today resembles many countries. As the table below shows, most countries do not establish a state religion. Until recently, however, Britain's Anglicanism guaranteed the right of Anglican bishops to sit in the House of Lords. Atheism is arguably the state religion of the People's Republic of China.

The Canadian, French, Japanese, and German constitutions all guarantee religious freedom. Reflecting the heavy American involvement in drafting Japan's current constitution, the guarantee of religious freedom in that document closely paraphrases Article I of the American Bill of Rights. Germany's Basic Law goes further than its American counterpart, guaranteeing the right of conscientious objection as part of religious freedom.

How states interact with religious organizations varies across countries. Many do not share the Jeffersonian insistence on a wall of separation between church and state. Many European countries, including Germany, have Christian democratic parties in their parliaments, most of which emerged out of Catholic parties. The German Basic Law, for example, lacks an establishment clause per se. The government subsidizes both the Catholic church and the Lutheran synods within its borders, and citizens may designate a portion of their income taxes for that purpose. While Indonesia's 1945 constitution does not acknowledge a state religion, the national ideology of Pancasila identifies monotheism as a component of national identity, and therefore of national policy. In practice, the state has supported Islamic organizations financially.

New or minority religions often find themselves at the forefront of civil liberties conflicts. The Church of Scientology has repeatedly complained that the German government discriminates against it by denying it official religious status. In France, the state has found itself in conflict with Muslims over a number of issues that touch on the heart of French understandings of national identity. In one case, a problem arose from the practice by some Muslim women of covering their heads when away from home. Muslim girls attending school were faced with expulsion because their head coverings were not part of the prescribed school uniform. What one side viewed as an issue of religious freedom, the other saw simply as a matter of enforcing national education policy.

The Establishment Clause in Comparative Perspective

Country	State Religion	Main Religion
Canada	None	Christianity
China	Atheism	Confucianism
France	None	Christianity (Catholicism)
Germany	None	Christianity
Indonesia	None	Islam
Italy	None	Christianity (Catholicism)
Japan	None	Buddhism, Shinto
Mexico	None	Christianity (Catholicism)
Russia	None	Orthodox Christianity
UK	Christianity (Church of England)	Christianity (Church of England)
USA	**None**	**Christianity**

Source: *L'Atlas Geopolitique et Cultural du Petit Robert des Noms Propres* (Paris: Diccionaires le Robert, 1999), 51.

Longman
Participate.com 2.0
Comparative
Comparing
Civil Liberties

the free exercise clause allowed Oregon to ban the use of sacramental peyote (an illegal hallucinogenic drug) in some Native American tribes' traditional religious services. The focus of the case turned on what standard of review the Court should use. Should the Court use the compelling state interest test? In upholding the state's right to deny unemployment compensation to two workers who had been fired by a private drug rehabilitation clinic because they had ingested an illegal substance, a majority of the Court held that the state did not need to show a compelling interest to limit the free exercise of religion.[23] This decision prompted a dramatic outcry. Congressional response was passage of the Religious Freedom Restoration Act, which reinstated strict scrutiny as the required judicial standard of review to make it harder for states to interfere with how citizens practice their religion. In 1997, however, the Supreme Court ruled that the act was unconstitutional.[24]

In contrast, in 1993, the Supreme Court ruled that members of the Santería Church, an Afro-Cuban religion, had the right to sacrifice animals during religious services. In upholding that practice, the Court ruled that a city ordinance banning such practices was unconstitutionally aimed at the group, thereby denying its members the right to free exercise of their religion.[25]

" TODAY IN SCHOOL WE PRAYED FOR A TAX-CUT. "

(Photo courtesy: Mick Stevens from cartoonbank.com. All rights Reserved.)

Although conflicts between religious beliefs and the government are often difficult to settle, the Court has attempted to walk the fine line between the free exercise and establishment clauses. In the area of free exercise, the Court often has had to confront questions of "What is a god?" and "What is a religious faith?"—questions that theologians have grappled with for centuries. In 1965, for example, in a case involving three men who had been denied conscientious objector deferments during the Vietnam War because they did not subscribe to "traditional" organized religions, the Court ruled unanimously that belief in a supreme being was not essential for recognition as a conscientious objector. Thus the men were entitled to the deferments because their views paralleled those who objected to war and who belonged to traditional religions. In contrast, despite the Court's having ruled that Catholic, Protestant, Jewish, and Buddhist prison inmates must be allowed to hold religious services,[26] in 1987 it ruled that Islamic prisoners could be denied the same right for security reasons.[27]

FIRST AMENDMENT GUARANTEES: FREEDOM OF SPEECH AND PRESS

Today some members of Congress criticize the movie industry and television talk shows, including *Ricki Lake* and *The Jerry Springer Show*, for pandering to the least common denominator of society. Other groups criticize popular performers, especially rap groups, for lyrics that promote violence in general and against women in particular. Despite the distastefulness of some talk show topics or rap lyrics, many civil libertarians have resisted even the suggestion that these things be regulated.

A democracy depends on a free exchange of ideas, and the First Amendment shows that the Framers were well aware of this fact. Historically, one of the most volatile areas of constitutional interpretation has been in the interpretation of the First Amendment's mandate that "Congress shall make no law . . . abridging the freedom of speech, or of the press." Like the establishment and free exercise clauses of the First Amendment, the speech and press clauses have not been interpreted as absolute bans against government regulation.

The popularity of Jerry Springer's nationally syndicated talk show is used by many to underscore declining morals and the need to regulate the airways. (Photo courtesy: Todd Buchanan/Black Star)

In fact, over the years the Court has used a hierarchical approach, with some items getting greater protection than others. Generally, thoughts have received the greatest protection, and actions or deeds the least. Words have come somewhere in the middle, depending on their content and purpose.

In the United States, thoughts are considered beyond the scope of governmental regulation but motives often are considered in assessing the legality of some activities such as hate crimes. Although people may experience a negative reaction for revealing their thoughts, the government has no legal right to punish or sanction Americans for what they think. Words, which stand between thoughts and deeds, are subject to some forms of restraint. Speech that is obscene, libelous (false and causing someone disrepute), or seditious (advocating violent overthrow of the government), or that could incite or cause injury to those to whom it is addressed has been interpreted as not protected by the First Amendment. Often, however, these exceptions to constitutional protection have troubled the Court. What is considered obscene in rural Mississippi, for example, may not offend someone in another part of the nation.

Actions, or deeds, are given the least constitutional protection. Thus actions are subject to the greatest governmental restrictions. For example, you may have a right to shoot a pistol in your back yard, but it is illegal to do so on most city streets. Over the years these competing rights have been balanced by the now classic observation that your "right to swing your arm ends at the tip of my nose."[28]

When the First Amendment was ratified in 1791, it was considered to protect only against **prior restraint** of speech or expression, that is, to guard against the prohibition of speech or publication before the fact. As was the case in Great Britain concerning free speech, the First Amendment was not considered to provide absolute immunity from governmental sanction for what speakers or publishers might say or print. Thus, over the years, the meaning of this amendment's mandate has been subject to thousands of cases seeking judicial interpretation of its meaning.

prior restraint
Government prohibition of speech or publication before the fact, generally held to be in violation of the First Amendment.

Attempts to Limit Speech

Although the Supreme Court has allowed few governmental bans on most types of speech, some forms of expression are not protected. In 1942, the Supreme Court set out the rationale by which it would distinguish between protected and unprotected speech. According to the Court, obscenity, lewdness, libel, and fighting words are not protected by the First Amendment because "such expressions are no essential part of any exposition of ideas, and are of such slight social value as a step to truth that any benefit that may be derived from them is clearly outweighed by the social interest in order and morality."[29]

The Alien and Sedition Acts.   In 1798, soon after passage of the Bill of Rights, a constitutional crisis arose when the Federalist Congress enacted the Alien and Sedition Acts. Designed to ban any political criticism by the growing numbers of Jeffersonian Democratic-Republicans, these acts made publication of "any false, scandalous writing against the government of the United States" a criminal offense. Overtly partisan Federalist judges imposed fines and even jail terms on at least ten Democratic-Republican newspaper editors for allegedly violating the acts. The acts became a major issue in the 1800 presidential election campaign, which led to the election of Thomas Jefferson, a vocal opponent of the acts. He quickly pardoned all who had been convicted under their provisions, and the new Democratic-Republican Congress allowed the acts to expire before the Supreme Court had an opportunity to rule on the constitutionality of these serious infringements of the First Amendment.

Slavery, the Civil War, and Rights Curtailments.   After the public outcry over the Alien and Sedition Acts, the national government largely got out of the business of regulating speech, but in its place the states began to prosecute those who published articles critical of governmental policies. In the 1830s, at the urgings of abolitionists, the publication or dissemination of any positive information about slavery became a punishable offense in the North. In the opposite vein, in the South, supporters of the "peculiar institution" of slavery enacted laws to prohibit publication of any anti-slavery sentiments. Southern postmasters refused to deliver Northern abolitionist papers throughout the South, which amounted to censorship of the mails.

During the Civil War, President Abraham Lincoln effectively suspended the free press provision of the First Amendment (as well as many other sections of the Constitution) and even went so far as to order the arrest of the editors of two New York papers that were critical of him. Far from protesting against these blatant violations of the First Amendment, Congress acceded to them. Right after the war, for example, Congress actually prevented the Supreme Court from issuing a judgment on a case because members feared its decision would be critical of the powers Lincoln had taken on during the war.[30] William McCardle, a Mississippi newspaper editor, had sought to arouse sentiment against Lincoln and the Union occupation. Even though he was a civilian, McCardle was jailed by a military court without having any charges brought against him. He appealed his detainment to the U.S. Supreme Court, arguing that he was being held unlawfully. Congress, fearing that a victory for McCardle would prompt other Confederate newspaper editors to follow his lead, enacted a law barring the Supreme Court from hearing appeals of cases involving convictions for publishing statements critical of the Union. Because Article III of the Constitution gives Congress the power to determine the jurisdiction of the Court, the Court was forced to conclude in *Ex Parte McCardle* (1869) that it had no authority to rule in the matter.

After the Civil War, states also began to prosecute individuals for seditious speech if they uttered or printed statements critical of the government. Between 1890 and 1900, for example, there were more than one hundred state prosecutions for sedition in state courts.[31] Moreover, by the dawn of the twentieth century, public opinion in the United States had become exceedingly hostile to the preachings of groups such as socialists and communists who attempted to appeal to the thousands of new and disheartened immigrants. Groups espousing socialism and communism became the targets of state laws curtailing speech and the written word. By the end of World War I, over thirty states had passed laws to punish seditious speech, and more than 1,900 individuals and over one hundred newspapers had been prosecuted for violations.[32]

Anti-Governmental Speech. The next major national efforts to restrict freedom of speech and the press, however, did not occur until congressional passage of the Espionage Act of 1917. Nearly 2,000 Americans were convicted of violating its various provisions, especially those that made it illegal to urge resistance to the draft and prohibiting the distribution of anti-war leaflets. In 1919, the Supreme Court interpreted the First Amendment to allow Congress to restrict speech that was "of such a nature as to create a clear and present danger that will bring about the substantive evils that Congress has a right to prevent."[33] Under the **clear and present danger test,** which allowed Congress to ban speech that could cause a clear and present danger to society, the circumstances surrounding the incident count, according to the Court. Anti-war leaflets, for example, may be permissible in peacetime, but they pose too much of a danger in wartime to be allowed.

For decades, the Supreme Court wrestled with what constituted a "danger." Finally, in 1969, the Court fashioned a new test for deciding whether certain kinds of speech could be regulated by the government: the **direct incitement test.** Now the government could punish the advocacy of illegal action only if "such advocacy is directed to inciting or producing imminent lawless action and is likely to incite or produce such action."[34] The requirement of "imminent harm" makes it more difficult for the government to punish speech and is consistent with the Framers' notion of the special role played by speech in a democratic society.

Longman
Participate.com 2.0
Timeline
Civil Liberties and National Security

clear and present danger test
Test used by the Supreme Court to draw the line between protected and unprotected speech; the Court looks to see if there is an imminent danger that illegal action would occur in response to the contested speech.

direct incitement test
A test used by the Court that holds that advocacy of illegal action is protected by the First Amendment unless imminent action is intended and likely to occur.

libel
False statements or statements tending to call someone's reputation into disrepute.

slander
Untrue spoken statements that defame the character of a person.

New York Times Co. v. Sullivan **(1964)**
The Supreme Court concluded that "actual malice" must be proved to support a finding of libel against a public figure.

Libel and Slander.   Today, national tabloid newspapers such as the *National Enquirer* and the *Star* boast headlines that cause many to shake their heads in disbelief. How can they get away with it, some may wonder. The Framers were very concerned that the press not be suppressed. The First Amendment works to allow all forms of speech, no matter how libelous. False or libelous statements are not restrained by the courts, yet the Supreme Court has consistently ruled that individuals or the press can be sued after the fact for untrue or libelous statements. **Libel** is a written statement that defames the character of a person. If the statement is spoken, it is **slander.** In many nations—such as Great Britain, for example—it is relatively easy to sue someone for libel. In the United States, however, the standards of proof are much more difficult. A person who believes that he or she has been a victim of libel, for example, must show that the statements made were untrue. Truth is an absolute defense against the charge of libel, no matter how painful or embarrassing the revelations.

It is often more difficult for individuals the Supreme Court considers to be "public persons or public officials" to sue for libel or slander. ***New York Times Co. v. Sullivan*** (1964) was the first major libel case considered by the Supreme Court.[35] An Alabama state court had found the *Times* guilty of libel for printing a full-page advertisement accusing Alabama officials of physically abusing African Americans during various civil rights protests (the ad was paid for by civil rights activists, including former First Lady Eleanor Roosevelt). The Supreme Court overturned the conviction, ruling that a finding of libel against a public official could stand only if there were a showing of "actual malice." Proof that the statements were false or negligent was not sufficient to prove "actual malice." The concept of actual malice (a burden of proof imposed on public officials and public figures suing for defamation and falsity requiring them to prove with clear and convincing evidence that an offending story was published with knowing falsehood or reckless disregard for the truth) can be difficult and confusing. In 1991, the Court directed lower courts to use the phrases "knowledge of falsity" and "reckless disregard of the truth" when giving instructions to juries in libel cases. Given the high degree of proof required, few public officials or public persons have been able to win libel cases.

Obscenity and Pornography.[36]   Although the Supreme Court has allowed few governmental bans on most types of speech, some forms of expression are not protected. In *Chaplinsky* v. *New Hampshire* (1942), the Supreme Court set out the rationale by which it would distinguish between protected and unprotected speech. According to the Court, obscenity, lewdness, libel, and fighting words are not protected by the First Amendment because "such expressions are no essential part of any exposition of ideas, and are of such slight social value as a step to truth that any benefit that may be derived from them is clearly outweighed by the social interest in order and morality."[37]

Through 1957, U.S. courts often based their decisions of what was obscene on an English common-law test that had been set out in 1868: "Whether the tendency of the matter charged as obscenity is to deprive and corrupt those whose minds are open to such immoral influences and into whose hands a publication of this sort might fall."[38]

In *Roth* v. *United States* (1957), the Court abandoned that approach and held that to be considered obscene, the material in question must be "utterly without redeeming social importance," and articulated a new test for obscenity: "whether to the average person, applying contemporary community standards, the dominant theme of the material taken as a whole appeals to the prurient interests."[39] In many ways the *Roth* test brought with it as many problems as it attempted to solve. Throughout the 1950s and 1960s, "prurient" remained hard to define, as the Court struggled to find a standard by which to judge actions or words. Moreover, it was very difficult to prove that a book or movie was "*utterly* without redeeming social value." In general, even some "hardcore" pornography passed muster under the *Roth* test, prompting some to argue that the Court fostered the increase in the number of sexually oriented publications designed to appeal to those living amidst what many called the "sexual revolution."

Richard M. Nixon made the growth in pornography a major issue when he ran for president in 1968, and he pledged to appoint to federal judgeships only those who would uphold "law and order" and stop coddling criminals and purveyors of porn. Once elected president, Nixon made four appointments to the Court, including Chief Justice Warren Burger. In *Miller* v. *California* (1973), the Supreme Court began to formulate rules designed to make it easier for states to regulate obscene materials and to return to communities a greater role in determining what is obscene.[40]

In *Miller* the Court set out a test that redefined obscenity. To determine whether or not material in question was obscene, the justices concluded that a lower court must ask "whether the work depicts or describes, in a patently offensive way, sexual conduct specifically defined by state law." Moreover, courts were to determine "whether the work, taken as a whole, lacks serious literary, artistic, political or scientific value." And in place of the contemporary community standards gauge used in earlier cases, the Court defined community standards to mean local, and not national, standards under the rationale that what is acceptable in Times Square in New York City might not be tolerated in San Antonio, Texas.

Time and contexts clearly have altered the Court's and, indeed, much of America's perceptions of what is obscene. But through the early 1990s, the Court allowed communities greater leeway in drafting statutes to deal with obscenity and, even more important, forms of non-obscene expression. In 1991, for example, the Supreme Court voted 5–4 to allow Indiana to ban totally nude erotic dancing, concluding that its statute did not violate the First Amendment's guarantee of freedom of expression and that it furthered an important or substantial governmental interest (thereby adopting the intermediate standard of review, discussed in detail in Chapter 6).[41]

Congress and Obscenity. While lawmakers have been fairly effective in restricting the sale and distribution of obscene materials, Congress has been particularly concerned with two obscenity and pornography issues: (1) federal funding for the arts; and (2) the distribution of obscenity and pornography on the Internet, which has "embroiled it in constitutional struggles over the proper balance between free expression and the interests of the majority."[42]

In 1990, concern over the use of federal dollars by the National Endowment for the Arts (NEA) for works with controversial religious or sexual themes led to passage of legislation requiring the NEA to "[take] into consideration general standards of decency and respect for the diverse beliefs and values of the American public" when it makes its annual awards. In a challenge brought by several performance artists, the Supreme Court ruled that decency standards could be considered by the arts funder as instructed by Congress.[43]

WEB EXPLORATION
For more information on the NEA, see
www.ablongman.com/oconnor

Congress recently turned to a more difficult task: monitoring the Internet, which some charge has become a vehicle for easy distribution of obscenity and pornography as well as a means for young children to be exposed to these kinds of materials. In 1996, Congress overwhelmingly passed the Telecommunications Reform Act. This act maintained the same ban on obscene material that already applied to the media and criminalized the transmission of "indecent" speech or images to people younger than eighteen years of age. Indecency was defined as any communication that depicts or describes in patently offensive terms any sexual or excretory activities or organs as measured by contemporary community standards. This definition makes no exceptions for materials that have serious literary, artistic, scientific, or other redeeming social value as spelled out in *Miller* v. *California* (1973).

Supporters of the act believed that barring the distribution of certain materials to those under eighteen years of age would protect the act from constitutional challenge.

HIGHLIGHT

POLITICAL SPEECH AND MANDATORY STUDENT FEES

In March 2000, the United States Supreme Court ruled unanimously in *Board of Regents* v. *Southworth* that public universities could charge students a mandatory activity fee that could be used to facilitate extracurricular student political speech so long as the programs are neutral in their application.[a]

Scott Southworth, while a law student at the University of Wisconsin, believed that the university's mandatory fee was a violation of his First Amendment right to free speech. He, along with several other law students, objected that their fees went to fund liberal groups. They particularly objected to the support of eighteen of the 125 various groups on campus that benefited from the mandatory activity, including the Lesbian, Gay, Bisexual, and Transgender Center, the International Socialist Organization, and the campus women's center.[b]

In ruling against Southworth and for the university, the Court underscored the importance of universities being a forum for the free exchange of political and ideological ideas and perspectives. The Southworth case performed that function on the Wisconsin campus even before it was argued before the Supreme Court. A student-led effort called the Southworth Project, for which over a dozen law and journalism students each earned two credits, was begun to make sure that the case was reported on campus in an accurate and sophisticated way. The Southworth Project, said a political science professor, gave "a tremendous boost to the visibility and the thinking process about the

case."[c] In essence, the case made the Constitution and what it means come alive on the Wisconsin campus as students pondered the effects of First Amendment protections on their ability to learn in a university atmosphere.

---

[a]*Board of Regents* v. *Southworth*, 529 U.S. 217 (2000).
[b]"U.S. Court Upholds Student Fees Going to Controversial Groups," *Toronto Star* (March 23, 2000), NEXIS.
[c]Mary Beth Marklein, "Fee Fight Proves a Learning Experience," *USA Today* (November 30, 1999): 8D.

Colleen Jungbluth, front, and other Wisconsin students await a ruling on a First Amendment lawsuit. (Photo courtesy: Tim Dillon/© 2000 *USA Today*. Reprinted with permission)

Nevertheless, the act was immediately challenged by the American Civil Liberties Union. The Supreme Court agreed with the ACLU in finding that Congress violated freedom of speech rights when it tried to limit smut on the Internet.[44] To get around this Supreme Court ruling, Congress enacted the Child Online Protection Act in late 1998. It forced commercial Web site operators to collect a credit card number as proof of age before allowing access to a site that could be considered "harmful to minors" without any sort of screening device that could render the material available only to adults. It also called for fines of up to $150,000 a day per offense as well as jail time. In June 2000, a federal appeals court ruled that the act, which had never been enforced, was unconstitutional. Pending appeals of this decision, many members of Congress are trying to find alternative solutions to this perceived problem, including proposals to cut off money to public libraries and schools that do not block children's access to Internet pornography.

WEB EXPLORATION
For more information on the *National Endowment for the Arts* v. *Finley* and *Reno* v. *ACLU*, see
www.ablongman.com/oconnor

(Photo courtesy: Dana Summers/© Tribune Media Services, Inc. All rights Reserved. Reprinted with permission.)

What Types of Speech Are Protected?

Not only will the Court not tolerate prior restraint of the press, but certain types of speech are protected, including symbolic speech, prior restraint, and hate speech. (See also Highlight: Political Speech and Mandatory Student Fees).

Prior Restraint.   With only a few exceptions, the Court has made it clear that it will not tolerate prior restraint of speech. In 1971, for example, in *New York Times Co.* v. *United States* (1971) (also called the "Pentagon Papers" case), the Supreme Court ruled that the U.S. government could not block the publication of secret Defense Department documents illegally furnished to the *Times* by antiwar activists.[45] In 1976, the Supreme Court went even further, noting that any attempt by the government to prevent expression carried "a 'heavy presumption' against its constitutionality."[46] In a Nebraska case, a trial court issued a "gag order" barring the press from reporting the lurid details of a crime. In balancing the defendant's constitutional right to a fair trial against the press's right to cover a story, the trial judge concluded that the defendant's right carried greater weight. The Supreme Court disagreed, holding the press's right to cover the trial paramount. Still, judges are often allowed to issue gag orders affecting parties to a lawsuit or to limit press coverage of a case.

Symbolic Speech.   In addition to the general protection accorded pure speech, the Supreme Court has extended the reach of the First Amendment to other means of expression often called **symbolic speech**—symbols, signs, and the like—as well as to activities like picketing, sit-ins, and demonstrations. In the words of Justice John Marshall Harlan, these kinds of "speech" are part of the "free trade in ideas."[47]

The Supreme Court first acknowledged that symbolic speech was entitled to First Amendment protection in *Stromberg* v. *California* (1931).[48] There the Court overturned the conviction of the director of a Communist youth camp under a state statute prohibiting the display of a red flag, a symbol of opposition to the U.S. government. In a similar vein, the right of high school students to wear black armbands to protest the Vietnam War was upheld in *Tinker* v. *Des Moines Independent Community School District* (1969).[49]

Burning the American flag has also been held to be a form of protected symbolic speech. In 1989, a sharply divided Supreme Court (5–4) reversed the conviction

Longman
Participate.com
2.0
Visual Literacy
What Speech Is Protected by the Constitution?

symbolic speech
Symbols, signs, and other methods of expression generally also considered to be protected by the First Amendment.

of Gregory Johnson, who had been found guilty of setting fire to an American flag during the 1984 Republican national convention in Dallas.[50] As a result, there was a major public outcry against the Court. President George Bush and numerous members of Congress called for a constitutional amendment to ban flag burning to overturn *Texas* v. *Johnson*. Others, including Justice William J. Brennan Jr. noted that if it had not been for acts like that of Johnson, the United States would never have been created nor would a First Amendment guaranteeing a right to political protest exist.

Instead of a constitutional amendment, Congress passed the Federal Flag Protection Act of 1989, which authorized federal prosecution of anyone who intentionally desecrated a national flag. Those who originally had been arrested burned another flag and were convicted. Their conviction was again overturned by the Supreme Court. As they had in *Johnson,* the justices divided 5–4 in holding that this federal law "suffered from the same fundamental flaw" as had the earlier state law that was declared in violation of the First Amendment.[51] Since that decision Congress has tried several times to pass a constitutional amendment to allow it to ban flag burning. Those efforts, however, have yet to be successful.

Hate Speech.　"As a thumbnail summary of the last two or three decades of speech issues in the Supreme Court," wrote the eminent First Amendment scholar Harry Kalven Jr. in 1966, "we may come to see the Negro as winning back for us the freedoms the Communists seemed to have lost for us."[52] Still, says noted African American scholar Henry Louis Gates Jr., Kalven would be shocked to see the stance that some blacks now take toward the First Amendment, which once protected protests, rallies, and agitation in the 1960s: "The byword among many black activists and black intellectuals is no longer the political imperative to protect free speech; it is the moral imperative to suppress 'hate speech.'"[53]

In the 1990s, a particularly thorny First Amendment area emerged as cities and universities attempted to prohibit what they viewed as offensive hate speech, and Congress moved to ban many forms of offensive speech on the Internet with passage of the Communications Decency Act. Since 1989, for example, hundreds of colleges and universities have banned a variety of forms of speech or conduct that creates or fosters an intimidating, hostile, or offensive environment on campus, such as racial slurs directed at minority groups. Other college codes ban conduct or speech that causes emotional distress.

While many commentators poke fun at what they call the "politically correct," or "PC movement," any possible infringements of constitutional protections are a serious matter. Universities, however, believe that offensive speech, in the wake of rising incidents of racism and anti-Semitism, require drastic measures. A series of court rulings, in fact, have found many state universities' speech codes to be unconstitutional; in contrast, private institutions can ignore public law rulings and enact whatever speech codes they desire. For example, at the University of Michigan in 1990, a student was accused of violating the university's regulation banning speech that stigmatizes individuals for their sexual orientation when he said during a classroom discussion that he considered homosexuality to be a disease treatable with therapy. The university's code was challenged by the American Civil Liberties Union and found unconstitutional by a federal district court. In contrast, at Brown University, a private institution, a student was expelled for shouting anti-Semitic, anti-black, and anti-homosexual obscenities at students in their dorm rooms at 2:00 A.M.

Supporters of speech codes see them as "morally essential" to the resolution of the conflict between civil rights (freedom from harmful stigma) and civil liberties (freedom of speech). Today, many cities and towns are trying to limit hate speech, and PBS has launched the program "Not in Our Town" to help cities and schools stamp out hate speech and make citizens more sensitive to its effects.

THE SECOND AMENDMENT: THE RIGHT TO KEEP AND BEAR ARMS

During colonial times, the English tradition of distrust of standing armies was evident: Most colonies required all white men to keep and bear arms, and all white men in whole sections of the colonies were deputized to defend their settlements against Indians and other European powers. These local militias were viewed as the best way to keep order and liberty.

The Second Amendment was added to the Constitution to ensure that Congress could not pass laws to disarm state militias. This amendment appeased Anti-Federalists, who feared that the new Constitution would cause them to lose the right to "keep and bear arms" as well as an unstated right—the right to revolt against governmental tyranny.

Through the early 1920s, few state statutes were passed to regulate firearms (and generally these laws dealt with the possession of firearms by slaves). The Supreme Court's decision in *Barron* v. *Baltimore* (1833), which limited the application of the Bill of Rights to the actions of Congress alone, prevented federal review of those state laws.[54] Moreover, in *Dred Scott* v. *Sandford* (1857) (see chapter 3), Chief Justice Taney listed the right to own and carry arms as a basic right of citizenship.[55]

In 1934, Congress passed the National Firearms Act in response to the increase in organized crime that occurred in the 1920s and 1930s as a result of Prohibition. The act imposed taxes on automatic weapons (such as machine guns) and sawed-off shotguns. In *United States* v. *Miller* (1939), a unanimous Court upheld the constitutionality of the act by stating that the Second Amendment was intended to protect a citizen's right to own ordinary militia weapons and *not* unregistered sawed-off shotguns, which were at issue in the *Miller* case.[56] *Miller* was the last time the Supreme Court directly addressed the Second Amendment. In *Quilici* v. *Village of Morton Grove* (1983), the Supreme Court refused to review a lower court's ruling upholding the constitutionality of a local ordinance banning handguns against a Second Amendment challenge.[57]

In the aftermath of the assassination attempt on President Ronald Reagan in 1981, many lawmakers called for passage of gun control legislation. At the forefront of that effort was Sarah Brady, the wife of James Brady, the presidential press secretary who was badly wounded and left partially disabled by John Hinckley Jr., President Reagan's assailant. In 1993, her efforts helped to win passage of the so-called Brady Bill, which imposed a federal mandatory five-day waiting period on the purchase of handguns.

In 1994, in spite of extensive lobbying by the powerful National Rifle Association (NRA), Congress passed and President Clinton signed the $30.2-billion Violent Crime Control and Law Enforcement Act. In addition to providing money to states for new prisons and law enforcement officers, the act banned the manufacture, sale, transport, or possession of nineteen different kinds of semi-automatic assault weapons.

In 1997, a sharply divided 5–4 U.S. Supreme Court ruled that the section of the Brady Act requiring state officials to conduct background checks of prospective handgun owners violated principles of state sovereignty.[58]

James and Sarah Brady being applauded for their efforts to win congressional approval of the Brady Bill after it was signed into law by President Clinton. (Photo courtesy: John Ficara/Corbis Sygma)

POINT / COUNTERPOINT

ZERO TOLERANCE V. DUE PROCESS: IS ZERO TOLERANCE TOLERABLE?

Zero tolerance is a policy established under the Reagan administration that originally dealt with adults and drugs and expanded during the late 1980s to include children and drugs as well as weapons violations and disciplinary infractions in schools. Proponents of the policy, such as police officers and the Drug Enforcement Agency, argue that the courts and prosecutors need additional power and prerogatives when dealing with the threat of drug usage and drug trafficking. Since drugs are often the cause of violence both at the societal and domestic level, powerful laws with no loopholes are needed to assure that drug kingpins and criminals are taken off the streets. Opponents of zero tolerance, such as the American Liberties Union (ACLU) and many Parent Teacher Associations (PTAs), argue that zero tolerance has taken away common sense and the discretion of judges and school administrators to look at extenuating circumstances and has led to some gross injustices and violations of civil liberties. Let's examine these points of view.

Because drugs are so often cited as the number one problem facing America, proponents of zero tolerance believe that drug use and trafficking are strongly related to violence and child abuse and constitute an enormous cost for society. The White House Office of Drug Policy promotes zero tolerance policies regarding the use of illegal drugs, alcohol, and tobacco within the family, school, workplace, and community. According to President Bill Clinton in his 1999 National Drug Control Strategy message to Congress, the threat of drugs costs our nation more than 14,000 lives and billions of dollars each year. In addition, since drug dealing is so lucrative, drug kingpins can afford the best lawyers. Zero tolerance laws make it easier to convict drug lords because there are no loopholes or room for negotiation—there is literally zero tolerance. Further, proponents argue this policy helps avoid litigation because it is evenhanded and cannot be manipulated by lawyers or judges. In essence, the problem of drugs is considered so severe that it merits special treatment.

In response to shooting in public schools, a 1994 federal law expanded zero tolerance to include guns in schools, while some districts adopted zero tolerance policies for sexual harassment as well. Proponents of zero tolerance argue that the safety of students in the public schools is para-

mount and the only way to get a handle on escalating school violence is through a virtually automatic policy: You get caught and the punishment is severe. Therefore, zero tolerance has a strong deterrent effect. The goal is to provide a safe learning environment for children in schools.

Opponents of zero tolerance argue that the policy allows no extenuating circumstances or common sense in drug and other cases. This policy allows the government to take away your property, search your car, and ignore your civil liberties, including the right to know the charges against you and the right to a hearing if drugs are suspected. There are countless stories about students being suspended or expelled from school for bringing a butter knife to school to cut brownies, having Midol in their backpack, and using water pistols. In one case, officials sought to suspend a six-year-old for kissing another child. Outside the classroom, there are numerous cases of the government confiscating large quantities of cash and luxury items such as yachts for the possession of an ounce of marijuana or suspicion of a drug-related crime.

Those opposed to zero tolerance argue that our basic civil liberties such as due process of law, established in the Fourth, Fifth, and Fourteenth Amendments, are so fundamental that the threat of drugs and weapons should not cause these rights to be trampled over. Zero tolerance also ignores the ideas of innocent until proven guilty and having the punishment fit the crime, while denying discretion and abdicating the responsibility of judges, school administrators, congressional representatives, and others. Opponents argue that lumping all possible cases together under a single rubric is mindless, thoughtless, unjust, and inflexible. It takes time to deal with problems on a case-by-case basis, but our personal liberties are so important that we must make time because if one innocent person is destroyed through a zero tolerance policy, all of our liberties are at stake. As Thomas Jefferson once said, "A society that will trade a little liberty for a little order will lose both, and deserve neither."

 What do you think? Should we enforce zero tolerance or not?
Go to www.ablongman. com/oconnor

The background check provision, while important, is not critical to the overall goals of the Brady Act because a federal record-checking system went into effect in late 1998. School shootings in Littleton, Colorado, Conyers, Georgia, and elsewhere heightened interest in gun control legislation.

The May 2000 Million Mom March was an attempt to highlight support for additional gun control measures, but by the November 2000 elections, gun control no longer appeared to be a key issue for many. By 2002, the Million Mom March was a thing of the past and the Republican-controlled Congress is not likely to favor further gun restrictions.

THE RIGHTS OF CRIMINAL DEFENDANTS

The Fourth, Fifth, Sixth, and Eighth Amendments provide a variety of procedural guarantees (often called **due process rights**) for those accused of crimes. Particular amendments, as well as other portions of the Constitution, specifically provide procedural guarantees to protect individuals accused of crimes at all stages of the criminal justice process. As is the case with the First Amendment, many of these rights have been interpreted by the Supreme Court to apply to the states.

due process rights
Procedural guarantees provided by the Fourth, Fifth, Sixth, and Eighth Amendments for those accused of crimes.

In interpreting the amendments dealing with what are frequently termed "criminal rights," the courts have to grapple not only with the meaning of the amendments, but also with how their protections are to be implemented. The Eighth Amendment, for example, prohibits "cruel and unusual punishments." The question of what is cruel and unusual, however, has vexed the Supreme Court for years. In 1972, in *Furman* v. *Georgia*, for example, the Supreme Court—by a vote of 5–4—for the first time struck down the death penalty under the cruel and unusual punishments clause of the Eighth Amendment.[59] Three justices for the majority concluded that the death penalty was imposed in an arbitrary and random pattern, and that this randomness was cruel and unusual. Two justices said it was always a violation. This decision sent the states back to the drawing boards to draft new, nonarbitrary death penalty laws. In 1976, the Court upheld Georgia's new, more specific standards and in 1999, thirty-eight states had capital punishment statutes.[60]

Today a more conservative Court routinely allows executions to be carried out. Perhaps even more than in the area of First Amendment guarantees, prevailing thoughts about the rights of criminal defendants are changing quickly and dramatically not only as the public becomes more intolerant of crime but as more conservative and moderate justices have been appointed to the Supreme Court, causing it to move away from what some view as the "excesses" of the Warren Court (1953–1969).

Over the years, many individuals criticized the liberal Warren Court's rulings, arguing that its rulings gave criminals more "rights" than their victims. The Warren Court made several provisions of the Bill of Rights dealing with the rights of criminal defendants applicable to the states through the Fourteenth Amendment. It is important to remember that most procedural guarantees apply to individuals *charged* with crimes, that is, before they have been tried. These rights were designed to protect those wrongfully accused, although, of course, they often have helped the guilty. But as Justice William O. Douglas once noted, "Respecting the dignity even of the least worthy citizen . . . raises the stature of all of us."[61]

Many continue to argue, however, that only the guilty are helped by the American system and that criminals should not go unpunished because of simple police error. The dilemma of balancing the rights of the individual against those of society permeates the entire debate, and often even judicial interpretations of the rights of criminal defendants.

The Fourth Amendment and Searches and Seizures

The Fourth Amendment to the Constitution declares:

> The right of the people to be secure in their persons, houses, papers, and effects, against unreasonable searches and seizures, shall not be violated, and no Warrants shall issue, but upon probable cause, supported by Oath or affirmation, and particularly describing the place to be searched, and the persons or things to be seized.

Rosie O'Donnell on stage at the "Million Mom March" May 14, 2000 in Washington, D.C. Tens of thousands of mothers, many accompanied by children and husbands, rallied in sight of the Capitol to demand strict control of handguns while memorializing loved ones and strangers killed by bullets. (Photo courtesy: Michael Smith/Liason Newsmakers/Online USA).

This amendment's purpose was to deny the national government the authority to make general searches. The English Parliament had often issued general "writs of assistance" that allowed such searches. These general warrants were often used against religious and political dissenters, a practice the Framers wanted banned in the new nation. But still, the language that they chose left numerous questions to be answered, including, what is an "unreasonable" search?

Over the years, in a number of decisions, the Supreme Court has interpreted the Fourth Amendment to allow the police to search:

1. The person arrested;
2. Things in plain view of the accused person; and
3. Places or things that the arrested person could touch or reach or are otherwise in the arrestee's "immediate control."

In 1995, the Court also resolved a decades-old constitutional dispute by ruling unanimously that police must knock and announce their presence before entering a house or apartment to execute a search. But, said the Court, there may be "reasonable" exceptions to the rule to account for the likelihood of violence or the imminent destruction of evidence.[62]

Warrantless searches often occur if police suspect that someone is committing or is about to commit a crime. In these situations, police may "stop and frisk" the individual under suspicion. In 1989, the Court ruled that there need be only a "reasonable suspicion" for stopping a suspect—a much lower standard than "probable cause."[63] Thus, a suspected drug courier may be stopped for brief questioning but only a frisk search (for weapons) is permitted. The answers to these questions may shift "reasonable suspicion" to "probable cause," thus permitting the officer to search. But except at international borders (or international airports), a *search* requires probable cause.

Searches can also be made without a warrant if consent is obtained, and the Court has ruled that consent can be given by a variety of persons. It has ruled, for example, that police can search a bedroom occupied by two persons as long as they have the consent of one of them.[64]

In situations where no arrest occurs, police must obtain search warrants from a "neutral and detached magistrate" prior to conducting more extensive searches of houses, cars, offices, or any other place where an individual would reasonably have some expectation of privacy.[65] Police can't get search warrants, for example, to require you to undergo surgery to remove a bullet that might be used to incriminate you, since your expectation of bodily privacy outweighs the need for evidence.[66] But courts don't require search warrants in possible drunk driving situations. Thus, the police can require you to take a Breathalyzer test to determine whether you have been drinking in excess of legal limits.[67]

Homes, too, are presumed to be private. Firefighters can enter your home to fight a fire without a warrant. But if they decide to investigate the cause of the fire, they must obtain a warrant before their reentry.[68] In contrast, under the "open fields doctrine" first articulated by the Supreme Court in 1924,[69] if you own a field, and even if you post "No Trespassing" signs, the police can search your field without a warrant to see if you are illegally growing marijuana, because you cannot reasonably expect privacy in an open field.

Cars have proven problematic for police and the courts because of their mobile nature. As noted by Chief Justice William Howard Taft as early as 1925, "the vehicle can quickly be moved out of the locality or jurisdiction in which the warrant must be sought."[70] Over the years the Court has become increasingly lenient about the scope of automobile searches. Today, even the belongings of automobile passengers can be searched without probable cause.

Drug Testing and DNA Sampling.   Testing for drugs has become an especially thorny search-and-seizure issue. If the government can require you to take a Breathalyzer test, can it require you to be tested for drugs? In the wake of growing public concern over drug use, in 1986 President Ronald Reagan signed an executive order requiring many federal employees to undergo drug tests. In 1997, Congress passed a similar law authorizing random drug searches of all congressional employees.

While many private employers and professional athletic organizations routinely require drug tests upon application or as a condition of employment, governmental requirements present constitutional questions about the scope of permissible searches and seizures. In 1989, the Supreme Court ruled that mandatory drug and alcohol testing of employees involved in accidents was constitutional.[71] And in 1995 the Court upheld the constitutionality of random drug testing of public high school athletes.[72]

But in *Chandler* v. *Miller* (1997), the U.S. Supreme Court refused to allow Georgia to require all candidates for state office to pass a urinalysis drug test thirty days before qualifying for nomination or election, concluding that its law violated the search-and-seizure clause.[73] In general, all employers can require pre-employment drug screening. Since the Supreme Court has ruled that drug tests are "searches" for the purposes of the Fourth Amendment, public employees enjoy more protections in this area than do employees of private enterprises.[74]

WEB EXPLORATION For more information on *Chandler* v. *Miller*, see www.ablongman.com/oconnor

The Fifth Amendment and Self-Incrimination

The Fifth Amendment provides that "No person shall be . . . compelled in any criminal case to be a witness against himself." "Taking the Fifth" is shorthand for exercising one's constitutional right not to self-incriminate. The Supreme Court has interpreted this guarantee to be "as broad as the mischief against which it seeks to guard,"[75] finding that criminal defendants do not have to take the stand at trial to answer questions, nor can a judge make mention of their failure to do so as evidence of guilt. Moreover, lawyers cannot imply that a defendant who refuses to take the stand must be guilty or have something to hide.

Use of "Voluntary" Confessions.   This right not to incriminate oneself also means that prosecutors cannot use as evidence in a trial any of a defendant's statements or confessions that were not "voluntary." As is the case in many areas of the law, however, judicial interpretation of the term "voluntary" has changed over time.

In earlier times, it was not unusual for police to beat defendants to obtain their confessions. In 1936, however, the Supreme Court ruled convictions for murder based solely on confessions given after physical beatings unconstitutional.[76] Police then began to resort to other measures to force confessions. Defendants, for example, were "given the third degree"—questioned for hours on end with no sleep or food, or threatened with physical violence until they were mentally "beaten" into a confession. In other situations family members were threatened. In one case a young mother was told that her welfare benefits would be terminated and her children taken away from her if she failed to talk.[77]

Miranda v. *Arizona* (1966) was the Supreme Court's response to these creative efforts to obtain confessions that were not truly voluntary. On March 3, 1963, an eighteen-year-old girl was kidnapped and raped on the outskirts of Phoenix, Arizona. Ten days later police arrested Ernesto Miranda, a poor, mentally disturbed man with a ninth-grade education. In a police-station lineup, the victim identified Miranda as her attacker. Police then took Miranda to a separate room and questioned him for two hours. At first he denied guilt. Eventually, however, he confessed to the crime and wrote and signed a brief statement describing the crime and admitting his guilt. At no time was he told that he did not have to answer any questions or that he could be represented by an attorney.

After Miranda's conviction, his case was appealed on the grounds that his Fifth Amendment right not to incriminate himself had been violated because his confession had been coerced. Writing for the Court, Chief Justice Earl Warren, himself a former district attorney and California state attorney general, noted that because police have a

Miranda v. *Arizona* (1966)
A landmark Supreme Court ruling that held the Fifth Amendment requires that individuals arrested for a crime must be advised of their right to remain silent and to have counsel present.

Even though Ernesto Miranda's confession was not admitted as evidence at his retrial, his ex-girlfriend's testimony and that of the victim were enough to convince the jury of his guilt. He served nine years in prison before he was released on parole. After his release, he routinely sold autographed cards inscribed with the Miranda rights now read to all suspects. In 1976, four years after his release, *Miranda* was stabbed to death in Phoenix in a bar fight during a card game. Two *Miranda* cards were found on his body, and the person who killed him was read his *Miranda* rights upon his arrest.
(Photo courtesy: Paul S. Howell/Liaison Agency/Getty Source)

tremendous advantage in any interrogation situation, criminal suspects must be given greater protection. A confession obtained in the manner of Miranda's was not truly voluntary; thus it was inadmissible at trial.

To provide guidelines for police to implement *Miranda,* the Court mandated that:

> Prior to any questioning, the person must be warned that he has a right to remain silent, that any statements he does make may be used as evidence against him, and that he has a right to the presence of an attorney, either retained or appointed.

Miranda rights

Statements that must be made by the police informing a suspect of his or her constitutional rights protected by the Fifth Amendment, including the right to an attorney provided by the court if the suspect cannot afford one.

In response to this mandate from the Court, police routinely began to read suspects their **Miranda rights,** a practice you undoubtedly have seen repeated over and over in movies and TV police dramas.

Although the Burger Court did not enforce the reading of *Miranda* rights as vehemently as had the Warren Court, Chief Justice Warren Burger, Warren's successor, acknowledged that they had become an integral part of established police procedures.[78] The Rehnquist Court, however, has been more tolerant of the use of coerced confessions and has employed a much more flexible standard to allow their admissibility. In 1991, for example, it ruled that the use of a coerced confession in a criminal trial does not automatically invalidate a conviction if its admission is deemed a "harmless error," that is, if the other evidence is sufficient to convict.[79]

But in 2000, in an opinion written by Chief Justice Rehnquist, the Court reaffirmed the central holding of *Miranda,* ruling that defendants must be read *Miranda* warnings. The Court went on to say, that despite an act of Congress that stipulated that voluntary statements made during custodial interrogations were admissable at trial, without *Miranda* warnings, no admissions could be trusted to be truly voluntary.[80]

The Fourth and Fifth Amendments and the Exclusionary Rule

exclusionary rule

Judicially created rule that prohibits police from using illegally seized evidence at trial.

In *Weeks* v. *United States* (1914), the U.S. Supreme Court adopted the **exclusionary rule,** which bars the use of illegally seized evidence at trial.[81] Thus, although the Fourth and Fifth Amendments do not prohibit the use of evidence obtained in violation of their provisions, the exclusionary rule is a judicially created remedy to deter constitutional violations. In *Weeks,* for example, the Court reasoned that allowing police and prosecutors to use the "fruits of a poisonous tree" (a tainted search) would only encourage that activity.

The Warren Court resolved the dilemma of balancing the goal of deterring police misconduct against the likelihood that a guilty individual would go free in favor of deterrence. In contrast, the Burger and Rehnquist Courts and, more recently, Congress have gradually chipped away at the exclusionary rule. In 1976, the Burger Court dramatically reduced the opportunities for defendants to appeal their convictions based on tainted evidence in violation of the Fourth Amendment.[82] The Court noted that the exclusionary rule "deflects the truth-finding process and often frees the guilty." Since then, the Court has carved out a variety of limited "good faith exceptions" to the exclusionary rule, allowing the use of "tainted" evidence in a variety of situations, especially when police have a search warrant, and "in good faith" conduct the search on the assumption that the warrant is valid—though it is subsequently found invalid. Since the purpose of the exclusionary rule is to deter police misconduct, and in this situation there is no police misconduct, the courts have permitted the introduction at trial of the seized evidence. Another exception to the exclusionary rule is "inevitable discovery." Evidence illegally seized may be introduced if it would have been discovered anyway in the course of continuing investigation.

The Sixth Amendment and the Right to Counsel

The Sixth Amendment guarantees to an accused person "the Assistance of Counsel in his defense." In the past this provision meant only that an individual could hire an attorney to represent him or her in court. Since most criminal defendants are impoverished, this provision was of little assistance to many who found themselves on trial. Recognizing this, Congress required federal courts to provide an attorney for defendants too poor to afford one. This was first required in capital cases (where the death penalty is a possibility); eventually, attorneys were provided to the poor in all federal criminal cases.[83] In 1932, the Supreme Court directed states to furnish lawyers to defendants in capital cases.[84] It also began to expand the right to counsel to other state offenses, but did so in a piecemeal fashion that gave the states little direction. Given the high cost of providing legal counsel, this ambiguity often made it cost-effective for the states not to provide counsel at all.

These ambiguities came to an end with the Court's decision in *Gideon* v. *Wainwright* (1963).[85] Clarence Earl Gideon, a fifty-one-year-old drifter, was charged with breaking into a Panama City, Florida, pool hall and stealing beer, wine, and some change from a vending machine. At his trial he asked the judge to appoint a lawyer for him because he was too poor to hire one himself. The judge refused, and Gideon was convicted and given a five-year prison term for petty larceny. The case against Gideon had not been strong, but as a layperson unfamiliar with the law and with trial practice and procedure, he was unable to point out its weaknesses.

The apparent inequities in the system that had resulted in Gideon's conviction continued to bother him. Eventually, he borrowed some paper from a prison guard, consulted books in the prison library, and then drafted and mailed to the U.S. Supreme Court a petition asking it to overrule his conviction.

In a unanimous decision, the U.S. Supreme Court agreed with Gideon and his court-appointed lawyer, Abe Fortas, a future associate justice of the Supreme Court. Writing for the Court, Justice Hugo Black explained that "lawyers in criminal courts are necessities, not luxuries." Therefore, the Court concluded, the state must provide an attorney to poor defendants in felony cases. Underscoring the Court's point, Gideon was acquitted when he was retried with a lawyer to argue his case.

In 1972, the Burger Court expanded the *Gideon* rule, holding that "even in prosecutions for offenses less serious than felonies, a fair trial may require the presence of a lawyer."[86] Seven years later, the Court clarified its decision by holding that defendants charged with offenses where imprisonment is authorized but not actually imposed do not have a Sixth Amendment right to counsel.[87] But the right to counsel *is* constitutionally required where any prison or jail term is imposed.

The Sixth Amendment and Jury Trials

The Sixth Amendment (and, to a lesser extent, Article III of the Constitution) provides that a person accused of a crime shall enjoy the right to a speedy and public trial by an impartial jury—that is, a trial in which a group of the accused's peers act as a fact-finding, deliberative body to determine guilt or innocence. It also provides defendants the right to confront witnesses against them. The Supreme Court has held that jury trials must be available if a prison sentence of six or more months is possible.

"Impartiality" is a requirement of jury trials that has undergone significant change, with the method of selecting jurors being the most frequently challenged part of the process. For example, whereas potential individual jurors who have prejudged a case are not eligible to serve, no groups can be systematically excluded from serving. In 1880, for example, the Supreme Court ruled that African Americans could not be excluded from state jury pools (lists of those eligible to serve).[88] And, in 1975, the Court ruled that to bar women from jury service violated the mandate that juries be a "fair cross section" of the community.[89]

In the 1980s the Court expanded the requirement that juries reflect the community by invalidating various indirect means of excluding African Americans. While noting that although lawyers historically had used peremptory challenges to select juries they believed most favorable to the outcome they desired, the use of peremptory challenges specifically to exclude African American jurors violated the equal protection clause of the Fourteenth Amendment.[90] In 1994, the Supreme Court answered the major remaining unanswered question about jury selection: Can lawyers exclude women from juries through their use of peremptory challenges? This question came up frequently because in rape trials and sex discrimination cases, one side or another often finds it advantageous to select jurors on the basis of their sex. The Supreme Court ruled that the equal protection clause prohibits discrimination in jury selection on the basis of gender. Thus lawyers cannot strike all potential male jurors based on the belief that males might be more sympathetic to the arguments of a man charged in a paternity suit, a rape trial, or a domestic violence suit, for example.

The right to confront witnesses at trial is also protected by the Sixth Amendment. In 1990, however, the Supreme Court ruled that this right was not absolute. In *Maryland v. Craig* (1990), the Court ruled that the testimony of a six-year-old alleged child abuse victim via one-way closed circuit television was constitutionally permissible. The clause's central purpose, said the Court, was to ensure the reliability of testimony by subjecting it to rigorous examination in an

When Clarence Earl Gideon wrote out his petition for a writ of *certiorari* to the Supreme Court (asking the Court, in its discretion, to hear his case), he had no way of knowing that his case would lead to the landmark ruling on the right to counsel, *Gideon* v. *Wainwright*. Nor did he know that Chief Justice Earl Warren had actually instructed his law clerks to be on the lookout for a *habeas corpus* petition (literally, "you have the body," which argues that the person in jail is there in violation of some statutory or constitutional right) that could be used to guarantee the assistance of counsel for defendants in criminal cases. (Photo courtesy: The Supreme Court Historical Society)

adversary proceeding.[91] In this case, the child was questioned out of the presence of the defendant, who was in communication with this attorney. The defendant, along with the judge and jury, watched the testimony.

The Eighth Amendment and Cruel and Unusual Punishment

The Eighth Amendment prohibits "cruel and unusual punishments," a concept rooted in the English common-law tradition. In the 1500s, religious heretics and those critical of the Crown were subjected to torture to extract confessions, and then were condemned to an equally hideous death by the rack, disembowelment, or other barbarous means. The English Bill of Rights and its safeguard against "cruel and unusual punishments" was a result of public outrage against those practices. The same language found its way into the U.S. Bill of Rights. Prior to the 1960s, however, little judicial attention was paid to the meaning of that phrase, especially in the context of the death penalty.

The death penalty was in use in all of the colonies at the time the Constitution was adopted, and its constitutionality went unquestioned. In fact, in two separate cases in the late 1800s, the Supreme Court ruled that deaths by public shooting[92] and electrocution were not "cruel and unusual" forms of punishment in the same category as "punishments which inflict torture, such as the rack, the thumbscrew, the iron boot, the stretching of limbs and the like."[93]

In the 1960s, the National Association for the Advancement of Colored People (NAACP) Legal Defense Fund, believing that the death penalty was applied more frequently to African Americans than to members of other groups, orchestrated a carefully designed legal attack on its constitutionality.[94] Public opinion polls revealed that in 1971, on the eve of the NAACP's first major death sentence case to reach the Supreme Court, support for the death penalty had fallen to below 50 percent of the American public. With the timing just right, in *Furman* v. *Georgia* (1972), the Supreme Court effectively put an end to capital punishment, at least in the short run.[95] The Court ruled that because the death penalty was often imposed in an arbitrary manner, it constituted cruel and unusual punishment in violation of the Eighth and Fourteenth Amendments. Following *Furman*, several state legislatures enacted new laws designed to meet the Court's objections to the arbitrary nature of the sentence. In 1976, in *Gregg* v. *Georgia*, Georgia's rewritten death penalty statute was ruled constitutional by the Supreme Court in a 7–2 decision.[96]

Unless the perpetrator of a crime was fifteen years old or younger at the time of the crime, the Supreme Court is currently unwilling to intervene to overrule state courts' imposition of the death penalty. In *McCleskey* v. *Kemp* (1987), a 5–4 Court ruled that imposition of the death penalty—even when it appeared to discriminate against African Americans—did not violate the equal protection clause.[97] Despite the testimony of social scientists and evidence that Georgia was eleven times more likely

Thousands of demonstrators took to the streets to protest against the death penalty during the 2000 Republican National Convention in Philadelphia. Earlier that year Illinois Republican Governor George Ryan declared a moratorium on executions because of flaws in the justice system. (Photo courtesy: AFP/Corbis)

A N A L Y Z I N G   T H E   D A T A

CAPITAL PUNISHMENT IN THE UNITED STATES

Since capital punishment was reinstated in 1976, over 650 people have been executed, mostly by lethal injection or electrocution. More than half of the accused (55 percent) were white, over a third (36 percent) were black, and almost a tenth were Latino, Native American, or Asian American. Today, over 3,600 inmates are sitting on death row. Of those inmates, 46.2 percent are white, 42.7 percent black, 8.9 percent Latino, 1.2 percent Native American, and 0.8 percent Asian American. The death-row population is overwhelmingly male, with females only accounting for 1.4 percent of inmates awaiting execution. It is also disproportionately African American. Seven states (New Mexico, Kansas, South Dakota, New York, New Hampshire, New Jersey, and Connecticut) have the death penalty but have had no executions.

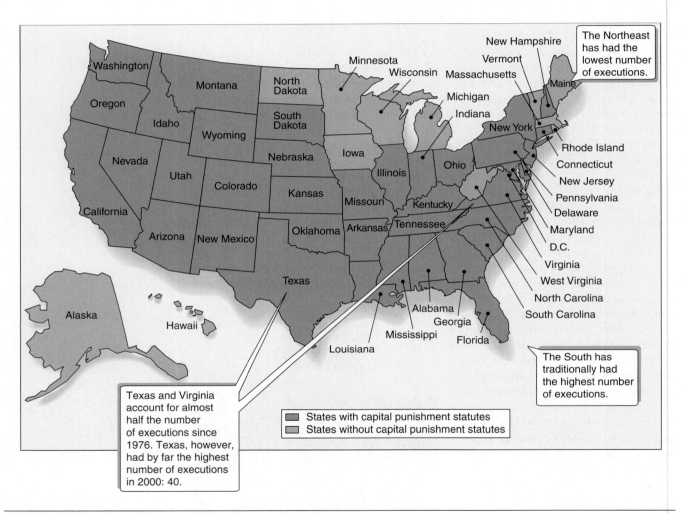

The Northeast has had the lowest number of executions.

Texas and Virginia account for almost half the number of executions since 1976. Texas, however, had by far the highest number of executions in 2000: 40.

The South has traditionally had the highest number of executions.

■ States with capital punishment statutes
■ States without capital punishment statutes

Source: Based on data from www.deathpenaltyinfo.org.

Longman
Participate.com 2.0
Visual Literacy
**Race and the
Death Penalty**

to seek the death penalty against a black defendant, the Court upheld Warren McCleskey's death sentence. It noted that even if statistics show clear discrimination, there must be a showing of racial discrimination in the specific case. Five justices concluded that there was no evidence of specific discrimination against McCleskey proved at his trial. Within hours of that defeat, McCleskey's lawyers filed a new appeal, arguing that the informant who gave the only testimony against McCleskey at trial had been placed in McCleskey's cell illegally.

Four years later McCleskey's death sentence challenge again produced an equally, if not more important, ruling on the death penalty and criminal procedure from the U.S. Supreme Court. In the second *McCleskey* case, *McCleskey* v. *Zant* (1991), the Court found that the issue of the informant should have been raised during the first appeal, in spite of the fact that McCleskey's lawyers were initially told by the state that the witness was not an informer. *McCleskey* v. *Zant* produced new standards designed to make it much more difficult for death-row inmates to file repeated appeals, a practice frequently decried by many of the justices.[98] Ironically, the informant against McCleskey was freed the night before McCleskey was electrocuted. Justice Powell, one of those in the majority, later said (after his retirement) that he regretted his vote and should have voted the other way. By 2000, executions were commonplace in the United States, as highlighted in Politics Now: DNA and the Death Penalty.

THE RIGHT TO PRIVACY

To this point, the rights and freedoms we have discussed have been derived fairly directly from specific guarantees contained in the Bill of Rights. In contrast, the Supreme Court has also given protection to rights not specifically enumerated in the Constitution or Bill of Rights.

There is no mention of a **right to privacy** in either the main body of the Constitution or the Bill of Rights. Nevertheless, as Justice William O. Douglas noted in 1965, the notion of privacy is "older than the Bill of Rights." It is questionable, however, whether the Framers would ever have considered birth control, surrogate motherhood, in vitro fertilization, or euthanasia, all defended under "right to privacy" claims, proper subjects of constitutional protection.

Although the Constitution is silent about the right to privacy, the Bill of Rights contains many indications that the Framers expected that some areas of life were "off limits" to governmental regulation. The right to freedom of religion guaranteed in the First Amendment implies the right to exercise private, personal beliefs. The guarantee against unreasonable searches and seizures contained in the Fourth Amendment similarly implies that persons are to be secure in their homes and should not fear that police will show up at their doorsteps without cause. As early as 1928, Justice Louis Brandeis hailed privacy as "the right to be left alone—the most comprehensive of rights and the right most valued by civilized men."[99] It was not until 1965, however, that the Court attempted to explain the origins of this right.

right to privacy
The right to be let alone; a judicially created doctrine encompassing an individual's decision to use birth control or secure an abortion.

Longman
Participate.com 2.0
Simulation
You Are a
Young Lawyer

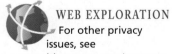
WEB EXPLORATION
For other privacy issues, see
www.ablongman.com/oconnor

Longman
Participate.com 2.0
Participation
Privacy and
Rights of the
Accused

Birth Control

Today most Americans take access to many forms of birth control as a matter of course. Condoms are sold in the grocery store, and some television stations air ads for them. Easy access to birth control, however, wasn't always the case. Many states often barred the sale of contraceptives to minors, prohibited the display of contraceptives, or even banned their sale altogether. One of the last states to do away with these kinds of laws was Connecticut. It outlawed the sale of all forms of birth control and even prohibited

POLITICS NOW

DNA AND THE DEATH PENALTY

On June 15, 2000, Paul Nuncio became the 134th prisoner put to death in Texas since Governor George W. Bush took office in 1995. Texas leads the nation in executions, as highlighted in Analyzing the Data: Capital Punishment in the United States, and Bush was questioned about this fact frequently during his presidential campaign. All during the 2000 campaign, study after study was released calling into question the appropriateness of the death penalty as administered. One study from Columbia University revealed that over two-thirds of all death sentences were overturned on appeal—most because of serious errors on the part of police officers, prosecutors, or low paid, often court-appointed defense attorneys.[a] The national average for overturned cases was 68 percent, and Kentucky led the nation with a 100 percent reversal rate.[b]

In March 2000, the Republican governor of Illinois, George Ryan, ordered a moratorium on all executions. Ryan, a death penalty proponent, was disturbed by new evidence collected by students at Northwestern University as part of a class project that led to the release of thirteen men in his state already on death row. The specter of presiding over an irreversible unjust punishment was just too much for Ryan. In May, the New Hampshire state legislature voted to abolish the death penalty, but that action was vetoed by the state's Democratic governor, Jeanne Shaheen.

Public support for the death penalty—now at 66 percent—is down from its high of 80 percent in 1994, and is actually at its lowest point since 1978, when it was 62 percent.[c] Because DNA evidence now can be used as a double check on guilty verdicts, many are clamoring to allow all of those on death row the opportunity to prove their guilt or innocence once and for all, although some public officials are against this. As people are less worried about crime, and at the same time have greater doubts about the fairness of the criminal justice system in light of several well-publicized cases of inmates proved innocent by DNA evidence, even Republicans in Congress are concerned. Senator Orrin Hatch, for example, introduced legislation in 2000 that would expand an inmate's right to seek DNA testing even if the time for his or her appeals had already expired. Under the Hatch bill, convicts would need to prove that identification was a critical issue at their trial and that DNA results could prove their innocence.

[a]This feature draws heavily from Judy Keen, "Death Penalty Issue Looms over Bush Campaign," *USA Today* (June 16, 2000): 17A.
[b]"Error in Courts," *The New York Times* (June 12, 2000): A1.
[c]Fox Butterfield, "Death Sentences Being Overturned in 2 of 3 Appeals," *The New York Times,* June 12, 2000, A1.

physicians from discussing it with their married patients until the Supreme Court ruled its restrictive laws unconstitutional.

Griswold v. *Connecticut* (1965) involved a challenge to the constitutionality of an 1879 Connecticut law prohibiting the dissemination of information about and/or the sale of contraceptives.[100] In *Griswold,* seven justices decided that various portions of the Bill of Rights, including the First, Third, Fourth, Fifth, and Fourteenth Amendments, cast what the Court called "penumbras" (unstated liberties on the fringes or in the shadow of more explicitly stated rights), thereby creating zones of privacy, including a married couple's right to plan a family. Thus the Connecticut statute was ruled unconstitutional because it violated marital privacy, a right the Court concluded could be read into the U.S. Constitution through interpreting several amendments.

Later, the Court expanded the right of privacy to include the right of unmarried individuals to have access to contraceptives. "If the right of privacy means anything," wrote Justice William J. Brennan, "it is the right of the individual, married or single, to be free from unwarranted governmental intrusion into matters so fundamentally affecting a person as the decision to bear or beget a child."[101] Contraceptive rights, however, are often limited to those under age eighteen by state or federal policy.

Abortion

In the early 1960s, two birth-related tragedies occurred: Severely deformed babies were born to women who had been given the drug thalidomide while pregnant, and a nationwide measles epidemic resulted in the birth of more babies with severe problems. The increasing medical safety of abortions and the growing women's rights movement combined with these tragedies to put pressure on the legal and medical establishments to enact laws that would guarantee a woman's access to a safe and legal abortion.

By the late 1960s, fourteen states had voted to liberalize their abortion policies, and four states decriminalized abortion in the early stages of pregnancy. But many women's rights activists wanted more. They argued that the decision to carry a pregnancy to term was a woman's fundamental constitutional right. In 1973, in one of the most controversial decisions ever handed down, seven members of the Court agreed with this position.

The woman whose case became the catalyst for pro-choice and anti-abortion groups was Norma McCorvey, an itinerant circus worker. The mother of one toddler she was unable to care for, McCorvey could not leave another child in her mother's care. So she decided to terminate her second pregnancy. Unable to secure a legal abortion and frightened by the conditions she found when she sought an illegal, back-alley abortion, McCorvey turned to two young Texas lawyers who were looking for a plaintiff to bring a lawsuit to challenge Texas's restrictive statute, which allowed abortions only when they were necessary to save the life of the mother. McCorvey, who was unable to obtain a legal abortion, later gave birth and put the baby up for adoption. Nevertheless, she allowed her lawyers to proceed with the case using her as their plaintiff, under the pseudonym Jane Roe, to challenge the Texas law as enforced by Henry Wade, the district attorney for Dallas County, Texas.

When the case finally came before the Supreme Court, Justice Harry A. Blackmun, a former lawyer at the Mayo Clinic, relied heavily on medical evidence to rule that the Texas law violated a woman's constitutionally guaranteed right to privacy, which he argued included her decision to terminate a pregnancy. Writing for the majority in ***Roe v. Wade,*** Blackmun divided pregnancy into three stages. In the first trimester, a woman's right to privacy gave her an absolute right (in consultation with her physician), free from state interference, to terminate her pregnancy. In the second trimester, the state's interest in the health of the mother gave it the right to regulate abortions—but only to protect the woman's health. Only in the third trimester—when the fetus becomes potentially viable—did the Court find that the state's interest in potential life outweighed the woman's privacy interests. Even in the third trimester, however, abortions to save the life or health of the mother were to be legal.[102]

Roe v. *Wade* unleashed a torrent of political controversy. Anti-abortion groups, caught off guard, scrambled to recoup their losses in Congress. Representative Henry Hyde (R–Ill.) persuaded Congress to ban the use of Medicaid funds for abortions for poor women, and the constitutionality of the Hyde Amendment was upheld by the Supreme Court in 1977 and again in 1980.[103] The issue also polarized both political parties.

From the 1970s through the present, the right to an abortion and its constitutional underpinnings in the right to privacy have been under attack by well-organized anti-abortion groups. The Reagan and Bush administrations were strong advocates of the anti-abortion position, regularly urging the Court to overrule *Roe*. They came close to victory in *Webster* v. *Reproductive Health Services* (1989).[104] In *Webster*, the Court upheld state-required fetal viability tests in the second trimester, even though these tests would increase the cost of an abortion considerably. The Court also upheld Missouri's refusal

WEB EXPLORATION
To compare the different sides of the abortion debate, see
www.ablongman.com/oconnor

Roe v. *Wade* (1973)
The Supreme Court found that a woman's right to an abortion was protected by the right to privacy that could be implied from specific guarantees found in the Bill of Rights applied to the states through the Fourteenth Amendment.

Anti-abortion group Operation Rescue has staged large-scale protests in front of abortion clinics across the nation. It now has a surprising new member—Norma McCorvey, the "Jane Roe" of *Roe* v. *Wade*, who announced in a 1995 press conference that she had become pro-life. (Photo courtesy: Tim Sharp/AP/Wide World Photos)

to allow abortions to be performed in state-supported hospitals or by state-funded doctors or nurses. Perhaps most noteworthy, however, were the facts that four justices seemed willing to overrule *Roe* v. *Wade*, and that Justice Antonin Scalia publicly rebuked his colleague Justice Sandra Day O'Connor, then the only woman on the Court, for failing to provide the critical fifth vote to overrule *Roe*.

After *Webster*, states began to enact more restrictive legislation. In the most important abortion case since *Roe*, *Planned Parenthood of Southeastern Pennsylvania* v. *Casey* (1992), Justices O'Connor, Anthony Kennedy, and David Souter, in a jointly authored opinion, wrote that Pennsylvania could limit abortions as long as its regulations did not pose "an undue burden" on pregnant women.[105]

The narrowly supported decision, which upheld a twenty-four-hour waiting period and parental consent requirements, did not overrule *Roe*, but clearly limited its scope by abolishing its trimester approach and substituting the "undue burden" standard. Since *Casey*, the Court has, for example, refused to find unconstitutional Mississippi's mandatory twenty-four-hour waiting period before an abortion. Mississippi has only three abortion clinics—all in Jackson. With this required waiting period, many women have to take time off work to drive over 100 miles, and then pay for a hotel. The number of abortions dropped 40 percent, and the clinics unsuccessfully argued that the waiting period posed an "undue burden." The U.S. Supreme Court refused to hear the appeal.[106]

In 1993, newly elected President Clinton, who ran on a pro-choice platform, ended bans on fetal tissue research, abortions at military hospitals, federal financing for overseas population control programs, and lifted the "gag" rule, a federal regulation enacted in 1987 which barred public health clinics receiving federal dollars from discussing abortion (policies later reversed by George W. Bush).[107] He also lifted the ban on testing of RU-486, the so-called French abortion pill, which ultimately was made available for public consumption late in 2000.

President Clinton used the occasion of his first appointment to the U.S. Supreme Court to select a longtime supporter of abortion rights, Ruth Bader Ginsburg, to replace Justice Byron White, one of the original dissenters in *Roe*. Most commentators believe that this was an important first step in shifting the Court away from any further curtailment of abortion rights, as was the later appointment of Justice Stephen Breyer in 1994.

While President Clinton was attempting to shore up abortion rights through judicial appointment, Republican Congresses made repeated attempts to restrict abortion rights. In March 1996, Congress passed and sent to President Clinton a bill that for the first time would ban a specific procedure used in late-term abortions.[108] The president vetoed the Partial Birth Abortion Act over the comments and pressure of the National Right to Life Committee, which had lobbied hard for the act. Many state legislatures, however, have passed their own versions of the act. The same measure was also vetoed by President Clinton in late 1998, and the Senate, again, was unable to override that veto. The election of George W. Bush virtually assured passage of this act.

In 2000, the Supreme Court, however, ruled 5–4 in *Stenberg* v. *Carhart* that a Nebraska "partial birth" abortion statute was unconstitutionally vague and therefore unenforceable, calling into question the laws of twenty-nine other states with their own bans on late-term procedures.[109] At the same time, it ruled that a Colorado law that prohibited protestors from coming within eight feet of women entering clinics was unconstitutional.[110] This "bubble law" was designed to create an eight-foot buffer zone around women as they walked through protesters into a clinic to receive an abortion.

Homosexuality

Although the Supreme Court has ruled that the right to privacy includes the right to decide whether "to bear or beget a child," it has declined to interpret the right of privacy to include the right to engage in homosexual acts. In 1985 the Court, in a 4–4 decision (Justice Powell was ill), upheld a lower-court decision that found unconstitutional an Oklahoma law allowing the dismissal of teachers who advocate homosexual relations.[111] The next year, a case involving the constitutionality of a Georgia law prohibiting consensual heterosexual and homosexual oral or anal sex, *Bowers* v. *Hardwick* (1986), was argued before the Court. The lawyer representing Michael Hardwick pitched his arguments toward Justice Powell, who he believed would be the crucial swing vote in this controversial area.[112]

In August 1982, in Atlanta, Georgia, Michael Hardwick was arrested in his bedroom by a police officer who was there to serve an arrest warrant on Hardwick for his failure to appear in court on another charge. One of his roommates let the officer in and directed him to Hardwick's room. After Hardwick's arrest on a sodomy charge, the local prosecutor decided not to prosecute. Nonetheless, Hardwick, a local gay activist, joined forces with the American Civil Liberties Union to challenge the constitutionality of the law under which he had been arrested. In a 5–4 decision, the Supreme Court upheld the law. At conference, Justice Powell reportedly seemed torn by the case. He believed that the twenty-year sentence that came with conviction was excessive, but he

WEB EXPLORATION
For more on gay rights, see
www.ablongman.com/oconnor

James Dale, a one-time Boy Scout leader who sued the organization after he was dismissed for being gay, talks to reporters following the Supreme Court's ruling allowing the Boy Scouts of America to deny entry of gays. A closely divided Court ruled that such a private group has the right to set its own moral code. (Photo courtesy: Archive Photos)

was troubled by the fact that Hardwick hadn't actually been (and never was) tried and convicted. Although he originally voted with the majority to overturn the law, Powell was bothered by the broadness of Justice Blackmun's original draft of the majority, opinion. Thus, he changed his mind and voted with the minority view to uphold the law, making it the new majority.[113] Like his change of heart in the *McCleskey* case, after his retirement Justice Powell confessed that he was wrong in *Bowers* and should have voted to overturn the Georgia law.

While the Court has refused to expand the right to privacy to invalidate state laws that criminalize some aspects of homosexual behavior, in 1996 it ruled that a state could not deny rights to homosexuals simply because they are homosexuals. Thus, as discussed in chapter 6, the Court ruled that the equal protection clause bars unreasonable state discrimination against gays and lesbians.[114]

Privacy rights and First Amendment associational rights came into conflict in *Boy Scouts of America* v. *Dale*.[115] The Court ruled that the Boy Scouts could exclude gay men from serving as scoutmasters, a move that disheartened gay rights activists and caused many public groups to withdraw their support from the Boy Scouts.

WEB EXPLORATION
To learn about the right to die movement, see
www.ablongman.com/oconnor

The Right to Die

While the current Supreme Court is unlikely to expand the scope of the privacy doctrine to include greater protections for homosexuals in the near future, it is likely to continue to get more cases involving claims for personal autonomy. In 1990, for exam-

FIGURE 5.1   Assisted-Suicide Laws in the United States

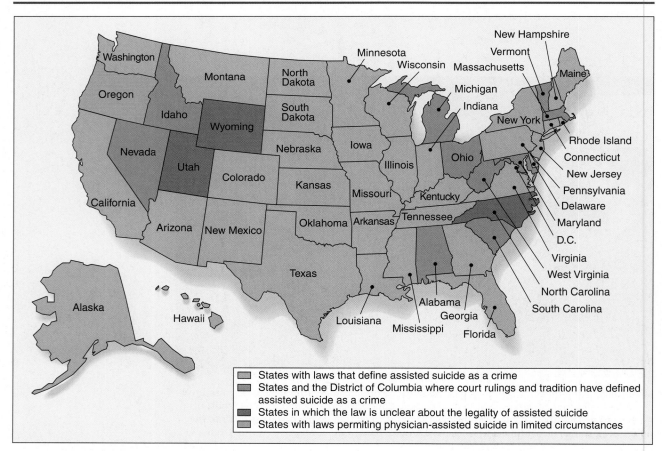

Source: Copyright 1997, USA TODAY. Reprinted with permission.

ple, in *Cruzan by Cruzan* v. *Director, Missouri Department of Health*, the Supreme Court sided with the state against the privacy claims of the parents of Nancy Cruzan, a brain-injured woman living in a comatose state who, according to her doctors, could live like that for many more years. Her parents sued to remove her feeding tube, and the Bush administration and numerous anti-abortion groups filed briefs supporting the state against the Cruzans.

Writing for a five-person majority, Chief Justice Rehnquist rejected any attempts to expand the right of privacy into this thorny area of social policy. The Court did note, however, that individuals could terminate medical treatment if they were able to express, or had done so in writing via a living will, their desire to have medical treatment terminated in the event they became incompetent.[116]

States, too, have entered into this arena. Even before the *Cruzan* case, the New Jersey Supreme Court allowed the parents of a comatose woman to withdraw her feeding tube.[117] More recently, in a different but related vein, states have legislated to prevent what is often called "assisted suicide." Jurors, however, often appear unwilling to find loved ones or even Dr. Jack Kervorkian guilty of helping the terminally ill carry out the decision to take their own lives. In 1999, however, after being acquitted in four other trials, Dr. Kevorkian represented himself and was found guilty of administering a lethal injection of chemicals to a fifty-two-year-old man.

In 1997, the U.S. Supreme Court ruled unanimously that terminally ill persons do not have a constitutional right to physician-assisted suicide. The Court's action upheld the laws of New York and Washington State that make it a crime for doctors to give life-ending drugs to mentally competent but terminally ill patients who wish to die.[118] As revealed in Figure 5.1, state laws concerning assisted suicide vary considerably. Nevertheless, 61 percent of the public believes that physicians should be able to assist terminally ill patients in pain to die.[119]

Dr. Jack Kevorkian, who was later found guilty of second degree murder, aired this videotape on *60 Minutes,* showing that he assisted the suicide of Thomas Youk, a fifty-two year-old man ravaged by Lou Gehrig's disease. (Photo courtesy: Sipa Press)

Continuity & Change

Conceptions of Civil Liberties

When the new Constitution was adopted by the citizens in the states, it lacked a Bill of Rights. This absence was a glaring one in the eyes of many Americans. Their state constitutions often protected their civil liberties, and they feared that they already were giving up too many rights to an untested national government. So, when the first Congress met in 1789, one of the first items on its agenda was the passage of a Bill of Rights to prevent the national government from infringing the liberties of the citizenry.

In the late 1700s, issues of political speech, freedom of the press, and the right to gather and petition the government were among the rights most cherished. After all, without these rights, the colonists never would have been able to organize and mobilize effectively enough to make the successful break with Great Britain.

Today, our conceptions of civil liberties, as well as their need for protection, are quite different. Poll after poll shows that if Americans were to vote on the Bill of Rights already contained in the Constitution, it would not garner enough votes in the states to be adopted. Over the years the role of the courts—especially the federal courts—in expanding the application of most of the Bill of Rights to the states, as well as in interpreting those provisions, has produced a panoply of rights never

envisioned by the Framers. Moreover, the provisions of the Constitution and the Bill of Rights have been interpreted to protect a variety of rights, and liberties that are not explicitly stated, such as protections for criminal defendants, the right to privacy, and reproductive rights.

Just think about how Americans' conceptions of rights have evolved in 200 years. New technologies from cars (police searches) to telephones (wiretaps) to e-mail have created new laws dealing with issues of civil liberties. The development of the Internet will undoubtedly produce even more civil liberties issues than those already addressed by Congress dealing with pornography.

1. As it becomes easier and easier to get more and more information about all of us, what kind of civil liberties protections do you think the government should institute?
2. Conversely, in a Hobbesian sense, what kinds of practices and policies that curtail some rights, such as DNA testing, but may contribute the betterment of life for the majority, should be permitted?

Cast Your Vote. Which civil liberties deserve protection? To cast your vote, go to **www.ablongman.com/oconnor**

SUMMARY

1. **The First Constitutional Amendments: The Bill of Rights**

   Most of the Framers originally opposed the Bill of Rights. Anti-Federalists, however, continued to stress the need for a Bill of Rights during the drive for ratification of the Constitution, and some states tried to make their ratification contingent on the addition of a Bill of Rights. Thus, during its first session, Congress sent the first ten amendments to the Constitution, the Bill of Rights, to the states for their ratification. Later, the addition of the Fourteenth Amendment allowed the Supreme Court to apply some of the amendments to the states through a process called selective incorporation.

2. **First Amendment Guarantees: Freedom of Religion**

   The First Amendment guarantees freedom of religion. The establishment clause, which prohibits the national government from establishing a religion, does not, according to Supreme Court interpretation, create an absolute wall between church and state. While the national and state governments may generally not give direct aid to religious groups, many forms of aid, espe-

cially many that benefit children, have been held to be constitutionally permissible. In contrast, the Court has generally barred prayer in public schools. The Court generally has adopted an accommodationist approach when interpreting the free exercise clause by allowing some governmental regulation of religious practices.

3. **First Amendment Guarantees: Freedom of Speech and Press**

   The First Amendment also guarantees freedom of speech and of the press. The Alien and Sedition Acts in 1798 were the first national efforts to curtail free speech, but they were never reviewed by the U.S. Supreme Court.

   Some forms of speech were punished during the Civil War, and the Supreme Court refused to address their constitutionality directly. By the twentieth century, several states, and later the national government, passed laws restricting freedoms of speech and of the press. These curtailments were upheld by the Court, using the clear and present danger test. Later, the Court used the more liberal direct incitement test, which required a stronger showing of imminent danger before speech could be restricted.

Symbolic speech has been afforded the same protection as other forms of speech. Historically, the Supreme Court has disfavored any attempts at prior restraint of speech or press; thus, so called hate speech and politically correct speech requirements have come under constitutional challenge.

Libel, slander, and obscenity (as well as some forms of pornography) are not protected by the First Amendment and the Supreme Court has upheld the authority of Congress to legislate in these areas.

4. The Second Amendment: The Right to Keep and Bear Arms

Initially, this right was envisioned as one dealing with state militias. Today, crime in the school in particular has led to a reexamination of this amendment's meaning with little Supreme Court interpretation as a guide.

5. The Rights of Criminal Defendants

The Fourth, Fifth, Sixth, and Eighth Amendments provide a variety of procedural guarantees to individuals accused of crimes. In particular, the Fourth Amendment prohibits unreasonable searches and seizures, and the Court has generally refused to allow evidence seized in violation of this safeguard to be used at trial.

Among other rights, the Fifth Amendment guarantees that "no person shall be compelled to be a witness against himself." The Supreme Court has interpreted this provision to require that the government inform the accused of his or her right to remain silent. This provision has also been interpreted to require that illegally obtained confessions must be excluded at trial.

The Sixth Amendment's guarantee of "assistance of counsel" has been interpreted by the Supreme Court to require that the government provide counsel to defendants unable to pay for it in cases where prison sentences may be imposed. The Sixth Amendment also requires an impartial jury, although the meaning of impartial continues to evolve through judicial interpretation.

The Eighth Amendment's ban against "cruel and unusual punishments" has been held not to bar imposition of the death penalty.

6. The Right to Privacy

The right to privacy is a judicially created right carved from the implications of several amendments, including the First, Third, Fourth, Fifth, and Fourteenth Amendments. Statutes limiting access to birth control and abortion rights have been ruled unconstitutional violations of the right to privacy. In contrast, the Supreme Court has not expanded the right to privacy to invalidate state statutes criminalizing homosexual acts.

KEY TERMS

Bill of Rights, p. 139
civil liberties, p. 138
clear and present danger test, p. 149
direct incitement test, p. 149
due process clause, p. 140
due process rights, p. 157
establishment clause, p. 142
exclusionary rule, p. 160

free exercise clause, p. 142
incorporation doctrine, p. 140
libel, p. 150
Miranda rights, p. 160
Miranda v. *Arizona* (1966), p. 159
New York Times Co. v. *Sullivan* (1964), p. 150
prior restraint, p. 148

right to privacy, p. 165
Roe v. *Wade* (1973), p. 167
selective incorporation, p. 141
slander, p. 150
substantive due process, p. 140
symbolic speech, p. 153

SELECTED READINGS

Abernathy, M. Glenn, and Barbara A. Perry, *Civil Liberties Under the Constitution.* Columbia: University of South Carolina Press, 1993.

Fiss, Owen M. *The Irony of Free Speech.* Cambridge, Mass.: Harvard University Press, 1996.

Friendly, Fred W. *Minnesota Rag: The Dramatic Story of the Landmark Case That Gave New Meaning to Freedom of the Press.* New York: Random House, 1981.

Gates, Henry Louis, Jr., ed. *Speaking of Race, Speaking of Sex: Hate Speech, Civil Rights, and Civil Liberties.* New York: New York University Press, 1995.

Greenawalt, Kent. *Fighting Words: Individuals, Communities, and Liberties of Speech.* Princeton, N.J.: Princeton University Press, 1995.

Kalven, Harry, Jr. *A Worthy Tradition: Freedom of Speech in America.* New York: Harper & Row, 1988.

Lewis, Anthony. *Gideon's Trumpet.* (reissue edition) New York: Vintage Books, 1989.

———. *Make No Law: The Sullivan Case and the First Amendment.* New York: Random House, 1991.

Manwaring, David R. *Render Unto Caesar: The Flag Salute Controversy.* Chicago: University of Chicago Press, 1962.

O'Brien, David M. *Constitutional Law and Politics, Vol. 2: Civil Rights and Civil Liberties,* 3rd ed. New York: Norton and Co., 1997.

O'Connor, Karen. *No Neutral Ground: Abortion Politics in an Age of Absolutes.* Boulder, Colo.: Westview Press, 1996.

Regan, Priscilla M. *Legislating Privacy: Technology, Social Values, and Public Policy.* Chapel Hill: University of North Carolina Press, 1995.

Weddington, Sarah. *A Question of Choice.* New York: Grosset/Putnam, 1993.

NOTES

1. This vignette draws heavily from on Jamie Ruskin, "In Defense of Students' Rights," *The Washington Post*, (August 27, 2000): B8.
2. The absence of a bill of rights led Mason to refuse to sign the proposed Constitution, noting that he "would sooner chop off his right hand than put it to the Constitution as it now stands." (Quoted in Eric Black, *Our Constitution: The Myth That Binds Us* [Boulder, Colo.: Westview Press, 1988], 75.)
3. Quoted in Jack N. Rakove, "Madison Won Passage of the Bill of Rights but Remained a Skeptic," *Public Affairs Report* (March 1991): 6.
4. 7 Pet. 243 (1833).
5. *Allgeyer* v. *Louisiana*, 165 U.S. 578 (1897).
6. 268 U.S. 652 (1925).
7. 283 U.S. 697 (1931). For more about *Near*, see Fred W. Friendly, *Minnesota Rag* (New York: Random House, 1981).
8. 302 U.S. 319 (1937).
9. Continental Congress to the People of Great Britain, October 21, 1774, in Philip Kurland and Ralph Lerner, eds., *The Founders' Constitution*, vol. 5 (Chicago: University of Chicago Press, 1987), 61.
10. *Reynolds* v. *U.S.*, 98 U.S. 145 (1879).
11. *Cantwell* v. *Connecticut*, 310 U.S. 296 (1940).
12. *Zobrest* v. *Catalina Foothills School District*, 506 U.S. 813 (1992).
13. 370 U.S. 421 (1962).
14. *Lee* v. *Weisman*, 505 U.S. 577 (1992).
15. *Santa Fe Independent School District* v. *Doe*, 530 U.S. 290 (2000).
16. *Widmar* v. *Vincent*, 454 U.S. 263 (1981).
17. *Board of Education* v. *Mergens*, 496 U.S. 226 (1990).
18. *Lamb's Chapel* v. *Center Moriches Union Free School District*, 508 U.S. 384 (1993).
19. *Rosenberger* v. *University of Virginia*, 515 U.S. 819 (1995).
20. *Rosenberger* v. *University of Virginia*, 515 U.S. 819 (1995).
21. *Agostini* v *Felton*, 521 US 203 (1997).
22. *Mitchell* v. *Helms*, 530 U.S. 793 (2000).
23. *Employment Division, Dept. of Human Resources of Oregon* v. *Smith*, 494 U.S. 872 (1990).
24. *City of Boerne* v. *Flores*, 521 U.S. 507 (1997).
25. *Church of the Lukumi Babalu Aye* v. *Hialeah*, 508 U.S. 525 (1993).
26. *Cruz* v. *Beto*, 405 U.S. 319 (1972).
27. *O'Lone* v. *Shabazz*, 482 U.S. 342 (1987).
28. See, for example, the opinion in *Boissonneault* v. *Flint City Council*, 392 Mich. 685 (1974).
29. *Chaplinsky* v. *New Hampshire*, 315 U.S. 568 (1942).
30. *Ex parte McCardle*, 74 U.S. 506 (1869).
31. David M. O'Brien, *Constitutional Law and Politics*, vol. 2 (New York: Norton, 1991), 345.
32. See Frederick Siebert, *The Rights and Privileges of the Press* (New York: D. Appleton-Century, 1934), 886, 931–40.
33. *Schenck* v. *United States*, 249 U.S. 47 (1919).
34. *Brandenburg* v. *Ohio*, 395 U.S. 444 (1969).
35. 376 U.S. 254 (1964).
36. *Masson* v. *New Yorker Magazine*, 501 U.S. 496 (1991).
37. 315 U.S. 568 (1942).
38. *Regina* v. *Hicklin*, L. R. 2 Q. B. 360 (1868).
39. 354 U.S. 476 (1957).
40. 413 U.S. 15 (1973).
41. *Barnes* v. *Glen Theater*, 501 U.S. 560 (1991).
42. Joan Biskupic, "Decency Can Be Weighed in Arts Funding," *The Washington Post* (June 26, 1998): A1, A18.
43. *National Endowment for the Arts* v. *Finley*, 524 U.S. 569 (1998).
44. *Reno* v. *ACLU*, 117 S.Ct. 2329 (1997).
45. 403 U.S. 713 (1971).
46. *Nebraska Press Association* v. *Stuart*, 427 U.S. 539 (1976).
47. *Abrams* v. *United States*, 250 U.S. 616 (1919).
48. 283 U.S. 359 (1931).
49. 393 U.S. 503 (1969).
50. *Texas* v. *Johnson*, 491 U.S. 397 (1989).
51. *U.S.* v. *Eichman*, 496 U.S. 310 (1990).
52. Harry Klaven Jr., *Negro and the First Amendment* (Chicago: University of Chicago Press, 1966).
53. Henry Louis Gates Jr., "Why Civil Liberties Pose No Threat to Civil Rights," *New Republic* (September 20, 1993).
54. 7 Peters 243 (1833).
55. 19 How. 393 (1857).
56. 307 U.S. 174 (1939).
57. 104 U.S. 194 (1983).
58. *Printz* v. *United States*, 514 U.S. 898 (1997).
59. *Furman* v. *Georgia*, 408 U.S. 238 (1972).
60. *Gregg* v. *Georgia*, 428 U.S. 153 (1976).
61. *Stein* v. *N.Y.*, 346 U.S. 156 (1953).
62. *Wilson* v. *Arkansas*, 514 U.S. 927 (1995).
63. *U.S.* v. *Sokolov*, 490 U.S. 1 (1989).
64. *U.S.* v. *Matlock*, 415 U.S. 164 (1974).
65. *Johnson* v. *U.S.*, 333 U.S. 10 (1948).
66. *Winston* v. *Lee*, 470 U.S. 753 (1985).
67. *South Dakota* v. *Neville*, 459 U.S. 553 (1983).
68. *Michigan* v. *Tyler*, 436 U.S. 499 (1978).
69. *Hester* v. *U.S.*, 265 U.S. 57 (1924).
70. *Carroll* v. *U.S.*, 267 U.S. 132 (1925).
71. *Skinner* v. *Railway Labor Executives' Association*, 489 U.S. 602 (1989).
72. *Vernonia School District* v. *Acton*, 515 U.S. 646 (1995).
73. *Chandler* v. *Miller*, 520 U.S. 305 (1997).
74. John Wefing, "Employer Drug Testing: Disparate Judicial and Legislative Responses," *Albany Law Review* 63 (2000): 799–801.
75. *Counselman* v. *Hitchcock*, 142 U.S. 547 (1892).
76. *Brown* v. *Mississippi*, 297 U.S. 278 (1936).
77. *Lynumm* v. *Illinois*, 372 U.S. 528 (1963).
78. *Rhode Island* v. *Innis*, 446 U.S. 291 (1980).
79. *Arizona* v. *Fulminante*, 500 U.S. 938 (1991).
80. Dickerson v. U.S., 121 S.Ct. 183 (2000) No. 99-5525 (June 26, 2000).
81. 232 U.S. 383 (1914).
82. *Stone* v. *Powell*, 428 U.S. 465 (1976).
83. *Johnson* v. *Zerbst*, 304 U.S. 458 (1938).
84. *Powell* v. *Alabama*, 287 U.S. 45 (1932).
85. 372 U.S. 335 (1963).
86. *Argersinger* v. *Hamlin*, 407 U.S. 25 (1972).
87. *Scott* v. *Illinois*, 440 U.S. 367 (1979).
88. *Strauder* v. *West Virginia*, 100 U.S. 303 (1880).
89. *Taylor* v. *Louisiana*, 419 U.S. 522 (1975).
90. *Batson* v. *Kentucky*, 476 U.S. 79 (1986).
91. 497 U.S. 836 (1990).
92. *Hallinger* v. *Davis*, 146 U.S. 314 (1892).
93. *O'Neil* v. *Vermont*, 144 U.S. 323 (1892).
94. See Michael Meltsner, *Cruel and Unusual: The Supreme Court and Capital Punishment* (New York: Random House, 1973).
95. 408 U.S. 238 (1972).
96. 428 U.S. 153 (1976).

97. 481 U.S. 279 (1987).

98. 501 U.S. 1224 (1991).

99. *Olmstead* v. *United States*, 277 U.S. 438 (1928).

100. 381 U.S. 481 (1965).

101. *Eisenstadt* v. *Baird*, 410 U.S. 113 (1972).

102. 410 U.S. 113 (1973).

103. *Beal* v. *Doe*, 432 U.S. 438 (1977) and *Harris* v. *McRae*, 448 U.S. 297 (1980).

104. 492 U.S. 490 (1989).

105. 502 U.S. 1056 (1992).

106. *Barnes* v. *Moore*, 506 U.S. 1013 (1992).

107. Karen O'Connor, *No Neutral Ground: Abortion Politics in an Age of Absolutes* (Boulder, Colo.: Westview Press, 1996).

108. "House Sends Partial Birth Abortion Bill To Clinton," *Politics USA* (March 28, 1996): 1.

109. *Stenberg* v. *Carhart*, 530 U.S. 914 (2000).

110. *Hill* v. *Colorado*, 530 U.S. 703 (2000).

111. *Board of Education of City of Oklahoma City* v. *National Gay Task Force*, 470 U.S. 903 (1985).

112. 478 U.S. 186 (1986).

113. Reported in O'Brien, *Constitutional Law and Politics*, 1223.

114. *Romer* v. *Evans*, 116 S. Ct. 1620 (1996).

115. 530 U.S. 640 (2000).

116. 110 S.Ct. 2841 (1990).

117. *In re Quinlan*, 70 N.J. 10 (1976).

118. *Vacco* v. *Quill*, 117 S.Ct. 2293 (1997).

119. *USA Today*/CNN Poll (November 22, 1999): 21A.

6 Civil Rights

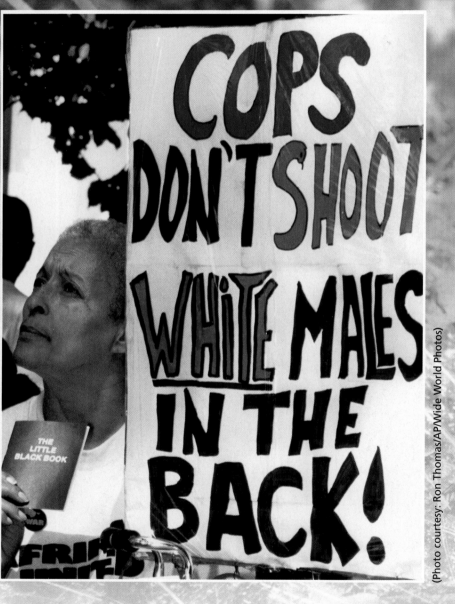

On February 4, 1999, just as Amadou Diallo, a twenty-two-year-old unarmed African immigrant, stood in the vestibule of his apartment building in the Bronx, New York, four white plainclothes police officers who were patrolling the neighborhood in an unmarked car opened fire on him, eventually firing forty-one shots. He died at the scene.[1] There were no witnesses. The four officers, who were eventually charged with second-degree murder, were members of the city's Street Crimes Unit. This unit was created by the mayor to help lower New York City's crime rate in the early 1990s. Known to have targeted black citizens, members of the unit admitted to stopping and searching as many as 225,000 citizens since its establishment.[2]

New York City's frightened minority community, African Americans and new immigrants alike, along with liberal activists and everyday citizens, turned their anger on city police and then Mayor Rudolph Giuliani, who they believed had used overly aggressive, and often racially biased, techniques to reduce crime. In the months after the shooting, citizens from all walks of life from actress Susan Sarandon to street cleaners protested at City Hall, and even marched from the federal courthouse over the Brooklyn Bridge and into Manhattan in a procession reminiscent of many 1960s civil rights marches.[3] Over 1,500 protesters were arrested at one demonstration, the largest New York City had seen in twenty-five years.[4] Eventually, all four police officers charged with Diallo's killing were acquitted at trial.

There is no question that in the 1980s, crime in the United States, and in particular New York City, was out of control and Americans demanded that their governments do something about it. Governments at all levels responded with more police and more prisons. But now that crime is on the wane and no longer even on Americans' list of top ten concerns, ordinary citizens are asking the question that troubled John Locke and Thomas Hobbes over three centuries ago: How much liberty should you give up to the government in return for safety? In the *Diallo* case, and many others, it is clear that black Americans, whether native- or foreign-born, are being targeted for civil rights deprivations at far higher rates than other identifiable groups. In 1999, for example, it was discovered that 40 percent of those strip-searched at the Chicago O'Hare airport by U.S. Customs officials were African American women.[5] In New Jersey and other states, allegations of the use by state troopers of what is called racial profiling to stop black drivers is under legal challenge.[6] Even African American college students recently filed suit when they were forced to pay higher room rates than white students in Daytona Beach during spring break.[7]

civil rights
Refers to the positive acts governments take to protect individuals against arbitrary or discriminatory treatment by governments or individuals based on categories such as race, sex, national origin, age, or sexual orientation.

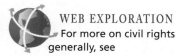

WEB EXPLORATION
For more on civil rights generally, see
www.ablongman.com/oconnor

Longman
Participate.com
2.0
Simulation
You Are the Mayor

The Declaration of Independence, written in 1776, boldly proclaims: "We hold these truths to be self-evident, that all men are created equal, that they are endowed by their Creator with certain inalienable rights." The Constitution, written eleven years later, is silent on the concept of equality. Only through constitutional amendment and Supreme Court definition and redefinition of the rights contained in that document have Americans come close to attaining equal rights. Even so, as our opening vignette highlights, some citizens still have yet to experience full equality and the full enjoyment of **civil rights** many Americans take for granted.

The term civil rights refers to the positive acts governments take to protect individuals against arbitrary or discriminatory treatment by governments or individuals. The Framers considered some civil rights issues. But as James Madison reflected in *Federalist No. 42*, one entire class of citizens—slaves—were treated in the new Constitution more like property than like people. Without the Three-Fifths Compromise, "No union could possibly have been formed" because the Southern states would not have agreed to join the union if slavery was prohibited by the national government.[8] In stipulating that slaves could be counted for purposes of fixing state population to determine congressional apportionment, slaves were counted as three-fifths of a person. The Constitution also stipulated that the importation of slaves could not be prohibited for twenty years. Delegates to the Constitutional Convention put political expediency before the immorality of slavery, and basic civil rights. Moreover, the Constitution considered white women full citizens for purposes of determining state population, but voting qualifications were left to the states and none allowed women to vote at the time the Constitution was ratified.

Since the Constitution was written, concepts of civil rights have changed dramatically. The addition of the Fourteenth Amendment, one of three amendments ratified after the Civil War, introduced the notion of equality into the Constitution by specifying that states could not deny "any person within its jurisdiction equal protection of the laws." The Fourteenth Amendment has generated more litigation to determine and specify its meaning than any other provision of the Constitution. Within a few years of its ratification, women—and later, African Americans and other minorities and disadvantaged groups—took to the courts to seek expanded civil rights in all walks of life. But the struggle to augment rights was not limited to the courts. Public protest, civil disobedience, legislative lobbying, and appeals to public opinion have all been part of the arsenal of those seeking equality. The *Diallo* case incorporates all of those actions. Ordinary citizens and celebrities took to the streets, legislators held hearings, police officers were put on trial, and the media reported it all.

Since passage of the Civil War amendments (1865–1870), there has been a fairly consistent pattern of the expansion of civil rights to more and more groups. In this chapter we will explore how notions of equality and civil rights have changed in this country. To do so we'll discuss slavery, its abolition, and the achievement of voting rights for African Americans and women by examining the evolution of African American rights and women's rights in tandem. To appreciate how each group has drawn ideas, support, and success from the other, throughout this chapter we discuss their parallel developments as well as those of other historically disadvantaged political groups, including Hispanics, now the largest minority group in the United States.

- First, we will discuss *slavery, abolition, and winning the right to vote*.
- Second, we will examine African Americans' and womens' next *push for equality from 1890 to 1954*, using two of the Supreme Court's most famous decisions, *Plessy* v. *Ferguson* and *Brown* v. *Board of Education* as bookends for our discussion.
- Third, we will analyze the *civil rights movement* and the Civil Rights Act of 1964 and its effects, including its facilitation of the development of a new women's rights movement and its push for an equal rights amendment to the U.S. Constitution.

■ Fourth, we will present the efforts of *other groups,* including Native Americans, Hispanic Americans, homosexuals, and disabled Americans, to mobilize for rights using methods often modeled after the actions of African Americans and women.

SLAVERY, ABOLITION, AND WINNING THE RIGHT TO VOTE, 1800–1890

Today, we take the rights of women and blacks to vote for granted. Since 1980, in fact, women generally have outvoted men; in the 1990s, African Americans and women became the core of the Democratic Party. But it wasn't always this way. The period from 1800 to 1890 was one of tremendous change and upheaval in America. Despite the Civil War and the freeing of the slaves, the promise of equality guaranteed to African Americans by the Civil War amendments failed to become a reality. Women's rights activists also began to make claims for equality, often using the arguments enunciated for the abolition of slavery, but they too fell far short of their goals.

Slavery and Congress

Congress banned the slave trade in 1808, after the expiration of the twenty-year period specified by the Constitution. In 1820, blacks made up 25 percent of the U.S. population and were in the majority in some Southern states. By 1840, that figure had fallen to 20 percent. After the invention of the cotton gin (a machine invented in 1793 that separated seeds from cotton very quickly), the South became even more dependent on agriculture and cheap slave labor as its economic base. At the same time, technological advances were turning the Northern states into an increasingly industrialized region, which intensified the cultural and political differences and animosity between North and South.

Ever since the first Africans had been brought to the New World in 1619, slavery had been a divisive issue. But as the nation grew westward in the early 1800s, conflicts between Northern and Southern states intensified over the admission of new states to the Union with "free" or "slave" status. The first major crisis occurred in 1820, when the Territory of Missouri applied for admission to the Union as a "slave state"—that is, one in which slavery would be legal. Missouri's admission would have weighted the Senate in favor of slavery and was therefore opposed by Northern senators. The resultant Missouri Compromise of 1820 allowed the admission of Missouri as a slave state, along with the admission of Maine (formed out of the territory of Massachusetts with the permission of Congress and Massachusetts) as a free state. Other compromises concerning slavery were eventually necessitated as the nation continued to grow and new states were added to the Union.

The Abolitionist Movement: The First Civil Rights Movement

The compromise of 1820 solidified the South in its determination to keep slavery legal, but it also fueled the fervor of those who opposed slavery. In the early 1800s, some private charities purchased slaves and transported them to the west coast of Africa, where, in the 1820s, eighty-eight former slaves formed the independent nation of Liberia. But this solution to the slavery problem was not all that practical. Few owners were willing to free their slaves, and the trip to Africa and conditions there were dangerous. The abolitionist movement might have fizzled had it not been for William Lloyd Garrison, a white New Englander who became active in the movement in the early 1830s. Garrison, a newspaper editor, founded the American Anti-Slavery Society in 1833; by 1838 it had more than 250,000 members—given the U.S. population today, the National

WEB EXPLORATION
For more on abolition, the American Anti-Slavery Society, and its leaders, see www.ablongman.com/oconnor

ROOTS OF GOVERNMENT

FREDERICK DOUGLASS

Frederick Douglass (1817–1895), a leading advocate of civil rights for blacks and women, was the son of a slave and an unidentified white man. Although born into slavery, Douglass learned how to read and write. Once he escaped to the North (where 250,000 free blacks lived), he became a well-known orator and journalist. He spoke to abolitionist groups about his experiences as a slave and included these experiences in his autobiography, *Narrative of the Life of Frederick Douglass.* His life was also romanticized in song.

In 1847, he started a newspaper, *The North Star,* in Rochester, New York, which quickly became a powerful voice against slavery. Douglass, a strong abolitionist, urged President Abraham Lincoln to emancipate the slaves and helped recruit black soldiers for the Union forces in the Civil War. His home in Rochester was a station along the Underground Railroad. Douglass was also a firm believer

in women's suffrage, and he attended the Seneca Falls Convention in 1848. He was a close friend of John Brown, whose raid at Harpers Ferry was a pivotal moment in the antislavery movement.

Douglass was appointed to several minor federal posts, including that of minister to Haiti from 1889 to 1891. He was considered the greatest black leader of his time. When he died in 1895, five states adopted resolutions of regret, and two U.S. senators and one Supreme Court justice were among honorary pallbearers.

(Photo courtesy: Library of Congress)

Association for the Advancement of Colored People (NAACP) would need 3.8 million members to have the same kind of overall proportional membership. (In 2000, it exceeds 500,000 members.)

The Women's Rights Tie-in.   Slavery was not the only practice that people began to question in the decades following adoption of the Constitution. In 1840, for example, Garrison and even Frederick Douglass, a well-known black abolitionist writer (see Roots of Government: Frederick Douglass), parted from the Anti-Slavery Society when it refused to accept their demand that women be allowed to participate equally in all its activities. Custom dictated that women not speak out in public, and most laws made women second-class citizens. In most states, for example, women could not divorce their husbands or keep their own wages and inheritances. And, of course, they could not vote.

Elizabeth Cady Stanton and Lucretia Mott, who were to found the women's movement, attended the 1840 meeting of the World's Anti-Slavery Society in London with their husbands. They were not allowed to participate because they were women. As they sat in the balcony apart from the male delegates, they paused to compare their status to that of the slaves they sought to free. They believed that women were not much better off than slaves, and resolved to address these issues. In 1848, they sent out a call for the first women's rights convention. Three hundred women and men, including Frederick Douglass, traveled to the sleepy little town of Seneca Falls, New York, to attend the first meeting for women's rights.

The Seneca Falls Convention (1848).   The Seneca Falls Convention attracted people from all over New York State who believed that all men and women should be able to enjoy all rights of citizenship equally. It passed resolutions calling for the abolition of legal, economic, and social discrimination against women. All of the resolutions reflected the attendees' dissatisfaction with contemporary moral codes, divorce and criminal laws, and the limited opportunities for women in education, the church, and in medicine, law, and politics. Only the call to extend the **franchise**—the legal right to vote—to women failed to win unanimous approval. Most who attended the Seneca Falls meeting continued to press for women's rights along with the abolition of slavery.

franchise
The right to vote.

The 1850s: The Calm Before the Storm.   By 1850, much was changing in America—the Gold Rush had spurred westward migration, cities grew as people were lured from their farms, railroads and the telegraph increased mobility and communication, and immigrants flooded into the United States. Reformers called for change, the women's movement gained momentum, and slavery continued to tear the nation apart. Harriet Beecher Stowe's *Uncle Tom's Cabin,* a novel that showed the evils of slavery by depicting a slave family torn apart, further inflamed the country. *Uncle Tom's Cabin* sold more than 300,000 copies in a single year, 1852.

The tremendous national reaction to Stowe's work, which later prompted Abraham Lincoln to call Stowe "the little woman who started the big war," had not yet faded when a new controversy over the 1820 Missouri Compromise became the lightning rod for the first major civil rights case to be addressed by the U.S. Supreme Court. As discussed in chapter 3, in *Dred Scott* v. *Sandford* (1857), the Supreme Court bluntly ruled unconstitutional the 1820 Missouri Compromise, which prohibited slavery north of the geographical boundary at 36 degrees latitude on a map of the United States, also known as the Mason–Dixon Line for the surveyors who made maps of the region. Furthermore, in that case the Court found that slaves were not U.S. citizens and therefore could not bring suits in federal court, and concluded that "the Negro might justly and lawfully be reduced to slavery for his benefit." Ironically, after the case was decided, Scott's owner freed him.

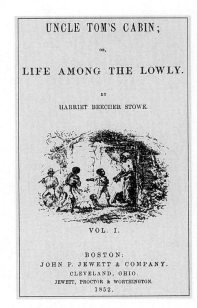

The original title page of *Uncle Tom's Cabin,* or *Life Among the Lowly,* by Harriet Beecher Stowe. (Photo courtesy: Library of Congress)

The Civil War and Its Aftermath: Civil Rights Laws and Constitutional Amendments

The Civil War had many causes, including (1) the political conflict between the North and the South over nullification, a doctrine allowing states to declare federal laws null and void, and secession, which involved the right of states to leave the Union; (2) the Northern states' increasing political strength in Congress, especially in the House of Representatives; (3) Southern agriculture versus Northern industry; and (4) the clash of conservative Southern culture with more progressive Northern ideas. Slavery, though, was clearly the key issue.

During the war (1861–1865), abolitionists kept their antislavery pressure on. They were rewarded when President Abraham Lincoln issued the Emancipation Proclamation, which provided that all slaves in states still in active rebellion against the United States would automatically be freed on January 1, 1863. Designed as a measure to gain favor for the war in the North, the Emancipation Proclamation did not free all slaves—it freed only those who lived in the Confederacy. Complete abolition of slavery did not occur until congressional passage and ultimate ratification of the Thirteenth Amendment in 1865.

The Civil War Amendments.   The **Thirteenth Amendment** was the first of the three so-called Civil War amendments. It banned all forms of "slavery [and] involuntary servitude." Although Southern states were required to ratify the Thirteenth Amendment as a condition of their readmission to the Union after the war, most of the former Confederate states quickly passed laws that were designed to restrict opportunities for newly freed slaves dramatically. These **Black Codes** prohibited African Americans from voting, sitting on juries, or even appearing in public places. Although Black Codes differed from state to state, all empowered local law-enforcement officials to arrest unemployed blacks, fine them for vagrancy, and hire them out to employers to satisfy their fines. Some state codes went so far as to require African Americans to work on

Thirteenth Amendment
One of the three Civil War amendments; specifically bans slavery in the United States.

Black Codes
Laws denying most legal rights to newly freed slaves; passed by Southern states following the Civil War.

plantations or to be domestics. The Black Codes laid the groundwork for Jim Crow laws, which would later institute segregation in all walks of life.

The outraged Reconstructionist Congress enacted the Civil Rights Act of 1866 to invalidate some state Black Codes. President Andrew Johnson vetoed the legislation, but—for the first time in history—Congress overrode a presidential veto. The Civil Rights Act formally made African Americans citizens of the United States and gave the Congress and the federal courts the power to intervene when states attempted to restrict male African American citizenship rights in matters such as voting. Congress reasoned that African Americans were unlikely to fare well if they had to file discrimination complaints in state courts, where judges were elected. Passage of a federal law allowed African Americans to challenge discriminatory state practices in the federal courts, where judges were appointed by the president.

Fourteenth Amendment
One of the three Civil War amendments; guarantees equal protection and due process of the laws to all U.S. citizens.

Because controversy remained over the constitutionality of the act (since the Constitution gives states the right to determine qualifications of voters), the **Fourteenth Amendment** was proposed simultaneously with the Civil Rights Act to guarantee, among other things, citizenship to all freed slaves. Other key provisions of the Fourteenth Amendment barred states from abridging "the privileges or immunities of citizenship" or depriving "any person of life, liberty, or property without due process of law."

Unlike the Thirteenth Amendment, which had near-unanimous support in the North, the Fourteenth Amendment was opposed by many women. During the Civil War, women's rights activists, including Elizabeth Cady Stanton and Susan B. Anthony, put aside their claims for expanded rights for women, most notably the right to vote, and threw their energies into the war effort. They were convinced that once slaves were freed and given the right to vote, women similarly would be rewarded with the franchise. They were wrong.

In early 1869, after ratification of the Fourteenth Amendment (which specifically added the word "male" to the Constitution for the first time), women's rights activists met in Washington, D.C., to argue against passage of any new amendment that would extend suffrage to black males and not to women. The convention resolved that "a man's government is worse than a white man's government, because, in proportion as you increase the tyrants, you make the condition of the disenfranchised class more hopeless and degraded."

Fifteenth Amendment
One of the three Civil War amendments; specifically enfranchised newly freed male slaves.

In spite of these arguments, the **Fifteenth Amendment** was passed by Congress in February 1869. It guaranteed the "right of citizens" to vote regardless of their "race, color or previous condition of servitude." Again, sex was not mentioned.

Women's rights activists were shocked. Abolitionists' continued support of the Fifteenth Amendment, which was ratified by the states in 1870, prompted many women's rights supporters to leave the abolition movement to work solely for the cause of women's rights. Twice burned, Anthony and Stanton decided to form their own National Woman Suffrage Association (NWSA) to achieve that goal. In spite of the NWSA's opposition, however, the Fifteenth Amendment was ratified by the states in 1870.

Civil Rights and the Supreme Court

While the Congress was clear in its wishes that the rights of African Americans be expanded and that the Black Codes be rendered illegal, the Supreme Court was not nearly so protective of those rights under the Civil War amendments. In the first two tests of the scope of the Fourteenth Amendment, the Supreme Court ruled that the citizenship rights guaranteed by the amendment applied only to rights of national citizenship and not to state citizenship. Ironically, neither case involved African Americans. In *The Slaughterhouse Cases* (1873), the Court upheld Louisiana's right to create a monopoly in the operation of slaughterhouses, despite the Butcher's Benevolent Association's claim that this action deprived its members of their livelihood and thus the privileges and immunities of citizenship guaranteed by the amendment.[9]

Similarly, in *Bradwell* v. *Illinois* (1873), when Myra Bradwell asked the U.S. Supreme Court to find that Illinois's refusal to allow her to practice law (although she had passed the bar examination) violated her citizenship rights guaranteed by the privileges and immunities clause of the Fourteenth Amendment, her arguments fell on deaf ears. In *Bradwell* one justice went so far as to declare that it was reasonable for the state to bar women from the practice of law because "the natural and proper timidity and delicacy which belongs to the female sex evidently unfits it for many of the occupations of civil life."[10]

The combined message of these two cases was that state and national citizenship were separate and distinct. In essence, the Supreme Court ruled that neither African Americans nor any others could be protected from discriminatory state action, because the Fourteenth Amendment did not enlarge the limited rights guaranteed by U.S. citizenship.

Claims for expanded rights and requests for a clear definition of U.S. citizenship rights continued to fall on deaf ears in the halls of the Supreme Court. In 1875, for example, the Court heard *Minor* v. *Happersett*, the culmination of a series of test cases launched by women's rights activists.[11] Virginia Minor, after planning with Anthony and other NWSA members, attempted to register to vote in her hometown of St. Louis, Missouri. When the registrar refused to record her name on the list of eligible voters, Minor sued, arguing that the state's refusal to let her vote violated the privileges and immunities clause of the Fourteenth Amendment. Rejecting her claim, the justices ruled unanimously that voting was not a privilege of citizenship. Until 1999, the Supreme Court never again addressed the possible scope of the privileges and immunities clause. (See chapter 3.)

Southern resistance to African American equality led Congress to pass the Civil Rights Act of 1875, designed to grant equal access to public accommodations such as theaters, restaurants, and transportation. The act also prohibited the exclusion of African Americans from jury service. After 1877, however, as Reconstruction was dismantled, national interest in the legal condition of African Americans waned. Most white Southerners had never believed in equality for "freedmen," as former slaves were called. Any rights freedmen received had been contingent on federal enforcement. Once federal troops were no longer available to guard polls and prevent whites from excluding black voters, Southern states moved to limit African Americans' access to the ballot. Other forms of discrimination were also allowed by judicial decisions upholding **Jim Crow laws,** which required segregation in public schools and facilities including railroads, restaurants, and theaters. Many Jim Crow laws also barred interracial marriage. All these laws, at first glance,

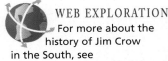

WEB EXPLORATION
For more about the history of Jim Crow in the South, see
www.ablongman.com/oconnor

Jim Crow laws
Laws enacted by Southern states that discriminated against blacks by creating "whites only" schools, theaters, hotels, and other public accommodations.

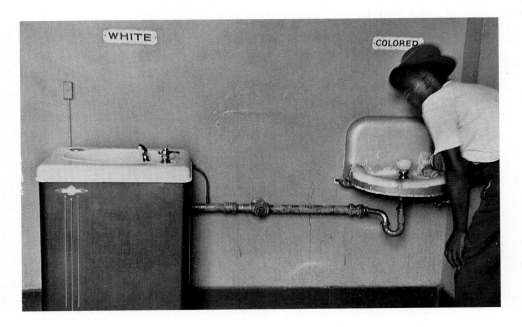

Throughout the South, examples of Jim Crow laws abounded. One such law required separate public drinking fountains, shown here. Notice the obvious difference in quality. (Photo courtesy: Bettmann/Corbis)

Civil Rights Cases (1883)
Name attached to five cases brought under the Civil Rights Act of 1875. In 1883 the Supreme Court decided that discrimination in a variety of public accommodations, including theaters, hotels, and railroads, could not be prohibited by the act because it was private, not state, discrimination.

appeared to conflict with the Civil Rights Act of 1875. In 1883, however, a series of cases decided by the Supreme Court severely damaged the vitality of the 1875 Act. The *Civil Rights Cases* (1883) were five separate cases involving the convictions of private individuals found to have violated the Civil Rights Act by refusing to extend accommodations to African Americans in theaters, a hotel, and a railroad.[12] In deciding these cases, the Supreme Court ruled that Congress could prohibit only state or governmental action and not private acts of discrimination. The Court thus seriously limited the scope of the Fourteenth Amendment by concluding that Congress had no authority to prohibit private discrimination in public accommodations.

The Court's opinion in the *Civil Rights Cases* provided a moral reinforcement for the Jim Crow system. Southern states viewed the Court's ruling as an invitation to gut the Thirteenth, Fourteenth, and Fifteenth Amendments.

In devising ways to make certain that African Americans did not vote, Southerners had to avoid the *intent* of the Fifteenth Amendment. This amendment did not guarantee suffrage; it simply said that states could not deny anyone the right to vote on account of race or color. To exclude African Americans in a seemingly racially neutral way, Southern states used two devices before the 1890s: (1) poll taxes (small taxes on the right to vote that often came due when poor African American sharecroppers had the least amount of money on hand) or some form of property-owning qualifications; and (2) "literacy" or "understanding" tests, which allowed local registrars to administer difficult reading-comprehension tests to potential voters whom they did not know.

These voting restrictions had an immediate impact. By the late 1890s, black voting fell by 62 percent from the Reconstruction period, while white voting fell by only 26 percent. To make certain that these laws didn't further reduce the numbers of poor or uneducated white voters, many Southern states added a **grandfather clause** to their voting qualification provisions, granting voting privileges to those who failed to pass a wealth or literacy test only if their grandfathers had voted before Reconstruction. Grandfather clauses effectively denied the descendants of slaves the right to vote.

grandfather clause
Voting qualification provision that allowed only those whose grandfathers had voted before Reconstruction to vote unless they passed a wealth or literacy test.

While African Americans continued to face wide-ranging racism on all fronts, women also confronted discrimination. During this period married women, by law, could not be recognized as legal entities. Women often were treated in the same category as juveniles and "imbeciles," and in many states were not entitled to wages, inheritances, or custody of their children.

THE PUSH FOR EQUALITY, 1890–1954

The Progressive Era (1889–1920) was characterized by a concerted effort to reform political, economic, and social affairs. Evils like child labor, the concentration of economic power in the hands of a few industrialists, limited suffrage, political corruption, business monopolies, and prejudice against African Americans were all targets of progressive reform efforts. Distress over the legal inferiority of African Americans was aggravated by the U.S. Supreme Court's decision in *Plessy* v. *Ferguson* (1896), a case that some commentators point to as the Court's darkest hour.

Plessy v. *Ferguson* (1896)
Plessy challenged a Louisiana statute requiring that railroads provide separate accommodations for blacks and whites. The Court found that separate but equal accommodations did not violate the equal protection clause of the Fourteenth Amendment.

In 1892 a group of African Americans in Louisiana decided to test the constitutionality of a Louisiana law mandating racial segregation on all public trains. They convinced Homer Adolph Plessy, a man of seven-eighths Caucasian and one-eighth African blood[13] to board a train in New Orleans and proceed to the "whites only" car. He was arrested when he refused to leave his seat and take one in the car reserved for African Americans. Plessy sued the railroad company, arguing that racial segregation was illegal under the provisions of the Fourteenth Amendment.[14]

The Supreme Court disagreed. After analyzing the history of African Americans in the United States, the majority concluded that the Louisiana law was constitutional. The justices based the decision on their belief that separate facilities for blacks and whites provided equal protection of the laws. After all, they reasoned, African Americans were not prevented from riding the train; the Louisiana statute required only that the races travel separately. Justice John Marshall Harlan (1877–1911) was the lone dissenter on the Court. He argued that "the Constitution is colorblind" and that it was senseless to hold constitutional a law "which, practically, puts the badge of servitude and degradation upon a large class of our fellow citizens."

Not surprisingly, the separate-but-equal doctrine enunciated in *Plessy* v. *Ferguson* soon came to mean only "separate," as new legal avenues to discriminate against African Americans were enacted into law throughout the South. The Jim Crow system soon became a way of life in the American South. In 1898 the Supreme Court upheld the constitutionality of literacy tests that were administered to African Americans and indicated its apparent willingness to allow the Southern states to define their own suffrage standards, whether or not they disproportionately affected blacks.[15] One year later, the Supreme Court upheld a school district's decision to maintain a whites-only high school but close a blacks-only high school to free up funds for a black elementary school.[16] The Supreme Court unanimously upheld the constitutionality of this disparate treatment.

By 1900, then, equality for African Americans was far from the promise first offered by the Civil War amendments. Again and again, the Supreme Court nullified the intent of the amendments and sanctioned racial segregation while the states avidly followed its lead. While discrimination was widely practiced in many parts of the North, Southern states passed laws legally imposing segregation in education, housing, public accommodations, employment, and most other spheres of life. Miscegenation laws, for example, prohibited blacks and whites from marrying.

Jim Crow laws were not the only practices designed to keep African Americans in a secondary position. Indeed, these laws established a way of life with strong social codes as well. Journalist Juan Williams notes in *Eyes on the Prize:*

> There were Jim Crow schools, Jim Crow restaurants, Jim Crow water fountains, and Jim Crow customs—blacks were expected to tip their hats when they walked past whites, but whites did not have to remove their hats even when they entered a black family's home. Whites were to be called "sir" and "ma'am" by blacks, who in turn were called by their first names by whites. People with white skin were to be given a wide berth on the sidewalk; blacks were expected to step aside meekly.[17]

Notwithstanding these degrading practices, by the early 1900s a small group of African Americans (largely from the North) had been able to attain some formal education and were ready to push for additional rights. They found some progressive white citizens and politicians amenable to their cause.

The Founding of the National Association for the Advancement of Colored People

In 1909 a handful of individuals active in a variety of progressive causes—including women's suffrage and the fight for better working conditions for women and children—met to discuss the idea of a group devoted to the problems of "the Negro." Major race riots had recently occurred in several American cities, and progressive reformers who sought change in political, economic, and social relations were concerned about these outbreaks of violence and the possibility of others. Oswald Garrison Villard, the influential publisher of the New York *Evening Post*—and grandson of William Lloyd Garrison—called a conference to discuss the problem. This group soon evolved into the National Association for the Advancement of Colored People (NAACP). Along with Villard, its first leaders included Jane Addams of Hull House, vice president of the National American Woman Suffrage Association; Moorfield Storey, a past president of the American Bar Association; and W. E. B. DuBois, a founder of the Niagara Movement, a group of educated African Americans who took

WEB EXPLORATION
To learn more about the NAACP, see
www.ablongman.com/oconnor

William E. B. DuBois (second from right in the second row, facing left) is pictured with the original leaders of the Niagara Movement in this 1905 photo taken on the Canadian side of Niagara Falls, where blacks did not face segregated facilities. (Photo courtesy: Photographs and Prints Division, Schomburg Center for Research in Black Culture, The New York Public Library, Astor, Lenox and Tilden Foundations)

their name from their first meeting place in Niagara Falls, Ontario, Canada. (The Niagara reformers met in Canada because no hotel on the U.S. side of the falls would accommodate them.)

Key Women's Groups

The NAACP was not the only group getting off the ground. The struggle for women's rights was revitalized by the formation of the National American Woman Suffrage Association (NAWSA) in 1890, when the National and American Woman Suffrage Associations merged, with Susan B. Anthony as its president. Unlike the National Woman Suffrage Association, which had sought a wide variety of expanded rights for women, this new association was devoted largely to securing women's suffrage. Its task was greatly facilitated by the proliferation of women's groups that emerged during the Progressive Era. In addition to the rapidly growing temperance movement—the move to ban the sale of alcohol, which many women blamed for a variety of social ills—women's groups were created to seek protective legislation in the form of maximum hour or minimum wage laws for women and to work for improved sanitation, public morals, education, and the like. Other organizations that were part of what was called the "club movement" were created to provide increased cultural and literary experiences for middle-class women. With increased industrialization, some women found for the first time that they had the opportunity to pursue activities other than those centered on the home.

One of the most active groups lobbying on behalf of women during this period was the National Consumers' League (NCL), which successfully lobbied for Oregon legislation limiting women to ten hours of work a day. When Curt Muller was then convicted of employing women more than ten hours a day in his small laundry and brought his appeal to the U.S. Supreme Court, the NCL sought permission from the state to conduct the defense of the statute.

At the urging of NCL attorney and future U.S. Supreme Court Justice Louis Brandeis, NCL members amassed an impressive array of sociological and medical data that were incorporated into what became known as the "Brandeis brief." This contained only three pages of legal argument, while more than a hundred pages were devoted to nonlegal, sociological data that were used to convince the

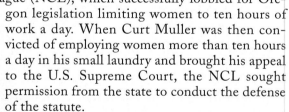

Suffragettes demonstrating for the franchise. Parades like this one took place in cities all over the United States. (Photo courtesy: Library of Congress)

Court that Oregon's statute was constitutional. In finding the law constitutional in *Muller* v. *Oregon* (1908), the Court relied heavily on these data to document women's unique status as mothers to justify their differential treatment.[18]

Women seeking the vote used reasoning reflecting the Court's opinion in *Muller*. Discarding earlier notions of full equality, NAWSA based its claim to the right to vote largely on the fact that women, as mothers, should be enfranchised. Furthermore, although many members of the **suffrage movement** were NAACP members, the new women's movement—called the suffrage movement because of its focus on the vote alone and not on broader issues of women's rights—took on racist overtones as women argued that if undereducated African Americans could vote, why couldn't women? Some NAWSA members even argued that "the enfranchisement of women would ensure immediate and durable white supremacy."

Diverse attitudes were clearly present in the growing suffrage movement, which often tried to be all things to all people. Its roots in the Progressive movement gave it an exceptionally broad base that transformed NAWSA from a small organization of just over 10,000 members in the early 1890s to a true social movement of more than 2 million members in 1917. By 1920, a coalition of women's groups led by NAWSA was able to secure ratification of the **Nineteenth Amendment** to the Constitution. It guaranteed *all* women the right to vote—fifty-five years after African American males had been enfranchised by the Fifteenth Amendment.

In 1908, the U.S. Supreme Court ruled that Oregon's law barring women from working more than ten hours a day in laundries was constitutional. Thus, the conviction of Curt Muller who owned the laundry where women worked twelve-and fourteen-hour days, (with arms folded) was upheld. (Photo courtesy: The Supreme Court Historical Society/Mrs. Neill Whisnant and Portland, Oregon, Chamber of Commerce)

suffrage movement
Term used to refer to the drive for votes for women that took place in the United States from 1890 to 1920.

After passage of the suffrage amendment in 1920, the fragile alliance of diverse women's groups that had come together to fight for the vote quickly disintegrated. Women returned to their "home" groups, such as the NCL or the Women's Christian Temperance Union, to pursue their individualized goals. In fact, after the tumult of the suffrage movement, widespread, organized activity on behalf of women's rights did not reemerge until the 1960s. In the meantime, however, the NAACP continued to fight racism and racial segregation. In fact, its activities and those of others in the civil rights movement would later give impetus to a new women's movement.

Litigating for Equality

During the 1930s leaders of the NAACP began to sense that the time was right to launch a full-scale challenge in the federal courts to the constitutionality of *Plessy*'s separate-but-equal doctrine. The NAACP mapped out a long-range strategy that would first target segregation in professional and graduate education. Clearly, the separate-but-equal doctrine and the proliferation of Jim Crow laws were a bar to any hope of full equality for African Americans. Traditional legislative channels were unlikely to work, given blacks' limited or nonexistent political power. Thus, the federal courts and a long range litigation strategy were the NAACP's only hope. The NAACP often relied on Brandeis-type briefs, so-called because they relied heavily on sociological data to support their legal arguments. In fact, the NAACP eventually hired a statistician to

Lloyd Gaines was the subject of the major test case, *Missouri ex rel. Gaines* v. *Canada*, which contested the principle of segregated schools. Gaines chose to attend the University of Michigan, from which he strangely disappeared, never to be heard from again. (Photo courtesy: AP/Wide World Photos)

help its lawyers amass data to help present evidence of discrimination to the courts.

Test Cases.   The NAACP opted first to challenge the constitutionality of Jim Crow law schools. In 1935, all Southern states maintained fully segregated elementary and secondary schools. Colleges and universities were also segregated, but most states did not provide for postgraduate education for African Americans. NAACP lawyers chose to target law schools because they were institutions that judges could well understand, and integration there could prove less threatening to most whites.

Lloyd Gaines, a graduate of Missouri's all-black Lincoln University, sought admission to the all-white University of Missouri Law School in 1936. He was immediately rejected. In the separate-but-equal spirit, the state offered to build a law school at Lincoln (although no funds were allocated for the project) or, if he didn't want to wait, to pay his tuition at an out-of-state law school. Gaines lost his appeal of this rejection in the lower court, and the case was appealed to the U.S. Supreme Court.

Gaines's case was filed at an auspicious time. As you may recall from chapter 3, a "constitutional revolution" of sorts occurred in Supreme Court decision making in 1937. Before this time, the Court was most receptive to and interested in the protection of economic liberties. In 1937, however, the Court reversed itself in a series of cases and began to place individual freedoms and personal liberties on a more protected footing. Thus, in 1938, Gaines's lawyers pleaded his appeal to a far more sympathetic Supreme Court. NAACP attorneys argued that the creation of a separate law school of any less caliber than that of the University of Missouri would not and could not afford Gaines an *equal* education. The justices agreed with the NAACP's contention and ruled that Missouri had failed to meet the separate-but-equal requirements of *Plessy*. The Court ordered Missouri either to admit Gaines to the school or to set up a law school for him.[19]

Recognizing the importance of the Court's ruling, in 1939 the NAACP created a separate, tax-exempt legal defense fund to devise a strategy to build on the Missouri case to bring about equal educational opportunities for all African American children. The first head of the NAACP Legal Defense and Educational Fund (LDF), as it was called, was Thurgood Marshall, who later became the first African American to serve on the U.S. Supreme Court (1967–1991). Sensing that the Court would be more amenable to the NAACP's broader goals if it was first forced to address a variety of less threatening claims to educational opportunity, Marshall and the NAACP LDF brought a series of carefully crafted test cases to the Court.

The first case involved H. M. Sweatt, a forty-six-year-old African American mail carrier, who in 1946 applied for admission to the all-white University of Texas Law School. Rejected on racial grounds, Sweatt sued. The judge gave the state six months to establish a law school or to admit Sweatt to the University of Texas. The university then rented a few rooms in downtown Houston and hired two local African American attorneys to be part-time faculty members. (At that time there was only one full-time African American law school professor in the United States.) The state legislature saw the handwriting on the wall and authorized $3 million for the creation of the Texas State University for Negroes. One hundred thousand dollars of that money was to be for a new law school in Austin across the street from the state capitol. It consisted of three small basement rooms,

WEB EXPLORATION
To learn more about the NAACP Legal Defense Fund, see
www.ablongman.com/oconnor

a library of more than 10,000 books, access to the state law library, and three part-time first-year instructors as the "faculty." Sweatt declined the opportunity to obtain an education there and instead chose to continue his legal challenge.

While working on the Texas case, the NAACP LDF and Marshall also decided to pursue another case. Thurgood Marshall chose to use the case of George W. McLaurin, a retired university professor who had been denied admission to the doctoral education program at the University of Oklahoma. Marshall reasoned that McLaurin, at sixty-eight years of age, would be immune from the charges that African Americans wanted integration in order to intermarry. After a lower court ordered McLaurin's admission, the university reserved a dingy alcove in the cafeteria for him to eat in during off-hours, and he was given his own table in the library behind a shelf of newspapers. In what surely "was Oklahoma's most inventive contribution to legalized bigotry since the adoption of the 'grandfather clause,' "[20] McLaurin was forced to sit outside classrooms while lectures were given and seminars were held.

The Supreme Court handled these two cases together.[21] The eleven Southern states filed an *amicus curiae* (friend of the court) brief, in which they argued that *Plessy* should govern both cases. The NAACP LDF received assistance, however, from an unexpected source—the U.S. government. In a dramatic departure from the past, the administration of Harry S Truman filed a friend of the court brief urging the Court to overrule *Plessy*. Since the late 1870s, the U.S. government had never sided against the Southern states in a civil rights matter and had never submitted an *amicus* brief supporting the rights of African American citizens. President Truman believed that because many African Americans had fought and died for their country in World War II, this kind of executive action was proper. The Court traditionally gives great weight to briefs from the U.S. government. The Court, however, again did not overrule *Plessy*, but the justices found that the measures taken by the states in each case failed to live up to the strictures of the separate-but-equal doctrine. The Court unanimously ruled that the "remedies" to each situation were inadequate to afford a sound education. In the *Sweatt* case, for example, the Court declared that the "qualities which are incapable of objective measurement but which make for greatness in a law school . . . includ[ing] the reputation of the faculty, experience of the administration, position and influence of the alumni, standing in the community, traditions and prestige" made it impossible for the state to provide an equal education in a segregated setting.

In 1950, after these decisions were handed down, the NAACP LDF concluded that the time had come to launch a full-scale attack on the separate-but-equal doctrine. The decisions of the Court were encouraging, and the position of the U.S. government and the population in general appeared to be more receptive to an outright overruling of *Plessy*.

Brown v. Board of Education (1954). *Brown* v. *Board of Education*, was actually four cases brought from different areas of the South and border states involving public elementary or high school systems that mandated separate schools for blacks and whites.[22]

In *Brown*, NAACP LDF lawyers, again headed by Thurgood Marshall, argued that *Plessy*'s separate-but-equal doctrine was unconstitutional under the **equal protection clause** of the Fourteenth Amendment, and that if the Court was still reluctant to overrule *Plessy*, the only way to equalize the schools was to integrate them. A major component of the NAACP LDF's strategy was to prove that the intellectual, psychological, and financial damage that befell African Americans as a result of segregation precluded any court from finding that equality was served by the separate-but-equal policy.

In *Brown*, the NAACP LDF presented the Supreme Court with evidence of the harmful consequences of state-imposed racial discrimination. To buttress its claims, the NAACP LDF introduced the now-famous "doll study," conducted by Kenneth Clark, a prominent African American sociologist who had long studied the negative effects of segregation on African American children. His research revealed that black children not only preferred white dolls when shown black dolls and white dolls, but that most liked the white doll better, many adding that the black doll looked "bad." This

Brown v. Board of Education (1954)
U.S. Supreme Court decision holding that school segregation is inherently unconstitutional because it violates the Fourteenth Amendment's guarantee of equal protection; marked the end of legal segregation in the United States.

equal protection clause
Section of the Fourteenth Amendment that guarantees that all citizens receive "equal protection of the laws"; has been used to bar discrimination against blacks and women.

WEB EXPLORATION
To read the full text of
Brown, see
www.ablongman.com/oconnor

information was used to illustrate the negative impact of racial segregation and bias on an African American child's self-image.

The NAACP LDF's legal briefs were supported by important *amicus curiae* briefs submitted by the U.S. government, major civil rights groups, labor unions, and religious groups decrying racial segregation. On May 17, 1954, Chief Justice Earl Warren delivered the fourth opinion of the day, *Brown* v. *Board of Education.* Writing for the Court, Warren stated:

> To separate [some school children] from others . . . solely because of their race generates a feeling of inferiority as to their status in the community that may affect their hearts and minds in a way very unlikely ever to be undone. We conclude, unanimously, that in the field of public education the doctrine of "separate but equal" has no place.

There can be no doubt that *Brown* was the most important civil rights case decided in the twentieth century.[23] It immediately evoked an uproar that shook the nation. Some called the day the decision was handed down "Black Monday." The governor of South Carolina decried the decision, saying, "Ending segregation would mark the beginning of the end of civilization in the South as we know it."[24] The NAACP LDF lawyers who had argued these cases and those cases leading to *Brown,* however, were jubilant.

Remarkable changes had occurred in the civil rights of Americans since 1890. Women had won the right to vote, and after a long and arduous trail of litigation in the federal courts, the Supreme Court had finally overturned its most racist decision of the era, *Plessy* v. *Ferguson.* The Court boldly proclaimed that separate but equal (at least in education) would no longer pass constitutional muster. The question then became how *Brown* would be interpreted and implemented. Could it be used to invalidate other Jim Crow laws and practices? Would African Americans be truly equal under the law?

THE CIVIL RIGHTS MOVEMENT

Our notion of civil rights has changed profoundly since 1954. First African Americans and then women have built upon existing organizations to forge successful movements for increased rights. *Brown* served as a catalyst for change, sparking the development of the modern civil rights movement. Women's work in that movement and the student protest movement that arose in reaction to the U.S. government's involvement in Vietnam gave women the experience needed to form their own organizations to press for full equality. As African Americans and women became more and more successful, they served as models for others who sought equality—Native Americans, Latino Americans, homosexuals, the disabled, and others.

School Desegregation After Brown

One year after *Brown,* in a case referred to as *Brown II,* the Court ruled that racially segregated systems must be dismantled "with all deliberate speed."[25] To facilitate implementation, the Court placed enforcement of *Brown* in the hands of appointed federal district court judges, who were considered more immune to local political pressures than were regularly elected state court judges.

The NAACP and its Legal Defense Fund continued to resort to the courts to see that *Brown* was implemented, while the South entered into a near-conspiracy to avoid the mandates of *Brown II.* In Arkansas, for example, Governor Orval Faubus, facing a reelection bid, announced that he would not "be a party to any attempt to force acceptance of change to which people are overwhelmingly opposed."[26] The day before school was to begin, Faubus announced that he would surround Little Rock's Central High School with National Guardsmen to prevent African American students from entering. While the federal courts in Arkansas continued to order the admission of African American children, the governor remained adamant. Finally, President Dwight D. Eisenhower sent federal troops to Little Rock to protect the rights of the nine students who had attempted to attend Central High.

In reaction to the governor's outrageous conduct, the Court broke with tradition and issued a unanimous decision in *Cooper* v. *Aaron* (1958), which was filed by the Little Rock School Board asking the federal district court for a two-and-one-half-year delay in implementation of its desegregation plans. Each justice signed the opinion individually, underscoring his individual support for the notion that "no state legislator or executive or judicial officer can war against the Constitution without violating his undertaking to support it."[27] The state's actions were thus ruled unconstitutional and its "evasive schemes" illegal.

A New Move for African American Rights

In 1955, soon after *Brown II*, the civil rights movement took another step forward—this time in Montgomery, Alabama. Rosa Parks, the local NAACP's Youth Council advisor, decided to challenge the constitutionality of the segregated bus system. First, Parks and other NAACP officials began to raise money for litigation and made speeches around town to garner public support. Then, on December 1, 1955, Rosa Parks made history when she refused to leave her seat on a bus to move to the back to make room for a white male passenger. She was arrested for violating an Alabama law banning integration of public facilities, including buses. After she was freed on bond, Parks and the NAACP decided to enlist city clergy to help her cause. At the same time, they distributed 35,000 handbills calling for African Americans to boycott the Montgomery bus system on the day of Parks's trial. Black ministers used Sunday services to urge their members to support the boycott. On Monday morning, African Americans walked, carpooled, or used black-owned taxicabs. That night, local ministers decided that the boycott should be continued. A twenty-six-year-old minister, Martin Luther King Jr., was selected to lead the newly formed Montgomery Improvement Association. King was new to town, and church leaders had been looking for a way to get him more involved in civil rights work.

Seven-year-old Linda Brown lived close to a good public school, but her race precluded her attendance there. When the NAACP sought plaintiffs to challenge this discrimination, her father, a local minister, offered Linda as one of several student plaintiffs named in the NAACP's case. Hers came first alphabetically, hence the case name. (Photo courtesy: Carl Iwasaki/ TimePix)

As the boycott dragged on, Montgomery officials and local business owners began to harass the city's African American citizens. But King urged Montgomery's African American citizens to continue their protest. The residents held out, despite suffering personal hardship for their actions, ranging from harassment to bankruptcy to job loss. In 1956, a federal court ruled that the segregated bus system violated the equal protection clause of the Fourteenth Amendment. After a year of walking, African Americans ended their protest as the buses were ordered to integrate. The first effort at nonviolent protest had been successful. Organized boycotts and other forms of nonviolent protest, including sit-ins at segregated restaurants and bus stations, were to follow.

WEB EXPLORATION
For more about the Montgomery bus boycott and Dr. Martin Luther King Jr., see
www.ablongman.com/oconnor

Formation of New Groups

The recognition and respect that King earned within the African American community helped him to launch the Southern Christian Leadership Conference (SCLC) in 1957, soon after the end of the Montgomery bus boycott. Unlike the NAACP, which had Northern origins and had come to rely largely on litigation as a means of

A prime objective of civil rights protesters in Birmingham, Alabama, was to focus national attention on their cause. For the first time in American history, a majority of the public owned television sets and could see the horrors of police brutality aimed at African Americans and supporters. But the print media continued to be a powerful tool. This picture was reprinted over and over again and even frequently mentioned on the floor of Congress during debates on the Civil Rights Act of 1964. (Photo courtesy: Charles Moore/Black Star)

achieving expanded equality, the SCLC had a Southern base and was rooted more closely in black religious culture. The SCLC's philosophy reflected King's growing belief in the importance of nonviolent protest.

On February 1, 1960, students at the all-black North Carolina Agricultural and Technical College participated in the first sit-in. Angered by their inability to be served at local lunch counters and heartened by the success of the Montgomery bus boycott, black students marched to the local Woolworth's store and ordered cups of coffee at the lunch counter there. They were refused service. So they sat at the counter until police came and carted them off to jail. Soon thereafter, African American college students around the South joined together to challenge Jim Crow laws. These mass actions immediately brought extensive attention from the national news media.

Over spring break 1960, with the assistance of an $800 grant from the SCLC, 200 student delegates—black *and* white—met at Shaw University in North Carolina to consider recent sit-in actions and to plan for the future. Later that year, two more meetings were held in Atlanta, Georgia, and the Student Nonviolent Coordinating Committee (SNCC) was formed.

Among SNCC's first leaders were Marion Barry, who would later serve as mayor of Washington, D.C. (1978–1990, 1995–1999); John Lewis, an eight-term Democratic member of the House of Representatives; and Marian Wright Edelman, who first became an NAACP lawyer and later the founder and head of the Children's Defense Fund. While the SCLC generally worked with church leaders in a community, the SNCC was much more of a grassroots organization. Always perceived as more radical than the SCLC, SNCC tended to focus its organizing activities on the young, both black and white.

In addition to joining the sit-in bandwagon, SNCC also came to lead what were called "freedom rides," designed to focus attention on segregated public accommodations. Bands of college students and other civil rights activists traveled by bus throughout the South in an effort to force bus stations to desegregate. Often these protesters were met by angry mobs of segregationists and brutal violence, as local police chose not to defend protesters' basic constitutional rights to free speech and peaceful assembly. African Americans were not the only ones to participate in freedom rides; increasingly, white college students from the North began to play an important role in the SNCC.

While the SNCC continued to sponsor sit-ins and freedom rides, in 1963, the Reverend Martin Luther King Jr. launched a series of massive nonviolent demonstrations in Birmingham, Alabama, long considered a major stronghold of segregation. Thousands of blacks and whites marched to Birmingham in a show of solidarity. Peaceful marchers were met there by the Birmingham police commissioner, who ordered his officers to use dogs, clubs, and fire hoses on the marchers. Americans across the nation watched in horror as they witnessed the brutality and abuse heaped on the protesters. As the marchers hoped, these shocking scenes helped convince President John F. Kennedy to propose important civil rights legislation.

The Civil Rights Act of 1964

The older faction of the civil rights movement, as represented by the SCLC, and the younger branch, represented by the SNCC, both sought a similar goal: full implementation of Supreme Court decisions and an end to racial segregation and discrimination. The cumulative effect of collective actions including sit-ins, boycotts, marches, and freedom rides—as well as the tragic bombings and deaths inflicted in retaliation—led Congress to pass the first major piece of civil rights legislation since the post–Civil War era.

In 1963, President Kennedy requested that Congress pass a law banning discrimination in public accommodations. Seizing the moment and recognizing the potency of a show of massive support, the Reverend Martin Luther King Jr. called for a monumental march on Washington, D.C., to demonstrate widespread support for legislation to ban discrimination in *all* aspects of life, not just public accommodations. The March on Washington for Jobs and Freedom was held in August 1963 only a few months after the Birmingham demonstrations. More than 250,000 people heard King deliver his famous "I Have a Dream" speech from the Lincoln Memorial. Before Congress had the opportunity to vote on any legislation, however, John F. Kennedy was assassinated on November 22, 1963, in Dallas, Texas.

It was clear that national laws outlawing discrimination were the only answer: Southern legislators would never vote to repeal Jim Crow laws. It was much more feasible for African Americans to first seek national laws and then their implementation from the federal judiciary. But through the 1960s, African Americans lacked sufficient political power or the force of public opinion to sway enough congressional leaders. Their task was further stymied by loud and strong opposition from Southern members of Congress. Many of these legislators, because of the Democratic Party's total control of the South, had been in office far longer than most, and therefore held powerful committee chairmanships that were awarded on seniority. The Senate Judiciary Committee was controlled by a coalition of Southern Democrats and conservative Republicans. The House Rules Committee was chaired by a Virginian opposed to any civil rights legislation, who by virtue of his position could block such legislation in committee.

When Vice President Lyndon B. Johnson, a Southern-born former Senate majority leader, succeeded Kennedy as president, he put civil rights reform at the top of his legislative priority list and civil rights activists gained a critical ally. Thus, through the 1960s, the movement subtly changed in focus from peaceful protest and litigation to legislative lobbying. Its focus broadened from integration of school and public facilities and voting rights to issues of housing, jobs, and equal opportunity.

The push for civil rights legislation in the halls of Congress was helped by changes in public opinion. Between 1959 and 1965, Southern attitudes toward integrated schools changed enormously. The proportion of Southerners who responded that they would not mind their child's attendance at a half-black school doubled.

In spite of strong presidential support and the sway of public opinion, the Civil Rights Act of 1964 did not sail through Congress. Southern senators, led by South Carolina's Strom Thurmond, a Democrat who later switched to the Republican Party, conducted the longest filibuster in the history of the Senate. For eight weeks they held up voting on the civil rights bill until cloture (see chapter 7) was invoked and the filibuster ended. Once passed, the **Civil Rights Act of 1964:**

1. Outlawed arbitrary discrimination in voter registration and expedited voting rights lawsuits.
2. Barred discrimination in public accommodations engaged in interstate commerce.

At this historic gathering on the Mall in Washington, D.C., in August, 1963, Rev. Martin Luther King Jr. delivered his famous "I Have a Dream" speech. (Photo courtesy: Flip Schulke/Black Star)

Civil Rights Act of 1964
Legislation passed by Congress to outlaw segregation in public facilities and racial discrimination in employment, education, and voting; created the Equal Employment Opportunity Commission.

3. Authorized the U.S. Justice Department to initiate lawsuits to desegregate public facilities and schools.
4. Provided for the withholding of federal funds from discriminatory state and local programs.
5. Prohibited discrimination in employment on grounds of race, color, religion, national origin, or sex.
6. Created the Equal Employment Opportunity Commission (EEOC) to monitor and enforce the bans on employment discrimination.

Other changes were sweeping the United States. Violence rocked the nation as ghetto riots broke out in the Northeast. Although Northern African Americans were not subject to Jim Crow laws, many lived in poverty and faced pervasive daily discrimination and its resultant frustration. Some, including Black Muslim leader Malcolm X, even argued that to survive, African Americans must separate themselves from white culture in every way. Given this growing "black power" movement and increased racial tension, it is not surprising that from 1964 to 1968, many African Americans in the North took to the streets, burning and looting to vent their rage.

Violence also marred the continued activities of civil rights workers in the South. During the summer of 1964 three civil rights workers—one black, two white—were killed in Neshoba County, Mississippi. In 1965 Martin Luther King Jr. again led his supporters on a massive march, this time from Selma, Alabama, to the state capital in Montgomery, in support of a pending voting rights bill. Again, Southern officials unleashed a reign of terror in Selma as they used whips, dogs, cattle prods, clubs, and tear gas on the protesters. Again, Americans watched in horror as they witnessed this brutality on their television screens. This march and the public's reaction to it led to quick passage of the Voting Rights Act of 1965.

The Impact of the Civil Rights Act of 1964

Many Southerners were adamant in their belief that the Civil Rights Act of 1964 was unconstitutional because it went beyond the scope of Congress's authority to legislate under the Constitution, and lawsuits were quickly brought to challenge the act. The first challenge to the act was heard by the Supreme Court on an expedited review (which bypasses the intermediate courts). The Court upheld its constitutionality when it found that Congress was within the legitimate scope of its commerce power as outlined in Article I.[28]

Education. One of the key provisions of the Civil Rights Act of 1964 authorized the U.S. Justice Department to bring actions against school districts that failed to comply with *Brown* v. *Board of Education*. In 1964, a full decade after *Brown*, fewer than 1 percent of African American children in the South attended integrated schools.

After *Brown*, the Charlotte-Mecklenburg School District had assigned students to the school closest to their homes without regard to race, leaving over half of African American students attending schools that were at least 99 percent black. In *Swann* v. *Charlotte-Mecklenburg School District* (1971), the Supreme Court ruled that all vestiges of state-imposed segregation, called *de jure* **discrimination,** or discrimination by law, must be eliminated at once and that lower federal courts had the authority to fashion a wide variety of remedies including busing, racial quotas, and the pairing of schools to end dual, segregated school systems.[29]

In *Swann* the Court was careful to distinguish *de jure* from *de facto* **discrimination,** unintentional discrimination often attributable to housing patterns and/or private acts. The Court noted that its approval of busing was a remedy for intentional, government imposed or -sanctioned discrimination only.

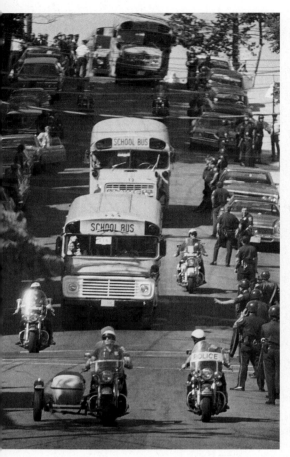

Court-ordered busing in the late 1960s frequently required by police escorts. (Photo courtesy: Bettmann/Corbis)

de jure **discrimination**
Racial segregation that is a direct result of law or official policy.

de facto **discrimination**
Racial discrimination that results from practice (such as housing patterns or other social factors) rather than the law.

Over the years, forced, judicially imposed busing has found less and less favor with the Supreme Court, even in situations where *de jure* discrimination had earlier been proven. In 1992, the U.S. Supreme Court even ruled that in situations where all-black schools still existed in spite of a 1969 court order to dismantle the *de jure* system, a showing that the persistent segregation was not a result of the school board's actions was sufficient to remove the district from court supervision. In 1995, the Court ruled 5–4 that city school boards can use plans to attract white suburban students to mostly minority urban schools only if both city and suburban schools still show the effects of segregation, thus reversing a lower court desegregation order.[30]

Employment. Title VII of the Civil Rights Act of 1964 prohibits employers from discriminating against employees for a variety of reasons, including race, sex, age, and national origin. (In 1978, the act was amended to prohibit discrimination based on pregnancy.)

In 1971, in one of the first major cases decided under the act, the Supreme Court found that employers could be found liable for discrimination if the *effect* of their employment practices was to exclude African Americans from certain positions.[31] African American employees were allowed to use statistical evidence to show that they had been excluded from all but one department of the Duke Power Company, because it required employees to have a high school education or pass a special test to be eligible for promotion.

The Supreme Court ruled that although the tests did not *appear* to discriminate against African Americans, their effects—that there were no African American employees in any other departments—were sufficient to shift the burden of proving lack of discrimination on the employer. Thus, the Duke Power Company would have to prove that the tests were "a business necessity" that had a "demonstrable relationship to successful performance" (of a particular job).

The notion of "business necessity," as set out in the Civil Rights Act of 1964 and interpreted by the federal courts, was especially important for women. Women had long been kept out of many occupations on the strength of the belief that customers preferred to deal with male personnel. Conversely, males were barred from flight-attendant positions because the airlines believed that passengers preferred to be served by young, attractive women. Similarly, many large factories, manufacturing establishments, and police and fire departments refused outright to hire women by subjecting them to arbitrary height and weight requirements, which also disproportionately affected Hispanics. Like the tests declared illegal by the Court, these requirements often could not be shown to be related to job performance and were eventually ruled illegal by the federal courts.

The Women's Rights Movement. Just as in the abolition movement in the 1800s, women from all walks of life also participated in the civil rights movement. Women were important members of both the SNCC and more traditional groups like the NAACP and the SCLC, yet they often found themselves treated as second-class citizens. At one point Stokely Carmichael, chair of the SNCC, openly proclaimed: "The only position for women in the SNCC is prone."[32] Statements and attitudes like these led some women to found early women's liberation groups that were generally quite radical, small in membership, and not intended to use more conventional political tactics.

As discussed earlier, initial efforts to convince the Supreme Court to declare women enfranchised under the Fourteenth Amendment were uniformly unsuccessful. The paternalistic attitude of the Supreme Court, and perhaps society as well, continued well into the 1970s. As late as 1961, Florida required women who wished to serve on juries to travel to the county courthouse and register for that duty. In contrast, all men who were registered voters were automatically eligible to serve. When Gwendolyn Hoyt was convicted of bludgeoning her adulterous husband to death with a baseball bat, she appealed her conviction, claiming that the exclusion of women from juries prejudiced her case. She believed that female jurors—her peers—would have been more sympathetic to her and the emotional turmoil that led to her attack on her husband and her claim of "temporary insanity." She therefore argued that her trial by an all-male jury violated her rights as guaranteed by the Fourteenth Amendment. In rejecting her contention, Justice John Harlan (the grandson of the lone dissenting justice in *Plessy*) wrote in *Hoyt* v. *Florida* (1961):

> Despite the enlightened emancipation of women from the restrictions and protections of bygone years, and their entry into many parts of community life formerly considered to be reserved to men, a woman is still regarded as the center of home and family life.[33]

These kinds of attitudes and decisions (*Hoyt* was later unanimously reversed in 1975) were not sufficient to forge a new movement for women's rights. Shortly after *Hoyt*, however, three events occurred to move women to action. In 1961, soon after his election, President John F. Kennedy created the President's Commission on the Status of Women. The Commission's report, *American Women*, released in 1963, documented pervasive discrimination against women in all walks of life. In addition, the civil rights movement and publication of Betty Friedan's *The Feminine Mystique* (1963),[34] which led some women to question their lives and status in society, added to their dawning recognition that something was wrong. Soon after, the Civil Rights Act of 1964 prohibited discrimination based not only on race, but also on sex. Ironically, that provision had been added to Title VII of the Civil Rights Act by Southern Democrats. These senators saw a prohibition against sex discrimination in employment as a joke, and viewed its addition as a means to discredit the entire act and ensure its defeat. Thus it was added at the last minute and female members of Congress seized the opportunity to garner support for the measure.

In 1966, after the **Equal Employment Opportunity Commission** failed to enforce the law as it applied to sex discrimination, women activists formed the National Organization for Women (NOW). From its inception, NOW was closely modeled on the NAACP. Women in NOW were quite similar to the founders of the NAACP; they wanted to work within the system to prevent discrimination. Initially, most of this activity was geared toward one goal: achievement of equality either through passage of an equal rights amendment to the Constitution, or by judicial decision. But because the Supreme Court failed to extend constitutional protections to women, the only recourse that remained was an amendment.

The Equal Rights Amendment (ERA). Not all women agreed with the notion of full equality for women. Members of the National Consumers' League, for example, feared that an equal rights amendment would invalidate protective legislation of the kind specifically ruled constitutional in *Muller* v. *Oregon* (1908). Nevertheless, from 1923 to 1972, a proposal for an equal rights amendment was made in every session of every Congress. Every president since Harry S Truman backed it, and by 1972 public opinion favored its ratification.

Finally, in 1972, in response to pressure from NOW, the National Women's Political Caucus, and a wide variety of other feminist groups, Congress passed the Equal Rights Amendment (ERA) by overwhelming majorities (84–8 in the Senate; 354–24 in the House). The amendment provided that:

- Equality of rights under the law shall not be denied or abridged by the United States or by any state on account of sex.
- The Congress shall have the power to enforce, by appropriate legislation, the provisions of this article.

Within a year, twenty-two states had ratified the amendment, most by overwhelming margins. But the tide soon turned. In *Roe* v. *Wade* (1973), the Supreme Court decided that women had a constitutionally protected right to privacy that included the right to terminate a pregnancy. Almost overnight *Roe* gave the ERA's opponents political fuel. Although privacy rights and the ERA have nothing to do with each other,

Equal Employment Opportunity Commission
Federal agency created to enforce the Civil Rights Act of 1964, which forbids discrimination on the basis of race, creed, national origin, religion, or sex in hiring, promotion, or firing.

WEB EXPLORATION
To learn more about NOW and the EEOC, see
www.ablongman.com/oconnor

opponents effectively persuaded many people in states that had yet to ratify the amendment that the two were linked. If abortion was legal, why not marriages between and adoptions by homosexuals? They also claimed that the ERA and feminists were antifamily and that the ERA would force women out of their homes and into the workforce because husbands would no longer be responsible for their wives' support.

These arguments and the amendment's potential to make women eligible for the military draft brought the ratification effort to a near standstill. In 1974 and 1975, the amendment only squeaked through the Montana and North Dakota legislatures, and two states—Nebraska and Tennessee—voted to rescind their earlier ratifications. By 1978, one year before the deadline for ratification was to expire, thirty-five states had voted for the amendment—three short of the three-fourths necessary for ratification. Efforts in key states such as Illinois and Florida failed as opposition to the ERA intensified. Faced with the prospect of defeat, ERA supporters heavily lobbied Congress to extend the deadline. Congress extended the time period for ratification by three years, but to no avail. No additional states ratified the amendment and three more rescinded their votes.

What began as a simple correction to the Constitution turned into a highly controversial proposed change. Even though large numbers of the public favored the ERA, opponents needed to stall ratification in only thirteen states while supporters had to convince legislators in thirty-eight. The success that women's rights activists were having in the courts was hurting the effort. When women first sought the ERA in the late 1960s, the Supreme Court had yet to rule that women were protected by the Fourteenth Amendment's equal protection clause from any kind of discrimination, thus clearly showing the need for an amendment. But as the Court widened its interpretation of the Constitution to protect women from some sorts of discrimination, in the eyes of many the need for a new amendment became less urgent.

Litigation for Equal Rights.   While several women's groups worked toward passage of the ERA, NOW and several other groups, including the Women's Rights Project of the American Civil Liberties Union (ACLU), formed litigating arms to pressure the courts. But women faced an immediate roadblock in the Supreme Court's interpretation of the equal protection clause of the Fourteenth Amendment.

The Equal Protection Clause and Constitutional Standards of Review

The Fourteenth Amendment protects all U.S. citizens from state action that violates equal protection of the laws. Most laws, however, are subject to what is called the rational basis or minimum rationality test. This lowest level of scrutiny means that governments must allege a rational foundation for any distinctions they make. Early on, however, the Supreme Court decided that certain rights were entitled to a heightened standard of review. As early as 1937, the Supreme Court recognized that certain rights were so fundamental that a very heavy burden would be placed on any government that sought to restrict those rights. As discussed in chapter 5, when fundamental rights such as First Amendment freedoms or **suspect classifications** such as race are involved, the Court uses a heightened standard of review called **strict scrutiny** to determine the constitutional validity of the challenged practices, as detailed in Table 6.1. Beginning with *Korematsu* v. *United States* (1944), which involved a constitutional challenge to the internment of Japanese Americans, Justice Hugo Black noted that "all legal restrictions which curtail the civic rights of a single racial group are immediately suspect," and should be given "the most rigid scrutiny."[35] In *Brown* v. *Board of Education* (1954), the Supreme Court again used the strict scrutiny standard to evaluate the constitutionality of race-based distinctions. In legal terms this means that if a statute or governmental practice makes a classification based on race, the statute is presumed to be unconstitutional unless the state can provide "compelling affirmative justifications"—that is, unless the state can prove the law in question is necessary to accomplish a permissible goal and that it is the least restrictive means through which that goal can be accomplished.

WEB EXPLORATION
To learn more about the ERA, see
www.ablongman.com/oconnor

Longman
Participate.com
2.0
Timeline
**The Struggle
for Equal
Protection**

suspect classification
Category or class, such as race, that triggers the highest standard of scrutiny from the Supreme Court.

strict scrutiny
A heightened standard of review used by the Supreme Court to determine the constitutional validity of a challenged practice.

TABLE 6.1   The Equal Protection Clause and Standards of Review Used by the Supreme Court to Determine Whether It Has Been Violated

TYPE OF CLASSIFICATION (What kind of statutory classification is at issue?)	STANDARD OF REVIEW (What standard of review will be used?)	TEST (What does the Court ask?)	EXAMPLE (How does the Court apply the test?)
Fundamental freedoms: religion, assembly, press, privacy, suspect classifications (including race)	Strict scrutiny or heightened standard	Is classification necessary to the accomplishment of a permissible state goal? Is it the least restrictive way to reach that goal?	*Brown* v. *Board of Education* (1954): Racial segregation not necessary to accomplish the state goal of educating its students
Gender	Intermediate standard	Does the classification serve an important governmental objective, and is it substantially related to those ends?	*Craig* v. *Boren* (1976): Keeping drunk drivers off the roads may be an important governmental objective, but allowing eighteen- to twenty-one-year-old women to drink alcoholic beverages while prohibiting men of the same age from drinking is not substantially related to that goal.
Others (including age, wealth, and sexual preference)	Minimum rationality standard	Is there any rational foundation for the discrimination?	*Romer* v. *Evans* (1996): Colorado constitutional amendment precluding any legislative, executive, or judicial action at any state or local level designed to bar discrimination based on sexual preference is not rational or reasonable.

WEB EXPLORATION
For more about the ACLU Women's Rights Project, see
www.ablongman.com/oconnor

During the 1960s and into the 1970s, the Court routinely struck down as unconstitutional practices and statutes that discriminated on the basis of race. "Whites-only" public parks and recreational facilities, tax-exempt status for private schools that discriminated, and statutes prohibiting racial intermarriage were declared unconstitutional. In contrast, the Court refused even to consider the fact that the equal protection clause might apply to discrimination against women. Finally, in a case brought in 1971 by Ruth Bader Ginsburg as director of the Women's Rights Project of the ACLU, the Supreme Court ruled that an Idaho law granting male parents automatic preference over female parents as the administrator of their deceased children's estates violated the equal protection clause of the Fourteenth Amendment.

Reed v. *Reed* (1971), the Idaho case, turned the tide in terms of constitutional litigation. While the Court did not rule that sex was a suspect classification, it concluded that the equal protection clause of the Fourteenth Amendment prohibited unreasonable classifications based on sex.[36] In 1976, the Court ruled that sex-discrimination complaints would be judged by a new, judicially created intermediate standard of review a step below strict scrutiny. In *Craig* v. *Boren* (1976), the owner of the Honk 'n' Holler Restaurant in Stillwater, Oklahoma, and Craig, a male under twenty-one, challenged the constitutionality of a state law prohibiting the sale of 3.2 percent beer to males under the age of twenty-one and to females under the age of eighteen.[37] The state introduced a considerable amount of evidence in support of the statute, including:

- Eighteen- to twenty-year-old males were more likely to be arrested for driving under the influence than were females of the same age.
- Youths aged seventeen to twenty-one were the group most likely to be injured or to die in alcohol-related traffic accidents, with males exceeding females.
- Young men were more inclined to drink and drive than females.

The U.S. women's 4x400 meters relay team celebrates victory at the 2000 Sydney Olympics. The United States won the relay ahead of Jamaica and Russia. And U.S. women, many who won college athletic scholarships mandated by Title IX, continued to win record numbers of medals. (Photo courtesy: Faugere/DPPI/SIPA Press)

The Supreme Court found that this information was "too tenuous" to support the legislation. In coming to this conclusion, the Court carved out a new "test" to be used in examining claims of sex discrimination, "[T]o withstand constitutional challenge, . . . classifications by gender must serve important governmental objectives and must be substantially related to achievement of those objectives." According to the Court an intermediate standard of review was created within what previously was a two-tier distinction—strict scrutiny/rational basis.

As *Craig* demonstrates, men, too, can use the Fourteenth Amendment to fight gender-based discrimination. Since 1976, the Court has applied the intermediate standard of constitutional review to most claims that it has heard involving gender. Thus, the following kinds of practices have been found to violate the Fourteenth Amendment:

- Single-sex public nursing schools.
- Laws that consider males adults at twenty-one years but females at eighteen years.
- Laws that allow women but not men to receive alimony.
- State prosecutors' use of preemptory challenges to reject men or women to create more sympathetic juries.
- Virginia's maintenance of an all-male military college, the Virginia Military Institute.

In contrast, the Court has upheld the following governmental practices and laws:

- Draft registration provisions for males only.
- State statutory rape laws that apply only to female victims.

The level of review used by the Court is crucial. Clearly, a statute excluding African Americans from draft registration would be unconstitutional. But because gender is not subject to the same higher standard of review that is used in racial discrimination cases, the exclusion of women from the requirements of the Military Selective Service Act was ruled permissible because the government policy was considered to serve "important governmental objectives."[38]

This history has perhaps clarified why women's rights activists continue to argue that until the passage of an equal rights amendment, women will never enjoy the same rights as men. An amendment would automatically raise the level of scrutiny that the Court applies to gender-based claims.

A N A L Y Z I N G   T H E   D A T A

EEOC SEXUAL HARASSMENT FILINGS

Sexual harassment filings have leveled off since 1995. Interestingly, however, the percentage of charges filed by males has increased steadily since the 1991 Clarence Thomas's Senate hearings on nomination to the Supreme Court concerning whether he had harassed Anita Hill: from 9.1% of the 10,500 total filings in 1992 to the 13.6% of 15,800 total filings in 2000.

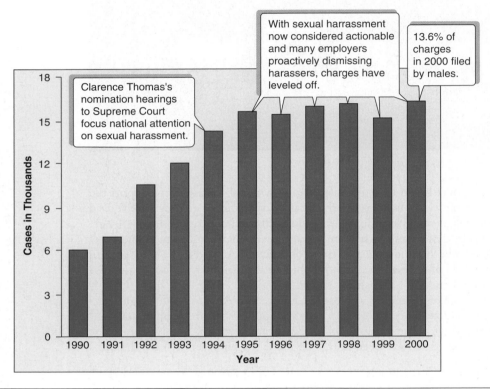

Clarence Thomas's nomination hearings to Supreme Court focus national attention on sexual harassment.

With sexual harrassment now considered actionable and many employers proactively dismissing harassers, charges have leveled off.

13.6% of charges in 2000 filed by males.

Source: Based on data from www.eeoc.gov/stats/harass. Accessed March 9, 2001.

Statutory Remedies for Sex Discrimination.   In part because of the limits of the intermediate standard of review and the fact that the equal protection clause applies only to *governmental* discrimination, women's rights activists began to bombard the courts with sex-discrimination cases. These cases have been filed under Title VII of the Civil Rights Act, which prohibits discrimination by private (and, after 1972, public) employers, or Title IX of the Education Amendments of 1972, which bars educational institutions receiving federal funds from discriminating against female students. Key victories under Title VII include:

- Consideration of sexual harassment as sex discrimination.
- Inclusion of law firms, which many argued were *private* partnerships, in the coverage of the act.
- A broad definition of what can be considered sexual harassment, which includes same-sex harassment.
- Allowance of voluntary affirmative action programs to redress historical discrimination against women.

After the hearings concerning whether or not Supreme Court justice nominee Clarence Thomas sexually harassed Anita Hill, sexual harassment claims skyrocketed

FIGURE 6.1 **The Wage Gap by Education, 1998**
Women's wages continue to fall short of men's although the gap is closing among all women except Hispanic women. What factors might account for these glaring inequities?

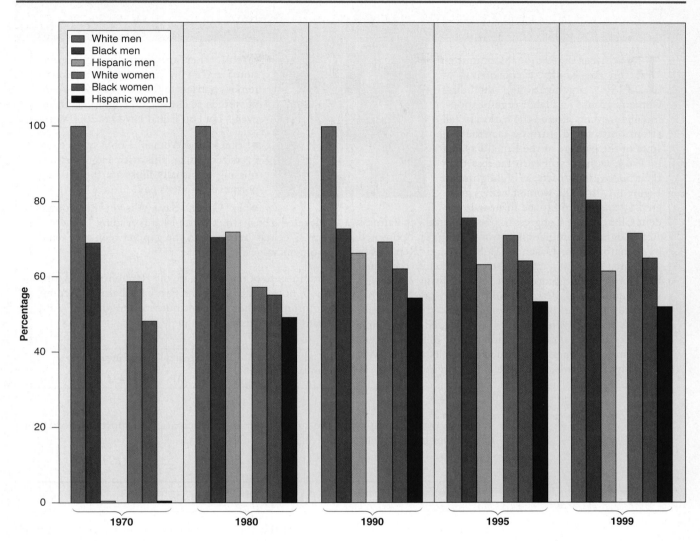

until 1995 and then leveled off. (See Analyzing the Data: EEOC Sexual Harassment Filings.) Claims more than doubled from 1990 to 1998. The Equal Employment Opportunity Commission (EEOC) was able to reach record settlements with employers rising from $7.7 million in 1990 to over $27 million in 1997. Complaints have begun to level off as more and more employers have begun education and training programs to avert workplace problems. Women also have won important victories under the Equal Pay Act, but a large wage gap between men and women continues to exist (see Figure 6.1), as underscored in Politics Now: Equal Pay for Women Workers.

Title IX, which parallels Title VII, also has expanded the opportunities for women in elementary, secondary, and postsecondary institutions greatly . Since women's groups, like the NAACP before them, saw eradication of educational discrimination as key to improving other facets of women's lives, they lobbied for it heavily. Most of today's college students did not go through school being excluded from home economics or shop classes because of their sex. Nor, probably, did many attend schools that had no team sports for females. Yet this was commonly the case in the United States prior to passage of Title IX.[39] The performance of American women athletes at recent Olympic

POLITICS NOW

EQUAL PAY FOR WOMEN WORKERS

Each year the National Committee on Pay Equity, a consortium of 180 organizations including women's groups and labor organizations, mobilizes events around the nation to call attention to the disturbing fact that, in spite of the passage of the Equal Pay Act in 1963, women still earn far less than their male counterparts, as highlighted in Figure 6.1. In 2000, women leaders gathered at the White House to hear President Clinton urge Congress to pass the Paycheck Fairness Act to fight discrimination in women's wages. Sponsored by Senator Tom Daschle (D-S.D.) and Rep. Rosa DeLauro (D-Conn.), its goal is to put teeth into the Equal Pay Act by prohibiting employers from firing employees who inquire about the salaries of their co-workers. At that same meeting, President Clinton announced his administration's Equal Pay initiative, which included the creation of an Equal Pay Task Force within the Equal Employment Opportunity Commission (the federal agency charged with enforcing the provisions of the Equal Pay Act, as well as several other antidiscrimination provisions), and an investment of $20 million to remove barriers to the career advancement of women scientists and engineers. Other events held on Equal Pay Day 2000 were:

- The Maine Women's Lobby handed out oversized dollar bills with large sections missing to visually illustrate the missing portion of women's pay.

- In Green Bay, Wisconsin, women picketed a busy street with placards reading "Where is my 27 cents?" referring to the gap between men's and women's wages.*

But in spite of the wage gap, the Republicans in Congress do not want to bring the Paycheck Fairness Act out of committee where it continues to languish in both Houses of Congress.

*National Committee on Pay Equity, http://www.feminist.com/fairpay/epd.htm.

games showed the impact of the law on women's participation in sports. Record numbers of women competed and won.

OTHER GROUPS MOBILIZE FOR RIGHTS

African Americans and women are not the only groups that have suffered unequal treatment under the law. Denial of civil rights has led many other disadvantaged groups to mobilize to achieve greater civil rights. Their efforts to achieve those rights have many parallels to the efforts made by African Americans and women. In the wake of the successes of those two groups in achieving enhanced rights, and sometimes even before, other traditionally disenfranchised groups have organized to gain fuller equality. Many of them have also recognized that litigation and the use of test-case strategies would be key to further civil rights gains. The Ford Foundation, which had heavily funded the NAACP LDF and some women's rights litigation, also helped interested Mexican Americans to found the Mexican American Legal Defense and Education Fund (MALDEF). Established in 1968, and modeled after the NAACP LDF, MALDEF has played and continues to play a major role in expanding civil rights for Hispanics. The Ford Foundation also facilitated the 1970 creation of the Native American Rights Fund to litigate for Indian rights.

Native Americans

Native Americans are the first "true" Americans, and their status under U.S. law is unique. Under the U.S. Constitution, "Indian tribes" are considered distinct governments, a situation that has affected Native Americans' treatment by the Supreme Court in contrast to other groups of ethnic minorities. And "minority" is a term that accurately describes American Indians. It is estimated that there were as many as 10 million Indians in the New World at the time it was discovered by Europeans in the 1400s, with 3 to 4 million living in what is today the United States. By 1900, the number of Indians in the continental United States had plummeted to less than 2 million.

Many commentators would agree that for years Congress and the courts manipulated Indian law to promote the westward expansion of the United States. The Northwest Ordinance of 1787, passed by the Continental Congress, specified that "the good faith should always be observed toward the Indians; their lands and property shall never be taken from them without their consent, and their property rights, and liberty, they shall never be invaded or disturbed, unless in just and lawful wars authorized by Congress." This is not what happened. Instead, over the years, "American Indian policy has been described as 'genocide-at-law' promoting both land acquisition and cultural extermination."[40] At first, during the eighteenth and nineteenth centuries, the U.S. government isolated Indians on reservations as it confiscated their lands and denied them basic political rights. Indian reservations were administered by the federal government and Native Americans often lived in squalid conditions.

With passage of the Dawes Act in 1887, however, the government switched policies to promote assimilation over separation. Each Indian family was given land within the reservation; the rest was sold to whites, thus reducing Indian lands from about 140 million acres to about 47 million. Moreover, to encourage Native Americans to assimilate, Indian children were sent to boarding schools off the reservation and native languages and rituals were banned. In 1924 Native Americans were made U.S. citizens and given the right to vote.

At least in part because tribes were small and scattered (and the number of Indians declining), they formed no protest movement in reaction to these drastic policy changes. It was not until the 1960s, at the same time that women were beginning to mobilize for greater civil rights, that Indians too began to mobilize to act. Like the civil rights and women's rights movements, it had a radical as well as a more traditional branch. In 1973, for example, national attention was drawn to the plight of Indians when members of the radical American Indian Movement took over Wounded Knee, South Dakota, the site of the massacre of 150 Indians by the U.S. Army in 1890. Just two years before the protest, the treatment of Indians had been highlighted in the best-selling *Bury My Heart at Wounded Knee*, which in many ways served to mobilize public opinion against the oppression of Native Americans in the same way *Uncle Tom's Cabin* had against slavery.[41]

At the same time, just as the growing number of women in the legal profession contributed to the push to secure greater rights for women through litigation, Indians, many attracted by the American Indian Law Center at the University of New Mexico, began to file hundreds of test cases in the federal courts involving tribal fishing rights, tribal land claims, and the taxation of tribal profits. Soon the Native American Rights Fund (NARF), founded in 1970, became the NAACP LDF of the Indian rights movement when the "courts became the forum of choice for Indian tribes and their members."[42]

Native Americans have won some very important victories concerning hunting, fishing, and land rights. Native American tribes all over America have begun to sue to reclaim lands they say were stolen from them by the United States, often more than 200 years ago. One of the largest Indian land claims was filed in 1972 on behalf of the Passamaquoddie and the Penobscot tribes, who were seeking return of 12.5 million acres in Maine—about two-thirds of the entire state—and $25 billion in damages. The suit was filed by the Native American Rights Fund and the Indian Service Unit of a legal services office that was funded by the U.S. Office of Economic Opportunity. It took intervention from the White House before a settlement was reached in 1980, giving each tribe over $40 million.

Native Americans are also litigating to gain access to their sacred places. All over the nation they have filed lawsuits to stop the building of roads and new construction on ancient burial grounds or other sacred spots. "We are in a battle for the survival

WEB EXPLORATION
For more about the Native American Rights Fund, see
www.ablongman.com/oconnor

HIGHLIGHT

THE CENSUS AND CIVIL RIGHTS

Since 1990, the U.S. government and demographers have estimated that Hispanics would become the largest minority in the United States by 2030. Thus, many were shocked by the preliminary results from the 2000 Census that indicated that the nation's Hispanic population grew by nearly 60 percent in the 1990s, an increase that may in part be due to undercounting in the 1990 Census. The right of individuals to select one or more races may also have had an impact. It is now expected that Hispanics will more than triple by 2050 and account for one-fourth of the total U.S. population and the U.S. will become a minority-majority population like California, New Mexico, and Hawaii. Texas will soon join their ranks and Dallas, Houston and San Antonio already have minority-majority populations.[a]

Hispanics are still largely concentrated in the Southwest, Florida, and New York. But in the 1990s, they also moved into North Carolina, Georgia, and Iowa, states that formerly had negligible Hispanic populations.

What does this mean in terms of civil rights? "It's an incentive for African Americans to move toward Latinos," said the vice president of the Tomas Rivera Policy Institute.[b] He went on to say, "It is not clear whether Hispanics feel it is clearer they need to work with blacks or think they are growing so fast, 'we don't need them.'"

States such as California no longer have majority white populations as the Hispanic population continues to increase at rates that far surpass African Americans and whites. Most of the American push for expanded rights, especially at the national level, has involved African Americans, who enjoy far greater electoral representation (although still vastly under represented) than do Hispanics. These new numbers may prompt Hispanic leaders to demand greater representation with the kind of fervor demonstrated by other disadvantaged groups in the past.

[a] Charles W. Holmes, "Hispanics Will Soon Be Largest Minority; New Census Data Show," *Austin American Statesman*, March 8, 2001, A1.
[b] Holmes, "Hispanics Will Soon."

---

of our very way of life," said one tribal leader. "The land is gone. All we've got left is our religion."[43]

But Native Americans have not fared nearly so well in areas such as religious freedom, especially where tribal practices come into conflict with state law. As noted in chapter 5, the Supreme Court used the rational basis test to rule that a state could infringe religious exercise (use of peyote as a sacrament in religious ceremonies) by a neutral law, and limited their access to religious sites during timber harvesting. Congress, however, quickly acted to restore some of those rights through passage of the Religious Freedom Restoration Act, although the law was later ruled unconstitutional by the Supreme Court. Native Americans continue to fight the negative stereotypes that continue to plague their progress. Indians contend that even the popular names of thousands of high school, college, and professional teams are degrading.

Hispanic Americans

Like women's efforts to garner expanded political rights, Hispanics, too, can date their first real push for equal rights to 1965–1975.[44] This civil rights movement included many tactics drawn from the African American civil rights movement, including sit-ins, boycotts, marches, and other activities designed to attract publicity to their cause.[45] Like blacks, women, and Native Americans, Hispanic Americans have some radical militant groups, but the movement has been dominated by more conventional organizations. The more conventional groups have pressed for Chicano and Latino studies programs and have built up ties with existing, powerful mainstream associations, including unions and the Roman Catholic church.

GLOBAL POLITICS

IMMIGRATION AND CIVIL RIGHTS

Americans are used to being a nation of immigrants, even as new immigration sparks public debate about how much is enough. Immigration into Western Europe and Japan has been an even more problematic issue. In the last decade or so, right-wing political parties in Western Europe have made immigration a national issue.

Immigration is a political issue in these countries for three reasons. First, European and Japanese nationalism since the nineteenth century is based on the notion of the nation as a common ethnic people. Second, most of the postwar immigration into Western Europe and Japan has been from developing countries in Asia, Africa, and the Middle East (many of them former colonies). Third, that immigration, which was assumed after World War II by many governments to be temporary, has been in many cases permanent. Large populations of Turkish "guest workers" in Germany, followed in the 1990s by refugees from Eastern Europe; North Africans in France; and Chinese and Koreans in Japan present problems of how to assimilate people from different backgrounds without radically altering national identity. In a number of ways, then, immigration issues in Europe and Japan resemble ethnic and racial issues in the United States.

More or less permanent outsider status invites civil rights abuses. Right-wing groups across Western Europe have made rhetorical as well as physical attacks on foreign residents. While the constitutions of these countries typically prohibit discrimination, immigrants who are not citizens often do not enjoy the full protection of the law.

Acquiring citizenship as a way to assimilate is not always easy. Japan and Germany provide a striking contrast to the United States on this point. The United States government subscribes to the doctrine of *jus soli*: People born on American soil automatically acquire citizenship even if their parents are not United States citizens. Moreover, American requirements for citizenship for permanent residents are comparatively lenient. The Japanese and German governments, in contrast, subscribe to the doctrine of *jus sanguinis*: Only the children of citizens (and therefore properly German or Japanese) automatically qualify for citizenship. In 2000, the German government eased this restriction to allow for dual citizenship for second-generation aliens, but preference in immigration and naturalization continues to go to ethnic German immigrants. Naturalization by second- and third-generation immigrants in Germany and Japan remains quite low.

Latinos have also relied heavily on litigation to secure greater rights. Key groups are the Mexican American Legal Defense and Educational Fund (MALDEF) and the Puerto Rican Legal Defense and Educational Fund.

MALDEF was founded in 1968 after members of the League of United Latin American Citizens (LULAC), the nation's largest and oldest Latino organization, met with NAACP LDF leaders and, with their assistance, secured a $2.2-million start-up grant from the Ford Foundation. It was created to bring test cases to force school districts to allocate more funds to schools with predominantly low-income minority populations, to implement bilingual education programs, to force employers to hire Hispanics, and to challenge election rules and apportionment plans that undercount or dilute Hispanic voting power. Just as Native American and women's rights groups had depended on the legal expertise of their own constituents, MALDEF quickly drew on the talent of Hispanic attorneys to staff offices in San Antonio and Los Angeles. It also started a scholarship fund to train more Hispanic attorneys, and established a New Mexico branch office in conjunction with the New Mexico Law School.

MALDEF lawyers quickly moved to bring major test cases to the U.S. Supreme Court, both to enhance the visibility of their cause and to win cases. MALDEF has been quite successful in its efforts to expand voting rights and opportunities to Hispanic Americans. In 1973, for example, it won a major victory when the Supreme Court

Longman
Participate.com 2.0
Comparative
Comparing Civil Rights

WEB EXPLORATION
To learn more about MALDEF, see
www.ablongman.com/oconnor

POINT/COUNTERPOINT

IS A CRIME JUST A CRIME, OR DO MOTIVES AND INTENTIONS MATTER?

A hate crime is an act of violence against a person or property based on the victim's race, color, gender, national origin, religion, sexual orientation, or disability. Every year, thousands of Americans are documented victims of hate crimes and it is suspected that many more go unreported. Many localities, states, and even the federal government are passing or considering special legislation to make hate crimes a separate type of crime that merits special punishment. But do crimes based on hatred deserve to be in a special category for punishment? Do motivations and intentions matter, or is a crime just a crime? Let's examine these two point of views.

Those who favor hate crimes legislation, including the Democratic Party and the NAACP, believe that hate crimes have a special emotional and psychological impact on the victim and the victim's community that causes the victim to withdraw from broader society. This kind of alienation can damage the very fabric of society by making people and groups feel isolated and untrusting of their fellow citizens. Proponents of hate crimes legislation argue that hate crimes are an assault not only to the victim but on the entire group to which that victim belongs and therefore merit additional attention and punishment because the state has a compelling interest in protecting its citizens against bias. The death of James Byrd Jr. in Texas is an example of a hate crime. Byrd was dragged several miles tied to the back of a pickup truck solely because he was an African American. This act of violence killed Byrd and injured his family and friends. However, many African Americans in and outside of Texas cite this crime as an act that makes them feel less secure and less trusting in society as a whole. In

Wyoming, two men cited Matthew Shepard's homosexuality as the reason they brutally beat him and left him tied to a fence. Shepard's murder is another example of a crime that had an impact beyond the immediate victims. These two examples, and many others, have left many people wondering what kind of society we live in and believing that the motivations behind these crimes are so heinous that they deserve extra punishment.

Other groups, such as Libertarians, Christian groups, Republicans, and the ACLU express opposition or reservations about hate crimes legislation. The basic arguments against hate crimes legislation are that legislating about motivations and intentions is a dramatic extension of government power. If the government can tell us we can't hate a certain group, can it also tell us we can't use certain words, watch certain movies, or associate with certain people? If a crime is committed, opponents say, there are already laws on the books to punish the guilty. A crime is a crime and should be treated as such. Why is murder worse if it is a hate crime? The victim is dead regardless of the motivations of the killer, so why add more laws? Why not prosecute using existing laws and use the punishments already prescribed, ranging from imprisonment to execution? Is the murder of James Byrd Jr. or Matthew Shepard worse than other murders because it is motivated by hate? Opponents of hate crimes legislation argue that it is not worse.

What do you think? Do hate crimes merit distinct treatment or is a crime simply a crime?
Go to www.ablongman.com/oconnor

---

ruled that multimember electoral districts (in which more than one person represents a single district) in Texas discriminated against African Americans and Hispanic Americans.[46] In multimember systems, legislatures generally add members to larger districts instead of drawing smaller districts in which a minority candidate could get a majority of the votes necessary to win.

While enjoying greater access to elective office, Hispanics still suffer discrimination. Language barriers and substandard educational opportunities continue to plague their progress. In 1973, the U.S. Supreme Court refused to find that a Texas law under which the state appropriated a set dollar amount to each school district per pupil, while allowing wealthier districts to enrich educational programs from other funds, violated the equal protection clause of the Fourteenth Amendment.[47] The lower courts had found that wealth was a suspect classification entitled to strict scrutiny. Using that test, the lower courts had found the Texas plan discriminatory. In contrast, a divided Supreme Court concluded that education was not a fundamental right (see chapter 5), and that a charge of discrimination based on wealth would be examined only under a minimal standard of review (the rational basis test).

Throughout the 1970s and 1980s, inter-school-district inequalities continued, and frequently had their greatest impact on poor Hispanic children, who often had inferior educational opportunities. Recognizing that the increasingly conservative federal courts (see chapter 10) offered no recourse, in 1984 MALDEF filed suit in state court alleging that the Texas school finance policy violated the Texas constitution. In 1989 it won a case in which a unanimous Texas Supreme Court declared the state's method of financing public schools to be unconstitutional under the state constitution.

MALDEF continues to litigate in a wide range of areas of concern to Hispanics. High on its agenda today are affirmative action, the admission of Hispanic students to state colleges and universities, health care for undocumented immigrants, and challenging unfair redistricting practices that make it more difficult to elect Hispanic legislators. Its highly successful Census 2000 educational outreach campaign, moreover, ought to make certain that all Hispanics were counted in 2000, as discussed in Highlight: The Census and Civil Rights.

Gays and Lesbians

Gays and lesbians have had an even harder time than African Americans, women, Native Americans, or Hispanics in achieving fuller rights.[48] Gays do, however, have on average far higher household incomes and educational levels than do these other groups. They are beginning to convert these advantages into political clout at the ballot box. As discussed in chapter 5, the cause of gay and lesbian rights, like that of African Americans and women early in their quest for greater civil rights, did not fare well in the Supreme Court initially. In the late 1970s, the Lambda Legal Defense and Education Fund, the Lesbian Rights Project, and Gay and Lesbian Advocates and Defenders were founded by gay and lesbian activists dedicated to ending legal restrictions on the civil rights of homosexuals.[49] Although these groups have won important legal victories concerning HIV/AIDS discrimination, insurance policy survivor benefits, and even some employment issues, they generally have not been as successful as other historically legally disadvantaged groups.[50]

In *Bowers* v. *Hardwick* (1986), for example, the Supreme Court ruled as constitutional a Georgia law that made private acts of consensual sodomy illegal (whether practiced by homosexuals or by heterosexual married adults). Gay and lesbian rights groups had argued that a constitutional right to privacy included the right to engage in consensual sex within one's home, but the Court disagreed. Although privacy rights may attach to relations of "family, marriage, or procreation," those rights did not extend to homosexuals, wrote Justice Byron White for the Court. In a concurring opinion—his last written on the Court— Chief Justice Warren Burger called sodomy "the infamous crime against nature."[51]

The public's and Congress's discomfort with gay and lesbian rights can be seen most clearly in the controversy that occurred after President Clinton attempted to lift the ban on gays in the armed services. Clinton tried to get an absolute ban on discrimination against homosexuals, who were subject to immediate discharge if their sexual orientation was discovered. Military leaders and then Senator Sam Nunn (D–Ga.), as head of the Senate Armed Services Committee, led the effort against Clinton's proposal. Eventually, Clinton and Senate leaders compromised on what was called the "Don't ask, don't tell" policy. It stipulated that gays and lesbians would no longer be asked if they were homosexual, but barred them from revealing their sexual orientation (under threat of discharge from the service). But when the Senate finally voted on the "compromise," its version of

WEB EXPLORATION
For more on gay and lesbian rights groups, see
www.ablongman.com/oconnor

the new policy labeled homosexuality "an unacceptable risk" to morale. In spite of gay and lesbian groups' labeling the new policy "lie and hide," the Clinton administration chose to back off on the issue, correctly sensing only minimal support in Congress.

The Supreme Court's unwillingness to expand privacy rights or special constitutional protections to homosexuals, and Congress's failure to end discrimination in the military, has led many gay and lesbian rights groups to other, potentially more responsive political forums: state and local governments. (See chapter 3 for a discussion of moves to recognize gay marriage and domestic partnerships.) Around the nation, such groups have lobbied for antidiscrimination legislation with mixed success. In 1992, for example, Colorado voters passed a state constitutional amendment that *rescinded* several local gay and lesbian rights ordinances and also prevented the adoption of any such measures. In 1996, however, the U.S. Supreme Court ruled that the amendment was unconstitutional. Although the Court used the rational basis test to invalidate the amendment, it was the first time ever that a majority of the justices applied the equal protection clause of the Fourteenth Amendment to prevent discrimination against homosexuals.[52] As discussed in chapter 5, however, the Court's decision allowing the Boy Scouts of America to bar homosexuals from becoming scout-masters had a chilling effect on gay rights activists' optimism about the Court as a source of continued rights expansion.

Disabled Americans

Disabled Americans also have lobbied hard for antidiscrimination legislation. In the aftermath of World War II, many veterans returned to a nation unequipped to handle their disabilities. The Korean and Vietnam Wars made the problems of disabled veterans all the more clear. These disabled veterans saw the successes of African Americans, women, and other minorities, and they too began to lobby for greater protection against discrim-

Longman
Participate.com
2.0
Participation
**Civil Rights
and Gay
Adoption**

WEB EXPLORATION
For more about disability advocacy groups, see
www.ablongman.com/oconnor

Former Senator Max Cleland (D–Ga.), shown here in a wheelchair, was a vocal proponent of the rights of those with disabilities. He knows firsthand the problems of noncompliance with the ADA. When he was elected to the U.S. Senate, it took him several months to find housing to accommodate his wheelchair. He lost his 2002 re-election bid.
(Photo courtesy: Mary Ann Chestain/AP/Wide World Photos)

ination.[53] In 1990, in coalition with other disabled people, veterans were finally able to convince Congress to pass the Americans with Disabilities Act. The statute defines a disabled person as someone with a physical or mental impairment that limits one or more "life activities," or who has a record of such impairment. It thus extends the protections of the Civil Rights Act of 1964 to all of those with physical or mental disabilities. It guarantees access to public facilities, employment, and communication services. It also requires employers to acquire or modify work equipment, adjust work schedules, and make existing facilities accessible. This means, for example, that buildings must be accessible to those in wheelchairs, and telecommunications devices be provided for deaf employees.

In 1999, the U.S. Supreme Court issued a series of four decisions redefining and significantly limiting the scope of the ADA. The cumulative impact of these decisions is to dramatically limit the number of people who can claim coverage under the act. Moreover, these cases "could profoundly affect individuals with a range of impairments—from diabetes and hypertension to severe nearsightedness and hearing loss—who are able to function in society with the help of medicines or aids but whose impairments—may still make employers consider them ineligible for certain jobs."[54] Thus, pilots who need glasses to correct their vision cannot claim discrimination when employers fail to hire them because of their correctable vision.

Simply changing the law, while often an important first step in achieving civil rights, is not the end of the process. Attitudes must also change. As history has shown, that can be a very long process and will be longer given the Court's decisions.

Continuity & Change

Race in America: Affirmative Action

When the Framers met in Philadelphia, they all recognized that the issue of slavery and how it was treated in the new Constitution could make or break their efforts to fashion a new nation and win acceptance in the Southern states. The Three-Fifths Compromise was their politically expedient solution. It got the Southern states on board, but only for a while. In 1861, the Civil War was fought largely over the issue of slavery. After slavery was abolished, the Southern states quickly acted to pass legislation to limit opportunities for newly freed slaves that persisted for nearly the next century.

Nearly one hundred years after the first shots rang out in the Civil War, African Americans and other civil rights supporters gained support for their efforts to attain fuller civil rights, including the right to vote, attend desegregated schools, and be treated fairly in the workplace. *Brown* v. *Board of Education* (1954) and passage of the Civil Rights Act of 1964, went a long way toward remedying many onerous forms of discrimination.

Since the mid-1960s, racial tolerance has increased, although discrimination still exists. In 1997, 77 percent of those surveyed by the Gallup organization said they approved of interracial marriage and 93 percent said that they would vote for a black president.[55] Nevertheless, while most Americans agree that discrimination is wrong, most whites—57 percent—today believe that **affirmative action** programs, policies designed to give special attention or compensatory treatment to members of a previously disadvantaged group, are no longer needed, although 86 percent thought that those programs were needed thirty years ago. As early as 1871, Frederick Douglass ridiculed the idea of racial quotas, arguing that they would promote "an image of blacks as privileged wards of the state." They were "absurd as a matter of practice" because some could use them to argue that blacks "should constitute one-eighth of the poets, statesmen, scholars, authors and philosophers."[54]

affirmative action
Policies designed to give special attention or compensatory treatment to members of a previously disadvantaged group.

The debate over affirmative action and equality of opportunity became particularly intense during the Reagan years. In 1978, the Supreme Court addressed the issue of affirmative action in the case of Alan Bakke, a thirty-one-year-old paramedic, who was

(continued)

(Photo courtesy: Mike Peters/©Tribune Media Services, Inc. All rights Reserved. Reprinted with permission)

wait-listed for admission by the University of California at Davis. The Davis Medical School maintained two separate admissions committees—one for white students and another for minority students. Bakke was not admitted, although his grades and standardized test scores were higher than those of all of the African American students admitted to the school. In *Regents of the University of California* v. *Bakke* (1978), a sharply divided Court concluded that Bakke's rejection had been illegal because the use of strict quotas was inappropriate.[57] The medical school, however, was free to "take race into account."

In 1979, the Court ruled that a factory and a union could voluntarily adopt a quota system in selecting black workers over more senior white workers for a training program. These kinds of programs outraged blue-collar Americans who had traditionally voted for the Democratic Party. In 1980, they abandoned the party in droves and supported Ronald Reagan, an ardent foe of affirmative action.

In subsequent affirmative action cases, the Reagan administration strongly urged the Court to invalidate the plans in question, but to no avail. With changes on the Court, however, including the 1986 elevation to Chief Justice of William Rehnquist, a strong opponent of affirmative action, the continued efforts of the Reagan administration finally began to pay off as the Court heard a new series of cases signaling an end to the advances in civil rights law. In a three-month period in 1989, the Supreme Court handed down five civil rights

decisions limiting affirmative action programs and making it harder to prove employment discrimination. In 1995, the U.S. Supreme Court ruled that all federal affirmative action programs based on racial classifications are "inherently suspect," virtually ending affirmative action programs.

The next year, the Court refused to review a challenge to a lower court ruling that upheld the constitutionality of a University of Texas practice that prohibited giving a "plus" to minorities applying to its state law school.[58] In the same year, California voters passed Proposition 209, which bans racial preferences throughout the state, including in college admissions. The University of California at Berkeley has seen its African American and Hispanic minority student populations plummet as a result.

1. With affirmative action now largely a thing of the past, do you see a need for new civil rights legislation to protect the growing minority population in the United States?

2. Do you see the Supreme Court as a vehicle to seek expanded rights or one likely to be curtailing civil rights in the future?

Cast Your Vote. What groups do you think need protection? To cast your vote, go to **www.ablongman.com/oconnor**

SUMMARY

While the Framers and other Americans basked in the glory of the newly adopted Constitution and Bill of Rights, their protections did not extend to all Americans. In this chapter we have shown how rights have been expanded to ever-increasing segments of the population. To that end, we have made the following points:

1. **Slavery, Abolition, and Winning the Right to Vote, 1800–1890**
   When the Framers tried to "compromise" on the issue of slavery, they only postponed dealing with a volatile question that was later to rip the nation apart. Ultimately, the Civil War was fought to end slavery. Among its results were the triumph of the abolitionist position and adoption of the Thirteenth, Fourteenth, and Fifteenth Amendments. During this period, women also sought expanded rights, especially the right to vote, but to no avail.

2. **The Push for Equality, 1890–1954**
   Although the Civil War amendments were added to the Constitution, the Supreme Court limited their application. As Jim Crow laws were passed throughout the South, the NAACP was founded in the early 1900s to press for equal rights for African Americans. Women's groups were also active during this period, successfully lobbying for passage of the Nineteenth Amendment, which assured them the right to vote.

   First women's groups such as the National Consumers' League (NCL), and then others, including NOW, began to view litigation as a means to their ends. The NCL was forced to court to argue for the constitutionality of legislation protecting women workers; in contrast, NOW sought the Court's help in securing equality under the Constitution.

3. **The Civil Rights Movement**
   In 1954, the U.S. Supreme Court ruled in *Brown* v. *Board of Education* that state-segregated school systems were unconstitutional. This victory empowered African Americans as they sought an end to other forms of pervasive discrimination. Bus boycotts and sit-ins were common tactics. As new groups were formed, freedom rides, pressure for voting rights, and massive nonviolent demonstrations became common "lobbying" tactics. This activity culminated in the passage of the Civil Rights Act of 1964 and the Voting Rights Act of 1965. These acts gave African American and women's rights groups two potential weapons in their legal arsenals: They could attack private discrimination under the Civil Rights Act, or state-sanctioned discrimination under the equal protection clause of the Fourteenth Amendment. Over the years the Supreme Court developed different tests to determine the constitutionality of various forms of discrimination. In general, strict scrutiny, the most stringent standard, was applied to race-based claims. An intermediate standard of review was developed to assess the constitutionality of sex discrimination claims.

4. **Other Groups Mobilize for Rights**
   Building on the successes of African Americans and women, other groups, including Native Americans, Hispanic Americans, gays and lesbians, and the disabled, organized to litigate for expanded civil rights as well as to lobby for antidiscrimination laws.

KEY TERMS

affirmative action, p. 209
Black Codes, p. 181
Brown v. *Board of Education* (1954), p. 189
civil rights, p. 178
Civil Rights Act of 1964, p. 193
Civil Rights Cases (1883), p. 184
de facto discrimination, p. 194

de jure discrimination, p. 194
Equal Employment Opportunity Commission, p. 196
equal protection clause, p. 189
Fifteenth Amendment, p. 182
Fourteenth Amendment, p. 182
franchise, p. 181
grandfather clause, p. 184

Jim Crow laws, p. 183
Plessy v. *Ferguson* (1896), p. 184
strict scrutiny, p. 197
suffrage movement, p. 187
suspect classification, p. 197
Thirteenth Amendment, p. 181

SELECTED READINGS

Bacchi, Carol Lee. *The Politics of Affirmative Action: 'Women,' Equality and Category Politics.* Thousand Oaks, Calif.: Sage, 1996.

Bergmann, Barbara R. *In Defense of Affirmative Action.* New York: Basic Books, 1996.

Bullock, Charles III, and Charles Lamb, eds. *Implementation of Civil Rights Policy.* Pacific Grove, Calif.: Brooks/Cole, 1984.

Eastland, Terry. *Ending Affirmative Action: The Case for Colorblind Justice.* New York: Basic Books, 1997.

Edley, Christopher, Jr. *Not All Black and White: Affirmative Action, Race, and American Values.* New York: Hill and Wang, 1996.

Freeman, Jo. *The Politics of Women's Liberation.* New York: Longman, 1975.

Kluger, Richard. *Simple Justice.* New York: Vintage, 1975.

Knobel, Dale T. *'America for the Americans': The Nativist Movement in the United States.* Old Tappan, N.J.: Twayne, 1996.

Mansbridge, Jane J. *Why We Lost the ERA.* Chicago: University of Chicago Press, 1986.

McClain, Paula D., and Joseph Stewart Jr. *"Can We All Get Along?" Racial and Ethnic Minorities in American Politics,* 2nd ed. Boulder, Colo.: Westview Press, 1998.

McGlen, Nancy E., and Karen O'Connor. *Women, Politics and American Society,* 2nd ed. Upper Saddle River, N.J.: Prentice Hall, 1998.

Nobles, Melissa. *Shades of Citizenship: Race and the Census in Modern America.* (Palo Alto, Calif.: Stanford University Press, 2000).

Reed, Adolph, Jr. *Without Justice for All: The New Liberalism and Our Retreat from Racial Equity.* Boulder, Colo.: Westview Press, 1999.

Rodriguez, Clara E. *Changing Race: Latinos, the Census, and the History of Ethnicity in the United States* (New York: New York University Press, 2000).

Rosales, Francisco A., and Arturo Rosales, eds. *Chicano! The History of the Mexican American Civil Rights Movement.* Houston, Tex.: Arte Publico Press, 1996.

Verba, Sidney, and Gary R. Orren. *Equality in America: The View from the Top.* Cambridge, Mass.: Harvard University Press, 1985.

Williams, Juan. *Eyes on the Prize: America's Civil Rights Years, 1954–1965.* New York: Penguin, 1987.

Wilson, William Julius. *The Bridge over the Racial Divide: Rising Inequality and Coalition Politics.* Berkeley: University of California Press, 1999.

NOTES

1. Michael Cooper, "Officers in Bronx Fire 41 Shots, and an Unarmed Man Is Killed," *The New York Times* (February 5, 1999): A1.

2. Amy Wilentz, "New York: The Price of Safety in a Police State," *The Los Angeles Times* (April 11, 1999): M1.

3. N. R. Kleinfield, "Veterans of 60's Protests Meet the Newly Outraged in a March," *The New York Times* (April 16, 1999): B8.

4. Kleinfield, "Veterans of 60's Protests."

5. Lee, Jessica. "Women Speak to House about Unwarranted Customs Strip-searches." *USA Today* (May 21 1999): 10A.

6. Edward Walsh, "The Racial Issue Looming in the Rear-View Mirror," *The Washington Post* (May 19, 1999): A3; and Ralph Siegel, "Turnpike Arrest Cases Explore Use of Racial Profiling Defenses," *The Record* (May 12, 1999): A3.

7. Judith Evans, "Suit Claims Race Bias at Fla. Hotel," *The Washington Post* (May 21, 1999): A1.

8. Catherine Drinker Bowen, *Miracle at Philadelphia: The Story of the Constitutional Convention May to September 1787* (Boston: Little, Brown, 1986), 201.

9. 83 U.S. (16 Wall.) 36 (1873).

10. 83 U.S. (16 Wall.) 130 (1873).

11. 88 U.S. (21 Wall.) 162 (1875). See also Karen O'Connor, *Women's Organizations' Use of the Courts* (Lexington, Mass.: Lexington Books, 1980).

12. 109 U.S. 3 (1883).

13. Jack Greenburg, *Judicial Process and Social Change: Constitutional Litigation* (St. Paul, Minn.: West, 1976), 583–86.

14. 163 U.S. 537 (1896).

15. *Williams* v. *Mississippi,* 170 U.S. 213 (1898).

16. *Cummins* v. *Richmond County Board of Education,* 175 U.S. 528 (1899).

17. Juan Williams, *Eyes on the Prize: America's Civil Rights Years, 1954–1965* (New York: Penguin, 1987), 10.

18. 208 U.S. 412 (1908).

19. *Missouri* ex rel. *Gaines* v. *Canada,* 305 U.S. 337 (1938).

20. Richard Kluger, *Simple Justice* (New York: Vintage, 1975), 268.

21. *Sweatt* v. *Painter,* 339 U.S. 629, and *McLaurin* v. *Oklahoma,* 339 U.S. 637 (1950).

22. 347 U.S. 483 (1954).

23. But see Gerald Rosenberg, *Hollow Hope: Can Courts Bring About Social Change* (Chicago: University of Chicago Press, 1991).

24. Quoted in Williams, *Eyes on the Prize,* 10.

25. 349 U.S. 294 (1955).

26. Quoted in Williams, *Eyes on the Prize,* 37.

27. *Cooper* v. *Aaron,* 358 U.S. 1 (1958).

28. *Heart of Atlanta Motel* v. *United States,* 379 U.S. 241 (1964).

29. 402 U.S. 1 (1971).

30. *Missouri* v. *Jenkins,* 115 S.Ct. 2038 (1995).

31. *Griggs* v. *Duke Power Co.,* 401 U.S. 424 (1971).

32. Jo Freeman, *The Politics of Women's Liberation* (New York: Longman, 1975), 57.

33. 368 U.S. 57 (1961).

34. Betty Friedan, *The Feminine Mystique* (New York: Dell, 1963).

35. 323 U.S. 214 (1944). This is the only case involving race-based distinctions applying the strict scrutiny standard where the Court has upheld the restrictive law.

36. 404 U.S. 71 (1971).

37. 429 U.S. 190 (1976).

38. *Rostker* v. *Goldberg,* 453 U.S. 57 (1981).

39. Joyce Gelb and Marian Lief Palley, *Women and Public Policies* (Charlottesville: University of Virginia Press, 1996).

40. Rennard Strickland, "Native Americans," in Kermit Hall, ed., *The Oxford Companion to the Supreme Court of the United States* (New York: Oxford University Press, 1992), 557.

41. Dee Brown, *Bury My Heart at Wounded Knee* (New York: Holt, Rinehart & Winston, 1971).

42. Strickland, "Native Americans," 579.

43. Hugh Dellios, "Rites by Law: Indians Seek Sacred Lands," *The Chicago Tribune* (July 4, 1993): C1.

44. Ernesto B. Virgil, *The Crusade for Justice* (Madison: University of Wisconsin Press, 1999).

45. F. Chris Garcia, *Latinos and the Political System* (Notre Dame, Ind.: University of Notre Dame Press, 1988), 1.

46. *White* v. *Register,* 412 U.S. 755 (1973).

47. *San Antonio Independent School District* v. *Rodriguez,* 411 U.S. 1 (1973).

48. Diane Helene Miller, *Freedom to Differ: The Shaping of the Gay and Lesbian Struggle for Civil Rights.* (New York: New York University Press, 1998).

49. Sarah Brewer, David Kaib, and Karen O'Connor, "Sex and the Supreme Court: Gays, Lesbians, and Justice," *The Politics of Gay Rights* (Chicago: University of Chicago Press, 2000).

50. Evan Gerstmann, *The Constitutional Underclass: Gays, Lesbians, and the Failure of Class-Based Equal Protection* (Chicago: University of Chicago Press, 1999).

51. 478 U.S. 186 (1986).

52. *Romer* v. *Evans,* 116 S.Ct. 1620 (1996).

53. David Pfeiffer, "Overview of the Disability Movement: History, Legislative Record and Political Implications," *Policy Studies Journal* (Winter 1993): 724–742; and "Understanding Disability Policy," *Policy Studies Journal* (Spring 1996): 157–174.

54. Joan Biskupic, "Supreme Court Limits Meaning of Disability," *The Washington Post* (June 23, 1999): A1.

7 Congress

Partisanship is alive and well in the U.S. Congress. Witness the political maneuverings that surrounded the ultimately unsuccessful attempts to enact gun control by Democrats in the 106th Congress and their abandonment of the issue by 2001. On April 21, 1999, two students dressed in long, baggy, black coats walked into Columbine High School in Littleton, Colorado, unleashing a bombing and shooting spree that left fourteen students and one teacher dead and shocked the nation. It was the fifth episode since 1997 in which one or more students opened fire on other students in a public school.[1]

In the days after the Columbine massacre, Senate Majority Leader Trent Lott (R–Miss.) promised quick Senate action on a gun control measure. The minority leader, Tom Daschle (D–S.D.), initially said more gun control is not the solution. Disagreeing with his party leader, Representative Edward J. Markey (D–Mass.) "predicted the public, angered over 'the toxic cocktail of media violence and easy availability of guns,'" would be quick to demand that their elected representatives take some action on gun control. Still, many wondered if Congress would bow to pressure from the powerful National Rifle Association (NRA), a 2.8-million-member group that spent over $3.4 million backing its preferred candidates in the 1998 congressional elections. The new House Speaker, Dennis Hastert (R–Ill.), as he expressed his condolences to the families of the dead and injured Columbine victims, called only for a National Conference on Youth and Culture, never mentioning possible legislation.[2]

Less than a month later, the Republican-controlled Senate turned down a Democratic-sponsored bill to require background checks on all firearms sales at gun shows by a vote of 51– 47.[3] It was a largely party-line vote, with 49 Republicans and 2 Democrats voting against the proposal. Republicans, however, underestimated the anger and concern of the American people over the gun control issue.

Within the week, in a "move that brought gun control forces their first big victory" since the Brady Bill five years earlier, with Vice President Al Gore casting the tie-breaking vote, the Senate approved the measure requiring background checks on gun show purchases on a 51–50 vote.[4] The House approved a scaled down version of the bill. The Judiciary conference committee met only once, in August 2000, where the bill died in spite of heavy lobbying and the pressure of the Million Mom March. In fact, by late 2000, the Democrats in the House had begun to play down their antigun position in an effort to attract white male voters in 2002, a tactic that proved to be largely unsuccessful.[5]

As each congressional representative pursues what appears to be his or her *individually* rational incentives to act on behalf of constituents, their actions can create centrifugal pressures that undermine Congress's *collective* capacity to get things done. Over the past three decades, changes inside and outside Congress have enhanced the ability of congressional representatives to be somewhat more individualistic than in the past; this arguably has weakened the institution's collective capacities even more. Is it any wonder that, before the 1994 midterm elections, public confidence in Congress was at only 8 percent? Although by March 2001, 55 percent of the public voiced approval about the way Congress was doing its job, in general, feelings about Congress as a whole are always much lower than the public's generally high level of support for their individual representatives. Various polls find that as many as 65 percent believe that their own representative deserves another term, (see Figure 7.1, page 223). Even more significant, the rate at which incumbents are reelected to the House continues to exceed 98 percent, despite the chamber's poor general standing with the public. Part of the public's strange split on these issues may stem from the dual roles that Congress plays—its members must combine and balance their roles as law and policy makers with their role as representatives selected to look after and serve the best interests of their constituents. Not surprisingly, this balancing act often results in role conflict. Moreover, recent studies by political scientists reveal many citizens hold Congress up to very high standards, which contributes to negative perceptions.[6] Increased media negativity doesn't help either.[7]

In this chapter we analyze the powers of Congress and the competing roles members of Congress play as they represent the interests of their constituents, make laws, and oversee the actions of the other two branches of government. We also see that, as these functions have changed throughout U.S. history, so has Congress itself.

- First, we will look at the *roots of the legislative branch* to better understand its place today.
- Second, we will examine what the *Constitution* has to say about Congress—*the legislative branch of government.*
- Third, we will look at the *members of Congress,* including how members get elected, and how they spend their days.
- Fourth, we will describe *how Congress is organized.* We compare the two chambers and how their differences affect the course of legislation.
- Fifth, we will outline the *lawmaking function of Congress.*
- Sixth, we will examine the various factors that influence *how members of Congress make decisions.*
- Seventh, we will discuss the ever-changing relationship between *Congress and the president.*

WEB EXPLORATION
To find out who your representative is and how he or she votes, see
www.ablongman.com/oconnor

THE ROOTS OF THE LEGISLATIVE BRANCH

As discussed in chapter 2, Congress's powers evolved from Americans' experiences in the colonies and under the Articles of Confederation. When the colonists came to the New World, their general approval of Britain's parliamentary system led them to adopt similar two-house legislative bodies in the individual colonies. One house was directly elected by the people; the other was a Crown-appointed council that worked under the authority of the colonial government.

The colonial assemblies were originally established as advisory bodies to the royal governors appointed by the king. Gradually, however, they assumed more power and authority in each colony, particularly over taxation and spending. The assemblies also legislated on religious issues and established quality standards for such colonial goods as flour, rice, tobacco, and rum. Before the American Revolution, colonists turned to their colonial legislatures (the only bodies elected directly by the "people") to represent and defend their interests against British infringement.

The first truly national legislature in the colonies, the First Continental Congress, met in Philadelphia in 1774 to develop a common colonial response to the Coercive Acts. All the colonies except Georgia sent a representative. Even though this Congress had no power to force compliance, it advised each colony to establish a militia and organized an economic boycott of British goods, among other things (see chapter 2).

By the time the Second Continental Congress met in Philadelphia in May 1775, fighting had broken out at Lexington and Concord. The Congress quickly helped the now-united colonies gear up for war, raise an army, and officially adopt the Declaration of Independence. During the next five years, the Congress directed the war effort and administered a central government. But it did so with little money or stability—because of the war, it had to move from city to city.

Although the Articles of Confederation were drafted and adopted by the Second Continental Congress in 1777, the states did not ratify them until 1781. Still, throughout the Revolutionary War, the Congress exercised the powers the Articles granted it: to declare war, raise an army, make treaties with foreign nations, and coin money. As described in chapter 2, however, the Congress had no independent sources of income; it had to depend on the states for money and supplies.

After the war the states began acting once again as if they were separate nations rather than parts of one nation, despite the national government that was created under the Articles of Confederation. The "national" government, moreover, was to serve the needs of the new nation. Discontent with the Articles and the government they created grew, and led eventually to the Constitutional Convention in Philadelphia in 1787.

THE CONSTITUTION AND THE LEGISLATIVE BRANCH OF GOVERNMENT

Article I of the Constitution created the legislative branch of government we know today. Any two-house legislature, such as the one created by the Framers, is called a **bicameral legislature.** All states except Nebraska, which has a one-house or *unicameral legislature,* follow this model. As discussed in chapter 2, the Great Compromise resulted in the creation of an upper house, the Senate, and a lower house, the House of Representatives. Each state is represented in the Senate by two senators, regardless of the state's population. The number of representatives each state sends to the House of Representatives, in contrast, is determined by that state's population.

The U.S. Constitution sets out the formal, or legal, requirements for membership in the House and Senate. House members must be at least twenty-five years of age; Senators, thirty. Members of the House must have resided in the United States for at least seven years; those elected to the Senate, nine. Representatives and senators must be legal residents of the states from which they are elected.

Members of each body were to be elected differently and would thus represent different interests and constituencies. Senators were to be elected to six-year terms by state legislatures, and one-third of them would be up for reelection every two years. Senators were to be tied to their state legislatures closely and were expected to represent those interests in the Senate. State legislators lost this influence with ratification of the Seventeenth Amendment in 1913, which provides for the direct election of senators by the voters.

In contrast to senators' six-year terms, members of the House of Representatives were to be elected to two-year terms by a vote of the eligible voters in each congressional district. It was expected that the House would be the more "democratic" branch of government because its members would be more responsible to the people (because they were directly elected by them) and more responsive to them (because they were up for reelection every two years).

bicameral legislature
A legislature divided into two houses; the U.S. Congress and the state legislatures are bicameral except Nebraska, which is unicameral.

WEB EXPLORATION
To see more about the legislative branch, see
www.ablongman.com/oconnor

Apportionment and Redistricting

The U.S. Constitution requires that a census, which entails the counting of all Americans, be conducted every ten years. Until the first census could be taken, the Constitution fixed the number of representatives in the House at sixty-five. In 1790, then, one member represented 37,000 people. As the population of the new nation grew and states were added to the Union, the House became larger and larger. In 1910, it expanded to 435 members, and in 1929 its size was fixed at that number by statute.

Because the Constitution requires that representation in the House be based on state population, congressional districts must be redrawn by state legislatures to reflect population shifts, so that each member in Congress will represent approximately the same number of residents. This process of redrawing congressional districts to reflect increases or decreases in seats allotted to the states, as well as population shifts within a state, is called **redistricting.** The effects of redistricting, which played an important, although less than initially anticipated, role in the 2002 elections, are discussed in chapter 13.

redistricting
The redrawing of congressional districts to reflect increases or decreases in seats allotted to the states, as well as population shifts within a state.

Constitutional Powers of Congress

The Constitution specifically gives to Congress its most important power—the authority to make laws. (See Table 7.1: The Powers of Congress.) This lawmaking power is shared by both houses. For example, no **bill** (proposed law) can become law without the consent of both houses. Examples of other constitutionally shared powers include the power to declare war, raise an army and navy, coin money, regulate commerce, establish the federal courts and their jurisdiction, establish rules of immigration and naturalization, and "make all Laws which shall be necessary and proper for carrying into Execution the foregoing Powers." As interpreted by the Supreme Court, the *necessary and proper clause,* when coupled with one or more of the specific powers enumerated in

bill
A proposed law.

TABLE 7.1   The Powers of Congress

The Powers of Congress, found in Article I, section 8, of the Constitution, include the power to:

- Lay and collect taxes and duties
- Borrow money
- Regulate commerce with foreign nations and among the states
- Establish rules for naturalization (that is, the process of becoming a citizen) and bankruptcy
- Coin money, set its value, and fix the standard of weights and measures
- Punish counterfeiting
- Establish a post office and post roads
- Issue patents and copyrights
- Define and punish piracies, felonies on the high seas, and crimes against the law of nations
- Create courts inferior to (that is, below) the Supreme Court
- Declare war
- Raise and support an army and navy and make rules for their governance
- Provide for a militia (reserving to the states the right to appoint militia officers and to train the militia under congressional rules)
- Exercise legislative powers over the seat of government (the District of Columbia) and over places purchased to be federal facilities (forts, arsenals, dock-yards, and "other needful buildings")
- "Make all Laws which shall be necessary and proper for carrying into Execution the foregoing Powers, and all other Powers vested by this Constitution in the government of the United States" (Note: This "necessary and proper," or "elastic," clause has been expansively interpreted by the Supreme Court, as explained in chapter 2.)

Article I, section 8, has allowed Congress to increase the scope of its authority, often at the expense of the states and into areas not necessarily envisioned by the Framers.

Congress alone is given formal lawmaking powers in the Constitution, but it is important to remember that presidents issue proclamations and executive orders with the force of law (see chapter 8), bureaucrats issue quasi-legislative rules (see chapter 9), and the Supreme Court renders opinions, as was the case with its redistricting decisions, which generate principles that also have the force of law (see chapter 10).

Reflecting the different constituencies and size of each house of Congress (as well as the Framers' intentions), Article I gives special, exclusive powers to each house in addition to their shared role in lawmaking. For example, as noted in Table 7.2, the Constitution specifies that all revenue bills must originate in the House of Representatives. Over the years, however, this mandate has been blurred, and it is not unusual to see budget bills being considered simultaneously in both houses, especially since each must approve all bills in the end, whether or not they involve revenues. In 1995, for example, when President Clinton submitted his budget deficit-reduction plan, both houses deliberated similar proposals simultaneously.

The House also has the power of **impeachment,** the authority to charge the president, vice president, or other "civil officers," including federal judges, with "Treason, Bribery, or other high Crimes and Misdemeanors." Only the Senate is authorized to conduct trials of impeachment, with a two-thirds vote being necessary before a federal official can be removed from office. (See The Impeachment Process, page 255.)

Only two presidents, Andrew Johnson in 1868 and Bill Clinton in 1998, were impeached by the House. Both were acquitted by the full Senate. President Richard M. Nixon resigned from office in 1974 after the House Judiciary Committee voted to impeach him for his role in the Watergate scandal.

The House and Senate share in the impeachment process, but the Senate has the sole authority to approve major presidential appointments, including federal judges, ambassadors, and Cabinet- and sub-Cabinet-level positions. The Senate, too, must approve by a two-thirds vote all treaties entered into by the president. Failure by the president to court the Senate can be costly. At the end of World War I, for example,

President Andrew Johnson, who was elected in 1865 and held office until 1869, died in 1875 after having been re-elected to the Senate in 1874. (Photo courtesy: AP/Wide World Photos)

impeachment
The power delegated to the House of Representatives in the Constitution to charge the president, vice president, or other "civil officers," including federal judges, with "Treason, Bribery, or other high Crimes and Misdemeanors." This is the first step in the constitutional process of removing such government officials from office.

TABLE 7.2   Key Differences Between the House and Senate

CONSTITUTIONAL DIFFERENCES	
House	*Senate*
Initiates all revenue bills	Offers "advice and consent" on many major presidential appointments
Initiates impeachment procedures and passes articles of impeachment	Tries impeached officials
Two-year terms	Six-year terms (one-third up for reelection every two years)
435 members (apportioned by population)	100 members (two from each state)
	Approves treaties

DIFFERENCES IN OPERATION	
House	*Senate*
More centralized, more formal; stronger leadership	Less centralized, less formal; weaker leadership
Rules Committee fairly powerful in controlling time and rules of debate (in conjunction with the Speaker)	No Rules Committee; limits on debate come through unanimous consent or cloture of filibuster
More impersonal	More personal
Power less evenly distributed	Power more evenly distributed
Members are highly specialized	Members are generalists
Emphasizes tax and revenue policy	Emphasizes foreign policy

CHANGES IN THE INSTITUTION	
House	*Senate*
Power centralized in the Speaker's inner circle of advisors	Senate workload increasing and informality breaking down; filibusters more frequent
House procedures are becoming more efficient	Becoming more difficult to pass legislation
Turnover is relatively high	Turnover is moderate

Representative Henry Hyde (R–Ill.) chaired the House Judiciary Committee as it conducted impeachment hearings. Later, Hyde managed the case against President Clinton in the Senate. Because committee chairs no longer can serve more than three terms, Hyde now chairs the House International Relations Committee. (Photo courtesy: Brad Markel/Liaison Agency/ Getty Source)

President Woodrow Wilson worked long and hard to get other nations to accept the Treaty of Versailles, which contained the charter of the proposed League of Nations. He overestimated his support in the Senate, however, and that body refused to ratify the treaty, thereby dealing Wilson and his international stature a severe setback.

THE MEMBERS OF CONGRESS

Today, many members of Congress find the job exciting in spite of public criticism of the institution. But it wasn't always so. Until D.C. got air-conditioning and drained the swamps, Washington was a miserable town. Most representatives spent as little time as possible there, viewing the Congress, especially the House, as a stepping stone to other political positions. Thus, after spending a brief tour of duty in D.C., most representatives went home to run for local or state political office or were rewarded for their service by party bosses with a federal judgeship. It is only after World War I that House members, in particular, became what were termed "congressional careerists" who viewed their work in Washington as rewarding and long term.[8]

Many members of Congress clearly relish their work, although there are indications that the high cost of living in Washington and maintaining two homes, political scandals, intense media scrutiny, the need to tackle hard issues, and a growth of partisan dissension is taking a toll on many members. Those no longer in the majority, in particular, often don't see their service in Congress as satisfying.

Members must attempt to appease two constituencies—party leaders, colleagues, and lobbyists in Washington, D.C., and constituents at home. As revealed in Table 7.3, members spend full days at home as well as in D.C. According to one study of House members in nonelection years, average representatives made thirty-five trips back home to their districts, and spent an average 138 days a year there.[9] Hedrick Smith, a Pulitzer Prize–winning reporter for *The New York Times*, has aptly described a member's days as a "kaleidoscopic jumble: breakfast with reporters, morning staff meetings, simultaneous committee hearings to juggle, back-to-back sessions with lobbyists and constituents, phone calls, briefings, constant buzzers interrupting office work to make quorum calls and votes on the run, afternoon speeches, evening meetings, receptions, fund-raisers, all

TABLE 7.3 A Day in the Life of a Member of Congress

Typical Member's At-Home Schedule[a]			*Typical Member's Washington Schedule*[b]	
Monday, March 20			**Wednesday, April 10**	
7:30 A.M.	Business group breakfast, 20 members of the business community leaders	(1 hour)	8:00 A.M.	Budget Study Group—Chairman Leon Panetta, Budget Committee, room 340 Cannon Building
8:45 A.M.	Hoover Elementary School, 6th grade class assembly	(45 min)	8:45 A.M.	Mainstream Forum Meeting, room 2344 Rayburn Building
9:45 A.M.	National Agriculture Day, speech, Holiday Inn South	(45 min)	9:15 A.M.	Meeting with Consulting Engineers Council of N.C. from Raleigh about various issues of concern
10:45 A.M.	Supplemental Food Shelf, pass foodstuffs to needy families	(1 hour)	9:45 A.M.	Meet with N.C. Soybean Assn. representatives re: agriculture appropriations projects
12:00 noon	Community College, student/faculty lunch, speech and Q & A	(45 min)	10:15 A.M.	WCHL radio interview (by phone)
1:00 P.M.	Sunset Terrace Elementary School, assembly 4, 5, 6 graders, remarks/Q & A	(45 min)	10:30 A.M.	Tape weekly radio show—budget
(Travel Time: 1:45 P.M.–2:45 P.M.)			11:00 A.M.	Meet with former student, now an author, about intellectual property issue
2:45 P.M.	Plainview Day Care Facility, owner wishes to discuss changes in federal law	(1 hour)	1:00 P.M.	Agriculture Subcommittee Hearing—Budget Overview and General Agriculture Outlook, room 2362 Rayburn Building
4:00 P.M.	Town Hall Meeting, American Legion	(1 hour)	2:30 P.M.	Meeting with Chairman Bill Ford and southern Democrats re: HR-5., Striker Replacement Bill, possible amendments
(Travel Time: 5:00 P.M.–5:45 P.M.)				
5:45 P.M.	PTA meeting, speech, education issues before Congress (also citizen involvement with national associations)	(45 min)	3:15 P.M.	Meet with Close-Up students from district on steps of Capitol for photo and discussions
6:30 P.M.	Annual Dinner, St. John's Lutheran Church Developmental Activity Center	(30 min)	3:45 P.M.	Meet with Duke professor re: energy research programs
7:15 P.M.	Association for Children for Enforcement of Support meeting to discuss problems of enforcing child support payments	(45 min)	4:30 P.M.	Meet with constituent of Kurdish background re: situation in Iraq
(Travel Time: 8:00 p.m.–8:30 p.m.)			5:30–7:00 P.M.	Reception—Sponsored by National Assn. of Home Builders, honoring new president Mark Tipton from Raleigh, H-328 Capitol
8:30 P.M.	Students Against Drunk Driving (SADD) meeting, speech, address; drinking age, drunk driving, uniform federal penalties	(45 min)	6:00–8:00 P.M.	Reception—Honoring retiring Rep. Bill Gray, Washington Court Hotel
9:30 P.M.	State University class, discuss business issues before Congress	(1 hour)	6:00–8:00 P.M.	Reception—Sponsored by Firefighters Assn., room B-339 Rayburn Building
			6:00–8:00 P.M.	Reception—American Financial Services Assn., Gold Room

Sources: [a]Craig Shultz, ed., *Setting Course. A Congressional Management Guide* (Washington, D.C.: American University, 1994), 335.

[b]David E. Price. *The Congressional Experience: A View from the Hill* (Boulder, Colo.: Westview Press, 1992), 38.

crammed into four days so they can race home for a weekend gauntlet of campaigning. It's a rat race."[10]

How do senators and representatives accomplish all that they must and also satisfy their constituents? They send newsletters to stay in touch, hold town meetings throughout their districts, and get important help from their staffs. **Casework,** although rarely indulged in by legislators themselves, is a major responsibility for selected staff members called caseworkers. Veterans who believe that they are getting the runaround at V.A. hospitals, retirees who experience delays in receiving Social Security checks, or entrepreneurs eager to start new businesses who need assistance from the Small Business Administration often seek help from their representative. Other citizens ask their legislators to intercede to overturn administrative decisions such as ones on eligibility for participation in a program or the receipt of benefits.

Increasingly, senators and representatives are placing most of their caseworkers back in their home district offices, where they are more accessible to constituents who can drop by and talk to a friendly face about their problems. In larger districts, caseworkers

casework

The process of solving constituents' problems dealing with the bureaucracy.

may "ride the circuit," taking the helping hand of the congressional office to county seats, crossroads, post offices, and mobile offices. The average House member has seventeen full-time staff members; the average size of a senator's office staff is forty-four, although this number varies with state population.[11]

Running for Office and Staying in Office

Despite the long hours, hard work, and sometimes even abuse, senators and representatives experience, thousands aspire to these jobs every year. Yet only 535 men and women actually serve in the U.S. Congress. Membership in one of the two major political parties is almost always a prerequisite for election, because election laws in various states often discriminate against independents (those without party affiliation) and minor-party candidates. As discussed in chapter 14, money is the mother's milk of politics—the ability to raise money is often key to any member's victory.

The **incumbency factor** helps members to stay in office once they are elected. Simply put, being in office helps you stay in office.[12] It's often very difficult for outsiders to win because they don't have the advantages (enumerated in Table 7.4) enjoyed by incumbents, including name recognition, access to media, and fund raising capabilites. As illustrated in Figure 7.1, which compares the way poll respondents feel about their own representatives to how they feel about Congress as an institution, most Americans approve of their *own* members of Congress.

It is not surprising, then, that from 1980 to 1990, an average of 95 percent of the incumbents who sought reelection actually won their primary and general election races.[13] More recent elections saw even higher proportions of incumbents returning to office. One study basically concluded that unless a member of Congress was involved in a serious scandal, his or her chances of defeat were minimal.[14]

Term Limits

A **term-limits** movement began sweeping the nation in the late 1980s because of voter frustration with gridlock and ethics problems in Congress and in state legislatures. Citizens and citizens groups approved referenda limiting the elected terms not only of their

---

incumbency factor
The fact that being in office helps a person stay in office because of a variety of benefits which go with the position.

Longman
Participate.com 2.0
Visual Literacy
Why Is It So Hard to Defeat an Incumbent?

---

term limits
Legislation designating that state or federal elected legislators can serve only a specified number of years.

TABLE 7.4   The Advantages of Incumbency

- Name recognition gained through previous campaigns and repeated visits to the district to make appearances at various public events.
- Credit claiming for bringing federal money into the district in the form of grants and contracts.
- Positive evaluations from constituents earned by doing favors (casework) such as helping cut red tape and tracking down federal aid, and tasks handled by publicly supported professional staff members.
- Distribution of newsletters and other noncampaign materials free through the mails by using the "frank" (an envelope that contains the legislator's signature in place of a stamp).
- Access to media—incumbents are news makers who provide reporters with tips and quotes.
- Greater ease in fundraising—their high reelection rates make them a good bet for people or groups willing to give campaign contributions in hopes of having access to powerful decision makers.
- Experience in running a campaign, putting together a campaign staff, making speeches, understanding constituent concerns, and connecting with people.
- Superior knowledge about a wide range of issues gained through work on committees, review of legislation, and previous campaigns.
- A record for supporting locally popular policy positions.

STILL THE BEST CONGRESSIONAL TERM-LIMITING DEVICE.

state representatives, but also of members of Congress. Given the power of incumbency, proponents of term limits argued that election to Congress, in essence, equaled life tenure. The concept of term limits is a simple one that appeals to many who oppose the notion of career politicians.

Term limits aren't a new idea. In 1787, the Framers considered, but rejected, a section of the Virginia Plan that called for members of the House to be restricted to one term. Still, many of the Framers believed in the regular rotation of offices among worthy citizens, and this was generally the practice in the early years of the republic.

In 1994, many Republicans running for Congress signed the Contract with America, which called for congressional passage of federal term limits; in 1995, the U.S. Supreme Court ruled that state-imposed limitations on the terms of members of Congress was unconstitutional.[15] Thus any efforts to enact congressional term limits would necessitate a constitutional amendment—not an easy feat. In the 104th Congress, a term-limits

WEB EXPLORATION
To evaluate your own representative, see
www.ablongman.com/oconnor

FIGURE 7.1   Approval of Congress and District Representatives

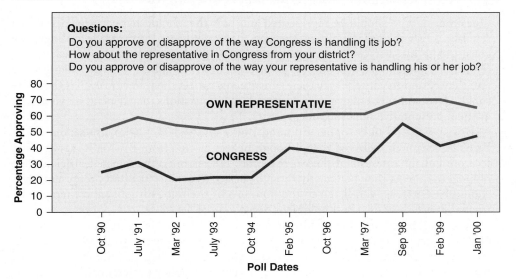

Questions:
Do you approve or disapprove of the way Congress is handling its job?
How about the representative in Congress from your district?
Do you approve or disapprove of the way your representative is handling his or her job?

Source: Data derived from R-Poll, LEXIS/NEXIS.

Susan Collins (R–ME), second term Senator, chats with members of the armed services. Collins sits on the Armed Services Committee. (Photo courtesy: Joel Page/AP/Wide World Photos.)

WEB EXPLORATION
To learn more about the members of the 108th Congress, go to www.ablongman.com/oconnor

amendment was brought to the floor for a vote. The proposal fell sixty votes short of the two-thirds vote needed to propose a constitutional amendment. In the Senate, Republicans failed to muster enough votes to cut off a Democratic filibuster. In 2000, seven of the ten members who made term limit pledges in 1994 did not seek reelection. Three broke those pledges; all of those members were reelected despite strong opposition from term-limits groups.

What Does Congress Look Like?

Congress is better educated, more white, more male, and richer than the rest of the United States. The Senate, in fact, is often called the "Millionaires' Club," and its members sport names like Rockefeller and Kennedy. The average age of House members in the 107th Congress was fifty-four; the average age of senators was sixty, and no senator was younger than forty. John Sununu (R–NH), is the youngest senator in the 108th Congress at thirty-eight.

As revealed in Figure 7.2, the 1992 elections saw a record number of women, African Americans, and other minorities elected to Congress. In 1992, for the first time ever, both senators elected from a single state—California—were women, Democrats Dianne Feinstein and Barbara Boxer. By the 108th Congress, the total number of women increased to seventy-five; sixty in the House and thirteen in the Senate. Two of these women serve as elected, but nonvoting, delegates in the House. The 2002 election also saw the election of Elizabeth Dole (R–NC), to the Senate, and the election of the first "sister act," Representative Loretta Sanchez (D–CA) and her younger sister, Linda (D–CA).

The number of African Americans in the House rose by one to thirty-nine. There are but twenty-five Hispanics in the 108th—all in the House. Almost all are Democrats. The number of Asian-Pacific Americans declined by one with the death of Patsy Mink (D-HI). There is but a lone Native American in each chamber of Congress.

The Representational Role of Members of Congress

Questions of who should be represented and how that should happen are critical in a republic. Over the years, political theorists have enunciated various ideas about how constituents' interests are best represented in any legislative body. Does it make a difference if the members of Congress come from or are members of a particular group? Are they bound to vote the way their constituents expect them to vote even if they personally favor another policy? Your answer to these questions may depend on your view of the representative function of legislators.

British political philosopher Edmund Burke (1729–1787), who also served in the British Parliament, believed that although he was elected from Bristol, it was his duty to represent the interests of the *entire* nation. He reasoned that elected officials were obliged to vote as they personally thought best. According to Burke, representatives should be **trustees** who listen to the opinions of their constituents and then can be trusted to use their own best judgment to make final decisions.

A second theory of representation holds that representatives are **delegates.** True delegates are representatives who vote the way their constituents would want them to, whether or not those opinions are the representative's. Delegates, therefore, must be ready and willing to vote against their conscience or policy preferences if they know

trustee
Role played by elected representatives who listen to constituents' opinions and then use their best judgment to make final decisions.

delegate
Role played by elected representatives who vote the way their constituents would want them to, regardless of their own opinions.

FIGURE 7.2 Numbers of Women and Minorities in Congress

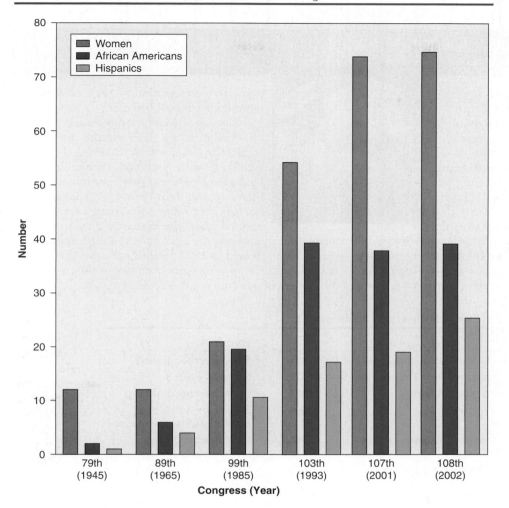

how their constituents feel about a particular issue. Not surprisingly, members of Congress and other legislative bodies generally don't fall neatly into either category. It is often unclear how constituents feel about a particular issue, or there may be conflicting opinions within a single constituency. With these difficulties in mind, a third theory of representation holds that **politicos** alternately don the hats of trustee or delegate, depending on the issue. On an issue of great concern to their constituents, representatives will most likely vote as delegates; on other issues, perhaps those that are less visible, representatives will act as trustees and use their own best judgment. Research by political scientists supports this view.[16]

How a representative views his or her role—as a trustee, delegate, or politico—may still not answer the question of whether or not it makes a difference if a representative or senator is male or female, African American or Latino or Caucasian, young or old, gay or straight. Burke's ideas about representation don't even begin to address more practical issues of representation. Can a man, for example, represent the interests of women as well as a woman? Can a rich woman represent the interests of the poor? The combinations are endless.

Female representatives historically have played prominent roles in efforts to expand women's rights. One such study by the Center for the American Woman and Politics,

politico
Role played by elected representatives who act as trustees or as delegates, depending on the issue.

GLOBAL POLITICS

REPRESENTATION IN THE INDONESIAN LEGISLATURE

As mentioned earlier, the representative function of legislatures is critical to a republic. In most of the industrialized democracies, the legislature is the only directly elected part of the national government. In the United States, members of Congress are first and foremost representatives of electoral districts, which is why district constituents play such a large role in what legislators do. The constitutional requirement that members of Congress reside in their districts reinforces that tendency. Other industrialized democracies such as Japan, Germany, and Italy mix single member districts with proportional representation, where candidates represent a political party, not a district.

Indonesia provides another form of representation. In the 1999 election for the Indonesian house of representatives, thirty-eight seats were reserved for the military. Under the New Order government that had been in power from 1966–1998, the number had been higher. Reserving seats had ensured that the Suharto dictatorship maintained control over the legislature, and the truncated version that followed in 1999 demonstrates the difficulties democratizing governments often face in eliminating the vestiges of powerful nondemocratic interests.

Electoral Rules and Representation in 11 Legislatures

Country	Lower House of Legislature	Seats	Electoral Rules
Canada	House of Commons	301	Single member districts
China	National People's Congress	2,979	Indirectly elected
France	National Assembly	577	Single member districts
Germany	Bundestag	669	Single member districts, proportional representation
Indonesia	House of Representatives	500	Multimember districts, reserved seats
Italy	Chamber of Deputies	630	Single member districts, proportional representation
Japan	House of Representatives	500	Single member districts, proportional representation
Mexico	Chamber of Deputies	500	Single member districts, proportional representation
Russia	State Duma	500	Single member districts, proportional representation
United Kingdom	House of Commons	652	Single member districts
United States	House of Representatives	435	Single member districts

Source: CIA World Factbook 2000 online, http://www.odci.gov/cia/publications/factbook/geos.

Longman
Participate.com 2.0
Comparative
Comparing
Legislatures

for example, found that most women in the 103rd Congress "felt a special responsibility to represent women, particularly to represent their life experiences. . . . They undertook this additional responsibility while first, and foremost, like all members of Congress, representing their own districts." Said Representative Nancy Johnson (R–CT), "We need to integrate the perspective of women into the policy-making process, just as we have now successfully integrated the perspective of environmental preservation, [and] the perspective of worker safety."[17] For more on the impact of women in Congress, see Politics Now: Seventy-Five and Counting.

POINT/COUNTERPOINT

IS PORK BARRELING WASTEFUL SPENDING OR LEGITIMATE EXPENDITURE?

The term "pork barrel" dates back to the early 1800s when pork was salted (as a preservative) and kept in a barrel. In the late 1800s, it became used as political slang to mean goodies for the local district paid for by the taxpayers at large. Today, Citizens Against Government Waste (CAGW), a nonpartisan, independent watchdog group, defines pork barreling as any government expenditure that meets at least one of these seven criteria:

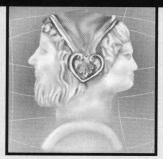

- Requested by only one member of Congress;
- Not specifically authorized;
- Not competitively awarded;
- Not requested by the president;
- Greatly exceeds the president's budget request from the previous year;
- Not the subject of congressional hearings; or
- Serves only a local or special interest.

This group argues that any spending that fits this definition is wasteful and should not be allowed. In fiscal year 2000, Citizens Against Government Waste (CAGW) estimated that the budget contained in excess of $14.6 billion in earmarks or pork barrel spending. Measured in the hundreds of millions or billions of dollars, pork barrel spending is not a huge part of the whole trillion dollar federal budget, however. To many members of Congress, one person's pork is another person's legitimate budgetary expenditure. Almost all members of Congress do it and a large number of them argue that what CAGW others call pork is not extravagant and wasteful spending but good constituent service. Let's examine these two points of view.

Opponents of pork barreling, such as CAGW and Common Cause, oppose pork barrel spending as illegitimate and against the national interest and the interests of the general taxpayers. The Libertarian Party even goes as far as defining most government spending as pork barrel and unnecessary. Opponents often cite examples of multi-million or billion dollar spending that is obviously wasteful or downright silly: the multi-million dollar study of cow flatulence, a one million dollar appropriation to determine why Americans don't ride their bikes to work, and, in 2000, the one million dollars given to Texas Tech University for an experiment on growing vegetables in outer space. Opponents of pork barrel spending argue that government monies ought to be spent on projects that benefit a large number of people and that all spending should go through a deliberative process not simply be added as a rider to a popular bill (which is how much pork gets signed into law). CAGW and others believe that irresponsible and reckless spending should be curbed through the implementation of the Grace Commission plan. The Grace Commission was impaneled by President Reagan in 1982 and after two years of analyzing government expenditures produced a 47-volume 21,000-page report on wasteful government spending and suggested numerous ways to reduce fraud, errors, and waste through better management, oversight, and enhanced accountability. The Grace Commission proposed cuts of over $141 million per year for three years without cutting any essential services.

Members of Congress, and the people who benefit from these projects, support these spending earmarks as legitimate expenditures as well as positive benefits. Members of Congress have staffs who do constituent service in order to help them get reelected as well as to help them represent the needs and views of their districts. These same members see what some have called "pork barrel" spending as another way of representing their constituents and benefiting their districts: Grand Rapids, Michigan, needed that highway to relieve local congestion; Savannah, Georgia, needed the harbor dredged so it could compete with other ports and maintain the local economy; California, hard hit by military base closures in the 1980s, was in desperate need of a refurbished naval base in San Diego; West Virginia is one of the poorest states in the union and needed the jobs provided by the FBI fingerprinting facility and the intelligence branch listening posts. These are instances of effective constituent service. Many members of Congress also argue that if they don't jockey for money for their own districts or states, those funds will go elsewhere.

What do you think? Is so-called pork barrel wasteful spending or legitimate expenditure?
Go to www.ablongman.com/oconnor

POLITICS NOW

SEVENTY-FIVE AND COUNTING: WOMEN IN THE U.S. CONGRESS

In 2000, the nine women in the United States Senate—three Republicans and six Democrats—came together to pen a book about their experiences in Congress and their efforts to work together to make a difference in the Senate.[a] By 2001, their numbers had grown to thirteen with the election of four additional women, all Democrats. Gains in the House were far more modest.

Study after study continues to find that women make a difference in all legislative bodies, especially when it comes to sponsoring legislation involving women's issues from health care to parental leave.[b] Still, their relatively low numbers continue to mean that women's interests are not always addressed. For example, in late 1999, Senate Foreign Relations Chairman Jesse Helms (R–N.C.) actually called Capitol police to remove nine female House members from a committee hearing after they tried to present him with a letter calling him as committee chair to hold hearings on Senate ratification of the 1979 United Nations Convention to Eliminate All Forms of Discrimination Against Women. Helms had refused to hold hearings on the treaty, which has been ratified by 160 nations. He also would not meet with House members who want the United States to ratify the treaty. After three months of Helms's dodging their request for a meeting, the women opted to confront him. "Now, please be a lady," Helms admonished Rep. Lynn C. Woolsey (D–Calif.), the leader of the House women who stood at the back of the room with blow-ups of the letter with one hundred House signatures. "If they want to be treated like members of Congress," said one Helms aide in defending his boss, "they ought to behave like members of Congress."[c]

While these women of the House were not able to prod Helms, the thirteen female senators are in an unusually advantageous position in the Senate because the Senate is so closely divided. As such, these thirteen women can provide a potential bloc of votes to urge the passage of policies of particular interest to women from education to health care to Social Security reform.

Rep. Lynn Woolsey (D–Calif.) is one of seventy-five female members of Congress. (Photo courtesy: Dudley M. Brooks, ©1998 *The Washington Post*. Reprinted by permission)

[a]*Nine and Counting: the Women of the Senate*. Barbara Mikulski et al. (New York: William Morrow, 2000.)
[b]Sue Thomas, *How Women Legislate* (New York: Oxford University Press, 1994).
[c]Helen Dewar, "Ladies of the House Rebuffed," *The Washington Post* (October 28, 1999): A31.

Actions of the one Native American and one African American in the Senate underscore the representative function that can be played in Congress. Ben Nighthorse Campbell (R–Colo.), for example, the only Native American in the Senate, also sits on the Committee on Indian Affairs. Earlier, as a member of the House, he led the fight to change the name of Custer Battlefield Monument in Montana to Little Bighorn Battlefield National Monument to honor the Indians who died in battle. He also fought successfully for legislation to establish the National Museum of the American Indian within the Smithsonian Institution.

Before her defeat in 1998, the only African American in the Senate, Senator Carol Moseley Braun, also tried to sensitize her colleagues about issues of race. In 1993 then Senator Jesse Helms (R–N.C.) sought to amend the national service bill in such a way to

Representative Carolyn Maloney (D–NY) is a regular in the House gym. Women members had to press to get equal access to all the facilities formerly enjoyed by their male colleagues.

preserve the design patent held by the United Daughters of the Confederacy that included the Confederate flag. Most senators had no idea what they were voting on, and the amendment to the bill passed by a vote of 52–48. Then, Senator Moseley Braun took to the floor to express her outrage at Helms's support of a symbol of slavery: "On this issue there can be no consensus. It is an outrage. It is an insult." Although Helms angrily insisted that slavery and race were not the issue, the Senate killed the Helms amendment by a vote of 75–25, as twenty-seven senators changed their votes. Said Senator Barbara Boxer (D–Calif.), "If there ever was proof of the value of diversity, we have it here today."[18]

Members of Congressional Black Caucus walk out in protest after trying to stop (symbolically) electoral college voting in a joint session of the House and Senate in January 2001. (Photo courtesy: Marshall/Liaison Agency/Getty Source)

Linda and Loretta Sanchez (D–CA) are the first two sisters elected to Congress. (Photo courtesy: Krista Niles/AP/Wide World Photos.)

HOW CONGRESS IS ORGANIZED

Every two years, a new Congress is seated. After ascertaining the formal qualifications of new members, the Congress organizes itself as it prepares for the business of the coming session. Among the first items on its agenda are the election of new leaders and the adoption of rules for conducting its business. As illustrated in Figure 7.3, each house has a hierarchical leadership structure.

The House of Representatives

Even in the first Congress in 1789, the House of Representatives was almost three times larger than the Senate. It is not surprising then, that from the beginning the House has been more tightly organized, more elaborately structured, and governed by stricter rules. Traditionally, loyalty to the party leadership and voting along party lines have been more common in the House than in the Senate. House leaders also play a key role in moving the business of the House along. Historically, the Speaker of the House, the majority and minority leaders, and the majority and minority House whips have made up the party leadership that runs Congress. This has now been expanded to include deputy minority whips of both parties.

Speaker of the House
The only officer of the House of Representatives specifically mentioned in the Constitution; elected at the beginning of each new Congress by the entire House; traditionally a member of the majority party.

majority party
The political party in each house of Congress with the most members.

minority party
Party with the second most members in either house of Congress.

The Speaker of the House.   The **Speaker of the House** is the only officer of the House of Representatives specifically mentioned in the Constitution. The office, the chamber's most powerful position, is modeled after a similar office in the British Parliament—the Speaker was the one who spoke to the king and conveyed the wishes of the House of Commons to the monarch.[19]

The Speaker is formally elected at the beginning of each new Congress by the entire House. Traditionally, the Speaker is a member of the **majority party,** the party in each house with the greatest number of members, as are all committee chairs. (The **minority party** is the party with the second most members in either House.) While typically not the member with the longest service, the Speaker generally has served in the House for a long time and in other House leadership positions as sort of an apprenticeship. J. Dennis Hastert spent twelve years in the House, and his predecessor Newt Gingrich (R–Ga.) took sixteen years to work his way to the gavel and dais. Generally, a Speaker is reelected until he chooses to retire or his party ceases to be in the majority.

FIGURE 7.3 Organizational Structure of the House of Representatives and the Senate Early in the 108th Congress

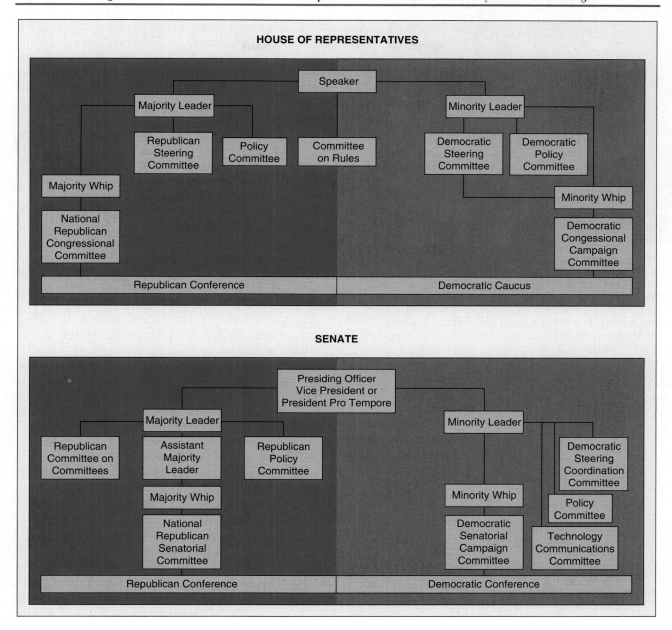

The Speaker presides over the House, oversees House business, is the official spokesperson for the House of Representatives, and is second in the line of presidential succession. Moreover, he is the House liaison with the president and generally has great political influence within the chamber. Through his parliamentary and political skills, he is expected to smooth the passage of party-backed legislation through the House.

The first "powerful" Speaker was Henry Clay. (See Roots of Government: Life on the Floor and in the Halls of Congress.) Serving in Congress at a time when turnover was high, he was elected to the position in 1810, his first term in office. He was Speaker of the House of Representatives for a total of six terms—longer than anyone else in the nineteenth century.

WEB EXPLORATION
For more on the Speaker and his activities, see
www.ablongman.com/oconnor

Representative Barney Frank (D–Mass.) has been in the rare position of having fun while being in the minority party. Says Frank, "I'm a counterpuncher, happiest fighting on the defensive. Besides, I really dislike what the Republicans are doing. I think they are bad for the country and for vulnerable people. I feel, 'Boy, this is a moral opportunity—you've got to fight this.' Also, I'm used to being in a minority. Hey, I'm a left-handed gay Jew. I've never felt, automatically, a member of any majority. So, I started swinging from the opening bell of this Congress." (Photo courtesy: Luke Frazza/AFP/Corbis)

Longman
Participate.com
2.0
Timeline
The Power of
the Speaker
of the House

majority leader
The elected leader of the party controlling the most seats in the U.S. House of Representatives or the Senate; is second in authority to the Speaker of the House and in the Senate is regarded as its most powerful member.

By the late 1800s, the House ceased to have a revolving door and average stays of members increased. With this professionalization of the House came professionalization in the speakership. Between 1896 and 1910, a series of Speakers initiated changes that brought more power to the Speaker's office. Filibusters could be broken, and Speakers largely took control of committee assignments and appointing committee chairs. Institutional and personal rule reached its height during the tenure of Speaker Joseph Cannon (1903–1910).

Negative reaction to those strong speakers eventually led to a revolt in 1910 and 1911 in the House and to a reduction of the formal powers of the Speaker. As a consequence, many Speakers between Cannon and Gingrich often relied on more informal powers that came from their personal ability to persuade.

Newt Gingrich, the first Republican Speaker in forty years, convinced fellow Republicans to return important formal powers to the Speaker. In return for a rule preventing Speakers from serving for more than four consecutive Congresses, the Speaker was given unprecedented authority, including the power to refer bills to committee, ending the practice of joint referral of bills to more than one committee, where they might fare better. These formal changes, along with his personal leadership skills, allowed Gingrich to exercise greater control over the House and its agenda than any other Speaker since the days of Joe Cannon.

In time, Gingrich's highly visible role as a revolutionary transformed him into a negative symbol outside the Beltway as his public popularity plunged. Exit polls conducted on election day 1996 revealed that 60 percent had an unfavorable opinion of the Speaker, although that dislike did not appear to translate into votes against incumbent House Republicans. But in 1998, Republicans were stung when they failed to win more seats in the House and Senate. Gingrich's general unpopularity with large segments of the public worked to reinforce Republican's discontent with Gingrich. The 105th Republican Congress had few legislative successes; members were forced to accept a budget advanced by the White House, and Republicans running for office in 1998 lacked the coherent theme that had been so successful for them in 1994. These were but two of many reasons that prompted several members to announce that they would run against the Speaker. Gingrich, who could read the writing on the wall, opted to resign as Speaker (later he resigned altogether from the House) rather than face the prospect that he might not be reelected to the position that he had coveted for so long.

Representative Bob Livingston (R–La.) quickly emerged as Gingrich's successor. But amid the Clinton impeachment fervor, news of a long-time Livingston extramarital affair broke and Livingston stunningly announced that he would give up his expected speakership and resign from the House altogether. Scandal-weary Republicans then turned to someone largely unknown to the public: a well-liked and respected one-time high school coach and social studies teacher, J. Dennis Hastert.

Since coming into his "accidental speakership," Hastert has shown himself to be a "pragmatic and cautious politician" as he tries to deal with his "whisker thin [ten-vote] majority."[20] Through the 106th Congress, Hastert boasted a remarkable record of mobilizing his majority. In fact, he never "lost a vote on the rule to govern floor debate, a feat not seen in at least a decade." Still, he and House Minority Leader Richard Gephardt (D–Mo.) enjoy a strained relationship and in 2000 the Speaker even campaigned for Gephardt's opponent, "a blatant departure from traditional leadership decorum."[21]

Other House Leaders.   After the Speaker, the next most powerful people in the House are the majority and minority leaders, who are elected in their individual party caucuses. The **majority leader** is the second most important person in the House; his counterpart on the other side of the aisle (the House is organized so that if you are standing on the podium, Democrats sit on the right side and Republicans on the left side of the center aisle) is the **minority leader.** Both work closely with the Speaker, and the majority leader helps the Speaker schedule proposed legislation for debate on the House floor.

The Speaker and majority and minority leaders are assisted in their leadership efforts by the majority and minority **whips,** who are elected by party members in caucuses. The concept of whips originated in the British House of Commons, where they were named after the "whipper in," the rider who keeps the hounds together in a fox hunt. Party whips—who were first designated in the House in 1899 and in the Senate in 1913—do, as their name suggests, try to "whip" fellow Democrats or Republicans into line on partisan issues. They try to maintain close contact with all members on important votes, prepare summaries of content and implications of bills, get "nose counts" during debates and votes, and in general get members to toe the

As House Speaker, Dennis Hastert was much more cautious than his predecessor, Newt Gingrich. (Photo courtesy: Robert Trippett/SIPA Press)

party line. Whips and their deputy whips also serve as communications links, distributing word of the party line from leaders to rank-in-file members and alerting leaders to concerns in the ranks. Whips can be extraordinarily effective. In 1998, for example, when President Clinton returned home from his trip to the Middle East amid calls for his impeachment, he was stunned to learn that moderate Republicans who he had counted on to vote against his impeachment were "dropping like flies." The reason? Powerful House Whip Tom DeLay (R–Tex.) threatened Republicans that they would be denied coveted committee assignments and would even face Republican challengers in the next primary season unless they voted the party line.

The Senate

The Constitution specifies that the presiding officer of the Senate is the vice president of the United States. Because he is not a member of the Senate, he votes only in the case of a tie. Briefly in 2001, Vice President Dick Cheney became the first vice president since 1881 to preside over an evenly divided Senate.

The official chair of the Senate is the president pro tempore, who is selected by the majority party and presides over the Senate in the absence of the vice president. The position of president pro tempore is today primarily an honorific office that generally goes to the most senior senator of the majority party. Once elected, the pro tem, as he is called, stays in that office until there is a change in the majority party in the Senate. Since presiding over the Senate can be a rather perfunctory duty, neither the vice president nor the president pro tempore performs the task often. Instead, the duty of actually presiding over the Senate rotates among junior members of the chamber, allowing more senior members to attend more important meetings unless a key vote is being debated.

The true leader of the Senate is the majority leader, elected to the position by the majority party. Because the Senate is a smaller and more collegial body, operating without many of the more formal House rules concerning debate, the majority leader is not nearly as powerful as the Speaker of the House, a more overtly partisan body that requires more control by the Speaker. The majority and minority whips round out the leadership positions in the Senate and perform functions similar to those of their House

minority leader
The elected leader of the party with the second highest number of elected representatives in either the House or the Senate.

whip
One of several representatives who keep close contact with all members and take "nose counts" on key votes, prepare summaries of bills, and in general act as communications links within the party.

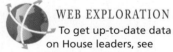 WEB EXPLORATION
To get up-to-date data on House leaders, see
www.ablongman.com/oconnor

ROOTS OF GOVERNMENT

LIFE ON THE FLOOR AND IN THE HALLS OF CONGRESS

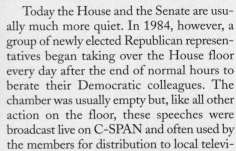

Throughout Congress's first several decades, partisan, sectional, and state tensions of the day often found their way onto the floors of the U.S. House and Senate. Many members were armed, and during one House debate thirty members showed their weapons. In 1826, for example, Senator John Randolph of Virginia insulted Henry Clay from the floor of the Senate, referring to Clay as "this being, so brilliant yet so corrupt, which, like a rotten mackerel by moonlight, shined and stunk." Clay immediately challenged Randolph to a duel on the Virginia side of the Potomac River. Both missed, although Randolph's coat fell victim to a bullet hole. Reacting to public opinion, however, in 1839 Congress passed a law prohibiting dueling in the District of Columbia.

Nevertheless, dueling continued. A debate in 1851 between representatives from Alabama and North Carolina ended in a duel, but no one was hurt. In 1856, Representative Preston Brooks of South Carolina, defending the honor of his region and family, assaulted Senator Charles Sumner of Massachusetts on the floor of the Senate. Sumner was disabled and unable to resume his seat in Congress for several years. Guns and knives were abundantly evident on the floor of both House and Senate, along with a wide variety of alcoholic beverages.

Today the House and the Senate are usually much more quiet. In 1984, however, a group of newly elected Republican representatives began taking over the House floor every day after the end of normal hours to berate their Democratic colleagues. The chamber was usually empty but, like all other action on the floor, these speeches were broadcast live on C-SPAN and often used by the members for distribution to local television stations back home. During a particularly strong attack on several Democrats' views on Central America, Representative Newt Gingrich paused suggestively mid-speech, as though waiting for an objection or daring the Democrats to respond. No other House member was on the floor at the time, but since C-SPAN cameras at that time focused only on the speaker, viewers were unaware of that fact.

Democratic House Speaker Thomas P. O'Neill (D–Mass.) angrily reacted by ordering C-SPAN cameras to span the empty chamber to expose Gingrich's and other Republicans' tactics, but what Republicans labeled "CAMSCAM" ignited a firestorm on the floor. Incensed by remarks made by Gingrich, O'Neill dropped his gavel, left his spot on the dais, and took to the floor, roaring at Gingrich, "You challenged their [House Democrats'] patriotism, and it is the lowest thing that I have ever seen in my thirty-two years in Congress!" Trent Lott (R–Miss.) then demanded that the Speaker be "taken down," the House term to call someone to order for violating House rules prohibiting personal attacks. The House Parliamentarian looked in the dictionary to see if the word "lowest" was a slur. As a hush fell on the House, the presiding officer told O'Neill that he had violated House rules. Bristled O'Neill, "I was expressing my views very mildly because I think much worse than I said."

O'Neill's penalty? The rarely invoked enforced silence for the remainder of the day's debate. So uncomfortable with that action was the House minority leader that he asked Lott to make a motion exempting O'Neill from the penalty, to which Lott agreed. No other House Speaker has ever been so reprimanded.*

---

*Alexander Stanley, "Tip Topped: O'Neill Tangles with Some Republican Turks over Camera Angles," *The Nation* (May 28, 1984): 36.

counterparts. But leading and whipping in the Senate can be quite a challenge. Senate rules have always given tremendous power to individual senators; in most cases senators can offer any kind of amendments to legislation on the floor, and an individual senator can bring all work on the floor to a halt indefinitely through a filibuster unless two-thirds of the senators vote to cut him or her off.[22]

Because of the Senate's smaller size, organization and formal rules have never played the same role in the Senate as they do in the House. Through the 1960s, it was a "Gentlemen's Club" whose folkways—unwritten rules of behavior—governed its operation. One such folkway, for example, stipulated that political disagreements not become personal criticisms. A senator who disliked another referred to that senator as "the able, learned, and distinguished senator." A member who really couldn't stand another called that senator "my very able, learned, and distinguished colleague."

In the 1960s and 1970s, senators became more and more active on and off the Senate floor in a variety of issues and extended debates that often occurred on the floor—without the rigid rules of courtesy that had once been the hallmark of the body. These changes weren't accompanied by giving additional powers to the Senate majority leader, who now often has difficulty controlling "the more active, assertive, and consequently less predictable membership" of the Senate.[23] Thus, while the majority leader sets the agenda, there's often not much he can formally do to control the other members of the Senate. This is especially true for Majority Leader Trent Lott (R–MS), who must try to keep liberal Republicans from bolting the party.

Vermont Representative Bernie Sanders (I–Vt.) is the only independent in the House, but he votes as a Democrat in its Caucus. Said Sanders of his election, "What Vermonters wanted is somebody to go down there and stand up and fight for ordinary people, rather than as the vast majority of members of Congress do—protect the interests of the wealthy and the powerful." In 2001, his fellow Vermonter, James Jeffords also became an Independent. Jeffords' actions, however, had far greater consequences as his defection and decision to ally himself with Democrats meant the Democrats took over control of the Senate. (Photo courtesy: Glen Russell/SIPA Press)

The Role of Political Parties in Organizing Congress

When the first Congress met in 1789 in the nation's temporary capital in New York City, it consisted of only twenty-two senators and fewer than sixty representatives. Those men faced the enormous task of creating much of the machinery of government as well as that of drafting a bill of rights, for which the Anti-Federalists had argued so vehemently. During their debates, the political differences that divided Americans during the early years of the Union were renewed. For example, when Alexander Hamilton, the first secretary of the treasury and a staunch Federalist, proposed to fund the national debt and create a national bank, he aroused the ire of those who feared vesting the national government with too much power. This conflict led Hamilton's opponents to create the Democratic–Republican Party to counter the Federalists, creating a two-party system in Congress. Control of the political parties quickly gave Congress far more powers. The Democratic–Republican **party caucus** (the name for a formal gathering of all party members in the House) nominated Thomas Jefferson (1804), James Madison (1808 and 1812), and James Monroe (1816) for president, all of whom were elected.

The organization of both houses of Congress is closely tied to political parties and their strength in each House. For the party breakdowns in the 108th Congress, see Figure 7.4. Parties play a key role in the committee system, an organizational feature of Congress that facilitates its lawmaking and oversight functions. The committees, controlled by the majority party in each house of Congress, often set the congressional agendas, although under Newt Gingrich's speakership, this power eroded substantially in the House of Representatives as the Speaker's power was enhanced.[24]

At the beginning of each new Congress—the 108th Congress, for example, will sit in two sessions, one in 2003 and one in 2004—the members of each party gather in its party caucus or conference. Historically, these caucuses have enjoyed varied powers, but

party caucus
A formal gathering of all party members.

FIGURE 7.4   The 108th Congress

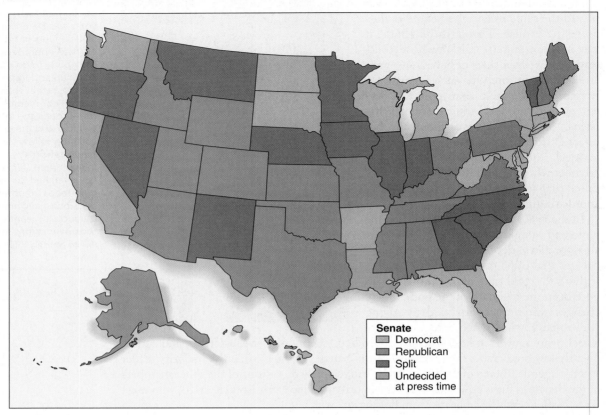

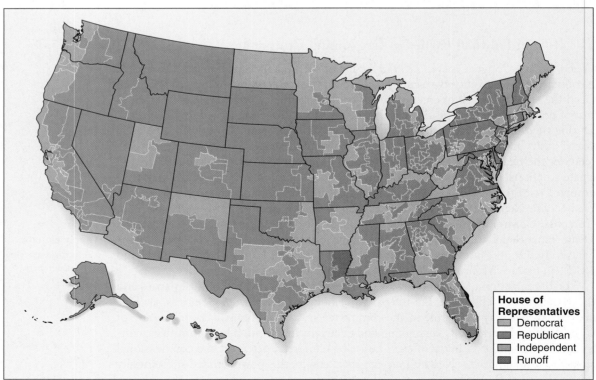

Source: Associated Press/*USA Today*.

today the party caucuses—called "caucus" by House Democrats and "conference" by House and Senate Republicans and Senate Democrats—have several roles, including nominating or electing party officers, reviewing committee assignments, discussing party policy, imposing party discipline, setting party themes, and coordinating media, including talk radio. Conference and caucus chairs are recognized party leaders who work with others who are part of the House or Senate leadership.[25]

Each caucus or conference has specialized committees that fulfill certain tasks. House Republicans, for example, have a Committee on Committees that makes committee assignments. The Democrats' Steering Committee performs this function. Each party also has a Congressional Campaign Committee to assist members in their reelection bids.

The Committee System

The saying "Congress in session is Congress on exhibition, whilst Congress in its committee rooms is Congress at work" may not be as true today as it was when Woodrow Wilson wrote it in 1885.[26] Still, "The work that takes place in the committee and subcommittee rooms of Capitol Hill is critical to the productivity and effectiveness of Congress."[27] **Standing committees** are the first and last places that most bills go. Usually committee members play key roles in floor debate in the full House or Senate about the merits of the proposed bill. When different versions of a bill are passed in the House and Senate, a **conference committee** with members of both houses meets to iron out the differences.

Committees are especially important in the House of Representatives because its size makes organization and specialization key, as noted in Table 7.5. The establishment of subcommittees allows for even greater specialization.

standing committee
Committee to which proposed bills are referred.

conference committee
Joint committee created to iron out differences between Senate and House versions of a specific piece of legislation.

TABLE 7.5   Committees of the 108th Congress (with a Subcommittee Example)*

STANDING COMMITTEES

House	Senate
Agriculture	Agriculture, Nutrition, and Forestry
Appropriations	Appropriations
Armed Services	Armed Services
Banking and Financial Services	Banking, Housing, and Urban Affairs
Budget	Budget
Commerce	Commerce, Science, and Transportation
Education and the Workforce	Energy and Natural Resources
Government Reform	Environment and Public Works
House Administration	Finance
International Relations	Foreign Relations
Judiciary	Governmental Affairs
Resources	Health, Education, Labor, and Pensions
Rules	Judiciary
Science	Judiciary Subcommittees:
Small Business	Administrative Oversight and the Courts
Standards of Official Conduct (Ethics)	Antitrust, Business Rights, and Competition
Transportation and Infrastructure	Constitution, Federalism, and Property Rights
Veterans' Affairs	Criminal Justice Oversight
Ways and Means	Immigration
	Technology, Terrorism, and Government Information
	Youth Violence
	Rules and Administration
	Small Business
	Veterans' Affairs

SELECT, SPECIAL, AND OTHER COMMITTEES

House	Senate	JOINT COMMITTEES
Select Intelligence	Special Aging	Economics
	Select Ethics	Library
	Select Intelligence	Printing
	Indian Affairs	Taxation

*As of press time.

WEB EXPLORATION
To get information on
specific committees, go to
www.ablongman.com/oconnor

An institutionalized committee system was created in 1816, and more and more committees have been added over time. So many committees resulted in duplication of duties and jurisdictional battles that the legislative process suffered. Changes were made to the committee system in the 103rd Congress. The growth of committees over the years greatly concerned House Republicans. Thus, when Republicans took control in 1995, they immediately targeted several committees and subcommittees (and the staffs of each of those committees) for cutting.

Types of Committees.   There are four types of congressional committees: (1) standing; (2) joint; (3) conference; and (4) ad hoc, special, or select.[28]

1. *Standing committees,* so called because they continue from one Congress to the next, are the committees to which proposed bills are referred for consideration. Fewer than 10 percent of the more than 8,000 measures sent to committees are ever reported out. Standing committees also conduct investigations, such as the Senate Banking Committee's investigation of Whitewater. These are permanent committees.
2. *Joint committees* include members from both houses of Congress who conduct investigations or special studies. They are set up to expedite business between the houses and to help focus public attention on major matters, such as the economy, taxation, or scandals. A joint committee, for example, investigated the Iran-Contra scandal.
3. *Conference committees* are a special kind of joint committee that reconciles differences in bills passed by the House and Senate. The conference committee is made up of members from the House and Senate committees that originally considered the bill.
4. *Ad hoc, special,* or *select committees* are temporary committees appointed for specific purposes, generally to conduct special investigations or studies and to report back to the chamber that established them.

The House and Senate standing committees listed in Table 7.5 were created by rule. In the 108th Congress, the House had nineteen standing committees, each with an average of thirty-one members. Together, they had a total of eighty-six subcommittees that collectively acted as the eyes, ears, and hands of the House. They considered issues roughly parallel to those of the departments represented in the president's Cabinet. For example, there were committees on agriculture, education, the judiciary, veterans' affairs, transportation, and commerce.

Although most committees in one house parallel those in the other, the House Rules Committee, for which there is no counterpart in the Senate, plays a key role in the lawmaking process. Indicative of the importance of Rules, majority party members are appointed directly by the Speaker. This committee reviews most bills after they come from a committee and before they go to the full chamber for consideration. Performing a "traffic cop" function, the House Rules Committee gives each bill what is called a *rule,* which contains the date the bill will come up for debate and the time that will be allotted for discussion, and often specifies what kinds of amendments can be offered. Bills considered under a *closed rule* cannot be amended.

Standing committees have considerable power. They can kill bills, amend them radically, or hurry them through the process. In the words of Woodrow Wilson, once a bill is referred to a committee, it "crosses a parliamentary bridge of sighs to dim dungeons of silence from whence it never will return." Thus a committee reports out to the full House or Senate only a small fraction of the bills assigned to it. Bills can be "forced" out of a House committee by a **discharge petition** signed by a majority (218) of the House membership, but legislators are reluctant to take this drastic measure.

Until the 107th Congress, a House rule kept the names of those signing discharge petitions secret. In late 1993, the system was targeted by House Republicans, who

discharge petition
Petition that gives a majority of the House of Representatives the authority to bring an issue to the floor in the face of committee inaction.

charged that the secrecy surrounding discharge petitions allowed members to claim that they supported legislation, yet assured that constituents could not learn whether a member indeed had tried to force a stalled bill out of committee. Under a new House rule, adopted in 1995, the clerk is required to publish the names of those who sign a discharge petition each week in the *Congressional Record* as well as to make that information available to the public electronically.

In the 108th Congress, the Senate had sixteen standing committees that ranged in size from twelve to twenty-eight members. It also had sixty-eight subcommittees, which allowed all majority party senators to chair one. For example, the Senate Judiciary Committee had seven subcommittees, as illustrated in Table 7.5.

In contrast to the House, whose members hold few committee assignments (an average of 1.8 standing and three subcommittees), senators are spread more thinly, with each serving on an average of three to four committees and seven subcommittees. Whereas the committee system allows House members to become policy or issue specialists, Senate members are often generalists. In the 108th Congress, Kay Bailey Hutchison (R–Tex.), for example, serves on nine committees including Appropriations, Defense, Armed Services, and Rules. She also serves on sixteen subcommittees and before the Republicans lost their majority, chaired two of those subcommittees.

Senate committees enjoy the same power over framing legislation as do House committees, but the Senate, being an institution more open to individual input than the House, gives less deference to the work done in committees. In the Senate, legislation is more likely to be rewritten on the floor, where all senators can participate and add amendments at any time.

Committee Membership.   Many newly elected members of Congress come into the body with their sights set on certain committee assignments. Others are more flexible. Many legislators seeking committee assignments inform their party's selection committee of their preferences. They often request assignments based on their own interests or expertise or on a particular committee's ability to help their prospects for reelection. Political scientist Kenneth Shepsle has noted that committee assignments are to members what stocks are to investors—they seek to acquire those that will add to the value of their portfolios.[29]

Representatives often seek committee assignments that have access to what is known as the **pork barrel.** Historically, pork barrel legislation has allowed representatives to "bring home the bacon" to their districts in the form of public works programs, military bases, or other programs designed to benefit districts directly. In the past a seat on the National Security Committee, for example, would allow a member to bring lucrative defense contracts back to his or her district, or discourage base closings within his or her district or state. The 1999 "emergency relief" bill for Kosovo well illustrates the pervasiveness of pork. The Senate version of that bill had something for everyone: In it was a $1 billion request for aid for ailing steel companies in Senator Robert Byrd's West Virginia (Byrd is known as the "King of Pork"), $500 million in loans for faltering oil and gas interests, and a provision to prevent the Mississippi sturgeon in the then Senate majority leader's home state, Mississippi, from being listed as an endangered species.[30]

Legislators who bring this kind of pork barrel back to their districts are hard to beat at the polls. But, ironically, these programs are the ones that attract much of the public criticism directed at the federal government in general and Congress in particular. Thus it is somewhat paradoxical that pork barrel improves a member's chances for reelection or for election to higher office. In 1984, Jesse Helms (R–N.C.), for example, turned down the chairmanship of the Senate Committee on Foreign Relations to stay on the less prestigious Committee on Agriculture, Nutrition, and Forestry, where he could better ensure continued support for the tobacco industry so vital to his home state's economy.

pork barrel
Legislation that allows representatives to "bring home the bacon" to their districts in the form of public works programs, military bases, or other programs designed to benefit their districts directly.

Pork isn't the only motivator for those seeking lush committee assignments. Some committees, such as Commerce, facilitate reelection by giving members influence over decisions that affect large campaign contributors. Other committees, such as Education and the Workforce or Judiciary, attract members eager to work on the policy responsibilities assigned to the committee even if the appointment does them little good at the ballot box. A third motivator for certain committee assignments is the desire to have power and influence within the chamber. The Appropriations and Budget Committees provide that kind of reward for some members.

In both the House and the Senate, committee membership generally reflects the party distribution within that chamber. For example, at the outset of the 108th Congress, Republicans held a narrow majority of House seats and thus claimed about a 54 percent share of the seats on several committees, including International Relations, Commerce, and Education and the Workforce. On committees more critical to the operation of the House or to setting national policy, the majority often takes a disproportionate share of the slots. Since the Rules Committee regulates access to the floor for legislation approved by other standing committees, control by the majority party is essential for it to manage the flow of legislation. For this reason, no matter how narrow the majority party's margin in the chamber, it makes up at least two-thirds of Rules's membership. In the Senate, during its brief 50–50 split in 2001, the leaders agreed to equal representation on committees, along with equal staffing, office space, and budget.

Committee Chairs.   Before recent changes giving the House Speaker more power, committee chairs long enjoyed tremendous power and prestige. Even today's House chairs may choose not to schedule hearings on a bill to kill it. (Senate power sharing rules allow either party to bring legislation to the floor, thereby diminishing its chairs' powers.) Chairs also carry with them the power to draft legislation, manage a million-plus dollar staff budget, and "hear pleas from lobbyists, Cabinet secretaries and even presidents who need something only a committee can provide."[31] Chairs may also convene meetings when opponents are absent, or they may adjourn meetings when things are going badly. Personal skill, influence, and expertise are a chair's best allies.

Historically, committee chairs have generally been the majority party member with the longest continuous service on the committee. Reforms made by Republicans in 1995 dramatically limited the long-term power of committee chairs. New rules prevent chairs from serving more than six years—three consecutive Congresses—or heading their own subcommittees. In return, committee chairs were, however, given some important powers. They are authorized to select all subcommittee chairs, call meetings, strategize, and recommend majority members to sit on conference committees. Committee chairs in the House no longer are selected by seniority, as is the case in the Senate. Thus, in the 107th Congress thirteen House committee chairs were new.[32]

THE LAWMAKING FUNCTION OF CONGRESS

The organization of Congress allows it to fulfill its constitutional responsibilities, chief among which is its lawmaking function. It is through this power that Congress affects the day-to-day lives of all Americans as well as sets policy for the future. Proposals for legislation—be they about education, violence against women, trade with China, gun control or foreign aid—can come from the president, executive agencies, committee staffs, interest groups, or even private individuals. Only members of the House or Senate, however, can formally submit a bill for congressional consideration. Once a bill is proposed, it usually reaches a dead end. Of the approximately 9,000 or so bills introduced during any session of Congress, fewer than 5 percent to 10 percent are made into law.

HIGHLIGHT

WHAT'S IN A NAME?

Naming a bill has become a not-so-subtle art of late. In times past, Franklin D. Roosevelt could propose a Social Security Act without calling it the "Dignity in Old Age Act" or the "Keep Grandma Out of the Poorhouse Act."* Since Republicans took over control of Congress in 1995, bills have been named much more creatively and usually have value-laden names. A tax-cutting bill, for example, was named the "American Dream Restoration Act," and the Omnibus Budget Reconciliation bill's name was changed to the "Balanced Budget" bill to garner more favorable attention.

Representative Barney Frank (D–Mass.) wondered aloud on the House floor if the immigration bill entitled the "Immigration in the National Interest Act" should be renamed the "Statue of Liberty Was Wrong Act." One Republican representative, in an attempt to promote a bill requiring football, baseball, basketball, and hockey to use instant replays, named his proposal the "What Really Happened Bill" after he rejected his first choice, "It Wasn't a Touchdown, Stupid, Bill."

The names of bills such as the "Partial Birth Abortion Bill" can be particularly value laden and put opponents on the defensive. Can you think of other examples?

*This highlight draws heavily from Adam Clymer, "When 'Ketchup' Is 'Tomato Achievement,'" *New York Times* (March 24, 1996): 4, 2.

It is probably useful to think of Congress as a system of multiple vetoes, which was what the Framers desired. They wanted to disperse power; and as Congress has evolved, it has come closer and closer to the Framers' intentions. As a bill goes through Congress, a dispersion of power occurs as roadblocks to passage must be surmounted at numerous steps in the process. In addition to realistic roadblocks, caution signs and other opportunities for delay abound. A member who sponsors a bill must get through *every* obstacle; in contrast, successful opposition means "winning" at only one of many stages, including: (1) the subcommittee, (2) the House full committee, (3) the House Rules Committee, (4) the House, (5) the Senate subcommittee, (6) the full Senate committee, (7) the Senate, (8) floor leaders in both Houses, (9) the House-Senate conference committee, and (10) the president.

The story of how a bill becomes a law in the United States can be told in two different ways. The first is the "textbook" method, which provides a greatly simplified road map of the process to make it easier to understand. We'll review this method first. But real life, of course, rarely goes according to plan, as underscored in Analyzing the Data: Gun Control Legislation Following Publicized Shootings Since 1968. So we will next look at an actual example of how a particular bill became a law, and explore the true complexities of the process.

How a Bill Becomes a Law: The Textbook Version

A bill must survive three stages before it becomes a law. It must be approved by one or more standing committees and both chambers, and, if House and Senate versions differ, a conference report resolving those differences must be accepted by each house. A bill may be killed during any of these stages, so it is much easier to defeat a bill than it is to get one passed. The House and Senate have parallel processes, and often the same bill is introduced in each chamber at the same time.

A N A L Y Z I N G   T H E   D A T A

GUN CONTROL LEGISLATION FOLLOWING PUBLICIZED SHOOTINGS SINCE 1968

Machine-gun violence during Prohibition and the attempted assassination of President Franklin D. Roosevelt in 1933 were followed by the National Firearms Act of 1934, which required registration of automatic weapons. Other gun control legislation has followed highly publicized shootings. As the gun control legislation saga described in our opening vignette underscores, the path a particular piece of legislation takes is often as varied as the content of the legislation itself. In the wake of so many school shooting tragedies, many Americans regard some form of gun control legislation as a must. Legislators, with their election campaigns always in sight, are mindful of this fact. With 64 percent of the American public responding that they would consider a candidate's position on gun control important when voting in the next election, it is reasonable to expect Congress to act. Congress frequently reacts to external stimuli that produces citizen demands for action. Still, gun control legislation was defeated in spite of public opinion, perhaps underscoring the potency of the gun lobby.

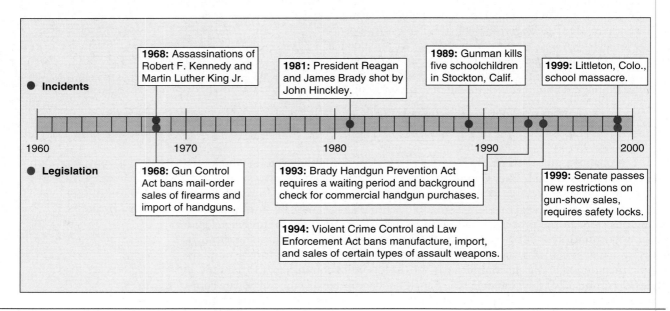

Source: USA Today (May 26, 1999): 2A. Reprinted with permission. Updated by authors.

A bill must be introduced by a member of Congress, but it is often sponsored by a whole list of other members in an early effort to show support for it. Once introduced, the bill is sent to the clerk of the chamber, who gives it a number (for example, HR 1 or S 1—indicating House or Senate bill number one for the session). The bill is then printed, distributed, and sent to the appropriate committee or committees for consideration.

The first action takes place within the committee, after it is referred there by the Speaker. The committee usually refers the bill to one of its subcommittees, which researches the bill and decides whether to hold hearings on it. The subcommittee hearings provide the opportunity for those on both sides of the issue to voice their opinions. Most of these hearings are now open to the public because of 1970s sunshine laws, which require open sessions. After the hearings, the bill is revised, and the subcommittee votes to approve or defeat the bill. If the subcommittee votes in favor of the bill, it is returned to the full committee, which then either rejects the bill or sends it to the House or Senate floor with a favorable recommendation (see Figure 7.5).

FIGURE 7.5   How a Bill Becomes a Law

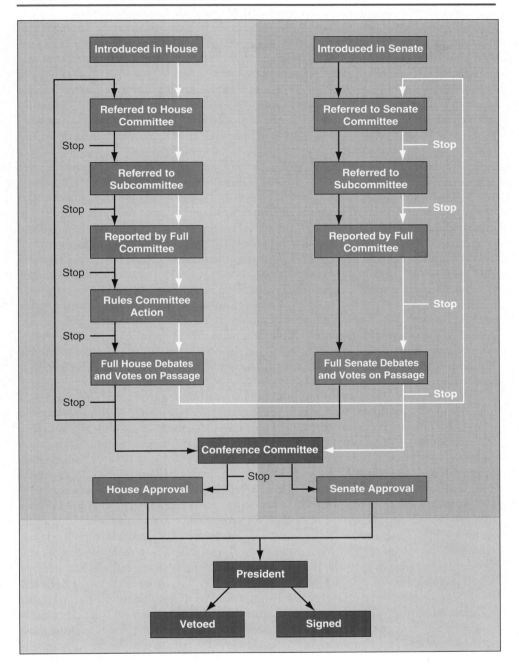

The second stage of action takes place on the House or Senate floor. In the House, before a bill may be debated on the floor, it must be approved by the Rules Committee and given a rule and a place on the calendar, or schedule. (House budget bills don't go to the Rules Committee.) In the House, the rule given to a bill determines the limits on the floor debate and specifies what types of amendments, if any, may be attached to the bill. Once the Rules Committee considers the bill, it is put on the calendar.

When the day arrives for floor debate, the House may choose to form a Committee of the Whole. This allows the House to deliberate with only 100 members present to expedite consideration of the bill. On the House floor, the bill is debated, amendments are offered, and a vote ultimately is taken by the full House. If the bill survives, it is sent to the Senate for consideration if it was not considered there simultaneously.

Unlike the House, where debate is necessarily limited given the size of the body, bills may be held up by a hold or a filibuster in the Senate. A **hold** is a tactic by which a senator asks to be informed before a particular bill is brought to the floor. This request signals the Senate leadership and the sponsors of the bill that a colleague may have objections to the bill and should be consulted before further action is taken. Because any single member can filibuster a bill or other action to death, the Senate leadership is very reluctant to bring actions with a hold on them to the floor. Explained one Senate staffer, "Four or five years ago it started to mean that if you put a hold on something, it would never come up. It became, in fact, a veto."[33]

In the first sessions of the 103rd and 104th Congresses, for example, holds were placed on more than two-thirds of the 250 bills reported out of committee in the Senate. In the 105th Congress, holds were also used to prevent votes on many judicial nominees, prompting criticism from Chief Justice Rehnquist. Since holds were not made public, it was difficult to know how many were actually placed and who exercised the privilege. The secrecy attached to holds made them particularly powerful as a personal means to stall action. In March 1999, however, the Senate changed its rules. Senators who want to place a hold on legislation now must notify a bill or nomination's sponsor and the committee with jurisdiction over the issue in writing. "What this means," said Senator Ron Wyden (D–Oreg.), long a critic of holds, "is that the fog is starting to lift over the Senate."[34] Still, holds are powerful tools. In late 2000, for example, Senate Foreign Relations Committee member Rod Grams (R–Minn.) put holds on the nominations of seven ambassadorial appointees to get the State Department to agree to change its handling of security violations. Once the State Department agreed, the hold was removed and the nominees approved.[35]

Filibusters, which allow for unlimited debate on a bill, grew out of the absence of rules to limit speech in the Senate and are often used to "talk a bill to death." In contrast to a hold, a filibuster is a more formal and public way of halting action on a bill by means of long speeches or unlimited debate in the Senate. The filibuster became an increasingly common feature of Senate life during the slavery debates. In 1917, eleven senators waged a filibuster against an important foreign policy matter supported by President Woodrow Wilson. The Senate then adopted a rule to avoid the potential disaster of tying the president's hands during World War I. Senate Rule 22 allows for unlimited debate on a motion before it is brought to a vote.[36] There are no rules on the content of a filibuster as long as the senator keeps on talking. A senator may read from a phone book, recite poetry, or read cookbooks in order to delay a vote. Often, a team of senators will take turns speaking to keep the filibuster going in the hope that a bill will be tabled or killed. In 1964, for example, a group of Northern liberal senators continued a filibuster for eighty-two days in an effort to prevent amendments that would weaken a civil rights bill. Still, filibusters often are more of a threat than an actual event on the Senate floor.

To end a filibuster, **cloture** must be invoked. To cut off debate, sixteen senators must first sign a motion for cloture, then sixty senators must vote to end debate. If cloture is invoked, no more than thirty additional hours can be devoted to debate before the legislation at issue is brought to a vote.

The third stage of action takes place when the two chambers of Congress approve different versions of the same bill. When this happens, a conference committee is established to iron out the differences between the two versions of a bill. The president is not given a multiple choice and allowed to select which version he prefers. The conference committee, whose members are from the original House and Senate committees, hammers out a compromise, which is returned to each chamber for a final vote. Sometimes, as was the case with gun control legislation discussed in our opening vignette, the conference committee fails to agree and the bill dies there. No changes or amendments to the compromise version are allowed. If the bill is passed it is sent to the president, who either signs it or vetoes it. If the bill is not passed in both houses, it dies.

hold
A tactic by which a senator asks to be informed before a particular bill is brought to the floor. This stops the bill from coming to the floor until the hold is removed.

filibuster
A formal way of halting action on a bill by means of long speeches or unlimited debate in the Senate.

cloture
Motion requiring sixty senators to cut off debate.

The president has ten days to consider a bill. He has four options: (1) He can sign the bill, at which point it becomes law. (2) He can veto the bill, which is more likely to occur when the president is of a different party from the majority in Congress. In the 103rd Congress, when Democrats controlled both houses of Congress, President Clinton became the first president in 140 years not to veto a single bill during a two-year Congress. Congress may override the president's veto with a two-thirds vote in each chamber, a very difficult task. (3) He can wait the full ten days, at the end of which time the bill becomes law without his signature if Congress is still in session. (4) If the Congress adjourns before the ten days are up, the president can choose not to sign the bill, and it is considered "pocket vetoed." A **pocket veto** figuratively allows bills stashed in the president's pocket to die. The only way for a bill then to become law is for it to be reintroduced in the next session and go through the process all over again. Because Congress sets its own date of adjournment, technically the session could be continued the few extra days necessary to prevent a pocket veto. Extensions are unlikely, however, as sessions are scheduled to adjourn close to the November elections or the December holidays. For a short while, the last action that the president could take was to exercise a **line-item veto.**

Presidents since Ulysses S. Grant urged Congress to give them a line-item veto as a way to curb wasteful spending, particularly in pork barrel projects added to bills to assure member support. As adopted by Congress on Ronald Reagan's eighty-fourth birthday, the line-item veto allowed the president to strike or reduce any discretionary budget authority or eliminate any targeted tax provision (the line item) in any bill sent to him by the Congress. The president was then required to prepare a separate rescissions package for each piece of legislation he wished to veto and then submit his proposal to Congress within twenty working days. The president's proposed recissions were to take effect unless both houses of Congress passed a disapproval bill by a two-thirds vote within twenty days of receiving the proposed deletions from the budget.[37]

President Clinton used the line-item veto to reject a range of pork barrel provisions in legislation that was sent to him for his approval. In 1998, however, the U.S. Supreme Court struck down the line-item veto as unconstitutional. In a 6–3 decision, a majority of the Court concluded that the provision violates a constitutional provision that mandates that legislation be passed by both houses of Congress and then be sent to the president—in its entirety—for his signature or veto.[38] Allowing the president to pick and choose among budget authorizations submitted to him by Congress gives the president the power "to enact, to amend or to repeal statutes," said the Court, a constitutional power the Framers never intended the president to have. Clinton, who had used the power eighty-two times, bemoaned the Court's decision.[39]

How a Bill *Really* Becomes a Law: The China Trade Act of 2000

For each bill introduced in Congress, enactment is a long shot. A bill's supporters struggle to get from filing in both houses of Congress to the president's signature, and each bill follows a unique course. The gun control legislation described in our opening vignette never was able to get a full hearing in one house, for example. The trade legislation described below followed a similar, yet unique course that is probably even quirkier than most bills that actually become law.

Under the Trade Act of 1974, part of a two-decades-old American Cold War policy, the president of the United States was empowered to grant any nation most favored trade status, a designation that brings favorable U.S. tariff treatment. By law, however, the president was limited to extending that status to communist countries on a year by year (instead of permanent) basis subject to congressional review. Thus, since passage of that act, China, as a communist nation, could receive this status only a year at a time although it provided a huge potential market for U.S. goods. President Clinton and many members of the business community wanted this year by year reauthorization dropped once China was scheduled to join the World Trade Organization. To do that required a new

pocket veto
If Congress adjourns during the ten days the president has to consider a bill passed by both houses of Congress, without the president's signature, the bill is considered vetoed.

line-item veto
The power to veto specific provisions of a spending bill without vetoing the bill in its entirety.

act of Congress. Ironically, the Clinton administration's push for this bill also allied President Clinton with many Republicans who favored opening trade to a nation with billions of new consumers. Many of the Republicans biggest financial and political supporters could benefit from opening Chinese markets and removing barriers to service providers such as banks and telecommunications companies. In contrast, unions, a traditionally Democratic constituency, feared further loss of jobs to foreign shores.

Legislation to extend what is called permanent normal trade relations (PNTR) was viewed by Clinton as a means of putting "his imprint on foreign policy [as] the president who cemented in place the post-cold-war experiment of using economic engagement to foster political change among America's neighbors and its potential adversaries."[40] He had begun this effort in 1993 after he pushed through Congress passage of the North American Free Trade Agreement (NAFTA) with Mexico and Canada. Now, as his time in office was coming to an end, he wanted Congress to act to allow him to cement PNTR with China.

As soon as the United States completed a bilateral agreement to make China a member of the World Trade Organization in November 1999 and early 2000, Clinton met with more than one hundred lawmakers individually or in groups, called scores more on the phone, and traveled to the Midwest and California to build support for the proposed legislation, which was necessary to implement this agreement. While Clinton was setting the stage for congressional action, the U.S. Chamber of Commerce and the Business Roundtable launched a $10 million ad campaign—the largest ever for a single legislative issue.[41]

WEB EXPLORATION
To learn about the details of Clinton's transmittal letter to Congress on permanent normal trade relations with China, go to www.ablongman.com/oconnor

On March 8, 2000, Clinton transmitted the text of legislation he was requesting to Congress. This proposed legislation, called S.2277, formally was introduced in the Senate on March 23 by Senator William V. Roth Jr. (R–Del.). It was then read twice and referred to the Finance Committee. In the House, hearings on the China trade policy were held throughout the spring, even before the Clinton legislation was formally introduced. Anticipating concern from colleagues about China's human rights abuses, labor market issues, and the rule of law, some members proposed that Congress create (under separate legislation) a U.S. Congressional-Executive Commission on China to monitor those issues. HR 4444, the bill that Clinton sought, was introduced formally in Congress on May 15, 2000, by Republican Bill Archer (R–Tex.). It was referred to the House Ways and Means Committee shortly thereafter and a mark-up session was held on May 17. It was reported out of committee on the same day by a vote of 34–4. On May 23, 2000, HR 4444 received a rule from the Rules Committee allowing for three hours of debate. The bill was closed to amendments except motions to recommit and the House Republican leadership "closed ranks behind the bill," claiming that economic change would foster political change.[42] But, they still had to sell this idea to their colleagues, many of whom balked at extending trade advantages to a communist government with a history of rights violations including religious persecution and the denial of political rights to many. The rights legislation was designed to assuage those fears.

While the House Committee on International Affairs was holding hearings (and even before), the Clinton administration sprang into action. Led by Secretary of Commerce William Daley, he and several other Cabinet members were sent out to say the same thing over and over again: The bill will mean jobs for Americans and stability in Asia. Republican leaders got Chinese dissidents to say that the bill would improve human rights in China,

Lobbyists fill the Senate reception area during the vote on permanently normalizing trade with China. (Photo courtesy: Ray Lustig, ©2000, The Washington Post. Reprinted with Permission.)

and televangelist Billy Graham was recruited by the leadership to endorse the measure. At the same time, interest groups on both sides of the debate rushed to convince legislators to support their respective positions. Organized labor, still stinging from its NAFTA loss, was the biggest opponent of the bill. Teamsters and members of the United Auto Workers roamed the halls of Congress, trying to lobby members of the House.[43] Vice President Al Gore, knowing that he would need union support in the upcoming presidential election, broke ranks with the president and said that the bill would only serve to move American jobs to China.

On the other side, lobbyists from large corporations, including Proctor & Gamble, TRW, and the Business Roundtable, used their cell phones and personal contacts to cajole legislators. "It's like a big wave hitting the shore," said one uncommitted Republican legislator from Staten Island, New York.[44] For the first time, he was lobbied by rank-and-file office workers at the request of their corporate offices, as well as union members. Another member of Congress was contacted by former President George Bush and Defense Secretary William Cohen, and he received a special defense briefing from the Central Intelligence Agency. The president of the AFL-CIO also personally visited him. All stops were out and this was the kind of treatment most undecided members received.

House debate on the bill began on May 24, 2000. That morning, House Majority Whip Tom DeLay (R–Tex.) didn't know if he had enough votes to support the measure to ensure its passage. The bare minimum he needed was 150 Republicans if he was to push the bill over the top.[45] DeLay lined up lots of assistance. Somewhat ironically, Governor George W. Bush and retired General Colin Powell were enlisted to help convince wavering Republicans to support the Democratic president's goals. Powell, in particular, was called on to assuage national security concerns of several conservative representatives. Scores of pro-trade lobbyists spread out over Capitol Hill like locusts looking to light on any wavering legislators. A last-minute amendment to create a twenty-three-member commission to monitor human rights and a second to monitor surges in Chinese imports helped garner the votes of at least twenty more legislators.

Debate then came on a motion from David Bonior (D–Mich.), the House minority whip, to recommit the bill to the Ways and Means and International Relations committees to give them the opportunity to add an amendment to the bill to provide conditions under which withdrawals of normal trade relations with China could occur should China attack or invade Taiwan. This motion failed on a vote of 176–258. As lobbyists stepped up their efforts, their actions and those of the Republican leadership and the Clinton administration bore fruit. Every single uncommitted Republican voted for the bill, joining seventy-three Democrats to grant China permanent normal trade status as the bill passed by a surprisingly large margin of 237–197. "Frankly, they surprised me a bit. Members in the last few hours really turned around and understood how important this was," said DeLay, who earned the nickname "The Hammer" for his efforts to have members vote his way. Stunned labor leaders admitted that they were outgunned. "The business community unleashed an unprecedented campaign that was hard for anyone to match," said the president of the United Auto Workers.[46]

As the bill was transmitted to the Senate, critics sprang into action. Senator Jesse Helms, chair of the Foreign Relations Committee and a major critic of the Beijing government, immediately put fellow Republicans on notice that he would not rubber stamp the actions of the House. Although amendments were not allowed in the House, Senate rules that permit amendment were seen as a way of changing the nature of the bill and causing the amended version to go back to the House for a vote. Secretary Daley immediately went to see the Senate majority leader and asked members of the Senate Finance Committee, which had jurisdiction over the bill, to ask their assistance in fending off amendments.

While hearings on China were being held in the House, the Senate Finance Committee had been considering the bill. Once it passed the House, however, it was reported out of the Senate Finance Committee immediately on May 25. On that day, Senators Fred Thompson (R–Tenn.) and Robert Torricelli (D–N.J.) held a press conference to announce that they would offer parallel legislation based on their concerns about Chinese proliferation of weapons of mass destruction to continue a yearly review of China as a condition of open trade with that nation. They viewed the opening of PNTR to China as a national security as well as a trade issue.

The Senate began debating S.2277 on July 26, 2000. The next day, after a filibuster was begun by several opponents of the bill including Senators Robert Byrd (D–W.Va.), Jesse Helms (R–N.C.), Barbara Mikulski (D–Md.), and Ben Nighthorse Campbell (R–Colo.), a move to invoke cloture was brought by the majority leader and several others. Cloture was then invoked by a vote of 86–12, well over the sixty votes required. The Senate recessed shortly thereafter. Debate on S.2277 began anew on September 5, after the Labor Day recess. At that time, until the final vote on September 19, 2000, scores of amendments were offered by senators; all failed by various margins. On September 19, 2000, the bill passed without amendment on a 83–15 vote with most senators voting as they had done on the cloture motion. Throughout that period, however, lobbyists kept up their pressure on the committed to make sure that no amendments were added to the bill that would require House reconsideration.

The bill was signed by President Clinton on October 10, 2000, amid considerable fanfare. Throughout the course of this bill becoming law, Clinton used his office in a way reminiscent of Lyndon B. Johnson's cajoling of recalcitrant legislators. One member got a new zip code for a small town and another got a natural gas pipeline for his district.[47] In the end, these kinds of efforts were crucial to House passage of the bill.

HOW MEMBERS MAKE DECISIONS

Longman
Participate.com 2.0
Simulation
You Are a Member of Congress

As a bill makes its way through the labyrinth of the lawmaking process described above, members are confronted with the question: How should I vote? Members often listen to their own personal beliefs on many matters, but those views can often be moderated by other considerations. To avoid making any voting mistakes, members look to a variety of sources for cues.

Constituents

Constituents—the people who live and vote in the home district or state—are always in the member's mind when casting a vote.[48] It is rare for a legislator to vote against the wishes of his or her constituency regularly, particularly on issues of welfare rights, domestic policy, or other highly salient issues such as civil rights, abortion, or war. Most constituents often have strong convictions on one or more of these issues. For example, during the 1960s, representatives from Southern states could not hope to keep their seats for long if they voted in favor of proposed civil rights legislation. But gauging how voters feel about any particular issue often is not easy. Because it is virtually impossible to know how the folks back home feel on all issues, a representative's *perception* of their preferences is important. Even when voters have opinions, legislators may get little guidance if their district is narrowly divided. Abortion is an issue about which many voters feel passionately; but a legislator whose district has roughly equal numbers of pro-choice and pro-life advocates can satisfy only a portion of his or her constituents.

If an issue affects their constituency, a representative often will try to determine how the people back home feel. Staff members often keep running tallies of the letters and phone calls for and against a policy that will be voted on soon. Only if a legislator has strong personal preferences will he or she vote against a clearly expressed desire of their constituents. Studies by political scientists show that members vote in conformity with prevailing opinion in their districts about two-thirds of the time.[49] On average, Congress passes laws that reflect national public opinion at about the same rate.[50] Legislators tend to act on their own preferences as trustees when dealing with topics that have come through the committees on which they serve or issues that they know about as a result of experience in other contexts, such as their vocation. On items of little concern to people back in the district or for which the legislator has little firsthand knowledge, the tendency is to turn to other sources for voting cues. The opinions of one's colleagues, especially those who belong to his or her party, often weigh heavily when casting a roll-call vote.

Colleagues

The range and complexity of issues confronting Congress means that no one can be up to speed on more than a few topics. When members must vote on bills about which they know very little, they often turn for advice to colleagues who have served on the committee that handled the legislation. On issues that are of little interest to a legislator, *logrolling,* or vote trading, often occurs. Logrolling often takes place on specialized bills targeting money or projects to selected congressional districts. A yea vote by an unaffected member often is given to a member in exchange for the promise of a future yea vote on a similar piece of specialized legislation.

Other appeals are of a more personal nature. During the China trade bill effort, for example, representatives often lobbied each other.

Party

Political parties are another important source of influence. Members often look to party leaders for indicators of how to vote. Indeed, it is the whips' job in each chamber to reinforce the need for party cohesion, particularly on issues of concern to party. From 1970 to the mid-1990s, the incidence of party votes in which majorities of the two parties took opposing sides roughly doubled to more than 60 percent of all roll-call votes. When the Republicans took control of Congress in 1995 with the Contract with America as its agenda, the parties divided over three-quarters of the time in both the House and the Senate, making 1995 the most partisan year in generations. Partisan voting decreased in 1999 to 47.1 percent,[51] its lowest in a decade. These numbers suprised many, given media attention to political acrimony on the Hill. Still, party makes a big difference, especially in times of **divided government**, the term used to describe the political condition in which different political parties control the White House and Congress (see Figure 7.6). Although the public opinion polls have found that Americans tend to like divided government, it does make it harder for either party to govern and often results in congressional leaders pulling out all the stops to keep their partisans together.[52]

divided government
The term used to describe the political condition in which different political parties control the White House and Congress.

FIGURE 7.6   Divided Government

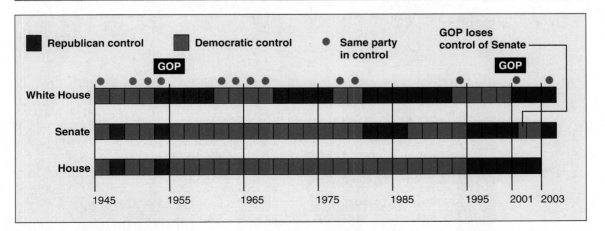

Today, many members of Congress elected on a partisan ticket feel a degree of obligation to their party and to the president if he is of the same party. The national political parties have little say in who gets a party's nomination for the U.S. Senate or the House. But once a candidate has emerged successfully from a primary contest (see chapter 13), both houses have committees that provide campaign assistance. It is to each party's advantage to win as many seats as possible in each house. If a member is elected with the financial support or campaign visits from popular members and party leaders, he or she is much more inclined to toe the party line.

Caucuses

Special-interest caucuses were created to facilitate member communication—often across party lines—over issues of common concern. Caucuses also complement and counterbalance the informational roles played by the committee system.[53] By 1994, there were at least 140 special-interest caucuses, including many formed to promote certain industries, such as textiles, tourism, wine, coal, steel, mushrooms, and cranberries, or to advance particular views or interests.

Before 1995, twenty-seven caucuses enjoyed special status as legislative service organizations (LSOs) and Congress provided staff, office space, and budgets for them. Included among these were the liberal Black Caucus, the Congressional Caucus for Women's Issues, and the Democratic Study Group. In 1995, the Republican majority voted to abolish LSOs.[54] Without institutional support, most of the caucuses have died while others have lost influence and members. Said Representative Charles Rangel (D–N.Y.) of the bipartisan Narcotics Abuse and Control Caucus, "We just couldn't keep it together."[55] The Congressional Caucus for Women's Issues disbanded and reorganized to form an informal caucus with the same name but without a paid staff or budget. Informal caucuses continue to be formed. One of the newer ones is the Internet Caucus, a bipartisan group devoted to helping educate members about the Internet. To join, members must agree to set up their own sites on the World Wide Web within ninety days.

State and regional caucuses are another important source of information exchange among members and across party lines. Large state delegations, such as those of California, New York, and Texas, often work together, regardless of party lines, to bring the

Organized labor has an impact on congressional elections, with most unions contributing to Democratic candidates. (Photo courtesy: Charlyn Zlotnik/Woodfin Camp & Associates)

bacon home to their states. Some state caucuses hold weekly meetings to assure that their interests are adequately represented on important committees and to keep abreast of pending legislation that might affect their states.

Interest Groups

The primary function of most interest group lobbyists is to provide information to supportive or potentially supportive legislators, committees, and their staffs.[56] It's likely, for example, that a representative knows the National Rifle Association (NRA) position on gun control legislation. What the legislator needs to get from the NRA is information and substantial research on the feasibility and impact of such legislation. How could the states implement such legislation? Is it constitutional? Will it really have an impact on violent crime or crime in schools? Interest groups can win over undecided legislators or confirm the support of their friends by providing information that legislators use to justify the position they have embraced. They also can supply direct campaign contributions, volunteers, and publicity to members seeking reelection.

Pressure groups also use grassroots appeals to pressure legislators by urging their members in a particular state or district to call, write, fax, or e-mail their senators or representatives. Lobbyists can't vote, but voters back home can and do.

Political Action Committees

While a link to a legislator's constituency may be the most effective way to influence behavior, that is not the only path of interest group influence on member decision making.[57] The high cost of campaigning has made members of Congress—especially those without huge personal fortunes—attentive to those who help pay the tab for tens of thousands of dollars worth of television commercials that have become staples in contested elections. The 4,000 or so political action committees (PACs) organized by interest groups are a major source of most members' campaign funding. When an issue comes up on which the legislator has no strong opinion and which is of little consequence to constituents, there is, not surprisingly, a tendency to support the stand taken by those nice folks who helped pay for the last campaign. After all, who wants to bite the hand that feeds him or her? (Interest groups and PACs are discussed in detail in chapter 16.)

Longman
Participate.com
2.0
Participation
The Debate
Over
Campaign
Finance
Reform

Staff and Support Agencies

Members of Congress rely heavily on members of their staffs for information on pending legislation.[58] Staff members prepare summaries of bills and brief the representative or senator based on their research. If the bill is nonideological or one on which the member has no real position, staff members can be very influential. Staff members also do research on and even draft bills that a member wishes to introduce.

Staff aides are especially crucial in the Senate. Because senators have so many committee assignments and are often spread so thin, they frequently rely heavily on aides. Every legislator has personal staff and other staff who work for each committee and subcommittee. The support personnel at the Congressional Budget Office and the Congressional Research Service at the Library of Congress are also considered to be staff working for Congress (see Table 7.6). Even with the reduction in House committee staffers enacted by Republicans in 1995, the ranks of Congressional staff total more than 15,000, albeit a number down from the 1980s.

The next time you see a televised Senate hearing, notice how each senator has at least one aide sitting behind him or her, ready with information and often even with questions for the senator to ask. Some believe that staff members have become too important, too powerful, and that their bosses are too dependent on them. As majority leader, Bob Dole, for example, came under intense criticism by many conservative

TABLE 7.6 Congressional Support Agencies

Congressional Research Service (CRS)	General Accounting Office (GAO)	Congressional Budget Office (CBO)
Created in 1914 as the Legislative Research Service (LRS), the CRS is administered by the Library of Congress and responds to more than a quarter of a million congressional requests for information each year. The service provides nonpartisan studies of public issues, compiling facts on both sides of issues, and it conducts major research projects for committees at the request of members. The CRS also prepares summaries of all bills introduced and tracks the progress of major bills.	The GAO was established in 1921 as an independent regulatory agency for the purpose of auditing the financial expenditures of the executive branch and federal agencies. Today, the GAO performs four additional functions: It sets government standards for accounting, it provides a variety of legal opinions, it settles claims against the government, and it conducts studies upon congressional request.	The CBO was created in 1974 to evaluate the economic effect of different spending programs and to provide information on the cost of proposed policies. It is responsible for analyzing the president's budget and economic projections. The CBO provides Congress and individual members with a valuable second opinion to use in budget debates.

members of Congress for the alleged influence of his chief aide, Sheila Burke, a moderate Republican, who ultimately was the subject of a Sunday *New York Times Magazine* cover story about the woman behind the man. Members also rely on the support agencies described in Table 7.6.

CONGRESS AND THE PRESIDENT

The Constitution envisioned that the Congress and the president would have discrete powers and that one branch would be able to hold the other in check. Over the years, and especially since the 1930s, the president has often held the upper hand. In times of crisis or simply when it was unable to meet public demands for solutions, Congress has willingly handed over its authority to the chief executive. Even though the chief executive has been granted greater latitude, legislators do, of course, retain ultimate legislative authority to question executive actions, and to halt administration activities by cutting off funds. Congress also wields the ultimate oversight power—the power to impeach and even remove the president from office.

The Shifting Balance of Power

The balance of power between Congress and the executive branch has seesawed over time. The post–Civil War Congress attempted to regain control of the vast executive powers that President Abraham Lincoln, recently slain, had taken from it. Angered at the refusal of Lincoln's successor, Andrew Johnson, to go along with its radical "reforms" of the South, Congress passed the Tenure of Office Act, which prevented the president, under the threat of civil penalty, from removing any Cabinet-level appointments of the previous administration. Johnson accepted the challenge and fired Lincoln's secretary of war, who many believed was guilty of heinous war crimes. The House voted to impeach Johnson, but only the desertion of a handful of Republican senators prevented him from being removed from office. (The effort fell short by one vote.) Nonetheless, the president's power had been greatly weakened, and the Congress again became the center of power and authority in the federal government.

Beginning in the early 1900s, however, a series of strong presidents acted at the expense of congressional power. Theodore Roosevelt, Franklin D. Roosevelt, and Lyndon B. Johnson, especially, all viewed the presidency as carrying with it enormous powers.

Over the years, especially since the presidency of Franklin D. Roosevelt, Congress has ceded to the president a major role in the legislative process. Today, for example,

Congress often finds itself responding to executive branch proposals. Critics of Congress point to its slow, unwieldy process and the complexity of national problems as reasons that Congress often doesn't seem to act on its own.

Individual members, especially if the president is popular with voters, often support White House initiatives. Legislators who are "on the fence" often find themselves targeted by the White House or inundated with invitations to state dinners or personal presidential appeals.

Congressional Oversight of the Executive Branch

According to political scientist Joel Aberbach, since 1961 there has been a substantial increase in the **oversight** activity by Congress.[59] Oversight subcommittees became particularly prominent in the 1970s and 1980s as a means of promoting investigation and program review,[60] to determine if an agency, department, or office is carrying out its responsibilities the way Congress intends. It also includes checking on possible abuses of power by governmental officials, including the president. In the 104th Congress, however, the House committee system was revamped by the new Republican leadership, which resulted in the elimination of more than half of the oversight subcommittees that existed in the 103rd.[61]

Key to Congress's performance of its oversight function is its ability to question members of the administration and the bureaucracy to see if they are enforcing and interpreting the laws passed by Congress as the members intended. These committee hearings, now routinely televised, are among Congress's most visible and dramatic actions. Millions, for example, tuned in to watch the House's investigations of Presidents Nixon and Clinton, the Senate's investigation of the Iran-Contra affair, and the Senate's trial of President Clinton. In contrast, despite the fact that 46 percent of those polled said they believed President Clinton and Vice President Gore broke campaign financing laws during the 1996 election, the Senate probe of campaign financing abuses drew little public interest.

By the late 1990s, a series of costly congressional investigations have led some to question the high cost of Senate oversight. Executive branch investigations by the Republican Congress cost over $200 million through 2000. In contrast, Congress allotted far less for the arts and job training programs.[62]

Hearings are not simply used to gather information. Hearings that focus on particular executive branch actions often signal that Congress believes changes in policy need to be made before an agency next comes before the committee to justify its budget. Recent research reveals that the more the legislative body sees the oversight committee as not representative of the House or Senate as a whole, the more likely it will allow the executive branch leeway in adopting regulations to implement congressional policy.[63]

Hearings are also used to improve the administration of programs. Since most members of House and Senate committees and subcommittees are interested in the issues under their jurisdiction, they often *want* to help bureaucrats and not hinder them.

Legislators augment their formal oversight of the executive branch by allowing citizens to appeal adverse bureaucratic decisions to agencies, Congress, and even the courts. **Congressional review,** a procedure adopted by the 104th Congress in 1996, by which agency regulations can be nullified by joint resolutions of legislative disapproval, is another method of exercising congressional oversight.[64] The act provides Congress with sixty days to disapprove newly announced agency regulations, often passed to implement some congressional action. A regulation is disapproved if the resolution is passed by both chambers and signed by the president, or when Congress overrides a presidential veto of a disapproving resolution. This act was not used until 2001 when Congress reversed Clinton administration ergonomics regulations.

Congressional review differs from another form of legislative oversight called the legislative veto. The **legislative veto,** a procedure by which one or both houses of Congress can disallow an act of an executive agency by a simple majority vote, was first

oversight
Congressional review of the activities of an agency, department, or office.

congressional review
The process by which Congress can nullify an executive branch regulation by a resolution jointly passed in both houses within sixty days of announcement of the regulation and accepted by the president.

legislative veto
A procedure by which one or both houses of Congress can disallow an act of the president or executive agency by a simple majority vote; ruled unconstitutional by the Supreme Court.

The War Powers Act, passed during the height of the Vietnam War, requires a president to obtain congressional approval before committing troops to a combat zone. (Photo courtesy: J.P. Fizet/Corbis Sygma)

War Powers Act

Passed by Congress in 1973, the president was limited in his deployment of troops overseas to a sixty-day period in peacetime (which could be extended for an extra thirty days to permit withdrawal) unless Congress explicitly gave its approval for a longer period.

added to statutes in 1932, but the vetoes were not used frequently until the 1970s. They were usually included in laws that delegated congressional powers to the executive branch while retaining the power of Congress to restrict their use. By 1981, more than 200 statutes contained legislative veto provisions. In *Immigration and Naturalization Service v. Chadha* (1983), however, the U.S. Supreme Court ruled that the legislative veto as it was used in many circumstances was unconstitutional because it violated separation of powers principles.[65] The Court concluded that although the Constitution gave Congress the power to make laws, the Framers were clear in their intent that Congress should separate itself from executing or enforcing the laws. It is the president's responsibility to sign or veto legislation, not the Congress's. In spite of *Chadha,* however, the legislative veto continues to play an important role in executive-legislative relations. In signing the Omnibus Consolidation Recision and Appropriation Act in April 1996, for example, President Clinton noted that Congress had included a legislative veto that the Supreme Court would in all likelihood find unconstitutional under *Chadha.* Nevertheless, he signed the bill. The continued use by Congress, and the acceptance by the president, of the legislative veto underscores the limits of judicial intervention without the cooperation of the other branches of government.

Foreign Affairs Oversight.   The Constitution divides foreign policy powers between the executive and the legislative branches. The president has the power to wage war and negotiate treaties, whereas the Congress has the power to declare war and the Senate has the power to ratify treaties. Throughout the twentieth century, the executive branch has become preeminent in foreign affairs despite the constitutional division of powers. This is partly due to the series of crises and the development of nuclear weapons in this century; both have necessitated quick decision making and secrecy, which are much easier to manage in the executive branch. Congress, with its 535 members, has a more difficult time reaching a consensus and keeping secrets.

After years of playing second fiddle to a series of presidents from Theodore Roosevelt to Richard M. Nixon, a "snoozing Congress" was "aroused"[66] and seized for itself the authority and expertise necessary to go head-to-head with the chief executive. In a delayed response to Lyndon B. Johnson's 1964–1969 conduct of the Vietnam War, Congress passed in 1973 the **War Powers Act** over President Nixon's veto. This act requires any president to obtain congressional approval before committing U.S. forces to a combat zone and to notify Congress within forty-eight hours of committing troops to foreign soil. In addition, the president must withdraw troops within sixty days unless Congress votes to declare war. The president is also required to consult with Congress, if at all possible, prior to committing troops.

The War Powers Act has been of limited effectiveness in claiming a larger congressional role in international crisis situations. Presidents Ford, Carter, and Reagan never consulted Congress in advance of committing troops, citing the need for secrecy and swift movement, although each president did notify Congress shortly after the incidents. They contended that the War Powers Act was probably unconstitutional because it limits presidential prerogatives as commander-in-chief. When Congress does try to get into the foreign affairs area, it often seems to botch it. In 1999, for example, the House voted to bar President Clinton from deploying ground troops to Kosovo without its approval. But ultimately it took six often contradictory votes on intervention in

Kosovo to formulate policy, as revealed in Table 7.7. With these kinds of confusing signals, it is not surprising that many presidents have insisted on quite a bit of autonomy in conducting foreign affairs, although President Clinton did pledge to consult Congress before he took action.

Confirmation of Presidential Appointments.   The Senate plays a special oversight function through its ability to confirm key members of the executive branch, as well as presidential appointments to the federal courts. As discussed in chapters 9 and 10, although the Senate generally confirms most presidential nominees, it does not always do so. A wise president considers senatorial reaction before nominating potentially controversial individuals to his administration or to the federal courts. In the case of federal district court appointments, senators often have a considerable say in the nomination of judges from their states through what is called **senatorial courtesy**, a process by which presidents generally defer selection of district court judges to the choice of senators of their own party who represent the state in which a vacancy occurs (see chapter 10).

> **senatorial courtesy**
> A process by which presidents, when selecting district court judges, defer to the senator in whose state the vacancy occurs.

Presidential appointees during the Clinton administration faced a particularly hostile Congress. "Appointments have always been the battleground for policy disputes," says political scientist G. Calvin MacKenzie, but now, "what's new is the rawness of it—all of the veneer is off."[67] Thus, while Congress's power seems to have waned over the years, its oversight function gives it a potent weapon to thwart presidential abuses of power. Most of the Bush executive appointments went much more smoothly in spite of the initial 50–50 Senate. His most controversial appointee, John Ashcroft, the former Republican senator from Missouri, withstood one of the closest votes in history—58–42. Still, Democrats in the Senate sent a clear message to the Bush administration. Although they were willing to allow the new president to fill his administration with like-minded conservatives, they would not allow him to appoint the same kind of individuals to the federal courts. A high priority of the lame-duck new Republican controlled Senate in 2002 was confirmation of the backlog of Bush nominees to the federal courts.

The Impeachment Process.   The impeachment process is Congress's ultimate oversight of the U.S. president (as well as federal court judges). The U.S. Constitution is quite vague about the impeachment process and much of the debate about it of late concerns what is an impeachable offense. The Constitution specifies that a president can be impeached for treason, bribery, or other "high crimes and misdemeanors." Most commentators agree that this phrase was meant to mean significant abuses of power. The question for the U.S.

TABLE 7.7   Congressional Action on Kosovo: An Exercise in Foreign Affairs Oversight

House

Adopted 249–180	Bill that prohibits funds for ground forces in Yugoslavia without prior congressional approval
Rejected 290–139	Resolution to direct removal of U.S. armed forces from Yugoslavian conflict
Rejected 427–2	Declaration of war against Yugoslavia
Rejected 213–213	Senate-passed resolution authorizing air operations in Yugoslavia

Senate

Adopted 58–41	Resolution authorizing air operations in Yugoslavia
Tabled 78–22	Further debate on resolution allowing "all necessary force" in Yugoslavia

Source: "Congress Votes Both Ways," *USA Today* (May 5, 1999): 26A.

Charged with serious misconduct in 1868, Andrew Johnson was acquitted by the Senate by a one-vote margin. (Photo courtesy: Bettman/Corbis)

House then in considering whether President Clinton should be removed from office was, were President Clinton's statements to the grand jury lies, and if so, did lying to a grand jury constitute a "high crime and misdemeanor" deserving of possible removal from office? In *The Federalist Papers* Alexander Hamilton noted his belief that impeachable offenses "are of a nature which may with peculiar propriety be denominated political, as they relate chiefly to injuries done immediately to society itself."

House and Senate rules control how the impeachment process operates. Yet, because the process is used so rarely, and under such disparate circumstances, there are few hard and fast rules. Until 1998, the U.S. House of Representatives had voted to impeach only sixteen federal officials—and only one of those was a president, Andrew Johnson. (Of those, seven were convicted and removed from office and three resigned before the process described below was completed.)

Until late 1998, only three resolutions against presidents had resulted in further action: (1) John Tyler, charged with corruption and misconduct in 1843; (2) Andrew Johnson, charged with serious misconduct in 1868; and (3) Richard M. Nixon, charged with obstruction and the abuse of power in 1974. The House rejected the charges against Tyler; Johnson was acquitted by the Senate by a one-vote margin; and Nixon resigned before the full House voted on the articles of impeachment. Four articles of impeachment were voted on in the House against President Clinton; two of these failed. The Senate acted on the remaining two and found the president not guilty on both articles.

The impeachment process itself has eight distinct stages as Illustrated in Table 7.8.

TABLE 7.8   The Eight Stages of the Impeachment Process

1. **The Resolution.** A resolution, called an inquiry of impeachment, is sent to the House Judiciary Committee. Members may also introduce bills of impeachment, which will be referred to the Judiciary Committee.

2. **The Committee Vote.** After the consideration of voluminous evidence, the Judiciary Committee votes on the resolution or bill of impeachment. A positive vote from the committee indicates its belief that there is sufficiently strong evidence for impeachment in the House.

3. **The House Vote.** If the articles of impeachment are recommended by the House Judiciary Committee, the full House votes to approve (or disapprove) a Judiciary Committee decision to conduct full-blown impeachment hearings.

4. **The Hearings.** Extensive evidentiary hearings are held by the House Judiciary Committee concerning the allegations of wrongdoing. Witnesses may be called and the scope of the inquiry may be widened at this time. The committee heard only from the independent counsel in the Clinton case.

5. **The Report.** The committee votes on one or more articles of impeachment. Reports supporting this finding (as well as dissenting views) are forwarded to the House and become the basis for its consideration of specific articles of impeachment.

6. **The House Vote.** The full House votes on each article of impeachment. A simple majority vote on any article is sufficient to send that article to the Senate for its consideration.

7. **The Trial in the Senate.** A trial is conducted on the floor of the Senate with the House Judiciary Committee bringing the case against the president, who is represented by his own private attorneys. The Senate, in essence, acts as the jury, with the chief justice of the United States presiding over the trial.

8. **The Senate Vote.** The full Senate votes on each article of impeachment. If there is a two-thirds vote on any article, the president is automatically removed from office and the vice president assumes the duty of the president. Both articles issued against President Clinton, charging him with lying to a grand jury and encouraging a grand jury witness to lie or mislead, were defeated in the Senate.

Continuity & Change

Representatives—In or Out of Touch?

When the Framers met in Philadelphia, they were concerned that their representatives not get too far away from the American people. Thus the House of Representatives was created with members to stand for election every two years. The House was truly to be "the people's house." The Framers envisioned those elected to this body would well represent the interests of their constituents, go back home frequently, and not view the House as their ultimate career.

Over time, not only did members come to represent more people, but the kinds of people who could vote for members changed. Thus, as those who didn't own property, blacks, and women were added to the rolls of voters, the kinds of interests that members were expected to represent should have changed, but did not necessarily.

Today, although women make up more than half of the population, they make up only about 13 percent of our national lawmakers. African Americans constitute more than 12 percent of the population but have no representation in the United States Senate. When members of the Congressional Black Caucus wanted to challenge the Joint Sessions' counting of the electoral college votes, they could not do so when they failed to get the signature of a single senator.

Hispanics, now the largest minority in the United States, suffer even poorer representation. Similarly, although they make up more than 13 percent of the population, they hold a small share of the seats in Congress and, like African Americans, none in the Senate.

As the nation becomes more diverse ethnically and racially and minorities as well as women hold so few seats in Congress, can that body still be seen as a representative body? Representative of whom, some might ask. Particularly when one sees the power of corporate interests, as evident in the section How a Bill *Really* Becomes a Law, one begins to wonder how much drastic change might take place before the interests of the citizens, as the citizenry has developed in this new century, are truly being represented.

1. Do you see the present racial, economic, and male/female composition of the Congress as a problem in truly representing the interests of "the people"?
2. What steps might be taken to make Congress more representative?

Cast Your Vote. Is Congress representative of the American people? To cast your vote, go to **www.ablongman.com/oconnor**

SUMMARY

The size and scope of Congress, and demands put on it, have increased tremendously over the years. In presenting the important role that Congress plays in American politics, we have made the following points:

1. **The Roots of the Legislative Branch**
   Congress was molded after the bicameral British Parliament, but with an important difference. The U.S. Senate is probably the most powerful upper house in any national legislature. The Senate has unique powers to ratify treaties and to approve presidential nominees.

2. **The Constitution and the Legislative Branch of Government**
   The Constitution created a bicameral legislature with members of each body to be elected differently, and thus to represent different constituencies. Article I of the Constitution sets forth qualifications for office, states age minimums, and specifies how legislators are to be distributed among the states. The Constitution also requires seats in the House of Representatives to be apportioned by population. Thus, after every census, district lines must be redrawn to reflect population shifts. The Constitution also provides a vast array of enumerated and implied powers to Congress. Some, such as lawmaking and oversight, are shared by each house of Congress; others are not.

3. **The Members of Congress**
   Members of Congress live in two worlds—in their home districts and in the District of Columbia. Casework is one way to keep in touch with the district, since members, especially those in the House, never stop running for office. Incumbency is an important factor in winning reelection. Thus many have called for limits on congressional terms of office.

4. **How Congress Is Organized**
   Political parties play a major role in the way Congress is organized. The Speaker of the House is always a member of the majority party, and members of the majority party chair all committees. In 1995, Speaker Newt Gingrich became the most powerful Speaker of the House since the first decade of this century. Because the House of Representatives is large, the Speaker enforces more rigid rules on the House than exist in the Senate.

   In addition to the party leaders, Congress has a labyrinth of committees and subcommittees that cover the entire range of government policies, often with a confusing tangle of shared responsibilities. Each legislator serves on one or more committees and multiple subcommittees. It is in these environments that many policies are shaped and that members make their primary contributions to solving public problems.

5. **The Lawmaking Function of Congress**
   The road to enacting a bill into law is long and strewn with obstacles, and only a small share of the proposals introduced become law. Legislation must be approved by committees in each house and on the floor of each chamber. In addition, most House legislation is initially considered by a subcommittee and must be approved by the Rules Committee before getting to the floor. Legislation that is passed in different forms by the two chambers must be resolved in a conference before going back to each chamber for a vote and then to the president, who can sign the proposal into law, veto it, or allow it to become law without his signature. If Congress adjourns within ten days of passing legislation, that bill will die if the president does not sign it.

6. **How Members Make Decisions**
   A multitude of factors impinge on legislators as they decide policy issues. The most important of the many considerations are constituents' preferred options and the advice given by better informed colleagues. When clear and consistent cues are given by voters back home, legislators usually heed their demands. In the absence of strong constituency preferences, legislators may turn for advice to colleagues who are experts on the topic or to interest group lobbyists, especially those who have donated to their campaigns.

7. **Congress and the President**
   The president can successfully twist arms or appeal to party loyalty when dealing with legislators who belong to his party. A president's influence both with fellow partisans and opponents is related to the chief executive's popularity with the public. Ronald Reagan, a popular president, succeeded in getting an economic package adopted by a House controlled by Democrats. Congressional oversight of the executive branch and the president takes many forms including hearings, appointments, and the ultimate weapon, impeachment.

KEY TERMS

bicameral legislature, p. 217
bill, p. 218
casework, p. 221
cloture p. 244
conference committee, p. 237
congressional review, p. 253
delegate, p. 224
discharge petition, p. 238
divided government, p. 249
filibuster, p. 244
hold, p. 244

impeachment, p. 219
incumbency factor, p. 222
legislative veto, p. 253
line-item veto, p. 245
majority party, p. 230
majority leader, p. 232
minority party, p. 230
minority leader, p. 233
oversight, p. 253
party caucus, p. 235
pocket veto, p. 245

politico, p. 225
pork barrel, p. 239
redistricting, p. 218
senatorial courtesy, p. 255
Speaker of the House, p. 230
standing committee, p. 237
term limits, p. 222
trustee, p. 224
War Powers Act, p. 254
whip, p. 233

SELECTED READINGS

Aberbach, Joel D. *Keeping a Watchful Eye.* Washington, D.C.: Brookings Institution, 1990.

Bianco, William T., ed. *Congress on Display, Congress at Work.* Ann Arbor: University of Michigan Press, 2000.

Deering, Christopher J., and Steven S. Smith, *Committees in Congress,* 3d ed. Washington, D.C.: Congressional Quarterly Press, 1997.

Dodd, Lawrence C., and Bruce Ian Oppenheimer, eds. *Congress Reconsidered,* 6th ed. Washington, D.C.: CQ Press, 1997.

Fenno, Richard F., Jr. *Home Style: House Members in Their Districts.* Boston: Little, Brown, 1978.

Fox, Richard Logan. *Gender Dynamics in Congressional Elections.* Beverly Hills, Calif.: Sage, 1996.

Gill, Laverne McCain. *African American Women in Congress: Forming and Transforming History.* New Brunswick, N.J.: Rutgers University Press, 1997.

Hammond, Susan Webb. *Congressional Caucuses in National Policy Making.* Baltimore, Md.: John Hopkins University Press, 1998.

Hibbing, John R., and Elizabeth Theiss-Morse. *Congress as Public Enemy: Public Attitudes Toward American Political Institutions.* New York: Cambridge University Press, 1996.

Kaptur, Marcy. *Women of Congress.* Washington, D.C.: CQ Press, 1996.

Mayhew, David R. *Congress: The Electoral Connection.* New Haven, Conn.: Yale University Press, 1986.

Oleszek, Walter J. *Congressional Procedures and the Policy Process,* 4th ed. Washington, D.C.: Congressional Quarterly Press, 1995.

Price, David E. *The Congressional Experience: A View from the Hill.* 2nd ed. Boulder, Colo.: Westview Press, 2000.

Thurber, James A., and Roger Davidson, eds. *Remaking Congress: Change and Stability in the 1990s.* Washington, D.C.: CQ, 1995.

NOTES

1. Valerie Richardson, "A Massacre in Colorado; Students Killed, Injured in Blood Bath," *The Washington Times* (April 21, 1999): A1.

2. Ceci Connolly, "Littleton Alters the Landscape of Debate on Guns," *The Washington Post* (May 5, 1999): A3.

3. Helen Dewar, "Senate Turns Down Rules to Tighten Gun Show Sales," *The Washington Post* (May 13, 1999): A1.

4. Helen Dewar and Juliet Eilperin, "Senate Backs New Gun Control, 51–50," *The Washington Post* (May 21, 1999): A1

5. Juliet Eilperin, "House Democrats Seek a New Edge, Members Look for Ways to Bet Votes of White Men," *The Washington Post,* (December 8, 2000): A28.

6. David C. Kimball and Samuel C. Patterson, "Living Up to Expectations: Public Attitudes toward Congress," *Journal of Politics* 59 (August 1997): 701–28.

7. John R. Hibbing and Elizabeth Theiss-Morse, "The Media's Role in Fomenting Public Disgust with Congress," *Extensions* (Fall 1996): 15–18.

8. Charles S. Bullock III, "House Careerists: Changing Patterns of Longevity and Attrition," *American Political Science Review* 66 (December 1972): 1295–1300.

9. Richard F. Fenno Jr., *Home Style* (Boston: Little, Brown, 1978), 32.

10. Hedrick Smith, *The Power Game* (New York: Ballentine Books, 1989), 108.

11. Norman Ornstein, ed. *Vital Statistics on Congress* (Washington, D.C.: CQ Press, 1998), 135.

12. Gary W. Cox and Jonathan N. Katz, "Why Did the Incumbency Advantage in U.S. House Elections Grow?" *American Journal of Political Science* 40 (May 1996): 478–97; and Kenneth N. Bickers and Robert M. Stein, "The Electoral Dynamics of the Federal Pork Barrel," *American Journal of Political Science* 40 (November 1996): 1300–1326.

13. Marjorie Randon Hershey, "Congressional Elections," in Gerald M. Pomper et al., *The Election of 1992: Reports and Interpretations* (Chatham, N.J.: Chatham House, 1993), 159.

14. Alan I. Abramowitz, "Incumbency, Congressional Spending, and the Decline of Competition in House Elections," *Journal of Politics* 53 (February 1991): 34–56.

15. *U.S. Term Limits, Inc.* v. *Thornton,* 115 U.S. 1842 (1995).

16. Warren E. Miller and Donald Stokes, "Constituency Influence in Congress," *American Political Science Review* 57 (March 1963): 45–57.

17. Center for the American Woman and Politics, *Voices, Views, Votes: The Impact of Women in the 103rd Congress* (New Brunswick, N.J.: Eagleton Institute of Politics, Rutgers, 1995), 15.

18. Adam Clymer, "Daughter of Slavery Hushes Senate," *The New York Times* (July 23, 1993): B6.

19. Barbara Hinckley, *Stability and Change in Congress,* 3d ed. (New York: Harper & Row, 1983), 166.

20. Katharine Seelye, "Congressional Memo; New Speaker, New Style, Old Problem," *The New York Times* (March 12, 1999): A18.

21. Karen Foerstel, "Hastert and the Limits of Persuasion," *CQ Weekly* (September 30, 2000): 2252.

22. Barbara Sinclair, "The Struggle Over Representation and Lawmaking in Congress: Leadership Reforms in the 1990s," in James A. Thurber and Roger H. Davidson, eds., *Remaking Congress: Change and Stability in the 1990s* (Washington, D.C.: CQ Press, 1995), 105.

23. Quoted in Donald R. Matthews, *U.S. Senators and Their Worlds* (Chapel Hill: University of North Carolina Press, 1960), 97–8.

24. Steven S. Smith and Eric D. Lawrence, "Party Control of Congress in the Republican Congress," in Lawrence C. Dodd and Bruce I. Oppenheimer, *Congress Reconsidered,* 6th ed. (Washington, DC: Congressional Quarterly, 1997), 163–164. For more on the role of parties in the organization of Congress, see Forrest Maltzman, *Competing Principals: Committees, Parties, and the Organization of Congress* (Ann Arbor: University of Michigan, 1997).

25. "A Short History of the Democratic Caucus," http://hillsource.house.gov.

26. Woodrow Wilson, *Congressional Government: A Study in American Government* (New York: Meridian Books, 1956, originally published in 1885), 79.

27. Roger H. Davidson, "Congressional Committees in the New Reform Era: From Combat to the Contract," in Thurber and Davidson, *Remaking Congress,* 28.

28. For more about committees, see Christopher Deering and Steven Smith, *Committees in Congress,* 3d ed. (Washington, D.C.: CQ Press, 1997).

29. Kenneth A. Shepsle, *The Giant Jigsaw Puzzle: Democratic Committee Assignments in the Modern House* (Chicago: University of Chicago Press, 1978).

30. Jack Anderson, "Subcontractor Oversight Absent," *Press Journal* (May 17, 1999): A8.

31. Guy Gugliotta, "Term Limits on Chairman Shake Up House," *The Washington Post* (March 22, 1999): A4.

32. Miles Benson, "New Faces Inevitable Amoung House Leadership," *Times Picayune* (June 15, 2000): A7.

33. Barbara Sinclair, *The Transformation of the U.S. Senate* (Baltimore, Md.: Johns Hopkins University Press, 1989).

34. Helen Dewar, "Senate Lifts Veil on Bill 'Holds'; Leaders Remove Anonymity from Long-Used Delay Tactic," *The Washington Post* (March 4, 1999): A8.

35. Miles Pomper, "Grams Ends Holds on Seven Nominees," *CQ Weekly* (September 23, 2000): 2229.

36. Sarah A. Binder and Steven S. Smith, *Politics or Principle Filibustering in the United States: Filibustering in the United States* (Washington, D.C.: Brookings Institution, 1997).

37. James A. Thurber, "If the Game Is Too Hard, Change the Rules: Congressional Budget Reform in the 1990s," in Thurber and Davidson, *Remaking Congress,* 140.

38. *Clinton* v. *City of New York,* 118 S. Ct. 2091 (1998).

39. Quoted in Helen Dewar and Joan Biskupic, "Line-Item Veto Struck Down." *The Washington Post* (June 26, 1998): A1.

40. David E. Sanger, "Rounding Out a Clear Clinton Legacy," *The New York Times* (May 25, 2000): A1.

41. Sanger, "Rounding Out," A1, A10.

42. Eric Schmitt, "How a Hard-Driving G.O.P. Gave Clinton a Trade Victory," *The New York Times* (May 26, 2000): A1.

43. John Burgess, "A Winning Combination: Money, Message, and Clout," *The Washington Post* (May 25, 2000): A4.

44. David E. Rosenbaum, "With Smiles and Cell Phones, a Last-Minute Assault on the Undecided," *The New York Times* (May 25, 2000): A11.

45. Schmitt, "How a Hard-Driving."

46. Schmitt, "How a Hard-Driving."

47. Sanger, "Rounding Out," A1, A10.

48. See L. Martin Overby, "The Senate and Justice Thomas: A Note on Ideology, Race, and Constituent Pressures," *Congress & the Presidency* 21 (Autumn 1994): 131–136.

49. John W. Kingdon, *Congressmen's Voting Decisions,* 3d ed. Ann Arbor: University of Michigan Press, 1989.

50. Kingon, *Congressmen's Voting Decisions.* See also Lee Sigelman, Paul J. Wahlbeck, and Emmett H. Buell Jr., "Vote Choice and the Preference for Divided Government: Lessons of 1992," *American Journal of Political Science* 41 (July 1997): 879–894.

51. Daniel Jo Parks, "Partisan Voting Holds Steady," *CQ Weekly,* (December 11, 1999): Vol.57, (48): 2975-7.

52. *National Journal* 26 (December 17, 1994): 2996.

53. Scott H. Ainsworth and Francis Akins. "The Informational Role of Caucuses in the U.S. Congress." *American Politics Quarterly* 25 (October 1997): 407–430.

54. Jonathan D. Salant, "LSOs Are No Longer Separate, the Work's Almost Equal," *Congressional Quarterly* 53 (May 27, 1995): 1483.

55. A. B. Stoddard, "Caucuses Lose Influence After LSOs Abolished," *The Hill* (February 14, 1996): 2.

56. Ken Kollman, "Inviting Friends to Lobby: Interest Groups, Ideological Bias, and Congressional Committees," *American Journal of Political Science* 41 (April 1997): 519–544.

57. Robert Beirsack, Paul Herrnson, and Clyde Wilcox, *After the Revolution: PACS, Lobbies and the Republican Congress* (Boston: Allyn and Bacon, 1999).

58. Barbara S. Romzek and Jennifer A. Utter, "Congressional Legislative Staff: Political Professionals or Clerks?" *American Journal of Political Science* 41 (October 1997): 1251–79; and Susan Webb Hammond, "Recent Research on Legislative Staffs," *Legislative Studies Quarterly* (November 1996): 543–76.

59. Joel D. Aberbach, *Keeping a Watchful Eye: The Politics of Congressional Oversight* (Washington, D.C.: Brookings Institution, 1990).

60. William F. West, "Oversight Subcommittees in the House of Representatives, *Congress & the Presidency* 25 (Autumn 1998): 147–160.

61. West, "Oversight Subcommittees."

62. Jonathan D. Salant, "GOP Reveals the Cost of Senate Oversight," *The Washington Post* (January 9, 1998): A19.

63. Steven J. Balla, "Legislative Organization and Congressional Review of Agency Regulations," paper delivered at the 1999 annual meeting of the Midwest Political Science Association.

64. This discussion draws heavily on Balla, "Legislative Organization and Congressional Review."

65. 462 U.S. 919 (1983).

66. *The Wall Street Journal* (April 13, 1973): 10.

67. Quoted in Stewart M. Powell, "Lee Fight Signals Tougher Battles Ahead on Nomination," *Commercial Appeal* (December 21, 1997): A15.

8 The Presidency

The shootings at Littleton, Colorado, and other schools around the nation. The bombing in Oklahoma City. The burning of churches throughout the South. The series of national floods, hurricanes, tornadoes, and other national disasters. The explosion of the space shuttle *Challenger.* The killing of 241 Marines in Beirut, Lebanon.

What do all of these horrific disasters have in common? All allowed a sitting president to show his ability to heal and lead the nation. President Bill Clinton, like President Ronald Reagan before him, showed himself to be a master in bringing the nation together in times of personal crisis. Clinton was always quick to hop on a plane to console the affected families in private and then to lead the nation in prayer. The ability to act as a national unifier often transcends partisan politics, usually to the dismay of the party that does not control the White House.

Not all presidents have this kind of ability to mold national tragedies into celebrations of heroes and American spirit, or the desire to do so. Without the personal charisma exercised by Presidents Clinton and Reagan, the bombings in Oklahoma City and in Beirut, Lebanon, could have turned into indictments of executive branch misfeasance.

Similarly, the *Challenger* explosion could have been the result of the Reagan administration's cost-cutting efforts, which led to faulty inspection procedures. But, that disaster was never cast in those terms. In sharp contrast, when Americans were held hostage in Iran, President Jimmy Carter took personal blame.

The ability to heal the nation is a natural talent that likely cannot be taught. The ability to use the symbols of office, and how a president uses the power, scope, and gravity of his office, often defines his administration. President George W. Bush opted not to greet servicemen and women detained in China upon their initial return to the United States. This revealed a far different style than presidents Clinton or Reagan, who in all likelihood, would have been there to greet the returning heros. The way presidents react to and even use crises underscores the importance of understanding the use of, as well as the sources of a president's unwritten powers in addition to his specific constitutional grants of authority.

The constitutional authority, statutory powers, and burdens of the presidency make it a powerful position and an awesome responsibility. Most of the men who have been president in the past two decades have done their best; yet, in the heightened expectations of the American electorate, most have come up short. Not only did the Framers not envision such a powerful role for the president, but they could not have foreseen the skepticism with which many presidential actions are now greeted in the press, on talk radio, and on the Internet. These expectations have also led presidents into policy areas never dreamed of by the Framers. Imagine, for example, what the Framers might have thought about President Clinton's 1998 State of the Union message, which advocated eighteen as a national norm for class size in the lower grades. But by the 2000 presidential campaign, both major party candidates embraced education and smaller class sizes as national priority, further underscoring the key role presidents can play in setting national policy agendas.

The modern media, used by successful presidents to help advance their agendas have brought us "closer" to our presidents, making them seem more human, a mixed blessing for those trying to lead. Only two photographs exist of Franklin D. Roosevelt in a wheelchair—his paralysis was a closely guarded secret. Five decades later, Bill Clinton was asked on national TV what kind of underwear he preferred (briefs). Later, revelations about his conduct with Monica Lewinsky made this exchange seem tame. This demythifying of the president, along with simultaneous increases in our general mistrust of government and in our expectations of it, have made governing a difficult job. A president does not rely only on the formal powers of office to lead the nation: Public opinion and public confidence are key components of his ability to get his programs adopted and his vision of the nation implemented. As political scientist Richard E. Neustadt has noted, the president's power often rests on his power to persuade.[1] To persuade, he must not only be able to forge links with members of Congress; he must also have the support of the American people and the respect of foreign leaders.

The ability to persuade and to marshal the unenumerated powers of the presidency have become more important over time. In fact, the presidency of George W. Bush and the times that surround it are dramatically different from the presidency of his father and the years 1989–1993. America is changing dramatically and so are the responsibilities of the president and people's expectations of the person who holds that office. Presidents in this century battled the Great Depression, fascism, communism, and several wars involving American soldiers. With the Cold War over, there are fewer episodic instances to demonstrate their clear leadership in the face of adversity, yet instances such as the 2001 terrorist attacks in New York City and Washington, D.C., challenge presidents to demonstrate their clear leadership in the face of adversity. Moreover, it is hard to lead on the domestic front when divided government or gridlock has become the norm. Still, there are myriad opportunities for what some call postmodern presidents, as we will discuss throughout this chapter.[2]

The tension between public expectations and the formal powers of the president permeate our discussion of how the presidency has evolved from its humble origins in Article II of the Constitution to its current stature. In this chapter,

- First, we will examine the *roots of the office of president of the United States* and discuss how the Framers created a chief executive officer for the new nation.
- Second, we will discuss Article II and the *constitutional powers of the president*.
- Third, we will examine the *development of presidential power* and a more personalized presidency: How well a president is able to execute the laws often depends strongly on his or her personality, popularity, and leadership style.
- Fourth, to help you understand more fully the development of the office of the president as a central focus of power and action in the American political system, we will also discuss the development of what is called the *presidential establishment*. Myriad departments, special assistants, and a staff of advisers help the president but also make it easier for a president to lose touch with the common citizen.
- Fifth, we will focus on the *role of the president in the legislative process*. Since the days of Franklin D. Roosevelt, most presidents have played major roles in setting the national policy agenda—a power that Congress is now trying to reclaim.

- Sixth, we will examine the *president and public opinion* including the effect that public opinion has on the American presidency as well as the role the president plays in molding public opinion.

THE ROOTS OF THE OFFICE OF PRESIDENT OF THE UNITED STATES

The earliest example of executive power in the colonies was the position of royal governor. The king of England appointed a royal governor to govern a colony. He was normally entrusted with the "powers of appointment, military command, expenditure, and—within limitations—pardon, as well as with large powers in connection with the powers of law making."[3] Royal governors often found themselves at odds with the colonists and especially with the elected colonial legislatures. As representatives of the Crown, the governors were distrusted and disdained by the people, many of whom had fled from Great Britain to escape royal domination. Others, generations removed from England, no longer felt strong ties to the king.

When the colonists declared their independence from England in 1776, their distrust of a strong chief executive remained. Most state constitutions reduced the office of governor to a symbolic post elected annually by the legislature. Governors were stripped of most rights we assume an executive must have today, including the right to call the legislature into session or to veto its acts. The constitution adopted by Virginia in 1776 illustrates prevailing colonial sentiment. It cautioned that "the executive powers of government" were to be exercised "according to the laws" of the state, and that no powers could be claimed by the governor on the basis of "any law, statute, or custom of England."[4]

Although most of the states opted for a more "symbolic" governor, some states did entrust wider powers to their chief executives. The governor of New York, for example, was elected directly by the people. Perhaps *because* he was directly accountable to the people, he was given the power to pardon, the duty to execute the law faithfully to the best of his ability, and to act as "commander-in-chief" of the state militia.

The Constitutional Convention

As we saw in chapter 2, the delegates to the Philadelphia Convention quickly decided to dispense with the Articles of Confederation and fashion a new government composed of three branches—the legislative (to make the laws), the executive (to execute, or implement, the laws), and the judicial (to interpret the laws). The Framers had little difficulty in agreeing that executive authority should be vested in one person, although some delegates suggested multiple executives to diffuse the power of the executive branch. Under the Articles of Confederation, there had been no executive branch of government; and the eighteen different men who served as the president of the Continental Congress of the United States of America were president in name only—they had no actual authority or power in the new nation. Yet, because the Framers were so sure that George Washington—whom they had trusted with their lives during the Revolutionary War—would become the first president of the new nation, many of their deepest fears were calmed. They agreed on the necessity of having one individual speak on behalf of the new nation, and they all agreed that one individual should be George Washington.

The Framers also had no problem in agreeing on a title for the new office. Borrowing from the constitutions of Pennsylvania, Delaware, New Jersey, and New Hampshire, the Framers called the new chief executive the president. How the president was to be chosen and by whom was a major stumbling block. James Wilson of Philadelphia suggested a single, more powerful president, who would be elected by the people and "independent of the legislature." Wilson also suggested giving the executive an absolute veto over the acts of Congress. "Without such a defense," he wrote, "the legislature can at any moment sink it [the executive] into non-existence."[5]

The manner of the president's election haunted the Framers for a while, and their solution to the dilemma is described in detail in chapter 13. We leave the resolution of that issue—the creation of the electoral college—aside for now and turn instead to details of the issues the Framers resolved quickly.

WEB EXPLORATION
To learn more about specific presidents, see www.ablongman.com/oconnor

Qualifications for Office.   The Constitution requires that the president (and the vice president, whose major function was to succeed the president in the event of his death or disability) be a natural-born citizen of the United States, at least thirty-five years old, and a resident of the United States for at least fourteen years. In the 1700s it was not uncommon for those engaged in international diplomacy to be out of the country for substantial periods of time, and the Framers wanted to make sure that prospective presidents spent some time on this country's shores before running for its highest elective office. Most presidents have prior elective experience, too, as revealed in Table 8.1.

TABLE 8.1   Personal Characteristics of the Men Who Became President

President	Place of Birth	Higher Education	Occupation	First Political Office/ Last Political Office	Years in Congress	Years as Governor	Years as Vice President	Age at Becoming President
George Washington	Va.	None	Farmer/ surveyor	County surveyor/ military general	2	0	0	57
John Adams	Mass.	Harvard	Farmer/lawyer	Highway surveyor/ vice president	5	0	4	61
Thomas Jefferson	Va.	William & Mary	Farmer/lawyer	State legislator/ vice president	5	3	4	58
James Madison	Va.	Princeton	Farmer	State legislator/ secretary of state	15	0	0	58
James Monroe	Va.	William & Mary	Farmer/lawyer	State legislator/ secretary of state	7	4	0	59
John Quincy Adams	Mass.	Harvard	Lawyer	Minister to Netherlands/ secretary of state	0[a]	0	0	58
Andrew Jackson	S.C.	None	Lawyer	Prosecuting attorney/ U.S. Senate	4	0	0	62
Martin Van Buren	N.Y.	None	Lawyer	County surrogate/ vice president	8	0	4	55
William H. Harrison	Va.	Hampden	Military	Territorial delegate/ minister to Colombia	0	0	0	68
John Tyler	Va.	William & Mary	Lawyer	State legislator/ vice president	12	2	0	51
James K. Polk	N.C.	North Carolina	Lawyer	State legislator/ governor	14	3	0	50
Zachary Taylor	Va.	None	Military	None/military general	0	0	0	65
Millard Fillmore	N.Y.	None	Lawyer	State legislator/ vice president	8	0	1	50
Franklin Pierce	N.H.	Bowdoin	Lawyer	State legislator/ district attorney	9	0	0	48
James Buchanan	Pa.	Dickinson	Lawyer	County prosecutor/ minister to Great Britain	20	0	0	65
Abraham Lincoln	Ky.	None	Lawyer	State legislator/ U.S. House	2	0	0	52
Andrew Johnson	N.C.	None	Tailor	City alderman/ vice president	14	4	0	57
Ulysses S. Grant	Ohio	West Point	Military	None/military general	0	0	0	47
Rutherford B. Hayes	Ohio	Kenyon	Lawyer	City solicitor/governor	3	6	0	55
James A. Garfield	Ohio	Williams	Educator/ lawyer	State legislator/ U.S. Senate	18	0	0	50
Chester A. Arthur	Vt.	Union	Lawyer	State engineer/ vice president	0	0	1	51
Grover Cleveland	N.J.	None	Lawyer	District attorney/ governor	0	2	0	48
Benjamin Harrison	Ohio	Miami (Ohio)	Lawyer	City attorney/ U.S. Senate	6	0	0	56

(continued)

Terms of Office.   While many recent presidents seem to have had considerable difficulty being reelected to a second term, at one time, the length of a president's term was controversial. Four-, seven-, and eleven-year terms with no eligibility for reelection were suggested by various delegates to the Constitutional Convention. Alexander Hamilton suggested that a president serve during "good behavior." The Framers of the Constitution reached agreement on a four-year term with eligibility for reelection.

The first president, George Washington (1789–1797), sought reelection only once, and a two-term limit for presidents became traditional. Although Ulysses S. Grant

TABLE 8.1   (continued)

President	Place of Birth	Higher Education	Occupation	First Political Office/ Last Political Office	Years in Congress	Years as Governor	Years as Vice President	Age at Becoming President
Grover Cleveland	N.J.	None	Lawyer	District attorney/ governor	0	2	0	53
William McKinley	Ohio	Allegheny	Lawyer	Prosecuting attorney/ governor	14	4	0	54
Theodore Roosevelt	N.Y.	Harvard	Lawyer/ author	State legislator/ vice president	0	2	1	43
William H. Taft	Ohio	Yale	Lawyer	Prosecuting attorney/ secretary of war	0	0	0	52
Woodrow Wilson	Va.	Princeton	Educator	Governor/governor	0	2	0	56
Warren G. Harding	Ohio	Ohio Central	Newspaper editor	State legislator/ U.S. Senate	6	0	0	56
Calvin Coolidge	Vt.	Amherst	Lawyer	City council/ vice president	0	2	3	51
Herbert Hoover	Iowa	Stanford	Engineer	Relief administrator/ secretary of commerce	0	0	0	55
Franklin D. Roosevelt	N.Y.	Harvard	Lawyer	State legislator/ governor	0	4	0	49
Harry S Truman	Mo.	None	Clerk/Store owner	County judge/ vice president	10	0	0	61
Dwight D. Eisenhower	Texas	West Point	Military	None/military general	0	0	0	63
John F. Kennedy	Mass.	Harvard	Lawyer/ U.S. Senate	U.S. House/	14	0	0	43
Lyndon B. Johnson	Texas	Southwest Texas State Teachers' College	Educator	U.S. House/ vice president	24	0	3	55
Richard M. Nixon	Calif.	Whittier/ Duke	Lawyer	U.S. House/ vice president	6	0	8	56
Gerald R. Ford	Nebr.	Michigan/ Yale	Lawyer	U.S. House/ vice president	25	0	2	61
Jimmy Carter	Ga.	Naval Academy	Farmer/ business owner	Member, county board of education/ governor	0	4	0	52
Ronald Reagan	Ill.	Eureka	Actor	Governor/governor	0	8	0	69
George Bush	Mass.	Yale	Business owner	U.S. House/ vice president	4	0	8	64
William Jefferson Clinton	Ark.	Georgetown/ Yale	Lawyer	State attorney general/governor	0	12	0	46
George W. Bush	Conn.	Yale/Harvard	Business owner	Governor	0	6	0	54

[a]Adams served in the U.S. House for six years after leaving the presidency.

Sources: Adapted from Presidential Elections Since 1789, 4th ed. (Washington, D.C.: Congressional Quarterly, 1987), 4; Norman Thomas, Joseph Pika, and Richard Watson, The Politics of the Presidency, 3rd ed. (Washington, D.C.: CQ Press, 1993), 490; Harold W. Stanley and Richard G. Niemi, eds., Vital Statistics on American Politics 1997–1998 (Washington, D.C.: CQ Press, 1998).

unsuccessfully sought a third term, the two terms established by Washington remained the standard for 150 years, avoiding the Framers' much-feared "constitutional monarch," a perpetually reelected tyrant. In the 1930s and 1940s, however, Franklin D. Roosevelt ran successfully in four elections as Americans fought first the Great Depression and then World War II. Despite Roosevelt's popularity, negative reaction to his long tenure in office ultimately led to passage (and ratification in 1951) of the Twenty-Second Amendment, which limited presidents to two four-year terms or a total of ten years in office, should a vice president assume a portion of a president's remaining term.

impeachment
Actual bringing of charges against a public official requiring a simple majority vote of the House of Representatives; not the hearings or trial on those charges.

WEB EXPLORATION For a chronology of the Clinton impeachment hearings, see www.ablongman.com/oconnor

articles of impeachment
The specific charges brought against a president or a federal judge by the House of Representatives.

Removal.   During the Constitutional Convention, Benjamin Franklin was a staunch supporter of **impeachment,** a process for removing an official from office. He noted that "historically, the lack of power to impeach had necessitated recourse to assassination."[6] Not surprisingly, then, he urged the rest of the delegates to formulate a legal mechanism to remove the president and vice president.

Just as the veto power was a check on Congress, the impeachment provision ultimately included in Article II was adopted as a check on the power of the president. Each house of Congress was given a role to play in the impeachment process to assure that the chief executive could be removed only for "Treason, Bribery, or other high Crimes and Misdemeanors."

The Constitution gives the House of Representatives the power to conduct a thorough investigation in a manner similar to a grand jury proceeding to determine whether or not the president has engaged in any of those offenses (see chapter 7). If the finding is positive, the House is empowered to vote to impeach the president by a simple majority vote. The Senate then acts as a court of law and tries the president for the charged offenses, which are called **articles of impeachment.** (The chief justice of the United States presides over the vote on the articles and the Senate hearing.) A two-thirds majority vote in the Senate on any count contained in the articles of impeachment is necessary to remove the president from office. Only two presidents, Andrew Johnson and Bill Clinton, were impeached by the House of Representatives. Neither man, however, was removed from office by the Senate. (For more on how the impeachment process works, see The Impeachment Process, Table 7.8, p. 257.)

Succession.   Through 2000, eight presidents died in office from illness or assassination. William Henry Harrison was the first president to die in office—he caught a cold at his inauguration in 1841 and died one month later. (John Tyler thus became the first vice president to succeed to the presidency.) In 1865, Abraham Lincoln became the first president to be assassinated. And in 1974, Richard M. Nixon, facing impeachment and likely conviction, became the first president to resign from office. The Framers were aware that a system of orderly transfer of power was necessary, so they created the office of the vice president. Moreover, the Constitution directs Congress to select a successor if the office of vice president is vacant. To clarify this provision, Congress passed the Presidential Succession Act of 1947, which lists—in order—those in line (after the vice president) to succeed the president:

1. Speaker of the House of Representatives
2. President pro tempore of the Senate
3. Secretaries of State, Treasury, and Defense, and other Cabinet heads in order of the creation of their department

The Succession Act has never been used because there has always been a vice president to take over when a president died in office. The Twenty-Fifth Amendment, in fact, was added to the Constitution in 1967 to assure that this will continue to be the case. Should a vacancy occur in the office of the vice president, the Twenty-Fifth Amendment directs the president to appoint a new vice president, subject to the approval (by a simple majority) of both houses of Congress.

The Twenty-Fifth Amendment has been used twice in its relatively short history. In 1973 President Richard M. Nixon selected the House minority leader, Gerald R. Ford, to replace Vice President Spiro T. Agnew after Agnew resigned in the wake of charges of bribe taking corruption and income tax evasion. Less than a year later, when Vice President Ford became the thirty-eighth president after Nixon's resignation, he appointed (and the Senate approved) former New York Governor Nelson A. Rockefeller to be vice president. This chain of events set up for the first time in U.S. history a situation in which neither the president nor the vice president had been elected to those positions.

The Twenty-Fifth Amendment also contains a section that allows the vice president and a majority of the Cabinet (or some other body determined by Congress) to deem a president unable to fulfill his duties. It sets up a procedure to allow the vice president to become "acting president" if the president is incapacitated. The president can also voluntarily relinquish his power. In 1985, following the spirit of the amendment, President Ronald Reagan sent Vice President George Bush a letter that made Bush the acting president for the eight hours that Reagan was incapacitated as he underwent surgery for colon cancer.

When President Lincoln was shot by John Wilkes Booth, he became the first of four presidents to be assassinated in office. (Photo courtesy: Museum of the City of New York)

The Vice President

The Framers paid little attention to the office of vice president beyond the need to have an immediate official "stand-in" for the president. Initially, for example, the vice president's one and only function was to assume the office of president in the case of the death of the president or some other emergency. After further debate, the delegates made the vice president the presiding officer of the Senate (except in cases of presidential impeachment). They feared that if the Senate's presiding officer was chosen from the Senate itself, one state would be short a representative. The vice president was given the authority to vote only in the event of a tie, however.

With so little authority, until recently, the office of vice president was considered a sure place for a public official to disappear into obscurity. When John Adams wrote to his wife, Abigail, about his position as America's first vice president, he said it was "the most insignificant office that was the invention of man . . . or his imagination conceived."[7]

Power and fame generally come only to those vice presidents who become president. Just "one heartbeat away" from the presidency, the vice president serves as a constant reminder of the president's mortality. In part, this situation has given rise to a trend of uneasy relationships between presidents and vice presidents that began as early as Adams and Thomas Jefferson. As historian Arthur M. Schlesinger, Jr., once noted, "The Vice President has only one serious thing to do: that is, to wait around for the President to die. This is hardly the basis for a cordial and enduring friendship."[8]

In the past, presidents chose their vice presidents largely to "balance"—politically, geographically, or otherwise—the presidential ticket, with little thought given to the possibility of the vice president becoming president. Franklin D. Roosevelt, for example, a liberal New Yorker, selected John Nance Garner, a conservative Texan, to be his running mate in 1932. After serving two terms, Garner—who openly disagreed with Roosevelt over many policies, including Roosevelt's Court-packing plan (see chapter 10) and his decision to seek a third term—unsuccessfully sought the 1940 presidential nomination himself.

In 1919, President Woodrow Wilson had what many believed to be a nervous collapse in the summer and a debilitating stroke in the fall that incapacitated him for several months. His wife, Edith Bolling Galt Wilson, refused to admit his advisers to his sickroom, and rumors flew about the "First Lady President," as many suspected it was his wife and not Wilson who was issuing the orders. (Photo courtesy: Stock Montage, Inc.)

WEB EXPLORATION
For more on the vice president, see
www.ablongman.com/oconnor

The Bush/Cheney and Gore/Lieberman tickets in 2000 also showed an effort to balance the ticket, but in ways different from the past. Many speculated that Gore selected Senator Joe Lieberman (D–Conn.), one of the first Democrats to speak out against President Clinton's moral lapses, to counter attacks on his own character and early support of Clinton. In contrast, most commentators agreed that Dick Cheney was chosen to provide "gravitas,"—i.e., a sense of national governmental experience, especially in foreign affairs, that Governor Bush neither had nor claimed.

How much power a vice president has depends on how much the president is willing to give him. Although Jimmy Carter, a Southerner, chose Walter F. Mondale, a Northerner, as his running mate in 1976 to balance the ticket, he was also the first president to give his vice president more than ceremonial duties. In fact, Mondale was the first vice president to have an office in the White House. (It wasn't until 1961 that a vice president even had an office in the Executive Office Building next door to the White House!) Mondale—a former senator from Minnesota with Washington connections—became an important adviser to President Carter, a former governor who had run for office as a Washington "outsider."

The "Mondale model" of an active vice president set the expectations for what the influence, powers, and limitations of modern vice presidents should be. Presidents Clinton and George W. Bush expanded tremendously on the Mondale model. Al Gore and Clinton forged a close working (and apparently personal) relationship when they traveled the country campaigning by bus in 1992. President George W. Bush's sharing of power with his vice president, Dick Cheney, a former secretary of defense in his father's administration, has been unprecedented. Cheney was at Bush's side when every major appointment to his new administration was announced. His greater interest and experience in foreign affairs have led to considerable speculation that Bush has delegated considerable authority to Cheney in the area of foreign affairs. No matter how much authority President Bush has opted to share with Vice President Cheney, it is clear that the days of inactive, out-of-the-loop vice presidents in America are over.

The question still exists, however, as to whether or not the vice presidency is a stepping stone to the presidency. As the 2000 campaign underscores, the vice president of a very popular president at a time of unprecedented economic prosperity was unable to translate that good will into election for himself. Since the presidency of Franklin D. Roosevelt, several vice presidents have become president, as revealed in Table 8.2. In fact, five of the twelve men who served as vice president from 1945 until 2001 became president.

TABLE 8.2   The Vice Presidency: A Modern Stepping Stone to the Presidency?

President	Vice President	President Through Death or Resignation	Ran for Office	Won
Franklin Roosevelt	Harry S Truman	Death		
Harry S Truman	(vacant 1945–49) Alben Barkley		1948	Won
Dwight D Eisenhower	Richard M. Nixon		1960 1968	Lost Won
John F. Kennedy	Lyndon B. Johnson	Death	1964	Won
Lyndon B. Johnson	Hubert H. Humphrey		1968	Lost
Richard M. Nixon	Spiro Agnew (resigned 1973) Gerald Ford	Resignation		
Gerald R. Ford	Nelson A. Rockefeller Ford ran as president		1976	Lost
Jimmy Carter	Walter Mondale		1984	Lost
Ronald Reagan	George Bush		1988	Won
George Bush	J. Danforth Quayle		Sought party nomination	Lost
Bill Clinton	Al Gore		2000	Lost

Three of those five, however—Presidents Truman, Johnson, and Ford—came to the office through the death or resignation of the president. (Truman and Johnson were then later elected in their own right.) Only two, Republican Presidents Nixon and Bush, were elected after serving as vice president. Richard M. Nixon actually was defeated by John F. Kennedy when he ran for president in 1960 while vice president; it wasn't until 1968 when he ran as a private citizen, that he was elected. Two vice presidents, Democrats Hubert H. Humphrey and Al Gore, ran for president and lost. Vice President J. Danforth Quayle sought the Republican Party nomination for the presidency but lost at that stage. Thus, since 1945 at least, the vice presidency can no longer be viewed as an especially advantageous place from which to make a run for the presidency.

THE CONSTITUTIONAL POWERS OF THE PRESIDENT

Though the Framers nearly unanimously agreed about the need for a strong central government and a greatly empowered Congress, they did not agree about the proper role of the president or the sweep of his authority. In contrast to Article I's laundry list of provisions for authority of the legislative branch, Article II details few presidential powers. Distrust of a powerful chief executive led to the Constitution's intentionally vague prescriptions for the presidency. Nevertheless, it is these constitutional powers, when coupled with a president's own personal style and abilities, that allow him to lead the nation.

Despite the Framers' faith in George Washington as their intended first president, it took considerable compromise to overcome their continued fear of a too-powerful president. The specific powers of the executive branch that the Framers agreed on are enumerated in Article II of the Constitution. Perhaps the most important section of Article II is its first sentence: "The executive Power shall be vested in a President of the United States of America." Just what the Framers meant by "executive power" was left intentionally vague.

Over the years, the expected limits of these specific constitutional powers have changed as individual presidents asserted themselves in the political process. Some presidents are powerful and effective; others just limp along in office. Much of the president's authority stems from his position as the symbolic leader of the nation and his ability to wield power, whether those powers are specifically enumerated in the Constitution or not. When the president speaks—especially in the area of foreign affairs—he speaks for the whole nation. *But* the base of all presidential authority is Article II, which outlines only a limited policy-making role for the president. Thus, as administrative head of the executive branch, the president is charged with taking "Care that the Laws be faithfully executed," but he has no actual power to make Congress enact legislation he supports. Nonetheless, the sum total of his powers, enumerated below, allow him to become a major player in the policy process.

The Appointment Power

To help the president enforce the laws passed by Congress, the Constitution authorizes him to appoint, with the advice and consent of the Senate, "Ambassadors, other public Ministers and Consuls, judges of the supreme Court, and all other Officers of the United States, whose Appointments are not herein otherwise provided for, and which shall be established by Law." Although this section of the Constitution deals only with appointments, behind that language is a powerful policy-making tool. Not only does the president have the authority to make more than 3,000 appointments to his administration (technically more than 75,000, if military officers are included), many of those appointees are in positions to wield substantial authority over the course and direction of public policy. Although Congress has the authority "to make all laws," through the president's enforcement power—and his

Longman
Participate.com
2.0
Simulation
**You Are
Appointing a
Supreme
Court Justice**

WEB EXPLORATION
To learn more about the number of confirmed presidential appointees in the Bush administration, go to
www.ablongman.com/oconnor

chosen assistants—he often can set the policy agenda for the nation. And, especially in the context of his ability to make appointments to the federal courts, his influence can be felt far past his term of office.

It is not surprising, then, that selecting the "right" people is often one of a president's most important tasks. Presidents look for a blend of loyalty, competence, and integrity. Identifying these qualities in people is a major challenge that every new president faces. Recent presidents, especially Bill Clinton and George W. Bush, have made an effort to make their Cabinets and staffs look, in President Clinton's terms, "more like America," as is underscored in Table 8.3). In fact, of the first five major appointments announced by then President-elect Bush, all but one were women and/or minorities: retired General Colin Powell to be secretary of state, Condoleezza Rice as his national security advisor, Texas Supreme Court Justice Alberto Gonzales as White House counsel, and long-time Bush adviser Karen Hughes as counselor to the president—two blacks, two women, and a Hispanic. By April 2001, 30 percent of his top appointments were women and 20 to 25 percent were minorities, although these account for only one-half of all appointments to be made.

In the past, when a president forwarded a nomination to the Senate for its approval, his selections were traditionally given great respect—especially those for the **Cabinet,** an advisory group selected by the president to help him make decisions and execute the laws. In fact, until the Clinton administration, the vast majority (97 percent) of all presidential nominations were confirmed.[9]

Rejections of presidential nominees can have a major impact on the course of an administration. Rejections leave a president without first choices, have a chilling effect on other potential nominees, affect a president's relationship with the Senate, and affect how the president is perceived by the public. George W. Bush's nomination of conservative John Ashcroft unleashed a torrent of liberal criticism and protacted hearings. But, in the end, Ashcroft was confirmed on a 58–42 vote.

The Power to Convene Congress

The Constitution requires the president to inform the Congress periodically of "the State of the Union," and authorizes the president to convene either or both houses of Congress on "extraordinary Occasions." In *Federalist No. 77,* Hamilton justified the latter by noting that because the Senate and the chief executive enjoy concurrent powers to make treaties, "It might often be necessary to call it together with a view to this object, when it would be unnecessary and improper to convene the House of Representatives." The power to convene Congress was important when Congress did not sit in nearly year-round sessions. Today this power has little more than symbolic significance.

The Power to Make Treaties

The president's power to make treaties with foreign nations is checked by the Constitution's stipulation that all treaties must be approved by at least two-thirds of the mem-

Cabinet

The formal body of presidential advisers who head the fourteen executive departments. Presidents often add others to this body of formal advisers.

WEB EXPLORATION
For more on President Bush's appointments, see
www.ablongman.com/oconnor

TABLE 8.3   **Presidential Teams (Senior Administrative Positions Requiring Senate Confirmation)**

	Total Appointments	Total Women	Percentage Women
Jimmy Carter	1,087	191	17.6%
Ronald Reagan	2,349	277	11.8%
George Bush	1,079	215	19.9%
Bill Clinton	1,257	528	42%

Sources: "Insiders Say White House Has Its Own Glass Ceiling," *Atlanta Journal Constitution* (April 10, 1995): A-4; and Judi Hasson, "Senate GOP Leader Lott Says He'll Work With Clinton," *USA Today* (December 4, 1996): 8A

bers of the Senate. The chief executive can also "receive ambassadors," wording that has been interpreted to allow the president to recognize the very existence of other nations.

Historically, the Senate ratifies about 70 percent of the treaties submitted to it by the president.[10] Only sixteen treaties that have been put to a vote have been rejected, often under highly partisan circumstances. Perhaps the most notable example of the Senate's refusal to ratify a treaty was its defeat of the Treaty of Versailles submitted by President Woodrow Wilson. The treaty was an agreement among the major nations to end World War I. At Wilson's insistence, it also called for the creation of the League of Nations—a precursor of the United Nations—to foster continued peace and international disarmament. In struggling to gain international acceptance for the league, Wilson had taken American support for granted. This was a dramatic miscalculation. Isolationists, led by Senator Henry Cabot Lodge (R–Mass.) opposed U.S. participation in the league on the grounds that the league would place the United States in the center of every major international conflict. Proponents countered that, league or no league, the United States had emerged from World War I as a world power and that membership in the League of Nations would enhance its new role. The vote in the Senate for ratification was very close, but the isolationists prevailed—the United States stayed out of the league, and Wilson was devastated.

The Senate also may require substantial amendment of a treaty prior to its consent. When President Carter proposed the controversial Panama Canal Treaties in 1977, for example, the Senate required several conditions to be ironed out between the Carter and Torrijos administrations before its approval was forthcoming.

When trade agreements are at issue, presidents are often also forced to be mindful of the wishes of Congress. The North American Free Trade Agreement (NAFTA) and the General Agreement on Tariffs and Trade (GATT) came to Congress after the president and his aides had negotiated these trade agreements under special rules referred to as "fast-track" procedures. These special rules are designed to protect a president's ability to negotiate with confidence that his accords will not be altered by Congress. The rules bar amendment and require an up or down vote in Congress within ninety days of introduction.

Presidents often try to get around the "advise and consent" requirement for ratification of treaties and the congressional approval required for trade agreements by entering into an **executive agreement,** which allows the president to enter into secret and highly sensitive arrangements with foreign nations without Senate approval. Presidents have used these agreements since the days of George Washington, and their use has been upheld by the courts. Although executive agreements are not binding on subsequent administrations, since 1900 they have been used far more frequently than treaties, further cementing the role of the president in foreign affairs.

Veto Power

Presidents can affect the policy process through the **veto power,** the authority to reject any congressional legislation. "Presidential vetoes have been vital to the development of the twentieth-century presidency."[11] The threat of a presidential veto often prompts members of Congress to fashion legislation that they know will receive presidential acquiescence, if not support. Thus, just threatening to veto legislation often gives a president another way to influence law making.

Proponents of a strong executive at the Constitutional Convention argued that the president should have an absolute and final veto over acts of Congress. Opponents of this idea, including Benjamin Franklin, countered that in their home states the executive veto "was constantly made use of to extort money" from the legislatures. James Madison made the most compelling argument for a compromise on the issue:

> Experience has proven a tendency in our governments to throw all power into the legislative vortex. The Executives of the States are in general little more than Ciphers, the legislatures omnipotent. If no effectual check be devised for restraining the instability and encroachments of the latter, a revolution of some kind or other would be inevitable.[12]

executive agreement
Secret and highly sensitive arrangement with a foreign nations entered into by the president; does not require a positive Senate vote.

veto power
The formal, constitutional authority of the president to reject bills passed by both houses of Congress, thus preventing their becoming law without further congressional action.

WEB EXPLORATION
To see the number of presidential vetoes from Washington to Clinton, go to
www.ablongman.com/oconnor

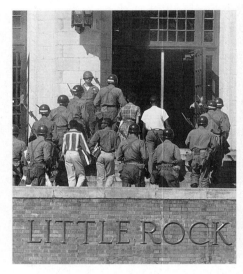

Chief law enforcer: National Guard troops sent by President Eisenhower enforce federal court decisions ordering the integration of public schools in Little Rock, Arkansas. (Photo courtesy: Bettman/Corbis)

Leader of the party: George W. Bush accepts his party's nomination for president at the 2000 Republican National Convention. (Photo courtesy: Mark Wilson/Newsmakers/Liaison Agency)

Commander-in-chief: President Bush and his wife, Barbara, with troops in the Persian Gulf. (Photo courtesy: Wally McNamee/ Folio, Inc.)

The President's Many Hats

Shaper of domestic policy: President Lyndon B. Johnson confers with the Reverend Martin Luther King, Jr. and Ralph Abernathy about Johnson's War on Poverty. (Photo courtesy: Bettman/Corbis)

Key player in the legislative process: President Bill Clinton proposes legislation to Congress and the nation. (Photo courtesy: Dirck Halstead/Liaison Agency/Getty Source)

Chief of state: President John F. Kennedy and his wife, Jacqueline, are greeted by the president of France and his wife during the Kennedys' widely publicized 1961 trip to that nation. (Photo courtesy: Bettman/Corbis)

In keeping with the system of checks and balances, then, the president was given the veto power, but only as a "qualified negative." Although the president was given the authority to veto any act of Congress (with the exception of joint resolutions that propose constitutional amendments), Congress was given the authority to override an executive veto by a two-thirds vote in each House. The veto is a powerful policy tool because Congress cannot usually muster enough votes to override a veto. Thus, in over 200 years, there have been approximately 2,500 presidential vetoes and only about a hundred have been overridden.

President George Bush was never reluctant to use his veto power: He often vetoed bills that were considered to enjoy wide popular support, and only one of his vetoes was overridden. During Bill Clinton's first two years in office, he became the first president since James A. Garfield (1881) not to veto any act of Congress. But, beginning in August 1995, when he exercised his first veto involving Congress's passage of legislation to require the United States to lift its embargo of arms sales to Bosnian Muslims, Clinton found himself at odds with the Republican-controlled Congress and was forced to veto thirty pieces of legislation through the end of his term. Only two were overridden.

The Line-Item Veto.   As early as 1873, in his State of the Union message, President Ulysses S. Grant proposed a constitutional amendment to give the president a **line-item veto,** a power enjoyed by many governors to disapprove of individual items within a spending bill and not just the bill in its entirety. Since then, over 150 resolutions calling for a line-item veto have been introduced in Congress. Franklin D. Roosevelt, Eisenhower, Ford, Carter, Reagan, Bush, and Clinton supported the concept. In 1994, congressional passage of a line-item veto was a key item in the Contract with America.

Finally, in 1996, Congress enacted legislation giving the president the authority to veto specific spending provisions of a bill without vetoing the bill in its entirety. This move allowed the president to project his policy priorities into the budget by vetoing any programs inconsistent with his policy goals. It also allowed President Clinton to do away with more outrageous examples of "pork" (legislators' pet projects which often find their way into a budget) and to eliminate what the president viewed as needless fat in the budget. In 1998, however, the state of New York challenged the line-item veto law when the president used the line-item veto to stop payment of some congressionally authorized funds to the state. The Supreme Court then ruled that the line-item veto was unconstitutional because it gave powers to the president denied him by the U.S. Constitution. Those kinds of alterations of power, said the Court, require constitutional amendments.[13]

line-item veto
The power to veto specific provisions of a bill without vetoing the bill in its entirety.

The Power to Preside over the Military as Commander-in-Chief

One of the most important constitutional executive powers is the president's authority over the military. Article II states that the president is "Commander-in-Chief of the Army and Navy of the United States." The Framers saw this power as consistent with state practices, and since the eighteenth century, it has proved to be wide-ranging. While the Constitution specifically grants Congress the authority to declare war, presidents since Abraham Lincoln have used the commander-in-chief clause in conjunction with the chief executive's duty to "take Care that the Laws be faithfully executed" to wage war (and to broaden various powers).

Modern presidents continually clash with Congress over the ability to commence hostilities. The Vietnam War, in which 58,000 American soldiers were killed and 300,000 were wounded, was conducted (at a cost of $150 billion) without a congressional declaration of war. In fact, acknowledging President Johnson's claim to war-making authority, in 1964 Congress passed—with only two dissenting votes—the Gulf of Tonkin Resolution, which authorized a massive commitment of U.S. forces in South Vietnam.

During that highly controversial war, presidents Johnson and then Nixon routinely assured members of Congress that victory was near. In 1971, however, publication of what were called *The Pentagon Papers* revealed what many had suspected all along—Lyndon B. Johnson had systematically altered casualty figures and distorted key facts

Longman
Participate.com 2.0
Simulation
You Are the President: Policy Toward Iran

War Powers Act
Law requiring presidents to obtain congressional approval before introducing U.S. troops into a combat situation; passed in 1973 over President Nixon's veto.

to place the conduct of the war in a more positive light. In 1973, Congress passed the **War Powers Act** to limit the president's authority to introduce American troops into hostile foreign lands without congressional approval. President Nixon's veto of the act was overridden by a two-thirds majority in both houses of Congress.

Presidents since Nixon have continued to insist that the War Powers Act is an unconstitutional infringement of their executive power. Thus, over and over again, presidents—Democratic and Republican—have ignored one or more provisions of the act. In 1980, Jimmy Carter failed to inform members of Congress before he initiated the unsuccessful effort to rescue American hostages at the U.S. Embassy in Iran. In 1983, President Reagan ordered the invasion of Grenada. In 1990, President Bush ordered 13,000 troops to invade Panama. And, in 1993, President Clinton sent U.S. troops to Haiti to restore its president to power. On each of these occasions, members of Congress have criticized the president. Yet the president's actions in each case have been judged in terms of his success and not on his possible abuse of power.

In 1999, Congress attempted to reassert itself in the foreign affairs process but managed only to give the president mixed signals. The House of Representatives was divided down the middle on a resolution showing simple support for the air war in Yugoslavia. Then, six weeks after the bombings began, the House took another vote. This time, it barred the president from sending ground troops to the former Yugoslavia without prior approval.[14]

The Pardoning Power

pardon
An executive grant providing restoration of all rights and privileges of citizenship to a specific individual charged or convicted of a crime.

Presidents can exercise a check on judicial power through their constitutional authority to grant reprieves or pardons. A **pardon** is an executive grant releasing an individual from the punishment or legal consequences of a crime before or after conviction, and restores all rights and privileges of citizenship. Presidents exercise complete pardoning power for federal offenses except in cases of impeachment, which cannot be pardoned. President Gerald R. Ford granted the most famous presidential pardon when he pardoned former President Richard M. Nixon—who had not been formally charged with any crime—"for any offenses against the United States, which he, Richard Nixon, has committed or may have committed while in office." This unilateral, absolute pardon, which prevented the former president from ever being tried for any crimes he may have committed, unleashed a torrent of public criticism against Ford and questions about whether or not Nixon had discussed the pardon with Ford before Nixon's resignation. Many attribute Ford's ultimate defeat in his 1976 bid for the presidency to that pardon.

In the waning days of his term, George Bush was showered with a torrent of criticism when he pardoned former Secretary of Defense Caspar Weinberger and five other administration officials on Christmas Eve 1992 for their conduct related to the Iran-Contra affair. Bush tried to place his pardons in the context of the historic use of the pardoning power to "put bitterness behind us and to look to the future."

Even though pardons are generally directed toward a specific individual, presidents have also used them to offer general amnesties. Presidents Washington, John Adams, Madison, Lincoln, Andrew Johnson, Theodore Roosevelt, Harry S Truman, and Jimmy Carter all used general pardons to grant amnesty to large classes of individuals for illegal acts. Carter, for example, incurred the wrath of many veterans' groups when he made an offer of unconditional amnesty to approximately 10,000 men who had fled the United States or gone into hiding to avoid being drafted to serve in the Vietnam War. While the pardoning power is not normally considered a key presidential power, its use by a president can get him in severe trouble with the electorate. Three presidents defeated in their reelection bids—Ford, Carter, and Bush—all incurred the wrath of the electorate for unpopular pardons. Thus, just as members of Congress are always on the lookout for potentially disastrous votes, it may be that presidents should be equally as wary of using their pardoning power.

It is politically much less risky for two-term presidents to use their pardon power. Still, president Clinton found himself in hot water over the number and kinds of pardons he issued on his last day in office: 140. Just as controversial were who got them. Critics were especially concerned with his pardon of financier Marc Rich, whose ex-wife was a major Clinton contributor. In reaction to this controversy, Senator

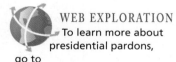

WEB EXPLORATION
To learn more about presidential pardons, go to
www.ablongman.com/oconnor

Hillary Rodham Clinton and others have co-sponsored legislation to require anyone lobbying for a pardon for themselves or a client to register as a lobbyist.

THE DEVELOPMENT OF PRESIDENTIAL POWER

Each person who has served as president of the United States has brought with him some expectation about the use of presidential authority and some vision (often outlined by campaign promises) of how the country could be improved through his guidance and leadership. Through 2001, the forty-two men who have held the nation's highest office have been a diverse lot. (While there have been forty-three presidents, only forty-two men have held the office—Grover Cleveland served as the twenty-second and twenty-fourth president because he was elected to nonconsecutive terms in 1884 and 1892.) Yet, most presidents have found accomplishing their goals much more difficult than they envisioned, even if they were elected with a sizable majority. After John F. Kennedy had been in office two years, for example, he noted publicly that there were "greater limitations upon our ability to bring about a favorable result than I had imagined."[15] Similarly, as he was leaving office, Harry S Truman mused about what surprises awaited his successor, Dwight D. Eisenhower, a former general: "He'll sit here and he'll say, 'Do this! Do that!' *And nothing will happen.* Poor Ike—it won't be a bit like the army. He'll find it very frustrating."[16]

A president's personal expectation of authority (and the public's expectations of him) are limited by the formal powers bestowed on the president by the Constitution and by the Supreme Court's interpretation of those constitutional provisions. These formal checks on presidential power are also affected by the times in which the president serves, by his selection of confidantes and advisers, and by the president's personality and leadership abilities. The postwar era of good feelings and economic prosperity presided over by the grandfatherly former war hero Dwight D. Eisenhower in the 1950s, for instance, called for a very different kind of leader from that needed by the Civil War–torn nation governed by Abraham Lincoln. Furthermore, not only do different times call for different kinds of leaders; they also often provide limits, or conversely, wide opportunities, for whoever serves as president at the time.

A president's authority can also be limited or expanded by the demands of the times in which he governs. Crises in particular have triggered expansions of presidential power. The danger to the Union posed by the Civil War in the 1860s required strong leaders to take up the reins of government. Because of his leadership during this crisis, Lincoln is generally ranked as the best president (see Table 8.4).

Longman
Participate.com 2.0
Participation
Rate the
Presidents

TABLE 8.4   The Best and the Worst Presidents

Who was the best president and who was the worst? Many surveys of scholars have been taken over the years to answer this question, and virtually all have ranked Abraham Lincoln the best. A 2000 C-SPAN survey of fifty-eight historians, for example, came up with these results:

Ten Best Presidents	Ten Worst Presidents
1. Lincoln (best)	1. Buchanan (worst)
2. F. Roosevelt	2. A. Johnson
3. Washington	3. Pierce
4. T. Roosevelt	4. Harding
5. Truman	5. W. Harrison
6. Wilson	6. Tyler
7. Jefferson	7. Fillmore
8. Kennedy	8. Hoover
9. Eisenhower	9. Grant
10. L. Johnson (10th best)	10. Arthur (10th worst)

Sources: Steve Neal, "Putting Presidents in their Place: Longtime Favorites Top the List," *Chicago Sun-Times* (November 19, 1995); and Susan Page, "Putting Presidents in Their Place," *The Washington Post* (February 21, 2000).

The First Three Presidents

The first three presidents, and their conception of the presidency, continue to have a profound impact on both the office and the public's expectations about the office and its inhabitants. When George Washington was sworn in as the first president of the United States on a cold, blustery day in New York City in April 1789, he took over an office and government that were really yet to be created. Eventually, a few hundred postal workers were hired and Washington appointed a small group of Cabinet advisers and clerks. During Washington's two terms, the entire federal budget was only about $40 million, or approximately $10 for every citizen in America. In contrast, in 1997, the federal budget was $1.6 trillion, or $6,065 for every man, woman, and child.

Like Washington (see Roots of Government: George Washington's Impact on the Presidency), the next two presidents, John Adams and Thomas Jefferson, acted in ways that were critical to the development of the office of the chief executive and the president's role in the political system. Adams's poor leadership skills, for example, heightened the divisions between Federalists and Anti-Federalists and probably quickened the development of political parties (see chapter 12). Soon thereafter, Jefferson used the party system to cement strong ties with the Congress and thereby expand the role of the president in the legislative process. He also expanded on the concept of **inherent powers** by taking the opportunity to expand the size of the nation dramatically through the **Louisiana Purchase** in 1803.

inherent powers
Powers of the president that can be derived or inferred from specific powers in the Constitution.

Louisiana Purchase
The 1803 land purchase authorized by Thomas Jefferson, which expanded the size of the United States dramatically.

Congressional Triumph: 1804–1933

The first three presidents made enormous contributions to the office of the chief executive and established important precedents to guide the conduct of those who came after them. But the very nature of the way government had to function in its formative years caused the balance of power to be heavily weighted in favor of a strong Congress. Americans routinely had intimate contacts with their representatives in Congress, while to most, the president seemed a remote figure. Members of Congress were frequently at home, where they could be seen by the voters; few ever even gazed on a president.

By the end of Jefferson's first term, it was clear that the Framers' initial fear of an all-powerful, monarchical president was unfounded. The strength of Congress and the relatively weak presidents who came after Jefferson allowed Congress quickly to assert itself as the most powerful branch of government. In fact, with but few exceptions, most presidents from Jefferson to Franklin Roosevelt failed to exercise the powers of the presidency in any significant manner.

Andrew Jackson was the first president to act as a strong *national* leader, representing more than just a landed, propertied elite. By the time Jackson ran for president in 1828, eleven new states had been added to the Union, and the number of white males eligible to vote had increased dramatically as property requirements for voting were removed by nearly all states. When Jackson, a Tennessean, was elected the seventh president, it signaled the end of an era: He was the first president not to be either a Virginian or an Adams. His election launched the beginning of "Jacksonian democracy," a label that embodied the Western, frontier, egalitarian spirit personified by Jackson, the first "common man" to be elected president. The masses loved him, and legends were built around his down-to-earth image. Jackson, for example, once was asked to give a postmastership to a soldier who had lost his leg on the battlefield and needed the job to support his family. When told that the man hadn't voted for him, Jackson responded: "If he lost his leg fighting for his country, that is vote enough for me."[17]

Jackson used his image and personal power to buttress the developing party system by rewarding loyal followers of his Democratic Party with presidential appointments. He frequently found himself at odds with Congress and made extensive use of the veto power. His veto of twelve bills surpassed the combined total of nine vetoes used by his six predecessors. Jackson also reasserted the supremacy of the national government (and the presidency) by facing down South Carolina's nullification of a federal tariff law.

ROOTS OF GOVERNMENT

GEORGE WASHINGTON'S IMPACT ON THE PRESIDENCY

In furtherance of his belief in the importance of the executive office to the development of the new nation, George Washington set several important precedents for future presidents:

- He took every opportunity to establish the primacy of the national government. In 1794, for example, Washington used the militia of four states to put down the Whiskey Rebellion, an uprising of 3,000 western Pennsylvania farmers opposed to the payment of federal excise tax on liquor. Leading those 1,500 troops was Secretary of the Treasury Alexander Hamilton, whose duty it was to collect federal taxes. Washington's action helped establish the idea of federal supremacy and the authority of the executive branch to collect the taxes levied by Congress.

- Washington began the practice of regular meetings with his advisers (called the Cabinet), thus establishing the Cabinet system.

- He asserted the prominence of the role of the chief executive in the conduct of foreign affairs. He sent envoys to negotiate the Jay Treaty with Great Britain. Then, over senatorial objection, he continued to assert his authority to negotiate treaties first and then simply submit them to the Senate for its approval. Washington made it clear that the Senate's function was limited to approval of treaties and did not include negotiation with foreign powers.

- He claimed the inherent power of the presidency as the basis for proclaiming a policy of strict neutrality when the British and French were at war. Although the Constitution is silent about a president's authority to declare neutrality, Washington's supporters argued that the Constitution granted the president inherent powers, that is, powers that can be derived or inferred from what is formally described in the Constitution. Thus, they argued, the president's power to conduct diplomatic relations could be inferred from the Constitution. Since neither Congress nor the Supreme Court later disagreed, this power was presumed added to the list of specific, enumerated presidential powers found in Article II.

Abraham Lincoln's approach to the presidency was similar to Jackson's. Moreover, the unprecedented emergency of the Civil War allowed Lincoln to assume powers that no president before him had claimed. Because Lincoln believed he needed to act quickly for the very survival of the Union, he frequently took action without first obtaining the approval of Congress. Among many of Lincoln's "questionable" acts:

- He suspended the writ of *habeas corpus,* which allows those in prison to petition to be released, citing the need to jail persons even suspected of disloyal practices.
- He expanded the size of the U.S. army above congressionally mandated ceilings.
- He ordered a blockade of Southern ports, in effect initiating a war without the approval of Congress.
- He closed the U.S. mails to treasonable correspondence.

Lincoln argued that the inherent powers of his office allowed him to circumvent the Constitution in a time of war or national crisis. Since the Constitution conferred on the president the duty to make sure that the laws of the United States are faithfully executed, reasoned Lincoln, the acts enumerated above were constitutional. He simply refused to allow the nation to crumble because of what he viewed as technical requirements of the Constitution. Noting the secession of the Southern states and their threat to the sanctity of the Union, Lincoln queried, "Are all of the laws *but one* to go unexecuted, and the Government itself go to pieces lest that one be violated?"[18]

Later, both Theodore Roosevelt (1901–1909) and Woodrow Wilson (1913–1921) expanded the powers of the presidency. Roosevelt worked closely with Congress, sending it several messages defining his legislative program. Roosevelt also followed the

stewardship theory
The theory that holds that Article II confers on the president the power *and* the duty to take whatever actions are deemed necessary in the national interest, unless prohibited by the Constitution or by law.

Taftian theory
The theory that holds that the president is limited by the specific grants of executive power found in the Constitution.

stewardship theory of executive-power, believing that Article II conferred on the president not only the power, but the duty to take whatever actions are deemed necessary in the national interest, unless prohibited by the Constitution or by law.[19] Wilson helped formulate bills and reinstated the practice of personally delivering the State of the Union message to Congress. World War I also forced him to take a pivotal role in international affairs.

Few presidents other than Jackson, Lincoln, Theodore Roosevelt, and Wilson subscribed to a broad and expansive interpretation of executive power prior to the administration of Franklin D. Roosevelt (1933–1945), possibly because the nation was not ready to submit to a series of strong presidents and because the times and national events did not seem to call for strong, charismatic leaders. Instead, most other presidents adopted what is known as the **Taftian theory** of presidential power, which holds that the president is limited by the specific grants of executive power found in the Constitution.[20] President Taft argued explicitly for this literalist view of presidential power, a view shared by Presidents Harding and Coolidge, among others.

The Growth of the Modern Presidency

Before the days of instantaneous communication, the nation could afford to allow Congress, with its relatively slow deliberative processes, to make most decisions. Furthermore, decision making might have been left to Congress because its members, and not the president, were closest to the people. As times and technology have changed, however, so have the public's expectations of anyone who becomes president. For example, the breakneck speed with which the electronic media such as the Cable News Network (CNN) report national and international events has intensified the public's expectation that in a crisis the president will be the individual to act quickly and decisively on behalf of the entire nation. Congress is often just too slow to respond to fast-changing events—especially in foreign affairs.

In the twentieth and twenty-first centuries, the general trend has been for presidential—as opposed to congressional—decision making to be more and more important. The start of this trend can be traced to the four-term presidency of Franklin D. Roosevelt (FDR), who led the nation through several crises, including the Great Depression and World War II. This growth of presidential power and the growth of the federal government and its programs in general are now criticized by many. To understand the basis for many of the calls for reform of the political system being made today, it is critical to understand how the growth of government and the role of the president occurred.[21]

FDR took office in 1933 in the midst of a major crisis—the Great Depression—during which a substantial portion of the U.S. workforce was unemployed. Noting the sorry state of the national economy in his inaugural address, FDR concluded, "This nation asks for action and action now." To jump-start the American economy, FDR asked Congress for *and was given* "broad executive powers to wage a war against the emergency, as great as the power that would be given to me if we were in fact invaded by a foreign foe."[22]

Just as Lincoln had taken bold steps on his inauguration, Roosevelt also acted quickly. He immediately fashioned a plan for national recovery called the **New Deal,** a package of bold and controversial programs designed to invigorate the failing American economy. As part of that plan, Roosevelt:

New Deal
The name given to the program of "Relief, Recovery, Reform" begun by President Franklin D. Roosevelt in 1933 designed to bring the United States out of the Great Depression.

- Declared a bank holiday to end public runs on the depleted resources of many banks;
- Persuaded Congress to pass legislation to provide for emergency relief, public works jobs, regulation of farm production, and improved terms and conditions of work for thousands of workers in a variety of industries;
- Made standard the executive branch practice of sending legislative programs to Congress for its approval; before, the executive branch had generally just reacted to congressional proposals;

- Increased the size of the federal bureaucracy from fewer than 600,000 to more than 1 million workers.

Throughout Roosevelt's unprecedented twelve years in office (he was elected to four terms but died shortly after beginning the last one), which saw the nation go from the economic "war" of the Great Depression to the real international conflict of World War II, the institution of the presidency changed profoundly and permanently. All kinds of new federal agencies were created to implement New Deal programs, and the executive branch became increasingly involved in implementing the wide variety of programs overseen by these agencies.

Not only did FDR create a new bureaucracy to implement his pet programs, but he also personalized the presidency by establishing a new relationship between the presidency and the people. In his radio addresses—or "fireside chats," as he liked to call them—he spoke directly to the public in a relaxed and informal manner about serious issues. He opened his radio addresses with the words, "My friends . . . ," which made it seem as though he were speaking directly to each listener. In response to these chats, Roosevelt began to receive about 4,000 letters per day, in contrast to the forty letters per day received by his predecessor, Herbert Hoover. The head of the White House correspondence section remembered that "the mail started coming in by the truckload. They couldn't even get the envelopes open."[23] One letter that found its way to the White House was simply addressed "My Friend, Washington, D.C."

President Franklin D. Roosevelt delivering one of his famous "fireside chats" to the American people. Roosevelt projected the voice and image of such a vigorous and active president that no one listening to him or seeing him in the newsreels would have guessed that he was confined to a wheelchair as a result of polio. (Photo courtesy: AP/Wide World Photos)

To his successors, FDR left the "modern presidency," including a burgeoning (many would say bloated) federal bureaucracy (see chapter 9), an active and usually leading role in both domestic and foreign policy and legislation, and a nationalized executive office that used technology—first radio and then television—to bring the president closer to the public than ever before.

The communication and leadership styles of post-FDR presidents are very different from those of eighteenth- and nineteenth-century presidents. George Washington believed that the purpose of public appearances was to "see and be seen," and not to discuss policy issues. Abraham Lincoln was applauded for refusing to speak about the impending Civil War. Today, presidents use every opportunity to sell their economic, domestic, and foreign programs. In addition, the modes of communication have changed greatly. The rhetoric of early presidents was written, formal, and addressed principally to Congress. Today press conferences and speeches addressed directly to the public are the norm.

THE PRESIDENTIAL ESTABLISHMENT

As the responsibilities and scope of presidential authority have grown over the years, especially since FDR's time, so has the executive branch of government and the number of people working directly for the president in the White House itself. While the U.S. Constitution makes no special mention of a Cabinet, it does imply that a president will be assisted by advisers. Just think of the differences in governance faced by two Georges—Washington and George W. Bush. George Washington supervised the

WEB EXPLORATION
For more on the modern White House, see
www.ablongman.com/oconnor

President George W. Bush selected retired General Colin Powell to serve as secretary of state, one of fourteen Cabinet-level departments. (Photo courtesy: AFP/Corbis)

nation from a temporary headquarters with a staff of but one aide—his nephew, paid out of Washington's own funds—and only four Cabinet members. In contrast, in 2001, George W. Bush presides over a White House staff of more than 500, a Cabinet of fourteen members, and an executive branch of government that employs more than 2.8 million people. Today a president is surrounded by policy advisers of all types—from the attorney general, who advises him on legal issues, to the surgeon general, who advises him on health matters. The White House staff, the first lady (see Highlight: First Ladies) and vice president and their staffs, the Cabinet, and the Executive Office of the President, all help the president fulfill his duties as chief executive.

The Cabinet

The Cabinet, which has no basis in the Constitution, is an informal institution based on practice and precedent whose membership is determined by tradition and presidential discretion. By custom, this advisory group selected by the president includes the heads of major executive departments. Presidents today also include their vice presidents in Cabinet meetings , as well as any other agency heads or officials to whom they would like to accord Cabinet-level status.

As a body, the Cabinet's major function is to help the president execute the laws and assist him in making decisions. Although the Framers had discussed the idea of some form of national executive council, they did not include a provision for one in the Constitution. They did, however, recognize the need for departments of government and departmental heads.

As revealed in Table 8.5, over the years the Cabinet has grown as departments have been added to accommodate new pressures on the president to act in areas that were not initially considered within the scope of concern of the national government. As interest groups, in particular, pressured Congress and the president to recognize their

TABLE 8.5   The U.S. Cabinet

Department	Date of Creation	Responsibilities
Department of State (DOS)	1789	Responsible for the making of foreign policy, including treaty negotiation
Department of the Treasury	1789	Responsible for government funds and regulation of alcohol, firearms,
Department of Defense (DOD)	1789, 1947	Created by consolidating the former Departments of War, the Army, the Navy, and the Air Force; responsible for national defense
Department of Justice (DOJ)	1870	Represents U.S. government in all federal courts, investigates and prosecutes violations of federal law
Department of the Interior (DOI)	1849	Manages the nation's natural resources, including wildlife and public lands
Department of Agriculture (USDA)	Created 1862; elevated to Cabinet status 1889	Assists the nation's farmers, oversees food-quality programs, administers food stamp and school lunch programs
Department of Commerce (DOC)	1903	Aids businesses and conducts the U.S. Census (originally the Department of Commerce and Labor)
Department of Labor (DOL)	1913	Runs labor programs, keeps labor statistics, aids labor through enforcement of laws
Department of Health and Human Services (HHS)	1953	Runs health, welfare, and Social Security programs; created as the Department of Health, Education, and Welfare (lost its education function in 1979)
Department of Housing and Urban Development (HUD)	1965	Responsible for urban and housing programs
Department of Transportation (DOT)	1966	Responsible for mass transportation and highway programs
Department of Energy	1977	Responsible for energy policy and research, including atomic energy
Department of Education	1979	Responsible for the federal government's education programs
Department of Veterans Affairs	1989	Responsible for programs aiding veterans

HIGHLIGHT

FIRST LADIES

From Martha Washington to Laura Bush, first ladies (a term coined during the Civil War) have made significant contributions to American society. Until recently, the only formal national recognition given to first ladies was an exhibit of inaugural ball gowns at the Smithsonian Institution. Not any more. Heightened interest—undoubtedly at least partially attributable to the highly visible role Hillary Rodham Clinton played in the Clinton administration—led the Smithsonian to launch an exhibit that highlights the personal accomplishments of first ladies since Martha Washington. The new exhibit is built around three themes: the political role of the first ladies, including how they were portrayed in the media and perceived by the public; their contributions to society, especially their personal causes; and, still, of course, their inaugural gowns.

Hillary Rodham Clinton was not the first instance of a first lady working for or with her husband.

- Martha Washington followed George to all the winter camps. At Valley Forge, she helped feed the troops and nurse the wounded.
- Abigail Adams was a constant sounding board for her husband. An early feminist, as early as 1776 she cautioned him "To Remember the Ladies" in any new code of laws.

- Edith Bolling Galt Wilson was probably the most powerful first lady. When Woodrow Wilson collapsed and was left partly paralyzed in 1919, she became his surrogate and decided who and what the stricken president saw. Her detractors dubbed her "Acting First Man."
- Eleanor Roosevelt also played a powerful and much criticized role in national affairs. Not only did she write a nationally syndicated daily newspaper column, she traveled and lectured widely, worked tirelessly on thankless Democratic Party matters, and raised six children. After FDR's death she shone in her own right as U.S. delegate to the United Nations, where she headed the commission that drafted the covenant on human rights. Later, she headed John F. Kennedy's Commission on the Status of Women.
- Rosalyn Carter also took an activist role by attending Cabinet meetings and traveling to Latin America as her husband's policy representative.

In sharp contrast to Hillary Rodham Clinton, who became the first first lady to seek and win election to the U.S. Senate, Laura Bush, a former librarian, initially followed the path of her mother-in-law, former First Lady Barbara Bush, more closely. Before 9/11, she adopted a more behind-the-scenes role and made literacy the focus of her activities.

demands for services and governmental action, they often were rewarded by the creation of an executive department. Since each was headed by a secretary who automatically became a member of the president's Cabinet, powerful groups including farmers (Agriculture), business people (Commerce), workers (Labor), and teachers (Education) saw the creation of a department as increasing their access to the president.

The size of the president's Cabinet has increased over the years at the same time that most presidents' reliance on their Cabinet secretaries has decreased, although some individual members of a president's Cabinet may be very influential. Because the Cabinet secretaries and high-ranking members of their departments are routinely subjected to congressional oversight and interest group pressures, they often have divided loyalties. In fact, Congress, through the necessary and proper clause, has the authority to reorganize executive departments, create new ones, or abolish existing ones altogether. For this reason most presidents now rely most heavily on members of their inner circle of advisers (the Executive Office of the President and the White House Office) for advice and information. (Chapter 9 provides a more detailed discussion of the Cabinet's role in executing U.S. policy.)

WEB EXPLORATION
For more on
first ladies, see
www.ablongman.com/oconnor

**Executive Office
of the President (EOP)**
Establishment created in 1939
to help the president oversee
the bureaucracy.

A former member of President
George Bush's foreign policy
team, Condoleezza Rice was
tapped as President George W.
Bush's national security advisor.
An expert on Russia, Rice will be
setting America's foreign policy
agenda. (Photo courtesy: Reuters
NewMedia, Inc./Corbis)

The Executive Office of the President (EOP)

The **Executive Office of the President (EOP)** was established by FDR in 1939 to oversee his New Deal programs. It was created to provide the president with a "general staff" to help him direct the diverse activities of the executive branch. In fact, it is a mini-bureaucracy of several advisers and offices located in the ornate Executive Office Building next to the White House on Pennsylvania Avenue, as well as in the White House itself, where his closest advisers often are located.

The EOP has expanded over time to include several advisory and policy-making agencies and task forces, each of which is responsible to the executive branch. Over time, the units of the EOP have become more responsive to individual presidents rather than to the executive branch as an institution. They are often now the prime policy makers in their fields of expertise as they play key roles in advancing the president's policy preferences. Among the EOP's most important members are the National Security Council, the Council of Economic Advisers, the Office of Management and Budget, the Office of the Vice President, and the U.S Trade Representative.

The National Security Council (NSC) was established in 1947 to advise the president on American military affairs and foreign policy. The NSC is composed of the president, the vice president, and the secretaries of state and defense. The president's national security adviser runs the staff of the NSC, coordinates information and options, and advises the president.

Although the president appoints the members of each of these bodies, they must still perform their tasks in accordance with congressional legislation. Thus, like the Cabinet, depending on who serves in key positions, these mini-agencies may not be truly responsible to the president.

Presidents can give clear indications of their policy preferences by the kinds of offices they include in the EOP. President Bush, for example, not only moved or consolidated several offices when he became president in 2001, he quickly moved to create a new Office of Faith-Based and Community Initiatives, which critics immediately attacked as an unconstitional mingling of the church and state.

White House Staff

Often more directly responsible to the president are the members of the White House staff: the personal assistants to the president, including senior aides, their deputies, assistants with professional duties, and clerical and administrative aides. As personal assistants, these advisers are not subject to Senate confirmation, nor do they have divided loyalties. Their power is derived from their personal relationship to the president and they have no independent legal authority.

George Washington's closest confidantes were Alexander Hamilton and Thomas Jefferson—both Cabinet secretaries—but that has often not been the case with modern presidents. As the size and complexity of the government grew, Cabinet secretaries had to preside over their own ever-burgeoning staffs, and presidents increasingly looked to a different inner circle of loyal informal advisers. By the 1830s, Andrew Jackson had chosen to rely on his own inner circle, nicknamed his "Kitchen Cabinet," instead of his department heads to advise him. FDR surrounded himself with New York political operatives and an intellectual "brain trust"; Jimmy Carter brought several Georgians to the White House with him; Ronald Reagan initially surrounded himself with fellow Californians.

Although each president organizes his staff in different ways, presidents typically have a chief of staff whose job is to facilitate the smooth running of the staff and the executive branch of government. Successful chiefs of staff have also protected the president from mistakes and helped implement their policies to obtain the maximum political advantage for the president. Other key White House aides include those who help plan domestic policy, maintain relations with Congress and interest groups, deal with the media, provide economic expertise, and execute political strategies.

As presidents have tried to consolidate power in the White House, and as public demands on the president have grown, so has the size of the White House staff—from fifty-one in 1943, to 247 in 1953, to a high of 583 in 1972. Since that time staffs have been trimmed, generally running around 4 to 500. During his 1992 presidential campaign, Bill Clinton promised to cut the size of the White House staff and that of the Executive Office of the President, and eventually he reduced the size of his staff by approximately 15 percent.

While White House staffers prefer to be located in the White House in spite of its small offices, many staffers are relegated to the old Executive Office Building next door because White House office space is limited. In Washington, the size of the office is not the measure of power it often is in corporations. Instead, power in the White House goes to those who have the president's ear and the offices closest to the Oval Office.

THE ROLE OF THE PRESIDENT IN THE LEGISLATIVE PROCESS: THE PRESIDENT AS POLICY MAKER

When FDR sent his first legislative package to Congress, he broke the traditional model of law making.[24] As envisioned by the Framers, it was to be Congress that made the laws. Now FDR was claiming a leadership role for the president in the legislative process. Said the president of this new relationship, "It is the duty of the President to propose and it is the privilege of the Congress to dispose."[25] With those words and the actions that followed, FDR shifted the presidency into a law- and policy-maker role. Now not only did the president and the executive branch *execute* the laws, he and his aides generally suggested them, too.

NBC's highly rated *The West Wing* has given the American Public a greater appreciation of the inner workings of the White House. (Photo courtesy: Reuters/HO/Archive Photos)

FDR's view of the role of the president in the lawmaking process of government is often called a **presidentialist** view. Thus a president such as FDR could claim that his power to oversee and direct the vast and various executive departments and their policies is based on the simple grant of executive power found in Article II that includes the duty to take care that the laws be faithfully executed. Presidentialists take an expansive view of their powers and believe that presidents should take a key role in policy making. For various reasons, Democratic presidents since FDR have tended to embrace this view of the president's role in law and policy making. In contrast, Republicans in the White House and in Congress have generally subscribed to what is called the **congressionalist** view, which holds that Article II's provision that the president should ensure "faithful execution of the laws" should be read as an injunction against substituting presidential authority for legislative intent.[26] These conflicting views of the proper role of the president in the lawmaking process should help you understand why presidents, especially Democratic presidents who have faced Republican majorities in the Congress or Republican presidents who have faced Democratic majorities, have experienced difficulties in governing in spite of public expectations.

From FDR's presidency to the Republican-controlled 104th Congress, the public routinely looked to the president to formulate concrete legislative plans to propose to Congress, which then adopted, modified, or rejected his plans for the nation. Then, in 1994, it appeared for a while that the electorate wanted Congress to reassert itself in the legislative process. In fact, the Contract with America was a Republican call for Congress to take the reins of the lawmaking process. But several Republican Congresses failed to pass many of the items of the Contract, and President Clinton's continued forceful presence in the budgetary process made a resurgent role for Congress largely

presidentialist
One who believes that Article II's grant of executive power is a broad grant of authority and power allowing a president wide discretionary powers.

congressionalist
A view of the president's role in the lawmaking process that holds Article II's provision that the president should ensure "faithful execution of the laws" should be read as an injunction against substituting presidential authority for legislative intent.

POINT/COUNTERPOINT

DOES THE PRESIDENT NEED A MANDATE TO GOVERN?

George W. Bush lost the popular vote in 2000 by about 500,000 votes and only won the electoral college after prolonged battles over the state of Florida's election process. According to conventional wisdom, and many media pundits, Bush should have had a difficult time governing the U.S. because he lacked a mandate—the authority to act on behalf of the people. In the United States, most people consider a mandate to be winning an overwhelming number, or at least a majority, of popular votes in an election. If a president has a mandate, he can govern authoritatively, using leverage with the Congress to get his policies enacted, holding news conferences to rally public support, and giving speeches to pressure the legislative branch to pass his agenda. In addition, the media tend to give the president more support and attack him less if he is popular with the people. Does a president need a mandate to govern, or can he run the country successfully without the popular vote majority? Let's examine these two points of view.

Democrats initially argued that Bush was going to have a hard time getting any of his programs passed because he lacked a mandate. Because Republicans lost seats in the House and the Senate during the 2000 elections as well as the presidential popular vote, Bush, they argued, needed to cooperate with Democrats and run the government in a bipartisan fashion. Many Democrats tried to block Bush's policies in Congress that they considered too conservative. They tried to force the Republicans to take up the Democratic agenda.

Democrats cite a number of presidents in history who have governed poorly due to their lack of a mandate. In 1827, the House of Representatives selected John Quincy Adams as president after no candidate managed to win a majority in the electoral college. He had nothing but trouble with Congress because many members viewed him as illegitimate. The 1876 election between Rutherford B. Hayes and Samuel Tilden was quite similar to the 2000 election. Tilden had won the popular vote by 250,000 votes, but South Carolina, Florida, and Louisiana were strongly divided and sent two sets of electors to the electoral college. A highly controversial commission chose the Republican contender, Hayes. The House rejected the commission's findings while the Senate accepted them. A political compromise was finally reached that allowed Hayes to take office. He is not remembered as a particularly good president, and many members of Congress referred to him as "his Fraudulency." In 1888, Benjamin Harrison won the electoral vote while Grover Cleveland won the popular vote. Harrison had an uneventful presidency and was beaten four years later in a rematch with Cleveland.

George W. Bush and the Republicans argue that winning the White House is its own mandate, regardless of the margin in the election. He is the legitimate president of the United States and will govern effectively. Because the Republican Party controls the House and won back the Senate in 2002, Bush should be able to push his programs through Congress. Historically speaking, several presidents have governed well despite their lack of a mandate as traditionally defined. In 1800, Thomas Jefferson became president when the House of Representatives selected him following an inconclusive vote in the electoral college, and most Americans today cite him as one of history's best presidents. In 1960, only 100,000 votes separated John F. Kennedy and Richard M. Nixon. The election hinged on the state of Illinois, where Kennedy won by 8,000 votes. Nixon was fond of saying that if one additional voter in each precinct in Illinois had voted for him, he would have won the presidency. Despite lacking a decisive voter mandate, however, Kennedy is also commonly listed as one of the best presidents in history. To most Republicans, these historical vignettes indicate that a traditional mandate is not necessary for a successful presidency.

What do you think? Does a president need a mandate to govern?
Go to www.ablongman.com/oconnor

---

illusory. Thus, modern presidents continue to play a major role in setting the legislative agenda especially in an era when the House and Senate are so narrowly divided along partisan lines. Without working majorities, "merely placing a program before Congress is not enough," as President Lyndon B. Johnson (LBJ) once explained. "Without constant attention from the administration, most legislation moves through the congressional process at the speed of a glacier."[27] The president's most important power (and often the source of his greatest frustration), then, in addition to support of the public, is his ability to construct coalitions within Congress that will work for passage

President Lyndon B. Johnson signs the long awaited Civil Rights Act of 1964. Immediately to his right is Senator Edward Brooke (R–Mass.), the first African American to be popularly elected as a U.S. Senator. On his left is Senator Walter Mondale (D–Minn.), who later served as vice president. (Photo courtesy: Bettmann/Corbis)

of his legislation. FDR and LBJ were among the best presidents at "working" Congress, but they were helped by Democratic majorities in both houses of Congress.[28]

On the whole, presidents have a hard time getting Congress to pass their programs.[29] Passage is especially difficult if the president presides over what is called a divided government, which occurs when the presidency and Congress are controlled by different political parties (see chapter 7). Recent research by political scientists, however, shows that presidents are much more likely to "win" on bills central to their announced agendas than to secure passage of legislation proposed by others.[30]

Presidents generally experience declining support for policies they advocate throughout their terms. That's why it is so important for a president to propose key plans early in his administration during the honeymoon period, a time when the goodwill toward the president often allows a president to secure passage of legislation that he would not be able to gain at a later period. Even LBJ, who was able to get about 57 percent of his programs through Congress, noted: "You've got to give it all you can, that first year . . . before they start worrying about themselves. . . . You can't put anything through when half the Congress is thinking how to beat you."[31]

George W. Bush moved quickly to take advantage of his honeymoon period, which was marred by a precipitous decline in the stock market. Still, he was able to sell his tax cut plan to the House and he took several decisive actions to reverse liberal Clinton era policies as discussed in Politics Now: What a Difference a President Makes. Said then Republican House Majority Leader Dick Armey (R–Tex.), "Our new president says he wants to take us in a new direction, and we should say, 'we're with you, Mr. President.'" While not a sentiment shared by all, many would agree that a new president deserves some time to act without rancorous partisan division.[32]

Presidential Involvement in the Budgetary Process

Since the 1970s, Congress has spent more time debating the budget than it has legislating.[33] The annual high-stakes showdowns that occur nearly every November are a way for presidents to exert their authority over Congress and to demonstrate leadership at the same time they drive home to the public and the Congress their policy priorities.

In addition to proposing new legislation or new programs, a president can also set national policy and priorities through his budget proposal and his continued insistence on their congressional passage. The budget proposal not only outlines the programs he proposes, it indicates the importance of each program by the amount of funding requested for each program and its associated agency or department. Because the Framers gave Congress the power of the purse, Congress had primary responsibility for the budget process until 1930. The economic disaster set off by the stock market crash of 1929, however, gave FDR the opportunity to assert himself in the congressional

WEB EXPLORATION
To try your hand at balancing the budget, see
www.ablongman.com/oconnor

budgetary process, just as he inserted himself into the legislative process. In 1939, the Bureau of the Budget, which had been created in 1921 to help the president tell Congress how much money it would take to run the executive branch of government, was made part of the newly created Executive Office of the President. In 1970, President Nixon changed its name to the Office of Management and Budget (OMB) to clarify its function in the executive branch.

OMB works exclusively for the president and employs hundreds of budget and policy experts. Key OMB responsibilities include preparing the president's annual budget proposal, designing the president's program, and reviewing the progress, budget, and program proposals of the executive department agencies. It also supplies economic forecasts to the president and conducts detailed analyses of proposed bills and agency rules. OMB reports allow the president to attach price tags to his legislative proposals and defend the presidential budget. The OMB budget is a huge document, and even those who prepare it have a hard time deciphering all of its provisions. Even so, the expertise of the OMB directors often gives them an advantage over members of Congress.

The importance of the executive branch in the budget process has increased in the wake of the Balanced Budget and Emergency Deficit Reduction Act of 1985 (often called Gramm-Rudman, for two of the three senators who sponsored it). This act outlined debt ceilings and targeted a balanced budget for 1993. To meet that goal, the act required that the president bring the budget in line by reducing or even eliminating cost-of-living and similar automatic spending increases found in programs such as Social Security. It also gave tremendous power to the president's director of the Office of Management and Budget, who was made responsible for keeping all appropriations in line with congressional understanding and presidential goals.

In 1990, Congress, recognizing that its goal of a balanced budget would not be met, gave OMB the authority to access each appropriations bill. Although this action gutted the Gramm-Rudman Balanced Budget Act, it "had the effect of involving [OMB] even more directly than it already is in congressional law-making."[34] Growing public (and even congressional) concern over the deficit contributed to the president's and executive branch's increasing role in the budget process. As a single actor, the president may be able to do more to harness the deficit and impose order on the federal budget and its myriad programs than the 535 members of Congress who are torn by several different loyalties.

Interestingly, many critics hailed the joint efforts of the president and Congress in coming up with a balanced budget in 1998—a goal that long eluded Bill Clinton's predecessors and earlier Congresses. The feat of avoiding a deficit budget was achieved without benefit of a balanced budget amendment. Although both parties to the budget dance have sought to take credit for their thriftiness, much of the surplus that occurred is a result of savings brought about by the end of the Cold War, which has led to much lower military spending, and a strong economy. Still, the president was happy to take credit for the balanced budget as he became the first president since Richard M. Nixon to sign a budget that had no red ink. Questions about what to do with the budget surplus came to the fore in every 2000 presidential debate and often seemed to define the Bush and Gore campaigns. President Bush cited the projected surplus as exhibit one that the federal government was taking too much of the people's money and therefore should give some back in the form of lower taxes across the board. The tax cuts, as well as many targeted tax cuts including the end of the marriage tax penalty supported by President Bush, may signal the first indications of his ability to wield the budget as a vehicle for policy change.

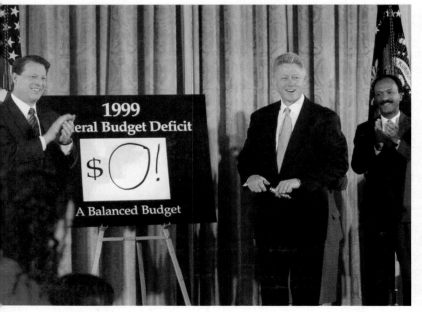

President Clinton and Vice President Gore celebrate the first balanced budget in years. (Photo courtesy: J. Scott Applewhite/AP/Wide World Photos)

Ruling Through Regulation

Proposing legislation and using the budget to advance policy priorities are not the only ways that presidents can affect the policy process, especially in times of highly divided government. Executive orders (further discussed in chapter 9) offer the president an opportunity to make policy without legislative approval. Major policy changes have been made when a president has issued an **executive order,** a rule or regulation issued by the president that has the effect of law. While many executive orders are issued to help clarify or implement legislation enacted by Congress, other executive orders have the effect of making new policy. President Harry S Truman ordered an end to segregation in the military through an executive order, and affirmative action was institutionalized as national policy through Executive Order 11246, issued by Lyndon B. Johnson in 1966.

A president's policies have been clearly evident in the use of executive orders to limit or advance access to abortion, depending on the views of the occupant of the White House. Ronald Reagan, for example, ordered a stop to federal funding of fetal tissue research and an end to federal monies to any group providing abortion counseling. When Bill Clinton took office in 1993, he immediately rescinded those orders. Over the course of his presidency, Clinton used the force of his office to set aside vast acreage of wilderness lands and to go after tobacco companies.

One of George W. Bush's first acts was to reinstate the ban on federal funds to groups providing abortion counseling. He also ordered his staff to stay Clinton's effort to set aside additional wilderness areas and investigate all of those last-minute regulations and rules. In the waning days of his presidency, Clinton marshaled the full force of the executive branch to issue thousands of regulations and executive orders, recognizing that the incoming Republican administration would have difficulty ferreting out all of the new directives. Among some of the midnight regulations issued by Clinton were regulations to limit emissions from diesel-powered trucks and buses, limits on the release of medical information by physicians and hospitals, and new requirements concerning workplace safety.[35]

Winning Support for Programs

As we have seen, the job of the president is ever expanding, a trend that makes it more and more difficult for any one individual to govern well enough to meet the rising expectations of the American public and their cynicism about politicians in general. Bill Clinton's lying to the public about his relationship with Monica Lewinsky didn't help his credibility with the public, either.

The ability to govern often comes down to a president's ability to get his programs through Congress. According to political scientist Thomas Cronin, a president has three ways to improve his role as a legislative lobbyist to get his favored programs passed.[36] The first two involve what you may think of as traditional political avenues.

Patronage and Party Ties.   Presidents can use patronage (jobs, grants, or other special favors that are given as rewards to friends and political allies for their support) and personal rewards to win support. Invitations to the White House and campaign visits to the home districts of members of Congress running for office are two ways to curry favor with legislators, and inattention to key members can prove deadly to a president's legislative program. House Speaker Thomas P. O'Neill reportedly was quite irritated when the Carter team refused O'Neill's request for extra tickets to Carter's inaugural. This did not exactly get the president off to a good start with the powerful Speaker.

A second way a president can bolster support for his legislative package is to call on his political party. As the informal leader of his party, he should be able to use that position to his advantage in Congress, where party loyalty is very important. This strategy works best when the president has carried members of his party into office on his coattails, as was the case in the Johnson and Reagan landslides of 1964 and 1984,

executive order
A rule or regulation issued by the president that has the effect of law. All executive orders must be published in the *Federal Register*.

Longman
Participate.com 2.0
Timeline
With the Stroke of a Pen: The Executive Order

Longman
Participate.com 2.0
Visual Literacy
Presidential Success in Polls and Congress

patronage
Jobs, grants, or other special favors that are given as rewards to friends and political allies for their support.

During the thousand days the Kennedys lived in the White House, it became a trendsetting center of culture and style, a royal palace, a "Camelot." John F. Kennedy and his family had looks, youth, and wealth, and JFK was a witty and gifted speaker. (Photo courtesy: Bettmann/Corbis)

respectively. In fact, many scholars regard LBJ as the most effective legislative leader. Not only had he served in the House and as Senate majority leader, he also enjoyed a comfortable Democratic Party majority in Congress.[37] As governor of Texas, President George W. Bush was able to work well with members of his own party as well as Democrats. This kind of across the aisle cooperation, however, is likely to be more difficult in a Congress where many of the leading Republicans are quite conservative and possibly less inclined to compromise with Democrats than is the president.

Presidential Style. The third way a president can influence Congress is a less "political" and far more personalized strategy. A president's ability to lead and to get his programs adopted or implemented depends on many factors, including his personality, his approach to the office, others' perceptions of his ability to lead, and his ability to mobilize public opinion to support his actions.

Some presidents have been modest in their approach to the office. Jimmy Carter, for example, adopted an unassuming approach to the presidency. During the energy crunch of the 1970s, he ordered White House thermostats set to a chilly 65 degrees and suggested that his advisers wear sweaters to work. Carter often appeared before the nation in cardigan sweaters instead of suits. He tried to build his "common man" image by carrying his own luggage and prohibiting the Marine band from playing the traditional fanfare, "Hail to the Chief," to signal his arrival on official occasions. In contrast, other presidents have been much more attuned to the trappings of office. Many believe that the Kennedys did it best.

Frequently, the difference between great and mediocre presidents centers on their ability to grasp the importance of leadership style. Truly great presidents, such as Lincoln and Franklin D. Roosevelt, understood that the White House was a seat of power from which decisions could flow to shape the national destiny. They recognized that their day-to-day activities and how they went about them should be designed to bolster support for their policies and to secure congressional and popular backing that could translate their intuitive judgment into meaningful action. Mediocre presidents, on the other hand, have tended to regard the White House as "a stage for the presentation of performances to the public" or a fitting honor to cap a career.[38]

Presidential Leadership. Leadership is not an easy thing to exercise, and it remains an elusive concept for scholars to identify and measure, but it is important to all presidents seeking support for their programs and policies. Moreover, ideas about the importance of effective leaders have deep roots in our political culture. The leadership abilities of the "great presidents"—Washington, Jefferson, Lincoln, and FDR—have been extolled over and over again, leading us to fault modern presidents who fail to cloak themselves in the armor of leadership. Americans thus have come to believe that "If presidential leadership works some of the time, why not all of the time?"[39] This attitude, in turn, directly influences what we expect presidents to do and how we evaluate them (see Table 8.6). Research by political scientists shows that presidents can exercise leadership by increasing their public attention to particular issues. Analyses of presidential State of the Union Addresses, for example, reveal that mentions of particular policies translate into more Americans mentioning those policies as the most important problems facing the nation.[40]

TABLE 8.6   Barber's Presidential Personalities

Does character seriously affect how a president handles his job? Many of the presidents ranked highest by historians had major flaws.

Not all discussions of presidential character center around lying, as was the case with Richard M. Nixon, or womanizing and draft evasion, as was the case with Bill Clinton. In an approach to analyzing and predicting presidential behavior criticized or rejected by many political scientists, political scientist James David Barber has suggested that patterns of behavior, many that may be ingrained during childhood, exist and can help explain presidential behavior. Barber believes that there are four presidential character types, based on (1) energy level (whether the president is active or passive) and (2) the degree of enjoyment a president finds in his job (whether the president has a positive or negative attitude about his job). Barber believes that active and positive presidents are more successful than passive and negative presidents. Active-positive presidents generally enjoyed warm and supportive childhood environments and are basically happy individuals open to new life experiences. They approach the presidency with a characteristic zest for life and have a drive to lead and succeed. In contrast, passive presidents find themselves reacting to circumstances, are likely to take direction from others, and fail to make full use of the enormous resources of the executive office. The table classifies presidents from Taft through George Bush according to Barber's categories. Where would you place Bill Clinton? George W. Bush?

	Active	*Passive*
Positive	F. Roosevelt	Taft
	Truman	Harding
	Kennedy	Reagan
	Ford	
	Carter[a]	
	Bush	
Negative	Wilson	Coolidge
	Hoover	Eisenhower
	L. Johnson	
	Nixon	

[a]Some scholars think that Carter better fits the active-negative typology.

Source: James David Barber, *The Presidential Character: Predicting Performance in the White House, 4th ed.* (Englewood Cliffs, N.J.: Prentice Hall, 1992).

The Power to Persuade.   In trying to lead against long odds, a president must not only exercise the constitutional powers of the chief executive but also persuade enough of the country that his actions are the right ones so that he can carry them out without national strife.[41] A president's personality and ability to persuade others are key to amassing greater power and authority.

Presidential personality and political skills often determine how effectively a president can exercise the broad powers of the modern presidency. To be successful, says political scientist Richard E. Neustadt, a president must not only have a will for power but must use that will to set the agenda for the nation. In setting that agenda, in effect, he can become a true leader. According to Neustadt, "Presidential power is the *power to persuade*," which comes largely from an individual's ability to bargain. Persuasion is key, Neustadt says, because constitutional powers alone don't provide modern presidents with the authority to meet rising public expectations.[42]

THE PRESIDENT AND PUBLIC OPINION

Presidents have long recognized the power of the "bully pulpit" and the importance of going public. Since the 1970s, however, the American public has been increasingly skeptical of presidential actions, and few presidents have enjoyed extended periods of the kind of popularity needed to help win support for programmatic change.

In 1974, President Richard M. Nixon resigned from office rather than face the certainty of impeachment, trial, and removal from office for his role in covering up details about a break-in at Democratic Party national headquarters in the Watergate office complex.

What came to be known simply as Watergate also produced a major decision from the Supreme Court on the scope of what is termed **executive privilege,** which later became an issue for Bill Clinton. In ***United States* v. *Nixon*** (1974) the Supreme Court ruled unanimously that there was no overriding executive privilege that sanctioned the president's refusal to comply with a court order to produce information to be used in the trial of the Watergate defendants.

Watergate forever changed the nature of the presidency. Because the president long had been held up as a symbol of the nation, the knowledge that corruption could exist at the highest levels of government changed how Americans viewed all institutions of government, and mistrust of government ran rampant. Watergate demystified the office and its occupant. As Richard M. Nixon toppled from office so did the prestige of the office itself. After Watergate, no longer was the president to be considered above the law or the scrutiny of the public or of the press.

Watergate not only forever changed the public's relationship to the president, it also spurred many reforms in how government and politics were run. Ethics and campaign finance laws were tightened up, and an independent counsel law, which allowed for independent investigation of the executive branch, was enacted. Perhaps even more than these changes, Watergate bruised Americans' optimism about what was good about America. Furthermore, intensive media attention to the president and the presidency brought him closer to the people (*and* to their intense public criticism) at the same time that the public expectations about the presidency itself increased. People began to look to the president rather than Congress to solve pressing and increasingly complex national problems even as their respect for the office—and often even its occupant—declined.

Writing in the 1940s, decades before Watergate, the great author John Steinbeck said, "We give the president more work than a man can do, more responsibility than a man should take, more pressure than a man can bear. We abuse him often, and rarely praise him. We wear him out, use him up, eat him up. And with all this, Americans have a love for the president that goes beyond party loyalty or nationality; he is ours, and we exercise the right to destroy him."[43]

executive privilege
An assertion of presidential power that reasons that the president can withhold information requested by the courts in matters relating to his office.

***United States* v. *Nixon* (1974)**
The Supreme Court ruled that there is no constitutional absolute executive privilege that would allow a president to refuse to comply with a court order to produce information needed in a criminal trial.

WEB EXPLORATION
For more details on Watergate, see
www.ablongman.com/oconnor

John Dean testifies before the Senate Watergate Committee, under the searching gaze of Senator Sam Ervin (D–N.C.). Dean's testimony as White House lawyer was pivotal in confirming Richard M. Nixon's participation in a coverup of the Watergate break-in. Dean later appeared as a frequent news commentator concerning the Clinton impeachment investigations. (Photo courtesy: Corbis/Bettmann)

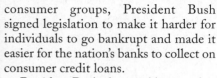

POLITICS NOW

WHAT A DIFFERENCE A PRESIDENT MAKES

Although George W. Bush came into office without any kind of clear mandate, down nearly a half million popular votes, he did not let that stop him from setting to work immediately to put his stamp on a wide array of bold public policies. One of his first actions found tremendous approval from the conservative wing of his party. On his third day in office he reimposed what is called the "Mexico City Policy" of the previous Reagan and Bush administrations, which bans federal aid to organizations that use their own money to perform or promote abortions, whether through counseling, public information campaigns, or lobbying to legalize abortions.

This change in policy was predicted by pro-choice activists in the campaign. Other quick steps by the new Bush administration, however, appeared to catch some—even members of his Cabinet—by surprise. During the 2000 presidential campaign, for example, President Bush pledged to seek reductions in carbon dioxide emissions from the nation's power plants. Christine Todd Whitman, the administrator of the Environmental Protection Agency, in fact, told her staff to come up with a plan to brand carbon dioxides as a pollutant, but her actions were suspended when the president announced that he had changed his mind because limits on carbon dioxide would cause energy costs to escalate further. His actions were hailed by industry lobbyists but triggered widespread condemnation from environmentalists.

President Bush's affinity with big business showed through loud and clear again with his support of bankruptcy reform legislation, which the Clinton administration opposed. Instead, over the strong objections of consumer groups, President Bush signed legislation to make it harder for individuals to go bankrupt and made it easier for the nation's banks to collect on consumer credit loans.

President Bush also quickly moved to create an Office of Faith Based Initiatives to allow for an increased participation in the nation's churches in implementing executive policies, a move that would have never happened during the Clinton administration. He also acted forcefully to support congressional efforts to overrule Clinton era ergonomics regulations hotly contested by big business, showing organized labor that they no longer had a friend in the White House.

President Bush also made it quickly evident that the United States was no longer to be a peace negotiator around the world. In meetings with Britain's Tony Blair, he made it clear that he would not take the kind of role that his predecessor did in the Northern Ireland peace process. Ditto to the administration's resolve to intervene in the Middle East peace process.

President Bush as we went to press also was considering ending the American Bar Association's fifty-year role in evaluating nominees to the federal bench, finding that the liberal ABA is often too critical in its evaluation of conservative judges of the kind that Mr. Bush expects to nominate to the federal courts.

Quick out of the starting gate in spite of a protracted election that shortened the time to put his administration in place, President Bush, the first president with an advanced degree in business administration, has shown himself to be an effective manager able to get policies he wants in place quickly.

The complex interaction of public opinion and the president are of considerable interest to scholars as well as members of the media and politicians. The president can mold public opinion and use public opinion to garner support for his favored programs. While all presidents try to manipulate public opinion to win support of their programs, they also are very mindful of their own standing in the polls.

Going Public

On average, President Bill Clinton spoke to the public in a variety of venues about 550 times a year. President Reagan, often remembered as a master of public relations and the media, averaged 320 appearances a year; the folksy President Truman, only 88 times a year.[44] What's the difference? The postmodern president has to try to govern amidst the din of several competing twenty-four-hour news channels, the Internet, and a news cycle that makes events of an hour ago old news. This rapid change provides presidents with rare opportunities while at the same time representing daunting challenges.

Historically, even before the days of radio and television, presidents tried to reach out to the public to gain support for their programs through what President Theodore Roosevelt (1901–1909) called "the bully pulpit." In this century, the development of commercial air travel and radio, news reels, television, and communication satellites have made direct communication to larger numbers of voters easier. Presidents no longer stay at home but instead travel all over the world to expand their views and to build personal support as well as support for their programs.

Bill Clinton and China's Jiang Zemin at a welcoming ceremony at Tiananmen Square in June 1998. (Photo courtesy: Fritz Hoffman/The Image Works)

Direct, presidential appeals to the electorate like those often made by Bill Clinton are referred to as "going public."[45] Going public means that a president goes over the heads of members of Congress to gain support from the people, who can then place pressure on their elected officials in Washington.

Like most presidents, Clinton was keenly aware of the importance of maintaining his connection with the public. Beginning with his 1992 campaign, Clinton often appeared on Larry King's TV talk show on CNN. Even after becoming president, Clinton continued to take his case directly to the people. He launched his health-care reform proposals, for example, on a prime-time edition of *Nightline* hosted by Ted Koppel. For an hour and a half, the president took audience questions about his health plan, impressing even those who doubted the plan with his impressive grasp of details. Moreover, at a black-tie dinner honoring radio and television correspondents, Clinton responded to criticisms levied against him for not holding traditional press conferences by pointing out how clever he was to ignore the traditional press. "You know why I can stiff you on the press conferences? Because Larry King liberated me from you by giving me to the American people directly," quipped Clinton.[46] In 1996, for example, President Clinton used the "bully pulpit" to convince television networks to get behind the idea of a rating system for television programs.

But some personal, direct appeals by a president appear to make no difference. In the case of health care, which the American public *seemed* to think was important in the 1992 presidential campaign, Clinton's personal approach had little apparent positive impact. The "people" didn't *really* rank health-care reform as a priority, so his direct appeal was a complete failure and a media disaster, which ultimately made it more difficult for the president to get other programs passed by Congress. Going public—unless the public clearly favors a policy not favored by Congress—is not a useful strategy.

Presidential Approval Ratings

Historically, a president has the best chances of convincing Congress to follow his policy lead when his public opinion ratings are high. Presidential popularity, however, generally follows a cyclical pattern. These "cycles" have occurred since 1938, when pollsters first began to track presidential popularity.

A N A L Y Z I N G   T H E   D A T A

PRESIDENTIAL APPROVAL SINCE 1938

Presidential approval ratings have generally followed a cyclical pattern. Presidents generally have enjoyed their highest ratings at the beginning of their terms and experienced lower ratings toward the end. First, Presidents Bush, and then President Clinton, however, enjoyed popularity surges during the course of their terms. Despite the Monica Lewinsky crisis and the threat of impeachment, Clinton's approval ratings continued to rise in 1998 and 1999. They peaked at 73% at the end of 1998—the highest rating of his administration. Clinton left office with a 66% approval rating.

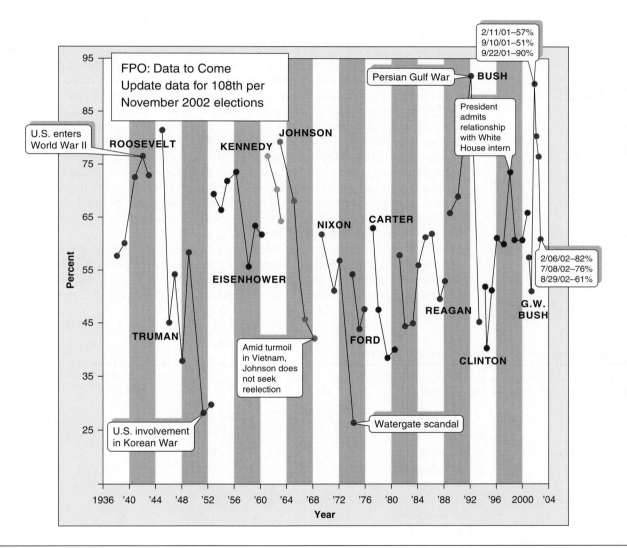

Source: *USA Today* (August 14, 2000) p. 6A. Copyright 2000, USA TODAY. Reprinted by permission.

Typically, presidents enjoy their highest level of popularity at the beginning of their terms and try to take advantage of this honeymoon period to get their programs passed by Congress as soon as possible. Each action a president takes, however, is divisive—some people will approve, and others will disapprove. Disapproval tends to have a cumulative effect. Inevitably, as a general rule, a president's popularity wanes, although Bill Clinton, who ended with a higher approval rating than any president in recent history, was a notable exception.

As revealed in Analyzing the Data, since Lyndon B. Johnson's presidency, only four presidents finished their term with approval rating of more than 50 percent. Many credit this trend to events such as Vietnam, Watergate, the Iran hostage crisis, and the Iran-Contra scandal, which have made the public increasingly skeptical of presidential performance. Presidents George Bush and Bill Clinton, however, experienced increases in their presidential performance scores during the course of their presidencies. Bush's rapid rise in popularity occurred after the major and, perhaps more important, quick victory in the 1991 Persian Gulf War. His popularity, however, plummeted as the good feelings faded and Americans began to feel the pinch of recession. In contrast, Bill Clinton's approval scores skyrocketed after the 1996 Democratic National Convention. More interestingly, Clinton's high approval ratings continued in the wake of allegations of wrongdoing in the Oval Office, his eventual admission of inappropriate conduct, and through his impeachment proceeding. In fact, when Clinton went to the American public and admitted that he misled them about his relationship with Monica Lewinsky, an ABC poll conducted immediately after his speech showed a 10-point jump in his job approval rating.[47]

Most presidents experience surges in popularity after major international events, but they generally don't last long. As revealed in Table 8.7, each of the last ten presidents before Bill Clinton experienced at least one "rallying" point based on a foreign event. Rallies lasted an average of ten weeks, with the longest being seven months.[48] These popularity surges have allowed presidents to make some policy decisions that they believe are for the good of the nation, even though the policies are unpopular with the public. This phenomenon has led some to ask if presidents launch bold international initiatives to distract critics of their personal (or domestic policy) problems and to enhance their popularity with the public.

Presidential popularity in domestic or foreign affairs is likely to hold some sway on the president's ability to build support for programs, although some political scientists question direct linkages between presidential support and policy influence.[49] Still, it is critical to remember that the president—whether you voted for him, like him, or agree

TABLE 8.7   Temporary Rises in Presidential Popularity

Gallup poll measurements of the size and duration of the largest increase in each president's approval rating before and after dramatic international events.

President	Event	Percentage Point Increase in Public Approval	Duration of the Increase in Weeks
Franklin D. Roosevelt	Pearl Harbor	12	30
Harry S Truman	Truman Doctrine;	12	N.A.[a]
	Korea invaded	9	10
Dwight D. Eisenhower	Bermuda Conf./Atoms for Peace speech	10	20
John F. Kennedy	Cuban Missile Crisis	13	31
Lyndon B. Johnson	Speech halting bombing of North Vietnam	14	19
Richard M. Nixon	Vietnam peace agreement	16	15
Gerald R. Ford	Mayaguez incident	11	25
Jimmy Carter	Hostages seized in Iran	19	30
Ronald Reagan	Beirut bombing/Grenada invasion;	8	N.A.[b]
	1st summit with Gorbachev	7	4
George Bush	Iraq invasion of Kuwait	18	30

[a]No polls conducted
[b]Overlapping events

Source: The New York Times, May 22, 1991 p. A10. information from the Gallup Organization. Reprinted by permission of NYT Graphics.

GLOBAL POLITICS

THE PRESIDENCY IN COMPARATIVE PERSPECTIVE

Presidents in the industrial democracies, faced with the difficulties of leading governments, often wish they had those powers exercised by the other kind of executive, the prime minister. Is the president of the United States more powerful than the prime ministers of the parliaments of Europe, Canada, and Japan?

In some ways, the president has significant powers that prime ministers do not. First, presidents typically appoint 3,000 positions in the executive branch and judiciary, two to three times the number prime ministers appoint. Second, presidents have larger staffs than prime ministers, a significant information-gathering resource. And third, the separation of powers places the president at the center of the political system, which gives him the ability to focus popular attention on key issues and to appeal to the public.

Presidents are harder to remove from office. Impeachment proceedings require that the president have committed "high crimes or misdemeanors." Prime ministers can be removed by a vote of no confidence, which requires only that a simple majority of the lower house of Parliament agrees that it does not support the prime minister's leadership.

Prime ministers, on the other hand, have powers American presidents often wish they had. Prime ministers do not face formal term limits and, with the exception of Germany's chancellor, can call for elections whenever they choose (within limits). Unlike recent American presidents, prime ministers have long prior experience in the legislature (an informal requirement for the position) and cabinet: "Outsiders" do not take over the reins of government. Finally, because the majority party or coalition in the lower house of parliament elects the prime minister, the latter are virtually assured of support from the legislature. Unlike both the American and French presidents in 1999, for example, no prime minister in the G-8 faced a hostile majority in the Parliament or Congress. As a result, prime ministers have a much easier time getting their legislative agendas passed into law; the success rate for cabinet-sponsored bills in the parliamentary systems is 80–90 percent, which no American president can match.

When we look farther afield, we run into a problem of comparison. "President" in countries like Mexico, China, and Indonesia means something rather different from what it means in the United States. In many developing countries, for different reasons, presidents typically have powers no American president enjoys. Among many of these presidencies, the chief executives are not faced with courts that can overturn executives' decisions. In China and Indonesia, the president is elected by the legislature, a device intended (until recently in Indonesia's case) to ensure that the incumbent remained in office. The domination of Mexican national politics by the Institutional Revolutionary Party until 1990s had similar consequences; President Vincente Fox represents a break from the domination. The existence of a president doesn't guarantee a government based on meaningful checks and balances.

China represents an extreme in this regard. Jiang Zemin is not chief executive because he is president so much as because he occupies a number of positions in the government and the Communist Party that enable him and his supporters to control government. Jiang's predecessor, Deng Xiao-Ping, was commonly referred to as "paramount leader," a term that fully conveys the idea that the executive power in China lies outside the constitutional provisions of any particular office.

Chief Executives, 2001

Country	Chief Executive	Office
Canada	Jean Chretien	Prime minister
China	Jiang Zemin	President
France	Jacques Chirac	President
Germany	Gerhard Schroder	Chancellor
Indonesia	Abdurrahim Wahid	President
Italy	Silvio Berlusconi	Prime minister
Japan	Junichiro Koizumi	Prime minister
Mexico	Vicente Fox	President
Russia	Vladimir Putin	President
United Kingdom	Tony Blair	Prime minister
United States	**George W. Bush**	**President**

with him on any particular issue or philosophical debate—is the elected leader of the nation and a key player in the policy process. A president is many things to many people: a symbol of the nation, a political organizer, a moral teacher. As we discussed in chapter 1, until the 1960s most Americans looked up to their president. Watergate heightened cynicism about the president and government in general. Nevertheless, until the 1990s it was highly unusual to see a sitting president vilified in the press or on radio or television talk shows. Never before have Americans known so much about the

Longman
Participate.com 2.0
Comparative
**Comparing
Chief
Executives**

WEB EXPLORATION
For more on the
White House Project, see
www.ablongman.com/oconnor

activities of their presidents, their background, who they dated in high school and college, what affairs they've had, and what they eat. Unlike the U.S. Supreme Court, whose members deliberate in secret and wear long, black judicial robes, Bill Clinton's legs, his running shorts (and even his undershorts) were often the frequent objects of public attention and comment. The Monica Lewinsky affair opened a whole new line of what is considered fair game. In fact, one of the strength's of George W. Bush's candidacy was there was no recent hint of scandal in his personal life.

Continuity & Change

A Woman President?

When the Constitution was first adopted, women could not vote, let alone dream of being president. By the mid-1800s, however, some women had begun to mobilize for expanded rights and opportunities, and the right to vote in particular. As early as 1871, Victoria Woodhull, an outspoken proponent of "free love" and editor of a weekly newspaper, tried to convince women suffrage leaders to form their own political party, the Cosmo-Political Party.[50] Woodhull would then run for president in the 1872 elections. Susan B. Anthony soon vetoed the idea because she was distrustful of Woodhull and her motives.[51]

Campaigning for Woodhull in 1872 was Belva Lockwood, who founded the first D.C. franchise group, the Universal Suffrage Association, in 1867. Lockwood was a strong believer in using publicity to serve the cause of women's rights. In 1884, Lockwood, along with a handful of other women, met in California and founded the National Equal Rights Party, which nominated Lockwood for president.[52] Her platform included equal rights for all, liquor restrictions, uniform marriage and divorce laws, and universal peace. Her run for the presidency was opposed by most women suffrage leaders; still, she received 4,149 votes in the six states where she was on the ballot. She ran again in 1888, but received even fewer votes.

In 1964, Senator Margaret Chase Smith (R–Maine), the only woman in the U.S. Senate, announced her candidacy for her party's nomination; her name was placed in nomination at the convention, but she garnered few votes. In 1984, the Democratic Party and its presidential candidate, former Vice President Walter Mondale, thought it could capitalize on its growing support from women voters and reenergize the party by nominating Geraldine Ferraro as his vice-presidential running mate.[53] Several women's groups, including the Women's Presidential Project, openly advocated that the Democrats add a woman to their party's ticket. The Mondale/Ferraro ticket was trounced by the popular incumbent Ronald Reagan. Still,

women's hopes to have a woman president did not die. In fact, in 1998, a nonpartisan group called the White House Project was founded to change the political climate so that the public would be more receptive to the idea of a woman president. In 2000, it cooperated with Mattel to produce "Madame President Barbie" to help socialize young girls to think about being president. In 2001, the Girl Scouts even added a Ms. President badge

Today, the idea of a woman president is becoming more and more accepted. In 1937, only 33 percent of those polled said they would vote for a woman for president.[54] By 1999, when Elizabeth Dole announced her exploratory committee for president, 92 percent of those polled said that they could vote for a woman, up 10 percentage points since 1987.[55] To facilitate the election of a woman to the White House by the year 2004, the White House Project launched a campaign in 1998 with a straw ballot in women's magazines offering twenty women as potential nominees. Over 100,000 people responded; the top five winners were Hillary Rodham Clinton, Elizabeth Dole, Senator Dianne Feinstein, New Jersey Governor Christine Todd Whitman, and General Claudia Kennedy, then the highest-ranking woman in the U.S. military.[56] The election of Elizabeth Dole to the U.S. Senate and the election of Representative Nancy Pelosi to the House leadership gives women more national exposure. Still, it is interesting to note that several other nations have been headed by women, yet in the United States, few see that happening soon.

1. What kind of barriers face women seeking the presidency?
2. Who will emerge as likely candidates in the future?

Cast Your Vote. What female candidate would you elect as President of the United States? To cast your vote, go to **www.ablongman.com/oconnor**

SUMMARY

Because the Framers feared a tyrannical monarch, they gave considerable thought to the office of the chief executive. Since ratification of the Constitution, the office has changed considerably—more through practice and need than from changes in the Constitution. In chronicling these changes, we have made the following points:

1. **The Roots of the Office of President of the United States**
   Distrust of a too-powerful leader led the Framers to create an executive office with limited powers. They mandated that a president be at least thirty-five years old and opted not to limit the president's term of office. To further guard against tyranny, they also made provisions for the removal of the president and created an office of vice president to provide for an orderly transfer of power.

2. **The Constitutional Powers of the President**
   The Framers gave the president a variety of specific constitutional powers in Article II, including the appointment power, the power to convene Congress, the power to make treaties, and the power to veto. The president also derives considerable power from being commander-in-chief of the military. The Constitution also gives the president the power to grant pardons.

3. **The Development of Presidential Power**
   The development of presidential power has depended on the personal force of those who have held the office. George Washington, in particular, took several actions to establish the primacy of the president in national affairs and as true chief executive of a strong national government. But, with only a few exceptions, subsequent presidents often let Congress dominate in national affairs. The election of FDR, however, forever changed all that, as a new era of the modern presidency began. A hallmark of the modern presidency is the close relationship between the American people and their chief executive.

4. **The Presidential Establishment**
   As the responsibilities of the president have grown, so has the executive branch of government. FDR established the Executive Office of the President to help him govern. Perhaps the most key policy advisers are those closest to the president—the White House staff and some members of the Executive Office of the President.

5. **The Role of the President in the Legislative Process: The President as Policy Maker**
   Since FDR, the public has looked to the president to propose legislation to Congress. The modern president also plays a major role in the budgetary process. To gain support for his programs or proposed budget, the president can use patronage, personal rewards, his party connections, and direct appeals to the public. How the president goes about winning support is determined by his leadership and personal style, affected by his character and his ability to persuade.

6. **The President and Public Opinion**
   Presidents have long recognized the power of the "bully pulpit" and the importance of going public. Since the 1970s, however, the American public has been increasingly skeptical of presidential actions, and few presidents have enjoyed extended periods of the kind of popularity needed to help win support for programmatic change.

KEY TERMS

articles of impeachment, p. 268
Cabinet, p. 272
congressionalist, p. 285
executive agreement, p. 273
Executive Office of the President (EOP), p. 284
executive order, p. 289

executive privilege, p. 292
impeachment, p. 268
inherent powers, p. 278
line-item veto, p. 275
Louisiana Purchase, p. 278
New Deal, p. 280
pardon, p. 276

patronage, p. 289
presidentialist, p. 285
stewardship theory, p. 280
Taftian theory, p. 280
United States v. *Nixon*, p. 292
veto power, p. 273
War Powers Act, p. 276

SELECTED READINGS

Barber, James David. *The Presidential Character: Predicting Presidential Performance in the White House,* 4th ed. Englewood Cliffs, N.J.: Prentice Hall, 1992.

Campbell, Karlyn Kohr, and Kathleen Hall Jamieson. *Deeds Done in Words: Presidential Rhetoric and the Genres of Governance.* Chicago: University of Chicago Press, 1990.

Corwin, Edwin S. *The Presidential Office and Powers,* 4th ed. New York: New York University Press, 1957.

Daynes, Byron W., and Glen Sussman. *The American Presidency and the Social Agenda.* Upper Saddle River, N.J.: Prentice Hall, 2001.

Edwards, George C., III. *Presidential Leadership: Politics and Policy Making,* 5th ed. New York: Bedford Books, 2000.

Kellerman, Barbara. *The Political Presidency.* New York: Oxford University Press, 1986.

Kernell, Samuel. *Going Public: New Strategies for Presidential Leadership,* 3rd ed. Washington, D.C.: CQ Press, 1997.

Levy, Leonard W., and Louis Fisher, eds. *Encyclopedia of the American Presidency*. Englewood Cliffs, N.J.: Prentice Hall, 1994.

Nelson, Michael, ed. *The Presidency and the Political System*, 6th ed. Washington, D.C.: CQ Press, 2000.

Neustadt, Richard E. *Presidential Power and the Modern Presidency*. New York: Free Press, 1991.

Pfiffner, James P. *Modern Presidency*. New York: Bedford Press, 2000.

Pious, Richard M. *The Presidency*. Boston: Allyn and Bacon, 1996.

Ragsdale, Lyn. *Vital Statistics on the Presidency: Washington to Clinton*. Washington, D.C.: CQ Press, 1998.

Rossiter, Clinton. *The American Presidency*. Baltimore, Md.: Johns Hopkins University Press, 1987.

Skowronek, Stephen. *The Politics Presidents Make: Leadership from John Adams to Bill Clinton*. Cambridge, Mass.: Harvard University Press, 1997.

Walcott, Charles E., and Karen Hult. *Governing the White House*. Lawrence: University Press of Kansas, 1995.

Warshaw, Shirley Anne. *The Domestic Presidency: Policy Making in the White House*. Boston: Allyn and Bacon, 1996.

———. *The Keys to Power: Managing the Presidency*. New York: Addison-Wesley, 1999.

NOTES

1. Richard E. Neustadt, *Presidential Power: The Politics of Power from FDR to Carter* (New York: Wiley, 1980).

2. Michael Waldman, "Bush's Presidential Power," *The Washington Post* (December 26, 2000): A29.

3. Edward S. Corwin, *The President: Office and Powers, 1787–1957*, 4th ed. (New York: New York University Press, 1957), 5.

4. F. N. Thorpe, ed., *American Charters, Constitutions, Etc.* (Washington, D.C., 1909), VIII, 3816–17.

5. Quoted in Corwin, *The President*, 11.

6. Winston Solberg, *The Federal Convention and the Formation of the Union of the American States* (Indianapolis, Ind.: Bobbs-Merrill, 1958), 235.

7. Alfred Steinberg, *The First Ten: The Founding Presidents and Their Administrations* (New York: Doubleday, 1967), 59.

8. "Is the Vice Presidency Necessary?" *Atlantic* 233 (May 1974): 37.

9. Benjamin I. Page and Mark P. Petracca, *The American Presidency* (New York: McGraw-Hill, 1983), 262.

10. Page and Petracca, *The American Presidency*, 268.

11. Todd Shields and Chi Huang, "Executive Vetoes: Testing Presidency Versus President Centered Perspectives of Presidential Behavior," *American Politics Quarterly* (October 1997): 431–32.

12. Quoted in Solberg, *The Federal Convention*, 91.

13. *Clinton* v. *City of New York*, 118 S.Ct. 2091 (1998).

14. Richard J. Newman, et al. "Making War from 15,000 ft." *U.S. News & World Report* (May 10, 1999): 32.

15. *Public Papers of the Presidents* (1963), 889.

16. Quoted in Richard E. Neustadt, *Presidential Power*, 9.

17. Quoted in Paul F. Boller Jr., *Presidential Anecdotes* (New York: Penguin Books, 1981), 78.

18. Abraham Lincoln, "Special Session Message," July 4, 1861, in Edward Keynes and David Adamany, eds., *Borzoi Reader in American Politics* (New York: Knopf, 1973), 539.

19. "The Stewardship Presidency," in James Pfiffner and Roger Davidson, *Understanding the Presidency* (Boston: Allyn and Bacon, 1995), 29–30.

20. "The Strict Constructionist Presidency," in Pfiffner and Davidson, *Understanding the Presidency*, 27–28.

21. Lyn Ragsdale and John Theis III, "The Institutionalization of the American Presidency, 1924–1992," *American Journal of Political Science* 41 (October 1997): 1280–1318.

22. Quoted in Page and Petracca, *The American Presidency*, 57.

23. Merlin Gustafson, "The President's Mail," *Presidential Studies Quarterly* 8 (1978): 36.

24. See Louis Fisher, *Constitutional Conflicts Between Congress and the President*, 4th ed. (Lawrence: University of Kansas Press, 1997).

25. Franklin D. Roosevelt, Press Conference, July 23, 1937.

26. See, generally, Richard Pious, *The American Presidency* (Boston: Allyn and Bacon, 1996), 213, 254, 255.

27. Lyndon B. Johnson, *The Vantage Point* (New York: Holt, Rinehart and Winston, 1971), 448.

28. Morris Fiorina, *Divided Government* (New York: Macmillan, 1992).

29. See Lance LeLoup and Steven Shull, *The President and Congress: Collaboration and Conflict in National Policymaking* (Boston: Allyn and Bacon, 1999).

30. See Cary Covington, J. Mark Wrighton, and Rhonda Kinney, "A 'Presidency-Augmented' Model of Presidential Success on House Roll Call Votes," *American Journal of Political Science* 39 (November 1995): 1001–24; and Wayne P. Steger, "Presidential Policy Initiation and the Politics of Agenda Control," *Congress & the Presidency* 24 (Spring 1997): 102–14.

31. Quoted in Thomas E. Cronin, *The State of the Presidency*, 2nd ed. (Boston: Little, Brown, 1980), 169.

32. "House Passes Bush's Budget and Tax Plan," *St. Louis Post-Dispatch*, March 29, 2001, A1.

33. Michael Waldman, "Bush's Presidential Power."

34. *Congressional Quarterly Weekly Report* (December 1, 1990): 4034.

35. Richard W. Stevenson, "Political Memo: Clinton Ending Term on a Busy Note," *The New York Times* (December 25, 2000): A27.

36. Thomas Cronin, *The State of the Presidency* (Boston: Little, Brown, 1975).

37. Paul C. Light, *The President's Agenda: Domestic Policy Choice from Kennedy to Carter* (Baltimore, Md.: Johns Hopkins University Press, 1983).

38. George Reedy, *The Twilight of the Presidency* (New York: New American Library), 38–9.

39. Samuel Kernell, *New Strategies of Presidential Leadership*, 2nd ed. (Washington, D.C.: CQ Press, 1993), 3.

40. Jeffrey Cohen, "Presidential Rhetoric and the Public Agenda," *American Journal of Political Science* 39 (February 1995): 87–107.

41. Reedy, *Twilight of the Presidency*, 33.

42. Neustadt, *Presidential Power*, 1–10.

43. Quoted in "Dear Abby," *Atlanta Journal and Constitution* (March 13, 1996): D11.

44. Michael Waldman, "Bush's Presidential Power."

45. Samuel Kernell, *Going Public: New Strategies of Presidential Leadership*, 3d ed. (Washington, D.C.: CQ Press, 1996).

46. Dan Balz, "Strange Bedfellows: How Television and Presidential Candidates Changed American Politics," *Washington Monthly* (July 1993).

47. William E. Gibson, "Job Approval Ratings Steady; Personal Credibility Takes a Hit," *News and Observer* (August 19, 1998): A16.

48. Michael R. Kagay, "History Suggests Bush's Popularity Will Ebb," *The New York Times* (May 22, 1991): A10.

49. See Kenneth Collier and Terry Sullivan, "New Evidence Undercutting the Linkage of Approval with Presidential Support and Influence," *Journal of Politics* 57 (February 1995): 197–209; and George C. Edwards III, "Aligning Tests with Theory: Presidential Approval as a Source of Influence in Congress," *Congress & the Presidency* 24 (Autumn 1997): 113–30.

50. *Woodhull & Clafin's Weekly* (April 22, 1871).

51. Carol Hymowitz and Michaele Weissman, *A History of Women in America* (New York: Bantam Books, 1978), 172.

52. Louis Filler, "Belva Lockwood," in Edward T. James, ed., *Notable American Women*, vol. 2 (Cambridge, Mass.: Harvard University Press, 1971), 413–16.

53. Nancy E. McGlen and Karen O'Connor, *Women, Politics, and American Society*, 2nd ed. (Upper Saddle River, NJ: Prentice Hall, 1998), 47–48.

54. Frank Newport, "Americans Today Much More Accepting of a Woman, Black, Catholic, or Jew as President," *Poll Releases*, Gallup Organization, March 29, 1999.

55. Newport, "Americans Today Much More Accepting of a Woman."

56. Gloria Negri, "Liswood's Goal: A Woman in the White House," *The Boston Globe* (May 2, 1999): *City Weekly*, 1.

9 The Executive Branch and the Federal Bureaucracy

From January through April of 2000, there was little that most Americans could do to avoid hearing about Elian Gonzalez. The story of a boy adrift in the ocean after his mother died attempting to flee Cuba pulled at the heartstrings of most Americans, regardless of whether or not they believed that he should be returned to his father or granted asylum in the United States and allowed to live with his relatives in Miami. While much of the action in this case took place in the courts as well as in the media, it was federal employees in the Immigration and Naturalization Services (INS), in consultation with Justice Department officials, who eventually made the decision to return Elian to his father, as well as to how they were to be reunited.

Federal bureaucrats made many of the important decisions in the Elian Gonzalez case and were charged with implementing directives from Attorney General Janet Reno, who presided over the Justice Department and its many branches, including one in Miami. Although many Americans often are critical of the federal government and those who work for it, even in the wake of the extraordinarily publicized armed raid on the Gonzales home and Elian's removal by INS officials, Americans overwhelmingly approved of the action. Neither did most Americans want members of Congress, who are charged with oversight of the executive branch, to launch into more hearings on the executive branch's handling of the entire Gonzalez matter. In fact, 68 percent of those polled opposed the proposed hearings.[1] Weary of the many highly partisan hearings over Whitewater, Travelgate, Filegate, Ruby Ridge, and Waco, many of them costing millions of dollars and leading to few concrete findings, the American public seemed sick of hearings and appeared to want Congress to let the executive branch get on with its function: executing the laws of the land and allowing bureaucrats to do their jobs. Still, it often seems as if every time the public rallies to support some action of the executive branch, some new revelation of misdoing appears as was the case with the FBI's failure to turn over thousands of pages of documents to Timothy McVeigh's lawyers.

bureaucracy
A set of complex hierarchical departments, agencies, commissions, and their staffs that exist to help a chief executive officer carry out his or her duty to enforce the law.

During the 2000 presidential race, George W. Bush painted Al Gore as a proponent of big federal government and federal programs, while he professed to want to devolve more power and money back to the states and the people. The bureaucracy is often called the "fourth branch of government" because of the tremendous power that agencies and bureaus can exercise, as was illustrated in the case of Elian Gonzalez. George W. Bush and many other Republicans charge that the **bureaucracy** the thousands of federal government agencies and institutions that implement and administer the laws and programs enacted by Congress or the president and the executive branch, is too large, too powerful, and too unaccountable to the people or even to elected officials. Often, many charge that the bureaucracy is too wasteful. Interestingly, few discuss the fact that laws and policies are also implemented by state and local bureaucracies and bureaucrats.

While many Americans are uncomfortable with the large role of the federal government in policy making, current studies show that most users of federal agencies rate the agencies and the services received quite favorably. Although many of those polled by the Pew Research Center as part of its efforts to assess America's often seemingly conflicting views about the federal government and its services were frustrated by complicated rules and the slowness of a particular agency, most gave most agencies overall high marks. Most of those polled drew sharp distinctions between particular agencies and the government as a whole, although the federal government, especially the executive branch, is largely composed of agencies, as we will discuss later in this chapter. For example, 84 percent of physicians and pharmacists rated the Food and Drug Administration favorably, while only one half were positive about the government.[2] Not surprisingly, the Internal Revenue Service got the lowest marks, but it even got a positive rating from 42 percent of the taxpayers surveyed. The survey also found that attitudes toward particular agencies were related to public support for their function. Thus, the public, which views clean air and water as a national priority, was much more likely to rate the Environmental Protection Agency highly. Since missions of the agencies aren't likely to change, most agencies are trying to improve their service to the public, and the public appears to be responding.

Harold D. Lasswell once defined political science as the "study of who gets what, when, and how."[3] It is by studying the bureaucracy that those questions can perhaps best be answered. To allow you to understand the role of the bureaucracy in the policy and governmental processes, this chapter explores the following issues:

- First, we will trace the *roots and development of the executive branch and the federal bureaucracy.*
- Second, we will examine the *modern bureaucracy* by discussing bureaucrats and the formal organization of the bureaucracy.
- Third, we will discuss *policy making,* including the role of rule making and adjudication.
- Fourth, we will analyze *how agencies are held accountable.*

THE ROOTS AND DEVELOPMENT OF THE EXECUTIVE BRANCH AND THE FEDERAL BUREAUCRACY

In the American system, the bureaucracy can be thought of as the part of the government that makes policy as it links together the three branches of the national government and the federal system. Although Congress makes the laws, it must rely on the executive branch and the bureaucracy to enforce them. Commissions such as the Equal Employment Opportunity Commission (EEOC) have the power not only to make rules, but also to settle disputes between parties concerning the enforcement and implementation of those rules. Often, agency determinations are challenged in the courts. Because most administrative agencies that make up part of the bureaucracy enjoy reputations for special expertise in clearly defined policy areas, the federal judiciary routinely defers to bureaucratic administrative decision makers.

German sociologist Max Weber believed bureaucracies were a rational way for complex societies to organize themselves. Model bureaucracies, said Weber, are characterized by certain features, including:

1. A chain of command in which authority flows from top to bottom.
2. A division of labor whereby work is apportioned among specialized workers to increase productivity.
3. A specification of authority where there are clear lines of authority among workers and their superiors.
4. A goal orientation that determines structure, authority, and rules.
5. Impersonality, whereby all employees are treated fairly based on merit and all clients are served equally, without discrimination, according to established rules.
6. Productivity, whereby all work and actions are evaluated according to established rules.[4]

Clearly, this Weberian idea is somewhat idealistic and even the best-run agencies don't always work this way, but most are trying.

In 2002, the executive branch had approximately 1.9 million civilian employees employed directly by the president or his advisers or in independent agencies or commissions. The Defense Department had an additional 723,000 employees, with most of those in the military. The Postal Service, which is a quasi-governmental corporation not part of the executive branch, has nearly 900,000 employees. In 1789, conditions were quite different. George Washington's bureaucracy consisted of only three departments, which had existed under the Articles of Confederation: State (called Foreign Affairs under the Articles of Confederation), War, and Treasury. Soon, the head of each department was called its *secretary*. To help the president with legal advice, Congress created the office of attorney general. The original status of the attorney general, however, was unclear—was he a member of the judicial or executive branch? That confusion was remedied in 1870 with the creation of the Justice Department as part of the executive branch, with the attorney general as its head. From the beginning, individuals appointed as Cabinet secretaries (as well as the attorney general) were subject to approval by the U.S. Senate but were removable by the president alone. Even the first Congress realized how important it was for a president to be surrounded by those in whom he had complete confidence and trust.

From 1816 to 1861, the size of the federal executive branch and the bureaucracy grew as increased demands were made on existing departments and new departments were created. The Post Office, for example, which Congress was constitutionally authorized to create in Article I, was forced to expand to meet the needs of a growing and westward-expanding population. In 1829, the Post Office was removed from the jurisdiction of the Treasury Department by Andrew Jackson, and the postmaster general was promoted to Cabinet rank, thereby giving him greater control over the separate office and its immense number of employees.

Longman
Participate.com 2.0
Timeline
Evolution of
the Federal
Bureaucracy

The Civil War

The Civil War (1861–1865) permanently changed the nature of the federal bureaucracy. As the nation geared up for war, thousands of additional employees were added to existing departments. The Civil War also spawned the need for new government agencies. A series of poor harvests and marketing problems led President Abraham Lincoln (who understood that one needs food in order to conduct a war) to create the Department of Agriculture in 1862, although it was not given full Cabinet-level status until 1889.

After the Civil War, the need for big government continued unabated. The Pension Office was established in 1866 to pay benefits to the thousands of Northern veterans who had fought in the war (more than 127,000 veterans were initially eligible for benefits). Justice was made a department in 1870, and other departments were added through 1900.

ANALYZING THE DATA

NUMBER OF FEDERAL EMPLOYEES IN THE EXECUTIVE BRANCH, 1900–2000

The federal government grew slowly until the 1930s, when Franklin D. Roosevelt's New Deal programs were created in response to the high unemployment and weak financial markets of the Great Depression. A more modest spike in the federal workforce occurred in the mid-1960s during Lyndon B. Johnson's Great Society program. Since that time, six executive branch departments have been created: Department of Housing and Urban Development (1965), Department of Transportation (1966), Department of Energy (1977), Depart-

ment of Education (1979) and Department of Health and Human Services (1979) (which were created out of the old Department of Health, Education and Welfare), and the Department of Veterans' Affairs (1989). Of all the federal departments, the Department of Defense is by far the largest, employing nearly 723,000 workers. In comparison, the smallest federal department—the Department of Education, until recently a branch frequently under fire by the Republican Congress—employs approximately 5,000 workers.

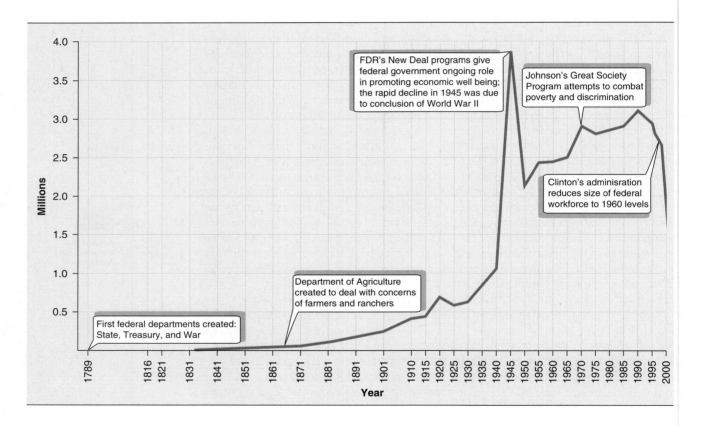

Sources: U.S. Department of Commerce, Bureau of the Census, *Historical Sate of U.S.: Colonial through 1970* (Washington, D.C.: Government Printing Office, 1975), U.S. Bureau of Labor Statistics, *Monthly Labor Review*, November 1988, and U.S. Office of Personnel Management, *The Fact Book*, http://www.opm.gov/feddata/factbook/html/fb-p08.html

patronage
Jobs, grants, or other special favors that are given as rewards to friends and political allies for their support.

Agriculture became a full-fledged department and began to play an important role in informing farmers about the latest developments in soil conservation, livestock breeding, and planting techniques. The increase in the types and nature of government services resulted in a parallel rise in the number of federal jobs, as illustrated in Analyzing the Data: Number of Federal Employees in the Executive Branch, 1900–2000. Many of the new jobs were used by the president or leaders of the president's political party for **patronage,** that is, jobs, grants, or other special favors given as rewards to friends and political allies for their support. Political patronage is often defended as an essential element of the party system because it provides rewards and inducements for party workers.

From Spoils to Merit

In 1831, describing a "rotation in office" policy for bureaucrats supported by President Andrew Jackson, Senator William Learned Marcy of New York commented, "To the victors belong the spoils." From his statement derives the phrase **spoils system** to describe the firing of public-office holders of the defeated political party and their replacement with loyalists of the new administration. Jackson, in particular, faced severe criticism for populating the federal government with his political cronies. But many presidents, including Jackson, argued that in order to implement their policies, they had to be able to appoint those who subscribed to their political views.

A political cartoonist's view of how President Andrew Jackson would be immortalized for his use of the spoils system. (Photo courtesy: Bettmann/Corbis)

spoils system
The firing of public-office holders of a defeated political party and their replacement with loyalists of the newly elected party.

The spoils system reached a high-water mark during Abraham Lincoln's presidency. By the time James A. Garfield, a former distinguished Civil War officer, was elected president in 1880, many reformers were calling publicly for changes in the patronage system. On his election to office, Garfield, like many presidents before him, was besieged by office seekers. Washington, D.C., had not seen such a demand for political jobs since Abraham Lincoln became the first president elected as a Republican. Garfield's immediate predecessor, Rutherford B. Hayes, had favored the idea of the replacement of the spoils system with a merit system based on test scores and ability. Congress, however, failed to pass the legislation he proposed. Possibly because potential job seekers wanted

An artist's interpretation of President Garfield's assassination at the hands of an unhappy office seeker. (Photo courtesy: Bettmann/Corbis)

to secure positions before Congress had the opportunity to act on an overhauled civil service system, thousands pressed Garfield for positions. This siege prompted Garfield to record in his diary: "My day is frittered away with the personal seeking of people when it ought to be given to the great problems which concern the whole country."[5] Garfield resolved to reform the civil service, but his life was cut short by the bullets of an assassin who, ironically, was a frustrated job seeker.

Public reaction to Garfield's death and increasing criticism of the spoils system prompted Congress to pass the Civil Service Reform Act in 1883, more commonly known as the **Pendleton Act,** named in honor of its sponsor, George H. Pendleton (D–Ohio). It established the principle of federal employment on the basis of open, competitive exams and created a bipartisan three-member Civil Service Commission, which operated until 1978. Initially, only about 10 percent of the positions in the federal **civil service system** were covered, but later laws and executive orders have extended coverage of the act to over 90 percent of all federal employees. This new system was called the **merit system,** one characteristic of Weber's model bureaucracy.

The civil service system as it has evolved today provides a powerful base for federal agencies and bureaucrats. Federal workers have tenure and the leverage of politicians is reduced. The good part is that the spoils system was reduced (but not eliminated). The bad part, however, is that federal agencies can and often do take on a life of their own making administrative law, passing judgments, and so on. With 90 percent of the federal workforce secure in their positions, some bureaucrats have been able to thwart reforms passed by legislators and wanted by the people. This often makes the bureaucracy the target of public criticism and citizen frustration.

National Efforts to Regulate the Economy

As the nation grew, so did the bureaucracy. In the wake of the tremendous growth of big business (especially railroads), widespread price fixing, and other unfair business practices that occurred after the Civil War, Congress created the Interstate Commerce Commission (ICC). It became the first **independent regulatory commission,** an agency outside of the major executive departments, generally concerned with particular aspects of the economy. Independent regulatory commissions such as the ICC are created by Congress to be independent of direct presidential authority. Commission members, although appointed by the president, hold their jobs for fixed terms and are not removable by the president unless they fail to uphold their oaths of office. In 1887 the creation of the ICC also marked a shift in the focus of the bureaucracy from service to regulation. Its creation gave the government—in the shape of the bureaucracy—vast powers over individual and property rights. In creating the ICC, Congress was reacting to public outcries over the exorbitant rates charged by railroad companies for hauling freight.

The 1900 election of Theodore Roosevelt, a progressive Republican, strengthened the movement toward governmental regulation of the economic sphere; the size of the bureaucracy was further increased when, in 1903, Roosevelt asked Congress to establish a Department of Commerce and Labor to oversee employer-employee relations. Roosevelt was motivated by the existence of intolerable labor practices, including low wages, long hours, substandard working conditions, the refusal of employers to recognize the rights of workers to join a union, and the fact that many businesses had grown so large and powerful that they could force workers to accept substandard conditions.

In 1913, President Woodrow Wilson divided the Department of Commerce and Labor and created a separate Department of Labor when it became clear that one agency could not well represent the interests of both employers and employees, factions with greatly differing perspectives. The creation of this department reflected the economic and societal changes that occurred as immigration increased and the economy became increasingly industrialized. One year later, in 1914, Congress created the Federal Trade Commission (FTC). Its function was to protect small businesses and the public from unfair competition, especially from big business. Bureaus within depart-

Pendleton Act
Reform measure that created the Civil Service Commission to administer a partial merit system. The act classified the federal service by grades, to which appointments were made based on the results of a competitive examination. It made it illegal for federal political appointees to be required to contribute to a particular political party.

civil service system
The system created by civil service laws by which many appointments to the federal bureaucracy are made.

merit system
The system by which federal civil service jobs are classified into grades or levels, to which appointments are made on the basis of performance on competitive examinations.

independent regulatory commission
An agency created by Congress that is generally concerned with a specific aspect of the economy.

ROOTS OF GOVERNMENT

MARY ANDERSON: THE FIRST HEAD OF THE FEDERAL WOMEN'S BUREAU

After pressure from women's groups, the Women in Industry Service, a wartime bureau originally established within the Department of Labor, was converted into a permanent Women's Bureau within the Labor Department by an act of Congress in 1920. Its first director was Mary Anderson, who migrated from Sweden with her younger sister to Michigan in the late 1880s in steerage. She soon moved to Chicago and found work in a variety of factories. In 1899, she was elected president of the woman stitchers, which was part of the International Boot and Shoe Workers Union.

After her years of union work, World War I brought a new role for Anderson when Samuel Gompers, labor's representative on the Advisory Commission on the U.S. Council of National Defense, appointed her to a subcommittee on women in industry. There she met Mary van Kleeck, who was chosen to head the women's branch in the Army's Ordnance Department; van Kleeck asked Anderson to join her staff. "Six months later, the Department of Labor set up a wartime bureau, the Women in Industry Service, with van Kleeck as director and Anderson as assistant director."* Later, when van Kleeck resigned, Anderson took her place. A few months later, when the Service was converted into a permanent Woman's Bureau, President Woodrow Wilson appointed her as director.

Under Anderson's directorship, the Women's Bureau began its long tradition of fact-finding and advocacy on behalf of women workers. During World War II, Anderson, relying on her World War I experiences, established governmental procedures to facilitate the influx of women workers into the defense industry and to enhance women's access to jobs and job training. She retired in 1944.

*Edward T. James, "Mary Anderson," in Barbara Sicherman and Carol Hurd Green, eds. *Notable American Women: The Modern Period* (Cambridge, Mass.: Harvard University Press, 1980), 23.

ments were also created to concentrate on a variety of issues including women in the workforce as discussed in Roots of Government: Mary Anderson.

The ratification of the Sixteenth Amendment to the Constitution in 1913 also affected the size of government and the possibilities for growth. It gave Congress the authority to implement a federal income tax to supplement the national treasury and provided an infusion of funds to support new federal agencies, services, and governmental programs.

WEB EXPLORATION
For more about the Women's Bureau in the Department of Labor, see
www.ablongman.com/oconnor

What Should Government Do?

During the early 1900s, while Progressives raised the public cry for governmental regulation of business, many Americans, especially members of the business community, continued to resist such moves. They believed that any federal government regulation was wrong. Instead they favored governmental facilitation of the national economy through a commitment to *laissez-faire,* a French term that means to leave alone. In America, the term was used to describe a governmental hands-off policy concerning the economy. This philosophical debate about the role of government in regulating the economy had major ramifications on the size of government and the bureaucracy. A *laissez-faire* attitude, for example, implied little need for the creation of new independent regulatory commissions or executive departments. In many ways, this philosophy guided the recent Republican Congress's efforts to downsize and deregulate the economy.

The New Deal and Bigger Government. In the wake of the high unemployment and weak financial markets of the Great Depression, Franklin D. Roosevelt planned to revitalize the economy by creating hundreds of new government agencies to regulate business practices and various aspects of the economy. Roosevelt proposed and the Congress

A political cartoonist satirizes President Roosevelt's criticisms of the Court's repeated rulings against the constitutionality of New Deal programs. (Photo courtesy: Richmont Times Dispatch)

enacted far-ranging economic legislation. The desperate mood of the nation supported these moves, as most Americans began to change their ideas about the proper role of government and the provision of governmental services. Formerly, Americans had believed in a hands-off approach; now they considered it the government's job to get the economy going and get Americans back to work.

Within the first hundred days of Roosevelt's administration, Congress approved every new regulatory measure proposed by the president. Other measures that Congress approved were the National Industrial Recovery Act (NIRA), an unprecedented attempt to regulate industry, and the Agricultural Adjustment Act (AAA), to provide government support for farm prices and to regulate farm production to ensure market-competitive prices. Congress also created the Federal Deposit Insurance Corporation (FDIC) to insure bank deposits, and it passed the Federal Securities Act, which gave the Federal Trade Commission the authority to supervise and regulate the issuance, buying, and selling of stocks and bonds.

Until 1937, the Supreme Court refused to allow Congress or the president to delegate to the executive branch or the bureaucracy such far-ranging authority to regulate the economy. *Laissez-faire* was alive and well at the Court, and attempts to end the economic slump through greater governmental involvement were repeatedly stymied by the justices. In a series of key decisions made through 1937, the Supreme Court repeatedly invalidated key provisions in congressional legislation designed to regulate various aspects of the economy. The Court and others who subscribed to *laissez-faire* principles of a free enterprise system argued that natural economic laws at work in the marketplace control the buying and selling of goods. Thus advocates of *laissez-faire* believed that the government had no right to regulate business in any way.

In response, FDR, frustrated by the decisions of the Court, proposed his famous Court-packing plan (see chapter 10), which would have allowed him to add appointees to the Court. In the wake of that institution-threatening proposal, the Court quickly fell into sync with public opinion. In a series of cases, the Supreme Court reversed a number of its earlier decisions and upheld what some have termed the "alphabetocracy." For example, the Court upheld the constitutionality of the National Labor Relations Act of 1935 (NLRA), which allowed recognition of unions and established formal arbitration procedures for employers and employees.[6] Subsequent decisions upheld the validity of the Fair Labor Standards Act (FLSA) and the Agricultural Adjustment Act (AAA).[7]

Once these new programs were declared constitutional, the proverbial floodgates were open to the creation of more governmental agencies. With the growth in the bureaucracy came more calls for reform of the system.

World War II and Its Aftermath.   During World War II, the federal government grew tremendously to meet the needs of a nation at war. Tax rates were increased to support the war, and they never again fell to prewar levels. After the war, this infusion of new monies and veterans' demands for services led to a variety of new programs and a much bigger government. The G.I. Bill, for example, provided college loans for returning veterans and reduced mortgage rates to allow them to buy homes. The national government's involvement in these programs not only affected more people but also led to its greater involvement in more regulation. Homes bought with Veterans' Housing Authority loans, for example, had to meet certain specifications. With these programs, Americans became increasingly accustomed to the national government's role in entirely new areas, such as middle-class housing.

After World War II, the civil rights movement and President Lyndon B. Johnson's War on Poverty produced additional growth in the bureaucracy. The Equal Employment Opportunity Commission (EEOC) was created in 1964, and the Departments of Housing and Urban Development (HUD) and Transportation were created in 1966. These expansions of the bureaucracy corresponded to increases in the president's power and his ability to persuade Congress that new agencies would be an effective way to solve pressing social problems. Remember from chapter 8 that most major expansions in the power of the presidency have occurred during times of war or economic emergency. Similarly, most of the important changes that have occurred in the size of the bureaucracy through the 1970s occurred in response to war, economic, or social crises.

THE MODERN BUREAUCRACY

Critics continually lament that the national government is not run like a business. But the national government differs from private business in ways too numerous to cover here adequately. Governments exist for the public good, not to make money. Businesses are driven by a profit motive; government leaders, but not bureaucrats, are driven by reelection. Businesses get their money from customers; the national government gets its money from taxpayers. Another difference between a bureaucracy and a business is that it is difficult to determine to whom bureaucracies are responsible. Is it the president? Congress? The citizenry? Still, governments can learn much from business and recent forms have tried to apply business solutions to create a government that works better and costs less.

These kinds of differences between government and business have a tremendous consequence on the way the bureaucracy operates. Because all of the incentive in government "is in the direction of not making mistakes," public employees view risks and rewards very differently than their private-sector counterparts.[8] The key to the modern bureaucracy is to understand how the bureaucracy is organized, who bureaucrats are, and how organization and personnel affect each other; but it is also key to understand that government cannot be run like a business. An understanding of these facts and factors can help in the search for ways to motivate positive change in the bureaucracy.

Who are the bureaucrats? Mulder and Scully, of Fox TV's *The X-Files*, a series about federal agents who investigate the paranormal, would be no one's idea of bureaucrats. But, as employees of the Federal Bureau of Investigation, that's exactly who they are supposed to be! (Photo courtesy: 20th Century Fox/Shooting Star)

Who Are Bureaucrats?

Federal bureaucrats are career government employees who work in the executive branch, in the fourteen Cabinet-level departments and the more than sixty independent agencies that comprise more than

FIGURE 9.1   Distribution of Federal Civilian Employment by Branch, July 2000

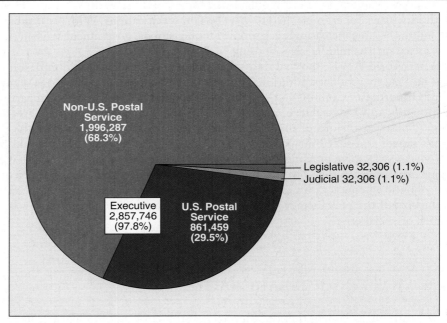

Note: The Department of Commerce employment rose by 184,745 employees (primarily temporary census enumerators) since December 1999.

2,000 bureaus, divisions, branches, offices, services, and other subunits of the federal government. There are approximately 1.9 million federal workers in the executive branch. Nearly one-third of all civilian employees work in the Postal Service as illustrated in Figure 9.1. The remaining federal civilian workers are spread out among the various executive departments and agencies throughout the United States. Most of these federal employees are paid according to what is called the "General Schedule" (GS). They advance within GS grades and onto higher GS levels and salaries as their careers progress.

As a result of reforms during the Truman administration that built on the Pendleton Act, most civilian federal governmental employees today are selected by merit standards, which include tests (such as civil service or foreign service exams) and educational criteria. Merit systems protect federal employees from being fired for political reasons. (For a description of how a federal employee can be fired, see Table 9.1.)

At the lower levels of the U.S. Civil Service, most positions are filled by competitive examinations. These usually involve a written test, although the same position in the private sector would not. Mid-level to upper ranges of federal positions don't normally require tests; instead, in the past, applicants had to fill out lengthy Form 171 job applications. Now, as a result of the Clinton administration's National Performance Review's call for the reduction of paperwork, they can simply submit a resume, or even apply by phone. Personnel departments then evaluate potential candidates and rank candidates according to how well they fit a particular job opening. Only the names of those deemed "qualified" are then forwarded to the official filling the vacancy. This can be a time-consuming process; it is not unusual for it to take six to nine months before a position can be filled in this manner.

The remaining 10 percent of the federal bureaucracy is made up of persons not covered by the civil service system. These positions generally fall into three categories:

1. Appointive policy-making positions. About 600 persons are appointed directly by the president. Some of these, including Cabinet secretaries, are subject to Senate confirmation. These appointees, in turn, are responsible for appointing the high-

WEB EXPLORATION
To examine the federal workforce by gender, race, and ethnicity, see
www.ablongman.com/oconnor

TABLE 9.1   How to Fire a Federal Bureaucrat

Firing a bureaucrat can be very difficult. Civil service rules make it easier to fire someone for misconduct than poor performance. Incompetent employees must be given notice by their supervisors and given an opportunity for remedial training.

To fire a member of the competitive civil service, explicit procedures must be followed:

1. At least thirty days' written notice must be given to an employee in advance of firing or demotion for incompetence or misconduct.

2. The written notification must contain a statement of reasons for the action and specific examples of unacceptable performance.

3. The employee has the right to reply both orally and in written form to the charges, and has the right to an attorney.

4. Appeals from any adverse action against the employee can be made to the three-person Merit Systems Protection Board (MSPB), a bipartisan body appointed by the president and confirmed by the Senate.

5. All employees have the right to a hearing and to an attorney in front of the MSPB.

6. All decisions of the MSPB may be appealed by the employee to the U.S. Court of Appeals.

level policy-making assistants who form the top of the bureaucratic hierarchy. These appointees are an exception to Weber's call for promotion by merit.

2. Independent regulatory commissioners. Although each president gets to appoint as many as one hundred commissioners, they become independent of his direct political influence once they take office.

3. Low-level, nonpolicy patronage positions. At one time, the U.S. Post Office was the largest source of these government jobs. In 1971, Congress reorganized the Post Office and removed positions such as local postmaster from the political patronage/rewards pool. Since then, these types of positions generally refer to secretarial assistants to policy makers.

Federal employees are stereotyped as "paper pushers," but more than 15,000 job skills are represented in the federal government, and its workers are perhaps the best trained and most skilled and efficient in the world. Government employees, whose average age is 45.9 years, with an average length of service at 16.9 years, include forest rangers, FBI agents, foreign service officers, computer programmers, security guards, librarians, administrators, engineers, plumbers, lawyers, doctors, postal carriers, and zoologists, among others. The diversity of government jobs mirrors the diversity of jobs in the private sector. The federal workforce, itself, is also diverse. As revealed in Figure 9.2, the federal workforce largely reflects the racial and ethnic composition of the United States as a whole, although the employment of women lags behind that of men. Women also appear to hit the same glass ceiling in the federal workforce that they find in the private sector. Not only do women make up over 70 percent of the lowest GS levels, but less than 25 percent of the positions at the highest levels of the federal General Service are held by women.

Only about 330,000 federal bureaucrats work in the nation's capital; the rest are located in regional, state, and local offices scattered throughout the country. The decentralization of the bureaucracy facilitates accessibility to the public. The Social Security Administration, for example, has numerous offices so that its clients may have a place nearby to take their paperwork, questions, and problems. Decentralization also helps distribute jobs and incomes across the country.

Many Americans believe that the federal bureaucracy is growing bigger each year, but they are wrong. Efforts to reduce the federal workforce have had an effect. Although it is true that the number of total government employees has been increasing until lately, most growth has taken place at the state and local levels. And, as more federal programs

Longman
Participate.com
2.0
Participation
Who Wants to
Be a
Bureaucrat?

FIGURE 9.2   Characteristics and Rank Distribution of Federal CivilianEmployees, 2000

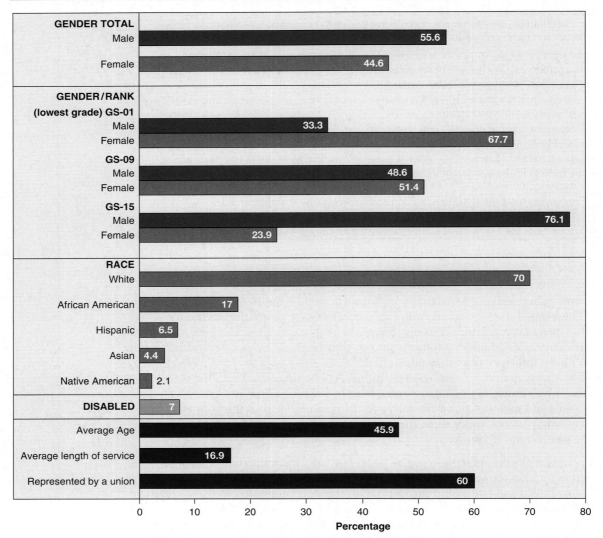

Source: "Government at Work," *Washington Post* (September 4, 2000): A23; and Demographic Profile of the Federal Work Force; Office of Workforce Information, n.d.

are shifted back to the states, the size of state payrolls and state bureaucracies are likely to rise to reflect these new responsibilities.

Formal Organization

While even experts can't agree on the exact number of separate governmental agencies, commissions, and departments that make up the federal bureaucracy, there are at least 1,149 civilian agencies.[9] A distinctive feature of the executive bureaucracy is its traditional division into areas of specialization. For example, one agency, the Occupational Safety and Health Administration, handles occupational safety, the Department of Education specializes in education, the State Department in foreign affairs, the Environmental Protection Agency in the environment, and so on. It is not unusual, however, for more than one agency to be involved in a particular issue or for one agency to be involved in myriad issues. In fact, numerous agencies often have authority in the same issue areas, making administration even more difficult. Agencies fall into four general types: (1) Cabinet departments, (2) government corporations, (3) independent agencies, and (4) regulatory commissions.

The Cabinet Departments. The fourteen Cabinet **departments** are major administrative units that have responsibility for conducting a broad area of government operations. Cabinet departments account for about 60 percent of the federal workforce.

As depicted in Figure 9.3, executive branch departments are headed by Cabinet members called secretaries (except the Justice Department, which is headed by the attorney general). The secretaries are responsible for establishing their department's general policy and overseeing its operations. As discussed in chapter 8, Cabinet secretaries are directly responsible to the president, but are often viewed as having two masters—the president and those affected by their department. Cabinet secretaries are also tied to Congress, from which they get their appropriations and the discretion to implement legislation and make rules and policy.

Although departments vary considerably in size, prestige, and power, they share certain features. Each department covers a broad area of responsibility generally reflected by its name. Each secretary is assisted by a deputy or undersecretary to take part of the administrative burden off the secretary's shoulders, as well as by several assistant secretaries, who direct major programs within the department. In addition, each secretary, like the president, has numerous assistants who help with planning, budgeting, personnel, legal services, public relations, and other key staff functions. Most departments are subdivided into bureaus, divisions, sections, or other smaller units, and it is at this level that the real work of each agency is done. Most departments are subdivided along functional lines, but the basis for division may be geography, work processes (for example, the Economic Research Service in the Department of Agriculture), or clientele (such as the Bureau of Indian Affairs in the Department of the Interior). In addition to national offices in Washington, D.C., or its immediate suburbs, each executive department has regional offices to serve all parts of the United States.

Departmental status generally signifies a strong permanent national interest to promote a particular function. Moreover, departments are organized to foster and promote the interests of a given clientele—that is, a specific social or economic group. Such departments are called **clientele agencies.** The Departments of Agriculture, Education, Energy, Labor, and Veterans' Affairs and the Bureau of Indian Affairs in the Department of the Interior are examples of clientele agencies/bureaus.

Because many of these agencies were created at the urging of well-organized interests to advance their particular objectives, it is not surprising that clientele groups are powerful lobbies with their respective agencies in Washington. The clientele agencies and groups are also active at the regional level, where the agencies devote a substantial part of their resources to program implementation. One of the most obvious examples of regional "outreach" is the Extension Service of the Department of Agriculture. Agricultural extension agents are scattered throughout the farm belt and routinely work with farmers on farm productivity and other problems. Career bureaucrats in the Agriculture Department know that farm interests will be dependable allies year in and year out. Congress and the president are not nearly so reliable, because they must balance the interests of farmers with those of other segments of society.

Government Corporations. **Government corporations** are the most recent addition to the bureaucratic maze. Dating from the early 1930s, they are businesses set up and created by Congress to perform functions that could be provided by private businesses. The corporations are formed when the government chooses to engage in activities that are primarily commercial in nature, produce revenue, and require greater flexibility than Congress generally allows regular departments. Some of the better-known government corporations include Amtrak and the Federal Deposit Insurance Corporation. Unlike

department
A major administrative unit with responsibility for a broad area of government operations. Departmental status usually indicates a permanent national interest in that particular governmental function, such as defense, health, or agriculture.

clientele agency
Executive department directed by law to foster and promote the interests of a specific segment or group in the U.S. population (such as the Department of Education).

government corporation
Business set up and created by Congress that performs functions that could be provided by private businesses (such as the U.S. Postal Service).

FIGURE 9.3   Department of the Executive Branch

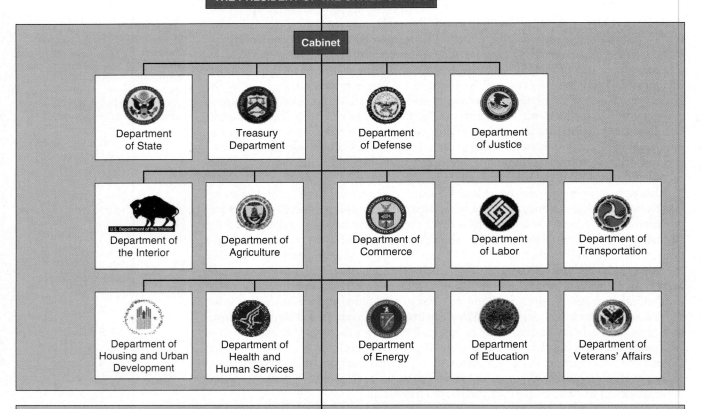

THE PRESIDENT OF THE UNITED STATES

Cabinet

Department of State

Treasury Department

Department of Defense

Department of Justice

Department of the Interior

Department of Agriculture

Department of Commerce

Department of Labor

Department of Transportation

Department of Housing and Urban Development

Department of Health and Human Services

Department of Energy

Department of Education

Department of Veterans' Affairs

Independent Establishments and Government Corporations

Advisory Council on Historic Preservation
African Development Foundation
Broadcasting Board of Governors
Central Intelligence Agency
Civil Air Patrol Great Lakes Region
Commission on Civil Rights
Commodity Futures Trading Commission
Consumer Product Safety Commission
Corporation for National Service
Defense Nuclear Facilities Safety Board
Environmental Protection Agency
Equal Employment Opportunity Commission
Export-Import Bank of the U.S.
Farm Credit Administration
Federal Communications Commission
Federal Deposit Insurance Corporation
Federal Election Commission
Federal Emergency Management Agency
Federal Housing Finance Board
Federal Labor Relations Authority

Federal Maritime Commission
Federal Mediation and Conciliation Service
Federal Mine Safety and Health Review Commission
Federal Reserve System
Federal Retirement Thrift Investment Board
Federal Trade Commission
General Services Administration
Inter-American Foundation
International Broadcasting Bureau
Merit Systems Protection Board
National Aeronautics and Space Administration
National Archives and Records Administration
National Capital Planning Commission
National Credit Union Administration
National Foundation of the Arts and the Humanities
National Labor Relations Board
National Mediation Board
National Performance Review
National Railroad Passenger Corporation (Amtrak)
National Science Foundation

National Transportation Safety Board
Nuclear Regulatory Commission
Occupational Safety and Health Review Commission
Office of Government Ethics
Office of Personnel Management
Office of Special Counsel
Overseas Private Investment Corporation
Peace Corps
Pension Benefit Guaranty Corporation
Postal Rate Commission
Railroad Retirement Board
Securites and Exchange Commission
Selective Service System
Small Business Administration
Social Security Administration
Tennesse Valley Authority
Trade Development Agency
U.S. Chemical Safety and Hazard Investigation Board
U.S. International Development Corporation Agency
U.S. International Trade Commission
U.S. Postal Service

Source: U.S. Government Agencies Directory. http://www.lib.lsu.edu/gov/fedgov.html
*As we went to press.

other governmental agencies, government corporations charge for their services. For example, the largest government corporation, the U.S. Postal Service—whose functions could be handled by a private corporation, such as Federal Express or the United Parcel Service (UPS)—exists today to ensure delivery of mail throughout the United States at cheaper rates than those a private business might charge. Similarly, the Tennessee Valley Authority (TVA) provides electricity at reduced rates to millions of Americans in the Appalachian region of the Southeast, generally a low-income area that had failed to attract private utility companies to provide service there.

In cases like that of the TVA, where the financial incentives for private industry to provide services are minimal, Congress often believes that it must act. In other cases, it steps in to salvage valuable public assets. For example, when passenger rail service in the United States no longer remained profitable, Congress stepped in to create Amtrak and thus nationalized the passenger-train industry to keep passenger trains running.

Independent Executive Agencies.   **Independent executive agencies** closely resemble Cabinet departments but have narrower areas of responsibility. Generally speaking, independent agencies perform service rather than regulatory functions. Many of these agencies are tied to the president and Congress as closely as executive departments because the heads of these agencies are appointed by the president and serve, like Cabinet secretaries, at his pleasure.

Independent agencies exist apart from executive departments for practical or symbolic reasons. The National Aeronautics and Space Administration (NASA), for example, could have been placed within the Department of Defense. That, however, could have conjured up thoughts of a space program dedicated solely to military purposes, rather than for civilian satellite communication or scientific exploration. Similarly, the Environmental Protection Agency (EPA) was created in 1970 to administer federal programs aimed at controlling pollution and protecting the nation's environment. It administers all congressional laws concerning the environment and pollution. Along with the Council on Environmental Quality, a staff agency in the Executive Office of the President, the EPA advises the president on environmental concerns. It also administers programs transferred to it along with personnel from the Departments of Agriculture, Energy, Interior, and Health and Human Services, as well as the Nuclear Regulatory Commission, among others. The expanding national focus on the environment, in fact, has brought about numerous calls to elevate the EPA to Cabinet-level status to reinforce a long-term national commitment to improved air and water and other environmental issues.

independent executive agency
Governmental unit that closely resembles Cabinet departments but has a narrower area of responsibility (such as the Central Intelligence Agency) and is not part of any Cabinet departments.

Independent Regulatory Commissions.   Independent regulatory commissions are agencies that were created by Congress to exist outside of the major departments to regulate a specific economic activity or interest. Because of the complexity of modern economic issues, Congress sought to create agencies that could develop expertise and provide continuity of policy with respect to economic issues because neither Congress nor the courts have the time or talent to do so. Examples include the National Labor Relations Board, the Federal Reserve Board, the Federal Communications Commission, and the Securities and Exchange Commission (SEC).[10] Congress started setting up regulatory commissions as early as 1887, recognizing the need for close and continuous guardianship of particular economic activities. Older boards and commissions, such as the Securities and Exchange Commission and the Federal Reserve Board, are generally charged with overseeing a certain industry. Regulatory agencies created since the 1960s are more concerned with how the business sector relates to public health and safety. The Occupational Safety and Health Administration (OSHA) promotes job safety.

Most of the older independent agencies were specifically created to be relatively free from immediate (partisan) political pressure. Each is headed by a board composed of five to seven members (always an odd number, to avoid tie votes) who are selected by the president and confirmed by the Senate for fixed, staggered terms to increase the chances of a bipartisan board. Unlike executive department heads, they cannot be easily removed by the president. In 1935, the U.S. Supreme Court ruled that in creating independent commissions, the Congress had intended that they be independent panels of experts as far removed as possible from immediate political pressures.[11]

Newer regulatory boards lack this kind of autonomy and freedom from political pressures; they are generally headed by a single administrator who can be removed by the president. These boards and commissions, such as the EEOC, are therefore far more susceptible to political pressure and the political wishes of the president who appoints them.

Politics and Government Workers

As an increasing proportion of the American workforce came to work for the U.S. government as a result of the New Deal recovery programs, many began to fear that the members of the civil service would play major roles not only in implementing public policy but also in electing members of Congress and even the president. Consequently, Congress enacted the Political Activities Act of 1939, commonly known as the **Hatch Act,** which was designed to prohibit federal employees from becoming directly involved in working for political candidates.

Although presidents as far back as Thomas Jefferson had advocated efforts to limit the opportunities for federal civil servants to influence the votes of others, over the years many criticized the Hatch Act as too extreme. Critics argued that it denied millions of federal employees the First Amendment guarantees of freedom of speech and association and discouraged political participation among a group of people who might otherwise be strong political activists. Critics also argued that civil servants *should* become more involved in campaigns, particularly at the state and local level, in order to understand better the needs of the citizens they serve.

In response to criticisms of the Hatch Act and at the urgings of President Bill Clinton, in 1993 Congress enacted the **Federal Employees Political Activities Act.** This liberalization of the Hatch Act among other things allows employees to run for public office in nonpartisan elections, contribute money to political organizations, and campaign for or against candidates in partisan elections. They still, however, are prohibited from engaging in political activity while on duty, soliciting contributions from the general public, or running for office in partisan elections. During the signing ceremony, Clinton said the law will "mean more responsive, more satisfied, happier, and more productive federal employees."[12] See Table 9.2 for more specifics about this law.

Hatch Act
Laws enacted in 1939 to prohibit civil servants from taking activist roles in partisan campaigns. This act prohibited federal employees from making political contributions, working for a particular party, or campaigning for a particular candidate.

Federal Employees Political Activities Act
1993 liberalization of the Hatch Act. Federal employees are now allowed to run for office in nonpartisan elections and to contribute money to campaigns in partisan elections.

TABLE 9.2   The Liberalized Hatch Act

Here are some examples of permissible and prohibited activities for federal employees under the Hatch Act, as modified by the Federal Employees Political Activities Act of 1993.

Federal employees

- **May** be candidates for public office in nonpartisan elections
- **May** assist in voter registration drives
- **May** express opinions about candidates and issues
- **May** contribute money to political organizations
- **May** attend political fund-raising functions
- **May** attend and be active at political rallies and meetings
- **May** join and be active members of a political party or club
- **May** sign nominating petitions
- **May** campaign for or against referendum questions, constitutional amendments, and municipal ordinances
- **May** campaign for or against candidates in partisan elections
- **May** make campaign speeches for candidates in partisan elections
- **May** distribute campaign literature in partisan elections
- **May** hold office in political clubs or parties

- **May not** use their official authority or influence to interfere with an election
- **May not** collect political contributions unless both individuals are members of the same federal labor organization or employee organization and the one solicited is not a subordinate employee
- **May not** knowingly solicit or discourage the political activity of any person who has business before the agency
- **May not** engage in political activity while on duty
- **May not** engage in political activity in any government office
- **May not** engage in political activity while wearing an official uniform
- **May not** engage in political activity while using a government vehicle
- **May not** solicit political contributions from the general public
- **May not** be candidates for public office in partisan elections

Source: U.S. Special Counsel's Office.

POLICY MAKING

One of the major functions of the bureaucracy is policy making—and bureaucrats can be, and often are, major policy makers.[13] When Congress creates any kind of department, agency, or commission, it is actually delegating some of its powers listed in Article I, section 8, of the U.S. Constitution. Therefore the laws creating departments, agencies, corporations, or commissions carefully describe their purpose and give them the authority to make numerous policy decisions, which have the effect of law. Congress recognizes that it does not have the time, expertise, or ability to involve itself in every detail of every program; therefore, it sets general guidelines for agency action and leaves it to the agency to work out the details. How agencies execute congressional wishes is called **implementation,** the process by which a law or policy is put into operation. Much of the policy-making process occurs in the form of what some call iron triangles or issue networks.

implementation
The process by which a law or policy is put into operation by the bureaucracy.

Iron Triangles and Issue Networks

The relatively stable relationships and patterns of interaction that occur among an agency, interest groups, and congressional committees or subcommittees as policy is made are often referred to as **iron triangles,** or subgovernments (see Figure 9.4).

Policy-making subgovernments are "iron" because they are virtually impenetrable to outsiders and are largely autonomous. Even presidents have difficulty piercing the workings of these subgovernments, which have endured over time. Examples of iron triangles abound. Senior citizens' groups (especially the American Association of Retired Persons), the Social Security Administration, and the House Subcommittee on Aging all are likely to agree on the need for increased Social Security benefits. Similarly, the Department of Veterans' Affairs, the House Committee on Veterans' Affairs, and the American Legion and Veterans' of Foreign Wars—the two largest organizations representing veterans—usually agree on the need for expanded programs for veterans.

The policy decisions made within these iron triangles often foster the interests of a clientele group and have little to do with the advancement of national policy goals.

iron triangle
The relatively stable relationship and pattern of interaction that occur among an agency, interest groups, and congressional committees or subcommittees.

FIGURE 9.4   An Iron Triangle

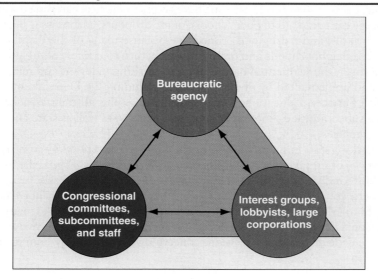

Senator John McCain (R–Ariz.) addresses a veterans group. The son and grandson of Navy admirals, McCain was shot down over Vietnam and held as a prisoner of war for five years. (Photo courtesy: M. Spencer Green/AP/Wide World Photos)

In part, subgovernmental decisions often conflict with other governmental policies and tend to tie the hands of larger institutions such as Congress and the president. The White House is often too busy dealing with international affairs or crises to deal with smaller issues like veterans' benefits. Likewise, Congress defers to its committees and subcommittees. Thus, these subgovernments decentralize policy making and make policy making difficult to control.[14]

Today, iron triangles no longer dominate most policy processes for three main reasons: an increasingly complex society, issues that cut across several policy areas, and the phenomenal increase in the number of Washington, D.C.–based interest groups. As these three changes have occurred, many iron triangles have become rusty, and new terms have been coined to describe the policy-making process and the bureaucracy's role in it. Hugh Heclo argues that this system of separate subgovernments is overlaid with an amorphous system of **issue networks,** that is, the fuzzy set of relationships among a large number of actors in broad policy areas.[15] In general, like iron triangles, issue networks are made up of agency officials, members of Congress (and committee staffers), and interest group lobbyists. But they also often include lawyers, consultants, academics, public relations specialists, and sometimes even the courts.[16] Unlike iron triangles, issue networks are constantly changing as members with technical expertise become involved in various issues.

issue network
The loose and informal relationships that exist among a large number of actors who work in broad policy areas.

Issue networks reflect the complexity of the issues that lawmakers and policy makers face. As an example, let's look at the plight of many American children. All kinds of complex and interrelated issues are involved. Improving their lives is, for example, a health issue, because many children don't have access to medical care; an education issue because many can't read, go to poor schools, or are dropouts; a labor issue because many have no job skills; and a drug and crime issue because many of these children live in drug-infested neighborhoods and often ultimately turn to crime, ending up in jail as a result. But given the segmented nature of policy making, relevant and related policies are made and implemented by myriad agencies, including the Departments of Health and Human Services, Education, Labor, and Justice—plus all their associated House and Senate subcommittees, interest groups, and experts, as well as state and local governmental agencies.

Policy making and implementation of the kind characterized by iron triangles or issue networks often take place on informal and formal levels. Practically, many decisions are left to individual government employees on a day-to-day basis. Justice Department lawyers, for example, make daily decisions about whether or not to prosecute someone. Similarly, street-level Internal Revenue Service agents make many decisions during personal audits. These street-level bureaucrats make policy on two levels. First, they exercise wide discretion in decisions concerning citizens with whom they interact.

Second, taken together, their individual actions add up to agency behavior.[17] Thus, how bureaucrats interpret and apply (or choose not to apply) various policies are equally important parts of the policy-making process. Administrative discretion allows decision makers (whether they are in a Cabinet-level position or at the lowest GS levels) a tremendous amount of leeway.

Administrative Discretion

Essentially, bureaucrats make as well as implement policy. They take the laws and policies made by Congress, the president, and the courts, and develop rules and procedures for making sure they are carried out. Most implementation involves what is called **administrative discretion,** the ability to make choices concerning the best way to implement congressional intentions. Administrative discretion is also exercised through two formal administrative procedures: rule making and administrative adjudication. This process is illustrated in Highlight: Enforcing Gender Equity in College Athletics.

Rule Making.   **Rule making** is a quasi-legislative administrative process that results in regulations and has the characteristics of a legislative act. **Regulations** are the rules that govern the operation of all government programs and have the force of law. In essence, then, bureaucratic rule makers often act as lawmakers as well as law enforcers when they make rules or draft regulations to implement various congressional statutes. Thus rule making is called a quasi-legislative process, and the process is illustrated in Figure 9.5. Some political scientists say that "[R]ulemaking is the single most important function performed by agencies of government."[18]

Because regulations often involve political conflict, the 1946 Administrative Procedure Act established rule-making procedures to give everyone the chance to participate in the process. The act requires that (1) public notice of the time, place, and nature of the rule-making proceedings be provided in the *Federal Register;* (2) interested parties be given the opportunity to submit written arguments and facts relevant to the rule; and (3) the statutory purpose and basis of the rule be stated. Once rules have been written, thirty days must generally elapse before they take effect.

Sometimes an agency is required by law to conduct a formal hearing before issuing rules. Evidence is gathered, and witnesses testify and are cross-examined by opposing interests. The process can take weeks, months, or even years, at the end of which agency administrators must review the entire record and then justify the new rules. Although cumbersome, the process has reduced criticism of some rules and bolstered the deference given by the courts to agency decisions.

Administrative Adjudication.   **Administrative adjudication** is a quasi-judicial process in which a bureaucratic agency settles disputes between two parties in a manner similar to the way courts resolve disputes. Administrative adjudication, like rule making, is referred to as "quasi" (Latin for "seemingly") judicial, because lawmaking by any body other than Congress or adjudication by any body other than the judiciary would be a violation of the constitutional principle of separation of powers.

Agencies regularly find that persons or businesses are not in compliance with the federal laws the agencies are charged with enforcing, or that they are in violation of an agency rule or regulation. To force compliance, some agencies resort to administrative adjudication, which is generally less formal than a trial. Several agencies and boards employ administrative law judges to conduct the hearings. Although these judges are employed by the agency, they are strictly independent and cannot be removed except for gross misconduct. Congress, for example, empowers the Federal Trade Commission (FTC) to determine what constitutes an unfair trade practice.[19] Its actions, however, are reviewable in the federal courts.

administrative discretion
The ability of bureaucrats to make choices concerning the best way to implement congressional intentions.

rule making
A quasi-legislative administrative process that has the characteristics of a legislative act.

regulation
Rule that governs the operation of a particular government program and has the force of law.

administrative adjudication
A quasi-judicial process in which a bureaucratic agency settles disputes between two parties in a manner similar to the way courts resolve disputes.

WEB EXPLORATION
To see federal agency rules and regulations contained in the *Federal Register,* see
www.ablongman.com/oconnor

FIGURE 9.5 How a Regulation Is Made

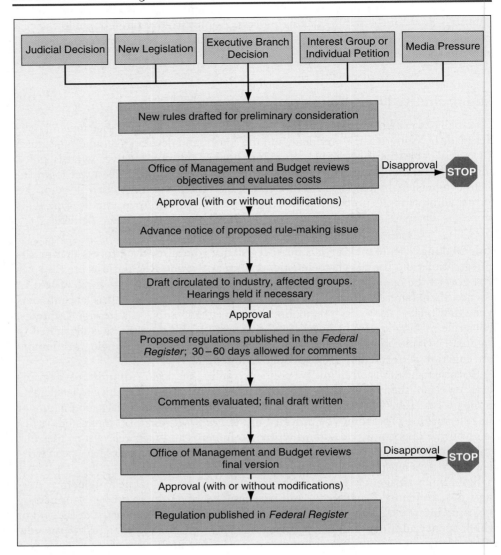

MAKING AGENCIES ACCOUNTABLE

The question of to whom bureaucrats should be responsible is one that continually comes up in any debate about governmental accountability. Should the bureaucracy be answerable to itself? To organized interest groups? To its clientele? To the president? To Congress? Or to some combination of all of these? As illustrated in *Politics Now: Can I Help You? It All Depends on Whether Congress Allocates Enough Money*, at times an agency becomes so removed from the public it serves that Congress must step in. While many would argue that bureaucrats should be responsive to the public interest, the public interest is difficult to define. As it turns out, several factors work to control the power of the bureaucracy, and, to some degree, the same kinds of checks and balances that operate among the three branches of government serve to check the bureaucracy (Table 9.3).

Longman
Participate.com
2.0
Simulation
**You Are a
Federal
Administrator**

HIGHLIGHT

ENFORCING GENDER EQUITY IN COLLEGE ATHLETICS

In 2000, there were approximately 148,802 female student-athletes,[a] a number up dramatically from 1971 when there were only 31,352 women participating in collegiate athletics.[b] A major source of that difference? The passage in 1972 of legislation popularly known as Title IX, which prohibits discrimination against girls and women in federally funded education, including athletics programs. This legislation mandates that "No person in the United States shall, on the basis of sex, be excluded from participation in, be denied the benefits of, or be subjected to discrimination under any education program or activity receiving federal financial assistance." It wasn't until December 1978—six years after passage of the Education Amendments—that the Office for Civil Rights in the Department of Health, Education and Welfare released a "policy interpretation" of the law, dealing largely with the section that concerned intercollegiate athletics.[c] More than thirty pages of text were devoted to dealing with a hundred or so words from the statute. Football was recognized as unique, because of the huge revenues it produces, so it could be inferred that male-dominated football programs could continue to outspend women's athletic programs. The more than sixty women's groups that had lobbied for equality of spending were outraged and turned their efforts toward seeking more favorable rulings on the construction of the statute from the courts.

Increased emphasis on Title IX enforcement has led many women to file lawsuits to force compliance. In 1991, in an effort to trim expenses, Brown University cut two men's and two women's teams from its varsity rosters. Several women on the downgraded gymnastics team filed a Title IX complaint against the school, arguing that it violated the act by not providing women varsity sport opportunities in relation to their population in the university. The women also argued that cutting the two women's program saved $62,000, whereas the men's cuts saved only $16,000. Thus the women's varsity programs took a bigger hit, in violation of federal law.

A U.S. district court refused to allow Brown to cut the women's programs. A U.S. court of appeals upheld that action, concluding that Brown had failed to provide adequate opportunities for its female students to participate in athletics.[d] In 1997, in *Brown University v. Cohen,* the U.S. Supreme Court declined to review the appeals court's decision.[e] This put all colleges and universities on notice that discrimination against women would not be tolerated, even when, as in the case of Brown University, the university had, since the passage of Title IX, tremendously expanded sports opportunities for women.

Women have made significant strides on all college campuses, but true equity in athletics is still a long way away at many colleges and universities. Since 1972, for every new dollar allocated to men's sports, women's teams have received but one dollar. While the number of women participating in college level sports is increasing, the proportion of women coaches is decreasing (at the same time the pool of women who could be coaches is increasing). Most colleges still provide far fewer opportunities to women given their numbers in most universities, and enforcement still lags. This has required groups including the National Women's Law Center to take the lead in the *Brown* case and to devote millions of dollars in legal fees to fuller enforcement.[f] Title IX is not self-enforcing. Individual colleges and universities must comply with the law, aggrieved students must complain of inequities, and the Department of Education's Office of Civil Rights must enforce the law.

[a] NCAA Homepage: http://www.ncaa.org.
[b] *Intercollegiate Athletics: Status of Efforts to Promote Gender Equity,* U.S. General Accounting Office, October 25, 1996.
[c] See Joyce Gelb and Marian Lief Palley, *Women and Public Policies* (Charlottesville: University of Virginia Press, 1996), ch. 5.
[d] *Cohen* v. *Brown University,* 101 F.3d 155 (1996).
[e] 117 S.Ct. 1469 (1997).
[f] http://www.edc.org/WomensEquity/resource/title9/report/athletic.html.

Many argue that the president should be in charge of the bureaucracy because it is up to him to see that popular ideas and expectations are translated into administrative action. But under our constitutional system, the president is not the only actor in the policy process. Congress creates the agencies, funds them, and establishes the broad rules of their operation. Moreover, Congress continually reviews the various agencies

TABLE 9.3   Making Agencies Accountable

The president has the authority to:
- Appoint and remove agency heads and a few additional top bureaucrats.
- Reorganize the bureaucracy (with congressional approval).
- Make changes in an agency's annual budget proposals.
- Ignore legislative initiatives originating within the bureaucracy.
- Initiate or adjust policies that would, if enacted by Congress, alter the bureaucracy's activities.
- Issue executive orders.
- Reduce an agency's annual budget.

Congress has the authority to:
- Pass legislation that alters the bureaucracy's activities.
- Abolish existing programs.
- Investigate bureaucratic activities and compel bureaucrats to testify about them.
- Influence presidential appointments of agency heads and other top bureaucratic officials.
- Write legislation to limit the bureaucracy's discretion.

The judiciary has the authority to:
- Rule on whether bureaucrats have acted within the law and require policy changes to comply with the law.
- Force the bureaucracy to respect the rights of individuals through hearings and other proceedings.
- Rule on the constitutionality of all rules and regulations.

through oversight committee investigations, hearings, and its power of the purse. And the federal judiciary, as in most other matters, has the ultimate authority to review administrative actions.

Executive Control

As the size and scope of the American national government in general, and of the executive branch and the bureaucracy in particular, have grown, presidents have delegated more and more power to bureaucrats. But most presidents have continued to try to exercise some control over the bureaucracy, although they have often found that task more difficult than they first envisioned. John F. Kennedy, for example, once lamented that to give anyone at the State Department an instruction was comparable to putting your request in a dead-letter box.[20] No response would ever be forthcoming.

Recognizing these potential problems, each president tries to appoint the best possible persons to carry out his wishes and policy preferences. Presidents may make thousands of appointments to the executive branch; in doing so, they have the opportunity to appoint individuals who share their views on a range of policies. Although presidential appointments make up less than 1 percent of all federal jobs, presidents usually fill most top policy-making positions.

Presidents can, with the approval of Congress, reorganize the bureaucracy. They can also make changes in an agency's annual budget requests and ignore legislative initiatives originating within the bureaucracy. Several presidents have made it a priority to try to tame the bureaucracy to make it more accountable. Thomas Jefferson was the first president to address the issue of accountability. He attempted to cut waste and bring about a "wise and frugal government." But it wasn't until the Progressive Era

POLITICS NOW

CAN I HELP YOU? IT DEPENDS ON WHETHER CONGRESS ALLOCATES ENOUGH MONEY

There are few letters that most Americans shudder to open: A letter from the Internal Revenue Service pointing to some problem with a recent tax return is one of them. Until recently, the cause for that nervousness was not necessarily unfounded. Throughout 1997 and 1998, Congress held extensive hearings about abuses at the Internal Revenue Service (IRS), one of the most hated and feared federal agencies in America. Senate hearings in particular exposed abuses of ordinary citizens who found themselves in a nightmare of bureaucratic red tape and agency employee abuse of power. As a result of these hearings, Congress ordered the new IRS Commissioner to overhaul the way the IRS deals with the public.[a]

To do this, a computer "whiz kid" was appointed to totally reorganize the agency. "We're going to burn the house down and build it back from the foundation," said a member of the reorganization team that proposed dispatching IRS vans to neighborhoods, using e-mail to communicate with taxpayers, and setting up anonymous Internet chatrooms for taxpayers to engage in a give and take with the IRS on a range of problems that affect their tax status.[b] Other changes include twenty-four-hour customer service help lines, allowing use of credit cards to pay tax bills, and stepped-up electronic filing and assistance, which resulted in record online filings in 2001.

Under the new reorganization, regional offices were abolished and replaced with four operating divisions to handle specific tax areas. This move was designed to create a more specialized workforce and allow employees to learn more about a single area, cutting down on the transmission of misinformation. "Early reports are that the agency's workers as well as its leadership are taking seriously Congress's and the public's demand for good manners and pleasant service."[c] One of its changes, however, has proven almost too good to be true. To help taxpayers settle their debts, the IRS created a new plan called the "offer in compromise" process, which allows the IRS to accept compromise offers before costly hearings. So many taxpayers, however, tried to take advantage of this process that the IRS was quickly overwhelmed, creating just the kind of logjam that the congressional investigations tried to get the IRS to fix. Tight budget restrictions won't allow the IRS to hire more staffers to handle the flood of requests, so the agency again is under attack for failing to fulfill its pledges to Congress to handle these complaints within six months.[d]

---

[a]Stephen Barr, "For IRS, a Deadline to Draft a Smile," *The Washington Post*, January 31, 1999, H1.

[b]Barr, "For IRS, a Deadline."

[c]Albert B. Crenshaw, "Another Tax Year, A Whole New Attitude at the IRS; Overhaul Produces Nicer Treatment, Better Service," *The Washington Post*, April 15, 1999, E9.

[d]Liz Pulliam Weston, "IRS Deluged over Tax-Debt Plan: Agency Can't Keep Up with the Applications," *The Milwaukee Journal Sentinel*, October 23, 2000, 10D.

(1890–1920) that calls for reform began to be taken seriously. Later, Calvin Coolidge urged spending cuts and other reforms. His Two Percent Club was created to cut staff, as its name implies, by 2 percent each year; his Correspondence Club was designed to reduce bureaucratic letter writing by thirty percent.[21]

All recent presidents since John F. Kennedy have tried to streamline the bureaucracy to make it smaller and thus more accountable. President Nixon, for example, proposed a plan to combine fifty domestic agencies and seven different departments into four large "super departments." But according to his former aide John Erlichman, this plan to "disrupt iron triangles" was dead on arrival. "Why? Because such a reorganization would have broken up the hoary congressional committee organization that corresponded to the existing departments and agencies." Said Erlichman, "A subcommittee chairman with oversight of the Agriculture Department would lose power, perks and status if we were authorized to fold Agriculture into a new Department of Natural Resources. The powerful farm lobbies were equally hostile to the idea."[22]

Longman
Participate.com
2.0
Visual Literacy
The Changing Face of the Federal Bureaucracy

POINT / COUNTERPOINT

The Central Intelligence Agency (CIA) is an independent government agency created in 1947 as an instrument for waging the Cold War between the United States and the Soviet Union through spying. But when the Cold War ended following the independence of eastern Europe and the fall of the Soviet Union in the early 1990s, the CIA's role in the post–Cold War world became uncertain. Because many different agencies collect intelligence, such as the Defense Intelligence Agency, the State Department Bureau of Research and Intelligence, the National Security Agency, and others, some believe the CIA—with its expensive intelligence operations—is no longer necessary. So why does the CIA still exist? Some believe that intelligence is even more important today, given the complexities of the world, the rise of terrorism, and the fact that nuclear and biological weapons still exist. Should the CIA be abolished? Let's examine these two points of view.

Opponents of the CIA, including the Libertarian Party and a number of groups on the far left as well as the far right, argue that the intelligence agency enjoys unlimited budgets with no accountability and little public scrutiny. The oversight that exists is minimal and is mostly congressional staff and members of Congress who have vested interests in maintaining huge expenditures for intelligence work. For example, members of Congress from Virginia favor spending on submarine-based intelligence work because it supports the ship-building industry, and the jobs that come with it, in that state. CIA opponents argue that there are plenty of other agencies collecting information and that the CIA is redundant and costly. Intelligence budgets are often top secret, but estimates are that all U.S. intelligence operations combined cost $28 billion per year. Some officials even wonder about the overall effectiveness of the agency in recent years. The CIA failed to predict the 1979 capture of American hostages in Iran, the fall of the Berlin Wall in 1989, or India's nuclear tests in 1999. The mission of the CIA was espoused during the height of the Cold War, and since the Cold War is over, the mission is also over.

Supporters of the CIA, including the Republican Party, argue that it is even more essential today than ever before to have accurate and timely intelligence about our adversaries and our allies. They see an expanded mission for intelligence agencies, not a need for cutting back. In the information age, the currency of the modern nation state and of security is intelligence. CIA advocates believe that congressional oversight provides adequate accountability while maintaining the need for security. Because the president must approve many of the riskier ventures the intelligence community pursues, the executive branch provides additional oversight. In defending rising intelligence budgets, CIA supporters argue that it is more expensive to keep tabs on the world today—with more than 200 states—than it was to watch the Soviet Union and its allies during the height of the Cold War. Technology such as satellites, specially outfitted submarines, and Internet surveillance used in collecting intelligence is more expensive and expansive today than ever before. In addition, the time leaders have to respond to crises has dramatically decreased. News sources such as CNN now report twenty-four hours a day, and leaders often have to respond immediately in crisis situations. During the Cuban Missile Crisis of 1961, John F. Kennedy had days and weeks in which to respond, while George W. Bush will have only hours or minutes to respond to a similar crisis. Thus, accurate and immediate intelligence information is even more crucial today.

What do you think? Should the CIA be abolished or retained and strengthened?
Go to www.ablongman.com/oconnor

The Clinton administration was especially bullish on reform. In 1993 Clinton created the President's Task Force on Reinventing Government and signed executive orders to:

- Cut the size of the federal workforce by 252,000 people within five years.
- Cut in half the growing number of federal regulations within three years.
- Set customer service standards to direct agencies to put the people they serve first.

The Environmental Protection Agency (EPA) is a bureaucracy charged with administering most of the federal government's environmental legislation. Here, EPA inspectors oversee the handling and storing of hazardous waste. (Photo courtesy: A. Ramey/Woodfin Camp & Associates)

These initiatives, and those of Congress, made dramatic bureaucratic reforms not seen since the New Deal.

Another way presidents can shape policy and provide direction to bureaucrats is by issuing **executive orders**.[23] These are presidential directives to an agency that provide the basis for carrying out laws or for establishing new policies. Even before Congress acted to protect women from discrimination by the federal government, for example, the National Organization for Women convinced President Lyndon B. Johnson to sign Executive Order 11375 in 1967. This amended an earlier order prohibiting the federal government from discriminating on the basis of race, color, religion, or national origin in the awarding of federal contracts, by adding to it the category of "gender." Nevertheless, although the president signed the order, the Office of Federal Contract Compliance (the executive agency charged with implementing the order) failed to draft appropriate guidelines for implementation of the order until several years later.[24] A president can direct an agency to act, but it may take some time for his orders to be carried out. Given the many "jobs" of any president, few can ensure that all their orders will be carried out or that they will like all the rules that are made.

executive order
Presidential directive to an agency that provides the basis for carrying out laws or for establishing new policies.

Congressional Control

Congress, too, plays an important role in checking the power of the bureaucracy. Constitutionally, it possesses the authority to create or abolish departments and agencies as well as to transfer agency functions. It can also expand or contract bureaucratic discretion. The Senate's authority to confirm (or reject) presidential appointments also gives Congress a check on the bureaucracy. Congress also exercises considerable oversight over the bureaucracy in several ways, as detailed in Table 9.4, which contains data from a study conducted by the Brookings Institution.

Title IX of the Education Amendments of 1972 mandated nondiscrimination in women's sports. Since its passage, there has been a dramatic increase in the number of high school and college women competing in school sports—from 80,000 college women in 1982 to nearly 150,000 in 2001. (Photo courtesy: Karen O'Connor)

TABLE 9.4   Frequency and Effectiveness of Oversight Techniques in a Single Congress

Oversight technique	Number of cases in which technique was used	Effectiveness ranking
Staff communication with agency personnel	91	1
Member communication with agency personnel	86	2
Program reauthorization hearings	73	3
Oversight hearings	89	4
Hearings on bills to amend ongoing programs	70	5
Staff investigations	90	6
Program evaluations done by committee staff	89	7
Program evaluations done by congressional support agencies	89	8
Legislative veto	82	9
Analysis of proposed agency rules and regulations	90	10
Program evaluations done by outsiders	88	11
Agency reports required by Congress	91	12
Program evaluations done by the agencies	87	13
Review of casework	87	14

Source: Joel Aberbach, *Keeping a Watchful Eye* (Washington, D.C.: Brookings Institution, 1990), 132, 135.

WEB EXPLORATION For more about the IRS and its modernization efforts, see www.ablongman.com/oconnor

Political scientists distinguish between two different forms of oversight: *police patrol* and *fire alarm* oversight.[25] As their names might imply, police patrol oversight is proactive and allows Congress to set its own agenda for programs or agencies to review. In contrast, fire alarm oversight is reactive and generally involves a congressional response to a complaint filed by a constituent or politically significant actor. The range of congressional responses can vary from simple inquiries about an issue to full-blown hearings. As illustrated in Politics Now: Can I Help You? It Depends on Whether Congress Allocates Enough Money, Congress at times even responds to constituent complaints about the bureaucracy. In that case, hearings resulted in total reorganization of the IRS.

Given the prevalence of iron triangles and issue networks, it is not surprising that the most frequently used form of oversight and the most effective is communication between house staffers and agency personnel. Various forms of program evaluations make up the next most commonly used forms of congressional control. Congress and its staff routinely conduct evaluations of programs and conduct oversight hearings.

Congress also uses many of its constitutional powers to exercise control over the bureaucracy. These include its *investigatory powers.* It is not at all unusual for a congressional committee or subcommittee to hold hearings on a particular problem, and then to direct the relevant agency to study the problem or find ways to remedy it. Representatives of the agencies also appear before these committees on a regular basis to inform members about agency activities, ongoing investigations, and so on.

Congress also has its *power of the purse.* To control the bureaucracy, Congress dangles its ability to fund or not fund an agency's activities like the sword of Damocles over the heads of various agency officials.[26] The House Appropriations Committee routinely holds hearings to allow agency heads to justify their budget requests. Authorization legislation originates in the various legislative committees that oversee particular agencies (such as Agriculture, Veterans' Affairs, Education, and Labor) and sets the maximum amounts that agencies can spend on particular programs. While some authorizations, such as those for Social Security, are permanent, others, including the State Department and Defense Department procurements, are watched closely and subject to annual authorizations.

GLOBAL POLITICS

BUREAUCRACIES IN SELECTED INDUSTRIALIZED COUNTRIES

The bureaucracy plays a significant role in European and Japanese government. Unlike in the United States, employment in the national bureaucracy is considered an elite career that competes for prestige with the best positions in the private sector. In Britain, France, and Japan, top civil servants are recruited from elite institutions of higher education and are recognized as having professional qualifications specifically to manage government and the economy.

Government Employment as a Proportion of Total Employment, 1995

Country	Percent
France	19.3
Germany	14.9
Japan	5.9
United Kingdom	19.3
United States	**14.5**

Source: From *European Politics Today*, 3rd ed., by Frank Wilson. Copyright ©1999. Reprinted by permission of Prentice-Hall, Inc., Upper Saddle River, N.J.

The higher civil service in the parliamentary systems is intimately involved in all aspects of policy making. Cabinet ministers drawn from the ranks of the legislature typically do not have expertise in the specific policy areas that their ministries oversee, so they rely on the higher civil service to draft the bills that will be introduced in their names. Top bureaucrats, of course, oversee the implementation of that legislation. In Germany and France, bureaucrats frequently run for election in the Parliament without giving up their civil service status; retired Japanese bureaucrats have often done the same. In these countries, the elite civil service is therefore represented not only in the bureaucracy, but in the legislature and executive as well.

France and Japan demonstrate that the size of the bureaucracy may be less important than the role it plays in society. France has one of the largest public sectors in the industrial democracies, Japan the smallest. Yet both are characterized by public policies that give the national civil service a great deal of power to manage the economy and lower levels of government.

Once funds are authorized, they must be appropriated before they can be spent. Appropriations originate with the House Appropriations Committee, not the specialized legislative committees. Often the Appropriations Committee allocates sums smaller than those authorized by the legislative committee. Thus, the Appropriations Committee, a budget cutter, has an additional oversight function.

Longman Participate.com 2.0
Comparative
Comparing Bureaucracies

To help Congress's oversight of the bureaucracy's financial affairs, in 1921 Congress created the General Accounting Office (GAO) at the same time that the Office of the Budget was created in the executive branch. With the establishment of the GAO, the Congressional Research Service, and later, the Congressional Budget Office (CBO), Congress essentially created its own bureaucracy to keep an eye on what the executive branch and *its* bureaucracy were doing. Today the GAO not only tracks how money is spent in the bureaucracy, but it also monitors how policies are implemented. The CBO also conducts oversight studies. If it or the GAO uncovers problems with an agency's work, Congress is notified immediately.

Legislators also augment their formal oversight of the executive branch by allowing citizens to appeal adverse bureaucratic decisions to agencies, Congress, and even the courts. Congressional review, a procedure adopted by the 104th Congress, by which agency regulations can be nullified by joint resolutions of legislative disapproval, is another method of exercising congressional oversight. This form of oversight is discussed in greater detail in chapter 7.

Judicial Control

While the president's and Congress's control over the actions of the bureaucracy is very direct, the judiciary's oversight function is less so. The federal judiciary, for example, can directly issue injunctions or orders to an executive agency even before a rule is formally promulgated. The courts have also ruled that agencies must give all affected individuals their due process rights guaranteed by the U.S. Constitution. A Social Security recipient's checks cannot be stopped, for example, unless that individual is provided with reasonable notice and an opportunity for a hearing. On a more informal, indirect level, litigation, or even the threat of litigation, often exerts a strong influence on bureaucrats. Injured parties can bring suit against agencies for their failure to enforce the law, and can challenge agency interpretations of the law. In general, however, the courts give great weight to the opinions of bureaucrats and usually defer to their expertise.[27]

Research by political scientists also shows that government agencies are strategic. They often implement Supreme Court decisions "based on the costs and benefits of alternative policy choices." Specifically, the degree to which agencies appear to respond to Supreme Court decisions is based on the "specificity of Supreme Court opinions, agency policy preferences, agency age, and *amicus curiae* support."[28]

The development of specialized courts has altered the relationship of some agencies with the federal courts, apparently resulting in less judicial deference to agency rulings. Research by political scientists reveals that specialized courts such as the Court of International Trade, because of their expertise, defer less to agency decisions than do more generalized federal courts. Conversely decisions from executive agencies are more likely to be reversed than those from more specialized independent regulatory commissions.[29]

Continuity & Change

Technology and the Bureaucracy

We rely on government bureaucrats to make sure that our cars are registered, to get our drivers' licenses, voter registration, and passports, and even to keep track of our contributions to the social security system. That is a far cry from what governments did in the late 1700s or what citizens expected of it. When the United States was first founded, there were but three departments in the executive branch, and an attorney general who provided the president with legal advice. The State Department, headed by Thomas Jefferson, a consistent opponent of big government, had but nine employees. The Treasury Department, headed by Federalist Alexander Hamilton, had a much larger staff. The bureaucracy continued to increase in size, albeit slowly. From 1816 to 1861, the size of the bureaucracy grew as demands on the national government increased. The Civil War and its aftermath greatly accelerated the growth of government.

Technology was barely existent. Ledgers and federal records were compiled and maintained with pen and ink. The development of the typewriter, carbon paper, and later, copying machines, while making the maintenance of records easier, also were to contribute tremendously to the red tape and paper woes of the bureaucracy. Computers totally revolutionized the way the federal government did business. Detailed records are now maintained about individuals by several different agencies, and some even fear that the government knows way too much about them. But even computers become obsolete.

(continued)

Today, local, state, and the national governments are adopting and embracing technology at breathtaking speed. States, in particular, are using the Internet to provide information and services to their citizens, cutting costs, increasing efficiency, and making government more responsive to the people, just as the Framers intended. "Well-run, efficiently organized Web sites [improve] the attitude of citizens toward government," concluded one major study of federal and state websites that ranked them according to twenty-seven factors, including the ability to register a vehicle online and access searchable records. In September 2000, the federal government went online with a new homepage to allow Americans to access all of its services from a single location. Firstgov.gov provides connections to over 27 million federal agency web pages on 20,000 sites.[30] Unlike the federal government, this site is accessible twenty-four hours a day. Better yet, for those who aren't familiar with federal bureaucratic structures, the site contains a search engine to allow the public to connect with the correct agency. This site contains connections to all branches of government and federal agencies, as well as to state and local governments.

It is not just governments that are making more information available to citizens to cut through the bureaucracy and red tape. Several Internet sites have sprung up to bring the government and the bureaucracy closer to the people. Govworks.com, now defunct, claimed that it could help you "take care of virtually all your government needs on line"[31] from locating the right office for reporting a pothole, paying property taxes, or registering to vote.

How technology can be used to make government more efficient and effective—especially as the number of federal employees decreases—may have important implications for how the federal government of the future operates.

1. What uses do you see for technology?
2. How could governmental services and accountability be improved through the use of new technologies?

Cast Your Vote. How would you modernize federal agencies? To cast your vote, go to **www.ablongman.com/oconnor**

SUMMARY

The bureaucracy plays a major role in America as a shaper of public policy, earning it the nickname the "fourth branch" of government. To explain the evolution and scope of bureaucratic power, in this chapter we have made the following points:

1. **The Roots and Development of the Executive Branch and the Federal Bureaucracy**

   According to Max Weber, all bureaucracies have similar characteristics. These characteristics can be seen in the federal bureaucracy as it developed from George Washington's time, when the executive branch had only three departments—State, War, and Treasury—through the Civil War. Significant gains occurred in the size of the federal bureaucracy as the government geared up to conduct a war. As employment opportunities within the federal government increased, concurrent reforms in the civil service system assured that more and more jobs were filled according to merit and not by patronage. By the late 1800s, reform efforts led to further increases in the size of the bureaucracy, as independent regulatory commissions were created. In the wake of the Depression, many new agencies were created to get the national economy back on course as part of President Franklin D. Roosevelt's New Deal.

2. **The Modern Bureaucracy**

   The modern bureaucracy is composed of nearly two million civilian workers from all walks of life. In general, bureaucratic agencies fall into four general types: departments, government corporations, independent agencies, and independent regulatory commissions.

3. **Policy Making**

   Bureaucrats not only make but implement public policy. Iron triangles or issue networks often can be used to describe how this policy making occurs. Much policy making occurs at the lowest levels of the bureaucracy, where administrative discretion can be exercised on an informal basis. More formal policy is often made through rule making and administrative adjudication.

4. **Making Agencies Accountable**

   Agencies enjoy considerable discretion, but they are also subjected to many formal controls. The president, Congress, and the judiciary all exercise various degrees of control over the bureaucracy.

KEY TERMS

administrative adjudication, p. 321
administrative discretion, p. 321
bureaucracy, p. 304
civil service system, p. 308
clientele agency, p. 315
department, p. 315
executive order, p. 327
Federal Employees Political Activities
    Act, p. 318

government corporation,
    p. 315
Hatch Act, p. 318
implementation, p. 319
independent executive agency,
    p. 317
independent regulatory commission,
    p. 308
iron triangle, p. 319

issue network, p. 320
merit system, p. 308
patronage, p. 306
Pendleton Act (Civil Services
    Reform Act of 1883), p. 308
regulation, p. 321
rule making, p. 321
spoils system, p. 307

SELECTED READINGS

Bennett, Linda L. M., and Stephen E. Bennett. *Living with Leviathan: Americans Coming to Terms with Big Government.* Lawrence: University of Kansas Press, 1990.

Brehm, John, and Scott Gates. *Working, Shirking, and Sabotage: Bureaucratic Response to a Democratic Public.* Ann Arbor: University of Michigan Press, 1997.

Derthick, Martha, and Paul J. Quirk. *The Politics of Deregulation.* Washington, D.C.: Brookings Institution, 1985.

Goodsell, Charles T. *The Case for Bureaucracy: A Public Administration Polemic.* Chatham, N.J.: Chatham House, 1994.

Gormley, William T., Jr. *Taming the Bureaucracy: Muscles, Prayers and Other Strategies.* Princeton, N.J.: Princeton University Press, 1989.

Handler, Joel F. *Down the Bureaucracy: The Ambiguity of Privatization and Empowerment.* Princeton, N.J.: Princeton University Press, 1996.

Ingraham, Patricia Wallace. *The Foundation of Merit: Public Service in American Democracy.* Baltimore, Md.: Johns Hopkins University Press, 1995.

Kerwin, Comelius M. *Rulemaking: How Government Agencies Write Law and Make Policy,* 2nd ed. Washington, D.C.: CQ Press, 1999.

Mackenzie, G. Calvin. *The Irony of Reform: Roots of Political Disenchantment.* Boulder, Colo.: Westview Press, 1996.

Osborne, David, and Peter Plastrik. *Banishing Bureaucracy: The Five Strategies for Reinventing Government.* Boston: Addison-Wesley, 1997.

Peters, B. Guy. *The Politics of Bureaucracy,* 4th ed. New York: Longman, 1995.

Richardson, William D. *Democracy, Bureaucracy and Character.* Lawrence: University of Kansas Press, 1997.

Rourke, Francis E. *Bureaucracy, Politics and Public Policy.* Boston: Little, Brown, 1988.

Wilson, James Q. *Bureaucracy: What Government Agencies Do and Why They Do It.* New York: Basic Books, 1991.

NOTES

1. Jack Kelly, "Poll: Most Support Elian Raid," *USA Today* (April 25, 2000): A1.

2. Stephen Barr, "Users Mostly Rate Agencies Favorably," *The Washington Post* (April 13, 2000): A29.

3. Harold D. Lasswell, *Politics: Who Gets What, When and How* (New York: McGraw-Hill, 1938).

4. H. H. Gerth and C. Wright Mills, *From Max Weber* (New York: Oxford University Press, 1958).

5. Quoted in Robert C. Caldwell, *James A. Garfield* (Hamden, Conn.: Archon Books, 1965).

6. *NLRB* v. *Jones & Laughlin Steel Corp.,* 301 U.S. 1 (1937).

7. *U.S.* v. *Darby Lumber Co.* 312 U.S. 100 (1941); and *Wickwood* v. *Filburn,* 317 U.S. 111 (1942).

8. David Osborne and Ted Gaebler, *Reinventing Government* (Reading, MA: Addison-Wesley, 1992), 20–21.

9. "A Century of Government Growth," *The Washington Post* (January 3, 2000): A17. But on the difficulty of counting the exact number of government agencies, see David Nachmias and David H. Rosenbloom, *Bureaucratic Government: U.S.A.* (New York: St. Martin's Press, 1980).

10. The classic work on regulatory commissions is Marver Bernstein, *Regulating Business by Independent Commission* (Princeton, N.J.: Princeton University Press, 1955).

11. *Humphrey's Executor* v. *U.S.,* 295 U.S. 602 (1935).

12. "Federal News: Hatch Act," *Inc.: Government Employee Relations Report* (October 11, 1993): 1317.

13. Deborah A. Stone, *Policy Paradox: The Art of Political Decision Making,* (New York: Norton, 1997).

14. For more on iron triangles, see Randall Ripley and Grace Franklin, *Congress, Bureaucracy and Public Policy,* 4th ed. (Homewood, Ill.: Dorsey Press, 1984). See also George Krauss, "The Institutional Dynamics of Policy Administration: Bureaucratic Influence over Securities Regulation," *American Journal of Political Science* 40 (November 1996): 1083–1121.

15. "Issue Networks and the Executive Establishment," in Anthony King, ed., *The New American Political System* (Washington, D.C.: American Enterprise Institute, 1978), 87–124.

16. Martin Shapiro, "The Presidency and the Federal Courts," in Arnold Meltsner, ed., *Politics and the Oval Office* (San Francisco: Institute for Contemporary Studies, 1981), ch. 8.

17. Michael Lipsky, *Street-Level Bureaucracy: Dilemmas of the Individual in Public Services* (New York: Russell Sage Foundation, 1980).

18. Cornelius M. Kerwin, *Rulemaking: How Government Agencies Write Law and Make Policy,* 2d ed. (Washington, D.C.: CQ Press, 1999), xv.

19. Jack C. Plano and Milton Greenberg, *The American Political Dictionary,* 6th ed. (New York: Holt, Rinehart and Winston, 1982), 236.

20. Quoted in Arthur Schlesinger Jr., *A Thousand Days* (Greenwich, Conn.: Fawcett Books, 1967), 377.

21. Thomas V. DiBacco, "Veep Gore Reinventing Government—Again!" *USA Today* (September 9, 1993): 13A.

22. John Erlichman, "Government Reform: Will Al Gore's Package of Changes Succeed Where Others Failed? Washington's 'Iron Triangles,'" *The Atlanta Journal and Constitution* (September 16, 1993): A15.

23. George A. Krause, "Presidential Use of Executive Orders, 1953–1994," *American Politics Quarterly* 25 (October 1997): 458–81.

24. Irene Murphy, *Public Policy on the Status of Women* (Lexington, Mass.: Lexington Books, 1974).

25. Matthew McCubbins and Thomas Schwartz, "Congressional Oversight Overlooked: Police Patrols Versus Fire Alarms," *American Journal of Political Science* 28 (1987): 165–79.

26. According to Greek legend, Damocles was a courtier and constant flatterer of Dionysus, King of Syracuse. Damocles coveted the happiness and glory of kings until Dionysus gave a banquet in his honor. Damocles enjoyed the banquet immensely until he looked up and saw a sword over his head, hung by a single thread. The sword was meant to teach him of the constant danger faced by the kings he so envied.

27. Rosemary O'Leary, *Environmental Change: Federal Courts and the EPA* (Philadelphia: Temple University Press, 1993).

28. James F. Spriggs III, "The Supreme Court and Federal Administrative Agencies: A Resource-Based Theory and Analysis of Judicial Impact," *American Journal of Political Science* 40 (November 1996): 1122.

29. Wendy Hansen, Renee Johnson, and Isaac Unah, "Specialized Courts, Bureaucratic Agencies, and the Politics of U.S. Trade Policy," *American Journal of Political Science* 39 (August 1995): 529–57.

30. Bob Dart, "Feds Open 'All-in-One' Web Site for Public," *Atlanta Journal and Constitution* (September 23, 2000): A1.

31. Full page advertisement, *The New York Times* (March 18, 2000): A19.

10 The Judiciary

On December 1, 2000, hundreds of protesters gathered outside the U.S. Supreme Court in spite of the bone-chilling temperatures, individuals had started lining up two days before to be one of the 250 lucky individuals who would be given tickets to hear the first of the two cases that ultimately would decide the outcome of the 2000 presidential election. All of the surrounding roads were closed by Court police to ensure public safety. Hundreds of media crews staked out positions outside the building.

As the new century dawned, Americans were accustomed to seeing Congress deliberate a full range of issues from the most mundane to presidential impeachment on C-SPAN or one or more of the other networks. Political junkies could get their fill of the 2000 presidential election contest as the trial, circuit, and Florida Supreme Court proceedings were televised in their entirety. But the U.S. Supreme Court hearings were not televised. In the first challenge, after Theodore Olson, a lawyer for the Bush campaign finished his presentation, Roger Cossack of CNN rushed out of the Court breathlessly to report on what had happened. Greta Van Sustern remained in the courtroom to cover the opposing arguments offered by Harvard University law professor Laurence Tribe on behalf of the Gore campaign.

Olson's arguments were dramatic as he attempted to fend off attacks from various justices who questioned whether Governor Bush even had a federal case. The mood and nature of the questioning then shifted during Tribe's turn at the lectern. But very few people in America were able to see either presentation, even though the gallery looked like a who's who in American politics—among the onlookers were retired Justice Byron White, several senators, and even Caroline Kennedy Schlossberg. The drama was similarly high when the second case involving the presidential contest was argued less than two weeks later.

Members of the news media, as well as the American Political Science Association, have been urging the U.S. Supreme Court to open its arguments to the public for years, to no avail. With the outcome of the presidential contest at stake, the call was raised anew, with C-SPAN and CNN leading the charge for a one-time deal. Still, it was a no go at the Court, where many of the justices have taken on an "over my dead body" stand on the issue of cameras in the Court while condoning their use in other courts. The Court's lone concession to the magnitude of the cases before it? Recordings of both sets of oral arguments were released in their entirety one hour after conclusion of the attorneys' presentations, instead of being made available two weeks later on the Court's Web site.

Even before the high-stakes presidential case was accepted by the Court, several members of the Senate were upset with the Court's refusal to make its "public" appearances more public. In fact, Senators Arlen Specter (R–Pa.) and Joseph Biden Jr. (D–Del.) of the Judiciary Committee have sponsored a bill to require television cameras in the Supreme Court. Nevertheless, although many commentators argued that the legitimacy of the Court was on the line because of *Bush* v. *Gore*, the justices remained undeterred in their commitment to keep their proceedings as private as possible.

In 1787, when Alexander Hamilton wrote to urge support of the U.S. Constitution, he firmly believed that the judiciary was the weakest of the three departments of government. In its formative years, the judiciary was, in Hamilton's words, "the least dangerous" branch. The judicial branch seemed so inconsequential that when the young national government made its move to the District of Columbia in 1800, Congress actually forgot to include any space to house the justices of the Supreme Court! Last-minute conferences with the Capitol architects led to the allocation of a small area in the basement of the Senate wing of the Capitol Building for a courtroom. No other space was allowed for the justices, however. Noted one commentator, "A stranger might traverse the darkest avenues of the Capitol for a week, without finding the remote corner in which justice is served in the American Republic."[1]

Today the role of the courts, particularly the U.S. Supreme Court, is significantly different from that envisioned in 1788, the year the national government came into being. The "least dangerous branch" is now perceived by many as having too much power.

During different periods of the judiciary's history, the role and power of the federal courts have varied tremendously. They have often played a key role in creating a strong national government and have boldly led the nation in social reform. Yet, at other times, the federal courts, especially the U.S. Supreme Court, have stubbornly stood as major obstacles to social and economic change.

In addition to being unaware of the expanded role of the federal judiciary, only recently have many Americans become aware of the political nature of the courts. They were raised to think of the federal courts, especially the Supreme Court, as above the fray of politics. That, however, is simply not the case. Elected presidents nominate judges to the federal courts and justices to the Supreme Court, often to advance their personal politics, and elected senators ultimately confirm (or decline to confirm) presidential nominees. Not only is the selection process political, but the process by which cases ultimately get heard—if they are heard at all—by the Supreme Court is often political as well. Interest groups routinely seek out good test cases to advance their policy positions. Even the U.S. government, generally through the Justice Department and the U.S. solicitor general (another political appointee), seeks to advance its version of the public interest in court. Interest groups then often line up on opposing sides to advance their positions, much in the same way lobbyists do in Congress.

Protesters gathered outside the U.S. Supreme Court during arguments in *Bush* v. *Gore*. (Photo courtesy: Sylvia Johnson/Woodfin Camp & Associates.)

In this chapter we explore these issues and the scope and development of judicial power:

■ First, we will look at the *Constitution and the creation of the national judiciary*. Article III of the Constitution created a Supreme Court but left it to Congress to create any other federal courts, a task it quickly took up.

■ Second, we will examine the *Judiciary Act of 1789* and explore the structure and the *creation of the federal judicial system*. The American legal system contains parallel courts systems for the fifty states and the national government. Each court system has courts of original and appellate jurisdiction.

■ Third, we will discuss the *American legal system* and the concepts of civil and criminal law.

■ Fourth, we will discuss the *federal court system*. The federal court system is composed of specialized courts, district courts, courts of appeals, and the Supreme Court, which is the ultimate authority on all federal law.

■ Fifth, we will see *how federal court judges are selected*. All appointments to the federal district courts, courts of appeals, and the Supreme Court are made by the president and are subject to Senate confirmation.

■ Sixth, we will take a look at the *Supreme Court today*. Only a few of the millions of cases filed in courts around the United States every year eventually make their way to the Supreme Court through the lengthy appellate process, as cases are filtered out at a variety of stages.

■ Seventh, we will learn *how justices vote and make decisions* and discuss how judicial decision making is based on a variety of legal and extra-legal factors.

■ Eighth, we will discuss *judicial policy making and implementation*.

A note on terminology: When we refer to the "Supreme Court," the "Court," or the "high Court" here, we always mean the U.S. Supreme Court, which sits at the pinnacle of the federal and state court systems. The Supreme Court is referred to by the name of the chief justice who presided over it during a particular period (for example, the Marshall Court is the Court presided over by John Marshall from 1801 to 1835). When we use the term "courts," we refer to all federal or state courts unless otherwise noted.

THE CONSTITUTION AND THE CREATION OF THE NATIONAL JUDICIARY

The detailed notes James Madison took at the Philadelphia Convention make it clear that the Framers devoted little time to the writing of or the content of Article III, which created the judicial branch of government. The Framers believed that a federal judiciary posed little of the threat of tyranny that they feared from the other two branches. One scholar has even suggested that, for at least some delegates to the Constitutional Convention,

> provision for a national judiciary was a matter of theoretical necessity…more in deference to the maxim of separation [of powers] than in response to clearly formulated ideas about the role of a national judicial system and its indispensability.[2]

Alexander Hamilton argued in *Federalist No. 78* that the judiciary would be the "least dangerous branch of government." Anti-Federalists, however, did not agree with Hamilton. They particularly objected to a judiciary whose members had life tenure and the ability to interpret what was to be "the supreme law of the land," a phrase that Anti-Federalists feared would give the Supreme Court too much power.

The Framers also debated the need for any federal courts below the level of the Supreme Court. Some argued in favor of deciding all cases in state courts, with only appeals going before the Supreme Court. Others argued for a system of federal courts. A compromise left the final choice to Congress, and Article III, section 1, begins simply by vesting "The judicial Power of the United States…in one supreme Court, and

judicial review
Power of the courts to review acts of other branches of government and the states.

in such inferior Courts as the Congress may from time to time ordain and establish." Although there is some debate over whether the Court should have the power of **judicial review,** which allows the judiciary to review acts of the other branches of government and the states, the question was left unsettled in Article III (and not finally resolved until *Marbury* v. *Madison* (1803), regarding acts of the national government, and *Martin* v. *Hunter's Lessee* (1816), regarding state law.)[3] This vagueness was not all that unusual, given the numerous compromises that took place in Philadelphia. Judicial review and its articulation in *Marbury* are discussed in greater detail in Highlight: *Marbury* v. *Madison* and Judicial Review.

Article III, section 1, also gave Congress the authority to establish other courts as it saw fit. Section 2 specifies the "judicial power" of the Supreme Court (see Table 10.1) and discusses the Court's original and appellate jurisdictions. This section also specifies that all federal crimes, except those involving impeachment, shall be tried by jury in the state in which the crime was committed. The third section of the article defines treason, and mandates that at least two witnesses appear in such cases.

Although it is the duty of the chief justice of the United States to preside over presidential impeachments, this is not noted in Article III. Instead, Article I, section 3, notes in discussing impeachment, "When the President of the United States is tried, the Chief Justice shall preside."

Had the Supreme Court been viewed as the potential policy maker it is today, it is highly unlikely that the Framers would have provided for life tenure with "good behavior" for federal judges in Article III. This feature was agreed on because the Framers did not want the justices (or any federal judges) subject to the whims of politics, the public, or politicians. Moreover, Alexander Hamilton argued in *Federalist No. 78* that the "independence of judges" was needed "to guard the Constitution and the rights of individuals." Because the Framers viewed the Court as quite powerless, Hamilton stressed the need to place federal judges above the fray of politics. Yet although there is no denying that judges are political animals and carry the same prejudices and preferences to the bench that others do to the statehouse, Congress, or the White House, the provision of life tenure for "good behavior" has generally functioned well.

Some checks on the power of the judiciary were nonetheless included in the Constitution. The Constitution gives Congress the authority to alter the Court's jurisdition (its ability to hear certain kinds of cases). Congress can also propose constitutional amendments that, if ratified, can effectively reverse judicial decisions, and it can impeach and remove federal judges. In one further check, it is the president who (with the "advice and consent" of the Senate) appoints all federal judges.

TABLE 10.1   The Judicial Power of the United States Supreme Court

The following are the types of cases the Supreme Court was given the jurisdiction to hear as initially specified in the Constitution:

- All cases arising under the Constitution and laws or treaties of the United States
- All cases of admiralty or maritime jurisdiction
- Cases in which the United States is a party
- Controversies between a state and citizens of another state
- Controversies between two or more states
- Controversies between citizens of different states
- Controversies between citizens of the same states claiming lands under grants in different states
- Controversies between a state, or the citizens thereof, and foreign states or citizens thereof
- All cases affecting ambassadors or other public ministers

HIGHLIGHT

MARBURY V. MADISON AND JUDICIAL REVIEW

Perhaps the most important power of the Supreme Court, although it is not mentioned in the Constitution, is that of judicial review, the authority of a court to determine the constitutional validity of acts of the legislature. During the Constitutional Convention, the Framers debated and rejected the idea of a judicial veto of legislation or executive acts, but they did approve Article VI, which contains the supremacy clause.

During its first decade, the Supreme Court reviewed acts of Congress, but it did not find any to be unconstitutional. The actual authority of the Supreme Court to review acts of Congress to determine their constitutionality thus was an unsettled question. But in *Marbury* v. *Madison* (1803), Chief Justice John Marshall claimed this sweeping authority for the Court by asserting the right of judicial review was a power that could be implied from the Constitution's supremacy clause.

Marbury v. *Madison* arose amidst a sea of political controversy. In the final hours of the Adams administration, William Marbury was appointed a justice of the peace for the District of Columbia. But in the confusion of winding up matters, Adams's secretary of state failed to deliver Marbury's commission. Marbury then asked James Madison, Thomas Jefferson's secretary of state, for the commission. Under direct orders from Jefferson, who was irate over the Adams administration's last-minute appointment of several federal judges (quickly confirmed by the Federalist Senate),

Madison refused to turn over the commission. Marbury and three other Adams appointees who were in the same situation then filed a writ of *mandamus* (a legal motion) asking the Supreme Court to order Madison to deliver their commissions.

Political tensions ran high as the Court met to hear the case. Jefferson threatened to ignore any order of the Court. Marshall realized that he and the prestige of the Court could be devastated by any refusal of the executive branch to comply with the decision. Responding to this challenge, in a brilliant opinion that in many sections reads more like a lecture to Jefferson than a discussion of the merits of Marbury's claim, Marshall concluded that although Marbury and the others were entitled to their commissions, the Court lacked the power to issue the writ sought by Marbury. In *Marbury* v. *Madison*, Marshall further ruled that the parts of the Judiciary Act of 1789 that extended the jurisdiction of the Court to allow it to issue writs were inconsistent with the Constitution and therefore unconstitutional.

Although the immediate effect of the decision was to deny power to the Court, its long-term effect was to establish the principle of judicial review, a power that Marshall concluded could be implied from the Constitution. Since *Marbury*, the Court has routinely exercised the power of judicial review, an implied power, to determine the constitutionality of acts of Congress, the executive branch, and the states.

THE JUDICIARY ACT OF 1789 AND THE CREATION OF THE FEDERAL JUDICIAL SYSTEM

In spite of the Framers' intentions, the pervasive role of politics in the judicial branch quickly became evident with the passage of the Judiciary Act of 1789. Congress spent nearly the entire second half of its first session deliberating the various provisions of the act to give form and substance to the federal judiciary. As one early observer noted, "The convention has only crayoned in the outlines. It left it to Congress to fill up and colour the canvas."[4]

The Judiciary Act of 1789 established the basic three-tiered structure of the federal court system. At the bottom are the federal district courts—at least one in each state—each staffed by a federal judge. If the people participating in a lawsuit (called litigants) are unhappy with the district court's verdict, they could appeal their case to one of three circuit courts. Each circuit court, initially created to function as a trial court for important cases, was composed of one district court judge and two itinerant Supreme Court

Judiciary Act of 1789
Established the basic three-tiered structure of the federal court system.

The Supreme Court held its first two sessions in this building, called the Exchange, located in New York City. (Photo courtesy: Bettmann/Corbis)

Justices who met as a circuit court twice a year. Thus, Supreme Court Justice Samuel Chase, in his capacity as a circuit court judge, presided over a Sedition Act trial resulting in the conviction of a Jeffersonian newspaper editor who was critical of the Federalist government. It wasn't until 1891 that circuit courts (also often called courts of appeals) as we know them today took on their exclusively appellate function.

The third tier of the federal judicial system fleshed out by the Judiciary Act of 1789 was the Supreme Court of the United States. Although the Constitution mentions "the supreme Court," it was silent on its size. In the Judiciary Act, Congress set the size of the Supreme Court at six—the chief justice plus five associate justices.

When the justices met in their first public session in New York City in 1790, they were magnificently garbed in black and scarlet robes in the English fashion, but they had discarded what Thomas Jefferson termed "the monstrous wig which makes English judges look like rats peeping through bunches of oakum!"[5] The elegance of their attire, however, could not make up for the relatively ineffective status of the Court. Its first session even had to be adjourned when a quorum of the justices failed to show up. That first session of the Court was presided over by John Jay, who was appointed chief justice of the United States by George Washington. It decided one key case—*Chisholm* v. *Georgia* (1793) (discussed on page 341). Moreover, in an indication of its lowly status, one associate justice left the Court to become chief justice of the South Carolina Supreme Court. (Although such a move would be considered a step down today, keep in mind that in the early years of the United States, many viewed the states as more important than the new national government.)

Hampered by frequent changes in personnel, limited space for its operations, no clerical support, and no system of reporting its decisions, the Court and its meager activities did not impress many people. From the beginning, the circuit court duties of the Supreme Court justices presented problems for the prestige of the Court. Few good lawyers were willing to accept nominations to the high Court because its circuit court duties entailed a substantial amount of travel—most of it on horseback over poorly maintained roads in frequently inclement weather. Southern justices often tallied up as much as 10,000 miles a year on horseback. George Washington tried to prevail on several friends and supporters to fill vacancies on the Court as they appeared, but most refused the "honor." John Adams, the second president of the United States, ran into similar problems. When he asked John Jay to resume the position of chief justice after he resigned to become governor of New York, Jay declined the offer. Jay had once remarked of the Court that it had lacked "energy, weight, and dignity" as well as "public confidence and respect." Given Jay's view of the Court and its performance statistics, his refusal was not surprising.

In spite of all its problems, in its first decade the Court took several actions to help mold the new nation. First, by declining to give George Washington advice on the legality of some of his actions, the justices attempted to establish the Supreme Court as an independent, nonpolitical branch of government. Although John Jay, as an individual, frequently gave the president advice in private, the Court refused to answer questions Washington posed to it concerning the construction of international laws and treaties. The justices wanted to avoid the appearance of prejudging an issue that could later arise before them.

The early Court also tried to advance principles of nationalism and to maintain the national government's supremacy over the states. As circuit court jurists, the justices rendered numerous decisions on such matters as national suppression of the Whiskey Rebellion and the constitutionality of the Alien and Sedition Acts, which made it a crime to criticize national governmental officials or their actions (see chapter 5).

During the ratification debates, Anti-Federalists had warned that Article III extended federal judicial power to controversies "between a State and Citizens of another State"—meaning that a citizen of one state could sue any other state in federal court, a prospect unthinkable to defenders of state sovereignty. Although Federalists, including Hamilton and Madison, had scoffed at the idea, the nationalist Supreme Court quickly proved them wrong in *Chisholm* v. *Georgia* (1793).[6] In *Chisholm* the justices interpreted the Court's jurisdiction under Article III, section 2, to include the right to hear suits brought by a citizen of one state against another state. For example, writing in *Chisholm,* Justice James Wilson denounced the "haughty notions of state independence, state sovereignty, and state supremacy." The states' reaction to this perceived attack on their authority led to passage and ratification (in 1798) of the Eleventh Amendment, which specifically limited judicial power by stipulating that the federal courts' authority could not "extend to any suit . . . commenced or prosecuted against one of the United States by citizens of another State."

Finally, in a series of circuit and Supreme Court decisions, the justices paved the way for announcement of the doctrine of judicial review by the third chief justice, John Marshall. (Oliver Ellsworth served from 1796 to 1800.) Justices "riding circuit" occasionally held state laws unconstitutional because they violated the U.S. Constitution. In 1796, the Court for the first time evaluated the constitutionality of an act of Congress.[7]

The Marshall Court (1801–1835)

John Marshall brought much-needed respect and prestige to the Court through his leadership in a progression of cases and a series of innovations. Marshall was appointed chief justice by President John Adams in 1801, three years after he declined to accept a nomination as associate justice (see Roots of Government: John Marshall). An ardent Federalist who also earlier had declined Washington's offer to become attorney general, Marshall later came to be considered the most important justice ever to serve on the high Court. Part of his reputation is the result of the duration of his service and the historical significance of this period in our nation's history.

As chief justice, Marshall instituted several innovations and led the Court to issue several important rulings to establish the Court as a co-equal branch of government:

- Discontinued the practice of *seriatim* (Latin for "in a series") opinions, which was the custom of the King's Bench in Great Britain. Prior to the Marshall Court, the justices delivered their individual opinions in order. There was no single "opinion of the Court," as we are accustomed to today. For the Court to take its place as an equal branch of government, Marshall strongly believed, the justices needed to speak as a *Court* and not as six individuals. In fact, during Marshall's first four years in office, the Court routinely spoke as one, and the chief justice wrote twenty-four of its twenty-six opinions.
- Claimed for the Court the right of judicial review, from which the Supreme Court derives much of its day-to-day power and impact on the policy process. This established the Court as the final arbiter of constitutional questions, with the right to declare congressional acts void (*Marbury* v. *Madison* [1803]).
- Established the authority of the Supreme Court over the judiciaries of the various states, including the Court's power to declare state laws invalid (*Fletcher* v. *Peck* [1810]; *Martin* v. *Hunter's Lessee* [1816]; *Cohens* v. *Virginia* [1821]).
- Established the supremacy of the federal government and Congress over state governments through a broad interpretation of the "necessary and proper" clause (*McCulloch* v. *Maryland* [1819]).

ROOTS OF GOVERNMENT

JOHN MARSHALL

A single person can make a major difference in the development of an institution. Such was the case with John Marshall, who dominated the Supreme Court during his thirty-four years as chief justice. As one commentator noted, "Marshall found the Constitution paper, and he made it power. He found a skeleton, and he clothed it with flesh and blood."

Who was this man still so revered today? John Marshall (1755–1835) was born in a log cabin in Virginia, the first of fifteen children of Welsh immigrants. Although tutored at home by two clergymen, Marshall's inspiration was his father, who introduced him to English literature and Sir William Blackstone's influential work *Commentaries on the Laws of England.* After serving in the Continental Army and acquiring the rank of captain, Marshall taught himself the law. He attended only one formal course at the College of William and Mary before being admitted to the bar. Marshall practiced law in Virginia, where he and his wife lived and raised a family. Of their ten children, only six survived childhood.

More of a politician than a lawyer, Marshall served as a delegate to the Virginia legislature from 1782 to 1785, 1787 to 1790, and 1795 to 1796, and played an instrumental role in Virginia's ratification of the U.S. Constitution in 1787. As the leading Federalist in Virginia, Marshall was offered several positions in the Federalist administrations of George Washington and John Adams—including attorney general and associate justice to the Supreme Court—but he refused them all. Finally, in 1799, Washington persuaded him to run for the House

of Representatives. Marshall was elected, but his career in the House was brief, for he became secretary of state in 1800 under John Adams. When Oliver Ellsworth resigned as chief justice of the United States in 1800, Adams nominated Marshall. Marshall was an ardent Federalist and a third cousin of Democratic–Republican President Thomas Jefferson, whose administration he faced head-on in *Marbury v. Madison.*

Marshall came to head the Court with little legal experience and *no* judicial experience, unlike the situation on the current Supreme Court, where all of the justices except Chief Justice Rehnquist had prior judicial experience. Still, it is unlikely that any contemporary justice will have anywhere near the impact that Marshall had on the Court and the course of U.S. politics.

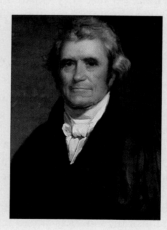

(Photo courtesy: Boston Athenaeum)

Asserting Judicial Review: *Marbury v. Madison*

During the Philadelphia Convention, the Framers debated and rejected the idea of judicial veto of legislation or executive acts, and they rejected the Virginia Plan's proposal to give the judiciary explicit authority over Congress. They did, however, approve Article VI, which contains the supremacy clause (see chapter 3).

In *Federalist No. 78,* Alexander Hamilton first publicly endorsed the idea of judicial review, noting, "Whenever a particular statute contravenes the Constitution, it will be the duty of the judicial tribunals to adhere to the latter and disregard the former." Nonetheless, because the power of judicial review is not mentioned in the U.S. Constitution, the actual authority of the Supreme Court to review the constitutionality of acts of Congress was an unsettled question. During its first decade, the Supreme Court (or justices riding circuit) had reviewed acts of Congress, but it had not found any unconstitutional. But in *Marbury v. Madison* (1803), John Marshall claimed this sweeping authority for the Court.[8] *Marbury's* long-term effect was to establish the rule that "it is emphatically the province and duty of the judicial department to say what the law is." Through judicial review, the

Marbury v. Madison (1803)
Supreme Court first asserted the power of judicial review in finding that the congressional statute extending the Court's original jurisdiction was unconstitutional.

Supreme Court most dramatically exerts its authority to determine what the Constitution means. Since *Marbury*, the Court has routinely exercised the power of judicial review to determine the constitutionality of acts of Congress, the executive branch, and the states. For more on *Marbury*, see Highlight: *Marbury* v. *Madison* and Judicial Review.

WEB EXPLORATION
To learn more about the workings of the U.S. justice system, go to www.ablongman.com/oconnor

THE AMERICAN LEGAL SYSTEM

The judicial system in the United States can best be described as a dual system consisting of the federal court system and the judicial systems of the fifty states. Cases may arise in either system. Both systems are basically three tiered. At the bottom of the system are **trial courts,** where litigation begins. In the middle are appellate courts in the state systems and the courts of appeals in the federal system. At the top of each pyramid sits a high court. (Some states call these supreme courts; New York calls it the Court of Appeals; Oklahoma and Texas call the highest state court for criminal cases the Court of Criminal Appeals.) The federal courts of appeals and Supreme Court as well as state courts of appeals and supreme courts are **appellate courts** that, with few exceptions, review on appeal only cases that already have been decided in lower courts. These courts generally hear matters of both civil and criminal law.

trial court
Court of original jurisdiction where a case begins.

appellate court
Court that generally reviews only findings of law made by lower courts.

Jurisdiction

Before a state or federal court can hear a case, it must have **jurisdiction**, which means the authority to hear and decide the issues in that case, which is called **jurisdiction.** The jurisdiction of the federal courts is controlled by the U.S. Constitution and by statute. Jurisdiction is conferred based on issues, money involved in a dispute, or the type of offense. Procedurally, we speak of two types of jurisdiction: original and appellate. **Original jurisdiction** refers to a court's authority to hear disputes as a trial court. O. J. Simpson's criminal and civil trials, for example, were heard in state trial courts of original jurisdiction. The case against "Unabomber" Theodore Kaczynski was begun in federal district court. More than 90 percent of all cases, whether state or federal, end at this stage. **Appellate jurisdiction** refers to a court's ability to review cases already decided by a trial court. Appellate courts do not ordinarily review the factual record; instead, they review legal procedures to make certain that the law was applied properly to the issues presented in the case. Table 10.2 shows the jurisdiction of the three major federal courts.

jurisdiction
Authority vested in a particular court to hear and decide the issues in any particular case.

original jurisdiction
The jurisdiction of courts that hear a case first, usually in a trial. Courts determine the facts of a case under their original jurisdiction.

appellate jurisdiction
The power vested in an appellate court to review and/or revise the decision of a lower court.

Criminal and Civil Law

Criminal law is the body of law that regulates individual conduct and is enforced by the government.[9] Crimes are graded as felonies, misdemeanors, or offenses, according to their severity. Some acts—for example, murder, rape, and robbery—are considered crimes in all states. Although all states outlaw murder, their penal, or criminal, codes treat the crime quite differently; the penalty for murder differs considerably from state to state. Other crimes—such as sodomy and some forms of gambling, such as lotteries or bingo—are illegal only in some states.

Criminal law assumes that society itself is the victim of the illegal act; therefore, the government prosecutes, or brings an action, on behalf of an injured party (acting as a plaintiff) in criminal but not civil cases. The murder charges against O. J. Simpson were styled as *The State of California* v. *Orenthal James Simpson.*

Criminal cases are traditionally in the purview of the states. But a burgeoning set of criminal laws is contributing significantly to delays in the federal courts.

Civil law is the body of law that regulates the conduct and relationships between private individuals or companies. Because the actions at issue in civil law do not constitute a

criminal law
Body of law that regulates individual conduct and is enforced by the government.

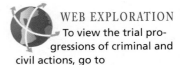

WEB EXPLORATION
To view the trial progressions of criminal and civil actions, go to www.ablongman.com/oconnor

civil law
Body of law that regulates the conduct and relationships between private individuals or companies.

TABLE 10.2   Federal Court Jurisdiction

The Supreme Court rarely exercises its original jurisdiction. Instead, most cases are heard by the Court under its appellate jurisdiction.

	Original Jurisdiction *(Approximately 2–5% of Cases Heard)*	*Appellate Jurisdiction* *(Approximately 95–97% of Cases Heard)*
The Supreme Court	Cases are heard in Supreme Court first when they involve: • Two or more states • The United States and a state • Foreign ambassadors and other diplomats • A state and a citizen of another state (if the action is begun by the state)	The Supreme Court can agree to hear cases first heard or decided on in lower courts or the state courts (generally the highest state court) involving appeals from: • U.S. courts of appeals • State highest courts (only in cases involving federal questions) • Court of Military Appeals
U.S. Courts of Appeals	None	Hears appeals of cases from: • Lower federal courts • U.S. regulatory commissions • Legislative courts, including the U.S. Court of Federal Claims and the U.S. Court of Veterans' Appeals
U.S. District Courts	Cases are heard in U.S. district courts when they involve: • The federal government • Civil suits under federal law • Civil suits between citizens of different states if the amount in issue is more than $75,000 • Admiralty or maritime disputes • Bankruptcy • Other matters assigned to them by Congress	None

threat to society at large, people who believe they have been injured by another party must take action on their own to seek judicial relief. Civil cases, then, involve lawsuits filed to recover something of value, whether it is the right to vote, fair treatment, or monetary compensation for an item or service that cannot be recovered. Most cases seen on *The People's Court* or *Judge Judy* are civil cases, as were the *Bush* v. *Gore* cases discussed in our opening vignette.

Before a criminal or civil case gets to court, much has to happen. In fact, most legal disputes that arise in the United States never get to court. Individuals and companies involved in civil disputes routinely settle their disagreements out of court. Often these settlements are not reached until minutes before the case is to be tried. Many civil cases that go to trial are settled during the course of the trial—before the case can be handed over to the jury or submitted to a judge for a decision or determination of guilt.

Each civil or criminal case has a plaintiff, who brings charges against a defendant. Sometimes the government is the plaintiff. The government may bring civil charges on behalf of the citizens of the state or the national government against a person or corporation for violating the law, but it is always the government that brings a criminal case. Cases are known by the name of the plaintiff first and the defendant second. So in *Marbury* v. *Madison*, William Marbury was the plaintiff, suing the defendants, the U.S. government and James Madison as its secretary of state, for not delivering his judicial commission.

During trials, judges must often interpret the intent of laws enacted by Congress and state legislatures as they bear on the issues at hand. To do so, they read reports, testimony, and debates on the relevant legislation and study the results of other similar legal cases. They also rely on the presentations made by lawyers in their briefs and at trial. If it is a jury trial, the jury ultimately is the finder of fact, while the judge is the interpreter of the law.

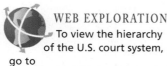

WEB EXPLORATION
To view the hierarchy of the U.S. court system, go to
www.ablongman.com/oconnor

THE FEDERAL COURT SYSTEM

The federal district courts, circuit courts of appeals, and the Supreme Court are called **constitutional** (or Article III) **courts** because Article III of the Constitution either established them (as is the case with the Supreme Court) or authorizes Congress to establish them. Judges who preside over these courts are nominated by the president (with the advice and consent of the Senate), and they serve lifetime terms, as long as they engage in "good behavior."

In addition to constitutional courts, **legislative courts** are set up by Congress, under its implied powers, generally for special purposes. The U.S. Territorial Courts (which hear federal cases in the territories) and the U.S. Court of Veterans' Appeals are examples of legislative courts, or what some call Article I courts. The judges who preside over these federal courts are appointed by the president (subject to Senate confirmation) and serve fixed, limited terms.

constitutional court
Federal court specifically created by the U.S. Constitution or by Congress pursuant to its authority in Article III.

legislative court
Court established by Congress for specialized purposes, such as the Court of Military Appeals.

District Courts

Congress recognized the need for federal trial courts of original jurisdiction soon after ratification of the Constitution. The district courts were created by the Judiciary Act of 1789. By 2001 there were ninety-four federal district courts staffed by a total of 653 active judges, assisted by more than 300 retired judges who still hear cases on a limited basis (see Figure 10.1). No district court cuts across state lines. Every state has at least one federal district court, and the most populous states—California, Texas, and New York—each have four (see Figure 10.2).[10]

Federal district courts, where the bulk of the judicial work takes place in the federal system, have original jurisdiction over only specific types of cases, as indicated in Table 10.2. (Cases involving other kinds of issues generally must be heard in state courts.) Although the rules governing district court jurisdiction can be complex, cases heard in

WEB EXPLORATION
To learn more about U.S. district courts, go to
www.ablongman.com/oconnor

FIGURE 10.1   **The Dual Structure of the American Court System**

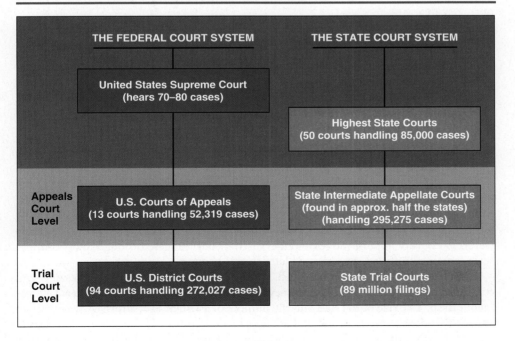

FIGURE 10.2   The Federal Court System

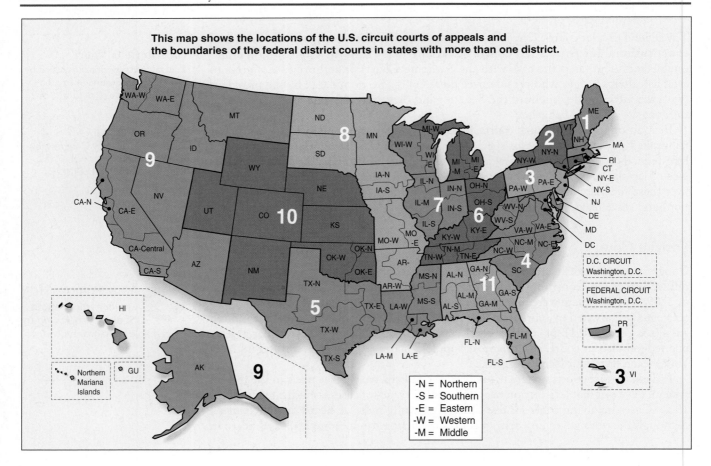

This map shows the locations of the U.S. circuit courts of appeals and the boundaries of the federal district courts in states with more than one district.

-N = Northern
-S = Southern
-E = Eastern
-W = Western
-M = Middle

federal district courts by a single judge (with or without a jury) generally fall into one of three categories:

1. They involve the federal government as a party.
2. They present a federal question based on a claim under the U.S. Constitution, a treaty with another nation, or a federal statute. This is called federal question jurisdiction and it can involve criminal or civil law.
3. They involve civil suits in which citizens are from different states, and the amount of money at issue is more than $75,000.[11]

Since 1789 the federal court system and the number of federal court judges who preside within it have grown tremendously. As illustrated in Figure 10.3, there were only thirteen federal judges and six Supreme Court Justices nominated and confirmed in 1789. By 2003, that number had grown to 812. Although John Adams and the lame-duck Federalist Congress created eighteen courts of appeals judgeships in 1801, those positions were quickly abolished by the Democratic-Republican Congress. It wasn't until 1869 that judges were selected specifically for the courts of appeals. By 2003, there were 179 court of appeals judges and 653 district court judges, although many of those seats remained unfilled, as discussed later in this chapter.

Each federal judicial district has a U.S. attorney, who is nominated by the president and confirmed by the Senate. The U.S. attorney in each district is that district's chief law enforcement officer. The size of the staff and the number of assistant U.S. attorneys who work in each district depend on the amount of litigation in each district. U.S. attorneys, like district attorneys within the states, have a considerable amount of discretion as to whether they pursue criminal or civil investigations or file charges against individuals or corporations.

FIGURE 10.3   **A Growing Federal Judiciary**
Since the 1950s the number of federal judges have been increased dramatically by Congress to help meet demands by litigants. Still, at the district court level, for example, 93 criminal cases per judge were filed in 1999.

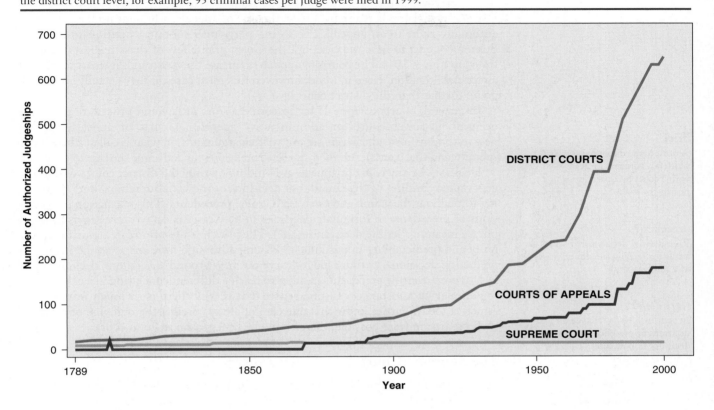

The Courts of Appeals

The losing party in a case heard and decided in a federal district court can appeal the decision to the appropriate court of appeals. The United States courts of appeals (known as the circuit courts of appeals prior to 1948) are the intermediate appellate courts in the federal system and were established in 1789 to hear appeals from federal district courts. The present structure of the appeals courts, however, dates from the Judiciary Act of 1891. There are eleven numbered circuit courts (see Figure 10.2). A twelfth, the D.C. Court of Appeals, handles most appeals involving federal regulatory commissions and agencies, including, for example, the National Labor Relations Board and the Securities and Exchange Commission. The thirteenth federal appeals court is the U.S. Court of Appeals for the Federal Circuit, which deals with patents and contract and financial claims against the federal government.

In 2003, the courts of appeals were staffed by 179 active and more than 80 senior judges, who were appointed by the president, subject to Senate confirmation. The number of judges within each circuit varies—depending on the workload and the complexity of the cases—and ranges from six to nearly thirty. Each circuit is supervised by a chief judge, the most senior judge in terms of service below the age of sixty-five, who can serve no more than seven years. In deciding cases, judges are divided into rotating three-judge panels, made up of the active judges within the circuit, visiting judges (primarily district judges from the same circuit), and retired judges. In rare cases, all the judges in a circuit may choose to sit together (*en banc*) to decide a case by majority vote.

The courts of appeals have no original jurisdiction. Rather, Congress has granted these courts appellate jurisdiction over two general categories of cases: appeals from criminal and civil cases from the district courts, and appeals from administrative agencies. Criminal and civil case appeals constitute about 90 percent of the workload of the courts of appeals, appeals from administrative agencies only about 10 percent. Because so many agencies are

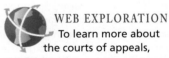

WEB EXPLORATION
To learn more about the courts of appeals, go to
www.ablongman.com/oconnor

located in Washington, D.C., the D.C. Circuit Court of Appeals hears an inordinate number of such cases. The D.C. Circuit Court of Appeals, then, is considered the second most important court in the nation because its decisions govern the regulatory agencies.

Once a decision is made by a federal court of appeals, a litigant no longer has an automatic right to an appeal. The losing party may submit a petition to the U.S. Supreme Court to hear the case, but the Court grants few of these requests, as illustrated in Figure 10.4. The courts of appeals, then, are the courts of last resort for almost all federal litigation. Keep in mind, however, that most cases, if they actually go to trial, go no further than the district court level.

In general, courts of appeals try to correct errors of law and procedure that have occurred in lower courts or administrative agencies. Courts of appeals hear no new testimony; instead, lawyers submit written arguments, in what is called a **brief** (also submitted in trial courts), and then appear to orally present and argue the case to the court.

Decisions of any court of appeals are binding on only the district courts within the geographic confines of the circuit, but decisions of the U.S. Supreme Court are binding throughout the nation and establish national **precedents.** This reliance on past decisions or precedents to formulate decisions in new cases is called *stare decisis* (a Latin phrase meaning "let the decision stand"). The principle of *stare decisis* allows for continuity and predictability in our judicial system. Although *stare decisis* can be helpful in predicting decisions, at times judges carve out new ground and ignore, decline to follow, or even overrule precedents in order to reach a different conclusion in a case involving similar circumstances. In one sense, that is why there is so much litigation in America today. Parties know that one cannot always predict the outcome of a case; if such prediction were possible, there would be little reason to go to court.

The Supreme Court

The U.S. Supreme Court is often at the center of the storm of highly controversial issues that have yet to be resolved successfully in the political process. As the court of last resort

brief
A document containing the legal written arguments in a case filed with a court by a party prior to a hearing or trial.

precedent
Prior judicial decision that serves as a rule for settling subsequent cases of a similar nature.

stare decisis
In court rulings, a reliance on past decisions or precedents to formulate decisions in new cases.

Longman
Participate.com
2.0
Visual Literacy
Case Overload

FIGURE 10.4   Supreme Court Caseload, 1950–2000 Terms
The caseload of the Supreme Court has remained fairly consistent from its 1992–1993 through 1998–1999 terms, although the Court accepted far fewer cases for its review than it did in earlier decades. In its 1999–2000 term, however, although the number of cases filed experienced a significant bump, in deciding only seventy-three cases, the Court hit a low not seen in fifty years.

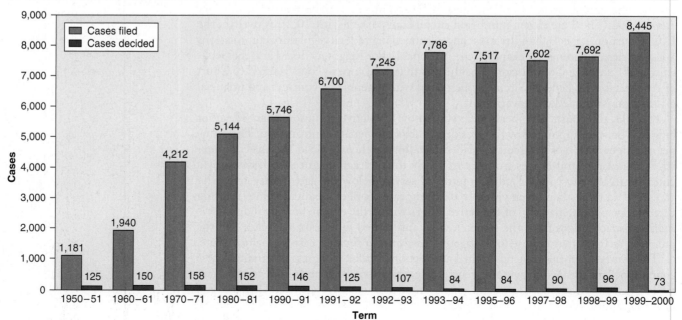

Source: Administrative Office of the Courts; Supreme Court Public Information Office.

TABLE 10.3 Chief Justices of the United States

Chief Justice	Nominating President	Years of Service
John Jay	Washington	1789–1795
John Rutledge*	Washington	1795
Oliver Ellsworth	Washington	1796–1800
John Marshall	Adams	1801–1835
Roger B. Taney	Jackson	1836–1864
Salmon P. Chase	Lincoln	1864–1873
Morrison R. Waite	Grant	1874–1888
Melville W. Fuller	Cleveland	1888–1910
Edward D. White	Taft	1910–1921
William Howard Taft	Harding	1921–1930
Charles Evans Hughes	Hoover	1930–1941
Harlan Fiske Stone	F. Roosevelt	1941–1946
Fred M. Vinson	Truman	1946–1953
Earl Warren	Eisenhower	1953–1969
Warren E. Burger	Nixon	1969–1986
William H. Rehnquist	Reagan	1986-

*Not confirmed by the Senate

at the top of the judicial pyramid, it reviews cases from the U.S. courts of appeals and state supreme courts and acts as the final interpreter of the U.S. Constitution. It not only decides many major cases with tremendous policy significance each year, but it also ensures uniformity in the interpretation of national laws and the Constitution, resolves conflicts among the states, and maintains the supremacy of national law in the federal system.

Since 1869 the U.S. Supreme Court has consisted of eight associate justices and one chief justice, who is nominated by the president specifically for that position. There is no special significance about the number nine, and the Constitution is silent about the size of the Court. Between 1789 and 1869, Congress periodically altered the size of the Court. The lowest number of justices on the Court was six; the most, ten. Through 2002, only 108 justices had served on the Court, and there had been fifteen chief justices (see Table 10.3).

The chief justice presides over public sessions of the Court, conducts the Court's conferences, and assigns the writing of opinions (if he is in the majority; otherwise, the most senior justice in the majority makes the assignment). By custom, he administers the oath of office to the president and the vice president on Inauguration Day (any federal judge can administer the oath, as has happened when presidents have died in office).

Compared with the president or Congress, the Supreme Court operates with few support staff. Along with the three of four clerks each justice employs, there are about 400 staff members at the Supreme Court.

WEB EXPLORATION To take a virtual tour of the Court and examine current cases on its docket, go to www.ablongman.com/oconnor

Longman Participate.com 2.0 Timeline **The Chief Justice of the United States**

HOW FEDERAL COURT JUDGES ARE SELECTED

Although specific, detailed provisions in Articles I and II specify the qualifications for president, Senator, and member of the House of Representatives, the Constitution is curiously silent on the qualifications for federal judges. This may have been because of an assumption that all federal judges would be lawyers, but to make such a requirement explicit might have marked the judicial branch as too elite for the tastes of common men and women. Also, it would have been impractical to require formal legal training, given that there were so few law schools in the nation, and that most lawyers became licensed after clerking or apprenticing with another attorney.[12]

The selection of federal judges is often a very political process with important political ramifications because judges are nominated by the president and must be confirmed by the U.S. Senate. During the Reagan-Bush years, for example, 553 basically conservative Republican judges were appointed to the lower federal bench, remolding it in a conservative image (see Figure 10.5). The cumulative impact of this conservative block of judges led many liberal groups to abandon their efforts to expand rights through the federal courts.

FIGURE 10.5   How a President Affects the Federal Judiciary
This figure depicts the number of judges appointed by each president and how quickly a president can make an impact on the makeup of the Court.

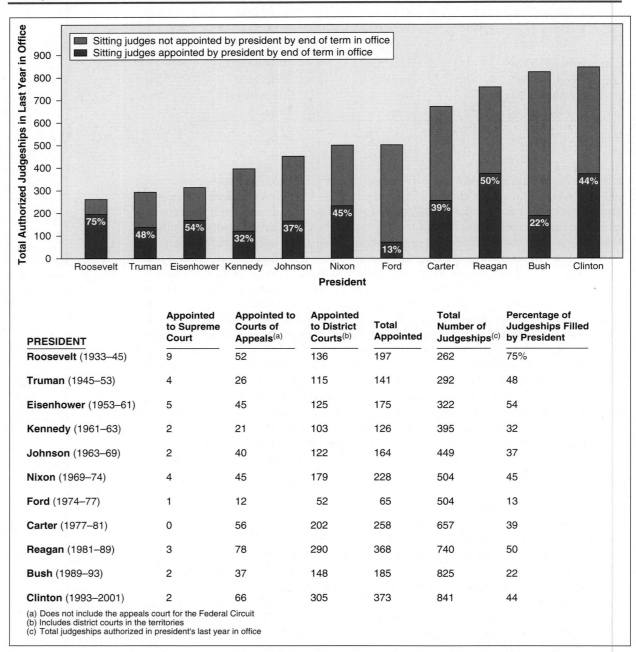

PRESIDENT	Appointed to Supreme Court	Appointed to Courts of Appeals[a]	Appointed to District Courts[b]	Total Appointed	Total Number of Judgeships[c]	Percentage of Judgeships Filled by President
Roosevelt (1933–45)	9	52	136	197	262	75%
Truman (1945–53)	4	26	115	141	292	48
Eisenhower (1953–61)	5	45	125	175	322	54
Kennedy (1961–63)	2	21	103	126	395	32
Johnson (1963–69)	2	40	122	164	449	37
Nixon (1969–74)	4	45	179	228	504	45
Ford (1974–77)	1	12	52	65	504	13
Carter (1977–81)	0	56	202	258	657	39
Reagan (1981–89)	3	78	290	368	740	50
Bush (1989–93)	2	37	148	185	825	22
Clinton (1993–2001)	2	66	305	373	841	44

(a) Does not include the appeals court for the Federal Circuit
(b) Includes district courts in the territories
(c) Total judgeships authorized in president's last year in office

Source: "Imprints on the Bench," *CQ Weekly Report* (January 19, 1991):, p. 173. Reprinted by permission of Copyright Clearance Center on behalf of Congressional Quarterly Inc.

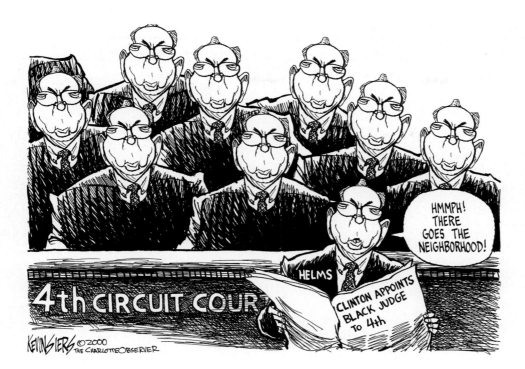

HMMPH! THERE GOES THE NEIGHBORHOOD!

HELMS

4th CIRCUIT COURT

CLINTON APPOINTS BLACK JUDGE TO 4th

KEVIN SIERS ©2000 THE CHARLOTTE OBSERVER

Jesse Helms (R–NC) originally blocked the nomination of Roger Gregory to the 4th Circuit Court of Appeals, headquartered in North Carolina. President Bill Clinton responded with a recess appointment of Gregory to be the first African American to sit on that court. Later, President George W. Bush surprised many when he formally nominated Gregory, a Democrat. for the seat. (Photo courtesy: Kevin Siers/Reprinted with special permission of North America Syndicate.)

Presidents, in general, try to select well-qualified men and women for the bench. But these appointments also provide a president with the opportunity to put his philosophical stamp on the federal courts. In the Clinton White House, candidates for district court generally came from recommendations by Democratic senators, "or in the absence of a Democratic senator, from the Democratic members of the House of Representatives or other high ranking Democratic Party politicians."[13] At least in part because of the conservative make-up of the Senate Judiciary Committee, President Clinton attempted to appoint moderates to the federal courts. But many of his nominations were met with unprecedented delay and obstruction in the Republican-controlled Senate, even though studies by political scientists found that his appointees were more moderate than earlier Republican or Democratic appointees.[14] In early 1998, Chief Justice Rehnquist spoke out, uncharacteristically criticizing the Senate for its failure to approve presidential nominees for the bench in a timely manner. These delays, charged Rehnquist, were contributing to lengthy delays in the federal courts, already overburdened by an "upward spiral" in case filings brought about, at least in part, by Congress's expanding federal jurisdiction over crimes involving drugs and firearms.

According to Rehnquist, in the 1990s the number of cases filed in courts of appeals rose 21 percent; district court filings increased by 24 percent. At the same time, not only did Congress refuse to expand the number of federal judges,[15] but the Senate refused to confirm many appointees to the federal courts. In 1998, the Court of Appeals for the Ninth Circuit, for example, had vacancies in nearly one-quarter of its seats, and five had been vacant for over eighteen months. The Senate confirmed only seventeen judges in 1996 and thirty-six in 1997, well below the 101 judges it confirmed in 1994.[16] The Senate, said Clinton White House Communications Director Ann Lewis, "has the right to advise and consent, but not to duck and delay, and what they have effectively done by a delaying process is causing some courts to almost grind to a halt."[17] When President Clinton left office in 2001, forty of his nominations to the federal courts had not been acted on by the Senate; he had made no nominations for an additional twenty-five vacancies, recognizing the futility of that effort. He did, however, make a recess appointment of Roger Gregory, the first African American to sit on the Fourth Circuit Court of Appeals.

WEB EXPLORATION
To learn about the U.S. Senate's Committee on the Judiciary and judicial nominations currently under review, go to
www.ablongman.com/oconnor

TABLE 10.4   Characteristics of District Court Appointees from Carter to Clinton

	Carter Appointees	*Reagan Appointees*	*Bush Appointees*	*Clinton Appointees*
Occupation				
Politics/gov't	5.0%	13.4%	10.8%	11.5%
Judiciary	44.6	36.9	41.9	48.2
Lawyer	49.9	49.0	45.9	38.7
Other	0.5	0.7	1.4	2.6
Experience				
Judicial	54.0%	46.2%	46.6%	52.1%
Prosecutorial	38.1	44.1	39.2	41.3
Neither	30.7	28.6	31.8	28.9
Political Affiliation				
Democrat	90.6%	4.8%	5.4%	87.5%
Republican	4.5	91.7	88.5	6.2
Independent	5.0	3.4	6.1	5.9
ABA Rating				
Extremely/Well Qualified	51.0%	53.5%	57.4%	59.0%
Qualified	47.5	46.6	42.6	40.0
Not Qualified	1.5	—	—	1.0
Net Worth				
Under $200,000	35.8%	17.6%	10.1%	13.4%
200,000–499,999	41.2	37.6	31.1	21.6
500,000–999,999	18.9	21.7	26.4	26.9
1,000,000+	4.0	23.1	32.4	32.4
Total number of appointees	202	290	148	305
Average age at nomination (years)	49.6	48.7	48.1	49.5

Source: Sheldon Goldman and Elliot E. Slotnick. "Clinton's first term judiciary: Many Bridges to Cross," *Judicature* (May–June 1997), p. 261. Reprinted by permission. Updated data from Sheldon Goldman. University of Massachusetts, Amherst.

Who Are Federal Judges?

Typically, federal district court judges have held other political offices, such as those of state court judge or prosecutor, as illustrated in Table 10.4. Most have been involved in politics, which is what usually brings them into consideration for a position on the federal bench. Griffin Bell, a former federal court of appeals judge, once remarked, "For me, becoming a federal judge wasn't very difficult. I managed John F. Kennedy's presidential campaign in Georgia."[18]

Increasingly, most judicial nominees have had prior judicial experience. White males continue to dominate the federal courts, but the Clinton administration sought to appoint nontraditional judges, as is revealed in Table 10.4. His female appointees, however, experienced far greater problems in their confirmation hearings than did white males.

Since the 1970s, in fact, most presidents have pledged (with varying degrees of success) to do their best to appoint more African Americans, women, and other groups traditionally underrepresented on the federal bench (see again, Table 10.4).

Appointments to the U.S. Supreme Court

The Supreme Court is not now, nor has it ever been, above politics, as its recent foray into settling the national election underscores. In fact, during the 2000 presidential campaign, commentators predicted that the new president would get from two to four opportunities to replace sitting justices. Much of that speculation was based on the ages of the justices. Politics permeates the selection process of federal court judges, including those on the Supreme Court. On occasion, some individuals or their friends have actively lobbied for the spot on the bench. In their classic insider's view on the Supreme Court, *The Brethren*, Bob Woodward and Scott Armstrong wrote critically of then Court

POINT / COUNTERPOINT

SHOULD JUDGES BE ELECTED OR APPOINTED

At both the federal and the state levels, judges are selected in a variety of ways. Some are elected in partisan election, some in nonpartisan election, others are appointed and then confirmed by elections, and others simply appointed. Basically, this boils down to two methods: election and appointment. Currently, twenty-nine states plus the District of Columbia use some form of appointment and twenty-one states some form of election. The goal in either method is an independent judiciary that is able to make impartial judgments on the meaning of the law and to pass judgment fairly. In addition, judges ought to be accountable to society at large and make rulings according to the laws, not their own wishes. How should we best balance the interests of an independent, and an accountable, judiciary? Let's examine both point viewpoints.

Advocates of judicial election, such as the Federalist Society for Law and Public Policy Studies, argue that it is more democratic to elect judges than to have some elite body choose them for us. Elections provide accountability so that judges cannot run amuck with our inalienable rights. In addition, judicial elections reinforce one of our most cherished ideals: self-government. Advocates of judicial election argue that the appointment process is riddled with partisan struggles, litmus tests, and bias so that it does not what advocates claim: assuring meritorious and independent judges. Instead, it gives U.S. judges chosen in smoke-filled rooms by a political elite. Appointments, then, replace open electoral processes with back-room elite manipulation. If a governor or president is the appointing party, that person's political affiliation comes to bear. If the appointing party is a committee, the committee is usually composed of experts who are lawyers. Why is this preferable to the will of voters?

Advocates of appointment, such as the American Judicature Society, argue that the appointment process allows qualified individuals and groups to carefully weigh the credentials of judicial aspirants and make selections based solely on merit to assure that judges are chosen from a pool of highly qualified candidates through the method of providing an appropriate balance between judicial independence and public accountability. Appointment minimizes the political considerations in the selection of judges and gets rid of the issues of campaign finance. How can a judge rule fairly in a case regarding one of his or her campaign contributors? Advocates of judicial appointment argue that the elections are merely popularity contests and reward name recognition, not wisdom and sagacity. In addition, elections tip the balance between judicial accountability so far in the direction of accountability that independence is often forfeit.

What do you think? Should judges be elected or appointed?
Go to www.ablongman.com/oconnor

---

of Appeals Judge Warren Burger's somewhat clumsy efforts to lobby Richard M. Nixon for the position of chief justice of the Supreme Court.[19] Burger's lobbying for the position was portrayed as unseemly.

The Constitution is silent on the qualifications for appointment to the Supreme Court (as well as to other constitutional courts), although Justice Oliver Wendell Holmes once remarked that a justice should be a "combination of Justinian, Jesus Christ and John Marshall."[20]

Like other federal court judges, the justices of the Supreme Court are nominated by the president and must be confirmed by the Senate. Few appointments, however, have been subject to the kind of lobbying that occurred when Court of Appeals Judge Ruth Bader Ginsburg was nominated to the U.S. Supreme Court in 1993. Ginsburg's husband, a prominent tax attorney and Georgetown University law professor, unabashedly orchestrated a letter-writing campaign on behalf of his wife's nomination. He contacted his wife's former students, the presidents of Stanford and Columbia Universities, academics, legal scholars, and even Texas Governor Ann Richards, urging them to call or write the White House to support his wife's nomination to the Court.

Longman
Participate.com 2.0
Simulation
You Are Appointing a Supreme Court Justice

Presidents have always realized how important their judicial appointments, especially their Supreme Court appointments, were to their ability to achieve all or many of their policy objectives. After all, Franklin D. Roosevelt proposed his infamous Court-packing plan because he wanted to add like-minded jurists to the Court to outweigh the votes of those opposed to federal governmental expansion and intervention into the economy. But, even though most presidents have tried to appoint jurists with particular political or ideological philosophies, they have often been wrong about their assumptions about their appointees. Eisenhower, a moderate/conservative, was appalled by the liberal opinions of the Warren Court concerning criminal defendants' rights, in particular. Similarly, Justices O'Connor, Kennedy, and Souter, appointed by Ronald Reagan (O'Connor) and George Bush, are not as conservative as some predicted. David Souter, in particular, has surprised many commentators with his moderate to liberal decisions in a variety of areas, including free speech, criminal rights, race and gender discrimination, and abortion.

Historically, because of the special place the Supreme Court enjoys in our constitutional system, its nominees have encountered more opposition than district or courts of appeals nominees. As the role of the Court has increased over time, so too has the amount of attention given to nominees. With this increased attention has come greater opposition, especially to nominees with controversial views.

Nomination Criteria

Justice Sandra Day O'Connor once remarked that "You have to be lucky" to be appointed to the Court.[21] Although luck is certainly important, over the years nominations to the bench have been made for a variety of reasons. Depending on the timing of a vacancy, a president may or may not have a list of possible candidates or even a specific individual in mind. Until recently, presidents often have looked within their

TABLE 10.5   The Supreme Court, 2001

Name	Year of Birth	Year of Appointment	Political Party	Law School	Appointing President	Religion	Prior Judicial Experience	Prior Government Experience
William H. Rehnquist	1924	1971/1986*	R	Stanford	Nixon	Lutheran	Associate Justice U.S. Supreme Court	Assistant U.S. Attorney General
John Paul Stevens	1920	1975	R	Chicago	Ford	Nondenominational Protestant	U.S. Court of Appeals	
Sandra Day O'Connor	1930	1981	R	Stanford	Reagan	Episcopalian	Arizona Court of Appeals	State Legislator
Antonin Scalia	1936	1986	R	Harvard	Reagan	Catholic	U.S. Court of Appeals	
Anthony Kennedy	1936	1988	R	Harvard	Reagan	Catholic	U.S. Court of Appeals	
David Souter	1939	1990	R	Harvard	Bush	Episcopalian	U.S. Court of Appeals	New Hampshire Assistant Attorney General
Clarence Thomas	1948	1991	R	Yale	Bush	Catholic	U.S. Court of Appeals	Chair, Equal Employment Opportunity Commission
Ruth Bader Ginsburg	1933	1993	D	Columbia	Clinton	Jewish	U.S. Court of Appeals	
Stephen Breyer	1938	1994	D	Harvard	Clinton	Jewish	U.S. Court of Appeals	Chief Counsel, Senate Judiciary Committee

*Promoted to Chief Justice by President Reagan in 1986.

circle of friends or their administration to fill a vacancy. Nevertheless, whether the nominee is a friend or someone known to the president only by reputation, at least six criteria are especially important: competence, ideology or policy preferences, rewards, pursuit of political support, religion, and race and gender.

Competence.   Most prospective nominees are expected to have had at least some judicial or governmental experience. John Jay, the first chief justice, was one of the authors of *The Federalist Papers* and was active in New York politics. Most have had some prior judicial experience. In 2001, eight sitting Supreme Court justices had prior judicial experience (see Table 10.5). If Chief Justice Rehnquist's service as associate justice is included, all nine justices have prior judicial experience.

Ideology or Policy Preferences.   Most presidents seek to appoint to the Court individuals who share their policy preferences, and almost all have political goals in mind when they appoint a justice. Presidents Franklin D. Roosevelt, Richard M. Nixon, and Ronald Reagan were very successful in molding the Court to their own political beliefs. Roosevelt was quickly able to appoint eight justices from 1937 to his death in 1945, solidifying support for his liberal New Deal programs. In contrast, Nixon and Reagan publicly proclaimed that they would nominate only conservatives who favored a **strict constructionist** approach to constitutional decision making—that is, an approach emphasizing the original intentions of the Framers.

strict constructionist
An approach to constitutional interpretation that emphasizes the Framers' original intentions.

Rewards.   Historically, many of those appointed to the Supreme Court have been personal friends of presidents. Abraham Lincoln, for example, appointed one of his key political advisers to the Court. Lyndon B. Johnson appointed his longtime friend Abe Fortas to the bench. Most presidents select justices of their own party affiliation. Chief Justice Rehnquist was long active in Arizona Republican Party politics, as was Justice O'Connor before her appointment to the bench; both were appointed by Republican presidents. Party activism can also be used by presidents as an indication of a nominee's commitment to certain ideological principles.

Pursuit of Political Support.   During Ronald Reagan's successful campaign for the presidency in 1980, some of his advisers feared that the "gender gap" would hurt him. Polls repeatedly showed that he was far less popular with female voters than with men. To gain support from women, Reagan announced during his campaign that should he win, he would appoint a woman to fill the first vacancy on the Court. When Justice Potter Stewart, a moderate, announced his early retirement from the bench, President Reagan nominated Sandra Day O'Connor of the Arizona Court of Appeals to fill the vacancy. It probably did not hurt President Clinton that his first appointment (Ruth Bader Ginsburg) was a woman and Jewish (at a time when no Jews served on the Court).

Religion.   Ironically, religion, which historically has been an important issue, was hardly mentioned during the most recent Supreme Court vacancies. Some, however, hailed Clinton's appointment of Ginsburg, noting that the traditionally "Jewish" seat on the Court had been vacant for over two decades.

Through 2002, of the 108 justices who have served on the Court, almost all have been members of traditional Protestant faiths.[22] Only nine have been Catholic and only seven have been Jewish.[23] Twice during the Rehnquist Court, more Catholics—Brennan, Scalia, and Kennedy, and then Scalia, Kennedy, and Thomas—served on the Court at one time than at any other period in history. Today, however, it is clear that religion cannot be taken as a sign of a justice's conservative or liberal ideology: When William Brennan was on the Court, he and fellow Catholic Antonin Scalia were at ideological extremes.

Race and Gender.   Only two African Americans and two women have served on the Court. Race was undoubtedly a critical issue in the appointment of Clarence Thomas

ANALYZING   THE   DATA

RACE AND GENDER OF DISTRICT COURT APPOINTEES, CARTER TO CLINTON

Traditionally, white males have dominated federal court appointments. Of Reagan's 290 appointees, for example, 92.4% were white males. By the end of Clinton administration, however, the percentage of white males federal appointees decreased significantly, comprising only 52.1% of his 305 court appointees. While most presidents in recent years have pledged to appoint more African Americans, women, and Hispanics to the federal bench, Clinton was the most succcessful.

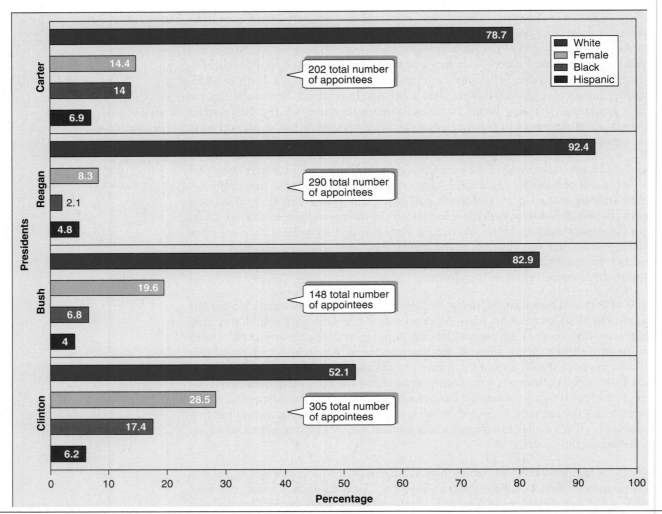

Source: Fordham Law Review (December 1992): 497–539, and Anne Marie Kilday, "Amendment Expert Agrees with Congressional Pay Ruling." *The Dallas Morning News* (February 14, 1993): 13A. Clinton data from Sheldon Goldman, University of Massachusetts, Amherst.

to replace Thurgood Marshall, the first African American justice. But President George Bush refused to acknowledge his wish to retain a "black seat" on the Court. Instead, he announced that he was "picking the best man for the job on the merits," a claim that was met with considerable skepticism by many observers.

In contrast, O'Connor was pointedly picked because of her gender. Ginsburg's appointment was more matter-of-fact, and her selection surprised many because the Clinton administration appeared to be considering seriously several men for the appointment first.

The Supreme Court Confirmation Process

The Constitution gives the Senate the authority to approve all nominees to the federal bench. Before 1900, about one-fourth of all presidential nominees to the Supreme Court were rejected by the Senate. In 1844, for example, President John Tyler sent six nominations to the Senate, and all but one were defeated. In 1866, Andrew Johnson nominated his brilliant attorney general, Henry Stanberry, but the Senate's hostility to Johnson led it to abolish the seat to prevent Johnson's filling it. Ordinarily, nominations are referred to the Senate Committee on the Judiciary. As detailed later, this committee investigates the nominees, holds hearings, and votes on its recommendation for Senate action. The full Senate then deliberates on the nominee before voting. A simple majority vote is required for confirmation.

Investigation.   As a president begins to narrow his list of possible nominees to the Supreme Court, those names are sent to the Federal Bureau of Investigation before a nomination is formally made. At the same time, until the current president, the president forwarded names of prospective nominees to the American Bar Association (ABA), the politically powerful organization that represents the interests of the legal profession. After its own investigation, the ABA rated each nominee, based on his or her qualifications, as Well Qualified (previously "Highly Qualified"), Qualified, or Not Qualified. (The same system was used for lower federal court nominees; over the years, however, the exact labels have varied.)

David Souter, George Bush's first nominee to the Court, received a unanimous rating of Highly Qualified from the ABA, as did both of Clinton's nominees, Ruth Bader Ginsburg and Stephen Breyer. In contrast, another Bush nominee, Clarence Thomas, was given only a Qualified rating (well before the charges of sexual harassment became public), with two members voting Not Qualified. Of the twenty-two previous successful nominees rated by the ABA, he was the first to receive less than at least a unanimous Qualified rating.

President George W. Bush has announced that the ABA would no longer play this key role. The 1996 Republican presidential candidate Bob Dole went so far as to pledge, if elected, he would remove the ABA from the selection process, viewing it as "another blatantly partisan liberal advocacy group."[24] Bush agreeing with this view, plans to look to the more conservative Federalist Society to vet his nominees. The ABA counters that it is "completely nonpartisan" and that its selection committee

WEB EXPLORATION
To learn the extent of the ABA's legislative and government advocacy, go to
www.ablongman.com/oconnor

The scrutiny by the public and press of President Reagan's Supreme Court nominee Robert H. Bork set a new standard of inquiry into the values—political and personal—of future nominees. Bork's nomination was rejected by the Senate in 1987. (Photo courtesy: Frank Fournier/Contact Press Images)

members are chosen for their "credibility and contacts in their communities, so lawyers and judges will speak frankly to them" about a prospective nominee's fitness for the federal bench.[25] ABA supporters argue that it is an independent check on the quality of judicial appointees who, once confirmed, serve for life.[26]

After a formal nomination is made and sent to the Senate, the Senate Judiciary Committee also begins its own investigation. (The same process is used for nominees to the lower federal courts, although such investigations generally are not nearly as extensive as for Supreme Court nominees.) To begin its task, the Senate Judiciary Committee asks each nominee to complete a lengthy questionnaire detailing previous work (dating as far back as high school summer jobs), judicial opinions written, judicial philosophy, speeches, and even all interviews ever given to members of the press. Committee staffers also contact potential witnesses who might offer testimony concerning the nominee's fitness for office.

Lobbying by Interest Groups.   While historically the ABA was the only organization that was asked formally to rate nominees, other groups are also keenly interested in the nomination process. Until recently, interest groups played a minor and backstage role in most appointments to the Supreme Court. Although interest groups generally have not lobbied *on behalf* of any one individual, in 1981 women's rights groups successfully urged President Reagan to honor his campaign commitment to appoint a woman to the high court.

It is more common for interest groups to lobby *against* a prospective nominee as revealed in Table 10.6. Even this, however, is a relatively recent phenomenon. In 1987, the nomination of Robert H. Bork to the Supreme Court produced an unprecedented amount of interest group lobbying on both sides of the nomination. The Democratic-controlled Senate Judiciary Committee delayed the hearings, thus allowing liberal interest groups time to mobilize the most extensive radio, television, and print media campaign ever launched against a nominee to the U.S. Supreme Court. This opposition was in spite of the fact that Bork sat with distinction on the D.C. Court of Appeals and was a former U.S. solicitor general, a top-ranked law school graduate, and a Yale Law School professor. His actions as solicitor general, especially his firing of the Watergate special prosecutor, made him a special target for traditional liberals.

The Senate Committee Hearings and Senate Vote.   As the relatively uneventful 1994 hearings of Stephen Breyer attest, not all nominees inspire the kind of intense reaction that kept Bork from the Court and, more recently, almost blocked the confirmation of Clarence Thomas. Until 1929, all but one Senate Judiciary Committee hearing on a

TABLE 10.6   Interest Groups Appearing in Selected Senate Judiciary Committee Hearings

Nominee	Year	INTEREST GROUPS Lib.	Cons.	ABA Rating	Senate Vote
Stevens	1976	2	3	Well-Q	98–0
O'Connor	1981	8	7	Well-Q	99–0
Scalia	1986	5	7	Well-Q	98–0
Rehnquist	1986	6	13	Well-Q	68–36
Bork	1987	18	68	Well-Q[a]	42–58
Kennedy	1987	12	14	Well-Q	97–0
Souter	1990	13	18	Well-Q	90–9
Thomas	1991	30	46	Q[b]	52–8
Ginsburg	1993	6	5	Well-Q	96–3
Breyer	1994	8	3	Well-Q	87–9

[a] Four ABA committee members evaluated him as not qualified.

[b] Two ABA committee members evaluated him as not qualified.

Source: From "Lobbying the Justices or Lobbying for Justice," by Karen O'Connor in *The Interest Group Connection,* edited by Paul S. Herrnson, Ronald G. Shaiko, and Clyde Wilcox, p. 273. Reprinted by permission of Chatham House Publishers, Inc.

Supreme Court nominee was conducted in executive session—that is, closed to the public. The 1916 hearings on Louis Brandeis, the first Jewish justice, were conducted in public and lasted nineteen days, although Brandeis himself was never called to testify. In 1939, Felix Frankfurter became the first nominee to testify in any detail before the committee. Subsequent revelations about Brandeis's secret financial payments to Frankfurter to allow him to handle cases of social interest to Brandeis (while Brandeis was on the Court and couldn't handle them himself) raise questions about the fitness of both Frankfurter and Brandeis for the bench. Still, no information about Frankfurter's legal arrangements with Brandeis was unearthed during the committee's investigations or Frankfurter's testimony.[27]

Until recently, modern nomination hearings were no more thorough in terms of the attention given to nominees' backgrounds. In 1969, for example, Chief Justice Warren E. Burger was confirmed by the Senate on a vote of 94–3, just nineteen days after he was nominated.

Since the 1980s it has become standard for senators to ask the nominees probing questions. Most nominees (with the notable exception of Robert H. Bork) have declined to answer most of them on the grounds that these issues might ultimately come before the Court. After hearings are concluded, the Senate Judiciary Committee usually makes a recommendation to the full Senate. Any rejections of presidential nominees to the Supreme Court generally occur only after the Senate Judiciary Committee has recommended against a nominee's appointment. Few recent confirmations have been close; prior to Clarence Thomas's 52–48 vote in 1991, Rehnquist's nomination in 1971 as associate justice (68–26) and in 1986 as chief justice (65–33) were the closest in recent history. (See Table 10.6)

THE SUPREME COURT TODAY

Given the judicial system's vast size and substantial, although often indirect, power over so many aspects of our lives, it is surprising that so many Americans know next to nothing about the judicial system in general and the Supreme Court in particular. Even today, at a time when all other institutions of government and government officials receive unprecedented media attention, the work of the Court proceeds in relative anonymity. Few Americans can correctly name the current chief justice, let alone the other eight justices. A poll conducted in 1990 for the Court's 200th anniversary revealed that only 23 percent of Americans queried knew how many justices sit on the Court, and nearly two-thirds could not name a single member of the Court.[28] A 1998 poll of teenagers found that only 2 percent know who the chief justice is. To fill in any gaps in your knowledge of the current Supreme Court, see Table 10.5.

Much of this ignorance can be blamed on the American public's lack of interest. But the Court itself has taken great pains to ensure its privacy and sense of decorum. Its rites and rituals contribute to the Court's mystique and encourage a "cult of the robe."[29] Consider, for example, the

The Supreme Court today. From left to right: Clarence Thomas, Antonin Scalia, Sandra Day O'Connor, Anthony Kennedy, David Souter, Stephen Breyer, John Paul Stevens, William Rehnquist, and Ruth Bader Ginsburg. (Photo courtesy: Ken Heinen/Pool/AP/Wide World Photos)

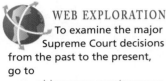

WEB EXPLORATION
To examine the major
Supreme Court decisions
from the past to the present,
go to
www.ablongman.com/oconnor

way Supreme Court proceedings are conducted. Oral arguments are not televised, and deliberations concerning the outcome of cases are conducted in utmost secrecy. In contrast, C-SPAN brings us daily coverage of various congressional hearings and floor debate on bills and important national issues, and Court TV (and sometimes other networks) provides gavel-to-gavel coverage of many important state court trials. The Supreme Court, however, remains adamant in its refusal to televise its proceedings—including public oral arguments, as discussed in the opening vignette.

Deciding to Hear a Case

Although more than 8,400 cases were filed at the Supreme Court in its 1999–2000 term, this was not always the case. From 1790 to 1801, the Court heard only eighty-seven cases under its appellate jurisdiction.[30] In the Court's early years, the bulk of the justices' workload involved their circuit-riding duties. From 1862 to 1866, only 240 cases were decided. Creation of the courts of appeals in 1891 resulted in an immediate reduction in Supreme Court filings—from 600 in 1890 to 275 in 1892.[31] As recently as the 1940s, fewer than 1,000 cases were filed annually. Since that time, filings increased at a dramatic rate until the 1993–1994 term. Filings then leveled off, but they skyrocketed during the 1999–2000 term, as revealed earlier in Figure 10.4, although that does not mean the Court is actually deciding more cases. In fact, of the 8,445 petitions it received during the 1999–2000 term, it handed down signed opinions in only seventy-four. The process by which cases get to the Supreme Court is outlined in Figure 10.6.

Just as it is up to the justices to "say what the law is," they can also exercise a significant role in policy making and politics by opting *not* to hear a case. The content of the Court's docket is, of course, every bit as significant as its size. Prior to the 1930s, the

FIGURE 10.6 How a Case Goes to the United States Supreme Court
This figure illustrates how cases get on the Court's docket; what happens after a case is accepted for review is detailed in Figure 10.7.

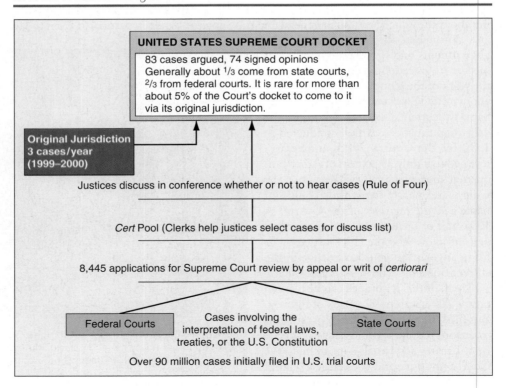

Court generally heard cases of interest only to the immediate parties. During the 1930s, however, cases requiring the interpretation of constitutional law began to take a growing portion of its workload, leading the Court to take a more important role in the policy-making process. At that time only 5 percent of the Court's cases involved questions concerning the Bill of Rights. By the late 1950s, one-third of filed cases involved such questions; and by the 1960s, half did.[32] In 1990, however, only 30 percent of the Court's caseload dealt with constitutional questions.

The Supreme Court's Jurisdiction

The Court has two types of jurisdiction, as indicated in Table 10.2. Its original jurisdiction is specifically set out in the Constitution. The Court has original jurisdiction in "all Cases affecting Ambassadors, other public Ministers and Consuls, and those in which a State shall be a party." Most cases arising under the Court's original jurisdiction involve disputes between two states, usually over issues such as ownership of offshore oil deposits, territorial disputes caused by shifting river boundaries, or controversies caused by conflicting claims over water rights, such as when a river flows through two or more states.[33] In earlier days, the Court would actually sit as a trial court and hear evidence and argument. Today, the Court usually appoints a Special Master—often a retired judge or an expert on the matter at hand—to hear the case in a district court on behalf of the Supreme Court and then report his or her findings and recommendations to the Court. It is rare for more than two or three of these cases to come to the Court in a year.

A second kind of jurisdiction enjoyed by the Court is appellate jurisdiction (see Table 10.2). The appellate jurisdiction of the Court can be changed by the Congress at any time, a power that has been a potent threat to the authority of the Court. The Judiciary Act of 1925 gave the Court discretion over its own jurisdiction, meaning that it does not have to accept all appeals that come to it. The idea behind the act was that the intermediate courts of appeals should be the final word for almost all federal litigants, thus freeing the Supreme Court to concentrate on constitutional issues, unless the Court decided that it wanted to address other matters. The Court, then, is not expected to exercise its appellate jurisdiction simply to correct errors of other courts. Instead, appeal to the Supreme Court should be taken only if the case presents important issues of law, or what is termed "a substantial federal question." Since 1988, nearly all appellate cases that had gone to the Supreme Court arrived there on a petition for a **writ of *certiorari*** (from the Latin "to be informed"), which is a request for the Supreme Court—at its discretion—to order up the records of the lower courts for purposes of review.

About one-third of all Supreme Court filings involve criminal law issues.[34] Many of these, in fact more than half of all petitions to the Court, are filed ***in forma pauperis*** (IFP) (literally from the Latin, "as a pauper"), which is a way for an indigent or poor person to appeal a case to the Supreme Court. About 80 percent of these are filed by indigent prison inmates seeking review of their sentences. Permission to proceed *in forma pauperis* allows the petitioner to avoid filing and printing costs. Any criminal defendant who has had a court-appointed lawyer in a lower court proceeding is automatically entitled to proceed in this fashion.

In recent years, the Court has tended more and more to deny requests to file *in forma pauperis*. In *In re Sindram* (1991), for example, the Rehnquist Court chastised Michael Sindram for filing his petition *in forma pauperis* to require the Maryland courts to expedite his request to expunge a $35 speeding ticket from his record. Sindram was no stranger to the Supreme Court: During the previous three years, he had filed forty-two separate motions on various legal matters, twenty-four of them in the 1990 term. In denying Sindram's request to file as an indigent, the majority noted that "[t]he goal of fairly dispensing justice . . . is compromised when the Court is forced to devote its limited resources to the processing of repetitious and frivolous requests." Along with the order denying the petition, the Court issued new rules to provide for denial of "frivolous" or "malicious" IFP motions.[35]

writ of *certiorari*
A request for the Court to order up the records from a lower court to review the case.

in forma pauperis
Literally, "as a pauper"; a way for an indigent or poor person to appeal a case to the U.S. Supreme Court.

The Rule of Four.   Unlike other federal courts, the Supreme Court controls its own caseload through the *certiorari* process, deciding which cases it wants to hear, and rejecting most cases that come to it. All petitions for *certiorari* must meet two criteria:

1. The case must come either from a U.S. court of appeals, a special three-judge district court, or a state court of last resort.
2. The case must involve a federal question. This means that the case must present questions of interpretation of federal constitutional law or involve a federal statute or treaty. The reasons that the Court should accept the case for review and legal argument supporting that position are set out in the petition (also called a brief).

The clerk of the Court's office transmits petitions for writs of *certiorari* first to the chief justice's office, where his clerks review the petitions, and then to the individual justices' offices. All the justices on the Rehnquist Court except Justice John Paul Stevens (for undisclosed reasons) participate in what is called the "*cert* pool."[36] As part of the pool, they review their assigned fraction of petitions and share their notes with each other. Those cases that the justices deem noteworthy are then placed on what is called the "discuss list"—a list of cases to be discussed—prepared by the chief justice's clerks and circulated to the chambers of the justices. All others are dead listed and go no further unless a justice asks that the case be removed from the dead list and discussed at conference. Only about 30 percent of submitted petitions make it to the discuss list. During one of the justices' weekly conference meetings, the cases on the discuss list are reviewed. The chief justice speaks first, then the rest of the justices, according to seniority. The decision process ends when the justices vote, and by custom, *certiorari* is granted according to the **Rule of Four**—when at least four justices vote to hear a case.

Rule of Four
At least four justices of the Supreme Court must vote to consider a case before it can be heard.

The Role of Clerks.   As early as 1850, the justices of the Supreme Court had beseeched Congress to approve the hiring of a clerk to assist each justice. Congress denied the request, so when Justice Horace Gray hired the first law clerk in 1882, he paid the clerk himself. Justice Gray's clerk was a top graduate of Harvard Law School whose duties included cutting Justice Gray's hair and running personal errands. Finally, in 1886, Congress authorized each justice to hire a "stenographer clerk" for $1,600 a year.

Clerks are typically selected from candidates at the top of the graduating classes of prestigious law schools. They perform a variety of tasks, ranging from searching for arcane facts to playing tennis or taking walks with the justices. Clerks spend most of their time researching material relevant to particular cases, reading and summarizing cases, and helping justices write opinions. The clerks also make the first pass through the petitions that come to the Court, undoubtedly influencing which cases get a second look. Just how much help they provide in the writing of opinions is unknown.[37]

Over time, the number of clerks employed by the justices has increased. Through the 1946 to 1969 terms, most justices employed two clerks. By 1970, most had three, and by 1980 all but three had four. In 2003, there were thirty-four clerks. This growth in clerks has had many interesting ramifications for the Court. "Between 1969 and 1972—the period during which the justices each became entitled to a third law clerk— . . . the number of opinions increased by about 50 percent and the number of words tripled."[38] And until recently, the number of cases decided annually increased as more help was available to the justices.

The relationship between clerks and the justices for whom they work is close and confidential, and many aspects of the relationship are kept secret. Clerks may sometimes talk among themselves about the views and personalities of their justices, but rarely has a clerk leaked such information to the press. In 1998, a former clerk to Justice Harry Blackmun broke the silence. Edward Lazarus published a book that shocked many Court watchers by penning an insider's account of how the Court really works.[39] He also charged that the justices give their young, often ideological clerks far too much power.

How Does a Case Survive the Process?

It can be difficult to determine why the Court decides to hear a particular case. Sometimes it involves a perceived national emergency, as was the case with appeals concerning the outcome of the 2000 presidential election. The Court does not offer reasons, and "the standards by which the justices decide to grant or deny review are highly personalized and necessarily discretionary," noted former Chief Justice Earl Warren, although sometimes individual justices publicly dissent from the Court's denial of *certiorari*. Moreover, he continued, "those standards cannot be captured in rules or guidelines that would be meaningful."[40] Political scientists have nonetheless attempted to determine the characteristics of the cases the Court accepts; not surprisingly, they are similar to those that help a case get on the discuss list. Among the cues are the following:

President George W. Bush nominated Theodore Olson to serve as his solicitor general. Olson represented Bush before the Supreme Court throughout the presidential election recount dispute. He narrowly won confirmation on a 51–47 vote in the Senate. (Photo courtesy: Reuters/NewMedia Inc./Corbis)

- The federal government is the party asking for review.
- The case involves conflict among the circuit courts.
- The case presents a civil rights or civil liberties question.
- The case involves ideological and/or policy preferences of the justices.
- The case has significant social or political interest, as evidenced by the presence of interest group ***amicus curiae*** briefs.

amicus curiae
"Friend of the court"; a third party to a lawsuit who files a legal brief for the purpose of raising additional points of view in an attempt to influence a court's decision.

solicitor general
The fourth-ranking member of the Justice Department; responsible for handling all appeals on behalf of the U.S. government to the Supreme Court.

The Federal Government.   One of the most important cues for predicting whether the Court will hear a case is the position the solicitor general takes on it. The **solicitor general,** appointed by the president, is the fourth-ranking member of the Justice Department and is responsible for handling all appeals on behalf of the U.S. government to the Supreme Court. The solicitor's staff is like a small, specialized law firm within the Justice Department. But because this office has such a special relationship with the Supreme Court, even having a suite of offices within the Supreme Court building, the solicitor general is often referred to as the Court's "ninth and a half member."[41] Moreover, the solicitor general, on behalf of the U.S. government, appears as a party or as an *amicus curiae* in more than 50 percent of the cases heard by the Court each term.

This special relationship with the Court helps explain the overwhelming success the solicitor general's office enjoys before the Supreme Court. The Court generally accepts 70 to 80 percent of the cases where the U.S. government is the petitioning party, compared with about 5 percent of all others.[42] But because of this special relationship, the solicitor general often ends up playing two conflicting roles: representing in Court both the president's policy interests and the broader interests of the United States. At times, solicitors find these two roles difficult to reconcile. Former Solicitor General Rex E. Lee (1981–1985), for example, noted that on more than one occasion he refused to make arguments in Court that had been advanced by the Reagan administration (a stand that ultimately forced him to resign his position). Said Lee, "I'm not the pamphleteer general; I'm the solicitor general. My audience is not 100 million people; my audience is nine people. . . . Credibility is the most important asset that any solicitor general has."[43]

WEB EXPLORATION
To examine the recent filings of the office of solicitor general, go to
www.ablongman.com/oconnor

Conflict Among the Circuits, Questions of Rights, and Ideological Preference.   Conflict among the lower courts is apparently another reason that the justices take cases. When interpretations of constitutional or federal law are involved, the justices seem to want consistency throughout the federal court system.

Often these conflicts occur when important civil rights or civil liberties questions arise. Political scientist Lawrence Baum has commented, "Justices' evaluations of lower court decisions are based largely on their ideological position."[44] Thus, it is not uncommon to see conservative justices voting to hear cases to overrule liberal lower court decisions, or vice versa.

Interest Group Participation.   A quick way for the justices to gauge the ideological ramifications of a particular case is by the amount of interest group participation. Richard C. Cortner has noted that "Cases do not arrive on the doorstep of the Supreme Court like orphans in the night."[45] Instead, most cases heard by the Supreme Court involve either the government or an interest group—either as the sponsoring party or as an *amicus curiae*. Liberal groups such as the ACLU, People for the American Way, the NAACP Legal Defense Fund, and conservative groups including the Washington Legal Foundation, Concerned Women for America, or Americans United for Life Legal Defense Fund routinely sponsor cases or file *amicus* briefs either urging the Court to hear a case or asking it to deny *certiorari*. Research by political scientists has found that "not only does [an *amicus*] brief in favor of *certiorari* significantly improve the chances of a case being accepted, but two, three and four briefs improve the chances even more."[46]

Clearly, it's the more the merrier, whether or not the briefs are filed for or against granting review.[47] Interest group participation may highlight lower court and ideological conflicts for the justices by alerting them to the amount of public interest in the issues presented in any particular case.

Starting the Case

Once a case is accepted for review, a flurry of activity begins (see Figure 10.7). If a criminal defendant is proceeding *in forma pauperis,* the Court appoints an expert lawyer to prepare and argue the case. Unlike the situation in many state courts, where appointed lawyers are often novices, it is considered an honor to be asked to represent an indigent before the Supreme Court even though such representation is on a *pro bono*, or no fee, basis.

Whether they are being paid or not, lawyers on both sides of the case begin to prepare their written arguments for submission to the Court. In these briefs, lawyers cite prior case law and make arguments as to why the Court should find in favor of their client.

FIGURE 10.7   How Supreme Court Decisions Get Made

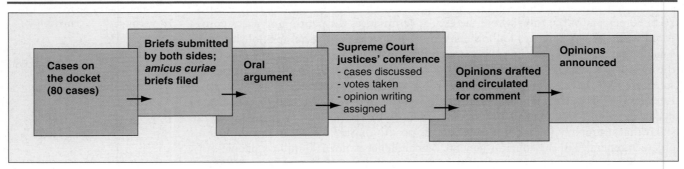

TABLE 10.7   *Amicus* Briefs in Support of a Plaintiff

Teresa Harris celebrates her victory after the Supreme Court ruled that her employer's conduct was illegal sexual harassment. (Photo courtesy: Fritz Hofmann/The Image Works)

In *Harris* v. *Forklift Systems* (1993), the U.S. Supreme Court unanimously ruled that federal civil rights law created a "broad rule of workplace equality." In *Harris*, the Court found that Title VII of the Civil Rights Act was violated when Teresa Harris was subjected to "intimidation, ridicule, and insults" of a sexually harassing nature by her supervisor. The following groups or governments filed *amicus* briefs:

In support of *Harris*

1. United States
   Equal Employment Opportunity Commission

2. National Conference of Women's Bar Associations
   Women's Bar Association of District of Columbia

3. National Organization for Women Legal Defense
      and Education Fund
   American Jewish Committee
   American Medical Women Association
   Asian American Legal Defense and Education Fund
   Association for Union Democracy
   Center for Women's Policy Studies
   Chicago Women in Trades
   Illinois Coalition Against Sexual Harassment
   National Organization for Women
   Northern Tradeswomen's Network
   Northern New England Tradeswomen Institute
   Puerto Rican Legal Defense and Education Fund
   Women's Law Project

4. NAACP Legal Defense and Education Fund
   National Conference of Jewish Women

5. Women's Legal Defense Fund
   National Women's Law Center
   AFL-CIO
   Ayuda, Inc.
   Bar Association of San Francisco
   California Women Lawyers
   Center for Women Policy Studies
   Coalition of Labor Union Women
   Committee for Justice for Women of North Carolina
   Federally Employed Women, Inc.
   Federation of Organizations for Professional Women
   Institute for Women's Policy Research
   Mexican American Women's National Association

   National Association of Female Executives
   National Association of Social Workers, Inc.
   National Center for Lesbian Rights
   National Council of Negro Women, Inc.
   National Association of Working Women
   9 to 5
   Older Women's League
   Trial Lawyers for Public Justice
   Wider Opportunities for Women
   Women Employed
   Women's Action Alliance
   Women's Bar Association of the District of Columbia
   Women's Law Center of Maryland
   YWCA of the U.S.A.

6. Employment Law Center
   California Women Lawyer's Committee
   Equal Rights Advocates

7. National Employment Lawyers Association

8. American Civil Liberties Union
   American Jewish Congress

9. Feminists for Free Expression

10. Southern States Police Benevolent Association
    North Carolina Police Benevolent Association

11. National Conference of Women's Bar Associations
    Women's Bar Association of the District of Columbia

In Support of Forklift Systems

1. Equal Employment Advisory Council

For Neither Party

1. American Psychological Association

More often than not, these arguments are echoed or expanded in *amicus curiae* briefs filed by interested parties, especially interest groups. (The vast majority of the cases decided by the Court in the 1990s had at least one *amicus* brief.)

Since the 1970s interest groups have increasingly used the *amicus* brief as a way to lobby the Court. Because litigation is so expensive, few individuals have the money (or time or interest) to pursue a perceived wrong all the way to the U.S. Supreme Court. All sorts of interest groups, then, find that joining ongoing cases through *amicus* briefs is a useful way of advancing their policy preferences. Major cases such as *Brown* v. *Board of Education* (1954), *Casey* v. *Planned Parenthood of Southeastern Pennsylvania* (1992), and *Harris* v. *Forklift Systems* (1993), which involved the degree of psychological damage a victim of sexual harassment must show, all attracted large numbers of *amicus* briefs as part of interest groups' efforts to lobby the judiciary and bring about desired political objectives[48] (see Table 10.7).

Interest groups also provide the Court with information not necessarily contained in the major-party briefs, help write briefs, and assist in practice moot-court sessions. In these sessions the lawyer who will argue the case before the nine justices goes through a complete rehearsal, with prominent lawyers and law professors playing the roles of the various justices.

Longman
Participate.com 2.0
Simulation
**You Are a
Young Lawyer**

Oral Arguments.   Once a case is accepted by the Court for full review, and after briefs and *amicus* briefs are submitted on each side, oral argument takes place. The Supreme Court's annual term begins the first Monday in October, as it has since the late 1800s, and runs through late June or early July. In the early 1800s, sessions of the Court lasted only a few weeks twice a year. Today, justices hear oral arguments from the beginning of the term until early April. Special cases, such as *U.S.* v. *Nixon* (1974), have been heard even later in the year.[49] During the term, "sittings," periods of about two weeks in which cases are heard, alternate with "recesses," also about two weeks long. Oral arguments are usually heard Monday through Wednesday during two-week sitting sessions.

Oral argument is generally limited to the immediate parties in the case, although it is not uncommon for the U.S. solicitor general to appear to argue orally as an *amicus curiae*. Oral argument at the Court is fraught with time-honored tradition and ceremony. At precisely ten o'clock every morning when the Court is in session, the Court Marshal (dressed in a cutaway—a formal morning coat) emerges to intone "Oyez! Oyez! Oyez!" as the nine justices emerge from behind a reddish-purple velvet curtain to take their places on the raised and slightly angled bench. (From 1790 to 1972, the justices sat on a straight bench. Chief Justice Burger modified it so that justices at either end could see and hear better.) The chief justice sits in the middle with the justices to his right and left, alternating in seniority.

Almost all attorneys are allotted one half hour to present their cases, and this allotment includes the time taken by questions from the bench. Justice John Marshall Harlan once noted that there was "no substitute for this method in getting at the heart of an issue and in finding out where the truth lies."[50] As the lawyer for the appellee approaches the mahogany lectern, a green light goes on, indicating that the attorney's time has begun. A white light flashes when five minutes remain. When a red light goes on, Court practice mandates that counsel stop immediately. One famous piece of Court lore told to all attorneys concerns a counsel who continued talking and reading from his prepared argument after the red light went on. When he looked up, he found an empty bench—the justices had quietly risen and departed while he continued to talk. On another occasion, Chief Justice Charles Evans Hughes stopped a leader of the New York bar in the middle of the word "if."

Although many Court watchers have tried to figure out how a particular justice will vote based on the questioning at oral argument, most find that the nature and number of questions asked does not help much in predicting the outcome of a case. Nevertheless, many believe that oral argument has several important functions. First, it is the only opportunity for even a small portion of the public (who may attend the hearings) and the press to observe the workings of the Court. Second, it assures lawyers that the justices have heard their case, and it forces lawyers to focus on arguments believed important by the justices. Last, it provides the Court with additional information, especially concerning the Court's broader political role, an issue not usually addressed in written briefs. For example, the justices can ask how many people might be affected by its decision or where the Court (and country) would be heading if a case were decided in a particular way. Justice Stephen Breyer also notes that oral arguments are a good way for the justices to try to highlight certain issues for other justices.

The Conference and the Vote. The Justices meet in closed conference once a week when the Court is hearing oral argument. Since the ascendancy of Chief Justice Roger B. Taney to the Court in 1836, the justices have begun each conference session with a round of handshaking. Once the door to the conference room closes, no others are allowed to enter. The Justice with the least seniority acts as the doorkeeper for the other eight, communicating with those waiting outside to fill requests for documents, water, and so on.

Conferences highlight the importance and power of the chief justice, who presides over them and makes the initial presentation of each case. Each individual justice then discusses the case in order of his or her seniority on the Court, with the most senior justice speaking next. Most accounts of the decision-making process reveal that at this point some justices try to change the minds of others, but that most enter the conference room with a clear idea of how they feel. Although other Courts have followed different procedures, on the Rehnquist Court the justices generally vote at the same time they discuss the case with each justice speaking only once. Initial conference votes are not final, allowing justices to change their minds before final votes are taken later.

Writing Opinions. There are basically five kinds of opinions that can be written:

1. A *majority opinion* is written by one member of the Court, and as such reflects the views of at least a majority of the justices. This opinion usually sets out the legal reasoning justifying the decision, and this legal reasoning becomes a precedent for deciding future cases.
2. A *concurring opinion* is one written by a justice who agrees with the outcome of the case but not with the legal rationale for the decision.
3. A *plurality opinion* is one that attracts the support of three or four justices. Generally, this opinion becomes the controlling opinion of the Court. Usually one or more justices agrees with the outcome of the decision in a concurring opinion, but there is no solid majority for the legal reasoning behind the outcome. Plurality opinions do not have the precedential value of majority opinions.
4. A *dissenting opinion* is one that is written by one or more justices who disagree with the opinion of a majority or plurality of the Court.
5. A *per curiam opinion* is an unsigned opinion issued by the Court. Justices may dissent from *per curiam* opinions but do so fairly rarely. The seventy-page, *Bush* v. *Gore* (2000) was an unsigned, *per curiam* opinion.

The chief justice, if he is in the majority, has the job of assigning the writing of the opinion. This privilege enables him to wield tremendous power. (If he is in the minority, the assignment falls to the most senior justice in the majority.)

The justice assigned to write the majority opinion circulates drafts of the opinion to all members of the Court. The Court must provide legal reasons for its positions. The reasoning behind any decision is often as important as the outcome. Under our system of *stare decisis*, both are likely to be relied on as precedent later by lower courts confronted with cases involving similar issues. The justice who drafts

WEB EXPLORATION
For an analysis of the Court's 2000 election decision by constitutional scholars, go to
www.ablongman.com/oconnor

the opinion can have an important impact on how any legal issues are framed. Informal caucusing and negotiation then often take place, as justices may "hold out" for word changes or other modifications as a condition of their continued support of the majority opinion. At the same time, dissenting opinions and/or concurring opinions also circulate through the various chambers. The justices are often assisted in their writing of opinions by their clerks, who also can serve as intermediaries between the justices as they talk among themselves.

A good example of how politics can be involved at the opinion-writing stage is evident in *Bowers* v. *Hardwick* (1986), the Georgia consensual sodomy case discussed in chapters 5 and 6.[51] Justices White and Burger voted for *certiorari* believing that the Constitution doesn't protect homosexual acts. The liberal Justices Marshall and Brennan thought they had enough votes to overturn the law, but when Brennan perceived he would lose, he withdrew his vote for *certiorari,* albeit too late. Once the case was argued, coalitions quickly shifted. According to papers kept by Justice Marshall, Justice Powell originally indicated at conference that he would vote with the majority to find the law unconstitutional. After drafts of the majority and minority opinions were circulated, however, he changed his mind, thus changing a 5–4 majority to strike down the law into a 5–4 majority to uphold it.[52]

This kind of communal work can result in poorly written opinions, as was the case with *U.S.* v. *Nixon* (1974).[53] Although the opinion involving President Nixon's refusal to turn over tape recordings of his conversations was issued under Chief Justice Burger's name, many believe that it was a combination of several justices' contributions and additions. Sensing the need for the Court to speak unanimously in such an important opinion—one that pitted two branches of government against each other—Chief Justice Burger apparently made concessions to get support.[54] This process led to some very confused prose in some sections of the opinion.

Recently, tensions have grown on the Court concerning some issues, and dissents or concurring opinions have become quite pointed. The protocol of the Court has always been characterized by politeness, but this has not stopped some justices from openly ridiculing their colleagues from the bench. Justice Scalia, for example, publicly criticized Justice O'Connor's opinion in *Webster* v. *Reproductive Health Services* (1989), saying that her "assertion that a fundamental rule of judicial restraint requires [the Court] to avoid reconsidering *Roe* [v. *Wade*] cannot be taken seriously."[55] This kind of ridicule was unprecedented and perhaps simply reflects how manners in politics are on the decline.

Not all cases result in split decisions from the justices. In *Clinton* v. *Jones* (1997), which involved President Clinton's attempt to defer Paula Jones's action for civil damages against him, a unanimous Court affirmed the lower court ruling allowing the case to go forward. Justice Breyer, who was appointed by Clinton, concurred with the opinion of the other eight justices, but did so only to underscore his belief that a federal judge could not schedule judicial proceedings that could interfere with the president's discharge of his public duties.[56] So here, in a decision that was to set the stage for debating articles of impeachment against the president, all nine justices—including two justices appointed by Clinton—were in agreement.

HOW THE JUSTICES VOTE

Justices are human beings, and they do not make decisions in a vacuum. Principles of *stare decisis* dictate that the justices follow the law of previous cases in deciding cases at hand. But more factors are usually operating. A variety of legal and extra-legal factors have been found to affect Supreme Court decision making. As Politics Now: Lobbying for Jurists indicates, there may be other ways too.

POLITICS NOW

LOBBYING FOR JURISTS

By now you should realize that judges, appointed and confirmed through an often highly political process, may reflect political or ideological biases. How else might we explain the growing number of 5–4 decisions including *Bush* v. *Gore* (2000) from the U.S. Supreme Court? Today some judges and justices lobby for spots on the federal bench, and interest groups bring cases to courts they believe are amenable to their causes. Interest groups are also involved in another form of perhaps more insidious lobbying that has received very little attention.

From 1992 to 1998, more than 230 federal judges took all-expenses-paid trips to resort locations (some might call these vacations) to attend legal seminars paid for by corporations and foundations that have interests in cases already in or likely to be soon in federal court. These seminars are always held in warm places and have been occurring since the early 1980s. The most recent seminars have been devoted to issues of environmental litigation, where the message from the seminar sponsors was that regula-

tion should be limited and that "the free market should be relied upon to protect the environment."*

In fact, judges who attended those seminars wrote ten of the most crucial rulings handed down during the 1990s dealing with curbing environmental protection, including decisions invalidating a provision of the Endangered Species Protection Act and another regulation that attempted to abate soot and smog. Although judges are asked each year to report outside sources of income, which itself is also controversial, many judges do not note these seminars on their financial disclosure forms. Whether undue influence is felt at these seminars, there is at least the appearance of a conflict of interest. Do you think that judges who go on these trips should rule on cases involving the parties hosting these events?

---

*Abner Mikva, "The Wooing of Our Judges," *The New York Times*, August 28, 2000, A17.

Legal Factors

Legal scholars long have argued that judges decide cases based on the Constitution and their reading of various statutes. Determining what the Framers meant—if that is even important today—often appears to be based on an individual jurist's philosophy.

Judicial Philosophy and Original Intent.   One of the primary issues concerning judicial decision making focuses on what is called the activism/restraint debate. Advocates of **judicial restraint** argue that courts should allow the decisions of other branches to stand, even when they offend a judge's own sense of principles.[57] Restraintists defend their position by asserting that the federal courts are composed of unelected judges, which makes the judicial branch the least democratic branch of government. Consequently, the courts should defer policy making to other branches of government as much as possible.

Restraintists refer to *Roe* v. *Wade* (1973), the case that liberalized abortion laws, as a classic example of **judicial activism** run amok. They maintain that the Court should have deferred policy making on this sensitive issue to the states or to the other branches of the federal government—the legislative and executive—because their officials are elected and therefore are more receptive to the majority's will.

Advocates of judicial activism contend that judges should use their power broadly to further justice, especially in the areas of equality and personal liberty. Activists argue that it is the courts' appropriate role to correct injustices committed by the other branches of government. Explicit in this argument is the notion that courts need to protect oppressed minorities.[58]

judicial restraint
A philosophy of judicial decision making that argues courts should allow the decisions of other branches of government to stand, even when they offend a judge's own sense of principles.

judicial activism
A philosophy of judicial decision making that argues judges should use their power broadly to further justice, especially in the areas of equality and personal liberty.

The "zipper" in New York's Time Square announces the Supreme Court's decision regarding the recounting of votes in Florida's presidential election. (Photo courtesy: Robert Mecea/AP/Wide World Photos)

Activists point to *Brown* v. *Board of Education* (1954) as an excellent example of the importance of judicial activism.[59] In *Brown,* the Supreme Court ruled that racial segregation in public schools violated the equal protection clause of the Fourteenth Amendment. Segregation was nonetheless practiced after passage of the Fourteenth Amendment. An activist would point out that if the Court had not reinterpreted its provisions of the amendment, many states probably would still have laws or policies mandating segregation in public schools.

The debate over judicial activism versus judicial restraint often focuses on how the Court should interpret the meaning of the Constitution. Advocates of judicial restraint generally agree that judges should be strict constructionists; that is, they should interpret the Constitution as it was written and intended by the Framers. They argue that in determining the constitutionality of a statute or policy, the Court should rely on the explicit meanings of the clauses in the document, which can be clarified by looking at the intent of the Framers.

Precedent.   Most Supreme Court decisions are laced with numerous references to previous Court decisions. Some justices, however, believe that *stare decisis* and adherence to precedent is no longer as critical as it once was. Chief Justice Rehnquist, for example, has noted that while "*stare decisis* is a cornerstone of our legal system . . . it has less power in constitutional cases."[60] In contrast, Justices O'Connor, Kennedy, and Souter explained their reluctance to overrule *Roe* v. *Wade* (1973) in *Planned Parenthood of Southeastern Pennsylvania* v. *Casey* (1992): "to overrule under fire in the absence of the most compelling reason to reexamine a watershed decision would subject this Court's legitimacy beyond any serious question."[61]

Interestingly, a 1990 study of the American public's knowledge and perceptions of the Court indicated that only 44 percent believed that the Court decides cases primarily on the basis of facts and law. Nearly 50 percent believe that the Court makes decisions based on other factors, including political pressures (28 percent), political/personal beliefs (18 percent), and religious beliefs (1 percent). More recently, a study conducted after *Bush* v. *Gore* found that 29 percent of those polled saw political reasons as motivating that decision. Although *theoretically* the Framers envisioned the Court to be above these pressures, the American public does not appear to be particularly upset about the role of politics and personal beliefs in the decision-making process. In fact, those polled want the Court to take a more active role in the areas of discrimination against women and minorities.

Extra-Legal Factors

Most political scientists who study what is called judicial behavior conclude that a variety of forces shape judicial decision making. Of late, many have attempted to explain how judges vote by integrating a variety of models to offer a more complete picture of how judges make decisions.[62] Many of those models attempt to take into account justices' behavioral characteristics and attitudes as well as the fact patterns of the case.

WEB EXPLORATION
To learn about ethics in the courts and view what some consider "outrageous" judicial rulings, go to www.ablongman.com/oconnor Which rulings do you consider most "outrageous"?

Behavioral Characteristics.   Originally, some political scientists argued that social background differences, including childhood experiences, religious values, education, earlier political and legal careers, and political party loyalties are likely to influence how a judge evaluates the facts and legal issues presented in any given case. Justice Harry A. Blackmun's service at the Mayo Clinic is often pointed to as a reason that his opinion for the Court in *Roe* v. *Wade* was so soundly grounded in medical evidence. Similarly, Justice Potter Stewart, who was generally considered a moderate on most civil liberties issues, usually took a more liberal position on cases dealing with freedom of the press. Why? It may be that Stewart's early job as a newspaper reporter made him more sensitive to these claims.

Ideology.   Critics of the social background approach argued that attitudes or ideologies can better explain the justices' voting patterns. Since the 1940s the two most prevailing ideologies in the United States have been conservative and liberal. On the Supreme Court, justices with "conservative" views generally vote against affirmative action, abortion rights, expanded rights for criminal defendants, and increased power for the national government. In contrast, "liberals" tend to support the parties advancing these positions.

Over time, scholars have generally agreed that identifiable ideological voting blocs have occurred on the Court. During Franklin D. Roosevelt's first term, for example, five justices, a critical conservative bloc, routinely voted to strike down the constitutionality of New Deal legislation. Traditionally, such voting blocs or coalitions have centered on liberal/conservative splits on issues such as states' rights (conservatives supporting and liberals opposing), economic issues (conservatives being pro-business; liberals, pro-labor), and civil liberties and civil rights (conservatives being less supportive than liberals). In death penalty cases, for example, Justices William Brennan and Thurgood Marshall (sometimes joined by John Paul Stevens) consistently voted against the imposition of capital punishment.

The Attitudinal and Strategic Models.   The attitudinal approach hypothesizes that there is a substantial link between judicial attitudes and decision making.[63] Simply stated, the attitudinal model holds that Supreme Court justices decide cases in light of the facts of the cases according to their personal preferences toward issues of public policy. Among some of the factors used to derive attitudes are a justice's party identification,[64] the party of the appointing president,[65] and the liberal/conservative leanings of a justice. Although by 1995 many judicial scholars were claiming that the attitudinal model could be used to explain all judicial decision making, by 2000 that was no longer the case. Now, several scholars who study the courts are advocating their belief that judges act strategically, meaning that they weigh and assess their actions against those of other justices to optimize the chances that their preferences will be adopted by the whole Court.[66] Moreover, this approach seeks to explain not only a justice's vote but also the range of forces such as congressional/judicial relations and judicial/executive relations that also affect the outcome of legal disputes.

Public Opinion.   Many political scientists also have examined the role of public opinion in Supreme Court decision making.[67] Not only do the justices read legal briefs and hear oral arguments, but they also read newspapers, watch television, and have some knowledge of public opinion—especially on controversial issues. According to Chief Justice Rehnquist,

> Judges, so long as they are relatively normal human beings, can no more escape being influenced by public opinion in the long run than can people working at other jobs. And if a judge on coming to the bench were to decide to hermetically seal himself off from all manifestations of public opinion, he would accomplish very little; he would not be influenced by current public opinion, but instead would be influenced by the state of public opinion at the time he came to the bench.[68]

Political scientist Thomas R. Marshall has discovered substantial variation in the degree to which particular justices' decisions were congruent with public opinion.[69] Whether or not public opinion actually influences some justices, public opinion can act as a check on the power of the courts as well as an energizing factor. Activist periods on the Supreme Court have generally corresponded to periods of social or economic crisis. For example, the Marshall Court supported a strong national government, much to the chagrin of a series of pro–states' rights Democratic–Republican presidents in the early crisis-ridden years of the republic. Similarly, the Court capitulated to political pressures and public opinion when, after 1936, it reversed many of its earlier decisions that had blocked President Roosevelt's New Deal legislation.

The courts, especially the Supreme Court, also can be the direct target of public opinion. During the spring of 1989, when the case of *Webster* v. *Reproductive Health Services* was about to come before the Supreme Court, the Court was subjected to unprecedented lobbying as groups and individuals on both sides of the abortion issue marched and sent appeals to the Court. Earlier, in the fall of 1988, Justice Harry A. Blackmun, author of *Roe* v. *Wade,* had warned a law school audience in a public address that he feared that the decision was in jeopardy. This in itself was a highly unusual move; until recently, it was the practice of the justices never to comment on cases or the Court.

Speeches like Blackmun's put pro-choice advocates on guard, and many took advantage of the momentum that had built around their successful campaign against the nomination of Robert H. Bork. In 1989, their forces mounted one of the largest demonstrations in the history of the United States—more than 300,000 people marched from the Mall to the Capitol building, just across the street from the Supreme Court. In addition, full-page advertisements appeared in prominent newspapers, and supporters of *Roe* v. *Wade* were urged to contact members of the Court to voice their support. Justice Sandra Day O'Connor, at the time the Court's lone woman, was targeted by many who viewed her as the crucial swing justice on the issue. Mail at the Court, which usually averages about 1,000 pieces a day, rose to an astronomical 46,000 pieces when *Webster* reached the Court, virtually paralyzing normal lines of communication. Several justices spoke out against this kind of "extra-judicial" communication and voiced their belief in its ineffectiveness. In *Webster* v. *Reproductive Health Services* (1989), Justice Scalia lamented,

> We can now look forward to at least another Term with carts full of mail from the public, and streets full of demonstrators, urging us—their unelected and life tenured judges

TABLE 10.8   The Court Versus the American Public

In recent years, the Court has agreed and disagreed with the public on various issues, such as:

Issue	Court	Public
Should TV and other recording devices be permitted in the Supreme Court?	No	Yes (59%)
Should a parent be forced to reveal the whereabouts of a child even though it could violate Fifth Amendment rights?	Yes	Yes (50%) No (39%) Don't know (11%)
Should a family be allowed to decide to end life-support systems?	Yes	Yes (88%)
Before getting an abortion, whose consent should a teenager be required to gain?	One parent	Both parents (38%) One parent (37%) Neither parent (22%)
Is the death penalty constitutional?	Yes	Yes (72% favor)
Should members of Congress be subject to term limits?	No	Yes (77% favor)

Source: Table compiled from General Social Surveys, Gallup Poll data, and a Tarrance Group Poll.

who have been awarded those extraordinary, undemocratic characteristics precisely in order that we might follow the law despite the popular will—to follow the popular will.

But the fact remains that the Court is very dependent on the public for its prestige as well as for compliance with its decisions. In times of war and other emergencies, for example, the Court frequently has decided cases in ways that commentators have attributed to the sway of public opinion and political exigencies. In *Korematsu* v. *The United States* (1944), for example, the high Court upheld the obviously unconstitutional internment of Japanese American citizens during World War II.[70] Moreover, Chief Justice Rehnquist himself has suggested that the Court's restriction on presidential authority in *Youngstown Sheet & Tube Co.* v. *Sawyer* (1952),[71] which invalidated President Harry S Truman's seizure of the nation's steel mills, was largely attributable to Truman's unpopularity and that of the Korean War.[72] As Table 10.8 reveals, the public and the Court often are in agreement on many controversial issues.

Public confidence in the Court, like other institutions of government, has ebbed and flowed. Public support for the Court was highest after the Court issued *U.S.* v. *Nixon* (1974). At a time when Americans lost faith in the presidency, they could at least look to the Supreme Court to do the right thing. Of late, however, the Court and the judicial system as a whole have taken a beating in public confidence. In the aftermath of the O. J. Simpson trial, many white Americans faulted the judicial system. This dissatisfaction was reflected in low levels of confidence in the judicial system, although the Supreme Court enjoys greater popular support than the other two branches of government. In 2000, 62 percent of those sampled by the Gallup Organization had a favorable opinion of the Supreme Court. Still, race seems to color an individuals' perceptions of the Court. Nearly 80 percent of blacks disagreed with the Court's decision in *Bush* v. *Gore*; only 18 percent of the whites polled did.

The Supreme Court also appears to affect public opinion. Political scientists have found that the court affects public opinion when it first rules in controversial cases such as those involving abortion or capital punishment but that subsequent decisions have little effect.[73]

JUDICIAL POLICY MAKING AND IMPLEMENTATION

Clearly, the American public regards the Supreme Court as a powerful policy maker. In a 1990 poll, most respondents said they believed that the Court was more powerful than the president (31 percent versus 21 percent), and that the Court was close to being as powerful as Congress (38 percent).

All judges, whether they like it or not, make policy. In 1996, when the U.S. Supreme Court ruled that Colorado could not prevent states and local governments from extending any constitutional protections to gay, lesbian, and bisexual citizens, the justices were making policy.[74] When the Court ruled that prayer at public school ceremonies was a violation of separation of church and state, the Court made policy.[75] It is through interpreting statutes or the Constitution that federal courts, and the Supreme Court in particular, make policy in several ways. Judges can interpret a provision of a law to cover matters not previously understood to be covered by the

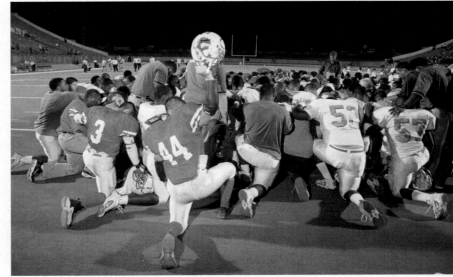

Football players at Odessa High School in Texas pray after their season opening game in September 2000. The players joined together for an unsanctioned prayer session as the Supreme Court's June ruling banning school-sanctioned pre-game prayer came into play. (Photo courtesy: Foe Raedle/Newsmakers/Liaison Agency/Getty Source)

law, or they can "discover" new rights, such as that of privacy, from their reading of the Constitution. They can also affect lives, with the extreme being death penalty cases.

This power of the courts to make policy presents difficult questions for democratic theory, as noted by Justice Scalia in *Webster*, because democratic theorists believe that the power to make law resides only in the people or their elected representatives. Yet court rulings, especially Supreme Court decisions, routinely affect policy far beyond the interests of the immediate parties.

Policy Making

One measure of the power of the courts and their ability to make policy is that more than one hundred federal laws have been declared unconstitutional. Although many of these laws have not been particularly significant, others have. For example, in *Immigration and Naturalization Service* v. *Chadha* (1983) (discussed in chapter 7), the Court found that legislative vetoes were unconstitutional.[76]

Another measure of the policy making power of the Supreme Court is its ability to overrule itself. Although the Court generally abides by the informal rule of *stare decisis,* by one count it has overruled itself in more than 140 cases since 1810. *Brown* v. *Board of Education* (1954), for example, overruled *Plessy* v. *Ferguson* (1896), thereby reversing years of constitutional interpretation concluding that racial segregation was not a violation of the Constitution. Moreover, in the past few years, the Court has repeatedly reversed earlier decisions in the areas of criminal defendants' rights, affirmative action, and the establishment of religion, thus revealing its powerful role in determining national policy.

A measure of the growing power of the federal courts is the degree to which they now handle issues that, after *Marbury* v. *Madison* (1803), had considered political questions more appropriately left to the other branches of government to decide. Prior to 1962, for example, the Court refused to hear cases questioning the size (and populations) of congressional districts, no matter how unequal they were.[77] The boundary of a legislative district was considered a political question. Then in 1962, writing for the Court, Justice William Brennan concluded that simply because a case involved a political issue it did not necessarily involve a political question. This opened up the floodgates to cases involving a variety of issues that the Court formerly had declined to address.[78]

Implementing Court Decisions

President Andrew Jackson, annoyed about a particular decision handed down by the Marshall Court, is alleged to have said, "John Marshall has made his decision; now let him enforce it." Jackson's statement raises a question: How do Supreme Court rulings translate into public policy? In fact, although judicial decisions carry legal and even moral authority, all courts must rely on other units of government to carry out their directives. If the president or Congress, for example, doesn't like a particular Supreme Court ruling, they can underfund programs needed to implement a decision or seek only lax enforcement. **Judicial implementation** refers to how and whether judicial decisions are translated into actual public policies affecting more than the immediate parties to the lawsuit.

How well a decision is implemented often depends on how well crafted or popular it is. Hostile reaction in the South to *Brown* v. *Board of Education* (1954) and the absence of precise guidelines to implement the decision meant that the ruling went largely unenforced for years. The *Brown* experience also highlights how much the Supreme Court needs the support of both federal and state courts as well as other governmental agencies to carry out its judgments. For example, you may have graduated from high school since 1992, when the Supreme Court ruled that public middle school and high school graduations could not include a prayer. Yet your own commencement ceremony may have included one.

judicial implementation
Refers to how and whether judicial decisions are translated into actual public policies affecting more than the immediate parties to a lawsuit.

(Photo courtesy: By permsission of Mike Luckovich and Creators Syndicate)

Charles Johnson and Bradley C. Canon suggest that the implementation of judicial decisions involves what they call an *implementing population* and a *consumer population*.[79] The implementing population consists of those people responsible for carrying out a decision. It varies, depending on the policy and issues in question, but can include lawyers, judges, public officials, police officers and police departments, hospital administrators, government agencies, and corporations. In the case of school prayer, the implementing population could include teachers, school administrators, or the school board. The consumer population consists of those people who might be directly affected by a decision, that is, students and parents.

For effective implementation of a judicial decision, the first requirement is that the members of the implementing population must act to show that they understand the original decision. For example, the Supreme Court ruled in *Reynolds* v. *Sims* (1964) that every person should have an equally weighted vote in electing governmental representatives.[80] This "one person, one vote" decision might seem simple enough at first glance,

TABLE 10.9　The Future Composition of the Supreme Court

In spite of these tables, many commentators speculate that it will be Chief Justice O'Connor who will depart the bench first.

Justice	Age in 2001	Philosophy	Projected Year of Retirement*
Stevens	81	Moderate	2002
Rehnquist	77	Conservative	2006
O'Connor	71	Conservative to Moderate	2012
Scalia	65	Conservative	2018
Kennedy	65	Conservative to Moderate	2018
Souter	62	Moderate	2021
Thomas	53	Conservative	2030
Ginsburg	69	Moderate to Liberal	2010
Breyer	63	Moderate	2020

*This is based on the age of the last six justices (Brennan, Burger, Marshall, Powell, White, and Blackmun) when they retired from 1986 to 1994—eighty-one years of age.

GLOBAL POLITICS

THE POWERS OF THE COURTS

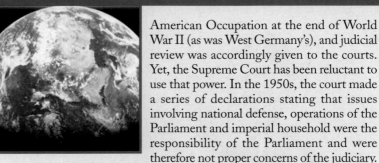

Judicial review is an American innovation that reflects the concern with balancing the branches of government under a system of separation of powers. It does not exist in all political systems, and how it is used in practice varies.

The United Kingdom and China occupy one extreme; these two countries do not afford the courts judicial review. In the British case, judicial review is seen as a violation of the principle of parliamentary sovereignty, that Parliament is the supreme organ of government. Consistent with this principle, the House of Lords, which combines a history of legislative and judicial functions, acts as the highest court. Judicial review is also inconsistent with socialist legality, which places the Communist Party above the law, so Chinese courts do not exercise judicial review.

A number of constitutions afford their courts limited powers of judicial review. In Russia and Mexico, the courts can overturn legislative acts but not executive actions. France stands out in this group because the Constitutional Council is not a court. It is a body of eminent persons appointed respectively by the president and the two houses of Parliament, and it rules only on the constitutionality of legislation current under debate. The deliberations of the council can be seen as part of the legislative process itself.

Japan's experience illustrates another aspect of judicial review. Japan's 1947 constitution was written during the American Occupation at the end of World War II (as was West Germany's), and judicial review was accordingly given to the courts. Yet, the Supreme Court has been reluctant to use that power. In the 1950s, the court made a series of declarations stating that issues involving national defense, operations of the Parliament and imperial household were the responsibility of the Parliament and were therefore not proper concerns of the judiciary. In so doing, the Supreme Court removed itself from the most controversial issues of the time, issues which had engendered numerous lawsuits by citizens.

Malapportionment of electoral seats in the Parliament illustrates the high court's reluctance to intervene in parliamentary operations. As the Japanese population shifted from the countryside to the cities in the postwar era, rural electoral districts became overrepresented at the expense of their urban counterparts. In extreme cases voters in some districts had the equivalent of nearly five times as many votes as did citizens in certain other districts, a violation of the constitutional principle of one person, one vote. The Supreme Court first ruled on suit brought in the wake of elections in 1976, ruling that while overrepresented rural districts violated the constitution, it was up to the Parliament to provide a remedy. Using similar arguments, the courts have continued to issue rulings that refuse to overturn the results of parliamentary elections. In the most recent case involving the 1998 House of Representatives election, plaintiffs sued the government alleging that malapportionment continues despite electoral reforms enacted in the mid-1990s (which had had the support of the judiciary): the Supreme Court again refused to nullify the results of the election.

Japan's case suggests that judicial activism is not necessarily part and parcel of judicial review. Whether the courts are active in shaping politics has to do with how the courts perceive their role in relation to other parts of government.

Judicial Review in 11 Countries

Country	Highest Court	Power of the Court
Canada	Supreme Court	judicial review
China	Supreme Peoples Court	no judicial review
France	Constitutional Council	limited judicial review
Germany	Federal Constitutional Court	judicial review
Indonesia	Supreme Court	judicial review
Italy	Constitutional Court	judicial review
Japan	Supreme Court	judicial review
Mexico	Supreme Court of Justice	limited judicial review
Russia	Constitutional Court	limited judicial review
United Kingdom	House of Lords	no judicial review
United States	**Supreme Court**	**judicial review**

Longman
Participate.com
2.0
Comparative
**Comparing
Judiciaries**

but in practice it can be very difficult to understand. The implementing population in this case consists chiefly of state legislatures and local governments, which determine voting districts for federal, state, and local offices (see chapter 7). If a state legislature draws districts in such a way that African American voters are spread thinly across a number of separate constituencies, the chances are slim that any particular district will elect a representative who is especially sensitive to blacks' concerns. Does that violate "equal representation"? (In practice, through the early 1990s, courts and the Justice Department intervened in many cases to ensure that elected officials would include minority representation, only ultimately to be overruled by the Supreme Court.)

The second requirement is that the implementing population must actually follow Court policy. Thus, when the Court ruled that men could not be denied admission to a state-sponsored nursing school, the implementing population—in this case, university administrators and the board of regents of the nursing school—had to enroll qualified male students.

Judicial decisions are most likely to be implemented smoothly if responsibility for implementation is concentrated in the hands of a few highly visible public officials, such as the president or a governor. By the same token, these officials can also thwart or impede judicial intentions. Recall from chapter 6, for example, the effect of Governor Orval Faubus's initial refusal to allow black children to attend all-white public schools in Little Rock, Arkansas.

The third requirement for implementation is that the consumer population must be aware of the rights that a decision grants or denies them. Teenagers seeking an abortion, for example, are consumers of the Supreme Court's decisions on abortion. They need to know that most states require them to inform their parents of their intention to have an abortion or to get parental permission to do so. Similarly, criminal defendants and their lawyers are consumers of Court decisions and need to know, for example, the implications of recent Court decisions for evidence presented at trial.

Continuity & Change

Participation in the Judicial Process

At the time the Constitution was adopted, women and African Americans were largely excluded from the judicial process. Neither could vote, and largely on that basis, both groups were excluded from jury service. Similarly, no women or African Americans were lawyers or judges. A handful of black lawyers practiced in the North in the mid-1880s, and John Swett Rock was admitted to practice before the Supreme Court in 1861. The first women lawyers were admitted to practice in the late 1860s. When Belva Lockwood's petition to be admitted to the Supreme Court bar was denied in 1876, she energetically lobbied Congress, which passed a law requiring the Court to admit qualified women to practice. In 1879, she became the first woman admitted to practice before the Supreme Court.

Women and blacks were often excluded from jury service because many states selected jurors from those registered to vote. African Americans were systematically excluded from the voter rolls throughout the South until after passage of the Voting Rights Act of 1965 (VRA). They have only recently begun to be part of the judicial system as the VRA has been implemented. As early as 1888, however, the Supreme Court ruled that Negro citizens could not be barred from serving as jurors.[81] It was not until 1975 that the Supreme Court was to rule that states could not exclude women from jury service.[82]

As a result of the civil rights and women's rights movements detailed in chapter 6, the number as well as percentage of women and minority lawyers and judges has grown tremendously. Today, 29 percent of all lawyers are women, and 7 percent are African American, Hispanic, or Native American. Similarly, beginning with President Carter's efforts to appoint more women and minorities to the federal courts, they have become a rising proportion of the federal judiciary. In 1993, when President Clinton took office, just 10 percent of the federal bench were minorities; 11 percent were women. He appointed more African Americans to judgeships than presidents serving in the last sixteen years combined. Similarly, he appointed three times as many female judges as Presidents Reagan and Bush before him. While no state can bar African Americans or women

(continued)

from serving on a jury, it was not all that unusual, until recently, for lawyers to use their peremptory challenges (those made without a reason) to systematically dismiss women or African Americans if they believed that they would be more hostile jurors to their side. In two cases, however, the Supreme Court ruled that race or gender could not be used as reasons to exclude potential jurors.[83] Thus, today, juries are much more likely to be truly representative of the community and capable of offering litigants in a civil or criminal matter a jury of their peers.

Many studies of the judicial process have concluded that male and female justices decide cases differently. Women and African American judges tend to be more liberal than their white male counterparts. Thus, the presence of more women and more minority judges could lead to enhanced public support for the judiciary.

The O. J. Simpson case brought home to most Americans quite vividly that whites and blacks view the judicial process quite differently, often based on group treatment within that process.

1. Will greater participation by women and minority judges affect how cases are decided and the ways that laws are interpreted?
2. As we move into a society with more minority and female jurists, lawyers, and jurors, what consequences will this have on public perceptions of the American legal system?

Cast Your Vote. What changes, if any, do you foresee in the judicial process? To cast your vote, go to **www.ablongman.com/oconnor**

SUMMARY

The judiciary and the legal process—on both the national and state levels—are complex and play a far more important role in the setting of policy than the Framers ever envisioned. To explain the judicial process and its evolution, we have made the following points:

1. **The Constitution and the Creation of the National Judiciary**

   Many of the Framers viewed the judicial branch of government as little more than a minor check on the other two branches, ignoring Anti-Federalist concerns about an unelected judiciary and its potential for tyranny.

2. **The Judiciary Act of 1789 and the Creation of the Federal Judicial System**

   The Judiciary Act of 1789 established the basic federal court system we have today. It was the Marshall Court (1801–1835), however, that interpreted the Constitution to include the Court's major power, that of judicial review.

3. **The American Legal System**

   Ours is a dual judicial system consisting of the federal court system and the separate judicial systems of the fifty states. In each system there are two basic types of courts: trial courts and appellate courts. Each type deals with cases involving criminal and civil law. Original jurisdiction refers to a court's ability to hear a case as a trial court; appellate jurisdiction refers to a court's ability to review cases already decided by a trial court.

4. **The Federal Court System**

   The federal court system is made up of constitutional and legislative courts. Federal district courts, courts of appeals, and the Supreme Court are constitutional courts.

5. **How Federal Court Judges Are Selected**

   District court and courts of appeals judges are nominated by the president and subject to Senate confirmation. Senators often play a key role in recommending district court appointees from their home state. Supreme Court justices are nominated by the president and must also win Senate confirmation. Presidents use different criteria for selection, but important factors include competence, standards, ideology, rewards, pursuit of political support, religion, race, and gender.

6. **The Supreme Court Today**

   Several factors go into the Court's decision to hear a case. Not only must the Court have jurisdiction, but at least four justices must vote to hear the case, and cases with certain characteristics are most likely to be heard. Once a case is set for review, briefs and *amicus curiae* briefs are filed and oral argument scheduled. The justices meet after oral argument to discuss the case, votes are taken, and opinions are written and circulated.

7. **How the Justices Vote**

   Several legal and extra-legal factors affect how the Court arrives at its decision. Legal factors include judicial philosophy, the original intent of the Framers, and precedent. Extra-legal factors include public opinion and the behavioral characteristics, ideology, and strategic preferences of the justices.

8. **Judicial Policy Making and Implementation**

   The Supreme Court is an important participant in the policy-making process. The process of judicial interpretation gives the Court powers never envisioned by the Framers.

KEY TERMS

SELECTED READINGS

Abraham, Henry J. *The Judicial Process,* 7th ed. New York: Oxford University Press, 1997.

Barrow, Deborah J., Gary Zuk, and Gerard S. Gryski, *The Federal Judiciary and Institutional Change.* Ann Arbor: University of Michigan Press, 1996.

Baum, Lawrence. *The Supreme Court,* 7th ed. Washington, D.C.: CQ Press, 2000.

———. *The Puzzle of Judicial Behavior.* Ann Arbor: University of Michigan Press, 1997.

Clayton, Cornell, and Howard Gillman, eds. *Supreme Court Decision-Making: New Institutionalist Approaches.* Chicago: University of Chicago Press, 1999.

Epstein, Lee, et al. *The Supreme Court Compendium: Data, Decisions, and Developments,* 2nd ed. Washington, D.C.: Congressional Quarterly Inc., 1996.

Goldman, Sheldon. *Picking Federal Judges: Lower Court Selection from Roosevelt Through Reagan.* New Haven, Conn.: Yale University Press, 1997.

Hall, Kermitt L., ed. *The Oxford Companion to the Supreme Court of the United States.* New York: Oxford University Press, 1992.

Lazarus, Edward. *Closed Chambers: The First Eyewitness Account of the Epic Struggles Inside the Supreme Court.* New York: Times Books, 1998.

Maveety, Nancy. *Justice Sandra Day O'Connor: Strategist on the Supreme Court.* Lanham, Md.: Rowman & Littlefield, 1996.

O'Brien, David M. *Storm Center: The Supreme Court in American Politics,* 5th ed. New York: Norton, 1999.

Perry, H. W. *Deciding to Decide: Agenda Setting in the United States Supreme Court.* Cambridge, Mass.: Harvard University Press, 1994.

Provine, Doris Marie. *Case Selection in the United States Supreme Court.* Chicago: University of Chicago Press, 1980.

Salokar, Rebecca Mae. *The Solicitor General: The Politics of Law.* Philadelphia: Temple University Press, 1992.

Slotnick, Elliot E., and Jennifer A. Segal. *Television News and the Supreme Court: All the News That's Fit to Air.* Boston: Cambridge University Press. 1998.

Sunstein, Cass R. *One Case at a Time: Judicial Minimalism on the Supreme Court.* Cambridge, Mass.: Harvard University Press, 1999.

Woodward, Bob, and Scott Armstrong. *The Brethren: Inside the Supreme Court.* New York: Avon, 1996.

NOTES

1. Bernard Schwartz, *The Law in America* (New York: American Heritage, 1974), 48.

2. Julius Goebel Jr., *History of the Supreme Court of the United States,* vol. 1: *Antecedents and Beginnings to 1801* (New York: Macmillan, 1971), 206.

3. 1 Wheat. 14 U.S. 304 (1816).

4. Quoted in Goebel, *History of the Supreme Court,* 280.

5. Schwartz, *The Law in America,* 11.

6. 2 Dall. 419 (1793).

7. 3 Dall. 171 (1796). In *Hylton* v. *United States* the Court ruled that a congressional tax on horse-drawn carriages was an excise tax and not a direct tax and therefore it need not be apportioned evenly among the states (as direct taxes must be, according to the Constitution).

8. 5 U.S. 137 (1803).

9. This discussion draws heavily on Jack C. Plano and Milton Greenberg, *The American Political Dictionary,* 10th ed. (Fort Worth, Tex.: Harcourt Brace, 1996), 247.

10. David W. Neubauer, *Judicial Process: Law, Courts and Politics* (Pacific Grove, Calif.: Brooks/Cole, 1991), 57.

11. Cases involving citizens from different states can be filed in state or federal court.

12. John R. Vile and Mario Perez-Reilly, "The U.S. Constitution and Judicial Qualifications: A Curious Omission," *Judicature* (December/January 1991): 198–202.

13. Sheldon Goldman and Elliot Slotnick, "Clinton's First Term Judiciary: Many Bridges to Cross," *Judicature* (May/June 1997): 254–55.

14. William H. Rehnquist, "The 1997 Year-End Report on the Federal Judiciary." http://www.uscourts.gov/cj97.html. Embargoed for release January 1, 1998, 12:01 A.M. EST.

15. "Rehnquist Sees Threat to Judicial System," *The Washington Post* (January 2, 1998): A21.

16. Thomas B. Edsall, "Clinton Plans Judicial Offensive," *The Washington Post* (January 16, 1998): A1.

17. Quoted in Edsall, "Clinton Plans."

18. Quoted in Nina Totenberg, "Will Judges Be Chosen Rationally?" *Judicature* (August/September 1976): 93.

19. Bob Woodward and Scott Armstrong, *The Brethren* (New York: Simon and Schuster, 1979).

20. Quoted in Judge Irving R. Kaufman, "Charting a Judicial Pedigree," *The New York Times* (January 24, 1981): 23.

21. Quoted in Lawrence Baum, *The Supreme Court,* 3rd. ed. (Washington, D.C.: CQ Press, 1989), 108.

22. See Barbara A. Perry, *A Representative Supreme Court? The Impact of Race, Religion and Gender on Appointments* (New York: Greenwood Press, 1991).

23. Clarence Thomas was raised a Catholic, but attended an Episcopalian church at the time of his appointment, having been barred from Catholic sacraments because of his remarriage. He again, however, is attending Roman Catholic services.

24. Saundra Torry, "ABA's Judicial Panel Is a Favorite Bipartisan Target," *The Washington Post* (April 29, 1996): F7

25. Torry, "ABA's Judicial Panel."

26. M. A. Stapleton, "Judicial Selection Process Survives Flaws," *Chicago Daily Law Bulletin* (February 7, 1996): 1.

27. See Bruce Allen Murphy, *The Brandeis/ Frankfurter Connection* (New York: Oxford University Press, 1982).

28. Marcia Coyle, "How Americans View High Court," *National Law Journal* (February 26, 1990): 1.

29. John Brigham, *The Cult of the Court* (Philadelphia: Temple University Press, 1987).

30. Stephen L. Wasby, *The Supreme Court in the Federal Judicial System,* 4th ed. (Chicago: Nelson-Hall, 1988), 194.

31. Wasby, *The Supreme Court,* 194.

32. Wasby, *The Supreme Court,* 199. Much of this change occurred as the result of an increase in state criminal cases, of which nearly 100 percent concerned constitutional questions.

33. Neubauer, *Judicial Process,* 370.

34. William P. McLauchan, "The Business of the United States Supreme Court, 1971–1983: An Analysis of Supply and Demand," paper presented at the 1986 annual meeting of the Midwest Political Science Association.

35. 498 U.S. 177 (1991).

36. Justice Stevens chooses not to join this pool. According to one former clerk, "He wanted an independent review," but Stevens himself examines only about 20 percent of the petitions, leaving the rest to his clerks. Tony Mauro, "Ginsburg Plunges into the Cert Pool," *Legal Times* (September 6, 1993): 8.

37. Paul Wahlbeck, James F. Spriggs II, and Lee Sigelman, "The Influence of Law Clerks on Supreme Court Opinions," paper delivered at the 1999 annual meeting of the Midwest Political Science Association.

38. Richard A. Posner, *The Federal Courts: Crisis and Reform* (Cambridge, Mass.: Harvard University Press, 1985), 114.

39. Edward Lazarus, *Closed Chambers: The First Eyewitness Account of the Epic Struggles Inside the Supreme Court* (New York: Random House, 1998).

40. "Retired Chief Justice Warren Attacks . . . Freund Study Group's Composition and Proposal," *American Bar Association Journal* 59 (July 1973): 728.

41. Kathleen Werdegar, "The Solicitor General and Administrative Due Process," *George Washington Law Review* (1967–68): 482.

42. Rebecca Mae Salokar, *The Solicitor General: The Politics of Law* (Philadelphia: Temple University Press, 1992), 3.

43. Quoted in Elder Witt, *A Different Justice: Reagan and the Supreme Court* (Washington, D.C.: CQ Press, 1986), 133.

44. Lawrence Baum, *The Supreme Court,* 4th ed. (Washington, D.C.: CQ Press, 1992), 106.

45. Richard C. Cortner, *The Supreme Court and Civil Liberties* (Palo Alto, Calif.: Mayfield, 1975), vi.

46. Gregory A. Caldeira and John R. Wright, "*Amicus Curiae* Before the Supreme Court: Who Participates, When and How Much?" *Journal of Politics* 52 (August 1990): 803.

47. See also John R. Hermann, "American Indians in Court: The Burger and Rehnquist Years," Ph.D. dissertation, Emory University, 1996.

48. 510 U.S. 17 (1993).

49. 418 U.S. 683 (1974).

50. Quoted in Wasby, *The Supreme Court,* 229.

51. 478 U. S. 186 (1986).

52. "Justices' Files Show Struggle over Georgia Sodomy Case," *The Atlanta Journal and Constitution* (May 25, 1993): A9. The Marshall papers also reveal politics at the *certiorari* stage.

53. 418 U.S. 683 (1974).

54. Bob Woodward and Scott Armstrong, *The Brethren* (New York: Simon and Schuster, 1979), 65, 288–347.

55. 492 U. S. 490 (1989).

56. *Clinton* v. *Jones,* 520 U.S. 681 (1997).

57. Stanley C. Brubaker, "Reconsidering Dworkin's Case for Judicial Activism," *Journal of Politics* 46 (1984): 504.

58. Donald L. Horowitz, *The Courts and Social Policy* (Washington, D.C.: Brookings Institution, 1977), 538.

59. 347 U.S. 483 (1954).

60. *Webster* v. *Reproductive Health Services,* 492 U.S. 518 (1989).

61. 112 S.Ct. 2791 (1992).

62. See, for example, Tracy E. George and Lee Epstein, "On the Nature of Supreme Court Decision Making," *American Political Science Review* 86 (1992): 323–37; Melinda Gann Hall and Paul Brace, "Justices' Responses to Case Facts: An Interactive Model," *American Politics Quarterly* (April 1996): 237–61; Lawrence Baum, *The Puzzle of Judicial Behavior* (Ann Arbor: University of Michigan Press, 1997); and Gregory N. Flemming, David B. Holmes, and Susan Gluck Mezey, "An Integrated Model of Privacy Decision Making in State Supreme Courts," *American Politics Quarterly* 26 (January 1998): 35–58.

63. Jeffrey A. Segal and Harold Spaeth, *The Supreme Court and the Attitudinal Model.* (Cambridge and New York: Cambridge University Press, 1993).

64. Gerard Gryski, Eleanor C. Main, and William Dixon, "Models of State High Court Decision Making in Sex Discrimination Cases," *Journal of Politics* 48 (1986): 143–55; and C. Neal Tate and Roger Handberg, "Time Binding and Theory Building in Personal Attribute Models of Supreme Court Voting Behavior, 1916–1988," *American Political Science Review* 35 (1991): 460–80.

65. Donald R. Songer and Sue Davis, "The Impact of Party and Region on Voting Decisions in the U.S. Courts of Appeals, 1955–86," *Western Political Quarterly* 43: 830–44.

66. See, generally, Lee Epstein and Jack Knight, "Field Essay: Toward a Strategic Revolution in Judicial Politics: A Look Back, A Look Ahead," *Political Research Quarterly* 53 (September 2000): 663–76.

67. Thomas R. Marshall, "Public Opinion, Representation and the Modern Supreme Court," *American Politics Quarterly* 16 (1988): 296–316.

68. William H. Rehnquist, "Constitutional Law and Public Opinion," paper presented at Suffolk University School of Law, Boston, April 10, 1986, 40–41.

69. Thomas R. Marshall, *Public Opinion and the Supreme Court* (Boston: Unwin and Hyman, 1989).

70. 323 U.S. 214 (1944).

71. 343 U.S. 579 (1952).

72. The Supreme Court ruled that President Truman's seizure and operation of U.S. steel mills in the face of a strike threat were

unconstitutional, because the Constitution implied no such broad executive power. See Alan Westin, *Anatomy of a Constitutional Law Case* (New York: Macmillan, 1958); and Maeva Marcus, *Truman and the Steel Seizure Case* (New York: Columbia University Press, 1977).

73. Timothy R. Johnson and Andrew D. Martin, "The Public's Conditional Response to Supreme Court Decisions," *American Political Science Review* 92 (June 1998): 299–309.

74. *Romer* v. *Evans*, 517 U.S. Ct. 620 (1996).

75. *Lee* v *Weisman*, 505 U.S. 577 (1992).

76. 462 U.S. 919 (1983).

77. See *Colegrove* v. *Green*, 328 U.S. 549 (1946), for example.

78. *Baker* v. *Carr*, 369 U.S. 186 (1962).

79. Charles Johnson and Bradley C. Canon, *Judicial Policies: Implementation and Impact*, 2nd ed. (Washington, D.C.: CQ Press, 1998), ch. 1.

80. 377 U.S. 533 (1964).

81. *Strauder* v. *West Virginia*, 100 U.S. 303 (1888).

82. *Duren* v. *Missouri*, 439 U.S. 357 (1979).

83. *Batson* v. *Kentucky*, 476 U.S. 79 (1986) (African Americans) and *J. E. B.* v. *Alabama*, 511 U.S. 127 (1994) (women).

11 Public Opinion and Political Socialization

At 2:18 A.M. November 9, 2000, one of the major television networks made the call that George W. Bush would become the forty-third president of the United States. All the major networks quickly followed suit. But as we all know now, that was not to be the end of it. As calls for recounts and litigation went on, one of the longest presidential elections in the nation's history became a field day for pollsters and their critics. Interestingly, the original call awarding Florida to Al Gore came early in the evening and was based not on actual vote totals, but on projections from the Voter News Service, an exit poll service used by a consortium of news organizations to hold down costs.

Pollsters sprang into action in the wake of Al Gore's decision to retract his concession to Governor Bush. The Gallup Organization polled Americans to determine if they favored or opposed the hand recounts favored by Al Gore. Nationwide, on November 11–12, 55 percent favored a recount, 85 percent of the Gore voters but only 20 percent of those who voted for Bush. Sixty percent believed that those votes should be included in the final totals.[1] On November 26, 2000, when asked who they considered the real winner in Florida to be, 51 percent said Bush but 32 percent were unsure. By then, only 15 percent thought Gore was the "real" winner. But after the U.S. Supreme Court's decision that stopped all further vote counting, and in essence declared George W. Bush the winner, voters were asked on December 15–17, "Just your best guess, if the Supreme Court had allowed the vote recount to continue in Florida, who do you think would have ended up with the most votes in Florida?" Of the national sample, 46 percent said Gore; 45 percent said Bush. As in the November 12 poll, there was a huge chasm between Bush and Gore voters. Nearly three-quarters (74 percent) of the Gore voters continued to believe that he was the rightful winner; 77 percent of the Bush voters believed that their man would have ended up the winner. The same poll found that only 51 percent of those sampled believed that the electoral college outcome was "fair." Again, huge gaps were evident in Bush and Gore voters. Eighty-five percent of the Bush voters through the election outcome was fair; only 23 percent of the Gore voters did. Nationally, 68 percent of black voters believed that their votes were less likely to have been counted fairly in Florida than whites. Still, 61 percent of the public reported their belief that George W. Bush would work hard to "represent the interests of all Americans," but only 22 percent of blacks polled agreed with this statement.

Polling gives us a unique view into the psyche of Americans. Politicians read the polls as do their advisers. George W. Bush, who prided himself on his good relations with Hispanic and African American communities in Texas, was undoubtedly shocked and troubled by the feelings of Gore supporters and African Americans. Some might even argue that the diversity of his first Cabinet appointments reflected his concern with American sentiment as he sought to lead the nation and establish the legitimacy of his victory in light of some continued public skepticism.

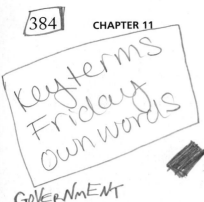

GOVERNMENT

(Photo courtesy: By permission of Mike Luckovich and Creators Syndicate)

The presidential candidates, news services, and the presidents are not the only ones in the United States looking at poll data. Professional pollsters routinely question Americans from all walks of life about their beliefs and opinions about a variety of things from washing detergent, to favorite television and radio programs, to their attitudes about government and democracy. Americans hold a variety of views on most issues presented to them by public opinion pollsters as reflected in Highlight, "Is There Too Much Polling?"

Over 200 years ago, in 1787, John Jay wrote glowingly of the sameness of the American people. He and other writers of *The Federalist Papers* believed that Americans had more in common than not. Wrote Jay in *Federalist No. 2,* we are "one united people—a people descended from the same ancestors, speaking the same language, professing the same religion, attached to the same principles of government, very similar in manners and customs." Many of those who could vote were of English heritage; almost all were Christian. Moreover, most believed that certain rights—such as freedom of speech, association, and religion—were unalienable rights. Jay also spoke of shared public opinion and of the need for a national government that reflected American ideals.

Today, however, Americans are a far more heterogeneous lot. Election after election and public opinion poll after poll reveal this diversity, but nonetheless, Americans appear to agree on many things. Most want less government, particularly at the national level. So did many citizens in 1787. Most want to leave a nation better for their children. So did the Framers. But the Framers did not have sophisticated public opinion polls to tell them this, nor did they have national news media to tell them the results of those polls. Today, many people wonder what shapes public opinion: poll results or people's opinions? Do the polls drive public opinion, or does public opinion drive the polls?

The role of public opinion in elections as well as the making of policy are just two issues we explore in this chapter. In analyzing the role of public opinion in a democracy, the development of polling, and how politicians respond to public opinion, in this chapter we'll look at the following issues:

- First, we will examine the question, *what is public opinion?* Here we offer a simple definition and then note the role of public opinion polls in determining public perception of political issues.
- Second, we will describe *early efforts to influence and measure public opinion.* From *The Federalist Papers* to the Republicans' Contract with America and the Democrats' Families First, parties and public officials have tried to sway as well as gauge public opinion for political purposes.
- Third, we will discuss *political socialization and other factors that influence opinion* formation about political matters. We also examine the role of political ideology in public opinion formation.
- Fourth, we will examine *how* Americans *form political opinions.*
- Fifth, we will analyze *how we measure public opinion* and note problems with various kinds of polling techniques.
- Sixth, we will look at *how polling and public opinion affect politicians* as well as how politicians affect public opinion.

WHAT IS PUBLIC OPINION?

public opinion
What the public thinks about a particular issue or set of issues at any point in time.

At first blush, **public opinion** seems to be a very straightforward term: It is what the public thinks about a particular issue or set of issues at a particular time. Since

H I G H L I G H T

IS THERE TOO MUCH POLLING?

Y ou may be one of those people who questions the polls because you have never been sampled. You need only to read a daily paper or watch television to recognize that polls are being conducted all the time. In the wake of this potential for too much information, the Gallup Organization has even polled Americans to see if there has been too much coverage of media events. They didn't ask, however, if there was too much polling about beliefs concerning those events.

What events did Gallup select to ask about? The 2000 post-election controversy, the Columbine High School shootings, the Clinton-Lewinsky scandal, and the death of Britain's Princess Diana. Gallup reports that 51 percent of the public thought that post-election coverage

was about right. Similar sentiments were reported about the shootings (50%) and the death of the princess (49%). Only the Clinton-Lewinsky affair was judged by the American public to be overreported by the news media—72 percent believed it was overdone; only 22 percent thought coverage was about right.

Clearly, there is a poll for every issue. What are the merits of these kinds of polls? Who might be swayed by their findings?

Source: All data reported here are from The Gallup Organization, "Poll Releases: Americans Divided Over Whether There is Too Much Media Coverage of the Election," http://www.gallup.cpm/poll/releases/pr001201.asp.

---

the 1930s, governmental decision makers have relied heavily on **public opinion polls**—interviews with a sample of citizens that are used to determine what the public is thinking. According to George Gallup, the founder of modern-day polling, polls have played a key role in defining issues of concern to the public, shaping administrative decisions, and helping "speed up the process of democracy" in the United States.[2] (See Roots of Government: George Gallup: The Founder of Modern Polling.)

According to Gallup, leaders must constantly take public opinion—no matter how short-lived—into account. Like the Jacksonians of a much earlier era, Gallup was distrustful of leaders who were not in tune with the "common man." According to Gallup,

> in a democracy we demand the views of the people be taken into account. This does not mean that leaders must follow the public's view slavishly; it does mean that they should have an available appraisal of public opinion and take some account of it in reaching their decision.[3]

Even though Gallup undoubtedly had a vested interest in fostering reliance on public opinion polls, his sentiments accurately reflect the feelings of many political thinkers concerning the role of public opinion and governance. Some, like Gallup, believe that the government should do what a majority of the public wants done. Others argue that the public as a whole doesn't have consistent opinions on day-to-day issues but that subgroups within the public often hold strong views on some issues. These *pluralists* (see chapter 1) believe that the government must allow for the expression of these minority opinions and that democracy works best when these different voices are allowed to fight it out in the public arena.

But, as we will see later in this chapter, what the public or even subgroups think about various issues is difficult to know with certainty, simply because public opinion can change so quickly. For example, two weeks before the United States bombed Iraq in January 1991, public opinion polls revealed that only 61 percent of the American public believed that the United States should engage in combat in Iraq. One week after the invasion, however, 86 percent reported that they approved of President George Bush's handling of the situation.

public opinion poll
Interviews or surveys with a sample of citizens that are used to estimate the feelings and beliefs of the entire population.

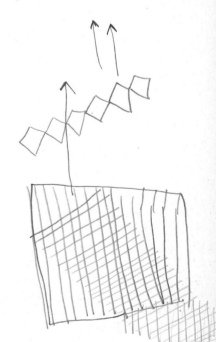

ROOTS OF GOVERNMENT

GEORGE GALLUP: THE FOUNDER OF MODERN POLLING*

George Gallup earned a Ph.D. in journalism from the University of Iowa with a dissertation that examined methods of measuring the readership of newspapers. He first became interested in polling when his mother-in-law ran for public office in 1932. She was running against a popular incumbent, and most observers considered her candidacy a lost cause. Nevertheless, because of the Democratic landslide of 1932, she was swept into office on Franklin D. Roosevelt's coattails.

Gallup's interest in politics, fostered by his experience in his mother-in-law's campaign and his academic background in journalism and advertising, led him to take a job at a New York advertising agency. In 1935, he founded the American Institute of Public Opinion, headquartered at Princeton University in New Jersey. At the institute, Gallup refined a number of survey and sampling techniques to measure the public's attitudes on social, political, and economic issues. Weekly reports called the Gallup Polls were sent to more than forty subscribing newspapers.

Gallup attracted considerable national attention when he correctly predicted the outcome of the 1936 presidential election. Recognizing many of the flaws of *Literary Digest's* poll, he relied on a sample of a few thousand people who represented the voting population in terms of important demographic variables, such as age, gender, political affiliation, and region.

(Photo courtesy: Bettmann/Corbis)

*Source: Benjamin Ginsberg, *The Captive Public* (New York: Basic Books, 1986).

EARLY EFFORTS TO INFLUENCE AND MEASURE PUBLIC OPINION

You can hardly read a newspaper or news magazine or watch television without hearing the results of the latest public opinion poll on social security, crime, or the president's performance. But long before modern polling, politicians tried to mold and win public opinion. *The Federalist Papers* were one of the first major attempts to change public opinion—in this case, to gain public support for the newly drafted U.S. Constitution. Even prior to publication of *The Federalist Papers*, Thomas Paine's *Common Sense* and later his *Crisis* papers were widely distributed throughout the colonies in an effort to stimulate patriotic feelings and increase public support for the Revolutionary War.

From the very early days of the republic, political leaders recognized the importance of public opinion and used all the means at their disposal to manipulate it for political purposes. By the early 1800s, the term "public opinion" was frequently being used by the educated middle class. As more Americans became educated, they became more vocal about their opinions and were more likely to vote. A more educated, reading public led to increased demand for newspapers, which in turn provided more information about the process of government. As the United States grew, there were more elections and more opportunities for citizens to express their political opinions through the ballot box. As a result of these trends, political leaders were more frequently forced to try to gauge public opinion in order to remain responsive to the wishes and desires of their constituents.

An example of the power of public opinion is the public's response to the 1851–1855 serialization of Harriet Beecher Stowe's *Uncle Tom's Cabin*. This novel was one of the most powerful propaganda statements ever issued about slavery. By the time the first shots of the Civil War were fired at Fort Sumter in 1861, more than one million copies of the book were in print. Even though Stowe's words alone could not have caused the public outrage over slavery that contributed to Northern support for the war, her book convinced the majority of the American people of the justness of the abolitionist cause and solidified public opinion in the North against slavery.

During World War I, some people argued that public opinion didn't matter at all. But President Woodrow Wilson (1913–1921) argued that public opinion would temper the actions of international leaders. Therefore, only eight days after the start of the war, Wilson created a Committee on Public Information. Run by a prominent journalist, the committee immediately undertook to unite U.S. public opinion behind the war effort. It used all of the tools available— pamphlets, posters, and speakers who exhorted the patrons of local movie houses during every intermission—in an effort to garner support and favorable opinion for the war. In the words of the committee's head, it was "the world's greatest adventure in advertising."[4]

As part of "the world's greatest adventure in advertising," the Committee on Public Information created a vast gallery of posters designed to shore up public support during World War I. (Photo courtesy: Bettmann/Corbis)

In the wake of World War I, Walter Lippmann, a well-known journalist and author who was extensively involved in propaganda activities during the war, openly voiced his concerns about how easily public opinion could be manipulated and his reservations about the weight it should be given. In his seminal work, *Public Opinion* (1922), Lippmann wrote, "Since Public Opinion is supposed to be the prime mover in democracies, one might reasonably expect to find a vast literature [examining it]. One does not find it."[5] By the 1920s, although numerous efforts had been made to manipulate public opinion, scientific measurement of public opinion had yet to occur.

Early Efforts to Measure Public Opinion

Public opinion polling as we know it today did not begin to develop until the 1930s. Researchers in a variety of disciplines, including political science, heeded Lippmann's call to learn more about public opinion. Some tried to use scientific methods to measure political thought through the use of surveys or polls. As methods for gathering and interpreting data improved, survey data began to play an increasingly important role in all walks of life, from politics to retailing.

Early Election Forecasting.   As early as 1824, one Pennsylvania newspaper tried to predict the winner of that year's presidential contest. Later, in 1883, the *Boston Globe* sent reporters to selected election precincts to poll voters as they exited voting booths, in an effort to predict the results of key contests. In 1916, *Literary Digest,* a popular magazine, began mailing survey postcards to potential voters in an effort to predict election outcomes. *Literary Digest* drew its survey sample from "every telephone book in the United States, from the rosters of clubs and associations, from city directories, lists of registered voters [and] classified mail order and occupational data."[6] Using the data it received from the millions of postcard ballots sent out throughout the United States, *Literary Digest* correctly predicted every presidential election from 1920 to 1932.

★ straw poll
Unscientific survey used to gauge
public opinion on a variety of issues
and policies.

Literary Digest used what were called **straw polls** to predict the popular vote in those four presidential elections. Its polling methods were widely hailed as "amazingly right" and "uncannily accurate."[7] In 1936, however, its luck ran out. *Literary Digest* predicted that Republican Alfred M. Landon would beat incumbent President Franklin D. Roosevelt by a margin of 57 percent to 43 percent of the popular vote. Roosevelt, however, won in a landslide election, receiving 62.5 percent of the popular vote and carrying all but two states.

Polling Matures.　Through the late 1940s, the number of polling groups and increasingly sophisticated polling techniques grew by leaps and bounds as new businesses and politicians relied on the information they provide to market products and candidates. In 1948, however, the polling industry suffered a severe, although fleeting, setback when Gallup and many other pollsters incorrectly predicted that Thomas E. Dewey would defeat President Harry S Truman.

What Went Wrong?　*Literary Digest* reached out to as many potential respondents as possible, with no regard for modern sampling techniques that require that respondents be selected or sampled according to strict rules of cross-sectional representation. Respondents, in essence, were like "straws in the wind," hence the term "straw polls."

Literary Digest's sample had three fatal errors. First, its sample was drawn from telephone directories and lists of automobile owners. This technique oversampled the upper middle class and the wealthy, groups heavily Republican in political orientation. Moreover, in 1936, voting polarized along class lines. Thus the oversampling of wealthy Republicans was particularly problematic, because it severely underestimated the Democratic vote.

Literary Digest's second problem was timing. Questionnaires were mailed in early September. Thus the changes in public sentiment that occurred as the election drew closer were not measured.

Its third error occurred because of a problem we now call self-selection. Only highly motivated individuals sent back the cards—a mere 22 percent of those surveyed responded. Those who respond to mail surveys are quite different from the general electorate; they often are wealthier and better educated and care more fervently about issues. *Literary Digest*, then, failed to observe one of the now well-known cardinal rules of survey sampling: "One cannot allow the respondents to select themselves into the sample."[8]

At least one pollster, however, correctly predicted the results of the 1936 election: George Gallup. Gallup had written his dissertation on how to measure the readership of newspapers, and then expanded his methods to study public opinion about politics. He was so confident about his methods that he gave all of his newspaper clients a money-back guarantee: If his poll predictions weren't closer to the actual election outcome than those of the highly acclaimed *Literary Digest*, he would refund them their money. The *Digest* predicted Alf Landon to win; Gallup predicted Roosevelt. Although he underpredicted Roosevelt's victory by nearly 7 percent, the fact that he got the winner right was what everyone remembered, especially given *Literary Digest*'s dra-

Not only did advance polls in 1948 predict that Republican nominee Thomas E. Dewey would defeat Democratic incumbent Harry S Truman, but based on early and incomplete vote tallies, some newspapers' early editions even on the day after the election declared Dewey to have won. Here a triumphant Truman holds aloft the *Chicago Daily Tribune*. (Photo courtesy: Bettmann/Corbis)

matic miscalculation. As revealed in Figure 11.1, the Gallup Organization, now run by George's Gallup's son, continues to be a successful predictor of the popular vote. But, as the 2000 presidential election reminded most Americans, it is the vote in the electoral college—not the popular vote—that ultimately counts. Thus, while George W. Bush's lead in the polls continued to shrink in the final days of polling, he won by a single vote in the electoral college as further detailed in chapter 13. On November 7, 2000, the Gallup Organization annouced what turned to be a major understatement, that the election was too close to call. Ultimately, Bush got 48 percent of the popular vote; Gore 49 percent.

WEB EXPLORATION
To learn more about the Gallup Organization and poll trends, see
www.ablongman.com/oconnor

The American Voter, Public Opinion, and Political Socialization

The American Voter was published in 1960.[9] This book "intellectually contributed the dominant model for thinking about mass attitudes and mass behavior in the social science research that followed."[10] Drawing on data from the 1952 and 1956 presidential elections, *The American Voter* showed how class coalitions, which were originally formed around social-welfare issues, led to party affiliations—the dominant force in presidential elections. This book also led directly to the "institutionalization of regular surveys of the American electorate, through a biennial series now recognized as the National Election Study (NES)."[11]

The NES surveys are conducted by social scientists at the Center for Political Studies of the Institute for Social Research at the University of Michigan. NES surveys focus only on political attitudes and behavior of the electorate. They include questions about how respondents voted, their party affiliation, and their opinions of major political parties and candidates. NES surveys also include questions about interest in political matters and political participation, including participation in non-election related activities, such as church attendance.

WEB EXPLORATION
To use NES data sets, see
www.ablongman.com/oconnor

NES surveys are conducted before and after midterm and presidential elections. A random sample of those eligible to vote on Election Day and living in the Continental United States is used. Some of the same questions are in used in each survey

FIGURE 11.1   The Success of the Gallup Poll in Presidential Elections, 1936–2000

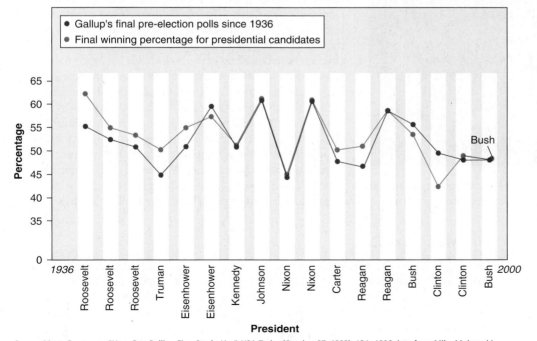

Source: Marty Baumann, "How One Polling Firm Stacks Up," *USA Today* (October 27, 1992): 13A. 1996 data from Mike Mokrzycki, "Pre-election Polls' Accuracy Varied," *Atlanta Journal and Constitution* (November 8, 1996): A12. 2000 data from *Gallup Organization*, "Poll Releases," (November 7, 2000).

to compile long-term studies of the electorate to facilitate political scientists' understanding of how and why peolpe vote and participate in politics.

POLITICAL SOCIALIZATION AND OTHER FACTORS THAT INFLUENCE OPINION FORMATION

political socialization
The process through which an individual acquires particular political orientations; the learning process by which people acquire their political beliefs and values.

Longman
Participate.com
2.0
Participation
Deciding on a Political Party

Political scientists believe that many of our attitudes about issues are grounded in our political values. We learn these values through a process called **political socialization,** "the process through which an individual acquires his particular political orientations—his knowledge, feeling and evaluations regarding his political world."[12] Family, the mass media, schools, and peers are often important influences or agents of political socialization. For example, try to remember your earliest memory of the president of the United States. It may have been Ronald Reagan or George Bush (older students probably remember earlier presidents). What did you think of him? Of the Republican or Democratic Party? It's likely that your earliest feelings or attitudes were shaped by what your parents thought about that particular president and his party. Similar processes also apply to your early attitudes about the flag of the United States, or the police. Other factors, too, often influence how political opinions are formed or reinforced. These include political events; the social groups you belong to, including your church; demographic group, including race, gender, and age; and even the region of the country in which you live.

The Family

The influence of the family can be traced to two factors: communication and receptivity. Children, especially during their preschool years, spend tremendous amounts of time with their parents; early on they learn their parents' political values, even though these concepts may be vague. One study, for example, found that the most important visible public figures for children under the age of ten were police officers and, to a much lesser extent, the president.[13] Young children almost uniformly view both as "helpful." But by the age of ten or eleven, children become more selective in their perceptions of the president. By this age children raised in Democratic households are much more likely to be critical of a Republican president than are those raised in Republican households. In 1988, for example, 58 percent of children in Republican households identified themselves as Republicans, and many had developed strong positive feelings toward Ronald Reagan, the Republican president. Support for and the popularity of Ronald Reagan translated into support for the Republican Party through the 1988 presidential election and also contributed to the decline of liberal ideological self-identification of first-year college students. (See Analyzing the Data: Idelogical Self-Identification of First-Year College Students, 2000.)

Political values are shaped in childhood. (Photo courtesy: Nancy O'Connor Zeigler)

The Mass Media

The media today are taking on a growing role as a socialization agent. Adult Americans spend nearly thirty hours a week in front of their television sets; children spend even more.[14] Television has a tremendous impact on how people view politics, government, and politicians. TV talk shows, talk radio, and now even online newsletters and magazines are important sources of information about politics for many, yet the information that people get from these sources is often skewed. One study, for example, found that 25 percent of all Americans learned about the 1996 presidential campaign from David Letterman and Jay Leno.[15] By 2000, another study was estimating that 51

A N A L Y Z I N G   T H E   D A T A

IDEOLOGICAL SELF-IDENTIFICATION OF FIRST-YEAR COLLEGE STUDENTS, 2000

Like the general population, many students who call themselves liberals or conservatives accept only part of the liberal or conservative ideology. During the Ronald Reagan era of the 1980s, those who considered themselves conservative increased. But by far, most considered their ideology middle-of-the-road. The Democratic response to this ideological shift was selecting presidential candidate Bill Clinton in 1992, a member of the party's more moderate wing.

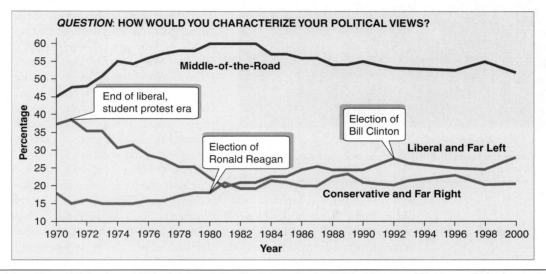

Source: Reprinted from Howard W. Stanley and Richard G. Niemi, *Vital Statistics on American Politics, 1997-1998* (Washington, D.C.: Congressional Quarterly, 1998), 113. 2000 data from Cooperative Institutional Research Program, "The American Freshman: National Norms for 2000," December 2000, Mimeo.

percent of all adults regularly got information about the election or candidates from alternative sources such as comedy shows like *Saturday Night Live* or MTV. For those younger than thirty, that figure soared to 79 percent.[16]

Television can serve to enlighten voters or encourage voter turnout. For example, MTV began coverage of presidential campaigns in 1992 and had reporters traveling with both major candidates to heighten young people's awareness of the stakes in the campaign. Its "Choose or Lose" campaign in the 1992, 1996, and 2000 elections was designed to enhance the abysmal turnout rates of young voters. When an MTV poll found only 33 percent of those age eighteen to twenty-four planned to vote, it stepped up its efforts.[17] Recognizing this, both candidates appeared on *Saturday Night Live* poking fun at themselves. Both also appeared on *Jay Leno, David Letterman, The Oprah Winfrey Show,* and *Live with Regis.* George W. Bush even donned a Regis-like monochromatic shirt and tie for the event. After his appearances on *Oprah* and *Regis,* Bush's poll numbers rose.[18] Only 22 percent of those under age thirty report that they watch nightly news; for 13 percent, MTV was the major source of their information about politics.[19] MTV's election features are designed to spur those under twenty-five to vote and to increase their knowledge about issues and candidates.[20] In 1992, Bill Clinton and his running mate, Al Gore, appeared on MTV to discuss issues and answer questions. The under-twenty-five vote went overwhelmingly for the more liberal candidate, Clinton, in contrast to the presidential elections in 1984 and 1988. In 2000, Vice President Al Gore attended MTV's youth forum and delegated his daughter Karenna Gore Schiff to attend youth-related functions. Similarly, Governor Bush used his young

ABC's *Politically Incorrect with Bill Maher* brings together four-guest panels to debate hot-button issues of the day. (Photo courtesy: Patricia Schroeder/©2000 ABC Inc.)

nephew George P. Bush to rally the youth and Hispanic vote and distribute "Generation W" stickers at campaign rallies. Both Karenna Gore Schiff and George P. Bush attended the MTV Video Music Awards.

All of the major candidates in the 2000 election also attempted to use another form of "media" to sway and inform voters: the Internet, a form of campaigning that was, believe it or not, still considered new in 1996. By 2000, although some still doubt its effectiveness, not only had each presidential and most other major and minor campaigns launched their own Internet sites, but all of the major networks and newspapers had their own Internet sites reporting on the election. There was even an Internet Alley at the Republican and Democratic National Conventions. On Election Night, millions of hits were counted on Election-related news sites as voters logged on to get the most up to date coverage. In fact, the outcome of the presidential election was first called online, prompting other forms of media to follow quickly. One poll conducted after the 2000 election found that one in three voters followed the campaign online—three times the number who did in 1996. Nationwide, 11 percent of voters listed the Internet as their major source of information about campaign news; an additional 19 percent reported that they got some of their information about the election online.[21] Forty-two percent of voters under age 30 reported that the net was their major source of information about the campaign.

School and Peers

Researchers report mixed findings concerning the role of schools in the political socialization process. There is no question that, in elementary school, children are taught respect for their nation and its symbols. Most school days begin with the Pledge of Allegiance, and patriotism and respect for country are important, although subtle, components of most school curricula. The terms "flag" and the "United States" evoke very positive feelings from a majority of Americans. Support for these two icons serves the purpose of maintaining national allegiance and underlies the success of the U.S. political system in spite of relatively negative views about Congress, the courts, and the current government. In 1991, for example, few schoolchildren were taught to question U.S. involvement in the Persian Gulf. Instead, at almost every school in the nation, children were encouraged or even required to write servicemen and servicewomen stationed in the Gulf, involving these children with the war effort and implying school support for the war.

In 1994, the Kids Voting Program was launched nationwide. This civic education project was designed to have a short-term impact on student political awareness *and* lead to a higher voter turnout among their parents. A study of the 2.3 million students who participated in 1994 revealed that the program met both goals.[22] Thus, a school-based program actually used children to affect their parents.

A child's peers—that is, children about the same age as a young person—also seem to have an important effect on the socialization process. Whereas parental influences are greatest during the tender years from birth to age five, a child's peer group becomes increasingly important as the child gets older, especially as he or she get into middle school or high school.[23]

High schools can also be important agents of political socialization. They continue the elementary school tradition of building good citizens and often reinforce textbook learning with trips to the state or national capital. They also offer courses on current

U.S. affairs. Many high schools impose a compulsory community service requirement, which some studies report positively affects later political participation.[24] Although the formal education of many people in the United States ends with high school, research shows that better-informed citizens vote more often as adults. Therefore, presentation of civic information is especially critical at the high school level.

At the college level, teaching style often changes. Many college courses and texts like this one are designed in part to provide you with the information necessary to think critically about issues of major political consequence. It is common in college for students to be called on to question the appropriateness of certain political actions or to discuss underlying reasons for certain political or policy decisions. Therefore, most researchers believe that college has a liberalizing effect on students. Since the 1920s, studies have shown, students become more liberal each year they are in college. As we show in Analizing the Data, however, this trend appeared to decline in the 1980s, as more and more students with conservative views entered colleges and universities during the Reagan era. The 1992 and 1996 victories of Bill Clinton and his equally youthful running mate Al Gore, who went out of their way to woo the youth vote, probably contributed to the small bump in the liberal ideological identification of first-year college students.

The Impact of Events

There is no doubt that parents—and, to a lesser degree, school and peers—play a role in a person's political socialization, but the role of key political events is also very important. You probably have some professors who remember what they were doing on the day that President John F. Kennedy was killed—November 22, 1963. This dramatic event is indelibly etched in the minds of virtually all people who were old enough to be aware of it. Similarly, most college students today remember where they were when the space shuttle *Challenger* exploded, or when they learned about the Oklahoma City bombing, or more recently the attack on the World Trade Center and the Pentagon.

Longman
Participate.com
2.0
Timeline
War, Peace,
and Public
Opinion

President Richard M. Nixon's fall from grace and forced resignation in 1974 also had a profound impact on the socialization process of all Americans. It made a particular impression on young people, who were forced to realize that their government was not always right or honest. This general distrust of politicians was reignited during the Starr investigation of President Clinton and his subsequent impeachment.

One problem in discussing political socialization is that many of the major studies on this topic were conducted in the aftermath of Watergate and other crucial events, including the civil rights movement and the Vietnam War, all of which produced a marked increase in Americans' distrust of government. The findings reported in Table 1.3 in chapter 1, reveal the dramatic drop-off of trust in government that began in the mid-1960s and continued through the election of Ronald Reagan in 1980. In a study of Boston children conducted in the aftermath of the Watergate scandal, for example, one political scientist found that children's perception of the president went from that of a benevolent to a "malevolent" leader.[25] These findings are indicative of the low confidence most Americans had in government in the aftermath of Watergate and President Nixon's ultimate resignation from office to avoid impeachment. Interestingly, confidence in government remained high during the Clinton scandal, although still down from the Watergate years. But the issues surrounding the Clinton impeachment raised concerns about their impact on young people, especially Generation Y. Some studies show that their views toward the president and political affairs are significantly more negative than ever seen before—including during and immediately after Watergate.[26] It is still probably too early to determine what impact the tumultuous 2000 presidential election will have on views toward the presidency and the electoral system more generally.

Social Groups

Group effects, that is, certain characteristics that allow persons to be lumped into categories, also affect the development and continuity of political beliefs and opinions. Among

The Amish are a religious group with distinct political views. (Photo courtesy: Dan Loh/AP/Wide World Photos)

the most important of these are religion, education level, income, and race. More recently, researchers have learned that gender and age are becoming increasingly important determinants of public opinion, especially on certain issues. Region, too, while not a social group, per se, appears to influence political beliefs and political socialization.

Religion.   Today religion plays a very important role in the life of Americans. Although only one in five citizens in 1776 belonged to a church or synagogue, today 67 percent of all Americans report such membership. Moreover, almost all Americans (96 percent) believe in God and 88 percent report that religion is "very" (61 percent) or "fairly" important in their own lives.[27] Nearly half of all Americans attend church regularly, and 62 percent believe that religion "can answer all or most of today's problems."[28]

In 1997, 58 percent of Americans identified themselves as Protestant, 27 percent as Catholic, 36 percent described themselves as born-again or evangelical Christians, 3 percent as Jewish, and 5 percent as other. Only 9 percent claimed to have no religious affiliation.[29] Over the years, analysts have found continuing ideological differences among these groups, with Protestants being the most conservative and Jews the most liberal, as shown in Figure 11.2.

Shared religious attitudes tend to affect voting and stances on particular issues. Catholics tend to vote Democratic more than do Protestants, and they tend to vote for other Catholics. For example, in 1960 Catholics overwhelmingly cast their ballots for John F. Kennedy, who became the first Catholic president. Catholics as a group also favor aid to parochial schools, and many fundamentalist Protestants support organized prayer in public schools. Seventy-eight percent of regular church-attending evangelicals voted Republican in the 1994 elections, contributing substantially to the Republican Revolution in Congress in 1995.[30] Jews, in contrast, tend to vote more Democratic. In 2000, for example, Al Gore and his running mate Joe Lieberman, the first Jew to run on a major party ticket, captured 79% of the Jewish vote. That proportion of the Jewish vote however, was actually slightly down from 80 percent of their vote captured by Bill Clinton in 1992. Figure 11.3 reveals other voting differences based on the factors discussed on this chapter.

Recent research by political scientists reveals that a new religious cleavage is emerging, as defined by the "orthodoxy of religious beliefs, affiliations, and practices on religious behavior." Thus conservative evangelical Christians are becoming increasingly Republican and more likely than less religious Protestants to vote for Republican candidates.[31]

FIGURE 11.2 The Ideological Self-Identification of Protestants, Catholics, and Jews

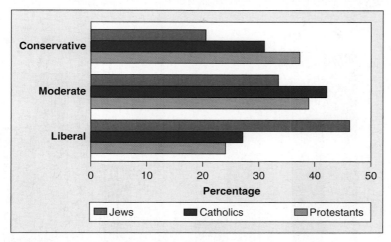

Source: Data compiled by Sarah Brewer from the General Social Survey Cumulative File, 1999.

FIGURE 11.3   Group Identified Voting Differences

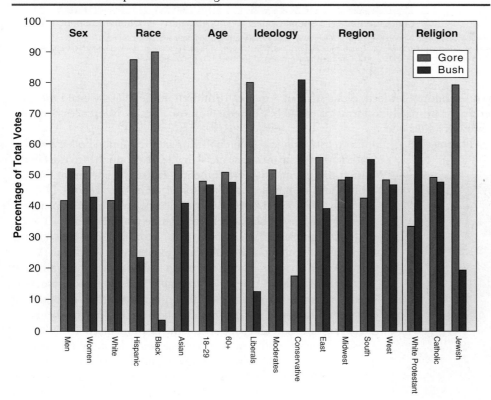

As revealed in Figure 11.2, Jews continue to be the most liberal religious group. When political scientists have compared the attitudes of Jews with non-Jews on a variety of issues, as revealed in Figure 11.4, Jews display very liberal attitudes on a range of issues from abortion to domestic spending on social programs.[32]

Race.   Differences in political socialization of African Americans and whites appear at a very early age. Young black children, for example, show "great affection for the national political community, [but] this attachment becomes seriously undermined with maturation." Black children fail to hold the president in the esteem accorded him by

FIGURE 11.4   Percent with Liberal Attitudes on Specific Issues Among Jews and Non-Jews

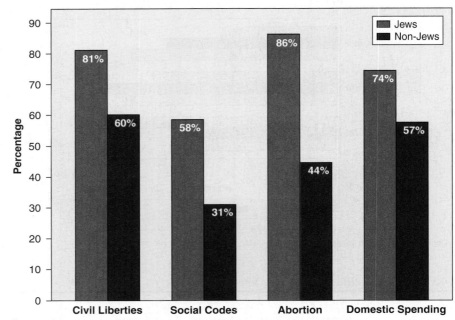

Social codes include support for liberal divorce laws, homosexual marriage, and premarital sex.
Source: Adapted from Steven M. Cohen and Charles S. Liebman, "American Jewish Liberalism: Unraveling the Strands," *Public Opinion Quarterly 61* (1997), p. 417. Reprinted by permission of The University of Chicago Press.

white children; indeed, older African American children in the 1960s viewed the government primarily in terms of the U.S. Supreme Court.[33] These differences continue through adulthood.

During the O. J. Simpson trial, public opinion poll after public opinion poll revealed in stark numbers the immense racial divide that continues to exist in the nation. Blacks distrust governmental institutions far more than do whites, and are much more likely to question police actions. Not surprisingly, then, while a majority of whites believed that Simpson was guilty, a majority of blacks believed that he was innocent.

Race is an exceptionally important factor in elections and in the study of public opinion. The direction and intensity of African American opinion on a variety of hot-button issues is often quite different from that of whites. As revealed in Figure 11.5, whites oppose affirmative action plans at significantly higher levels than do blacks or Hispanics. Likewise, significant differences can be seen in other areas, including abortion and support for the death penalty. Other issues, however, such as gun control, show much smaller racial dimensions.

Latinos, Asians/Pacific Islanders, and American Indians are other identifiable ethnic minorities in the United States who often respond differently to issues than do whites. Generally, Latinos and American Indians hold similar opinions on many issues largely because many of them have low incomes and find themselves targets of discrimination. Within the Hispanic community, however, existing divisions often depend on national origin. Generally, Cuban Americans who cluster in Florida (and in the Miami-Dade County area in particular) are more likely to be conservative. They fled from communism and Fidel Castro in Cuba, and they generally vote Republican. In contrast, Chicanos (people of Mexican origin) voting in California, New Mexico, Arizona, Texas, and Colorado are more likely to vote Democratic.[34]

Vice Presidential candidate Joseph Lieberman became the first Jewish candidate to run for national office. Al Gore and Lieberman were defeated by George W. Bush and Dick Cheney in one of the closest presidential elections in American History. (Photo courtesy: Arnold Gold/New Haven Register/The Image Works)

FIGURE 11.5   Racial Attitudes on Selected Issues

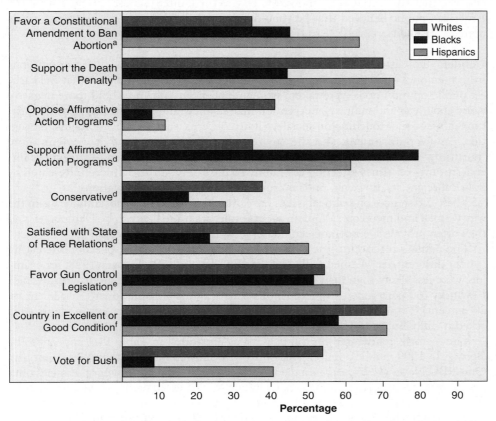

Source: Compiled by authors from 1999 National Election Study. Data on Bush from Marjorie Connelly, "Who voted: A Portrait of American Politics, 1976–2000," *The New York Times,* November 12, 2000, C4. Questions from the Roper Center, *Public Opinion Online.*
[a]December 1996   [b]August 1997   [c]March 1998   [d]April 1998   [e]December 1998   [f]January 1999

TABLE 11.1   Gender Differences on Political Issues

Favored or Supporting	Males	Females
Initial sending of troops to Gulf (1991)	62	41
Contract with America (1994)	72	54
Approve of Bill Clinton's handling of the presidency (2000)	58	70
Approve of George W. Bush's handling of the presidency (2001)	54	44
Return Elian Gonzales to his father	63	32
Favor affirmative action for women and minorities (1998)	49	63
Favor the death penalty (2000)	72	60
Favor gun control legislation (2000)	55	77
Health care important in 2000 presidential vote	76	89

Source: Data from CNN/*USA Today* (December 28–30, 1994); *The Public Perspective* (June/July 1995): 38; and (April/May 1996): 39; Roper Center, *Public Opinion Online*, 1998; The Gallup Organization, *The Washington Post*/ABC poll, May 7–10, 2000, and The Harris Poll, February 22–March 3, 2001.

On issues directly affecting a particular group, sentiments are often markedly different. As our opening vignette illustrated, black voters perceived the fairness of Florida vote counting procedures very differently from whites. Similarly, public sentiment in the Cuban community about the proper fate of Elian Gonzales was quite different from the rest of the nation. Although nearly 90 percent of the Cuban community in Miami believed that Elian should be allowed to stay in the United States,[35] 56 percent of the American public believed that he should be returned.[36] Figure 11.5 highlights some more of these differences.

Gender. Poll after poll continues to reveal that women hold very different opinions from men on a variety of issues, as shown in Table 11.1. From the time that the earliest public opinion polls were taken, women have been known to hold more negative views about war and military intervention than do men, and more strongly positive attitudes about issues touching on social-welfare concerns, such as education, juvenile justice, capital punishment, and the environment. Some suggest that women's more "nurturing" nature and their prominent role as mothers lead women to have more liberal attitudes on issues affecting the family or the safety of their children. Research by political scientists, however, finds no support for a maternal explanation.[37]

These differences on political issues have often translated into substantial gaps in the way women and men vote. Women, for example, are more likely to be Democrats, and they often provide Democratic candidates with their margin of victory.[38]

The public's reaction to the Monica Lewinsky affair reveals especially interesting gender differentials. Women polled by the *Washington Post* in January 1998, for example, were less likely than men to believe that the president had an affair with Monica Lewinsky (60 percent vs. 46 percent) or sexually harassed Paula Jones (35 percent vs. 29 percent).[39] But, interestingly, polls showed no gender gap when respondents were asked if Bill Clinton should be impeached.[40]

The historic gender gap on military issues illustrated in Table 11.1 appears to be closing. In 1999, public opinion polls on Kosovo showed no more than a 10-point gap. One NBC News/*Wall Street Journal* poll showed only a 4-point difference. Experts offer several reasons for this shrinking gap, including the increased participation of women in the workforce and in the military, the "sanitized nature of much of the war footage" shown on TV, and the humanitarian reasons offered for NATO involvement in Yugoslavia.[41]

Age. As Americans live longer, senior citizens are becoming a potent political force. In states such as Florida, to which many Northern retirees have flocked seeking relief from cold winters and high taxes, the elderly have voted as a bloc to defeat school tax increases and to pass tax breaks for themselves. As a group, senior citizens are much more likely to favor an increased governmental role in the area of medical insurance and to oppose any cuts in Social Security benefits.

In the future, the "graying of America" will have major social and political consequences. As we discuss in chapter 13, the elderly under age seventy vote in much larger numbers than do their younger counterparts. Moreover, the fastest-growing age group in the United States is that of citizens over the age of sixty-five. Thus not only are there more people in this category, but they are more likely to be registered to vote, and often vote conservatively.

The elderly continue to be a potent voting bloc with high concern about particular issues, but the youth vote that was mobilized in 1992 appeared to have burned itself out by 1996. Then, turnout among those eighteen to twenty one dropped from 38 to 31 percent; for those twenty–one to twenty–four the drop was from 45 to 33 percent.[42] Young voters are least likely to follow campaigns, with only 15 percent of those under thirty years of age reporting that they followed campaigns "very closely" compared with 43 percent for those over sixty years of age.[43] One 1996 poll found that only 28 percent thought that "keeping up with politics" was "important"; in 1966, 57 percent believed it was important.[44]

Polls and focus groups conducted for MTV find that younger voters believe that "politics and real life are not in sync. Their main beef is that the candidates are not talking about issues, they're talking about politics."[45] The under-thirty generation, or Generation X, also holds strong views on certain issues, as revealed in Figure 11.6. The vast majority want stronger environmental laws, a higher minimum wage, and a balanced budget amendment.

Age also seems to have a decided effect on one's view of the proper role of government, with older people continuing to be affected by having lived through the Depres-

FIGURE 11.6   Comparing Two Age Cohorts on Political Issues

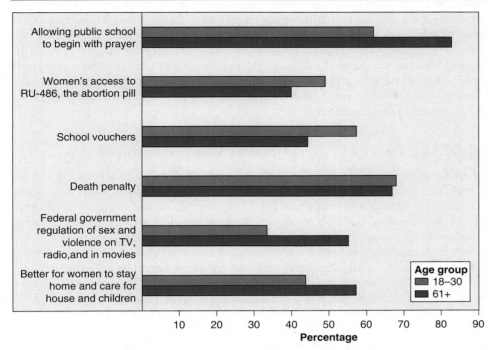

Source: *Washington Post* Poll conducted September 7–17, 2000. margin of error + or – 3%. On Politics at
http://www.washingtonpost.com/cgi-bin/gx.cgi/applogictftcontent.server.

sion and World War II. One political scientist predicts that as baby boomers age, the age gap in political beliefs about political issues, especially governmental programs, will increase.[46] Young people, for example, resist higher taxes to fund Medicare, while the elderly resist all efforts to limit it or Social Security.

Region.   Regional and sectional differences have been important factors in the development and maintenance of public opinion and political beliefs since colonial times. As the United States grew and developed into a major industrial nation, waves of immigrants with different religious traditions and customs entered the United States and often settled in areas they viewed as hospitable to their way of life. For example, thousands of Scandinavians settled in cold, snowy, rural Minnesota, and many Irish settled in the urban centers of the Northeast, as did many Italians and Jews. All brought with them unique views about many issues, as well as about the role of government. Many of these regional differences continue to affect public opinion today and sometimes result in conflict at the national level.

Recall, for example, that during the Constitutional Convention most Southerners staunchly advocated a weak national government. Nearly a hundred years later, the Civil War was fought in part because of basic differences in philosophy toward government (states' rights in the South versus national rights in the North). As we know from the results of modern political polling, the South has continued to lag behind the rest of the nation on support for civil rights, while continuing to favor return of power to the states at the expense of the national government.

The South is also much more religious than the rest of the nation, as well as more Protestant. Sixty-four percent of the South is Protestant (versus 39 percent for the rest of the nation), and 45 percent identify themselves as born-again Christians. Nearly half of all Southerners believe that "the United States is a Christian country, and the government should made laws to keep it that way."[47] Church attendance is highest in the South, where 38 percent report weekly visits. In contrast, only 26 percent of those living in the Midwest and 19 percent of those residing in the West go to church or synagogue on a weekly basis.[48] Given the South's higher churchgoing rates, it is not surprising that the Christian Coalition has been very successful at mobilizing voters in that region.

Southerners also are much more supportive of a strong national defense. They accounted for 41 percent of the troops in the Persian Gulf in the early days of that war, even though they made up only 28 percent of the general population.

The West, too, now appears "different" from other sections of the nation. Some people have moved there to avoid city life; other residents have an anti-government bias. Many who have sought refuge there are staunchly against any governmental action, especially on the national level.

Political Ideology and Public Opinion About Government

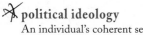

political ideology
An individual's coherent set of values and beliefs about the purpose and scope of government.

As discussed in chapter 1, an individual's coherent set of values and beliefs about the purpose and scope of government is called his or her **political ideology.** Americans' attachment to strong ideological positions has varied over time. In sharp contrast to spur-of-the-moment responses, these sets of values, which are often greatly affected by political socialization, can prompt citizens to favor a certain set of policy programs and adopt views about the proper role of government in the policy process.

Conservatives are generally likely to support smaller, less activist governments, limited social-welfare programs, and reduced government regulation of business. In contrast, liberals generally believe that the national government has an important role to play in a wide array of areas, including helping the poor and disadvantaged. Unlike most conservatives, they generally favor activist governments. Most Americans today, however, identify themselves as moderates.

Political scientists and politicians often talk in terms of conservative and liberal ideologies, and most Americans believe that they hold a political ideology. When asked by the Roper Center, most Americans (42 percent) responded that their political beliefs were moderate, although a substantial number called themselves conservatives (39 percent) with 17 percent describing themselves as liberal. Only 2 percent of those polled "didn't know" or refused to label themselves.

WEB EXPLORATION
For the most recent
Roper Center polls, see
www.ablongman.com/oconnor

Longman
Participate.com 2.0
Participation
**Are You a
Liberal or a
Conservative?**

Longman
Participate.com 2.0
Visual Literacy
**Who Are
Liberals and
Conservatives?
What's the
Difference?**

HOW WE FORM POLITICAL OPINIONS

Many of us hold opinions on a wide range of political issues, and our ideas can be traced to our social group and the different experiences each of us has had. Some individuals (called ideologues) think about politics and vote strictly on the basis of liberal or conservative ideology. Others use the party label. Most people, however, do neither. Most people filter their ideas about politics through the factors discussed above, but they are also influenced by (1) personal benefits, (2) political knowledge, and (3) cues from various leaders or opinion makers.

Personal Benefits

Most polls reveal that Americans are growing more and more "I" centered. This perspective often leads people to choose policies that best benefit them personally. You've probably heard the adage, "People vote with their pocketbooks." Taxpayers generally favor lower taxes; hence, the popularity of candidates pledging "No new taxes." Similarly, an elderly person is likely to support Social Security increases, while a member of Generation X, worried about the continued stability of the Social Security program, is not likely to be very supportive of federal retirement programs. Those born in what is now being called Generation Y, or Generation X, appear even less willing to support retirement programs. Similarly, an African American is likely to support strong civil rights laws and affirmative action programs, while a majority of nonminorities will not.

Some government policies, however, don't really affect us individually. Legalized prostitution and the death penalty, for example, are often perceived as moral issues that few citizens experience. Individuals' attitudes on these issues are often based on underlying values they have acquired through the years.

When we are faced with policies that don't affect us personally and don't involve moral issues, we often have difficulty forming an opinion. Foreign policy is an area in which this phenomenon is especially true. Most Americans often know little of the world around them. Unless moral issues such as ethnic cleansing in Kosovo are involved, American public opinion is likely to be volatile in the wake of any new information.

Political Knowledge

Americans enjoy a relatively high literacy rate, and most Americans (82 percent) graduate from high school. Most Americans, moreover, have access to a range of higher education opportunities. In spite of that access to education, however, Americans' level of actual political knowledge is low. As illustrated in Table 11.2, Americans generally don't know much about politics. One need only watch Jay Leno interview person after person on the street concerning well-publicized issues to recognize that. These kinds of differences have persisted for more than fifty years. It may be that women simply talk less about politics, or are less interested in some of its aspects. For example, on issues of campaign finance reform, women scored much higher than they did on issues such as the test ban treaty or ethanol tax breaks. In discussing this information gap, Ellen Malcolm, the head of EMILY'S List, noted, "women tend to learn, decide and vote." Thus, it was not surprising to her that women were the largest segment of undecided voters close to the 2000 election. Swamped with working and running their families, women, said Malcolm, wait until the last minute to focus on the election and to collect the information they need to cast their votes.[49]

In 1996, 94 percent couldn't identify the chief justice of the United States and nearly 50 percent didn't know that Newt Gingrich was the Speaker of the House. Moreover, only 33 percent of people surveyed could correctly identify their representative in Congress. There is, however, some evidence that the 2000 election raised political knowledge about government, from the electoral college to the composition of the Supreme Court.

Americans don't appear to know much about foreign policy, and some would argue that many Americans are geographically illiterate. One Gallup study done in 1988, for example, found that 75 percent of all Americans were unable to locate the Persian Gulf on a map. Two-thirds couldn't find Vietnam. Americans age eighteen to twenty-four scored the lowest, with two-thirds not being able to point to France on an outline map.[50]

There are also significant gender differences in political knowledge. One 2000 survey found that only 27 percent of the women polled knew that Republicans controlled the House and the Senate; 46 percent of the men did. Another 1996 study found that 75 percent of the women scored well below men on political information questions.[51] Moreover, in a survey one month before the 2000 presidential election, MTV found that one quarter of those age eighteen to twenty-four could not name both presidential candidates; 70 percent couldn't name the running mates.[52] Knowledge, however, is

WEB EXPLORATION
To test your own political knowledge, see
www.ablongman.com/oconnor

TABLE 11.2   American Political Knowledge

Percentage Unable to Identify	
Party with most members in Senate (1996)	38
Name of vice president (1996)	40
Name of the Speaker of the House (1996)	47
Both senators from their state (1996)	54
Chief justice of the United States (1996)	94

Source: Richard Morin, "Who's in Control: Many Don't Know or Care," *Washington Post* (January 29, 1996): A1, A6.

often related to interest. Given both major candidates emphasis on issues of concern to the elderly such as social security, Medicare and prescription drugs, it may be that young people, turned off, tuned out.

In 1925, Walter Lippmann critiqued the American democratic experience and highlighted the large but limited role the population plays. Citizens, said Lippmann, cannot know everything about candidates and issues but they can, and often do, know enough to impose their views and values as to the general direction the nation should take.[53] This generalized information often stands in contrast and counterbalance to the views held by more knowledgeable political elites "inside the Beltway."

As early as 1966, V. O. Key argued in his book *The Responsible Electorate* that voters "are not fools."[54] Since then, many political scientists have argued that generalizable knowledge is enough to make democracy work. Research, for example, shows citizens' perception "of the policy stands of parties and candidates were considerably more clear and accurate when the stands themselves were more distinct: in the highly ideological election of 1964, for example, as opposed to that of 1957, or in the primaries rather than the general election of 1968."[55] In elections with sharper contrasts between candidates, voters also seemed to pay more attention to issues when they cast their ballots, and to have more highly structured liberal–conservative belief systems.[56] In addition, the use of more sophisticated analytical methods involving perceived issue distances between candidates and voters seems to reveal more issue voting in general than had previously been discovered.[57]

Cues from Leaders

Low levels of knowledge, however, can lead to rapid opinion shifts on issues. The ebb and flow of popular opinion can be affected dramatically (some might say "manipulated") by political leaders. Given the visibility of political leaders and their access to the media, it is easy to see the important role they play in influencing public opinion. Political leaders, members of the news media, and a host of other experts have regular opportunities to influence public opinion because of the lack of deep conviction with which most Americans hold many of their political beliefs.[58]

The president, especially, is often in a position to mold public opinion through effective use of the "bully pulpit," as discussed in chapter 8.[59] Political scientist John E. Mueller concludes, in fact, that there is a group of citizens—called *followers*—who are inclined to rally to the support of the president no matter what he does.[60]

According to Mueller, the president's strength, especially in the area of foreign affairs (where public information is lowest), derives from the "majesty" of his office and his singular position as head of state. Recognizing this phenomenon, presidents often take to television in an effort to drum up support for their programs.[61] President Bush, borrowing a page from Presidents Reagan and Clinton, clearly realizes the importance of mobilizing public opinion. He took his case for his tax cut directly to the public, urging citizens to support his plan.

HOW WE MEASURE PUBLIC OPINION

Public officials at all levels use a variety of measures as indicators of public opinion to guide their policy decisions. These measures include election results; the number of telephone calls, faxes, or e-mail messages received pro and con on any particular issue; letters to the editor in hometown papers; and the size of demonstrations or marches. But the most commonly relied-on measure of public sentiment continues to be the public opinion survey, more popularly called a public opinion poll. Opinion polls are big news—especially during an election year. But even the most accurate polls can be very deceiving. In the past sixty years, polls have improved so much that we may be dazzled—and fooled—by their statistical precision.

Polls, however, can often mislead. "Slight differences in question wording or in the placement of the questions in the interview can have profound consequences," says David Moore, vice president of the Gallup Organization. He points out that poll findings "are very much influenced by the polling process itself."[62] Consider, for instance, what researchers discovered in a 1985 national poll: Only 19 percent of the public agreed that the country wasn't spending enough money on "welfare." But when the question contained the phrase "assistance to the poor" instead of "welfare," affirmative responses jumped to 63 percent.

That 44 percent shift explains how people can make opposite—and equally vehement—claims about what "polls show." The truth is that, at best, polls offer us flat snapshots of a three-dimensional world.

Traditional Public Opinion Polls

The polling process most often begins when someone says, "Let's find out about X and Y." Xs and Ys can be many things. Potential candidates for local office may want to know how many people have heard of them (the device used to find out is called a *name recognition survey*). Better-known candidates contemplating running for higher office might want to know how they might fare against an incumbent. Polls can also be used to gauge how effective particular ads are or if a candidate is being well (or negatively) perceived by the public. Even incumbent presidents use polls. According to the Federal Election Commission, President Clinton spent millions on polling. Remember, this was money for polls taken while in office—not running for office. These polls and others have several key phases, including (1) determining the content and phrasing the questions, (2) selecting the sample and (3) contacting respondents.

Determining the Content and Phrasing the Questions. Once a candidate, politician, or news organization decides to use a poll to measure the public's attitudes, special care has to be taken in constructing the questions to be asked. For example, if your professor asked you, "Do you think my grading procedures are fair?" rather than asking, "In general, how fair do you think the grading is in your American Politics course?" you might give a slightly different answer. The wording of the first question tends to put you on the spot and personalize the grading style; the second question is more neutral. Even more obvious differences appear in the real world of polling, especially when interested groups want a poll to yield particular results. Responses to highly emotional issues such as abortion, busing, and affirmative action are often skewed depending on the wording of a particular question.

Selecting the Sample. Once the decision is made to take a poll, pollsters must determine the *universe,* or the entire group whose attitudes they wish to measure. This universe could be all Americans, all voters, all city residents, all women, or all Democrats. Although in a perfect world each individual would be asked to give an opinion, this kind of polling is simply not practical. Consequently, pollsters take a sample of the universe in which they are interested. One way to obtain this sample is by **random sampling.** This method of selection gives each potential voter or adult the same chance of being selected. In theory, this sounds good, but it is actually impossible to achieve because no one has lists of every person in any group. This is why the method of poll taking is extremely important in determining the validity and reliability of the results.

random sampling
A method of selection that gives each potential voter or adult the same chance of being selected.

Nonstratified Sampling. *Literary Digest* polls suffered from an oversampling of voters whose names were drawn from telephone directories and car registrations; this group was hardly representative of the general electorate in the midst of the Depression. Thus the use of a nonstratified or nonrepresentative sample led to results that could not be used to predict accurately how the electorate would vote.

(Photo courtesy: Copyright ©1998 News World Communications. Reprinted with permission from the Washington Times.)

WEB EXPLORATION
To see an example of a nonstratified poll, see
www.ablongman.com/oconnor

A typical polling instrument.
(Photo courtesy: Council for Marketing and Opinion Reasearch [CMOR])

Model Introduction

Hello, my name is _____ and I'm calling from (company). Today/Tonight we are calling to gather opinions regarding (general subject), and are not selling anything. This study will take approximately (length) and may be monitored (and recorded) for quality purposes. We would appreciate your time. May I include your opinions?

Closing

- At the conclusion of the survey, thank the respondent for his/her time.

- Express the desired intention that the respondent had a positive survey experience and will be willing to participate in future market research projects.

- Remind the respondent that his/her opinions do count.

MODEL CLOSING

Thank you for your time and cooperation. I hope this experience was a pleasant one and you will participate in other market research projects in the future. Please remember that your opinion counts! Have a good day/evening.

Alternative: Participate in collecting respondent satisfaction data to improve survey quality.

Thank you very much for taking part in this survey. Because consumers like you are such a valued part of what we do, I'd like you to think about the survey you just participated in. On a scale from 1 to 10 where ten means "it was a good use of my time", and one means "it was not a good use of my time", which number between 1 and 10 best describes how you feel about your experience today? That's all the questions I have. Please remember that your opinion counts! Have a good day/evening.

Perhaps the most common form of unrepresentative sampling is the kind of straw poll used today by local television news programs or online services. Many have regular features asking viewers to call in their sentiments (with one phone number for pro and another for con) or asking those logged on to indicate their preferences. The results of these unscientific polls vary widely because those who feel very strongly about the issue often repeatedly call in to vote more than once. One poll taken by *Mother Jones* magazine online, for example, recorded a slightly different outcome from the general presidential election. Al Gore led the field with 32.6 percent of the vote, followed by Green Party candidate Ralph Nader at 28.1 percent. George W. Bush drew only 23.2 percent of the vote. Results of a survey net poll were 51.9 percent for Bush but only 33.6 percent for Gore

A more reliable method is a quota sample, in which pollsters draw their sample based on known statistics. Assume that a citywide survey has been commissioned. If the city is 30 percent African American, 15 percent Hispanic, and 55 percent white, interviewers will use those statistics to determine the proportion of particular groups to be questioned. These kinds of surveys are often conducted in local shopping malls. Perhaps you've wondered why the man or woman with the clipboard has let you pass by but has stopped the next shopper. Now you know it is likely that you did not match the profile of the subjects that the interviewer was instructed to locate. Although this kind of sampling technique can produce relatively accurate results, the degree of accuracy falls short of those surveys based on probability samples. Moreover, these surveys generally oversample the visible population, such as shoppers, while neglecting the stay-at-homes who may be glued to the Home Shopping Network or prefer to buy online.

stratified sampling
A variation of random sampling; census data are used to divide a country into four sampling regions. Sets of counties and standard metropolitan statistical areas are then randomly selected in proportion to the total national population.

Stratified Sampling.   Most national surveys and commercial polls use samples of from 1,000 to 1,500 individuals and use a variation of the random sampling method called **stratified sampling.** Simple random, nonstratified samples aren't very useful at predicting voting because they may undersample (or oversample) key populations that are not likely or particularly likely to vote.

To avoid these problems, reputable polling organizations use stratified sampling based on census data that provide the number of residences in an area and their loca-

Doonesbury

BY GARRY TRUDEAU

tion. Researchers divide the country into four sampling regions. They then randomly select a set of counties and standard metropolitan statistical areas in proportion to the total national population. Once certain primary sampling units are selected, they are often used for many years, because it is cheaper for polling companies to train interviewers to work in a fixed area.

About twenty respondents from each primary sampling unit are selected to be interviewed. Generally four or five city blocks or areas are selected, and then four or five target families from each district are used. Large, sophisticated surveys like the National Election Study and General Social Survey, which produce the data commonly used by political scientists, attempt to sample from lists of persons living in each household. The key to the success of the stratified sampling method is not to let people volunteer to be interviewed—volunteers as a group often have different opinions from those who don't volunteer.

Stratified sampling (the most rigorous sampling technique) is generally not used by those who do surveys reported in the *New York Times* and *USA Today* or on network news programs. Instead, those organizations or pollsters working for them randomly survey every tenth, hundredth, or thousandth person or household. If those individuals are not at home, they go to the home or apartment next door.

Contacting Respondents.   After selecting the methodology to conduct the poll, the next question is how to contact those to be surveyed. Television stations often ask people to call in, and some surveyors hit the streets. Telephone polls, however, are becoming the most frequently used mechanism by which to gauge the temper of the electorate.

Telephone Polls.   The most common form of telephone polls are random-digit dialing surveys, in which a computer randomly selects telephone numbers to be dialed. Because it is estimated that as many as 95 percent of the American public have telephones in their homes, samples selected in this manner are likely to be fairly representative.

In spite of some problems (such as the fact that many people don't want to be bothered, especially at dinner time), most polls done for newspapers and news magazines are conducted this way. Most polls, in fact, contain language similar to that used by the Gallup Organization in reporting its survey results:

> The current results are based on telephone interviews with a randomly selected national sample of 1,008 adults, conducted _____ to _____. For results based on a sample of this size, one can say with 95 percent confidence that the error attributable to sampling and other random effects could be plus or minus 3 percentage points. In addition to sampling error, question wording and practical difficulties in conducting surveys can introduce error or bias into the findings of public opinion polls.[63]

In-Person Polls.   Individual, in-person interviews are conducted by some groups, such as by the University of Michigan for the National Election Studies. Some analysts favor such in-person surveys, but others argue that the unintended influence of

the questioner or pollster is an important source of errors. How the pollster dresses, relates to the person being interviewed, and even asks the questions can affect responses. (Some of these factors, such as tone of voice, can also affect the results of telephone surveys.)

Political Polls

As polling has become increasingly sophisticated and networks, newspapers, and magazines compete with each other to report the most up-to-the-minute changes in public opinion on issues or political candidates, new types of polls have been suggested and put into use. Each type of poll has contributed much to our knowledge of public opinion and its role in the political process.

tracking poll
Continuous surveys that enable a campaign to chart its daily rise or fall in support.

Tracking Polls.   During the 1992 presidential elections, **tracking polls,** which were taken on a daily basis by some news organizations (see Figure 11.7), were first introduced to allow presidential candidates to monitor short-term campaign developments and the effects of their campaign strategies.

Tracking polls involve small samples and are conducted every twenty-four hours (usually of registered voters contacted at certain times of day). They are usually combined with some kind of a moving statistical average to boost the sample size and therefore the statistical reliability.[64] Even though such one-day surveys are fraught with reliability problems, many major news organizations continued their use as they reported subsequent presidential campaigns. As revealed in Figure 11.7, the 2000 tracking polls failed to pick up the upswing in Vice President Gore's popular vote, although the differences between the two candidates were well within the margin of error of the poll.

exit poll
Poll conducted at selected polling places on Election Day.

Exit Polls.   **Exit polls** are polls conducted at selected polling places on Election Day. Generally, large news organizations send pollsters to selected precincts to sample every tenth voter as he or she emerges from the polling place. The results of these polls are used to help the television networks predict the outcome of key races, often just a few minutes after the polls close in a particular state and generally before voters in other areas—sometimes in a later time zone—have cast their ballots. They also provide an independent assessment of why voters supported particular candidates "free from the spin that managers and candidates alike place on the 'meaning of an election.'"[65]

In 1980, President Jimmy Carter's own polling and the results of network exit polls led him to concede defeat three hours before the polls closed on the West Coast. Many Demo-

FIGURE 11.7:   A Daily Update Tracking Poll of the 2000 Presidential Election

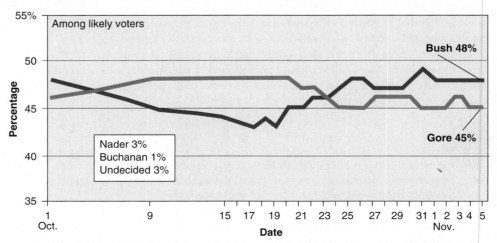

Source: "Washington Post Daily Tracking Poll," *The Washington Post,* November 7, 2000, p. A17. Copyright © 2000, The Washington Post. Reprinted with permission.

POLITICS NOW

EXIT POLLING AND THE 2000 ELECTIONS

When the *Literary Digest* miscalled the 1948 presidential election, its call went into the error hall of fame. The Voter News Service (VNS), however, is likely to take the overall prize for bad judgment although it never actually called the 2000 race for either candidate. Instead, the networks and news services looked at data provided by VNS and made their own calls. None, however, were aware of the problems below.

In 1990, the major television networks consolidated their polling operations under the VNS umbrella in a major cost-saving effort. But, the construction of a single questionnaire and one data set meant that problems could arise.

According to a confidential report of VNS, its polling was plagued with errors all night long in Florida. The polling firm had no reliable way of estimating the number of Florida's absentee ballots, which were nearly double the expected number. It estimated that the absentee ballots would make up 7.2 percent of all of the ballots cast; instead, they were 12 percent. VNS also misprojected how many of those absentee votes would go to Governor Bush, estimating 22.4 percent when it actually was 23.7. "That mistake alone accounted for 1.3 percentage points of the 7.3 percent lead that Gore was projected to hold at 7:50 that night."*

Prior to the election, VNS failed to conduct any telephone polling in Florida as it had done in traditionally absentee-heavy states such as California, Oregon, and Washington, in an effort to estimate the magnitude or direction of absentee voting. Essentially, it overlooked the politics of the state where the Republican Party was headed by the brother of one of the candidates. Phone polling is labor intensive and expensive, and according to VNS, its budget simply didn't allow it to sample every state.

An additional part of Gore's projected lead—2.8 percent—was inflated because of results from forty-five sample polls. This error, while in the range of acceptable error for exit polls, added to the inaccuracy of VNS's actions on Election Night. The rest of its error—3.2 percent—came from the exit poll model that it used. Instead of relying on the vote model of 1996 Republican presidential candidate Bob Dole, VNS used the 1998 Florida gubernatorial vote for Jeb Bush as an indicator of how his older brother would fare in 2000. Critics charge that since more voters turn out in presidential elections, 1996 should have been used as a baseline instead of 1998 when comparisons were being made to project the winner in 2000. Finally, to correct exit poll errors, VNS turned to actual vote data. At 7:50 P.M., the Tampa exit poll was off by 16 percentage points, but no actual votes were yet reported there or in Miami. Thus, VNS was unable to modify any of its exit poll errors in Tampa and Miami, where its polls were the most inaccurate.

VNS's own quality control was also off. It failed to reject, for example, an early report that 95 percent of Duval County's votes were for Gore. Moreover, because it used far smaller samples than the networks had used before creation of VNS, it overestimated the size of the black vote and underestimated the Cuban vote. It got worse in 2002. VNS, in spite of efforts to improve its act, had to admit grievous errors, and the networks were left with no exit polls on Election Day.

What other effects do you think the failures of this polling firm will have?

Do you see problems with all major media outlets relying on a single source for their election night polling?

---

*This account of errors in the VNS poll draws heavily on "New Group Admits Poll Errors: Probe Also Reveals Use of Risky Techniques," *The Washington Post* (December 24, 2000): A7.

cratic Party officials and candidates criticized Carter and network predictions for harming their chances at victories, arguing that with the presidential election already "called," voters were unlikely to go to the polls. In the aftermath of that controversy, all networks agreed not to predict the results of presidential contests until all polling places were closed, a vow they unintentionally broke in 2000 when they initially called Florida for Vice President Gore before the polls closed in the Florida panhandle, which is in a different time zone from the rest of the state. For more on the troubles with that call and exit polls, see Politics Now: Exit Polling and the 2000 Elections. Exit polls have also been faulted because it appears that not all voters are willing to reply truthfully to pollsters' questions, especially in biracial contests.[66]

David Duke, the controversial Louisiana politician with ties to the Ku Klux Klan, ran in a special election in 1999 for the seat vacated by Rep. Bob Livingston. Duke came in third. (Photo courtesy: J. Pat Carter/AP/Wide World Photos)

sampling error or margin of error
A measure of the accuracy of a public opinion poll.

Shortcomings of Polling

In 1990, the networks consolidated their polling operations under the umbrella of Voter News Service (VNS), which was a major cost-saving measure for all involved. But the construction of a single questionnaire and one data set meant that problems could arise, as was evident in the 2000 election night projections. In 1992 the VNS data significantly overpredicted the support for Republican candidate Patrick Buchanan in the New Hampshire primary, and showed President George Bush to be in much more trouble than he was. Armed with these erroneous survey results, commentator after commentator (all relying on the same data) predicted a narrow victory for Bush—who actually went on to win by a healthy sixteen-point margin. Nevertheless, "[M]any Americans went to bed believing that the president had been badly damaged."[67] This kind of reporting based on inaccurate polls can skew the rest of a campaign, particularly in an era when campaigns are viewed as horse races and everyone wants to know who's winning and by how much. VNS also provided all of the major networks with exit poll data that prompted them to call Florida, and then the entire presidential contest, too early. (See Point/Counterpoint: Should Politics Be Driven by Polls?)

Sampling Error. The accuracy of any poll depends on the quality of the sample that was drawn. Small samples, if properly drawn, can be very accurate if each unit in the universe has an equal opportunity to be sampled. If a pollster, for example, fails to sample certain populations, his or her results may reflect that shortcoming. Often the opinions of the poor and homeless are underrepresented because insufficient attention is given to making certain that these groups are representatively sampled. In the case of tracking polls, if you choose to sample only on weekends or from 5 P.M. to 9 P.M., you may get more Republicans, who are less likely to have jobs that require them to work in the evening or on weekends. There comes a point in sampling, however, where increases in the size of the sample have little effect on a reduction of the **sampling error** (also called **margin of error**), the difference between the actual universe and the sample.

All polls contain errors. Standard samples of approximately 1,000 to 1,500 individuals provide fairly good estimates of actual behavior (in the case of voting, for example). Typically, the margin of error in a sample of 1,500 will be about 3 percent. If you ask 1,500 people "Do you like ice cream?" and 52 percent say "yes" and 48 percent say "no," the results are too close to tell whether more people like ice cream than not. Why? Because the margin of error implies that somewhere between 55 percent (52 + 3) and 49 percent (52 - 3) of the people like ice cream, while between 51 percent (48 + 3) and 45 percent (48 - 3) do not. The margin of error in a close election makes predictions very difficult.

The introduction of tracking polls into the 1992 election scenario brought more criticism of political polling. According to one political scientist, their advent "played upon the worst tendencies of journalists to focus almost entirely upon who is ahead and by how much."[68] Moreover, the one-day polls were fraught with other problems. Sampling is conducted with limited or no callbacks and may be skewed because certain groups may not be at home at certain times. The 1992 CNN/Gallup poll, for example, used two different time periods—weekdays 5 P.M. to 9 P.M. and all day on the weekends.

POINT / COUNTERPOINT

SHOULD POLITICS BE DRIVEN BY POLLS?

Polling is everywhere. Every newspaper and TV station seems to run polls about everything from your preference on toilet tissue to your attitude toward immigration policies. The Internet is awash with polls, some scientific and some not so scientific. Good polls can help us understand the world around us, and bad polls can confuse us. The use of polling in politics is controversial in part because there are good and bad polls, but also because polls are being used today as a means of governance and not just for information. Since FDR, all American presidents have used polls in some way, but their use has become more controversial in the last ten years. Bill Clinton was an avid and frequent user of polls. George W. Bush says he will not be guided by polls but by principle. Should a president use polls on a frequent basis, or should a president be guided more by principle and ideology? Let's examine these two points of view.

Advocates of poll-driven politics, such as former President Bill Clinton believe that it can help the public good. During his presidency, Clinton relied on techniques designed to constantly gauge public opinion and respond to it in a variety of ways. According to *The Washington Post*, "no previous president read public opinion surveys with the same hypnotic intensity." Clinton's administration took hundreds of polls, ranging from daily polls during the campaign or crises to weekly polls during quieter times. Policy decisions that were heavily polling driven include devoting the surplus to "save Social Security first," protecting the privacy of medical and financial records, and prohibiting needle exchanges for drug addicts to combat AIDS. Phrases such as "risky tax scheme" were tested and refined through polling. Mark Penn, Clinton's primary pollster, argued that polls are all about democracy, allowing voices to be heard that might otherwise be silent. Clinton said that polling is a tool that a president ought to use to find out what the people want. According to supporters of this use for polls, polling helps politicians find consensus and is democratic because those polled are the people themselves. They claim that the alternative to polling is relying heavily on special interest groups and people with lots of money, access, and influence.

Opponents of governing through polls, such as George Bush and former U.S. Senator Bob Dole, argue that too heavy a reliance on polls drains politics of meaning and encourages cynicism. Many of Clinton's political opponents believe that the manipulation of public opinion by the former president increased public cynicism about government and harmed the public good. They argue that elected officials ought to lead the people, not follow polls that often twitch and change with the political winds; sometimes the right thing to do is the unpopular thing. Leaders should educate the people and inform them about their ideas, not simply ask everyone their opinion. A president should not aim to be popular but should accomplish something and maintain his principles. According to comments made during the 2000 campaign, George W. Bush seemed to agree with these sentiments, although as president, he also relies on polls.

In the wake of continued poll errors, there seems to be skepticism about the accuracy of polls. Many opponents of governing by polls question whether polls measure public opinion or simply give a snapshot of a certain point in time. Accurate polling is very difficult, and political polling can often be deliberately inaccurate.

 What do you think? Should politics be driven by polls? *Go to* www.ablongman.com/oconnor

Midweek surveys produced candidate distributions that disproportionately favored Bush, while weekend surveys showed the reverse.

This problem was exacerbated by two shifts in the way data were collected. First, pollsters moved from surveying "registered" voters to surveying "likely" voters[69]; second, Gallup changed the way it allocated "undecided" voters. All of these methodologies created the impression that the race was closer than it was and gave a boost to George Bush. Thus, some argue that the danger of tracking polls needs to be highlighted and discussed before more emphasis is placed on them.

Limited Respondent Options.   Polls can be inaccurate when they limit responses. If you are asked, "How do you like this class?" and are given only like or dislike options, your full sentiments may not be tapped if you like the class very much or feel only so-so about it.

Lack of Information.   Public opinion polls may also be off when they attempt to gauge attitudes about issues that some or even many individuals don't care about or about which the public has little information. For example, until the 2000 election, few Americans cared about the elimination of the electoral college. If a representative sample were polled prior to 2000, many would answer pro or con without having given much consideration to the question. Of course, all of this changed in the wake of public attention to the electoral college.

Most academic public opinion research organizations, such as the National Election Study, use some kind of filter question that first asks respondents whether or not they have thought about the question. These screening procedures generally allow surveyors to exclude as many as 20 percent of their respondents, especially on complex issues like the federal budget. Questions on more personal issues such as moral values, drugs, crime, race, and women's role in society get far fewer "no opinion" or "don't know" responses.

Intensity.   Another shortcoming of polls concerns their inability to measure intensity of feeling about particular issues. Whereas a respondent might answer affirmatively to any question, it is likely that his or her feelings about issues such as abortion, the death penalty, or support for U.S. troops in the Gulf are much more intense than are his or her feelings about the electoral college or even types of voting machines.

HOW POLLING AND PUBLIC OPINION AFFECT POLITICIANS, POLITICS, AND POLICY

Longman
Participate.com 2.0
Simulation
**You Are a
Polling
Consultant**

As early as the founding period the authors of *The Federalist Papers* noted that "all government rests on public opinion," and as a result, public opinion inevitably influences the actions of politicians and public officials. (For a broader perspective, see Global Politics: Public Opinion on Government Responsibilities.) The public's perception of crime as a problem, for example, was the driving force behind the comprehensive crime bill President Clinton submitted to Congress in 1994 and congressional passage of the Brady gun control bill in 1993. The public's concern with crime skyrocketed to an all-time high in 1994, when 37 percent of the public rated crime as the nation's most important problem, and politicians at all levels were quick to convert that concern into a campaign issue. In 1996, during the presidential campaign, Bill Clinton even called for the passage of a constitutional amendment to protect crime victims' rights. But action by Clinton and Congress and dropping crime rates actually pushed concern with crime way down; in 2000, only 12 percent of those polled thought it was the most important problem.[70]

Politicians and government officials spend millions of dollars each year taking the pulse of the public. Even the federal government spends millions annually on polls and surveys designed to evaluate programs and to provide information for shaping policies. But as political scientist Benjamin Ginsberg noted, "the data reported by opinion polls are actually the product of an interplay between opinion and the survey instrument." They interact with each other and, in essence, often change the "character of the views receiving public expression."[71] Polls can thus help transform public opinion.

We know that politicians rely on polls, but it's difficult to say to what degree. Several political scientists have attempted to study whether public policy is responsive to public opinion, with mixed results.[72] As we have seen, public opinion can fluctuate, making it difficult for a politician or policy maker to assess. Some critics of polls

G L O B A L   P O L I T I C S

PUBLIC OPINION ON
GOVERNMENT RESPONSIBILITIES

The notions of limited government and individual liberty are two major components of political culture in the United States. The public opinion effects of these notions is clear in the table below: In a 1990 survey, the percentage of American respondents who definitely agreed that their government is responsible for providing health care and full employment was well below that of citizens polled in Germany, Italy, and Britain. Other polls show similar figures for other European countries. Polls also demonstrate that these public preferences are not limited to health care and employment but extend to other issue areas. Americans are less likely to agree that government should guarantee basic incomes, for example, or work to reduce inequality.

The difference can be traced to two related phenomena. First, Americans tend to agree with the Jeffersonian

dictum that small government is better than big government. While Americans may not distrust government any more than Europeans do (polls show that Italians trust their government less than citizens in other European governments, and even a significant number of British citizens do not trust theirs), they have been less willing to put up with what they perceive as big government to the extent that Europeans and Japanese have. Unlike the United States, Canada, and Britain, the countries of continental Europe and Japan have had modern histories in which the state has taken a major role in shaping national society and has actively competed with the private sector.

Second, these public predispositions have affected what governments have actually been able to do. While the size of government in every industrial democracy has grown since World War II, it has grown less in important policy areas in the United States than it has in its counterparts. In particular, the postwar welfare state (of which healthcare and employment are a part) in the United States has not developed to the extent that it has in Japan, Canada, and Europe.

Citizen Attitudes About Appropriate Government Services

Country	Agree Government Is Responsible for Health Care (%)	Agree Government Is Responsible for Jobs (%)
Germany	57	30
Italy	88	38
United Kingdom	85	24
United States	**40**	**16**

Source: From *European Politics Today*, 3rd ed, by Frank Wilson. Copyright © 1999. Reprinted by permission of Prentice-Hall, Inc., Upper Saddle River, N.J.

Longman
Participate.com
2.0
Comparative
Comparing
Public
Opinion

and of their use by politicians argue that polls hurt democracy and make leaders weaker. Benjamin Ginsberg, one of these critics, argues that these polls weaken democracy.[73] He claims that these polls allow governments and politicians to say they have considered public opinion even though polls don't always measure the intensity of feeling on an issue or might overreflect the views of the responders who lack sufficient information to make educated choices. Ginsberg further argues that democracy is better served by politicians' reliance on telephone calls and letters—active signs of interest—than on the passive voice of public opinion. Some say that politicians are simply driven by the results of polls that do not reflect a serious debate of issues. In response to this argument, George Gallup retorted, "One might as well insist that a thermometer makes the weather."[74]

Polls can clearly distort the election process by creating what are called "bandwagon" and "underdog" effects. In a presidential campaign, an early victory in the Iowa caucuses or the New Hampshire primary, for example, can boost a candidate's standings in the polls as the rest of the nation begins to think of him or her in a more positive light. New supporters jump on the bandwagon. A strong showing in the polls, in turn, can generate more and larger donations, the lifeblood of any campaign. Political scientist Herbert Asher has noted that "bad poll results, as well as poor primary and caucus standings, may deter potential donors from supporting a failing campaign."[75]

Continuity &Change

Election Forecasting

The first attempts to measure public opinion were quite crude.[76] While politicians attempted to influence how Americans would vote, as well illustrated by the Federalist/Anti-Federalist debates in local newspapers and in political tracts circulated among the thirteen states, the true test of public opinion was the election results. It wasn't until the development of more sophisticated methods of communication such as mass-circulation magazines and a reliable mail service that organizations such as the *Literary Digest* even attempted to tap the pulse of American voters in any systematic fashion.

The development of the telephone truly revolutionized the polling industry. While social scientists still recognize the value of face-to-face interviews with respondents, as more and more households in all regions of the nation got telephone service, the ability to use sampling techniques to draw representative samples, and quickly administer surveys and polls, proved a real boon to the political polling industry. The telephone changed fundamentally how most political polls were conducted. Since their widespread use in the 1970s, "telephone polls, on the whole, have proved to be remarkably accurate predictors of voter behavior—the gold standard of all polling research." Problems with telephone polls are rapidly increasing, however. Over 40 percent of those contacted now refuse to participate, and such polls get more and more costly each year.[77]

In the 1990s, American pollsters and social scientists began to experiment with a variety of other kinds of polls, often spurred on by news agencies' desire to be the "first" with the "news." Sophisticated exit polls, often conducted to allow a network to be the first on the air with a prediction, and tracking polls, often conducted to make political races seem closer than they are thereby enhancing their "newsworthiness," are particularly popular today. While these polls utilized new techniques, they didn't utilize a new medium.

A variety of new forms of measuring public sentiment are now being devised using the Internet as a new medium. One company, DiscoveryWhy.com, used Internet polling to measure the instantaneous responses of potential voters to the 2000 Democratic nomination acceptance speech of Al Gore.[78] Participants rated his performance with mouse clicks as they watched the address on television and the results could be known almost instantaneously. The 300 watchers—a smaller sample than used for phone polls—were drawn from lists created by the company and were by invitation only. Thus, DiscoveryWhy.com attempts to approximate the same kind of reliability as phone surveys.

Harris Interactive, an Internet-based marketing firm, used the Internet to achieve a 99 percent accuracy rate in seventy-three political contests in November 2000.[79] Harris's margin of error was 1.9 percent; conventional polling was off by 3.9 percent for Gore and 3.9 percent for Bush. They even predicted that Gore would win the popular vote but lose the electoral college vote. How did they do it? Over 300,000 members of the voting-age public participated in the poll online from October 30 through November 6, 2000. The company processed over 40,000 online interviews per hour, including 7,800 simultaneous interviews. The final data were then weighted and tabulated. The results were remarkable and could change the face of polling as we know it, especially in light of the errors in traditional methods that occurred in 2000.

1. What potential problems do you see with Internet polling?
2. Can huge sample sizes reduce polling problems regardless of the way the sample was drawn?

Cast Your Vote. Will the Internet serve as an effective and accurate tool for political polling? To cast your vote, go to **www.ablongman.com/oconnor**

SUMMARY

Public opinion is a subject constantly mentioned in the media, especially in presidential election years or when important policies (such as health care, balancing the budget, race, or crime) are under consideration. What public opinion is, where it comes from, how it's measured, and how it's used are aspects of a complex subject. To that end, this chapter has made the following points:

1. **What Is Public Opinion?**
   Public opinion is what the public thinks about an issue or a particular set of issues. Public opinion polls are used to estimate public opinion.

2. **Early Efforts to Influence and Measure Public Opinion**
   Almost since the beginning of the United States, various attempts have been made to influence

public opinion about particular issues or to sway elections. Modern-day polling did not begin until the 1930s, however. Over the years, polling to measure public opinion has become increasingly sophisticated and more accurate because pollsters are better able to sample the public in their effort to determine their attitudes and positions on issues. Pollsters recognize that their sample must reflect the population whose ideas and beliefs they wish to measure.

3. **Political Socialization and Other Factors That Influence Opinion Formation**
The first step in forming opinions occurs through a process called political socialization. The family, school, peers, the impact of events, the social group of which one is a member—including religion, race, gender, and age—as well as where one lives all affect how one views political events and issues, as do the major events themselves. Our political ideology—whether we are conservative, liberal, or moderate—also provides a lens through which we filter our political views, as does our level of personal benefit from and our political knowledge of issues and events. Even the views of

other people a...
of issues, includ...
abortion, and fede...

4. **How We Form Polit...**
Myriad factors enter ...
about political matters. ...
about the personal benef...
sonal political knowledge, a...

5. **How We Measure Public Opi...**
Measuring public opinion can b... ..cult. The most frequently used measure is the public opinion poll. Determining the content, phrasing the questions, selecting the sample, and choosing the right kind of poll are critical to obtaining accurate and useful data.

6. **How Polling and Public Opinion Affect Politicians, Politics, and Policy**
Knowledge of the public's views on issues is often used by politicians to tailor campaigns or to drive policy decisions. Polls, however, have several shortcomings including sampling error and inadequate respondent information.

KEY TERMS   *due friday*

exit poll, p. 406
margin of error, p. 408
political ideology, p. 399
political socialization, p. 390

public opinion, p. 384
public opinion poll, p. 385
random sampling, p. 403
sampling error, p. 408

stratified sampling, p. 404
straw poll, p. 388
tracking poll, p. 406

SELECTED READINGS

Asher, Herbert. *Polling and the Public: What Every Citizen Should Know,* 4th ed. Washington, D.C.: CQ Press, 1998.

Bennet, W. Lance, and David L. Paletz, ed,. *Taken by Storm: The Media, Public Opinion, and U.S. Foreign Policy in the Gulf War.* Chicago: University of Chicago Press, 1994.

Carmines, Edward G., and James A. Stimson. *Issue Evolution.* Princeton, N.J.: Princeton University Press, 1990.

Crespi, Irving. *Public Opinion, Polls, and Democracy.* Boulder, Colo.: Westview Press, 1989.

Erikson, Robert S., and Kent L. Tedin. *American Public Opinion: Its Contents, Origins and Impact.* Englewood Cliffs, N.J.: Prentice Hall, 1995.

Fishkin, James S. *The Voice of the People: Public Opinion and Democracy.* New Haven, Conn.: Yale University Press, 1996.

Ginsberg, Benjamin. *The Captive Public.* New York: Basic Books, 1986.

Herbst, Susan. *Numbered Voices: How Opinion Polling Has Shaped American Politics.* Chicago: University of Chicago Press, 1993.

Jamieson, Kathleen Hall. *Everything You Think You Know About Politics ... and Why You Were Wrong.* New York: Basic Books, 2000.

Jennings, M. Kent, and Richard Niemi. *Generations and Politics: A Panel Study of Young Adults and Their Parents.* Princeton, N.J.: Princeton University Press, 1981.

Key, V. O., Jr. *Public Opinion and American Democracy.* New York: Alfred E. Knopf, 1961.

Mutz, Diana Carole. *Impersonal Influence: How Perceptions of Mass Collectives Affect Political Attitudes.* New York: Cambridge University Press, 1998.

Rubenstein, Sondra Miller. *Surveying Public Opinion.* Belmont, Calif.: Wadsworth Publishing, 1994.

Shafer, Bryon E., and William J. M. Claggett. *The Two Majorities: The Issue Context of Modern American Politics.* Baltimore, Md.: Johns Hopkins University Press, 1995.

Stimson, James A. *Public Opinion in America: Moods, Cycles, and Swings.* 2nd ed. Boulder, Colo.: Westview Press, 1998.

Zaller, John. *The Nature and Origins of Mass Opinions.* New York: Cambridge University Press, 1992.

up Organization, "Poll Releases: The Florida Re-
Controversy From the Public's Perspective: 25 Insights,"
http://www.gallup.com/poll/releases. All data discussed here are
drawn from this compendium of polls concerning the Florida
recount.

2. Allan M. Winkler, "Public Opinion," in Jack Greene, ed., *The Encyclopedia of American Political History* (New York: Charles Scribner's Sons, 1988), 1038.

3. Quoted in *Public Opinion Quarterly* 29 (Winter 1965–66): 547.

4. Winkler, "Public Opinion," 1035.

5. Quoted in Winkler, "Public Opinion," 1035.

6. *Literary Digest* 122 (August 22, 1936): 3.

7. *Literary Digest* 125 (November, 14 1936): 1.

8. Robert S. Erikson, Norman Luttbeg, and Kent Tedin, *American Public Opinion: Its Origin, Content and Impact* (New York: Wiley, 1980), 28.

9. Angus Campbell, Philip Converse, Warren Miller, and Donald Stokes, *The American Voter* (New York: Wiley, 1960).

10. Byron E. Shafer and William J. M. Claggett, *The Two Majorities: The Issue Context of Modern American Politics* (Baltimore, Md.: Johns Hopkins University Press, 1995), 12.

11. Shafer and Claggett, *The Two Majorities*, 13.

12. Richard Dawson, et al. *Political Socialization*, 2nd ed. (Boston: Little, Brown, 1977), 33.

13. Robert D. Hess and David Easton, "The Child's Changing Image of the President," *Public Opinion Quarterly* 14 (Winter 1960): 632–42; and Fred I. Greenstein, *Children and Politics* (New Haven, Conn.: Yale University Press, 1965).

14. *Statistical Abstract of the United States, 1997*, 117th ed. (Government Printing Office, Washington, D.C., 1997), 1011.

15. Sandor M. Polster, "Bad News for Much TV News," *Bangor Daily News* (May 18, 1996): NEXIS.

16. Peggy Fikas, "A Funny Thing Happened on the Way to the White House," *San Antonio Express* (October 31, 2000): 1F.

17. Anne Miller, "Students Fighting National Apathy Trend," *San Antonio Express* (November 1, 2000): 3H.

18. Julie Mason, "Avalanche of Politico-tainment Seems to Benefit Presidential Candidates," *Houston Chronicle* (October 1, 2000): A38; and Lois Romano, "For the Candidates, It's Showtime," *The Washington Post* (October 20, 2000): A11.

19. Sandor Polster, "Bad News for Much TV News," *Bangor Daily News*, May 18, 1996.

20. David Buckingham, "News Media, Political Socialization, and Popular Citizenship: Towards a New Agenda," *Critical Studies in Mass Communication* 14:1 (December 1997): 344–66.

21. Andrew Glass, "News About the Net," *The Atlanta Journal and Constitution* (November 17, 2000): 2D.

22. Miranda Yates and James Youniss, "Communication and Age in Childhood Political Socialization: An Interactive Model of Political Development," *Journalism and Mass Communication Quarterly* (Winter 1998): 699–718.

23. James Simon and Bruce D. Merrill, "Political Socialization in the Classroom Revisited: The Kids Voting Program," *Social Science Journal* 35 (1998): 29–42.

24. Simon and Merrill, "Political Socialization."

25. F. Christopher Arterton, "The Impact of Watergate on Children's Attitudes Toward Political Authority," *Political Science Quarterly* 89 (June 1974): 273.

26. Diana Owen and Jack Dennis, "Kids and the Presidency: Assessing Clinton's Legacy," *Public Perspective* (April 1999): NEXIS.

27. "Church Membership Trend," http://www.gallup.com/POLL_ARCHIVES/970329.html.

28. "Basic Religious Beliefs," *Public Perspective* (October/November 1995): 4–5.

29. "America's Religious Makeup," http:// www.gallup.com/POLL_ARCHIVES/970329.html.

30. Lyman A. Kellstedt, et al., "Has Godot Finally Arrived? Religion and Realignment," *Public Perspective* (June/July 1995): 19.

31. Geoffrey C. Layman, "Religion and Political Behavior in the United States: The Impact of Beliefs, Affiliations, and Commitment from 1980 to 1994," *Public Opinion Quarterly* 61 (1997): 288.

32. Steven M. Cohen and Charles S. Liebman, "American Jewish Liberalism," *Public Opinion Quarterly* 61 (1997): 405–30.

33. Edward S. Greenberg. "The Political Socialization of Black Children," in Edward S. Greenberg, ed., *Political Socialization* (New York: Atherton Press, 1970), 181.

34. Alejandro Portest and Rafael Mozo, "The Political Adaptation Process of Cubans and Other Ethnic Minorities in the United States: A Preliminary Analysis," in F. Chris Garcia, ed., *Latinos and the Political System* (Notre Dame, Ind.: University of Notre Dame Press, 1988), 161.

35. Wes Allison and David Adams, "Family to Dad: Elian Stays with Us," *St. Petersburg Times* (April 1, 2000): 1A.

36. The Gallup Organization, "Poll Releases: Americans Approve of U.S. Government Decision to Return Boy to Cuba," http://www.gallup.com/poll/releases/pr000112.asp.

37. Pamela Johnson Conover and Virginia Sapiro, "Gender, Feminist Consciousness and War," *American Journal of Political Science* 37 (November 1993): 1079–99.

38. Margaret Trevor, "Political Socialization, Party Identification, and the Gender Gap," *Public Opinion Quarterly* 63: (Spring 1999): 62–89.

39. "Number Crunching," *The Washington Post* (March 22, 1998): C2.

40. "*Newsweek:* No Gender Gap on Impeachment Question," *Hotline* (December 14, 1998).

41. Alexandra Marks, "Gender Gap Narrows over Kosovo," *The Christian Science Monitor* (April 30, 1999): 1.

42. Danny Goldberg, "As Politicians Demonize Pop Culture, Young Voters Tune Out," *The Los Angeles Times*, (September 3, 2000): M3.

43. William Booth, "Younger Voters Reflect Rise in Apathy, Discontent with Politics," *The Washington Post* (November 5, 1996): A10.

44. Tanya Bricking, "Young Voters May Not," *The Cincinnati Enquirer* (October 19, 1996): A1.

45. Booth, "Younger Voters Reflect Rise in Apathy."

46. Susan A. MacManus, *Young v. Old: Generational Combat in the 21st Century* (Boulder, Colo.: Westview Press, 1995).

47. Richard Morin, "Southern Exposure," *The Washington Post* (July 14, 1996): A18.

48. "Church Pews Seat More Blacks, Seniors, and Republicans," http://www.gallup.com. 6A.POLL_ARCHIVES/970329.html.

49. Scripps Howard News Service, April 2, 2000.

50. "Geography: A Lost Generation," *The Nation* (August 8, 1988): 19.

51. Kate O'Bierne, "Clueless: What Women Don't Know About Politics," *National Review* (October 9, 2000): NEXIS.

52. David Bauder, "Young Voters Turning Out in Droves, MTV Says," *Dayton Daily News* (October 20, 2000): 6A.

53. Quoted in Everett Carl Ladd, "Fiskin's 'Deliberative Poll' Is Flawed Science and Dubious Democracy," *Public Perspective* (December/January 1996): 41.

54. V. O. Key, Jr. *The Responsible Electorate: Rationality in Presidential Voting, 1936–1960* (Cambridge, Mass.: Belknap Press of Harvard University, 1966).

55. Gerald M. Pomper, *The Performance of American Government,* (New York: Free Press, 1972); and Benjamin I. Page, *Choices and Echoes in Presidential Elections* (Chicago: University of Chicago Press, 1978).

56. Norman H. Nie, Sidney Verba, and John R. Petrocik. *The Changing American Voter* (Cambridge, Mass.: Harvard University Press, 1976).

57. Ladd, "Fiskin's 'Deliberative Poll,'" 42.

58. Richard Nodeau, et al., "Elite Economic Forecasts, Economic News, Mass Economic Judgments and Presidential Approval," *Journal of Politics* 61 (February 1999): 109–135.

59. Micheal Towle, Review of Jeffrey E. Cohen's "Presidential Responsiveness and Public Policy-making: The Public and the Policies," *Journal of Politics* 61 (February 1999): 230–32.

60. John E. Mueller, *War, Presidents and Public Opinion* (New York: Wiley, 1973), 69.

61. Roderick P. Hart, *The Sound of Leadership: Presidential Communication in the Modern Age* (Chicago: University of Chicago Press, 1987).

62. David W. Moore, *The Superpollsters: How They Measure and Manipulate Public Opinion in America*, 2nd ed. (New York: Four Walls Eight Windows, 1995).

63. David W. Moore, "Public Opposes Gay Marriages," Gallup Organization, April 4, 1996.

64. Michael W. Traugott, "The Polls in 1992: Views of Two Critics: A Good General Showing, but Much Work Needs to Be Done," *Public Perspective* 4 (November/December 1992): 14–16.

65. Michael W. Traugott, "The Polls in 1992: It Was the Best of Times, It Was the Worst of Times," *Public Perspective* (December/January 1992): 14.

66. Adam Berinsky, "A Tale of Two Elections: An Investigation of Pre-election Polling in Biracial Contests," paper presented at the 1999 annual meeting of the Midwest Political Science Association.

67. Traugott, "The Polls in 1992."

68. Traugott, "The Polls in 1992."

69. Michael W. Traugott and Clyde Tucker, "Strategies for Predicting Whether a Citizen Will Vote and Estimation of Electoral Outcomes," *Public Opinion Quarterly* (Spring 1984): 330–43.

70. "Most Important Problem," The Gallup Organization, 6/19/99.

71. Benjamin Ginsberg, "How Polls Transform Public Opinion," in Michael Margolis and Gary A. Mauser, eds., *Manipulating Public Opinion* (Pacific Grove, Calif.: Brooks/Cole, 1989), 273.

72. See, for example, Benjamin Page and Robert Shapiro, "Effects of Public Opinion on Policy," *American Political Science Review* 57 (March 1983): 175–90.

73. Benjamin Ginsberg, *The Captive Public* (New York: Basic Books, 1986), ch. 4.

74. Quoted in Pace, "George Gallup Is Dead at 82," *The New York Times*, (July 28, 1984): A1.

75. Herbert Asher, *Polling and the Public: What Every Citizen Should Know* (Washington, D.C.: CQ Press, 1988), 109.

76. For an interesting discussion of measuring public opinion before surveys, see Karen Hoffman, "Going Public in the Eighteenth and Nineteenth Centuries: Measuring the Influence of Public Opinion Before Surveys," paper prepared for delivery at the 1999 annual meeting of the Midwest Political Science Association.

77. Gordon S. Black and George Terhanian, "Using the Internet for Election Forecasting," http://www.pollingreport.com./internet.html.

78. Steve Marantz, "Dotcom Finds a Future Cyber Polling," *The Boston Herald* (September 25, 2000): 21.

79. "2000 Election Winners: George W. Bush and Online Polling," *Business Wire* (December 14, 2000).

12 Political Parties

The difficulty inherent in sustaining a third party in a traditional two-party political culture is nowhere better exemplified than the current fractured state of the Reform Party. Once a challenger to the two parties in the early 1990s, the Reform Party was in shambles by 2000. In 1992, Ross Perot, the diminutive Texas billionaire who founded the party, seemed on the verge of capturing the White House. Capitalizing on economic and political dissatisfaction in the nation, Perot's message made such a favorable impression that at various points during the campaign, polls showed him winning 40 percent of the popular vote (nearly as much as Clinton would later win to take the presidency from Bush). But Perot's erratic behavior—including withdrawing from the race and then re-entering—sunk his campaign, and he ultimately secured only 19 percent of the popular vote.

While Perot's 19 percent in 1992 was far less than he had hoped to secure at the zenith of his campaign, it was still substantially more than the 5 percent required by the federal government to secure matching funds during the next campaign. Perot ran again in 1996, but with the economy good and Clinton's public image still largely intact, Perot was able to secure only 8 percent of the popular vote, and it was clear that both the man and the moment had passed once and for all, even if the party he created still retained some vital energy.

But after eight years in the spotlight, the Reform Party had clearly reached the end of its run. Desperately in search of a compelling candidate, but deprived in economic good times of a populist or reformist mandate, the party fell prey in 2000 to the ambition of the one man who ironically had the least in common with its basically nonpartisan, non-ideological nature: the divisive and ultra-conservative Pat Buchanan. Buchanan, of course, wanted only to secure access to the party's war chest, and thus packed the national party convention with his supporters. The convention nearly became riotous as Buchanan supporters refused to allow access to supporters of his only opponent, Natural Law Party candidate John Hagelin. Ultimately the two groups physically fractured and met in different venues amidst accusations of unscrupulous behavior on all parts. Buchanan ultimately secured the nomination, but his reactionary message has been diminishing in appeal for years, and his failure to secure the magic 5 percent means effectively that the party is over.

The story of the Reform Party does offer one ironic insight into party structure and American democracy: Given the difficulties of holding together a third party, it is remarkable indeed that the two major parties have remained relatively stable for nearly 150 years, since the Republican Party came together in its modern shape in 1856.

It is difficult to reject the assertion that we are now entering a new, more fluid era of party politics. But, while some maintain that our two-party system is likely to be replaced by a chaotic multiparty system, or that a system in which presidential hopefuls bypass party nominations altogether and compete on their own is on the horizon, it is important to remember that political parties have been staples of American life since the late 1700s and, in one form or another, they will most likely continue to be. As this chapter explains, political scientist E. E. Schattschneider was not exaggerating when he wrote, "Modern democracy is unthinkable save in terms of the parties."[1]

The chapter addresses contemporary party politics and attempts to help you understand political parties by examining them from many vantage points. Our examination of political parties traces their development from their infancy in the late 1700s to today:

- First, we will discuss *what a political party is.*
- Second, we will look at the *parties' evolution* through U.S. history.
- Third, we will examine the *roles of the American parties* in our political system.
- Fourth, we will analyze the phenomena of *one-partyism and third-partyism.*
- Fifth, we will present the *basic structure of American political parties.*
- Sixth, we will explore the *party in government,* the office holders and candidates who run under the party's banner.
- Seventh, we will examine the *modern transformation of the parties,* paying special attention to how political parties have moved from the labor-intensive, person-to-person operations of the first half of the century toward the use of technology and communication strategies.
- Eighth, we will look at the *party in the electorate,* showing that a political party's reach extends well beyond the relative handful of men and women who are the party in government.
- Finally, we will discuss independent and third-party candidates and the history of party alignment.

WHAT IS A POLITICAL PARTY?

Any definition of "political party" must be kept general because there are so many kinds of parties in the United States. In some states and localities, party organizations are strong and well entrenched, whereas in other places the parties exist more on paper than in reality. A definition of "party" might also be shaped by what people expect of parties. Some people expect parties to seek policy changes, while others expect them to win elections. This distinction flavors some of the debate over the effectiveness of political parties. If you expect parties to help candidates win office, then you might conclude that they are healthy. But if you believe that the main goal of political parties should be to promote and accomplish policy changes, then you might believe they frequently fail. We will be concerned here primarily with the electoral functions served by political parties, but it is important to remember these distinctions.[2]

political party
A group of office holders, candidates, activists, and voters who identify with a group label and seek to elect to public office individuals who run under that label.

At the most basic level, a **political party** is a group of office holders, candidates, activists, and voters who identify with a group label and seek to elect to public office individuals who run under that label. Notice how pragmatic this concept of party is. The goal is to win office, not just compete for it. This objective is in keeping with the practical nature of Americans and the country's historical aversion to most ideologically driven, "purist" politics (as we discuss later in this chapter). Nevertheless, the group label, also called party identification for the voters who embrace the party as their own, can carry with it clear messages about ideology and issue positions. Although this is especially true of minor, less broad-based parties that have little chance of electoral success, it also applies to the national, dominant political parties in the United States, the Democrats and the Republicans.

In recent years women have made serious inroads as party delegates, candidates, and office holders. Here, Democratic women of the United States House of Representatives gather during the 2000 Democratic National Convention. (Photo courtesy: Paul J. Richards/AFP/Corbis)

When it comes to providing a formal definition of political parties, however, political scientists have often disagreed.[3] Some political scientists, for example, conceive of political parties as being made up of three separate but related entities: (1) the office holders and candidates who run under the party's banner (the **governmental party**), (2) the workers and activists who staff the party's formal organization (the **organizational party**), and (3) the voters who consider themselves to be allied or associated with the party (the **party in the electorate**).[4] Other political scientists take issue with this definition, arguing that, especially in the American political system, voters should not be included in the definition of political parties. Voters, they note, are not part of the parties but choosers among them, in much the same way that fans of a sports team are not actually part of the team.[5] In this chapter, we examine all three components of political parties—the governmental party, the organizational party, and the party in the electorate—including voters if only because they are so important in driving the actions of the other two components. First, however, we turn to the history and development of political parties in the United States.

governmental party
The office holders and candidates who run under a political party's banner.

organizational party
The workers and activists who staff the party's formal organization.

party in the electorate
The voters who consider themselves to be allied or associated with the party.

THE EVOLUTION OF AMERICAN PARTY DEMOCRACY

It is one of the great ironies of the early republic that George Washington's public farewell, which warned the nation against parties, marked the effective end of the brief era of partyless politics in the United States (see Figure 12.1). Washington's unifying influence ebbed as he stepped off the national stage, and his vice president and successor, President John Adams, occupied a much less exalted position. Adams was allied with Alexander Hamilton. To win the presidency in 1796, he narrowly defeated Thomas Jefferson, Hamilton's former rival in Washington's Cabinet. Before ratification of the Constitution, Hamilton and Jefferson had been leaders of the Federalists and Anti-Federalists, respectively (see chapter 2). Over the course of Adams's single term, two competing congressional party groupings (or caucuses) gradually organized around these clashing men and their principles: Hamilton's Federalists supported a strong central government; the Democratic–Republicans of Thomas Jefferson and his ally James Madison inherited the mantle of the Anti-Federalists and preferred a federal

FIGURE 12.1 American Party History at a Glance

This table shows the transformations and evolution of the various parties that have always made up the basic two-party structure of the American political system.

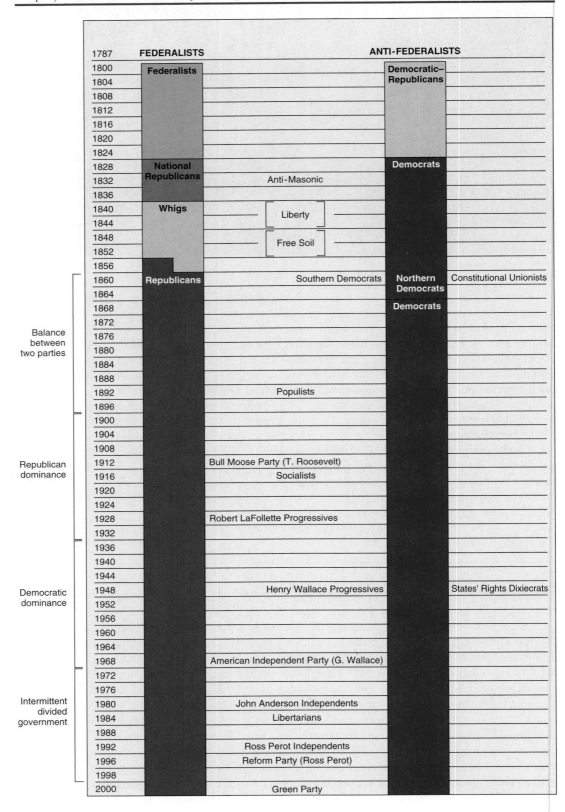

system in which the states were relatively more powerful. (Jefferson actually preferred the simpler name "Republicans," a very different group from today's party of the same name, but Hamilton insisted on calling them "Democratic–Republicans" to link them to the radical democrats of the French Revolution.) In the presidential election of 1800, the Federalists supported Adams's bid for a second term, but this time the Democratic–Republicans prevailed with their nominee, Jefferson, who became the first U.S. president elected as the nominee of a political party.

Jefferson was deeply committed to the ideas of his party, but not nearly as devoted to the idea of a party system. He regarded his party as a temporary measure necessary to defeat Adams and Hamilton. Neither Jefferson's party nor Hamilton's enjoyed widespread "party identification" among the citizenry akin to that of today's Democrats and Republicans. Although Southerners were overwhelmingly partial to the Democratic–Republicans and New Englanders to the Federalists, no broad-based party organizations existed on either side to mobilize popular support. Rather, as political scientist John H. Aldrich observes, the congressional factions organized around Hamilton and Jefferson were primarily governmental parties designed to settle the dispute over how strong the new federal government would be.[6] Just as the nation was in its infancy, so, too, was the party system, and attachments to both parties were weak at first.

The Early Parties Fade

After the spirited confrontations of the republic's early years, political parties faded somewhat in importance for a quarter of a century. The Federalists ceased nominating presidential candidates by 1816, having failed to elect one of their own since Adams's victory in 1796, and by 1820 the party had dissolved. James Monroe's presidency from 1817 to 1825 produced the so-called Era of Good Feelings, when party politics was nearly suspended at the national level. Even during Monroe's tenure, though, party organizations continued to develop at the state level. Party growth was fueled in part by the enormous increase in the electorate that took place between 1820 and 1840, as the United States expanded westward and most states abolished property requirements as a condition of white male suffrage. During this twenty-year period, the number of votes cast in presidential contests rose from 300,000 to more than 2 million.

At the same time, U.S. politics was being democratized in other ways. By the 1820s all the states except South Carolina had switched from state legislative selection of presidential electors to popular election of electoral college members. This change helped transform presidential politics. No longer just the concern of society's upper crust, the election of the president became a matter for all qualified voters to decide.

The party base broadened along with the electorate. Small caucuses of congressional party leaders had previously nominated candidates, but after much criticism of the process as elitist and undemocratic, this system gave way to nominations at large party conventions. The country's first major national presidential nominating convention was held in 1832 by the Democratic Party,[7] the successor to the old Jeffersonian Democratic–Republicans (the shortened name had gradually come into use in the 1820s). Formed around the charismatic populist President Andrew Jackson, the Democratic Party attracted most of the newly enfranchised voters, who were drawn to Jackson's style. His strong personality helped to polarize politics, and opposition to the president coalesced into the Whig Party. The Whig Party was descended from the Federalists; its early leaders included Henry Clay, the Speaker of the House from 1811 to 1820. The incumbent Jackson defeated Clay in the 1832 presidential contest. He became the first chief executive who won the White House as the nominee of a truly national, popularly based political party.

The Whigs and the Democrats continued to strengthen after 1832, establishing state and local organizations almost everywhere. Their competition was usually fierce and closely matched, and they brought the United States the first broadly supported two-party system in the Western world.[8] Unfortunately for the Whigs, the issue of slavery sharpened the many existing divisive internal party tensions that led to its gradual dissolution and replacement by the new Republican Party. Formed in 1854 by antislavery activists, the Republican Party set its sights on the abolition (or at least the containment) of slavery. After a losing presidential effort for John C. Fremont in 1856, the party was able to assemble enough support primarily from the Whigs and antislavery Northern Democrats to win the presidency for Abraham Lincoln in a fragmented 1860 vote. In that year the South voted solidly Democratic, beginning a habit so strong that not a single Southern state voted Republican for president again until 1920.

It should also be recognized that, between 1838 and 1890, many minor parties engaged in the political activities developed by the major parties. Minor parties, that is, organized themselves, nominated candidates, and attempted to mobilize the support of voters.[9] Thus, despite the self-imposed "outsider" image of minor parties in this era, they clearly adhered to the tactics and strategies deployed by the major parties.

The British political system, which has been characterized by competition between two main political parties with significant third-party activity, provides an interesting contrast to the American case. In Britain the massive extension of suffrage in 1867 prompted the emergence of two modern, mass political parties (the Liberals and the Conservatives), which were needed to organize and mobilize the now unwieldy electorate. In the aftermath of World War I, the Liberals gave way to the Labour Party as the Conservatives' principal contender for power.

Democrats and Republicans: The Golden Age

From the presidential election of 1860 to this day, the same two major parties, the Republicans and the Democrats, have dominated elections in the United States, and control of an electoral majority has seesawed between them. The dominance of the Republicans (now often called the Grand Old Party, or GOP) in the post–Civil War Reconstruction era eventually gave way to a closely competitive system from 1876 to 1896, in part because the Democrats were more successful at integrating new immigrants into U.S. society in port cities like New York, Boston, and Chicago. In the later years of the nineteenth century, however, the Republicans skillfully capitalized on fears of a growing anti-establishment, anti–big business sentiment in the Democratic Party. They fashioned a dominant and enduring majority of voters that essentially lasted until the early 1930s, when the Great Depression created the conditions for a Democratic resurgence.

President Franklin D. Roosevelt's New Deal coalition of 1932 consisted of the South, racial and ethnic groups, organized labor, farmers, liberals, and big-city "machines," as well-oiled party organizations are sometimes called. This coalition characterized both the Democratic Party and the prevailing national majority until at least the late 1960s. Since 1970, neither party has been clearly dominant, as more and more voters have seemed to be less committed to either of the two parties. In this same period, the Republicans have dominated presidential elections and Democrats have won most congressional contests, a pattern that was broken in 1994 when the Republicans won control of both congressional houses. (The development of a "divided government" is discussed later in this chapter.)

The Modern Era Versus the Golden Age

The modern era seems very distant from the "golden age" of parties that existed from the 1870s to the 1920s. Emigration from Europe (particularly from Ireland, Italy, and Germany) fueled the development of big-city party organizations that ruled their domains with an iron hand. Party and government were virtually interchangeable, and the parties were the providers of much-needed services, entertainment, and employment. These big-city party organizations were called **machines.** A political machine is a party

machine
A party organization that recruits its members with tangible incentives and is characterized by a high degree of control over member activity.

ROOTS OF GOVERNMENT

PLUNKITT OF TAMMANY HALL

Tammany Hall was a powerful New York City political organization during the mid-nineteenth and early twentieth centuries. Originally formed as a social club in 1797, it had been transformed into an influential political machine by 1850, with membership including most of the city's prominent Democrats.

Of all the organization's politicians, one of the most renowned at the turn of the twentieth century was ward boss George Washington Plunkitt. Starting as a teenager, this son of Irish immigrants worked his way up through the ranks of the organization to become the leader of the city's Fifteenth Assembly District. (An assembly district is made up of many smaller units, called election districts.) He is remembered as one of the shrewdest politicians of his time. Plunkitt was born poor but died a millionaire, acquiring most of his wealth through what he called "honest graft," a term best described in his own candid words:

> My party's in power in the city, and its goin' to make a lot of public improvements. Well, I'm tipped off, say, that they're going to lay out a new park at a certain place.
>
> I see my opportunity and I take it. I go to that place and I buy up all the land I can in the neighborhood. Then the board of this or that makes it public, and there is a rush to get my land, which nobody cared particular for before.
>
> Ain't it perfectly honest to charge a good price and make a profit on my investment and foresight? Of course, it is. Well, that's honest graft.

For Plunkitt there was a difference between dishonest and honest graft, "between [dishonest] political looters and [honest] politicians who make a fortune out of politics by keepin' their eyes wide open":

> The looter goes in for himself alone without considerin' his organization or his city. The politician looks after his own interests, the organization's interests, and the city's interests all at the same time.

Plunkitt certainly looked after his constituents' interests. During Tammany's reign, the population of New York City was made up predominantly of poor immigrants, mostly Irish, for whom Plunkitt and his fellow district leaders served as a bridge between the Old and New Worlds and also as a way out of the slums. Besides assimilating these newcomers to life in the United States and acquainting them with the processes of self-government, the ward bosses used the patronage at their disposal to provide tangible benefits. Be it a job, liquor, a pushcart license, or even cash, the ward boss was always happy to help out a needy constituent—in exchange, of course, for loyalty at the ballot box during election time.

In contrast to the issue-oriented or image-appeal politics we know today, Plunkitt's politics were *personal*. As Plunkitt put it, "[I] learned how to reach the hearts of the great mass of voters. I don't bother about reaching their heads." Plunkitt understood the value of this personalized, community-oriented politics to both voters and leaders. His advice to aspiring politicians was simply to know and study the members of their communities and to "study human nature and act accordin'."

Plunkitt's brand of politics had all but disappeared by the mid-twentieth century. First, a drastic decline of immigration during the 1920s strangled the fuel line that fed the fires of city machines. Second, many of the services the parties provided gradually came to be viewed as rights of citizenship rather than as rewards for supporting a particular party; therefore, government replaced party organizations as the dispensers of benefits. Most important, however, and much to the chagrin of Plunkitt himself, were the new civil service laws passed by reformers in the 1920s to combat the alleged corruption of machine politics. These laws, which struck at the heart and soul of machine politics—patronage and the spoils system—induced Plunkitt to deem the civil service laws "the biggest fraud of the age" and the ruin of the nation:

> There can't be no real patriotism while it lasts. How are you goin' to interest our young men in their country if you have no offices to give them when they work for their party? . . . I know more than one man in the past years who worked for the ticket and was just overflowin' with patriotism, but when he was knocked out by the civil service humbug he got to hate his country and became an anarchist.

For better or worse, however, the reformers prevailed, and by the mid-twentieth century, civil service had come to dominate government at every level, consigning Plunkitt's brand of politics to America's past.

Source: William L. Riordon, ed., *Plunkitt of Tammany Hall* (New York: Dutton, 1963), 11, 89.

organization that recruits its members with tangible incentives—money, political jobs, an opportunity to get favors from government—and that is characterized by a high degree of leadership control over member activity. Machines were a central element of life for millions of people: They sponsored community events, such as parades and picnics, and provided social services, such as helping new immigrants settle in and giving food and temporary housing to those in immediate need, all in exchange for votes.

The parties offered immigrants not just services, but also the opportunity for upward social mobility as they rose in the organization. Because they held the possibility of social advancement, the parties engendered among their supporters and office holders intense devotion that helped to produce startlingly high voter turnouts—75 percent or better in all presidential elections from 1876 to 1900, compared with only about 50 percent to 55 percent today.[10] They also fostered the greatest party-line voting ever achieved in Congress and many state legislatures[11] (see Roots of Government: Plunkitt of Tammany Hall).

As several political scientists have observed, political machines have not been exclusive to urban areas.[12] Although the most prominent and colorful political machines existed in cities, political machines could be found in some rural and suburban areas as well. Even today, for example, a traditional, machine-style Republican Party organization continues to exist in Nassau County, New York—a wealthy suburb of New York City situated on Long Island.[13]

Is the Party Over?

In the twenty-first century, many social, political, technological, and governmental changes have contributed to party decline. Historically, the government's gradual assumption of important functions previously performed by the parties, such as printing ballots, conducting elections, and providing social welfare services, had a major impact. Social services began to be seen as a right of citizenship rather than as a privilege extended in exchange for a person's support of a party. Also, as the flow of immigrants slowed dramatically in the 1920s, party organizations gradually withered in most places.

The **direct primary,** whereby party nominees were determined by the ballots of qualified voters rather than at party conventions, was widely adopted by the states in the first two decades of the twentieth century. The primary removed the power of nomination from party leaders and workers and gave it instead to a much broader and more independent electorate, thus loosening the tie between the party nominee and the party organization. **Civil service laws** also removed much of the patronage used by the parties to reward their followers. Civil service laws require appointment on the basis of merit and competitive examinations, whereas **patronage**—also called the **spoils system**—awards jobs on the basis of party loyalty. These changes were encouraged by the Progressive movement (consisting of politically liberal reformers), which flourished in the first two decades of the twentieth century.

In the post–World War II era, extensive social changes led the movement away from strong parties. Broad-based education gave rise to **issue-oriented politics,** politics that focuses on specific issues, such as civil rights, tax cutting, environmentalism, or abortion, rather than on party labels. Issue politics tends to cut across party lines and encourages voters to **ticket-split,** that is, to vote for candidates of different parties for various offices in the same election. Recent studies by political scientists indicate that split-ticket voting is not the result of a conscious effort on behalf of voters to moderate the government by pitting the parties against each other. It is rather a result of decisions made by individual voters about individual candidates' positions on specific issues important to them. This issue-based vote, combined with often lopsided congressional campaigns favoring well-funded and well-known candidates over little-known upstarts, contributes greatly to split ticket voting.[14] Another post–World War II social change that has affected the parties is the shift in the population. Millions of people have moved out of the cities, which are easily organizable because of population density, and into the sprawling suburbs, where a sense of privacy and detachment can deter the most energetic organizers. One example of this is the voter mobilization activities of the

direct primary
The selection of party candidates through the ballots of qualified voters rather than at party nomination conventions.

civil service laws
These acts removed the staffing of the bureaucracy from political parties and created a professional bureaucracy filled through competition.

patronage
Jobs, grants, or other special favors that are given as rewards to friends and political allies for their support.

spoils system
The firing of public-office holders of a defeated political party and their replacement with loyalists of the newly elected party.

issue-oriented politics
Politics that focuses on specific issues rather than on party, candidate, or other loyalties.

ticket-split
To vote for candidates of different parties for various offices in the same election.

Senior members of Republican presidential candidate George W. Bush's campaign staff watch the televised Florida Supreme Court hearing on the vote recounts at the Bush 2000 Campaign head-quarters in Austin, Texas. From left are Chief Strategist Karl Rove, Campaign Chairman Don Evans, and Karen Hughes, Communications Director. (Photo courtesy: Harry Cabluck/AP/Wide World Photos)

Christian Coalition in the 1990s. When first organized, Pat Robertson's conservative evangelical Christian organization relied on the traditional political precinct-level method of organizing communities to turn out and vote. By the middle of the 1990s, however, Robertson retired this method in favor of a church-based model of literature distribution and voter activation. In modern suburbs, the Christian Coalition found it easier to reach their target audience in church on Sunday rather than in sprawling neighborhoods on other days of the week.[15]

Politically, many other trends have contributed to the parties' decline. Television, which has come to dominate U.S. politics, naturally emphasizes personalities rather than abstract concepts such as party labels. In addition, the modern parties have many rivals for the affections of their candidates, including **political consultants,** the hired guns who manage campaigns and design television advertisements. Both television and consultants have replaced the party as the intermediary between candidate and voter. It is little wonder that many candidates and office holders who have reached their posts without much help from their parties remain as free as possible of party ties.

political consultant
Professional who manages campaigns and political advertisements for political candidates.

The Parties Endure

The parties' decline can easily be exaggerated. Viewing parties in the broad sweep of U.S. history, it becomes clear that first, although political parties have evolved considerably and changed form from time to time, they usually have been reliable vehicles for mass participation in a representative democracy. In fact, the gradual but steady expansion of suffrage itself was orchestrated by the parties. As political scientist E. E. Schattschneider concluded, "In the search for new segments of the populace that might be exploited profitably, the parties have kept the movement to liberalize the franchise well ahead of the demand. . . . The enlargement of the practicing electorate has been one of the principal labors of the parties, a truly notable achievement for which the parties have never been properly credited."[16]

Second, the parties' journey through U.S. history has been characterized by the same ability to adapt to prevailing conditions that is often cited as the genius of the Constitution. Flexibility and pragmatism are characteristics of both and help ensure their survival and the success of the society they serve.

Third, despite massive changes in political conditions and frequent dramatic shifts in the electorate's mood, the two major parties have not only achieved remarkable longevity, but they also have almost consistently provided strong competition for each other and the voters at the national level. Of the twenty-nine presidential elections from

WEB EXPLORATION
To evaluate how the "Big Two" political parties portray their platform issues and use political language to present their policies, go to
www.ablongman.com/oconnor

1884 to 1996, for instance, the Republicans won fifteen and the Democrats fourteen. Even when calamities have beset the parties—the Great Depression in the 1930s or the Watergate scandal of 1973–1974 for the Republicans (see chapter 8), and the Civil War or left-wing McGovernism in 1972 for the Democrats—the two parties have proved tremendously resilient, sometimes bouncing back from landslide defeats to win the next election. After losing the presidential election badly in 1988, for example, the Democrats managed to win the presidency in 1992 and 1996, demonstrating again that the only constant in politics is change. Indeed, political scientist Philip A. Klinkner argues that the national committees have been at their most innovative in adapting to changing political conditions precisely when they are responding to electoral defeat.[17]

Perhaps most of all, history teaches us that the development of parties in the United States (outlined in Figure 12.1) has been inevitable, as James Madison feared. Human nature alone guarantees conflict in any society; in a free state, the question is simply how to contain and channel conflict productively without infringing on individual liberties. The Founders' utopian hopes for the avoidance of partisan faction, Madison's chief concern, have given way to an appreciation of the parties' constructive contributions to conflict definition and resolution during the years of the American republic.

THE ROLES OF THE AMERICAN PARTIES

For 150 years the two-party system has served as the mechanism American society uses to organize and resolve social and political conflict. Although political parties are arguably less popular today than in previous times, it is important both to remember that political parties often are the chief agents of change in our political system and to discuss the vital services to society the parties provide and how difficult political life would be without them.

Mobilizing Support and Gathering Power

Party affiliation is enormously helpful to elected leaders. They can count on disproportionate support among their partisans in times of trouble and in close judgment calls. Therefore the parties aid office holders by giving them room to develop their policies and by mobilizing support for them. When the president addresses the nation and requests support for his policies, for example, his party's activists are usually the first to respond to the call, perhaps by flooding Congress with telegrams urging action on the president's agenda. Additionally, a recent study found that the more liberal and competitive the Democratic Party is in a state, the greater the level of mobilization and voter turnout among the lower classes. The lower classes, after activation by the Democrats, presumably then vote and participate in ways favorable to the Democratic Party or their position on issues.[18]

Because there are only two major parties, pragmatic citizens who are interested in politics or public policy are mainly attracted to one or the other standard, creating natural majorities or near-majorities for party office holders to command. The party creates a community of interest that bonds disparate groups over time into a **coalition.** This continuing mutual interest eliminates the necessity of creating a new coalition for every campaign or every issue. Imagine the constant chaos and mad scrambles for public support that would ensue without the continuity provided by the parties.

coalition
A group of interests or organizations that join forces for the purpose of electing public officials.

A Force for Stability

As mechanisms for organizing and containing political change, the parties are a potent force for stability. They represent continuity in the wake of changing issues and personalities, anchoring the electorate in the midst of the storm of new political policies and people. Because of its unyielding, practical desire to win elections (not just to contest them), each party in a sense acts to moderate public opinion. The party tames its own extreme elements by pulling them toward an ideological center in order to attract a majority of votes on Election Day.

Another aspect of the stability the parties provide is found in the nature of the coalitions they forge. There are inherent contradictions in these coalitions that, oddly enough, strengthen the nation even as they strain party unity. Franklin D. Roosevelt's Democratic New Deal coalition, for example, included many African Americans and most Southern whites, opposing elements nonetheless joined in common political purpose. This party union of the two groups, as limited a context as it may have been, provided a framework for acceptance of change and contributed to reconciliation of the races in the civil rights era. Nowhere can this reconciliation be more clearly seen than in the South, where most state Democratic parties remained predominant after the mid-1960s by building on the ingrained Democratic voting habits of both whites and blacks to create new, moderate, generally integrated societies.

In fact, a recent study of the voting patterns of Southern Democratic senators from 1960 to 1995 found that, as the years progressed, the senators became more and more liberal in their policy positions compared to their predecessors. The study determined that the liberalization of the formally conservative Southern Democratic Party was a direct result of the growth of the viable and conservative Southern Republican Party, and the extension of greater voting rights to African Americans.[19]

Unity, Linkage, and Accountability

Parties provide the glue that holds together the disparate elements of the fragmented U.S. governmental and political apparatus. The Framers designed a system that divides and subdivides power, making it possible to preserve individual liberty but difficult to coordinate and produce action in a timely fashion. Parties help compensate for this drawback by linking all the institutions of power one to another. Although rivalry between the executive and legislative branches of U.S. government is inevitable, the partisan affiliations of the leaders of each branch constitute a common basis for cooperation, as any president and his fellow party members in Congress usually demonstrate daily. Each time President Bill Clinton proposed a major new program (such as health care and crime control), for instance, Democratic members of the Congress were the first to speak up in favor of the program and to orchestrate efforts at its passage. Furthermore, political scientist Kelly D. Patterson shows that presidential candidates continue to advocate policies similar to those advocated by their party's congressional leaders, suggesting that the diminished power of party elites in the presidential nomination process has not weakened parties' linkage function.[20]

Even within each branch there is intended fragmentation, and the party once again helps narrow the differences between the House of Representatives and the Senate, or between the president and his chiefs in the executive bureaucracy. Similarly, the division of national, state, and local governments, while always an invitation to conflict, is made more workable and easily coordinated by the intersecting party relationships that exist among office holders at all levels. Party affiliation, in other words, is a basis for mediation and negotiation laterally among the branches and vertically among the layers.

One of the last of the big-city party bosses, Chicago Mayor Richard J. Daley controlled a powerful political machine for more than twenty-five years. (Photo courtesy: Bettman/Corbis)

The party's linkage function does not end there. Party identification and organization are natural connectors and vehicles for communication between the voter and the candidate, as well as between the voter and the office holder. The party connection is one means of increasing accountability in election campaigns and in government. Candidates on the campaign trail and elected party leaders in office are required from time to time to account for their performance at party-sponsored forums, nominating primaries, and conventions.

Political parties, too, can take some credit for unifying the nation by dampening sectionalism. Because parties must form national majorities in order to win the presidency, any single, isolated region is guaranteed minority status unless it establishes ties with other areas. The party label and philosophy build the bridge that enables regions to join forces; in the process, a national interest, rather than a merely sectional one, is created and served.

The Electioneering Function

The election, proclaimed author H. G. Wells, is "democracy's ceremonial, its feast, its great function," and the political parties assist this ceremony in essential ways. First, the parties funnel eager, interested individuals into politics and government. Thousands of candidates are recruited each year by the two parties, as are many of the candidates' staff members—the people who manage the campaigns and go on to serve in key governmental positions once the election has been won.

This function is even more crucial in the British parliamentary system. In the postwar period, the only avenue to national power (that is, the prime minister's office or a choice seat on the cabinet) has been through either the Conservative Party or the Labour Party. Ambitious politicians must work their way up through the party hierarchy and build a supporting coalition along the way.

Elections can have meaning in a democracy only if they are competitive, and in the United States they probably could not be competitive without the parties. Even in the South, traditionally the least politically competitive U.S. region, the parties today regularly produce reasonably vigorous contests at the state (and, increasingly, the local) level.

Party as a Voting and Issue Cue

A voter's party identification acts as an invaluable filter for information, a perceptual screen that affects how he or she digests political news. Therefore party affiliation provides a useful cue for voters, particularly for the least informed and least interested, who can use the party as a shortcut or substitute for interpreting issues and events they may not fully comprehend. But even better-educated and more involved voters find party identification helpful. After all, no one has the time to study every issue carefully or to become fully knowledgeable about every candidate seeking public office.

Policy Formulation and Promotion

U.S. Senator Huey Long (D–La.), one of the premier spokesmen for "the people" of this century, was usually able to capture the flavor of the average person's views about politics. Considering an independent bid for president before his assassination in 1935, Long liked to compare the Republican and Democratic parties to the two patent medicines offered by a traveling salesman. Asked the difference between them, the salesman explained that the "High Populorum" tonic was made from the bark of the tree taken from the top down, while "Low Populorum" tonic was made from bark stripped from the root up. The analogous moral, according to Long, was this: "The only difference I've found in Congress between the Republican and Democratic leadership is that one of 'em is skinning us from the ankle up and the other from the ear down!"[21]

Long would certainly have insisted that his fable applied to the **national party platform,** the most visible instrument by which parties formulate, convey, and promote

Longman
Participate.com 2.0
Visual Literacy
State Control
and National
Platforms

national party platform
A statement of the general and specific philosophy and policy goals of a political party, usually promulgated at the national convention.

public policy. Every four years, each party writes for the presidential nominating conventions a lengthy platform explaining its positions on key issues. Most citizens in our own era undoubtedly still believe that party platforms are relatively undifferentiated, a mixture of pabulum and pussyfooting. Yet political scientist Gerald M. Pomper's study of party platforms from 1944 through 1976 has demonstrated that each party's pledges were consistently and significantly different, a function in part of the varied groups in their coalitions.[22] Interestingly, about 69 percent of the specific platform positions were taken by one party but not the other. The trend observed by Pomper continues: on abortion, for example, the Democrats are strongly for abortion rights while the Republicans are firmly against them in their most recent platforms.

Granted, then, party platforms are quite distinctive. Does this elaborate party exercise in policy formulation mean anything? One could argue that the platform is valuable, if only as a clear presentation of a party's basic philosophy and as a forum for activist opinion and public education. But platforms have much more impact than that. About two-thirds of the promises in the victorious party's presidential platform have been completely or mostly implemented; even more

Senator Huey Long (D–La.) campaigned for the presidency in 1935 on a populist platform, arguing in fiery speeches that neither of the major parties' policies had the people's best interests at heart. (Photo courtesy: Bettman/Corbis)

astounding, one-half or more of the pledges of the losing party find their way into public policy (with the success rate depending on whether the party controls one, both, or neither house of Congress).[23] The party platform also has great influence on a new presidential administration's legislative program and on the president's State of the Union address. While party affiliation is normally the single most important determinant of voting in Congress and in state legislatures,[24] the party–vote relationship is even stronger when party platform issues come up on the floor of Congress. Gerald M. Pomper concludes: "We should therefore take platforms seriously, because politicians appear to take them seriously."[25] More recent analyses of the role of party platforms, however, tend to discount their electoral significance in the 1990s. L. Sandy Maisel, for instance, states that in the 1990s and beyond, party platforms "really are not party platforms" anymore. They are instead "presidential candidate-centered platforms." They are documents written to be generally noncontroversial and acceptable to broad coalitions of voters, not to set the national policy agenda nor spur debate on the direction of government. They are written by and for the candidate seeking office, not as representations of the party positions on current and philosophical issues.[26] (For differences in party platforms, see chapter 13, Highlight: Selected Contrasts in the 2000 Party Platforms, page 482).

Besides mobilizing Americans on a permanent basis, then, the parties convert the cacophony of hundreds of identifiable social and economic groups into a two-part semi-harmony that is much more comprehensible, if not always on key and pleasing to the ears. The simplicity of two-party politics may be deceptive, given the enormous variety in public policy choices, but a sensible system of representation in the American context might be impossible without it. The people who would suffer most from its absence would not be the few who are individually or organizationally powerful; their voices would be heard under almost any system. As political scientist Walter Dean Burnham has pointed out, the losers would be the many individually powerless for whom the parties are the only effective devices yet created that can generate collective power on their behalf.[27]

ONE-PARTYISM AND THIRD-PARTYISM

The two-party system has not gone unchallenged. At the state level, two-party competition was severely limited or nonexistent in much of the country for most of the twentieth century.[28] Formerly in the one-party Democratic states of the Deep South and the rock-ribbed Republican states of Maine, New Hampshire, and Vermont, the dominant party's primary nomination was often equivalent to election, and the only real contest was an unsatisfying intraparty one in which colorful personalities often dominated and a half-dozen major candidacies in each primary proved confusing to voters.[29] Even in most two-party states, many cities and counties had a massive majority of voters aligned with one or the other party and thus were effectively one-party in local elections. In Britain, one-partyism at the subnational level is a relatively common phenomenon; for example, certain regions like the Northeast have voted overwhelmingly for the Labour Party in general election after general election.

Historical, cultural, and sectional forces primarily accounted for the concentration of one party's supporters in certain areas. The Civil War's divisions, for instance, were mirrored for the better part of a century in the Democratic predisposition of the South and the Republican proclivities of the Yankee Northern states. Whatever the combination of factors producing **one-partyism**—a political system in which one party dominates and wins virtually all contests—the condition has certainly declined precipitously in the last quarter century.[30]

The spread of two-party competition, especially in the South, is one of the most significant political trends of recent times, and virtually no one-party states are left. The once solidly Democratic South has been reduced to, at most, Louisiana and Arkansas. (Note, though, that even in each of these two states, one or more Republicans have been elected to the governorship or U.S. Senate since 1970, and the Deep South states usually vote Republican in presidential contests, as well, unless a Southerner heads the Democratic ticket.) At the same time, there are no longer any purely Republican states.

Ironically, the growth of two-party competition has been spurred less by the developing strength of the main parties than by party weakness, as illustrated by the decline in partisan loyalty among the voters. In other words, citizens now are somewhat more inclined to cross party lines in order to support an appealing candidate regardless of party affiliation, thus making a victory for the minority party possible whether or not it has earned the victory through the party's own organizational hard work. It should also be noted that the elimination of pockets of one-party strength adds an element of instability to the system, since at one point, even in lean times of national electoral disaster, each party was assured of a regional base from which a comeback could be staged. Nonetheless, the increase in party competitiveness can be viewed positively, since it eliminates the effects of one-partyism and guarantees a comprehensible and credible partisan choice to a larger segment of the electorate than ever before.

Minor Parties: Third-Partyism

Third-Partyism has proved more durable than one-partyism, though its nature is sporadic and intermittent, and its effects on the political system are on the whole less weighty. Given all the controversy third parties generate, one could be excused for thinking that they were extraordinarily important on the American scene. But as Frank J. Sorauf has concluded, third parties in fact "have not assumed the importance that all the [academic] attention lavished on them suggests."[31] No minor party has ever come close to winning the presidency, and only eight minor parties have won so much as a single state's electoral college votes (see Table 12.1). Eight third parties (including the farmer-backed Populists in 1892, Theodore Roosevelt's Bull Moose Party in 1912, the reform-minded Progressives in 1924, former Alabama Governor George Wallace's racially based American Independent Party in 1968, and Ross Perot's Independents in

one-partyism
A political system in which one party dominates and wins virtually all contests.

WEB EXPLORATION
Independents proliferate, but finding one that represents your views on several issues is difficult. To compare the planks of several different independent parties, go to www.ablongman.com/oconnor

third-partyism
The tendency of third parties to arise with some regularity in a nominally two-party system.

TABLE 12.1   Third-Party and Independent Presidential Candidates
Receiving 5 Percent or More of Popular Vote

Candidate (Party)	Year	Percentage of Popular Vote	Electoral Votes
Ross Perot (Reform Party)	1996	8.5	0
Ross Perot (Independent)	1992	18.9	0
John B. Anderson (Independent)	1980	6.6	0
George C. Wallace (American Independent)	1968	13.5	46
Robert M. LaFollette (Progressive)	1924	16.6	13
Theodore Roosevelt (Bull Moose)	1912	27.4	88
Eugene V. Debs (Socialist)	1912	6.0	0
James B. Weaver (Populist)	1892	8.5	22
John C. Breckinridge (Southern Democrat)	1860	18.1	72
John Bell (Constitutional Union)	1860	12.6	39
Millard Fillmore (Whig-American)	1856	21.5	8
Martin Van Buren (Free Soil)	1848	10.1	0
William Wirt (Anti-Masonic)	1832	7.8	7

Source: Congressional Quarterly Weekly Report (October 18, 1980): 3147 (as adapted), and official election returns for 1992, 1996.

1992) have garnered more than 10 percent of the popular vote for president. Theodore Roosevelt's 1912 effort was the most successful; the Bull Moose Party won 27 percent of the popular vote for president (although only 17 percent of the electoral college votes). Roosevelt's is also the only third party to run ahead of one of the two major parties (the Republicans). Roosevelt, incidentally, abandoned the Republican Party, under whose banner he had won the presidency in 1904, in order to form the Bull Moose Party, composed mainly of reformist Republicans.

Third parties find their roots in sectionalism (as did the South's states' rights Dixiecrats, who broke away from the Democrats in 1948); in economic protest (such as the agrarian revolt that fueled the Populists, an 1892 prairie-states party); in specific issues (such as the Green Party's support of the environment); in ideology (the Socialist, Communist, and Libertarian Parties are examples); and in appealing, charismatic personalities (Theodore Roosevelt is perhaps the best case). Many of the minor parties have drawn strength from a combination of these sources. The American Independent Party enjoyed a measure of success because of a dynamic leader (George Wallace), a firm geographic base (the South), and an emotional issue (civil rights). In 1992 Ross Perot, the billionaire with a folksy Texas manner, was a charismatic leader whose campaign was fueled by the deficit issue (as well as by his personal fortune).

The 2000 election saw Green Party nominee Ralph Nader, the environmentalist and consumer advocate who ran for president in 1996, lead a nationwide grassroots, anti-establishment campaign to oppose the corporate-backed main party candidates, Vice President Al Gore and Texas Governor George W. Bush. Although Nader collected just 2.86 million votes (or 2.72 percent nationwide, well below the 5 percent required for the Green Party to receive matching federal funding in 2004), there is little question that

Longman
Participate.com
2.0
Timeline
**Third Parties
in American
History**

Minnesota Governor Jesse Ventura spoke to the media during a press conference while attending the national governors association seminar for new governors, November 1998. His unconventional image and enthusiasm for contact with the general public made him one of the most conspicuous candidates of the 1998 election year. (Photo courtesy: John Gillis/AP/Wide World Photos)

Nader cost Democrat Al Gore the presidency in 2000. In the critical state of Florida—the state that effectively decided the presidential election—Nader received 97,488 votes, while the official margin between Al Gore and George W. Bush in that state was 537 votes out of 5,963,070 votes cast. At least half of all Nader voters indicated in exit polls that they would have voted for Gore in a two-way race, while most of the rest said they would not have voted at all, and only a small percentage of Nader voters said that they would have voted for Bush over Gore. Nader's 22,188 votes in New Hampshire also cost Gore that state which Bush won by a mere 7,211 votes out of 567,795 cast.

Gore came to the brink of winning the presidential election and carried, albeit closely, some states where Nader did well: Wisconsin, Oregon, New Mexico, and Washington. Nader did relatively well in California, but Gore won there anyway, with a landslide 53 percent of the vote. Democratic Party anger at Ralph Nader was intense, especially after the election, when the full impact of his run for office became clear. Despite this resentment, it is important to note that no party has the right to take anyone's vote for granted. Under the American electoral system, any candidate qualifying for the ballot is eligible for any vote, and if the Democrats had been more attentive to certain liberal environmental issues over the course of the Clinton-Gore administration, it is possible that Gore would have fared better with Nader voters, or that Nader himself might not have run. While recent research in political science raises the chicken-or-egg question of which comes first, political dissatisfaction leading to third parties[32] or third-party movements leading to political dissatisfaction,[33] the conclusion that third parties are at some point linked to discontent with government and party leaders is widely accepted.

Importantly, minor-party and independent candidates are not limited to presidential elections; many also run in congressional elections, and the numbers appear to be growing. In the 2000 congressional elections, for example, more than 850 minor-party and independent candidates ran for seats in the House and Senate—almost eight times as many as in 1968 and nearly three times the number that ran in 1980. In 2001, Vermont Senator James Jeffords switched from the Republican Party to Independent. A recent study shows that minor party candidates for the House are most likely to emerge under three conditions: (1) when a House seat becomes open, (2) when a minor party candidate has previously competed in the district, and (3) when partisan competition between the two major parties in the district is close.[34]

Above all, third parties make electoral progress in direct proportion to the failure of the two major parties to incorporate new ideas or alienated groups or to nominate attractive candidates as their standard-bearers. One study, for instance, found that in 1992, the independent candidacy of Ross Perot increased voter turnout by three percentage points. Perot presumably activated previous non-voters who were ignored, disenchanted, or frustrated with the current two-party system.[35] Other recent studies have found that third parties do best when declining trust in the two major political parties plagues the electorate.[36] Usually, though, third parties are eventually co-opted by one of the two major parties, each of them eager to take the politically popular issue that gave rise to the third party and make it theirs in order to secure the allegiance of their supporters. For example, the Republicans of the 1970s absorbed many of the "states' rights" planks of George Wallace's 1968 presidential bid. Both parties have also more recently attempted to attract independent voters by sponsoring reforms of the governmental process, such as limitations on the activities of Washington lobbyists.

Why Third Parties Tend to Remain Minor

Third parties in the United States are akin to shooting stars that appear briefly and brilliantly but do not long remain visible in the political constellation. In fact, the United

States is the only major Western nation that does not have at least one significant, enduring national that does not have at least one significant, enduring national third party. There are a number of explanations for this. Unlike many European countries that use **proportional representation** (awarding legislative seats in proportion to the number of votes received), the United States has a "single-member, plurality" electoral system. The U.S. system requires a party to get one more vote than any other party in a legislative district or in a state's presidential election in order to win. In contrast, countries that use proportional representation often guarantee parliamentary seats to any faction securing as little as 5 percent of the vote. To paraphrase the legendary football coach Vince Lombardi, finishing first is not everything, it is the *only* thing in U.S. politics; placing second, even by a smidgen, doesn't count. This condition encourages the grouping of interests into as few parties as possible (the democratic minimum being two). Moreover, the two parties will often move to the left or right on issues in order to gain popular support. Some observers go so far as to say that parties in the United States have no permanent positions at all, only permanent interests—winning elections. Regardless of one's position on this issue, it is clear that the adaptive nature of the two parties further forestalls the growth of third parties in the United States. Nonetheless, we should not write off the possibility that an enduring third party will emerge.

Other institutional factors also undergird the two-party system:

■ Most states have laws that require third parties to secure a place on the ballot by gathering large numbers of signatures, whereas the Democratic and Republican Parties are often granted automatic access.

■ Democrats and Republicans in the state legislatures may have little in common, but both want to make sure that the political pie is cut into only two sizable pieces, not three or more smaller slices.

■ The public funding of campaigns (financing from taxpayer dollars), where it exists, is much more generous for the two major parties. At the national level, for instance, third-party presidential candidates receive money only after the general election, if they have garnered more than 5 percent of the vote, and only in proportion to their total vote; the major-party candidates, by contrast, get large, full general-election grants immediately upon their summer nominations. (This funding difference does not affect wealthy politicians like Perot.)

■ The news media give relatively little coverage to minor parties compared with that given to major-party nominees. The media's bias is legitimate—it only reflects political reality, and it would be absurd to expect them to offer equal time to all comers. Still, this is a vicious cycle for minor-party candidates: A lack of broad-based support produces slight coverage, which minimizes their chances of attracting more adherents. Of course, once a third-party candidate such as Ross Perot becomes prominent, the media flock to his appearances and clamor to schedule him on their news shows.

Beyond the institutional explanations are historical, cultural, and social theories of two-partyism in the United States. The **dualist theory,** frequently criticized as overly simplistic, suggests that there has always been an underlying binary nature to U.S. politics. Whether it was the early conflict between Eastern financial interests and Western frontiersmen, the sectional division of North and South, the more current urban-versus-rural or urban-versus-suburban clashes, or even the natural tensions of democratic institutions (the government against the opposition, for instance), dualists believe that the processes and interests of politics inevitably push the players into two great camps.

Other political scientists emphasize the basic social consensus existing in American life. Despite great diversity in our heritage, the vast majority of Americans accept without serious question the fundamental structures of our system: the Constitution, the governmental setup, a lightly controlled free enterprise economy, for example. This consensus, when allied with certain American cultural characteristics developed over time (pragmatism, acceptance of the need for compromise, a lack of extreme and divisive social-class consciousness), produces the conditions necessary for relatively

proportional representation
The practice of awarding legislative seats in proportion to the number of votes received.

dualist theory
The theory claiming that there has always been an underlying binary party nature to U.S. politics.

POINT / COUNTERPOINT

SHOULD AMERICANS HAVE MORE CHOICES ON THE BALLOT?

While it is technically possible for a third party to appear on a national ballot, supporters of a multiparty system complain that the hurdles—both legal and cultural—are simply to high to allow their candidates a reasonable chance of appearing on all the ballots of the fifty states, giving the United States a de facto two-party political system. Supporters of the two-party system counter that because the platforms of third-party candidates are more narrow, they lack widespread support. Should Americans have more choices on the ballot? Let's examine these two points of view.

Citizens who favor easing the restrictions required to place minor-party candidates on the national ballot tend to feel that their views are not considered strongly enough by either of the major parties. These voters also tend to disagree with corporate-financed candidates who are "beholden" to their biggest donors. Consider the case of Ralph Nader and the Green Party. Nader had been a major figure in American life since the 1960s, and after appearing on some states' ballots in the 1996 election, he ran an energetic and well-funded presidential campaign in 2000. Despite his relative prominence, however, he failed to appear on every state's ballot and received less than 3 percent of the vote nationally. Furthermore, he was not invited to participate in the mainstream presidential debates, and he was unable to secure significant media coverage for his convention and campaign. Those who vote for minor-party candidates often are single-issue voters (e.g., the environment), or voters attracted to a charismatic, reform-minded candidate (e.g., Huey Long as a Populist in the 1920s).

Although minor-party candidates can receive federal funds for their campaigns (the Reform Party in 1996 and 2000 received federal money based on Ross Perot receiv-

ing more than 5 percent of the national vote in the previous elections), many claim that it still is not enough money to effectively compete with the Democratic and Republican candidates. By having more parties and more candidates, many voters who may be turned off by the electoral process or by the two major candidates may feel more compelled to vote for a candidate that reflects their beliefs more accurately. This, in turn, could increase voter turnout in presidential elections.

Opponents of a multiparty system claim that the two-party model has provided stability for American democracy for over two centuries, and that America should take care lest it encourage a splintering of the electorate as has become a pervasive and normal state of affairs in many countries. According to this view, nations such as Italy, Russia, and Israel—riven by factionalism and power-sharing between as many as thirty parties—can only form governments through coalitions of minute special interests, which in addition to being politically short-lived and unstable, are often unprepared for the task of providing strong, reliable leadership in times of national or international crisis. Those who support the two-party system also suggest minor-party candidates like Ralph Nader espouse platforms that lack widespread support among the electorate; if they want to compete, then they must broaden their platforms and attract a more national rather than regional or single-issue following.

What do you think? Would multiple parties on the national ballot make a difference in elections and voter turnout, or is the two-party system still the tried and true method for selecting candidates? *Go to* www.ablongman.com/oconnor

nonideological, centrist politics that can naturally support two moderate alternative parties but has little need for more.

The passion for power and victory that drives both Democrats and Republicans overrides ideology and prevents rigidity. Unless a kind of rigor mortis takes hold in the future in one or both major parties—with, say, the capture of the party organization by unyielding extremists of right or left—it is difficult to imagine any third party becoming a major, permanent force in U.S. politics. The corollary of this axiom, though, is that the major parties must be eternally vigilant if they are to avoid ideologically inspired takeovers.

For the foreseeable future, however, third parties likely will continue to play useful supporting roles similar to their historically sanctioned ones: They can popularize ideas that might not receive a hearing otherwise. They can serve as vehicles of popular dis-

FIGURE 12.2   Political Party Organization in America: From Base to Pinnacle

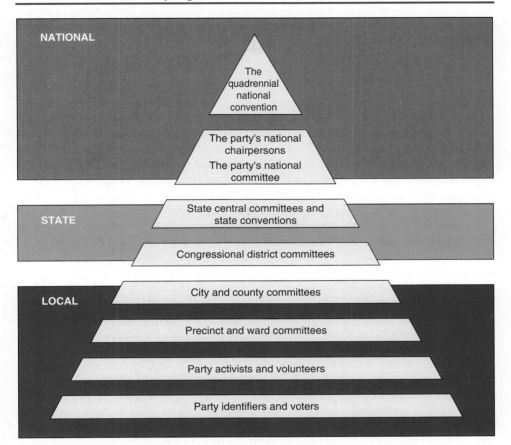

content with the major parties and thereby induce change in major-party behavior and platforms, such as in 1992 when Ross Perot forced the two major parties to acknowledge and address the deficit issue. They may presage and assist party realignments in the future as they have sometimes done in the past. In a few states, third parties will also continue to take a unique part in political life, as the Conservative and Liberal Parties of New York State do. But in a two-party system that is supplemented by generous means of expressing dissent and registering political opposition in other ways (court challenges and interest group organizing, for example), third parties will probably continue to have a limited future in the United States.

THE BASIC STRUCTURE OF AMERICAN POLITICAL PARTIES

While the distinctions might not be as clear today as they were two or three decades ago, the two major parties remain fairly simply organized, with national, state, and local branches (Figure 12.2). The different levels of each party represent diverse interests in Washington, D.C., state capitols, and local governments throughout the nation.

The pyramid shown in Figure 12.2 illustrates the hierarchy of party organization in the United States, and it will help you to see how parties operate in a general sense. It is also important to remember that this very simple diagram is deceptive in one important way: The national, state, and local parties overlap. Frequently, state and local parties have more influence than the national party in their region, and their decisions can override the national party. This is especially true in the Republican Party. A diagram this simple cannot fully represent the dynamic and complex federal interrelationships of national, state, and local parties.

National Committees

national convention

A party conclave (meeting) held in the presidential election year for the purposes of nominating a presidential and vice presidential ticket and adopting a platform.

The first national party committees were skeletal and formed some years after the creation of the presidential nominating conventions in the 1830s. Every four years, each party holds a **national convention** to nominate its presidential and vice presidential candidates. First the Democrats in 1848 and then the Republicans in 1856 established national governing bodies (the Democratic National Committee, or DNC, and the Republican National Committee, or RNC) to make arrangements for the conventions and to coordinate the subsequent presidential campaigns. The DNC and RNC were each composed of one representative from each state; this was expanded to two in the 1920s after the post of state committeewoman was established. The states had complete control over the selection of their representatives to the national committees. In addition, to serve their interests, the congressional party caucuses in both houses organized their own national committees, loosely allied with the DNC and RNC. The National Republican Congressional Committee (NRCC) was started in 1866 when the Radical Republican congressional delegation was feuding with Abraham Lincoln's moderate successor, President Andrew Johnson, and wanted a counterweight to his control of the RNC. At the same time, House and Senate Democrats set up a similar committee.

After the popular election of U.S. Senators was initiated in 1913 with the ratification of the Seventeenth Amendment to the Constitution, both parties organized separate Senate campaign committees. This three-part arrangement of national party committee, House party committee, and Senate party committee has persisted in both parties to the present day, and each party's three committees are located together in Washington, D.C. There is, however, an informal division of labor among the national committees. Whereas the DNC and RNC focus primarily on aiding presidential campaigns and conducting general party-building activities, the congressional campaign committees work primarily to maximize the number of seats held by their respective parties in Congress. In the past two decades, all six national committees have become major, service-oriented organizations in American politics.[37]

Leadership

The key national party official is the chairperson of the national committee. Although the chair is formally elected by the national committee, he or she is usually selected by the sitting president or newly nominated presidential candidate, who is accorded the right to name the individual for at least the duration of his or her campaign. Only the post-campaign out-of-power party committee actually has the authority to appoint a chairperson independently. The committee-crowned chairpersons generally have the greatest impact on the party, because they come to their posts at times of crisis when a leadership vacuum exists. (A defeated presidential candidate is technically the head of the national party until the next nominating convention, but the reality is naturally otherwise as a party attempts to shake off a losing image.) The chair often becomes the prime spokesperson and arbitrator for the party during the four years between elections. He or she is called on to damp down factionalism, negotiate candidate disputes, raise money, and prepare the machinery for the next presidential election. Balancing the interests of all potential White House contenders is a particularly difficult job, and strict neutrality is normally expected from the chair.

In recent times both parties have benefited from adept leadership while out of power. William Brock, RNC chair during the Carter presidency, and Ron Brown, the first African American to chair the DNC (during the Bush term), both skillfully used their positions to strengthen their parties organizationally and to polish the party images. Brock and Brown frequently appeared on news shows to give the out-of-power party's viewpoint. By contrast, party chairpersons selected by incumbent presidents and presidential candidates tend to be close allies of the presidents or candidates and often subordinate the good of the party to the needs of the campaign or White House. During the Carter presidency, for example, DNC Chairman Kenneth Curtis and his successor John White were creatures of the White House; they acted as cheerleaders for their chief executive but did little to keep the Democratic Party competitive with the strengthening GOP organization.

Because of their command of presidential patronage and influence, a few national party chairpersons selected by presidents have become powerful and well known, such as Republican Mark Hanna during the McKinley presidency (1897–1901) and Democrat James Farley under President Franklin D. Roosevelt. Most presidentially appointed chairs, however, have been relatively obscure; the chance for a chairperson to make a difference and cut a memorable figure generally comes when there is no competition from a White House nominee or occupant.

National Conventions

Much of any party chairperson's work involves planning the presidential nominating convention, or national convention, the most publicized and vital event on the party's calendar. Until 1984, gavel-to-gavel coverage was standard practice on all national television networks. Even after the recent cutbacks by some news organizations, a substantial block of time is still devoted to the conventions. (In 2000, for example, all the networks devoted a prime-time hour per night to convention coverage.) Although the nomination of the presidential ticket naturally receives the lion's share of attention, the convention also fulfills its role as the ultimate governing body for the party itself. The rules adopted and the platform passed at the quadrennial conclave are durable guidelines that steer the party for years after the final gavel has been brought down.

Most of the recent party chairpersons, in cooperation with the incumbent president or likely nominee, have tried to orchestrate every minute of the conventions in order to project just the right image to voters. By and large, they have succeeded, though at the price of draining some spontaneity and excitement from the convention process.

States and Localities

Although national committee activities of all kinds attract most of the media attention, the party is structurally based not in Washington, D.C., but in the states and localities. Except for the campaign finance arena, virtually all governmental regulation of political parties is left to the states, for example, and most elected officials give their allegiance to the local party divisions they know best. Most important, the vast majority of party leadership positions are filled at subnational levels.

The pyramidal arrangement of party committees provides for a broad base of support. The smallest voting unit, the precinct, usually takes in a few adjacent neighborhoods and is the fundamental building block of the party. Each of the more than 100,000 precincts in the United States potentially has a committee member to represent it in each party's councils. The

A participant in the 2000 Republican National Convention. In an effort to appear inclusive, Republicans and Democrats alike sought endorsements from women and minorities in their respective parties. (Photo courtesy: Sal DiMarco/Black Star)

In the 2000 presidential campaign, Green Party candidate Ralph Nader attracted liberals, environmentalists, and campaign finance reformers, among others, to his cause. As a third-party candidate, the former consumer advocate garnered 3 percent of the popular vote. (Photo courtesy: AFP/Corbis)

precinct committee members are the key foot soldiers of any party, and their efforts are supplemented by party committees above them in the wards, cities, counties, towns, villages, and congressional districts.

The state governing body supervising this collection of local party organizations is usually called the state central (or executive) committee. It comprises representatives from all major geographic units, as determined by and selected under state law. Generally, state parties are free to act within the limits set by their state legislatures without interference from the national party, except in the selection and seating of presidential convention delegates. National Democrats have been particularly inclined to regulate this aspect of party life. With the decline of big-city political machines, few local parties have the clout to object to the national party's dictates.

Research conducted by political scientists shows that state and local parties have become significantly stronger over the past three decades. Comparing the same county parties in 1964 and 1980, for example, a team of political scientists found considerable increases in several important campaign activities: fundraising, campaign events, registration drives, publicity of party and candidate activity, and the distribution of campaign literature.[38] A subsequent study indicates that local parties have continued to increase their levels of activity in these areas.[39] While all this renewed party activity surely helps the parties' candidates, recent research indicates that higher levels of party organizational strength also leads to greater public support for political parties as institutions.[40]

Many states have also seen the emergence of state legislative campaign committees.[41] These party committees resemble the congressional campaign committees at the national level in that they are run by a party's legislative incumbents and exist primarily to help maximize the number of legislative seats held by the party of which they are part. (For example, the Democratic Assembly Campaign Committee in the New York State assembly seeks primarily to maximize the number of Democrats elected to the assembly.) Importantly, legislative campaign committees are playing an increasingly important role in the financing of state legislative elections.[42] One scholar, however, makes the important point that these committees care little about the overall party ticket and thus resemble big political consulting firms more than they do traditional political parties.[43]

Examining separately the national, state, and local parties should not lead us to overlook the increasing integration of these committees. The national parties have become fundraising powerhouses during the last two decades, and they now channel significant financial support—much of it in soft money (see chapter 13)—to state parties. This financial support has given the national parties considerable leverage over the state committees—many of which have become dependent on the funding—and the national parties have increasingly used the state committees to help execute national campaigns. As such, the growing reliance of state parties on national party funding has changed fundamentally the balance of power in the American party system. Whereas power previously flowed up from the state and local parties to the national committees, the national committees now enjoy considerable leverage over state and local parties.[44]

Informal Groups

The formal structure of party organization is supplemented by numerous official, semi-official, and unaffiliated groups that combine and clash with the parties in countless ways. Both the DNC and RNC have affiliated organizations of state and local party women (the National Federation of Democratic Women and the National Federation of Republican Women). The youth divisions (the Young Democrats of America and the Young Republicans' National Federation) have a generous definition of "young," up to and including age thirty-five. The state governors in each party have their own party associations, too.

Just outside the party orbit are the supportive interest groups and associations that often provide money, labor, or other forms of assistance to the parties. Labor unions, progressive political action committees (PACs), teachers, African American and liberal women's groups, and the Americans for Democratic Action are some of the Democratic Party's organizational groups. Business PACs, the Chamber of Commerce of the United States, fundamentalist Christian organizations, and some anti-abortion agencies work closely with the Republicans. Similar party–interest group pairings occur in Britain. Trade unions have aligned themselves with the Labour Party, providing the bulk of the party's contributions, and business has been closely allied with the Conservatives.

Each U.S. party also has several institutionalized sources of policy ideas. Though unconnected to the parties in any official sense, these so-called *think tanks* (institutional collections of policy-oriented researchers and academics) are quite influential. During the Reagan administration, for instance, the right-wing Heritage Foundation placed many dozens of its conservatives in important governmental positions, and its issue studies on subjects ranging from tax reform to South Africa carried considerable weight with policy makers. The more moderate and bipartisan American Enterprise Institute also supplied the Reagan team with people and ideas. On the Democratic side, liberal think tanks proliferated during the party's Reagan- and Bush-induced exile. More than a half-dozen policy institutes formed after 1980 in an attempt to nurse the Democrats back to political health. The Center for National Policy and the Progressive Policy Institute, to cite two, sponsored conferences and published papers on Democratic policy alternatives.

Finally, there are extra-party organizations that form for a wide variety of purposes, including "reforming" a party or moving it ideologically to the right or left. In New York City, for example, Democratic reform clubs were established in the late 1800s to fight the Tammany Hall machine, the city's dominant Democratic organization at the time. About seventy clubs still prosper by attracting well-educated activists committed to various liberal causes. More recently, both national parties have been favored (or bedeviled) by the formation of new extra-party outfits. The Democrats have been pushed by both halves of the ideological continuum. The Democratic Leadership Council (DLC) was launched in 1985 by moderate and conservative Democrats concerned about what they perceived as the leftward drift of their party and its image as the captive of liberal special-interest groups. It is composed of more than one hundred current and former Democratic office holders (such as Senator Sam Nunn of Georgia and House Minority Leader Richard Gephardt of Missouri). The DLC has not always been popular with the national party leadership, which has sometimes viewed it as a potential rival, but it nurtured and strongly backed Bill Clinton's candidacy in 1992 and 1996. Several DLC leaders were appointed to positions in the Clinton administration.

The DLC formed in part to counter a left-leaning force organizing from within the partisan ranks, Jesse Jackson's National Rainbow Coalition. The coalition is partly a vehicle for Jackson's ambitions. Beyond that, its goals of mass membership, hundreds of state and local charter affiliates, and endorsements of independent candidates when Democratic nominees are found to be "unacceptable" present a challenge to the Democratic Party in the eyes of at least some party officials.

GOPAC was prominent throughout the 1990s but dissolved after the resignation and disgrace of its leader, Newt Gingrich. The void in the Republican organization is now being filled less formally by leading conservative congressmen such as House GOP Whip Tom DeLay of Texas and House Republican Committee Chairman Tom Davis of Virginia.

Over the past decade, informal groups allied with the two parties have become more fully (if informally) integrated into the increasingly complex party network, often working closely with the national and state parties in conducting campaigns. Indeed, as political scientist John F. Bibby observes, parties and interest group allies now work together so closely that "the traditional lines of demarcation between parties and interest groups are no longer clear."[45]

Senator Tom Daschle (D–SD) lost his role as majority leader to Trent Lott (R–MS) after Republicans regained control of the Senate in the 2002 midterm elections.

WEB EXPLORATION
To explore the partisan and ideological agendas of unaffiliated think tanks and search for connections to specific parties or politicians, go to
www.ablongman.com/oconnor

WEB EXPLORATION
To learn about the informal factions and interest groups that strive for influence with the major parties, go to
www.ablongman.com/oconnor

THE PARTY IN GOVERNMENT

Political parties are not restricted to their role as grassroots organizations of voters; they also have another major role inside government institutions. Parties are the organizing mechanisms for the branches and layers of American government.

The Congressional Party

In no segment of U.S. government is the party more visible or vital than in the Congress. In this century, the political parties have dramatically increased the sophistication and impact of their internal congressional organizations. Prior to the beginning of every session, each party in both houses of Congress gathers (or "caucuses") separately to select party leaders (House Speaker or minority leader, Senate majority and minority leaders, party whips, and so on) and to arrange for the appointment of members of each chamber's committees. In effect, then, the parties organize and operate the Congress. Their management systems have grown quite elaborate; the web of deputy and assistant whips for House Democrats now extends to about one-fourth of the party's entire membership. Although not invulnerable to pressure from the minority, the majority party in each house generally holds sway, even fixing the size of its majority on all committees—a proportion frequently in excess of the percentage of seats it holds in the house as a whole.

Discipline.   Congressional party leaders have some substantial tools at their disposal to enforce a degree of discipline in their troops. Even though seniority usually determines most committee assignments, an occasional choice plum may be given to the loyal or withheld from the rebellious. For example, House Speaker for the 104th and 105th Congresses Newt Gingrich rewarded his most loyal freshmen representatives with plum slots on major committees, such as Ways and Means, when he took the reins in January 1995. Gingrich also took the unprecedented step of appointing committee chairs, and on several committees he disregarded seniority altogether and awarded chairmanships to members he believed would fight most aggressively for the GOP's program.[46] A member's bill can be lovingly caressed through the legislative process, or it can be summarily dismissed without so much as a hearing. Pork barrel—government projects yielding rich patronage benefits that sustain many a legislator's electoral survival—may be included or deleted during the appropriations process. Small favors and perquisites (such as the allocation of desirable office space or the scheduling of floor votes for the convenience of a member) can also be useful levers. Then, too, there are the campaign aids at the command of the leadership: money from party sources, endorsements, appearances in the district or at fund-raising events, and so on. On rare occasions the leaders and their allies in the party caucus may even impose sanctions of various sorts (such as the stripping of seniority rights or prized committee berths) in order to punish recalcitrant lawmakers.[47]

There are, however, limits to coordinated, cohesive party action. For example, the separate executive branch, the bicameral power-sharing, and the extraordinary decentralization of Congress's work all constitute institutional obstacles to effective party action. Moreover, party discipline is hurt by the individualistic nature of U.S. politics: campaigns that are candidate-centered rather than party-oriented; diverse electoral constituencies to which members of Congress must understandably be responsive; the largely private system of election financing that indebts legislators to wealthy individuals and nonparty interest groups more than to their parties; and the importance to lawmakers of attracting the news media's attention—often more easily done by showmanship than by quiet, effective labor within the party system.

Despite all of the barriers to cohesive party action, events occasionally move a party in that direction. One such example occurred in 1994, when most Republican U.S.

House candidates signed onto the so-called "Contract with America," a party platform for Congressional campaigns similar in some respects to a formal presidential platform. The Contract included such popular items as tax relief, term limits for members of Congress, and welfare reform, and it became the basis for the House of Representatives' legislative activity in early 1995. While not all of these items were passed by the legislature or signed into law by the president, in debating and voting on the Contract both the Republicans and Democrats showed that cohesive party action can still be achieved.

The above are formidable barriers to the operation of responsible, potent legislative parties. Therefore it is impressive to discover that party labels have consistently been the most powerful predictor of congressional roll-call voting, and in the last few years even more votes have closely followed the partisan divide. While not invariably predictive, as in strong parliamentary systems, a member's party affiliation has proven to be the indicator of his or her votes more than 70 percent of the time in recent years; that is, the average representative or senator sides with his or her party on about 70 percent of the votes that divide a majority of Democrats from a majority of Republicans. In most recent years, more than half of the roll-call votes in the House and Senate also found majorities of Democrats and Republicans on opposite sides.

In the past several years, party voting has increased noticeably, as reflected in the upward trend in party voting by both Democrats and Republicans shown in Figure 12.3. In 1993, for instance the average Democratic member and the average Republican member voted with his or her party (on votes dividing party majorities) about 88 percent of the time. President Clinton's economic programs in his first year in office clearly polarized the Congress, and the proportion of party voting jumped considerably from the already high (79 percent) level recorded in 1992. Partisanship in 1994 was less evident than in 1993, but still high, 83 percent among Democrats and 82 percent among Republicans. In 1995 partisans among Republicans took a major jump up; following their big election triumph, the GOP unity percentage was 91. Among Democrats it was 80 percent in 1995. The year 2001 saw a continuation of the current partisan divide in Congress, with the GOP scoring 90 percent and the Democrats scoring 85 percent. This high level of party unity is especially impressive in the light of one recent research study which concluded that party unity scores are highest during times of unified government, when one party controls both houses of Congress and the presidency. The high scores between 1995 and 1997 prevailed despite split control of the federal government between the Democratic president and Republican House and Senate.[48]

There are many reasons for the recent growth of congressional party unity and cohesion. Some are the result of long-term political factors. Both congressional parties, for

FIGURE 12.3 Congressional Party Unity Scores, 1959–2001
Note how party-based voting has increased conspicuosly since the 1970s.

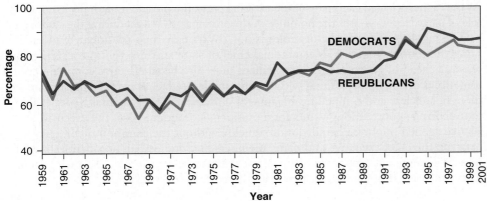

Source: Congressional Quarterly Almanacs (Washington, D.C.: Congressional Quarterly, Inc); Source for 2001; "Party Unity Background" *CQ Weekly*, vol. 60, no. 2, January 12, 2002, p. 142.

instance, have gradually become more ideologically homogeneous and internally consistent. Southern Democrats today are more moderate and much closer philosophically to their Northern counterparts than the South's legislative barons of old ever were. Similarly, there are few liberal Republicans left in either chamber of Congress, and GOP House members from all regions of the country are—with a few exceptions—moderately to solidly conservative. As each party became more ideologically homogenous, rank-and-file members of Congress (especially in the House) delegated to party leaders enhanced powers with which to push through the party's agenda.[49] At the same time, strong two-party competition has come to almost all areas of the nation. The electoral insecurity produced by vigorous competition seems to encourage party unity and cooperation in a legislature (perhaps as a kind of "circling the wagons" effect).[50]

The circumstances of contemporary politics are also producing greater party cohesion. The militancy of Speaker of the House for the 104th and 105th Congresses Newt Gingrich of Georgia raised the partisan hackles of many Democrats, polarizing the House a bit more along party lines. In fact, Gingrich's Contract with America generated very strong party voting in the House in early 1995; most floor votes found virtually all Republicans supporting the provisions of the Contract, with most Democrats voting in opposition. The recent defections from both parties ironically strengthens party cohesion. Conservative Democratic Representative Virgil Goode (D–Va.) bolted the Democratic party in January 2000. Similarily, Republican Senator Jim Jeffords left the GOP in spring 2001, shifting the Senate to Democratic control. These, and other defections, underscore the polarizing trend among an electorate that is less tolerant of dissent.

Each national party committee has been recruiting and training House and Senate candidates as never before, and devising common themes for all nominees in election seasons, work that may help to produce a consensual legislative agenda for each party. Party money and campaign services, such as media advertisements and polling, may also help convert candidates into team players. The evidence for this, however, is mixed, with some research showing that party money increases party loyalty among House members[51] while other research reveals no such effect.[52]

The Presidential Party

Political parties may be more central to the operation of the legislative branch than the executive branch, but it is the presidential party that captures the public imagination and shapes the electorate's opinion of the two parties. In our very personalized politics, voters' perceptions of the incumbent president and the presidential candidates determine to a large extent how citizens perceive the parties.

A chief executive's successes are his party's successes; the president's failures are borne by the party as much as by the individual. The image projected by a losing presidential candidate is incorporated into the party's contemporary portrait, whether wanted or not. As the highest elected candidate of the national party, the president naturally assumes the role of party leader, as does the nominee of the other party (at least during the campaign).

The juggling of contradictory roles is not always easy for a president. Expected to bring the country together as ceremonial chief of state and also to forge a ruling consensus as head of government, the president must also be an effective commander of a sometimes divided party. Along with the inevitable headaches party leadership brings, though, are clear and compelling advantages. Foremost among them is a party's ability to mobilize support among voters for a president's program. Also, the executive's legislative agenda might be derailed more quickly without the common tie of party label between the chief executive and many members of Congress; all presidents appeal for some congressional support on the basis of shared party affiliation, and they generally receive it depending on circumstances and their executive skill.

These party gifts to the president are reciprocated in many ways. In addition to compiling a record for the party and giving substance to its image, presidents appoint many activists to office, recruit candidates, raise money for the party treasury, campaign extensively for party nominees during election seasons, and occasionally provide some "coattail" help to fellow office seekers who are on the ballot in presidential election years.

Pro-Party Presidents.   Some presidents take their party responsibilities more seriously than others. Democrats Woodrow Wilson and Franklin D. Roosevelt were exceptionally party-oriented and dedicated to building their party electorally and governmentally. Republican Gerald R. Ford, during his brief tenure from 1974 to 1977, also achieved a reputation as a party builder. He was willing to undertake campaign and organizational chores for the GOP (especially in fund raising and in barnstorming for nominees) that most other presidents minimized or shunned. Perhaps Ford's previous role as House minority leader made him more sensitive to the needs of his fellow party office holders.

More recently, Ronald Reagan and George Bush exemplified the "pro-party" presidency. Ronald Reagan was one of the most party-oriented presidents of recent times.[53] In 1983 and 1984, during his own reelection effort, Reagan made more than two dozen campaign and fund-raising appearances for all branches of the party organization and candidates at every level. He taped more than 300 television endorsements as well, including one for an obscure Honolulu city council contest. Reagan also showed a willingness to get involved in the nitty-gritty of candidate recruitment, frequently calling strong potential candidates to urge them to run. Unlike Eisenhower, Reagan was willing to attempt a popularity transfer to his party and to campaign for Republicans whether or not they were strongly loyal to him personally. Unlike Johnson, Reagan was willing to put his prestige and policies to the test on the campaign trail. Unlike Nixon, Reagan spent time and effort helping underdogs and long-shot candidates, not just likely winners. Unlike Carter, Reagan signed more than seventy fund-raising appeals for party committees and took a personal interest in the further strengthening of the GOP's organizational capacity. George Bush, a former RNC chairman, emulated the Reagan model during his own presidency.

However, neither Reagan nor Bush had long enough coattails to help elect their party's nominees lower down on the ballot. Reagan's initial victory in 1980 was one factor in the election of a Republican Senate, but his landslide reelection in 1984 had, like Nixon's in 1972, almost no impact on his party's congressional representation. Bush provided no coattails at all to the GOP in 1988. There is little question that the **coattail effect,** the tendency of lesser-known or weaker candidates lower on the ballot to profit in an election by the presence on the party's ticket of a more popular candidate, has diminished sharply compared with a generation ago.[54] Partly, the decreased competitiveness of congressional elections has been produced by artful redistricting and the growing value of incumbency.[55] But voters are also less willing to think and cast ballots in purely partisan terms, a development that limits presidential leadership and hurts party development. (We return to this subject in the next chapter.) One study for example, concluded that the coattails of Ross Perot in 1992 benefited challengers to House incumbents, regardless of party. In this case, Perot's coattails went toward a general feeling of anti-incumbency, not toward (or against) any one party.[56]

coattail effect
The tendency of lesser-known or weaker candidates lower on the ballot to profit in an election by the presence on the party's ticket of a more popular candidate.

Recent Presidents.   Because Bill Clinton won with such a small plurality (43 percent) in 1992, he also produced little coattail for his party's candidates. Like Reagan and Bush, though, he campaigned vigorously for many Democrats across the country after taking office. Unlike his predecessors, however, Clinton enjoyed little success in transferring popularity. Democrats lost both governor's races in 1993 and a special Senate election in Texas since Clinton won the presidency. Then came the Republican deluge in 1994, when the GOP won fifty-two House seats and nine Senate seats in an election widely regarded as a repudiation of Clinton's presidency.

But before the ink was dry on the obituaries penned by journalists and political pundits, Clinton and his party rose from the ashes of the 1994 elections. After outmaneuvering congressional Republicans during the costly government shutdowns of late 1995 and early 1996, Clinton and congressional Democrats saw their popularity ratings climb. Meanwhile, the Republicans tried to regroup, a task made difficult by an acrimonious presidential primary season. Two months later, Clinton was returned to the White House and Democrats significantly cut into the Republican Party's hold on the U.S. House of Representatives, proving again that we should not be too quick to write off any politician, let alone an entire political party. Underlining this conclusion is the remarkable survival of Bill Clinton during 1998, when scandals of various sorts sprouted like daisies in spring. The final proof came in the November pudding, when Clinton's party defied all the rules and predictions. Profiting from the unpopular partisan antagonism between the Republican Congress and Democratic White House, Clinton's party did not lose, but actually won, five seats in the House of Representatives!

After the divisive 2000 election, Bush's tiny margin of victory gave his party—its representatives and senators, its very platform and public reception—the weakest and most bitterly contested mandate any party has received in recent history. Bush was redeemed in the 2002 midterm elections, gaining historic pick-ups in both houses of Congress and creating a legislative and executive majority that will likely allow him to push through a strong legislative agenda during the remained of his first term.

Nonpartisan Presidents.   Most modern American chief executives have been cast in an entirely different mold from the pro-party presidents of more recent times. Dwight D. Eisenhower elevated "nonpartisanship" to a virtual art form; while this may have preserved his personal popularity, it proved a disaster for his party. Despite a full two-term occupancy of the White House, the Republican Party remained mired in minority status among the electorate, and Eisenhower never really attempted to transfer his high ratings to the party. Lyndon B. Johnson kept the DNC busy with such trivial tasks as answering wedding invitations sent to the first family. When many of the Democratic senators and representatives elected on his presidential coattails were endangered in the 1966 midterm election, LBJ canceled a major campaign trip on their behalf lest his policies get tied too closely to their possible defeats. Democrats lost forty-seven House seats, three Senate seats, and eight governorships in the 1966 debacle.

In 1972 Richard M. Nixon discouraged the GOP from nominating candidates against conservative Southern Democrats in order to improve his own electoral and congressional position, since the grateful unopposed legislators would presumably be less likely to cause Nixon trouble on the campaign trail or in Congress. Nixon also subordinated the party's agenda almost wholly to his own reelection. Shunting aside the Republican National Committee, Nixon formed the Committee to Re-Elect the President, which became known by the acronym CREEP. So removed were party leaders from the committee's abuses that the Republican Party organization escaped blame during the Watergate investigations.

Jimmy Carter also showed little interest in his national party. Elected as an outsider in 1976, Carter and his top aides at first viewed the party as another extension of the Washington establishment they had pledged to ignore. Carter and his DNC chairmen failed to develop the Democratic Party organizationally and financially in order to keep it competitive during a critical period, while the Republicans were undergoing a dramatic revitalization stimulated by their desire to recover from the Watergate scandal. Later, during his unsuccessful 1980 reelection campaign, Carter was properly criticized for diverting DNC personnel and resources to his presidential needs, such as travel and Christmas cards, rather than permitting them to pursue essential partywide electoral tasks.

Clearly, then, some presidents have taken their party responsibilities more seriously than have others. In general, argues political scientist Sidney Milkis, most presidents since Franklin D. Roosevelt have been less supportive of their respective political parties than have been earlier presidents.[57]

The Parties and the Judiciary

Many Americans view the judiciary as "above politics" and certainly as nonpartisan, and many judges are quick to agree. Yet not only do members of the judiciary sometimes follow the election returns and allow themselves to be influenced by popular opinion, but they are also products of their party identification and possess the same partisan perceptual screens as all other politically aware citizens.

Legislators are much more partisan than judges, but it is wrong to assume that judges reach decisions wholly independent of partisan values. First, judges are creatures of the political process, and their posts are considered patronage plums. Judges who are not elected are appointed by presidents or governors for their abilities but also as members of the executive's party and increasingly as representatives of a certain philosophy of or approach to government. In this century every president has appointed judges overwhelmingly from his own party; Jimmy Carter and Ronald Reagan, for instance, drew 95 percent or more of their judicial choices from their respective parties. Furthermore, Democratic executives are naturally inclined to select for the bench liberal individuals who may be friendly to the welfare state or critical of some business practices. Republican executives generally lean toward conservatives for judicial posts, hoping they will be tough on criminal defendants, anti-abortion, and restrained in the use of court power. During the Clinton administration when Republicans were in charge of both Houses of Congress, the GOP strongly opposed many of President Clinton's judicial nominations and refused to confirm a fair number of them or even to bring the nominations to a vote. As a result, there were many judicial vacancies across the country. Unfortunately, this was an inevitable result of divided government in a very partisan and ideologically polarized era marked by a mutual lack of trust. Even the strongly Republican Chief Justice, William H. Rehnquist, was moved to criticize the Republican Senate's failure to confirm Clinton nominees.

Research has long indicated that party affiliation is in fact a moderately good predictor of judicial decisions, at least in some areas.[58] One specific example involves judicial approval of new congressional districts created by state legislatures every ten years after the United States census. Randall D. Lloyd found that judges "vote against [redistricting] plans presented from legislatures of their own party at a much lower rate than in cases where the party opposite their own controls the district drawing process."[59] In other words, party matters in the judiciary just as it does in the other two branches of government, although it certainly matters less on the bench than in the legislature and in the executive.

Many judges appointed to office have had long careers in politics as loyal party workers or legislators. Supreme Court Justice Sandra Day O'Connor, for example, was an active member of the National Republican Women's Club and is a former Republican state legislator. Some jurists are even more overtly political, since they are elected to office. In a majority of states at least some judicial positions are filled by election, and seventeen states hold outright partisan elections, with both parties nominating opposing candidates and running hard-hitting campaigns. In some rural counties across the United States, local judges are not merely partisanly elected figures; they are the key public officials, controlling many patronage jobs and the party machinery itself.

Clearly, in many places in the United States, judges by necessity and by tradition are not above politics but are in the thick of it. Although election of the judiciary is a questionable practice in light of its specially sanctioned role as impartial arbiter, partisan influence exerted both by jurists' party loyalties and by the appointment (or election) process is useful in retaining some degree of accountability in a branch often accused of being arrogant and aloof.

The Parties and State Governments

Most of the conclusions just discussed about the party's relationship to the legislature, the executive, and the judiciary apply to those branches on the state level as well. The national parties, after all, are organized around state units, and the basic structural arrangement of party and government is much the same in Washington and the state capitals. Remarkably, too, the major national parties are the dominant political forces in all fifty states. This has been true consistently; unlike Great Britain or Canada, the United States has no regional or state parties that displace one or both of the national parties in local contests. Occasionally in U.S. history a third party has proven locally potent, as did Minnesota's Farmer-Labor Party and Wisconsin's Progressives, both of which elected governors and state legislative majorities in the twentieth century. But over time, no such party has survived,[60] and every state's two-party system mirrors national party dualism, at least as far as labels are concerned.

Parties and Governors.   The partisan makeup of the governors in the United States is heavily Republican, with Republicans in 2001 holding twenty-nine governorships, Democrats holding nineteen, and independents holding two (in Maine and Minnesota). The powerful position of governor is a natural launching pad for a presidential candidacy. Just since 1900, Woodrow Wilson, Franklin D. Roosevelt, Jimmy Carter, Ronald Reagan, Bill Clinton, and most recently, George W. Bush have all gone from statehouses to the White House. In 2000, governors played a very prominent auxiliary role in George W. Bush's victory. During his bid for office, Bush relied heavily on his fellow GOP governors, who were among his principle surrogates and stalwart supporters on the campaign trail. During the resolution of the contested vote in Florida, the Republican governorship of that state under Bush's brother Jeb loomed as a constant background presence in the associated political maneuvering. Shortly after Bush's victory was confirmed, a prized presidential appointment went to another governor: Jim Gilmore of Virginia was appointed chairman of the Republican National Committee in recognition of his rising status in the Republican ranks and in appreciation of his efforts on Bush's behalf, which included an address at the Republican National Convention in Philadelphia. Governors in many states tend to possess even greater influence over their parties' organizations and legislators than do presidents. Many governors have more patronage positions at their command than does a president, and these material rewards and incentives give governors added clout with activists and office holders. In addition, tradition in some states permits the governor to play a role in selecting the legislature's committee chairs and party floor leaders, and some state executives even attend and help direct the party legislative caucuses, activities no president would ever undertake. Moreover, forty-three governors possess a power denied the national executive until 1997: the line-item veto, which permits the governor to veto single items (such as individual pork barrel projects) in appropriations bills. Whereas many presidents prior to Clinton accepted objectionable measures as part of a bill too urgent or important to be vetoed, a governor could gain enormous leverage with legislators by means of the line-item veto. A Republican-sponsored measure in the 104th Congress gave the president this potent tool, beginning in January 1997. Subsequently, however, the presidential line-item veto was ruled unconstitutional in federal court.

In 1998, Arizona elected an unprecedented slate of female legislators, shown here waving to the crowd at their swearing-in ceremony at the State Capitol in Phoenix, January 4, 1999. From left are Governor Jane D. Hull, Secretary of State Betsey Bayless, Attorney General Janet Napolitano, Treasurer Carol Springer, and Superintendent of Public Instruction Lisa Graham Keegan. (Photo courtesy: Roy Dabner/AP/Wide World Photos)

Parties and State Legislatures.   Unlike the partisan makeup of state executives, state legislatures are nearly evenly split, with neither party having a significant advantage. Similar to state executives, however, the party role in the legislature tends to be more high-profile and effective at the state level. Most state legislatures surpass the U.S. Congress in partisan unity and cohesion. Even though fewer than half of congressional roll calls in the post–World War II era have produced majorities of the two parties on opposite sides, a number of state legislatures (including Massachusetts, New York, Ohio, and Pennsylvania) have achieved party voting levels of 70 percent or better in some years. Not all states display party cohesion of this magnitude, of course. Nebraska has a nonpartisan legislature, elected without party labels on the ballot. In the South the lack of two-party competition has left essentially one-party legislatures split into factions, regional groupings, or personal cliques. As real interparty competition reaches the legislative level in Southern states, however, party cohesion in the legislatures is likely to increase.

One other party distinction is notable in many state legislatures. Compared with the Congress, state legislative leaders have much more authority and power; this is one reason party unity is higher in the state capitols.[61] The strict seniority system that usually controls committee assignments in Congress is less absolute in most states, and legislative leaders often have considerable discretion in appointing the committee chairs and members. The party caucuses, too, are usually more active and influential in state legislatures than in their Washington counterparts. In some legislatures, the caucuses meet weekly or even daily to work out strategy and count votes, and nearly one-fourth of the caucuses bind all the party members to support the group's decisions on key issues (such as appropriations measures, tax issues, and procedural questions).

Not just the leaders and caucuses but the party organizations as well have more influence over legislators at the state level. State legislators are much more dependent than their congressional counterparts on their state and local parties for election assistance. Whereas members of Congress have large government-provided staffs and lavish perquisites to assist (directly or indirectly) their reelection efforts, state legislative candidates need party workers and, increasingly, the party's financial support and technological resources at election time.

THE MODERN TRANSFORMATION OF PARTY ORGANIZATION

Political parties have moved from the labor-intensive, person-to-person operations of the first half of the century toward the utilization of modern high technologies and communication strategies. Nevertheless, the capabilities of each party's organization vary widely.

Republican Strengths

Until 1992 the modern Republican Party thoroughly outclassed its Democratic rival in almost every category of campaign service and fund raising. There are a number of explanations for the disparity between the two major parties: From 1932 until 1980, the Republicans were almost perennially disappointed underdogs, especially in congressional contests; they therefore felt the need to give extra effort. The GOP had the willingness, and enough electoral frustrations, to experiment with new campaign technologies that might hold the key to elusive victories. Also, since Democrats held most of the congressional offices and thus had most of the benefits of incumbency and staff, Republican nominees were forced to rely more on their party to offset built-in Democratic advantages. The party staff, in other words, compensated for the Democratic congressional staff, and perhaps also for organized labor's divisions of election troops, which were usually at the beck and call of Democratic candidates. Then, too, one can argue that the business and middle-class base of the modern GOP has a natural managerial and entrepreneurial flair demonstrated by the party officers drawn from that talented pool.

Whatever the causes, the contemporary national Republican Party has organizational prowess unparalleled in American history. The Republicans have surpassed the Democrats in fund raising by large margins in recent election cycles—never by less than two to one and usually by a considerably higher ratio (see Figure 12.4). Democrats must struggle to raise enough money to meet the basic needs of most of their candidates, while, in the words of a past chairman of the Democratic Senatorial Campaign Committee, "The single biggest problem the Republicans have is how to legally spend the money they have."[62]

FIGURE 12.4   Political Party Finances, 1976–2002: Total Receipts

Note how the Republican Party has consistently taken in substantially higher receipts than their Democratic competitors—especially during the 1980s, when the Republican Party consolidated and prospered during Ronald Reagan's administration. Not until 1996 did Democrats reach levels long enjoyed by the Republicans.

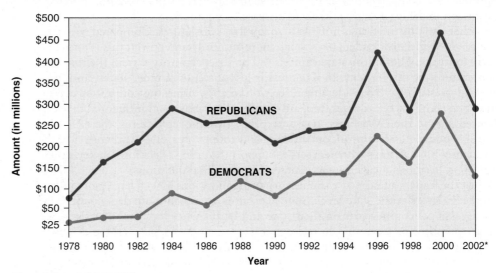

*Amounts through Oct. 16, 2002
Source: Federal Election Commission.

In 2000, Republicans still outspent the Democrats in Senate and House races, but the Democrats came closer to matching the Republicans than in any other modern election season. In the presidential race, George W. Bush became the object of considerable public attention and criticism as a result of the huge war chest which he raised very early in the campaign and used to defeat his main challenger in the primaries, John McCain.

Most of the Republican money is raised through highly successful mail solicitation. This procedure started in the early 1960s and accelerated in the mid-1970s, when postage and production costs were relatively low. From a base of just 24,000 names in 1975, for example, the national Republican Party has expanded its mailing list of proven donors to several million in the 1990s. Mailings produce about three-fourths of total revenue, and they do so with an average contribution of less than $35. In this fashion the GOP may have broadened its committed base, because contributing money usually strengthens the tie between a voter and any organization. Most of the rest of the GOP's funds come from donors of larger amounts who secure membership in various Republican contributor groups. For instance, the Republican National Committee designates any $10,000 annual giver an "Eagle."

The Republican cash is used to support a dazzling variety of party activities and campaign services. These include party staff, voter contact, polling, media advertising, and campaign staff training and research. Recently calculated empirical evidence also shows that large campaign war chests of incumbents act to deter high-quality challengers from entering political races. Faced with the prospect of raising huge sums of money to match incumbents, many potentially competitive opposition candidates simply decide to sit races out.[63]

Party Staff.   Several hundred operatives are employed by the national GOP in election years, and even in the off years many more than one hundred people hold full-time positions. There is great emphasis on field staff, that is, on staff members sent to and stationed in key districts and states who maintain close communication between local and national party offices.

positions. There is great emphasis on field staff, that is, on staff members sent to and stationed in key districts and states who maintain close communication between local and national party offices.

Voter Contact. The Republicans frequently conduct massive telephone canvassing operations to identify likely Republican voters and to get them to the polls on Election Day. In 1986, for instance, the GOP used paid callers in seventeen phone centers across the country to reach 10.5 million prospective voters in twenty-five states during the general election campaign. Nearly 5.5 million previously identified Republicans were called again just before Election Day. Many of them heard an automated message from the president that began: "This is Ronald Reagan and I want to remind you to go out and vote on Tuesday." In addition, 12 million pieces of "persuasive" (non-fund-raising) mail were sent to households in the last two weeks of the campaign.

The Republican National Committee also pioneered the use of interactive technologies to attract voters. The RNC's award winning "Main Street" Internet site has offered "chats" with the RNC chair and links to a variety of sites of interest to voters.

Polling. The national Republican committees have spent millions of dollars for national, state, and local public opinion surveys, and they have accumulated an enormous storehouse of data on American attitudes in general and on marginal districts in particular. Many of the surveys are provided to GOP nominees at a cut-rate cost. In important contests, the party will frequently commission tracking polls, continuous surveys that enable a campaign to chart its daily rise or fall. The information provided in such polls is invaluable in the tense concluding days of an election.

Media Advertising. The national Republican Party operates a sophisticated in-house media division that specializes in the design and production of television advertisements for party nominees at all levels. About seventy to one hundred candidates are helped in an election cycle. They obtain expert and technically superior media commercials, and the party also offers its wares for a minimal fee, often including the actual buying of time, that is, the purchase of specific time slots on television shows for broadcasting the advertising spots. The candidates thus save the substantial commissions and fees usually charged by independent political consultants for the same services.

The Republican Party was also the first to pioneer the use of "morphing" in campaign advertising. The negative campaigning technique, which was first used in the 1994 congressional elections, transformed faces of Democratic candidates for Congress into Bill Clinton.

The GOP's party advertising is even more significant. Since 1978 the Republicans have aired spots designed to support not specific candidates, but the generic party label. Beginning with the 1980 election, the GOP has used institutional advertising to establish basic election themes. "Vote Republican, for a Change" spots attacked the Democratic Congress in 1980. In another spot House Speaker Thomas P. O'Neill was lampooned by an actor lookalike who ignored all warning signs and drove a car until it ran out of fuel. ("The Democrats are out of gas," announced the narrator as the "Speaker" futilely kicked the automobile's tire.) In 1996, Republicans used a television spot to revive the issue of Clinton's draft-dodging and attack his Achilles' heel by asking if he could be trusted to tell the truth.

Campaign Staff Training and Research. The party trains many of the political volunteers and paid operatives who manage the candidates' campaigns. Since 1976 the Republicans have held annually about a half-dozen week-long "Campaign Management Colleges" for staffers. In 1986 the party launched an ambitious million-dollar "Congressional Campaign Academy" that offers two-week, all-expenses-paid training courses for prospective campaign managers, finance directors, and press relations staff. Early in each election cycle, the national party staff also prepares voluminous research reports on Democratic opponents, analyzing their public statements, votes, and attendance records. The reports are made available to GOP candidates and their aides.

Staffers call on the party faithful to vote on Election Day. Phone banks, like the ones shown here, have become a major part of party-related activity around election time. (Photo courtesy: Bob Daemmrich/The Image Works)

Despite its noted financial edge and service sophistication, all is not well in the Republican organization. Success has bred self-satisfaction and complacency, encouraged waste, and led the party to place too much reliance on money and technology, and not enough on the foundation of any party movement—people. As former U.S. Senator Paul Laxalt (R–Nev.), outgoing general chair of the national Republican Party, was forced to admit in 1987: "We've got way too much money, we've got way too many political operatives, we've got far too few volunteers. . . . We are substituting contributions and high technology for volunteers in the field. I've gone the sophisticate route, I've gone the television route, and there is no substitute for the volunteer route."[64]

As Laxalt's comments imply, technology and money can probably add only two or three percentage points to a candidate's margin, and one recent study even put the advantage of higher spending for Senate incumbents at about six percentage points.[65] The rest is determined by the nominee's quality and positions, the general electoral tide prevailing in any given year, and the energy of party troops in the field. Republicans were to learn this anew in 1992, when George Bush's large war chest could not stave off defeat. Similarly, many Democratic senators and representatives outspent their opponents by a wide margin in the 1994 elections, but they tasted defeat nonetheless. Similarly in 1996, Senate candidates in South Carolina and Virginia outspent their incumbent opponents and yet failed to win. Have the two major parties learned that while money helps, having more than your opponent by no means guarantees electoral success, especially when running against incumbents? Only time and future elections will tell.

Democratic Party Gains

Parties, like people, change their habits slowly. The Democrats were reluctant to alter a formula that had been a winning combination for decades of New Deal dominance. The prevailing philosophy was, "Let a thousand flowers bloom"; candidates were encouraged to go their own way, to rely on organized labor and other interest groups allied with the Democrats, and to raise their own money, while the national party was kept subservient and weak.

The massive Democratic defeats suffered in 1980 forced a fundamental reevaluation of the party's structure and activities. Democrats, diverse by nature, came to an unaccustomed consensus that the party must change to survive, that it must dampen internal ideological disputes and begin to revitalize its organization. Thus was born the commitment to technological and fund-raising modernization, using the Republican Party's accomplishments as a model, that drives the Democratic Party today.

Comprehension of the task is the first step to realization of the goal, so even after more than a decade, Democrats still trail their competitors by virtually every significant measure of party activity. Yet the figures of party finances (receipts), graphed in Figure 12.4, can be read a different way. While the GOP has consistently maintained an enormous edge, the Democrats have considerably increased their total receipts, now raising many times more than just a few years ago. More importantly, Democrats are contributing much more to their candidates and have actually come close to the GOP's larger total recently (see Analyzing the Data: Political Party Finances, 1976–2000). Several national party chairs (Paul Kirk, Ron Brown, David Wilhelm, and Roy Romer) have aggressively sought more funds from party supporters and friendly interest groups.

Running on one of the most liberal platforms in the 2000 election, Democratic candidate Jon Corzine spent some $60 million to win the New Jersey U.S. Senate seat, defeating four-term Congressman Bob Franks. (Photo courtesy: Laura Pedrick/Corbis Sygma)

A N A L Y Z I N G   T H E   D A T A

POLITICAL PARTY FINANCES, 1976–2000: TOTAL PARTY CONTRIBUTIONS TO AND EXPENDITURES FOR CANDIDATES

The Republican Party has historically raised and spent far more campaign money than the Democratic Party (notice the especially large difference in the 1980s). Since the early 1990s, however, the Democrats have made tremendous strides in fundraising and are now fully competitive with their opponents. Democrats also receive an invisible boost from labor unions, which are not required to disclose or report politically oriented expenditures.

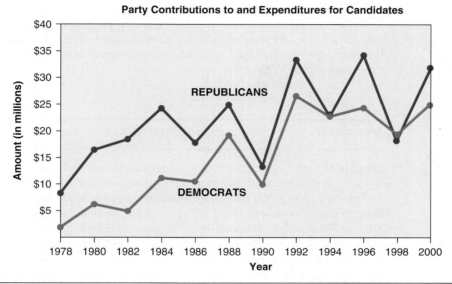

Party Contributions to and Expenditures for Candidates

Numbers represent monies spent between Jan. 1, 1999 and Oct. 18, 2000. Substantial spending took place by both parties after June 30, 1998. Includes total for national senatorial and congressional committees as well as all other reported national, state, and local spending; all presidential, Senate, and House candidates are included. Not included are "soft money" expenditures.
Source: Federal Election Commission.

efforts as the midterm elections of 1994 approached, and their exertions again made the Democrats more competitive with the Republicans. In the 2000 presidential race, Bush outspent Gore, but significantly, independent liberal groups such as pro-choice and environmental organizations and labor unions spent more to support Gore than partisan conservative organizations spent in support of Bush.

The decision in 1981 to begin a direct-mail program for the national party was a turning point. From a list of only 25,000 donors before the program began, the DNC's support base has grown to 500,000. The Democrats have imitated the Republicans not just in fund raising but also in the uses to which the money is put. For instance, in 1986 the party opened a $3-million media center that produces television and radio spots at rates much lower than those charged by independent political consultants. The Democratic Party is attempting to do more for its candidates and their campaign staffs, too, creating the Democratic National Training Institute in 1985. The Institute coordinates campaign schools for party workers from around the country. "Smart money" is a term used to describe campaign contributions that flow to the candidates and political party expected to win in an election year. With Bill Clinton leading every public opinion poll taken after mid-July during the 1992 campaign and almost every public opinion poll taken during the 1996 campaign, Democrats were flooded with smart money. The Democratic Party dramatically increased both its receipts and expenditures in 1992 and then again in 1996. The Republicans did equally well, but the GOP's well-oiled fund-raising machinery has regularly produced massive war chests. For the Democrats, being financially well-off was a new and delightful experience.

Interestingly, the party campaign committees in Congress have also begun to raise significant sums of money from their own congressional incumbents. For example, under former campaign committee chair Vic Fazio (D–Calif.), the DCCC began in 1991 requesting a $5,000 contribution from all House Democratic incumbents.[66] During the 1993–1994 election cycle, the NRCC instituted a similar program to encourage financial support from incumbents.[67] Both parties' efforts to raise funds from incumbents have been remarkably successful. Indeed, the NRCC collected more than $4 million from House GOP members during the 1995–1996 election cycle.[68]

Thus both party organizations have grown mightier in recent years, at the time when political parties have seemed to be in decline in some other ways. Most important, many voters appear to have less a sense of partisan identification and loyalty today than in generations past. Why is this so?

THE PARTY IN THE ELECTORATE

A political party is much more than its organizational shell, however dazzling the technologies at its command, and its reach extends well beyond the relative handful of men and women who are the party in government. In any democracy, where power is derived directly from the people, the party's real importance and strength must come from the citizenry it attempts to mobilize. The party in the electorate—the mass of potential voters who identify with the Democratic or Republican labels—is the most significant element of the political party, providing the foundation for the organizational and governmental parties. But in some crucial respects, it is the weakest of the components of the U.S. political party system. In recent decades fewer citizens have been willing to pledge their fealty to the major parties, and many of those who have declared their loyalties have done so with less intensity. Also, voters of each partisan stripe are increasingly casting ballots for some candidates of the opposing party, and partisan identification is a less reliable indicator of likely voting choices today than it once was. Notice, in Figure 12.5, the recent merging of party identification toward the political center (Politics Now: The Move Toward the Center discusses the effect of centrism on political candidates.)

Party Identification

party identification
A citizen's personal affinity for a political party, usually expressed by his or her tendency to vote for the candidates of that party.

Most American voters identify with a party but do not belong to it. There is no universal enrolled party membership; there are no prescribed dues, no formal rules concerning an individual's activities, and no enforceable obligations to the party assumed by the voter. The party has no real control over or even an accurate accounting of its adherents, and the party's voters subscribe to few or none of the commonly accepted tenets of organizational membership, such as regular participation and some measure of responsibility for the group's welfare. Rather, **party identification** or affiliation is an informal and impressionistic exercise whereby a citizen acquires a party label and accepts its standard as a summary of his or her political views and preferences. To see which party you identify with, see Highlight: Are You a Democrat, Republican, or Independent?

However, just because the acquisition is informal does not mean that it is unimportant. The party label becomes a voter's central political reference symbol and perceptual screen, a prism or filter through which the world of politics and government flows and is interpreted. For many Americans, party identification is a significant aspect of

FIGURE 12.5   Party Identification, 1952–2002

Simply defined, party identification is the response a voter gives to the poll question, "With what political party do you identify?" Notice how, despite the varying party of the president over time, party identification has remained fairly stable from the 1950s to the early 1990s. Not until an era of acute partisan strife in the mid-1990s have the independents made significant gains in party identification.

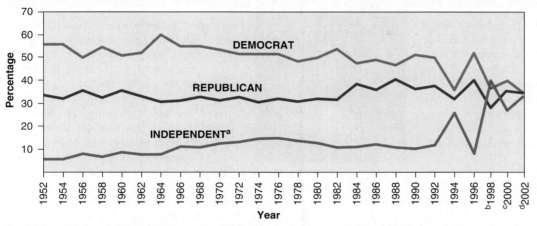

Note: Partisan totals do not add up to 100% because "apolitical" and "other" responses were deleted. Sample size varied from poll to poll, from a low of 1,130 to a high of 2,850.

[a]Pure Independents only. Independent "leaners" have been added to Democratic and Republican totals.

[b]1998 figures were provided from a Gallup poll. Due to differences in wording from the Center for Political Studies Poll, the Gallup Poll may overstate the number of Independents.

[c]2000 figures based on Voter News Service exit poll.

[d]Data for 2002 from Gallop Poll, Nov. 4, 2002.

Source: Center for Political Studies/Survey Research Center of the University of Michigan, made available through the Inter-University Consortium for Political and Social Research. Also, Leon D. Epstein, *Political Parties in the American Mold* (Madison: University of Wisconsin Press, 1986), Table 8.1, p. 257. Data for 1996 provided by election-day exit poll conducted by Voter Research and Surveys.

their political personality and a way of defining and explaining themselves to others. The loyalty generated by the label can be as intense as any enjoyed by sports teams and alma maters; in a few areas of the country, "Democrat" and "Republican" are still fighting words. Some studies of aggregate personal party identification in the electorate, such as one conducted by Michael MacKuen, Robert S. Erikson, and James A. Stimson, argue that a great variability of individual partisan leanings exists, stemming from short-term evaluations of the state of the economy, approval of the incumbent president, and other factors.[69] Other, more recent studies of a greater amount of polling data, however, support the traditional view of partisanship, finding much smaller permanent variability in party identification. Donald Green, Bradley Palmquist, and Eric Schickler, for example, claim that the partisanship of the electorate changes in response to temporal features only in the short term. Long-term partisanship remains stable after the condition causing the shock subsides.[70]

On the whole, Americans regard their partisan affiliation as a convenience rather than a necessity. The individual identifications are reinforced by the legal institutionalization of the major parties. Because of restrictive ballot laws, campaign finance rules, the powerful inertia of political tradition, and many other factors, voters for all practical purposes are limited to a choice between a Democrat and a Republican in virtually all elections—a situation that naturally encourages the pragmatic choosing up of sides. The party registration process that exists in about half of the states, requiring a voter to state a party preference (or independent status) when registering to vote and thus restricting voter participation in primaries to party registrants, also is an incentive for voters to affiliate themselves with a party.[71]

Sources of Party Identification.   Whatever the societal and governmental forces undergirding party identification, the explanations of partisan loyalty at the individual's level are understandably more personal. Not surprisingly, parents are the single greatest influence in establishing a person's first party identification. Politically active parents with

POLITICS NOW

THE MOVE TOWARD THE CENTER

The 2000 election played itself out in a most unconventional manner, but one aspect of the campaign proceeded pretty much by the book: a move toward centrism—a convergence of candidate platforms around the center of the political-ideological spectrum—resulting almost entirely from the open nature of the election (i.e., the fact that neither candidate was an incumbent).

Open contests for the presidency are almost always more competitive than elections contested by an incumbent president (there are of course exceptions, such as the elections of 1980 and 1992). Basically, the Democrats and the Republicans each control between roughly 33 and 40 percent of the electorate based on nationwide party identification numbers, while the remaining 20 to 33 percent of the electorate considers themselves independents. Independents tend to be more center-oriented or moderate in some views, so if a candidate can secure his or her base, he or she will then articulate a moderate position to capture more of the independent, moderate voters. The first politician to define the "move to the center" in such a way was Richard M. Nixon, who advised Republican candidates to run to the right for the primaries, and to the center for the general election. For Democrats, the reverse is true: run to the left for the primaries, then run to the middle for the general election.

In 2000, true to form, centrism offered the key to victory. However widely mocked by skeptical liberals, Bush's centrist platform of "compassionate conservatism" enabled him to make some improvements in his ratings with women and Hispanics. Bush still lost both groups to Gore, but he did considerably better than his predecessor in 1996, Bob Dole, and this slight gain was one of many small things that made the critical difference for Bush.

Al Gore, on the other hand, declined to make similar centrist gestures and paid the penalty accordingly. In a close-running and open election, his strong advocacy of gun control, environmentalism, and reproductive freedom likely failed to endear him to moderate voters. The best evidence of this failure was the loss of both his home state, Tennessee, and the usually heavily Democratic West Virginia. Why did Gore lose two states that he almost certainly should have carried? The answer is simple: his liberal position on guns, coal, and abortion.

the same party loyalty raise children who will be strong party identifiers, whereas parents without party affiliations or with mixed affiliations produce offspring more likely to be independents (see chapter 11).

Early socialization is hardly the last step in the acquisition and maintenance of a party identity; marriage and other aspects of adult life can change one's loyalty. So can charismatic political personalities, particularly at the national level (such as Franklin D. Roosevelt and Ronald Reagan), cataclysmic events (the Civil War and the Great Depression are the best examples), and maybe intense social issues (for instance, abortion). Interestingly, social class is not an especially strong indicator of likely partisan choice in the United States, at least in comparison with Western European democracies. Not only are Americans less inclined than Europeans to perceive class distinctions, preferring instead to see themselves and most other people as members of an exceedingly broad middle class, but other factors, including sectionalism and candidate-oriented politics, tend to blur class lines in voting.

Declining Loyalty

Over the past two decades, many political scientists as well as other observers, journalists, and party activists have become increasingly anxious about a perceived decline in partisan identification and loyalty. Many public opinion surveys have shown a significant growth in independents at the expense of the two major parties. The Center for Political Studies/Survey Research Center (CPS/SRC) of the University of Michigan,

H I G H L I G H T

ARE YOU A DEMOCRAT, REPUBLICAN, OR INDEPENDENT?

Choosing a political party can be easy or quite difficult. The answer depends on you and your values.

Republicans since the 1980s are generally identified as more conservative than Democrats and tend to be associated with free market economics, lower taxes, family values, hawkish foreign policy, and devolution of power from the federal government to the states.

Democrats of the last two decades, on the other hand, are associated with greater economic intervention, protection of minorities, a social safety net, including Social Security and Medicare, government regulation, protection of the environment, a less aggressive foreign policy, and the cause of poor and working-class people.

Of course, the descriptions of the political parties above are generalizations of their views. Clearly, many people are concerned about a combination of issues that are associated with both of the political parties. In addition, third parties perennially, if often fleetingly, emerge to appeal to highly focused voters, or to average voters when circumstances make urgent issues out of what are usually secondary concerns. For example, the Green Party's primary plank is based predominantly on environmentalism; the Reform Party's, on the need for nonpartisan reform of government corruption and inefficacy; the Libertarian Party's, on the

philosophical conviction that democracy functions best with the least intervention from the state. These choices can be tempting for voters with strong opinions but without strong major-party affiliation, or voters who happen to place a great deal of importance on a third party's one key issue. The difficult question is: *How do you decide which party is generally more in line with your values?*

Try this exercise. Think about an issue or set of issues that is important to you. Ask yourself, are the positions taken by well-known politicians from the Republican and Democratic parties different? In what ways? If there are independent or minor-party candidates, do their views differ greatly from those of major-party candidates?

Of course, the choice of a political party is not usually made on the basis of one issue but on the basis of *many* issues taken together. Parties are not made up of one type of person but many diverse groups of people combined. The people who make up the membership of these parties have compromised on some issues and emphasized others in their choice of party. The bottom line is that it is up to you to choose the combination of issues that concern you the most and the party you believe best represents your values.

Do you consider yourself a Democrat, Republican, or Independent? Does it matter?

for instance, has charted the rise of self-described independents from a low of 19 percent in 1958 to a peak of 38 percent twenty years later. Before the 1950s (although the evidence for this research is more circumstantial because of the scarcity of reliable survey research data), there are indications that independents were fewer in number, and party loyalties considerably firmer.

Yet the recent decline of party identification can be exaggerated, and in some ways there has been remarkable stability in the voters' party choices. Over more than thirty years, during vast political, economic, and social upheavals that have changed the face of the nation, the Democratic Party has nearly consistently drawn the support of a small majority and the Republican Party has attracted a share of the electorate in the low to mid-30-percent range. Granted, there have been peaks and valleys for both parties. The Lyndon B. Johnson landslide of 1964 helped Democrats top the 60 percent mark, and the Reagan landslide of 1984 and the post–Persian Gulf War glow of 1991 sent Democratic stock below the majority midpoint. Yet these sorts of gradations are more akin to rolling foothills than towering mountain ranges. The steady nature of modern partisanship goes beyond the fortunes of each party. Identification with the two parties in modern times has never dipped below 83 percent of the U.S. electorate (recorded during the disillusionment spawned by Watergate in 1974) and can usually be found in the mid-to-upper-80-percent range. Finally, political scientist Martin Wattenberg suggests that

Simple messages and catchy phrases have earned campaign buttons a permanent place in American politics. These popular campaign novelties serve to increase candidate name recognition in the general public and to reinforce the support of the button wearer. (Photo courtesy: Sally Anderson-Bruce/Museum of Political Life, University of Hartford)

Americans' attitudes about political parties are not so much negative as they are neutral—leaving the door open for strengthened party attachments in the American electorate.[72]

When pollsters ask for party identification information, they generally proceed in two stages. First, they inquire whether a respondent considers himself or herself a Democrat, Republican, or independent. Then the party identifiers are asked to categorize themselves as "strong" or "not very strong" supporters, while the independents are pushed to reveal their leanings with a question such as, "Which party do you normally support in elections, the Democrats or the Republicans?" It may be true that some independent respondents are thereby prodded to pick a party under the pressure of the interview situation, regardless of their true feelings. But research has demonstrated that independent "leaners" in fact vote very much like real partisans, in some elections more so than the "not very strong" party identifiers. There is reason to count the independent leaners as closet partisans, though voting behavior is not the equivalent of real partisan identification.

In fact, the reluctance of "leaners" to admit their real party identities is in itself worrisome, because it reveals a change in attitudes about political parties and their role in our society. Being a socially acceptable, integrated, and contributing member of one's community once almost demanded partisan affiliation; it was a badge of good citizenship, signifying that one was a patriot. Today, the labels are avoided as an offense to a thinking person's individualism, and a vast majority of Americans insist that they vote for "the person, not the party."

The reasons for these anti-party attitudes are not hard to find. The growth of issue-oriented politics that cuts across party lines for voters who feel intensely about certain policy matters is partly the cause. So, too, is the emphasis on personality politics by the mass media (especially television) and political consultants. Party splits have also played a role. Fiscal conservatives in the GOP often have little in common with social conservatives who care most about the abortion issue, for example. Underlying these causes, though, are two much more disturbing and destructive long-term phenomena: the perceived loss of party credibility, and the decline of the party's tangible connections to the lives of everyday citizens. Although the underlying partisanship of the American people has not declined significantly since 1952, voter-admitted partisanship has dropped considerably. About three-fourths or more of the electorate volunteered a party choice without prodding from 1952 to 1964, but since 1970 an average of less than two-thirds has been willing to do so. Professed independents (including leaners) have increased from around one-fifth of the electorate in the 1950s to one-third or more during the last three decades. Also cause for concern is the marginal decline in strong Democrats and strong Republicans. Strong partisans are a party's backbone, the source of its volunteer force, candidates, and dependable voters. Even a slight shrinkage in these ranks can be troublesome.

Group Affiliations.   Just as individuals vary in the strength of their partisan choice, so, too, do groups vary in the degree to which they identify with the Democratic Party or the Republican Party. There are enormous variations in party identification from one region or demographic group to another, particularly in geographic region, gender, race and ethnicity, age, social and economic factors, religion, marital status, and ideology.

Geographic Region.   While all other geographic regions in the United States are relatively closely contested between the parties, the South still exhibits some of the Democratic Party affinity cultivated in the nineteenth century and hardened in the fires of the Civil War. This is only still true in local elections, however, and even there, it is changing rapidly. In the 1994 election, for instance, Southerners elected Republicans to a majority of the U.S. House seats in the states of the old Confederacy, and dozens of sheriffs won under the GOP banner, too. This increase in the number of Southern elected officials matches changes in party identification in the South as calculated by Alan I. Abramowitz and Kyle L. Saunders. Abramowitz and Saunders found that Democratic Party identification among white southerners fell by sixteen percentage points between 1987 and 1994, from 64 percent to 48 percent. For the first time since

GLOBAL POLITICS

POLITICAL PARTIES IN SELECTED DEMOCRACIES

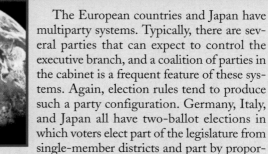

The United States has a limited range of political parties at the national level. While there are many parties in this country, the Reform Party is currently the most prominent third party. Since the Civil War, the Republican and Democratic parties have always controlled the federal government. Currently only one member of Congress, Bernie Sanders of Vermont, is a member of a third party.

Election rules offer a partial explanation for this. The "winner-take-all" single-member district system found here tends to produce a two-party system. Yet Canada and the United Kingdom also use the winner-take-all election rule, with two parties dominating their parliaments, but other parties also have at least a few members representing them in the legislature. In Britain's House of Commons, for example, even the Sinn Fein, the political arm of the Irish Republican Army, now has two seats (currently vacant because the party opposes British government policy in Northern Ireland). Canada and the United Kingdom are thus better described as two-plus party systems. In the United States and the United Kingdom, the two dominant parties are far larger than any of their rivals, consistent with the understanding of the effects of single-member districts. The near destruction of the once-dominant Progressive Liberal Party in Canada has evened out the distribution of parliamentary seats.

The European countries and Japan have multiparty systems. Typically, there are several parties that can expect to control the executive branch, and a coalition of parties in the cabinet is a frequent feature of these systems. Again, election rules tend to produce such a party configuration. Germany, Italy, and Japan all have two-ballot elections in which voters elect part of the legislature from single-member districts and part by proportional representation based on party lists. Proportional representation tends to benefit smaller parties, because their electoral bases are not confined to districts. Not only do these countries' parliaments have several medium-sized parties (Japan is a bit different because the conservative party is far larger than any of its rivals), but they have parties that span the political spectrum. On the left, social democratic parties are represented in every legislature. France, Germany, and Japan have communist parties (a reformed one in Germany's case). In France, the reactionary National Front has emerged in the last decade as a powerful alternative to the mainstream conservative Union for French Democracy and the Rally for the Republic.

China, Mexico, and Indonesia challenge American assumptions about what the term "political party" means. China is a one-party state in which the Communist Party is guaranteed the leading role in politics by the constitution. The eight other parties represented in the National People's Congress form a token opposition that publicly acknowledges the Communist Party's preeminent position as the price for being allowed to exist. Until the 1999 elections, Indonesian legislative politics was dominated by GOLKAR, an official party created and supported by the military and the civil service. Since 1999, the once dominant GOLKAR finds itself in the uncomfortable position of being the second largest of twenty parties but it still dwarfs the smaller parties in the legislature. The Institutional Revolutionary Party (PRI) in Mexico dominated politics there until recently, although less by statutory provision than by skillful manipulation of patronage.

Number of Political Parties in the Lower House of National Legislatures, 1999

Country	Number of Parties
Canada	5
China	9
France	6
Germany	6
Indonesia	20
Italy	8
Japan	8
Mexico	5
Russia	11
United Kingdom	11
United States	3

the Civil War, a majority of Southern whites no longer identify with the Democratic Party, either nationally or within their own state.[73] In all regions, party strengths vary by locality, with central cities almost everywhere heavily Democratic, the swelling suburbs serving as the main source of GOP partisans, and the small town and rural areas split evenly between the two major parties.

Gender. Some political scientists argue that the difference in the way men and women vote first emerged in 1920, when newly enfranchised women registered overwhelmingly as Republicans. It was not until the 1980 presidential election, however, that a

Longman
Participate.com
2.0
Comparative
**Comparing
Political
Parties**

noticeable and possibly significant *gender gap* emerged. This time, the Democratic Party was the apparent beneficiary. While Ronald Reagan trounced incumbent Democratic President Jimmy Carter, he did so with the votes of only 46 percent of the women, compared with 54 percent of the men.

This gender gap continues to persist at all levels of elections. In 1990 exit polls conducted after seventy races revealed a gender gap in 61 percent of the races analyzed. In 1992, as in previous elections, more voters were women (54 percent) than men (46 percent). Again, more women—47 percent—voted for the Democrat (Clinton) than men—41 percent. Among working women the gap was even more pronounced—51 percent voted for Clinton, only 31 percent for George Bush.

In 2000, the gender gap persisted. Women favored Gore by anything from a seven- to a twelve-point margin in polls taken during the summer leading up to the Democratic and Republican conventions, while men favored Bush by margins ranging from eight to sixteen points. Two months later, the largest gender gap in the nation's history was recorded. While men split their vote evenly between the two candidates (Bush received 45 percent of the male vote and Gore 44 percent), according to exit polls women supported Clinton by a 54–37 margin!

In 2000, women preferred Gore by a fairly constant margin that hovered around seven points throughout the last two months of the election. Men clearly favored Bush, although the gap between his and Gore's preference among men closed from a high of 17 points in October to a mere 9 on Election Day. One of the biggest challenges then facing Republicans is how to gain the support of women without alienating their male base. Besides abortion and women's rights issues, female concerns for peace and social compassion may provide much of the gap's distance. For instance, women are usually much less likely than men to favor American military action, and they are less inclined to support cuts in government funding of social welfare programs. This is not, however, the only explanation for the gender gap. One recent study has pointed the finger not at Republican Party difficulties in attracting female voters, but rather at the Democratic Party's inability to attract the votes of males. In other words, the gender gap exists because of the lack of support for the Democratic Party among men, and the corresponding male preference for the Republican Party, stemming from the same differences in opinions about social welfare and military issues identified above.[74]

Race and Ethnicity.   African Americans are the most dramatically different population subgroup in party terms. The 80-percent-plus advantage they offer the Democrats dwarfs the edge given to either party by any other segment of the electorate, and their proportion of strong Democrats (about 40 percent) is three times that of whites. African Americans account almost entirely for the slight lead in party affiliation that Democrats normally enjoy over Republicans, since the GOP has recently been able to attract a narrow plurality of whites to its standard. Perhaps as a reflection of the massive party chasm separating blacks and whites, the two races differ greatly on many policy issues, with blacks overwhelmingly on the liberal side and whites closer to the conservative pole. Two recent studies of African American voting behavior show this, contending that whites of middle to upper income are most concerned with issues of the economy and defense, while blacks of all income levels nearly uniformly identify health care and problems of the poor as their key voting issues. Both Michael Dawson and Louis Bolce therefore conclude that while whites tend to vote differently depending on their socio-economic class interest, African Americans' policy concerns are the same regardless of their socio-economic class. The belief of most blacks that their fate is linked causes upper income blacks to vote the same as lower income blacks. Whites see no such class-based obligation.[75] An exception, incidentally, is abortion, where religious beliefs may lead African Americans to the more conservative stance. The much smaller population group of Hispanics supplements this group as a Democratic stalwart; by more than three to one, Hispanics prefer the Democratic label. An exception is the Cuban-American population, whose anti–Fidel Castro tilt leads to Republicanism.

Age.   Young people are once again becoming more Democratic. Polls in 1972 indicated that the group of eighteen- to twenty-four-year-olds, and particularly students, was the only age group to support Democratic presidential nominee George McGovern. But by the 1990s the eighteen-to-twenty-four-year-old age group was the most Republican of all. Much of this margin was derived from strong student affiliation with the Republicans. Perhaps because of the bad economy from 1990 to 1992, which limited job availability for college graduates, young people swung back to the Democrats in 1992. Bill Clinton ran strongly among eighteen- to twenty-four-year-olds, and they were among his best groups in the electorate. In 2000, Gore and Bush split the young vote fairly evenly in the mid-40-percent range, while Green Party candidate Ralph Nader not suprisingly found his best support among the under-30s, from whom he managed to secure around 8 percent of the vote.

Social and Economic Factors.   Some traditional strengths and weaknesses persist for each party by occupation, income, and education. The GOP remains predominant among executives, professionals, and white-collar workers, whereas the Democrats lead substantially among blue-collar workers and the unemployed. Labor union members are also Democratic by two-and-a-half to one. The more conservative, retired population leans Republican. Women who do not work outside the home are less liberal and Democratic than those who do. Occupation, income, and education are closely related, of course, so many of the same partisan patterns can be detected in all three classifications. Democratic support usually drops steadily as one climbs the income scale. Similarly, as years of education increase, identification with the Republican Party climbs; in graduate school, however, the Democrats rally a bit and only narrowly trail GOP partisans.

Religion.   The party preferences by religion are also traditional, but with modern twists. Protestants—especially Methodists, Presbyterians, and Episcopalians—favor the Republicans, whereas Catholics and, even more so, Jews are predominantly Democratic in affiliation. Decreased polarization is apparent all around, though.[76] Democrats have made inroads among many Protestant denominations over the past three decades, and Republicans can now sometimes claim up to 25 percent of the Jewish population and nearly 40 percent of the Catholics. Recent studies have confirmed this, finding empirical evidence of liberal Protestants leaving their traditional home in the Republican Party, and conservative Catholics and conservative Protestants remaining relatively stable, if not voting more for the Republicans, between 1960 and 1992.[77] The "born again" Christians, who have received much attention in recent years, are somewhat less Republican than commonly believed. The GOP usually has just about a 10 percent edge among them, primarily because so many blacks classify themselves as members of this group.

Marital Status.   Even marital status reveals something about partisan affiliation. People who are married, a traditionally more conservative group, and people who have never married, a segment weighted toward the premarriage young who currently lean toward the Republicans, are closely divided in party loyalty. But the widowed are Democratic in nature, probably because there are many more widows than widowers; in this, the gender gap is again expressing itself. Proof of the "marriage gap" is found in a study that determined married people vote 10–15 percent more for Republicans than their unmarried counterparts. This difference, the study says, is key, for the proportion of unmarried people, including divorcees, has doubled since 1964.[78] The divorced and the separated, who may be experiencing economic hardship and appear to be more liberal than the married population, are a substantially Democratic group.

Ideology.   Ideologically, there are few surprises. Lending credence to the belief that both parties are now relatively distinct philosophically, liberals are overwhelmingly Democratic and conservatives are staunchly Republican in most surveys and opinion studies.

As party identification has weakened, so, too, has the likelihood that voters will cast ballots predictably and regularly for their party's nominees. (Chapter 13 discusses this in some detail.) In the present day, as at the founding of the republic, Americans are simply not wedded to the idea or the reality of political parties. Said one Democratic pollster: "It took a lot of years for the trust and loyalty to dissipate, and it will take a lot of years to bring it back."[79] If this is true, then the dealigning patterns we have witnessed in recent times are likely to remain the norm in the foreseeable future.

PARTISAN ALIGNMENTS

While the independent or third-party candidate is often talked about as a new phenomenon, most of the presidential elections since 1832 have included a third-party or independent candidate. Unfortunately for today's hopefuls, no route to the White House has proved more daunting than that of the independent candidate. No one has ever made it all the way; in fact, no one has ever even come close. Since 1831, only eight independent or third-party candidates have obtained more than 10 percent of the popular vote. Of the eight individuals who have broken the 10 percent plateau, the high-water mark was set by the former Republican president Theodore Roosevelt in 1912. Running as a representative of the Progressive "Bull Moose" Party, Roosevelt won 88 electoral votes and 27.4 percent of the popular vote. Twelve years later Robert LaFollette, also running as a Progressive, garnered 16.6 percent of the popular vote. But from 1924 to 1992, no independent or third-party candidate, save for George Wallace in 1968, was able to surpass the 10 percent mark. Furthermore, if you were to add every electoral vote that went for anyone other than a nominee of the Democratic or Republican party in the twentieth century, the total would still fall short of the 270 needed to win a single election!

In 1992, Texas billionaire Ross Perot spent $60 million of his personal fortune and won nearly one in five votes. In 1996, several individuals considered following his lead (for example, Harry Browne of the Libertarian Party and consumer advocate Ralph Nader of the Green Party) but only Perot, in his second attempt, came close to mounting a serious third-party challenge. In 2000, Ralph Nader hoped to break the 5 percent barrier but fell short by several points, due clearly to the remarkable closeness of the presidential contest, in which every vote for one of the two major-party candidates carried extra weight.

While some political pundits, focusing on the fact that a growing number of voters deem themselves "independents," have openly predicted the demise of Democratic and Republican dominance of the presidential selection process and the concurrent rise of a "third way," before we rush to support these opinions, we must remember that independent and third-party candidacies collide head-on with some forces of modern history:

- Voters tend to flirt with independent candidates early in the election process, but they routinely return to the two-party fold by late fall.
- In the twentieth century, only thirteen states have voted for a third-party candidate even once, and none have since 1968. Theodore Roosevelt proved to be the most successful, carrying six states; in 1980 John Anderson failed to carry any, as did Perot in 1992 and 1996, and Nader in 2000.
- Independent or third-party candidates suffer from a "can't win" syndrome. Voters tell pollsters that they like the non-major-party candidate but ultimately decide not to cast their vote for him or her if they suspect the candidate cannot win.
- Raising money and getting on the ballot in all fifty states poses a significant obstacle to third-party and independent candidates.

Over the course of our country's history, these hurdles have proved daunting to independent and third-party challengers. Thus, for the time being, we might conclude that until a charismatic, moderate, well-heeled candidate who appeals to a wide array of voters emerges and steals the show from the usual stars, independent and third-party candidates are most likely doomed to failure. The hurdles of history await such a challenger.

Continuity & Change

The Rise and Fall of the Reform Party

In 1992, the economy was in a slump and voters were angry. Their discontent coalesced behind the Reform Party, in the form of party founder Ross Perot's presidential candidacy. Perot announced that he would run for president if citizens would get the necessary signatures to the petitions required to put him on the ballot in every state, and from this populist beginning, his clever and idiosyncratic campaign was as unconventional as any of the twentieth century. In the end, Perot gained an astonishing 19 percent of the popular vote and the Reform Party became a major player in American politics. Unfortunately for Perot, the economy had improved by 1996 and his message, falling on prosperous ears, earned him only 8 percent of the vote. Jesse Ventura's successful Reform Party bid for the Minnesota governorship gave the party a boost in 1998, but his departure from the party a few years later clearly stole back that energy. Internecine struggles among various contenders to be the party's 2000 presidential nomination—ultimately and preposterously won by Pat Buchanan—unmistakably signaled the end of the Reform Party, which was promptly confirmed at the polls.

But in 2000, the dramatic change in the fortunes of the Reform Party was matched by a very significant sign of continuity in the role of a third party in American politics. Just as Perot's 19 percent of the popular vote may have deprived George Bush of some crucial votes against newcomer Bill Clinton in 1992, so did Green Party candidate Ralph Nader's share of the vote likely play a tiny but critical role in taking the 2000 election from Clinton's vice president, Al Gore, and giving it to George Bush's son, George W. Bush. Nader's 3 percent of the popular vote was only a fraction of Perot's record, but the unprecedented closeness of the election meant that every vote had exceptional importance in key states such as Florida. Had Nader's third-party appeal cost Gore only a few hundred votes less in Florida, the 2000 election might have told a very different story.

Despite the decline and fall of the Reform Party, the rise of the Green Party offers hope to those who believe the American system needs a strong third party. The Green Party may fair better than previous third parties because it seems to recognize that the only way to build a party is from the ground up. In the near future, Green Party leaders are likely to focus not so much on the presidential races as on local races, for city councils and resources management officials, in more liberal areas across the country, including New Mexico, California, Oregon, Washington, Wisconsin, Vermont, and Minnesota. So while a changing state of third-party candidates rises and falls but rarely attains to the highest office, the existence of third parties continues to play an erratic and unpredictable, but very important, role in American politics.

1. Many people would argue that America is currently suffering from a political disease in which there is a real or perceived gap between our political leaders and the electorate, between the obvious need for action and strong, effective, and prompt action itself. What connection, if any, do you find between our traditional binary (two-party) political system and the current political malaise?
2. Despite their best efforts, no third-party candidate has ever been elected to the White House. Would you ever consider voting for a third-party candidate, even if you didn't think he or she had a good chance to win? Why, and what is the significance of such a vote?

Cast Your Vote. Do you think a third party candidate will win the presidential election in your lifetime? To cast your vote, go to **www.ablongman.com/oconnor**

SUMMARY

A political party is a group of office holders, candidates, activists, and voters who identify with a group label and seek to elect to public office individuals who run under that label. They encompass three separate components: (1) the governmental party comprises office holders and candidates who run under the party's banner; (2) the electoral party comprises the workers and activists who staff the party's formal organization; (3) the party in the electorate refers to the voters who consider themselves to be allied or associated with the party. In this chapter we have made the following points:

1. **What Is a Political Party?**
   The goal of American political parties is to win office. This objective is in keeping with the practical nature of Americans and the country's longstanding aversion to most ideologically driven, "purist" politics.

2. **The Evolution of American Party Democracy**

The evolution of U.S. political parties has been remarkably smooth, and the stability of the Democratic and Republican groupings, despite name changes, is a wonder, considering all the social and political tumult in U.S. history.

3. **The Roles of the American Parties**

For 150 years, the two-party system has served as the mechanism American society uses to organize and resolve social and political conflict. The Democratic and Republican parties, through lengthy nominating processes, provide a sort of screening mechanism for those who aspire to the presidency, helping to weed out unqualified individuals, expose and test candidates' ideas on important policy questions, and ensure a measure of long-term continuity and accountability.

4. **One-Partyism and Third-Partyism**

The U.S. party system is uniquely a two-party system. While periods of one-partyism, third-partyism, or independent activism (such as the Perot phenomenon) can prevail, the greatest proportion of all federal, state, and local elections are contests between the Republican and Democratic parties only.

5. **The Basic Structure of American Political Parties**

While the distinctions might not be as clear today as they were two or three decades ago, the basic structure of the major parties remains simple and pyramidal. The state and local parties are more important than the national ones, though campaign technologies and fund raising concentrated in Washington are invigorating the national party committees.

6. **The Party in Government**

Political parties are not restricted to their role as grass-roots organizations of voters; they also have another major role *inside* government institutions. The party in government comprises the office holders and candidates who run under the party's banner.

7. **The Modern Transformation of Party Organization**

Political parties have moved from the labor-intensive, person-to-person operations of the first half of the century toward the utilization of modern high technologies and communication strategies. Nevertheless, the capabilities of the party organizations vary widely from place to place.

8. **The Party in the Electorate**

The party in the electorate refers to the voters who consider themselves to be allied or associated with the party. This is the most significant element of the political party, providing the foundation for the organizational and governmental parties.

KEY TERMS

civil service laws, p. 424
coalition, p. 426
coattail effect, p. 443
direct primary, p. 424
dualist theory, p. 433
governmental party, p. 419
issue-oriented politics, p. 424

machine, p. 422
national convention, p. 436
national party platform, p. 428
one-partyism, p. 430
organizational party, p. 419
party identification, p. 452
party in the electorate, p. 419

patronage, p. 424
political consultant, p. 425
political party, p. 418
proportional representation, p. 433
spoils system, p. 424
third-partyism, p. 430
ticket-split, p. 424

SELECTED READINGS

Abramowitz, Alan. *Senate Elections.* Ann Arbor: University of Michigan Press, 1992.

Aldrich, John Herbert. *Why Parties? The Origin and Transformation of Political Parties in America.* Chicago: University of Chicago Press, 1995.

Brady, David W. *Critical Elections and Congressional Policy-Making.* Stanford, Calif.: Stanford University Press, 1988.

Broder, David S. *The Party's Over.* New York: Harper & Row, 1971.

Ceaser, James W. *Reforming the Reformers: A Critical Analysis of the Presidential Selection Process.* Cambridge, Mass.: Ballinger, 1982.

Chambers, William Nisbet, and Walter Dean Burnham, eds. *The American Party Systems: Stages of Political Development,* 2nd ed. New York: Oxford University Press, 1975.

Cox, Gary, and Mathew McCubbins. *Legislative Leviathan: Party Government in the House.* Berkeley: University of California Press, 1993.

Epstein, Leon. *Political Parties in the American Mold.* Madison: University of Wisconsin Press, 1986.

Fiorina, Morris P. *Divided Government.* Boston: Allyn and Bacon, 1996.

Gierzynski, Anthony. *Legislative Party Campaign Committees in the American States.* Lexington: University of Kentucky Press, 1992.

Kayden, Xandra, and Eddie Mahe. *The Party Goes On.* New York: Basic Books, 1985.

Key, V. O., Jr., *Politics, Parties, and Pressure Groups,* 5th ed. New York: Thomas Y. Crowell, 1964.

Klinkner, Philip A. *The Losing Parties: Out-Party National Committees, 1956–1993.* New Haven, Conn.: Yale University Press, 1994.

Maisel, L. Sandy, ed. *The Parties Respond.* 2d ed. Boulder, Colo.: Westview Press, 1994.

Mayhew, David R. *Placing Parties in American Politics.* Princeton, N.J.: Princeton University Press, 1986.

Milkis, Sidney M. *The President and the Parties: The Transformation of the American Party System Since the New Deal.* New York: Oxford University Press, 1993.

Patterson, Kelly D., *Political Parties and the Maintenance of Liberal Democracy.* New York, Columbia University Press, 1996.

Polsby, Nelson W. *Consequences of Party Reform.* New York: Oxford University Press, 1983.

Pomper, Gerald M. *Passions and Interests: Political Party Concepts of American Democracy.* Lawrence: University Press of Kansas, 1992.

Price, David E. *Bringing Back the Parties.* Washington, D.C.: CQ Press, 1984.

Ranney, Austin. *Curing the Mischiefs of Faction: Party Reform in America.* Berkeley: University of California Press, 1975.

Reichley, James. *The Life of the Parties: A History of American Political Parties.* New York: Free Press, 1992.

Riordan, William L., ed. *Plunkitt of Tammany Hall.* New York: Dutton, 1963.

Rohde, David W. *Parties and Leaders in the Postreform House.* Chicago: University of Chicago Press, 1991.

Sabato, Larry J. *The Party's Just Begun: Shaping Political Parties for America's Future.* Glenview, Ill.: Scott, Foresman/Little, Brown, 1988.

Schattschneider, E. E. *Party Government.* New York: Holt, Rinehart and Winston, 1942.

Shafer, Byron E. *Quiet Revolution: The Struggle for the Democratic Party and the Shaping of Post-Reform Politics.* New York: Russell Sage Foundation, 1983.

Shea, Daniel M. *Transforming Democracy: Legislative Campaign Committees and Political Parties.* Albany: SUNY Press, 1995.

Sorauf, Frank J., and Paul Allen Beck. *Party Politics in America,* 7th ed. New York: Harper/Collins, 1995.

Sundquist, James L. *Dynamics of the Party System,* rev. ed. Washington, D.C.: Brookings Institution, 1983.

Wattenberg, Martin P. *The Decline of American Political Parties, 1952–1994.* Cambridge, Mass.: Harvard University Press, 1996.

NOTES

1. E. E. Schattschneider, *Party Government* (New York: Holt, Rinehart and Winston, 1942), 1. This book stands as one of the most eloquent arguments for a strong political party system ever penned.

2. For more information on this topic, see Larry J. Sabato, *The Party's Just Begun: Shaping Political Parties for America's Future* (Glenview, Ill.: Scott, Foresman/Little, Brown, 1988).

3. For a sampling of some alternative definitions of political parties put forth by political scientists, see Paul Allen Beck, *Party Politics in America,* 8th ed. (New York: Longman, 1998), 8–9.

4. This conception of a political party was originally put forth by V. O. Key in *Politics, Parties, and Pressure Groups* (New York, Crowell, 1958).

5. Joseph Schlesinger, *Political Parties and the Winning of Office* (Ann Arbor: University of Michigan, 1991). Mildred A. Schwartz, *The Party Network: The Robust Organization of Illinois Republicans* (Madison: University of Wisconsin, 1990).

6. John H. Aldrich, *Why Parties? The Origin and Transformation of Party Politics in America* (Chicago: University of Chicago Press, 1995).

7. The National Republican (one forerunner of the Whig Party) and the Anti-Masonic parties each had held more limited conventions in 1831.

8. By contrast, Great Britain did not develop truly national, broad-based parties until the 1870s.

9. Joel H. Silbey, "The Rise and Fall of American Parties, 1790–2000," in L. Sandy Maisel, ed., *The Parties Respond, Changes in American Parties and Campaigns,* 3rd ed. (Boulder, Colo.: Westview, 1998), 11.

10. See *Historical Statistics of the United States: Colonial Times to 1970,* part 2, series Y-27-28 (Washington, D.C.: Government Printing Office, 1975), based on unpublished data prepared by Walter Dean Burnham.

11. Frank J. Sorauf, *Party Politics in America,* 5th ed. (Boston: Little, Brown, 1984), 22.

12. Leon Esptein, *Political Parties in the American Mold* (Madison: University of Wisconsin, 1986), 135. Paul Allen Beck, *Party Politics in America,* 8th ed. (New York: Longman, 1998), 75.

13. Tom Watson, "All Powerful Machine of Yore Endures in New York's Nassau," *Congressional Quarterly Weekly Report* 43 (August 17, 1985), 1623–25.

14. Lee Sigelman, Paul J. Wahlbeck, and Emmett H. J. Buell Jr., "Vote Choice and the Preference for Divided Government: Lessons of 1992," *American Journal of Political Science* 41 (July 1997): 879–94. Barry C. Burden and David C. Kimball, "A New Approach to the Study of Ticket-Splitting," *American Political Science Review* 92 (September 1998): 533–44. Paul Frymer, Terri Bimes, and Thomas Kim, "Party Elites, Ideological Voters, and Divided Party Government," *Legislative Studies Quarterly* 22 (May 1997): 195–216.

15. Robert Boston, "How to Eat an Elephant: The Christian Coalition's Precinct-Based Political Strategy," *Church and State* 52 (November 1999): 9.

16. Schattschneider, *Party Government,* 48.

17. Philip A. Klinkner, *The Losing Parties: Out-Party National Committees, 1956–1993* (New Haven, Conn.: Yale University Press, 1994).

18. Kim Hill and Jan Leighley, "Political Parties and Class Mobilization in Contemporary United States Elections," *American Journal of Political Science* 40 (August 1996): 787–804.

19. M. V. Hood, Quentin Kidd, and Irwin L. Morris, "Of Byrds and Bumpers: Using Democratic Senators to Analyze Political Change in the South, 1960–1995," *American Journal of Political Science* 43 (April 1999): 465–87.

20. Kelly D. Patterson, *Political Parties and the Maintenance of Liberal Democracy* (New York, Columbia University Press, 1996).

21. As quoted in Ken Bode, "Hero or Demagogue?" *New Republic* 195 (March 3, 1986): 28.

22. Gerald M. Pomper with Susan Lederman, *Elections in America,* 2nd ed. (New York: Longman, 1980), 145–50, 167–73.

23. See David E. Price, *Bringing Back the Parties* (Washington, D.C.: CQ Press, 1984), 284–88.

24. See, for example, Sarah McCally Morehouse, "Legislatures and Political Parties," *State Government* 59 (1976): 23.

25. Pomper with Lederman, *Elections in America*, 150.

26. L. Sandy Maisel, "The Platform-Writing Process: Candidate-Centered Platforms in 1992," *Political Science Quarterly* 108 (Winter 1993–94): 671–98.

27. Walter Dean Burnham, *Critical Elections and the Mainsprings of American Politics* (New York: Norton, 1970), 132–33.

28. See V. O. Key Jr., *American State Politics: An Introduction* (New York: Knopf, 1956).

29. See V. O. Key Jr., *Southern Politics in State and Nation* (New York: Knopf, 1949).

30. See Bibby et al., "Parties in State Politics," in Virginia Gray, Herbert Jacob, and Kenneth Vines, eds., *Politics in the American States*, 4th ed. (Boston: Little, Brown, 1983), Table 3.3, 66; also see Larry J. Sabato, *Goodbye to Good-Time Charlie: The American Governorship Transformed*, 2d ed. (Washington, D.C.: CQ Press, 1983), 116–38.

31. Sorauf, *Party Politics in America*, 51.

32. Todd Donovan, Shaun Bowler, and Tammy Terrio, "Support for Third Parties in California," *American Politics Quarterly* 28 (January 2000): 50–71.

33. Jeffrey Koch, "The Perot Candidacy and Attitudes Toward Government and Politics," *Political Research Quarterly* 51 (March 1998): 141–54.

34. Christian Collet and Martin P. Wattenberg, "Strategically Unambitious: Minor Party and Independent Candidates in the 1996 Congressional Elections," in John C. Green and Daniel M. Shea, eds. *The State of the Parties: The Changing Role of Contemporary American Parties*, 3rd ed. (Lanham, Md.: Rowman and Littlefield, 1999)

35. Dean Lacy and Barry C. Burden, "The Vote-Stealing and Turnover Effects of Ross Perot in the 1992 U.S. Presidential Election," *American Journal of Political Science* 43 (January 1999): 233–55.

36. Mark J. Hetherington, "The Effect of Political Trust on the Presidential Vote, 1968–1996," *American Political Science Review* 93 (June 1999): 311–26.

37. Paul S. Herrnson, "National Party Organizations at Century's End," in L. Sandy Maisel, ed. *The Parties Respond, Changes in American Parties and Campaigns*, 3rd ed. (Boulder, Colo.: Westview, 1998).

38. Cornelius P. Cotter, James L. Gibson, John F. Bibby, and Robert J. Huckshorn, *Party Organizations in American Politics* (Pittsburgh: University of Pittsburgh Press, 1989).

39. Paul Allen Beck, Russell J. Dalton, Audrey Haynes, and Robert Huckfeldt, "Local Party Organizations in the 1992 Presidential Elections," paper presented at the 1993 Annual Meeting of the Southern Political Science Association. See also Paul Allen Beck, Russell J. Dalton, Audrey Haynes, and Robert Huckfeldt, "Party Efforts at the Grass Roots: Local Presidential Campaigning in 1992," paper presented at the 1994 Annual Meeting of the Midwest Political Science Association.

40. John J. Coleman, "Party Organization Strength and Public Support for Parties," *American Journal of Political Science* 40 (August 1996), 805–24.

41. Anthony Gierzynski, *Legislative Party Campaign Committees in the American States* (Lexington: University of Kentucky Press, 1992).

42. Anthony Gierzynski and David A. Breaux, "The Financing Role of Parties," in Joel A. Thompson and Gary Moncrief, eds. *Campaign Finance in State Legislative Elections* (Washington D.C.: Congressional Quarterly Press, 1998).

43. Daniel M. Shea, *Transforming Democracy: Legislative Campaign Committees and Political Parties* (Albany: SUNY Press, 1995).

44. John F. Bibby, "Party Networks: National-State Integration, Allied Groups, and Issue Activists," in John C. Green and Daniel M. Shea, eds. *The State of the Parties: The Changing Role of Contemporary American Parties*, 3rd. ed. (Lanham, Md.: Rowman and Littlefield, 1999).

45. Bibby, "Party Networks."

46. Steven S. Smith and Eric D. Lawrence, "Party Control of Committees in the Republican Congress," in Lawrence C. Dodd and Bruce I. Oppenheimer, eds., *Congress Reconsidered*, 6th ed. (Washington, D.C.: Congressional Quarterly Press, 1997).

47. Such cases are few, but a deterrent nonetheless. Several U.S. senators were expelled from the Republican Caucus in 1925 for having supported the Progressive candidate for president the previous year. In 1965 two Southern House Democrats lost all their committee seniority because of their 1964 endorsement of GOP presidential nominee Barry Goldwater, as did another Southerner in 1968 for backing George Wallace's third-party candidacy. In early 1983 the House Democratic Caucus removed Texas Representative Phil Gramm from his Budget Committee seat because of his "disloyalty" in working more closely with Republican committee members than with his own party leaders. (Gramm resigned his seat in Congress, changed parties, and was reelected as a Republican. He then used the controversy to propel himself into the U.S. Senate in 1984.)

48. Gregory R. Thorson, "Divided Government and the Passage of Partisan Legislation, 1947–1990," *Political Research Quarterly* 51 (September 1998): 751–65.

49. David W. Rohde, *Parties and Leaders in the Postreform House*. (Chicago: University of Chicago Press, 1991). John A. Aldrich and David W. Rohde, "The Transition to Republican Rule in the House: Implications for Theories of Congressional Politics," *Political Science Quarterly* 112 (1997–98), 541–67.

50. Joseph A. Schlesinger, "The New American Political Party," *American Political Science Review* 79 (1985): 1168.

51. Kevin M. Leyden and Stephen A. Borrelli, "An Investment in Goodwill: Party Contributions and Party Unity Among U.S. House Members in the 1980s," *American Politics Quarterly* 22 (1994): 421–52.

52. Richard A. Clucas, "Party Contributions and the Influence of Campaign Committee Chairs on Roll-Call Voting," *Legislative Studies Quarterly* 22 (1997): 179–94. David M. Cantor and Paul S. Herrnson, "Party Campaign Activity and Party Unity in the U.S. House of Representatives," *Legislative Studies Quarterly* 22 (1997): 393–415.

53. Rhodes Cook, "Reagan Nurtures His Adopted Party to Strength," *Congressional Quarterly Weekly* 43 (September 28, 1985): 1927–30.

54. George C. Edwards III, *Presidential Influence in Congress* (New York: Freeman, 1980); and Herbert M. Kritzer and Robert B. Eubank, "Presidential Coattails Revisited: Partisanship and Incumbency Effects," *American Journal of Political Science* 23 (1979): 615–26.

55. Lyn Ragsdale, "The Fiction of Congressional Elections as Presidential Events," *American Politics Quarterly* 8 (1980): 375–98;

and Thomas E. Mann and Raymond E. Wolfinger, "Candidates and Parties in Congressional Elections," *American Political Science Review* 74 (1980): 617–32.

56. Gregory R. Thorson and Stephen J. Stambough, "Anti-Incumbency and the 1992 Elections: The Changing Face of Presidential Coattails," *Journal of Politics* 57 (February 1995): 210–20.

57. Sidney M. Milkis, *The President and the Parties: The Transformation of the American Party System Since the New Deal* (New York: Oxford University Press, 1993).

58. See S. Sidney Ulmer, "The Political Party Variable on the Michigan Supreme Court." *Journal of Public Law* 11 (1962): 352–62; Stuart Nagel, "Political Party Affiliation and Judges' Decisions," *American Political Science Review* 55 (1961): 843–50; David W. Adamany, "The Party Variable in Judges' Voting: Conceptual Notes and a Case Study," *American Political Science Review* 63 (1969): 57–73; Sheldon Goldman, "Voting Behavior on the United States Courts of Appeals, 1961–1964," *American Political Science Review* 60 (1966): 374–83; and Robert A. Carp and C. K. Rowland, *Policymaking and Politics in the Federal District Courts* (Knoxville: University of Tennessee Press, 1983).

59. Randall D. Lloyd, "Separating Partisanship from Party in Judicial Research: Reapportionment in the U.S. District Courts," *American Political Science Review* 89 (June 1995): 413–20.

60. The Farmer-Labor Party did survive in a sense; having endured a series of defeats, it merged in 1944 with the Democrats, and Democratic candidates still officially bear the standard of the Democratic-Farmer-Labor (DFL) Party. At about the same time, also having suffered severe electoral reversals, the Progressives stopped nominating candidates in Wisconsin. The party's members either returned to the Republican Party, from which it had split early in the century, or became Democrats.

61. Morehouse, "Legislatures and Political Parties," 19–24.

62. Senator George J. Mitchell (D–Maine), as quoted in *The Washington Post* (February 9, 1986): A14.

63. Janet M. Box-Steffensmeier, "A Dynamic Analysis of the Role of War Chests in Campaign Strategy," *American Journal of Political Science* 40 (May 1996): 352–71.

64. As quoted in a speech to the RNC by the Associated Press, January 24, 1987, and in *The Washington Post* (January 24, 1987): A3.

65. Alan Gerber, "Estimating the Effect of Campaign Spending on Senate Election Outcomes Using Instrumental Variables," *American Political Science Review* 92 (June 1998): 401–12.

66. Tim Kenworthy, "Collaring Colleagues for Cash," *The Washington Post* (14 May 1991): A17.

67. Jennifer Babson and Beth Donovan, "GOP Fundraiser Raises Sights and Tightens Belt," *Congressional Quarterly Weekly Report* (2 April 1994): 809–11.

68. Bruce A. Larson, "Ambition and Money in the U.S. House of Representatives: Analyzing Campaign Contributions from Incumbents' Leadership PACs and Reelection Committees" (Ph.D. dissertation, University of Virginia, 1998). Paul S. Herrnson, "Money and Motives: Spending in House Elections," in Lawrence C. Dodd and Bruce I. Oppenheimer, eds., *Congress Reconsidered*, 6th ed. (Washington, DC: Congressional Quarterly Press, 1997). Bibby, "Party Networks."

69. Michael B. McKuen, Robert S. Erikson, and James A. Stimson, "Macropartisanship," *American Political Science Review*, 83 (December 1989): 1125–42.

70. Donald Green, Bradley Palmquist, and Eric Schickler, "Macropartisanship: A Replication and Critique," *American Political Science Review* 92 (December 1998): 883–900.

71. See Steven E. Finkel and Howard A. Scarrow, "Party Identification and Party Enrollment: The Difference and the Consequence," *Journal of Politics* 47 (May 1985): 620–42.

72. Martin P. Wattenberg, *The Decline of American Political Parties, 1952–1994* (Cambridge, Mass.: Harvard University Press, 1996).

73. Alan I. Abramowitz and Kyle L. Saunders, "Ideological Realignment in the U.S. Electorate," *Journal of Politics* 60 (August 1998): 634–52.

74. Karen M. Kaufmann, and John R. Petrocik, "The Changing Politics of American Men: Understanding the Sources of the Gender Gap," *American Journal of Political Science* 43 (July 1999): 864–87.

75. Michael Dawson, *Behind the Mule: Race and Class in African-American Politics* (Princeton, N.J.: Princeton University Press, 1994). Louis Bolce, Gerald DeMaio, and Douglas Muzzio, "Blacks and the Republican Party: The 20 Percent Solution," *Political Science Quarterly* 107 (Spring 1992): 63–79.

76. The presidential election of 1960 may be an extreme case, but John F. Kennedy's massive support among Catholics and Nixon's less substantial but still impressive backing by Protestants demonstrates the polarization that religion could once produce. See Philip E. Converse, "Religion and Politics: The 1960 Election," in Angus Campbell et al., *Elections and the Political Order* (New York: Wiley, 1966), 96–124.

77. Jeff Manza and Clem Brooks, "The Religious Factor in U.S. Presidential Elections, 1960–1992," *American Journal of Sociology* 103 (July 1997): 38–81.

78. Herbert F. Weisberg, "The Demographics of a New Voting Gap: Marital Differences in American Voting," *Public Opinion Quarterly* 51 (Autumn 1987): 335–43.

79. Richard Benedetto, "Fed-Up Voters in Search of a Better Candidate," *USA Today* (August 11, 1995): A4.

13 Voting and Elections

(REPUBLICAN)
GEORGE W. BUSH - PRESIDENT
DICK CHENEY - VICE PRESIDENT
3➤

(DEMOCRATIC)
AL GORE - PRESIDENT
JOE LIEBERMAN - VICE PRESIDENT
5➤

(LIBERTARIAN)
HARRY BROWNE - PRESIDENT
ART OLIVIER - VICE PRESIDENT
7➤

(GREEN)
RALPH NADER - PRESIDENT
WINONA LaDUKE - VICE PRESIDENT
9➤

(SOCIALIST WORKERS)
JAMES HARRIS - PRESIDENT
MARGARET TROWE - VICE PRESIDENT
11➤

(NATURAL LAW)
JOHN HAGELIN - PRESIDENT
NAT GOLDHABER - VICE PRESIDENT
13➤

◄ 4
(REFORM)
PAT BUCHANAN - PRESIDENT
EZOLA FOSTER - VICE PRESIDENT

◄ 6
(SOCIALIST)
DAVID McREYNOLDS - PRESIDENT
MARY CAL HOLLIS - VICE PRESIDENT

◄ 8
(CONSTITUTION)
HOWARD PHILLIPS - PRESIDENT
J. CURTIS FRAZIER - VICE PRESIDENT

◄10
(WORKERS WORLD)
MONICA MOOREHEAD - PRESIDENT
GLORIA La RIVA - VICE PRESIDENT

WRITE-IN CANDIDATE
To vote for a write-in candidate, follow the
directions on the long stub of your ballot card.

For what should have been a relatively tame election, the 2000 presidential contest turned out to be one of the most historic elections in United States history. The race between Democratic Vice President Al Gore and Texas Governor George W. Bush was not a banner contest because of the charisma of the candidates, the strength of their platforms, or a particularly exciting campaign season. The real drama began to unfold after Election Day, as a near tie between the candidates developed into a near crisis. With the entire country and the rest of the world watching, the election struggle waged for thirty-six days after November 7 as Americans waited to learn who the new chief executive would be. Those who witnessed the 2000 election will never forget the chaos, intrigue, and indecision wrought by it. Historians and analysts likened the election to the fabled 1876 contest between Rutherford B. Hayes and Democrat Samuel L. Tilden, in which Hayes was delivered a controversial win despite clearly losing the popular vote. In addition, 2000 marked the first election since 1888 where the man who would eventually become president did not receive the plurality of the national vote. Gore won the popular vote by about 540,000 votes out of 105 million ballots cast. This amount, incidentally, is about the same as the margin by which Richard Nixon defeated Hubert Humphrey in 1972 and nearly five times the margin by which John F. Kennedy bested Nixon in 1968. But as Americans learned anew in 2000, the popular vote matters much less than the vote of the electors in the electoral college.

With most election prognosticators targeting Florida and its 25 electoral votes as the key to the election, the Sunshine State did not disappoint. Even before all of the polls were closed in Florida, the networks declared Gore the winner of the state. Several hours after calling the state for Gore, then recanting, and announcing Bush the winner, the major media outlets were forced to once again retract their projection, as the election returns showed a margin of less than 1,000 votes between the two candidates. With no precedent to draw on, the country entered a virtually uncharted moment in history and the outcome came down to the judicial system, bouncing from court to court within Florida and eventually ending up in the Supreme Court. In a close 5–4 vote, the justices ruled to shut down manual recount efforts, and accept the votes that were certified by Florida Secretary of State Katherine Harris, a Republican who had been appointed by the Republican governor and brother of the victor, Jeb Bush. The Supreme Court's decision effectively elected George W. Bush the forty-third president of the United States. It was an inauspicious start to a presidential term for Bush, but he was grateful for the decision. The ruling and subsequent victory of Bush was met with mixed reactions. The country had been eager for an outcome and most were just glad the ordeal was over. There was, however, strong resentment from many Democrats, especially African American voters who felt that their vote had been invalidated by overt political maneuvering on the part of the Republicans.

While every race is not as close or as controversial as the 2000 presidential election, each is important in the way it dictates the course that the country will take in the coming years. Whether the contest is for commander-in-chief or county clerk, each represents an opportunity for the voice of the American people to be heard.

Recall for a moment Election Day, November 5, 1996. A plurality of the voting electorate, simply by casting ballots peacefully across a continent-sized nation, reelected or replaced politicians at all levels of government—from the president of the United States, to members of the U.S. Congress, to state legislators. Other countries do not have the luxury of a peaceful transition of political power. We tend to take this process for granted, but in truth it is a marvel. Fortunately, most Americans, though not enough, understand why and how elections serve their interests. Elections take the pulse of average people and gauge their hopes and fears; the study of elections permits us to trace the course of the American revolution over 200 years of voting.

Today the United States of America is a democrat's paradise in many respects, because it probably conducts more elections for more offices more frequently than any nation on earth. Moreover, in recent times the U.S. electorate (those citizens eligible to vote) has been the most universal in the country's history; no longer can one's race or sex or creed prevent participation at the ballot box. But challenges still remain. After all the blood spilled and energy expended to expand the suffrage (as the right to vote is called), little more than half the potentially eligible voters bother to go to the polls!

This chapter focuses on the purposes served by elections, the various kinds of elections held in the United States, and patterns of voting over time. We concentrate in particular on presidential and congressional contests, both of which have rich histories that tell us a great deal about the American people and their changing hopes and needs. We conclude by returning to contemporary presidential elections and addressing some topics of electoral reform.

The home page of Al Gore's presidential campaign Website. Campaign web sites were substantially more widespread and sophisticated in the 2000 election than when they first appeared in 1996. (Photo courtesy: Gore 2000 Campaign)

- First, we will examine the *purposes served by elections,* pointing out that they confer a legitimacy on regimes better than any other method of change.
- Second, we will analyze *different kinds of elections,* including the many different types of elections held at the presidential and congressional levels.
- Third, we will take a closer look at the elements of *presidential elections,* including primaries, conventions, and delegates.
- Fourth, we will explore how *congressional elections,* although they share similarities with presidential elections, are really quite different.
- Fifth, we will discuss *how voters behave* in certain distinct ways and exhibit unmistakable patterns each election cycle.
- Finally, we will present arguments for *reforming the electoral process* for the most powerful official in the world, the president of the United States.

THE PURPOSES SERVED BY ELECTIONS

Both the ballot and the bullet are methods of governmental change around the world, and surely the former is preferable to the latter. Although the United States has not escaped the bullet's awful effects, most change has come to this country through the election process. Regular free elections guarantee mass political action and enable citizens to influence the actions of their government. Election campaigns may often seem unruly, unending, harsh, and even vicious, but imagine the stark alternatives: violence and social disruption. Societies that cannot vote their leaders out of office are left with little choice other than to force them out by means of strikes, riots, or coups d'état.

Popular election confers on a government the legitimacy that it can achieve no other way. Even many authoritarian and Communist systems around the globe recognize this. From time to time, they hold "referenda" to endorse their regimes or one-party elections, even though these so-called elections offer no real choice that would ratify their rule. The symbolism of elections as mechanisms to legitimize change, then, is important, but so is their practical value. After all, elections are the means to fill public offices and staff the government. The voters' choice of candidates and parties helps to organize government as well. Because candidates advocate certain policies, elections also involve a choice of platforms and point the society in certain directions on a wide range of issues, from abortion to civil rights to national defense to the environment.

Regular elections also ensure that government is accountable to the people it serves. At fixed intervals the **electorate,** citizens eligible to vote, is called on to judge those in power. If the judgment is favorable, and the incumbents are reelected, the office holders may continue their policies with renewed resolve. Should the incumbents be defeated and their challengers elected, however, a change in policies will likely result. Either way, the winners will claim a **mandate** (literally, a command) from the people to carry out their platform.

Sometimes the claim of a mandate is suspect because voters are not so much endorsing one candidate and his or her beliefs as rejecting his or her opponent. Frequently, this occurs because the electorate is exercising **retrospective judgment;** that is, voters are rendering judgment on the performance of the party in power. This judgment makes sense because voters can evaluate the record of office holders much better than they can predict the future actions of the out-of-power challengers.

At other times, voters might vote using **prospective judgment,** that is, they vote based on what a candidate pledges to do about an issue if elected. This forward-looking approach to choosing candidates voters believe will best serve their interests requires that the electorate examine the views that the rival candidates have on the issues of the day and then cast a ballot for the person they believe will best handle these matters. Unfortunately, prospective voting requires lots of information about issues and candidates. Voters who cast a vote prospectively must be willing to spend a great deal of time seeking out information and learning about issues and how each candidate stands on them. As the authors of a classic study on the American electorate note, three requirements exist in order for voters to engage in prospective voting: (1) voters must have an opinion on an issue, (2) voters must have an idea of what action, if any, the government is taking on the issue, and (3) voters must see a difference between the two parties on the issue.[1] Only a small minority of voters, the authors concluded, could meet these requirements, although scholars studying more recent elections have found voters better equipped to engage in prospective voting.[2] Consider for a moment how voters retrospectively and prospectively judged recent presidential administrations in reaching their ballot decisions:

- *1972:* The American people were satisfied with Nixon's stewardship of foreign affairs, especially his good relationship with the Soviet Union, the diplomatic opening of China, and the "Vietnamization" of the war. Thus they retrospectively judged his administration to have been a success and looked to the future, believing that he, rather than Democrat George McGovern, could best lead the country. The Watergate scandal (involving Nixon's coverup of his campaign committee's bugging of the Democrats' national headquarters) was only in its infancy, and the president was rewarded with a forty-nine-state sweep.

- *1976:* This year retrospective judgments clearly prevailed over prospective considerations. Despite confusion about Jimmy Carter's real philosophy and intentions, the relatively unknown Georgia Democrat was elected president as voters held President Gerald R. Ford responsible for an economic recession and deplored his pardon of Richard M. Nixon for Watergate crimes.

- *1980:* Burdened by difficult economic times and the Iranian hostage crisis (one year before Election Day, Iranian militants had seized fifty-three Americans, whom they held until January 20, 1981, Inauguration Day), Carter became a one-term president as the electorate rejected the Democrat's perceived weak leadership. At age sixty-nine, Ronald Reagan was not viewed as the ideal replacement by many voters, and neither did a majority agree with some of his conservative principles. But the retrospective judgment on Carter was so harsh and the prospective outlook of four

electorate
Citizens eligible to vote.

mandate
A command, indicated by an electorate's votes, for the elected officials to carry out their platforms.

retrospective judgment
A voter's evaluation of the performance of the party in power.

prospective judgment
A voter's evaluation of a candidate based on what he or she pledges to do about an issue if elected.

more years under his stewardship so glum that an imperfect alternative was considered preferable to another term of the Democrat.

■ *1984:* A strong economic recovery from a midterm recession and an image of strength derived from a defense buildup and a successful military venture in Grenada combined to produce a satisfied electorate that retrospectively and prospectively decided to grant Ronald Reagan four more years. The result: A forty-nine-state landslide reelection for Reagan over Jimmy Carter's vice president, Walter Mondale.

■ *1988:* Continued satisfaction with Reagan, a product of strong economic expansion and superpower summitry, produced an electoral endorsement of Reagan's vice president, George Bush. Bush was seen as Reagan's understudy and natural successor; the Democratic nominee, Michael Dukakis, offered too few convincing reasons to alter the voters' considered retrospective judgment.

■ *1992:* A prolonged economic recession and weak growth in jobs plus Ross Perot's candidacy, which split the Republican base, denied a second term to George Bush, despite his many significant triumphs in foreign policy (the Persian Gulf War victory and arms control agreements, for example). In the end, voters decided to vote retrospectively, gambling on a little-known governor, Bill Clinton, rather than order up more of the same by reelecting Bush.

■ *1996:* Similar to 1984, only with the party labels reversed, a healthy economy prompted Americans to retrospectively support President Bill Clinton in his quest for reelection. Voters also looked prospectively at the two candidates and again registered their support for President Clinton. Clinton then received relatively high marks by voters both for his stewardship during the first four years of his administration and his vision for the country's future.

■ *2000:* According to most political models, eight years of peace and record economic prosperity, coupled with the advantage of semi-incumbency, should have worked in favor of Vice President Al Gore. Gore's Clinton-era baggage and questioning of his credibility, however, helped to nullify any advantage over Texas Governor George W. Bush, an opponent with an undistinguished record but no significant liabilities. Ultimately, given the unusual circumstances of the actual election itself, it is difficult to say more precisely to what extent the outcome of the election represents a retrospective or prospective political opinion.

Whether one agrees or disagrees with these election results, there is a rough justice at work here. When parties and presidents please the electorate, they are rewarded; when they preside over hard times, they are punished. A president is usually not responsible for all the good or bad developments that occur on his watch, but the voters nonetheless hold him accountable, not an unreasonable way for citizens to behave in a democracy.

On rare occasions, off-year congressional elections can produce mandates. In 1974 a tidal wave for Democrats produced a mandate to clean up politics after Watergate, while in 1994 Republicans enjoyed a similar wave and claimed a mandate for limiting government.

Controversy over vote counting in the 2000 presidential election brought people to West Palm Beach, Florida, to protest on behalf of Al Gore and George Bush. (Photo courtesy: Kirk Condyles/ Impact Visuals)

DIFFERENT KINDS OF ELECTIONS

So far we have referred mainly to presidential elections, but in the U.S. system, elections come in many varieties.

Primary Elections

In **primary elections,** voters decide which of the candidates within a party will represent the party's ticket in the general elections. The primaries themselves vary in kind. For example, **closed primaries** allow only a party's registered voters to cast a ballot, and **open primaries** allow independents and sometimes members of the other party to participate. (Figure 13.1 shows the states with open and closed primaries for presidential delegate selection.) Closed primaries are considered healthier for the party system ballot because they prevent members of one party from influencing the primaries of the opposition party. Studies of open primaries indicate that **crossover voting**—participation in the primary of a party with which the voter is not affiliated—occurs frequently.[3] On the other hand, little evidence exists that much **raiding** occurs—an *organized* attempt by voters of one party to influence the primary results of the other party.[4] In the **blanket primary,** voters are permitted to vote in either party's primary (but not both) on an office-by-office basis. When none of the candidates in the initial primary secures a majority of the votes, there is a **runoff primary,** a contest between the two candidates with the greatest number of votes. One final type of primary, used in Nebraska, Louisiana, and hundreds of cities large and small across America, is the **nonpartisan primary,** which is used to select candidates without

primary election
Election in which voters decide which of the candidates within a party will represent the party in the general election.

closed primary
A primary election in which only a party's registered voters are eligible to vote.

open primary
A primary in which party members, independents, and sometimes members of the other party are allowed to vote.

crossover voting
Participation in the primary of a party with which the voter is not affiliated

raiding
An organized attempt by voters of one party to influence the primary results of the other party

blanket primary
A primary in which voters may cast ballots in either party's primary (but not both) on an office-by-office basis.

FIGURE 13.1   Methods of Selecting Presidential Delegates

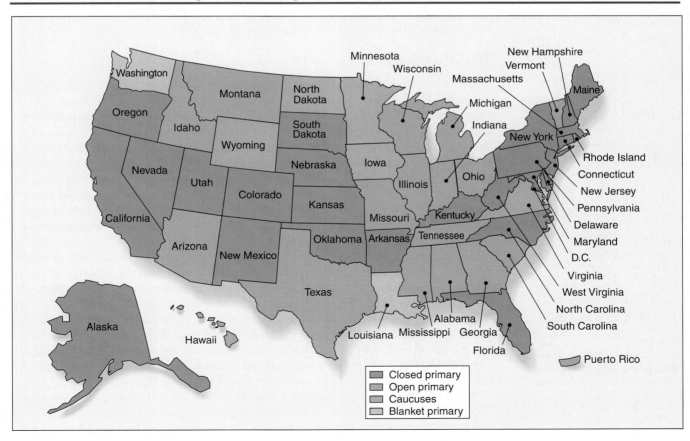

runoff primary
A second primary election between the two candidates receiving the greatest number of votes in the first primary.

nonpartisan primary
A primary used to select candidates regardless of party affiliation.

general election
Election in which voters decide which candidates will actually fill elective public offices.

WEB EXPLORATION
Select, evaluate, and debate upcoming referendum or initiatives currently under consideration in California, the "Referendum State." Go to
www.ablongman.com/oconnor

initiative
A process that allows citizens to propose legislation and submit it to the state electorate for popular vote.

Longman
Participate.com
2.0
Timeline
The Initiative
and the
Referendum

referendum
A procedure whereby the state legislature submits proposed legislation to the state's voters for approval.

regard to party affiliation, whether in the initial slate of contenders or the final choice presented to the voters. For example, a nonpartisan primary would be used to select two final candidates, perhaps both of the same party, from a slate of several candidates, also perhaps from many parties, to run for some local elected office.

General Elections

Once the party candidates for various offices are chosen, general elections are held. In the **general election,** voters decide which candidates will actually fill the nation's elective public offices. These elections are held at many levels, including municipal, county, state, and national. While primaries are contests between the candidates within each party, general elections are contests between the candidates of opposing parties.

General elections come in many varieties, because Americans perceive the various offices as substantially different from one another. In sizing up presidential candidates, voters look for leadership and character, and they base their judgments partly on foreign policy and defense issues that do not arise in state and local elections. Leadership qualities are vital for gubernatorial and mayoral candidates, as are the nuts-and-bolts issues (such as taxes, schools, and roads) that dominate the concerns of state and local governments. Citizens often choose their congressional representatives very differently than they select presidents. Knowing much less about the candidates, people will sometimes base a vote on simple name identification and visibility. This way of deciding one's vote obviously helps incumbents and therefore to some degree explains the high reelection rates of incumbent U.S. representatives: Since World War II, 92 percent of all U.S. House members seeking another term have won, and in several recent election years the proportion has been above 95 percent. But in 1996, it again approached recent election averages when fully 94 percent of the lawmakers who sought reelection won; even higher figures in 2000 only confirmed the pattern again. Still, as political scientist Gary Jacobson observes, greater name recognition *per se* is probably not the most important factor driving the incumbency advantage. More important is that incumbents are typically able to cultivate more favorable public images than are challengers.[5]

Initiative, Referendum, and Recall

Three other types of elections are the initiative, the referendum (plural, referenda), and the recall. Used in twenty-four states and the District of Columbia, initiatives and referenda involve voting on issues (as opposed to voting for candidates). An **initiative** is a process that allows citizens to propose legislation and submit it to the state electorate for popular vote, as long as they get a certain number of signatures on petitions supporting the proposal. Ballot initiatives have been the subject of growing controversy in the past decades, as critics charge that the process—which was intended to give citizens more direct control over policy-making—is now unduly influenced by interest groups and "the initiative industry"—"law firms that draft legislation, petition management firms that guarantee ballot access, direct-mail firms, and campaign consultants who specialize in initiative contests."[6]

For example, Proposition 209, one of the more famous and controversial initiatives, passed in 1996. This initiative eliminated state and local affirmative action programs in California for women and minorities in the areas of education, public employment, and contracting that give preferential treatment on the basis of sex, race, color, ethnicity, or national origin. A **referendum** is a procedure whereby the state legislature submits proposed legislation to the state's voters for approval. Although both of these electoral devices provide for more direct democracy, they are not problem-free. In the 1990 elections, for instance, California had so many referenda and initiatives on its ballot that the state printed a lengthy two-volume guide in an attempt to explain them all to voters.

Other problems with initiatives and referenda are identified in a recent study by Edward L. Lascher. Lascher and his co-researchers found, among other things, that referenda are imperfect representations of the public will because only a small, self-selected portion of the voting public choose to participate in the referenda voting process. Those who decide to study and form an opinion on the numerous questions are generally of higher socio-economic class, and therefore the votes of the lower classes are underrepresented. Additionally, Lascher found that because the process of first getting thousands of signatures to place a question on the ballot, and then waging a political campaign for it, is so expensive, private citizens are dissuaded from taking part in the process. He therefore concludes referenda are not the voice of the people, but rather the voice of well-funded special interest groups who can afford the cost and time commitment of a major campaign.[7]

The third type of election (or "deelection") found in many states is the **recall,** whereby an incumbent can be removed from office by popular vote. Recall elections are very rare, and sometimes they are thwarted by the official's resignation or impeachment prior to the vote. For example, Arizona Governor Evan Mecham was impeached and ousted in 1988 by the state legislature for mishandling campaign finances (among other offenses) just a few weeks before a recall election had been scheduled.

recall
Removal of an incumbent from office by popular vote.

PRESIDENTIAL ELECTIONS

Variety aside, no U.S. election can compare to the presidential contest. This spectacle, held every four years, brings together all the elements of politics and attracts the most ambitious and energetic politicians to the national stage. The election itself, though altered by a front-loaded primary season, remains a collection of fifty separate state elections within each party in which delegates to each party's national convention are allotted. The election of delegates is followed in midsummer by the parties' grand national conventions and then by a final set of fifty separate state elections all held on the Tuesday after the first Monday in November. This lengthy process exhausts candidates and voters alike, but it allows the diversity of the United States to be displayed in ways a shorter, more homogeneous presidential election process could not. Every state has its moment in the sun, every local and regional problem a chance to be aired, every candidate an opportunity to break away from the pack.

The state party organizations use a number of methods to elect national convention delegates:

1. *Winner-take-all:* Under this system the candidate who wins the most votes in a state secures all of that state's delegates. The Democrats moved away from this mode of delegate selection in 1976 and no longer permit its use because of the arguable unfairness to all candidates except the primary winner. Republicans do not prohibit winner-take-all contests, thus enabling a GOP candidate to amass a majority of delegates more quickly.

2. *Proportional representation:* Under this system, candidates who secure a threshold percentage of votes (usually around 15 percent) are awarded delegates in proportion to the number of popular votes won. This system is now strongly favored by the Democrats and is used in many states' Democratic primaries. Although proportional representation is probably the fairest way of allocating delegates to candidates, its downfall is that it renders majorities of delegates more difficult to accumulate and thus can lengthen the contest for the nomination.

3. *Proportional representation with bonus delegates; beauty contest with separate delegate selection; delegate selection with no beauty contest:* Used rarely, the first of these awards delegates to candidates in proportion to the popular vote won and then gives one bonus delegate to the winner of each district. The second serves as an indication of popular sentiment for the conventions to consider as they choose the actual delegates. Finally, under the "delegate selection with no beauty contest" system, the primary election chooses delegates to the national conventions who are not linked on the ballot to specific presidential contenders.

4. *The caucus:* The caucus is the oldest, most party-oriented method of choosing delegates to the national conventions. Traditionally, the caucus was a closed meeting

WEB EXPLORATION
To see how presidential candidates presented themselves in the technology age of the 2000 race, go to www.ablongman.com/oconnor

of party members in each state that selected the party's choice for presidential candidate. In the late nineteenth and early twentieth centuries, however, these caucuses came to be viewed by many people as elitist and antidemocratic, and reformers succeeded in replacing them with direct primaries in most states. While there are still presidential nominating caucuses today, as in Iowa, they are now more open and attract a wider range of the party's membership. Indeed, political scientists Elaine Ciulla Kamarck and Kenneth M. Goldstein note that the new participatory caucus more closely resembles primary elections than they do the old, exclusive party caucuses.[8]

Primaries Versus Caucuses

WEB EXPLORATION
To learn about the functions of the Federal Election Commission, the government agency that monitors and enforces campaign finance and election laws, go to
www.ablongman.com/oconnor

The mix of preconvention contests has changed over the years, with the most pronounced trend being the shift to primaries: Only seventeen states held presidential primaries in 1968, compared with thirty-eight in 1992, and forty-two in 1996, and forty-three in 2000. Figure 13.1 shows which states use primaries (open and closed) and which use caucuses to select presidential delegates.

The increase in the number of primaries is supported by some people who claim that this type of election is more democratic. The primaries are open not only to party activists, but also to anyone, wealthy or poor, urban or rural, Northern or Southern, who wants to vote. Theoretically, then, representatives of all these groups have a chance of winning the presidency. Related to this idea, advocates argue that presidential primaries are the most representative means by which to nominate presidential candidates. They are a barometer of a candidate's popularity with the party rank and file. Recent research also posits that primaries help nominate more moderate and appealing candidates—those that primary voters believe can win in the general election. Paul Abramson, for instance, describes "sophisticated voting," where primary voters vote for their second or third choice because they believe he or she will more easily win in November than will their first choice candidate, perhaps because of less extreme policy positions.[9] Finally, the proponents of presidential primaries claim that they constitute a rigorous test for the candidates, a chance to display under pressure some of the skills needed to be a successful president.

Critics of presidential primaries, however, see the situation somewhat differently. First, they argue that although it may be true that primaries attract more participants than do caucuses, this quantity is more than matched by the quality of caucus participation. Compared with the unenlightening minutes spent at the primary polls, caucus attendees spend several hours learning about politics and the party, listening to speeches by candidates or their representatives, and taking cues from party leaders and elected officials. Moreover, voters may not know very much about any of the field of candidates in a primary, or they may be excessively swayed by popularity polls, television ads, and other media presentations, such as newspaper and magazine coverage.

Critics also argue that the scheduling of primaries unfairly affects their outcomes. For example, the earliest open primary is in the small, atypical state of New Hampshire, which is heavily white and conservative, and it receives much more media coverage than it warrants simply because it is first. Such excessive coverage undoubtedly skews the picture for more populous states that hold their primaries later. The critics also argue that the qualities tested by the primary system are by no means a complete list of those a president needs to be successful. For instance, skill at playing the media game is by itself no guarantee of an effective presidency. Similarly, the exhausting schedule of the primaries may be a better test of a candidate's stamina than of his or her brain power.

The primary proponents have obviously had the better of the arguments so far, though the debate continues, as do efforts to experiment with the schedule of primaries. From time to time, proposals are made for **regional primaries.** Under this system, the nation would be divided into five or six geographic regions (such as the South or the Midwest). All the states in each region would hold their primary elections on the same day, with perhaps one regional election day per month from February through June of

regional primary
A proposed system in which the country would be divided into five or six geographic areas and all states in each region would hold their presidential primary elections on the same day.

presidential election years. This change would certainly cut down on candidate wear and tear. Moreover, candidates would be inspired to focus more on regional issues. On the other hand, regional primaries would probably cost candidates at least as much as the state-by-state system, and the system might needlessly amplify the differences and create divisive rifts among the nation's regions.

Occasionally, a regional plan is adopted. In 1988, for instance, fourteen Southern and border South states joined together to hold simultaneous primaries on "Super Tuesday" (March 8) in order to maximize the South's impact on presidential politics. This was an attempt by conservative Democrats to influence the choice of the party nominee. Their effort failed, however, since the two biggest winners of Super Tuesday were liberals Jesse Jackson (who won six Southern states) and Michael Dukakis, who carried the megastates of Texas and Florida. This outcome occurred because, in general, the kinds of citizens who vote in Democratic primaries in the South are not greatly different from those who cast ballots in Northern Democratic primaries—most tend toward the liberal side of the ideological spectrum. This trend was repeated in 1996 with the construction of the so-called "Yankee Primary," with five of the six New England states holding their contests on March 5 (Massachusetts, Connecticut, Rhode Island, Vermont, and Maine) plus New York on March 7, and the continuation of a scaled-down Super Tuesday on March 12.

The primary schedule has also been altered, as we saw earlier in the chapter, by a process called **front-loading,** the tendency of states to choose an early date on the primary calendar. Seventy percent of all the delegates to both party conventions are now chosen before the end of March. This trend is hardly surprising, given the added press emphasis on the first contests and the voters' desire to cast their ballots before the competition is decided. The focus on early contests (such as the Iowa caucus and the New Hampshire primary), coupled with front-loading, can result in a party's being saddled with a nominee too quickly, before press scrutiny and voter reflection are given enough time to separate the wheat from the chaff. Front-loading has also had other important effects on the nomination process. First, a front-loaded primary schedule generally benefits the front-runner, since opponents have little time to turn the contest around once they fall behind. Second, front-loading advantages the candidate who can raise the bulk of the money *before* the nomination season begins, since there will be little opportunity to raise money once the process begins and since candidates will need to finance campaign efforts simultaneously in many states. Finally, front-loading has amplified the importance of the "invisible primary"—the year or so prior to the start of the official nomination season when candidates begin raising money and unofficially campaigning.[10]

Pat Buchanan announcing his third run for the presidency, March 1999, before obtaining the Reform Party nomination. Buchannan has never had any real chance of success in recent years, though he has shown remarkable skill and determination in promoting his reactionary platform. (Photo courtesy: Rick Friedman/Black Star)

front-loading
The tendency of states to choose an early date on the primary calendar.

THE PARTY CONVENTIONS

The seemingly endless nomination battle does have a conclusion: the national party convention held in the summer of presidential election years. The out-of-power party traditionally holds its convention first, in late July, followed by the party holding the White House in mid-August. Preempting some of prime-time television for four nights, these remarkable conclaves are difficult for the public to ignore; indeed, they are pivotal events in shaping the voters' perceptions of the candidates.

Yet the conventions once were much more: They were deliberative bodies that made actual decisions, where party leaders held sway and deals were sometimes cut in "smoke-filled rooms" to deliver nominations to little-known contenders called "dark horses" (see Roots of Government: The Party Conventions of 1920). But this era predated the modern emphasis on reform, primaries, and proportional representation, all of which have combined to make conventions mere ratifying agencies for preselected nominees.[11]

The first national convention was held in 1831 by the Anti-Masonic Party. In 1832 Andrew Jackson's nomination for reelection was ratified by the first Democratic National Convention. Just four years later, in 1836, Martin Van Buren became the first nonincumbent candidate nominated by a major party convention (the Democrats) to win the presidency.

From the 1830s to the mid-twentieth century, the national conventions remained primarily under the control of the important state and local party leaders, the so-called bosses or kingmakers, who would bargain within a splintered, decentralized party. During these years, state delegations in the convention consisted mostly of *uncommitted delegates* (that is, delegates who had not pledged to support any particular candidate). These delegates were selected by party leaders, a process that enabled the leaders to broker agreements with prominent national candidates. Under this system, a state party leader could exchange delegation support for valuable political plums—for instance, a Cabinet position or even the vice presidency—for an important state political figure.

Today the convention is fundamentally different. First, its importance as a party conclave, at which compromises on party leadership and policies can be worked out, has diminished. Second, although the convention still formally selects the presidential ticket, most nominations are settled well in advance. New preconvention political processes have lessened the role of the convention in three areas.

Delegate Selection.   The selection of delegates to the conventions is no longer the function of party leaders but of primary elections and grassroots caucuses. Moreover, recent reforms, especially by the Democratic Party, have generally weakened any remaining control by local party leaders over delegates. A prime example of such reform is the Democrats' abolition of the **unit rule,** a traditional party practice under which the majority of a state delegation (say, twenty-six of fifty delegates) could force the minority to vote for its candidate. Another new Democratic Party rule decrees that a state's delegates be chosen in proportion to the votes cast in its primary or caucus (so that, for example, a candidate who receives 30 percent of the vote gains about 30 percent of the convention delegates). This change has had the effect of requiring delegates to indicate their presidential preference at each stage of the selection process. Consequently, the majority of state delegates now come to the convention already committed to a candidate. Again, this diminishes the discretionary role of the convention and the party leaders' capacity to bargain.

In sum, the many complex changes in the rules of delegate selection have contributed to the loss of decision-making powers by the convention. Even though many of these changes were initiated by the Democratic Party, the Republicans were carried along as many Democrat-controlled state legislatures enacted the reforms as state laws. There have been new rules to counteract some of these changes, however. For instance, since 1984 the number of delegate slots reserved for elected Democratic Party officials—called **superdelegates**—has been increased in the hope of adding stability to the Democratic convention. Before 1972 most delegates to a Democratic National Convention were not bound by primary results to support a particular candidate for president. This freedom to maneuver meant that conventions could be exciting and somewhat unpredictable gatherings, where last-minute events and deals could sway wavering delegates. Superdelegates are supposed to be party professionals concerned with winning the general election contest, not simply amateur ideologues concerned mainly with satisfying their policy appetites. All Democratic governors and 80 percent of the congressional Democrats, among others, are now included as voting delegates at the convention. Two recent studies of the role of superdelegates in the Democratic Party offer differing conclusions about

unit rule
A traditional party practice under which the majority of a state delegation can force the minority to vote for its candidate.

superdelegate
Delegate slot to the Democratic Party's national convention that is reserved for an elected party official.

ROOTS OF GOVERNMENT

THE PARTY CONVENTIONS OF 1920

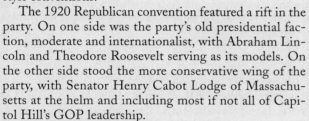

The national party convention of the present day is a different animal from that of the past. No longer is it a deliberative forum for choosing the party presidential nominee; rather, the convention now merely ratifies the choices of the preconvention state caucuses and primaries. A look at the Republican and Democratic Party conventions of 1920 illuminates the contrast between the old-style and new-style conventions.

The 1920 Republican convention featured a rift in the party. On one side was the party's old presidential faction, moderate and internationalist, with Abraham Lincoln and Theodore Roosevelt serving as its models. On the other side stood the more conservative wing of the party, with Senator Henry Cabot Lodge of Massachusetts at the helm and including most if not all of Capitol Hill's GOP leadership.

The "presidential" party during those days usually exerted more influence in presidential nominations than did the congressional party. But this changed in 1920, because Lodge's congressional party had garnered more power and influence during the latter part of Democratic President Woodrow Wilson's White House tenure (1913–1921), when Wilson was seriously ill and his policies were under attack. Could the two wings of the party compromise on a presidential candidate for 1920? Any such compromise would undoubtedly be difficult to come by, because most potential candidates were aligned firmly with one wing of the party or the other.

Senator Warren G. Harding of Ohio was one possible compromise candidate. A small-town politician and onetime editor of a staunchly Republican Ohio newspaper, Harding had a reputation in the Senate based primarily on his ability to win allies in all factions of the Republican Party. But Harding's chances appeared bleak at the outset of the convention, and after the first ballot, he was considerably behind a number of other Republican hopefuls. Yet several frontrunners continued to deadlock in ballot after ballot, testing the patience of the delegates, who were baking in the hot Chicago summer.

The weather, combined with the seemingly unresolvable convention impasse, spurred a group of influential Senate leaders to meet at a nearby hotel room to attempt to hammer out a compromise—the classic gathering of party leaders behind the closed doors of a smoke-filled room. At the meeting, Harding's name continued to be floated. Although most of the party leaders questioned the Ohioan's convictions and leadership abilities, he did have some attractive qualities: He was handsome (it was said that Harding "looked like a president"), he hailed from a politically important state, and he could be expected to work with leaders of both party factions. The GOP kingmakers therefore decided to test the waters with Harding, but agreed to reconvene later in the more likely event that the delegates rejected him. Harding soon went to work to ensure that no new meeting would be needed, however; he campaigned vigorously for his candidacy throughout the evening, roaming the halls and trying to convince any delegate he could find of his credibility as a candidate.

The deadlock at the convention continued for a few more ballots, but the frazzled delegates gradually realized that Harding perhaps was the only candidate with the potential to secure a majority. This realization sent frontrunners scurrying around the convention to build a coalition to stop Harding. They failed, however, and dark-horse candidate Harding—on the tenth ballot—secured enough votes to win the nomination.

The Democrats also needed a candidate to unite the party in 1920, one who could emphasize Wilson's successes yet downplay his failures. After thirty-eight ballots at the Democratic National Convention, no majority candidate had yet emerged, instilling in Wilson a hope that the party might again turn to him as the nominee, despite his deteriorated physical condition. It was one thing for the Democrats to remain loyal to Wilson—which they did by endorsing his policies and paying him homage in the party platform—and another for the party to nominate him for a third term. A return to Wilson was ultimately unnecessary, as Ohio Governor James M. Cox finally secured the nomination on the forty-fourth ballot.

Conditions are very different today. Nominations are no longer decided in smoke-filled back rooms at the conventions; instead, the critical moments occur well beforehand in the highly visible primary-and-caucus obstacle course that creates not dark horses but wornout horses by convention time.

The 2000 presidential candidates and their running mates. On the left, Joseph Lieberman and Al Gore Jr. On the right, George W. Bush and Dick Cheney. (Photos courtesy: left, Doug Mills/AP/Wide World Photos; right, M. Spencer Green/AP/Wide World Photos)

the usefulness of those party insiders in the nomination process. Priscilla Southwell posits that if the superdelegate rule were relaxed in 1984, as it was in 1992, "the 1984 [Democratic primary] race could have changed the outcome of the Democratic nomination," as the eventual nominee, Walter Mondale, was the overwhelming choice of the party insiders who were unpledged superdelegates. Without support among this numerous group for Mondale, the nomination fight would have been much tighter.[12] Contrasting this conclusion is that of Richard Herrera. Using data on the views of both regular and superdelegates to the 1988 Democratic convention, Herrera concludes that that the common belief (and fear) that the regularly chosen delegates are amateurs who do not understand the true interests of the party is overstated. Regular delegates and superdelegates are more similar to each other than previously believed, according to Herrera.[13]

National Candidates and Issues.   The political perceptions and loyalties of voters are now influenced largely by national candidates and issues, a factor that has undoubtedly served to diminish the power of state and local party leaders at the convention. The national candidates have usurped the autonomy of state party leaders with their preconvention ability to garner delegate support. Issues, increasingly national in scope, are significantly more important to the new, issue-oriented party activists than to the party professionals, who, prior to the late 1960s, had a monopoly on the management of party affairs.

The News Media.   The mass media have helped to transform the national conventions into political extravaganzas for the television audience's consumption. They have also helped to preempt the convention, by keeping count of the delegates committed to the candidates; as a result, the delegates and even the candidates now have much more information about nomination politics well before the convention. From the strategies of candidates to the commitments of individual delegates, the media cover it all. Even the bargaining within key party committees, formerly done in secret, is now subject to some public scrutiny, thanks to open meetings. The business of the convention has been irrevocably shaped to accommodate television: desirous of presenting a unified image to kick off a strong general election campaign, the parties assign important roles to attractive speakers, and most crucial party affairs are saved for prime-time viewing hours. During the 1990s, the networks gradually began to reduce their convention coverage, citing low viewer ratings. In 2000, the networks cut their coverage back from two hours to one hour—reflecting perhaps a lack of public interest in the political process, perhaps a change in the political culture away from meaningful convention activity, or perhaps both.

Extensive media coverage of the convention has its pros and cons. On the one hand, such exposure helps the party launch its presidential campaign with fanfare. On the other hand, it can expose rifts within a party, as happened in 1968 at the Democratic convention in Chicago. Dissension was obvious when "hawks," supporting the Vietnam War and President Lyndon B. Johnson, clashed with the antiwar "doves" both on the convention floor and in street demonstrations outside the convention hall. Whatever the case, it is obvious that saturation media coverage of preelection events has led to the public's loss of anticipation and exhilaration about convention events.

Some reformers have spoken of replacing the conventions with national direct primaries, but it is unlikely that the parties would agree to this. Although its role in nominating the presidential ticket has often been reduced to formality, the convention is still a valuable political institution. After all, it is the only real arena where the national political parties can command a nearly universal audience while they celebrate past achievements and project their hopes for the future.

Who Are the Delegates? In one sense, party conventions are microcosms of the United States: every state, most localities, and all races and creeds find some representation there. (For some historic "firsts" for women and the conventions, see Table 13.1.) Yet delegates are an unusual and unrepresentative collection of people in many other ways. It is not just their exceptionally keen interest in politics that distinguishes delegates. These activists also are ideologically more pure and financially better off than most Americans.

In 2000, for example, both parties drew their delegates from an elite group that had income and educational levels far above the average American's. The distinctiveness of each party was also apparent. Democratic delegates tended to be younger and were more likely to be African American, female, divorced or single, and a member of a labor union. Because of George W. Bush's "compassionate conservatism," the GOP in 2000 made a special effort (but with mixed results) to attract minorities and open delegates to its convention.

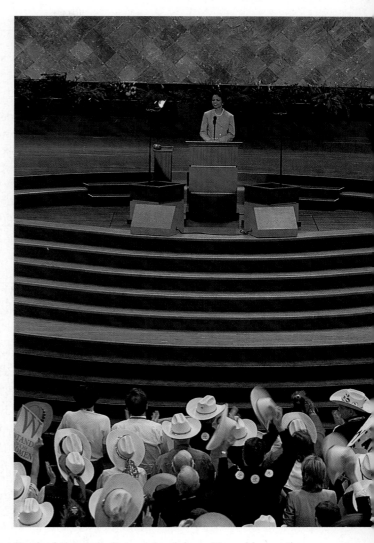

Stanford University Provost Condoleeza Rice addresses the 2000 Republican National Convention. Rice would later be tapped by President George W. Bush to serve as national security advisor. (Photo courtesy: Steve Liss/Corbis Sygma)

The contrast in the two parties' delegations is no accident; it reflects not only the differences in the party constituencies, but also conscious decisions made by party leaders. After the tumultuous 1968 Democratic National Convention (which, as noted, was torn by dissent over the Vietnam War), Democrats formed a commission to examine the condition of the party and to propose changes in its structure. As a direct consequence of the commission's work, the 1972 Democratic convention was the most broadly representative ever of women, African Americans, and young people, because the party required these groups to be included in state delegations in rough proportion to their numbers in the population of each state. (State delegations failing this test were not seated.) This new mandate was very controversial, and it has since been watered down considerably. Nonetheless, women and blacks are still more fully represented at Democratic conventions than at Republican conventions. GOP leaders have placed much less emphasis on proportional representation, and instead of procedural reforms, Republicans have concentrated on strengthening their state organizations and fund-raising efforts, a strategy that has clearly paid off at the polls in the elections of 1980, 1984, and 1988, which saw Republicans elected as president.

TABLE 13.1   Women and the Conventions

Since 1980, Democratic Party rules have required that women comprise 50 percent of the delegates to its national convention. The Republican Party has no similar quotas. Nevertheless, both
parties have tried to increase the role of women at the convention. Some "firsts" for women at
conventions include:

1876	First woman to address a national convention
1890	First women delegates to conventions of both parties
1940	First woman to nominate a presidential candidate
1951	First woman asked to chair a national party
1972	First woman keynote speaker
1984	First major party woman nominated for vice president (Democrat Geraldine Ferraro)
1996	Wives of both nominees make major addresses
2000	Daughter of a presidential candidate nominates her father

Source: Center for the Study of American Women in Politics.

The delegates in each party also exemplify the philosophical gulf separating the two
parties. Democratic delegates are well to the left of their own party's voters on most
issues, and even farther away from the opinions held by the nation's electorate as a
whole. Republican delegates are a mirror image of their opponents—considerably to
the right of GOP voters and even more so of the entire electorate. Although it is sometimes said that the two major parties do not present U.S. citizens with a "clear choice"
of candidates, it is possible to argue the contrary. Our politics are perhaps too polarized, with the great majority of Americans, moderates and pragmatists overwhelmingly,
left underrepresented by parties too fond of ideological purity. Political scientists James
L. Hutter and Steven E. Schier conducted a study of 1980 Iowa caucus and convention delegates for both the Republican and Democratic parties that confirms the above
conclusion. Hutter and Schier found that, among the Democrats, the delegates to the
state convention were the most liberal of the group of voters studied, followed closely
by Democratic caucus attenders. Republican delegates, similarly, were the most conservative members of the group studied, followed closely by Republican caucus attenders. Hutter and Schier also found that while both groups of party decision makers were
more ideological than other party members, Republican Party leaders were "closer to
their followers in representativeness of opinions than were Democratic leaders and followers,"[14] although the difference was small.

The philosophical divergence is usually reflected in the party platforms, even in years
such as 1996, when both parties attempted to water down their rhetoric and smooth over
ideological differences (see Highlight: Selected Contrasts in the 2000 Party Platforms). (The
Democrats did so in 1996; the Republicans have done so in earlier years, as in 1968.)

The Electoral College: How Presidents Are Elected

Given the enormous amount of energy, money, and time expended to nominate two
major-party presidential contenders, it is difficult to believe that the general election
could be more arduous than the nominating contests, but it usually is. The actual campaign for the presidency (and other offices) is described in chapter 14, but the object of
the exercise is clear: winning a majority of the **electoral college.** This uniquely American institution consists of representatives of each state who cast the final ballots that
actually elect a president.

The electoral college was the result of a compromise between Framers like Roger
Sherman and Elbridge Gerry, who argued for selection of the president by the Congress, and those such as James Madison, James Wilson, and Gouverneur Morris, who
favored selection by direct popular election. The electoral college compromise, while
not a perfect solution, had practical benefits. Since there were no mass media in those
days, it is unlikely that common citizens, even reasonably informed ones, would know

electoral college
Representatives of each state who
cast the final ballots that actually
elect a president.

Longman
Participate.com 2.0
Participation
**The Electoral
College**

much about a candidate from another state. This situation could have left voters with no choice but to vote for someone from their own state, thus making it improbable that any candidate would secure a national majority. On the other hand, the **electors** (members of the electoral college) would be men of character with a solid knowledge of national politics who were able to identify, agree on, and select prominent national statesmen. There are three essentials to understanding the Framers' design of the electoral college: (1) It was meant to work without political parties, (2) it was designed to cover both the nominating and electing phases of presidential selection, and (3) it was constructed to produce a nonpartisan president.

The machinery of the electoral college was somewhat complex. Each state designated electors (through appointment or popular vote) equal in number to the sum of its representation in the House and Senate. (Figure 13.2 shows a map of the United States drawn in proportion to each state's 2000 electoral college votes.) The electors met in their respective states. Each elector had two votes to cast in the electoral college's selection for the president and vice president. The rules of the college stipulated that each elector was allowed to cast only one vote for any single candidate, and by extension obliged each elector to use his second vote for another candidate. There was no way to designate votes for president or vice president; instead, the candidate with the most votes (provided he also received votes from a majority of the electors) won the presidency and the runner-up won the vice presidency. If two candidates received the same number of votes and both had a majority of electors, the election was decided in the House of Representatives, with each state delegation acting as a unit and casting one vote. In the event that no candidate secured a majority, the election would also be decided in the House, with each state delegation casting one vote for any of the top five electoral vote-getters. In both these scenarios, a majority of the total number of states was necessary for victory.

This system seems almost insanely unpredictable, complex, and unwieldy until one remembers that the Framers devised it specifically for the type of political system that existed when they framed the Constitution and which they (erroneously) foresaw for America in perpetuity: a nonpartisan (one-party), consensus-based, indirectly representative, multi-candidate system. In such a system, the electoral college would function admirably, as indeed it did for several elections. In practice, electors with a common basic political understanding would arrive at a consensus preference for president, and most, if not all, would plan to cast one of their votes for that candidate, thereby virtually guaranteeing one clear winner, who would then become president; a tie was an unlikely and unhappy outcome. Each would then plan to cast his remaining vote for another candidate, the one whom the elector implicitly preferred for vice president. Consensus on the vice presidency would presumably be less clear than for the more important position of president, so there might be a closer spread among the runners-up, but in any case, the eventual president and vice president—indeed, all the candidates—would still have been members of the same one party.

But the Framers' idea of nonpartisan presidential elections lasted barely a decade, ending for the most part after George Washington's two terms. In 1796 their arrangement for presidential selection produced a president and vice president with markedly different political philosophies, a circumstance much less likely in modern times.

The Election of 1800

The republic's fourth presidential election revealed a flaw in the Framers' plan. In 1800 Thomas Jefferson and Aaron Burr were, respectively, the presidential and vice presidential candidates advanced by the Democratic–Republican Party, and supporters of the Democratic–Republican Party controlled a majority of the electoral college. Accordingly, each Democratic–Republican elector in the states cast one of his two votes for Jefferson and the other one for Burr, a situation that resulted in a tie for the presidency between Jefferson and Burr, since there was no way under the constitutional arrangements for electors to earmark their votes separately for president and vice president.

elector
Member of the electoral college chosen by methods determined in each state.

HIGHLIGHT

SELECTED CONTRASTS IN THE 2000 PARTY PLATFORMS

DEMOCRATS

State of the Economy

Democrats responsible for "longest economic expansion in American history"

Taxes

Tax cuts for middle class families; enable families to "live their values by helping them save for college, invest in their job skills and lifelong learning, pay for health insurance, afford child care, eliminate the marriage penalty for working families, care for elderly or disabled loved ones."

REPUBLICANS

State of the Economy

"Inspired by Presidents Reagan and Bush, Republicans hammered into place the framework for today's prosperity and surpluses."

Taxes

Replace the five current tax brackets with four lower ones; help families by doubling the child tax credit to $1000; encourage entrepreneurship and growth by capping the top marginal rate, ending the death tax.

Abortion

Support a woman's right to choose to have an abortion in all circumstances currently legal. "Respect the individual conscience of each American on this difficult issue."

Support a constitutional amendment that would outlaw abortion in all circumstances. No specific mention of tolerance for other views on abortion.

Social Security

"Democrats believe in using our prosperity to save Social Security."

"Personal savings accounts must be the cornerstone of restructuring."

Immigration

Permit the children of illegal immigrants to attend public schools; allow legal immigrants to receive welfare and other benefits; make it easier for eligible immigrants to become United States citizens. Support restoration of basic due process protections and essential benefits for legal immigrants.

"Prohibit the children of illegal immigrants from attending public schools; restrict welfare to legal immigrants; support a constitutional amendment denying automatic citizenship to children born in the United States to illegal immigrants and legal immigrants who are in this country for a short time."

Balanced Budget

"In the next 12 years, Democrats vow to wipe out the publicly held national debt."

"Support a constitutional amendment requiring a balanced budget."

Education

Support strengthening public schools. "Advocate raises for teachers and accountability for under-performing schools."

Favor using federal money to help parents pay private school tuition. "Support increased local and state control of education."

Homosexual Rights

"We support continued efforts ... to end workplace discrimination against gay men and lesbians. We support the full inclusion of gay and lesbian families in the life of the nation."

"We do not believe sexual preference should be given special legal protection of standing in the law."

Trade

Insist that international trade agreements include standards to protect children, workers, and the environment.

Oppose using trade policy to pursue "social agenda items." "Insist on free trade in global marketplace."

Gun Control

Support mandatory child safety locks, a photo license I.D., a full background check, and a gun safety test to buy a new handgun in America.

"Defend the constitutional right to keep and bear arms" and favor mandatory penalties for crimes committed with guns.

Environment

Emphasize government regulation to protect the environment.

Emphasize consideration of private property rights and economic development in conjunction with environmental protection.

Star Wars

Oppose revival of the landbased missile defense system known as Star Wars.

Favor development of the missile defense system.

Source: 2000 Democratic and Republican Party Platforms.

FIGURE 13.2   **The States Drawn in Proportion to their Electoral College Votes, 2000 Election**
This table visually represents the electoral "weight" of the fifty states.

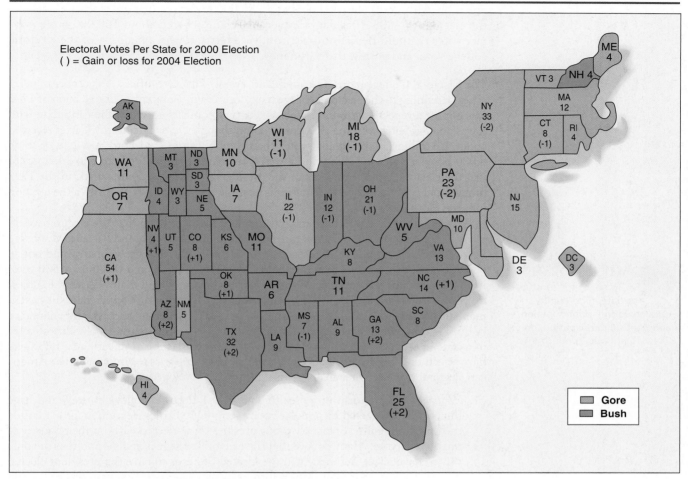

Note: States drawn in proportion to number of electoral votes. Total electoral votes: 538
Source: U.S. National Archives & Records Administration.

Even though most understood Jefferson to be the actual choice for president, the Constitution mandated that a tie be decided by the House of Representatives. It was, of course, and in Jefferson's favor, but only after much energy was expended to persuade lame-duck Federalists not to give Burr the presidency.

The Twelfth Amendment, ratified in 1804 and still the constitutional foundation for presidential elections, was an attempt to remedy the confusion between the selection of vice presidents and presidents that beset the election of 1800. The amendment provided for separate elections for each office, with each elector having only one vote to cast for each. In the event of a tie or when no candidate received a majority of the total number of electors, the election still went to the House of Representatives; now, however, each state delegation would have one vote to cast for one of the three candidates who had received the greatest number of electoral votes.

The electoral college modified by the Twelfth Amendment has fared better than the college as originally designed, but it has not been problem-free. For example, in the 1824 election between John Quincy Adams and Andrew Jackson, neither presidential candidate secured a majority of electoral votes, once again throwing the election into the House. Despite the fact that Jackson had more electoral and popular votes than Adams, the House voted for the latter as president. On two other occasions in the nineteenth century, the presidential candidate with fewer popular votes than his opponent won the presidency. In the 1876 contest between Republican

Rutherford B. Hayes and Democrat Samuel J. Tilden, no candidate received a majority of electoral votes; the House decided in Hayes's favor even though he had only one more (disputed) electoral vote and 250,000 fewer popular votes than Tilden. In the election of 1888, President Grover Cleveland secured about 100,000 more popular votes than did Benjamin Harrison, yet Harrison won a majority of the electoral college vote, and with it the presidency.

The Electoral College in the Twentieth and Twenty-First Centuries.   A number of near-crises pertaining to the electoral college have occurred more recently. The election of 1976 was almost a repeat of those nineteenth-century contests in which the candidate with fewer popular votes won the presidency: Even though Democrat Jimmy Carter received about 1.7 million more popular votes than Republican Gerald Ford, a switch of some 8,000 popular votes in Ohio and Hawaii would have secured for Ford enough votes to win the electoral college, and hence the presidency. Had Ross Perot stayed in the 1992 presidential contest without a hiatus, it is possible that he could have thrown the election into the House of Representatives.

Throughout the 2000 presidential campaign, many foresaw that the election would likely be the closest since the 1960 race between John F. Kennedy and Richard M. Nixon. Few realized, however, that the election would be so close that the winner would not be officially declared for more than five weeks after Election Day, and that a mere 500 votes in Florida would effectively decide the presidency of the United States. With the subject of third parties in mind, it is worth remarking that the existing winner-take-all system mandated by the Constitution is a major obstacle to the creation, success, and endurance of third parties, which have a uniquely high hurdle to clear in securing a plurality of votes in a state in order to secure any electoral votes. In such a time of uncertainty, reformers have seized the opportunity to bring forward several proposals for improving the American electoral system. Three major reform ideas have developed:

WEB EXPLORATION
To access the most up-to-date, high-quality data on voting, public opinion, and political participation, go to www.ablongman.com/oconnor

1. *Abolition.* This reform proposes to abolish the electoral college entirely and have the president selected by popular vote. George W. Bush's election in 2000 marked the fourth time in U.S. history that a president was elected without the majority of the popular vote. Many believe that the electoral college is archaic and that the only way to have a true democracy in the United States is to have the president elected directly by a popular vote. This reform is by far the most unlikely to succeed, given that the Constitution of the United States would have to be amended to change the electoral college. Even assuming that the House of Representatives could muster the two-third majority necessary to pass an amendment, the proposal would almost certainly never pass the Senate. This is because small states have the same representation in the Senate as populous ones, and the Senate thus serves as a bastion of equal representation for all states, regardless of population—a principle generally reinforced by the existing configuration of the electoral college, which ensures a minimum of electoral influence for even the smallest states.

2. *Congressional district plan.* Under this plan, each candidate would receive one electoral vote for each congressional district that he wins in a state, and the winner of the overall popular vote in each state would receive two bonus votes (one for each senator) for that state. Take for example Virginia, which has eleven representatives and two senators for a total of thirteen electoral votes. If the Democratic candidate wins five congressional districts, and the Republican candidate wins the other six districts and also the statewide majority, the Democrat wins five electoral votes and the Republican wins a total of eight. The interesting fact about this reform is that it can be adopted without a constitutional amendment. This electoral system currently exists only in Maine and Nebraska, but any state can adopt this system on its own because the Constitution gives states the right to determine the place and manner by which electors are selected. There are, however, some unintended consequences to this reform. First, the winner of the overall election might change in some circumstances. Richard Nixon would have won the 1960 election instead of John F. Kennedy under a congres-

sional district plan. George W. Bush would have likely won by a wider margin if the entire nation used this system in 2000. Second, this reform would further politicize the redistricting process that takes place every ten years according to census results. Fair and objective redistricting already suffers at the hands of many political interests, and if electoral votes were at stake, it would suffer further as the parities made nationwide efforts to maximize the number of safe electoral districts for their presidential nominee while minimizing the number of competitive districts. The third consequence of state-by-state adoption is that the nation would quickly come to resemble a patchwork of different electoral methods, with some states being awarded by congressional districts and some states awarded solely by popular vote. California, for example, would be unlikely to adopt this system because it would tremendously reduce the power of the state that comes with have fifty-four electoral votes in one package and induces California legislators to keep their electoral votes together. In the end, the United States and its democracy might be better served by preserving the more uniform system that currently prevails, despite its other shortcomings.

3. *Keep the college, abolish the electors.* This proposal calls for the preservation of the college as a statistical electoral device but would remove all voting power from actual human electors and their legislative appointers. This would eliminate the threat of so-called faithless electors—that is, electors who are appointed by state legislators to vote for the candidate who won that state's vote, but who then choose, for whatever reason, to vote for the other candidate. This reform is widely accepted, although—perhaps even because—the problem of faithless electors is only a secondary and little-realized liability of the electoral college.

While the fate of these reform proposals has yet to be determined, any change in the existing system would inevitably have a profound impact on the way that candidates go about the business of seeking votes for the U.S. presidency.

Patterns of Presidential Elections

The electoral college results reveal more over time than simply who won the presidency. They show which party and which regions are coming to dominance and how voters may be changing party allegiances in response to new issues and generational changes.

Party Realignments.   Usually such movements are gradual, but occasionally the political equivalent of a major earthquake swiftly and dramatically alters the landscape. During these rare events, called **party realignments,**[15] existing party affiliations are subject to upheaval: Many voters may change parties, and the youngest age group of voters may permanently adopt the label of the newly dominant party. Until recent times, at least, party realignments have been spaced about thirty-six years apart in the U.S. experience.

A major realignment is precipitated by one or more **critical elections,** which may polarize voters around new issues and personalities in reaction to crucial developments, such as a war or an economic depression. In Britain, for example, the first postwar election held in 1945 was critical, since it ushered the Labour Party into power for the first time and introduced to Britain a new interventionist agenda in the fields of economic and social welfare policies.

In the entire history of the United States, there have been six party realignments; three tumultuous eras in particular have produced significant critical elections (see Figure 13.3). First, during the period leading up to the Civil War, the Whig Party gradually dissolved and the Republican Party developed and won the presidency. Second, the populist radicalization of the Democratic Party in the 1890s enabled the Republicans to greatly strengthen their majority status and make lasting gains in voter attachments. Third, the Great Depression of the 1930s propelled the Democrats to power, causing large numbers of voters to repudiate the GOP and embrace the Democratic Party. In each of these cases, fundamental and enduring alterations in the party equation resulted.

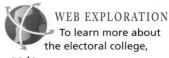
WEB EXPLORATION
To learn more about the electoral college, go to
www.ablongman.com/oconnor

party realignment
A shifting of party coalition groupings in the electorate that remains in place for several elections.

critical election
An election that signals a party realignment through voter polarization around new issues.

The last confirmed major realignment, then, happened in the 1928–1936 period, as Republican Herbert Hoover's presidency was held to one term because of voter anger about the Depression. In 1932 Democrat Franklin D. Roosevelt swept to power as the electorate decisively rejected Hoover and the Republicans. This dramatic vote of "no confidence" was followed by substantial changes in policy by the new president, who demonstrated in fact or at least in appearance that his policies were effective. The people responded to his success, accepted his vision of society, and ratified their choice of the new president's party in subsequent presidential and congressional elections.

With the aid of timely circumstances, realignments are accomplished in two main ways.[16] Some voters are simply converted from one party to the other by the issues and candidates of the time. New voters may also be mobilized into action: Immigrants, young voters, and previous nonvoters may become motivated and then absorbed into a new governing majority. However vibrant and potent party coalitions may be at first, as they age, tensions increase and grievances accumulate. The majority's original reason for existing fades, and new generations neither remember the traumatic events that originally brought about the realignment nor possess the stalwart party identifications of their ancestors. New issues arise, producing conflicts that can be resolved only by a breakup of old alignments and a reshuffling of individual and group party loyalties. Viewed in historical perspective, party realignment has been a mechanism that ensures stability by controlling unavoidable change.

A critical realigning era is by no means the only occasion when changes in partisan affiliation are accommodated. In truth, every election produces realignment to some degree, since some individuals are undoubtedly pushed to change parties by events and by their reactions to the candidates. Recent research suggests that partisanship is much more responsive to current issues and personalities than had been believed earlier, and that major realignments are just extreme cases of the kind of changes in party loyalty registered every year.[17]

secular realignment
The gradual rearrangement of party coalitions, based more on demographic shifts than on shocks to the political system.

Secular Realignment.   Although the term *realignment* is usually applied only if momentous events such as war or depression produce enduring and substantial alterations in the party coalitions, political scientists have long recognized that a more gradual rearrangement of party coalitions could occur.[18] Called **secular realignment,** this piecemeal process depends not on convulsive shocks to the political system, but on slow, almost barely discernable demographic shifts—the shrinking of one party's base of support and the enlargement of the other's, for example—or simple generational replacement (that is, the dying off of the older generation and the maturing of the younger generation). A recent version of this theory, termed "rolling realignment,"[19] argues that in an era of weaker party attachments (such as we currently are experiencing), a dramatic, full-scale realignment may not be possible. Still, a critical mass of voters may be attracted for years to one party's banner in waves or streams, if that party's leadership and performance are consistently exemplary.

Some scholars and political observers also contend that the decline of party affiliation has in essence left the electorate dealigned and incapable of being realigned as long as party ties remain tenuous for so many voters.[20] Voters shift with greater ease between the parties during dealignment, but little permanence or intensity exists in identifications made and held so lightly. If nothing else, the obsolescence of realignment theory may be indicated by the calendar; if major realignments occur roughly every thirty-six years, then we are long overdue. The last major realignment took place between 1928 and 1936, and so the next one might have been expected in the late 1960s and early 1970s.

As the trends toward ticket-splitting, partisan independence, and voter volatility suggest, there is little question that we have been moving through an unstable and somewhat "dealigned" period at least since the 1970s. The foremost political question today is whether dealignment will continue (and in what form) or whether a major realignment is in the offing. Each previous dealignment has been a precursor of realignment,[21] but realignment need not succeed dealignment, especially under modern conditions.

FIGURE 13.3   Electoral College Results for Three Realigning Presidential Contests
This figure shows the electoral votes in three crucial elections of our century.

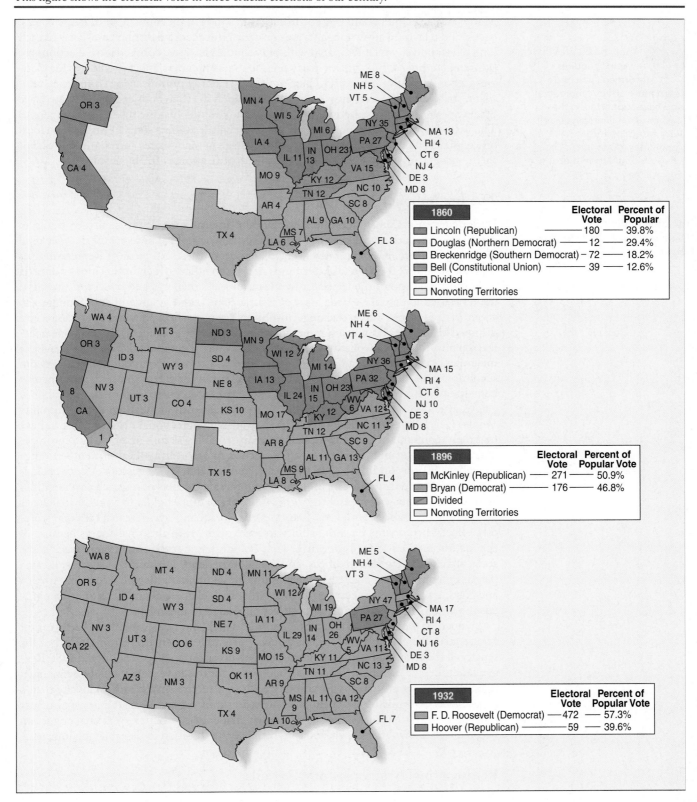

WEB EXPLORATION
Voting requires informed choices. To learn more about candidates you have supported in the past or to familiarize yourself with future political candidates, go to
www.ablongman.com/oconnor

incumbency
The condition of already holding elected office.

CONGRESSIONAL ELECTIONS

Many similar elements are present in different kinds of elections: Candidates, voters, issues, and television advertisements are constants. But there are distinctive aspects of each kind of election as well. Compared with presidential elections, congressional elections are a different animal. Unlike major-party presidential contenders, most candidates for Congress labor in relative obscurity. There are some celebrity nominees for Congress—television stars, sports heroes, even local TV news anchors. (See Politics Now: Senate Race Steals Spotlight for First Lady Hillary Rodham Clinton's historic senatorial compaign.) The vast majority of party nominees, however, are little-known state legislators and local office holders who receive remarkably little coverage in many states and communities. For them, just getting known, establishing name identification, is the biggest battle.

The Incumbency Advantage

Under current circumstances the advantages of **incumbency** (that is, already being in office) are enhanced, and a kind of electoral inertia takes hold: Those people in office tend to remain in office. Every year, the average member of the U.S. House of Representatives expends about $750,000 in taxpayer funds to run the office. Much of this money directly or indirectly promotes the legislator by means of mass mailings and *constituency services,* the term used to describe a wide array of assistance provided by a member of Congress to voters in need (for example, tracking a lost Social Security check, helping a veteran receive disputed benefits, or finding a summer internship for a college student). Indeed, one political scientist found that constituents for whom a House incumbent did casework gave the incumbent considerably higher evaluations than constituents who did not benefit from such casework.[22] In addition to these institutional means of self-promotion, most incumbents are highly visible in their districts. They have easy access to local media, cut ribbons galore, attend important local funerals, and speak frequently at meetings and community events. Nearly a fourth of the people in an average congressional district claim to have met their representative, and about half recognize their legislator's name without prompting. This spending and visibility pay off: reelection rates for sitting House members range well above 90 percent in most election years, and research shows district attentiveness is at least partly responsible for incumbents' electoral safety.[23] Recent research also identifies an indirect advantage of incumbency: the ability of the office holder to fend off challenges from strong opposition candidates. Gary Cox and Jonathan Katz's research calls it a "scare-off" effect. Incumbents have the ability to scare off high-quality challengers because of the institutional advantages of office, such as high name recognition, large war chests, staffs attached to legislative offices, and overall experience in running a successful campaign. Potential strong challengers facing this initial uphill battle will, according to Cox and Katz, wait until the incumbent retires rather than challenge him. This only strengthens the arguments for advantages to reelection related to incumbency.[24]

Frequently, the reelection rate for Senators is as high, but not always. In a "bad" year for House incumbents, "only" 88 percent will win (as in the Watergate year of 1974), but the senatorial reelection rate can drop much lower on occasion (to 60 percent in the 1980 Reagan landslide, for example). There is a good reason for this lower senatorial reelection rate. A Senate election is often a high-visibility contest; it receives much more publicity than a House race. So while House incumbents remain protected and insulated in part because few voters pay attention to their little known challengers, a Senate-seat challenger can become well known more easily and thus be in a better position to defeat an incumbent.

Redistricting, Scandals, and Coattails

For the relatively few incumbent members of Congress who lose their reelection bids, three explanations are paramount: redistricting, scandals, and coattails. Every ten years, after the census, all congressional district lines are redrawn (in states with more than one congressperson) so that every legislator represents about the same number of citizens. The U.S. Constitution requires that a census, which entails the counting of all Americans, be conducted every ten years. Until the first census could be taken, the Constitution fixed the number of representatives in the House at sixty-five. In 1790, then, one member represented 37,000 people. As the population of the new nation grew and states were added to the Union, the House became larger and larger. In 1910 it expanded to 435 members, and in 1929 its size was fixed at that number by statute.

Because the Constitution requires that representation in the House be based on state population, congressional districts must be redrawn by state legislatures to reflect population shifts, so that each member in Congress will represent approximately the same number of residents. This process of redrawing congressional districts to reflect increases or decreases in seats allotted to the states, as well as population shifts within a state, is called **redistricting.** When shifts occur in the national population, states gain or lose congressional seats. In the spring of 2000, the U.S. Census Bureau announced its results from the 2000 Census, which showed the largest population growth in American history. Since the 1990 Census, the U.S. population has increased 13.2 percent from 248.7 million people to an estimated 281.4 million people, with Western and Southern states (the sunbelt) gaining residents at the expense of the Northeast. This has been a trend since the 1960 Census, causing the Northeast to lose Congressional seats in every recent decade. It is also important to consider that the substantial increase in the Hispanic population (from 9 percent in 1990 to 13 percent in 2000) has magnified its collective political clout and will play an important role in redistricting and politics in general in the twenty-first century.

Redistricting is a largely political process that is used in many cases by majority party to insure formation of voting districts conducive to retaining or expanding their majority. Some states, however, including Iowa and Arizona, appoint nonpartisan commissions or use some independent means of drawing district lines. Although the processes vary in detail, most states require legislative approval of the plans.

This redistricting process, which has gone on since the first census in 1790, often involves what is called **gerrymandering** (see Figure 13.4). Recent research has added yet another actor into the redistricting process: the individual member. In an analysis of 1992 redistricting in North Carolina, Paul Gronke maintains that members' partisanship is balanced with their own ambition. He finds that "individual ambition generally outweighs partisan loyalty." If, in other words, voting for the other party's district lines will help the individual member obtain higher office, he will vote his own self-interest over the better interests of his party.[25]

Creative redistricting and the actions of state legislators have often created problems that have ended up in litigation. Over the years, the Supreme Court has ruled that:

- Congressional as well as state legislative districts must be apportioned on the basis of population.[26]
- Purposeful gerrymandering of a congressional district to dilute minority strength is illegal under the Voting Rights Act of 1965.[27]
- Redrawing of districts for obvious racial purposes to enhance minority representation is unconstitutional because it denies the constitutional rights of white citizens.[28]

Redistricting inevitably puts some incumbents in the same districts as other incumbents, and weakens the base of other congresspersons by adding territory favorable to the opposition party. In 1992 ten incumbents were paired together—five therefore lost—and about a dozen more incumbents were defeated in part because of unfavorable redistricting. The number of incumbents who actually lose their reelections because of redistricting is lessened by the strategic behavior of redistricted members—who often choose to retire rather than wage an expensive (and likely unsuccessful) reelection battle.[29–30]

Scandals come in many varieties in this age of the investigative press. The old standby of financial impropriety (bribery and payoffs, for example) has been supplemented by other forms of career-ending incidents, such as personal improprieties (sexual escapades, for instance). As with redistricting, the number of incumbents who actually lose their reelections because of a scandal is reduced by the propensity of implicated members to

Longman
Participate.com 2.0
Simulation
You Are Redrawing the Districts in Your State

redistricting
The redrawing of congressional districts to reflect increases or decreases in seats allotted to the states, as well as population shifts within a state.

gerrymandering
The legislative process through which the majority party in each statehouse tries to assure that the maximum number of representatives from its political party can be elected to Congress through the redrawing of legislative districts.

U.S. Senator Edward Kennedy (D–Mass.) knows full well the advantages of incumbency. Elected to the Senate in 1962 to complete the term of his brother, President John F. Kennedy, Edward Kennedy has been reelected every term since. His name recognition and campaign war chest enabled him to handily defeat Republican challenger Jack Robinson 73% to 13% in the 2000 election. (Photo courtesy: David McNew/Newsmakers/Liason Agency/Getty Source)

POLITICS NOW

SENATE RACE STEALS SPOTLIGHT

Every now and then, a race for a governorship or U.S. Senate seat becomes the headline race of an election season, defining the political year or providing an exceptionally memorable match-up. It was clear from the moment that First Lady Hillary Rodham Clinton expressed interest in an open New York Senate seat that 2000 would be such a year and the contest in the Empire State would be the race. It was not simply that a first lady had never in American history run for any public office, nor that her likely Republican opponent, New York City Mayor Rudolph Giuliani, was almost as well known as Clinton and an exceptionally feisty campaigner. Rather, the Senate contest would top the charts because it would inevitably encapsulate all of the important current issues and personalities in American politics today, from President Clinton and his scandals to splits within the Republican Party and the voracity of the press.

The situation was further complicated by Giuliani's unexpected withdrawal following his diagnosis of cancer in the summer before the election. Representative Rick Lazio, whose name had briefly been mentioned in the Republican nominating process, reappeared to carry the Republican torch. As a relatively young and unknown congressman,

Lazio had a hard time filling Giuliani's shoes, although his campaign did profit from the direct inheritance of all the anti-Clinton vote.

The immediate question was whether New York would support a carpetbagger. In fact, in an earlier headline race that helped define an election year, New Yorkers had already done so, by voting former U.S. Attorney General Robert Kennedy to a handy victory over a Republican incumbent in 1964. One difference between the two cases is that Kennedy was revered as the inheritor of his assassinated brother's political legacy, whereas Mrs. Clinton presumably hopes not to inherit many parts of Bill Clinton's baggage.

Nevertheless, the press are likely to tear into a candidate in a New York minute and were certain to review and revive all the issues of the Clinton era. As the campaign drew to a close, record expenditures for a Senate race and a series of telephone attack calls by both sides revealed that it was a very expensive and very nasty race. In the end, Clinton easily took the election by a 12-point margin. It remains to be seen how easily Clinton, as a junior senator with a high profile and considerable political baggage, will find the transition to and pursuit of her new career.

Longman
Participate.com 2.0
Simulation
You Are Redrawing the Districts in Your State

retire rather than seek reelection.[31] The power of incumbency is so strong, however, that many legislators survive even serious scandal to win reelection. An aide to Congressman Barney Frank (D–Mass.), an acknowledged homosexual, ran a prostitution service out of Frank's apartment in Washington, which became public knowledge in 1989. Though Frank claimed ignorance of the man's activities, he admitted having some of his parking tickets "fixed." Despite the scandal, most of Frank's constituents were satisfied with his representation of them and easily reelected him in 1990.

Sometimes the scandal factor comes into play because of national rather than local conditions. In 1998 the accumulation of many scandals in the Clinton administration resulted in the appointment of seven separate independent counsels. These scandals and the investigations they spawned energized at least a few Republican campaigns, while damaging strong Democratic defenders of Clinton. This was most clearly the case in states where Clinton was weak (for example, Idaho and Texas).

The defeat of a congressional incumbent can also occur as a result of the presidential coattail effect. As Table 13.2 shows, successful presidential candidates usually carry into office congressional candidates of the same party in the year of their election. Notice the overall decline in the strength of the coattail effect in modern times, however, as party identification has weakened and the powers and perks of incumbency have grown. Whereas Harry S Truman's party gained seventy-six House seats and nine additional Senate seats in 1948, George Bush's party actually lost three House seats and one Senate berth in 1988, despite Bush's handsome 54 percent majority. The gains can be minimal even in presidential landslide reelection years, such as 1972 (Nixon) and 1984 (Reagan). Occasionally, though, when the issues are emotional and the voters' desire for change is strong enough, as in Reagan's original 1980 victory, the coattail effect can still be substantial.

Off-Year Elections

Elections in the middle of presidential terms, **off-year elections,** present a different threat to incumbents. This time it is the incumbents of the president's party who are most in jeopardy. Just as the presidential party usually gains seats in presidential election years, it usually loses seats in off years. The problems and tribulations of governing normally cost a president some popularity, alienate key groups, or cause the public to want to send the president a message of one sort or another. An economic downturn or a scandal can underline and expand this circumstance, as the Watergate scandal of 1974 and the recession of 1982 demonstrated. The 2002 midterm elections, however, bucked that trends, marking the first time since Franklin D. Roosevelt in 1934 that a first-term president gained seats for his party in a midterm election. The historic election yielded President Bush a Republican sweep, wresting control of the Senate from Democrats and expanded the GOP majority in the House.

What is most apparent from the off-year statistics of Table 13.2, however, is the frequent tendency of voters to punish the president's party much more severely in the sixth year of an eight-year presidency, a phenomenon associated with retrospective voting (1958, 1966, 1974).[32] After only two years, voters are still willing to "give the guy a chance"; but after six years, voters are often restless for change. To their credit, Democrats, despite the scandals that plagued Clinton's presidency, avoided all second six-year itching 1998. During this midterm election, Democrats actually gained five seats in the U.S. House of Representatives. Finally, as Table 13.3 shows, Senate elections are less inclined to follow these rules than are House elections. The idiosyncratic nature of Senate contests is due to both their intermittent scheduling (only one-third of the seats come up for election every two years) and the existence of well-funded, well-known candidates who can sometimes swim against whatever political tide is rising. Also worth remembering is that midterm elections in recent history have a much lower voter turnout than presidential elections. A midterm election may draw only 35 percent to 40 percent of adult

off-year election
Election that takes place in the middle of a presidential term.

FIGURE 13.4   Gerrymandering
Two drawings—one a mocking cartoon, the other all too real—showing the bizarre geographical contortions involving in gerrymandering.

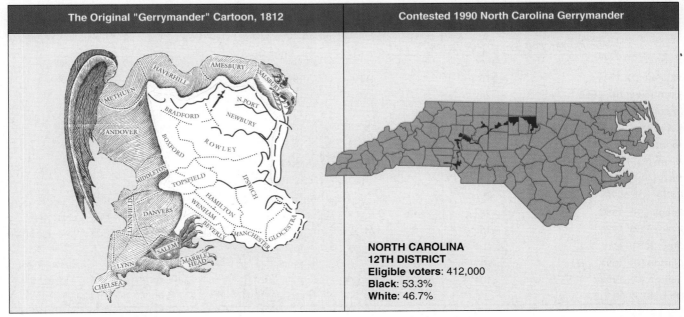

The Original "Gerrymander" Cartoon, 1812

Contested 1990 North Carolina Gerrymander

NORTH CAROLINA
12TH DISTRICT
Eligible voters: 412,000
Black: 53.3%
White: 46.7%

Source: From "Snakes or Ladders?" by David Van Biema, *Time*, July 12, 1993. Copyright © 1993 Time Inc. Reprinted by permission.

Americans to the polls, whereas a presidential contest attracts between 50 percent and 55 percent. (See Analyzing the Data: Voter Turnout in American Presidential and Midterm Congressional Elections.) (1996 was obviously an exception, producing the lowest voter turnout in a presidential general election since 1924.)

As noted, the 1994 congressional elections were extraordinary, a massacre for the Democrats and a dream come true for the Republicans. Not since Harry Truman's loss in 1946 had a Democratic president lost both houses of Congress in a midterm election, but such was President Clinton's fate. For the first time since popular elections for the U.S. Senate began in the early 1900s, the entire freshman Senate class (that is, all newly elected senators) was Republican. Moreover, every incumbent House member, senator, and governor who was defeated for reelection was a Democrat. Even the House Speaker, Thomas Foley (D–Wash.), fell in the onslaught. Republican George Nethercutt became the first person to unseat a House Speaker since 1862. Looking specifically at the House, political scientist Gary C. Jacobson concludes that Republicans scored their impressive victory in 1994 "by fielding (modestly) superior candidates who were on the right side of the issues that were important to voters in House elections and by persuading voters to blame a unified Democratic government for government's failures."[33]

Republicans had just as much success at the state level. The GOP took control of nineteen houses in state legislatures, securing a majority of the legislative bodies. From just nineteen governors before the election, Republicans wound up with thirty governorships, including eight of the nine largest. (Only Florida, which reelected Democratic Governor Lawton Chiles, resisted the trend.)

Where did the GOP margins at the polls come from? Men voted strongly Republican, overwhelming women's narrow preference for Democrats. Whites cast 58 percent of their ballots for the GOP, overwhelming the 88 percent of African Americans and 70 percent of Hispanics who voted Democratic. Americans who backed Ross Perot in 1992 also shifted heavily to the GOP column in 1994. Moreover, the once solidly Democratic South continued a decades-long trend toward the Republican Party. For the first time since Reconstruction, the GOP captured a majority of all Southern U.S. House seats, Senate seats, and governorships. All across the United States, but in the South in particular, voters seemed to be rejecting the Clinton presidency. Of the majority of Americans who disapproved of Clinton's performance as president, 82 percent cast ballots for GOP candidates for Congress, according to the networks' exit polls on Election Day.

TABLE 13.2   Congressional Election Results, 1948–2002

| | GAIN (+) OR LOSS (−) FOR PRESIDENT'S PARTY | | | | |
| PRESIDENTIAL ELECTION YEARS | | | OFF-YEAR ELECTIONS | | |
President/Year	House	Senate	Year	House	Senate
Truman (D): 1948	+76	+9	1950	-29	-6
Eisenhower (R): 1952	+24	+2	1954	-18	-1
Eisenhower (R): 1956	-2	0	1958	-48	-13
Kennedy (D): 1960	-20	-2	1962	-4	+3
Johnson (D): 1964	+38	+2	1966	-47	-4
Nixon (R): 1968	+7	+5	1970	-12	+2
Nixon (R): 1972	+13	-2	Ford: 1974	-48	-5
Carter (D): 1976	+2	0	1978	-15	-3
Reagan (R): 1980	+33	+12	1982	-26	+1
Reagan (R): 1984	+15	-2	1986	-5	-8
Bush (R): 1988	-3	-1	1990	-9	-1
Clinton (D): 1992	-10	0	1994	-52	-9*
Clinton (D): 1996	+10	-2	1998	+5	0
Bush (R): 2000	-2	-4	2002	+6	+2

Includes the switch from Democrat to Republican of Alabama U.S. Senator Richard Shelby.

While the 1994 congressional elections were extraordinary, the 1996 congressional elections were immediately dubbed the "Status Quo" election by political observers. Far less hostile than they were in 1992, when voters ousted Republicans from the White House for the first time since 1976, and in 1994, when those same voters booted the Democrats from Capitol Hill, this time the White House, Senate, and House all remained in the previous proprietors' hands. Perhaps the most important fact about the 1996 congressional election is that it reinforced the GOP's electoral hold on the South—where only a few decades ago the Democratic Party dominated.[34]

The 1996 election results confirmed preelection conventional wisdom. In the U.S. House of Representatives, Democrats were able to knock off a handful of vulnerable Republican freshmen in states like Illinois, New York, North Carolina, Maine, and New Jersey. Republicans offset some of these losses by taking nine seats from Democrats, most of which had been relinquished by retiring Democratic lawmakers. In the Senate, Republicans posted a net gain of two seats.

Cynics frequently say that elections do not matter, but the 1998 midterm elections effectively and dramatically refuted the cynics. A loss of just five seats for the Republicans in the U.S. House of Representatives toppled a speaker, and not just any speaker of the House, but one of the most powerful speakers of the twentieth century—Newt Gingrich of Georgia. The Republicans were expected to gain seats in both the House of Representatives and, especially, in the Senate, as well as a few governorships. They, however, did not do so for several reasons. First, Republicans had pushed hard for severe punishment against President Clinton because of the Monica Lewinsky scandal. While the public disapproved of President Clinton's embarrassing and demeaning behavior in that scandal, most Americans believed that impeachment was simply too severe a penalty. Second, the Republicans made a strategic miscalculation in the election by shifting into neutral governmentally; that is, Republicans accomplished virtually nothing in the second session of the 105th Congress. Their assumption was that the Clinton scandal would be enough to deliver substantial gains for the GOP, and they bet wrong. President Clinton's Democratic Party scored a moral victory by actually gaining five seats in the U.S. House of Representatives and maintaining their share of seats in the Senate. The most surprising election result of all, however, occurred on the Friday after the November third election, when Speaker Gingrich shocked the nation by announcing his resignation from the speakership and from Congress itself.

The 2002 Congressional Elections

As discussed earlier, the presdient's party historically loses congressional seats in midterm electrons, espcially during the first term in office. George W. Bush's first midterm election, however, was a remarkable exception. In the previous fourteen midterms, the opposing party has lost an average of twenty-six seats in the House and four in the Senate. It was more than a statistical anomaly, however, when the Republicans gained a handful of seats in House and Senate races. This year marks the first time since 1934 that a first-term president has picked up seats in both houses of Congress. How did this occur? While there is no definitive answer, the remarkable time and energy Presdient George W. Bush devoted to stumping for Republican candidates in key battleground states (under White House strategist Karl Rove's watchful direction) cannot be overlooked. Between April and November, Bush and Vice President Dick Cheney raised more than $141 million campaigning for Republican candidates, capitalizing on his approval ratings, which remained high more than a year after 9/11 terrorist attacks. Some Democrats felt that the War on Terrorism and the administration's focus on impending hostility with Iraq constrained the voice of opposition by monopolizing the political agenda, preventing Democratic candidates from gaining ground on a weak economy, corporate scandals, and traditionally Democratic domestic issues. In addition, the D.C.-area snipers dominated media coverage, quite justifiably becoming a fixture of public consciousness that eclipsed virtually all political discourse until the final twelve days before the election.

TABLE 13.3   Results of Selected Elections, 2002

STATE	CONTEST	WINNER	LOSER	SIGNIFICANCE
Arkansas	Senate	Mark Pryor (D)	Tim Hutchinson (R)	AG Pryor defeats scandal-ridden, one-term Senator; only Senate seat to change from Republican to Democrat
Florida	Governor	Jeb Bush (R)	Bill McBride (D)	President's brother overcomes last minute surge from McBride
Georgia	Governor	Sonny Perdue (R)	Roy Barner (D)	Perdue upsets Barnes to become the first Republican governor of Georgia since Reconstruction
Georgia	Senate	Saxby Chambliss (R)	Max Cleland (D)	Cleland, a triple-amputee Vietnam veteran, defeated by Rep. Chambliss
Maryland	Governor	Bob Ehrlich (R)	Kathleen Kennedy Townsend (D)	Lt. Gov. Townsend, saddled with baggage from an unpopular governor, runs poor campaign and loses in a heavily Democratic state
Massachusetts	Governor	Mitt Romney (R)	Shannon O'Brien (D)	2002 Olympic organizer Romney pulls upset in strong Democratic state
Minnesota	Senate	Norm Coleman (R)	Walter Mondale (D)	Sen. Paul Wellstone, who was tragically killed in a plane crash a few days before the election, replaced on ballot by former Vice President Walter Mondale
Missouri	Senate	Jim Talent (R)	Jean Carnahan (D)	Carnahan, who was named Senator after her husband was elected posthumously in 2000, loses to Bush candidate Talent
New Jersey	Senate	Frank Lautenberg (D)	Doug Forrester (R)	Despite protest from Republicans, Lautenberg replaces corrupt Senator Torricelli on the ballot when it becomes clear he will lose; Lautenberg coasts to win
New Hampshire	Senate	John Sununu (R)	Jeanne Shaheen (D)	Rep. Sununu beats Republican Sen. Bob Smith in primary and three-term Democratic governor Shaheen in general election
North Carolina	Senate	Elizabeth Dole (R)	Erskine Bowles (D)	Wife of former Senator and presidential nominee Bob Dole defeats former Clinton chief of staff

Following the 2000 election, the Senate was tied at 50–50 with Republicans holding leadership capacity because of Vice President Cheney's tie-breaking vote. In May 2001, the defection of Sen. Jim Jeffords of Vermont allowed Democrats to take a control of the Senate by the smallest of margins, while Republicans narrowly held a six-vote majority in the House. The near parity of the balance of power in the Senate and House produced an election where even marginal gains for either side made a crucial difference. In 2002, thirty-four Senate seats, thirty-six governorships, and the entire House were up for grabs. Republicans capitalized on a late wave that expanded their House majority by four seats and regained control of the Senate, 51–48, possibly giving Bush the mandate that eluded him in the 2000 election. At the time of publication, the Louisiana senate election was undecided, as Democratic incumbent Mary Landrieu was facing a December 7 runoff against Republican Suzanne Haik Terrell, a result of Louisiana election law that requires winners to post 50 percent or more of the vote; Landrieu only secured 46 percent of the vote in an election that featured nine candidates.

Consistent with the historical norm, most contests tended to favor incumbents regardless of party. Only four incumbent governors lost, and only three incumbent senators who were on the Election Day ballot lost: Democrats Jean Carnahan of Missouri and Max Cleland of Georgia, and Republican Tim Hutchinson of Arkansas. (In adition, Republican Sen. Bob Smith of New Hampshire was defeated in the primary). Because many of the Republican governors elected in the 1994 GOP landslide and reelected in 1998 were term-limited, Democrats were expected to make big gains in several open govenorship races. Wins by Republicans in heavily GOP states Massachusetts and Maryland, as well as the surprise victory of Republican Sonny Perdue for Georgia governor helped mute the number of Democratic pick-ups, leaving the parties tied at twenty-five governorships apiece when the dust settled.

A N A L Y Z I N G   T H E   D A T A

VOTER TURNOUT IN AMERICAN PRESIDENTIAL AND MIDTERM CONGRESSIONAL ELECTIONS

The twentieth century has seen a gradual and erratic but generally consistent decline in voter turnout. Various factors influence turnout: the high percentages of 1876 and 1960 both occurred in open races (i.e., when no incumbent was running), and in the latter, the new TV debates ener-gized and engaged the electorate. The low midterm election turnout of 1998 is unfortunately all too typical of off-year (i.e., nonpresidential) elections. Following the historic 2000 election, many anticipate high voter turnout in the 2004 presidential election.

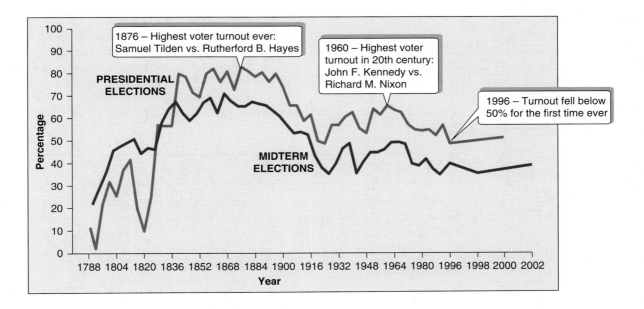

Source: Adopted from Harold W. Stanley and Richard G. Niemi, *Vital Statistics on American Politics,* 2001-2002, 5th ed. (Washington, DC: CQ Press, 2002, p. 14; 2002 turnout: Curtis Gans, Committee for the Study of the American Electorate.

The 2002 elections were unique not only for delivering big wins for the incumbent president, but also for the unusual and unexpected conditions that preceded a number of contests. In Minnesota, Senator Paul Wellstone, along with his family and several staff members, died tragically in a plane crash while campaigning on October 25, only days before the November elections. Amid the disbelief, Minnesotans desperately scanned the political landscape for a qualified replacement. Former Vice President Walter Mondale accepted the Democratic Party's appointment, but lost the race to Republican Norm Coleman, who capitalized on a remarkable backlash to Sen. Wellstone's memorial service, which was seen by some as a Democratic pep rally. In New Jersey, former Senator Frank Lautenberg became the Democrat's late nominee when Senator Robert Toricelli abruptly withdrew his candidacy after a wave of criticism over professional ethics made it clear that he was not likely to win the election. Following the decisive ruling by the New Jersey Supreme Court, Lautenberg was permitted to replace Toricelli on the ballot, ultimately defeating his Republican opponent Douglas Forrester.

ALL THOSE APATHETIC AMERICANS WHO DID NOT VOTE IN THE LAST ELECTION TODAY SPENT FIFTY CENTS APIECE TO DIAL IN THEIR OPINIONS TO "ENTERTAINMENT TONIGHT" ON THE QUESTION OF WHETHER JOHN TRAVOLTA SHOULD HAVE A CHIN TUCK.

turnout

The proportion of the voting-age public that votes.

WEB EXPLORATION
What voters say before going to the polls and whom they actually vote for are sometimes different. To look at poll questions and answers that were asked before and after national elections, go to.
www.ablongman.com/oconnor

By and large, control by the Republicans over the two branches of elected government should hasten the flow of legislative business and improve the ability of the White House to promote and control the agenda. Senator Trent Lott (R-Miss.), returned to power as Majority Leader in the Senate, will be able to help President Bush promote legislature for the remainder of his term. They must not forget, however, the lessons learned from 1994—the last time the GOP held both houses of Congress—when Newt Gingrich's overconfidence hurt Republicans in 1996. Under the leadership of new House Minority Leader Nancy Pelosi, a liberal from San Francisco, Democrats will retain the ability to block discussion on the Senate floor with filibusters that cannot be defeated by a simple majority. However, it remains to be seen how they will regroup and recover from such a devasting election season without a national leader and consistant message as the focus now turns toward 2004 and the presdiential race.

VOTING BEHAVIOR

Whether they are casting ballots in congressional or presidential elections, voters behave in certain distinct ways and exhibit unmistakable patterns to political scientists who study them.

Participation

Turnout is the proportion of the voting-age public that votes. The first clear division is between citizens who turn out and those who do not. About 40 percent of the eligible adult population in the United States vote regularly, whereas 25 percent are occasional voters. Thirty-five percent rarely or never vote. Turnout is important because voters have the ability to influence election outcomes. The presidential election of 2000 will forever be the classic example of the power of an individual's single vote. As recounts succeeded recounts in several states and the fate of the presidency rested on razor-thin margins representing perhaps a handful of ballots, many voters in Florida, New Mexico, and Oregon must have wished they had taken the trouble to exercise their rights to choose their leader.

There are many differences, including socioeconomic and attitudinal, between voters and nonvoters. First, people who vote are usually more highly educated than nonvoters. Other things being equal, college graduates are much more likely to vote than those with less education. People with more education tend to learn more about politics, are less hindered by registration requirements, and are more self-confident about their ability to affect public life. Therefore, one might argue that institutions of higher education provide citizens with opportunities to learn about and become interested in politics.

Income

There is also a relationship between income and voting. A considerably higher percentage of citizens with annual incomes over $40,000 vote than do citizens with incomes under $10,000. Income level is, to some degree, connected to education level, as wealthier people tend to have more opportunities for higher education and more education also may lead to higher income. Wealthy citizens are also more likely than poor ones to think that the "system" works for them and that their votes make a difference.

People with higher income also find the opportunity cost of participation cheaper than do the poor and are more likely to have a direct financial stake in the decisions of the government, thus spurring them into action.[35]

By contrast, lower-income citizens often feel alienated from politics, possibly believing that conditions will remain the same no matter for whom they vote. A factor that contributes to this feeling of alienation is that American political parties, unlike parties in many other countries that tend to associate themselves with specific social classes, do not attempt to link themselves intimately to one major class (such as the "working class"). Therefore, the feelings of alienation and apathy about politics prevalent among many lower-income Americans should not be unexpected.

Age

There is also a correlation between age and voter participation rates. The Twenty-Sixth Amendment, ratified in 1971, lowered the voting age to eighteen. While this amendment obviously increased the number of *eligible* voters, it did so by enfranchising the group that is least likely to vote. A much higher percentage of citizens age thirty and older vote than do citizens younger than thirty, although voter turnout decreases over the age of seventy, primarily because of physical infirmity, which makes it difficult to get to the polling location. Regrettably, less than half of eligible eighteen- to twenty-four-year-olds are even registered to vote. The most plausible reason for this is that younger people are more mobile; they have not put down roots in a community. Because voter registration is not automatic, people who relocate have to make an effort to register. Therefore, the effect of adding this low-turnout group to the electorate has been to lower the overall turnout rate. As young people marry, have children, and settle down in a community, their likelihood of voting increases.[36]

Gender

There have been elections throughout the twentieth century in which gender was a factor, although precise data are not always available to prove the conventional wisdom. For example, journalists in 1920 claimed that women—in their first presidential election after the passage of the Nineteenth Amendment granted women suffrage—were especially likely to vote for Republican presidential candidate Warren G. Harding. In the sexist view of the day, women were supposedly taken in by the handsome Harding's charm. Recent evidence is more clear that women act and react differently than men to some candidacies, including those of other women. For instance, Democratic women were more likely than Democratic men to support Walter Mondale's presidential ticket in 1984 because of former Vice President Mondale's selection of New York Representative Geraldine Ferraro for the second slot on his presidential ticket. However, Republican women at the time were more likely than GOP men to support Ronald Reagan's candidacy because of Ferraro's presence on the Democratic ticket; Republican women were opposed to Ferraro's liberal voting record and views. Since 1980 the so-called "gender gap" (the difference between the voting choices of men and women) has become a staple of American politics.

Simply put, in most elections today, women are more likely to support the Democratic candidate and men are more likely to support the Republican candidate. The size of the gender gap varies considerably from election to election, though normally the gender gap is between 5 and 7 percentage points. That is, women support the average Democrat 5 to 7 percent more than men support the average Republican candidate. Some elections result in an expanded gender gap though, such as the presidential election of 1996 where the gender gap was an enormous 17 percentage points, about 10 points larger than in 1992 (Bob Dole narrowly won men, while Bill Clinton scored a landslide among women). Of importance here is the fact that women now comprise a majority of the adult population in all the American states, and they are a majority of the registered electorate in virtually all of those states. This means it has become increasingly important for both Democrats and Republicans to seek the votes and support of women.

TABLE 13.4   **How America Votes**
The U.S. voting system relies on a patchwork of machines to tally voter's choices. The number of punch-card systems similar to the ones involved in the 2000 ballot dispute in Florida has declined to 16 percent since the 2000 election.

	How they work	*Percentage of precincts that use them*
Optical scan	Shade in area next to candidate's name.	43%
Punch cards	Punch holes in a card next to a candidate's name.	16%
Electronic	Use keyboard or touch-screen to record votes.	16%
Lever machine	Inside booth, voters pull levers to choose candidate.	11%
Paper ballots	Voters mark ballots with pen or pencil.	11%
Mixed	More than one system.	4%

Source: "How it Looked Inside the Booth," *New York Times*, November 6, 2002.

Race

Another voter difference is related to race: Whites tend to vote more regularly than do African Americans. This was evident in the most recent presidential election. While turnout was up for both races—from the 49 percent of 1996 to a little over 51 percent in 2000—turnout increased less among African Americans than among whites. Turnout among whites was slightly over 50 percent in 2000; among African Americans, it hovered in the mid-40s depending on the locality.

This difference is due in part to the relative income and educational levels of the two racial groups. African Americans tend to be poorer and have less formal education than whites; as mentioned earlier, both of these factors affect voter turnout. Significantly, though, highly educated and wealthier African Americans are at least equally likely to vote, and sometimes more so, than whites of similar background.

Race also helps explain why the South has long had a lower turnout than the rest of the country (see Figure 13.5). In the wake of Reconstruction, the Southern states made it extremely difficult for African Americans to register to vote, and only a small percentage of the eligible African American population was registered throughout the South. The Voting Rights Act of 1965 (VRA) helped to change this situation. The VRA was intended to guarantee voting rights to African Americans nearly a century after passage of the Fifteenth Amendment. Often now heralded as the most successful piece of civil rights legislation ever passed, the VRA targeted states that had used literacy or morality tests or poll taxes to exclude blacks from the polls. The act has two key provisions: (1) Section 2, which makes it illegal to use any voting device or procedure that denies or hinders minority registration was not in proportion to the racial composition of the district to obtain approval from the Justice Department concerning any proposed changes in voting qualifications or procedures. It also authorized the federal government to monitor all elections in areas where discrimination was found to be practiced or where less than 50 percent of the voting-age public was registered to vote in the 1964 election.

The impact of the act was immediate. African American voter registration skyrocketed and the number of African Americans elected to office skyrocketed. For example, in 1965 there were 280 black elected officials at any level in the United States. Since 1965, African American voters have used their strength at the ballot box to elect black officials at all levels of government. But while the results have been encouraging, the percentage of elected offices held by African Americans in the eleven southern states covered by the VRA remains relatively small.

The Asian American segment of the electorate is less monolithic and more variable in its voting than either the Hispanic or the African American communities. Even so, it is worth noting the considerable political diversity within this group: Chinese Americans tend to prefer Democratic candidates, but Vietnamese Americans, with a strong anticommunist leaning, tend to support Republicans. A typical voting split for the Asian American community in general, though, might run about 60 percent Democratic and 40 percent Republican, though it can reach the extreme of a 50–50 split, depending on the election.

FIGURE 13.5   **The South Versus the Non-South for Presidential Voter Turnout**
After a century-long discrepancy caused by discrimination against African-American voters in the South, regional voting turnouts have grown much closer together with the increasing enfranchisement of these voters.

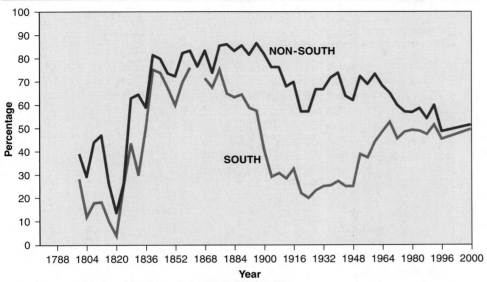

Source: Adopted from Harold W. Stanley and Richard G. Niemi, *Vital Statistics on American Politics,* 1997–1998, 5th ed. (Washington, D.C.: CQ Press, 1998), Figure 3-2, p. 86.

Interest in Politics

Although socioeconomic factors undoubtedly weigh heavily in voter participation rates, an interest in politics must also be included as an important factor. Many citizens who vote have grown up in families interested and active in politics, and they in turn stimulate their children to take an interest. Additionally, recent research has determined that interest in politics is not dependent on any one especially mobilizing candidate. Those citizens involved in the process remain so even if their favored candidate loses. Political scientist James McCann, for instance, found that "preconvention mobilization into presidential politics tends to increase participation on behalf of House candidates," even if the candidate for which the individual was mobilized lost their party's presidential nomination.[37] Likewise, based on data from 1984 presidential nomination caucus attenders, Walter Stone says that voters become mobilized for later party work and support after participating in presidential nominating campaigns, whether their favored candidate won or lost. Such workers, Stone maintains, care more about the outcome of elections and the political process than they do about individual candidates.[38] Conversely, many nonvoters simply do not care about politics or the outcome of elections, never having been taught their importance at a younger age.

People who are highly interested in politics constitute only a small minority of the U.S. populace. For example, the most politically active Americans—party and issue-group activists—make up less than 5 percent of the country's 250 million people. Those who contribute time or money to a party or a candidate during a campaign make up only about 10 percent of the total population. On the other hand, although these percentages appear low, they translate into millions of Americans who contribute more than just votes to the system.

Why Is Voter Turnout So Low?

There is no getting around the fact that the United States has one of the lowest voter participation rates of any nation in the industrialized world. In 1960, 62 percent of the eligible electorate voted in the 1960 presidential election, but by 1996, American voter

FIGURE 13.6   **Why People Don't Vote**
Nonvoters give a variety of reasons why they do not vote. Being too busy is the most popular excuse, but most answers are likely a byproduct of overall apathy and disenchantment with the political process.

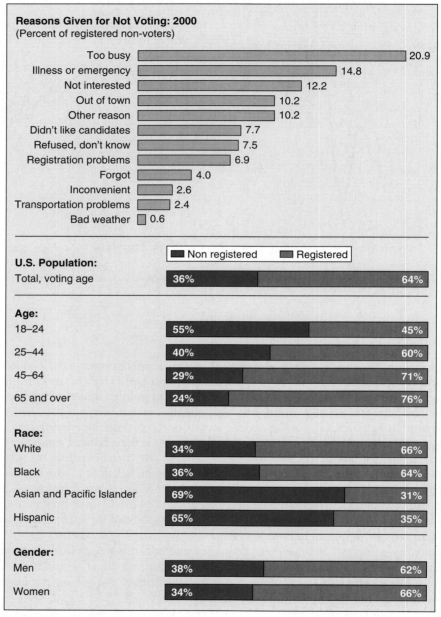

Source: U.S. Census Bureau, Current Population Survey, 2000.

participation had fallen to a record low of 48.8 percent—the lowest general presidential election turnout since 1824. In 2000, despite the closeness of the race and the consequent importance of a single vote, participation only touched 51 percent. In contrast, turnout for post war British elections has fluctuated between 72 percent and 84 percent. Figure 13.6 lists several reasons nonvoters give for not voting in the United States.

Difficulty of Registration.   Interestingly, of those who are registered, the overwhelming majority vote. The real source of the participation problem in the United States seems to be that a relatively low percentage of the adult population is registered to vote. There are a number of reasons for the low U.S. registration rates. First, while nearly every other democratic country places the burden of registration on the government rather than on the individual, in the United States the registration process requires individual initiative—a daunting impediment in this age of political apathy. Thus, the cost (in terms of time and effort) of registering to vote is higher in the United States than it is in other industrialized democracies. Second, many nations automatically register all of their citizens to vote. In the United States, however, citizens must jump the extra hurdle of remembering on their own to register. Indeed, it is no coincidence that voter participation rates dropped markedly after reformers pushed through strict voter registration laws in the early part of the twentieth century. Correspondingly, several recent studies of the effects of relaxed state voter registration laws show that easier registration leads to higher levels of turnout. Stephen Knack, for instance, found that when states adopted Election Day registration of new voters, large and significant improvements in turnout occurred among younger voters and the poor.[39] Similarly, Daniel Franklin, in a 1992 study of states with a "motor voter" law (allowing citizens to register to vote at the Department of Motor Vehicles), found that those states had levels of registration and turnout that were significantly higher than in states lacking such a law.[40]

A major mobilizer of the youth vote, Rock the Vote registers new voters and lobbies for legislation of interest to young people and the record industry. The band Angry Salad performs here at a 2000 event in Philadelphia. (Photo courtesy: Rock the Vote. www.rockthevote.org)

Difficulty of Absentee Voting.   Stringent absentee ballot laws are another factor in the United States' low voter turnout. Many states, for instance, require citizens to apply in person for absentee ballots, a burdensome requirement given that one's inability to be present in his or her home state is often the reason for absentee balloting in the first place. Recent literature in political science links liberalized absentee voting rules and higher turnout. One study, for instance, concluded that lax absentee voting restrictions reduced the "costs of voting" and increased turnout when the parties mobilized their followers to take advantage of new lenient absentee voting laws.[41]

Number of Elections.   Another explanation for low voter turnout in this country is the sheer number and frequency of elections, which few if any other democracies can match. Yet an election cornucopia is the inevitable result of federalism and the separation of powers, which result in layers of often separate elections on the local, state, and national levels.

Longman
Participate.com 2.0
Participation
The Prepared Voter Kit

Voter Attitudes.   Although some of the reasons for low voter participation are due to the institutional factors we have just reviewed, voter attitudes play an equally important part. Some nations try to get around the effects of voter attitudes with compulsory voting laws (Australia and Belgium), or by taxing citizens who do not vote. Not surprisingly, voter turnout rates in Australia and Belgium are often greater than 95 percent.

As noted previously, alienation afflicts some voters, and others are just plain apathetic, possibly because of a lack of pressing issues in a particular year, satisfaction with the status quo, or uncompetitive (even uncontested) elections. Furthermore, many citizens may be turned off by the quality of campaigns in a time when petty issues and personal mudslinging are more prevalent than ever. Additionally, one recent study

Longman
Participate.com 2.0
Visual Literacy
Voter Turnout: Who Votes? Do Americans Vote as Much as Other Citizens?

GLOBAL POLITICS

VOTER TURNOUT AND THE SUCCESS OF INDONESIA

The problem of declining voter turnout over the last two decades has been a cause of concern across the industrial democracies. Nowhere is the issue seen as more acute than in the United States, which has the lowest voter turnout of any country surveyed here. Why do other countries have higher voter turnouts?

One explanation has to do with when elections are held. Every other government holds elections on weekends, usually on Sunday, when voters are not at work. Another explanation is that parliamentary systems require their voters to vote less often. Elections for the parliament typically happen every three to four years. Prime ministers are elected by the lower house of Parliament, so a vote for a legislative candidate is also an indirect vote for a chief executive. By definition, there are no midterm legislative elections, when turnout in the United States drops from presidential election levels.

Most important, voter registration is automatic, or nearly so, in the other countries. Voters are placed on the election rolls when they register their residence at the local government office. The Canadian government actively canvasses citizens of voting age to ensure their inclusion on the rolls. This is significant because the percentage recorded for the United States in the table shows voter turnout as a proportion of the voting-age population (including people ineligible to vote); the proportion of actual voters to registered voters is nearly two-thirds, close to the other industrial democracies levels. Automatic registration would undoubtedly

increase the number of registered voters, and therefore turnout, as it does in Europe, Canada, and Japan.

The high voter turnout in the 1999 election for the Indonesian House of Representatives highlights another issue. That election, and the presidential election that took place the same year, was the first democratic election since the 1950s. The number of new political parties that contested that election suggests a broad public enthusiasm for the turn to democracy. We may see that election as a repudiation of the previous dictatorship as well as support for a new political system. Given the magnitude of the shift in government, we may also conclude that the stakes were much higher in that election than in any American election in recent history, with a correspondingly high voter participation.

Voter Turnout in Recent National Elections

Country	Year, Election	Turnout (%)
Canada	1997, parliamentary	69.6
France	1997, parliamentary	71.4
Germany	2002, parliamentary	77.9
Indonesia	1999, parliamentary	93.3
Italy	1996, parliamentary	82.9
Japan	2000, parliamentary	62.4
Mexico	2000, presidential	64.0
Russia	2000, presidential	68.6
United Kingdom	2001, parliamentary	54.9
United States	2000, presidential	50.7

Sources: Elections Around the World, http://www.Agora.stm.it/election; and selected national government sites.

Longman
Participate.com
2.0
Comparative
Comparing Voting and Elections

finds that divided government affects voter turnout, with turnout declining by 2 percent in each consecutive election conducted when the presidency and Congress are controlled by different parties.[42] Finally, perhaps turnout has declined due to rising levels of distrust of government. More and more people are telling pollsters that they lack confidence in political leaders. In the past, some scholars argued that there is no correlation between distrust of political leaders and nonvoting. But as the levels of distrust rise, these preliminary conclusions might need to be revisited.

Weak Political Parties. Political parties today are no longer as effective as they once were in mobilizing voters, ensuring that they are registered, and getting them to the polls. As we discussed in chapter 12, the parties once were grassroots organizations which forged strong party-group links with their supporters. Today these bonds have been stretched to the breaking point for many. Candidate-centered campaigns and the growth of expansive party bureaucracies have resulted in a somewhat more distant party with which most people do not identify very strongly.

How Can the United States Improve Voter Turnout?

Reformers have suggested many ideas to increase voter turnout in the United States. Always on the list is raising the political awareness of young citizens, a reform that inevitably must involve our nation's schools. Political scientists Steven J. Rosenstone and John Marc Hansen's research show that the rise in formal education levels among Americans played a significant role in preventing an even greater decline in voter turnout.[43] No less important, and perhaps simpler to achieve, are the institutional reforms, though many of these reforms, if enacted, may result in only a marginal increase in turnout.

Easier Registration and Absentee Voting.   Registration laws vary by state; but in every state except North Dakota, registration is required in order to vote. Many observers believe that voter turnout could be increased if registering to vote were made simpler for citizens. The typical thirty-days-before-an-election registration deadline could be shortened to a week or ten days. After all, most people become more interested in voting as Election Day nears. Indeed, one political scientist calculated that allowing citizens to register on the same day as they vote would boost national turnout by five percentage points.[44] Better yet, all U.S. citizens could be registered automatically at the age of eighteen. Absentee ballots could also be made easier to obtain by eliminating the in-person requirement.

In 1993 a major advance toward easier registration was achieved with the passage by Congress of the so-called motor-voter bill, which required states to permit individuals to register by mail, not just in person. The law, strongly backed by President Clinton, also allows citizens to register to vote when they visit any motor vehicles office, public assistance agency, or military recruitment division. Proponents of the law say it will result in the registration of the roughly 49 million Americans of voting age with driver's licenses or identification cards but who have failed to register to vote. Opponents claim the new law is yet another in a long line of intrusive and costly federal mandates that do not appropriate money to pay for the costs involved in implementing the programs. The motor-voter bill took effect in 1995, so it will be some time before we know how many people it will add to the registration rolls. However, research on motor-voter laws passed by states prior to the passage of federal legislation indicates that such laws indeed have a positive impact on voter registration levels.[45]

Make Election Day a Holiday.   Besides removing an obstacle to voting (the busy workday), making Election Day a holiday might focus more voter attention on the contests in the critical final hours.

Strengthen Parties.   Reformers have long argued that strengthening the political parties would increase voter turnout, because parties have historically been the organizations in the United States best suited for and most successful at mobilizing citizens to vote. During the late 1800s and early 1900s, the country's "Golden Age" of powerful political parties, one of their primary activities was getting out the vote on Election Day. Even today, the parties' Election Day get-out-the-vote drives increase voter turnout by as many as several million in national contests.

Other Suggestions.   Other ideas to increase voter turnout are less practical or feasible. For example, holding fewer elections might sound appealing, but it is difficult to see how this could be accomplished without diluting many of the central tenets of federalism and separation of powers that the Founders believed essential to the protection of liberty. Political scientist Arend Lijphart suggests other changes that he believes could increase voter turnout, including proportional representation of the congressional vote to encourage third parties and combat voter apathy toward the two major parties, changing Election Day to Saturday or Sunday, and making voting mandatory, which he contends has benefits which far outweigh most Americans' aversion to it.[46]

A state registry of motor vehicles worker displays the form that makes it easy for those visiting the registry also to register to vote. (Photo courtesy: Dennis Brack/Black Star)

Does Low Voter Turnout Matter?

Some political observers have argued that nonvoting is not a critical problem. For example, some feel that the preferences of nonvoters are not much different from those who do vote. If this is true, the results would be about the same if everyone voted. Others contend that since legal and extralegal denial of the vote to previously disfranchised groups—African Americans, women, Hispanics,—have now been outlawed, nonvoting is voluntary. Nonvoters are said to be indicating their acceptance of things as they are. Therefore we should not attempt to make it easier for these people, often characterized as apathetic and lazy, to vote. Finally, some even claim that low voter turnout is a positive benefit, based on the dubious supposition that less-educated people are more easily swayed. Thus low turnout supposedly increases the stability of the system and discourages demagogic, populist appeals.

We should not be too quick to accept these arguments, which have much in common with the early nineteenth-century view that the Nineteenth Amendment to the Constitution (which enfranchised women) need not be passed because husbands could protect the interests of their wives. First, the social makeup and attitudes of present-day nonvoters are significantly different from those of voters. Nonvoters tend to be low income, younger, blue collar, less educated, and more heavily minority. Even if their expressed preferences about politics do not look very distinctive, their objective circumstances as well as their need for government services differ from the majority of those who do vote. These people—those who require the most help from government—currently lack a fair share of electoral power. A political system that actively seeks to include and mobilize these people might well produce broader-based policies that differ from those we have today.

In 2000, nationwide voter turnout was approximately 51 percent of the eligible population, slightly up from 49 percent in 1996. The 2 percent increase should be lauded and praised, but it is certainly not sufficient. The low turnout is even more frustrating given the closeness and magnitude of the 2000 election: the presidency, the House, the Senate, numerous state legislatures (and consequent redistricting battles), and even the Supreme Court hung on the outcome of the historic election of 2000. It is regrettable that more people did not familiarize themselves with the issues and candidates and exercise their constitutional right to participate in the election. Ironically, after years of failing to vote on the grounds that "my vote doesn't count," this was the year in which every vote counted, with painful significance. If more Americans had known how close this election actually would be, they almost certainly would have voted on November 7th but of course it is the very impossibility of this foreknowledge that makes it so essential to vote—always, every time.

There is a stark contradiction in the results of the 2000 election. One interpretation offers a message of idealism, and the other a message of cynicism. On the one hand, we have learned anew how one vote really can make a difference. An older generation of Americans learned this in 1960 in the extremely close election where one vote per precinct in the United States made John F. Kennedy the president of the United States. This was so few votes in a handful of states that clearly the power of the individual vote became clear, and perhaps this is a lesson that Americans need to learn and relearn.

On the other hand, the carelessness with which the media handled the election in its early stages, especially in Florida, did nothing to dispel the doubly false belief of many

Americans that their votes would be no more important than usual. Of course, there is bitterness from the realization that for many Americans who did trouble to vote, their vote went uncounted. Thousands of ballots were discarded due to machine or human error, several thousand ballots from Americans living overseas or serving in the military were not counted in the initial tabulation; some polling stations may even have unfairly turned away rightful voters. The turnout in several states during the 2002 elections challenged apathy and cynicism. Following Sen. Paul Wellstone's tragic death, the intrigue surrounding the last few weeks of the Minnesota senate race led to a turnout of over 60 percent. In South Dakota, where the senate race was viewed as a proxy for President Bush versus Senate Majority Leader Tom Daschle, turnout also topped 60 percent of voters. Unfortunately, these states were the exceptions, not the norms. While national turnout increased slightly from 1998's record low, breaking a steady decline, only 39 percent of voters turned out on November 5, 2002.

Ticket-Splitting

Citizens have been increasingly deserting their party affiliations in the polling booths. The practice of **ticket-splitting,** voting simultaneously for candidates of both parties for different offices, has soared dramatically. The evidence of this development abounds. As already reviewed in this chapter, Republican presidential landslides in 1956, 1972, 1980, and 1984 were accompanied by the election of substantial Democratic majorities in the House of Representatives. Divided government, with the presidency held by one party and one or both houses of Congress held by the other party, has never been as frequent in U.S. history as it has been recently. From 1920 to 1944, about 15 percent of the congressional districts voted for presidential and House candidates of different parties. But from 1960 to 1996, at least 25 percent of the districts cast split tickets in any presidential year; and in 1984 nearly 50 percent of the districts did so. Similarly, at the statewide level, only 17 percent of the states electing governors in presidential years between 1880 and 1956 elected state and national executives from different parties. Yet from 1960 to 1992, almost 40 percent of states holding simultaneous presidential and gubernatorial elections recorded split results. (In 1992 and 1996, this proportion was somewhat lower, just 25 percent and 27 percent, respectively.) Final data on ticket-splitting in the 2000 election were not available at press time, but preliminary results suggest that while there have been variations from state to state, the national average indicates a drop in ticket-splitting and an increased tendency in 2000 to vote a straight party ticket.

These percentages actually understate the degree of ticket-splitting by individual voters. The Gallup Poll has regularly asked its respondents, "For the various political offices, did you vote for all the candidates of one party, that is, a straight ticket, or did you vote for the candidates of different parties [ticket-splitting]?" Since 1968 the proportion of voters who have ticket-split in presidential years has consistently been around 60 percent of the total.[47] Other polls and researchers have found reduced straight-ticket balloting and significant ticket-splitting at all levels of elections, especially since 1952.

Not surprisingly, the intensity of party affiliation is a major determinant of a voter's propensity to split the ticket. Strong party identifiers are the most likely to cast a straight-party ballot; pure independents are the least likely. Somewhat greater proportions of ticket-splitters are found among high-income and better-educated citizens, but there is little difference in the distribution by gender or age. African Americans exhibit the highest straight-party rate of any population subgroup; about three-quarters of all black voters stay in the Democratic Party column from the top to the bottom of the ballot.

Scholars have posited several potential explanations for ticket splitting. For example, political scientist Morris P. Fiorina argues that voters split their tickets, consciously or not, because they trust neither party to govern.[48] Under this interpretation, ticket-splitters are aware of the differences between the two parties and split their tickets to augment the checks and balances already present in the Constitution. Alternatively—and in contrast to Fiorina—political scientist Martin P. Wattenberg argues that voters split their

ticket-splitting
Voting simultaneously for candidates of both parties for different offices.

tickets because party has become less relevant as a voting cue.[49] Other explanations for ticket splitting abound. The growth of issue-oriented politics, the mushrooming of single-interest groups, the greater emphasis on candidate-centered personality politics, and broader-based education are all often cited. A strong independent presidential candidacy also helps to loosen party ties among many voters. So, too, does the marked gain in the value of incumbency. Thanks in part to the enormous fattening of congressional constituency services, incumbent U.S. representatives and senators have been able to attract a steadily increasing share of the other party's identifiers.[50]

REFORMING THE ELECTORAL PROCESS

Most proposals for electoral reform in America center on the electoral college, as discussed earlier. Abolition of the electoral college, the establishment of a congressional district plan, and the elimination of electors are at once the most dramatic and apparently urgent reforms, especially in light of the events of the 2000 election, and the least likely to succeed, given the many entrenched interests they serve and the difficulty of amending the Constitution. Changes to the electoral college, however, are not the only ways in which the election of public officials in America might be improved.

Another possible electoral reform, one which focuses on the nomination rather than the general election stage of presidential elections, is the idea of holding a series of regional primaries throughout the United States during the first week of each month beginning in February of a presidential election year. Under this system the country would be divided into five regions: the Southeast, Southwest, Far West, Midwest, and Northeast. In December of the year prior to the presidential election, a lottery would be held to determine the order in which the regions would hold their nomination races, with all regional contests held on the first of every month from February through June. The goals of this reform would be twofold: First, to end the current "permanent campaign" by preventing candidates from "camping out" in Iowa and New Hampshire for one to two years in the hopes of winning or doing better-than-expected in these small, unrepresentative states. Second, some rational order would be imposed on the electoral process, allowing candidates to focus on each region's concerns and people in turn.

(Photo courtesy: Bruce Plante/*The Chatanooga Times*)

The final suggestion for reform to be touched on here deals with campaign finance. Ross Perot in 1992 and Steve Forbes in 1996, one a billionaire and the other close to it, were able to bypass all campaign finance laws because they were able to bankroll their respective bids for the presidency independent of federal matching funds. Consequently, they were freed of both the spending and contribution limits, limits that still applied to the other presidential hopefuls. While neither was successful, the inherent problems posed by these sorts of candidates are clear. In

POINT / COUNTERPOINT

SHOULD VOTERS BE ALLOWED TO CAST THEIR VOTES ON THE INTERNET?

The prospect of national online voting has garnered attention as the Internet continues to increase its presence in the daily lives of Americans. In March 2000, Internet voting became a reality, as Arizona made history by allowing Democrats to vote via the Internet during the statewide presidential primary. Following the 2000 election, the nation appears primed for a complete revamping of voting methods. Should voters be allowed to cast their votes on line?

Supporters of Internet voting, including technology leaders and younger voters, believe that the ease of casting a ballot electronically from a personal computer at home or work would combat voter apathy and would increase turnout, especially among overseas military, business executives, and the young—all groups that have typically low participation rates. Voters would not be deterred by inclement weather or long lines at voting booths if they could instead cast their votes from home with a click of a mouse. It is also possible to set up online voting stations at specified polling locations for those without Internet access, either using desktop computers with monitors or computers set up like familiar touch-screen ATM machines. Establishing an infrastructure to facilitate online voting would reduce public expenses associated with running polling stations and compensating election judges who monitor them. Also, given the chaos of the 2000 election caused by outdated punch-card machines that created countless dangling chads, counting and recounting ballots would be swifter and more reliable. With increasingly powerful encryption, greater technological experience in handling secure transactions, the falling costs of Internet hardware, and the increasing availability of Internet access in public places, supporters of Internet voting believe that implementation of national balloting via the Internet is only a few years away.

Opponents of Internet voting believe that this type of voting opens up enormous potential for electoral fraud. Hackers, domestic and foreign, might be able to tinker with registration rolls and votes and thereby corrupt the results of the election, or even crash an entire computer system in mid-election. A virus unleashed on the Internet voting system could wreck havoc. The "Love Bug" virus, for example, infected 45 million computers in 20 countries and caused an estimated $8 billion in damage in 2000. Elections would also be completely vulnerable to a "denial of service" attack such as those that brought down Yahoo, CNN, Ebay, and other giant web portals in 2000. If something devastating happened, there would be no paper trail by which a recount could take place. Likewise, external agencies—governmental, commercial, or private—might find ways to electronically eavesdrop on voting and thereby compromise the cherished privacy associated with an individual's right to vote in the United States.

The complex issue of the "digital divide" might also disenfranchise those Americans—including the elderly, the poor, and minorities—who do not have any, much less regular, access to the Internet. The implementation of Internet voting might skew turnout of minorities and the poor—perhaps reducing their representation as prosperous, better educated, Americans claim the polls.

What do you think? Should the United States work toward online voting?
Go to www.ablongman.com/oconnor

response, some have argued that should a Ross Perot or Steve Forbes a presidential contest, then those candidates who rely on matching funds to finance their campaigns should be freed of the proscribed spending and contribution limits. This would allow all the candidates to compete on a more level financial playing field. Whether this specific reform is adopted or not, we can certainly expect campaign financing as we now know it to be reworked in some fashion sooner or later.

These possible reform ideas should convince you that although individual elections may sometimes be predictable, the electoral system in the United States is anything but static. New generations, and party-changers in older generations, constantly remake the political landscape. At least every other presidential election brings a change of administration and a focus on new issues. Every other year at least a few fresh personalities and perspectives infuse the Congress, as newly elected U.S. senators and representatives claim mandates and seek to shake up the established order. Each election year the same tumult and transformation can be observed in the fifty states and in thousands of localities.

The welter of elections may seem like chaos, but from this chaos comes the order and often explosive productivity of a democratic society. For the source of all change in the United States, just as Hamilton and Madison predicted, is the individual citizen who goes to the polls and casts a ballot.

Continuity & Change

Election Technology—Past, Present, Future

In the nineteenth century, political parties ran the elections, supplying not only paper ballots but also many of the poll-watchers and election judges. This was a formula for fraud, of course—there was not even a truly secret ballot, as people voted on different colors of ballot depending on their choice of party! The twentieth century saw widespread improvements in election practices and technology. The states now oversee the election process through official state boards of election, and the use of voting machines, nearly universal in American by the 1970s, permit truly secret mechanical voting. These measures helped effect enormous reductions in fraud and electoral ambiguity—though as the irregularities of the election of 2000 proved, there is still a long way to go.

As more and more Americans become computer savvy and as computer technology continues to evolve, Internet voting has become the likely way to cast votes in the coming years. Rightly or wrongly, Internet voting equates in the minds of many Americans with the ideals of instant democracy and greater citizen input in major decisions. Many states are formally studying the feasibility and impact of Internet voting. In 2000, Arizona pioneered online balloting by allowing citizens to vote via the Internet in the state's Democratic presidential primary. Opponents and proponents alike recognize potential problems, but technical solutions draw ever nearer.

The use of mail-in ballots, whereby registered voters are mailed ballots and given several weeks to mail them back in with their votes, increases participation but delays final tabulation of the ballots for several weeks. Oregon, the only state that votes entirely by mail-in ballots, did not have its 2000 presidential results finalized until several weeks after Election Day. Washington, which has extremely liberal laws regarding mail-in votes, was also much later than the rest of the country in announcing its presidential and senatorial winners.

The nation also lacks a standardized method by which votes should be recounted in close elections. Many reformers favor a national uniform ballot system for the entire country—a single ballot that would list the appropriate candidates for each voting locale. A national ballot is highly unlikely, however. If the federal government mandates a ballot form, it would almost certainly have to pay for it at a price tag of up to several billion dollars. In addition, there are over 41,000 voting localities in states and jurisdictions across the United States electing hundreds of thousands of officials, making it extremely difficult to create a uniform ballot.

Another change likely to result from the chaos of the 2000 election addresses the technology of the ballot itself. Prior to the 2002 midterm elections Florida outlawed the "butterfly ballot," which featured prominently in the heavily contested county of Palm Beach, Florida. Although the ballot was approved for use, it gained national attention because of its confusing layout. Despite the punch card bar and a $30 million investment in new touch screen voting systems, the tragic scene of election 2002 was replayed in south Florida on September 12, 2002 Democratic gubernatorial primary.

Many Americans believe that the federal government should assist states in updating outdated and faulty voting equipment. Some localities across the country use computerized touch-screen machines, which are expensive but much more secure and accurate than the older mechanical devices still in widespread use. An analysis of Florida's voting machines found that older, punch-card machines failed to indicate a vote for president on 1.5 percent of the ballots, while newer, optical-scanning machines failed on only 0.3 percent of the ballots. Additionally, older, error-ridden machines are commonly assigned to low-income

(continued)

and African American precincts, which reintroduces a troublesome discriminatory dimension into the voting process. Although updating equipment across the country would cost billions of dollars, it seems a small price to pay to modernize our democracy. As Charles M. Vest, the president of the Massachusetts Institute of Technology, said, "A nation that can send a man to the moon, that can put a reliable ATM machine on every corner, has no excuse not to deploy a reliable, affordable, easy-to-use voting system."

1. What kind of voting machine does your precinct use? What about the precincts of your friends and family? Did you or someone you know vote by mail? Ask around, and then determine how the perceived experience of voting, especially after the

year 2000, differs depending on the technology one uses.

2. We tend to take fair elections and private voting for granted in the United States, but in many countries such conditions are still not widespread. What do the lessons of election reform in America teach us about ways of improving the integrity of elections in other nations? What can a country without a long stable democratic tradition do to ensure fraud-free elections and private voting?

Cast Your Vote. How can America improve voter turnout? To cast your vote, go to www.ablongman.com/oconnor

SUMMARY

The explosion of elections we have experienced in over 200 years of voting has generated much good and some harm. But all of it has been done, as Hamilton insisted, "on the solid basis of the consent of the people." In our efforts to explain the complex and multilayered U.S. electoral system, we covered these points in this chapter:

1. **The Purposes Served by Elections**
   Regular elections guarantee mass political action and governmental accountability. They also confer legitimacy on regimes better than any other method of change.

2. **Different Kinds of Elections**
   When it comes to elections, the United States has an embarrassment of riches. There are various types of primary elections in the country, as well as general elections, initiatives, referenda, and recall elections. In presidential elections, primaries are sometimes replaced by caucuses, in which party members choose a candidate in a closed meeting, but recent years have seen fewer caucuses and more primaries.

3. **Presidential Elections**
   Variety aside, no U.S. election can compare to the presidential contest. This spectacle, held every four years, brings together all the elements of politics and attracts the most ambitious and energetic politicians to the national stage.

4. **The Party Conventions**
   No longer closed affairs dominated by deals cut in "smoke-filled rooms," today's conventions are more open made-for-television events in which the party platform is drafted and adopted, and the presidential ticket is formally nominated.

5. **Congressional Elections**
   Many similar elements are present in different kinds of elections: Candidates, voters, issues, and television advertisements are constants. But there are distinctive aspects of each kind of election as well. Compared with presidential elections, congressional elections are a different animal.

6. **Voting Behavior**
   Whether they are casting ballots in congressional or presidential elections, voters behave in certain distinct ways and exhibit unmistakable patterns to political scientists who study them.

7. **Reforming the Electoral process**
   The American political system uses indirect electoral representation in the form of the electoral college. Events of the 2000 election have renewed a long-standing debate over the legitimacy and efficacy of this institution and sparked controversial calls for change.

KEY TERMS

blanket primary, p. 471
closed primary, p. 471
critical election, p. 485
crossover voting, p. 471
elector, p. 481
electoral college, p. 480
electorate, p. 469
front-loading, p. 475
general election, p. 472
gerrymandering p. 489
incumbency, p. 488
initiative, p. 472
mandate, p. 469
nonpartisan primary, p. 472
off-year election, p. 492

SELECTED READINGS

Bartels, Larry M. *Presidential Primaries and the Dynamics of Public Choice.* Princeton, N.J.: Princeton University Press, 1988.

Berelson, Bernard R., Paul F. Lazarsfeld, and William N. McPhee. *Voting: A Study of Opinion Formation in a Presidential Campaign.* Chicago: University of Chicago Press, 1954.

Burnham, Walter Dean. *Critical Elections and the Mainsprings of American Politics.* New York: Norton, 1970.

Campbell, Angus, Philip E. Converse, Warren E. Miller, and Donald E. Stokes. *The American Voter.* New York: Wiley, 1960.

Carroll, Susan J. *Women as Candidates in American Politics.* Bloomington: Indiana University Press, 1994.

Conway, M. Margaret. *Political Participation in the United States,* 2nd ed. Washington, D.C.: CQ Press, 1990.

Darcy, Robert, Susan Welch, and Janet Clark. *Women, Elections, and Representation,* 2nd ed. Lincoln: University of Nebraska Press, 1994.

Fiorina, Morris P. *Retrospective Voting in American National Elections.* New Haven, Conn.: Yale University Press, 1981.

Herrnson, Paul S. *Congressional Elections: Campaigning at Home and in Washington.* Washington, D.C.: Congressional Quarterly Press, 1995.

Jacobson, Gary C. *The Politics of Congressional Elections,* 2nd ed. New York: Harper Collins, 1992.

———. *The Electoral Origins of Divided Government.* Boulder, Colo.: Westview Press, 1990.

Key, V. O., Jr., with the assistance of Milton C. Cummings. *The Responsible Electorate.* Cambridge, Mass.: Harvard University Press, 1966.

Nie, Norman H., Sidney Verba, and John R. Petrocik. *The Changing American Voter.* Cambridge, Mass.: Belknap Press of Harvard University, 1976.

Polsby, Nelson W., and Aaron Wildavsky. *Presidential Elections: Strategies and Structures of American Politics,* 7th ed. Chatham, N.J.: Chatham House, 1996.

Sundquist, James L. *Dynamics of the Party System: Alignment and Realignment of Political Parties in the United States.* Washington, D.C.: Brookings Institution, 1983.

Teixeira, Ruy. *The Disappearing American Voter.* Washington, D.C.: Brookings Institution, 1992.

Verba, Sidney, Norman H. Nie, and Jae-on Kim. *Participation and Political Equality.* Cambridge, England: Cambridge University Press, 1978.

Verba, Sidney, Kay Lehman Schlozman, and Henry E. Brady. *Voice and Equality: Civic Voluntarism in American Politics.* Cambridge, Mass.: Harvard University Press, 1995.

Wayne, Stephen J. *The Road to the White House,* 6th ed. New York: St. Martin's Press, 1997.

Weisberg, Herbert F., ed. *Democracy's Feast: Elections in America.* Chatham, N.J.: Chatham House, 1995.

NOTES

1. Angus Cambell, Philip E. Converse, Warren E. Miller, and Donald E. Stokes, *The American Voter* (New York: Wiley, 1960).

2. Paul Abramson, John H. Aldrich, and David W. Rohde, *Change and Continuity in the 1996 Elections* (Washington, D.C.: Congressional Quarterly Press, 1998).

3. Paul Allen Beck, *Party Politics in America,* 8th ed. (New York: Longman, 1998). David Adamany, "Cross-over Voting and the Democratic Party's Reform Rules," *American Political Science Review* 70 (1976): 536–41. Ronald Hedlund and Meredith W. Watts, "The Wisconsin Open Primary: 1968 to 1984," *American Politics Quarterly* 14 (1986): 55–74. Gary D. Wekkin, "The Conceptualization and Measurement of Crossover Voting," *Western Political Quarterly* 41 (1988) 105–14.

4. Beck, *Party Politics in America.* Alan Abromowitz, John McGlennon, and Ronald Rapoport, "A Note on Strategic Voting in a Primary Election," *Journal of Politics* 43 (1981): 899–904. Gary D. Wekken, "Why Crossover Voters Are Not 'Mischievous' Voters," *American Politics Quarterly* 19 (1991): 229–47.

5. Gary C. Jacobson, *The Politics of Congressional Elections* (New York: Longman, 1997), 107–8.

6. Shaun Bowler, Todd Donovan, and Caroline Tolbert, eds, *Citizens as Legislators: Direct Democracy in the United States* (Columbus: Ohio State University Press, 1998).

7. Edward L. Lascher Jr., Michael G. Hagen, and Steven A. Rochlin, "Gun Behind the Door?" *Journal of Politics* 58 (August 1996): 766–75.

8. Elaine Ciulla Kamarck and Kenneth M. Goldstein, "The Rules Matter: Post-Reform Presidential Nominating Politics," in L. Sandy Maisel, *The Parties Respond: Changes in American Parties and Campaigns* (Boulder, Colo.: Westview Press, 1994), 174.

9. Paul R. Abramson, John H. Aldrich, Phil Paolino, and David W. Rohde, "'Sophisticated' Voting in the 1998 Presidential Primaries," *American Political Science Review* 86 (March 1992): 55–69.

10. Larry J. Sabato, "Presidential Nominations: The Front-loaded Frenzy of 1996," in Larry J. Sabato, ed., *Toward the Millennium: The Elections of 1996* (New York: Allyn and Bacon, 1997).

11. Byron Shafer, *Bifurcated Politics: Evolution and Reform in the National Party Convention* (Cambridge, Mass: Harvard University Press, 1988).

12. Priscilla Southwell, "Rules as 'Unseen Participants'" *American Politics Quarterly* 20 (January 1992): 54–68.

13. Richard Herrera, "Are 'Superdelegates' Super?" *Political Behavior* 16 (March 1994): 79–92.

14. James L. Hutter and Steven E. Schier, "Representativeness: From Caucus to Convention in Iowa," *American Politics Quarterly* 12 (October 1984): 431–48.

15. On the subject of party realignment, see Walter Dean Burnham, *Critical Elections and the Mainsprings of American Politics* (New York: Norton, 1970); Kristi Andersen, *The Creation of a Democratic Majority* (Chicago: University of Chicago Press, 1979); and John R. Petrocik, "Realignment: New Party Coalitions and the Nationalization of the South," *Journal of Politics* 49 (May 1987): 347–75.

16. Barbara Farah and Helmut Norpoth, "Trends in Partisan Realignment, 1976–1986: A Decade of Waiting," paper prepared for delivery at the annual meeting of the American Political Science Association, Washington, D.C., August 27–31, 1986.

17. Morris P. Fiorina, *Retrospective Voting in American National Elections* (New Haven, Conn.: Yale University Press, 1981); and Charles H. Franklin and John E. Jackson, "The Dynamics of Party Identification," *American Political Science Review* 77 (1983): 957–73.

18. See, for example, V. O. Key Jr., "A Theory of Critical Elections," *Journal of Politics* 17 (February 1955): 3–18.

19. The less dynamic term "creeping realignment" is also sometimes used by scholars and journalists.

20. Everett Carl Ladd, "Like Waiting for Godot: The Uselessness of 'Realignment' for Understanding Change in Contemporary American Politics," in Byron Shafer, ed. *The End of Realignment? Interpreting American Electoral Eras* (Madison: Wisconsin, 1991).

21. See Paul Allen Beck, "The Dealignment Era in America," in Russell J. Dalton et al., *Electoral Change in Advanced Industrial Democracies: Realignment or Dealignment?* (Princeton, N.J.: Princeton University Press, 1984), 264. See also Philip M. Williams, "Party Realignment in the United States and Britain," *British Journal of Political Science* 15 (January 1985): 97–115.

22. George Serra, "What's in It for Me? The Impact of Congressional Casework on Incumbent Evaluation," *American Politics Quarterly* 22 (1994): 403–20.

23. Glenn R. Parker and Suzanne L. Parker, "Correlates and Effects of Attention to District by U.S. House Members," *Legislative Studies Quarterly* 10 (May 1985): 223–42.

24. Gary W. Cox and Jonathan N. Katz, "Why Did the Incumbency Advantage in U.S. House Elections Grow?" *American Journal of Political Science* 40 (May 1996): 478–97.

25 Paul Gronke and J. Wilson, "Competing Plans as Evidence of Political Motives: The North Carolina Case," *American Politics Quarterly* 27 (April 1999): 147–76.

26. *Wesberry* v. *Sanders,* 376 U.S. 1 (1964).

27. *Thornburg* v. *Gingles,* 478 U.S. 30 (1986).

28. *Shaw* v. *Reno,* 113 S.Ct. 2816 (1993).

29. Sunhil Ahuja, et al., "Modern Congressional Election Theory Meets the 1992 House Elections," *Political Research Quarterly* 47 (1994): 909–21. Paul S. Herrnson, *Congressional Elections: Campaigning at Home and in Washington,* 2nd ed. (Washington, D.C.: Congressional Quarterly Press, 1998).

30. John W. Swain, Stephen A. Borrelli, and Brian C. Reed, "Partisan Consequences of the Post-1990 Redistricting for the U.S. House of Representatives," *Political Research Quarterly* 51 (December 1998): 945–67.

31. Gary C. Jacobson and Michael A. Dimock, "Checking Out: The Effects of Bank Overdrafts on the 1992 House Elections," *American Journal of Political Science* 38 (1994): 601–24. Herrnson, *Congressional Elections: Campaigning at Home and in Washington.*

32. The Kennedy-Johnson years (1961–1969) and the Nixon-Ford years (1969–1977) are each considered an eight-year unit for our purposes here.

33. Gary C. Jacobson, "The 1994 House Elections in Perspective," *Political Science Quarterly* 111 (1996): 203–23.

34. Richard E. Cohen, "Campaigning for Congress: The Echo of '94," in Larry J. Sabato, ed., *Toward the Millennium: The Elections of 1996* (New York: Allyn and Bacon, 1997).

35. Steven J. Rosenstone and John Mark Hanson, *Mobilization, Participation, and Democracy in America* (New York: Macmillan, 1993).

36. See, for example, Laura Stoker and M. Kent Jennings, "Life-Cycle Transitions and Political Participation: The Case of Marriage," *American Political Science Review* 89 (1995): pp. 421–36, and Abramson, et al., *Change and Continuity in the 1996 Elections.*

37. James A. McCann, Randall W. Partin, Ronald B. Rapoport, and Walter J. Stone, "Presidential Nomination Campaigns and Party Mobilization: An Assessment of Spillover Effects," *American Journal of Political Science* 40 (August 1996): 756–67.

38. Walter Stone, Lonna Rae Atkeson, and Ronald B. Rapoport, "Turning On or Turning Off? Mobilization and Demobilization Effects of Participation in Presidential Nomination Campaigns," *American Journal of Political Science* 36 (August 1992): 665–91.

39. Stephen Knack and J. White, "Election-Day Registration and Turnout Inequality," *Political Behavior* 22 (March 2000): 29–44.

40. Daniel Franklin and Eric Grier, "Effects of Motor Voter Legislation: Voter Turnout, Registration, and Partisan Advantage in the 1992 Presidential Election," *American Politics Quarterly* 25 (January 1997): 104–17.

41. J. Eric Oliver, "The Effects of Eligibility Restrictions and Party Activity on Absentee Voting and Overall Turnout," *American Journal of Political Science* 40 (May 1996): 498–513.

42. Marg N. Franklin and Wolfgang P. Hirczy, "Separated Powers, Divided Government, and Turnout in U.S. Presidential Elections," *American Journal of Political Science* 42 (January 1998): 316–26.

43. Steven J. Rosenstone and John Marc Hansen, *Mobization, Participation, and Democracy in America* (New York: Macmillan, 1993).

44. Mark J. Fenster, "The Impact of Allowing Day of Registration Voting on Turnout in U.S. Elections from 1960 to 1992: A Research Note," *American Politics Quarterly* 22 (January 1994), 74–87

45. Stephen Knack, "Does 'Motor Voter' Work? Evidence from State-Level Data," *Journal of Politics* 57 (1995): 796–811.

46. Arend Lijphart, "Unequal Participation: Democracy's unsolved dilemma," American Political Science Review 91 (March 1997):1–14

47. Cited in Everett Carl Ladd Jr., "On Mandates, Realignments, and the 1984 Presidential Election," *Political Science Quarterly* 100 (Spring 1985): 23.

48. Morris P. Fiorina, *Divided Government* (Boston: Allyn and Bacon, 1996).

49. Martin P. Wattenberg, *The Decline of American Political Parties, 1952–1994* (Cambridge, Mass.: Harvard University Press, 1996).

50. Thomas E. Mann and Raymond E. Wolfinger, "Candidates and Parties in Congressional Elections," *American Political Science Review* 74 (September 1980): 617–32; Albert D. Cover, "One Good Term Deserves Another: The Advantage of Incumbency in Congressional Elections," *American Journal of Political Science* 21 (August 1977): 535; and Gary C. Jacobson, The Politics of Congressional Elections, 2nd ed. (Boston: Little, Brown, 1987), 86.

14 The Campaign Process

Contrary to appearances upon occasion, serious presidential candidates do not simply materialize out of thin air. Rather, they are often a product of a lifetime's work in careful strategy and campaign planning. The case of Al Gore, Democratic candidate for president in 2000, is an excellent case in point. With a family history of political distinction; with a record of military service that distinguished him from his opponent, George W. Bush; and with respectable career experience in journalism and the U.S. Senate, the semi-incumbency of the vice presidency seemed like the crowning touch on an extremely eligible candidate for president of the United States.

The advantage of the vice presidential incumbency, in fact, was historically quite significant, since almost all modern vice presidents have won their party's nomination at the expiration of their president's term (Truman, Nixon, Johnson, Humphrey, Ford, Mondale, and George Bush) and the exceptions—Spiro Agnew, who resigned in disgrace, and Dan Quayle, who was never taken seriously—only prove the rule

In the Republican camp, however, two straight defeats for the presidency had eliminated any of the inevitability that might have followed from a recent or current vice presidency, and like a royal family searching for a distant relative to occupy the throne, the GOP found itself looking far and wide for someone with viable credentials. Perhaps anticipating that the campaign of 2000 would be as much about personality and character as about issues and ideology, the Republicans turned to the son of a former president. Bush's rhetoric and persona seemed appealing to many voters, despite his relatively unremarkable record as a Texas governor, businessman, and Yale student. The process by which Bush came to accept the Republican nomination was almost reminiscent of William McKinley's Front Porch Campaign in 1896—delegations of Republican governors and state legislators came to the governor's mansion in Austin to beg Bush to accept the party's nomination

Gore and Bush both suffered from various liabilities which briefly offered advantages to their opponents in the primaries, especially in the form of enthusiastic support from independent, crossover, and undecided "swing" votes. In the end, however, the conventional logic of party selection held fast, and regular party activists carried Gore and Bush to the final election contest.

U p to this point in the book, we have focused on the election decision itself and have said little about the campaign conducted prior to the balloting. Many today denounce electioneering and politicians for their negative use of the airwaves and the perceived disproportionate influence of a few wealthy donors and a handful of well-endowed and well-organized political action committees and interest groups. Nonetheless, the basic purpose of modern electioneering remains intact: one person asking another for support, an approach unchanged since the dawn of democracy.

The art of campaigning involves the science of polls, the planning of sophisticated mass mailings, and the coordination of electronic telephone banks to reach voters. More importantly, it also involves the diplomatic skill of unifying disparate individuals and groups to achieve a fragile but election-winning majority. How candidates perform this exquisitely difficult task is the subject of this chapter, in which we discuss the following topics:

- First, we will explore the *structure of a campaign,* the process of seeking and winning votes in the run-up to an election, which consists of five separate components: the nomination campaign, the general election campaign, the personal campaign, the organizational campaign, and the broadcast media campaign.

- Second, we will look at the question of *which we vote for: the candidate or the campaign.* Although campaign methods have clearly become very sophisticated, in most cases the candidate wins or loses the race according to his or her abilities, qualifications, communication skills, issues, and weaknesses.

- Third, we will see how the modern candidate faces two major *modern campaign challenges:* communicating through the media and raising the money needed to stay in the race.

- Fourth, we will see *where campaign contributions* come from and *how those funds are spent.*

- Fifth, we will discuss the *2000 presidential campaign and election.* After some initial excitement early in the primary season, George Bush and Al Gore triumphed over John McCain and Bill Bradley much as expected. During the course of the campaign Bush avoided significant missteps while Gore's advantages slowly eroded. By Election Day, the two candidates were dead even, and the election itself fell victim to numerous disorders, including media misreporting and irregularities in the casting and counting of ballots. Bush's lawyers succeeded in the ensuing and protracted legal battles, which went all the way to the U.S. Supreme Court, and when he accepted the presidency in January 2001, he triumphed in one of the most contentious elections in United States history.

- Sixth, we will look at *campaign finance laws,* exploring ways that these might be changed so that their effect can be strengthened.

THE STRUCTURE OF A CAMPAIGN

A campaign for high office (such as the presidency, a governorship, or a U.S. Senate seat) is a highly complex effort akin to running a multi-million-dollar business, while campaigns for local offices are usually less complicated. But all campaigns, no matter what their size, have certain aspects in common. Indeed, each campaign really consists of several campaigns run simultaneously:

1. The **nomination campaign.** The target is the party elite, the leaders and activists who choose nominees in primaries or conventions. Party leaders are concerned with electability, while party activists are often ideologically and issue oriented, so a candidate must appeal to both bases.

WEB EXPLORATION
To compare the development of presidential candidates, go to
www.ablongman.com/oconnor

Longman
Participate.com
2.0
Visual Literacy
American
Electoral Rules:
How Do They
Influence
Campaigns?

"Next time, why don't you run? You're a well-known figure, people seem to like you, and you haven't had an original idea in years." (Photo courtesy: Reproduced by Special Permission of Playboy magazine. Copyright ©1992 by Playboy.)

2. The **general election campaign.** A farsighted candidate never forgets the ultimate goal: winning the general election. Therefore the candidate tries to avoid taking stands that, however pleasing to party activists in the primary, will alienate a majority of the larger general election constituency.

3. The **personal campaign.** This is the public part of the campaign. The candidate and his or her family and supporters make appearances, meet voters, hold press conferences, and give speeches.

4. The **organizational campaign.** Behind the scenes, another campaign is humming. Volunteers telephone voters and distribute literature, staffers organize events, and everyone raises money to support the operation.

5. The **media campaign.** On television and radio the candidate's advertisements (termed *paid media*) air frequently in an effort to convince the public that the candidate is the best person for the job. Meanwhile, campaigners attempt to influence the press coverage of the campaign by the print and electronic news reporters—the *free media.*

British election campaigns are very different from those in the United States. In the first place, candidate selection is controlled by local party organizations, not by any sort of primary system. Second, the national parties control key facets of the campaign. For example, they provide all the financing, which is regulated by national statute, and execute the campaign strategy. As a result, national party platforms—not candidate personalities—play a dominant role in British campaigns. Finally, the power of the prime minister to call elections at his or her discretion—literally at a moment's notice—produces campaigns of a mere four to five weeks in duration instead of the two-year (for a Senate seat) to four-year campaigns (for president) we endure in the United States.

To better comprehend the various campaigns, let's examine a few aspects of each, remembering that they must all mesh successfully for the candidate to win.

The Nomination Campaign

New candidates get their sea legs early on, as they adjust to the pressures of being in the spotlight day in and day out. This is the time for the candidates to learn that a single careless phrase could end the campaign or guarantee a defeat. This is also the time to seek the support of party leaders and interest groups and to test out themes, slogans, and strategies. The press and public take much less notice of shifts in strategy at this time than they will later in the general election campaign.

This is a critical time for gaining and maintaining the aura of support both within the party and with the larger electorate. Patrick Kenney and Tom Rice explain this in a study of momentum and the "bandwagon effect" in the 1988 Republican presidential primary. They found that Vice President George Bush, the eventual nominee, converted support from other Republican candidates through a variety of means. Some party members switched their allegiance from their favored candidate to Bush because they became caught up in his media-driven sense of upward momentum. Others switched to him simply because they perceived him to be the eventual nominee and liked the feeling of supporting a winner. Still others voted for Bush in the later primaries because they perceived him as the strongest Republican candidate heading into the November general election. Much of Bush's eventual support, therefore, grew out of his previous success and a sense of inevitability, not necessarily out of support for his issue positions or campaign themes or slogans.[1]

At this time there is a danger not widely recognized by candidates: Surrounded by friendly activists and ideological soulmates in the quest to win the party's nomination, a candidate can move too far to the right or the left and become too extreme for the November electorate. Conservative Barry Goldwater, the 1964 Republican nominee for president, and liberal George McGovern, the 1972 Democratic nominee for president, both fell victim to this phenomenon in seeking their party's nomination, and they were handily defeated in the general elections by Presidents Lyndon B. Johnson and Richard M. Nixon, respectively.

nomination campaign
That part of a political campaign aimed at winning a primary election.

general election campaign
That part of a political campaign following a primary election, aimed at winning a general election.

personal campaign
That part of a political campaign concerned with presenting the candidate's public image.

organizational campaign
That part of a political campaign involved in fund raising, literature distribution, and all other activities not directly involving the candidate.

media campaign
That part of a political campaign waged in the broadcast and print media.

The General Election Campaign

Once the choice between the two major-party nominees is clear, both candidates can get to work. Most significant interest groups are courted for money and endorsements, although the results are mainly predictable: liberal, labor, and minority groups usually back Democrats, while conservative and business organizations support Republicans. The most active and intense groups are often coalesced around emotional issues such as abortion and gun control, and these organizations can produce a bumper crop of money and activists for favored candidates. Race and class divisions can often play an important role in general elections, although this tends not to be true in the United States.

Virtually all candidates adopt a brief theme, or slogan, to serve as a rallying cry in their quest for office. The first to do so was William Henry Harrison in 1840, with the slogan "Tippecanoe and Tyler, Too." Tippecanoe was a nickname given to Harrison, a reference to his participation in the battle of Tippecanoe, and Tyler was Harrison's vice presidential candidate, John Tyler of Virginia. Some presidential campaign slogans have entered national lore, like Herbert Hoover's

Right-wing 1964 Republican candidate Barry Goldwater's famous slogan, "in your heart, you know he's right," was quickly lampooned by incumbent Democratic opponent President Lyndon B. Johnson's campaign as "in your guts, you know he's nuts." (Photo courtesy: Bettman/Corbis)

1928 slogan "A chicken in every pot, a car in every garage." President Clinton used two memorable slogans: "Time for a change" and "Building a bridge to the twenty-first century." Most slogans can fit many candidates ("She thinks like us," "He's on our side," "She hears you," "You know where he stands"). Candidates try to avoid controversy in their selection of slogans, and some openly eschew ideology. (An ever-popular one of this genre: "Not left, not right—forward!") The clever candidate also attempts to find a slogan that cannot be lampooned easily. In 1964 Barry Goldwater's handlers may have regretted their choice of "In your heart, you know he's right" when Lyndon B. Johnson's supporters quickly converted it into "In your guts, you know he's nuts." (Democrats were trying to portray Goldwater as a warmonger after the Republican indicated a willingness to use nuclear weapons in Vietnam and elsewhere under some conditions.)

The Personal Campaign

In the effort to show voters that they are hard-working, thoughtful, and worthy of the office they seek, candidates try to meet personally as many citizens as possible in the course of a campaign. A candidate for high office may deliver up to a dozen speeches a day, and that is only part of the exhausting schedule most contenders maintain. The day may begin at 5 A.M. at the entrance gate to an auto plant with an hour or two of handshaking, followed by similar gladhanding at subway stops until 9 A.M. Strategy sessions with key advisers and preparation for upcoming presentations and forums may fill the rest of the morning. A luncheon talk, afternoon fund raisers, and a series of television and print interviews crowd the afternoon agenda. The light fare of cocktail parties is followed by a dinner speech, perhaps telephone or neighborhood canvassing of voters, and a civic-forum talk or two. More meetings with advisers and planning for the next day's events can easily take a candidate past midnight. Following only a few hours of sleep, the candidate starts all over again. After months of this grueling pace, the candidate may be functioning on automatic pilot and unable to think clearly.

Beyond the strains this fast-lane existence adds to a candidate's family life, the hectic schedule leaves little time for reflection and long-range planning. Is it any wonder that under these conditions many candidates commit gaffes and appear to have foot-in-mouth disease?

It's not all drudgery, however. The considerable rewards to be had on the campaign trail can balance the personal disadvantages. A candidate can affect the course of the government and community, and in so doing become admired and respected by peers. Meeting all kinds of people, solving problems, gaining exposure to every facet of life in one's constituency—these experiences help a public person live life fully and compensate for the hardships of campaigning.

The Organizational Campaign

If the candidate is the public face of the campaign, the organization behind the candidate is the private face. Depending on the level of the office sought, the organizational staff can consist of a handful of volunteers or hundreds of paid specialists supplementing and directing the work of thousands of volunteers. The most elaborate structure is found in presidential campaigns. Tens of thousands of volunteers distribute literature and visit neighborhoods. They are directed by paid staff that may number 300 or more, including a couple of dozen lawyers and accountants.

At the top of the organizational chart is the **campaign manager,** who coordinates and directs the various aspects of the campaign. Beside the manager is the **political consultant,** whose position is one of the most important developments in campaigning for office in this century. The political consultant is a private-sector individual (or, more often now, a team of individuals or a firm) who sells to a candidate the technologies, services, and strategies required to get that candidate elected to his or her office of choice. The number of consultants has grown exponentially since they first appeared in the 1930s, and their specialties and responsibilities have increased accordingly, to the point that they are now an obligatory part of campaigns at almost any level of government. Candidates hire generalist consultants to oversee their entire campaign from beginning to end, which often include responsibilities ranging from defining campaign objectives to formulating strategy, developing tactics, and fighting individual battles alongside the candidate. Alongside the generalist consultant, or perhaps hired by the generalist in turn, are more specialized consultants who focus on the new and complex technologies for only one or two specialties such as fund raising, polling, mass mailings, media relations, advertising, and speech writing.

The best-known consultants for any campaign are usually the **media consultant,** who produces the candidate's television and radio advertisements; the **pollster,** who takes the public opinion surveys that guide the campaign; and the **direct mailer,** who supervises direct-mail fund raising. After the candidate, however, the most important person in the campaign is probably the **finance chair** who is responsible for bringing in the large contributions that pay most of the salaries of the consultants and staff.

Many critics claim that consultants strip campaigns of substance and reduce them to a clever bag of tricks for sale, even blaming the degeneration of American politics in the latter half of this century on the rise of the political consultant. Disappointed office seekers sometimes blame their loss entirely on their consultants, while successful candidates often retain their consultants after the election as political advisers, thereby lending even more credibility to the claim that politics now is all about appearance and not about issues. Candidates, always busy with making public appearances and canvassing, often entrust the entire management of campaigns to their consultants without understanding entirely what those consultants do. Sometimes, as in the notable case of Mary Matalin and James Carville (see chapter 12), the consultants become media stars in their own right.

Yet there are others who insist that despite the consultants, running for office is still about the bread and butter of campaigns: shaking hands, speaking persuasively, and

WEB EXPLORATION
To find out what Americans have to say on a range of political issues and to experience poll taking firsthand, go to www.ablongman.com/oconnor

Longman Participate.com 2.0 Simulation
You Are a Professional Campaign Manager

campaign manager
The individual who travels with the candidate and coordinates the many different aspects of the campaign.

political consultant
A hired individual, team, or firm that advises the campaign on strategies and techniques to win an election.

media consultant
A professional who produces political candidates' television, radio, and print advertisements.

pollster
A professional who takes public opinion surveys that guide political campaigns.

direct mailer
A professional who supervises a political campaign's direct-mail fund-raising strategies.

finance chair
A volunteer who coordinates the fund-raising efforts for the campaign.

listening to the voters. Voters, they say, are smart enough to tell the difference between a good candidate and a bad one, regardless of the smoke and mirrors erected by their consultants. Nevertheless, consultants do make a difference. Recent research on political consultants conducted by political scientists indicates that consultants have a significant impact in elections. In campaigns for the U.S. House, for example, the use of professional campaign consultants has been shown to have a positive impact on candidates' fund-raising ability[2] and on candidates' final vote shares.[3]

In addition to raising money, the most vital work of the candidate's organization is to get in touch with voters. Some of this is done in person by volunteers who walk the neighborhoods, going door to door to solicit votes. Some is accomplished by volunteers who use computerized telephone banks to call targeted voters with scripted messages. (See Politics Now: High-Tech Campaigning for a discussion of the types of technologies contemporary campaigns rely on.) Both contact methods are termed **voter canvass.** Most canvassing takes place in the month before the election, when voters are paying attention. Close to Election Day, the telephone banks begin the vital **get-out-the-vote (GOTV)** effort, reminding supporters to vote and arranging for their transportation to the polls if necessary.

The Media Campaign

What voters actually see and hear of the candidate is primarily determined by the **paid media** (such as television advertising) accompanying the campaign and the **free media** (newspaper and television coverage). The two kinds of media are fundamentally different: Paid advertising is completely under the control of the campaign, whereas the press is independent. Great care is taken in the design of the television advertising, which takes many approaches. (See Roots of Government: The Television Advertising Campaign of 1952 for information on the first national political ad campaign.) **Positive ads** stress the candidate's qualifications, family, and issue positions with no direct reference to the opponent. These are usually favored by the incumbent candidate. **Negative ads** attack the opponent's character and platform and (except for a brief, legally required identification at the ad's conclusion) may not even mention the candidate who is paying for their airing. In 2000, Republicans attempted to capitalize on Al Gore's ethical liabilities by running a series of ads that in different ways effectively called Gore a liar. Nor were the Democrats and their allies innocent of mud-slinging: The NAACP ran an anti-Bush ad featuring the daughter of James Byrd (the victim of a notorious racist hate crime in Texas) in which Byrd's daughter implicitly attributed her father's death to the governorship of George W. Bush. **Contrast ads** compare the records and proposals of the candidates, with a bias toward the sponsor. Whether the public likes them or not, all three kinds of ads can inject important (as well as trivial) issues into a campaign. Incidentally, some of the negative ads aired in modern campaigns are sponsored *not* by candidates but by interest groups. These ads usually focus on issues and are independent of the actual campaigns, though it may be easy to tell which candidate the interest group favors.

Occasionally, advertisements are relatively long (ranging from four-and-one-half-minute ads up to thirty-minute documentaries). Usually, however, the messages are short **spot ads,** sixty, thirty, or even ten seconds long.

While there is little question that negative advertisements have shown the greatest growth in the past two decades, they have been a part of American campaigns for some time. In 1796 Federalists portrayed Thomas Jefferson, a Founding Father and one of the chief authors of our Constitution, as an atheist and a coward. In 1800 Federalists again attacked Jefferson, spreading a rumor that Jefferson was dead! Clearly, although negative advertisements are more prevalent today, they are not solely the function of the modern media. Furthermore, their effects are well documented. While voters normally need a reason to vote for a candidate, they also fre-

voter canvass
The process by which a campaign gets in touch with individual voters: either by door-to-door solicitation or by telephone.

get-out-the-vote (GOTV)
A push at the end of a political campaign to encourage supporters to go to the polls.

paid media
Political advertisements purchased for a candidate's campaign.

free media
Coverage of a candidate's campaign by the news media.

positive ad
Advertising on behalf of a candidate that stresses the candidate's qualifications, family, and issue positions, without reference to the opponent.

negative ad
Advertising on behalf of a candidate that attacks the opponent's platform or character.

contrast ad
Ad that compares the records and proposals of the candidates, with a bias toward the sponsor.

spot ad
Television advertising on behalf of a candidate that is broadcast in sixty-, thirty-, or ten-second duration.

POLITICS NOW

HIGH-TECH CAMPAIGNING: THE CHANGING NATURE OF RUNNING FOR OFFICE

The age of modern technology has brought many changes to the traditional campaign. Labor-intensive community activities have been replaced by carefully targeted messages disseminated through the mass media, and candidates today are able to reach voters more quickly than at any time in our nation's history. Consequently, the well-organized party machine is no longer essential to winning an election. The results of this technological transformation are candidate-centered campaigns in which candidates build well-financed, finely tuned organizations centered around their personal aspirations.

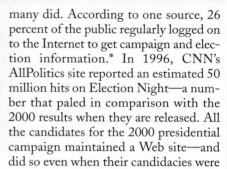

At the heart of the move toward today's candidate-centered campaigns is an entire generation of technological improvements. Contemporary campaigns have an impressive new array of weapons at their disposal: faster paper printing technologies, instantaneous Internet publishing and mass e-mail, fax machines and video technology, and enhanced telecommunications and teleconferencing. As a result, candidates can gather and disseminate information better than ever.

One outcome of these changes is the ability of candidates to employ "rapid-response" techniques: the formulation of prompt and informed responses to changing events on the campaign battlefield. In response to breaking news of a scandal or issue, for example, candidates (as well as journalists) can conduct background research, implement an opinion poll and tabulate the results, devise a containment strategy and appropriate "spin," and deliver a reply. This makes a strong contrast with the campaigns of the 1970s and early 1980s, which were dominated primarily by radio and TV advertisements, which took much longer to prepare and had little of the flexibility enjoyed by contemporary campaigners.

The first widespread use of the Internet in national campaigning came in 1996. Republican presidential candidate Bob Dole urged voters to log onto his Web site, and many did. According to one source, 26 percent of the public regularly logged on to the Internet to get campaign and election information.* In 1996, CNN's AllPolitics site reported an estimated 50 million hits on Election Night—a number that paled in comparison with the 2000 results when they are released. All the candidates for the 2000 presidential campaign maintained a Web site—and did so even when their candidacies were only in the exploratory stage, before their formal declarations. These sites have always presented platforms, offered easily accessible information on how to get involved in the campaign, and, for the very enthusiastic Web-surfer, information on how to contribute money.

As bandwidth on the Internet continues to improve, real-time video clips enable Web-users to view speeches, press conferences, state-of-the-nation addresses, and other typically "live" events at their own convenience, independent of the schedule of the original television coverage or rebroadcast. Campaign sites often offer the text of the speech as well as multiple video and audio versions of the real public event. Whatever the real benefit of such an embarrassment of riches, the goal is to suggest a candidate's technological mastery, sophistication, and depth of resources. The new media appear to be serving the current paradigm of mass-media, candidate-centered campaigns, but it is possible that with time they may reshape the campaign landscape. One possibility is that political parties might use new technologies to organize and manage massive voter bases, in an effort to return to an older mode of campaign that supports the party, rather than just one individual candidate. Another possible outcome is that with increasing ease of public access, the number of candidates or parties might increase, while elections and voting become increasingly private, solitary events.

*The Public Perspective (December/January 1997): 42.

quently vote *against* the other candidate—and negative ads can provide the critical justification for such a vote.

Before the 1980s well-known incumbents usually ignored negative attacks from their challengers, believing that the proper stance was to be above the fray. But after some well-publicized defeats of incumbents in the early 1980s in which negative television advertising played a prominent role,[4] incumbents began attacking their challengers in earnest. The new rule of politics became "An attack unanswered is an attack agreed to." In a further attempt to stave off brickbats from challengers, incumbents even began anticipating the substance of their opponents' attacks and airing **inoculation advertising** early

inoculation advertising
Advertising that attempts to counteract an anticipated attack from the opposition before the attack is even launched.

ROOTS OF GOVERNMENT

THE TELEVISION ADVERTISING CAMPAIGN OF 1952

The initial, landmark year for political television was 1952. Television had become truly national, not just regional, and portions of the political parties' national conventions were telecast for the first time. With 45 percent of the nation's households owning television sets, the presidential campaign was forced to take notice. Republican presidential nominee Dwight D. Eisenhower's advisers were particularly intrigued with the device, seeing it as a way to counter Eisenhower's stumbling press-conference performances and to make him appear more knowledgeable.

Eisenhower's advertising campaign was a glimpse of the future. The three primary themes of the commercials (corruption, high prices, and the Korean War) were chosen after consultation with pollster George Gallup. There was an extraordinarily large number of spots (forty-nine produced for television, twenty-nine for radio). Most spots were twenty seconds in length; the rest, sixty seconds. They played repeatedly in forty-nine selected counties in twelve non-Southern states as well as in a few targeted Southern states. The GOP's media strategy appeared to have been successful, and the Nielsen ratings showed that Eisenhower's telecasts consistently drew higher ratings than those of his Democratic opponent, Adlai Stevenson.

The commercials themselves were simplistic and technically very primitive in comparison with modern fare. Eisenhower had a peculiarly stilted way of speaking while reading cue cards, and his delivery was amateurish, albeit sincere and appealing. If nothing else, the GOP commercials from 1952 reveal that the issues in U.S. politics never seem to change. Eisenhower's slogan, "It's Time for a Change," for example is a perennial production. One advertisement was a clever adaptation of the "March of Time" newsreel series that preceded the main features in U.S. movie theaters of the period, and various news clips of Eisenhower accompanied the audio.

Narrator: The man from Abilene. Out of the heartland of America, out of this small-frame house in Abilene, Kansas, came a man, Dwight D. Eisenhower. Through the crucial hours of historic D-Day, he brought us to the triumph and peace of VE-Day. Now, another crucial hour in our history. The big question…

Man's voice: General, if war comes, is this country really ready?

Eisenhower: It is not. The administration has spent many billions of dollars for national defense. Yet today we haven't enough tanks for the fighting men in Korea. It is time for a change.

Narrator: The nation, haunted by the stalemate in Korea, looks to Eisenhower. Eisenhower knows how to deal with the Russians. He has met with Europe's leaders, has got them working with us. Elect the number-one man for the number-one job of our time. November fourth, vote for peace, vote for Eisenhower.

Yet this spot had an odd ring to it, perhaps because the approach ignored the intimate nature of television, which reaches its viewers in the home's cozy quarters as opposed to the blare of a newsreel in an auditorium.

By the best estimates, this first media blitz cost the Republicans close to $1.5 million. During that campaign, the Democrats spent only about $77,000 on television, and the new spots they produced played on New Deal themes and Republican responsibility for the Great Depression: "Sh-h-h-h. Don't mention it to a soul, don't spread it around … but the Republican party was in power back in 1932 … 13 million people were unemployed . . . bank doors shut in your face …." The Democrats, who had wanted to run an ad blitz but could not raise the money to pay for it, turned instead to broadsides about the GOP's "soap campaign." Stevenson's supporters charged that the Republican ad managers conceived a multimillion-dollar production designed to sell a political party ticket to the American people in precisely the way they sell soap.

The poet Marya Mannes was moved to write "Sales Campaign" in reaction to the Eisenhower advertising effort. Her poem read, in part: "Philip Morris, Lucky Strike, Alka Seltzer, I Like Ike." For better or worse, the pattern was set for future campaigns.

TIMELINE
Presidential Candidates and Their Television Ads

in the campaign to protect themselves in advance of the other side's spots. (Inoculation advertising attempts to counteract an anticipated attack from the opposition before the attack is even launched.) For example, a senator who fears a broadside about her voting record on Social Security issues might air advertisements featuring senior citizens praising her support of Social Security.

There has been significant debate among political scientists about the impact of negative advertising on American electoral politics. Particularly prominent have been studies investigating the influence of negative advertising on voter turnout. In an important study, political scientists Stephen Ansolabehere and Shanto Iyengar concluded that negative advertising decreases voter turnout (especially among political independents), and, worse yet, that political consultants use negative advertising precisely for such purposes.[5] However, this study by no means constitutes the last word on the subject. Indeed, several studies have cast doubt on the demobilizing effect of negative advertising. Steven Finkel and John Geer, for instance, find no demobilizing effects of negative ads, even among independent voters, and suggest that negative advertising might actually increase turnout by increasing knowledge and a sense of urgency about the campaign.[6] Similarly, Paul Freedman and Ken Goldstein also suggest a mobilizing effect of negative ads when they took into account viewing behavior and the total mix of positive, negative, and contrast ads actually broadcast, something that previous studies had omitted.[7] Hence the only conclusion we can arrive at here is that there is presently little consensus among scholars regarding the impact of negative advertising on voter turnout.

President George W. Bush held his first White House press conference approximately a month after he was officially sworn into office. Rather than meeting with members of the media in the East Room of the White House, with its moldings and chandeliers, Bush chose the unadorned briefing room, with its fluorescent lights. Many observers felt that it reflected the president's folksy sense of himself and unpretentious demeanor. (Photo courtesy: Jamal A. Wilson/Liaison Agency/Getty Source)

THE CANDIDATE OR THE CAMPAIGN: WHICH DO WE VOTE FOR?

Much is said and written about media and organizational techniques during the campaign, and they are often presented as political magic. Despite their sophistication, however, the technologies often fail the candidates and their campaigns. The political consultants who develop and master the technologies of polling, media, and other techniques frequently make serious mistakes in judgment. Despite popular lore and journalistic legend, few candidates are the creations of their clever consultants and dazzling campaign techniques. Partly, this is because politics always has been (and always will be) much more art than science, not subject to precise manipulation or formulaic computation. Of course, campaign techniques can enhance the candidate's strengths and downplay his or her weaknesses, and in that respect, technique certainly matters. In the end—in most cases—the candidate wins or loses the race according to his or her abilities, qualifications, communication skills, issues, and weaknesses. Although this simple truth is warmly reassuring, it has been remarkably overlooked by election analysts and reporters seemingly mesmerized by the exorbitant claims of consultants and the flashy computer lights of their technologies.[8]

The voter deserves much of the credit for whatever encouragement we can draw from this candidate-centered view of politics. Granted, citizens are often inattentive to politics, almost forcing candidates to use empty slogans and glitz to attract their attention. But it is also true that most voters want to take the real measure of candidates, and they retain a healthy skepticism about the techniques of running for office. Political cartoonist Tom Toles suggested as much when he depicted the seven preparatory steps the modern candidate takes: (1) Set out to discover what voters want, (2) conduct extensive polling, (3) study demographic trends, (4) engage in sophisticated interpretation of in-depth voter interviews, (5) analyze results, (6) discover that what the voters want is a candidate who doesn't need to do steps one through five, and (7) pretend you didn't. The chastened politician then tells his assembled throng, "I follow my conscience."[9]

Not all political scientists believe that the campaign or even the candidate matters to a great degree, however. A strain of thought in political science contends that citizens vote for the president based on their evaluations of past, current, or prospective states of the economy. This is based on the early work of political scientist V. O. Key, who posited, "voters are not fools"—that they may not understand the details of economic policy, but they know its effects on them and vote accordingly.[10] Later, Morris Fiorina analyzed election results from 1964 to 1972 and found that voters choose candidates based on retrospective evaluations of changes in their economic welfare under the incumbent party. If it went up, they voted for the status quo. If it went down, they voted for a change in government.[11] To this end, much of the recent literature in political science proposes to be able to predict election outcomes based on measures of economic growth and incumbent popularity measured prior to the start of the campaign. Robert S. Erikson, for instance, asserts from his analysis of post–World War II election outcomes that the change in per capita income measured prior to the election is a better predictor of presidential election outcomes than the affect in the electorate for the Democratic or Republican Parties or their candidates.[12] Likewise, Steven Finkel finds that the overwhelming majority of individual vote decisions are accounted for by party identification and presidential approval measured before the start of the fall campaign. The campaigns do not make a difference in individual vote choice or the outcome of most elections, except to remind people of their pre-existing preferences and activate them to vote on those preconceived notions.[13]

HIGHLIGHT

FAMOUS SOUND BYTES FROM PRESIDENTIAL CAMPAIGNS

2000

"That's Adam Clymer over there...he's a major-league asshole."

"Oh, yeah. Big-time."

—*Presidential candidate George W. Bush commenting on a* New York Times *political reporter to running mate Dick Cheney, unaware that his microphone was on, and Cheney's response.*

1996

"I ask for your help and if you really want to get involved, just tap into my homepage, www.dole/kemp96.org."

—*Senator Robert Dole (R), speaking during the second presidential debate.*

1992

"Message: I care"

—*George Bush (R), attempting to connect with New Hampshire's economically devastated voters.*

"Let's clean out the barn!"

—*Ross Perot (I)*

"Who am I? Why am I here?"

—*Retired Adm. James Stockdale, Ross Perot's 1992 vice presidential running mate, during a televised debate.*

1988

"Read my lips: no new taxes."

—*George Bush (R)*

"Stop lying about my record!"

—*Senator Robert Dole (R–Kans.), speaking to George Bush during their campaign for the Republican nomination.*

"I knew Jack Kennedy; he was a friend of mine. And, Senator, you're no Jack Kennedy."

—*Democratic vice presidential nominee, Senator Lloyd Bentsen (D–Tex.), responding in an October debate to Republican nominee Dan Quayle's comparison of himself to John F. Kennedy.*

1984

"Where's the beef?"

—*Walter Mondale to his Democratic rival Gary Hart, who claimed to have "new ideas."*

1980

"There you go again ...."

—*Ronald Reagan (R) to President Jimmy Carter (D), in response to some of Carter's charges against Reagan in a debate.*

"Are you better off today than you were four years ago?"

—*Reagan's oft-repeated question to the voters.*

MODERN CAMPAIGN CHALLENGES

The modern candidate faces two major challenges: communicating through the media and raising the money needed to stay in the race. We consider each challenge in turn.

The News Media

The news media present quite a challenge to candidates. Although politicians and their staffs cannot control the press, they nonetheless try to manipulate press coverage. They use three techniques to accomplish this aim. First, the staff often seeks to isolate the candidate from the press, thus reducing the chances that reporters will bait a candidate into saying something that might damage the candidate's cause. Naturally, the media are frustrated by such a tactic and insist on as many open press conferences as possible.

Second, the campaign stages media events—activities designed to include brief, clever quotes called *sound bytes* and staged with appealing backdrops so that they are all but irresistible, especially to television news (see Highlight: Famous Sound Bytes from Presidential Campaigns). In this fashion the candidate's staff can successfully fill the news hole reserved for campaign coverage on the evening news programs and in the morning papers.

candidate debates
Forums in which political candidates face each other to discuss their platforms, records, and character.

Third, the handlers and consultants have cultivated the technique termed *spin*—that is, they put the most favorable possible interpretation for their candidate on any circumstance occurring in the campaign, and they work the press to sell their point of view or at least to ensure that it is included in the reporters' stories. The two would-be Democratic contenders offered a classic example of spin after the 2000 New Hampshire primary. Gore was the favorite, but he won the primary with a relatively narrow margin. This led Bradley's handlers to proclaim a moral victory over the powerful pro-Gore party apparatus, while Gore's team took very public advantage of the chance to celebrate what they chose to call a miraculous victory over a candidate who might have profitted from the advantage of regional affiliations (Bradley is from New Jersey and so might conceivably be lumped with New Hampshirites as a northeasterner). Luckily for Gore, events rendered his spin closer to the truth as Bradley rapidly faded from contention. **Candidate debates,** especially the televised presidential variety, are also showcases for the consultants' spin patrol, and teams of staffers from each side swarm the press rooms to declare victory even before the candidates finish their closing statements.

Televised Debates.   Candidate debates are media extravaganzas that are a hybrid of free and paid media. As with ads, much of the candidate dialogue (jokes included) is canned and prepackaged. Yet spontaneity cannot be completely eliminated, and gaffes, quips, and slips of the tongue can sometimes be revealing. President Gerald Ford's insistence during an October 1976 debate with Jimmy Carter that Poland was not under Soviet domination may have cost him a close election. Ronald Reagan's refrain, "Are you better off today than you were four years ago?" neatly summed up his case against Carter in 1980. Moreover, Reagan's easygoing performance reassured a skeptical public that wanted Carter out of the White House but was not certain it wanted Reagan in.

Senator John F. Kennedy's visually impressive showing in the first 1960 presidential debate dramatically reduced the edge that experience gave two-term Vice President Richard M. Nixon. Not only was Nixon ill at the time, but he also was poorly dressed and poorly made up for television. Interestingly, most of those who heard the debate on radio—and therefore could not see the contrast between the pale, anxious, sweating Nixon and the relaxed, tanned Kennedy—thought that Nixon had won.

The importance of debates can easily be overrated, however. A weak performance by Reagan in his first debate with Walter Mondale in 1984 had little lasting effect, in part because Reagan did better in the second debate. Most of the debates in 1960, 1976, 1980,

Presidential debates have come a long way—at least in terms of studio trappings—since the ill-at-ease Richard M. Nixon was visually bested by John F. Kennedy in the first televised debate. In the first of three 2000 debates, Al Gore's aggressive debating style contrasted sharply with that of George W. Bush. (Photos courtesy: left, Bettman/Corbis; right, Al Behrman/AP/Wide World Photos)

and 1988 were unmemorable and electorally inconsequential. Debates usually just firm up voters' predispositions and cannot change the fundamentals of an election (the state of the economy, scandal, and presidential popularity, for example). This is what appeared to happen in 1992 and 1996 when none of the three presidential debates and one vice presidential debate changed the underlying pro-Clinton trends in the election. In 2000, Gore was universally expected to dispatch Bush readily, on the basis of his greater experience in both foreign and domestic policy. However, although Gore did have a better command of the facts, he defeated himself on the stage by sighing, rolling his eyes, and giving an impression of impatience and disdain. While the debates did not radically alter the larger course of the campaign, they did nothing to help voters feel any affection toward Gore as a person. Thus, while debates do not usually remake an election, they are potentially educational and focus the public's mind on the upcoming election.

Political scientists have recently found some effects resultant from presidential debates. John Geer, for instance, using panel-study poll data, finds that "a sizable minority of the public altered their preferences for president" after watching debates. In 1976, he found that 16 percent of viewers altered the intensity of their choice for president, and 10 percent switched candidate allegiance altogether, with the largest changes occurring among undecided voters and those weakly allied to a candidate.[14] Similarly, David Lanoue, in a study of the 1980 debates, finds significant shifts occurred in candidate preference among viewers with low levels of political knowledge.[15] So while debates do not appear to alter the results of elections, they do tend to increase knowledge about the candidates and their respective personalities and issue positions, especially among voters who have not previously paid attention to the campaign. Since they have been held in every presidential campaign since 1976, debates are now likely to be an expected and standard part of the presidential election process. They are also an established feature of campaigns for governor, U.S. senator, and many other offices.

Can the Press Be "Handled"?   Candidates and their consultants constantly try to "spin" (or influence) the thinking of the press. For example, campaigns today will often fax a dozen or more statements or releases a day to key journalists. Efforts by candidates to manipulate the news media often fail because the press is wise to their tactics and determined to thwart them. Not even the candidates' paid media are sacrosanct anymore. Major newspapers throughout the country have taken to analyzing the accuracy of the television advertisements aired during the campaign—a welcome and useful addition to journalists' scrutiny of politicians.

Less welcome are some other news media practices in campaigns. Many studies have shown that the media are obsessed with the horse race aspect of politics—who's ahead, who's behind, who's gaining—to the detriment of the substance of the candidates' issues and ideas. Public opinion polls, especially tracking polls, many of them taken by the news outlets themselves, dominate coverage, especially on network television, where only a few minutes a night are devoted to politics. (Tracking polls were discussed in chapter 11.)

Related to the proliferation of polls is the media's expectations game in presidential primary contests. With polls as the objective backdrop, journalists set the margins by which contenders are expected to win or lose—so much so that even a clear victory of 5 percentage points can be judged a setback if the candidate had been projected to win by 12 or 15 points. Additionally, research in political science shows that media coverage of the horse race in presidential primaries affects campaign contributions to candidates at this critical time. The tone of the media coverage—that a candidate is either gaining or losing support in polls—can affect, positively or negatively, the frequency with which citizens decide to give money and other types of support to a candidate.[16] Finally, the news media often overemphasize trivial parts of the campaign, such as a politician's minor gaffe, and give too much attention to the private lives of candidates. This superficial coverage and the resources needed to generate it are displacing serious journalism on the issues. These subjects are taken up again in the next chapter, which deals with the news media.

WEB EXPLORATION
To get an insider's look at the detail and urgency with which campaigns are now covered, go to www.ablongman.com/oconnor

Campaign Financing

To run all aspects of a campaign successfully requires a great deal of money. In 2000 alone, more than $1 billion was raised and spent in U.S. House and Senate races.[17] This amount was an increase of greater than 34 percent over the 1998 elections. On average, an incumbent Democrat in the House spent nearly $670,000; Republican incumbents in the House spent an average of $782,000. Their challengers, in contrast, spent an average of $59,000. In contests with open seats, usually the most expensive races, candidates spent on average of almost $1 million. As humorist Will Rogers once remarked early in the twentieth century, "Politics has got so expensive that it takes lots of money even to get beat with."

Political money is regulated by the federal government under the terms of the Federal Election Campaign Act of 1971, first passed in 1971 and substantially strengthened after Watergate in 1974, 1976, and 1979. In March of 2002, however, President George W. Bush signed into law the Bipartisan Campaign Finance Reform Act of 2002, which, while substantial, did not take effect until after the 2002 congressional elections. Table 14.1 summarizes some of the important provisions of this law, which limits what individuals, interest groups, and political parties can give to candidates for president, U.S. senator, and U.S. representative. The goal of all limits is the same: to prevent any single group or individual from gaining too much influence over elected officials, who naturally feel indebted to campaign contributors.

Given the cash flow required by a campaign and the legal restrictions on political money, raising the funds necessary to run a modern campaign is a monumental task. Consequently, presidential and congressional campaigns have squads of fund raisers on staff. These professionals rely on several standard sources of campaign money.

Individual Contributions.   Individual contributions are donations from individual citizens. The maximum allowable contribution under federal law for congressional and presidential elections is $1,000 per election to each candidate, with primary and general elections considered separately. Individuals are also limited to a total of $25,000 in gifts to all candidates combined in each calendar year. Most candidates receive a majority of all funds directly from individuals, and most individual gifts are well below the maximum level.

political action committee (PAC)

Federally mandated, officially registered fund-raising committee that represents interest groups in the political process.

Political Action Committee (PAC) Contributions.   Donations from **political action committees (PACs)** are those from interest groups (labor unions, corporations, trade associations, and ideological and issue groups). Under federal law these organizations are required to establish officially recognized fund-raising committees, called PACs, in order to participate in federal elections. (Some but not all states have similar requirements for state elections.) Approximately 4,000 PACs are registered with the Federal Election Commission—the governmental agency charged with administering the election laws. In 1994 all PACs together gave $179 million to Senate and House candi-

TABLE 14.1   Contribution Limits for Congressional Candidates Before and After Bipartisan Campaign Finance Reform Act, 2002

Contributions From	Given to Candidate (per election)[a]	Given to National Party (per calendar year)	Total Allowable Contributions (per calendar year)
	Before/After	**Before/After**	**Before/After**
Individual	$1,000/$2,000	$20,000/$25,000	$25,000/$95,000 per two-year cycle
Political action committee[b]	$5,000/$5,000	$15,000/$15,000	No limit/No limit
Any political party committee[c]	$5,000/$10,000	No limit/No limit	No limit/No limit
All national and state party committees taken together	To House candidates: $30,000 plus "coordinated expenditures"[d] To Senate candidates: $27,500 plus "coordinated expenditures"[d]		

Note: The regulations under the Bipartisan Campaign Finance Reform Act did not take effect until *after* the 2002 election.
[a]Each of the following is considered a separate election: primary (or convention), runoff, general election.
[b]Multi-candidate PACs only. Multi-candidate committees have received contributions from at least fifty persons and have given to at least five federal candidates.
[c]Multi-candidate party committees only. Multi-candidate committees have received contributions from at least fifty persons and have given to at least five federal candidates.
[d]Coordinated expenditures are party-paid general election campaign expenditures made in consultation and coordination with the candidate under the provisions of section 441(a)(d) of the Federal Code.

dates. (By contrast, individual citizens donated nearly $336 million.) In 1998 PACs contributed $207 million to Senate and House candidates, while individuals donated $420 million. On average, PAC contributions account for 32 percent of the war chests (campaign funds) of House candidates and 17 percent of the treasuries of Senate candidates. Because a small number of PACs make up such a large proportion of campaign war chests, they have influence disproportionate to that of individuals. Recent studies, in fact, show that PACs effectively use contributions to punish legislators and affect policy, at least in the short run.[18] Legislators who vote contrary to the wishes of a PAC see their donations withheld, but those who are successful in legislating in the PAC's wishes are rewarded with even greater donations.[19] (Interest groups are treated in more detail in chapter 16.) In 2002, PACs and other committees contributed $420 million of the $890 million raised by House and Senate candidates.

Longman
Participate.com
2.0
Timeline
**Interest
Groups and
Campaign
Finance**

Political Party Contributions.   Candidates also receive donations from the national and state committees of the Democratic and Republican Parties. As mentioned in chapter 12, political parties can give substantial contributions to their congressional nominees. In 1996 the Republicans and the Democrats funneled over $25 million to their standard-bearers. In competitive races, the parties may provide 15 percent to 17 percent of their candidates' total war chests. In addition to helping elect party members, campaign contributions from political parties have another, less obvious benefit: helping to ensure party discipline in voting. One study of congressional voting behavior in the 1980s, for instance, found that those members who received a large percentage of their total campaign funds from their party voted with their party more often than they were expected to.[20] Much of the activity of national party committees in recent election cycles has shifted towards transfers of funds from the national committees to various states. In total, the national committees of the Democratic Party transferred $226.9 million to various states in the 2000 election cycle, while the national committee of the Republican Party transferred $184.9 million.

Member-to-Candidate Contributions.   In Congress and in state legislatures, well-funded, electorally secure incumbents now often contribute campaign money to their party's needy incumbent and nonincumbent legislative candidates.[21] This activity has long occurred in some state legislatures (notably California), but it has recently become increasingly important at the congressional level.[22] Generally, members contribute to other candidates in one of two ways. First, some members have established their own PACs—informally dubbed "leadership" PACs—through which they distribute campaign support to candidates. For example, through the 2002 general election cycle, then Senate Minority Leader Trent Lott's (R–Miss.) PAC, the New Republican Majority Fund, not only helped him become the new Majority Leader, it allowed him to contribute to eleven House and twenty-nine Senate candidates. In total, his PAC spent $5.6 million in his efforts to help win back the Senate and maintain the House. Members, however, are limited by campaign finance law to giving no more than $1,000 per candidate (this will be $2,000 in 2004) per election and $10,000 per candidate for each cycle: $5,000 for the primary and $5,000 for the general election from a leadership PAC.

Collectively, these contributions can add up. For example, in 1996 fifty-four House Republicans contributed a total of $111,242 to the campaign of Randy Tate, an electorally vulnerable Republican House incumbent running for reelection in Washington State's Ninth Congressional District. Astonishingly, the amount contributed to Tate by his colleagues was $41,167 *greater* than that contributed in cash and coordinated expenditures by the National Republican Congressional Committee (NRCC), the primary fund-raising arm of the House Republican Conference. In general, members give their contributions to the same candidates who receive the bulk of congressional campaign committee resources. As such, member contributions at the congressional level have emerged as a major supplement to the campaign resources contributed by the party campaign committees.[23] In an interesting twist on member-to-candidate contribution activity in congressional elections, it now appears that some leadership PACs are raising and spending soft money.[24]

Senator John McCain (R–AZ) and Senator Russ Feingold (D–WI) co-authored the Bipartisan Campaign Finance Reform Act of 2002, legislation that bans unregulated soft money contributions. The crusade to reform the campaign finance system was aided significantly by McCain's 2000 presidential candidacy. (Photo courtesy: Robert Trippett/SIPA Press.)

public funds
Donations from the general tax revenues to the campaigns of qualifying presidential candidates.

matching funds
Donations to presidential campaigns from the federal government that are determined by the amount of private funds a qualifying candidate raises.

Candidates' Personal Contributions. Candidates and their families may donate to the campaign. The Supreme Court ruled in 1976 in *Buckley* v. *Valeo* that no limit could be placed on the amount of money candidates can spend from their own families' resources, since such spending is considered a First Amendment right of free speech.[25] For wealthy politicians such as U.S. Senators John D. Rockefeller IV (D–W.Va.) or Herbert H. Kohl (D–Wisc.), this allowance may mean personal spending in the millions. Most candidates, however, commit much less than $100,000 in family resources to their election bids. In 1994 House and Senate candidates loaned or contributed almost $123 million to their own campaigns. In 1996 House and Senate candidate contributions to their own campaigns was $107 million, a decrease due mostly to 1996 senatorial candidates spending less of their own funds. John Corzine (D–N.J.), however, spent over $60 million of his vast personal fortune in 2000 to capture a U.S. Senate seat. In all, 18 candidates for House or Senate seats spent over $1 million of their own money to finance their campaigns; interestingly, only five of the candidates were victorious.

Public Funds. **Public funds** are donations from general tax revenues. Only presidential candidates (and a handful of state and local contenders) receive public funds. Under the terms of the Federal Election Campaign Act of 1971 (which first established public funding of presidential campaigns), a candidate for president can become eligible to receive public funds during the nominating contest by raising at least $5,000 in individual contributions of $250 or less in each of twenty states. Once the receipt of this money is certified, the candidate can apply for federal **matching funds,** whereby every dollar raised from individuals in amounts less than $251 is matched by the federal treasury on a dollar-for-dollar basis. This assumes there is enough money in the Presidential Election Campaign Fund to do so. The fund is accumulated by taxpayers who designate $3 of their taxes for this purpose each year when they send in their federal tax returns. (Only about 20 percent of taxpayers check off the appropriate box, even though participation does not increase their tax burden.)

For the general election, the two major-party presidential nominees are given a lump-sum payment in the summer before the election ($62 million each in 1996), from which all their general election campaign expenditures must come. A third-party candidate receives a smaller amount proportionate to his or her November vote total if that candidate gains a minimum of 5 percent of the vote. Note that in such a case the money goes to third-party campaigns only *after* the election is over; no money is given in advance of the general election. The only third-party candidate to qualify for general election funds before Ross Perot did so was John Anderson, the Independent candidate for president in 1980, who garnered 7 percent of the national vote. While Ross Perot chose not to take public funds for his campaign in 1992, a campaign which was largely self-financed, in 1996 Perot did accept public funding. He qualified for this funding by securing 19 percent of the popular vote in the 1992 presidential election.

Independent Expenditures. In the landmark case of *Buckley* v. *Valeo* (1976), the Supreme Court ruled that it is unconstitutional for Congress to limit the amount of money that an individual or a political committee may spend supporting or opposing a candidate if the expenditures are made independently of the candidate's campaign.[26] (See Figure 14.1.) In a 1996 case, *Colorado Republican Federal Campaign Committee* v. *Federal*

FIGURE 14.1   Expenditures by PACs in 2000

Notice how PACS use a majority of their expenditures to support congressional candidates positively, and only a small fraction to attack opponents in presidential campaigns. Notice how PAC spending has a slight bias towards Republican candidates and a strong bias toward incumbents.

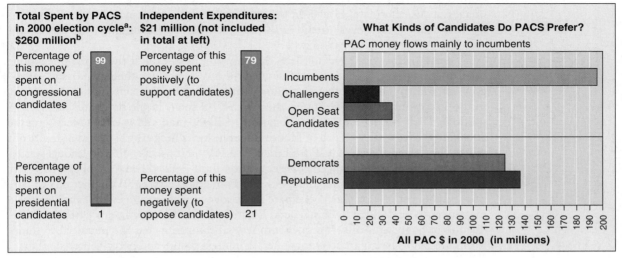

Source: Federal Election Commission.

Election Commission, the Supreme Court extended this ruling to political parties.[27] Hence, individuals, PACs and now political parties may spend unlimited amounts of money directly advocating the election or defeat of a candidate as long as these expenditures are not made in coordination with the candidate's campaign. Often, when a group spends independently of a candidate, it will do so for television advertisements urging voters to support or defeat a particular candidate. However, because independent expenditure advertisements expressly advocate the election or defeat of a specific federal candidate, they must be paid for with **hard money**—that is, with money raised under the guidelines of the Federal Election Campaign Act (see Table 14.1). This stands in direct contrast to issue advocacy ads financed by soft money, which are considered next.

Soft Money/Issue Advocacy Advertisements.   **Soft money** is campaign money raised and spent by political parties and interest groups that is not subject to the regulations of the Federal Election Campaign Act. In a 1978 advisory opinion, the Federal Election Commission ruled that political parties could raise these unregulated funds in order to pay for expenses—such as overhead and administrative costs—and grassroots activities that did not directly influence campaigns for federal elections. In 1979 Congress passed an amendment to the Federal Elections Campaign Act allowing parties to *spend* unlimited sums on these same activities.[28] In the years immediately following the rule changes, the national parties began raising five- and six-figure sums from individuals and interest groups to pay for expenses such as rent, employee salaries, and building maintenance. The national parties also began transferring large sums of soft money to state parties in order to help pay for grassroots activities (such as get-out-the-vote drives) and campaign paraphernalia (such as yard signs and bumper stickers).

However, the line separating expenditures that influence federal elections from those that do not has proved to be quite blurry, and this blurriness has resulted in a significant campaign finance loophole. The largest controversy has come in the area of campaign advertisements. The federal courts have ruled that only campaign advertisements that use explicit words—for example, "vote for," "vote against," "elect," or "support"— qualify as *express-advocacy* advertisements. Political advertisements that do not use these words are considered *issue-advocacy* advertisements.[29] The distinction here is crucial. Because express-advocacy advertisements are openly intended to influence federal

hard money

Legally specified and limited contributions that are clearly regulated by the Federal Election Campaign Act and by the Federal Election Commission.

soft money

The virtually unregulated money funneled by individuals and political committees through state and local parties.

elections, they must be paid for with strictly regulated hard money. Issue-advocacy advertisements, on the other hand, can be paid for with unregulated soft money. The parties' response to these rules has been to create issue-advocacy advertisements that very much resemble express-advocacy ads. Typically, for such advertisements call attention to the voting record of the candidate supported or opposed and are replete with images of the candidate. However, the parties ensure that the magic words "vote for" or "vote against" are never uttered in the advertisements, allowing them to be paid for with soft rather than hard money.

The national parties have not been the only groups to exploit the soft-money loophole; interest groups have increasingly joined the fray by running their own "issue"-advocacy ads and conducting other soft money–financed campaign activities. For example, in the 1996 congressional elections, the AFL–CIO spent in the neighborhood of $35 million in soft money on "voter education"—direct-mail and media advertisements attacking the legislative record of House Republicans. These efforts played a significant role in the defeat of many GOP freshmen.[30] In 1999, House Republican leaders started their own soft money–financed voter education fund—called the Republican Majority Issues Campaign—to counter the AFL–CIO's ongoing efforts.[31] Whether or not parties and interest groups may coordinate issue-advocacy campaigns with candidates is a matter yet to be decided by the Federal Election Commission.[32] In any case, the introduction of huge sums of soft money into federal campaigns has the potential to transform campaigns from candidate-centered to interest group–and party-centered affairs.[33]

Some argue that the recent proliferation of soft money (in 2002, the Republican and Democratic Party committees raised $511 million and $328 million in non-federal fund, respectively—a 135 percent increase over 2000 for the Republicans, and 70 percent increase for the Democrats) is not to be lamented. They maintain that political parties deserve more fund-raising freedom, which would give these critical institutions a more substantial role in elections. But when individual contributors are able to donate as much money as they like via the soft money route, they at least theoretically gain a heightened level of access to politicians not enjoyed by the electorate as a whole. The money itself was the cause of great concern during the 2000 presidential campaign and has increased public outcry for reform. Government watchdog groups such as Common Cause and Public Campaign argued that the soft-money/issue-advocacy loophole has created a complete meltdown of federal campaign laws, and they successfully argued that political parties should be banned from raising soft money.

The Internet and Campaign Finance

The Internet has the potential to alter radically the way candidates raise funds for their campaigns. After all, making an online appeal for campaign contributions costs significantly less than raising funds through expensive direct-mail campaigns or pricey fund-raising events—the standard means of raising campaign resources. Still, it's not clear that online fund-raising appeals would be all that successful. The Internet, veteran political consultant Hal Malchow reminds us, is a self-directed medium, and "it is not human nature to seek out places to give money."[34] Nevertheless, the potential weaknesses of Internet fund raising are unlikely to stop candidates from experimenting with it. Republican presidential nominee John McCain became the first political candidate to raise over $1 million in forty-eight hours after his victory in the 2000 New Hampshire primary.

The Internet also promises to create headaches for the Federal Election Commission. Already, the FEC has been forced to rule on issues such as whether a business site link to a campaign site constitutes in-kind contribution from the business to the campaign, and whether funds raised online by presidential candidates are eligible to be matched with public funds from the Presidential Election Campaign Fund. (In the first case, the FEC ruled yes; in the second case, it ruled no.) Clearly, these issues are only the beginning of a seemingly limitless plethora of concerns regarding the Internet and campaign finance that the FEC will be asked to address. "Every day," noted former FEC Chair

Trevor Potter, "I'm running into people in my practice who are saying, 'This is what I want to do on the Internet—are there any Federal Election law implications?'" Indeed, campaign finance experts have wondered aloud whether the agency has the resources to regulate and monitor the newly unfolding campaign activity on the Internet.[35]

Are PACs a Good or Bad Part of the Process?

Of all these forms of spending, probably the most controversial is that involving PAC money. Some PACs, due to the amount of money they are able to raise and their ability to get their supporters to the polls on Election Day, are more influential than others; but there are few poor, noninfluential PACs. Some observers claim that PACs are the embodiment of corrupt special interests that use campaign donations to buy the votes of legislators. Furthermore, they argue that the less affluent and minority members of our society do not enjoy equal access to these political organizations.

These charges are serious and deserve consideration. Although the media relentlessly stresses the role of money in determining policy outcomes, the evidence that PACs buy votes is less than overwhelming.[36] Political scientists have conducted a multitude of studies regarding the impact of interest group PAC contributions on legislative voting, and the conclusions reached by these studies have varied widely.[37] Whereas some studies have found that PAC money affects members' voting behavior, other studies have uncovered no such correlation. It may be, of course, that interest group PAC money has an impact on members' behavior at earlier stages of the legislative process. Along these lines, one innovative study found that PAC money had a significant effect on members' participation in committee on legislation important to the contributing group.[38] Thus, interest group PAC money may mobilize something more important than votes—the valuable time and energy of members themselves.

Also serious is the charge that some interests are significantly better represented by the PAC system than are others. This view was put forth most recently by political scientist Thomas Gais, who argues that laws regulating PAC activity inherently favor PACs with parent organizations—corporate, labor, and trade PACs—over citizen-based PACs without parent organizations.[39] Although Gais's argument is complex, a simple example of the biases of federal law illustrates his point. As Gais points out, federal campaign finance law allows corporate, labor, and trade PACs to use general treasury funds from the PAC's parent organization to pay for the (often formidable) overhead and administrative costs of running the PAC, whereas PACs without parent organizations are forced to rely on voluntary contributions to pay their overhead and administrative costs. The result of these laws, argues Gais, is that citizen-based PACs have a more difficult time organizing than do PACs with a well-established, wealthy parent organization. Consequently, the PAC system, in Gais's view, aids some interests more than others. Gais argues that any campaign finance reform should raise substantially the limits on the amount of money an individual may contribute to a PAC—to the point where a single person could underwrite a citizen group's formation and maintenance costs.

Still, for all their faults, many political scientists view PACs as a natural manifestation of interest group politics in a diverse democracy. Also, many political scientists point out that a person need not belong to a PAC to wield electoral and political influence. The Democrats' best-known external resources—and the ones that most pain Republicans—are the PACs associated with organized labor, and minority groups as a whole. While organized labor has for decades provided Democrats with an army of volunteers and huge amounts of financial support, minorities have been the single most loyal Democratic voting bloc—in raw vote terms even more indispensable to the Democrats than labor.

Although a good number of PACs of all persuasions existed prior to the 1970s, it was during this decade—the decade of campaign reform—that the modern PAC era began. Spawned by the Watergate-inspired revisions of the campaign-finance laws, PACs grew in number from 113 in 1972 to 4,599 by the late 1990s (see Figure 14.2),

FIGURE 14.2   **Growth in Total Number of PACs**
Note how the first PACs appeared in the early 1970s and how their numbers grew substantially
in the decade after Watergate.

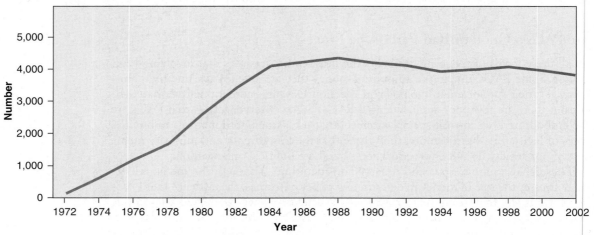

Note: Numbers are as of December 31st of every other year, starting in 1972.
Source: Federal Election Commission.

FIGURE 14.3   **Growth in Total Contributions by PACs to House and Senate Candidates**
The growth of campaign spending by PACs has roughly paralleled the increasing number of PACs over their
30-year history.

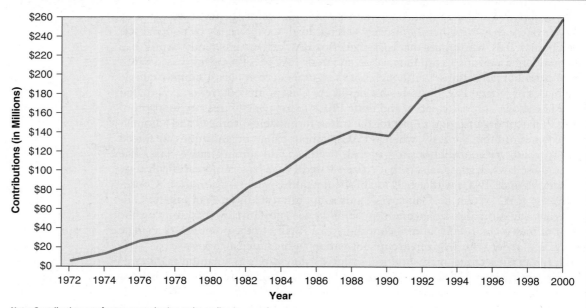

Note: Contributions are for two-year election cycles ending in years shown.
Source: Federal Election Commission.

Longman
Participate.com
2.0
Visual Literacy
**PACs and the
Money Trail**

and their contributions to congressional candidates multiplied nearly thirtyfold, from
$8.5 million in 1971 and 1972 to $254 million in 2000 (see Figure 14.3). But these
numbers should not obscure a basic truth about the PAC system: that a very small
group of PACs conducts the bulk of total PAC activity. Indeed, as political scientist
Paul Herrnson observes, a mere 4 percent of all PACs contributed a full 57 percent of
the total dollars given to congressional candidates by PACs during the 1995–1996 election cycle.[40]

Some people argue that PACs are newfangled inventions that have flooded the political system with money. Although the widespread use of the PAC structure is new, the fact remains that special interest money of all types has always found its way into politics. Before the 1970s it did so in less traceable and much more disturbing and unsavory ways, because little of the money given to candidates was regularly disclosed to public inspection. Although it is true that PACs contribute a massive sum to candidates in absolute terms, it is not clear that there is proportionately more interest group money in the system than before. The proportion of House and Senate campaign funds provided by PACs has certainly increased since the early 1970s, but individuals, most of whom are unaffiliated with PACs, together with the political parties, still supply more than 60 percent of all the money spent by or on behalf of House candidates, 75 percent of the campaign expenditures for Senate contenders, and 85 percent of the campaign expenditures for presidential candidates. So while the importance of PAC spending has grown, PACs clearly remain secondary as a source of election funding and therefore pose no overwhelming threat to the system's legitimacy.

It can be argued that contemporary political action committees are another manifestation of what James Madison called "factions." Through the flourishing of competing interest groups or factions, said Madison in *Federalist No. 10*, liberty would be preserved. In any democracy, and particularly in one as pluralistic as that of the United States, it is essential that groups be relatively unrestricted in advocating their interests and positions. Not only is unrestricted political activity by interest groups a mark of a free society, but it also provides a safety valve for the competitive pressures that build on all fronts in a democracy and supplies a way to keep representatives responsive to legitimate needs.

The election outlays of PACs, like the total amount expended in a single election season, seem huge. But the cost of elections in the United States is less than or approximately the same as in some other nations, measured on a per-voter basis.[41] Moreover, the cost of all elections in the United States taken together is less than the amount many individual private corporations spend on advertising cereals, dog food, cars, and toothpaste. These days it is expensive to communicate, whether the message is political or commercial. The costs of television time, polling, consultants, and other items have soared over and above the inflation rate.

A SUMMARY OF CONTRIBUTIONS AND EXPENSES

A typical U.S. Senate candidate in 2002 received most of his or her war chest (about 67 percent) from relatively small individual donations. PACs supplied about 26 percent, and 7 percent came from the political party committees and the candidates themselves. (See Analyzing the Data: Campaign for Senate, 2002.)

The single greatest outlay (38 percent of the total) was for television and radio advertising; the next-largest item, fundraising, was half that cost (18 percent). The other 44 percent of the budget was spent on everything from polls to travel expenses. Keep in mind that in a large state with a dozen or more media markets (concentrated population centers with many television and radio stations), expenditures often balloon to $5 million, $10 million, and even more.

Some candidates have more difficulty than others in raising the necessary dollar amounts. Those in power—the incumbents—have the least trouble, although challengers who face incumbents weakened by scandal can also find the task of financing the campaign relatively easy. The size of a challenger's war chest is really the key variable. There is a point of diminishing returns for incumbent spending, since most office holders are already well known to the voters. But the challenger's name and platform are likely to be obscure. If the challenger can raise and spend enough to get his or her basic message across, there is a reasonable chance that the election will be at least moderately competitive. As is more common, though, if the challenger is starved for funds, the contest will probably turn into a romp for the well-heeled incumbent.

A N A L Y Z I N G   T H E   D A T A

CAMPAIGN FOR SENATE, 2000: A "TYPICAL" CANDIDATE'S BUDGET OF $7 MILLION

The breakdown of a sample budget for a typical senate campaign. Notice how most of the revenues come from individual contributions, although the rising cost of running for office now often favors wealthy candidates who can help finance their campaigns with their own dollars. Notice also how media—TV, radio, and increasingly the Internet—are the single greatest expense, as candidates seek to discredit their opponents through negative ads.

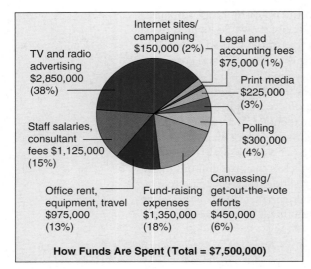

How Funds Are Spent (Total = $7,500,000)

TV and radio advertising $2,850,000 (38%)

Staff salaries, consultant fees $1,125,000 (15%)

Office rent, equipment, travel $975,000 (13%)

Fund-raising expenses $1,350,000 (18%)

Internet sites/campaigning $150,000 (2%)

Legal and accounting fees $75,000 (1%)

Print media $225,000 (3%)

Polling $300,000 (4%)

Canvassing/get-out-the-vote efforts $450,000 (6%)

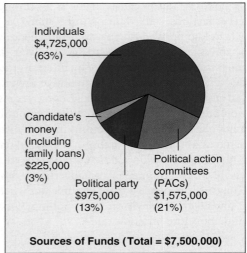

Sources of Funds (Total = $7,500,000)

Individuals $4,725,000 (63%)

Candidate's money (including family loans) $225,000 (3%)

Political party $975,000 (13%)

Political action committees (PACs) $1,575,000 (21%)

BRINGING IT TOGETHER: THE 2000 PRESIDENTIAL CAMPAIGN AND ELECTION

The 2000 election for president will go down as the closest election in modern United States history. Despite a strong economy, low unemployment, peace abroad, remarkable domestic prosperity, and semi-incumbency, Vice President Al Gore faced an incredibly difficult race against Texas Governor George W. Bush, son of the former president. At the most basic level, Americans generally thought that Gore was the most qualified candidate, but he lacked strong personal appeal and carried baggage associated with unethical events of the Clinton administration. On the other hand, Bush was personable and likable, but aided by the humor of the late night talk shows, few Americans thought that he was experienced enough or even competent enough to serve in the highest office in the nation.

The Party Nomination Battle

Both Gore and Bush were considered the front-runners for their respective party's nominations for well over a year prior to the November 2000 election. Gore, the vice president, former Tennessee senator, and son of a Tennessee senator, had served with Bill Clinton since 1992. Gore was challenged by former New Jersey senator and New York Knick Bill Bradley. Bradley, who was very popular with independents and more liberal members of the Democratic Party, espoused the need for campaign finance reform and universal health care coverage. Senator John McCain sought the nomination against Bush on a platform of campaign finance reform. McCain was very popular with many independents and moderate Republicans. (See Figure 14.4 for a timeline of Campaign 2000).

Despite momentum in the early rounds, Bill Bradley never seriously challenged Vice President Gore's bid for the 2000 Democratic nomination. In Iowa, the primary equivalent of a litmus test, the results showed that voters considered Gore a "stronger leader with better ideas" on campaign finance and health care reform: the two issues most central to the Bradley campaign. Iowa also evidenced that voters in every age and nearly every income group supported Gore, who carried the state with a 28 percent lead. While New Hampshire solidified the belief that although Bill Bradley could win the support of such anti-Clinton voters as well-educated white males, he could not garner the support of the core Democrats. Gore won easily, buoyed by Clinton supporters, union workers, and the voters who traditionally form the heart of the party. Even after these two substantial defeats and a declining fund-raising effort, the Democratic Party did not put substantial pressure on Bradley to drop out of the race. Nevertheless, after losing California, New York, and other big primaries, Gore emerged as the clear front-runner for the Democratic Party.

In contrast, George W. Bush faced a much tougher road to the Republican National Convention. While Bush won the first Iowa caucus, many were stunned at how far below expectations his performance fell. New Hampshire, however, delivered the sharpest blow to Bush's run for the GOP nomination. In an outcome some compared to that of 1996, when Pat Buchanan bested Bob Dole in the New Hampshire primary, Senator John McCain pulled ahead of Bush by 18 points to win the state. This blowout was attributed to the fact that up to that point, Bush's campaign had been endorsement-laden while lacking in issues. Additional factors pointed at were the continued presence of billionaire publisher Steve Forbes and conservative African American talk-show host Alan Keyes. Nevertheless, McCain's clear victory placed pressure on the Texas governor to sharpen his message, boost his energy as a candidate, and confront McCain directly.

Bush did just that in South Carolina, abandoning his "compassionate conservatism" and winning the Republican vote by a margin of 9 percent. Forbes had disappeared by this time, leaving Alan Keyes with the remaining 4 percent. Although Bush's victory was slightly marred by his visit to conservative Bob Jones University, a school that prohibited interracial dating among students, this much-needed victory gave Bush the momentum he needed to win the primaries in Michigan, California, and New York. After alienating himself from Michigan voters by attacking Christian conservatives, McCain continued to slide downward, finally leaving the race (but not the political landscape) after losses in the large state primaries.

Once the dust from the primaries settled around the two remaining candidates, both parties decisively backed their choices. Bush supporters believed he needed to renew his appeal to independent and moderate voters after being pushed to the right by McCain, but they wholeheartedly backed the Texas governor's bid for the White House. Gore's camp believed that despite a somewhat negative primary season, Bradley had left Gore relatively unscarred, and they eagerly awaited the coming months which would pit Democrats against Republicans in the most hotly contested presidential race since 1960.

Longman
Participate.com 2.0
Timeline
Third Parties
in American
History

The Third Force

The year 1992 seemed to mark a turning point in two-party history. Ross Perot's Reform Party garnered nearly 20 percent of the national vote, ensuring federal funding for a third party. The 1996 elections gave the Texas billionaire and his party 8 percent, a substantial decrease, but still enough to continue the flow of federal money into Reform party coffers. These two results appeared as evidence to the rise of a direct challenge to the traditional presidential electoral system. However, the 2000 elections showed that third parties still have a long road ahead.

The draw of federal funding for the Reform Party produced two legitimate candidates for the party: Pat Buchanan and John Hagelin. The Christian conservative Buchanan continued to make extremist statements as well as support what some called "bigoted policies" such as closing American borders to Mexico. The official Reform Party candidate on the national ballot, Buchanan emerged with zero percent of the national vote. Hagelin, a former professor and Natural Law Party candidate, could not muster support for the Reform Party either; the majority of his support came from pro-Perot, anti-Buchanan voters.

As both candidates stood at opposite ends of the political spectrum, neither candidate was able to accrue a substantial following for the Reform Party and therefore, provided no threat to either of the two main candidates. The Reform Party's inability to rally its support behind one candidate evidenced deep-seated divisions within the party and ultimately resulted in its downfall. Additionally, due to the failure of either candidate to achieve the required 5 percent of the national vote, the Reform Party will not receive federal matching funds in the 2004 election.

The presidential nominee of the Green Party, Ralph Nader, emerged as the real threat to both of the traditional parties. A staunch advocate of "government of, by, and for the people ... not monied interests," Nader promoted universalizing health care, abolishing child poverty, and rejecting big businesses and consumerism. These issues carried enough weight with American voters to give Nader strong support in both Minnesota and Oregon. However, unlike Perot, Nader did not garner enough public support to force either of the two main candidates to truly acknowledge his issues. In fact, the Committee on Presidential Debates completely prevented Nader from participating in the debates, not only as a candidate, but also as observer. As a result of being blocked from the national debates, in addition to his lack of federal funding, Nader relied heavily on personal appearances to promote his campaign. In the end, Ralph Nader gathered 3 percent of the national vote, 2 percent short of that needed to receive federal funding, but possibly played the spoiler in key states, including Florida.

Looking back at the 2000 election, the role of third parties could be described as numerically insignificant, since none managed to gain the 5 percent needed to receive federal money in upcoming years. However, one could also argue that the continued presence of third parties and their direct or indirect effects on the national parties could be the reflection of national desire for reform of the presidential electoral system and possibly the impetus for change.

The Party Conventions

Republicans and Democrats, as well as the fledgling Reform Party, each held conventions in the month of August.

Republican Convention. Several days prior to the Republican convention, Bush tapped Dick Cheney, former White House chief of staff and former secretary of defense, to be his running mate. Cheney, a conservative from Wyoming, also served in the U.S. House of Representatives and was a part of both the Ford-Bush wing of the GOP and the party's more conservative Reagan wing. What Cheney brought to Bush's campaign, more than anything, was *gravitas*, and certain experience in foreign policy and domestic matters that Bush sorely lacked. Bush had received criticism that he was under-qualified for

Paul Traux, a founding member of the Reform Party, watches as the final e-ballot vote count is posted at the party's national convention. John Hagelin lost the nomination to opposing faction candidate Patrick Buchanan. (Photo courtesy: Reuters NewMedia Inc./Corbis)

the job and that he was riding his famous name into the White House, but his selection of such as seasoned veteran satisfied many Republicans. Although political Cheney would not bring Bush additional votes (as Pennsylvania Governor Tom Ridge would likely have), he would make an excellent statesman and adviser.

On July 31, 2000, thousands of faithful Republicans kicked off the Republican National Convention in the "City of Brotherly Love." Held at the Comcast-Spectator's First Union Center, the 2000 Republican Convention marks the tenth time that Philadelphia has hosted a presidential nominating convention. Though lacking the suspense of many of the previous conventions, Republicans planned an impressive celebration for their anointing of George W. Bush as the GOP presidential nominee.

Two noticeable themes of the 2000 Republican Convention were diversity and inclusiveness, topics on which Republicans are trying to gain credibility. The first night featured a diverse cast of speakers who hailed the "compassionate conservatism" of George W. Bush and a rousing challenge from former chairman of the Joint Chiefs of Staff, General Colin L. Powell, who forcefully urged them to do more to live up to their legacy as the party of Abraham Lincoln. On a night devoted to the theme of leaving no child behind, Powell delivered a stirring call to arms, asking his party "to bring the promise of America to everyone" and praising Bush as a Republican who could "bridge the racial divides in America."

The second night focused on energizing the Republican base across the country by recognizing the achievements of the three living Republican presidents, starting off with a video tribute to former president and GOP icon Ronald Reagan. Former Senate majority leader and 1996 presidential candidate Bob Dole and retired General H. Norman Schwarzkopf spoke about the importance of military readiness and honored veterans of American wars. Condoleezza Rice, an African American woman serving as foreign policy advisor to Governor Bush, discussed international relations. Rice was followed by Elizabeth Dole, the former secretary of transportation who had been considering her own presidential bid a few months earlier.

The highlight of the evening, however, was a speech by Senator John McCain, who had challenged Bush through the primary season. McCain's speech carried the greatest political significance of the entire convention. The Arizona senator had a higher approval rating in the polls than either Bush or Gore and was especially favored by independents and ticket-splitters, whose votes would likely decide the election. McCain enthusiastically offered his support to Bush, telling cheering delegates and a national television audience that his erstwhile rival was a man "of courage and character" who would "confidently defend our interests and values wherever they are threatened."

Day three of the convention began on a somber note. Media reported that Gerald Ford suffered a mild stroke in the early hours of August 2, shortly after his convention appearance. Ford's condition improved throughout the week, and he was released several days later. That evening, House Speaker Dennis Hastert and the World Wrestling Federation champion The Rock (an incredibly popular figure among the youth of America) called the delegates to their seats, and former San Fransisco 49er quarterback Steve Young delivered the invocation. The Republicans continued to stress their primary issues throughout the night.

Later that night, former Secretary of Defense Richard B. Cheney officially accepted the Republican vice presidential nomination and immediately took aim at Vice President Gore, tying Gore to President Clinton and holding them both responsible for making Washington "a scene of bitterness and ill will and partisan strife." Calling Bush "a man without pretense, without cynicism, a man of principle, a man of honor," Cheney said that "on the first hour of the first day, he will restore decency and integrity to the Oval Office." Cheney's speech, the most partisan to be delivered at the convention, was an attack more on Clinton than on Gore, reflecting the determination of Republicans to turn the fall campaign into a referendum on the president's personal behavior.

The final night was reserved for the official nomination of Texas Governor George W. Bush as the Republican Party candidate for president. Governor Tom Ridge of Pennsylvania, the man many Americans thought would be the vice presidential nominee a few weeks before, profiled Governor Bush, and after an introductory biographical video, the Texas governor took center stage for the first time. Bush portrayed himself as a fresh force in the White House, promising to "change the tone of Washington" while seizing "this moment of American promise" to reform Social Security and Medicare, improve the nation's schools, rebuild its defenses, and cut taxes dramatically. Throughout the speech, Bush bluntly criticized the Clinton-Gore administration as "so much promise, to no great purpose," and took advantage of the fact that most Americans strongly disapproved of Clinton's inappropriate personal behavior while in the White House.

Against the backdrop of Independence Hall and the Liberty Bell, Republicans left Philadelphia energized by their new nominee and remarkably confident about their chances of recapturing the White House.

Democratic Convention.   Four days after the Republican Convention closed, Vice President Al Gore made public his selection for vice presidential running mate: Connecticut Senator Joe Lieberman, a longtime leader of the centrist Democratic Leadership Council and the first Jewish major-party nominee in United States history. Pundits emphasized the religious precedent as well as Lieberman's integrity and reputation as a strong moral leader. Just as Cheney was chosen to help Bush overcome his shortcomings in foreign policy experience, Lieberman was given the vice presidential nomination in an effort to help address Gore's weaknesses. He was one of the few Democratic senators who openly chastised Clinton during the impeachment trials, and many believe that he was chosen as a "moral compass" to help Gore distance himself from the perceived immorality of the Clinton years in the White House. Lieberman also brought energy and enthusiasm to the party on the eve of the Democratic National Convention.

With Gore still trailing George W. Bush in most national polls (with increased margins following the Republican National Convention), Gore and Lieberman gave the Democrats across America their time to shine during the Democratic National Convention, held in Los Angeles, California, from August 14 to August 17. The only other Democratic convention that was held in California was in 1960, when Massachusetts Senator John F. Kennedy was chosen as the nominee in a nail-biter against Lyndon Johnson from Texas.

The first night started with a tribute to former President Jimmy Carter, as well as a profile of the women members of the Senate. Many analysts believed that the Democrats were going to make a concerted effort to reach out to middle-class female voters, much as the Republicans appeared to reach out to minorities during their convention. The night belonged, however, to William Jefferson Clinton, who symbolically passed the torch to his vice president, Al Gore. In a moving and impassioned speech, Clinton delivered a sharp rebuttal to Republican criticism that he had squandered his presidency, claiming the nation's prolonged economic boom was "a matter of choice ... not a matter of chance" while praising Vice President Gore as someone who would "keep our prosperity going." Following the speech, Clinton left to continue campaigning in selected areas for Gore and other Democratic candidates. Party officials denied that he was stealing the spotlight away from Gore while in Los Angeles, but there was no question that Clinton was the center of attention until his departure.

Just as the Republicans used the second night to energize their base voters, the Democrats brought out the lions of the liberal wing to encourage the party faithful. From Massachusetts Senator Edward M. Kennedy to Reverend Jesse L. Jackson to former New Jersey Senator Bill Bradley, the man Gore defeated in the primaries, Gore received a powerful push toward the fall campaign. Kennedy remarked that Gore was only the third Democratic nominee that he had supported for president as early and as strongly; the other two were his brothers, John and Robert Kennedy. Bradley roused the crowd with his speech, saying, "We don't window-dress diversity; we're the party of diversity," in reference to the Republican convention in Philadelphia. "We don't declare ourselves to be compassionate; we've been acting compassionately for decades. We don't just talk about prosperity; we make it happen. Don't read our lips. Watch what we do."

Four members of the Kennedy family addressed the convention, including Caroline Kennedy Schlossberg, John F. Kennedy's daughter, who provided the most poignant moment of the night as she made a rare public appearance to introduce her uncle Ted. When her father accepted the Democratic nomination here in 1960, she said, his goal was "not only to make better the world that surrounds us, but to dream of something more." In the only piece of official business at the convention, the delegates approved a generally centrist party platform pitched toward swing voters but reaffirming the party's traditional stands on abortion, gay rights, and affirmative action. The platform endorsed Gore's policies on education reform, trade, Social Security, Medicare, and health care, and it reinforced the issue distinctions the Democrats hoped to draw with Bush and the Republicans.

The next night, Senator Joe Lieberman addressed delegates. In a passionate yet often humorous speech, Lieberman promised to "work my heart out to make Al Gore the president of the United States." He also drew laughs and applause from the delegates with his assertion that "Not since Tom Hanks won an Oscar has there been that much acting in Philadelphia," continuing the Democratic criticism of the Republican Convention. Al Gore also took the stage that night, much to the surprise of many of the delegates and the audience watching across the country. Following the remarks of his daughter and campaign adviser, Karenna Gore Schiff, the vice president appeared on stage and hugged his daughter prior to the ritual roll call.

Thursday night, the convention came to a close with the acceptance of the nomination by Vice President Gore. After speeches by Kweisi Mfume, president of the NAACP, and Iowa Senator Tom Harkin, Tipper Gore took the stage to introduce her husband. In an effort to humanize Gore and make him seem less rigid, Tipper used a video album of family pictures that also included testimonials of family friends who have known Gore for years. When the vice president took the stage, he embraced his wife and planted what was soon to be known across the country and on the late-night talk shows as "the kiss," a passionate display that distanced him further from Clinton by emphasizing that he was in love with and entirely faithful to his wife. Gore stood before the crowd, claiming that he was his own man and that he would help continue the prosperity by fighting for all Americans as president. He drew sharp contrasts between himself and his opponent on key issues like tax cuts and Social Security. Animated and energetic that night, Gore cast himself as a serious if sometimes unexciting politician who would battle against powerful special interests to ensure "that our prosperity enriches not just the few, but all working families." Lieberman and his wife Hadassah joined the Gores on stage as balloons and confetti fell from the rafters onto the frenzied crowd. Following the convention, Gore and Lieberman surged in the polls while visiting key battleground states on a riverboat tour on the Mississippi River.

The Presidential Debates

In an up-and-down campaign season, the candidate debates promised a rare decisive moment. Conventional wisdom suggests that debates rarely alter the complexion of a contest, but the three meetings between Texas Governor George W. Bush and Vice President Al Gore proved a modest exception to the rule.

The weeks and months preceding these face-offs were filled with traditional jockeying and posturing by the Democrats and Republicans. Both Green Party candidate Ralph Nader and Reform Party candidate Patrick Buchanan protested persistently, yet unsuccessfully, for inclusion in the debates.

Much of the back-and-forth regarding debates occurred via the news media, with both campaigns publicly proposing formats and

On the campaign trail, candidates frequently rely on sound bytes and media devices to convey their messages. Here, George W. Bush uses dollar bills to illustrate how the budget surplus could be used to finance an across-the-board tax cut and save Social Security. (Photo courtesy: Iikka Uimonen/Corbis sygma)

venues. In the end, the details of the debates were brokered through the bipartisan Commission on Presidential Debates. The nation would see three meetings between the Bush and Gore and one featuring vice presidential candidates Dick Cheney and Joe Lieberman. All of these forums would run ninety minutes and each would present a different format. The presidential debates would be moderated by public television's Jim Lehrer, and the vice presidential debate would be run by CNN's Bernard Shaw.

While Gore remained behind in the tracking polls during the months before the conventions, his supporters and surrogates often pointed to the vice president's reputation as a tenacious, effective debater as a possible key to victory. This optimistic anticipation was based upon the high marks Gore had earned in prior showdowns in 1992 and 1996. Leading up to campaign 2000, Al Gore put his debating prowess on display in several fierce match-ups with Democratic nomination rival Bill Bradley. The Bush campaign, on the other hand, seemed more reluctant heading into the debates. Typically, the candidate with lower poll numbers seeks more opportunities to face his opponent. In the weeks following the conventions, however, the Bush strategy was to balk when it came to the issue of debates, this despite Gore's steady lead in the polls after Labor Day.

Bush's growing reputation for grammatical missteps and a tenuous grasp on issue detail had many postulating that he would not be able to hold his own against the aggressive and sometimes wonkish vice president. The differing campaign strategies regarding debates and universal predictions of a mismatch had lowered expectations substantially for Bush and raised them for Gore.

The first debate took place on October 3 in Boston, Massachusetts. The format for this event featured questions posed by the moderator, with responses and rebuttals by the candidates. Gore and Bush clashed sharply on issues ranging from taxes, Medicare, and Social Security to U.S. policy in the Balkans. The vice president was notably aggressive, asserting himself repeatedly, even when it was not his turn to speak. He focused heavily on details, repeatedly citing numerous facts and figures, with an almost pedantic air. Gore portrayed his opponent's plans as risky and argued that Bush would spend the nation's projected surplus on a tax cut for the wealthy at the expense of economic stability and programs like Social Security and Medicare. The Texas governor, on the other hand, discussed broader philosophical issues. He described himself as someone who could inspire unity and cut through partisanship in Washington. Bush also depicted his opponent as a proponent of big federal government. While many instant polls and numerous pundits gave a slight edge to Gore in this first debate, Bush had managed to survive intact by exceedingd expectations.

Two days later, vice presidential candidates Joe Lieberman and Dick Cheney faced off in Danville, Kentucky. The format for this debate was conversational, with each candidate answering questions from the moderator while seated at a table. The dialogue in this debate was highly substantive and very cordial. Both candidates performed well in a discussion that ranged from foreign policy to education.

The second presidential debate took place in Winston-Salem, North Carolina, on October 11. This contest featured a conversational format like that of the vice presidential debate. This debate was characterized by a near lack of conflict between the two candidates. Bush came across as relaxed and confident. Gore, however, seemed shell shocked and overly passive, his performance and strategy clearly affected by the criticism of political analysts and late-night comedians of his behavior during the first debate. Gore also had to deal with the fact that he had exaggerated several points during the first debate. This blunder had added to questions regarding his credibility, an issue that had plagued him throughout the campaign. Gore openly apologized for getting some of the details wrong in Boston. The evening's result was a victory for Bush that brought on an increase in his momentum.

The candidates met for the last time in Saint Louis, Missouri, on October 17. This debate featured a town-hall format, with the candidates answering questions from a room full of undecided voters. Both candidates sought to use this final opportunity to draw distinctions between themselves. Gore was in old form and once again on the offensive. The two candidates seemed to duel for the upper hand in style, substance, and physical

FIGURE 14.4   Landmarks in the 2000 Campaign

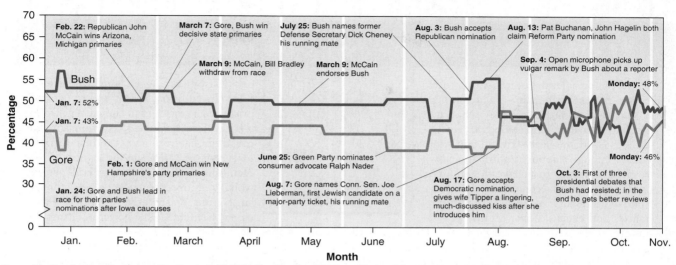

Source: "Tracking the Campaign that was Too Close to Call," *USA Today,* November 8, 2000, p. 15A. Copyright 2000, USA TODAY. Reprinted with permission.

control of the stage. Gore again sought to portray himself as a champion of middle-class families and a check on the influence of big business. Bush presented his opponent as a big-government liberal who embodied inside-the-Beltway partisan bickering, and he described himself as a consensus builder who could transcend party lines. While this debate was widely regarded as Gore's best performance, the lack of a clear knock-out blow may have once again favored Bush, who still benefited from an expectation gap.

The 2000 presidential debates managed to change public opinion in a campaign that had previously failed to attract a great deal of attention. Bush entered the debate season down in the polls, and he finished it with a lead. He had managed to exceed expectations and quiet some doubts, while the vice president had rekindled some questions regarding his own credibility and come across as knowledgeable, yet at times abrasive.

The Fall Campaign and General Election

As the campaign headed into its last month, national polls consistently showed an incredibly tight race. In the final month of the campaign, the two candidates maintained furious campaign schedules, visiting the key swing states dozens of time in a last-ditch effort to secure the requisite 270 electoral votes.

Stumping on issues of Social Security reform, military readiness and restoring integrity to the Oval Office, Governor Bush campaigned heavily in the waning days of the campaign in the vice president's home state of Tennessee, President Bill Clinton's home state of Arkansas, and the key swing states of Florida, Pennsylvania, Minnesota, Missouri, Wisconsin, and Michigan. Gore also campaigned heavily in those states, especially in Florida, where he attempted to steal the state governed by Jeb Bush, the brother of the Republican presidential nominee. The vice president appealed to the state's numerous elderly voters by promising to deliver changes in the Medicare system, including prescription drug benefits.

Also in the last weeks of the race, media attention began to focus even more on Green Party candidate Ralph Nader, who was polling well enough in states such as Oregon, Wisconsin, and Minnesota to take the states out of the Gore column and potentially give them to Bush. Nader appealed to liberal Democrats and independents and was seen as a potential spoiler for Gore. In fact, Democrats unsuccessfully attempted to persuade Nader to drop out of the race, and Internet sites offered opportunities for Nader voters in hotly contested states to trade votes with Democrats in heavily Democratic states.

POINT/COUNTERPOINT

SHOULD THE PRESIDENTIAL NOMINATION AND CAMPAIGN PROCESS BE SHORTENED?

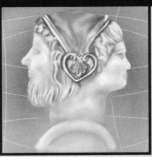

The presidential nomination process is the first hurdle a politician must clear in order to have a chance at holding the nation's top elected office. Candidates court the party faithful and try to secure enough support within their own respective parties to receive the endorsement at the national convention. Individual states hold Republican and Democratic primaries and caucuses over a four- or five-month span, with New Hampshire and Iowa as the traditional kick-off states, followed by the summer conventions and then the intense general campaign and election in the fall. The real campaigning, however, begins long before the primaries and continues well beyond Election Day. Campaigns for president are practically on a four-year cycle; the newly elected president is hardly sworn in before candidates from his or her own party and the opposing party begin jockeying for position among the party elite in hopes of becoming anointed the next presidential candidate. At the same time, the long campaign enables the public to become acquainted with candidates who are vying for the most powerful office in the world. Should the presidential nomination and campaign process be shortened? Let's examine these two points of view.

Many reform-minded citizens and legislators believe that shortening the nomination and campaign process would reduce the exorbitant spending (over nearly $360 million in the 2000 presidential election) involved in campaigns and benefit the democratic process by encouraging participation. Many European nations have a much more abbreviated political season, and most have higher turnout and lower campaign spending than the United States. Under the British system, for example, campaigns and elections are held in a period of six weeks after the election is called. Shortening the nomination and campaign process in the United States into a series of regional primaries held shortly before the conventions, an idea with a wide range of support from political organizations, could reduce the cost involved in campaigning and might keep people from tuning out during the elections. In addition, many see set regional primaries as fairer than the current front-loaded system. Due to tradition and the constitutional freedom to set their own primary dates, first-in-the-nation New Hampshire (whose population is 98 percent white) and Iowa (97 percent white), though largely unrepresentative of America as a whole, yield incredible power in setting the course of presidential elections.

On the other hand, many political practitioners and elected officials are hesitant to reduce the formal processes of nomination and campaigning. The political parties have a responsibility for the nominating process, although it is often shared with state governments, who actually set the dates of primary elections. Congress has been hesitant to take the authority away from the states and mandate a set primary and caucus schedule. Supporters say that the apparently chaotic nature of the primary system and general election is by design—candidates are forced to appeal not only to members of their own party, but to a broad base of Americans that does not necessarily reflect all of their views. Candidates try out slogans and develop their message over the course of the primary, and they build on those positions during the general campaign. True, the selection system is not perfect, but attempts to reduce the formal apparatuses of the nomination process would likely have little impact on the tendency for politicians to begin their presidential bids earlier and earlier. In addition, reform opponents suggest that there is not necessarily cause to believe that shortening the campaign process will have any effect on voter education or participation.

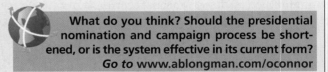

What do you think? Should the presidential nomination and campaign process be shortened, or is the system effective in its current form? *Go to* www.ablongman.com/oconnor

---

With the nation in a period of economic prosperity, Americans turned to other issues—including character and integrity—to decide their vote. Then, on November 2, just five days before the election, a television station in Maine reported that Bush had been arrested for driving under the influence of alcohol in 1976. The revelation, which was confirmed by the Bush campaign, had Republicans pointing to dirty campaign tactics on the part of the Democrats and the Gore campaign declining to comment. Though the DUI story broke so closely before the election, the vast majority of voters said Bush's arrest would not affect their choice for the forty-third president of the United States.

FIGURE 14.5   Exit Poll Results for 2000 Elections

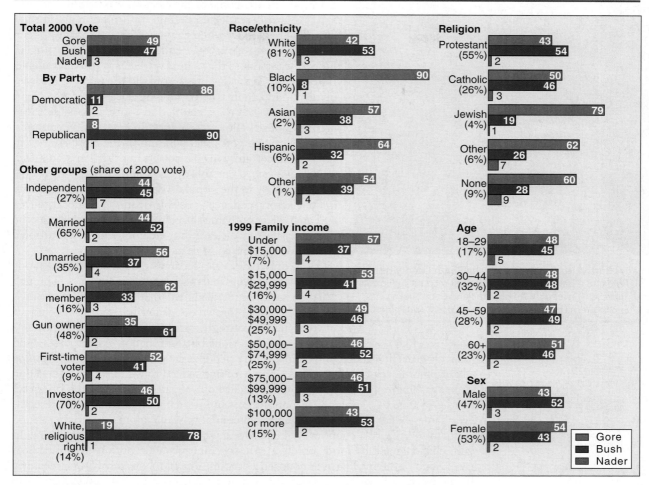

In the final days before the November 7 election, national polls showed Vice President Gore cutting into Governor Bush's already slim margin. The election would certify what the polls had said all along—Americans were having an incredibly difficult time deciding who should next occupy the White House.

Election Results

On November 7, just over half of all eligible Americans cast their votes for their next president and went home to watch the election returns on TV. Exit polls showed the two candidates running neck and neck, and as results trickled in after polls (see Figure 14.5) closed across the nation, audiences were on the edge of their seat as precinct after precinct, state after state, fell alternately to Bush and to Gore. Around mid-evening, the major networks placed the all-important state of Florida in Gore's "win" column and, coupled with a victory in Pennsylvania, Gore seemed to be pulling ahead, even as continually arriving results started to show Bush retaking the lead in Florida. News of Hillary Clinton's victory in the New York senatorial race broke as states continued to fall one after the other to Bush and Gore, and the nation was stunned when the networks retracted their verdict on Florida and the entire election was suddenly wide open again. Late that night, Gore conceded to Bush, only to learn of the closeness of the race and call Bush to

Judge Charles Burton, chairman of the Palm Beach County canvassing board, holds up a ballot during the manual recount in Florida. The recounts were overseen by Democratic and Republican lawyers. (Photo courtesy: Charles Rex Arbogast/AP/Wide World Photos)

Longman
Participate.com 2.0
Timeline
And the Winner Is . . .
Close Calls in Presidential Elections

retract his concession! When America went to bed on Tuesday night, the outcome of the election was utterly unclear.

If Americans expected definite information about their president's identity when they read their morning paper, however, they awoke to a rude surprise: The voting in Florida was so close that a final verdict was still unavailable. Indeed, only as the day progressed did the number of issues involved, and their true complexity, begin to come clear: absentee votes yet to be counted in Florida; possible irregularities in the ballot presentation in key Florida counties; critical absentee votes still pending in the close contest in Oregon; uncertainty in vote counts in other key states such as New Mexico; a possible discrepancy between one candidate's majority in the popular vote and the other's majority in the electoral college; a possible tie in the electoral college and an unclear outcome should Congress have to break the tie; and a host of other minor electoral and constitutional issues not confronted in decades.

With only 1,725 votes separating Bush and Gore, Florida began a legally mandated machine recount of votes. Through the process, it was revealed that 30,000 ballots in Palm Beach County had been thrown out as invalid, and that thousands of voters had unwittingly miscast their votes after being confused by the notorious butterfly ballot. As the media and countless lawyers descended on Florida, Bush acted like the presumed winner, beginning to talk of preliminary Cabinet selections and seeking federal funds to set up a transition office in Washington, D.C. Both campaigns called on veteran statesmen and former U.S. secretaries of state to oversee the recount process in Florida: The Republican representative was James Baker, and the Democratic representative was Warren Christopher. Hand recounts in four Florida counties were approved, while citizen organizations filed eight lawsuits challenging the Florida results. As the machine recounts continued, Florida Secretary of State Katherine Harris announced a deadline of 5 P.M. November 14 for recounts.

In the weeks following the election, more court actions were filed by both sides to stop or extend the recounts. The Florida Supreme Court decided recounts could continue, but did not say Harris had to accept the results. Palm Beach County missed the 5 P.M. deadline for Florida counties to submit amended tallies. Harris rejected a partial recount from Palm Beach and declared Bush the winner of Florida's popular vote by 537 votes, giving Bush Florida's twenty-five electoral votes. Winning Florida gave Bush 271 total electoral votes, one more than the 270 required to be elected president.

On November 27, the Gore legal team, led by attorney David Boise, contested the November 26 results that had been certified by Secretary of State Harris, challenging results in Miami-Dade, Nassau, and Palm Beach Counties. The case, *Gore* v. *Harris*, was assigned to Leon County Circuit Court Judge N. Sanders Sauls. After more than twenty-two hours of testimony and arguments, Judge Sauls rejected Gore's contest of the election results. In response, the Gore team swiftly appealed to the Florida Supreme Court, whereupon Sauls's decision was reversed and a manual recount of the undervote ballots that were not counted by voting machines was ordered.

One day after the December 8 Florida Supreme Court reversal, the U.S. Supreme Court granted the Bush campaign's request for a stay of the Florida Supreme Court order, thereby stopping any recounts in Florida. The U.S. Supreme Court also accepted Bush's appeal of the Florida Supreme Court ruling ordering the recount. On December 11, the Supreme Court of the United States heard oral arguments in *Bush* v. *Gore*.

In the evening of December 12, the high Court ruled 5–4 that there was no constitutionally acceptable way for a new recount to be finished by Tuesday's midnight deadline for selection of presidential electors—effectively declaring Bush the president-elect. Many Americans believed that the Supreme Court's decisive role in the process to select

TABLE 14.2   2000 Election Results

State	Bush	Gore	State	Bush	Gore
Alabama	56%	42%	Montana	58%	33%
Alaska	60	27	Nebraska	63	33
Arizona	50	45	Nevada	50	46
Arkansas	51	46	New Hampshire	48	47
California	41	54	New Jersey	40	56
Colorado	51	42	New Mexico	48	48
Connecticut	39	55	New York	35	60
Delaware	42	55	North Carolina	56	43
District of Columbia	9	85	North Dakota	61	33
Florida	49	49	Ohio	50	46
Georgia	55	43	Oklahoma	60	38
Hawaii	37	56	Oregon	47	47
Idaho	68	28	Pennsylvania	46	51
Illinois	41	56	Rhode Island	32	61
Indiana	57	41	South Carolina	57	41
Iowa	48	49	South Dakota	60	38
Kansas	58	47	Tennessee	51	47
Kentucky	56	41	Texas	59	38
Louisiana	53	45	Utah	71	23
Maine	44	49	Vermont	41	51
Maryland	40	57	Virginia	52	45
Massachusetts	33	60	Washington	45	50
Michigan	48	49	West Virginia	52	46
Minnesota	46	48	Wisconsin	48	48
Mississippi	58	41	Wyoming	69	28
Missouri	50	47			

Source: *The New York Times* (Monday, November 13, 2000).

the president exceeded the Court's legal powers and set a poor judicial precedent. To many, the Court's decision seemed based on political ideology, with justices voting along partisan lines. As Justice John Paul Stevens noted in his dissent, "Although we may never know with complete certainty the identity of the winner of this year's presidential election, the identify of the loser is perfectly clear. It is the nation's confidence in the judge as an impartial guardian of the rule of law."

Bush very narrowly won Florida, the electoral college, and the Supreme Court ruling. He actually lost the popular vote to Al Gore by over half a million votes. The African American community was particularly displeased with the results of the election and its aftermath; exit polls in Florida showed that nine out of ten blacks voted for Gore, but thousands of ballots were thrown out in areas with large minority populations. Many believed that Florida's Governor Jeb Bush, brother of the president-elect, and Florida Republicans conspired to disenfranchise blacks and in effect stole the election from Vice President Al Gore. Protests by African American leaders including Jesse Jackson and Al Sharpton brought more attention to the alleged disenfranchisement.

On December 13, Vice President Al Gore officially conceded the 2000 election to George W. Bush. In Gore's gracious and humorous concession, he stated, "While I strongly disagree with the Court's decision, I accept it ... and tonight, for the sake of our unity of the people and the strength of our

Florida Secretary of State Katherine Harris certified the Florida elections and declared George W. Bush the winner of the presidential election of November 26. However, it was the U.S. Supreme Court who became the final arbiter in the contested election. (Photo courtesy: Bruce Brewer/The Image Works)

democracy, I offer my concession." Immediately following Gore's address, President-elect George W. Bush gave his acceptance speech to the nation from the chambers of the Texas legislature. Thirty-six days after Election Day, the longest period of post-election uncertainty since 1876, when Rutherford B. Hayes was confirmed only forty-eight hours before Inauguration Day, and fully aware of the divisiveness caused by the tumultuous nature of the election, Bush embarked upon his transition by remarking optimistically, "Our nation must rise above a house divided. Americans share hopes and goals and values far more than any political disagreements."

The debate over whether or not Bush had actually won the populat vote in Florida waged on several months into the new administration. On April 4, 2001, *The Miami Herald* and *USA Today* released the results from their comprehensive three-month review of 64,248 ballots in all 67 Florida counties which showed that by using even the most generous counting standards favored by Al Gore, George W. Bush would have tripled his margin of victory in Florida from 537 votes to 1,665 votes. The *Herald/USA Today* recount considered every dimple, pinprick, or hanging chad on a punch-card ballot a valid vote, and answered the question: What would have happened if the U.S. Supreme Court had not stopped the sweeping recount of undervotes ordered by the Florida Supreme Court on December 8, 2000? The answer: Under almost every imaginable scenario, Bush would have won.

Most Americans had already accepted that George W. Bush had won the election, and this apparent final count was intended to settle the dispute once and for all. Some Gore backers, however, remained unconvinced. Doug Hattaway, a former Gore campaign spokeman surmised, "If you count every vote, Gore wins." This study confirms that Floridas election system failed the voters.[42]

CAMPAIGN FINANCE LAWS

Longman
Participate.com
2.0
Participation
**The Debate
Over
Campaign
Finance
Reform**

In response to growing concerns about the amounts of money spent on federal elections, both Republicans and Democrats have sponsored major campaign finance reform bills in Congress. But changing the rules of the game can alter the results of elections. Not surprisingly, Democratic proposals tend to favor Democratic candidates while Republican proposals tend to favor Republican candidates. For many years now, as a consequence, Congress has created more smoke than fire on campaign reform.

Prior to the 1994 congressional elections, Democrats supported setting a limit on the amount of money congressional candidates could spend in an effort to win office. (For the House, a candidate would have been limited to $600,000; the Senate limit would have depended on each state's population, with a more heavily populated state having a higher limit.) Republicans, long the congressional minority, were adamantly against these spending caps. They argued that the limits mainly hurt challengers who are not as well known as incumbents and who need to spend more money to increase their name identification. For example, from 1978 to 1988, only seven of the thirty-two winning Senate challengers remained within the spending limits proposed by the Democrats. The Democrats responded that without limits on total campaign spending, personally wealthy candidates, like Steve Forbes, have an advantage over less affluent candidates. This advantage results from the present federal contribution limits and the Supreme Court decision in *Buckley* v. *Valeo*, which ruled that limits on a candidate's spending of personal funds violates his or her constitutional right to free speech. In the spring of 1992, the proposed legislation was passed by the Democratic legislative majority only to be vetoed by then Republican President George Bush.

In the time since President Bush's veto, Democratic President Bill Clinton and Republican lawmakers have championed campaign finance reform only to later renege on their pledges. Prior to the 1992 presidential election, candidate Bill Clinton pledged to support and sign strong campaign finance reform legislation. Once in office, this promise fell by the wayside. In 1994 Democratic legislators were swept out of office and replaced with Republicans, who had also campaigned on the promise of change. Yet campaign finance reform was conspicuously absent from the Republican Contract with America. In June 1995, President Clinton and Republican Speaker of the House of Representatives Newt Gingrich, in a joint appearance, were asked by an audience member whether they would support the formation of a commission to reform the campaign finance system. Both men said yes—shaking hands in mutual agreement for the cameras. Finally, after months of stalling by the House Republican leadership, the House passed the Shays–Meehan campaign finance reform bill in the 105th Congress (1995–1996), which, among other provisions, banned the national parties from raising soft money. Unfortunately for reform proponents, however, senators could not muster enough votes to stop a filibuster on the Senate version of the Shays–Meehan bill (authored by Senators John McCain and Russ Feingold), and campaign finance reform died still another death.

Of course, both parties' positions on this issue are rooted in self-interest. The Republicans are usually more successful than are Democrats at raising money, and the Democrats want to limit that advantage. Moreover, the cost to either party of conceding too much on this issue is the possibility of relinquishing control of Congress. This makes campaign spending an issue that does not easily lend itself to compromise.

In the wake of the 2000 election, however, reform of campaign finance law has become a staple of debate in Washington. To the surprise of many observers, Senator John McCain (R–Ariz.) and Russ Feingold (D–Wisc.) managed to get the U.S. Senate to pass a somewhat watered down version of their long-standing bill on campaign finance in late March 2001. The bill as passed by the Senate bans all corporate, labor, and individual "soft money," which had been previously unregulated. President Bush signed the bill into law in March 2002, entitled The Bipartisan Campaign Finance Reform Act (BCFRA).

In addition, the BCFRA doubled the amount of money an individual could contribute to a candidate (from $1,000 to $2,000 per election) with the primary and the general election counted separately. This act also requires disclosure of donors and spending on issue ads run before an election. The rules apply to anyone who spends more than $10,000 on broadcast ads that name or show the likeness of a candidate for federal office within sixty days of a general election or thirty days of a primary. While supporters heralded its passage as a major victory in lessening the influence of big money on politics, a number of problems remain.

Various provisions relating to television advertising by interest groups close to an election, which are banned or limited in the BCFRA, may be considered an infringement on the First Amendment. So the final outcome is indeterminate, but it is significant that at last some kind of campaign finance reform appeared to be meeting with congressional approval after a decade of scandal. Unfortunately, political consultants have already found ways around the new legislation leaving many voters to wonder what change the legislation will effect.

WEB EXPLORATION
To get involved and find out what you can do about campaign reform, go to
www.ablongman.com/oconnor

Perhaps not coincidentally, the election saw the defeat of all the candidates who made campaign finance an issue—John McCain, Bill Bradley, and Al Gore—while the well-funded George Bush won the contest. To be sure, Bush had little incentive or obligation to advocate reform, as he was able to sell himself to the nation as an untarnished newcomer to national campaign finance, even though his exceptional nationwide fund raising earned him much scrutiny—and significant advantage—early in his campaign. As a Republican, Bush also had historical and ideological reasons to be relatively content with the existing structure of campaign finance laws. McCain and Bradley, however, had clear practical incentives to advocate reform as they found their primary challenges quickly outspent by their major-party opponents, and of course McCain had long been associated with the cause. Al Gore, for his part, was obliged to make an issue of his desire for reform in an attempt to insulate himself from the finance scandals of the Clinton campaigns, in which he was directly implicated.

While most discussions of campaign finance reform focus on spending and contribution limits, many experts inside and outside of Congress argue that there are other ideas concerning campaign finance that would create a more wholesome system without

GLOBAL POLITICS

THE AMERICANIZATION OF PARLIAMENTARY CAMPAIGNS

Election campaigns in the United States have the distinction of being the longest and most expensive of any in the industrial democracies. Institutions like Political Action committees (PACs), the horse race media coverage of presidential campaigns, and the concentration on momentum in presidential primaries are unknown in the other six democracies.

Observers in the European countries have worried in recent years about the "Americanization" of parliamentary campaigns, by which they mean in particular the growing use of television as a campaign tool. In the most recent rounds of parliamentary elections in Great Britain and Germany, the winning parties' campaign teams closely studied how the Clinton campaign had used media techniques to deliver effective messages. In 1998, Gerhard Schröder's winning team used focus groups and speeches deliberately geared to television during the campaign for the German Bundestag. It is not clear, however, how far American-style campaigning can go; in France and Japan, the government carefully regulates media coverage of campaigns, and candidates are prohibited from buying television and radio time. Polling, a key tool in any national campaign in the United States, is less widely used in other democracies. In France, Italy, and Canada, the government prohibits public dissemination of poll results in the days prior to an election.

In most parliamentary systems (Japan until recently was an exception) the parties are the candidates' major source of funding. Sympathetic interest groups channel their campaign contributions through the parties. Not only do PACs not exist, but pronouncements such as U.S. Senator Russ Feingold's that one way to lessen the expense of campaigns is to refuse "soft money" from the national parties and their committees* would baffle a candidate in any of the other six countries.

In addition, no other major democratic political system has primaries (Mexico's PRI experimented with presidential primaries in the mid-1990s). Candidates are selected by the political party organizations, not the rank-and-file voters in all other countries surveyed in this book. The public does not have to go to the polls twice in a year to elect a government.

Parliamentary general election campaigns in other countries are short. The campaign season typically lasts less than a month. Japan's 1996 and 2000 parliamentary election campaigns each lasted less than two weeks, and prompted some observers to ask whether the campaigns were too short to allow the public to make informed candidate choices. Election dates are not fixed in the parliamentary systems. Except for Germany and France, elections occur whenever the prime minister calls for them (the French president has that power). Moreover, the Parliament elects the prime minister, so direct election of the executive (except for the presidents of France and Russia) is not possible.

*Russ Feingold, "Running and Winning a 'Restrained' Campaign," *Extensions* (Spring 1999): 4.

Longman
Participate.com 2.0
Comparative
**Comparing
Political
Campaigns**

resorting to limits. One idea is to limit the influence of political action committees (PACs). Critics charge that PACs reduce political competition by giving overwhelmingly to incumbents—usually about two-thirds to three-quarters of their war chests—while at the same time they corrupt the system by indebting legislators to the special interests that form PACs. Supporters argue that PACs better represent the "little guys" in American politics by allowing them to pool their funds and have a greater impact on campaigns and elections. Abolishing PACs altogether, however, is probably unconstitutional, since doing so would violate the First Amendment's guarantee of free political association. Restricting their contribution limits too greatly would only divert their money into other forms of political spending that are not easily revealed (such as funneling cash to state and local parties in states that do not require full campaign finance disclosure). As reformers through the years have discovered, it is nearly impossible to dam the flow of political money in a free and open democratic system in which participation is encouraged.

A better way to control PACs and special interest groups is to increase the influence and level of spending by political parties. This would limit PACs indirectly by augmenting the power of a rival source of campaign funds. As discussed in chapter 12, parties can be strengthened in many ways, especially by loosening or eliminating current restrictions on what citizens may give to a party or what a party may donate to its candidates. In addition, parties ought to receive some free broadcast time on all television and radio stations. This air time could then be allocated to the most needy nominees—incumbents who are in trouble, as well as promising challengers. Since candidates spend a major portion of their campaign funds for media advertising time—up to 60 percent in some Senate races—such a reform could conceivably help to cut the burgeoning costs of campaigns. It would aid challengers and less wealthy candidates in particular, balancing some of the advantages of incumbency. Of course, this reform also has First Amendment problems because, along with the "free" air time, candidates would likely be required to agree on total television advertising time. The United States, incidentally, is the only major democratic country that does not provide some free media time to parties or candidates. Moreover, while increasing party spending limits may augment party power, it is unlikely to cleanse the campaign finance system of interest group influence. After all, parties would presumably raise much of the money they spend from interest groups, which—in return for their contributions—would likely have the ear of party leaders who set the legislative agenda.[43]

There is one other possible workable solution to the campaign finance ills, one that takes advantage of both current realities and the remarkable self-regulating tendencies of a free-market democracy. Consider the American stock market. Most government oversight simply makes sure that publicly traded companies accurately disclose vital information about their finances. The philosophy is that buyers, given the information they need, are intelligent enough to look out for themselves. There will be winners and losers, of course, both among companies and the consumers of their securities, but it is not the government's role to guarantee anyone's success. The notion that people are smart enough—and indeed have the duty—to think and choose for themselves also underlies our basic democratic arrangement. There is no reason that the same principle cannot be successfully applied to a free market for campaign finance. In this scenario, disclosure laws would be broadened and strengthened, and penalties for failure to disclose would be ratcheted up, while rules on other aspects—such as sources of funds and sizes of contributions—could be greatly loosened or even abandoned altogether.

Call it *deregulation plus*. Let a well-informed marketplace, rather than a committee of federal bureaucrats, be the judge of whether someone has accepted too much money from a particular interest group or spent too much to win an election. Reformers who object to money in politics would lose little under such a scheme, since the current system has already utterly failed to inhibit special-interest influence. On the other hand, reform advocates might gain substantially by bringing all financial activity out into the open where the public can see for itself the truth about how campaigns are conducted.

Campaign finance reform is a favorite Washington topic, but for all the good (and bad) ideas that are proposed, little legislation is ever passed. Many incumbents prefer not to alter the system that—whatever its faults—elected them. Democrats and Republicans are also at loggerheads over the partisan effects of various reforms. The American people also remain skeptical of political parties, and little popular support can be found for strengthening them. The last set of campaign finance reforms passed in the wake of Watergate, and it may take more scandal to generate enough momentum to pass a successor package of reforms in the Congress.

As analyses of recent elections suggest, the campaign process in the United States is far from perfect. Campaigns seem to stretch out interminably. Moreover, trivialities rather than the important issues of the day often determine the success or failure of campaigns, voters cast many ballots for the lesser of two evils, and some contenders for lower office never raise enough money to get a fair hearing. But those who follow campaigns would also do well to remember the wise words of one of this century's greatest political scientists, V. O. Key Jr. Key's central observation was simple but powerful: "Voters are not fools." Not every citizen devotes enough time to politics, and many people are woefully uninformed at times. But virtually all voters know their basic interests and cast their ballots accordingly. They are not always right in their judgments, yet over time there is a rough justice to election results. Parties and office holders who produce a measure of prosperity and happiness for the electorate are usually rewarded, and those who do not keep the home folks satisfied may be forced to find another line of work (see chapter 13).

Continuity & Change

Campaign Ethics in American Politics

American politics has never been particularly clean or ethical, and even the Founders were much maligned in their campaigns. The rumors about Jefferson's black mistress, Sally Hemings, first came to prominence during his presidential campaign in 1800, and Jefferson's campaigns were the subject of much acrimonious and partisan strife in newly emerging American newspapers.

When Andrew Jackson campaigned for president in 1828, his opponents widely published the fact that the divorce of his wife's first marriage had not been finalized by the time of their marriage, though this was unbeknownst to her or Jackson at the time. Rachel Jackson was completely humiliated by the ensuing public scandal, and historians have read this as a major contribution to the physical and emotional breakdown that took her life between the time of Jackson's election and his swearing-in as president.

America did not leave campaign corruption behind in the nineteenth century. The country's greatest political scandal, Watergate, is still well within the nation's living memory. The Watergate scandal centered precisely around Richard Nixon's flagrantly illegal measures to investigate anti-Vietnam activists and to ensure his reelection in 1972—including misusing the CIA, FBI, and IRS; accepting huge concealed campaign contributions; and bugging and breaking into the Democratic National Committee, headquartered in the Watergate Building that gave the scandal its name. Laws passed after Watergate to compel campaign finance reform have had some limited success in cleaning up the campaign process in America, although the disguising and misreporting of fund raising inevitably continues in new forms.

Personal political attacks, especially in TV advertising, are still par for the course today. The most egregious example of negative campaigning occurred in 1988, when George Bush ran the infamous "Willie Horton ad." This ad featured the face of Willie Horton—a convicted African American criminal who had committed a rape while on a weekend furlough program advocated by Bush's Democratic presidential opponent, Massachusetts Governor Michael Dukakis. The advertisement was extremely effective in casting doubt on some of Dukakis's policies, though many criticized it for brazenly exploiting racial and cultural prejudices to asperse Dukakis.

Push-polling, the dissemination of negative and often inaccurate information about a candidate under the guise of asking opinion-poll questions, is a dirty but increasingly popular campaign tactic that remains unregulated and can only worsen in upcoming campaigns. In push-polling, a pollster for Candidate Y might make a phone call and ask the respondent, "Would you be less likely to vote for [Candidate X] if you found out that she had voted for six consecutive tax increases?" (Notice how the question implies that Candidate X actually has voted for six increases whether she really has or, more likely, has not voted for them.) As Americans become increasingly immersed in the Internet, it is not hard to imagine how push-polling might rear its ugly head in the form of e-mail messages.

In the 2000 election, electoral ethics and integrity ultimately came to play a larger role than campaign ethics. But to be sure, the 2000 campaign had its moments of ethical misgivings, just as all campaigns do. Gore continued to be haunted by references to the Buddhist Temple campaign scandal of 1996, but the most dramatic and suspicious campaign incident was the last-minute revelation of George Bush's DUI charge, in which Democrats claimed they had no hand, but which threw Bush's campaign into confusion and nearly cost him the election. If the Democrats really are blameless, so much the better; if not, the move, while perhaps not illegal, suggests a truly unappealing political cunning. Some candidates will always push the letter of the law, and sometimes even break it, in their attempts to win elected office—it will always be true that campaign ethics is an oxymoron for many. The public can only keep a close eye on their antics and do its best to keep the political arena as clean as possible.

(continued)

1. Campaign finance reform is a perennially popular topic for congressional debate, but little action has resulted from recent discussions of the issue. What reasons, if any, do politicians have to pass laws regulating their own campaign behavior? What do they stand to gain (or lose) by policing their own activity? What is the role of party affiliation in supporting campaign finance reform? How can one ethically justify a partisan vote opposing another party's proposal for reform legislation?
2. Debate the specific merit of the "no-limits, full-disclosure" system of campaign finance, in which unlimited campaign contributions are allowed if they are fully declared in a publicly accessible manner.

Will it ever be possible to close all the loopholes in laws governing campaign ethics? What would be the particular advantages and disadvantages of such an open system—not only to politicians, but to PACs and other lobbyists, and to the interest of the general public? Do you believe that the general public is smart enough to track political contributions and take them into account when voting for a candidate?

Cast Your Vote. Should there be a limit on campaign contributions, or should there be no limits, but full disclosure on the contributors? To cast your vote, go to **www.ablongman.com/oconnor**

SUMMARY

With this chapter we switched our focus from the election decision itself and turned our attention to the actual campaign process. What we have seen is that while modern campaigning makes use of dazzling new technologies and a variety of strategies to attract voters, campaigns still tend to rise and fall on the strength of the individual candidate. In this chapter we have stressed the following observations:

1. **The Structure of a Campaign**
   Campaigns, the process of seeking and winning votes in the run-up to an election, consist of five separate components: the nomination campaign or "invisible primary," in which party leaders and activists are courted to ensure that the candidate is nominated in primaries or conventions; the general election campaign, in which the goal is to appeal to the nation as a whole; the personal campaign, in which the candidate and his or her family make appearances, meet voters, hold press conferences, and give speeches; the organizational campaign, in which volunteers telephone voters, distribute literature, organize events, and raise money; and the broadcast media campaign waged on television and on the radio.
   Campaign staffs combine volunteers, a manager to oversee them, and key political consultants—including media consultants, a pollster, and a direct mailer. In recent years media consultants have assumed greater and greater importance, partly because the cost of advertising has skyrocketed, so that campaign media budgets consume the lion's share of available resources.

2. **The Candidate or the Campaign: Which Do We Vote For?**
   Despite the dazzle of technology and the celebrity of well-known consultants, the candidate remains the most important component of any campaign. The candidate's strengths, weaknesses, and talents are central to the success or failure of the campaign.

3. **Modern Campaign Challenges**
   Candidates tell their story directly in paid broadcast media advertising. They are much less successful in managing and directing their press coverage.

4. **A Summary of Contributions and Expenses**
   Receiving the majority of their financial war chest from individuals, and spending most of these funds for television advertising, today's senatorial candidates struggle to keep pace with the rising costs associated with campaigning for a seat in the U.S. Senate.

5. **Bringing It Together: The 2000 Presidential Campaign and Election**
   After some initial excitement early in the primary season, George Bush and Al Gore triumphed over John McCain and Bill Bradley much as expected. During the course of the campaign Bush avoided significant missteps while Gore's advantages slowly eroded. By Election Day, the two candidates were dead even, and the election itself fell victim to numerous disorders, including media misreporting and irregularities in the casting and counting of ballots. Bush's lawyers succeeded in the ensuing and protracted legal battles, which went all the way to the U.S. Supreme Court, and when he accepted the presidency in January 2001, he triumphed in one of the most contentious elections in United States history.

6. **Campaign Finance Laws**
   Campaign finance is regularly a reform issue because candidates who outspend their opponents tend to win and raising money is easier for some candidates than for others. Incumbents enjoy a fund-raising edge as well as advantages related to name recognition and some perks of office, such as mailing privileges.

KEY TERMS

campaign manager, p. 517
candidate debates, p. 524
contrast ad, p. 518
direct mailer, p. 517
finance chair, p. 517
free media, p. 518
general election campaign, p. 515
get-out-the-vote (GOTV), p. 518
hard money, p. 529

inoculation advertising, p. 519
matching funds, p. 528
media campaign, p. 515
media consultant, p. 517
negative ad, p. 518
nomination campaign, p. 515
organizational campaign, p. 515
paid media, p. 518
personal campaign, p. 515

political action committee (PAC),
   p. 526
political consultant, p. 517
pollster, p. 517
positive ad, p. 518
public funds, p. 528
soft money, p. 529
spot ad, p. 518
voter canvass, p. 518

SELECTED READINGS

Abramson, Paul R., John H. Aldrich, and David W. Rohde. *Change and Continuity in the 1992 Elections.* Washington, D.C.: CQ Press, 1995.

Ansolabehere, Stephen, and Shanto Iyengar. *Going Negative: How Attack Ads Shrink and Polarize the Electorate.* New York: Free Press, 1995.

Ceaser, James W., and Andrew E. Busch. *Losing to Win: The 1996 Elections and American Politics.* Lanham, Md.: Rowman & Littlefield, 1997.

Fenno, Richard F. *Senators on the Campaign Trail: The Politics of Representation.* Norman: University of Oklahoma Press, 1996.

Goldenberg, Edie, and Michael W. Traugott. *Campaigning for Congress.* Washington, D.C.: CQ Press, 1984.

Greive, R. R. Bob. *The Blood, Sweat, and Tears of Political Victory—and Defeat.* Lanham, Md.: University Press of America, 1996.

Herrnson, Paul S. *Congressional Elections: Campaigning at Home and in Washington.* Washington, D.C.: CQ Press, 1995.

Hertzke, Allen D. *Echoes of Discontent: Jesse Jackson, Pat Robertson, and the Resurgence of Populism.* Washington, D.C.: CQ Press, 1993.

Holbrook, Thomas M. *Do Campaigns Matter?* Thousand Oaks, Calif.: Sage Publications, 1996.

Jackson, Brooks. *Honest Graft: Big Money and the American Political Process.* Washington, D.C.: Farragut, 1990.

Kern, Montague. *30-Second Politics: Political Advertising in the Eighties.* New York: Praeger, 1989.

Mayer, William G., ed. *In Pursuit of the White House: How We Choose Our Presidential Nominees.* Chatham, N.J.: Chatham House Publishers, 1996.

Nelson, Michael, ed. *The Elections of 1996.* Washington, D.C.: CQ Press, 1997.

Orren, Gary R., and Nelson W. Polsby, eds. *Media and Momentum: The New Hampshire Primary and Nomination Politics.* Chatham, N.J.: Chatham House, 1987.

Patterson, Thomas E. *The Mass Media Election.* New York: Praeger, 1980.

Pika, Josepha A. and Richard A. Watson. *The Presidential Contest,* 5th ed. Washington, D.C.: CQ Press, 1995.

Pomper, Gerald M., ed. *The Election of 1992: Reports and Interpretations.* Chatham, N.J.: Chatham House, 1993.

Sabato, Larry J., ed. *Campaigns and Elections: A Reader in Modern American Politics.* Glenview, Ill.: Scott, Foresman, 1989.

———. *PAC Power: Inside the World of Political Action Committees.* New York: Norton, 1985.

———. *Paying for Elections: The Campaign Finance Thicket.* New York: Priority Press for the Twentieth Century Fund, 1989.

———. *The Rise of Political Consultants: New Ways of Winning Elections.* New York: Basic Books, 1981.

———. *Toward the Millennium: The Elections of 1996.* Boston: Allyn and Bacon, 1997.

Sabato, Larry J., and Glenn R. Simpson. *Dirty Little Secrets: The Persistence of Corruption in American Politics.* New York: Times Books, 1996.

Salmore, Barbara G., and Stephen Salmore. *Candidates, Parties, and Campaigns,* 2d ed. Washington, D.C.: CQ Press, 1989.

Sorauf, Frank J. *Inside Campaign Finance.* New Haven, Conn.: Yale University Press, 1992.

Troy, Gil. *See How They Ran: The Changing Role of the Presidential Candidate.* Cambridge, Mass.: Harvard University Press, 1996.

NOTES

1. Patrick J. Kenney and Tom W. Rice, "The Psychology of Political Momentum," *Political Research Quarterly* 47 (December 1994): 923–38.

2. Paul S. Herrnson, "Campaign Professionalism and Fundraising in Congressional Elections," *Journal of Politics* 54 (1992): 859–70.

3. Stephen K. Medvic and Silvo Lenart, "The Influence of Political Consultants in the 1992 Congressional Elections," *Legislative Studies Quarterly* 22 (February 1997): 61–77.

4. Five liberal Democratic U.S. senators, including George McGovern of South Dakota, were defeated in this way in 1980, for example.

5. Stephen Ansolabehere and Shanto Iyengar, *Going Negative: How Political Advertisements Shrink and Polarize the Electorate* (New York: Free Press, 1995).

6. Steven E. Finkel and John G. Geer, "A Spot Check: Casting Doubt on the Demobilizing Effect of Attack Advertising," *American Journal of Political Science* 42 (April 1998): 573–95.

7. Paul Freedman and Ken Goldstein, "Measuring Media Exposure and the Effects of Negative Campaign Ads," *American Journal of Political Science* 43 (October 1999): 1189–1208.

8. See Larry J. Sabato, ed., *Campaigns and Elections: A Reader in Modern American Politics* (Glenview, Ill.: Scott, Foresman, 1989), 3–4.

9. From a 1987 cartoon by Tom Toles, copyrighted by the *Buffalo News*.

10. V. O. Key Jr., with the assistance of Milton C. Cummings Jr., *The Responsible Electorate: Rationality in Presidential Voting, 1936–1960* (Cambridge, Mass.: Harvard University Press, 1966).

11. Morris Fiorina, *Retrospective Voting in American National Elections* (New Haven, Conn.: Yale University Press, 1981).

12. Robert S. Erikson, "Economic Conditions and the Presidential Vote," *American Political Science Review* 82 (June 1989): 567–73.

13. Steven E. Finkel, "Reexamining the 'Minimal Effects' Model in Recent Presidential Campaigns," *Journal of Politics* 55 (February 1993): 1–21.

14. John G. Geer, "The Effects of Presidential Debates on the Electorate's Preferences for Candidates," *American Politics Quarterly* 16 (October 1988): 486–501.

15. David J. Lanoue, "One That Made a Difference: Cognitive Consistency, Political Knowledge, and the 1980 Presidential Debate," *Public Opinion Quarterly* 56 (Summer, 1992): 168–84.

16. Diana C. Mutz, "Effects of Horse-Race Coverage on Campaign Coffers: Strategic Contributing in Presidential Primaries," *Journal of Politics* 57 (November 1995): 1015–42.

17. Data provided by the Federal Election Commission.

18. Steven T. Engel and David J. Jackson, "Wielding the Stick Instead of Its Carrot: Labor PAC Punishment of Pro-NAFTA Democrats," *Political Research Quarterly* 51 (September 1998): 813–28.

19. Janet M. Box-Steffensmeier and J. Tobin Grant, "All in a Day's Work: The Financial Rewards of Legislative Effectiveness," *Legislative Studies Quarterly* 24 (November 1999): 511–23.

20. Kevin M. Leyden and Stephen A. Borrelli, "An Investment in Goodwill: Party Contributions and Party Unity Among U.S. House Members in the 1980s," *American Politics Quarterly* 22 (October 1994): 421–52.

21. Amy Keller, "Helping Each Other Out: Members Dip into Campaign Funds for Fellow Candidates," *Roll Call*, June 15, 1998, 1.

22. For member contribution activity at the state level, see Jay K. Dow, "Campaign Contributions and Intercandidate Transfers in the California Assembly," *Social Science Quarterly* 75 (1994): 867–80. For member contribution activity at the congressional level, see Bruce A. Larson, "Ambition and Money in the U.S. House of Representatives: Analyzing Campaign Contributions from Incumbents' Leadership PACs and Reelection Committees" (Ph.D. dissertation, University of Virginia, 1998). For a briefer account, see Paul S. Herrnson, "Money and Motives: Spending in House Elections," in *Congress Reconsidered*, Lawrence C. Dodd and Bruce I. Oppenheimer, eds, 6th ed. (Washington, D.C.: Congressional Quarterly Press, 1997).

23. Larson, "Ambition and Money in the U.S. House of Representatives."

24. Susan B. Glasser and Julie Eilperin, "A New Conduit for Soft Money: Critics Decry Big, Largely Untraceable Donations to Lawmakers' 'Leadership PACs,'" *The Washington Post* (May 16, 1999) A1.

25. 424 U.S. 1 (1976).

26. 424 U.S. 1 (1976).

27. 116 S.Ct. 2309 (1996).

28. Anthony Corrado, "Party Soft Money," in Anthony Corrado et al., eds., *Campaign Finance Reform: A Sourcebook* (Washington, D.C.: Brookings Institution, 1997).

29. Trevor Potter, "Issue Advocacy and Express Advocacy," in Anthony Corrado et al., eds., *Campaign Finance Reform: A Sourcebook* (Washington, D.C.: Brookings Institution, 1997).

30. Gary Jacobson, "The Effect of the AFL-CIO's 'Voter Education' Campaigns on the 1996 House Elections," *Journal of Politics* 61 (1999): 185–94.

31. Julie Eilperin, "In Divided House, All Eyes on 2000," *The Washington Post* (June 3, 1999): A3, A11.

32. Potter, "Issue Advocacy and Express Advocacy."

33. David Magleby and Marianne Holt, "The Long Shadow of Soft Money and Issue Advocacy Ads," *Campaigns and Elections* (May 1999): 22.

34. Michael Cornfield, "The On-Line Campaigner: Interacting for Campaign Dollars," *Campaigns and Elections* (June 1999): 31.

35. Amy Keller, "Experts Wonder about FEC's Internet Savvy: Regulating Web Is a Challenge for Watchdog Agency," *Roll Call*, May 6, 1999, 1, 21.

36. Frank Sorauf, *Inside Campaign Finance: Myths and Realities* (New Haven, Conn.: Yale University Press, 1992), ch 6.

37. Richard A. Smith, "Interest Group Influence in the U.S. Congress," *Legislative Studies Quarterly* 20 (1995): 89–139. See also Janet Grenzke, "PACs and the Congressional Supermarket: The Currency Is Complex," *American Journal of Political Science* 33 (1989): 1–24.

38. Richard L. Hall and Frank W. Wayman, "Buying Time: Moneyed Interests and the Mobilization of Bias in Congressional Committees," *American Political Science Review* 84 (1990): 797–820.

39. Thomas Gais, *Improper Influence: Campaign Finance Law, Political Interest Groups, and the Problem of Equality* (Ann Arbor: University of Michigan Press, 1996).

40. Paul S. Herrnson, *Congressional Elections: Campaigning at Home and in Washington*, 2nd ed. (Washington, D.C.: Congressional Quarterly Press, 1998), 105.

41. See Howard Penniman, "U.S. Elections: Really a Bargain?" *Public Opinion* (June/July 1984): 51.

42. Martin Merzer, Review Shows Ballots Say Bush, Miami Herald (April 4, 2001).

43. Frank J. Sorauf, "Political Parties and Campaign Finance," in L. Sandy Maisel, ed., *The Parties Respond: Changes in American Parties and Campaigns* (Boulder, Colo.: Westview Press, 1998): 238–39.

15 The News Media

The difference between the coverage of the Persian Gulf War of 1990–1991 and that of the NATO–Yugoslav conflict of 1999 aptly demonstrates the dramatic changes that took place in news coverage during the decade of the 1990s. During the Persian Gulf War, television coverage was extensive on the major commercial networks and CNN, but the coverage was primarily factual and centered on the military activities of the moment. Commentary at that time was provided mostly by retired military officers hired by the networks to explain weapons systems and military terminology unfamiliar to both journalists and the general public.

By 1999, however, the talk-show mentality of television had taken over even the coverage of military conflict. The networks certainly covered the facts of the Yugoslav war, but the recent additions of cable networks such as the Fox News Channel, MSNBC, and CNBC, combined with the usual extensive coverage on CNN, meant that the long-standing talk shows such as Chris Matthews's *Hardball, Geraldo Live,* and John Hockenberry's program on MSNBC ran almost full-time coverage of the war. With only a limited supply of hard breaking news, the networks and cable channels filled the remainder of their airtime with constant speculation and second-guessing of the military strategy, even when they lacked sound or certain knowledge of the proceedings from either the battlefield or the war room.

Furthermore, the commentary conspicuously came from journalists whose experience extended little further than running talk shows, let alone military operations. Such televised discussion, which sometimes approaches kibitzing, makes it exceedingly difficult for public leaders to control the presentation and reception of military operations and their outcomes. Some would argue that this keeps leadership open and accountable; others would argue that it interferes with the government's ability to conduct its appointed business with the required security. President Clinton spoke for the second opinion during the Yugoslav war when he criticized the current state of affairs with a touch of sarcastic humor. At a dinner of the White House Correspondents' Association, referring to prominent journalist and lawyer-by-training Howard Fineman, Clinton said he would not know what to do without the "second-guessing" and "continual critiquing of Retired General Howard Fineman."

The media have the potential to exert enormous influence over Americans. Not only does the press tell us what is important by setting the agenda for what we will watch and read, but they can also influence what we think about issues through the content of the news stories. The simple words of the Constitution's First Amendment, "Congress shall make no law . . . abridging the freedom of the speech, or of the press" have shaped the American republic as much as or more than any others in the Constitution and its amendments. With the Constitution's sanction, as interpreted by the Supreme Court over two centuries, a vigorous and highly competitive press has emerged. This freedom has been crucial in facilitating the political discourse and education necessary for the maintenance of democracy. But does this freedom also entail responsibility on the part of the press? Has the press, over the years, met its obligation to provide objective, issue-based coverage of our politicians and political events, or do the media tend to focus on the trivial and sensational, ignoring the important issues and contributing to voter frustration with their government and their politicians? How this freedom evolved, the ways in which it is manifested, and whether press freedom is used responsibly, are subjects we examine further in this chapter.

The chapter reviews the historical development of the press in the United States, and then explores the contemporary media scene. Does the press go too far in their coverage of public figures and issues, and are they biased in their reporting? Does the press really influence public opinion, and does the press allow itself to be manipulated by skilled politicians? We also explore the ways in which the government controls the organization and operation of the press, attempting to promote a balance between freedom and responsibility on the one hand, and competitiveness and consumer choice on the other. In discussing the changing role and impact of the media, we will address the following:

- First, we will discuss the *evolution of the press,* from the founding of the country up to modern times.
- Second, we will examine the *current structure and role of the media.*
- Third, we will discuss the *contemporary trends in media attention* toward investigative journalism during the Watergate era and, more recently, toward character issues and intrusive examination of the private lives of public figures.
- Fourth, we will investigate the *media's influence on the public,* and whether public opinion is significantly swayed by media coverage.
- Fifth, we will observe the *ways politicians use the media* and attempt to influence press coverage for their own ends.
- Sixth, we will explain how the *government regulates the electronic media,* and identify the motivations for and evolution of such control.

THE AMERICAN PRESS OF YESTERYEAR

Journalism—the process and profession of collecting and disseminating the news (that is, new information about subjects of public interest)—has been with us in some form since the dawn of civilization (see Table 15.1 for a history of the media in the United States).[1] Yet its practice has often been remarkably uncivilized, and it was much more so at the beginning of the American republic than it is today.

The first newspapers were published in the American colonies in 1690. The number of newspapers grew throughout the 1700s, as colonists began to realize the value of a press free from government oversight and censorship. Thus it was not surprising that one of the most important demands made by Anti-Federalists (see chapter 2) during our country's constitutional debate was that an amendment guaranteeing the freedom of the press be included in the final version of the Constitution. When beginning a discussion of the media in American history, it is important to remember that by and large

TABLE 15.1 Landmarks of the Amercan Media

1760	First newspaper published	1960	televised presidential campaign debates		the news, allowing candidates to go around journalists to reach the voting public directly.
1789	First party newspapers circulated	1979	The Cable Satellite Public Affairs Network (C-SPAN) is founded, providing live round-the-clock coverage of politics and government.	1996	Official candidate home pages containing, among other things, candidate profiles, issue positions, campaign strategy and slogans, and e-mail addresses appear on the World Wide Web.
1833	First penny press				
1890	Yellow journalism spreads				
1900	Muckraking in fashion				
1928	First radio broadcast of an election	1980	Cable News Network (CNN) is founded by media mogul Ted Turner, making national and international events available instantaneously around the globe.		
1948	First election results to be covered by television			2000	Explosion of World Wide Web as a primary campaign tool for candidates, and a continuous twenty-four hour news cycle.
1952	First presidential campaign advertisements aired on television	1992	Talk-show television circumvents		

that history is one of private enterprise, and that the reference to the media as "the fourth branch of government," while a provocative notion, is a complete fiction. In other words, an American media outlet might choose, or have chosen, stridently to support a particular political party, platform, issue or official, but it would do so as an independent voice of private citizens or a private organization, not as the concealed organ of the government in power (contrast this system with those of totalitarian regimes, in which a state news agency is often the only, and inevitably a highly biased, source of information). This distinction can be difficult to maintain under some circumstances, as this chapter will discuss, but its basic reliability continues to provide the basis for journalistic integrity in America.

During his presidency, George Washington escaped most press scrutiny but detested journalists nonetheless; his battle tactics in the Revolutionary War had been much criticized in print, and an early draft of his "Farewell Address to the Nation" at the end of his presidency (1796) contained a condemnation of the press that has often been described as savage.[2] Thomas Jefferson was treated especially harshly by elements of the early U.S. press. For example, one Richmond newspaper editor, angered by Jefferson's refusal to appoint him as postmaster, printed a rumor that started a debate that continues to this day: that Jefferson kept a slave as his concubine and had several children by her.[3] One can understand why Jefferson, normally a defender of a free press, commented that "even the least informed of the people have learned that nothing in a newspaper is to be believed." Jefferson, of course, probably did not intend that statement literally, since he himself was instrumental in establishing the *National Gazette*, the newspaper of his political faction and viewpoint.

The partisan press eventually gave way to the penny press. In 1833 Benjamin Day founded the *New York Sun*, which cost a penny at the newsstand. Because it was not tied to one party, it was politically more independent than the party papers. The *Sun* was the forerunner of the modern press built on mass circulation and commercial advertising to produce profit. By 1861 the penny press had so supplanted partisan papers that President Abraham Lincoln announced that his administration would have no favored or sponsored newspaper.

The press thus became markedly less partisan but not necessarily more respectable. Mass-circulation dailies sought wide readership, and readers were clearly attracted by the sensational and the scandalous. The sordid side of politics became the entertainment of the times. One of the best-known examples occurred in the presidential campaign of 1884, when the *Buffalo Evening Telegraph* headlined "A Terrible Tale" about Grover Cleveland, the Democratic nominee.[4] In 1871, while sheriff of Buffalo, the bachelor Cleveland had allegedly fathered a child. Even though the woman in question had been seeing other men, Cleveland willingly accepted responsibility since all the other men were married, and he had dutifully paid child support for years. Fortunately for Cleveland, another newspaper, the *Democratic Sentinel*, broke a story that helped to

yellow journalism
A form of newspaper publishing in vogue in the late nineteenth century that featured pictures, comics, color, and sensationalized, oversimplified news coverage.

muckraking
A form of newspaper publishing, in vogue in the early twentieth century, concerned with reforming government and business conduct.

WEB EXPLORATION
For examples of nineteenth-century yellow journalism, go to
www.ablongman.com/oconnor

offset this scandal: Republican presidential nominee James G. Blaine and his wife had had their first child just three months after their wedding.

In the late 1800s and early 1900s, the era of the intrusive press was in full flower. First yellow journalism and then muckraking were in fashion. Pioneered by prominent publishers such as William Randolph Hearst and Joseph Pulitzer, **yellow journalism**[5] featured pictures, comics, and color designed to capture a share of the burgeoning immigrant population market. These newspapers also oversimplified and sensationalized many news developments. The front-page editorial crusade became common, the motto for which frequently seemed to be, "Damn the truth, full speed ahead."

After the turn of the century, the muckrakers—so named by President Theodore Roosevelt after a special rake designed to collect manure[6]—took charge of a number of newspapers and nationally circulated magazines. **Muckraking** journalists such as Upton Sinclair and David Graham Phillips searched out and exposed real and apparent misconduct by government, business, and politicians in order to stimulate reform.[7] There was no shortage of corruption to reveal, of course, and much good came from these efforts. But an unfortunate side effect of the emphasis on crusades and investigations was the frequent publication of gossip and rumor without sufficient proof.

The modern press corps may also be guilty of this offense, but it has achieved great progress on another front. Throughout the nineteenth century, payoffs to the press were not uncommon. Andrew Jackson, for instance, gave one in ten of his early appointments to loyal reporters;[8] and during the 1872 presidential campaign, the Republicans slipped cash to about 300 newsmen.[9] Wealthy industrialists also sometimes purchased editorial peace or investigative cease-fire for tens of thousands of dollars. Examples of such press corruption are exceedingly rare today, and not even the most extreme of the modern media's critics believe otherwise.

As the news business grew, its focus gradually shifted from passionate opinion to corporate profit. Newspapers, hoping to maximize profit, were more careful to avoid alienating the advertisers and readers who produced their revenues, and the result was less harsh, more objective reporting. Meanwhile, media barons such as Joseph Pulitzer and William Randolph Hearst became pillars of the establishment; for the most part, they were no longer the antiestablishment insurgents of yore.

"Uncle Sam's Next Campaign—the War Against the Yellow Press." In this 1898 cartoon in the wake of the Spanish-American War, yellow journalism is attacked for its threats, insults, filth, grime, blood, death, slander, gore, and blackmail, all of which are "lies." The cartoonist suggests that, after winning the foreign war, the government ought to attack its own yellow journalists at home. (Photo courtesy: Stock Montage, Inc.)

Technological advances had a major impact on this transformation in journalism. High-speed presses and more cheaply produced paper made mass-circulation dailies possible. The telegraph and then the telephone made news gathering easier and much faster, and nothing could compare to the invention of radio and television. When radio became widely available in the 1920s, millions of Americans could hear national politicians instead of merely reading about them. With television—first introduced in the late 1940s, and nearly a universal fixture in U.S. homes by the mid-1950s—citizens could see and hear candidates and presidents. The removal of newspapers and magazines as the foremost conduits between politicians and voters had profound effects on the electoral process, as we discuss shortly.

Longman
Participate.com 2.0
Timeline
300 Years of Media

THE CONTEMPORARY MEDIA SCENE

The editors of the first partisan newspapers could scarcely have imagined what their profession would become more than two centuries later. The number and diversity of media outlets existing today are stunning: the **print press**—many thousands of daily and weekly newspapers, periodicals, magazines, newsletters, and journals; and the **electronic media**—radio and television stations and networks, computerized information services, and the Internet. In some ways the news business is more competitive now than at any time in history; yet, paradoxically, the news media have expanded in some ways and contracted in others, dramatically changing the ways in which they cover politics.

The growth of the political press corps is obvious to anyone familiar with government or campaigns. Since 1983, for example, the number of print (newspaper and magazine) reporters accredited at the U.S. Capitol has jumped from 2,300 to more than 4,100; the gain for broadcast (television and radio) journalists was equally impressive and proportionally larger, from about 1,000 in 1983 to an average of 3,000 by 1999.[10] On the campaign trail, a similar phenomenon has been occurring. In the 1960s a presidential candidate in the primaries would attract a press entourage of at most a couple of dozen reporters, but in the 1990s a hundred or more print and broadcast journalists can be seen tagging along with a front-runner. Consequently, a politician's every public utterance is reported and intensively scrutinized and interpreted in the media. (See Politics Now: The Press and the Bush DUI.)

Although there are more journalists, they are not necessarily attracting a larger audience, at least on the print side. Daily newspaper circulation has been stagnant for twenty years at 60 million to 62 million papers per day (see Analyzing the Data: Circulation of Daily Newspapers, 1850–2002). On a per-household basis, circulation has actually fallen 47 percent from 1976 to 1998.[11] Barely half of the adult population reads a newspaper every day. Among young people age eighteen to twenty-nine, only one-third are daily readers—a decline of 50 percent in two decades.

Along with the relative decline of readership has come a drop in the overall level of competition. In 1880, 61 percent of U.S. cities had at least two competing dailies, but by 1990 a mere 2 percent of cities did so. Not surprisingly, the number of dailies has declined significantly, from a peak of 2,600 in 1909 to around 1,500 today.[12] Most of the remaining dailies are owned by large media conglomerates called chains such as Gannett, Hearst, Knight-Ridder, and Newhouse. In 1940, 83 percent of all daily newspapers were independently owned, but by 1990 just 24 percent remained independent of a chain. Chain ownership usually reduces the diversity of editorial opinions and can result in the homogenization of the news.

Part of the cause of the newspapers' declining audience has been the increased numbers of television sets and cable subscribers (see Figure 15.1) and the increased popularity of television as a news source. At the dawn of the 1960s, a substantial majority of Americans reported that they got most of their news from newspapers;

print press
The traditional form of mass media, comprising newspapers, magazines, and journals.

electronic media
The newest form of broadcast media, including television, radio, cable, and the Internet.

A N A L Y Z I N G   T H E   D A T A

CIRCULATION OF DAILY NEWSPAPERS, 1850–

In the second half of the nineteenth century , newpapers were the primary news medium, and circulation expanded dramatically as the penny press reduced the cost of newspapers and universal public education boosted literacy rates. In the second half of the twentieth century—with the advent of new media from television to the Internet—newspaper circulation has dropped just as dramatically. This does not mean necessarily that people are less well informed; they may simply be getting their news from other sources.

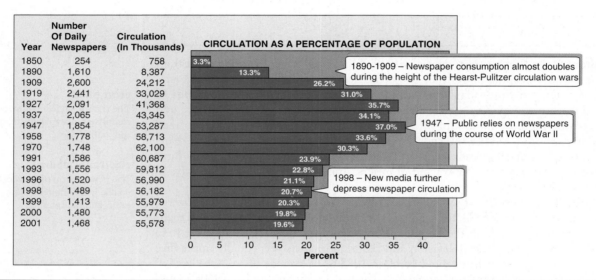

Year	Number Of Daily Newspapers	Circulation (In Thousands)
1850	254	758
1890	1,610	8,387
1909	2,600	24,212
1919	2,441	33,029
1927	2,091	41,368
1937	2,065	43,345
1947	1,854	53,287
1958	1,778	58,713
1970	1,748	62,100
1991	1,586	60,687
1993	1,556	59,812
1996	1,520	56,990
1998	1,489	56,182
1999	1,413	55,979
2000	1,480	55,773
2001	1,468	55,578

CIRCULATION AS A PERCENTAGE OF POPULATION

1890-1909 – Newspaper consumption almost doubles during the height of the Hearst-Pulitzer circulation wars

1947 – Public relies on newspapers during the course of World War II

1998 – New media further depress newspaper circulation

Source: Adapted from Harold W. Stanley and Richard G. Niemi, *Vital Statistics on American Politics, 1997-1998 (6th ed.)* (Washington, D.C.: Congressional Quarterly, Inc., 2001), Table 4-2, pp. 171–172, *Editor & Publisher Yearbook 1999; NAA.*

but by the latter half of the 1980s, television was the people's choice by an almost two-to-one margin.[13] Moreover, by a margin of 55 percent to 21 percent, Americans now say that they are inclined to believe television over newspapers when conflicting reports about the same story arise. Of course, most individuals still rely on both print *and* broadcast sources,[14] but there can be little question that television news is increasingly important. Despite its many drawbacks (such as simplicity, brevity, and entertainment orientation), television news is "news that matters." It has the power to greatly effect which issues viewers say are important.[15]

Although not totally eclipsing newspapers, television frequently overshadows them, even though it often takes its agenda and lead stories from the headlines produced by print reporters (especially those working for the print elite—papers such as the *New York Times, Washington Post,* and *Wall Street Journal;* wire services such as the Associated Press and United Press International; and journals such as *Time, Newsweek,* and *U.S. News & World Report*). Regrettably, busy people today appear to have less time to review the printed word, and consequently they rely more on television's brief headline summaries to stay in touch. Additionally, at least one study of television and print news finds differences in the level of independence each shows in their reporting. Television news was less questioning of the "government line" during the Gulf War, while newspapers exhibited a greater deal of journalistic autonomy and diversity of opinion about the conduct of the war in their coverage.[16] Perhaps over time, the Internet will nudge Americans back to the printed word—not in newspapers but on Web sites sponsored by the major news organizations.

FIGURE 15.1   Television in the American Home

The growth of cable television has been tremendous over the last thirty years. Today, the majority of American households possess access to cable television. Moreover, satellite television, bring literally hundreds of channels to viewers, is also on the rise. Smaller satellite dishes and lower prices are sure to make satellite television a more attractive media source in the future.

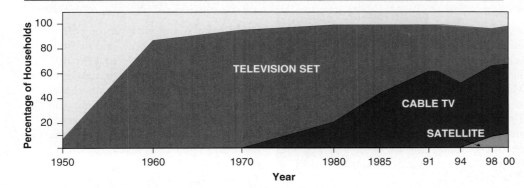

Source: Adapted from Harold W. Stanley and Richard G. Niemi, *Vital Statistics on American Politics,* 2001–2002 (Washington, DC: Congressional Quarterly, Inc., 2002), Table 4-1, p. 170, Television Bureau of Advertising.

The television news industry differs from its print counterpart in a variety of ways. The number of outlets has been increasing, not declining, as with newspapers. The three major networks now receive broadcast competition from Cable News Network (CNN), Headline News, Cable Satellite Public Affairs Network (C-SPAN), and PBS's *News-Hour/Jim Lehrer.* Although the audiences of all the alternative shows are relatively small compared with those of the network news shows, they are growing while the networks' audience shares contract. The potential for cable expansion is large: nearly half of all U.S. households are currently wired for cable. In addition, the rise of cable has had important implications for the political system. For instance, political scientists Matthew Baum and Samuel Kernell suggest that the splintering of television audiences caused by cable makes it much more difficult for the president to drum up support for his favored policies. Whereas the president could at one time command the attention of all television consumers by appearing on network television, this is no longer possible.[17]

Adding to television's diversity, the national television news corps is often outnumbered on the campaign trail by local television reporters. Satellite technology has provided any of the 1,300 local stations willing to invest in the hardware an opportunity to beam back reports from the field. On a daily basis, local news is watched by more people (67 percent of adults) than is network news (49 percent), so increased local attention to politics has some real significance. Unfortunately, however, studies also show that local news, compared to newspapers and network reports, contains the least substantive coverage. Criticism and analysis of policy positions and candidates are much more likely to be found in national news reports than local broadcasts.[18]

The decline of the major networks' audience shares and the local stations' decreasing reliance on the major networks for news—coupled with stringent belt tightening ordered by the networks' corporate managers—resulted in severe news staff cutbacks at NBC, CBS, and ABC during the 1980s and 1990s. These economy measures have affected the quality of broadcast journalism. Many senior correspondents bemoan the loss of desk assistants and junior reporters, who did much of the legwork necessary to get less superficial, more in-depth pieces on the air. As a consequence, stories requiring extensive research are often discarded in favor of simplistic, eye-catching, "sexy" items that increasingly seem to dominate campaign and government coverage.

There has also been a substantial increase in the number of media mergers in recent years, so that each national television network now is only a piece of a massive corporation. These mergers have had at least two important effects. One effect is that the large corporations have their financial bottom line as the alpha and the omega of their

POLITICS NOW

THE PRESS AND THE BUSH DUI

On November 2, 2000, a mere 100 hours before the presidential election, reporters launched a media feeding frenzy by revealing that George W. Bush had been arrested in Maine in 1976 for driving under the influence of alcohol. The story was disclosed by Tom Connolly, a lawyer and Democratic activist in Maine who had no apparent connection to the Gore campaign. Earlier in the campaign for president, Bush had admitted a history of drinking and reckless youthful indiscretions but swore that he gave up drinking entirely after his fortieth birthday. During a hastily called press conference in Wisconsin that evening, Bush acknowledged the charge and said that he had kept it a secret to protect his twin daughters from embarrassment. The Gore campaign vehemently denied any involvement with the story.

Most media analysts, both Republicans and Democrats, suggested that Bush's character would not be seriously damaged by the revelation. Instead, what hurt Bush the most in the end was constant dogging by the media for the next three days. Not a single press conference or event could take place without questions about the DUI, and Bush and his staff were completely unable to keep the focus on Bush's campaign message. The radio and television talk shows were swamped with calls about the arrest, and Internet news sites covered the DUI heavily. Stories about the 1962 and 1963 DUI arrests of Bush's running mate Dick Cheney resurfaced and only further prevented the Bush team from discussing the issues in the crucial five days before the election.

In the end, it is difficult to say how much the DUI revelations and the ensuing feeding frenzy damaged Bush. On one hand, Americans tend to be more forgiving if the candidate is sincerely remorseful, as was Bush, and if the indiscretion took place many years ago. On the other hand, it is very likely that Bush, who campaigned strongly on returning integrity and strong moral character to the White House, did much to convince undecided voters that he was no more credible than his opponent or his predecessor.

---

existence. As a consequence, if news shows cannot be profitable, the corporate executives will either cut the news divisions back or force the news divisions to do virtually anything to expand the audience. Unfortunately, what expands the audience is sleazy, tabloid coverage of gossip, innuendo, and sex (see Highlight: The Punditocracy).

Another suspected effect is that the media megacorporations are censoring news that reflects badly on products created by the nonnews divisions of those corporations.[19] While conservative critics say that media bias is mainly liberal—and in coverage of politics this criticism may well be valid—it is also true that another form of bias in the news media is conservative since these corporations are making sure that the coverage of their own products stays positive.

Every newspaper, radio station, and television station is influential in its own area, but only a handful of media outlets are influential nationally. The United States has no nationwide daily newspapers to match the influence of Great Britain's the *Times,* *Guardian,* and *Daily Telegraph,* all of which are avidly read in virtually every corner of the United Kingdom. The national orientation of the British print media can be traced to the smaller size of the country and also to London's role as both the national capital and the largest cultural metropolis. The vastness of the United States and the existence of many large cities, such as New York, Los Angeles, and Chicago, effectively preclude a nationally united print medium in this country.

However, national distribution of the *New York Times, Wall Street Journal, USA Today,* and *Christian Science Monitor* does exist, and other newspapers, such as the *Washington Post* and *Los Angeles Times,* have substantial influence from coast to coast. These six newspapers also have a pronounced effect on what the five major national **networks** (ABC, CBS, NBC, CNN, and Fox) broadcast on their evening news programs—or, in the case

WEB EXPLORATION
To see how media is diversifying and repackaging itself through the use of pundits, go to
www.ablongman.com/oconnor

network
An association of broadcast stations (radio or television) that share programming through a financial arrangement.

HIGHLIGHT

THE PUNDITOCRACY

The Constitution specifies three branches of government, but many observers of modern American politics would add an informal fourth branch—the news media. Within the world of the media, the role of so-called pundits (media commentators who dissect and interpret daily political affairs) is increasingly controversial as the media, especially television, becomes even more pervasive and influential.

The pundits appearing in the media today come in many forms. Some are relatively neutral academics who have studied American history, government, and politics. Others come from the partisan and ideological world, where they have worked for candidates and parties for years prior to becoming media experts.

Once limited to a handful of key reporters and television anchors, the punditocracy now numbers in the hundreds. This is largely due to the expansion of cable television. The advent of CNN, MSNBC, Fox News Network, and other cable outlets, as well as the proliferation of network news magazines such as *20/20, Dateline,* and *60 Minutes,* has created an ever-growing platform from which pundits operate. Today, the pundits are everywhere, all the time. Although only a relatively small fraction of the American public watches any particular channel at any particular time, another audience, small but loyal, made up of politicians and fellow opinion-shapers, pays a great deal of attention to pundits.

Bias in the punditocracy is often assumed, since so many of the pundits come from a particular partisan or ideological background. In many cases, the pundits' most important objective is to project their side's spin—the interpretation of real events and issues in the light most favorable for their preferred party or ideology. Spin is a constant fixture on TV, as partisan operatives battle to frame issues in a way that benefits their political objectives.

Many of us will recognize the dramatic displays of punditry that occur on organized shouting matches such as CNN's *Crossfire* and *The Capital Gang.* These programs deliberately produce talk-show fireworks by pairing up hosts and guests of different political orientations to debate current and controversial issues. While it is often difficult to hear the guests, the points made in this process have an undeniable impact. (For more information, check out http://www.cnn.com/CNN/Programs/crossfire/ and http:// www.cnn.com/CNN/Programs/capital.gang/)

The cacophony of competing perspectives can confuse and even mislead the average citizen. Negativity and intense partisanship within the punditocracy may actually contribute to the public's apathetic and skeptical view of politics.* Some argue that the spectacle of pundits picking fights can easily disillusion thoughtful citizens and cheapen political discourse, while others claim that pundits offer important insights and opinions that would otherwise go unreported by traditional news coverage.

*James Fallows, *Breaking the News: How the Media Undermine American Democracy* (New York: Vintage Press, 1997).

---

of CNN, air on cable around the clock. A major story that breaks in one of these papers is nearly guaranteed to be featured on one or more of the network news shows. These news shows are carried by hundreds of local stations—called **affiliates**—that are associated with the national networks and may choose to carry their programming. A **wire service,** such as the Associated Press (AP) (established in 1848), also nationalizes the news. Most newspapers subscribe to the service, which not only produces its own news stories but also puts on the wire major stories produced by other media outlets.

The national newspapers, wire services, and broadcast networks are supplemented by a number of national news magazines, whose subscribers number in the millions. *Time, Newsweek,* and *U.S. News & World Report* bring the week's news into focus and headline one event or trend for special treatment. Other news magazines stress commentary from an ideological viewpoint, including the *Nation* (left-wing), *New Republic* (moderate-liberal), and *National Review* (conservative). These last three publications have much smaller circulations, but because their readerships are composed of activists and opinion leaders, they have disproportionate influence.

affiliates
Local television stations that carry the programming of a national network.

wire service
An electronic delivery of news gathered by the news services' correspondents and sent to all member news media organizations.

TABLE 15.2 Younger Americans: Turned On by Information, Off by News

	18–29 %	30–49 %	50–64 %	65+ %
Like having so many information sources to choose from	77	70	64	52
Enjoy keeping up with the news a lot	33	48	59	68

WEB EXPLORATION
What does it mean for a television station or a newspaper to have a Web site? To see which newspapers, magazines, and networks have a Web presence, and how that coverage differs from or complements its standard coverage, go to
www.ablongman.com/oconnor

In politics, as in every other field, the World Wide Web is truly the wave of the future. Already, Web-based information has become standard fare for anyone interested in politics. Three Web sites among the dozens now available are those of the *National Journal*, which includes its famous Hotline report (www.nationaljournal.com); the *Washington Post*, whose site is widely considered the best political site on the Web (www.washingtonpost.com); and an all-politics collaboration between CNN, *Time* magazine, and other media sources (www.cnn.com/ALLPOLITICS). Virtually every major newspaper, opinion magazine, and news magazine now has a site, as well as all the television networks, which endlessly offer not only the pieces that appear on the evening news, but also additional commentary and information too lengthy to include on the original thirty-minute broadcast.

Many people wonder if the media is cutting into its own subscription revenues, since it is not feasible to charge for the use of a public site associated with a newspaper or TV network. Interestingly, there is very little evidence that this is happening. By and large, the people who use media Web sites are highly informed voters who devour additional information about politics and government and use the Web for updates and supplements to their traditional media services. Web sites thus appear to be building interest in traditional media rather than detracting from them. As the current generation of computer-literate children and young people become adult voters, the Web is likely to become the primary means by which America informs itself about politics and government on a regular and current basis. (See Table 15.2.)

HOW THE MEDIA COVER POLITICIANS AND GOVERNMENT

Much of the media's attention is focused on our politicians and the day-to-day operations of our government. In this section we will discuss how the press covers the three constitutionally created branches of government (Congress, the president, and the courts), and show how the tenor of this coverage has changed since the Watergate scandal of the early 1970s.

Covering the Presidency

The three branches of the U.S. government—the executive, the legislative, and the judicial—are roughly equal in power and authority, but in the world of media coverage, the president is first among equals. All television cables lead to the White House, and a president can address the nation on all networks almost at will. On television, Congress and the courts appear to be divided and confused institutions—different segments contradicting others—whereas the commander-in-chief is in clear focus as chief of state and head of government. The situation is scarcely different in other democracies. In Great Britain, all media eyes are on No. 10 Downing Street, the office and residence of the prime minister.

FIGURE 15.2   **Presidential News Conferences, 1929–2002**
The modern president has less need to give frequent presidential news conferences than was the case in the past. Today, presidents prefer to give a limited number of well planned news conferences rather than make more regular appearances. The modern president relies on advisors and a press team to provide the media with daily briefings.

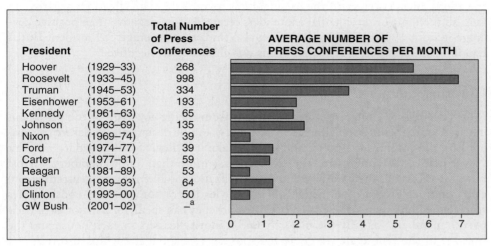

President		Total Number of Press Conferences	AVERAGE NUMBER OF PRESS CONFERENCES PER MONTH
Hoover	(1929–33)	268	
Roosevelt	(1933–45)	998	
Truman	(1945–53)	334	
Eisenhower	(1953–61)	193	
Kennedy	(1961–63)	65	
Johnson	(1963–69)	135	
Nixon	(1969–74)	39	
Ford	(1974–77)	39	
Carter	(1977–81)	59	
Reagan	(1981–89)	53	
Bush	(1989–93)	64	
Clinton	(1993–00)	50	
GW Bush	(2001–02)	—[a]	

Note: Any count of news conferences is only an approximation, given the variety of contacts presidents have with the press.
[a]On March 28, 2001, White House spokesman Ari Fleischer said President George W. Bush planned to conduct no formal news conferences but intended to be accessible to reporters during public appearances.
Source: Adapted from Harold W. Stanley and Richard G. Niemi, *Vital Statistics on American Politics,* 2001–2002 (Washington, DC: Congressional Quarterly, Inc., 2002), Table 4–3, p. 170.

Since Franklin D. Roosevelt's time, chief executives have used the presidential press conference to shape public opinion and explain their actions (see Figure 15.2). The presence of the press in the White House enables a president to appear even on very short notice and to televise live, interrupting regular programming. The White House's press-briefing room is a familiar sight on the evening news, not just because presidents use it so often, but also because the presidential press secretary has almost daily question-and-answer sessions there.

It is useful to distinguish between several terms associated with the release and discussion of information by elected officials, public figures, and their staff. A **press release** is a written document offering an official comment or position on an issue or news event; it is usually printed on paper and handed directly to reporters, or, increasingly, released by e-mail or fax. A **press briefing** is a relatively restricted live engagement with the press, in which the range of questions accepted is limited to one or two specific topics and a public figure or elected official is usually represented by his or her press secretary or other aides but does not appear in person. In a full-blown **press conference**, an elected official appears in person to talk with the press at greater length about an unrestricted range of topics. Press conferences are still significant media events, providing a field on which reporters struggle to get the answers they need and public figures attempt to retain control of their message and "spin" the news and issues in ways favorable to them.

The press secretary's post has existed only since Herbert Hoover's administration (1929–1933), and the individual holding it is the president's main disseminator of information to the press. For this vital position, a number of presidents have chosen close aides who were very familiar with their thinking. For example, John F. Kennedy had Pierre Salinger (now an ABC News foreign correspondent), Lyndon B. Johnson had Bill Moyers (who now hosts many PBS documentaries), and Jimmy Carter chose his longtime Georgia associate Jody Powell. Probably the most famous recent presidential press secretary is James Brady, who was wounded and disabled in the March 1981 assassination attempt on President Ronald Reagan.

On any given day, presidents, their advisers, and their families do any number of things that might become news. In deciding what *does* become news, presidents and the press engage in a continuous "negotiation of news worthiness." This negotiation

press release
A document offering an official comment or position.

press briefing
A relatively restricted session between a press secretary or aide and the press.

press conference
An unrestricted session between an elected official and the press.

occurs not only between the White House and the news media but within the two entities as well, and it involves "what get covered, who gets asked about a story, and how and for how long the story is covered."[20]

Finally, although the president receives the lion's share of the press's attention, political scientist Thomas Patterson suggests that much of this focus is unfavorable. Since the 1960s, press coverage of the president has become dramatically more negative. In fact, all three major presidential contenders received more negative than positive coverage in both 1992 and 1996. Patterson also finds that coverage of President Bush's handling of important national problems was almost solely negative.[21]

Covering Congress

Press coverage of Congress is very different from media coverage of the president. The size of the institution alone (535 members) and its decentralized nature (bicameralism, the committee system, and so on) make it difficult for the media to survey. Nevertheless, the congressional press corps has more than 3,000 members.[22] Most news organizations solve the size and decentralization problems by concentrating coverage on three groups of individuals. First, the leaders of both parties in both houses receive the lion's share of attention because only they can speak for a majority of their party's members. Usually the majority and minority leaders in each house and the Speaker of the House are the preferred spokespersons, but the whips also receive a substantial share of air time and column inches. Second, key committee chairs command center stage when subjects in their domain are newsworthy. Heads of the most prominent committees (such as Ways and Means or Armed Services) are guaranteed frequent coverage, but even the chairs and members of minor committees or subcommittees can achieve fame when the time and issue are right. Third, local newspapers and broadcast stations will normally devote some resources to covering their local senators and representatives, even when these legislators are junior and relatively lacking in influence. Most office holders, in turn, are mainly concerned with meeting the needs of their local media contingents, since these reporters are the ones who directly and regularly reach the voters in their home constituencies. Political scientist Timothy Cook showed this in his 1984 survey of congressional press secretaries. Local print and television news, if applicable, occupied much of the House members' time when dealing with the press. Members only contacted the national news media when they sought to become a national spokesperson on some issue.[23]

One other kind of congressional news coverage is worth noting: investigative-committee hearings. Occasionally, a sensational scandal leads to televised congressional committee hearings that transfix and electrify the nation. In the early 1950s, Senator Joseph R. McCarthy (R–Wisc.) held a series of hearings to expose and root out what he claimed were Communists in the State Department and other U.S. government agencies, as well as Hollywood's film industry. The senator's style of investigation, which involved many wild charges made without proof and the smearing and labeling of some innocent opponents as Communists, gave rise to the term *McCarthyism.*

The Watergate hearings of 1973 and 1974—which stemmed from White House

During the Clinton impeachment hearings C-SPAN provided extensive live Congressional coverage for cable viewers across the United States. (Photo courtesy: C-SPAN)

efforts to eavesdrop on officials of the Democratic National Committee and then to cover up presidential involvement in the scheme—made heroes out of two committee chairs, Senator Sam Ervin (D–N.C.) and U.S. Representative Peter Rodino (D–N.J.). They uncovered many facts behind the Watergate scandal and then pursued the impeachment of President Richard M. Nixon. (Nixon resigned in August 1974, before the full House could vote on his impeachment.)

In 1987 the Iran-Contra hearings—set up to investigate a complicated Reagan administration scheme in which arms were sold to Iran and the profits were then diverted to the anti-Communist Nicaraguan Contras—also created a popular hero. This time, however, the hero was not the committee chair but a witness, Lieutenant Colonel Oliver North, a White House aide deeply involved in the plot. North's boyish appeal and patriotic demeanor projected well on television, on which all the hearings were carried live (as were the McCarthy and Watergate hearings). North capitalized on his fame and in 1994 launched an unsuccessful campaign for a U.S. Senate seat from Virginia. In October 1991, the nation viewed another televised committee spectacle when Supreme Court nominee Clarence Thomas was accused of sexual harassment

More recently, throughout the latter months of 1995 and 1996, Whitewater hearings led by Senator Alfonse D'Amato (R–N.Y.) questioned the actions of President Clinton and Hillary Rodham Clinton in a failed investment venture while Clinton was governor of Arkansas. On much the same subject, even more sensational hearings were convened by the Senate under Tennessee Senator Fred Thompson in 1997 concerning the financing of President Clinton's 1996 reelection campaign. Though containing much sound and fury and a number of very serious charges, the hearings seemed to fizzle as the year wore on, as hard evidence was difficult to come by. Similar hearings were held on the House side headed by Representative Dan Burton (R–Ind.) in 1998. Burton was a highly controversial choice as chairman because of his staunchly anti-Clinton perspective and was not viewed as credibly as the moderate Thompson. In 2002, congressional committees were heavily covered by an attentive media as they investigated several high profile corporate scandals, including the collapse of Enron and WorldCom.

Coverage of Congress has been greatly expanded through use of the cable industry channel C-SPAN and C-SPAN2 provide gavel-to-gavel coverage of House and Senate sessions as well as many committee hearings. For the first time, Americans can watch their representatives in action (or inaction, as the case may be), and do so twenty-four hours a day. As with coverage of the president, press coverage of Congress is disproportionately negative. Much media attention given to the House and Senate focuses on conflict between members. Political scientists John Hibbing and Elizabeth Theiss-Morse believe that such reporting is at least partially responsible for the public's negative perceptions of Congress.[24]

Covering the Courts

The branch of government that is the most different, in press coverage as in many other respects, is the judicial branch. Cloaked in secrecy—because judicial deliberations and decision making are conducted in private—the courts receive scant coverage under most circumstances. However, a volatile or controversial issue, such as abortion, can change the usual type of coverage, especially when the Supreme Court is rendering the decision. Each network and major newspaper has one or more Supreme Court reporters, people who are usually well schooled in the law and whose instant analysis of court opinions interprets the decisions for the millions of people without legal training. Gradually, the admission of cameras into state and local courtrooms across the United States is offering people a more in-depth look at the operation of the judicial system. As yet, though, the Supreme Court does not permit televised proceedings. While the proceedings of the U.S. Supreme Court are conducted in public, the justices continue to resist attempts to have oral arguments televised. State courts, however, often allow television cameras in the courtroom. First the Palm Beach rape trial of William Kennedy

WEB EXPLORATION
Should television cameras be allowed in the courtroom, particularly the Supreme Court? To learn more about both sides of the debate, go to
www.ablongman.com/oconnor

Longman
Participate.com
2.0
Simulation
You Are a
News Editor

Smith and then the O. J. Simpson trial attracted millions of viewers. The Simpson trial even spawned two new legal-oriented television programs: *Burden of Proof*, a CNN program hosted by Greta Van Sustern and Roger Cossack (who had served as commentators during the Simpson trial), and *Geraldo Live*, on CNBC. Court TV, which provides full televised coverage of many highly publicized trials, such as that of Winona Ryder, also draws significant viewership.

The work of Independent Counsel Kenneth Starr and the grand juries investigating Whitewater and the president's relationship with Monica Lewinsky also attracted the attention of the mass media, overshadowing the pope's historic visit to Cuba in almost all media outlets. The operations of the federal and state courts, as well as the judges and attorneys who appear in them, are now regular fodder for media pundits and legal experts.

Watergate and the Era of Investigative Journalism

The Watergate scandal of the Nixon administration had the most profound impact of any modern event on the manner and substance of press conduct. In many respects Watergate began a chain reaction that today allows for intense scrutiny of public officials' private lives. Moreover, coupled with the civil rights movement and the Vietnam War, Watergate shifted the orientation of journalism away from mere description (providing an account of happenings) and toward prescription—helping to set the campaign's (and society's) agenda by focusing attention on the candidates' shortcomings as well as on certain social problems.

A new breed and a new generation of reporters were attracted to journalism, particularly to its investigative role. As a group they were idealistic, although aggressively mistrustful of authority, and they shared a contempt for "politics as usual." The Vietnam and Watergate generation dominates journalism today. They and their younger colleagues hold sway over most newsrooms, with two-thirds of all reporters now under the age of thirty-six and an ever-increasing number of editors and executives who had their start in journalism in the Watergate era.[25]

The Post-Watergate Era

A volatile mix of guilt and fear is at work in the post-Watergate press. The guilt stems from regret that experienced Washington reporters failed to detect the telltale signs of the Watergate scandal early on; that even after the story broke, most journalists underplayed the unfolding disaster until forced to take it more seriously by two young *Post* reporters; that over the years journalism's leading lights had become too close to the politicians they were supposed to check and therefore for too long failed to tell the public about dangerous excesses in the government. The press's ongoing fear is deep-seated and complements the guilt. Every political journalist is apprehensive about missing the next big story, of being left on the platform when the next scandal train leaves Union Station.

In the post-Watergate era, the sizable financial and personnel investments many major news organizations have made in investigative units almost guarantee that greater attention will be given to scandals and that probably more of them—some real and some manufactured—will be uncovered.

Washington Post reporters Bob Woodward, right, and Carl Bernstein won a Pulitzer Prize for their reporting of the Watergate case. (Photo courtesy: AP/Wide World Photos)

The Character Issue in Media Coverage of Politicians. Another clear consequence of Watergate has been the increasing emphasis by the press on the character of candidates. The issue of character has always been present in U.S. politics—George Washington was not made the nation's first president for his policy positions—but rarely if ever has character been such an issue as it has in elections from 1976 onward. (See Roots of Government: The Presidency in the Television Age.) Jimmy Carter's 1976 presidential campaign was characterized by moral posturing in the wake of Watergate. Edward M. Kennedy's 1980 presidential candidacy was destroyed in part by lingering character questions. The 1988 race witnessed an explosion of character concerns so forceful that several candidates (including Gary Hart) were badly scarred by it, and the 1992 contest for the White House became a tawdry debate about the alleged mistresses of Bill Clinton and George Bush.

The character issue may in part have been an outgrowth of the "new journalism" popularized by author Tom Wolfe in the 1970s.[26] Contending that conventional journalism was sterile and stripped of color, Wolfe and others argued for a reporting style that expanded the definition of news and, novel-like, highlighted all the personal details of the newsmaker.

During his 2000 presidential campaign, George W. Bush promised to restore character and honor to the presidency. In recent years, the press has focused more and more on character issues rather than on policy proposals during presidential elections. (Photo courtesy: Jenny Warburg/Impact Visuals)

Then, too, reporters had witnessed the success of such books as Theodore H. White's *The Making of the President* series and Joe McGinniss's *The Selling of the President 1968*, which offered revealing, behind-the-scenes vignettes of the previous election's candidates.[27] Why not give readers and viewers this information before the election? the press reasoned. There was encouragement from academic quarters as well. "Look to character first" when evaluating and choosing among presidential candidates, wrote Duke University political science professor James David Barber in a widely circulated 1972 volume, *The Presidential Character* (see chapter 8).[28]

Communications scholar Roderick Hart believes that this shift in focus from issues to character is the result of the shift from newspaper to television news. Unlike print, television is a visual medium, which best portrays faces and images. As a result, voters who receive their political information from television are significantly more likely to rely on candidate traits (rather than issue positions) in casting their ballots than are voters who receive their political information primarily from newspapers.[29]

Whatever the precise historical origins of the character trend in reporting, it is undergirded by certain assumptions. First, the press sees that it has mainly replaced the political parties as the screening committee that winnows the field of candidates and filters out the weaker or more unlucky contenders. (This fact may be another reason to support the strengthening of the political parties. Politicians are in a much better position than the press to provide professional peer review of colleagues who are seeking the presidency.) Second, many journalists believe it necessary to tell people about any of a candidate's foibles that might affect his or her public performance. The press's third supposition is that it is giving the public what it wants and expects, more or less. Perhaps television has conditioned voters to think about the private lives of the rich and famous. The rules of television prominence now seem to apply to all celebrities equally, whether they reside in Hollywood or Washington. Perhaps more important, scandal sells papers and attracts television viewers.

Loosening of the Libel Law. Another factor permits the modern press to undertake character investigations. In the old days, a reporter would think twice about filing a story critical of a politician's character, and the editors probably would have killed the

ROOTS OF GOVERNMENT

THE PRESIDENCY IN THE TELEVISION AGE

We have come to expect most of our presidential candidates to be media-genic—that is, able to look good on television and use their media appearance to achieve their political ends. From their hairstyles and suits to their televised personas, candidates aim to please the unblinking eye of the camera. But what of the period when television was first emerging as a mass medium? How did the presidency adapt to this strange and forbidding new medium?

Television first became a phenomenon for the mass public at the end of Harry Truman's presidency in the early 1950s. While historians now rate Truman as a near-great president—that is, among our top fifteen presidents—he was clearly not cut out for the cathode ray tube. He was not a gifted public speaker, and his looks were pedestrian. Had television been universal in those days, it is doubtful that Truman could have been elected without great difficulty. Democrat Truman was replaced by Republican Eisenhower, but while their policies and outlooks were very different, they shared the same aversion to television. Eisenhower was, if anything, an even worse public speaker than Truman. While the former World War II general had a dazzling smile that inspired Americans to like and trust him (thus the famous slogan, "I like Ike"), he was particularly inarticulate when delivering official speeches. Eisenhower's inadequacy in communicating with the American people may have been one reason why, despite his enormous personal popularity, he was unable to pass the presidency along to his chosen successor, Richard Nixon, in 1960.

Television ultimately had its inevitable effect upon politics in 1960. In that famous presidential campaign, John F. Kennedy clearly loved the television camera, and it loved him. His vigor (he pronounced it "vigah," with a Massachusetts accent), the Kennedy family touch football games, his beautiful wife, and his handsome young family all combined to give Kennedy an intangible but powerful media edge against the jowly Richard Nixon. In the famous televised Nixon-Kennedy debate, which probably tipped an extremely close election in JFK's favor, Kennedy's tanned and handsome visage was as much a part of his victory as any argument he employed. In contrast to television viewers, many radio listeners, judging the performance without visual aid, actually thought that Nixon had won the debate. Kennedy's time in office was brief, but he set the style that has dominated the presidency in the media ever since. All presidents have tried to live up to the Kennedy standard, some with more success than others, but it is difficult to imagine a talented but TV-phobic president like Truman or Eisenhower coming to the fore of the American political system again.

story had the reporter been foolish enough to do so. The reason? Fear of a libel suit. (Recall from chapter 5 that libel is published defamation of character that unjustly injures a person's reputation.) The first question editors would ask about even an ambiguous or suggestive phrase about a public official was, "If we're sued, can you prove beyond a doubt what you've written?"

Such inhibitions were ostensibly lifted in 1964, when the Supreme Court ruled in ***New York Times Co. v. Sullivan***[30] that simply publishing a defamatory falsehood is not enough to justify a libel judgment. Henceforth a public official would have to prove "actual malice," a requirement extended three years later to all public figures, such as Hollywood stars and prominent athletes.[31] The Supreme Court declared that the First Amendment requires elected officials and candidates to prove that the publisher either believed the challenged statement was false or at least entertained serious doubts about its truth and acted recklessly in publishing it in the face of those doubts. The actual malice rule has made it very difficult for public figures to win libel cases.

Despite *Sullivan*, the threat of libel litigation (and its deterrent effect on the press) persists for at least two reasons. First, the *Sullivan* protections do little to reduce the expense of defending defamation claims. The monetary costs have increased enormously, as have the required commitments of reporters' and editors' time and energy. Small news organizations without the financial resources of a national network or the *New York Times* are sometimes reluctant to publish material that might invite

New York Times Co. v. Sullivan (1964)
Supreme Court decision ruling that simply publishing a defamatory falsehood is not enough to justify a libel judgment.

a lawsuit because the litigation costs could threaten their existence. The second reason for the continuing libel threat is a cultural phenomenon of heightened sensitivity to the harm that words can do to an individual's emotional tranquility. As a result, politicians are often more inclined to sue their press adversaries, even when success is unlikely.

But high costs and the politicians' propensity to sue cut both ways. The overall number of libel suits filed in recent years has dropped because plaintiffs also incur hefty legal expenses, and—perhaps more important—they have despaired of winning. Some news outlets have added another disincentive by filing countersuits charging their antagonists with bringing frivolous or nuisance actions against them.

In practice, then, the loosening of libel law has provided journalists with a safer harbor from liability in their reporting on elected officials and candidates. Whether it has truly diminished press self-censorship, especially for financially less well-endowed media outlets, is a more difficult question to answer. However, at least for the wealthy newspapers and networks, the libel laws are no longer as severe a restraint on the press as they once were.

The Question of Bias.   Whenever the media break an unfavorable story about a politician, the politician usually counters with a cry of "biased reporting"—a claim that the press has told an untruth, has told only part of the truth, or has reported facts out of the complete context of the event. Who is right? Are the news media biased? The answer is simple and unavoidable: Of course they are. Journalists are fallible human beings who inevitably have values, preferences, and attitudes galore—some conscious, others subconscious, but all reflected at one time or another in the subjects selected for coverage or the slant of that coverage. Given that the press is biased, it is important to know in what ways it is biased and when and how the biases are shown.

Truth be told, most journalists lean to the left. First of all, those in the relatively small group of professional journalists (not many more than 100,000, compared with more than 4 million teachers in the United States) are drawn heavily from the ranks of highly educated social and political liberals, as a number of studies, some conducted by the media themselves, have shown.[32] Journalists are substantially Democratic in party affiliation and voting habits, progressive and antiestablishment in political orientation, and well to the left of the general public on most economic, foreign policy, and social issues (such as abortion, affirmative action, gay rights, and gun control). Second, dozens of the most influential reporters and executives entered (or reentered) journalism after stints of partisan involvement in campaigns or government, and a substantial majority worked for Democrats.[33]

Third, this liberal press bias does indeed show up frequently on screen and in print. A study of reporting on the abortion issue, for example, revealed a clear slant to the pro side on network television news, matching in many ways the reporters' own abortion-rights views.[34]

Conservative bias exists in the media as well. One example is the world of AM radio talk shows. Some studies have indicated that liberal programs actually enjoy more airtime than conservative ones, but there is no question that conservatives host by far the most popular shows, as exemplified by Rush Limbaugh, G. Gordon Liddy (of Watergate infamy), and Oliver North (of the Iran–Contra affair). These radio hosts are the political equivalent of "shock jocks." They strive for controversy and attack liberals (especially the Clinton family and administration) with ferocious and inflammatory rhetoric.

Of course, these conservative hosts are within their First Amendment rights, and their programs only exist because an audience exists to support them. The Limbaugh show, for example, attracts millions of listeners every day and is tremendously profitable and successful in increasing voter preferences for Republican candidates, according to one analysis of panel-study data.[35] At the same time, others worry that these programs have a corrosive effect on political discourse and are simply unfair to their appointed targets. However, it must be said that these conservative organs provide some balance to the liberal orientation of much of the other media, especially in the evening news programs televised on the major networks and cable channels.

Longman
Participate.com
2.0
Participation
**Are the Media
Biased?**

WEB EXPLORATION
Compare news coverage on a particular news story for evidence of political bias. Go to
www.ablongman.com/oconnor

Other Sources of Bias.   From left to right, all of these media criticisms have some validity in different times and circumstances, in one media forum or another. But these critiques ignore some nonideological factors probably more essential to an understanding of press bias. Owing to competition and the reward structure of journalism, the deepest bias most political journalists have is the desire to get to the bottom of a good campaign story—which is usually negative news about a candidate. The fear of missing a good story, more than bias, leads all media outlets to develop the same headlines and to adopt the same slant.

A related nonideological bias is the effort to create a horse race where none exists. Newspeople, whose lives revolve around the current political scene, naturally want to add spice and drama, minimize their boredom, and increase their audience. Other human, not just partisan, biases are also at work. Whether the press likes or dislikes a candidate personally is often vital. Former Governor Bruce Babbitt and U.S. Representative Morris K. Udall, both wisecracking, straight-talking Arizona Democrats, were press favorites in their presidential bids (in 1988 and 1976, respectively), and both enjoyed favorable coverage. Richard M. Nixon, Jimmy Carter, and Gary Hart—all aloof politicians—were disliked by many reporters who covered them, and they suffered from a harsh and critical press. More recently, as House Speaker, Newt Gingrich was the favorite target of the press. Repeatedly, the stories newspaper editors decide to print about Gingrich when he was Speaker of the House cast him in a negative light. This treatment has contributed to his negative popularity ratings. Some research even suggests that claims of bias in the media are candidate strategies for dealing with the press. Bias claims are simply part of the dynamic between elected officials and reporters. If a candidate can plausibly and loudly decry bias in the media as the source of his negative coverage, for example, reporters might temper future negative stories or give the candidate favorable coverage to mitigate the calls of bias.[36]

Conservative talk-show host Rush Limbaugh became the symbol for the talk-radio phenomenon of the 1990s. In addition to his daily three-hour radio broadcast, Limbaugh also had a nightly syndicated television show. (Photo courtesy: Lennox McLendon/AP/Wide World Photos)

One other source of bias, or at least of non-objectivity, in the press is the increasing celebrity status of many people involved in reporting the news. In an age of media stardom and blurring boundaries between forms of entertainment, journalists in prominent media positions have unprecedented opportunities to attain fame and fortune, of which they often take full advantage. Already commanding multimillion-dollar salaries, journalists can often secure lucrative speaker's fees by addressing corporations, trade societies, private political organizations, universities, and media gatherings. Especially in the case of journalists with highly ideological perspectives, close involvement with wealthy or powerful special interest groups can blur the line between reporting on policy and issues and influencing them. Some journalists even find work as political consultants or members of government—which seems reasonable, given their prominence, abilities, and expertise, but which can become problematic when they move between spheres not once, but repeatedly. A good example of this troublesome revolving-door phenomenon is the case of Pat Buchanan, who has repeatedly and alternately enjoyed prominent positions in both media (as host of CNN's *Crossfire*) and government (as perennial presidential candidate). If American journalism is to retain the watertight integrity for which it is justly renowned, it is essential that key distinctions between private and media enterprise and conscientious public service continue to command our respect.

But does press bias affect election outcomes? Perhaps. Political scientist Eric Veblen shows that the net advantage that the *Manchester Union-Leader,* New Hampshire's most influential newspaper, provides its favored candidate can increase that candidate's vote share significantly. On the other hand, media darlings such as Bruce Babbitt and Morris Udall failed in their quest to become president, while those less popular with the media, such as Jimmy Carter and Richard Nixon, succeeded. Clearly, bias is not the be-all and end-all that critics on both the right and left often insist. Press tilt has a marginal to moderate effect, and it is but one piece in the media's new mosaic.[37]

THE MEDIA'S INFLUENCE ON THE PUBLIC

How much influence do the media have on the public? In most cases the press has surprisingly little effect. To put it bluntly, people tend to see what they want to see; that is, human beings will focus on parts of a report that reinforce their own attitudes and ignore parts that challenge their core beliefs. Most of us also selectively tune out and ignore reports that contradict our preferences in politics and other fields. Therefore, a committed Democrat will remember certain portions of a televised news program about a current campaign—primarily the parts that reinforce his or her own choice—and an equally committed Republican will recall very different sections of the report or remember the material in a way that supports the GOP position. In other words, most voters are not empty vessels into which the media can pour their own beliefs. This fact dramatically limits the ability of news organizations to sway public opinion.

Yet this is not the only view. Some political scientists find that the content of network television news accounts for a large portion of the volatility and change in policy preferences of Americans, when measured over relatively short periods of time.[38] These changes are called **media effects.** Let's examine how these media-influenced changes might occur.

First, reporting can sway people who are uncommitted and have no strong opinion in the first place. So, for example, the media has a greater influence on political independents than on strong partisans.[39] Indeed, many studies from the 1940s and 1950s, an era when partisanship was very strong, suggested that the media had no influence at all on public opinion. The last forty years, however, have seen the rapid decline in political partisanship,[40] thereby opening the door to greater media influence. On the other hand, the sort of politically unmotivated individual who is open to media effects is probably unlikely to vote in a given election, and therefore the media influence is of no particular consequence.

Second, the press has a much greater impact on topics far removed from the lives and experiences of its readers and viewers. News reports can probably shape public opinion about events in foreign countries fairly easily. Yet what the media say about domestic issues such as rising prices, neighborhood crime, or child rearing may have relatively little effect, because most citizens have personal experience of and well-formed ideas about these subjects.

Third, news organizations can help tell us what to think about, even if they cannot determine what we think. As mentioned earlier, the press often sets the agenda for government or a campaign by focusing on certain issues or concerns. For example, in the weeks following the Littleton, Colorado, school massacre in 1999, every national network devoted extensive coverage to the incident. Sure enough, concern about gun control, school safety, and cultural violence began to top the list of national problems considered most pressing by the public, as measured in opinion polls. Without the dramatic pictures and lavish attention that accompanied the shooting, it is doubtful that these issues would have risen so quickly to the forefront of the national agenda.

Longman
Participate.com
2.0
Visual Literacy
**Use of Media
by the
American
Public**

media effects
The influence of news sources on public opinion.

The media's premature call on Election Night in 2000 damaged the credibility of the news networks. (Photo courtesy: Wilfredo Lee/AP/Wide World Photos)

Thus, perhaps not so much in *how* they cover an event, but in *what* they choose to cover, the media make their effect felt. By deciding to focus on one event while ignoring another, the media can determine to a large extent the country's agenda, an awe-inspiring power.

The media's power to shape citizens' perceptions—though limited—can have important implications for the success of politicians. For example, voters' choice in presidential elections is often related to their assessments of the economy. In general, a healthy economy motivates voters to reelect the incumbent president, whereas a weak economy motivates voters to choose the challenger. Hence, if the media paint a consistently dismal picture of the economy, that picture may well hurt the incumbent president seeking reelection. In fact, political scientist Marc Hetherington convincingly shows that the media's relentlessly negative coverage of the economy in 1992 negatively shaped voters' retrospective assessments of the economy, which in turn helped lead to George Bush's defeat in the 1992 presidential election.[41]

Finally, in light of the debacle of the media coverage of election night in 2000, it is worth remarking on one very particular way in which the media can influence public behavior. On election night 2000, all the networks assigned Florida to Gore's list of wins fairly early in the evening. In fact, their call was extremely premature, and their actions had disastrous consequences for the dignity and credibility of both the networks and the election. Unbeknownst to most viewers, the networks had given Florida to Gore based purely on exit-poll predictions, before any Florida precincts had reported a single actual return, and the ensuing reversal, counter-reversal, and confusion—reminiscent of the famous *Chicago Daily Tribune's* "Dewey Defeats Truman"—have become legendary. (For a complete description of the media debacle, see chapter 13, "Election Results.") It was later discovered that a series of errors had contributed to the debacle, including: network over-eagerness to break the news; underestimating the number of absentee ballots in Florida; network projections based on inadequate poll data in key Florida cities; and flaws in the sampling techniques of exit-pollers in Florida. Many of these errors can be laid at the feet of Voter News Services, a company created and owned by the major networks and the Associated Press for the specific purpose of reporting uniform and reliable election results. For their part, VNS blames budget limitations for their inability to do their job accurately.[42]

In the end, the networks must shoulder the blame for hasty, premature reporting, with all the ensuing implications. Network executives have apologized repeatedly, and even if no legal constraints are imposed on their Election Night conduct, Americans can expect to see significant internal reforms in their future practice. At the very least, networks would be well advised to refrain from predicting elections until all polls have closed across the country.

HOW POLITICIANS USE THE MEDIA

President Clinton was an acknowledged master of media manipulation. Despite all of the negative coverage he endured over his long political career, or perhaps because of it, Clinton knows how to push the right media buttons. For example, in his initiative to encourage better race relations, which he labeled a prime goal of his second term, President Clinton staged a series of town meetings and televised encounters among people of all colors. Most of these events were carefully stage managed and resulted in little frank talk, something experts in the field of race relations believe is a necessity if real progress is to be made. Yet reams of positive publicity resulted; so, at least from a public relations perspective, the race initiative could be termed a success. The president was not always the leader in getting the media to focus attention on a particular issue, however. Indeed, often the relationship was exactly the opposite—the president *reacted* to attention given to an issue by the news media. This seemed to be especially true in foreign policy.[43]

Politics once again met policy on the day before President Clinton was scheduled to be impeached by the House of Representatives, when the president decided to launch the largest attack on Iraq since the Gulf War. While Clinton's military advisers urged this action, the timing was naturally highly suspicious to many on the Republican side of the aisle as well as in the press. Some went so far as to suggest that the president was following the script of a recent movie, *Wag the Dog,* in which a president attempts to detract attention from his sex scandal by starting a war. This was but the latest example of real-life politics imitating the art and entertainment of our time.

On a lighter note, Bill Clinton's most positive publicity in 1997 came when he decided to adopt a dog once his daughter Chelsea left for college. This became a major news focus for weeks, with the media highlighting each insignificant detail during a "slow news" period. Incredibly, the dog received more coverage over a month's time than any major national issue, according to the Center for Media and Public Affairs. Journalists from the major news organizations understood full well that they were being manipulated by the Buddy "story." A president and his dog, however, was an irresistible human interest account, sure to increase ratings or sell newspapers. Presidents are not, however, the only politicians to try to manipulate the press to advance their own ends. Recent research by political scientist Douglas Harris finds a growing inclination among recent United States House Speakers to use the media as a part of their overall legislative and public relations strategies. Speaker Newt Gingrich, for example, aggressively used the news media during his tenure in office. Harris says Gringrich's behavior is not an aberrant case—it was only part of the larger trend toward this type of behavior.[44]

Among recent politicians, John McCain rediscovered a brilliant political gambit: attract copious, free, and favorable media coverage by wooing the journalists themselves. McCain was so straightforward, candid, accessible, and generous with his time that the reporter pool collectively fell in love with him even as he out-endured them in the media game, exhausting their questions but never running short of answers. McCain even named his campaign bus "The Straight Talk Express," and it soon became famous for hosting regular, intimate, on-the-road interviews. McCain had a popular issue in campaign finance reform, but only his skill in delivering that message through the media enabled him to overcome tight funding and win the New Hampshire primary over George W. Bush in a landslide upset not anticipated in the polls.

VISUAL LITERACY
What's in an Ad?

During the 2000 presidential campaign, George W. Bush appeared on talk shows such as *Oprah Winfrey.* (Photo courtesy: Wilfredo Lee/AP/Wide World Photos)

The new president, George W. Bush, seems to have ingratiated himself with the media, too, at least at this early point in his tenure. While the media lean toward more liberal positions on social and economic issues, which might have made them more receptive to Al Gore, they seemed to like Bush as a person and at least in some news organizations extended softer treatment to him than to many of his opponents in the primaries and general election.

On some occasions, candidates and their aides will go on background to give trusted newspersons juicy morsels of negative information about rivals. **On background**—meaning that none of the news can be attributed to the source—is one of several journalistic devices used to solicit and elicit information that might otherwise never come to light. **Deep background** is another such device; whereas background talks can be attributed to unnamed senior officials, deep background news must be completely unsourced, with the reporter giving the reader no hint about the origin of the information. An even more drastic form of obtaining information is the **off-the-record** discussion, in which nothing the official says may be printed. (If a reporter can obtain the same information elsewhere, however, he or she is free to publish it.) By contrast, in an **on-the-record** session, such as a formal press conference, every word an official utters can be printed—and used against that official. It is no wonder that office holders often prefer the nonpublishable alternatives!

Clearly, these rules are necessary for reporters to do their basic job—informing the public. But ironically, the same rules keep the press from fully informing their readers and viewers. Every public official knows that journalists are pledged to protect the confidentiality of their sources, and therefore the rules can sometimes be used to an official's own benefit.

on background
A term for when sources are not included in a news story.

deep background
Information gathered for news stories that must be completely unsourced.

off the record
Term applied to information gathered for a news story that cannot be used at all.

on the record
Term applied to information gathered for a news story that can be used and cited.

GOVERNMENT REGULATION OF THE ELECTRONIC MEDIA

Not only do politicians manipulate the media, but the U.S. government also regulates the electronic component of the media. Unlike radio or television, the print media are exempt from most forms of government regulation, although even print media must not violate community standards for obscenity, for instance. There are two reasons for this unequal treatment. First, the airwaves used by the electronic media are considered public property; they are leased by the federal government to private broadcasters. Second, those airwaves are in limited supply, and without some regulation, the nation's many radio and television stations would interfere with one another's frequency signals. It was not, in fact, the federal government but rather private broadcasters, frustrated by the numerous instances in which signal jamming occurred, that initiated the call for government regulation in the early days of the electronic media. Newspapers, of course, are not subject to these technical considerations.

The first government regulation of the electronic media came in 1927, when Congress enacted the Federal Radio Act, which established the Federal Radio Commission (FRC) and declared the airwaves to be public property. In addition, the act required that all broadcasters be licensed by the FRC. In 1934 the Federal Communications Commission (FCC) replaced the FRC as the electronic media regulatory body. The FCC is composed of five members, of whom not more than three can be from the same political party. These members are selected by the president for five-year terms on an overlapping basis. Because the FCC is shielded from direct, daily control by the president or Congress—although both have influence over the FCC commissioners—it is an independent regulatory agency (see chapter 9). In addition to regulating public and commercial radio and television, the FCC oversees telephone, telegraph, satellite, and foreign communications in the United States.

POINT/COUNTERPOINT

SHOULD TELEVISION NETWORKS PROVIDE FREE CAMPAIGN ADVERTISING?

In an age when the majority of Americans learn more about presidential candidates from Jay Leno and Jon Stewart than Tom Brokaw and Dan Rather, and presidential candidates and their parties pay over $160 million on largely negative political ads, reforming the way political information is delivered is becoming increasingly important. As the costs of campaigns rise dramatically despite fewer and fewer Americans feeling connected to the system, one reform proposal that has gained recognition is either convincing or forcing by government mandate network television companies to provide free airtime for candidates to discuss the issues of the elections. Opponents of free broadcast campaign advertising worry about the First Amendment implications of such a proposal. Should television networks provide free campaign advertising? Let's examine these two points of view.

Championed by public interest organizations like the Alliance for Better Campaigns, the call to increase political coverage and candidate-centered discourse or provide free airtime for candidate commercials is grounded in the fact that the airwaves belong to the public. Television companies are becoming very wealthy from campaign commercials, yet provide very little for the public good in return. In addition to the $160 million taken in from the 2000 presidential race, stations are estimated to have received an additional $500 million to $800 million from political ads in other federal, state, and local races, while airing on average sixty-four seconds of candidate-centered discourse per night. According to the proponents of free airtimes, increased information about the candidates and issues is essential to effective political participation. News networks focus too much on the horse race aspect of campaigns, describing who's leading in the polls but not where the candidates stand on the issues. The networks own the most powerful information medium in the United States, and they are not living up to their responsibility to inform the public.

The network stations largely oppose government regulation of how much political discourse they air. They claim that mandating stations to show a certain amount of political coverage violates the First Amendment and imposes on their civil liberties. Many stations claim that they are providing more than enough coverage of candidates and campaigns—the problem is that people are not interested in politics. Stations point to studies that show their viewers would much rather see the upcoming weather forecast than a segment on politics. In addition, because the networks and the stations are private businesses, they are therefore in the business of making money. In an age when exciting big-budget programs like *Who Wants to Be a Millionaire* and *Survivor* bring in high advertising revenue and dominate the water-cooler conversation in the workplace, providing free airtime to candidates, even if it is to just the two major-party candidates, would cost them millions of dollars. This is a loss they are obviously less than willing to take, especially knowing that the majority of Americans would not tune in to watch the candidates or commercials anyway.

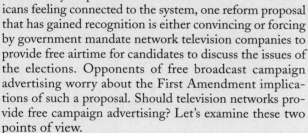

What do you think? Do the major networks have an obligation to the public to air candidate commercials or provide more candidate-centered discourse on the news?
Go to www.ablongman.com/oconnor

In 1996 Congress passed the sweeping Telecommunications Act, deregulating whole segments of the electronic media. The goal of the legislation was to break down the barriers required by federal and state laws and by the legal settlement that broke up the AT&T/Bell monopoly in 1984, which separated local phone service, long-distance service, and cable television service. The hope was that such deregulation and increased competition will create cheaper and better programming options for consumers and increase the global competitiveness of U.S. telecommunications firms. Under the new law, consumers might soon receive phone service from their cable provider, television programming from their local phone company, or local phone service from their long-distance phone provider. Besides more flexible service options, the legislation is expected to spur the development of new products and services such as unlimited movie selections, interactive television, and advanced computer networking that would permit more people to work from their homes.

The core of the new legislation is the federal preemption of state and local laws that grant monopolies to local telephone carriers. The seven "baby Bells," the regional phone companies that have been allowed to monopolize local telephone service since the 1984 breakup of AT&T, would be required to allow competitors to use their local networks. In return for opening their local networks to competition, the regional Bells would be allowed to enter the long-distance service market, from which they have been barred since the AT&T breakup.

There are also significant changes in the regulations for private ownership of broadcast stations. First, there is no longer a cap on how many FM and AM stations a single company can own. In the 1950s, under the 7-7-7 rule, companies were limited to seven each of television, AM, and FM stations that they could own throughout the nation. By the 1990s, however, this limit had been progressively raised to twelve television stations and twenty each of FM and AM stations. Despite eliminating the cap, there are still limits on how many stations any one firm can own in each market. The FCC will examine on a case-by-case basis whether an owner should be allowed to have two television stations in the same local market, which is currently prohibited.

The legislation has provoked criticism by civil libertarian groups that objected to provisions designed to curb "cyberpornography." The act would ban the dissemination of "indecent" material on the Internet and online services. Indecency is a very broad legal standard that includes use of profanity. While it has been applied to broadcasting in a limited way, it has not been used in recent years as a standard for written material. The act also requires all large-screen televisions to include built-in "V-chips" that permit parents to block objectionable material they do not wish their family to view.

Content Regulation

content regulation
Governmental attempts to regulate the electronic media.

equal time rule
The rule that requires broadcast stations to sell campaign air time equally to all candidates if they choose to sell it to any.

fairness doctrine
Rule in effect from 1949 to 1985 requiring broadcasters to cover events adequately and to present contrasting views on important public issues.

The government also subjects the electronic media to substantial **content regulation** that, again, does not apply to the print media. Charged with ensuring that the air waves "serve the public interest, convenience, and necessity," the FCC has attempted to promote equity in broadcasting. For example, the **equal time rule** requires that broadcast stations sell campaign air time equally to all candidates if they choose to sell it to any, which they are under no obligation to do. An exception to this rule is a political debate: Stations may exclude from this event less well-known and minor-party candidates.

Until 2000, broadcasters also were required to give candidates the opportunity to respond to personal attacks and political endorsements by the station under FCC rules. In October 2000, however, a federal court of appeals found these rules, long attacked by broadcasters as having a chillling effect on free speech, to be unconstitutional when the FCC was unable to justify these regulations to its satisfaction.

Perhaps the most controversial FCC regulation was the **fairness doctrine.** Implemented in 1949 and in effect until 1985, the fairness doctrine required broadcasters to be "fair" in their coverage of news events—that is, they had to cover the events adequately and present contrasting views on important public issues. Many broadcasters disliked this rule, however, claiming that fairness is simply too difficult to define and that the rule abridged their First Amendment freedoms. They also argued that it ultimately forced broadcasters to decrease coverage of controversial issues out of fear of a deluge of requests for air time from interest groups involved in each matter.

In a hotly debated 1985 decision, the FCC, without congressional consent, abolished the fairness doctrine, arguing that the growth of the electronic media in the United States during the preceding forty years had created enough diversity among the stations to render unnecessary the ordering of diversity within them. In 1986 a federal circuit court of appeals vindicated the FCC decision, holding that the FCC did not need congressional approval to abolish the rule. Seeking to counter the FCC's decision,

GLOBAL POLITICS

MEDIA FREEDOM

What role the media plays in politics is partly determined by how free the media are. In 2000, Freedom House, an independent civil liberties organization, rated the degree of media freedom in 186 countries of the world. Using as criteria the degree of government ownership of the media, pressures on media, and actual violations of media freedom, the organization rated countries on a 100-point scale. The lower the score, the freer the media is from government interference. Countries rated between 0 and 30 are considered to have free media, those between 31 and 60 partly free, and those between 61 and 100 not free.

The United States in this respect is in good company. All industrial democracies are considered to have free presses, although they vary in degree. The U.S. and German media are rated freest among the group. State restrictions on the media are highest in Italy and France, which are close to the partly free threshold. The press in Russia, Mexico, and Indonesia are considered partly free because recent trends toward independent, competitive media institutions still face governments that control significant media resources and which continue to try to control the content of private media.

Restrictions on the media vary. All the industrial democracies have public media outlets, most of which are more visible and influential than National Public Radio or the Public Broadcasting Service are in the United States, but the degree of government editorial control varies. In the late 1990s, Japan and the United Kingdom adopted freedom of information acts, but restrictions on the press remain. The British, American, and German governments have passed legislation that makes certain kinds of media communications illegal (i.e., libel in Britain, Internet pornography in the United States, and hate speech and Nazi propaganda in Germany). The Russian government includes a ministry, directly responsible to the president, which supervises the media. China ranks near the bottom of Freedom House's ratings, with near universal control over media outlets and routine harassment of journalists critical of the government.

Media self-censorship is a problem in many countries. Corporate ownership of media outlets in Italy and the United States is acknowledged as potentially restrictive because corporate-owned media outlets are tempted to try to suppress news that is critical of their owners. Mexico's Institutional Revolutionary Party (PRI) owns the major television station, allowing it to dominate the country's main news outlet. The press club system in Japan is an example of self-censorship in a society generally considered to have a free press. Nearly every government agency has a press club, access to which is limited by the agencies themselves. Press clubs exercise informal restraints on the media because they control the flow of official information and because they can deny membership to journalists who are too critical of the agency. This can have an impact on the coverage of Japanese government. In contrast to the sensational coverage of Britain's royal family, similar coverage is absent in Japan in no small part because the Imperial Household Agency manages the flow of information about the imperial family and denies tabloid journalists access to its press club.

Freedom House Scores for Media Freedom

Country	Freedom House Score (1–100)	Freedom House Rating
Canada	14	Free
China	80	Not Free
France	24	Free
Germany	13	Free
Indonesia	49	Partly Free
Italy	27	Free
Japan	19	Free
Mexico	50	Partly Free
Russia	60	Partly Free
United Kingdom	20	Free
United States	**13**	**Free**

Source: Freedom House, *Press Freedom Survey* 2000. http://freedomhouse.org/pfs2000/reports.html.

Congress attempted to write the fairness doctrine into law, which, if successful, would have forced the FCC to implement it. Although both the House and the Senate passed the bill, President Reagan temporarily ended the controversy by vetoing it, citing his First Amendment concerns about government regulation of the news media.

Longman
Participate.com 2.0
Comparative
Comparing
News Media

Political news coverage often involves "talking heads" in the studio and on the spot press conferences. On the left, Sam Donaldson and Cokie Roberts interview Representatives F. James Sensenbrenner (R–Wisc.) and Asa Hutchinson (R–Ark.) with commentator George Will on ABC's *This Week,* one of the many political talk shows that celebrate the "talking heads." On the right, Helen Thomas (center) veteran UPI correspondent and dean of the White House press corps, looks on as Sam Donaldson questions White House Press Secretary Mike McCurry. (Photos courtesy: left, © 2000 ABC Inc.; right, Susan Walsh/AP/Wide World photos)

The abolition of the fairness doctrine has by no means ended debate over its merit, however. Proponents, still trying to reinstate the doctrine, argue that its elimination results in a reduction of quality programming on public issues. In their view deregulation means more advertisements, soap operas, and situation comedies wasting airtime and leaving less room for public discourse on important matters. Opponents of the fairness doctrine, on the other hand, continue to call for decreased regulation, arguing that the electronic media should be as free as the print media—especially because the electronic media are now probably more competitive than are the print media.

Censorship

The media in the United States, while not free of government regulation, enjoy considerably more liberty than do their counterparts in Great Britain. One of the world's oldest democracies, Great Britain nonetheless owns that nation's main electronic medium, the British Broadcasting Company (BBC). And the BBC, along with the privately owned media, is subjected to unusually strict regulation on the publication of governmental secrets. For example, the sweeping Official Secrets Acts of 1911 makes it a criminal offense for a Briton to publish any facts, material, or news collected in that person's capacity as a public minister or civil servant. The act was invoked most recently when the British government banned the publication of *Spy Catcher,* a 1987 novel written by Peter Wright, a former British intelligence officer, who undoubtedly collected much of the book's information while on the job.

In the United States, only government officials can be prosecuted for divulging classified information; no such law applies to journalists. Nor can the government, except under extremely rare and confined circumstances, impose prior restraints on the press—that is, the government cannot censor the press. This principle was clearly established in *New York Times* v. *United States* (1971).[45] In this case the Supreme Court ruled that the government could not prevent publication by the *New York Times* of the Pentagon Papers, classified government documents about the Vietnam War that had been stolen, photocopied, and sent to the *Times* and the *Washington Post* by Daniel Ellsberg, an antiwar activist. "Only a free and unrestrained press can effectively expose deception in the government," Justice Hugo Black wrote in a concurring opinion for the Court. "To find that the President has 'inherent power' to halt the publication of news by resort to the courts would wipe out the first Amendment."

To assist the media in determining what is and is not publishable, Great Britain provides a system called D-notice, which allows journalists to submit questionable material to a review committee before its publication. But D-notice has not quelled argument over media freedom in the United Kingdom. Indeed, the debate came to the fore during the 1982 Falkland Islands war between Great Britain and Argentina, when it centered on questions of how much information the public had a right to know and whether the media should remain neutral in covering a war in which the nation is involved. Once again, however, the British government prevailed in arguing for continued strict control of the media, declaring, "There can be sound military reasons for withholding the whole truth from the public domain, [or] for using the media to put out 'misinformation.' "[46]

Similar questions and arguments arose in the United States during the 1991 Persian Gulf War. Reporters were upset that the military was not forthcoming about events on and off the battlefield, while some Pentagon officials and many persons in the general public accused the press of telling the enemy too much in their dispatches. Unlike the case in Great Britain, however, the U.S. government had little recourse but to attempt to isolate offending reporters by keeping them away from the battlefield. Even this maneuver was highly controversial and very unpopular with news correspondents because it directly interfered with their job of reporting the news.

Such arguments are an inevitable part of the landscape in a free society. Whatever their specific quarrels with the press, most Americans would probably prefer that the media tell them too much rather than not enough. Totalitarian societies have a tame journalism, after all, so press excesses may be the price of unbridled freedom. Without question, a free press is of incalculable value to a nation, as the recent revolution in the former Soviet Union has shown. The 1991 coup against then Soviet President Mikhail Gorbachev failed in part because the coup leaders could not smother the public's continued desire for freedom, stoked by the relatively uncensored television and print journalism that existed in the final years of Gorbachev's rule.

In the United States, freedom is secured mainly by the Constitution's basic guarantees and institutions. But freedom is also ensured by the thousands of independently owned and operated newspapers, magazines, and broadcast stations. The cacophony of media voices may often be off-key and harsh, but its very lack of orchestration enables us all to continue to sing the sweet song of freedom.

Continuity & Change

How TV Transformed Our Politics

Whether one views television as good or evil, this technological marvel of the twentieth century has transformed all aspects of American society, especially government and politics. When televisions were first mass-produced in the late 1940s and early 1950s, television news was primitive. Broadcasts were limited to fifteen minutes or less, announcers simply read headlines from the Associated Press, and there were frequently no pictures or moving images of any sort used in the broadcast. The first half-hour broadcast appeared only in the early 1960s, hosted on CBS by anchor Walter Cronkite, and television remained very stilted and entirely respectful toward public figures.

As with American society, Vietnam and Watergate transformed television news coverage of politics from an entirely positive, passive, and boring project into an agent of change. The key broadcast in all of television's early years may have occurred in 1968, when Cronkite traveled to Vietnam after the Tet Offensive, in which North Vietnamese forces surprised Americans at home and abroad with widespread military offensives. Cronkite covered this crucial psychological setback and critically scrutinized President Lyndon B. Johnson's claim that there was "light at the end of the tunnel" (that is, a clear prospect of military and political success in

(continued)

Vietnam). Cronkite all but concluded that there was little hope for victory, and Johnson himself, sitting in the White House and watching Cronkite's report, turned to an aide and said, "We've lost the war, now that we've lost Walter Cronkite."

The phenomenal growth of cable television during the past three decades has given new competition to the major commercial television networks (ABC, CBS, NBC, and Fox). With over half of all U.S. households now wired for cable television, the networks' share of the national television audience has declined steadily. Today, fewer than six in every ten viewers are watching network stations during prime-time hours, compared with the networks' near-monopoly thirty years ago. In addition to increased competition, the rise of cable television has brought with it a new breed of political talk show. Cable talk shows like *Larry King Live, Rivera Live, Hardball, Beltway Boys,* and *Capitol Gang* provide near-constant media scrutiny and commentary on the latest political events. While many of the cable news shows have come and gone in this highly competitive market, the fast-moving and combative format of these shows appears here to stay.

As recent events remind us, TV also has a sometimes disastrous ability to interfere with political events even as they are happening. The Gulf War and the Balkan conflict showed us that information released to the media by the American armed forces and then broadcast to the public during a military conflict can sometimes provide the enemy with more current and accurate information than their own intelligence services. The instantaneous live reporting of incoming election returns has long been feared to bias the decisions of voters who see election coverage from polls in other time zones before they have cast their own ballots—whether by influencing those voters to vote strategically in response to emerging poll trends, or by misleading voters into thinking that the election has already been decided and

that their vote could no longer make a difference. When an election runs as close as it did in 2000, even such small factors can make a huge difference in the final outcome. TV is a powerful tool for communications, but it must be managed with discretion.

One of the vital differences between television's conventional role and its role in the future will undoubtedly be the growth of interactive systems—systems that allow two-way communication between the sender and the consumer. As computer and cable technologies merge in the future, interactive systems will permit viewers to immediately voice their opinions regarding breaking news and policy issues. Potentially, such arrangements could lead to televised town meetings on issues of general interest. (Both Ross Perot and Bill Clinton talked about holding electronic "town halls" in the future.) In a very real sense, not only does this technological development have the potential to change the way politics is covered in this country, but it might also actually help change the role of citizenship—making television viewers more active political players in American democracy.

1. A recent trend in American media has been the concentration of commercial and cable television ownership into the hands of a relatively small number of corporate owners. Do you believe that this trend is likely to continue in the future and, if so, what are the implications for media coverage of politics?

2. Is the likely increased interactivity of the media in the future necessarily a positive trend? What are some of the negative consequences of injecting the public voice more directly into the political process? Do the potential benefits outweigh the likely costs?

Cast Your Vote. What role do you think media should play in the political process? To cast your vote, go to **www.ablongman.com/oconnor**

SUMMARY

The simple words of the Constitution's First Amendment, that "Congress shall make no law . . . abridging the freedom of speech, or of the press," have shaped the American republic as much as or more than any others in the Constitution and its amendments. With the Constitution's sanction, as interpreted by the Supreme Court over two centuries, a vigorous and highly competitive press has emerged. In this chapter we examined the following topics:

1. **The American Press of Yesteryear**
   Journalism—the process and profession of collecting and disseminating the news—was introduced in America in 1690 with the publication of the nation's

first newspaper. Until the mid- to late 1800s, when independent papers first appeared, newspapers were partisan; that is, they openly supported a particular party. In the twentieth century, first radio in the late 1920s and then television in the late 1940s revolutionized the transmission of political information, leading to more candidate-centered, entrepreneurial politics in the age of television.

2. **The Contemporary Media Scene**
   The modern media consist of print press (many thousands of daily and weekly newspapers, magazines, newsletters, and journals) and electronic media (tele-

vision and radio stations and networks as well as computerized information services). In the United States the media are relatively uncontrolled and free to express many views, although that has not always been the case here and remains a problem in other countries.

3. **How the Media Cover Politicians and Government**
The media have shifted focus in recent years, first toward investigative journalism in the Watergate era and then toward character issues. While there are useful aspects to both kinds of coverage, excesses have occurred, especially unnecessary invasions of privacy and the publication and broadcast of unsubstantiated rumor.

4. **The Media's Influence on the Public**
Studies have shown that by framing issues for debate and discussion, the media have clear and recognizable effects on voters. For example, people who are relatively uninformed about a topic can be more easily swayed by press coverage about that topic. However, in most cases the press has surprisingly little effect on people's views.

5. **How Politicians Use the Media**
Politicians constantly try to manipulate and influence press coverage. One method many officials use is passing along tips (information) on an off-the-record basis in the hopes of currying favor or producing stories favorable to their interests. However regrettable the manipulation might be at times, it is an unavoidable part of the political process.

6. **Government Regulation of the Electronic Media**
The press is a business—big business, in the case of the networks and large newspapers—and as such it is regulated to some extent by the government. The government has gradually loosened its restrictions on the media. Officially, the Federal Communications Commission (FCC) licenses and regulates broadcasting stations, although in practice it has been quite willing to grant and renew licenses, and recently it has reduced its regulation of licensees. Additionally, cable transmission was first allowed on a widespread basis in the late 1970s, from whence it has grown into a large supplier of information. Finally, content regulations have loosened, with the courts using a narrow interpretation of libel. All of these trends toward deregulation were accelerated by the enactment of the Telecommunications Act of 1996, which further deregulated the communications landscape.

KEY TERMS

affiliates, p. 563
content regulation, p. 578
deep background, p.576
electronic media, p. 559
equal time rule, p. 578
fairness doctrine, p. 578
media effects, p. 573

muckraking, p. 558
network, p. 562
New York Times Co. v. *Sullivan*
    (1964),p. 570
off the record, p. 576
on background, p. 576
on the record, p. 576

press briefing, p. 565
press conference, p. 565
press release, p. 565
print press, p. 559
wire service, p. 563
yellow journalism, p. 558

SELECTED READINGS

Arterton, F. Christopher. *Media Politics: The News Strategies of Presidential Campaigns.* Lexington, Mass.: Lexington Books, 1984.

Bartels, Larry A. "Message Received: The Political Impact of Media Exposure." *American Political Science Review* (June 1993).

Berkman, Ronald, and Laura W. Kitch. *Politics in the Media Age.* New York: McGraw-Hill, 1986.

Broder, David S. *Behind the Front Page.* New York: Simon & Schuster, 1987.

Cook, Timothy E. *Making Laws and Making News: Media Strategies in the U.S. House of Representatives.* Washington, D.C.: Brookings Institution, 1989.

Crouse, Timothy. *The Boys on the Bus.* New York: Ballantine, 1973.

Entman, Robert M. *Democracy Without Citizens: Media and the Decay of American Politics.* New York: Oxford University Press, 1989.

Garment, Suzanne. *Scandal.* New York: Random House, 1991.

Graber, Doris A. *Mass Media and American Politics,* 5th ed. Washington, D.C.: CQ Press, 1996.

————. *Media Power in Politics,* 3rd ed. Washington, D.C.: CQ Press, 1992.

Grossman, Michael Baruch, and Martha Joynt Kumar. *Portraying the President: The White House and the News Media.* Baltimore, Md.: Johns Hopkins University Press, 1981.

Hamilton, John Maxwell. *Hold the Press: The Inside Story on Newspapers.* Baton Rouge: Louisiana State University Press, 1996.

Iyengar, Shanto, and Donald R. Kinder. *News That Matters.* Chicago: University of Chicago Press, 1987.

Kerbel, Matthew Robert. *Remote and Controlled: Media Politics in a Cynical Age.* Boulder, Colo.: Westview Press, 1995.

Kurtz, Howard. *Media Circus: The Trouble with America's Newspapers.* New York: Times Books, 1993.

Lichter, S. Robert, Stanley Rothman, and Linda S. Lichter. *The Media Elite.* Bethesda, Md.: Adler & Adler, 1986.

Linsky, Martin. *Impact: How the Press Affects Federal Policymaking.* New York: Norton, 1986.

Patterson, Thomas E. *Out of Order.* New York: Vintage, 1993.

Press, Charles, and Kenneth VerBurg. *American Politicians and Journalists.* Glenview, Ill.: Scott, Foresman, 1988.

Ranney, Austin. *Channels of Power: The Impact of Television on American Politics.* New York: Basic Books, 1983.

Sabato, Larry J. *Feeding Frenzy: How Attack Journalism Has Transformed American Politics,* updated ed. New York: Macmillan/The Free Press, 1993.

Stephens, Mitchell. *A History of News: From the Drum to the Satellite.* New York: Viking, 1989.

West, Darrell M. *Air Wars: Television Advertising in Election Campaigns, 1952–1992.* Washington, D.C.: CQ Press, 1993.

Zaller, John. *The Nature and Origins of Mass Opinion.* Cambridge, England: Cambridge University Press, 1992.

NOTES

1. See Mitchell Stephens, *A History of News: From the Drum to the Satellite* (New York: Viking, 1989).

2. Charles Press and Kenneth VerBurg, *American Politicians and Journalists* (Glenview, Ill.: Scott, Foresman, 1988), 8–10.

3. See Merrill D. Peterson, *Thomas Jefferson and the New Nation* (New York: Oxford University Press, 1970), 185–87.

4. For a delightful rendition of this episode, see Shelley Ross, *Fall from Grace* (New York: Ballantine, 1988), ch. 12.

5. The name strictly derived from printing the comic strip "Yellow Kid" in color.

6. Doris A. Graber, *Mass Media and American Politics,* 3rd ed. (Washington, D.C.: CQ Press, 1989), 12.

7. See Thomas C. Leonard, *The Power of the Press: The Birth of American Political Reporting* (New York: Oxford University Press, 1986), ch. 7.

8. Richard L. Rubin, *Press, Party, and Presidency* (New York: Norton, 1981), 38–39.

9. Stephen Bates, *If No News, Send Rumors* (New York: St. Martin's Press, 1989), 185.

10. Barbara Matusow, "Washington's Journalism Establishment," *Washingtonian* 23 (February 1989): 94–101, 265–70.

11. See Eleanor Randolph, "Extra! Extra! Who Cares?" *The Washington Post* (April 1, 1990): C1, 4.

12. Sunday newspapers are exceptions to the trend. More than 100 new Sunday papers were created in the 1980s, and Sunday circulation as a whole has increased 25 percent since 1970.

13. Harold W. Stanley and Richard G. Niemi, *Vital Statistics on American Politics* (Washington, D.C.: CQ Press, 1988), Table 2–8, 58.

14. See Evans Witt, "Here, There, and Everywhere: Where Americans Get Their News," *Public Opinion* 6 (August/September 1983): 45–48; and June O. Yum and Kathleen E. Kendall, "Sources of Political Information in a Presidential Primary Campaign," *Journalism Quarterly* 65 (Spring 1988): 148–51, 177.

15. This was the fundamental conclusion of Shanto Iyengar and Donald R. Kinder, *News That Matters* (Chicago: University of Chicago Press, 1987).

16. L. Peer and B. Chestnut, "Deciphering Media Independence: The Gulf War Debate in Television and Newspaper News," *Political Communication* 12 (January 1995): 81–95.

17. Matthew Baum and Samuel Kernell, "Has Cable Ended the Golden Age of Television?" *American Political Science Review* 93 (June 1999): 99–114.

18. M. Just, T. Buhr, and A. Crigler, "Voice, Substance, and Cynicism in Presidential Campaign Media," *Political Communication* 16 (January 1999): 25–44.

19. Ben Bagdikan, *The Media Monopoly,* 4th ed. (Boston: Beacon Press, 1992).

20. Timothy E. Cook and Lyn Ragsdale, "The President and the Press: Negotiating Newsworthiness at the White House," in Michael Nelson, ed., *The Presidency and the Political System,* 5th ed. (Washington D.C.: Congressional Quarterly Press, 1998), 323.

21. Thomas Patterson, *Out of Order* (New York: Vintage, 1994).

22. Harold W. Stanley and Richard G. Niemi, *Vital Statistics on American Politics,* 4th ed. (Washington, D.C.: CQ Press, 1994), 28.

23. Timothy E. Cook, "Press Secretaries and Media Strategies in the House of Representatives: Deciding Whom to Pursue," *American Journal of Political Science* 32 (November 1998): 1047–69.

24. John Hibbing and Elizabeth Theiss-Morse, *Congress as Public Enemy: Political Attitudes Toward American Political Institutions* (New York: Cambridge University Press, 1995).

25. American Society of Newspaper Editors, *The Changing Face of the Newsroom* (Washington, D.C.: ASNE, May 1989), 29.

26. See Tom Wolfe, *The New Journalism* (New York: Harper & Row, 1973), especially 9–32.

27. The first and best in White's series was *The Making of the President 1960* (New York: Atheneum, 1961). See also Joe McGinniss, *The Selling of the President 1968* (New York: Trident, 1969).

28. See James David Barber, *The Presidential Character* (Englewood Cliffs, N.J.: Prentice Hall, 1972), 445.

29. Roderick Hart, *Seducing America: How Television Charms the Modern Voter* (New York: Oxford University Press, 1995).

30. 376 U.S. 254 (1964). See also Steven Pressman, "Libel Law: Finding the Right Balance," *Editorial Research Reports* 2 (August 18, 1989): 462–71.

31. *Curtis Publishing Co.* v. *Butts,* 388 U.S. 130 (1967); *Associated Press* v. *Walker,* 388 U.S. 130 (1967).

32. American Society of Newspaper Editors, "The Changing Face," 33; William Schneider and I. A. Lewis, "Views on the News," *Public Opinion* 8 (August/September 1985): 6–11, 58–59; and S. Robert Lichter, Stanley Rothman, and Linda S. Lichter, *The Media Elite* (Bethesda, Md.: Adler & Adler, 1986).

33. See Dom Bonafede, "Crossing Over," *National Journal* 21 (January 14, 1989): 102; Richard Harwood, "Tainted Journalists," *The Washington Post* (December 4, 1988): L6; Charles Trueheart, "Trading Places: The Insiders Debate," *The Washington Post* (January 4, 1989): D1, 19; and Kirk Victor, "Slanted Views," *National Journal* 20 (June 4, 1988): 1512.

34. "*Roe* v. *Webster,*" *Media Monitor* 3 (October 1989): 1–6. See also David Shaw, "Abortion and the Media" (four-part series), *The Los Angeles Times* (July 1, 1990): A1, 50–51; (July 2, 1990): A1, 20; (July 3, 1990): A1, 22–23; (July 4, 1990): A1, 28–29.

35. David C. Barker, "Rushed Decisions: Political Talk Radio and Vote Choice, 1994–1996," *Journal of Politics* (May, 1999): 527–39.

36. David Domke, David P. Fan, Dhavan V. Shah, and Mark D. Watts, "The Politics of Conservative Elites and the 'Liberal Media' Argument," *Journal of Communication* 49 (Fall 1999): 35–58.

37. Eric Veblen, *The Manchester Union-Leader in New Hampshire Elections* (Hanover, N.H.: University of New England Press, 1975).

38. Benjamin I. Page, Robert Y. Shapiro, and Glenn R. Dempsey, "What Moves Public Opinion?" *American Political Science Review* 81 (March 1987): 23–44.

39. Iyengar and Donald Kinder, *News That Matters*.

40. Martin P. Wattenberg, *The Decline of American Political Parties, 1952–1994* (Cambridge, Mass.: Harvard University Press, 1996).

41 Marc Hetherington, "The Media's Role in Forming Voters' National Economic Evaluations in 1992," *American Journal of Political Science* 40 (May 1996): 372–95.

42. For a thorough and intelligent discussion of the chain of errors in the media coverage, see Howard Kurtz, "Errors Plague Election Night Polling Service," *The Washington Post* (December 22, 2000).

43. George C. Edwards III and Dan Wood, "Who Influences Whom? The President, Congress, and the Media," *American Political Science Review* 93 (June 1999): 327–44.

44. Douglas B. Harris, "The Rise of the Public Speakership," *Political Science Quarterly* 113 (Summer 1998): 193–212.

45. 403 U.S. 713 (1971).

46. House of Commons, Defense Committee, *The Handling of the Press and Public Information During the Falklands Conflict* (London: Her Majesty's Stationery Office, 1982).

16 Interest Groups

How many offers for a new credit card at a "special introductory rate" have you received this year? If you are a traditional first-year college student, maybe not many. But, by the end of your college career, you will probably get as many as one hundred. In all likelihood, promoters even had tables set up during your college orientation. Open an account, get a free airplane ticket, water bottle, or watch. In the past few years, credit card companies have extended credit to millions of unemployed college students or ones with limited incomes. Seventy percent of all four-year college undergraduates have at least one credit card; from 1990 to 1995, the average credit card debt for college students rose from $900 to $2,100.[1]

After a few years of heavy spending, many students don't have enough money to pay back the credit card companies. To remedy this, those same companies are lobbying Congress intensely to pass bankruptcy laws to make it easier for them to collect the money charged by those who should not have been extended credit in the first place.

According to Senator Russ Feingold (D–Wisc.), bankruptcy reform "has become special-interest legislation" and campaign money is "a central component of the lobbying effort."[2] In 1998, the National Consumer Bankruptcy Coalition, an industry lobbying group with members like Visa and Mastercard as well as big banks and retailers, contributed more than $4.5 million to both political parties and candidates in addition to harder-to-track soft money contributions.[3] Their expenditures were especially well timed. For example, on the day that the House passed a bankruptcy reform bill in 1998 and sent it to the Senate, "Mastercard gave a $200,000 soft money contribution to the Republican Senatorial Committee." Later, during the month that the Judiciary Committee began debating the bill, coalition members contributed an additional $227,000 to the campaign coffers of key committee members.[4] These kinds of contributions are designed to reward friends in the legislature and to remind lawmakers about who can help them in the future.

In October 2000, this bill passed the House on a voice vote. In December, the Senate voted 70–28 to make it harder for people to avoid their credit card debts through bankruptcy. President Clinton, however, opposed the bill in part because it would have allowed violent protesters at abortion clinics to use bankruptcy laws to avoid fines. Once the bill was sent to him, however, he had to do nothing. Because Congress wasn't in session long enough, the bill was pocket vetoed when President Clinton left the bill unsigned. The 107th Congress immediately took up the bill again when it convened in January 2001 with a more friendly president, but it became bogged down over Democrat's insistence that abortion protesters fined for clinic violence not be allowed to declare bankruptcy. The 108th Congress, controlled by Republicans, should have the votes, finally, to pass the act.

The face of interest group politics in the United States is changing as quickly as laws, political consultants, and technology allow. The activities of big business and trade groups like the Bankruptcy Coalition are increasing at the same time that there is conflicting evidence concerning whether on not ordinary citizens even join political groups. In an influential essay, "Bowling Alone: America's Declining Social Capital," political scientist Robert Putnam argues that fewer Americans are joining groups,[5] while political scientist Everett Carll Ladd, as executive director of the Roper Center for Public Opinion, concluded that America is in the midst of an "explosion of voluntary groups, activities and charitable, donations [that] is transforming our towns and cities."[6] While bowling leagues have withered, said Ladd, other groups such as soccer associations, health clubs, and environmental groups are flourishing. Old groups like the Elks Club and the League of Women Voters, whose membership was tracked by Putnam, no longer are attracting members, according to Ladd. At the same time, people are reporting more *individual* acts—many of them designed to pressure policy makers at all levels of government.

Today, community soccer associations may be playing the same role that bowling leagues once played in the United States. Or, as Ladd notes, political scientists, many trained in the 1960s and 1970s, overlook the kinds of contributions most frequently made by young people today: involvement in voluntary community service work (as opposed to that often required by many school districts). Young people often don't see involvement in groups such as Habitat for Humanity or working in a soup kitchen as political, but it frequently is.

Interest groups often fill voids left by the traditional political parties and give Americans another opportunity to take their claims directly to the government (see Table 16.1). Interest groups give the unrepresented or underrepresented an opportunity to have their voices heard, thereby making the government and its policy-making process more representative of diverse populations and perspectives. Additionally, interest groups often offer powerful and wealthy interests even greater access to, or influence

TABLE 16.1   Reported Acts Designed to Influence Policy Makers (in percentages)

Political Activity	18–34	35–44	45–54	55–64	65+
			AGE GROUP		
Direct Contacting					
Written a letter to any elected official	21.1	32.6	41.2	28.3	33.8
Called or sent a letter to your Congress member	23.5	42.9	48.0	50.1	53.9
Indirect Contacting					
Written a letter to the editor of a newspaper	11.0	16.0	16.6	12.9	12.7
Tried to call in to a talk show to discuss views on a public or political issue	7.9	14.7	5.9	7.8	7.6
Dialed a toll-free or 900 number to register an opinion on some issue of public concern	14.2	20.6	13.8	15.3	10.1
Joining/Attending					
Joined an organization in support of a particular cause	19.9	24.9	27.1	20.1	15.2
Attended a city or town meeting in your community	21.7	27.5	33.4	39.8	38.6
Attended a public hearing	27.7	34.3	43.9	40.6	35.6
Participated in a "town meeting" or public affairs discussion group	17.7	28.1	30.6	32.8	24.5
Contributing					
Contributed money to a PAC	8.9	17.5	16.3	18.0	17.0
Contributed money to a candidate running for public office	10.7	21.4	26.9	23.1	26.9

Respondents were asked: "People express their opinions about politics and current events in a number of ways besides voting. I'm going to read a list of some of these ways. Please just tell me if you have or have not ever done each. Have you ever [X]?"

Source: Compiled from a telephone survey by the Times Mirror Center for The People & The Press, conducted May 18–24, 1993 as appeared in *Young v. Old* by Susan A. MacManus, Westview Press, 1996. Reprinted by permission of The Pew Research Center for The People and The Press.

on, policy makers at all levels of government. To explore this phenomenon, in this chapter we'll look at the following issues:

- First, we will answer the question, *what are interest groups?*
- Second, we will explore the historical *roots and development of interest groups* in America.
- Third, we will discuss *what interest groups do* by looking at the various strategies and tactics used by organized interests.
- Fourth, we will analyze *what makes an interest group successful.*

WHAT ARE INTEREST GROUPS?

Interest groups go by a variety of names: special interests, pressure groups, organized interests, political groups, lobby groups, and public interest groups are among the common ones. These various terms have produced a diverse collection of operational definitions:

- "Any association of individuals, whether formally organized or not, that attempts to influence public policy."[7]
- "An organization which seeks or claims to represent people or organizations which share one or more common interests or ideals."[8]
- "Any group that, on the basis of one or more shared attitudes, makes certain claims upon other groups in society for the establishment, maintenance, or enhancement of forms of behavior that are implied by the shared attitudes."[9]

Some definitions stress what a group does. This definition is offered by political scientist Robert H. Salisbury:

- "An interest group is an organized association which engages in activity relative to governmental decisions."[10]

Distinguished political scientist V. O. Key Jr. tried to differentiate political parties from interest groups by arguing that:

- "[Interest groups] promote their interests by attempting to influence government rather than by nominating candidates and seeking responsibility for the management of government."[11]

David B. Truman, one of the first political scientists to study interest groups, posed what he termed **disturbance theory** to explain why interest groups form.[12] He hypothesized that groups form in part to counteract the activities of other groups or of organized special interests. According to Truman, the government's role is to provide a forum in which the competing demands of groups and the majority of the U.S. population can be heard and balanced. He argued that the government's role in managing competing groups is to balance their conflicting demands.

Political scientist Robert H. Salisbury expanded on Truman by arguing that groups are formed when resources—be they clean air, women's rights, or rights of the unborn, for example are inadequate or scarce.[13] Unlike Truman, Salisbury stresses the role that leaders, or what he terms "entrepreneurs," play in the formation of groups.

disturbance theory
The theory offered by political scientist David B. Truman that posits that interest groups form in part to counteract the efforts of other groups.

(Photo courtesy: Toles © *The Buffalo News.* Reprinted with permission of Universal Press Syndicate. All rights reserved.)

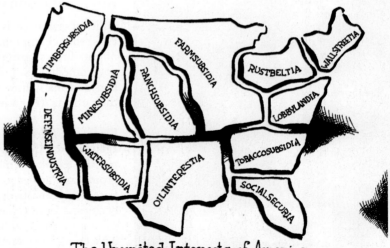

The Ununited Interests of America

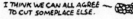

I THINK WE CAN ALL AGREE — TO CUT SOMEPLACE ELSE.

Originally, most political scientists used the term "pressure group" because it best described what these groups do. Today most political scientists use the terms *interest group* or *organized interest*. In this book we use **interest group** as a generic term to describe the numerous organized groups that try to influence government policy. Thus, interest groups can be what we normally think of as organized interests as well as state and local governments, political action committees, and individual businesses and corporations. We also consider less formal groups as interest groups. Although these groups are more nebulous in form than interest groups traditionally studied by political scientists, they, too, engage in concerted action to influence government policy.

interest group
An organized group that tries to influence public policy.

WEB EXPLORATION
For more on the Christian Coalition of America, see
www.ablongman.com/oconnor

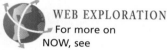

WEB EXPLORATION
For more on NOW, see
www.ablongman.com/oconnor

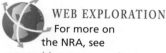

WEB EXPLORATION
For more on the NRA, see
www.ablongman.com/oconnor

Multi-Issue Versus Single-Issue Interest Groups

Political scientists often talk of interest groups as single-issue or multi-issue. Many organizations, while founded around a single guiding principle such as the NAACP's interest in advancing the cause of civil rights, or the Christian Coalition's concern with Christian family values, are actually involved in a wide range of issue areas including education (school vouchers, prayer in school), television ratings, and abortion. Thus, they must divide some of their energies as they lobby for varied policies in diverse forums. Similarly, the National Organization for Women (NOW) deals in issues of abortion and reproductive rights, affirmative action, economic equity, and lesbian rights, among others. Multi-issue groups often must have expertise in a wide array of areas and be prepared to work on the local, state, and national levels to advance their interests.

Single-issue groups differ from multi-issue groups in both the range and intensity of their interests. Concentration on one area generally leads to greater zeal in a group's lobbying efforts. Probably the most visible single-issue groups today are those organized on either side of the abortion and gun control debates. Right-to-life groups like the Army of God and pro-choice groups like the National Abortion and Reproductive Rights Action League (NARAL) are good examples of single-issue groups, as are the National Rifle Association (NRA) and Handgun Control, Inc. Today people singlemindedly pursue all kinds of interests. Drug- or AIDS-awareness groups, and anti-nuclear power groups, for example, can be classified as single-issue groups. Table 16.2 categorizes a number of prominent interest groups by their issue concentration.

Charlton Heston, the legendary actor, now serves as president of the National Rifle Association.
(Photo courtesy: Eric Gay/AP/Wide World Photos)

Kinds of Organized Interests

Political scientists also categorize organized interests by the type of interest(s) they champion. The major types of organized interests are (1) economic interest groups; (2) public interest groups; and increasingly, (3) governmental units. Most of these groups lobby on behalf of their members and many hire D.C.-based lobbying firms to lead or supplement their efforts. (For a list of top lobbying firms, see Table 16.2.)

Economic Interest Groups.   Most groups have some sort of "economic" agenda, even if it only involves acquiring enough money in donations to pay the telephone bill or send out the next mailing. **Economic interest groups** are, however, a special type of interest group: Their primary purpose is to promote the economic interests of their members. Historically, business groups (including trade and professional groups), labor organizations (unions), and organizations representing the interests of farmers have been considered the "big three" of economic interest groups. The National Consumer Bankruptcy Coalition discussed in the chapter opening vignette is a good example of an economic interest group.

Groups that mobilize to protect particular economic interests generally are the most fully and effectively organized of all the types of inter-

TABLE 16.2   Profiles of Selected Interest Groups

Name (Founded)	Single- or Multi-Issue	Members	PAC	2002 Election Cycle PAC Donation
Economic Groups				
AFL–CIO (1886)	M	13.4 million	AFL–CIO PAC	$1.6 million
American Medical Association (AMA) (1847)	M	300,000	AMA PAC	$4.5 million
Association of Trial Lawyers of America (1946)	M	60,000	Association of Trial Lawyers of America PAC	$6.3 million
National Association of Manufacturers (NAM) (1895)	M	12,500	no	
U.S. Chamber of Commerce (1912)	M	180,000 companies	U.S. Chamber of Commerce PAC	$187,000
Public Interest Groups				
American Association of Retired Persons (AARP) (1958)	M	32,000,000	no	
Amnesty International U.S.A. (1961)	S	386,000	no	
League of United Latin American Citizens (LULAC) (1929)	M	110,000	no	
National Abortion and Reproduction Rights Action League (NARAL) (1969)	S	450,000	NARAL PAC	$2.1 million
National Association for the Advancement of Colored People (NAACP) (1909)	M	500,000	no	
Human Rights Campaign Fund (1980)	S	17,000	yes	$1.1 million
National Right to Life Committee (1973)	S	400,000	National Right to Life PAC	$279,000
Environmental Groups				
Environmental Defense Fund (EDF) (1967)	S	150,000	no	
Greenpeace USA (1971)	S	1,690,500 (1996)	no	
Sierra Club (1892)	S	550,000 (1996)	Sierra Club Political Committee	$687,000
Good Government Groups				
Common Cause (1970)	S	270,000	no	
Public Citizen, Inc. (1971)	M	100,000	no	

Sources: http://www.opensecrets.org

est groups.[14] They exist to make profits and to obtain economic benefits for their members. To achieve these goals, however, they often find that they must resort to political means rather than trust the operation of economic markets to produce outcomes favorable for their members.

Public Interest Groups.   Political scientist Jeffrey M. Berry defines **public interest groups** as organizations "that seek a collective good, the achievement of which will not selectively and materially benefit the membership or activists of the organization."[15] Unlike economic interest groups, public interest groups do not tend to be particularly motivated by the desire to achieve goals that would benefit their members. As Berry notes, the public interest has many faces. In the past, for example, many Progressive Era groups were created in the late 1800s and early 1900s to solve the varied problems of new immigrants and the poor. Today civil and constitutional rights groups, environmental groups, good government groups such as Common Cause, peace groups, church groups, and groups that speak out for those who cannot (such as children, the mentally ill, or animals) are examples of public interest groups.

Governmental Units.   State and local governments are becoming strong organized interests as they lobby the federal government or even charitable foundations for money for a vast array of state and local programs. The Big Seven intergovernmental associations and state and local governments want to make certain that they get their fair share of federal dollars in the form of block grants or pork barrel projects. Most states retain lobbyists in Washington, D.C., to advance their interests or to keep them informed

economic interest group
A group with the primary purpose of promoting the financial interests of its members.

public interest group
An organization that seeks a collective good that will not selectively and materially benefit the members of the group.

about legislation that could affect them. They want to make sure that they will get their share (if not more) of the federal budget designated to go back to the states in a variety of forms including money for roads, schools, and poverty programs.

THE ROOTS AND DEVELOPMENT OF AMERICAN INTEREST GROUPS

Political scientists have long debated how and why interest groups arise, their nature, and their role in a democratic society. Do they contribute to the betterment of society, or are they an evil best controlled by government? From his days in the Virginia Assembly, James Madison knew that factions occurred in all political systems and that the struggle for influence and power among such groups was inevitable in the political process. This knowledge led him and the other Framers to tailor a governmental system of multiple pressure points to check and balance these factions, or what today we call interest groups, in the natural course of the political process. As we discuss in chapter 2, Madison and many of the other Framers were intent on creating a government of many levels—local, state, and national—with the national government consisting of three branches. It was their belief that this division of power would prevent any one individual or group of individuals from becoming too influential. They also believed that decentralizing power would neutralize the effect of special interests, who would not be able to spread their efforts throughout so many different levels of government. Thus the "mischief of faction" could be lessened. But, farsighted as they were, the Framers could not have envisioned the vast sums of money or technology that would be available to some interest groups.

Ironically, however, *The Federalist Papers* were a key component of one of the most skillful and successful examples of interest group activity in the history of this nation. If "the Federalists [themselves an interest group] had not been as shrewd in manipulation as they were sound in theory, their arguments could not have prevailed."[16]

As with the many different definitions of interest groups, a variety of sound reasons have been offered to explain why interest groups form. Generally, however, interest groups tend to arise in response to changes. These can be political or economic changes, changes in the population, technological changes, or even changes in society itself.

National Groups Emerge (1830–1889)

Although all kinds of local groups proliferated throughout the colonies and in the new states, it was not until the 1830s, as communications networks improved, that the first groups national in scope began to emerge. Many of these first national groups were single-issue groups deeply rooted in the Christian religious revivalism that was sweeping the nation. Concern with humanitarian issues such as temperance (total abstinence from alcoholic beverages), peace, capital punishment, education, and most important, slavery led to the founding of numerous groups dedicated to solving these problems. Among the first of these groups was the American Anti-Slavery Society, founded in 1833 by William Lloyd Garrison.

After the Civil War, more groups were founded. For example, the Women's Christian Temperance Union (WCTU) was created in 1874 with the goal of outlawing the sale of liquor. Its members, many of them quite religious, believed that the consumption of alcohol was an evil injurious to family life because many men drank away their paychecks, leaving no money to feed or clothe their families. The WCTU's activities took conventional and nonconventional forms: organizing prayer groups, lobbying for prohibition legislation, conducting peaceful marches, and engaging in more violent protests that included destruction of saloons. Like the WCTU, the Grange was also formed during the period following the Civil War, as an educational society for farmers to teach them about the latest agricultural developments. Although its charter formally stated that the Grange was not to become involved in "politics," in 1876 it formulated a detailed plan to pressure Congress to enact legislation favorable to farmers.

Perhaps the most effective interest group of the day was the railroad industry. In a move that couldn't take place today because of its clear impropriety, the Central Pacific Railroad sent its own **lobbyist** to Washington, D.C., in 1861, where he eventually became the clerk (staff administrator) of the committees of both houses of Congress that were charged with overseeing regulation of the railroad industry. Subsequently, the Central Pacific Railroad (later called the Southern Pacific) received from Congress vast grants of lands along its route and large subsidized loans from the national government. The railroad became so important that it later went on to have nearly total political control of the California state legislature.

After the Civil War, business interests began to play even larger roles in both state and national politics. A popular saying of the day noted that the Standard Oil Company did everything to the Pennsylvania legislature except refine it. Increasingly large trusts, monopolies, business combinations, and corporate conglomerations in the oil, steel, and sugar industries became sufficiently powerful to control many representatives in the state and national legislatures.

lobbyist
Interest group representative who seeks to influence legislation that will benefit his or her organization through political persuasion.

The Progressive Era (1890–1920)

By the 1890s, a profound change had occurred in the nation's political and social outlook. Rapid industrialization and an influx of immigrants created a host of problems, including crime, poverty, squalid and unsafe working conditions, widespread political corruption, and high prices caused by monopolistic business practices. Many Americans began to believe that new measures would be necessary to impose order on this growing chaos and to curb some of the more glaring problems brought on by industrialization and immigration. The political and social movement that grew out of these concerns was called the Progressive movement.

Not even the Progressives themselves could agree on what the term "progressive" actually meant, but their desire for reform led to an explosion of all types of interest groups: single-issue, trade, labor, and the first public interest groups. Politically, the movement took the form of the Progressive Party, which sought on many fronts to limit or end the power of the industrialists' near-total control of the steel, oil, railroad, and other key industries.

In response to the pressure applied by Progressive groups, the national government began to regulate business. Because businesses had a vested interest in keeping wages low and costs down, more business groups organized to consolidate their strength and to counter Progressive moves. Not only did governments have to mediate Progressive and business demands, but they also had to accommodate the role of organized labor which often allied itself with Progressive groups against big business.

Organized labor groups into national unions, it was not until the creation of the American Federation of Labor (AFL) in 1886 that there was any real national union activity. The AFL for the first time brought skilled workers from several trades together into one stronger national organization. Its effectiveness in mobilizing for higher wages for workers triggered more and better business organization. As business interests pushed states for "open shop" laws (which would outlaw unions in their factories), the AFL became increasingly political. It was also forced to react to the success of big businesses' use of legal injunctions to prohibit union organization. In 1914, massive lobbying by the AFL and its members led to passage of the Clayton Act, which the labor leader Samuel Gompers hailed as the "Magna Carta" of the labor movement. This law allowed unions to organize free from prosecution and also guaranteed their right to strike, a powerful weapon against employers.

Business Groups and Trade Associations.   The National Association of Manufactur- ers (NAM) was founded in 1895 by manufacturers who had suffered business reverses in the economic panic of 1893 and who believed that they were being affected adversely by the growth of organized labor. NAM first became politically active in 1913 when a major tariff bill was under congressional consideration. NAM's tactics were "so insis- tent and abrasive" and its expenditures of monies so lavish that President Woodrow Wilson was forced to denounce its lobbying tactics as an "unbearable situation."[17] Con- gress immediately called for an investigation of NAM's activities but found no mem- ber of Congress willing to testify that he had ever even encountered a member of NAM (probably because many of them had been "bought" with illegal contributions and gifts).

The second major business organization came into being in 1912, when the National Chamber of Commerce was created with the assistance of the Secretary of Commerce and Labor. (This was before that Cabinet post was split into the Department of Com- merce and the Department of Labor.)

trade association
A group that represents specific industries.

NAM, the Chamber of Commerce, and other **trade associations** representing spe- cific industries were effective spokespersons for their member companies. They were unable to defeat passage of the Clayton Act, but groups such as the Cotton Manufac- turers planned elaborate and successful court campaigns to overturn key provisions of the act in the courts.[18] Aside from the Clayton Act, innumerable pieces of pro-business legislation were passed by Congress, whose members continued to insist that they had never been contacted by business groups.

In 1928, the bubble burst for some business interests. At the Senate's request, the Federal Trade Commission (FTC) undertook a massive investigation of the lobbying tactics of the business community. The examination of Congress by the FTC revealed extensive illegal lobbying by yet another group, the National Electric Light Associa- tion (NELA). Not only did the NELA lavishly entertain members of Congress, it also went to great expense to educate the public on the virtues of electric lighting. Books and pamphlets were produced and donated to schools and public libraries to sway pub- lic opinion. Needy teachers and ministers who were willing to advocate electricity were helped with financial grants. These tactics were considered unethical by many, and busi- ness was held in public disfavor. It was these kinds of activities that led the public to view lobbyists in a negative light.

The Rise of the Interest Group State

During the 1960s and 1970s, the Progressive spirit found renewed vigor in the rise of pub- lic interest groups. Generally, these groups devoted themselves to representing the inter- ests of African Americans, women, the elderly, the poor, and consumers, or to working on behalf of the environment. Many of their leaders and members had been active in the civil rights and anti–Vietnam War movement of the 1960s. Other groups, like the Amer- ican Civil Liberties Union (ACLU) and the NAACP, which had survived for nearly a cen- tury, gained renewed vigor. Many of them had as their patron the liberal Ford Foundation, which helped to bankroll numerous groups, including the Women's Rights Project of the ACLU, the Mexican American Legal Defense and Education Fund, the Puerto Rican Legal Defense and Education Fund, and the Native American Rights Fund.[19] Another group that came to prominence in this era was the American Association of Retired Per- sons (AARP). The elderly are the fastest-growing group in the United States, and AARP is the largest single interest group in the country, with 32 million members in 2000.

The civil rights and anti-war struggles left many Americans feeling cynical about a government that they believed failed to respond to the will of the majority. They also believed that if citizens banded together, they could make a difference. Thus two major new public interest groups—Common Cause and Ralph Nader's Public Citizen, Inc.— were founded. Common Cause, a "good government" group similar to some of the early Progressive movement's public interest groups, has effectively challenged aspects of the congressional seniority system, successfully urged the passage of sweeping campaign financing reforms, and played a major role in the enactment of legislation authorizing

WEB EXPLORATION
For more about Common Cause and Public Citizen, Inc., see
www.ablongman.com/oconnor

federal financing of presidential campaigns. It continues to lobby for accountability in government and for more efficient and responsive governmental structures and practices.

Perhaps more well known than Common Cause is the collection of groups headed by Ralph Nader under the name Public Citizen, Inc. In 1965, Nader, a young lawyer, was thrust into the limelight with the publication of his book *Unsafe at Any Speed.* In it he charged that the Corvair, a General Motors (GM) car, was unsafe to drive; he produced voluminous evidence of how the car could flip over at average speeds on curved roads. In 1966, he testified about auto safety before Congress and then learned that General Motors had spied on him in an effort to discredit his work. The $250,000 that GM subsequently paid to Nader in an out-of-court settlement allowed him to establish the Center for the Study of Responsive Law in 1969. The center analyzed the activities of regulatory agencies and concluded that few of them enforced antitrust regulations or cracked down on deceptive advertising practices. Nader then turned again to lobbying Congress, which led him to create Public Citizen, Inc., which would act as an umbrella organization for what was to be called the "Nader Network" of groups. In 1996, and again in 2000, Nader was the unsuccessful Green Party candidate for president.

Conservative Backlash: Religious and Ideological Groups.   The growth and successes that various public interest groups and the civil rights and women's rights movements had in the 1960s and 1970s (see chapter 5) ultimately led to a conservative backlash. Conservatives became very concerned about the successes liberal groups had in shaping and defining the public agenda, and religious and ideological conservatives became a potent force in U.S. politics. The first major new religious group was the Reverend Jerry Falwell's Moral Majority, founded in 1978. It was widely credited with assisting Ronald Reagan's 1980 presidential victory as well as the defeats of several liberal Democratic senators that same year. Falwell claimed to have sent from 3 million to 4 million newly registered voters to the polls.[20] In June 1989, Falwell announced that he was terminating the Moral Majority after the group suffered from a series of financial and sexual scandals involving television evangelists.

In 1990, televangelist Pat Robertson, host of the popular television program *The 700 Club,* formed a new group, the Christian Coalition, to fill the void left by the demise of the Moral Majority. Since then, it has grown in power and influence by leaps and bounds. Its exit polls showed that religious conservatives accounted for one-third of all votes cast in 1994 and provided the margin of victory for all Republicans who won with 53 percent of the vote or less.[21]

After the important role the Christian Coalition played in the Republicans' winning control of the Congress, some of its members became disenchanted when many of its favorite issues failed to gain support in Congress. James Dobson, leader of the fundamentalist group Focus on the Family, met with Republican House leaders in May 1998 to protest their inaction and to seek assurances that the House would act on several conservative legislative policy priorities.[22]

Concern with the outcome of the 1998 elections, steeply declining revenues, a ruling from the Internal Revenue Service revoking its tax-exempt status led Pat Robertson to reassert his authority as the Christian Coalition's founder and to restructure the group to step up its lobbying presence in Congress. A for-profit corporation, Christian Coalition International, was created "to endorse political candidates on a state and local level [and] to make financial contributions to candidates," and a second organization, Christian Coalition of America, was created to replace the old Christian Coalition.[23]

WEB EXPLORATION
For more on *The 700 Club* and other conservative groups, see www.ablongman.com/oconnor

To inform voters of issues of concern during the 2000 election, the Christian Coalition distributed millions of voting guides in churches throughout the United States. (Photo courtesy: Christian Coalition of America)

2000 Christian Coalition

VOTER GUIDE

PRESIDENTIAL Election

George Bush (R)	ISSUES	Al Gore (D)
Supports	Emphasizing Free Enterprise Solutions to Social Problems	Opposes
Opposes	Control of Public Education by Powerful Unions	Supports
Supports	Educational Choice for Parents (Vouchers)	Opposes
Opposes	Unrestricted Abortion on Demand	Supports
Opposes	Increased Taxes on Coal & Oil (BTU Tax)	Supports
Supports	Elimination of the Marriage Penalty Tax	Opposes
Supports	Elimination of the Death Tax	Opposes
Supports	Banning Partial Birth Abortions	Opposes
Opposes	Public Financing of Abortions	Supports
Opposes	Federal Firearms Registration & Licensing of Gun Owners	Supports
Opposes	Adoption of Children by Homosexuals	No Response*
Supports	Prescription Drug Benefits For Medicare Recipients	Supports
Opposes	Placing US Troops Under UN Control	No Response*
Supports	Federal Tort Reform & Conservative Judges	Opposes
Supports	Allowing Younger Workers to Invest a Portion of Their Social Security Tax in a Private Account	Opposes

*Each candidate was sent a 2000 Federal Issues Survey by certified mail and/or facsimile machine. When possible, positions of candidates on issues were verified or determined using voting records and/or public statements.

Paid for and authorized by the Christian Coalition of America: 499 South Capital St., SW, Washington DC. 20003. The Christian Coalition of America is a pro-family citizen action organization. This voter guide is provided for educational purposes only and is not to be construed as an endorsement of any candidate or political party.

Please visit our website@www.cc.org

★ Vote on November 7 ★

AA—1

The reorganized coalition continued its efforts to inform voters of issues of concern to it without specifically endorsing candidates. In the November 2000 elections, the Christian Coalition distributed more than 70 million voter guides in churches throughout the United States the weekend before the election. In Florida, it passed out more than 3 million voter guides; 1 million of them were in Spanish.[24]

The Christian Coalition is not the only conservative interest group to play an important role in the policy process as well as in elections at the state and national level. The National Rifle Association (NRA) has been an active opponent of gun control legislation and of late has seen its membership rise, as well as its importance in Washington, D.C. (see Analyzing the Data). Its political action committee raised $11.4 million and spent $1.6 million to help elect President George W. Bush. Before the 2000 election, an NRA vice president boasted: "We'll have a president … where we work out of their office—unbelievably friendly relations."[25] To motivate voters, NRA President Charlton Heston barnstormed through close states, including Tennessee and West Virginia, recognizing that the election of a president sympathetic to its cause would make ultimate passage of NRA-supported legislation more likely.[26]

Longman
Participate.com
2.0
Participation
Gun Rights
and Gun
Control

Business Groups, Trade and Professional Associations.   Conservative, religious-based groups were not the only ones organized in the 1970s to advance conservative views. Many business people, dissatisfied with the work of the National Association of Manufacturers or the Chamber of Commerce, decided to start new, more politically oriented organizations to advance their political and financial interests in Washington, D.C. The Business Roundtable, for example, was created in 1972. The Roundtable, say some, is "a fraternity of powerful and prestigious business leaders that tells 'business's side of the story' to legislators, bureaucrats, White House personnel, and other interested public officials."[27] It urges its members to engage in direct lobbying to influence the course of policy formation. In 1998, for example, the Business Roundtable's Environment Task Force lobbied hard against the Kyoto Protocol on Climate Change out of concern over its impact on American businesses. These efforts ultimately paid off when the Bush administration announced it would not support it.

Businesses and corporations, too, can be powerful individually or collectively as organized interests, as highlighted at the beginning of this chapter. Most large corporations, for example, employ Washington, D.C.–based lobbyists to keep them apprised of legislation that may affect them, or to lobby for the consideration of legislation that could help them. Corporations also hire D.C.-based lobbyists to lobby bureaucrats for government contracts.

Large corporations also give large sums to favored politicians or political candidates. In 1998, for example, when Senate Majority Leader Trent Lott (R–Miss.) sought reelection to his Senate seat, he received $367,498 from the National Association of Realtors, $333,126 from Auto Dealers and Drivers for Free Trade (manufacturers of Japanese cars), $33,000 from Federal Express, and $58,202 from National Security PAC (defense interest advocacy). In the 2000 election, the 1,000 biggest companies gave a record $187 million to candidates for president and other national offices. Microsoft was number one. After recognizing the importance of having friends in Washington, D.C., Microsoft gave a total of $3.7 million; it gave only $237,000 to candidates in 1996. Philip Morris, the large tobacco company, contributed $3 million, with over three-quarters going to Republicans.[28]

Unlike public interest groups, organizations like the Chamber of Commerce and the Business Roundtable, as well as trade associations, enjoy many of the benefits other businesses do as lobbyists: They already have extensive organization, expertise, large numbers, a strong financial base, and a long-standing relationship with key actors in government. Such natural advantages have led to a huge number of business groups. One observer describes their proliferation this way:

> If you want to understand government, don't begin by reading the Constitution. It conveys precious little of today's statecraft. Instead, read selected portions of the Washington Telephone Directory, such as pages 354–58, which contain listings for all of the organizations with titles beginning with the word "National." . . . There

A N A L Y Z I N G   T H E   D A T A

HOW THE NRA MEMBERSHIP HAS RISEN

The National Rifle Association (NRA), a single-issue interest group, lobbies against any law that it considers a restriction on an individual's right to bear arms. NRA membership has spiked in recent years in reaction to proposed gun control legislation. Interestingly, following the Columbine High School shooting in 1999, in which twelve people were killed, membership has increased dramatically.

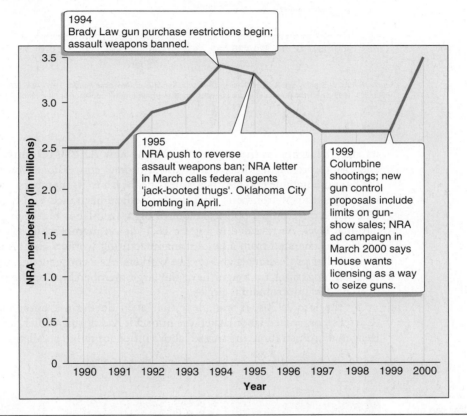

1994
Brady Law gun purchase restrictions begin; assault weapons banned.

1995
NRA push to reverse assault weapons ban; NRA letter in March calls federal agents 'jack-booted thugs'. Oklahoma City bombing in April.

1999
Columbine shootings; new gun control proposals include limits on gun-show sales; NRA ad campaign in March 2000 says House wants licensing as a way to seize guns.

Source: "How the NRA Membership Has Risen" by Genevieve Lynn, *USA Today,* May 18, 2000, p. A1. Copyright 2000, USA TODAY. Reprinted with permission.

are, of course, the big ones, like the National Association of Manufacturers, and the National Association of Broadcasters. But the pages teem with others, National Cigar Leaf Tobacco Association, National Association of Mirror Manufacturers, National Association of Miscellaneous Ornamental and Architectural Product Contractors, National Association of Margarine Manufacturers.[29]

Many of these national groups, businesses, and corporations devote tremendous resources to fighting government regulation. Rock the Vote, described in Politics Now: Rock the Vote, is an example of a quasi-trade association. It was begun by industry officials and then recruited younger members as well as affected recording artists.

Organized Labor.   As revealed in Figure 16.1, membership in labor unions held steady throughout the early and mid-1900s and then skyrocketed toward the end of the Depression. By then, organized labor began to be a potent political force as it was able to turn out its members in support of particular political candidates.

Labor became a stronger force in U.S. politics when the American Federation of Labor merged with the Congress of Industrial Organizations in 1955. Concentrating

FIGURE 16.1   Labor Union Membership, 1900 to 1999

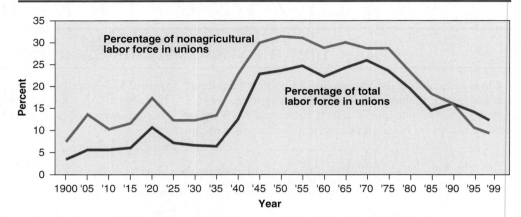

Source: Harold W. Stanley and Richard G. Niemi, eds. *Vital Statistics on American Politics, 1997–1998* (Washington, D.C.: CQ Press, 1998), 399. 1999 data from Bureau of Labor Statistics, updates from Current Population Survey, January 19, 2001.

its efforts largely on the national level, the new AFL-CIO immediately turned its energies to pressuring the government to protect concessions won from employers at the bargaining table and to other issues of concern to its members, including minimum wage laws, the environment, civil rights, medical insurance, and health care.

But the once fabled political clout of organized labor has been on the wane at the national level. As revealed in Figure 16.1, union membership has plummeted as the nation has changed from a land of manufacturing workers and farmers to a nation of white-collar professionals and service workers. As a consequence, unions and agricultural organizations no longer have the large memberships or the political clout they once held in governmental circles.

By the late 1970s, it was clear that even during a Democratic administration (Carter's), organized labor lacked the impact it had during earlier decades.[30] During the Reagan administration, organized labor's influence fell to an all-time modern-day low.

As part of a union, pilots can also threaten a strike, as this group of Delta Airline pilots did when they were dissatisfied with the progress of their contract talks. (Photo courtesy: Erik S. Lesser/AP/Wide World Photos)

P O L I T I C S   N O W

ROCK THE VOTE

Rock the Vote was a major mobilizer of the youth vote in the 2000 elections by holding forums in fifteen cities to gather young people to talk about important issues.

By registering new voters and then getting those new voters and others to the polls, it hopes to help young people see "that ACTIVISM is an ESSENTIAL part of the political process."[a] While Rock the Vote is closely associated in the minds of most with MTV, it actually was founded in 1990 by several people involved in the recording industry. After court rulings finding 2 Live Crew's music obscene, Congress began debating censorship of the record industry. In response, a coalition of recording industry executives from Warner Bros., Capitol, Geffen, MCA, A & M, Virgin, and Giant Records created Rock the Vote to stir grassroots support from music listeners to make their voices heard at the ballot box. MTV pitched in with $1 million in free airtime for Rock the Vote ads. The first sixty-second MTV spot featured Madonna in a red bikini with an American flag furled around her shoulders quipping: "If you don't vote, you're going to get a span-

ing."[b] Over the years, a variety of artists including Whoopi Goldberg, Hootie and the Blowfish, Dave Matthews Band, and the Fugees recorded public service announcements on behalf of Rock the Vote.

Rock the Vote lobbies for legislation of interest to young people and the record industry. In 1996, it began the first program to register by phone, 1-800-REGISTER, and became the first Web site to offer online voter registration. It also gives callers the necessary numbers to obtain absentee ballots. Rock the Vote registered over 250,000 new voters in 1998 and an additional 500,000 in 2000—160,000 of them online. It also e-mailed reminders to vote to those it registered.[c]

---

[a]"Rock the nation one community at a time," http://www.rockthevote.org/National/intro.html
[b]John Hiscock, "Madonna Rocks Censorship Vote," *The Daily Telegraph* (October 22, 1990): 3.
[c]Bruce Horowitz, "Rock the Vote Aims to Click with Young Electorate," *USA Today* (October 23, 2000): 5B.

In spite of the tremendous resources behind the AFL-CIO and other unions, membership dropped through 1998 but remained constant in 1999, prompting union leaders to hope. As revealed in Figure 16.1, in 1970, over 25 percent of workers were unionized; in 1999, only 13.9 percent were.

Organized labor recognizes its troubles and has tried to recapture some of its lost political clout. Since 1996, the AFL-CIO has ambitiously campaigned to return Congress into the hands of the Democratic Party, long a good friend to organized labor. Targeted TV and radio ads were run in districts of members who voted against the minimum wage increase that was later signed into law by President Clinton.

In 2002, labor unions spent over $43 million, with 89 percent going to Democrats. Not only did unions around the nation contribute substantial sums to elect pro-labor candidates, but they also launched a massive effort to get fellow workers to the polls. Members also made more than 8 million phone calls and distributed 12 million pieces of literature. The AFL-CIO alone had 2,000 full-time coordinators working to mobilize union households.[31] Labor was particularly evident in Walter Mondale's unsuccessful five-day race for the U.S. Senate after Paul Wellstone died.

Although organized labor's clout on the national level continues to fall well short of what it once was, labor unions are making a visible difference in state-level policies. Recent research reveals that "labor organization profoundly affects public policy."[32] In fact, the greater the organizational strength of labor, "the more states spend on welfare, education and other activities."[33]

WEB EXPLORATION
To join Rock the Vote, see
www.ablongman.com/oconnor

WEB EXPLORATION
For more on the AFL-CIO, see
www.ablongman.com/oconnor

WHAT DO INTEREST GROUPS DO?

As illustrated by the discussion of groups above, "In Washington, money talks, and it is foolish for anyone to pretend it is irrelevant to this debate," as the director of the Center for Public Integrity, a nonprofit research center financed by foundations, corporations, and unions, underscored in discussing the wide range of expensive policy-oriented activities engaged in by many interest groups.[34] For example, more than $100 million was spent in campaign contributions, television ads, and expense-paid trips for lawmakers as interests on both sides of the health-care reform issue reacted to reform initiatives by President Clinton soon after he took office in 1993. Twenty-five million dollars alone went to campaign contributions, and $8.2 million went to members of five health-related committees.

All in all, 650 health-related organizations made campaign contributions. Forty bought airtime to broadcast their views on the health-care debate. The AMA sponsored fifty-five trips—largely to California and Florida—where lawmakers addressed groups, golfed, and sunned. Moreover, at least eighty ex-lawmakers and former White House officials went to work for well-heeled health-related interests. Hiring lobbyists to sway policy thus "remains the bedrock of the Washington landscape."[35]

Not all interest groups are political, but they may become politically active when their members feel that a government policy threatens or affects group goals. Interest groups also enhance political participation by motivating like-minded individuals to work toward a common goal. Legislators are often much more likely to listen to or be concerned about the interests of a group as opposed to the interests of any one individual. Still, the congressional testimony of actor Michael J. Fox brought considerable attention to the underfunding of research for Parkinson's disease.

Just as members of Congress are assumed to represent the interests of their constituents in Washington, D.C., interest groups are assumed to represent the interests of their members to policy makers at all levels of government. In the 1950s, for example, the National Association for the Advancement of Colored People (NAACP) was able to articulate and present the interests of African Americans to national decision makers even though as a group they had little or no electoral clout, especially in the South. Without the efforts of the civil rights groups discussed in chapter 6, it is unlikely that either the courts or Congress would have acted as quickly to make discrimination illegal. All sorts of individuals—from railroad workers to women to physical therapists to campers to homosexuals to mushroom growers—have found that banding together with others who have similar interests can advance their collective interests. Getting celebrity support or hiring a lobbyist to advocate those interests in Washington, D.C., or a state capital also increases the likelihood that issues of concern to them will be addressed and acted on favorably.

There is also a downside to interest groups. Because groups make claims on society, they can increase the cost of public policies. The elderly can push for more costly health-care and Social Security programs, people with disabilities for improved access to public buildings, industry for tax loopholes, and veterans for improved benefits. Many Americans believe that interest groups exist simply to advance their own selfish interests, with

Actor Christopher Reeve is one of many celebrities who have actively lobbied Congress to support their interests or causes.
(Photo courtesy: Richard Ellis/Corbis/Sygma)

G L O B A L   P O L I T I C S

L A B O R   U N I O N S   I N
C O M P A R A T I V E   P E R S P E C T I V E

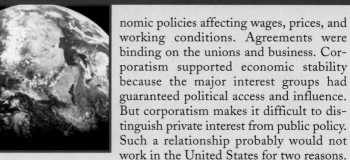

A survey of major interest groups in the industrial democracies would reveal a list familiar to students of American politics. Business, labor, and professional interest groups are well represented. New social movements focusing on the environment, gender equality, and other post-industrial issues have emerged across Europe, North America, and Japan in the last twenty-five years although they often lack the political resources of the traditional lobbies.

In the postwar period, labor unions represented one constellation of powerful interest groups in the industrial democracies. As the table above reveals, labor unions have been powerful because they have represented significant numbers of workers, typically in the manufacturing sector. The relatively low rate of unionization in the United States contrasts with the relative size, and therefore influence, of the labor movement in Europe.

Access to government is the centerpiece of interest group activity everywhere, but how groups get access differs from one country to the next. In Germany, where postwar unionization rates approached 50 percent, big labor has been an essential element of corporatist economic policy making. At certain times in the postwar Federal Republic, representatives from big business, labor, and the economic bureaucracy formally negotiated eco-nomic policies affecting wages, prices, and working conditions. Agreements were binding on the unions and business. Corporatism supported economic stability because the major interest groups had guaranteed political access and influence. But corporatism makes it difficult to distinguish private interest from public policy. Such a relationship probably would not work in the United States for two reasons. First, it requires a great deal of centralized control by national interest group representatives over their members, which has not been a feature of American labor (nor of French, Japanese, or Italian unions). Second, such a close relationship would almost certainly raise a public outcry about conflict of interest.

The table reveals the decline of big labor across the developed countries. There are several reasons for this. First, the shift in employment from the manufacturing sector to the service sector has undermined labor membership. The service sector is harder to organize, and in many cases unions did not try to reach out to workers outside of manufacturing. Second, privatization of public corporations in the last decade in Britain, France, and Japan has undermined a key bastion of labor strength. Finally, the shift in the 1980s and early 1990s toward conservative, pro-business governments undermined the Left, historically sympathetic to unions. In Japan, the near-destruction of the Socialist Party and realignment of the moderate left in the 1990s has been accompanied by the emergence of a moderate new labor federation, *Rengo*. A key feature of Rengo's new approach to management has been the abandonment of confrontation, including the postwar institution of the spring offensive, in which unions had attempted to synchronize wage bargaining by carrying out short strikes at the same time.

Labor Union Strength

Country	Unionization Rate, 1995 (%)	% Change, 1985–1995
Canada	31.0	-0.6
France	6.1	na
Germany	29.6	-3.5
Italy	30.6	-7.0
Japan	18.6	-4.0
United Kingdom	26.2	-27.2
United States	**12.7**	**-15.2**

Source: From Immanuel Ness and James Ciment, *Encyclopedia of Global Population and Demographics,* Vols. 1 and 2, (1999). Reprinted by permission of M.E. Sharpe, Inc., Armonk, N.Y. 10504.

little regard for the rights of other groups or, more important, of people not represented by any organized group.

Whether good or bad, interest groups play an important role in U.S. politics. In addition to enhancing the democratic process by providing increased representation and participation, they increase public awareness about important issues, help frame the public agenda, and often monitor programs to guarantee effective implementation. Most often, they accomplish these things through some sort of lobbying or informational campaign.

Lobbying

Most interest groups put lobbying at the top of their agendas. **Lobbying** is the process by which interest groups attempt to assert their influence on the policy-making process. The term lobbyist refers to any representative of a group that attempts to influence a policy maker by one or more of the tactics illustrated in Table 16.3. It is important to note that not only do large, organized interests have their own lobbyists (see Figure 16.2), but other groups, including colleges, trade associations, cities, states, and even foreign nations, also hire lobbying firms (some law firms have lobbying specialists) to represent them in the halls of Congress or to get through the bureaucratic maze.

Most politically active groups use lobbying to make their interests heard and understood by those who are in a position to influence or cause change in governmental policies. (See Roots of Government: Pressure Politics of the Past.) Depending on the type of group and on the role it is looking to play, lobbying can take many forms. You probably have never thought of the Boy Scouts or Girl Scouts of America as "political." Yet, when Congress began debating the passage of legislation dealing with discrimination in private clubs, representatives of both organizations testified in an attempt to persuade Congress to allow each one to remain a single-sex organization. Similarly, you probably don't often think of garden clubs as political. Yet, when issues of highway beautification come before a legislature, representatives from numerous garden clubs are likely to be there to lobby for, or to advance, their interests.

As Table 16.3 indicates, there are at least twenty-three ways for lobbyists and organizations to lobby on the state and national level. Lobbying allows interest groups to try to convince key governmental decision makers and the public of the correctness of their positions. Almost all interest groups lobby by testifying at hearings and contacting legislators. Other groups also provide information that decision makers might not have the time, opportunity, or interest to gather on their own. Of course, information these groups provide is designed to present the group's position in a favorable light,

TABLE 16.3   Percentage of Groups and Lobbyists Using Each Lobbying Technique

Technique	STATE-BASED GROUPS		D.C.-BASED GROUPS
	Lobbyists (n = 595)	Organizations (n = 301)	(n = 175)
1. Testifying at legislative hearings	98	99	99
2. Contacting government officials directly to present point of view	98	97	98
3. Helping to draft legislation	96	88	85
4. Alerting state legislators to the effects of a bill on their districts	96	94	75
5. Having influential constituents contact legislator's office	94	92	80
6. Consulting with government officials to plan legislative strategy	88	84	85
7. Attempting to shape implementation of policies	88	85	89
8. Mounting grassroots lobbying efforts	88	86	80
9. Helping to draft regulations, rules, or guidelines	84	81	78
10. Shaping government's agency by raising new issues and calling attention to previously ignored problems	85	83	84
11. Engaging in informal contacts with officials	83	81	95
12. Inspiring letter-writing or telegram campaigns	82	83	84
13. Entering into coalitions with other groups	79	93	90
14. Talking to media	73	74	86
15. Serving on advisory commissions and boards	58	76	76
16. Making monetary contributions to candidates	—	45	58
17. Attempting to influence appointment to public office	44	42	53
18. Doing favors for officials who need assistance	41	36	56
19. Filing suit or otherwise engaging in litigation	36	40	72
20. Working on election campaigns	—	29	24
21. Endorsing candidates	—	24	22
22. Running advertisements in media about position	18	21	31
23. Engaging in protests or demonstrations	13	21	20

Sources: State-Based Groups: Anthony J. Nownes and Patricia Freeman, "Interest Group Activity in the States," *Journal of Politics* (February 1998): 92. D.C.-Based Groups: Kay Lehman Schlozman and John Tierney, "More of the Same: Washington Pressure Group Activity in a Decade of Change," *Journal of Politics* 45 (1983): 358.

ROOTS OF GOVERNMENT

PRESSURE POLITICS OF THE PAST

The exact origin of the term "lobbying" is disputed. In mid-seventeenth-century England, there was a room located near the floor of the House of Commons where members of Parliament would congregate and could be approached by their constituents and others who wanted to plead a particular cause. Similarly, in the United States, people often waited outside the chambers of the House and Senate to speak to members of Congress as they emerged. Because they waited in the lobbies to argue their cases, by the nineteenth century they were commonly

referred to as "lobbyists." Another piece of folklore explains that when Ulysses S. Grant was president, he would frequently walk from the White House to the Willard Hotel on Pennsylvania Avenue just to relax in its comfortable and attractive lobby. Interest group representatives and those seeking favors from Grant would crowd into that lobby and try to press their claims. Soon they were nicknamed "lobbyists."

Lobbying reached an infamous peak in the late 1800s, when railroads and other big businesses openly bribed state and federal legislators to obtain favorable legislation. Congress finally got around to regulating some aspects of lobbying in 1946 with the Regulation of Lobbying Act, which required paid lobbyists to register with the House and Senate and to file quarterly financial reports, including an account of all contributions and expenditures as well as the names and addresses of those to whom they gave $500 or more. Organizations also were required to submit financial reports, although they did not have to register officially. The purpose of the act was to publicize the activities of lobbyists and remove some of the uncertainty surrounding the influence of lobbying on legislation. In 1954, however, a lower court ruled the act unconstitutional. Although the Supreme Court reversed the decision, it ruled that the act was applicable only to persons or organizations who solicited, collected, or received money for the principal purpose of influencing legislation by directly lobbying members of Congress. Consequently, many lobbyists did not register at all. The National Association of Manufacturers, for example, was formed in 1895 but did not register as a lobbying group until 1975.

FEMALE LOBBYISTS.

(Photo courtesy: Bettmann/Corbis)

although a good lobbyist for an interest group will also note the downside to proposed legislation. Interest groups also file lawsuits to lobby the courts, and some even engage in protests or demonstrations as a form of lobbying public opinion or decision makers.

Lobbying Congress.   Members of Congress are the targets of a wide variety of lobbying activities: congressional testimony on behalf of a group, individual letters from interested constituents, campaign contributions, trips, speaking fees, or the outright payment of money for votes. Of course, the last item is illegal, but there are numerous documented instances of money changing hands for votes. Many lobbying firms pay millions yearly to former lawmakers to lobby their old colleagues. Former Senators Robert Dole and George Mitchell, as well as former Texas Governor Ann Richards, earn well over a half-million dollars a year as lobbyists for national lobbying firms that are hired by interest groups and other special interests to advance their causes.[36]

POINT / COUNTERPOINT

DO INTEREST GROUPS HURT
OR HELP DEMOCRACY?

Since the 1960s, interest groups have proliferated dramatically, and some people claim that this explosion of interest groups harms democracy. Others claim that the number of interest groups today show the health of our democracy and enhance the representation of the people. Do interest groups help or hurt democracy? Let's examine these two points of view.

Opponents of interest group political influence, like the Reform Party and populists, argue that James Madison was right in *Federalist No. 10* when he warned of the factions. The proliferation of single-issue interest groups has tipped the governmental balance in favor of the minority—be it ideological or other—at the expense of the majority. They believe that minority groups, ranging from ultra-conservative to ultra-liberal hold the political system hostage. The result is gridlock and an ever-expanding role for the government as it gives in to ever more strident demands from all of these groups. Opponents of interest group influence argue that none of these groups think about the public good, only about their own little issue area. Labor unions demand more money and more benefits without regard for the needs of business owners. At the same time, business owners, represented by chambers of commerce or the National Association of Manufacturers, demand to make maximum profits and pay minimum wages at the expense of workers. Neither extreme position is in the best interest of the nation.

Advocates of the interest group system, including many interest group like AARP, AFL–CIO, Right-to-Life groups, chambers of commerce, and the Business Roundtable, argue that interest groups have an important and healthy role to play in modern society. They agree that interest groups make many demands but that the political system is designed to balance those demands and tends to do a pretty good job of it. For example, in the 1960s, conservative groups sought to maintain a wholly private system of health care and liberal groups lobbied for national health care; the result was Medicaid and Medicare—medical help from the government for those most in need, the poor and elderly—and everyone else had private health care.

Supporters maintain that interests groups are not evil pressure groups seeking to destroy the national interest, but groups with similar interests who get together to make their voices louder (strength in numbers) and advocate for their position. This is true democracy. Members of Congress and government officials are lobbied by advocates and opponents of environmental regulations, and so on. It is through this clash of interests that we arrive at good policy and true public good.

What do you? Do interest groups hurt or help democracy?
Go to www.ablongman.com/oconnor

Lobbying Congress and issue advocacy are skills that many people have developed over the years. In 1869, for example, women meeting in Washington, D.C., for the second annual meeting of the National Woman Suffrage Association marched to Capitol Hill to hear one of their members (unsuccessfully) ask Congress to pass legislation to enfranchise women under the terms of the Fourteenth Amendment.

Practices such as these floor speeches are no longer permitted. Some interest groups, however, still try mass marches to Congress. For example, after the Supreme Court ruled in 1976 that discrimination against a pregnant women was not prohibited by the Civil Rights Act of 1964, hordes of lobbyists from various women's rights groups descended on Congress at one time. In response, Congress quickly enacted the Pregnancy Discrimination Act of 1978.

Today lobbyists try to develop close relationships with senators and House members in an effort to enhance their access to the policy-making process. A symbiotic relationship between members of Congress, interest group representatives, and affected bureaucratic agencies often develops. In these iron triangles, congressional representatives and their staff members, who face an exhausting workload and legislation they know little about, frequently look to lobbyists for information. "Information is the currency on Capitol Hill, not dollars," said one lobbyist.[37] According to one aide:

> My boss demands a speech and a statement for the *Congressional Record* for every bill we introduce or co-sponsor—and we have a lot of bills. I just can't do it all myself. The better lobbyists, when they have a proposal they are pushing, bring it to me along with a couple of speeches, a *Record* insert, and a fact sheet.[38]

Not surprisingly, lobbyists work most closely with representatives who share their interests. A lobbyist from the National Rifle Association (NRA), for example, would be unlikely to try to influence a liberal representative who was on record as strongly in favor of gun control. It is much more effective for a group like the NRA to provide useful information for its supporters and to those who are undecided. Good lobbyists can also encourage members to file amendments to bills favorable to their interests. They can also urge their supporters in Congress to make speeches (often written by the group) and to pressure their colleagues in the chamber.

A lobbyist's effectiveness depends largely on his or her reputation for fair play and provision of accurate information. No member of Congress wants to look uninformed. As one member noted:

> It doesn't take very long to figure out which lobbyists are straightforward, and which ones are trying to snow you. The good ones will give you the weak points as well as the strong points of their case. If anyone ever gives me false or misleading information, that's it—I'll never see him again.[39]

Because lobbying plays such an important role in Congress, many effective lobbyists often are former members of that body, former staff aides, former White House officials or Cabinet officers, or Washington insiders. This type of lobbyist frequently drops in to visit members of Congress or their staff members and often takes them to lunch, golf, or parties. Although much of that activity may be ethically questionable, most is not illegal (see Table 16.4).

Attempts to Reform Congressional Lobbying.   In 1946, in an effort to limit the power of lobbyists, Congress passed the Federal Regulation of Lobbying Act, which required anyone hired to lobby any member of Congress to register and file quarterly financial reports. Few lobbyists actually file these reports. For years, numerous good government groups argued that lobbying laws should be strengthened. Civil liberties groups such as

TABLE 16.4   The Ethics in Government Act

In 1978, in the wake of Watergate, Congress passed the Ethics in Government Act. Its key provisions dealt with (1) financial disclosure, and, (2) employment after government service.

(1) Financial disclosure: The president, vice president, and top-ranking executive employees must file annual public financial disclosure reports that list:

- The source and amount of all earned income; all income from stocks, bonds, and property; any investments or large debts; and the source of a spouse's income, if any.

- Any position or offices held in any business, labor, or nonprofit organizations.

(2) Employment after government services: Former executive branch employees may not:

- Represent anyone before any agency for two years after leaving government service on matters that came within the former employees' sphere of responsibility (even if they were not personally involved in the matter).

- Represent anyone on any matter before their former agency for one year after leaving it, even if the former employees had no connection with the matter while in the government.

Sources: National Journal (November 19, 1977): 1796–1803; and *Congressional Quarterly Weekly Report* (October 28, 1978): 3121–327.

★ HOW a bill becomes law in Congress ★

Mike Luckovich ATLANTA CONSTITUTION (c)98

(Photo courtesy: By permission of Mike Luckovich and Creators Syndicate.)

the American Civil Liberties Union (ACLU), however, argue that registration provisions violate the First Amendment's freedom of speech and the right of citizens to petition the government.

But public opinion polls continued to reveal that many Americans believed that the votes of numerous members of Congress were often available to the highest bidder. In late 1995, after nearly fifty years of inaction, Congress passed the first effort to regulate lobbying since the 1946 act. The new act, the 1995 Lobbying Disclosure Act, was passed overwhelmingly in both houses of Congress. The new act employs a strict definition of lobbyist (one who devotes at least 20 percent of a client's or employer's time to lobbying activities), which should trigger far greater reporting of lobbyist activities. It also requires lobbyists to:

1. Register with the Clerk of the House and the Secretary of the Senate.
2. Report their clients and issues and the agency or house they lobbied.
3. Estimate the amount they are paid by each client.

The reporting of clients and issues should make it easier for those kinds of activities to be monitored by watchdog groups or the media. In fact the first comprehensive analysis by the Center for Responsible Politics revealed that by June 1999, 20,512 lobbyists were registered—a 35 percent jump from just two years earlier. The number of organizations reporting spending more than one million dollars a year on lobbying also jumped dramatically to 117. In 1998, $2.7 million was spent on lobbying for every member of Congress.[40]

As revealed in Figure 16.2, not only did ten large firms spend millions to lobby Congress and the executive branch, they also contributed heavily to political campaigns, with the majority of those funds going to Republicans.[41]

Lobbying the Executive Branch. As the scope of the federal government has expanded, lobbying the executive branch has increased in importance and frequency. Groups often target one or more levels of the executive branch because there are so many potential access points—the president and White House staff, and the numerous levels of the executive branch bureaucracy. Groups try to work closely with the administration in an effort to influence policy decisions at their formulation and implementation stages. Like the situation with congressional lobbying, the effectiveness of a group often lies in its ability to provide decision makers with important information and a sense of where the public stands on the issue.

Historically, group representatives have met with presidents or their staff members to urge policy directions. In 1992, representatives of the auto industry even accompanied President George Bush to lobby the Japanese for more favorable trade regulations. According to political scientist Thomas Cronin, most presidents specifically set up staff positions "explicitly to serve as brokerages or clearinghouses to provide greater access to presidential attention for professional, demographic, or specialized organizations." Cronin has suggested that "presidents have appointed either an aide or an office for every American dilemma."[42] Many of these offices, such as those dealing with consumer affairs, the environment, and minority affairs, are routinely the target of organized interests. At various times, even more interest-oriented special liaison offices have been created to deal with women, Jews, African Americans, and bankers, among others.

An especially strong link exists between interest groups and regulatory agencies (see chapter 8). While these agencies are ostensibly independent of Congress and the president, interest groups often have clout there. Because of the highly technical aspects of much regulatory work, many groups employ Washington attorneys and lobbying firms to deal directly with the agencies. So great is interest group influence in the decision-

WEB EXPLORATION
To experience how the lobbying process works, go to
www.ablongman.com/oconnor

FIGURE 16.2   Top Lobbying Expenditures

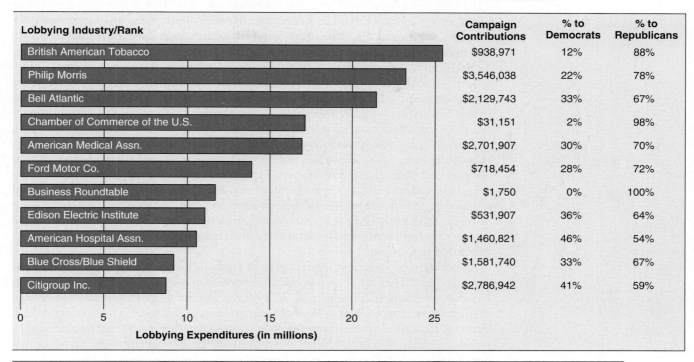

Lobbying Industry/Rank	Campaign Contributions	% to Democrats	% to Republicans
British American Tobacco	$938,971	12%	88%
Philip Morris	$3,546,038	22%	78%
Bell Atlantic	$2,129,743	33%	67%
Chamber of Commerce of the U.S.	$31,151	2%	98%
American Medical Assn.	$2,701,907	30%	70%
Ford Motor Co.	$718,454	28%	72%
Business Roundtable	$1,750	0%	100%
Edison Electric Institute	$531,907	36%	64%
American Hospital Assn.	$1,460,821	46%	54%
Blue Cross/Blue Shield	$1,581,740	33%	67%
Citigroup Inc.	$2,786,942	41%	59%

Lobbying Expenditures (in millions)

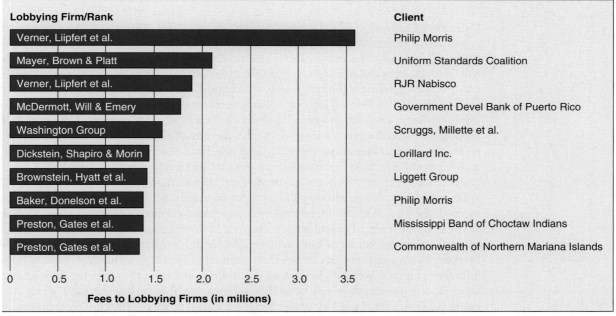

Lobbying Firm/Rank	Client
Verner, Liipfert et al.	Philip Morris
Mayer, Brown & Platt	Uniform Standards Coalition
Verner, Liipfert et al.	RJR Nabisco
McDermott, Will & Emery	Government Devel Bank of Puerto Rico
Washington Group	Scruggs, Millette et al.
Dickstein, Shapiro & Morin	Lorillard Inc.
Brownstein, Hyatt et al.	Liggett Group
Baker, Donelson et al.	Philip Morris
Preston, Gates et al.	Mississippi Band of Choctaw Indians
Preston, Gates et al.	Commonwealth of Northern Mariana Islands

Fees to Lobbying Firms (in millions)

Sources: http://www.opensecrets.org/pubs/lobby98/topspend.html and http://www.opensecrets.org/pubs/lobby98/topfees.html

making process of these agencies that many people charge that the agencies have been captured by the interest groups.

Groups often monitor how the laws or policies they advocated are implemented. Once a law is passed or a regulation written that affects an interest group, it often finds it useful to monitor how that law or regulation is implemented. The National Women's Law Center, for example, has been instrumental in seeing that Title IX be enforced fully. It has successfully sued several colleges and universities that have failed to provide equity in athletic funding for men and women.

Lobbying the Courts.   The courts, too, have proved a useful target for interest groups.[43] Although you might think that the courts decide cases that affect only the parties involved or that they should be immune from political pressures, interest groups have for years recognized the value of lobbying the courts, especially the Supreme Court, and many political scientists view it as a form of political participation.[44] As shown in Table 16.3, 72 percent of the Washington-based groups surveyed participated in litigation as a lobbying tool. Richard C. Cortner has noted that "Cases do not arrive on the doorstep of the Supreme Court like orphans in the night."[45] Most major cases noted in this book either have been sponsored by an interest group or one or both of the parties in the case have been supported by an *amicus curiae* (friend of the court) brief.

Generally, interest group lobbying of the courts can take two forms: direct sponsorship or the filing of *amicus curiae* briefs. When cases come to the Supreme Court that raise issues a particular organization is interested in but not actually sponsoring, often the organization will file an *amicus* brief—either alone or with other like-minded groups—to inform the justices of their policy preference, generally offered in the guise of legal arguments. Over the years, as the number of both liberal and conservative groups viewing litigation as a useful tactic has increased, so has the number of briefs submitted to the Court.

In addition to litigating, interest groups try to influence who is nominated to the federal courts. They also have played an important role of late in Senate confirmation hearings, as discussed in chapter 10. In 1991, for example, 112 groups testified or filed prepared statements for or against the nomination of Clarence Thomas to the U.S. Supreme Court.[46] Thomas's nomination was unusual in that it attracted so much opposition, including that of the NAACP. In contrast, the subsequent nominations of Justices Ginsburg and Breyer attracted the attention of far fewer interest groups.

Grassroots Lobbying.   As the term implies, *grassroots lobbying* is a form of pressure-group activity that attempts to involve those people at the bottom level of the political system.[47] Although it often involves door-to-door informational or petition drives—a tried and true method of lobbying—the term also can be used to encompass more modern forms of grassroots lobbying such as fax and Internet lobbying of lawmakers. As early as the 1840s, women (who could not vote) used petition campaigns to persuade state legislators to enact Married Women's Property Acts that gave women control of their earnings and a greater legal say in the custody of their children. Petitioning has come a long way since then. In 1996, the Fund for a Feminist Majority held a weekend symposium to teach women how to use the Internet to contact lawmakers.

Interest groups regularly try to stir up their members to inspire grassroots activity, hoping that lawmakers will respond to those pressures and the attendant publicity. In essence, the goal of many organizations is to persuade ordinary voters to serve as their advocates. In the world of lobbying, there are few things more useful than a list of committed supporters. Radio talk-show hosts like Rush Limbaugh also try to stir up their listeners by urging them to contact their representatives in Washington, D.C. Those undefined masses, however, are not an interest group; but as they join together on the Internet or via faxes, they may be mobilized into one or more groups. Grassroots lobbying is often a term used by professional lobbyists for their activities "to camouflage an unpopular or unsympathetic client."[48] Typically, in these kinds of grassroots campaigns, a "large business hires a Washington firm to organize a coalition of small business, nonprofit groups, and individuals across the nation." This coalition (or better yet, arranged marriage) then draws public attention and sympathy to the proposed policy or legislation sought by the lobbyists' initial client—who, by the time the issue gets on the public agenda, has faded from the public. This kind of grassroots lobbying occurs on most major pieces of legislation.

Interest groups' use of electronic technologies to reach and recruit thousands of Americans at the grassroots level quickly has caused "Congress to govern more by fear and an intense desire for simple, easy answers," said Representative Steve Gunderson (R–Wisc.) before he left office.[49] Today the simple grassroots campaigns of just a few years ago (fill-in-the-blank postcards and forms torn out of the newspaper) have grown much more sophisticated and become much more effective.

Many interest groups and trade groups have installed banks of computerized fax machines to send faxes automatically around the country overnight, instructing each member to ask his or her employees, customers, or other people to write, call, or fax their members of Congress. Other interest groups now run carefully targeted and costly television advertisements pitching one side of an argument. Their opponents must generally respond or lose. Many of these advertisements end with a toll-free phone number that viewers can call if they find the pitch convincing. New telemarketing companies answer these calls and transfer the callers directly to the offices of the appropriate members of Congress.[50]

The Internet is the newest weapon in the arsenal of interest groups and lobbyists. Each major party's political convention had Internet Alleys, with "dot-com delegates participating in virtual conventions." Many see this as a way of encouraging grassroots political involvement that politicians and political parties will soon need to respond to. E-mail is a way for groups to connect with supporters as well as to urge supporters to connect with policy makers. Digital activism can be especially effective at the local level. "Flash campaigns," as they are called, can be generated with the click of a mouse to contact hundreds or thousands of concerned citizens.[51]

Anti-Bush protesters lined the Inaugural parade route to show their dissatisfaction with the 2000 election outcome. (Photo courtesy: Christy Bowe/Corbis Sygma)

Protest Activities.   Most groups have few members so devoted as to put everything on the line for their cause. Some will risk jail or even death, but it is much more usual for a group's members to opt for more conventional forms of lobbying or to influence policy through the electoral process. When these forms of pressure group activities are unsuccessful or appear to be too slow to achieve results, however, some groups (or individuals within groups) resort to more forceful legal and illegal measures to attract attention to their cause. Since the Revolutionary War, violent, illegal protest has been one tactic of organized interests. The Boston Tea Party, for example, involved breaking all sorts of laws, although no one was hurt physically. Other forms of protest, such as Shays's Rebellion, ended in tragedy for some participants.

During the civil rights movement, as discussed in chapter 6, the Reverend Martin Luther King Jr. and his followers frequently resorted to nonviolent marches to draw attention to the plight of African Americans in the South. These forms of organized group activity were legal. Proper parade permits were obtained, and government officials notified. The protesters who tried to stop the freedom marchers, however, were engaging in illegal protest activity.

Groups on both ends of the political spectrum historically have resorted to violence in the furtherance of their objectives. Abolitionists, anti–nuclear power activists, anti-war activists, animal-rights advocates, and other groups on the "left" have broken laws, damaged property, and even injured or killed people, as have groups on the "right" such as The Army of God (an anti-abortion group) and the Ku Klux Klan (KKK). From the early 1900s until the 1960s, African Americans were routinely lynched by KKK members. Today some radical anti-abortion groups regularly block the entrances to abortion clinics; others active in the anti-abortion movement have taken credit for clinic bombings.

Other protest activities are less violent, sometimes tasteless, and often also illegal. After New York Mayor Rudy Giuliani announced that he had prostate cancer, People for the Ethical Treatment of Animals (PETA) put up controversial billboards linking prostate cancer to milk. PETA activists also have trespassed on private property to free animals from testing by humans and have thrown cans of red paint on women sporting fur coats.

Election Activities

In addition to trying to achieve their goals (or at least draw attention to them) through the conventional and unconventional forms of lobbying and protest activity, many interest groups also become involved more directly in the electoral process. The 2000 Republican and Democratic presidential nominating conventions were the targets of significant organized interest group protest concerning each party's stance on a variety of issues, including U.S. involvement in Colombian drug wars, support for Iraqi sanctions, the death penalty, abortion, and third world sweatshops.

Endorsements.   Many groups claim to be nonpartisan, that is, nonpolitical. Usually they try to have friends in both political parties to whom they can look for assistance and access. Some organizations, however, routinely endorse candidates for public office, pledging money, group support, and often even campaign volunteers. However, some spenders tend to give more to Republicans.

EMILY's List, a women's group (EMILY stands for "Early Money Is Like Yeast— it makes the dough rise"), not only endorses candidates but contributes heavily to races of pro-choice Democratic women. In 2002, EMILY's list raised more than $20 million. Still, very few of its endorsed candidates won election or re-election. Of the eight women it endorsed for House seats, only one was victorious. In 2000, the National Abortion and Reproductive Rights Action League was significantly involved in 110 races. It spent $7.5 million to make 3.4 million calls to pro-choice households, mailed 4.6 million pieces of mail to pro-choice households, and spent more than $1.5 million on television advertisements to encourage the election of pro-choice representatives and Al Gore.[52]

Once groups become overly political, however, their tax-exempt status is jeopardized. Federal law precludes tax-exempt organizations from taking partisan positions. The Christian Coalition for years claimed to be nonpartisan, although the FEC charged that it used money to promote specific candidates, causing it to redesign its scorecards into voters guides.

Endorsements from some groups may be used by a candidate's opponent to attack a candidate. While labor union endorsements can add money to a candidate's campaign coffers, for example, they risk being labeled a "tool of the labor unions" by their opponents.

Rating the Candidates or Office Holders.   Many liberal and conservative ideological groups rate candidates to help their members (and the general public) evaluate the voting records of members of Congress. The American Conservative Union (conservative) and the Americans for Democratic Action (liberal)—two groups at ideological polar extremes—routinely rate candidates and members of Congress based on their votes on key issues of importance to the group, as illustrated in Table 16.5. So do groups including the ACLU, and the Christian Coalition. These scores help voters to know more about their representatives' votes on issues that concern them.

Creating Political Parties.   Another interest group strategy is to form a political party to publicize a cause and even possibly win a few public offices. In 1848, the Free Soil Party was formed to publicize the crusade against slavery; twenty years later the Prohibition Party was formed to try to ban the sale of alcoholic beverages. Similarly, in the early 1970s, the National Right-to-Life Party was formed to publicize the anti-abortion position, and it ran its own candidate for president in 1976.

TABLE 16.5   Interest Group Ratings of Selected Members of Congress, 2002

Member	ACU	ACLU	ADA	AFL-CIO	CC	CoC	LCV
Senate							
Dianne Feinstein (D–Calif.)	12	50	85	94	15	54	75
Trent Lott (R–Miss.)	96	25	0	0	92	93	0
Kay Bailey Hutchison (R–Tex.)	96	25	0	0	92	93	0
Edward M. Kennedy (D–Mass.)	4	50	100	100	15	80	88
House							
Tom DeLay (R–Tex.)	100	0	0	0	100	84	0
Sheila Jackson-Lee (D–Tex.)	8	100	100	100	14	50	71
John Conyers (D–Mi.)	4	100	90	100	0	30	93
Mary Bono (R–Calif.)	68	33	15	17	80	100	0

Key

ACU = American Conservative Union

ACLU = American Civil Liberties Union

ADA = Americans for Democratic Action

AFL–CIO = American Federation of Labor– Congress of Industrial Organizations

CC = Christian Coalition

CoC = Chamber of Commerce

Lev = League of Conservation Voters

Members are rated on a scale from 1 to 100, with 1 being the lowest and 100 being the highest support of a particular group's policies.

In 1995, many in the Ross Perot–founded group United We Stand established the Reform Party to highlight the group's goals, including government reform (in particular, passage of new campaign finance laws) and fiscal responsibility. Similarly, consumer advocate Ralph Nader was the 1996 and 2000 nominee of the Green Party, created to bring attention to environmental issues. Groups often see forming political parties as a way to draw attention to their legislative goals and to drive one of the major political parties to give their demands serious attention.

The effectiveness of an interest group in the election arena has often been overrated by members of the news media. In general, it is very difficult to assess the effect of a particular group's impact on any one election because of the number of other factors present in any election or campaign. However, the one area in which interest groups do seem able to affect the outcome of elections directly is through a relatively new device called the political action committee.

Interest Groups and Political Action Committees.   Throughout most of history, powerful interests and individuals have often used their money to "buy" politicians or their votes. Even if outright bribery was not involved, huge corporate or other interest group donations certainly made some politicians look as if they were in the "pocket" of certain special interests. Congressional passage of the Federal Election Campaign Act began to change most of that. The 1971 act required candidates to disclose all campaign contributions and limited the amount of money that they could spend on media advertising.

In 1974, in the wake of the Watergate scandal (see chapter 8), amendments to the act made it more far-reaching by sharply limiting the amount of money any interest group could give to a candidate for federal office. However, the act also made it legal for corporations, labor unions, and interest groups to form what were termed **political action committees** (**PACs**), which could make contributions to candidates for national elections. (See chapter 14 for more on this subject.)

Technically, a PAC is a political arm of a business, labor, trade, professional, or other interest group legally authorized to raise funds on a voluntary basis from employees or members in order to contribute to a political candidate or party. PAC money has changed the face of U.S. elections. Unlike some contributions to interest groups, however, contributions to PACs are not tax deductible, and PACs generally don't have members who call legislators; instead, PACs have contributors who write checks specifically for the purpose of campaign donations. PAC money plays a significant role in the campaigns of many congressional incumbents, often averaging over half a House candidate's total campaign spending. PACs generally contribute to those who have helped them before and who serve on committees or subcommittees that routinely consider legislation of concern to that group.

WEB EXPLORATION To examine the specific values and platforms of these new political parties, see www.ablongman.com/oconnor

WEB EXPLORATION To learn more about the issue position of each of the groups in Table 16.5, see www.ablongman.com/oconnor

political action committee (PAC)
A federally registered fund-raising committee that represents an interest group in the political process through campaign donations.

Longman Participate.com 2.0
Visual Literacy
PACs and the Money Trail

WHAT MAKES AN INTEREST GROUP SUCCESSFUL?

Throughout our nation's history, all kinds of interests in society have organized to pressure the government for policy change. Some have been successful, and some have not. E. E. Schattschneider once wrote, "Pressure politics is essentially the politics of small groups. . . . Pressure tactics are not remarkably successful in mobilizing general interests."[53] He was correct; historically, corporate interests often prevail over the concerns of public interest groups such as environmentalists.

All of the groups discussed in this chapter have one thing in common: They all want to shape the public agenda, whether by winning elections, maintaining the status quo, or obtaining favorable legislation or rulings from Congress, executive agencies, or the courts.[54] For powerful groups, simply making sure that certain issues never get discussed may be the goal. Gun manufacturers dread incidents such as the school shooting in Littleton, Colorado, because it propels the issue of gun regulation out of their hands. Similarly, the bank card companies profit when students and other consumers don't know about proposed changes in bankruptcy legislation that could hurt consumers. In contrast, those opposed to random stops of African American drivers on the roads win when the issue becomes front-page news and law enforcement officials feel pressured to investigate, if not stop altogether, the discriminatory practice of racial profiling.

Groups often claim credit for "winning" legislation, court cases, or even elections individually or in coalition with other groups.[55] They also are successful when their leaders become elected officials or policy makers themselves. Each administration is often loaded with former group activists. In the Reagan administration, the secretary of the interior and the solicitor general were former leaders of a conservative public interest law firm, the Mountain States Legal Foundation. In the Clinton administration, Supreme Court appointee Ruth Bader Ginsburg was a former ACLU board member and the director of its Women's Rights Project. New York Senator Hillary Rodham Clinton was a former leader of the Children's Defense Fund and her election was hailed by its staff.

Political scientists have studied several phenomena that contribute in varying degrees—individually and collectively—to particular groups' successes. These include (1) leaders and patrons, (2) adequate funding, and (3) a solid membership base.

Leaders and Patrons.   Interest group theorists such as Robert Salisbury frequently acknowledge the key role that leaders play in the formation, viability, and success of interest groups, a fact underscored in Highlight: "Perfect Patron?" Jack L. Walker contends that without what he terms **patrons** (those who often finance a group), few organizations could begin.[56]

patron
Individual who finances an interest group.

Without the powerful pen of William Lloyd Garrison in the 1830s, who knows whether the abolitionist movement would have been as successful. Similarly, Frances Willard was the prime mover behind the WCTU, as were Marian Wright Edelman of the Children's Defense Fund in 1968, and the Reverend Jerry Falwell of the Moral Majority in the 1980s. Most successful groups, especially public interest groups, are led by charismatic individuals who devote most of their energies to "the cause." The role of an interest group leader is similar to that of an entrepreneur in the business world. As in the marketing of a new product, an interest group leader must have something attractive to offer to persuade members to join. Potential members of the group must be convinced that the benefits of joining outweigh the costs. Union members, for example, must be persuaded that the cost of their union dues will be offset by the union's winning higher wages for them.

Funding.   Funding is crucial to all interest groups to build their memberships as well as to advance their policy objectives. Government, foundations, and wealthy individuals can serve as patrons providing crucial start-up funds for groups, especially public interest groups. Advertising, litigating, and lobbying all are expensive.

During the 1980s, conservative groups relied on the direct-mail skills of marketing wizard Richard Viguerie to raise monies for a variety of conservative causes. In the early

Longman
Participate.com
2.0
Timeline
**Interest
Groups and
Campaign
Finance**

H I G H L I G H T

PERFECT PATRON?

On August 24, 1994, billionaire Richard Mellon Scaife told those assembled at a luncheon on Nantucket, "We're going to get Clinton, and you'll be much happier because Al Gore will be president."[a] Well, Scaife was wrong, but the money he spent to "get Clinton" underscores the powerful role that patrons can play in the political system. Not only did Scaife give $2.3 million to the conservative magazine the *American Spectator* to dig up negative information on Clinton and his associates, but over the past forty years he and members of his family have contributed $620 million in current dollars to conservative interest groups and causes.

Scaife's first foray into philanthropy was a 1962 contribution to the American Bar Association's Fund for Public Education, whose purpose was to educate against communism. Later he funded conservative research institutes at Stanford and Georgetown Universities and then became an important contributor to the conservative American Enterprise Institute. He also became a major contributor to the Heritage Foundation, which compiles a *Directory of Public Policy Conservative Organizations*. In 1998, it listed 300 groups; Richard Scaife has funded 111 of them; 76 in 1998.[b] Scaife has been particularly instrumental in providing support to conservative public interest law firms that were begun in part to counter the ACLU and environmental groups, and he is an important patron of the oldest and largest conservative public interest law firm, the Pacific Legal Foundation. The Southeastern Legal Foundation, another target of his largess, won the Supreme Court case barring the Census Bureau from using statistical sampling. Even on the eve of the November 2000 election, Scaife's patronage of conservative causes was in evidence. As publisher of the *Pittsburgh Tribune-Review*, Scaife ordered his top editors to make certain that no photos appeared of Vice President Al Gore, the Democratic Party's candidate for president. He even had editors rework an Associated Press story to downplay its reference to Gore.[c]

[a]This highlight draws heavily from Robert G. Kaiser and Ira Chinoy, "How Scaife's Money Powered a Movement," *The Washington Post* (May 2, 1999): A1.
[b]Kaiser and Chinoy, "How Scaife's Money Powered a Movement."
[c]Dennis B. Roddy, "Tribune–Reviews" Election Coverage Vice President Gore's Campaign," *Pittsburgh Post Gazette* (November 8, 2000): A26.

1990s, pro-choice groups appealed to supporters by requesting funds to campaign for legislation in anticipation of the Supreme Court's reversal of *Roe* v. *Wade*. When the Supreme Court did not overrule *Roe* in 1992, and Ruth Bader Ginsburg was appointed to the Supreme Court, contributions to pro-choice groups such as NARAL and Planned Parenthood dropped precipitously.

Some groups, particularly political action committees (PACs), measure their successes by the number of candidates supported who won. In 1996, for example, tobacco companies contributed an estimated $11.3 million on the targeted races and received $50 billion in tax breaks as a result of congressional legislation. Similarly, the airlines individually and through several trade associations contributed $3.2 million. By 1997, they had won a 2.5 percent tax reduction on each plane ticket.[57]

Members. Alexis de Tocqueville, a French aristocrat and philosopher, toured the United States extensively during 1831 and 1832. A keen observer of American politics, he was very much impressed by the tendency of Americans to join groups in order to participate in the policy-making process. "Whenever at the head of some new undertaking you see government in France, or a man of rank in England, in the United States you will be sure to find an association,"[58] wrote de Tocqueville.

The United States is still a nation of joiners. As a college student, think of the number of interest groups or voluntary associations to which you belong. It's likely that you belong to some kind of organized religion; to a political party; or to a college, or university social, civic, athletic, or academic group, at a bare minimum. You may also belong to a more general special-interest group, such as Greenpeace, People for the Ethical

Treatment of Animals, the National Right-to-Life Committee, or Amnesty International, as well as being involved in local literacy or poverty groups.

Organizations are usually composed of three kinds of members. At the top are a relatively small number of leaders who devote most of their energies to the single group. The second tier of members is generally involved psychologically as well as organizationally. They are the workers of the group—they attend meetings, pay dues, and chair committees to see that things get done. In the bottom tier are the rank and file, members who don't actively participate. They pay their dues and call themselves group members, but they do little more. Most group members fall into this last category.

Political scientist E. E. Schattschneider has noted that the interest group system in the United States has a decidedly "upper-class bias," and he concluded that 90 percent of the population does not participate in an interest group, or what he called the pressure group system.[59] Since the 1960s, survey data have revealed that group membership is drawn primarily from people with higher income and education levels. Individuals who are wealthier can afford to belong to more organizations because they have more money and, often, more leisure time. Money and education are also associated with greater confidence that one's actions will bring results, a further incentive to devote time to organizing or supporting interest groups. These elites are often more involved in politics and hold stronger opinions on many political issues.

People who do belong to groups often belong to more than one. Overlapping memberships can often affect the cohesiveness of a group. Imagine, for example, that you are an officer in the college Young Republicans. If you call a meeting, people may not attend because they have academic, athletic, or social obligations. Divided loyalties and multiple group memberships can often affect the success of a group, especially if any one group has too many members who simply fall into the dues-paying category.

Groups vary tremendously in their ability to enroll what are called potential members (see Table 16.6). Economist Mancur Olson Jr. notes that all groups provide some **collective good**—that is, something of value, such as money, a tax write-off, a good feeling, or a better environment—that can't be withheld from a non–group member.[60] If one union member at a factory gets a raise, for example, all other workers at that factory will, too. Therefore, those who don't join or work for the benefit of the group still reap the rewards of the group's activity. This phenomenon is called the **free rider** problem. Consequently, Olson asserts, potential members are unlikely to join a group because they realize that they will receive many of the benefits the group achieves regardless of their participation. Not only is it irrational for free riders to join any group, but the bigger the group, the greater the free rider problem. Thus, groups need to pro-

collective good
Something of value that cannot be withheld from a non–interest group member, for example, a tax write-off, a good feeling.

free rider
A person who doesn't join or work for the benefit of the group the rewards of the group's activity.

TABLE 16.6   Potential Versus Actual Interest Groups

The goal of most groups is to mobilize all potential members. Often, that task is impossible. As Mancur Olson Jr. points out, the larger the group, the more difficult it is to mobilize. To illustrate the potential versus actual membership phenomenon, here are several examples of groups and their potential memberships.

Population	Group	Number of Potential Members	Number of Actual Members
Governors	National Governors' Association	55	55 (includes territories)
Political Science Faculty	American Political Science Association	17,000	13,000
Physicians	American Medical Association (AMA)	548,000	300,000
Women	National Organization for Women (NOW)	127,000,000	500,000
African Americans	National Association for the Advancement of Colored People (NAACP)	30,600,000	500,000

vide a variety of other incentives to convince potential members to join. These can be newsletters, discounts, or simply a good feeling.

Small groups often have an organizational advantage because, in a small group such as the National Governors' Association, any individual's share of the collective good may be great enough to make it rational to join. Patrons, be they large foundations such as the Ford Foundation or individuals such as Jane Fonda, who donated $500,000 to the Georgia Campaign for Adolescent Pregnancy Prevention in 1995, often eliminate the free rider problem for public interest groups. They make the costs of joining minimal because they contribute much of the group's necessary financial support.[61]

Continuity & Change

A Nation of Joiners?

Interest groups long have been a factor in the course of American political history. Members of many discrete religious groups first settled in America seeking religious freedom. Later, after the Revolutionary War was fought and a new nation was created, political factions or groups—Federalists and Anti-Federalists—emerged with strong leaders and even publications clearly setting forth their goals and political philosophies.

When Alexis de Tocqueville toured the United States in the 1830s, he was struck by the tendency of Americans to join groups of all kinds. Interest groups, particularly labor and big business, also played a critical role in the development of the new nation, especially after the Civil War and into the Progressive Era.

The development of what some term the modern interest group society began in the 1960s with the development of myriad civil rights and public interest groups reminiscent of the kinds of interest group formation and activity that occurred during the Progressive movement. Environmental groups, were a new interest group phenomenon, whose formation and successes in part spurred the development of new conservative groups and public interest law firms to counter their claims in the legislature, before executive agencies, and in the courts. In many ways, however, the power exerted by big business through trade associations, the hiring of pro-

fessional lobbyists, and PACs is still quite reminiscent of the power it enjoyed just before and well into the Progressive movement.

By the year 2001, technology-based firms and corporations will contribute as much if not more to the economy than major U.S. car manufacturers. This new wealth will create with it new interests. In addition, the Internet is becoming an increasingly effective tool for grassroots mobilization for existing groups and may be usurping the role of patrons in the formation of new groups, whose start-up costs are now much lower. While Robert Putnam may be correct that people are no longer bowling in leagues, they are spending more and more time on the Internet.

1. What kinds of interest groups do you believe would be particularly amenable to start up on the Internet?
2. Will the research and conventional wisdom about organized interests and their effectiveness have to be rewritten in light of the growth of the Internet?

Cast Your Vote. In what ways will the Internet succeed as a mobilizing tool for interest groups ? In what ways will it fail? To cast your vote, go to **www.ablongman.com/oconnor**

SUMMARY

Interest groups lie at the heart of the American social and political system. National groups first emerged in the 1830s. Since that time the type, nature, sophistication, and tactics of groups have changed dramatically. To that end we have made the following points:

1. **What Are Interest Groups?**
   Those who study interest groups have offered a variety of definitions to explain what they are. Most definitions

revolve around notions of "associations or groups of individuals" who "share" some sort of "common" "interest" or "attitude" and who try to "influence" or "engage in activity" to affect "governmental policies" or the people in "government." Political scientists find it helpful to categorize interest groups in several ways. They study multi-issue versus single-issue groups. They also examine economic, public interest and governmental units as participants in the interest group process.

2. The Roots and Development of American Interest Groups

Interest groups, national in scope, did not begin to emerge until around the 1830s. Later, from 1890–1920, the Progressive movement emerged. The 1960s saw the rise of a wide variety of liberal interest groups. By the 1970s through the 1980s, legions of conservatives were moved to form new groups to counteract those efforts. Professional associations, too, became an active presence in Washington, D.C.

3. What Do Interest Groups Do?

Interest groups often fill voids left by the major political parties and give Americans opportunities to make claims, as a group, on government. The most common activity of interest groups is lobbying, which takes many forms. Groups routinely pressure members of Congress and their staffs, the president and the bureaucracy, and the courts; they use a variety of techniques to educate and stimulate the public to pressure key governmental decision makers. Interest groups also attempt to influence the outcome of elections; some even run their own candidates for office. Others rate elected officials to inform their members how particular legislators stand on issues of importance to them. Political action committees (PACs), a way for some groups to contribute money to candidates for office, are another method of gaining support from elected officials and ensuring that their "friends" stay in office. Reaction to public criticism of this influence led Congress to pass the first major lobbying reforms in fifty years.

4. What Makes an Interest Group Successful?

Interest group success can be measured in a variety of ways, including a group's ability to get its issues on the public agenda, winning key pieces of legislation in Congress or executive branch or judicial rulings, or backing successful candidates. Several factors contribute to interest group success, including leaders and patrons, funding, and committed members.

KEY TERMS

collective good, p. 614
disturbance theory, p. 589
economic interest group, p. 591
free rider, p. 614

interest group, p. 590
lobbying, p. 602
lobbyist, p. 602
patron, p. 612

political action committee (PAC), p. 611
public interest group, p. 591
trade association, p. 594

SELECTED READINGS

Berry, Jeffrey M. *The Interest Group Society*, 3rd ed. New York: Longman, 1997

———. *Lobbying for the People: The Political Behavior of Public Interest Groups*. Princeton, N.J.: Princeton University Press, 1977.

Cigler, Allan J., and Burdett A. Loomis, eds. *Interest Group Politics*, 5th ed. Washington, D.C.: CQ Press, 1998.

Herrnson, Paul S., Ronald G. Shaiko, and Clyde Wilcox. *The Interest Group Connection*. Chatham, N.J.: Chatham House, 1998.

Kollman, Ken. *Outside Lobbying: Public Opinion and Interest Group Strategies*. Princeton, N.J.: Princeton University Press, 1998.

McGlen, Nancy E., and Karen O'Connor. *Women, Politics and American Society*. 2nd ed. Upper Saddle River, N.J.: Prentice Hall, 1998.

Olson, Mancur Jr. *The Logic of Collective Action: Public Good and the Theory of Groups*. Cambridge, Mass.: Harvard University Press, 1965.

Sabato, Larry J. *PAC Power: Inside the World of Political Action Committees*. New York: Norton, 1984.

Schlozman, Kay Lehman, and John T. Tierney. *Organized Interests and American Democracy*. New York: Harper & Row, 1986.

Truman, David B. *The Governmental Process: Political Interests and Public Opinion*. New York: Knopf, 1951.

Walker, Jack L., ed. *Interest Groups in America: Patrons, Professions and Social Movements*. Ann Arbor: University of Michigan Press, 1991.

Wilson, James Q. *Political Organizations*. Princeton, N.J.: Princeton University Press, 1995.

Woliver, Laura. *From Outrage to Action: The Politics of Grassroots Dissent*. Urbana: University of Illinois Press, 1993.

Wolpe, Bruce C, and Bertram J. Levine. *Lobbying Congress: How the System Works*, 2nd ed. Washington, D.C.: CQ Press, 1996.

NOTES

1. "Students Binge on Credit," *USA Today* (September 14, 2000): 26A.
2. Russ Feingold, "Lobbyists' Rush for Bankruptcy Reform," *The Washington Post* (June 7, 1999): A19.
3. Feingold, "Lobbyists' Rush."
4. Feingold, "Lobbyists' Rush."
5. Robert D. Putnam, "Bowing Alone: America's Declining Social Capital" *Journal of Democracy* 6(1): 650-665.
6. Richard Morin, "Who Says We're Not Joiners," quoting Everett Carll Ladd, *The Washington Post* (May 2, 1999): B5.
7. Clive Thomas and Ronald Hrebenar, "Changing Patterns of Interest Group Activity: A Regional Perspective," in Mark Petracca, ed., *The Politics of Interests* (Boulder, Colo.: Westview Press, 1992), 4.
8 Graham Wilson, *Interest Groups in the United States* (New York: Oxford University Press, 1981), 4.

9. David B. Truman, *The Governmental Process: Political Interests and Public Opinion* (New York: Knopf, 1951), 33.

10. Robert H. Salisbury, "Interest Groups," in Fred I. Greenstein and Nelson W. Polsby, eds., *Handbook of Political Science*, vol. 4 (Reading, Mass.: Addison-Wesley, 1975), 175.

11. V. O. Key Jr., *Politics, Parties and Pressure Groups* (New York: T. J. Crowell, 1942), 23.

12. Truman, *The Governmental Process*, ch. 16.

13. Robert H. Salisbury, "An Exchange Theory of Interest Groups," *Midwest Journal of Political Science* 13 (1969): 1–32.

14. Salisbury, "An Exchange Theory of Interest Groups," 1–32.

15. Jeffrey M. Berry, *Lobbying for the People: The Political Behavior of Public Interest Groups* (Princeton, N.J.: Princeton University Press, 1977), 7.

16. Samuel Eliot Morrison and Henry Steel Commager, *The Growth of the American Republic* (New York: Oxford University Press, 1930), 163.

17. Quoted in Grant McConnell, "Lobbies and Pressure Groups," in Jack Greene, ed., *Encyclopedia of American Political History*, vol. 2 (New York: Macmillan, 1984), 768.

18. Lee Epstein, *Conservatives in Court* (Knoxville: University of Tennessee Press, 1985).

19. Jack L. Walker, "The Origins and Maintenance of Interest Groups in America," *American Political Science Review* 77 (June 1983): 390–406.

20. Peter Steinfels, "Moral Majority to Dissolve; Says Mission Accomplished," *The New York Times* (June 12, 1989): A14.

21. Steve Goldstein, "The Christian Right Grows in Power," *The Atlanta Journal* (November 11, 1994): A8.

22. Richard S. Dunham, "Corporate America vs. the Religious Right?" *Business Week* (May 18, 1998): 46.

23. Thomas B. Edsall and Hanna Rosin, "Christian Coalition, Denied Tax-Exempt Status, Will Reorganize," *The Washington Post* (June 11, 1999): A4.

24. Matthew Vita and Susan Schmidt, "The Interest Groups: Religious Right Mutes Voice, Not Efforts," *The Washington Post* (November 2, 2000): A20.

25. Robert Scheer, "The NRA-Friendly Candidate: Bush's Stance on Guns Proves That He Is No Compassionate Conservative," *The Pittsburgh Post-Gazette* (May 11, 2000): A29.

26. Juliet Eilperin, "A Pivotal Election Finds NRA's Wallet Open," *The Washington Post* (November 1, 2000): A16.

27. David Mahood, *Interest Groups Participation in America: A New Intensity* (Englewood Cliffs, N.J.: Prentice Hall, 1990), 23.

28. Tom Walker, "Business Press: Microsoft Tops Political Donations," *The Atlanta Journal and Constitution* (November 7, 2000): 6D.

29. Quoted in Ronald J. Hrebenar and Ruth K. Scott, *Interest Group Politics in America*, 2nd ed. (Englewood Cliffs, N.J.: Prentice Hall, 1990), 263.

30. See Taylor E. Dark, *The Unions and the Democrats: An Enduring Alliance* (Ithaca, N.Y.: ILR Press, 1999).

31. Nancy Cleeland, "Decision 2000: Unions Mobilize to Get out Vote," *The Los Angeles Times* (November 8, 2000): A3.

32. Benjamin Radcliff and Martin Saiz, "Labor Organizations and Public Policy in the American States," *Journal of Politics* (February 1998): 121.

33. Radcliff and Saiz, "Labor Organizations and Public Policy."

34. Brenda Rios, "Big Blitz from TV to the Hill: A $100 Million Whirlwind of Spin Control," *The Atlanta Journal* (July 22, 1994): A4.

35. Rios, "Big Blitz."

36. Sam Loewenberg, "Now, The Tricky Part: Dividing Profits," *Legal Times* (May 31, 1999): 4.

37. Michael Wines, "For New Lobbyists, It's What They Know," *The New York Times* (November 3, 1993): B14.

38. Quoted in Kay Lehman Schlozman and John T. Tierney, *Organized Interests and American Democracy* (New York: Harper & Row, 1986), 85.

39. Quoted in Norman J. Ornstein and Shirley Elder, *Interest Groups, Lobbying and Policy Making* (Washington, D.C.: CQ Press, 1978), 77.

41. Bill McAllister, "No Death of Lavish Lobbying in 1999," *The Washington Post* (May 11, 1998): A19.

42. Thomas Cronin, *The State of the Presidency* (Boston: Little, Brown, 1975), 123.

43. Some political scientists speak of "iron rectangles," reflecting the growing importance of a fourth party, the courts, in the lobbying process.

44. Clement E. Vose, "Litigation as a Form of Pressure Group Activity," *Annals* 319 (September 1958): 20–31.

45. Richard C. Cortner, "Strategies and Tactics of Litigation in Constitutional Cases," *Journal of Public Law* 17 (1968): 287.

46. Karen O'Connor, "Lobbying the Justices or Lobbying for Justice?" in Paul Herrnson, Ronald G. Shaiko and Clyde Wilcox, *The Interest Group Connection* (Chatham, N.J.: Chatham House Publishers, 1998), 267–88.

47. Robert A. Goldberg, *Grassroots Resistance: Social movements in Twentieth Century America* (Belmont, Calif.: Wadsworth, 1991).

48. Jane Fritsch, "Sometimes, Lobbyists Strive to Keep Public in the Dark," *The New York Times* (March 19, 1996): A1.

49. Joel Brinkley, "Cultivating the Grass Roots to Reap Legislative Benefits," *The New York Times* (November 1, 1993): A1.

50. Brinkley, "Cultivating the Grass Roots."

51. Marilyn J. Cohodas, "Digital Activism," *Governing Magazine* (August 2000): 70.

52 NARAL Memorandum to Interested Parties, November 14, 2000.

53. E. E. Schattschneider, *The Semi-Sovereign People* (New York: Holt, Rinehart and Winston, 1960), 51.

54. Ken Kollman, *Outside Lobbying: Public Opinion and Interest Group Strategies* (Princeton, N.J.: Princeton University Press, 1998); and Karen O'Connor, *Women's Organizations' Use of the Courts* (Lexington, Mass.: 1980).

55. Marie Hojnacki, "Interest Groups' Decisions to Join Alliances or Work Alone," *American Journal of Political Science* 41 (January 1997): 61–87.

56. Walker, "The Origins and Maintenance of Interest Groups in America."

57. Ceci Connolly, "Donors to Campaigns Fared Well in Budget," *The Washington Post* (August 22, 1997): A20.

58. Alexis de Tocqueville, *Democracy in America*, vol. 1, trans. Phillips Bradley (New York: Knopf, Vintage Books, 1945; orig. published in 1835), 191.

59. E. E. Schattschneider, *The Semi-Sovereign People*, 35.

60. Mancur Olson Jr. *The Logic of Collective Action: Public Goods and the Theory of Groups* (Cambridge, Mass.: Harvard University Press, 1965).

61. Walker, "The Origins and Maintenance of Interest Groups," 390–406.

APPENDIX I

The Declaration of Independence

In Congress, July 4, 1776

The Unanimous Declaration of the Thirteen United States of America

When in the Course of human events it becomes necessary for one people to dissolve the political bands which have connected them with another, and to assume, among the powers of the earth, the separate and equal station to which the Laws of Nature and of Nature's God entitle them, a decent respect to the opinions of mankind requires that they should declare the causes which impel them to the separation.

We hold these truths to be self-evident, that all men are created equal, that they are endowed by their Creator with certain unalienable Rights, that among these are Life, Liberty and the pursuit of Happiness. That to secure these rights, Governments are instituted among Men, deriving their just powers from the consent of the governed. That whenever any Form of Government becomes destructive of these ends, it is the Right of the People to alter or to abolish it, and to institute new Government, laying its foundation on such principles and organizing its powers in such form, as to them shall seem most likely to effect their Safety and Happiness. Prudence, indeed, will dictate that Governments long established should not be changed for light and transient causes; and accordingly all experience hath shewn that mankind are more disposed to suffer, while evils are sufferable, than to right themselves by abolishing the forms to which they are accustomed. But when a long train of abuses and usurpations, pursuing invariably the same Object evinces a design to reduce them under absolute Despotism, it is their right, it is their duty, to throw off such Government, and to provide new Guards for their future security.—Such has been the patient sufferance of these Colonies; and such is now the necessity which constrains them to alter their former Systems of Government. The history of the present King of Great Britain is a history of repeated injuries and usurpations, all having in direct object the establishment of an absolute Tyranny over these States. To prove this, let Facts be submitted to a candid world.

He has refused his Assent to Laws, the most wholesome and necessary for the public good.

He has forbidden his Governors to pass Laws of immediate and pressing importance, unless suspended in their oper-ation till his Assent should be obtained; and when so suspended, he has utterly neglected to attend to them.

He has refused to pass other Laws for the accommodation of large districts of people, unless those people would relinquish the right of Representation in the Legislature, a right inestimable to them and formidable to tyrants only.

He has called together legislative bodies at places unusual, uncomfortable, and distant from the depository of their Public Records, for the sole purpose of fatiguing them into compliance with his measures.

He has dissolved Representative Houses repeatedly, for opposing with manly firmness his invasions on the rights of the people.

He has refused for a long time, after such dissolutions, to cause others to be elected; whereby the Legislative Powers, incapable of Annihilation, have returned to the People at large for their exercise, the State remaining in the mean time exposed to all the dangers of invasion from without, and convulsions within.

He has endeavored to prevent the population of these States; for that purpose obstructing the Laws of Naturalization of Foreigners; refusing to pass others to encourage their migration hither, and raising the conditions of new Appropriations of Lands.

He has obstructed the Administration of Justice, by refusing his Assent to Laws for establishing Judiciary powers.

He has made Judges dependent on his Will alone, for the tenure of their offices, and the amount and payment of their salaries.

He has erected a multitude of New Offices, and sent hither swarms of Officers to harass our people, and eat out their substance.

He has kept among us, in times of peace, Standing Armies without the Consent of our legislatures.

He has affected to render the Military independent of and superior to the Civil power.

He has combined with others to subject us to a jurisdiction foreign to our constitution, and unacknowledged by our laws, giving his Assent to their Acts of pretended Legislation:

For quartering large bodies of armed troops among us:

For protecting them, by a mock Trial, from punishment for any Murders which they should commit on the Inhabitants of these States:

For cutting off our Trade with all parts of the world:

For imposing Taxes on us without our Consent:

For depriving us in many cases, of the benefits of Trial by Jury:

For transporting us beyond Seas to be tried for pretended offences:

For abolishing the free System of English Laws in a neighboring Province, establishing therein an Arbitrary government, and enlarging its Boundaries so as to render it at once an example and fit instrument for introducing the same absolute rule into these Colonies:

For taking away our Charters, abolishing our most valuable Laws, and altering fundamentally the Forms of our Governments:

For suspending our own Legislatures, and declaring themselves invested with power to legislate for us in all cases whatsoever.

He has abdicated Government here, by declaring us out of his Protection and waging War against us.

He has plundered our seas, ravaged our Coasts, burnt out towns, and destroyed the lives of our people.

He is at this time transporting large Armies of foreign Mercenaries to compleat the works of death, desolation and tyranny, already begun with circumstances of Cruelty and perfidy scarcely paralleled in the most barbarous ages, and totally unworthy the Head of a civilized nation.

He has constrained our fellow Citizens taken Captive on the high Seas to bear Arms against their Country, to become the executioners of their friends and Brethren, or to fall themselves by their Hands.

He has excited domestic insurrections amongst us, and has endeavored to bring on the inhabitants of our frontiers, the merciless Indian Savages, whose known rule of warfare, is an undistinguished destruction of all ages, sexes and conditions.

In every stage of these Oppressions We have Petitioned for Redress in the most humble terms: Our repeated Petitions have been answered only by repeated injury: A Prince, whose character is thus marked by every act which may define a Tyrant, is unfit to be the ruler of a free people.

Nor have We been wanting in attention to our British brethren. We have warned them from time to time of attempts by their legislature to extend an unwarrantable jurisdiction over us. We have reminded them of the circumstances of our emigration and settlement here. We have appealed to their native justice and magnanimity; and we have conjured them by the ties of our common kindred to disavow these usurpations, which would inevitably interrupt our connections and correspondence. They too have been deaf to the voice of justice and consanguinity. We must, therefore, acquiesce in the necessity, which denounces our Separation, and hold them, as we hold the rest of mankind, Enemies in War, in Peace Friends.

We, therefore, the Representatives of the United States of America, in General Congress, Assembled, appealing to the Supreme Judge of the world for the rectitude of our intentions, do, in the Name, and by Authority of the good People of these Colonies, solemnly publish and declare, That these United Colonies are, and of Right ought to be Free and Independent States; that they are Absolved from all Allegiance to the British Crown, and that all political connection between them and the State of Great Britain, is and ought to be totally dissolved: and that as Free and Independent States, they have full power to levy War, conclude Peace, contract Alliances, establish Commerce, and to do all other Acts and Things which Independent States may of right do. And for the support of this Declaration, with a firm reliance on the protection of divine Providence, we mutually pledge to each other our Lives, our Fortunes and our sacred Honor.

JOHN HANCOCK,
Attest.

CHARLES THOMSON,
Secretary.

NEW HAMPSHIRE
Josiah Bartlett,
Wm. Whipple,
Matthew Thornton.

MASSACHUSETTS BAY
Saml. Adams,
John Adams,
Robt. Treat Paine,
Elbridge Gerry.

RHODE ISLAND
Step. Hopkins,
William Ellery.

CONNECTICUT
Roger Sherman,
Samuel Huntington,
Wm. Williams,
Oliver Wolcott.

NEW YORK
Wm. Floyd,
Phil. Livingston,
Frans. Lewis,
Lewis Morris

NEW JERSEY
Richd. Stockton,
J. Witherspoon,
Fras. Hopkinson,
John Hart,
Abra. Clark.

PENNSYLVANIA
Robt. Morris,
Benjamin Rush,
Benjamin Franklin,
John Morton,
Geo. Clymer,
Jas. Smith,
Geo. Taylor,
James Wilson,
Geo. Ross.

DELAWARE
Caesar Rodney,
Geo. Read,
Tho. McKean.

MARYLAND
Samuel Chase,
Wm. Paca,
Thos. Stone,
Charles Caroll
  of Carollton.

VIRGINIA
George Wythe,
Richard Henry Lee,
Th. Jefferson,
Benjamin Harrison,
Thos. Nelson, jr.,
Francis Lightfoot Lee,
Carter Braxton.

NORTH CAROLINA
Wm. Hooper,
Joseph Hewes,
John Penn.

SOUTH CAROLINA
Edward Rutledge,
Thos. Heyward, Junr.,
Thomas Lynch, jnr.,
Arthur Middleton.

GEORGIA
Button Gwinnett,
Lyman Hall,
Geo. Walton.

APPENDIX II

THE CONSTITUTION OF THE UNITED STATES OF AMERICA

We the People of the United States, in Order to form a more perfect Union, establish Justice, insure domestic Tranquility, provide for the common defence, promote the general Welfare, and secure the Blessings of Liberty to ourselves and our Posterity, do ordain and establish this Constitution for the United States of America.

ARTICLE I

SECTION 1. All legislative Powers herein granted shall be vested in a Congress of the United States, which shall consist of a Senate and House of Representatives.

SECTION 2. The House of Representatives shall be composed of Members chosen every second Year by the People of the several States, and the Electors in each State shall have the Qualifications requisite for Electors of the most numerous Branch of the State Legislature.

No person shall be a Representative who shall not have attained to the Age of twenty five Years, and been seven Years a Citizen of the United States, and who shall not, when elected, be an Inhabitant of that State in which he shall be chosen.

Representatives and direct Taxes shall be apportioned among the several States which may be included within this Union, according to their respective Numbers which shall be determined by adding to the whole Number of free Persons, including those bound to Service for a Term of Years, and excluding Indians not taxed, three fifths of all other Persons. The actual Enumeration shall be made within three Years after the first Meeting of the Congress of the United States, and within every subsequent Term ten Years, in such Manner as they shall by Law direct. The Number of Representatives shall not exceed one for every thirty Thousand, but each State shall have at Least one Representative; and until such enumeration shall be made, the State of New Hampshire shall be entitled to chuse three, Massachusetts eight, Rhode-Island and Providence Plantations one, Connecticut five, New-York six, New Jersey four, Pennsylvania eight, Delaware one, Maryland six, Virginia ten, North Carolina five, South Carolina five, and Georgia three.

When vacancies happen in the Representation from any State, the Executive Authority thereof shall issue Writs of Election to fill such Vacancies.

The House of Representatives shall chuse their speaker and other Officers; and shall have the sole Power of Impeachment.

SECTION 3. The Senate of the United States shall be composed of two Senators from each State chosen by the Legislature thereof, for six Years; and each Senator shall have one Vote.

Immediately after they shall be assembled in Consequence of the first Election, they shall be divided as equally as may be into three Classes. The Seats of the Senators of the first Class shall be vacated at the Expiration of the second year, of the second Class at the Expiration of the fourth Year, and of the third Class at the Expiration of the sixth Year, so that one third may be chosen every second Year and if Vacancies happen by Resignation, or otherwise, during the Recess of the Legislature of any State, the Executive thereof may make temporary Appointments until the next Meeting of the Legislature, which shall then fill such Vacancies.

No Person shall be a Senator who shall not have attained to the Age of thirty Years, and been nine Years a Citizen of the United States, and who shall not, when elected, be an Inhabitant of that State for which he shall be chosen.

The Vice President of the United States shall be President of the Senate, but shall have no Vote, unless they be equally divided.

The Senate shall chuse their other Officers, and also a President pro tempore, in the Absence of the Vice President, or when he shall exercise the Office of President of the United States.

The Senate shall have the sole Power to try all Impeachments. When sitting for that Purpose, they shall be on Oath or Affirmation. When the President of the United States is tried, the Chief Justice shall preside: And no Person shall be convicted without the Concurrence of two thirds of the Members present.

Judgment in Cases of Impeachment shall not extend further than to removal from Office, and disqualification to hold and enjoy any Office of honor, Trust or Profit under the United States; but the Party convicted shall nevertheless be liable and subject to Indictment, Trial, Judgment and Punishment, according to Law.

SECTION 4. The Times, Places and Manner of holding Elections for Senators and Representatives, shall be prescribed in each State by the Legislature thereof; but the Congress may at any time by law make or alter such Regulations, except as to the Places of chusing Senators.

The Congress shall assemble at least once in every Year, and such Meeting shall be on the first Monday in December, unless they shall by Law appoint a different Day.

SECTION 5. Each House shall be the Judge of the Elections, Returns and Qualifications of its own Members, and a Majority of each shall constitute a Quorum to do Business; but a smaller Number may adjourn from day to day, and may be authorized to compel the Attendance of absent Members, in such Manner, and under such Penalties as each House may provide.

Each House may determine the Rules of its Proceedings, punish its Members for disorderly Behaviour, and with the Concurrence of two thirds, expel a Member.

Each House shall keep a journal of its Proceedings, and from time to time publish the same, excepting such Parts as may in their judgment require Secrecy; and the Yeas and Nays of the Members of either House on any question shall, at the Desire of one fifth of those present, be entered on the Journal.

Neither House, during the Session of Congress, shall, without the Consent of the other, adjourn for more than three days, nor to any other Place than that in which the two Houses shall be sitting.

SECTION 6. The Senators and Representatives shall receive a Compensation for their Services, to be ascertained by Law, and paid out of the Treasury of the United States. They shall in all Cases, except Treason, Felony and Breach of the Peace, be privileged from Arrest during their Attendance at the Session of their respective Houses, and in going to and returning from the same; and for any Speech or Debate in either House, they shall not be questioned in any other Place.

No Senator or Representative shall, during the Time for which he was elected, be appointed to any civil Office under the Authority of the United States, which shall have been created, or the Emoluments whereof shall have been encreased during such time; and no Person holding any Office under the United States, shall be a Member of either House during his Continuance in Office.

SECTION 7. All Bills for raising Revenue shall originate in the House of Representatives; but the Senate may propose or concur with Amendments as on other Bills.

Every Bill which shall have passed the House of Representatives and the Senate, shall, before it become a Law, be presented to the President of the United States; If he approves he shall sign it, but if not he shall return it, with his Objections to that House in which it shall have originated, who shall enter the Objections at large on their journal, and proceed to reconsider it. If after such Reconsideration two thirds of that House shall agree to pass the Bill, it shall be sent, together with the Objections, to the other House, by which it shall likewise be reconsidered, and if approved by two thirds of that House, it shall become a Law. But in all such Cases the Votes of both Houses shall be determined by Yeas and Nays, and the Names of the Persons voting for and against the Bill shall be entered on the Journal of each House respectively. If any Bill shall not be returned by the President within ten Days (Sundays excepted) after it shall have been presented to him, the Same shall be a Law, in like Manner as if he had signed it, unless the Congress by their Adjournment prevent its Return, in which Case it shall not be a Law.

Every Order, Resolution, or Vote to which the Concurrence of the Senate and House of Representatives may be necessary (except on a question of Adjournment) shall be presented to the President of the United States; and before the Same shall take Effect, shall be approved by him, or being disapproved by him, shall be repassed by two thirds of the Senate and House of Representatives, according to the Rules and Limitations prescribed in the Case of a Bill.

SECTION 8. The Congress shall have Power To lay and collect Taxes, Duties, Imposts and Excises, to pay the Debts and provide for the common Defence and general Welfare of the United States; but all Duties, Imposts and Excises shall be uniform throughout the United States;

To borrow Money on the credit of the United States;

To regulate Commerce with foreign Nations, and among the several States, and with the Indian Tribes;

To establish a uniform Rule of Naturalization, and uniform Laws on the subject of Bankruptcies throughout the United States;

To coin Money, regulate the Value thereof, and of foreign Coin, and fix the Standard of Weights and Measures;

To provide for the Punishment of counterfeiting the Securities and current Coin of the United States;

To establish Post Offices and post Roads;

To promote the Progress of Science and useful Arts, by securing for limited Times to Authors and Inventors the exclusive Right to their respective Writings and Discoveries;

To constitute Tribunals inferior to the supreme Court;

To define and punish Piracies and Felonies committed on the high Seas, and Offences against the Law of Nations;

To declare War, grant Letters of Marque and Reprisal, and make Rules concerning Captures on Land and Water;

To raise and support Armies, but no Appropriation of Money to that Use shall be for a longer Term than two Years;

To provide and maintain a Navy;

To make Rules for the Government and Regulation of the land and naval Forces;

To provide for calling forth the Militia to execute the Laws of the Union, suppress Insurrections and repel Invasions;

To provide for organizing, arming, and disciplining, the Militia, and for governing such Part of them as may be employed in the Service of the United States, reserving to the States respectively, the Appointment of the Officers, and the Authority of training the Militia according to the discipline prescribed by Congress;

To exercise exclusive Legislation in all Cases whatsoever, over such District (not exceeding ten Miles square) as may, by Cession of particular States, and the Acceptance of Congress, become the Seat of the Government of the United States, and to exercise like Authority over all Places purchased by the Consent of the Legislature of the State in which the Same shall be for the Erection of Forts, Magazines, Arsenals, dock-Yards, and other needful Buildings;—And

To make all Laws which shall be necessary and proper for carrying into Execution the foregoing Powers, and all other Powers vested by this Constitution in the Government of the United States, or in any Department or Officer thereof.

SECTION 9. The Migration or Importation of such Persons as any of the States now existing shall think proper to admit, shall not be prohibited by the Congress prior to the Year one thousand eight hundred and eight, but a Tax or duty may be imposed on such Importation, not exceeding ten dollars for each Person.

The Privilege of the Writ of Habeas Corpus shall not be suspended, unless when in Cases of Rebellion or Invasion the public Safety may require it.

No Bill of Attainder or ex post facto Law shall be passed.

No Capitation, or other direct, Tax shall be laid, unless in Proportion to the Census or Enumeration herein before directed to be taken.

No Tax or Duty shall be laid on Articles exported from any State.

No Preference shall be given by any Regulation of Commerce or Revenue to the Ports of one State over those of another; nor shall Vessels bound to, or from, one State, be obliged to enter, clear, or pay Duties in another.

No Money shall be drawn from the Treasury, but in Consequence of Appropriations made by Law; and a regular Statement and Account of the Receipts and Expenditures of all public Money shall be published from time to time.

No Title of Nobility shall be granted by the United States: And no Person holding any Office of Profit or Trust under them, shall, without the Consent of the Congress, accept of any present, Emolument, Office, or Title, of any kind whatever, from any King, Prince, or foreign State.

SECTION 10. No state shall enter into any Treaty, Alliance, or Confederation; grant Letters of Marque and Reprisal; coin Money; emit Bills of Credit; make any Thing but gold and silver Coin a Tender in Payment of Debts; pass any Bill of Attainder, ex post facto Law, or Law impairing the Obligation of Contracts, or grant any Title of Nobility.

No State shall, without the Consent of the Congress, lay any Imposts or Duties on Imports or Exports, except what may be absolutely necessary for executing its inspection Laws: and the net Produce of all Duties and Imposts, laid by any State on Imports or Exports, shall be for the Use of the Treasury of the United States, and all such Laws shall be subject to the Revision and Controul of the Congress.

No State shall, without the Consent of Congress, lay any Duty of Tonnage, keep Troops, or Ships of War in time of Peace, enter into any Agreement or Compact with another State, or with a foreign Power, or engage in War, unless actually invaded, or in such imminent Danger as will not admit of delay.

ARTICLE II

SECTION 1. The executive Power shall be vested in a President of the United States of America. He shall hold his Office during the Term of four Years, and, together with the Vice President, chosen for the same Term, be elected as follows.

Each State shall appoint, in such Manner as the Legislature thereof may direct, a Number of Electors, equal to the whole Number of Senators and Representatives to which the State may be entitled in the Congress; but no Senator or Representative, or Person holding an Office of Trust of Profit under the United States, shall be appointed an Elector.

The Electors shall meet in their respective States, and vote by Ballot for two Persons, of whom one at least shall not be an Inhabitant of the same State with themselves. And they shall make a List of all the Persons voted for, and, of the Number of Votes for each; which List they shall sign and certify, and transmit sealed to the Seat of the Government of the United States, directed to the President of the Senate. The President of the Senate shall, in the Presence of the Senate and House of Representatives, open all the Certificates, and the Votes shall then be counted. The Person having the greatest Number of Votes shall be the President, if such Number be a Majority of the whole Number of Electors appointed; and if there be more than one who have such Majority, and have an equal Number of Votes, then the House of Representatives shall immediately chuse by Ballot one of them for President; and if no Person have a Majority, then from the five highest on the List the said House shall in like Manner chuse the President. But in chusing the President, the Votes shall be taken by States, the Representation from each State having one Vote; A quorum for this Purpose shall consist of a Member or Members from two thirds of the States, and a Majority of all the States shall be necessary to a Choice. In every Case, after the Choice of the President, the Person having the greatest Number of Votes of the Electors shall be the Vice President. But if there should remain two or more who have equal Votes, the Senate shall chuse from them by Ballot the Vice President.

The Congress may determine the Time of chusing the Electors, and the Day on which they shall give their Votes; which Day shall be the same throughout the United States.

No Person except a natural born Citizen, or a Citizen of the United States, at the time of the Adoption of this Constitution, shall be eligible to the Office of President; neither shall any Person be eligible to that Office who shall not have attained to the Age of thirty five Years, and been fourteen Years a Resident within the United States.

In Case of the Removal of the President from Office, or of his Death, Resignation, or Inability to discharge the Powers and Duties of the said Office, the Same shall devolve on the Vice President, and the Congress may by Law provide for the Case of Removal, Death, Resignation or Inability, both of the President and Vice President, declaring what Officer shall then act as President, and such Officer shall act accordingly, until the Disability be removed, or a President shall be elected.

The President shall, at stated Times, receive for his Services, a Compensation, which shall neither be encreased nor diminished during the Period for which he shall have been elected, and he shall not receive within that Period any other Emolument from the United States, or any of them.

Before he enter on the Execution of his Office, he shall take the following Oath or Affirmation—"I do solemnly swear (or affirm) that I will faithfully execute the Office of President of the United States, and will to the best of my Ability, preserve, protect and defend the Constitution of the United States."

Section 2. The President shall be Commander in Chief of the Army, and Navy of the United States, and of the Militia of the several States, when called into the actual Service of the United States; he may require the Opinion, in writing, of the principal Officer in each of the executive Departments, upon any Subject relating to the Duties of their respective Offices, and he shall have Power to grant Reprieves and Pardons for Offences against the United States, except in Cases of Impeachment.

He shall have Power, by and with the Advice and Consent of the Senate, to make Treaties, provided two thirds of the Senators present concur; and he shall nominate, and by and with the Advice and Consent of the Senate, shall appoint Ambassadors, other public Ministers and Consuls, Judges of the supreme Court, and all other Officers of the United States, whose Appointments are not herein otherwise provided for, and which shall be established by Law: but the Congress may by Law vest the Appointment of such inferior Officers, as they think proper, in the President alone, in the Courts of Law, or in the Heads of Departments.

The President shall have Power to fill up all Vacancies that may happen during the Recess of the Senate, by granting Commissions which shall expire at the end of their next Session.

Section 3. He shall from time to time give to the Congress Information of the State of the Union, and recommend to their Consideration such Measures as he shall judge necessary and expedient; he may, on extraordinary Occasions, convene both Houses, or either of them, and in Case of Disagreement between them, with Respect to the Time of Adjournment, he may adjourn them to such Time as he shall think proper; he shall receive Ambassadors and other public Ministers; he shall take Care that the Laws be faithfully executed, and shall Commission all the Officers of the United States.

Section 4. The President, Vice President and all civil Officers of the United States, shall be removed from Office on Impeachment for, and Conviction of, Treason, Bribery, or other high Crimes and Misdemeanors.

ARTICLE III

Section 1. The judicial Power of the United States, shall be vested in one supreme Court, and in such inferior Courts as the Congress may from time to time ordain and establish. The Judges, both of the supreme and inferior Courts, shall hold their Offices during good Behaviour, and shall, at stated Times, receive for their Services, a Compensation, which shall not be diminished during their Continuance in Office.

Section 2. The judicial Power shall extend to all Cases, in Law and Equity, arising under this Constitution, the Laws of the United States, and Treaties made, or which shall be made, under their Authority;—to all Cases affecting Ambassadors, other public Ministers and Consuls;—to all Cases of admiralty and maritime Jurisdiction;—to Controversies to which the United States shall be a Party;—to Controversies between two or more States;—between a State and Citizens of another State;—between Citizens of different States,—between Citizens of the same State claiming Lands under Grants of different States,—and between a State, or the Citizens thereof, and foreign States, Citizens of Subjects.

In all Cases affecting Ambassadors, other public Ministers and Consuls, and those in which a State shall be Party, the supreme Court shall have original Jurisdiction. In all the other Cases before mentioned, the supreme Court shall have appellate Jurisdiction, both as to Law and Fact, with such Exceptions, and under such Regulations as the Congress shall make.

The Trial of all Crimes, except in Cases of Impeachment, shall be by Jury; and such Trial shall be held in the State where the said Crimes shall have been committed; but when not committed within any State, the Trial shall be at such Place or Places as the Congress may by Law have directed.

Section 3. Treason against the United States, shall consist only in levying War against them, or in adhering to their Enemies, giving them Aid and Comfort. No Person shall be convicted of Treason unless on the Testimony of two Witnesses to the same overt Act, or on Confession in open Court.

The Congress shall have Power to declare the Punishment of Treason, but no Attainder of Treason shall work Corruption of Blood, or Forfeiture except during the Life of the Person attainted.

ARTICLE IV

Section 1. Full Faith and Credit shall be given in each State to the public Acts, Records, and judicial Proceedings of every other State. And the Congress may by general Laws prescribe the Manner in which such Acts, Records and Proceedings shall be proved, and the Effect thereof.

Section 2. The Citizens of each State shall be entitled to all Privileges and Immunities of Citizens in the several States.

A Person charged in any State with Treason, Felony, or other Crime, who shall flee from Justice, and be found in another State, shall on Demand of the executive Authority of the State from which he fled, be delivered up, to be removed to the State having Jurisdiction of the Crime.

No Person held to Service or Labour in one State under the Laws thereof, escaping into another, shall, in Consequence of any Law or Regulation therein, be discharged from such Service or Labour, but shall be delivered up on Claim of the Party to whom such Service or Labour may be due.

SECTION 3. New States may be admitted by the Congress into this Union; but no new State shall be formed or erected within the Jurisdiction of any other State; nor any State be formed by the Junction of two or more States, or Parts of States, without the Consent of the Legislatures of the States concerned as well as of the Congress.

The Congress shall have Power to dispose of and make all needful Rules and Regulations respecting the Territory or other Property belonging to the United States; and nothing in this Constitution shall be so construed as to Prejudice any Claims of the United States, or of any particular State.

SECTION 4. The United States shall guarantee to every State in this Union a Republican Form of Government, and shall protect each of them against Invasion, and on Application of the Legislature, or of the Executive (when the Legislature cannot be convened) against domestic Violence.

ARTICLE V

The Congress, whenever two thirds of both Houses shall deem it necessary, shall propose Amendments to this Constitution, or, on the Application of the Legislatures of two thirds of the several States, shall call a Convention for proposing Amendments, which, in either Case, shall be valid to all Intents and Purposes, as Part of this Constitution, when ratified by the Legislatures of three fourths of the several States, or by Conventions in three fourths thereof, as the one or the other Mode of Ratification may be proposed by the Congress; Provided that no Amendment which may be made prior to the Year One thousand eight hundred and eight shall in any Manner affect the first and fourth Clauses in the Ninth Section of the first Article; and that no State, without its Consent, shall be deprived of its equal Suffrage in the Senate.

ARTICLE VI

All Debts contracted and Engagements entered into, before the Adoption of this Constitution, shall be as valid against the United States under this Constitution, as under the Confederation.

This Constitution, and the laws of the United States which shall be made in Pursuance thereof; and all Treaties made, or which shall be made, under the Authority of the United States, shall be the supreme Law of the Land; and the Judges in every State shall be bound thereby, any Thing in the Constitution or Laws of any State to the Contrary notwithstanding.

The Senators and Representatives before mentioned, and the Members of the several State Legislatures, and all executive and judicial Officers, both of the United States and of the several States, shall be bound by Oath or Affirmation, to support this Constitution; but no religious Test shall ever be required as a Qualification to any Office or public Trust under the United States.

ARTICLE VII

The Ratification of the Conventions of nine States, shall be sufficient for the Establishment of this Constitution between the States so ratifying the Same.

Done in Convention by the Unanimous Consent of the States present the Seventeenth Day of September in the Year of our Lord one thousand seven hundred and Eighty seven and of the Independence of the United States of America the Twelfth. IN WITNESS whereof we have hereunto subscribed our Names,

Go. WASHINGTON,
Presid't. and deputy from Virginia

Attest
WILLIAM JACKSON,
Secretary.

DELAWARE
Geo. Read,
Gunning Bedford jun,
John Dickinson,
Richard Basset,
Jaco. Broom.

MASSACHUSETTS BAY
Nathaniel Gorham,
Rufus King.

CONNECTICUT
Wm. Saml. Johnson,
Roger Sherman.

NEW YORK
Alexander Hamilton.

NEW JERSEY
Wi. Livingston,
David Brearley,
Wm. Paterson,
Jona. Dayton.

PENNSYLVANIA
B. Franklin,
Thomas Mifflin,
Robt. Morris,
Geo. Clymer,
Thos. FitzSimons,
Jared Ingersoll,
James Wilson,
Gouv. Morris

NEW HAMPSHIRE
John Langdon,
Nicholas Gilman.

MARYLAND
James McHenry,
Dan of St. Thos. Jenifer,
Danl. Carroll.

VIRGINIA
John Blair,
James Madison, Jr..

NORTH CAROLINA
Wm. Blount,
Richd. Dobbs Spaight,
Hu. Williamson.

SOUTH CAROLINA
J. Rutledge,
Charles Cotesworth Pinckney,
Charles Pinckney.
Pierce Butler

GEORGIA
William Few,
Abr. Baldwin

Articles in addition to, and amendment of the Constitution of the United States of America, proposed by Congress and ratified by the Legislatures of the several states, pursuant to the Fifth Article of the original Constitution.

(The first ten amendments were passed by Congress on September 25, 1789, and were ratified on December 15, 1791.)

AMENDMENT I

Congress shall make no law respecting an establishment of religion, or prohibiting the free exercise thereof; or abridging the freedom of speech, or of the press; or the right of the people peaceably to assemble, and to petition the Government for a redress of grievances.

AMENDMENT II

A well regulated Militia, being necessary to the security of a free State, the right of the people to keep and bear Arms, shall not be infringed.

AMENDMENT III

No Soldier shall, in time of peace be quartered in any house, without the consent of the Owner, nor in time of war, but in a manner to be prescribed by law.

AMENDMENT IV

The right of the people to be secure in their persons, houses, papers, and effects, against unreasonable searches and seizures, shall not be violated, and no warrants shall issue, but upon probable cause, supported by Oath or affirmation, and particularly describing the place to be searched, and the persons or things to be seized.

AMENDMENT V

No person shall be held to answer for a capital, or otherwise infamous crime, unless on a presentment or indictment of a Grand Jury, except in cases arising in the land or naval forces, or in the Militia, when in actual service in time of War or public danger; nor shall any person be subject for the same offence to be twice put in jeopardy of life or limb; nor shall be compelled in any criminal case to be a witness against himself, nor be deprived of life, liberty, or property, without due process of law; nor shall private property be taken for public use, without just compensation.

AMENDMENT VI

In all criminal prosecutions, the accused shall enjoy the right to a speedy and public trial, by an impartial jury of the State and district wherein the crime shall have been committed, which district shall have been previously ascertained by law, and to be informed of the nature and cause of the accusation; to be confronted with the witnesses against him; to have compulsory process for obtaining witnesses in his favor, and to have the assistance of counsel for his defence.

AMENDMENT VII

In Suits at common law, where the value in controversy shall exceed twenty dollars, the right of trial by jury shall be preserved, and no fact tried by a jury, shall be otherwise reexamined in any Court of the United States, than according to the rules of the common law.

AMENDMENT VIII

Excessive bail shall not be required, nor excessive fines imposed, nor cruel and unusual punishments inflicted.

AMENDMENT IX

The enumeration in the Constitution, of certain rights, shall not be construed to deny or disparage others retained by the people.

AMENDMENT X

The powers not delegated to the United States by the Constitution, nor prohibited by it to the States, are reserved to the States respectively, or to the people.

AMENDMENT XI *(Ratified on February 7, 1795)*

The Judicial power of the United States shall not be construed to extend to any suit in law or equity, commenced or prosecuted against one of the United States by Citizens of another State, or by Citizens or Subjects of any Foreign State.

AMENDMENT XII *(Ratified on June 15, 1804)*

The Electors shall meet in their respective states, and vote by ballot for President and Vice-President, one of whom, at least, shall not be an inhabitant of the same state with themselves; they shall name in their ballots the person voted for as President, and in distinct ballots the person voted for as Vice-President, and they shall make distinct lists of all persons voted for as President, and of all persons voted for as Vice-President, and of the number of votes for each, which lists they shall sign and certify, and transmit sealed to the seat of the government of the United States, directed to the President of the Senate;—The President of the Senate shall, in the presence of the Senate and House of Representatives, open all the certificates and the votes shall then be counted;—The person having the greatest number of votes for President, shall be the President, if such number be a majority of the whole number of Electors appointed; and if no person have such majority, then from the persons having the highest numbers not exceeding three on the list of those voted for as President, the House of Representatives shall choose immediately, by ballot, the President. But in choosing the President, the votes shall be taken by states, the representation from each state having one vote; a quorum for this purpose shall consist of a member or members from two-thirds of the states, and a majority of all the states shall be necessary to a choice. And if the House of Representatives shall not choose a President whenever the right of choice shall devolve upon them, before the fourth day of March next following, then the Vice-President shall act as President, as in the case of the death or other constitutional disability of the President.—The person having the greatest number of votes as Vice-President, shall be the Vice-President, if such number be a majority of the whole number of Electors appointed, and if no person have a majority, then from the two highest numbers on the list, the Senate shall choose the Vice-President; a quorum for the purpose shall consist of two-thirds of the whole number of Senators, and a majority of the whole number shall be necessary to a choice. But no person constitutionally ineligible to the office of President shall be eligible to that of Vice-President of the United States.

AMENDMENT XIII *(Ratified on December 6, 1865)*

SECTION 1. Neither slavery nor involuntary servitude, except as a punishment for crime whereof the party shall have been duly convicted, shall exist within the United States, or any place subject to their jurisdiction.

SECTION 2. Congress shall have power to enforce this article by appropriate legislation.

AMENDMENT XIV *(Ratified on July 9, 1868)*

SECTION 1. All persons born or naturalized in the United States, and subject to the jurisdiction thereof, are citizens of the United States and of the State wherein they reside. No State shall make or enforce any law which shall abridge the privileges or immunities of citizens of the United States; nor shall any State deprive any person of life, liberty, or property, without due process of law; nor deny to any person within its jurisdiction the equal protection of the laws.

SECTION 2. Representatives shall be apportioned among the several States according to their respective numbers, counting the whole number of persons in each State, excluding Indians not taxed. But when the right to vote at any election for the choice of electors for President and Vice President of the United States, Representatives in Congress, the Executive and Judicial officers of a State, or the members of the Legislature thereof, is denied to any of the male inhabitants of such State, being twenty-one years of age, and citizens of the United States, or in any way abridged, except for participation in rebellion, or other crime, the basis of representation therein shall be reduced in the proportion which the number of such male citizens shall bear to the whole number of male citizens twenty-one years of age in such State.

SECTION 3. No person shall be a Senator or Representative in Congress, or elector of President and Vice President, or hold any office, civil or military, under the United States, or under any State, who, having previously taken an oath, as a member of Congress, or as an officer of the United States, or as a member of any State legislature, or as an executive or judicial officer of any State, to support the Constitution of the United States, shall have engaged in insurrection or rebellion against the same, or given aid or comfort to the enemies thereof. But Congress may by a vote of two-thirds of each House, remove such diability.

SECTION 4. The validity of the public debt of the United States, authorized by law, including debts incurred for payment of pensions and bounties for services in suppressing insurrection or rebellion, shall not be questioned. But neither the United States nor any State shall assume or pay any debt or obligation incurred in aid of insurrection or rebellion against the United States, or any claim for the loss or emancipation of any slave, but all such debts, obligations and claims shall be held illegal and void.

SECTION 5. The Congress shall have power to enforce, by appropriate legislation, the provisions of this article.

AMENDMENT XV *(Ratified on February 3, 1870)*

SECTION 1. The right of citizens of the United States to vote shall not be denied or abridged by the United States or by any State on account of race, color, or previous condition of servitude.

SECTION 2. The Congress shall have power to enforce this article by appropriate legislation.

AMENDMENT XVI *(Ratified on February 3, 1913)*

The Congress shall have power to lay and collect taxes on incomes, from whatever source derived, without apportionment among the several States, and without regard to any census or enumeration.

AMENDMENT XVII *(Ratified on April 8, 1913)*

The Senate of the United States shall be composed of two Senators from each State, elected by the people thereof, for six years; and each Senator shall have one vote. The electors in each State shall have the qualifications requisite for electors of the most numerous branch of the State legislatures.

When vacancies happen in the representation of any State in the Senate, the executive authority of such State shall issue writs of election to fill such vacancies: Provided, That the legislature of any State may empower the executive thereof to make temporary appointments until the people fill the vacancies by election as the legislature may direct.

This amendment shall not be so construed as to affect the election or term of any Senator chosen before it becomes valid as part of the Constitution.

AMENDMENT XVIII *(Ratified on January 16, 1919)*

SECTION 1. After one year from the ratification of this article the manufacture, sale, or transportation of intoxicating liquors within, the importation thereof into, or the exportation thereof from the United States and all territory subject to the jurisdiction thereof for beverage purposes is hereby prohibited.

SECTION 2. The Congress and the several States shall have concurrent power to enforce this article by appropriate legislation.

SECTION 3. This article shall be inoperative unless it shall have been ratified as an amendment to the Constitution by the legislatures of the several States, as provided in the Constitution, within seven years from the date of the submission hereof to the States by the Congress.

AMENDMENT XIX *(Ratified on August 18, 1920)*

The right of citizens of the United States to vote shall not be denied or abridged by the United States or by any State on account of sex.

Congress shall have power to enforce this article by appropriate legislation.

AMENDMENT XX *(Ratified on February 6, 1933)*

SECTION 1. The terms of the President and Vice President shall end at noon on the 20th day of January, and the terms of Senators and Representatives at noon on the 3d day of January, of the years in which such terms would have ended if this article had not been ratified; and the terms of their successors shall then begin.

SECTION 2. The Congress shall assemble at least once in every year, and such meeting shall begin at noon on the 3d day of January, unless they shall by law appoint a different day.

SECTION 3. If, at the time fixed for the beginning of the term of the President, the President elect shall have died, the Vice President elect shall become President. If a President shall not have been chosen before the time fixed for the beginning of his term, or if the President elect shall have failed to qualify, then the Vice President elect shall act as President until a President shall have qualified; and the Congress may by law provide for the case wherein neither a President elect nor a Vice President elect shall have qualified, declaring who shall then act as President, or the manner in which one who is to act shall be selected, and such person shall act accordingly until a President or Vice President shall have qualified.

SECTION 4. The Congress may by law provide for the case of the death of any of the persons from whom the House of Representatives may choose a President whenever the rights of choice shall have devolved upon them, and for the case of the death of any of the persons from whom the Senate may choose a Vice President whenever the right of choice shall have devolved upon them.

SECTION 5. Sections 1 and 2 shall take effect on the 15th day of October following the ratification of this article.

SECTION 6. This article shall be inoperative unless it shall have been ratified as an amendment to the Constitution by the legislatures of three-fourths of the several States within seven years from the date of its submission.

AMENDMENT XXI *(Ratified on December 5, 1933)*

SECTION 1. The eighteenth article of amendment to the Constitution of the United States is hereby repealed.

SECTION 2. The transportation or importation into any State, Territory, or possession of the United States for delivery or use therein of intoxicating liquors, in violation of the laws thereof, is hereby prohibited.

SECTION 3. This article shall be inoperative unless it shall have been ratified as an amendment to the Constitution by conventions in the several States, as provided in the Constitution, within seven years from the date of the submission hereof to the States by the Congress.

AMENDMENT XXII *(Ratified on February 27, 1951)*

No person shall be elected to the office of the President more than twice, and no person who has held the office of President, or acted as President, for more than two years of a term to which some other person was elected President shall be elected to the office of the President more than once. But this Article shall not apply to any person holding the office of President when this Article was proposed by the Congress, and shall not prevent any person who may be holding the office of President, or acting as President, during the term within which this Article becomes operative from holding the office of President or acting as President during the remainder of such term.

AMENDMENT XXIII *(Ratified on March 29, 1961)*

SECTION 1. The District constituting the seat of Government of the United States shall appoint in such manner as the Congress may direct:

A number of electors of President and Vice President equal to the whole number of Senators and Representatives in Congress to which the District would be entitled if it were a State, but in no event more than the least populous State; they shall be in addition to those appointed by the States, but they shall be considered, for the purposes of the election of President and Vice President, to be electors appointed by a State; and they shall meet in the District and perform such duties as provided by the twelfth article of amendment.

SECTION 2. The Congress shall have power to enforce this article by appropriate legislation.

AMENDMENT XXIV *(Ratified on January 23, 1964)*

SECTION 1. The right of citizens of the United States to vote in any primary or other election for President or Vice President, for electors for President or Vice President, or for Senator or Representative in Congress, shall not be denied or abridged by the United States or any State by reason of failure to pay any poll tax or other tax.

SECTION 2. The Congress shall have power to enforce this article by appropriate legislation.

AMENDMENT XXV *(Ratified on February 10, 1967)*

SECTION 1. In case of the removal of the President from office or of his death or resignation, the Vice President shall become President.

SECTION 2. Whenever there is a vacancy in the office of the Vice President, the President shall nominate a Vice President who shall take office upon confirmation by a majority vote of both Houses of Congress.

SECTION 3. Whenever the President transmits to the President pro tempore of the Senate and the Speaker of the House of Representatives his written declaration that he is unable to discharge the powers and duties of his office, and until he transmits to them a written declaration to the contrary, such powers and duties shall be discharged by the Vice President as Acting President.

SECTION 4. Whenever the Vice President and a majority of either the principal officers of the executive departments or of such other body as Congress may by law provide, transmit to the President pro tempore of the Senate and the Speaker of the House of Representatives their written declaration that the President is unable to discharge the powers and duties of his office, the Vice President shall immediately assume the powers and duties of the office as Acting President.

Thereafter, when the President transmits to the President pro tempore of the Senate and the Speaker of the House of Representatives his written declaration that no inability exists, he shall resume the powers and duties of his office unless the Vice President and a majority of either the principal officers of the executive department or of such other body as Congress may by law provide, transmit within four days to the President pro tempore of the Senate and the Speaker of the House of Representatives their written declaration that the President is unable to discharge the powers and duties of his office. Thereupon Congress shall decide the issue, assembling within forty-eight hours for that purpose if not in session. If the Congress, within twenty-one days after receipt of the latter written declaration, or, if Congress is not in session, within twenty-one days after Congress is required to assemble, determines by two-thirds vote of both Houses that the President is unable to discharge the powers and duties of his office, the Vice President shall continue to discharge the same as Acting President; otherwise, the President shall resume the powers and duties of his office.

AMENDMENT XXVI *(Ratified on July 1, 1971)*

SECTION 1. The right of citizens of the United States, who are eighteen years of age or older, to vote shall not be denied or abridged by the United States or by any State on account of age.

SECTION 2. The Congress shall have power to enforce this article by appropriate legislation.

AMENDMENT XXVII *(Ratified on May 7, 1992)*

No law varying the compensation for the services of Senators and Representatives shall take effect until an election of Representatives shall have intervened.

APPENDIX III

FEDERALIST NO. 10

November 22, 1787

James Madison

TO THE PEOPLE OF THE STATE OF NEW YORK.

Among the numerous advantages promised by a well constructed Union, none deserves to be more accurately developed than its tendency to break and control the violence of faction. The friend of popular governments, never finds himself so much alarmed for their character and fate, as when he contemplates their propensity to this dangerous vice. He will not fail therefore to set a due value on any plan which, without violating the principles to which he is attached, provides a proper cure for it. The instability, injustice and confusion introduced into the public councils, have in truth been the mortal diseases under which popular governments have every where perished; as they continue to be the favorite and fruitful topics from which the adversaries to liberty derive their most specious declamations. The valuable improvements made by the American Constitutions on the popular models, both ancient and modern, cannot certainly be too much admired; but it would be an unwarrantable partiality, to contend that they have as effectually obviated the danger on this side as was wished and expected. Complaints are every where heard from our most considerate and virtuous citizens, equally the friends of public and private faith, and of public and personal liberty; that our governments are too unstable; that the public good is disregarded in the conflicts of rival parties; and that measures are too often decided, not according to the rules of justice, and the rights of the minor party; but by the superior force of an interested and over-bearing majority. However anxiously we may wish that these complaints had no foundation, the evidence of known facts will not permit us to deny that they are in some degree true. It will be found indeed, on a candid review of our situation, that some of the distresses under which we labor, have been erroneously charged on the operation of our governments; but it will be found, at the same time, that other causes will not alone account for many of our heaviest misfortunes; and particularly, for that prevailing and increasing distrust of public engagements, and alarm for private rights, which are echoed from one end of the continent to the other. These must be chiefly, if not wholly, effects of the unsteadiness

and injustice, with which a factious spirit has tainted our public administrations.

By a faction I understand a number of citizens, whether amounting to a majority or minority of the whole, who are united and actuated by some common impulse of passion, or of interest, adverse to the rights of other citizens, or to the permanent and aggregate interests of the community.

There are two methods of curing the mischiefs of faction: the one, by removing its causes; the other, by controlling its effects.

There are again two methods of removing the causes of faction: the one by destroying the liberty which is essential to its existence; the other, by giving to every citizen the same opinions, the same passions, and the same interests.

It could never be more truly said than of the first remedy, that it is worse than the disease. Liberty is to faction, what air is to fire, an aliment without which it instantly expires. But it could not be a less folly to abolish liberty, which is essential to political life, because it nourishes faction, than it would be to wish the annihilation of air, which is essential to animal life, because it imparts to fire its destructive agency.

The second expedient is as impracticable, as the first would be unwise. As long as the reason of man continues fallible, and he is at liberty to exercise it, different opinions will be formed. As long as the connection subsists between his reason and his self-love, his opinions and his passions will have a reciprocal influence on each other; and the former will be objects to which the latter will attach themselves. The diversity in the faculties of men from which the rights of property originate, is not less an insuperable obstacle to a uniformity of interests. The protection of these faculties is the first object of Government. From the protection of different and unequal faculties of acquiring property, the possession of different degrees and kinds of property immediately results: and from the influence of these on the sentiments and views of the respective proprietors, ensues a division of the society into different interests and parties.

The latent causes of faction are thus sown in the nature of man; and we see them every where brought into different degrees of activity, according to the different circumstances of civil society. A zeal for different opinions concerning religion, concerning Government and many other points, as well of speculation as of practice; an attachment to different leaders ambitiously contending for pre-eminence and power; or to persons of other descriptions whose fortunes have been interesting to the human passions, have in turn divided mankind into parties, inflamed them with mutual animosity, and rendered them much more disposed to vex and oppress each other, than to cooperate for their common good. So strong is this propensity of mankind to fall into mutual animosities, that where no substantial occasion presents itself, the most frivolous and fanciful distinctions have been sufficient to kindle their unfriendly passions, and excite their most violent conflicts. But the most common and durable source of factions, has been the various and unequal distribution of property. Those who hold, and those who are without property, have ever formed distinct interests in society. Those who are creditors, and those who are debtors, fall under a like discrimination. A landed interest, a manufacturing interest, a mercantile interest, a monied interest, with many lesser interests, grow up of necessity in civilized nations, and divide them into different classes, actuated by different sentiments and views. The regulation of these various and interfering interests forms the principal task of modern Legislation, and involves the spirit of party and faction in the necessary and ordinary operations of Government.

No man is allowed to be a judge in his own cause; because his interest would certainly bias his judgment, and, not improbably, corrupt his integrity. With equal, nay with greater reason, a body of men, are unfit to be both judges and parties, at the same time; yet, what are many of the most important acts of legislation, but so many judicial determinations, not indeed concerning the rights of single persons, but concerning the rights of large bodies of citizens, and what are the different classes of legislators, but advocates and parties to the causes which they determine? Is a law proposed concerning private debts? It is a question to which the creditors are parties on one side, and the debtors on the other. Justice ought to hold the balance between them. Yet the parties are and must be themselves the judges; and the most numerous party, or, in other words, the most powerful faction must be expected to prevail. Shall domestic manufactures be encouraged, and in what degree, by restrictions on foreign manufactures? are questions which would be differently decided by the landed and the manufacturing classes; and probably by neither, with a sole regard to justice and the public good. The apportionment of taxes on the various descriptions of property, is an act which seems to require the most exact impartiality; yet, there is perhaps no legislative act in which greater opportunity and temptation are given to a predominant party, to trample on the rules of justice. Every shilling with which they over-burden the inferior number, is a shilling saved to their own pockets.

It is in vain to say, that enlightened statesmen will be able to adjust these clashing interests, and render them all subservient to the public good. Enlightened statesmen will not always be at the helm: Nor, in many cases, can such an adjustment be made at all, without taking into view indirect and remote considerations, which will rarely prevail over the immediate interest which one party may find in disregarding the rights of another, or the good of the whole.

The inference to which we are brought, is, that the *causes* of faction cannot be removed; and that relief is only to be sought in the means of controlling its *effects*.

If a faction consists of less than a majority, relief is supplied by the republican principle, which enables the majority to defeat its sinister views by regular vote: It may clog the administration, it may convulse the society; but it will be unable to execute and mask its violence under the forms of the Constitution. When a majority is included in a faction, the form of popular government on the other hand enables it to sacrifice to its ruling passion or interest, both the public good and the rights of other citizens. To secure the public good, and private rights, against the danger of such a faction, and at the same time to preserve the spirit and the form of popular government, is then the great object to which our enquiries are directed: Let me add that it is the great desideratum, by which alone this form of government can be rescued from the opprobrium under which it has so long labored, and be recommended to the esteem and adoption of mankind.

By what means is this object attainable? Evidently by one of two only. Either the existence of the same passion or interest in a majority at the same time, must be prevented; or the majority, having such co-existent passion or interest, must be rendered, by their number and local situation, unable to concert and carry into effect schemes of oppression. If the impulse and the opportunity be suffered to coincide, we well know that neither moral nor religious motives can be relied on as an adequate control. They are not found to be such on the injustice and violence of individuals, and lose their efficacy in proportion to the number combined together; that is, in proportion as their efficacy becomes needful.

From this view of the subject, it may be concluded, that a pure Democracy, by which I mean, a Society, consisting of a small number of citizens, who assemble and administer the Government in person, can admit of no cure for the mischiefs of faction. A common passion or interest will, in almost every case, be felt by a majority of the whole; a communication and concert results from the form of Government itself; and there is nothing to check the inducements to sacrifice the weaker party, or an obnoxious individual. Hence it is, that such Democracies have ever been spectacles of turbulence and contention; have ever been found incompatible with personal security, or the rights of property; and have in general been as short in their lives, as they have been violent in their deaths. Theoretic politicians, who have patronized this species of Government, have erroneously supposed, that by reducing mankind to a perfect equality in their political rights, they would, at the same time, be perfectly equalized and assimilated in their possessions, their opinions, and their passions.

A republic, by which I mean a government in which the scheme of representation takes place, opens a different prospect, and promises the cure for which we are seeking. Let us examine the points in which it varies from pure democracy, and we shall comprehend both the nature of the cure and the efficacy which it must derive from the union.

The two great points of difference, between a democracy and a republic, are, first, the delegation of the government, in the latter, to a small number of citizens, elected by the rest; secondly, the greater number of citizens, and greater sphere of country, over which the latter may be extended.

The effect of the first difference is, on the one hand, to refine and enlarge the public views, by passing them through the medium of a chosen body of citizens, whose wisdom may best discern the true interest of their country, and whose patriotism and love of justice, will be least likely to sacrifice it to temporary or partial considerations. Under such a regulation, it may well happen, that the public voice, pronounced by the representatives of the people, will be more consonant to the public good, than if pronounced by the people themselves, convened for the purpose. On the other hand the effect may be inverted. Men of factious tempers, of local prejudices, or of sinister designs, may by intrigue, by corruption, or by other means, first obtain the suffrages, and then betray the interest of the people. The question resulting is, whether small or extensive republics are most favorable to the election of proper guardians of the public weal, and it is clearly decided in favor of the latter by two obvious considerations.

In the first place, it is to be remarked that, however small the republic may be, the representatives must be raised to a certain number, in order to guard against the cabals of a few; and that however large it may be, they must be limited to a certain number, in order to guard against the confusion of a multitude. Hence, the number of representatives in the two cases not being in proportion to that of the constituents, and being proportionally greatest in the small republic, it follows, that if the proportion of fit characters be not less in the large than in the small republic, the former will present a greater option, and consequently a greater probability of a fit choice.

In the next place, as each Representative will be chosen by a greater number of citizens in the large than in the small Republic, it will be more difficult for unworthy candidates to practise with success the vicious arts, by which elections are too often carried; and the suffrages of the people being more free, will be more likely to center on men who possess the most attractive merit, and the most diffusive and established characters.

It must be confessed, that in this, as in most other cases, there is a mean, on both sides of which inconveniences will be found to lie. By enlarging too much the number of electors, you render the representatives too little acquainted with all their local circumstances and lesser interests; as by reducing it too much, you render him unduly attached to these, and too little fit to comprehend and pursue great and national objects. The Federal Constitution forms a happy combination in this respect; the great and aggregate interests being referred to the national, the local and particular, to the state legislatures.

The other point of difference is, the greater number of citizens and extent of territory which may be brought within the compass of Republican, than of Democratic Government; and it is this circumstance principally which renders factious combinations less to be dreaded in the former, than in the latter. The smaller the society, the fewer probably will be the distinct parties and interests composing it; the fewer the distinct parties and interests, the more frequently will a majority be found of the same party; and the smaller the number of individuals composing a majority, and the smaller the compass within which they are placed, the more easily will they concert and execute their plans of oppression. Extend the sphere, and you take in a greater variety of parties and interests; you make it less probable that a majority of the whole will have a common motive to invade the rights of other citizens; or if such a common motive exists, it will be more difficult for all who feel it to discover their own strength, and to act in unison with each other. Besides other impediments, it may be remarked, that where there is a consciousness of unjust or dishonorable purposes, communication is always checked by distrust, in proportion to the number whose concurrence is necessary.

Hence it clearly appears, that the same advantage, which a Republic has over a Democracy, in controlling the effects of faction, is enjoyed by a large over a small Republic—is enjoyed by the Union over the States composing it. Does this advantage consist in the substitution of Representatives, whose enlightened views and virtuous sentiments render them superior to local prejudices, and to schemes of injustice? It will not be denied, that the Representation of the Union will be most likely to possess these requisite endowments. Does it consist in the greater security afforded by a greater variety of parties, against the event of any one party being able to outnumber and oppress the rest? In an equal degree does the increased variety of parties, comprised within the Union, increase this security? Does it, in fine, consist in the greater obstacles opposed to the concert and accomplishment of the secret wishes of an unjust and interested majority? Here, again, the extent of the Union gives it the most palpable advantage.

The influence of factious leaders may kindle a flame within their particular States, but will be unable to spread a general conflagration through the other States: a religious sect, may degenerate into a political faction in a part of the Confederacy but the variety of sects dispersed over the entire face of it, must secure the national Councils against any danger from that source: a rage for paper money, for an abolition of debts, for an equal division of property, or for any other improper or wicked project, will be less apt to pervade the whole body of the Union, than a particular member of it; in the same proportion as such a malady is more likely to taint a particular county or district, than an entire State.

In the extent and proper structure of the Union, therefore, we behold a Republican remedy for the diseases most incident to Republican Government. And according to the degree of pleasure and pride, we feel in being Republicans, ought to be our zeal in cherishing the spirit, and supporting the character of Federalists.

PUBLIUS

APPENDIX IV

FEDERALIST NO. 51

February 6, 1788

James Madison

TO THE PEOPLE OF THE STATE OF NEW YORK.

To what expedient then shall we finally resort for maintaining in practice the necessary partition of power among the several departments, as laid down in the constitution? The only answer that can be given is, that as all these exterior provisions are found to be inadequate, the defect must be supplied, by so contriving the interior structure of the government, as that its several constituent parts may, by their mutual relations, be the means of keeping each other in their proper places. Without presuming to undertake a full development of this important idea, I will hazard a few general observations, which may perhaps place it in a clearer light, and enable us to form a more correct judgment of the principles and structure of the government planned by the convention.

In order to lay a due foundation for that separate and distinct exercise of the different powers of government, which to a certain extent, is admitted on all hands to be essential to the preservation of liberty, it is evident that each department should have a will of its own; and consequently should be so constituted, that the members of each should have as little agency as possible in the appointment of the members of the others. Were this principle rigorously adhered to, it would require that all the appointments for the supreme executive, legislative, and judiciary magistracies, should be drawn from the same fountain of authority, the people, through channels, having no communication whatever with one another. Perhaps such a plan of constructing the several departments would be less difficult in practice than it may in contemplation appear. Some difficulties however, and some additional expense, would attend the execution of it. Some deviations therefore from the principle must be admitted. In the constitution of the judiciary department in particular, it might be inexpedient to insist rigorously on the principle; first, because peculiar qualifications being essential in the members, the primary consideration ought to be to select that mode of choice, which best secures these qualifications; secondly, because the permanent tenure by

which the appointments are held in that department, must soon destroy all sense of dependence on the authority conferring them.

It is equally evident that the members of each department should be as little dependent as possible on those of the others, for the emoluments annexed to their offices. Were the executive magistrate, or the judges, not independent of the legislature in this particular, their independence in every other would be merely nominal.

But the great security against a gradual concentration of the several powers in the same department, consists in giving to those who administer each department, the necessary constitutional means, and personal motives, to resist encroachments of the others. The provision for defense must in this, as in all other cases, be made commensurate to the danger of attack. Ambition must be made to counteract ambition. The interest of the man must be connected with the constitutional right of the place. It may be a reflection on human nature, that such devices should be necessary to control the abuses of government. But what is government itself but the greatest of all reflections on human nature? If men were angels, no government would be necessary. If angels were to govern men, neither external nor internal controls on government would be necessary. In framing a government which is to be administered by men over men, the great difficulty lies in this: You must first enable the government to control the governed; and in the next place, oblige it to control itself. A dependence on the people is no doubt the primary control on the government; but experience has taught mankind the necessity of auxiliary precautions.

This policy of supplying by opposite and rival interests, the defect of better motives, might be traced through the whole system of human affairs, private as well as public. We see it particularly displayed in all the subordinate distributions of power; where the constant aim is to divide and arrange the several offices in such a manner as that each may be a check on the other; that the private interest of every individual, may be a sentinel over the public rights. These inventions of prudence cannot be less requisite in the distribution of the supreme powers of the state.

But it is not possible to give to each department an equal power of self defense. In republican government the legislative authority, necessarily, predominates. The remedy for this inconveniency is, to divide the legislature into different branches; and to render them by different modes of election, and different principles of action, as little connected with each other, as the nature of their common functions, and their common dependence on the society, will admit. It may even be necessary to guard against dangerous encroachments by still further precautions. As the weight of the legislative authority requires that it should be thus divided, the weakness of the executive may require, on the other hand, that it should be fortified. An absolute negative, on the legislature, appears at first view to be the natural defense with which the executive magistrate should be armed. But perhaps it would be neither altogether safe, nor alone sufficient. On ordinary occasions, it might not be exerted with the requisite firmness; and on extraordinary occasions, it might be prefidiously abused. May not this defect of an absolute negative be supplied, by some qualified connection between this weaker department, and the weaker branch of the stronger department, by which the latter may be led to support the constitutional rights of the former, without being too much detached from the rights of its own department?

If the principles on which these observations are founded be just, as I persuade myself they are, and they be applied as a criterion, to the several state constitutions, and to the federal constitution, it will be found, that if the latter does not perfectly correspond with them, the former are infinitely less able to bear such a test.

There are moreover two considerations particularly applicable to the federal system of America, which place that system in a very interesting point of view.

First. In a single republic, all the power surrendered by the people, is submitted to the administration of a single government; and usurpations are guarded against by a division of the government into distinct and separate departments. In the compound republic of America, the power surrendered by the people, is first divided between two distinct governments, and then the portion allotted to each, subdivided among distinct and separate departments. Hence a double security arises to the rights of the people. The different governments will control each other; at the same time that each will be controlled by itself.

Second. It is of great importance in a republic, not only to guard the society against the oppression of its rulers; but to guard one part of the society against the injustice of the other part. Different interests necessarily exist in different classes of citizens. If a majority be united by a common interest, the rights of the minority will be insecure. There are but two methods of providing against this evil: The one by creating a will in the community independent of the majority, that is, of the society itself, the other by comprehending in the society so many separate descriptions of citizens, as will render an unjust combination of a majority of the whole, very improbable, if not impracticable. The first method prevails in all governments possessing an hereditary or self appointed authority. This at best is but a precarious security; because a power independent of the society may as well espouse the unjust views of the major, as the rightful interests, of the minor party, and may possibly be turned against both parties. The second method will be exemplified in the federal republic of the United States. While all authority in it will be derived from and dependent on the society, the society itself will be broken into so many parts, interests and classes of citizens, that the rights of individuals or of the minority, will be in little danger from interested combinations of the majority. In a free government, the security for civil rights must be the same as for religious rights. It consists in the one case in the multiplicity of interests, and in the other, in the multiplicity of sects. The degree of security in both cases will depend on the number of interests and sects; and this may be presumed to depend on the extent of country and number of people comprehended under the same government. This view of the subject must particularly recommend a proper federal system to all the sincere and considerate friends of republican government: Since it shows that in exact proportion as the territory of the union may be formed into more circumscribed confederacies or states, oppressive combinations of a majority will be facilitated, the best security under the republican form, for the rights of every class of citizens, will be diminished; and consequently, the stability and independence of some member of the government, the only other security, must be proportionally increased. Justice is the end of government. It is the end of civil society. It ever has been, and ever will be pursued, until it be obtained, or until liberty be lost in the pursuit. In a society under the forms of which the stronger faction can readily unite and oppress the weaker, anarchy may as truly be said to reign, as in a state of nature where the weaker individual is not secured against the violence of the stronger: And as in the latter state even the stronger individuals are prompted by the uncertainty of their condition, to submit to a government which may protect the weak as well as themselves: So in the former state, will the more powerful factions or parties be gradually induced by a like motive, to wish for a government which will protect all parties, the weaker as well as the more powerful. It can be little doubted, that if the state of Rhode Island was separated from the confederacy, and left to itself, the insecurity of rights under the popular form of government within such narrow limits, would be displayed by such reiterated oppressions of factious majorities, that some power altogether independent of the people would soon be called for by the voice of the very factions whose misrule had proved the necessity of it. In the extended republic of the United States, and among the great variety of interests, parties and sects which it embraces, a coalition of a majority of the whole society could seldom take place on any other principles than those of justice and the general good; and there being thus less danger to a minor from the will of the major party, there must be less pretext also, to provide for the security of the former, by introducing into the government a will not dependent on the latter; or in other words, a will independent of the society itself. It is no less certain than it is important, notwithstanding the contrary opinions which have been entertained, that the larger the society, provided it lie within a practicable sphere, the more duly capable it will be of self government. And happily for the *republican cause,* the practicable sphere may be carried to a very great extent, by a judicious modification and mixture of the *federal principle.*

PUBLIUS

APPENDIX V

Presidents, Congresses, and Chief Justices: 1789–2001

Term	President and Vice President	Party of President	Congress	Majority Party		Chief Justice of the United States
				House	**Senate**	
1789–1797	**George Washington** John Adams	None	1st 2d 3d 4th	(N/A) (N/A) (N/A) (N/A)	(N/A) (N/A) (N/A) (N/A)	John Jay (1789–1795) John Rutledge (1795) Oliver Ellsworth (1796–1800)
1797–1801	**John Adams** Thomas Jefferson	Federalist	5th 6th	(N/A) Fed	(N/A) Fed	Oliver Ellsworth (1796–1800) John Marshall (1801–1835)
1801–1809	**Thomas Jefferson** Aaron Burr (1801–1805) George Clinton (1805–1809)	Democratic-Republican	7th 8th 9th 10th	Dem-Rep Dem-Rep Dem-Rep Dem-Rep	Dem-Rep Dem-Rep Dem-Rep Dem-Rep	John Marshall (1801–1835)
1809–1817	**James Madison** George Clinton (1809–1812)[a] Elbridge Gerry (1813–1814)[a]	Democratic-Republican	11th 12th 13th 14th	Dem-Rep Dem-Rep Dem-Rep Dem-Rep	Dem-Rep Dem-Rep Dem-Rep Dem-Rep	John Marshall (1801–1835)
1817–1825	**James Monroe** Daniel D. Tompkins	Democratic-Republican	15th 16th 17th 18th	Dem-Rep Dem-Rep Dem-Rep Dem-Rep	Dem-Rep Dem-Rep Dem-Rep Dem-Rep	John Marshall (1801–1835)
1825–1829	**John Quincy Adams** John C. Calhoun	National-Republican	19th 20th	Nat'l Rep Dem	Nat'l Rep Dem	John Marshall (1801–1835)
1829–1837	**Andrew Jackson** John C. Calhoun (1829–1832)[b] Martin Van Buren (1833–1837)	Democrat	21st 22d 23d 24th	Dem Dem Dem Dem	Dem Dem Dem Dem	John Marshall (1801–1835) Roger B. Taney (1836–1864)
1837–1841	**Martin Van Buren** Richard M. Johnson	Democrat	25th 26th	Dem Dem	Dem Dem	Roger B. Taney (1836–1864)
1841	**William H. Harrison**[a] John Tyler (1841)	Whig				Roger B. Taney (1836–1864)
1841–1845	**John Tyler** (VP vacant)	Whig	27th 28th	Whig Dem	Whig Whig	Roger B. Taney (1836–1864)
1845–1849	**James K. Polk** George M. Dallas	Democrat	29th 30th	Dem Whig	Dem Dem	Roger B. Taney (1836–1864)
1849–1850	**Zachary Taylor**[a] Millard Fillmore	Whig	31st	Dem	Dem	Roger B. Taney (1836–1864)
1850–1853	**Millard Fillmore** (VP vacant)	Whig	32d	Dem	Dem	Roger B. Taney (1836–1864)

Term	President and Vice President	Party of President	Congress	House	Senate	Chief Justice of the United States
1853–1857	**Franklin Pierce** William R.D. King (1853)[a]	Democrat	33d 34th	Dem Rep	Dem Dem	Roger B. Taney (1836–1864)
1857–1861	**James Buchanan** John C. Breckinridge	Democrat	35th 36th	Dem Rep	Dem Dem	Roger B. Taney (1836–1864)
1861–1865	**Abraham Lincoln**[a] Hannibal Hamlin (1861–1865) Andrew Johnson (1865)	Republican	37th 38th 38th	Rep Rep Rep	Rep Rep Rep	Roger B. Taney (1836–1864) Salmon P. Chase (1864–1873)
1865–1869	**Andrew Johnson** (VP vacant)	Republican	39th 40th	Union Rep	Union Rep	Salmon P. Chase (1864–1873)
1869–1877	**Ulysses S. Grant** Schuyler Colfax (1869–1873) Henry Wilson (1873–1875)[a]	Republican	41st 42d 43d 44th	Rep Rep Rep Dem	Rep Rep Rep Rep	Salmon P. Chase (1864–1873) Morrison R. Waite (1874–1888)
1877–1881	**Rutherford B. Hayes** William A. Wheeler	Republican	45th 46th	Dem Dem	Rep Dem	Morrison R. Waite (1874–1888)
1881	**James A. Garfield**[a] Chester A. Arthur	Republican	47th	Rep	Rep	Morrison R. Waite (1874–1888)
1881–1885	**Chester A. Arthur** (VP vacant)	Republican	48th	Dem	Rep	Morrison R. Waite (1874–1888)
1885–1889	**Grover Cleveland** Thomas A. Hendricks (1885)[a]	Democrat	49th 50th	Dem Dem	Rep Rep	Morrison R. Waite (1874–1888) Melville W. Fuller (1888–1910)
1889–1893	**Benjamin Harrison** Levi P. Morton	Republican	51st 52d	Rep Dem	Rep Rep	Melville W. Fuller (1888–1910)
1893–1897	**Grover Cleveland** Adlai E. Stevenson	Democrat	53d 54th	Dem Rep	Dem Rep	Melville W. Fuller (1888–1910)
1897–1901	**William McKinley**[a] Garret A. Hobart (1897–1899)[a] Theodore Roosevelt (1901)	Republican	55th 56th	Rep Rep	Rep Rep	Melville W. Fuller (1888–1910)
1901–1909	**Theodore Roosevelt** (VP vacant, 1901–1905) Charles W. Fairbanks (1905–1909)	Republican	57th 58th 59th 60th	Rep Rep Rep Rep	Rep Rep Rep Rep	Melville W. Fuller (1888–1910)
1909–1913	**William Howard Taft** James S. Sherman (1909–1912)[a]	Republican	61st 62d	Rep Dem	Rep Rep	Melville W. Fuller (1888–1910) Edward D. White (1910–1921)
1913–1921	**Woodrow Wilson** Thomas R. Marshall	Democrat	63d 64th 65th 66th	Dem Dem Dem Rep	Dem Dem Dem Rep	Edward D. White (1910–1921)
1921–1923	**Warren G. Harding**[a] Calvin Coolidge	Republican	67th	Rep	Rep	William Howard Taft (1921–1930)
1923–1929	**Calvin Coolidge** (VP vacant, 1923–1925) Charles G. Dawes (1925–1929)	Republican	68th 69th 70th	Rep Rep Rep	Rep Rep Rep	William Howard Taft (1921–1930)
1929–1933	**Herbert Hoover** Charles Curtis	Republican	71st 72d	Rep Dem	Rep Rep	William Howard Taft (1921–1930) Charles Evans Hughes (1930–1941)
1933–1945	**Franklin D. Roosevelt**[a] John N. Garner (1933–1941) Henry A. Wallace (1941–1945)	Democrat	73d 74th 75th	Dem Dem Dem	Dem Dem Dem	Charles Evans Hughes (1930–1941) Harlan F. Stone (1941–1946)

Term	President and Vice President	Party of President	Congress	House	Senate	Chief Justice of the United States
1933–1945	**Franklin D. Roosevelt**[a] Harry S Truman (1945)	Democrat	73d 76th 77th 78th	Dem Dem Dem Dem	Dem Dem Dem Dem	Charles Evans Hughes (1930–1941)
1945–1953	**Harry S Truman** (VP vacant, 1945–1949) Alben W. Barkley (1949–1953)	Democrat	79th 80th 81st 82d	Dem Rep Dem Dem	Dem Rep Dem Dem	Harlan F. Stone (1941–1946) Frederick M. Vinson (1946–1953)
1953–1961	**Dwight D. Eisenhower** Richard M. Nixon	Republican	83d 84th 85th 86th	Rep Dem Dem Dem	Rep Dem Dem Dem	Frederick M. Vinson (1946–1953) Earl Warren (1953–1969)
1961–1963	**John F. Kennedy**[a] Lyndon B. Johnson (1961–1963)	Democrat	87th	Dem	Dem	Earl Warren (1953–1969)
1963–1969	**Lyndon B. Johnson** (VP vacant, 1963–1965) Hubert H. Humphrey (1965–1969)	Democrat	88th 89th 90th	Dem Dem Dem	Dem Dem Dem	Earl Warren (1953–1969)
1969–1974	**Richard M. Nixon**[c] Spiro T. Agnew (1969–1973)[b] Gerald R. Ford (1973–1974)[d]	Republican	91st 92d	Dem Dem	Dem Dem	Earl Warren (1953–1969) Warren E. Burger (1969–1986)
1974–1977	**Gerald R. Ford** Nelson A. Rockefeller	Republican	93d 94th	Dem Dem	Dem Dem	Warren E. Burger (1969–1986)
1977–1981	**Jimmy Carter** Walter Mondale	Democrat	95th 96th	Dem Dem	Dem Dem	Warren E. Burger (1969–1986)
1981–1989	**Ronald Reagan** George Bush	Republican	97th 98th 99th 100th	Dem Dem Dem Dem	Rep Rep Rep Dem	Warren E. Burger (1969–1986) William H. Rehnquist (1986–)
1989–1993	**George Bush** Dan Quayle	Republican	101st 102d	Dem Dem	Dem Dem	William H. Rehnquist (1986–)
1993–2001	**Bill Clinton** Al Gore	Democrat	103d 104th 105th 106th	Dem Rep Rep Rep	Dem Rep Rep Rep	William H. Rehnquist (1986–)
2001–	**George W. Bush** Dick Cheney	Republican	107th 108th	Rep Rep	Dem Rep	William H. Rehnquist (1986–)

[a]Died in office.
[b]Resigned from the vice presidency.
[c]Resigned from the presidency.
[d]Appointed vice president.

MAJOR SUPREME COURT CASES

- **Brown v. Board of Education (1954):** U.S. Supreme Court decision holding that school segregation is inherently unconstitutional because it violates the Fourteenth Amendment's guarantee of equal protection; marked the end of legal segregation in the United States.

- **Civil Rights Cases (1875):** Name attached to five cases brought under the Civil Rights Act of 1875. In 1883 the Supreme Court decided that discrimination in a variety of public accommodations, including theaters, hotels, and railroads, could not be prohibited by the act because it was private and not state discrimination.

- **Gibbons v. Ogden (1824):** The Court upheld broad congressional power over interstate commerce.

- **Immigration and Naturalization Service v. Chadha (1983):** Legislative veto ruled unconstitutional by the Supreme Court.

- **Marbury v. Madison (1803):** Supreme Court case in which the Court first asserted the power of judicial review in finding that a congressional statute extending the Court's original jurisdiction was unconstitutional.

- **McCulloch v. Maryland (1819):** Supreme Court upheld the power of the national government and denied the right of a state to tax the bank. The Court's broad interpretation of the necessary and proper clause paved the way for later rulings upholding expansive federal powers.

- **Miranda v. Arizona (1966):** The Fifth Amendment requires that individuals arrested for a crime must be advised of their right to remain silent and to have counsel present.

- **New York Times Co. v. Sullivan (1964):** Supreme Court decision ruling that simply publishing a defamatory falsehood is not enough to justify a libel judgment. "Actual malice" must be proved to support a finding of libel against a public figure.

- **Plessy v. Ferguson (1896):** *Plessy* challenged a Louisiana statute requiring that railroads provide separate accommodations for blacks and whites. The Court found that separate but equal accommodations did not violate the equal protection clause of the Fourteenth Amendment.

- **Roe v. Wade (1973):** The Supreme Court found that a woman's right to an abortion was protected by the right to privacy that could be implied from specific guarantees found in the Bill of Rights and the Fourteenth Amendment.

- **United States v. Nixon (1974):** There is no constitutional absolute executive privilege that would allow a president to refuse to comply with a court order to produce information needed in a criminal trial.

GLOSSARY

administrative adjudication: A quasi-judicial process in which a bureaucratic agency settles disputes between two parties in a manner similar to the way courts resolve disputes.

administrative discretion: The ability of bureaucrats to make choices concerning the best way to implement congressional intentions.

advisory referendum: A process in which voters cast nonbinding ballots on an issue or proposal.

affiliates: Local television stations that carry the programming of a national network.

amicus curiae: "Friend of the court"; a third party to a lawsuit who files a legal brief for the purpose of raising additional points of view in an attempt to influence a court's decision.

Anti-Federalists: Those who favored strong state governments and a weak national government; opposed the ratification of the U.S. Constitution.

appellate court: Court that generally reviews only findings of law made by lower courts.

appellate jurisdiction: The power vested in an appellate court to review and/or revise the decision of a lower court.

aristocracy: A system of government in which control is based on rule of the highest.

Articles of Confederation: The compact among the thirteen original states that was the basis of their government. Written in 1776, the Articles were not ratified by all the states until 1781.

articles of impeachment: The specific charges brought against a president or a federal judge by the House of Representatives.

at-large elections: Elections in which candidates for office must compete throughout the jurisdiction as a whole.

ℬ

bicameral legislature: A legislature divided into two houses; the U.S. Congress and the state legislatures are bicameral except Nebraska, which is unicameral.

bill: A proposed law.

bill of attainder: A law declaring an act illegal without a judicial trial.

Bill of Rights: The first ten amendments to the U.S. Constitution, which guarantee specific rights and liberties.

Black Codes: Laws denying most legal rights to newly freed slaves; passed by Southern states following the Civil War.

blanket primary: A primary in which voters may cast ballots in either party's primary (but not both) on an office-by-office basis.

block grant: Broad grant with few strings attached are given to states by the federal government for specified activities, such as secondary education or health services.

brief: A document containing the legal written arguments in a case filed with a court by a party prior to a hearing or trial.

Brown v. Board of Education (1954): U.S. Supreme Court decision holding that school segregation is inherently unconstitutional because it violates the Fourteenth Amendment's guarantee of equal protection; marked the end of legal segregation in the United States.

bureaucracy: A set of complex hierarchical departments, agencies, commissions, and their staffs that exist to help a chief executive officer carry out his or her duty to enforce the law.

Cabinet: The formal body of presidential advisers who head the fourteen executive departments. Presidents often add others to this body of formal advisers.

campaign manager: The individual who travels with the candidate and coordinates the many different aspects of the campaign.

candidate debates: Forums in which political candidates face each other to discuss their platforms, records, and character.

capitalism: The economic system that favors private control of business and minimal governmental regulation of private industry.

casework: The process of solving constituents' problems dealing with the bureaucracy.

categorical grant: Grant for which Congress appropriates funds for a specific purpose.

charter: A document that, like a constitution, specifies the basic policies, procedures, and institutions of a municipality.

charter school: Public schools sanctioned by a specific agreement that allows the program to operate outside the usual rules and regulations.

checks and balances: A governmental structure that gives each of the three branches of government some degree of oversight and control over the actions of the others.

city council: The legislature in a city government.

civil law: Codes of behavior related to business and contractual relationships between groups and individuals.

civil liberties: The personal rights and freedoms that the federal government cannot abridge by law, constitution, or judicial interpretation.

civil rights: Refers to the positive acts governments take to protect individuals against arbitrary or discriminatory treatment by governments or individuals based on categories such as race, sex, national origin, age, or sexual orientation.

Civil Rights Act of 1964: Legislation passed by Congress to outlaw segregation in public facilities and racial discrimination in employment, education, and voting; created the Equal Employment Opportunity Commission.

Civil Rights Cases (1883): Name attached to five cases brought under the Civil Rights Act of 1875. In 1883 the Supreme Court decided that discrimination in a variety of public accommodations, including theaters, hotels, and railroads, could not be prohibited by the act because it was private, not state, discrimination.

civil service laws: These acts removed the staffing of the bureaucracy from political parties and created a professional bureaucracy filled through competition.

civil service system: The system created by civil service laws by which many appointments to the federal bureaucracy are made.

clear and present danger test: Test used by the Supreme Court to draw the line between protected and unprotected speech; the Court looks to see if there is an imminent danger that illegal action would occur in response to the contested speech.

clientele agency: Executive department directed by law to foster and promote the interests of a specific segment or group in the U.S. population (such as the Department of Education).

closed primary: A primary election in which only a party's registered voters are eligible to vote.

cloture: Motion requiring 60 Senators to cut off debate.

coalition: A group of interests or organizations that join forces for the purpose of electing public officials.

coattail effect: The tendency of lesser-known or weaker candidates lower on the ballot to profit in an election by the presence on the party's ticket of a more popular candidate.

collective good: Something of value that cannot be withheld from a non–interest group member, for example, a tax write-off, a good feeling.

commission: Form of local government in which several officials are elected to top positions that have both legislative and executive responsibilities.

Committees of Correspondence: Organizations in each of the American colonies created to keep colonists abreast of developments with the British; served as powerful molders of public opinion against the British.

common law: Legal traditions of society that are for the most part unwritten but based on the aggregation of rulings and interpretations of judges beginning in thirteenth-century England.

communism: An economic system in which workers own the means of production and control the distribution of resources.

commute: The authority of a governor to cancel all or part of the sentence of someone convicted of a crime, while keeping the conviction on the record.

concurrent powers: Powers shared by the national and state governments.

confederation: Type of government in which the national government derives its powers from the states; a league of independent states.

conference committee: Joint committee created to iron out differences between Senate and House versions of a specific piece of legislation.

congressional review: The process by which Congress can nullify an executive branch regulation by a resolution jointly passed in both houses within sixty days of announcement of the regulation and accepted by the president.

congressionalist: A view of the president's role in the lawmaking process that holds Article II's provision that the president should ensure "faithful execution of the laws" should

be read as an injunction against substituting presidential authority for legislative intent.

conservative: One thought to believe that a government is best that governs least and that big government can only infringe on individual, personal, and economic rights.

constitutional court: Federal court specifically created by the U.S. Constitution or by Congress pursuant to its authority in Article III.

content regulation: Governmental attempts to regulate the electronic media.

Contract with America: Campaign pledge signed by most Republican candidates in 1994 to guide their legislative agenda.

contrast ad: Ad that compares the records and proposals of the candidates, with a bias toward the sponsor.

cooperative federalism: A term used to characterize the relationship between the national and state governments that began with the New Deal.

county: A geographic district created within a state with a government that has general responsibilities for land, welfare, environment, and, where appropriate, rural service policies.

criminal law: Codes of behavior related to the protection of property and individual safety.

critical election: An election that signals a party realignment through voter polarization around new issues.

crossover voting: Participation in the primary of a party with which the voter is not affiliated.

D

de facto discrimination: Racial discrimination that results from practice (such as housing patterns or other social factors) rather than the law.

de jure discrimination: Racial segregation that is a direct result of law or official policy.

Declaration of Independence: Document drafted by Thomas Jefferson in 1776 that proclaimed the right of the American colonies to separate from Great Britain.

deep background: Information gathered for news stories that must be completely unsourced.

delegate: Role played by elected representatives who vote the way their constituents would want them to, regardless of their own opinions.

democracy: A system of government that gives power to the people, whether directly or through their elected representatives.

department: A major administrative unit with responsibility for a broad area of government operations. Departmental status usually indicates a permanent national interest in that particular governmental function, such as defense, health, or agriculture.

Dillon's Rule: A court ruling that local governments do not have any inherent sovereignty, but instead must be authorized by state government.

direct democracy: A system of government in which members of the polity meet to discuss all policy decisions and then agree to abide by majority rule.

direct incitement test: A test used by the Court that holds that advocacy of illegal action is protected by the First Amendment unless imminent action is intended and likely to occur.

direct initiative: A process in which voters can place a proposal on a ballot and enact it into law without involving the legislature or the governor.

direct mailer: A professional who supervises a political campaign's direct-mail fund-raising strategies.

direct (popular) referendum: A process in which voters can veto a bill recently passed in the legislature by placing the issue on a ballot and expressing disapproval.

direct primary: The selection of party candidates through the ballots of qualified voters rather than at party nomination conventions.

discharge petition: Petition that gives a majority of the House of Representatives the authority to bring an issue to the floor in the face of committee inaction.

district-based elections: Elections in which candidates run for an office that represents only the voters of a specific district within the jurisdiction.

disturbance theory: The theory offered by political scientist David B. Truman that posits that interest groups form in part to counteract the efforts of other groups.

divided government: The term used to describe the political condition in which different political parties control the White House and Congress.

domestic dependent nation: A type of sovereignty that makes an Indian tribe in the United States outside the authority of state governments but reliant on the federal government for the definition of tribal authority.

dual federalism: The belief that having separate and equally powerful levels of government is the best arrangement.

dualist theory: The theory claiming that there has always been an underlying binary party nature to U.S. politics.

due process clause: Clause contained in the Fifth and Fourteenth Amendments. Over the years, it has been construed to guarantee to individuals a variety of rights ranging from economic liberty to criminal procedural rights to protection from arbitrary governmental action.

due process rights: Procedural guarantees provided by the Fourth, Fifth, Sixth, and Eighth Amendments for those accused of crimes.

E

economic interest group: A group with the primary purpose of promoting the financial interests of its members.

elector: Member of the electoral college chosen by methods determined in each state.

electoral college: Representatives of each state who cast the final ballots that actually elect a president.

electorate: Citizens eligible to vote.

electronic media: The newest form of broadcast media, including television, radio, cable, and the Internet.

enumerated powers: Seventeen specific powers granted to Congress under Article I, section 8, of the U.S. Constitution; these powers include taxation, coinage of money, regulation of commerce, and the authority to provide for a national defense.

Equal Employment Opportunity Commission: Federal agency created to enforce the Civil Rights Act of 1964, which forbids discrimination on the basis of race, creed, national origin, religion, or sex in hiring, promotion, or firing.

equal protection clause: Section of the Fourteenth Amendment that guarantees that all citizens receive "equal protection of the laws"; has been used to bar discrimination against blacks and women.

equal time rule: The rule that requires broadcast stations to sell campaign air time equally to all candidates if they choose to sell it to any.

establishment clause: The first clause in the First Amendment. It prohibits the national government from establishing a national religion.

ex post facto **law:** Law passed after the fact, thereby making previously legal activity illegal and subject to current penalty; prohibited by the U.S. Constitution.

exclusionary rule: Judicially created rule that prohibits police from using illegally seized evidence at trial.

executive agreement: Secret and highly sensitive arrangements with foreign nations entered into by the president that do not require a positive Senate vote.

Executive Office of the President (EOP): Establishment created in 1939 to help the president oversee the bureaucracy.

executive order: Presidential directive to an agency that provides the basis for carrying out laws or for establishing new policies.

executive privilege: An assertion of presidential power that reasons that the president can withhold information requested by the courts in matters relating to his office.

exit poll: Poll conducted at selected polling places on Election Day.

extradite: The authority of a governor to send someone against his or her will to another state to face criminal charges.

F

fairness doctrine: Rule in effect from 1949 to 1985 requiring broadcasters to cover events adequately and to present contrasting views on important public issues.

Federal Employees Political Activities Act: 1993 liberalization of the Hatch Act. Federal employees are now allowed to run for office in nonpartisan elections and to contribute money to campaigns in partisan elections.

federal system: Plan of government created in the U.S. Constitution in which power is divided between the national government and the state governments and in which independent states are bound together under one national government.

federalism: The philosophy that describes the governmental system created by the Framers; see also federal system.

Federalists: Those who favored a stronger national government and supported the proposed U.S. Constitution; later became the first U.S. political party.

The Federalist Papers: A series of eighty-five political papers written by John Jay, Alexander Hamilton, and James Madison in support of ratification of the U.S. Constitution.

Fifteenth Amendment: One of the three Civil War amendments; specifically enfranchised newly freed male slaves.

filibuster: A formal way of halting action on a bill by means of long speeches or unlimited debate in the Senate.

finance chair: A volunteer who coordinates the fund-raising efforts for the campaign.

First Continental Congress: Meeting held in Philadelphia from September 5 to October 26, 1774, in which fifty-six delegates (from every colony except Georgia) adopted a resolution that opposed the Coercive Acts.

Fourteenth Amendment: One of the three Civil War amendments; guarantees equal protection and due process of the laws to all U.S. citizens.

franchise: The right to vote.

free exercise clause: The second clause of the First Amendment. It prohibits the U.S. government from interfering with a citizen's right to practice his or her religion.

free market economy: The economic system in which the "invisible hand" of the market regulates prices, wages, product mix, and so on.

free media: Coverage of a candidate's campaign by the news media.

free rider: A person who doesn't join or work for the benefit of the group the rewards of the group's activity.

front-loading: The tendency of states to choose an early date on the primary calendar.

G

general election: Election in which voters decide which candidates will actually fill elective public offices.

general election campaign: That part of a political campaign following a primary election, aimed at winning a general election.

gerrymandering: The legislative process through which the majority party in each statehouse tries to assure that the maximum number of representatives from its political party can be elected to Congress through the redrawing of legislative districts.

get-out-the-vote (GOTV): A push at the end of a political campaign to encourage supporters to go to the polls.

Gibbons v. *Ogden* (1824): The Court upheld broad congressional power over interstate commerce.

government corporation: Business set up and created by Congress that performs functions that could be provided by private businesses (such as the U.S. Postal Service).

governmental party: The office holders and candidates who run under a political party's banner.

governor: Chief elected executive in state government.

grandfather clause: Voting qualification provision that allowed only those whose grandfathers had voted before Reconstruction to vote unless they passed a wealth or literacy test.

Great Compromise: A decision made during the Philadelphia Convention to give each state the same number of representatives in the Senate regardless of size; representation in the House was determined by population.

hard money: Legally specified and limited contributions that are clearly regulated by the Federal Election Campaign Act and by the Federal Election Commission.

Hatch Act: Laws enacted in 1939 to prohibit civil servants from taking activist roles in partisan campaigns. This act prohibited federal employees from making political contributions, working for a particular party, or campaigning for a particular candidate.

hold: A tactic by which a senator asks to be informed before a particular bill is brought to the floor. This stops the bill from coming to the floor until the hold is removed.

I

impeachment: Actual bringing of charges against a public official requiring a simple majority vote of the House of Representatives; not the hearings or trial on those charges.

implementation: The process by which a law or policy is put into operation by the bureaucracy.

implied power: A power derived from an enumerated power and the necessary and proper clause. These powers are not stated specifically but are considered to be reasonably implied through the exercise of delegated powers.

implied powers: Powers given to the national government through the interference from enumerated powers.

in forma pauperis: Literally, "in the form of a pauper"; a way for an indigent or poor person to appeal a case to the U.S. Supreme Court.

inclusion: The principle that state courts will apply federal laws when those laws directly conflict with the laws of a state.

incorporation doctrine: An interpretation of the Constitution that holds that the due process clause of the Fourteenth Amendment requires that state and local governments also guarantee those rights.

incumbency: The condition of already holding elected office.

incumbency factor: The fact that being in office helps a person stay in office because of a variety of benefits which go with the position.

independent executive agency: Governmental unit that closely resembles Cabinet departments but has a narrower area of responsibility (such as the Central Intelligence Agency) and is not part of any Cabinet departments.

independent regulatory commission: An agency created by Congress that is generally concerned with a specific aspect of the economy.

indirect initiative: A process in which the legislature places a proposal on a ballot and allows voters to enact it into law, without involving the governor or further action by the legislature.

indirect (representative) democracy: A system of government that gives citizens the opportunity to vote for representatives who will work on their behalf.

inherent powers: Powers of the president that can be derived or inferred from specific powers in the Constitution.

initiative: A process that allows citizens to propose legislation and submit it to the state electorate for popular vote.

inoculation advertising: Advertising that attempts to counteract an anticipated attack from the opposition before the attack is even launched.

interest group: An organized group that tries to influence public policy.

intergovernmental lobby: The pressure group or groups that are created when state and local governments hire lobbyists to lobby the national government.

iron triangle: The relatively stable relationship and pattern of interaction that occur among an agency, interest groups, and congressional committees or subcommittees.

issue network: The loose and informal relationships that exist among a large number of actors who work in broad policy areas.

issue-oriented politics: Politics that focuses on specific issues rather than on party, candidate, or other loyalties.

J

Jim Crow laws: Laws enacted by Southern states that discriminated against blacks by creating "whites only" schools, theaters, hotels, and other public accommodations.

judicial activism: A philosophy of judicial decision making that argues judges should use their power broadly to further justice, especially in the areas of equality and personal liberty.

judicial implementation: Refers to how and whether judicial decisions are translated into actual public policies affecting more than the immediate parties to a lawsuit.

judicial restraint: A philosophy of judicial decision making that argues courts should allow the decisions of other branches of government to stand, even when they offend a judge's own sense of principles.

judicial review: Power of the courts to review acts of other branches of government and the states.

Judiciary Act of 1789: Established the basic three-tiered structure of the federal court system.

jurisdiction: Authority vested in a particular court to hear and decide the issues in any particular case.

L

legislative court: Court established by Congress for specialized purposes, such as the Court of Military Appeals.

legislative veto: A procedure by which one or both houses of Congress can disallow an act of the president or executive agency by a simple majority vote; ruled unconstitutional by the Supreme Court.

libel: False statements or statements tending to call someone's reputation into disrepute.

liberal: One considered to favor extensive governmental involvement in the economy and the provision of social services and to take an activist role in protecting the rights of women, the elderly, minorities, and the environment.

libertarian: One who favors a free market economy and no governmental interference in personal liberties.

line-item veto: The power to veto specific provisions of a bill without vetoing the bill in its entirety.

lobbying: The activities of groups and organizations that seek to influence legislation and persuade political leaders to support a group's position.

lobbyist: Interest group representative who seeks to influence legislation that will benefit his or her organization through political persuasion.

Louisiana Purchase: The 1803 land purchase authorized by Thomas Jefferson, which expanded the size of the United States dramatically.

M

machine: A party organization that recruits its members with tangible incentives and is characterized by a high degree of control over member activity.

majority leader: The elected leader of the party controlling the most seats in the U.S. House of Representatives or the Senate; is second in authority to the Speaker of the House and in the Senate is regarded as its most powerful member.

majority party: The political party in each house of Congress with the most members.

majority rule: The central premise of direct democracy in which only policies that collectively garner the support of a majority of voters will be made into law.

manager: A professional executive hired by a city council or county board to manage daily operations and to recommend policy changes.

mandate: A command, indicated by an electorate's votes, for the elected officials to carry out their platforms.

mandates: National laws that direct states or local governments to comply with federal rules or regulations (such as clean air or water standards) under threat of civil or criminal penalties or as a condition of receipt of any federal grants.

Marbury v. Madison (1803): Supreme Court first asserted the power of judicial review in finding that the congressional statute extending the Court's original jurisdiction was unconstitutional.

matching funds: Donations to presidential campaigns from the federal government that are determined by the amount of private funds a qualifying candidate raises.

mayor: Chief elected executive of a city.

McCulloch v. Maryland (1819): The Supreme Court upheld the power of the national government and denied the right of a state to tax the bank. The Court's broad interpretation of the necessary and proper clause paved the way for later rulings upholding expansive federal powers.

media campaign: That part of a political campaign waged in the broadcast and print media.

media consultant: A professional who produces political candidates' television, radio, and print advertisements.

media effects: The influence of news sources on public opinion.

mercantile system: A system that binds trade and its administration to the national government.

merit system: The system by which federal civil service jobs are classified into grades or levels, to which appointments are made on the basis of performance on competitive examinations.

minority leader: The elected leader of the party with the second highest number of elected representatives in either the House or the Senate.

minority party: Party with the second most members in either house of Congress.

Miranda rights: Statements that must be made by the police informing a suspect of his or her constitutional rights protected by the Fifth Amendment, including the right to an attorney provided by the court if the suspect cannot afford one.

Miranda v. Arizona (1966): A landmark Supreme Court ruling that held the Fifth Amendment requires that individuals arrested for a crime must be advised of their right to remain silent and to have counsel present.

Missouri Plan: A method of selecting judges in which a governor must appoint someone from a list provided by an independent panel. Judges are then kept in office if they get a majority of "yes" votes in general elections.

monarchy: A form of government in which power is vested in hereditary kings and queens.

muckraking: A form of newspaper publishing, in vogue in the early twentieth century, concerned with reforming government and business conduct.

municipality: A government with general responsibilities, such as a city, town, or village government, that is created in response to the emergence of relatively densely populated areas.

N

national convention: A party conclave (meeting) held in the presidential election year for the purposes of nominating a presidential and vice-presidential ticket and adopting a platform.

national party platform: A statement of the general and specific philosophy and policy goals of a political party, usually promulgated at the national convention.

natural law: A doctrine that society should be governed by certain ethical principles that are part of nature and, as such, can be understood by reason.

necessary and proper clause: Found in the final paragraph of Article I, section 8, of the U.S. Constitution, it gives Congress the authority to pass all laws "necessary and proper" to carry out the enumerated powers specified in the Constitution.

negative ad: Advertising on behalf of a candidate that attacks the opponent's platform or character.

network: An association of broadcast stations (radio or television) that share programming through a financial arrangement.

New Deal: The name given to the program of "Relief, Recovery, Reform" begun by President Franklin D. Roosevelt in 1933 designed to bring the United States out of the Great Depression.

New Jersey Plan: A framework for the Constitution proposed by a group of small states; its key points were a one-house legislature with one vote for each state, a multiperson "executive," the establishment of the acts of Congress as the "supreme law" of the land, and a supreme judiciary with limited power.

New York Times Co. v. Sullivan **(1964):** The Supreme Court concluded that "actual malice" must be proved to support a finding of libel against a public figure.

nomination campaign: That part of a political campaign aimed at winning a primary election.

nonpartisan election: A contest in which candidates run without formal identification or association with a political party.

nonpartisan primary: A primary used to select candidates regardless of party affiliation.

O

off the record: Term applied to information gathered for a news story that cannot be used at all.

off-year election: Election that takes place in the middle of a presidential term.

oligarchy: A form of government in which the right to participate is always conditioned on the possession of wealth, social status, military position, or achievement.

on background: A term for when sources are not included in a news story.

on the record: Term applied to information gathered for a news story that can be used and cited.

one-partyism: A political system in which one party dominates and wins virtually all contests.

one-person, one-vote: The principle that each legislative district within a state should have the same number of eligible voters so that representation is equitably based on population.

open primary: A primary in which party members, independents, and sometimes members of the other party are allowed to vote.

organizational campaign: That part of a political campaign involved in fund raising, literature distribution, and all other activities not directly involving the candidate.

organizational party: The workers and activists who staff the party's formal organization.

original jurisdiction: The jurisdiction of courts that hear a case first, usually in a trial. Courts determine the facts of a case under their original jurisdiction.

oversight: Congressional review of the activities of an agency, department, or office.

P

package or general veto: The authority of a chief executive to void an entire bill that has been passed by the legislature. This veto applies to all bills, whether or not they have taxing or spending components, and the legislature may override this veto, usually with a two-thirds majority of each chamber.

paid media: Political advertisements purchased for a candidate's campaign.

pardon: An executive grant providing restoration of all rights and privileges of citizenship to a specific individual charged or convicted of a crime.

parole: The authority of a governor to release a prisoner before his or her full sentence has been completed and to specify conditions that must be met as part of the release.

party caucus: A formal gathering of all party members.

party identification: A citizen's personal affinity for a political party, usually expressed by his or her tendency to vote for the candidates of that party.

party in the electorate: The voters who consider themselves to be allied or associated with the party.

party realignment: A shifting of party coalition groupings in the electorate that remains in place for several elections.

patron: Individual who finances an interest group.

patronage: Jobs, grants, or other special favors that are given as rewards to friends and political allies for their support.

Pendleton Act: Reform measure that created the Civil Service Commission to administer a partial merit system. The act classified the federal service by grades, to which appointments were made based on the results of a competitive examination. It made it illegal for federal political appointees to be required to contribute to a particular political party.

personal campaign: That part of a political campaign concerned with presenting the candidate's public image.

personal liberty: A key characteristic of U.S. democracy. Initially meaning freedom from governmental interference, today it includes demands for freedom to engage in a variety of practices free from governmental discrimination.

Plessy v. *Ferguson* **(1896):** Plessy challenged a Louisiana statute requiring that railroads provide separate accommodations for blacks and whites. The Court found that separate but equal accommodations did not violate the equal protection clause of the Fourteenth Amendment.

pocket veto: If Congress adjourns during the ten days the president has to consider a bill passed by both houses of Congress, without the president's signature, the bill is considered vetoed.

political action committee (PAC): Federally mandated, officially registered fund-raising committee that represents interest groups in the political process.

political consultant: A hired individual, team, or firm that advises the campaign on strategies and techniques to win an election.

political culture: Attitudes toward the political system and its various parts, and attitudes toward the role of the self in the system.

political ideology: An individual's coherent set of values and beliefs about the purpose and scope of government.

political machine: An organization designed to solicit votes from certain neighborhoods or communities for a particular political party in return for services and jobs if that party wins.

political party: A group of office holders, candidates, activists, and voters who identify with a group label and seek to elect to public office individuals who run under that label.

political socialization: The process through which an individual acquires particular political orientations; the learning process by which people acquire their political beliefs and values.

politico: Role played by elected representatives who act as trustees or as delegates, depending on the issue.

politics: The process by which policy decisions are made.

pollster: A professional who takes public opinion surveys that guide political campaigns.

popular consent: The idea that governments must draw their powers from the consent of the governed.

popular sovereignty: The right of the majority to govern themselves.

pork barrel: Legislation that allows representatives to "bring home the bacon" to their districts in the form of public works programs, military bases, or other programs designed to benefit their districts directly.

positive ad: Advertising on behalf of a candidate that stresses the candidate's qualifications, family, and issue positions, without reference to the opponent.

precedent: Prior judicial decision that serves as a rule for settling subsequent cases of a similar nature.

preemption: A concept derived from the Constitution's supremacy clause that allows the national government to override or preempt state or local actions in certain areas.

presidentialist: One who believes that Article II's grant of executive power is a broad grant of authority and power allowing a president wide discretionary powers.

press briefing: A relatively restricted session between a press secretary or aide and the press.

press conference: An unrestricted session between an elected official and the press.

press release: A document offering an official comment or position.

primary election: Election in which voters decide which of the candidates within a party will represent the party in the general election.

print press: The traditional form of mass media, comprising newspapers, magazines, and journals.

prior restraint: Government prohibition of speech or publication before the fact, generally held to be in violation of the First Amendment.

Progressive Movement: Advocate of measures to destroy political machines and instead have direct participation by voters in the nomination of candidates and the establishment of public policy.

progressive tax: The level of tax increases with the wealth or ability of an individual or business to pay.

prospective judgment: A voter's evaluation of a candidate based on what he or she pledges to do about an issue if elected.

public corpoations (authorities): Government organizations established to provide a particular service or to run a particular facility that are independent of other city or state agencies and supposed to be operated like a business. Examples include a port authority or a mass transit system.

public funds: Donations from the general tax revenues to the campaigns of qualifying presidential candidates.

public interest group: An organization that seeks a collective good that will not selectively and materially benefit the members of the group.

public opinion: What the public thinks about a particular issue or set of issues at any point in time.

public opinion poll: Interviews or surveys with a sample of citizens that are used to estimate the feelings and beliefs of the entire population.

R

raiding: An organized attempt by voters of one party to influence the primary results of the other party

random sampling: A method of selection that gives each potential voter or adult the same chance of being selected.

recall: Removal of an incumbent from office by popular vote.

redistricting: The redrawing of congressional districts to reflect increases or decreases in seats allotted to the states, as well as population shifts within a state.

referendum: A procedure whereby the state legislature submits proposed legislation to the state's voters for approval.

regional primary: A proposed system in which the country would be divided into five or six geographic areas and all states in each region would hold their presidential primary elections on the same day.

regressive tax: The level of tax increases as the wealth or ability of an individual or business to pay decreases.

regulation: Rule that governs the operation of a particular government program and has the force of law.

republic: A government rooted in the consent of the governed; a representative or indirect democracy.

reservation land: Land designated in a treaty that is under the authority of an Indian nation and is exempt from most state laws and taxes.

reserve (or police) powers: Powers reserved to the states by the Tenth Amendment that lie at the foundation of a state's right to legislate for the public health and welfare of its citizens.

retrospective judgment: A voter's evaluation of the performance of the party in power.

right-of-rebuttal rule: A Federal Communications Commission regulation that people attacked on a radio or television broadcast be offered the opportunity to respond.

right to privacy: The right to be let alone; a judicially created doctrine encompassing an individual's decision to use birth control or secure an abortion.

Roe v. Wade (1973): The Supreme Court found that a woman's right to an abortion was protected by the right to privacy that could be implied from specific guarantees found in the Bill of Rights applied to the states through the Fourteenth Amendment.

rule making: A quasi-legislative administrative process that has the characteristics of a legislative act.

Rule of Four: At least four justices of the Supreme Court must vote to consider a case before it can be heard.

runoff primary: A second primary election between the two candidates receiving the greatest number of votes in the first primary.

S

sampling error or margin of error: A measure of the accuracy of a public opinion poll.

Second Continental Congress: Meeting that convened in Philadelphia on May 10, 1775, at which it was decided that an army should be raised and George Washington of Virginia was named commander-in-chief.

secular realignment: The gradual rearrangement of party coalitions, based more on demographic shifts than on shocks to the political system.

segregated funds: Money that comes in from a certain tax or fee and then is restricted to a specific use, such as a gasoline tax that is used for road maintenance.

selective incorporation: A judicial doctrine whereby most but not all of the protections found in the Bill of Rights are made applicable to the states via the Fourteenth Amendment.

senatorial courtesy: A process by which presidents, when selecting district court judges, defer to the senator in whose state the vacancy occurs.

separation of powers: A way of dividing power among three branches of government in which members of the House of Representatives, members of the Senate, the president, and the federal courts are selected by and responsible to different constituencies.

Shays's Rebellion: A 1786 rebellion in which an army of 1,500 disgruntled and angry farmers led by Daniel Shays marched to Springfield, Massachusetts, and forcibly restrained the state court from foreclosing mortgages on their farms.

slander: Untrue spoken statements that defame the character of a person.

social contract theory: The belief that people are free and equal by God-given right and that this in turn requires that all people give their consent to be governed; espoused by John Locke and influential in the writing of the Declaration of Independence.

socialism: An economic system that advocates for collective ownership and control of the means of production.

soft money: The virtually unregulated money funneled by individuals and political committees through state and local parties.

solicitor general: The fourth-ranking member of the Justice Department; responsible for handling all appeals on behalf of the U.S. government to the Supreme Court.

sovereign immunity: The right of a state to be free from lawsuit unless it gives permission to the suit. Under the Eleventh Amendment, all states are considered sovereign.

Speaker of the House: The only officer of the House of Representatives specifically mentioned in the Constitution; elected at the beginning of each new Congress by the entire House; traditionally a member of the majority party.

special district: A local government that is responsible for a particular function, such as K–12 education, water, sewerage, or parks.

spoils system: The firing of public-office holders of a defeated political party and their replacement with loyalists of the newly elected party.

spot ad: Television advertising on behalf of a candidate that is broadcast in sixty-, thirty-, or ten-second duration.

Stamp Act Congress: Meeting of representatives of nine of the thirteen colonies held in New York City in 1765, during which representatives drafted a document to send to the king listing how their rights had been violated.

standing committee: Committee to which proposed bills are referred.

stare decisis: In court rulings, a reliance on past decisions or precedents to formulate decisions in new cases.

state constitution: The document that describes the basic policies, procedures, and institutions of the government of a specific state, much like the U.S. Constitution does for the federal government.

stewardship theory: The theory that holds that Article II confers on the president the power *and* the duty to take whatever actions are deemed necessary in the national interest, unless prohibited by the Constitution or by law.

stratified sampling: A variation of random sampling; census data are used to divide a country into four sampling regions. Sets of counties and standard metropolitan statistical areas are then randomly selected in proportion to the total national population.

straw poll: Unscientific survey used to gauge public opinion on a variety of issues and policies.

strict constructionist: An approach to constitutional interpretation that emphasizes the Framers' original intentions.

strict scrutiny: A heightened standard of review used by the Supreme Court to determine the constitutional validity of a challenged practice.

substantive due process: Principle in which the Supreme Court has held that most, but not all, of the specific guarantees in the Bill of Rights limit state and local governments by making those guarantees applicable to the states through the due process clause of the Fourteenth Amendment.

suffrage movement: Term used to refer to the drive for votes for women that took place in the United States from 1890 to 1920.

superdelegate: Delegate slot to the Democratic Party's national convention that is reserved for an elected party official.

supremacy clause: Portion of Article VI of the U.S. Constitution that mandates that national law is supreme to (that is, supersedes) all other laws passed by the states or by any other subdivision of government.

suspect classification: Category or class, such as race, that triggers the highest standard of scrutiny from the Supreme Court.

symbolic speech: Symbols, signs, and other methods of expression generally also considered to be protected by the First Amendment.

Taftian theory: The theory that holds that the president is limited by the specific grants of executive power found in the Constitution.

term limits: Legislation designating that state or federal elected legislators can serve only a specified number of years.

third-partyism: The tendency of third parties to arise with some regularity in a nominally two-party system.

Thirteenth Amendment: One of the three Civil War amendments; specifically bans slavery in the United States.

Three-Fifths Compromise: Agreement reached at the Constitutional Convention stipulating that each slave was to be counted as three-fifths of a person for purposes of determining population for representation in the U.S. House of Representatives.

ticket-split: To vote for candidates of different parties for various offices in the same election.

ticket-splitting: Voting simultaneously for candidates of both parties for different offices.

totalitarianism: An economic system in which the government has total control over the economy.

town meeting: Form of local government in which all eligible voters are invited to attend a meeting at which budgets and ordinances are proposed and voted on.

tracking poll: Continuous surveys that enable a campaign to chart its daily rise or fall in support.

trade association: A group that represents specific industries.

trial court: Court of original jurisdiction where a case begins.

trust land: Land owned by an Indian nation and designated by the federal Bureau of Indian Affairs as exempt from most state laws and taxes.

trustee: Role played by elected representatives who listen to constituents' opinions and then use their best judgment to make final decisions.

turnout: The proportion of the voting-age public that votes.

unit rule: A traditional party practice under which the majority of a state delegation can force the minority to vote for its candidate.

United States v. Nixon **(1974):** The Supreme Court ruled that there is no constitutional absolute executive privilege that would allow a president to refuse to comply with a court order to produce information needed in a criminal trial.

veto power: The formal, constitutional authority of the president to reject bills passed by both houses of Congress, thus preventing their becoming law without further congressional action.

Virginia Plan: The first general plan for the Constitution, proposed by James Madison. Its key points were a bicameral legislature, an executive chosen by the legislature, and a judiciary also named by the legislature.

voter canvass: The process by which a campaign gets in touch with individual voters: either by door-to-door solicitation or by telephone.

War Powers Act: Law requiring presidents to obtain congressional approval before introducing U.S. troops into a combat situation; passed in 1973 over President Nixon's veto.

whip: One of several representatives who keep close contact with all members and take "nose counts" on key votes, prepare summaries of bills, and in general act as communications links within the party.

wire service: An electronic delivery of news gathered by the news services' correspondents and sent to all member news media organizations.

writ of certiorari: A request for the Court to order up the records from a lower court to review the case.

yellow journalism: A form of newspaper publishing in vogue in the late nineteenth century that featured pictures, comics, color, and sensationalized, oversimplified news coverage.

INDEX